D8686783

Engineering Education

IEEE Press
445 Hoes Lane
Piscataway, NJ 08854

IEEE Press Editorial Board
Mohamed E. El-Hawary, *Editor in Chief*

M. Akay	T. G. Croda	M. S. Newman
J. B. Anderson	R. J. Herrick	F. M. B. Periera
R. J. Baker	S. V. Kartalopoulos	C. Singh
J. E. Brewer	M. Montrose	G. Zobrist

Kenneth Moore, *Director of IEEE Book and Information Services (BIS)*
Catherine Faduska, *Senior Acquisitions Editor*

Engineering Education

Research and Development
in Curriculum and Instruction

John Heywood

IEEE

IEEE PRESS

WILEY-INTERSCIENCE

A JOHN WILEY & SONS, INC., PUBLICATION

Copyright © 2005 by the Institute of Electrical and Electronics Engineers, Inc. All rights reserved.

Published by John Wiley & Sons, Inc., Hoboken, New Jersey.
Published simultaneously in Canada.

No part of this publication may be reproduced, stored in a retrieval system, or transmitted in any form or by any means, electronic, mechanical, photocopying, recording, scanning, or otherwise, except as permitted under Section 107 or 108 of the 1976 United States Copyright Act, without either the prior written permission of the Publisher, or authorization through payment of the appropriate per-copy fee to the Copyright Clearance Center, Inc., 222 Rosewood Drive, Danvers, MA 01923, (978) 750-8400, fax (978) 750-4470, or on the web at www.copyright.com. Requests to the Publisher for permission should be addressed to the Permissions Department, John Wiley & Sons, Inc., 111 River Street, Hoboken, NJ 07030, (201) 748-6011, fax (201) 748-6008, or online at http://www.wiley.com/go/permission.

Limit of Liability/Disclaimer of Warranty: While the publisher and author have used their best efforts in preparing this book, they make no representations or warranties with respect to the accuracy or completeness of the contents of this book and specifically disclaim any implied warranties of merchantability or fitness for a particular purpose. No warranty may be created or extended by sales representatives or written sales materials. The advice and strategies contained herein may not be suitable for your situation. You should consult with a professional where appropriate. Neither the publisher nor author shall be liable for any loss of profit or any other commercial damages, including but not limited to special, incidental, consequential, or other damages.

For general information on our other products and services or for technical support, please contact our Customer Care Department within the United States at (800) 762-2974, outside the United States at (317) 572-3993 or fax (317) 572-4002.

Wiley also publishes its books in a variety of electronic formats. Some content that appears in print may not be available in electronic format. For information about Wiley products, visit our web site at www.wiley.com.

Library of Congress Cataloging-in-Publication Data is available.

ISBN-13 978-0-471-74111-4
ISBN-10 0-471-74111-6

Printed in the United States of America.

10 9 8 7 6 5 4 3 2 1

To Dick Culver, Sandy Courter, Karl Smith, John Sharp, and Eddie Gould
whose help and encouragement sustained me in the completion of this study

CONTENTS

FOREWORD

Those of us who regularly attend the Frontiers in Education conference (jointly sponsored by the Education Research and Methods division of the American Society for Engineering Education, the IEEE Education Society, and the IEEE Computer Society) have benefited for years from John Heywood's wisdom. With the publication of this volume, the culmination of many years of hard work, others will similarly benefit. In my opinion, this is a vitally important contribution to engineering education literature, which comes at a most propitious time. Engineering education research is gaining respect as the field becomes increasingly scholarly and adopts more stringent standards. For example, the *Journal of Engineering Education* has declared its mission to serve as an archival record of scholarly research in engineering education. Other signs of the increasing importance of engineering education research include the establishment of schools of engineering education at Purdue University and Virginia Polytechnic and State University, the proliferation of centers for engineering education in universities, the NSF-sponsored Center for the Advancement of Engineering Education (CAEE) headquartered at the University of Washington, and the founding of the Center for the Advancement of Scholarship on Engineering Education (CASEE) at the National Academy of Engineering.

John Heywood's review is an excellent complement to all of these efforts. It is an impressive compendium of the research and practice related to curriculum, instruction, and leadership in engineering education over the past forty years. I am convinced that only Professor Heywood, with his encyclopedic knowledge and astounding memory, could have accomplished such a feat. While each of us who works in engineering education will no doubt quibble about a favorite study that has been omitted, the volume as a whole provides an excellent overview of several decades of theory and practice. An especially attractive feature is its international focus. John Heywood's review will be an excellent general resource, but will be a "must" for any serious engineering education researcher. It will also be invaluable as a resource for graduate-level courses on teaching engineering.

All of us who are interested in providing the best education possible for our engineering students owe John Heywood a debt of gratitude for this important and timely book. It is a strong contribution to the field.

BARBARA OLDS
Professor of Liberal Arts and International Studies
Colorado School of Mines
ASEE Board of Directors 2002–2004
Chair, Educational Research and Methods (ERM) Division, ASEE 1999–2001

PREFACE

Historically the Education Research and Methods Division (ERM) of the American Society for Engineering Education (ASEE) has provided leadership in research and innovation in teaching engineering. Five or so years ago the Division began to review its role and to look to the future. This book arose out of these discussions.

As part of my contribution to the debate, as a result of discussions with the group, I produced a paper on the need for instructional leadership in engineering education. It was used as a background paper for a seminar organized by the ERM Division at the Kansas City Frontiers in Education Conference (AD 2000), and it was published in the conference proceedings.

When I revised and extended this paper I replaced the term *instructional leader* with that of *curriculum leader*. This extended version of the paper was used as a background report for the Forum on Engineering Education Leadership that resulted from the Kansas City seminar.

Dick Culver, in his introduction to the Forum, used Astin's recently published definition of leadership to focus on the purposes of the Forum. He summarized it as follows:

"Leadership involves fostering change, implies intentionality, is inherently value-based, is by definition a group process, and thus depends on collaboration"[1]

Or, to put it in the way of the *New Shorter Oxford Dictionary* (1993) it is the ability *"to lead or influence."* Culver took the view that this necessarily involved change, thus by definition a leader is a change agent.

Culver argued that while there was a substantial body of research that supported the need for new approaches to teaching in higher education, this knowledge remained the preserve of educational researchers and a few dedicated teachers. The first objective of this book is to make the knowledge accumulated from research and innovation in the curriculum and instruction in engineering education more generally available.

He quoted from John T. Bruer's *The Minds Journey. From Novice to Expert* to support his case. *"Teaching methods based on research in cognitive science are the educational equivalents of polio vaccine and penicillin. Yet few outside the educational research community are aware of these breakthroughs or understand the research that makes them possible."*

This is the case worldwide, irrespective of the drive in some countries to evaluate university teaching. If evaluations are done by peers, then it is the case of the ignorant (I do not mean to deprecate) leading the ignorant, and such assessments are often carried out within a very limited notion of what constitutes good or effective teaching.

Teachers in higher education are accountable, if only to their profession. If they believe they are an expert profession, then they have obligation not only to ensure that beginning teachers have an adequate training but to be aware of the pedagogical knowledge that is available to inform the curriculum process.

But there is another argument. It stems from the fact that teachers in higher education value research in their own subjects. It is, therefore, surprising that the notion that teaching and learning should be informed by research has not pervaded the teaching profession in higher education. Patricia Cross has argued that teaching will not become a respectable activity until teachers treat their classrooms as laboratories for research.[2]

To encourage the development of this idea, Tom Angelo and Patricia Cross worked with teachers to develop and evaluate 50 techniques of classroom assessment. They are intended to help *"individual college teachers obtain useful feedback on what, how much and how well their students are learning. Faculty can then use this information to refocus their teaching to help students make their learning more efficient and more effective."*[3]

Another approach is to learn through more formal research into one's classroom practices, and even more generally into other dimensions of the curriculum process. Among others, Patricia Cross and Mimi Steadman as well as this writer have illustrated how this can be done.[4] There are several examples of such research in recent publications of the *Proceedings of the ASEE Annual Conferences* and the *Proceedings of the Frontiers in Education* conferences. Some provide major contributions to educational knowledge. While the first objective of this study is to provide an illustrative review of research and development in engineering education since 1960; the second objective is with the examples given to encourage the practice of classroom assessment and research.

Classroom assessment and classroom research require different levels of expertise. In the case of classroom assessment, teachers need not be necessarily exposed to a formal course of training since learning about learning is accomplished through the implementation of classroom assessment techniques. It is a level 1 of teaching expertise.

Classroom research requires more knowledge before one can begin. This might be related to a specialist topic (e.g., cooperative learning, student ratings), or it may be of a more general kind (e.g. the redesign of a curriculum). In either case the teacher(s) may require help from educational specialists, and there are examples of such collaboration in the recent literature of engineering education. These teachers acquire a level 2 of expertise and leadership. The third

---

[1] Astin, A.W., Astin, H. S., and others (2001). *Leadership Reconsidered: Engaging Higher Education in Social Change*. W. K. Kellog Foundation, Battele Creek, MI.

[2] Cross, K. P. (1986) A proposal to improve teaching. *AAHE* (American Association for Higher Education) *Bulletin*. September. Pp 9-15.

[3] Angelo, T and. Cross, K. P. *Classroom Assessment*. Jossey Bass, San Francisco

[4] Cross, K. P. and M. Steadman (1996). Classroom Research. Jossey Bass, San Francisco.

objective is therefore to promote the idea of curriculum leadership. That is the idea that in departments and schools there will be persons who can be consulted about classroom assessment and research and are acknowledged as such.

Leading implies following. To the extent that we set ourselves goals, and to the extent that we set about obtaining those goals, we both lead and follow. In this sense, every individual is a leader, even at the level 1 of teaching expertise. Because this is the case, each individual has within him or herself the attributes of leadership. What distinguishes one person from another as a leader is the use to which they put the attributes of leadership in the varying situations in which they find themselves.[5] To acknowledge the findings of educational research and not to do anything about them is a neglect of professional responsibility. It is also a denial of the professional's responsibility to lead. Transformational leadership is required to create an environment in which teaching is valued as much as research.

Those faculty members who, in an ethos that values research above teaching, spend time on classroom assessment strategies are leading themselves, and by example, others. If they try to persuade others that such activities are worthwhile and lead to better practice, they are leading in the traditional understanding of leadership. The same is true of classroom research, the second level of expertise.

More generally, part of the role of the professional teacher is to lead beginning teachers into the pedagogy of higher education. In Ralph Tyler's words, they have the goal of *"helping practitioners who want to improve the curriculum of the schools* (engineering departments) *in which they work."*[6]

There will be those who have acquired the capability to do this at the first level of expertise. There will be others who can do it at the second level of expertise. Those who take on these leadership roles can help create a climate of cultural change from the bottom up. By themselves such activities cannot be expected to maintain cultural change since they are often due to the initiatives of individuals. In any event, those individuals also need support from the top, and this means that those at the top will have to have an understanding of the professional pedagogy. While they may wish to act as curriculum leaders themselves, given the scope of the knowledge required, there would seem to be the need to recognize a faculty, school, or departmental position of curriculum leader whose promotion prospects are not diminished because of the task. This is a third level of curriculum leadership.[7] A fourth level of leadership is involved in the external politics that determine the program.

Philip Jackson's summary of Joseph Schwab's view of the role of the curriculum specialist is as good a description of the role of a curriculum leader in any context as there is.[8] It read as follows,

- Skillful use of the rhetoric of persuasion (which includes knowing how to elicit participation in small group settings and person to person encounters). (*The first stage of curriculum leadership*).
- Experience in deliberation (*and causing people to deliberate at greater levels than they have before*).
- Ability to read learned journals and the habit of doing so.
- Ability to guide colleagues to the use of the journals, *and to encourage them to believe that their classrooms are laboratories for valid research.*
- Knowledge of curricular practices (*their design and improvement*).
- Knowledge of the behavioral sciences which contribute to the guidance of educational *policy and* practice (*e.g., branches of psychology and sociology*).
- *Knowledge of the humanities which contribute to the guidance of educational policy and practice (e.g., philosophy).*
- "nodding", and *sometimes detailed* acquaintance with some of the academic fields from which other *engineering* subjects are drawn.

There are difficulties with this list as with all lists. My comments are shown in italics. The first item would pre-suppose that the person is a propagandist for a particular model, but the real need is that all professional teachers should have defensible theories of learning, and sociology for it is in these domains of knowledge where the aims of education reside. This implies that professional teachers and curriculum leaders in particular should have a training that is at least in scope similar to a good quality course of training provided for graduates who wish to teach in high school.

Discussion of the idea of training university teachers is no longer anathema. In the United Kingdom the Government wishes to make the training of new teachers in higher education compulsory. Thus, an Institute for Teaching and Learning (ILT) has been established by legislation and university teachers are encouraged to become members. Some universities require all newly appointed teachers to take certificate courses accredited by the Institute for Teaching and Learning.[9]

---

[5] Taken from Heywood, J. (1989). *Learning, Adaptability and Change*. Paul Chapman (Sage), London.

[6] Ralph Tyler is quoted thus by P. W. Jackson (1992). Conceptions of the curriculum and curriculum specialists. In P. W. Jackson (ed). *Handbook of Research on Curriculum*. American Educational Research Association. Macmillan, New York.

[7] Culver has suggested that the level 0 person be called a lecturer, the level 1 a practitioner, the level 2 a researcher and level 3 a leader.

[8] *Ibid* P. W. Jackson (1992)

[9] The ILT has been subsumed into a Higher Education Academy.

Cropley, writing from an Australian perspective, considered *"that, unless the requirements for faculty to have a formal teaching qualification become mandated, improvements in the quality of teaching and learning at universities will remain elusive and fractured. If universities wish to be competitive in the future and if they seek to have a reputation for quality, then the compulsory accreditation of teaching in higher education, both generally, and in education specifically, is a proactive step that is unequivocal about the commitment to that change."*[10] Governance of this kind could have a profound influence on the how, what, and why of accreditation.

Prior to that, both in Australia and the United Kingdom there had been a considerable amount of training, generally in the form of short courses, and a substantial amount of research had created a basic pedagogy of higher education. There have also been substantive contributions to this research effort in Canada and the United States.[11]

As in the rest of the world many short courses are on offer in North America, and many of these are provided for the induction of new teachers. Some courses are provided that offer credits. One or two universities are providing mentoring programs.[12]

Within engineering some 20 or so centers for engineering education and professional development have been created at universities in the United States. Several are of long standing. They are engaged in major research and faculty development. Some offer courses with credits for persons in doctoral programs who are graduate teaching assistants.[13] The National Academy of Engineering has now established a Center for the Advancement of Scholarship on Engineering Education. It seeks to *"enhance faculty awareness of challenges, opportunities, and standards for the conduct, evaluation and communication of research on engineering education. Reduce barriers to faculty engagement in such research, and speed the transition of education research results."*[14]

Worldwide, since the early 1960s, there has been an increasing flow of papers in the engineering education journals and conferences. They number around 10,000 since 1964. There are at least 1500 articles that a tutor of students in a post-graduate education course would consider provide a framework for the discussion of pedagogical principles. The first purpose of this book is to examine that collection of papers from the perspective of the curriculum process. The second purpose is to have in mind the need for professional teachers, especially those who would lead the curriculum, to acquire defensible theories of learning, philosophy, sociology, and history as they apply to the process of curriculum improvement and evaluation.

Dr. Sandra Courter of the University of Wisconsin-Madison agreed to ask the students in two of her courses for TA's on Teaching and Learning in Engineering to evaluate the 14 chapters that had been written by asking them to critique them and give short papers about them in class. Some major changes were made as a result of these seminars.

Encouraged by these 20 or so TA's, and taking into account their advice as well as that of the aforementioned and other colleagues, I continue with the task. My purpose is to provide a resource for engineering educators working at each of these levels of expertise. It is based on the wide range of knowledge available in the literature of engineering education. I draw attention to its limitations, and where appropriate I point out relevant work in other fields of knowledge. It is comparable with the level of knowledge required by graduate trainees for teaching in high schools. While the language of the book may be challenging at times, and on occasion all too brief, it is hoped that the organization of this material within a single text will provide a substantial resource for those who wish to lead. This means that the more challenging chapters, so the TA's told us, come in the first part. Since the text is intended as a resource reader, each chapter is relatively self contained, and may be read independently of the others.

Doubtless some will argue that I should have included articles that are not included and excluded some that are. I shall have achieved my purpose if it is agreed that I have given the flavor of a field and the debates within it, together with sufficient information to guide further reading. For this reason I have tried to draw out examples issues from the authors themselves.

The report was concluded during a period when it was evident that an explosion in the number of reports on the evaluation of on-line learning in all its many forms had begun.[15] On-line learning is opening up many possibilities for inter-university collaboration in an international framework.[16] But, the first reports suggest that the same principles of learning that were established from traditional contexts for learning will apply. They also suggest that it is possible to establish effective communities of learning in the on-line contest.

---

[10]Cropley, D. H. (2003). A case for compulsory teaching accreditation of engineering faculty. *IEEE Transactions on Education*, 46, (4), 460 – 463.

[11]For summary of much of this work especially in engineering see Stice, J., Felder, R.M., Woods, D. R., and A. Rugarcia (2000). The Future of Engineering Education 1V. Learning how to teach. *Chemical Engineering Education*, 34, (2), 118-127.

[12] *Ibid,*

[13] For example the Engineering Learning Center at the University of Madison-Wisconsin where some of the evaluation of this text was done. Descriptions of the work of some of these centres were given at the ERM division breakfast at the 2001 annual conference of ASEE.

[14] Fortenberry, N. L. (2003). Work-in-progress: Designing a support system for research on engineering education. *Proceedings Frontiers in Education Conference*, 3, S1A-p12.

[15] For example Ellis, T (2004). Animating to build higher cognitive understanding: a model for studying multimedia effectiveness' in education. *Journal of Engineering Education*, 93, (1), 59–64.

[16] See, for example J. Hamilton-Jones and T. Svane (2003). Developing research using reflective diaries. *Proceedings Frontiers in Education Conference*, 1, T3A-14 to 19.

For convenience the text is divided into four main parts. The first is about aims and objectives and their screening. It is about the curriculum process and how the foundation subjects of education (History, Philosophy, Psychology, and Sociology) are used to determine the aims and objectives of the curriculum and the internal structure that integrates assessment, content, teaching, and learning. Part II is about the curriculum *per se*, and it considers content organization, trends, and change. Chapter 7 is about change and the problems of changing the curriculum. This is followed by a chapter (8) on interdisciplinary and integrated study and a chapter on project and problem based models of the curriculum. Part III focuses on problem solving, creativity, and design. For convenience, in spite of some overlap between them, each of these concepts is dealt with in a separate chapter. Part IV focuses on teaching, assessment, and evaluation. Following on from the chapter on design in the previous section, this part begins with a chapter (13) on the lecture, cooperative learning, and teamwork. This is followed by a discussion of other approaches to teaching including case studies, PSI, laboratory work, and electronic assisted learning, a term that is meant to be all embracing (Chapter 14). Various definitions of the meaning of assessment are given, and the value of the traditional distinction between assessment and design is highlighted (Chapter 15). Chapter 17 draws together the lessons learnt from research, development, and experience for attrition and retention. The study concludes with a brief epilogue on the future of engineering education.

It is not expected that readers will approach this text linearly. Even though it contains its own logic each chapter may be treated as free standing, although inevitably there will be relationships with material in other chapters, some of which have been cross-referenced. This approach means that some overlaps are unavoidable.

Many of the activities and innovations referred to in this text are due to individuals apparently working on their own. Because nothing further has been reported about them, it is not known if they have continued with or stopped the innovation. For this reason the past tense is used throughout the text. In addition to the opening summaries, italics have been used for quotations.

JOHN HEYWOOD

Dublin, Ireland
August 2005

ACKNOWLEDGMENTS

I am particularly grateful to Sandra Courter for her patience. The structure owes much to her wisdom and insight. Her students, to whom I am most grateful, also provided me with many insights. John Cowan's criticisms were of great value, as were those of Sheri Sheppard, Don Evans, Sharon Fellows, John Sharp, Jim Stice, Karl Smith, Norman Fortenberry, and Charles Yokomoto. The origins of this work lie in many discussions with Dick Culver, and without his encouragement I would never have embarked on or continued with the task.

Over the forty year period of this study I was involved as team leader in several major projects into the education of engineers and technologists in the UK I also supervised post-graduates undertaking research in engineering education topics. These activities gave me the grounding in the literature that formed the background for the review. But one's understanding is influenced by the colleagues with whom one worked and they merit a specific thank you. I thank therefore, George Carter and Deryk Kelly with whom I conducted a 15 year longitudinal evaluation (action research) of an engineering science curriculum. To Michael Youngman, Bob Oxtoby, and the late Denis Monk with whom I developed new methods for deriving objectives for the training of engineers and technologists. To John Sharp and Jim Freeman for allowing me to collaborate with them in developing approaches to course evaluation, and to my postgraduates for their many insights especially Sam Lee, Joe Moon and Paul McElwee. In the area of school technology I thank Michael Murray, Glyn Price and Stan Owen. Finally to John Cowan with whom I regularly debated these issues

I am very grateful to Ed Gould of the University of Salford who prepared the camera copy and to his wife Margaret who provided the cover piece. Emma Balfe and Mary Weafer of the University of Dublin (Trinity College) who have provided me with much secretarial assistance over the years for which I am very grateful.

More than anyone, I am grateful to my wife Pauline, who had to put up with the four year day and night struggle to produce this work.

No acknowledgment would be complete without a thank you to all the authors whose work I have read, and whose contributions gave me so much pleasure. I regret that the scale of the exercise prevented me from drawing attention to many other studies that merited mention. The principal sources of reference were *Engineering Education* subsequently *The Journal of Engineering Educatio;, Engineering Science and Education Journal; The European Journal of Engineering Education; The IEEE Transaction on Education; The International Journal of Applied Engineering Education,* subsequently the *International Journal of Engineering Education; The International Journal of Technology and Design Education; The International Journal of Electrical Engineering Education;* the *Bulletin of Mechanical Engineering Education,* subsequently the *International Journal of Mechanical Engineering Education; and Research in Science and Technological Education.* These were scrutinised from 1966 or from their inception.

Other journals consulted included *ASEE Annual Conference Proceedings; Assessment and Evaluation in Higher Education; Chartered Mechanical Engineer; Chemical Engineering Education; IEE Proceedings; Journal of Technology Education; Nature; Physics Education; and Studies in Higher Education.*

By far the most number of citations come from the *Proceedings of the ASEE/IEEE Frontiers in Education Conferences,* and in very many respects this study is a tribute to the members of the ERM Division of ASEE, and the IEEE Education and Computer Societies. These proceedings were scrutinized from 1973.

J. H.

PART I: AIMS AND OBJECTIVES (OUTCOMES) AND THEIR SCREENING

Chapter 1: Curriculum Design, Implementation and Evaluation

Summary

This Chapter begins with a definition of the curriculum. The curriculum is always subject to minor changes as teachers take up the prevailing ideas and respond to technological change. Sometimes it is necessary to formalize these changes. Formalization has to take into account the mission, aims and objectives of the institution in which the department resides. Engineering departments are also subject to the requirements of their profession. Change is often caused by external factors. It often demands substantial changes in the culture of the organizational unit responsible for delivering the curriculum.

A theoretical model of the curriculum process derived from a proposal by Tyler is discussed. Since Tyler's proposal the terminology has become very confused. An example of the application of the model to the problem of curriculum overload is discussed.

It is noted that there are many variations of this model but, the implications of all these models for the role of the teacher and the institution are similar. Taking into account any professional requirements, the role of the teacher is to determine (a) the aims and objectives (outcomes) of the course (program) to be given, (b) the best methods of achieving those aims and objectives (outcomes), (c) the sequence of learning and instruction, and, if as a result of (b) and (c) they have been achieved. Traditionally the last process has been called evaluation. A distinction is made between the assessment of student learning and evaluation. Evaluation embraces the assessment of student learning. It would detect mismatches between the formal learning environment and the experiences of students in that environment achieving desired outcomes. It would also include the evaluation of teaching performance, the continuing appraisal of goals in response to sociotechnical change, and the attention to the core values of the course (program).

The Chapter concludes that the determination of aims and objectives (outcomes) is an important but difficult process that involves their screening using the philosophy, sociology, and psychology of education.

1. The Curriculum

In order to understand the curriculum process, it is necessary to offer a definition of the curriculum. Here, it is taken to be *the formal mechanism through which intended educational aims are achieved*. Since educational aims are achieved through learning, the curriculum process is described by those factors that bring about learning. Thus, both learning and instruction are central to the curriculum process. *Informal* changes may be made to the curriculum by teachers without the formal assent of the accrediting agency, and often are. Teachers may leave out or add to the material, or change the way in which it is taught and assessed by them. In technological subjects, teachers' often have to make changes to the content. Rather like automobiles the curriculum is subject to a continuing process of minor change. But these changes, which while from the teachers' perspective provide for continuous quality improvement, do not form the *formal* perspective that is the subject of quality assurance. Every now and again the accumulation of these changes makes necessary a major review of the curriculum and some departments do this irrespective of external pressures. More often than not it is external agencies that cause such a review, as for example those caused by ABET (Accreditation Board for Engineering and Technology) in the United States and SARTOR in the United Kingdom (Brown, 1998). Other agencies can intervene and influence the professional organizations in one way or another may, for example, the NSF (National Science Foundation) sponsored coalitions in the United States and the United Kingdom Employment Department's Enterprise in Higher Education Initiative. Sometimes the demands of professional organizations require substantial changes in the approach to the curriculum that have a bearing on how the curriculum is taught. Moreover, these changes may require a substantial change in the culture of the department or unit that has to initiate change. Bringing about change is not an easy exercise as a recent step by step study by Walkington (2002) shows. Those who would bring about change have to have an understanding of the system and the culture that they wish to change (i.e. its external and internal dynamics). While this Chapter is concerned with a general explanation of the curriculum process, a more detailed study of the curriculum and change is left to Chapter 7, understanding of the curriculum process requires an understanding of institutional structures, practices and procedures. It is with these that the Chapter begins.

1.1. The Curriculum, the Institution, and Accountability

For its delivery the curriculum is dependent upon teachers who function within some kind of unit that gives coherence to the subject being taught. More often than not, the unit is a department. Where, however, the subject is interdisciplinary, then it may be a team. For its delivery the curriculum is dependent on cohesion among the members of the team, and if there are tensions between team members learning may be impeded. There can, for example, be conflicts of interest between the subject areas for time within courses. *"My subject requires this amount of time!"* This is not to say that conflicts among the members of departments are avoided. Far from it! Such conflicts can be about the utilization of scarce resources, particularly if there is a shortage of teachers. Shortages of teachers will more often than not be due to decisions taken at a higher level, that is, the School (College, Faculty), the institution, and/or government. Hidden agendas play a powerful role in advancing or preventing change.

The institution has aims and objectives that it wishes to achieve, and to some extent their achievement will depend on the exchanges that it has with its external and internal environments. A diagram of some of the interactions it has to make is shown in Figure 1.1. It is considerably simplified.

It will be evident that if the taxpayer is unwilling to increase funding, or at least believed by the legislators not to be willing to pay, then the achievement of institutional goals may be hampered. One consequence is likely to be a cost-cutting exercise and since the most expensive item on any campus is person power, teachers may not be replaced when they leave. The making of such cuts, in the face of internal opposition, is a formidable exercise, and for some departments it may mean having to lose an elective, reduce the teaching in certain subjects, or find other ways to teach them (e.g., Midwinter, 2000).

The diagram also shows how the structures of an organization are not only affected by the social system but influence the practices and procedures that the institution develops to respond exchanges with its external environment. Because higher education institutions are slow to change, change is often forced on them from the outside. For example, the belief in the value of computer-assisted learning, probably backed up by a belief that it will reduce the number of teachers, can lead legislators to vote extensive funds for that purpose across the university. Teachers who might not have considered using computer-assisted learning find that they have to use it whether they like it or not. Perhaps, in the United Kingdom the biggest imposition from the outside during the last 20 years was the demand for greater and greater accountability. It demanded the utilization of one of the two most scarce resources in a university, time (Williams, 2002; Midwinter, 2000)[1]T.

The world wide demand for accountability has meant that institutions have had to put in place mechanisms and structures for quality assurance at all levels of the institution. Given that quality assurance is the degree to which these aims and objectives are achieved, then everyone in the institution has to be seen to be contributing to that goal. While engineering is not exempt from these conditions, it has like all professional subjects, its professional requirements to meet, and in institutional debates about funding it will use those requirements to try and protect its resources. ("If you insist on that, then we will not be able to meet the educational requirements of the profession.") Thus, one of the factors that worries engineering departments, is the supply of students. As engineering departments have found in the United Kingdom, if they do not have sufficient students they will be closed. For this reason, much attention is paid to mission statements. Aims and goals for such statements both at the institutional and professional levels are important for the marketing of the

institution. They are also the criteria against which their performance can be judged.

1.2. Mission Statements, Aims and Goals

Unfortunately, there is no agreed terminology about the use of these terms. They are often used interchangeably (Heywood, 2000; Yokomoto and Bostwick, 1999). Even the term *objective* may be used instead of aim or goal. Those who use them seem to be agreed that they are fairly general and to be used to focus on where an institution or a department should go (or be going). One of the reasons for seeking a sharper focus was that many of the statements of aims became a pious list of platitudes that academics used when they had to defend what they did. In fact they had no means of judging whether, what they did was achieving the goals they believed in. Therefore, if we were to establish what academics achieved in their teaching, it would be necessary to have some criteria against which the performance of students could be judged. These criteria have to be derived from the aims that the institution has.

1.2.1. The Importance of Mission Statements

A mission statement should be the emotional hook on which an institution hangs its clothing. Because mission statements lacked substance they came to be disregarded by both faculty and students. The linkage between them and the reality of the institution was broken. Sometimes they were expressions of hope about how students would develop. But such hopes, as for example, those shown in Exhibit 1.1, did not necessarily find an appropriate response in the curriculum. Yet as Knight pointed out, aims that are related to attitudes are important (private communication). Unlike the examination objectives related to the knowledge and abilities to be tested, not all of these attitudes can be directly measured. They can, however, be detected in the way students tackle problems based on both syllabus content and the way they behave in coursework, as for example, in teamwork. As Nichols (1991) wrote *"Instead of 'assuming' their accomplishments, institutions are being challenged to demonstrate their overall effectiveness through assessment of departmental program outcomes and objectives linked closely to the institution's statement of purpose. This requirement changes the mission statement of purpose from a shelf-document with little practical use to the basis for institutional action and that is what it was intended to be"*(p,13).

But, as Swaim and Moretti (1991) commented, programs too have missions. When they argued the case for a more limited B.S. degree, they said that it was important to identify the mission of each level of education (i.e., B.S./M.S.), and once that had been done, curriculum questions can be addressed. In a short paper in Chemical Engineering Education Rugarcia et al, (2000) demonstrated this point in the first of six papers that considered the future of engineering education.

---

[1] See Chapter 15 for a detailed discussion of the mechanisms for evaluation (quality) assurance in the United Kingdom.

Nichols (1991) went on to argue that most mission statements are not substantial enough to provide a basis for institutional effectiveness. They will have to be to be expanded considerably and a *"working relationship between the revised statement of purpose and the intended outcomes and objectives at departmental and programme levels, must be established"* (p,13).

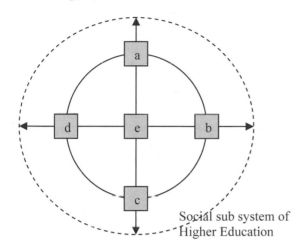

Social sub system of Higher Education

a = Aims and objectives b – Resources
c = Evaluation accountability
d = Practice and procedures e = Structures

Figure 1.1: A model of the institutional evaluation process within a sub system of higher education

He called for an expanded statement of institutional purpose. His examples, which also described linkages for various programs, listed what are sometimes called aims or goals, and, in the case of the linkages, broad outcomes or non-behavioural objectives. These lists of goals should provide statements against which the achievement of institutional goals can be measured.

1.2.2. The Importance of Aims

The trouble is that like all movements there was a danger of throwing the baby out with the bath water. In this case, the move to "objectivity", as this increasing focus on aims was called, carried with it the danger that it removed the emotional props that supported academics in their everyday work (Heywood, 1977). The language of higher education is a language of aims and goals, not a language of objectives and outcomes, however important they may be. It is a language of broad terminology about motivation, interest, intelligence, critical thought, willingness to learn, and in engineering-analytical thought and problem solving. It is a mix of cognitive and affective. Some aims are more tangible from a measurement perspective than others. The role of objectives and outcomes is in the interpretation of aims into practice, and that practice involves the way that students learn. Therefore, discussion of aims is important

and several seminal texts continue to be relevant.[2] Such aims have to generate a dynamic for change or renewal or both, and take into account that learning in higher education is a complex process (Knight, 2001).

1.3. The Mission of Engineering Education

Like all systems, engineering education has to adjust, albeit slowly, to changes in the socioeconomic system in which it functions. Periodically it reviews its mission and goals, and sometimes such reviews are government inspired. In the past, American Society for Engineering Education (ASEE) has commissioned substantial reports into aspects of engineering education's future, as, for example, the Grinter Report (1955), see also ASEE 1968 (a, b). In the United Kingdom, the government sponsored an enquiry into engineering that resulted in the Finniston Report (1980), and many recent major developments in engineering education in the United Kingdom find their stimulus in that report. At the present time, in the United States, the current state of engineering education is the subject of an enquiry by the Carnegie Foundation (Sheppard, 2001).

Grayson (1978) summarized the goals proposed by the Grinter Committee as follows: The first, the technical goal, *"was the preparation of the student to perform analysis and creative design, or construction, production or operation where a full knowledge of the analysis and design of the structure, machine or process is essential."*

The second, the social goal:, *"was to develop an understanding of the evolution of Society and of the impact of technology on it, an acquaintance with an appreciation of the heritage of other cultural fields, and the development of a personal philosophy, which will ensure satisfaction in the pursuit of a productive life, and a sense of moral and ethical values consistent with the career of a professional engineer."*

The authors of ABET 2000 would surely claim that their aims are no different, and they might have pointed out that although the Grinter Committee had profound effects on the development of engineering education in the United States, there was still a long way to go to achieve perfection.

How to achieve the second goal is still a matter of controversy (Haws, 2001).

In Great Britain the cultural formation of engineers arises from a somewhat different tradition in which industry was expected to play a key part, even if for the most part it did not.[3] The Finniston Committee wrote that, *"we lay special emphasis on the role of employers in structuring and supervising the experience gained by young engineers in their first years work, which are in many ways the most critical in the*

---

[2] For example Newman's *Idea of a University* especially in that he interpreted his idea in the practical reality of establishing the catholic University of Dublin (Culler, 1955; McGrath, 1962), and Whitehead's *The Aims of Education and Other Essays* in which, among other things, the science and mathematics curriculum is discussed.

[3] See Heywood (1969). See also Finniston (1980) paragraph 4.23, p 85.

package." (i.e., the formation of engineers). *"The academic years should seek best to develop in students the analytical and scientific foundations on which they will build their practical skills and also to prepare them to begin synthesizing and applying what they have learnt from the time they enter employment".* (Finniston, 1980, p, 77).

This is in contrast to the Grinter report where an important component of the education of an engineer was in creative design. The only mention of a government report on engineering design (Feilden, 1963) that made recommendations about engineering design education in the Finniston Report comes as a footnote to a section on market trends for manufacturing economies! [4]

(i)	The recognition of the need for a method which is organized, careful and intellectually honest in respect of experimental observation.
(ii)	The acceptance of the need to consider the parallel social and economic bases of engineering.
(iii)	An awareness of the need to derive the more particular relationships from basic concepts.
(iv)	An awareness of the advantage of seeking parallels in other fields to relate one kind of phenomenon to another.
(v)	An awareness of the advantage of attempting to reduce a social, economic or situation to a simple system.
(vi)	The recognition of the fact that it may be necessary to exercise judgment as well as reason when dealing with a problem.
(vii)	The recognition that a perfect answer to a problem may not exist, and that the best available answer must be sought.
(viii)	The recognition of the fact that not all the information necessary to tackle a problem may be available, and that some information which is available may not be relevant.
(ix)	The acceptance of the fact that more than one way of thinking exists, and that different ways may be more appropriate to different problems or different stages of the same problem.
(x)	The recognition of the fact that the required exactness of a calculation may vary from case to case (for example from a preliminary quick order of magnitude estimate to a precise forecast of performance).

Exhibit 1.1. The attitudes and interests that it was hoped students studying engineering science at the Advanced level of the General Certificate of Education would acquire. (*From Notes for the Guidance of Schools for Engineering Science at the Advanced level of the General Certificate of Education.* Joint Matriculation Board, Manchester)

The cultural press on institutions is considerable, and it is very difficult for them to stand aside from this culture and examine the inevitable contradictions through which practice is mediated. The same is true of departments and their teachers. Nevertheless, outside influences such as changing technology are forcing departments to make changes, and it seems from the engineering literature that research and new practices are having an impact on the curriculum process. Demands for accountability by legislators and especially by professional organizations are causing the curriculum to be reviewed at site level (Programme assessment (United

States); subject review (United Kingdom)[5]. Such requirements provide the opportunity for fundamental curriculum change if the educational community is versed in the curriculum process and in the philosophical, psychological, and sociological foundations upon which it is based.

1.4.   The Curriculum Process in Theory

A variety of models of the curriculum process have been proposed. There are many similarities between them. The models shown in Figures 1.2 to 1.5 have their origins in the work of Tyler (1949). Figures 1.2, 1.3, and 1.4 are characterized by the fact that they incorporate the syllabus (list of content).   But the models shown in Figures 1.2 and 1.3 fail to take into account the entering characteristics of the learner. These are the characteristics that indicate the learner's potential to learn within the particular context to be faced.

There is really no adequate way to demonstrate the complexity of the curriculum process in either its static or dynamic form. Indeed Culver (private communication) has told the author that he prefers Figure 1.3 to the model in Figure 1.4 that attempted to demonstrate both the static (design) and dynamic (implementation) nature of the curriculum. An American model due to Cronbach (Figure.1.5) had to be adapted for use in the United Kingdom because, at the time, it omitted a component for assessment. This would no longer be the case in engineering education in the United States, because the ABET criteria are now focused on outcomes and their assessment. But it would still be necessary to distinguish between program and student learning assessment.

Kerns et al, (1998) described the six-step approach to the medical curriculum shown in Figure 1.6.

---

[5] The statement from the Finniston Committee arises from the fact that until the 1970's the major route for the education and training of engineers was by part-time study at a technical college while working in industry (see Payne, 1960). The Finniston report compared the system of education and training for engineers in Great Britain with the systems in France, Germany, Japan and the United States and came to the conclusion that these systems were "generally superior" to the British. *"This deficiency to a large extent reflects the relatively restricted and narrow British conception of engineering as a branch of applied science, which militates against an effective marriage between theory and application. The British system does not give students sufficient grounding in the technical, human and financial considerations nor does it adequately encourage the development of the wider skills and outlook required of engineers within the engineering dimension. In consequence employers have often taken the attitude that few engineers are properly equipped to take on broader managerial responsibilities and have employed them instead as providers of technical services, thereby closing the vicious circle"* (p 91). In arriving at this statement the Committee was greatly influenced by the view that there was no dichotomy between theory and practice in Germany because *" the philosophy of Technik which places everything taught firmly in the context of economic performance"* (p90).
The point to be made here is that while engineering courses have been extended to take into account these other considerations there is little evidence that the attitudes of engineering educators have changed. Moreover, there is nothing in the introductory statement of what the academic years should aim to do, that could be said to generate any dynamic that would lead to change.

---

[4] Finniston (1980, p 17).

The six steps are problem identification; and general needs assessment; needs assessment of targeted learners; goals and objectives; educational strategies; mplementation; and evaluation and feedback. Another model, due to Cowan and Harding (1986), that had its origins in engineering, is shown in Figure 1.7.

These models have many similarities with one developed by Grayson (1978) for engineering education. This is shown in Figure 1.8. Like the model in Figure 1.5 it is presented, for convenience, as a linear flow. But like the author of the models in Figures 1.3 and 1.4, Grayson recognised that the curriculum process is a complex ctivity. *"Each stage involves an iterative procedure, the output of which is evaluated before being used as part of the input to the next stage"*. This approach differs from that of the author of Figures 1.3 and 1.4, who used, as indicated above, a separate model to show the institutional processes at work in designing the curriculum (Figure 1.1). Grayson combined these in the one model.

Grayson pointed out that *"curricula may be organized at two levels. The first approach may be at a broad or macro level, in which decisions are made about the type of courses to be offered, the amount of time to be devoted to each, the way they will be arranged over the program and so forth. Second, the particular content elements and learning activities can be selected and organized to optimize the knowledge gained by the student. This latter approach usually deals with materials within and the relationship between courses and can be based on certain principles of teaching and learning and of curriculum design. The two types of organization may be compared to the adjustment made in tuning a mechanism or an instrument: first gross adjustments are made, and then fine-tuning is carried out."*

Fine-tuning applies to groups of courses as a whole, and is similar to the process implicit in the model in Figure 1.4. Like that model, it requires the application of learning theory. Both models recognize that there is no single theory of learning, and for that reason it is incumbent on a teacher to adopt a defensible theory of learning. Over and above that, it will be argued that teachers should also have a defensible epistemology. While Grayson is one of a few engineers who in the 1960's and 1970's recognized that knowledge of human learning was such that it was no longer possible to concentrate on what the students should know without taking into account how they learn. He evidently saw the latter as part of fine-tuning. In the models in Figures 1.4 and 1.5, it has equal precedence with all the other elements, and it is the iterative interplay with them that makes curriculum design a complex activity. Figure 1.5 is intended to not only illustrate the complexity of the model but also its dynamic nature. In present day language the model is not static and something that is returned to every now and again but something that is continually done.

Shor and Robson (2000) took much the same kind of approach as Grayson to the continuous improvement required by ABET. They pointed out that in the traditional system the student's achievement in relation to outcomes *"is not used to adjust the sequence or nature of the student's educational experiences"*. There is no feedback in the system. However, if there is feedback in the system the process is adjusted to ensure that the output matches the desired output. Clearly, this has implications for both design of assessment and the design of instruction.

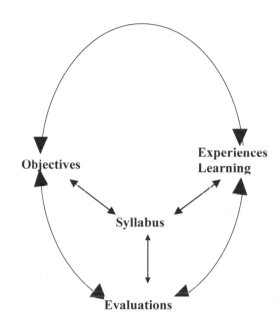

Figure 1.2. The syllabus as the result of the curriculum development and evaluation process. (Reprinted from *Assessment in Mathematics* (PEEP, 1976))

The first implication of the application of these models for the curriculum process, and thus for curriculum design, is that instruction should be designed to achieve specified aims and objectives and that different methods of instruction are more likely to obtain some objectives than others.

As indicated, the models in the illustrations have their origins in the work of Tyler, whose book *The Basic Principles of Curriculum and Instruction* has been described by Jackson (1992) as the Bible of the curriculum.[6] Tyler took the designer away from listing content in the first instance. He proposed that the curriculum designer had to begin, not by listing content,

---

[6] Tyler was not the first educationalist to believe that the curriculum should be defined by objectives. Bobbitt (1924) devised a model that was in many respects similar to Tyler's. It is of interest to engineers because he derived his objectives from human experience. As described by Jackson (1992) Bobbitt's first step was to analyze the broad range of human experience into major fields. (In the case of this text engineering would be a major field). The second step was to take these fields, one after the other, and analyze them into their specific activities. For example, in respect of engineering see Meuwese (1969) and Youngman et al (1978). *"One starts with rather large activities and breaks them up into smaller ones. This process is to continue until the curriculum makers have found the quite specific activities that are to be performed"*. In the activities once discovered one can see the objectives of education (Jackson, 1992).

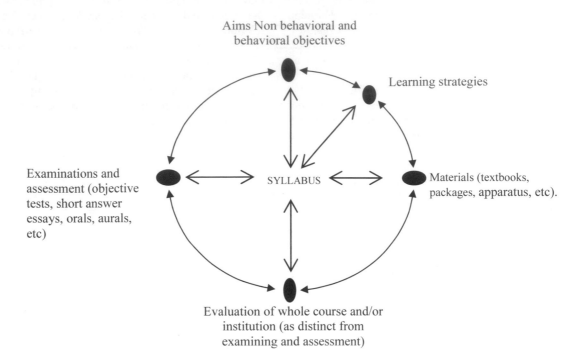

Aims Non behavioral and
behavioral objectives

Learning strategies

Examinations and
assessment (objective
tests, short answer
essays, orals, aurals,
etc)

SYLLABUS

Materials (textbooks,
packages, apparatus, etc).

Evaluation of whole course and/or
institution (as distinct from
examining and assessment)

Figure 1.3. A development of the model in Figure 1.2 to show more fully the assessment curriculum instruction process.

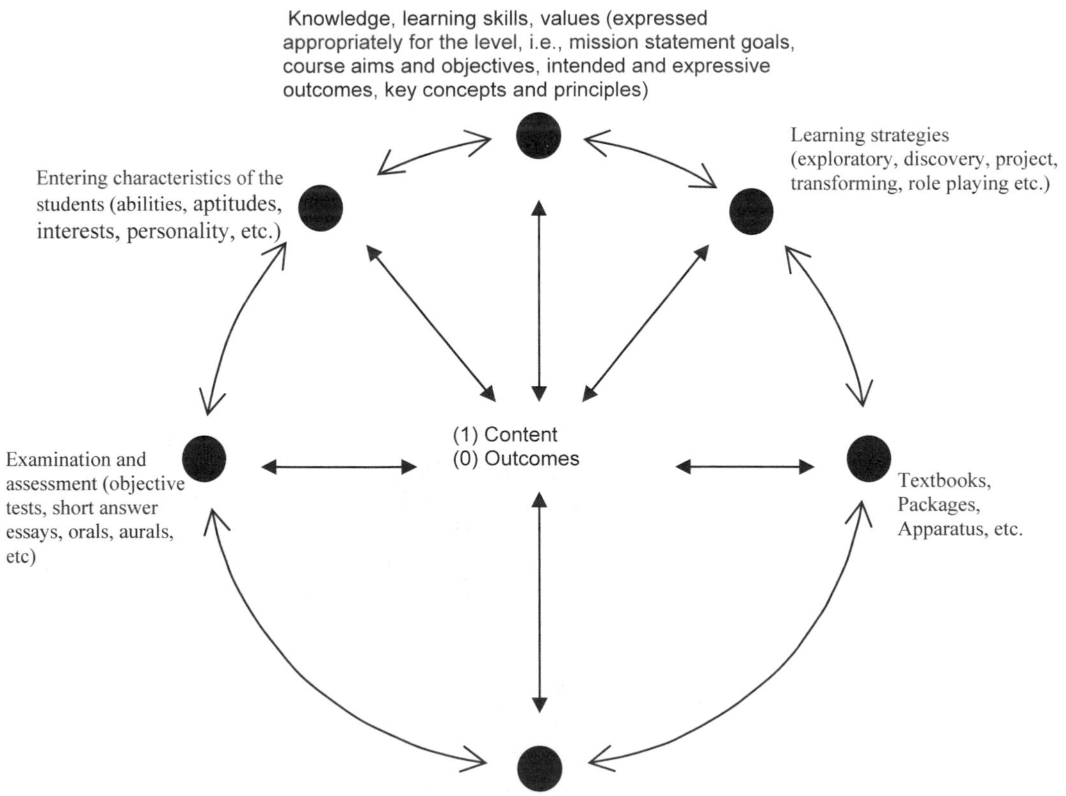

Knowledge, learning skills, values (expressed
appropriately for the level, i.e., mission statement goals,
course aims and objectives, intended and expressive
outcomes, key concepts and principles)

Entering characteristics of the
students (abilities, aptitudes,
interests, personality, etc.)

Learning strategies
(exploratory, discovery, project,
transforming, role playing etc.)

(1) Content
(0) Outcomes

Examination and
assessment (objective
tests, short answer
essays, orals, aurals,
etc)

Textbooks,
Packages,
Apparatus, etc.

Figure 1.4. A development of Figure 1.3 to show the dynamic nature of the process. A model of the assessment, curriculum, learning, teaching process (1) The first phase in which the structure of the syllabus content is derived and (2) how the intended learning outcomes are a function of a complex interaction between all the parameters and allowing that there will also be unintended outcomes. The original model in *Enterprise Learning and Its Assessment in Higher Education* (Technical Report No. 20, Employment Department, Sheffield) referred only to the design of the syllabus while indicating that evaluation took care of the dynamic nature of the model. Professor Georgine Loacker of Alverno College suggested that this dynamism would be better expressed if the model also recorded the outcomes of the on going activity in the centre

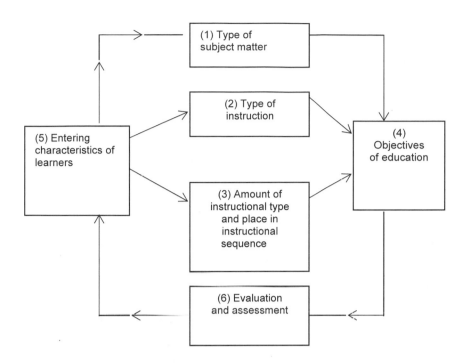

Figure 1.5 Theoretical generalization about the nature of instruction. (Shulman's, 1970, generalization of Cronbach's view of the nature of instruction). Block 6 has been added by this writer. Examples of the variables given by Shulman, (1) content of subject defined in task terms; (2) expository discovery (degree of guidance), inductive, deductive; (3) number of minutes or hours of instruction, position in sequence of instructional types; (4) products, processes, attitudes, self-perception; (5) prior knowledge, aptitude, cognitive style, values; (6) knowledge, comprehension, problem solving skills, etc.

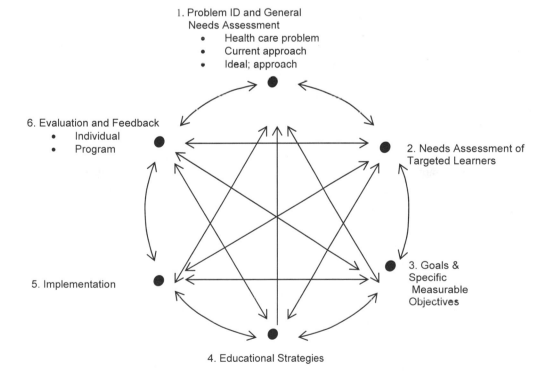

Figure 1.6. A six step approach to curriculum design for medical education (Kewrns, D. E., Thomas, P. A., Howard, D. M and E. B. Bass (1998). *Curriculum Development for Medical Education. A Six-Step Approach.* Reproduced by kind permission The Johns Hopkins University Press.)

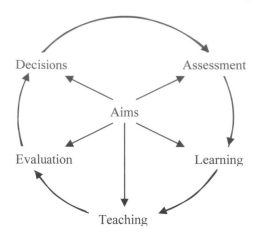

Figure 1.7. A model of the curriculum due to Cowan and Harding (1986). (Reproduced with the permission of J. Cowan)

but by declaring the aims and objectives to be achieved. Once these were understood it would be possible to determine the instructional methods that would create the learning that would achieve those aims and objectives. These are systems models. For example, when they applied the principles of guided design to the design of the curriculum Wales and Stager (1972) were clearly influenced by Tyler among other educators of that era as Waina (1969) acknowledged. The psychological principles they listed are shown in Exhibit 1.2.

Tabulations of method against objectives, method against learning styles, and method against cognitive development have been made by Weston and Cranton (1986), Svinicki and Dixon (1987), and Culver and Hackos (1982). Fromm and Quinn (1989), add the salutary reminder, that revamping a curriculum requires significant changes in attitudes, goals, curriculum content, and teaching methods. And that may not be palatable to many teachers. Hence the requirement that those who would change the curriculum should have an understanding of change and diffusion processes. They would be helped in this matter if those who apply educational theories would agree a common terminology, but sadly this is not the case as the brief section that follows and Chapter 2 will show.

1.5.   Confusion in Terminology

For example, the heading in Figure 1.4 relating to aims and objectives serves to illustrate two points. First is the confusion in terminology that has arisen during the 50 years since Tyler first enunciated his principles of the curriculum. What, for example, are the differences between aims, goals and mission statements? These will be explored below, and in Chapter 2. Second, as will be explained, there has been a marked reluctance to stick to the terminology related to objectives. Today, the term *outcome* is preferred to objectives. Some writers infer differences between objectives and outcomes that were not in the minds of those with   whom the so-called '*objectives movement*' is associated.   In any event the terminology has become thoroughly confused (Heywood,

2000). Yokomoto and Bostwick (1999) summarized the position with respect to ABET's criteria for Ec 2000 as follows: *"Dissimilar words are used as synonyms, such as "outcomes," "attributes," and "competencies to describe what students must demonstrate." Sometimes the term "performance outcome" is used.*

The same applies to the terms assessment and evaluation. In the models, evaluation is now commonly called program assessment. In this way the assessment of student learning becomes confused with programme evaluation (see Chapters 15 and 16).

The second point is that discussion about aims and objectives has been very restricted to the developments associated with Tyler and his colleagues. It tends to ignore content in favor of learning skills in the cognitive, affective and psychomotor domains, yet the understanding of a key concept is as much a learning objective as are the development of skills in analysis and synthesis. It also undervalued statements of aims or goals, and in consequence, the effects of the institutional mission on the curriculum, and it caused teachers to ignore process in favor of product (Knight, 2001).

1.6. The Curriculum Process in Action. An Illustration

As indicated previously, these models are unusual in that they incorporate the syllabus (content). They are intended to illustrate the syllabus as being the outcome of a complex design activity involving the declaration of objectives and the simultaneous design of assessment and instruction procedures that will cause those objectives to be obtained.

The process may be illustrated by consideration of the student complaint that courses are overloaded. By this they mean that the syllabuses are so detailed that they cannot be covered adequately by the teacher or themselves in the time allowed. This does not, however, mean that they would want the course lengthened. Seymour and Hewitt (1997) found that science and engineering students in the United States, (in the sample they interviewed), already felt that the courses were long enough. All of this raises the question as to whether all the material that is put into courses is essential. Very occasionally engineering tutors have suggested that the length of courses might be reduced (e.g. Swaim and Moretti, 1991).Van Valkenburg (1991) had an article entitled *"Too many topics, covered too fast."* But, it is this writer's experience that those concerned with the design of new courses tend to overload them with content and subsequently face the task of reducing them. He has been found guilty of this offense (Heywood, 2000). There is also the problem of information overload (Rockland, 2000).

At the same time, length of course has been a key factor in the professional judgment of the standard of courses. Thus, when in the 1980's comparisons were made between engineering courses in England and Germany, there was a demand in England for enhanced courses of 4 years duration instead of 3. (Jordan and

Carter, 1986).[7] By contrast, at least one American comparative study of programs in Europe concluded that American programs were too short (Dorato and Abdallah, 1993), although there has been at least one plea for a reduction in the credit hours for the BS degree in the United States (Swaim and Moretti, 1991). The Goals of Engineering Education Final Report (ASEE, 1968a) said: *Engineering education...has attempted to provide within the confines of a traditional four-year period both a broad general education and a specialized technical education of great and growing complexity.*

The point here is that it is only by following the curriculum design procedures outlined below that a satisfactory teaching, learning syllabus can be defined within the time constraints available.

To determine whether or not a course would be overloaded the estimates of times taken for each instructional procedure required for the learning of a key concept or a higher-order thinking skill are summed. If the sum of the periods required to complete all these strategies comes to more than the time allowed for the course, then the course is overloaded. This is irrespective of any overloading caused by home study requirements. Therefore, the tutor should be prepared to reduce the number of key concepts, and/or higher order skills taught. This will involve him or her in a ranking exercise.

Tutors have to cope with the reality of learning, which is, that the rate of internalization necessary for understanding is, relatively slow for many students.

Stice (1976) quoted in full in Chapter 2 reported that the use of objectives helped him distinguish between essential and nice-to know knowledge. This enabled him to cover a course that had never been fully covered before.

Mansfield (1979) writing about the design of mini courses said, *"try to be as realistic as possible, total up the times for all activities on your mini-course outline. Adjust any item to meet the overall goal within the allotted time trading, deleting activities or even reducing the number of realizable objectives.*

Alternatively, consider providing more total time for the course ... .be brutally honest in your time estimates."[8] This is why the syllabus (content) has been put at the centre of these models because it is the outcome of the design process and not its beginning (e.g., Figure 1.4). It is also the reason why the key concepts to be

considered are as much a component of the objectives as are the statement of skills that have come to be associated with objectives (e.g., problem solving, critical thinking). Transfer of learning will not be obtained without an understanding of the appropriate principles and concepts. For this reason a teacher should concentrate on ensuring that these concepts and principles are understood even if that means that some parts of the course cannot be covered. Wales and Stager (1972) recognized the importance of concept learning, as well as higher-order thinking as the illustrations taken from their paper in Exhibit 1.3 show. How concepts are learned will be discussed in Chapter 4. The selection of key concepts for the curriculum is a critical stage in the process of curriculum design, as is the evaluation of whether or not they have been learned (see Chapter 4).

The same general principles apply to the development of a program. It is possible to fit the models so that they will derive the subjects that would make up a whole discipline-based program, as, for example the work undertaken in Thailand by Yeomans and Atrens (2001). They derived their objectives from those stated by the Institute of Engineers of Australia. The same can be said of the course development matrix suggested by Sinclair and Bordeaux (1999).

1.7.   Assessment and Evaluation

As indicated above assessment and evaluation are also terms that have had a chequered history. In present-day parlance assessment is sometimes used in place of evaluation (see Chapter 15). In Figures 1.3 and 1.4 assessment has been separated from evaluation. Assessment is taken to mean the assessment of student learning by tests of some form another for the purposes of grading. It may include both summative and formative components.[9] The inclusion of the term examinations reflects the different educational cultures prevailing in the United Kingdom including those countries whose education systems derive from the United Kingdom (e.g. Australia, Ireland), and the United States. Evaluation is intended to indicate something that is broader in intent and takes into account all the factors that contribute to course design and student learning including the quality of teaching. It would embrace the term program assessment which is now in common usage. The term evaluation is preferred because there is a very substantial literature on the theory and practice of evaluation. The theory and practice of evaluation will be considered in detail in Chapters 15 and 16. A key role for evaluation in these models is to ensure that there are no mismatches between (a) the assessment strategies for checking that outcomes have been obtained, and (b) the learning

---

[7]Monograph published from The University of Salford circa 1986. Contains detailed discussion of the meaning of enhancement. Initially eight universities were selected to offer enhanced courses. Now it is expected that a chartered engineer will have pursued a 4 year course resulting in an M.Eng degree.

[8]On the assumption that the syllabus must remain the same Felder, Stice and Rugarcia (2000) cite Felder and Brent who argued that much of the material that is used in lectures can be assigned to handouts or even a coursework pack. The handouts should have spaces for the students to fill in missing steps. I have used this technique, but at the appropriate point I told the students what to put in the space. The blanks were always for key concepts or important principles. In another course a self-study guide was designed to accompany the lectures (Heywood and Montagu Pollock, 1977).

---

[9]Summative refers to what is often termed the final exam. In some systems, feedback about performance might be given to a student. In other systems, no information is given. In systems that make performance assessments during the course, feedback is likely to be given, and sometimes this may be diagnostic. In any case, such information is formative.

strategies implemented to bring about these outcomes. Often innovations are made in assessment that are not reflected in the learning strategies desired to bring about improvements in performance (e.g. Segers and Dochy 2001, see Chapter 16). The expertise that is required will depend on the level at which it is practiced.

Accrediting institutions often require that the student participants evaluate the course. There have been two consequences of this requirement. The first has been a massive research effort to discover the validity and: reliability of student rating questionnaires. The second has been that teacher's and program designers feel that all that is necessary for the evaluation of an innovation is the collection of student opinion by means of either a discussion or a questionnaire. Many of the innovations described in the engineering education literature report evaluations of this kind. However, such evaluation is inadequate more often than not.

There is, of course, a point at which there is a conjunction between the assessment of student learning and evaluation. In this respect a first level of evaluation is exemplified by the classroom assessment techniques (CAT's) developed by Angelo and Cross (1993). They described 52 such techniques. A distinction was, however, made between these techniques and classroom research, which is a more substantial exercise (Cross and Steadman, 1996). To illustrate this point, they suggested a number of simple ideas for "probing" the prior knowledge that students have. Responses to the "probes" were not meant to be graded. This meant that the teacher could hope to ask questions that would yield "thoughtful answers." Another example is the use of concept maps to evaluate the student's ability to think holistically.

A second level of evaluation is classroom research. Neither classroom assessment techniques nor classroom research are solely concerned with the evaluation of cognitive achievement. They are equally concerned with, for example, the assessment of attitudes. However, classroom research and more generally research that is able to obtain data from engineering students as a group is more likely to be able to evaluate in more depth those factors that contribute to performance. The first two levels of curriculum leadership correspond with these levels of evaluation.

1.8. The Role of the Teacher Institution in the Curriculum Process

If the instructional methods should be designed to meet objectives, so too should the procedures for assessment. It is for this reason that a single method of assessment is unlikely to assess whether all the objectives are being obtained. In these models assessment is an integral part of the curriculum process. These models are multiple-strategy in their approach. Whether they focus on the design of the curriculum, or a method of instruction, or an assessment procedure, or learning, or even the evaluation of an institution, the starting point is the same. It is the understanding and expression of what we are trying to do in the parlance of the day (e.g.

outcomes). Whether it is at the level of the program, a specific course, a topic, or a classroom session their objectives (outcomes) derive from the mission statement of the institution. In its turn the institution is responsible for the resources and organizational structure that will bring about these ends. This point was illustrated in Figure 1.1.

Given this understanding of the curriculum process then, subject to the rules of the department, institution or professional body the role of the teacher is to:

1. Determine the aims and objectives (outcomes) that are to be obtained by screening.
2. Determine the instructional methods to be used to obtain the aims and objectives (outcomes).
3. Determine the sequence of instruction.
4. Evaluate the extent to which the aims and objectives (outcomes) have been achieved.

At the department level this model implies that the following questions should be addressed:

- What educational purposes should the school (engineering department) seek to obtain?
- What educational experiences can be provided which are likely to attain these purposes?
- How can these educational experiences be effectively organized?
- How can we determine whether these purposes are being attained?

1.9. Establishing Aims and Objectives (outcomes). The Process of Screening

As Furst (1958) recognized the problem with lists of aims and objectives is that it is very easy to generate long lists. These can become as self-defeating as a long list of content and may end up being just that. Unless objectives, or outcomes, call them what you will, are strictly limited, their number is likely to overload courses as teachers struggle to obtain them. Applied to the goals of an institution, Furst (1958) pointed out that *"some of these goals will be more important than others; and some will be inconsistent in the sense that they call for contradictory patterns of behaviour. Clearly the school (institution) must choose a small number of important and consistent goals that can be attained in the time available."* (p, 39).

This applies at all levels of the educational process be it at the level of policy or the level of the curriculum. Helsby (1999) has shown how government policies to school education in the United Kingdom have been contradictory. With respect to engineering programs and course design, it has been argued that the number of domain objectives should be limited to only those that are significant, and that within them the sub-abilities to be tested should also be limited (Heywood, 1989).

Furst (1958) argued that in order to choose these domains, the lists that are developed have to be screened for consistency and significance. He argued that the

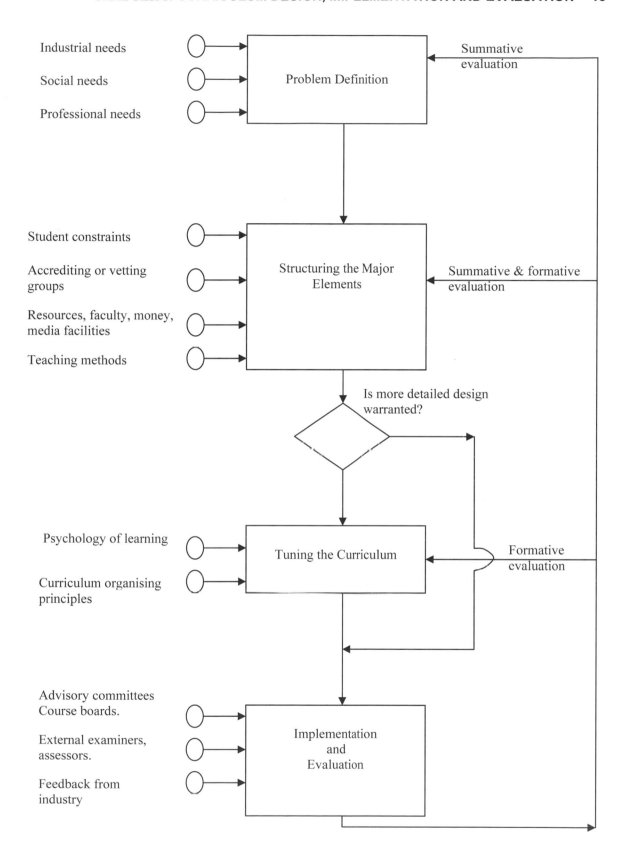

Figure 1.8: Grayson's model of the curriculum process. (Reproduced with the permission of Lawrence, P. Grayson).

Organize the Subject Matter for Presentation to the Student.

    1.   Identify the specific concepts and principles the student must learn.
    2.   Arrange the concepts and principles in sequence from simple to complicated.
    3.   Provide Organizers (9a) verbal, and visual, and (b) concrete empirical illustrations and analogies.

Organize the Student's Practice of the Intellectual Modes and Abilities.

    1.   Identify the specific modes and abilities the student will practice.
    2.   Integrate these modes and abilities with content.

Organize the Student's Intellectual Development.

    1.   Guide the student as he/she learns.
        (a)   Demonstrate or model and/or provide a situation in which the student can experiment
            and/or discover the desired behavior.
        (b)   Supervise the student's initial trials.
        (c)   Use the necessary prompts. Withdraw this support gradually as the student's ability develops.
        (d)   Describe to the student the intellectual modes and abilities involved in his work and relate each to specific
            activities.
        (e)   Help the student to learn to evaluate his own performance.

    2   Provide for practice.
        (f)   Ensure that the student is active.
        (g)   Pace his work, spaced practice is best.
        (h)   Vary the context.

    3   Evaluate and provide feedback.
        (a)   To reinforce correct responses.
        (b)   To correct inadequate responses.
        (c)   Immediately during initial learning.
        (d)   Frequently thereafter.
        (e)   Formative: provide the student with diagnostic progress information about his performance.
        (f)   Summative: Determine if the student has mastered stated objectives and is ready to move on.

    4   Motivate.
        (a)   Encourage the desired behaviour.
        (b)   Show the value of (1) learning, (2) the concepts and principles to be learned by showing their relevance to
            meaningful work.
        (c)   Help the student achieve success.

    5   Individualize.
        (a)   Provide for students who learn at different rates.
        (b)   Enrichment for the fast learner.
        (c)   Extra help for the slow learner.

Exhibit 1.2. The late Wales and Stager's (1972) list of psychological principles involved in curriculum and instruction.

Intellectual Ability	Action
Recall	Write the concept.
Manipulation	Restate the concept in a new form
Translate.	Convert the concept from verbal to graphical or symbolic form.
Interpret.	State the results derived from the use of the concept.
Predict.	State the expected effect of the concept.
Choose	Independently select the concept and use it to solve a problem.
(b) Content-performance objectives for decision making;	
At the end of a period of study, each student should be able to solve an open-ended problem using: **Decision- making skill**	**Action**
Gather information	Gather required information from appropriate sources
Problem identification.	State the basic objective of the project
Basic objective	State the basic objective of the project.
Constraints/assumptions	List the constraints assumptions which affect the project.
Possible solutions	
Analysis	Generate possible solutions which appear to meet the objective.
Synthesis	Combine elements from many sources into a pattern not previously known to the student.
Evaluation	Make purposeful judgements about the value of ideas, methods, designs of defects.
Report	Report the results and make recommendations.
Action.	Implement decision.

Exhibit 1.3. The late C.E.Wales and R.A. Stager's (1972) concept performance objectives for a concept and decision making.

educational and social philosophy to which the school (department or institution) is committed should provide.the first screen. In the first instance, it is concerned with the mission statement that should raise key questions

His examples of such questions for schools (presented in italics) are highly relevant to engineering education, as the text in normal type shows, even though they do not use today's terminology. The questions included, *Should the school prepare young people to accept the present social order?* (Should engineering students be prepared to accept the current mores of the engineering profession, or should they be enabled to review and challenge them?) *Should different social groups or classes receive different kinds of education?* (Should minorities receive different kinds of engineering education? Should engineering

education be designed to cater for different personality types?)

Should the school (engineering department) *try to make people alike or should it cultivate idiosyncrasy?* (Should an engineering department encourage creative and innovative behaviour among its students?)

Should the school emphasize general education or should it aim at specific vocational education? (What is the role of general/liberal education in engineering education?)

There is much in the engineering literature that deals with such issues. Furst's point was that the education that will be provided is a function of the stance taken on such issues. He pointed out that if a school prepares students for the present social order, it should emphasize conformity and emphasize mastery of fairly stable and well organized bodies of knowledge Whereas if a school wants to encourage students to improve society, it will emphasize sensitivity to social problems, skills in analysing problems and proposing solutions, independence and self direction, freedom of inquiry, and self-discipline (p, 40). Answers to these questions have to be consistent and not contradictory. He described in great detail how philosophy functioned in the formulation of content in the program of general education in the University of Chicago, at that time

Furst also argued that the psychology of learning and human development should serve as a second screen for selecting and eliminating goals. As with philosophy he offered a series of questions that might be asked. Three of these follow:
At what level of maturity are particular objectives obtained?

What is the optimum growth that may be expected of different kinds of student with respect to the objectives? (Should an engineering school design its curriculum to take into account the cognitive and emotional development of students?)

What is the transfer value of different kinds of outcome? (Answers to this question should be helpful in evaluating a curriculum that is said to be overloaded.

In a different context the National Post-Secondary Education Cooperative (NEPC, 1977) suggested criteria for the screening of policy performance indicators. The conceptual criteria for their first screen were relevance, utility and applicability. The conceptual criteria for their second screen were interpretability, credibility, and fairness. Their methodological criteria for the third screen were scope, availability, measurability and costs. They said that, *"conceptual criteria involve philosophical and political considerations. They can be thought of as a set of questions relating to the question 'Why should this outcome be included in the data set under development?' Methodological criteria involve technical issues of measurement availability and data collection design.. methodological questions ask 'How sound is the data likely to be?*

It is evident from the foregoing, and as at least one illustration of its use in engineering showed, that screening is by no means an easy task (Heywood, 1981; see also Staiger, 1983). It should also be evident that satisfactory answers to these questions will entail knowledge of philosophy, sociology, and psychology as they are applied to pedagogy. In so far as the design and implementation of the curriculum is concerned Furst (1958) argued, that every teacher should have a defensible theory of learning, and that must go for philosophy as well. The need to screen aims and objectives provides the rationale for including the study of appropriate philosophy, psychology, and sociology in the student teacher's curriculum. Similarly, it is the rationale for curriculum leaders in engineering education to be conversant in these areas in order that they can advise and lead in the design and evaluation of the curriculum and its renewal.

As Furst's illustration of the curriculum in general education at the University of Chicago showed, curriculum designers should approach the curriculum from the perspective of philosophy, sociology and psychology and not from the perspective of the syllabus. There are many curriculum frameworks. The most appropriate one should result from the exercise of screening. It is a substantial process as a group of designers in the engineering curriculum have shown (Heywood et al, 1966). In general education the recent report of the development of the assessment led curriculum at Alverno College more than adequately illustrates the process (Mentkowski and associates, 2000). The general idea is well illustrated by Sherren and Long (1972), who argued that engineering educators must take into account philosophy, alternative educational theories, and alternative psychological theories of learning (see Chapter 3). It is a complex process. It is not simply a matter of defining outcomes that can be tested or of relating teaching methods and assessments to those outcomes. Strong support for this thesis is provided by Felder and Brent's (2003) paper on the design of teaching courses to satisfy ABET criteria.[10] This discussion continues in Chapter 2.

It is part of the purpose of this book to, (a) explore the knowledge required for this to be achieved, and (b) illustrate from research and practice in the engineering curriculum.

1.10.   Conclusion

Irrespective of the model that is used

1. Curriculum design, assessment and evaluation begin at the same point. That is the understanding and expression of what it is we are trying to do.
2. For each general objective there will be an appropriate method of testing, and that may not be of a traditional kind.
3. Specific learning strategies will be required if the objectives are to be successfully obtained, and this requires an understanding of the complexity of learning.
4. A multiple strategy approach to teaching, learning and assessment will be required
5. The combination of all these elements may lead to a substantial reorganization of the syllabus and approaches to teaching and learning.
6. This may require a substantial change in culture of the organizational unit responsible for the delivery of the curriculum

An integrated approach of this kind demands a considerable change on the part of the teacher to the planning and implementation of the curriculum. While curriculum design and change require knowledge of philosophy, sociology, and psychology as they are applied to education, change is unlikely to be accomplished, unless it is shown to follow from the notional aims to which teachers in higher education are attached. (Yeomans and Atrens; 2001).

In the Chapters that follow in part 1, the concern is with how we arrive at statements of aims and objectives (outcomes). In Chapter 2 the so-called 'objectives' approach is discussed and some methods for deriving objectives considered. Since, the danger is that long lists are produced, the question arises as to how they might be screened for relative importance and also avoid any internal contradictions. How this may be accomplished by applying philosophy, sociology, and history[11] is the subject of Chapter 3, and psychology as it is applied to the learning of concepts and principles, the understanding of our learning dispositions and cognitive development is considered in Chapters, 4, 5,and 6.

References

Angelo, T. and P. K. Cross (1993). *Classroom Assessment Techniques.* Jossey Bass, San Francisco.
ASEE (1968a). *Goals of Engineering Education.* Final Report. American Society for Engineering Education, Washington, DC.
ASEE (1968b).Liberal Learning for the Engineer. *Engineering Education,* 59, (4),303-340.

Bobbitt, F.J. (1924). *How to Make a Curriculum.* Houghton Mifflin, Boston, MA.
Brown, K (1998) SARTOR 97: the background and looming shake-up for university engineering departments. *Engineering Science and Education Journal.* Feb. pp 41-48

Carter, G., and T. R. Jordan (1986) *Student Centred Learning. Engineering Enhancement in Higher Education.* Monograph. University of Salford.

---

[10] The reader interested in the history of curriculum change in engineering will find a paper on managing engineering education by Staiger (1983) of interest Like Felder and Brent he included a bibliography relevant to the design of the curriculum.

[11] The recent publication of *Retooling: A Historian Confronts Technological Change* by R. Williams (2002) (MIT Press) proposes a thesis that would have profound implications for engineering education

Cowan, J and A. G. Harding (1986). A logical model for curriculum development. *British Journal of Educational Technology*. 2, (17), 103 – 109.

Cronbach, L (1957). The two disciplines of scientific psychology. *American Psychologist*, 671-684.

Cross, P. K., and M. Steadman (1996) *Classroom Research. Implementing the Scholarship of Teaching*. Jossey Bass, San Francisco.

Culler, A .D. (1955). *The Imperial Intellect. A Study of Newman's Educational Ideal*. Yale U.P., New Haven, Conn.

Culver, R.S. and J.T. Hackos (1982). Perry's model of intellectual development. *Engineering Education*. 73, (2), 221-226.

Dorato, P. and C. Abdallah (1993). A survey of engineering education outside the United States: Implications for the ideal engineering program. *Journal of Engineering Education*. 82, (4), 212-215.

Feilden, G (1963). (Chairman of a Committee). *Engineering Design*. Department of Scientific and Industrial Research. HMSO, London.

Felder, R. M and R. Brent (2003). Designing and teaching courses to satisfy the ABET engineering criteria. *Journal of Engineering Education*, 92, (1), 7 – 28.

Felder, R. M., Stice, J., and A. Rugarcia. The future of engineering education VI. Making reform happen. *Chemical Engineering Education*. 34, (3), 208-215.

Finniston, M. (1980). *Engineering our Future*. Report of a Committee of Enquiry into the Engineering Profession. Cmnd 7794. Her Majesty's Stationery Office, London.

Fromm, E. G. and R. G. Quinn (1989). An experiment to enhance the educational experience of engineering students. *Engineering Education*, 79, (3), 424 – 429.

Furst, E.J (1958). *The Construction of Evaluation Instruments*. David McKay, New York

Grayson, L (1978). On a methodology for curriculum design. *Engineering Education*. 69, (3), 285-295.

Grinter, L. E (1955). *Report on the Evaluation of Engineering Education*. American Society for Engineering Education. Washington, DC

Haws, E. D (2001) Ethics instruction in engineering education: a (mini) meta-analysis. *Journal of Engineering Education*. 90, (2), 223-231.

Helsby, G. (1999). *Changing Teachers Work*. Open University Press, Buckingham.

Heywood, J (1969). An Evaluation of Certain Post-War Developments in Technological Education. Thesis. University of Lancaster, Lancaster. UK

Heywood, J (1977). *Assessment in Higher Education*. 1st Edition Wiley, Chichester.

Heywood, J (1981). The Academic versus practical debate: a case study in screening. *Institution of Electrical Engineers Proceedings*. PART A, 128, (7), 511-519.

Heywood, J (1989). Problems in the evaluation of focussing objectives and their implications for the design of systems models of the curriculum with special reference to comprehensive examinations. *Proceedings of the Frontiers in Education Conference*. pp. 235-241.

Heywood, J (2000). *Assessment in Higher Education. Student Learning, Teaching, Programmes and Institutions*. Jessica Kingsley, London.

Heywood, J., Lee, L. S., Monk, J. D., Rowley, B. G. H., Turner, B. T. and J. Vogler (1966). The Education of Professional Engineers for Design and manufacture. *Lancaster Studies in Higher Education*, No 1. pp. 1-104.

Heywood, J. and H. Montagu Pollock (1977). *Science for Arts Students. A Case Study in Curriculum Development*. Society for Research into Higher Education, London.

Jackson, P. W. (1992). Conceptions of the curriculum and curriculum specialists. In P. W. Jackson (ed). *Handbook of Research on the Curriculum*. American Educational Research Association, Macmillan, New York.

Kerns, D. E., Thomas, P. A., Howard, D. M., and E. B. Bass (1998). *Curriculum Development for Medical Education. A Six-Step Approach*. The Johns Hopkins University Press, Baltimore.

Knight, P.T (2001) Complexity and curriculum: a process approach to curriculum making. *Teaching in Higher Education*. 6, (3), 236-251.

McGrath, F (1962). *The Consecration of Learning*, Gill, Dublin.

Mansfield, G (1979). Designing your own mini course. *Engineering Education*. 70, (2), 205-207.

Mentkowski, M and Associates (2000). *Learning that Lasts. Integrating Learning, Development, and Performance in College and Beyond*. Jossey Bass, San Fransisco.

Meuwese, W (1968). Measurement of Industrial Engineering Objectives. 16th International Congress of Applied Psychology, Amsterdam.

Midwinter, J. E (2000). Something old, somethoing new and something just in time: dilemmas for EE education and training. *Engineering Science and Education Journal*. October (5, 219 –230

NEPC. (1977). *Student Outcomes Information Policy*. Council for National Post-Secondary Cooperative. Washington, DC.

Nichols, J.O. (1991). *A Practitioners Handbook for Institutional Effectiveness and Student Outcomes Assessment Implementation*. Agathon Press, New York.

Payne, G. L (1960) *Britain's Scientific and Technological Manpower*. Oxford University Press, Oxford.

PEEP (1976). *Assessment in Mathematics*. Report No 2. Public Examinations Evaluations Project. School of Education, University of Dublin, Dublin.

Rockland, R. H (2000). Reducing the information overload: a method on helping students research engineering topics using the internet. *IEEE Transactions on Education*, 43, (4), 420- 425.

Rugarcia, A., Felder, R. M.., Woods, D. R., and J. E. Stice (2000). The future of engineering education. I. A vision for a new century. *Chemical Engineering Education*, 34, (1), 16-25.

Segers, M and F. Dochy (2001). New assessment forms in problem-based learning: the value added of the students perspective. *Studies in Higher Education*, 26, (3), 327 – 343.

Seymour, E and N.M. Hewitt.(1997). *Talking About Leaving. Why Undergraduates Leave the Science*. Westview Press, Boulder, Co.

Sherren, D. C. and T. R. Long (1972). The educator's dilemma: What makes Clyde want to learn? *Engineering Education*, 63, (3), 188-190.

Sheppard, S (2001) Status Report on- Taking Stock- Engineering Education at the end of the twentieth century and beyond. Carnegie Foundation for the Advancement of Teaching. Menlo Park, CA

Sinclair, J. B., and J. D. Bordeaux. (1999) The course development matrix. A tool for improving programme development. *Proceedings Frontiers in Education Conference* 13b1-14 to 19.

Shor, M. H and R. Robson (2000) A student-centred feedback control model of the educational process. *Proceedings Frontiers in Education Conference*, 3, S1A- 14 to 19.

Shulman, L. S (1970) Psychology and mathematics education in E. Begle (ed) *Mathematics in Education*. 69th Year book of the National Society for the Study of education. University of Chicago Press, Chicago.

Staiger, E. H. (1983). Managing engineering education. *Engineering Education*, December, 152- 156.

Stice, J. E (1976) A first step towards improved teaching. *Engineering Education* 70, (2), 175-180.

Svinicki, M. D and N. M. Dixon (1987). The Kolb Model modified for classroom activities. *College Teaching*, 35, (4), 141-146.

Swaim. M. and P. M. Moretti (1991). The case for the 120 credit-hour B.S. *Engineering Education*, 81, (5), 463-465.

Tyler, R. W (1949) *Basic Principles of Curriculum and Instruction*. University of Chicago Press, Chicago.

van Valkenburg, M (1991). Too many topics, covered too fast. *Engineering Education*, 81, (3), 394.

Waina, R. H (1969). System design of the curriculum. *Engineering Education.* 60, (2), 97-99.

Wales, C. E. and R. A. Stager (1972). The design of an educational system. *Engineering Education*, 62, (5), 456-459.

Walkington, J (2002). Curriculum change in engineering. *European Journal of Engineering Education* 27, (2), 133 - 148

Weston, C. .A. and P. A. Cranton (1986). Selecting instructional strategies. *Journal of Higher Education*, 57, (3), 259-288.

Whitehead, A. .N. (1932). *The Aims of Education and other Essays.* Benn, Edinburgh.

Williams, R (2002). *Retooling: A Historian Confronts Technological Change.* MIT Press, Cambridge, MA.

Yeomans, S. R and A. Atrens (2001). A methodology for discipline-specific curriculum development. *International Journal of Engineering education*, 17, (6), 518 – 524.

Yokomoto, C. F., and W. D. Bostwick (1999). Modeling the process of writing measurable outcomes for Ec 2000. *Proceedings Frontiers in Education Conference*, 2, 11b1, 18 to 22.

Youngman, M.B., Oxtoby, R., Monk, J. D. and J. Heywood (1978) *Analysing Jobs.* Gower Press, Aldershot.

CHAPTER 2: AIMS AND OBJECTIVES (OUTCOMES)

Summary and introduction

Engineering educators the world over are now required to state the aims and objectives, or 'outcomes' as they have come to be known, of their programs and courses. As explained in Chapter 1 this is the beginning of the curriculum process, and whether it is the design of assessment or instruction or the curriculum as a whole the first step is to declare aims and objectives-behavioral and non-behavioral. There are many sources of aims and objectives that can lead to statements of performance outcomes. The first purpose of this Chapter is to outline the sources of objectives, (and methods for their derivation) that are pertinent to engineering education. To achieve this goal,, some cognisance, of what is sometimes known as the "objectives movement," is appropriate because work undertaken in the 1950's continues to influence engineering educators. It will also help to achieve a second objective, namely to account for the confusion in terminology that has arisen. This, as will be shown, has considerable implications for the educator since it is full of ambiguities.

Arguments for approaching curriculum design in this way can be traced back to the nineteenth century. However, in this text the point of entry is the same as that taken in Chapter 1, namely with the seminal study of Ralph Tyler (1949) on the curriculum. By 1954 a group of educators, who counted Tyler among their number, had produced The Taxonomy of Educational Objectives for the cognitive domain (Bloom, 1956). Its purpose was to provide a common framework for testing. Its authors proposed that there is, beyond the acquisition of knowledge and comprehension, a hierarchy of skills involved in all learning. They were application, analysis, synthesis, and evaluation. Many engineering educators have been influenced by his Taxonomy, and some continue to use it in its original form.

A third purpose of this Chapter is to illustrate how engineers have used or been influenced by The Taxonomy, the limitations they have found, and the developments of this idea that they have made. These include a study of its relation to the ABET EC 2000 criteria (Besterfield-Sacre et al, 2000), and a study of its use in the development of a curriculum in engineering science illustrates how the idea of multiple strategy assessment and instruction was conceived in Britain (Carter, Heywood, and Kelly, 1986).[1]

The authors of The Taxonomy recognized that it could not apply to every subject, and this has been the experience of some engineering educators when they came to design a curriculum. Geometrical and Engineering Drawing in the United Kingdom is a case in point. At the same time the idea that there are ability domains within the cognitive skill category has been acknowledged, although surveys of alumni and task analyzes of engineers at work have led to different conceptualizations of what these domains might be.

More generally, in the world of education, The Taxonomy has been subject to considerable criticism. It was argued, for example, that all education should proceed from pre-formulated goals. Teachers should be able to plan for the expressive in the curriculum (Eisner, 1979). The relevance of this point to creativity in engineering will be apparent. But the achievement of an expressive end is an objective, and if this view is accepted, it broadens what is understood by objectives. As indicated in Chapter 1, just such a broad view is taken, although it is predicated on the proposition that teachers should be able to declare where they are going in order that they may evaluate (assess) when they have arrived.

However, there are many sources of objectives. Among them are alumni surveys and analyzes of what engineers do. These are considered in part 2 of the Chapter. That part also takes account of the transition from college to work. Preparation for work is reinforced if the curriculum attends to (a) the development of the generic skills revealed in these studies of engineers at work, and (b) their attitudes to the curriculum they received. Alumni studies are also important since they take into account the general environment in which learning takes place.

The data reveal other important domains of communication, diagnosis, management and organizing, team work and problem solving. Although the authors of The Taxonomy showed how it covered problem solving, there are teachers who prefer to think of problem solving as an identifiable category. Necessarily, it would involve the higher order thinking skills of The Taxonomy. The role of the curriculum designer is to select the generic skills on which the proposed curriculum is to be based. It is evident that those listed above encompass cognitive and affective behaviors.

Part 3 gives a brief summary of the Taxonomy of Educational Objectives in the affective domain. Although educators took very little notice of this domain and concentrated on the cognitive dimension, it is not, in reality, possible to separate the domains in this way. The affective domain is becoming increasingly important with the emphasis that is being placed in engineering curricula on group and teamwork and the development of professional attitudes.

It is evident that there are many sources of aims and objectives. It may be argued that for the most part, program and learning objectives should be intimately related, and that program objectives should be presented as domains with sub-abilities that clearly indicate the learning objectives to be obtained. More general objectives should relate the general experience of college as it should enhance learning.

The danger is that curriculum designers will, whether of programs, courses or instructional periods, choose too many aims and objectives, and in overloading the students achieve none of them. The Chapter ends therefore, with the view that the derivation of objectives

---

[1] Its use in the United States is described in Chapter 15.

(outcomes) is not a simple matter and requires the application of philosophy, sociology and psychology as they are applied to education to their determination. Each of these dimensions is reviewed in Chapters, 3, 4, 5, and 6 from the perspective of the literature of engineering education. It also benefits from an understanding of the historical process that has brought the curriculum to where it is.

For convenience, as indicated above, this Chapter is divided into three parts, each with its own summary.

Part 1: Summary

The origins of The Taxonomy are described. A few examples of its use in engineering classrooms are given, and engineering's contribution to the terminological confusion is discussed. The advantages and disadvantages of behavioral objectives are listed, and the significance of the "expressive" in education is considered.

The fourth section considers the influence of The Taxonomy on engineering education and shows how it has been used directly, and adapted. Reference is made to its relation to the ABET EC2000 criteria. The development of a multiple strategy examination in engineering science is described and the integrated relationships between the methods of teaching and learning has been discussed.

2. Origins

Although the idea that schools should declare their objectives has a long history (e.g. Bobbitt, 1924 cited by Jackson, 1992), the starting point for this section is based on Ralph Tyler's (1949) *Basic Principles of the Curriculum and Instruction*. As we have seen in Chapter 1 he proposed that the curriculum designer and/or teacher should begin by declaring the aims and objectives that were to be achieved. Tyler took part in a number of conferences with a group of educators which took place between 1949 and 1953 to develop a taxonomy that would help educators *"evaluate the learning of students systematically"* (Bloom, 1994). It was aimed at college and university examiners, although it would apply at school level. This group believed *"that some common framework used by all college and university examiners could do much to promote the exchange of test materials and ideas for testing ... .After considerable discussion there was agreement that the framework might be best obtained through a system of classifying goals of the educational process using objectives"* (Bloom, 1994).

As this group developed the taxonomy they became aware, "that too much emphasis was being placed on the lowest level of the taxonomy-'knowledge'. Frequently as much as 90% of instructional time was spent at this level, with very little time spent on the higher mental processes that would enable students to apply their knowledge creatively."

Since the cognitive domain of the taxonomy was published in 1956 it has had a profound influence on many educators and educational practices both at school and post-school levels. Some engineering teachers have used it, and continue to use it in its original form (e.g., Hoyt and Prince, 2002; Kashy et al, 2001). The Wave Concepts Inventory is based on The Taxonomy (Rhoads and Roedel, 1999). Others have adapted the idea directly while others have wanted to change the vocabulary. In any event, the vocabulary has become thoroughly confused and confusing as was indicated in Chapter 1.

There is little doubt that the so-called "outcomes movement" has its origins in *The Taxonomy of Educational Objectives*. As such, it remains of considerable interest to engineering educators, and many continue to use it as a base for curriculum understanding (e.g., Apple et al, 2002; Prince and Hoyt, 2002; Striegel and Rover, 2002). An understanding of its development may help resolve some of the terminological inexactitudes that Yokomoto and Bostwick described (see Chapter 1).

2.1. Introducing the Idea of the Taxonomy of Educational Objectives

The group had the intention of developing taxonomies in the affective, cognitive and psychomotor domains. While they achieved separate reports on the affective and cognitive domains, it was left to Harrow (1972) to describe a taxonomy for the psychomotor domain. Subsequently, Steinaker and Bell (1969) described a taxonomy for experiential education. The first report to be produced was on the cognitive domain, and it is commonly known as the *Bloom Taxonomy* after the lead editor (Bloom et al, 1956). It was this volume that created the stir.

An outline of the major categories in the *Taxonomy of Educational Objectives* in the cognitive domain is shown in Exhibit 2.1. To be a taxonomy, the categories have to be hierarchically ordered and independent of each other, but at the same time build on each other. One way of understanding its intention is to imagine the mental processes that one goes through when reading an editorial in a quality newspaper. This faces one with having to make a judgment about the validity of the article. Clearly, it is impossible to be critical unless one has the knowledge with which to comprehend the article. It is also clear that one cannot criticize without comprehension, and in that sense, our thinking is hierarchical. Analysis and synthesis follow. One cannot synthesize without analyzing, and we cannot judge without analysis and synthesis.

Apple et al (2002), whose examples are shown in Exhibit 2.1, argued that level 4 is working expertise. They noted that teaching commonly follows the hierarchy in that it begins with simple problems and then moves to more complex ones, and they suggested a process for arriving at skill in analysis in engineering (level 4). The sequence begins with vocabulary and the collection of information (level 1), the creation of a plan for learning, modeling, and critical thinking (level 2), skill exercises and application (level 3), problem solving (level 4), and research (level 5) all of which is highly controversial especially the inclusion of critical thinking in level 2 (see

Chapter 2). But then *The Taxonomy*, in spite of its undoubted value, is controversial, as will be shown. Each of the sub sections in *The Taxonomy* was described in great detail, and examples of test questions were provided. These were intended to describe what a person was "able to do" in terms of a particular category.

Several British philosophers argued that *The Taxonomy* was based on an inadequate epistemology, and Furst (1994) admitted that the committee paid little attention to the philosophic dimension. *"Instead they placed much of the burden of defining educational goals and cognitive levels on test items, the correct response to which was taken as necessary evidence of the attainment at issue. Thus, the authors took as the only viable alternative the operational definition in which the intended student behavior was implicit (Wilhoyte, 1965). They did recognize, however, that the operational definition was not sufficient; one also had to know or assume the nature of the students' educational experience."* [2]

The problem arose from the fact that the committee had chosen Ralph Tyler's definition of an educational objective. For him, an educational objective represented a change in behavior in ways of acting, thinking, and feeling. *"A behavioral objective expresses what a person will be able to do. It is action oriented. At the end of a class or course a student will be able to define, discriminate between..., identify..., etc."*

The difference between a non behavioral objective and a behavioral objective is well illustrated by St. Clair and Baker (2000) in relation to engineering graphics. Their first example (below) is that of a non behavioral objective (some investigators might call it an aim).

Example 1. At the end of this course in Engineering Graphics, the student will know how to use a computer-aided-design software package.

Example 2. At the end of this course in Engineering Graphics, the student will be able to draw a multi-view representation of a solid object using a computer-aided-design software package.

In lesson planning Cohen and Manion (1977) distinguished between aim, non behavioral objective and behavioral objective). Mansfield (1979) defined objectives by their condition, behavior and standard.[3] Thus the objectives for the application of Laplace Transforms were as follows:

Objective 1
Condition- At the end of the one class period, the student
Behavior- will be able to transform linear differential equations.
Standard- Up to fourth year.
Objective 2

Condition- At the end of two class periods, the student
Behavior-will find inverses to Laplace transforms.
Standard- With non repeated linear and quadratic equations.

Waina (1969) suggested that the behavioral objectives of a course in the basic concepts of electricity and magnetism would be "that the student should be able to:

Predict the performance of a specified simple system. Design a simple system to achieve a specified performance."

The committee used the term behavioral in a broad sense. It is, wrote Furst (1994), a broad concept rather than the usual (overt) behavioral one, because it includes covert as well as overt states. It is that which creates the philosophical difficulty because tests measure something that is overt, hence the need to know or assume the nature of the students' educational experience. Many other criticisms of *The Taxonomy* were made on anti-behaviorist grounds. There was an unwillingness to accept the broad use intended by the group. Had the authors been behaviorist then *The Taxonomy* would have produced a curriculum based on drill and practice. An important criticism made by a mathematics educator in England was that some of the demands for knowledge were more complex than the demands for analysis and evaluation (Ormell, 1974).

The authors foreshadowed what has come to be known as outcomes-based assessment since they declared that *"The Taxonomy is designed to be a classification of the student behaviors which represent the intended outcomes of the educational process. It is assumed that essentially the same classes of behavior may be observed in the usual range of subject-matter content of different levels of education (elementary, high school, college). Thus a single set of classifications should be applicable in all these circumstances."*

"What we are classifying is the intended behaviors of students-the ways in which individuals are to think, act or feel, as a result of participating in some unit of instruction. (Only such of those intended behaviors as are related to mental acts of thinking are included in the part of The Taxonomy developed in the handbook for the cognitive domain.)"

It is recognized that actual behaviors of the students after they have completed a unit of instruction may differ in degree as well as kind from the intended behavior specified by the objectives. That is the effects of instruction may be such that students do not learn a skill to any given degree."

There is still much confusion about outcomes. For example, one assessment specialist went so far as to propose that objectives were used by course designers whereas specifications of learning outcomes were made by teachers (Otter, 1991). It is, however, difficult to see what the differences between objectives and outcomes are when they are statements of what is expected that students will be able to do as a result of this or that learning activity.

---

[2] For a detailed review of these criticisms see Anderson, L.W. and L.A. Sosniak (1994) (eds). *Bloom's Taxonomy. A Forty-year Retrospective,* and in particular the Chapter by Furst.. A summary of this text is contained in Heywood (2000)

[3] derived from learning theory "Conditioned behavior standard". Mansfield cites Borg (1972).

Yokomoto and Bostwick (1999) wrote that *"Secondary meanings of some words are sometimes used, such as using the term "criteria" to describe the level of performance that students must achieve and "outcomes" to describe the learning behaviors students must demonstrate. A more common definition of "outcome" is "result" or "consequence", and anyone attaching meaning to the word will surely become confused in a discussion on writing measurable outcomes."* They go on to point out that ABET also confused the issue. It described its statement (a), (k) in criterion 3 (see Exhibit 2.2) as "outcomes." They are *"considered by experts to be too broad to be assessed directly and should be broken down into smaller, more easily measurable units."* In some ways the British requirements for a Chartered Engineer, provide such a breakdown. They use the term "competence" and describe the qualities that give rise to competence as abilities. The competence shown in Exhibit 2.3 corresponds approximately to (k) in the ABET list. This list of abilities belongs to the Domain of Problem Solving, and in abstraction, would be found in any list of skills that contribute to problem solving.[4] The other competencies in the British list are as follows:

"Utilise a combination of general and specialist engineering knowledge and understanding; optimise the application of existing and emerging technology. Provide technical and managerial leadership; utilise effective communication and interpersonal skills; and, make a professional commitment to live by the appropriate code of professional conduct, recognizing obligations to society, the profession and the environment."

It should be noted that these are requirements for registration as an engineer. They are not necessarily the same as those that would be required for a degree program. This is explained in Chapter 15, Section 4. One might ask, if the last one is a competence or an attitude? And that is to reinforce the point made by Yokomoto and Bostwick, because, in the language of objectives the ABET list is a list of aims.[5] They are too broad to be described as non-behavioral objectives, because such objectives generally relate to what is being taught (Cohen and Manion, 1997), and they still have to be turned into behavioral objectives that are measurable. And, this is true of the British list. If one wishes to use the term outcome or objective then it might best be preceded by the term "domain".

As indicated, the abilities in the British competence are within the domain of problem solving. Yokomoto and Bostwick distinguished between course outcomes, and course instructional objectives. They differed little from what was intended by those writers who distinguished between aims, non-behavioral objectives, and behavioral objectives. Nevertheless, as Yokomoto and Bostwick made clear, it behooves accrediting agencies to use consistent terminology and explain the terms used in them.

The story does not end. For example, two engineering educators, Adams and Munsterman (1977) made a distinction between instructional goals and behavioral objectives, thus: *"Instructional goals are the objectives the teacher seeks to achieve; behavioral objectives are the instructional outcomes the student is expected to display as evidence of learning".*

Mager (1962), whose work on preparing instructional objectives has been cited by several engineering educators, wrote that *"an objective is an intent communicated by a statement describing a proposed change in the learner-a statement of what the learner is to be like when he has successfully completed a learning experience."* Thus, an instructional objective must (i) describe what the learner will be doing when demonstrating that he has reached the objective (ii) describe the conditions under which the learner will demonstrate his or her competence and (iii) show how an acceptable performance will be assessed. As Stice (1976) says it causes an instructor to ask, *"Where am I going? How shall I get there? How will I know I have arrived?"* It is possible to describe course objectives without reference to *The Taxonomy,* but it is not possible to escape from the need to declare objectives if teaching is to be made more effective (Stice, 1976; Svinicki, 1976).

Adams and Munsterman (1977) argued (as did Stice and Svinicki, 1976) that, *"Since a student's performance is at least partially dependent on understanding the behavioral objectives, the instructor has to make every effort to provide objectives in a way that will effectively aid the student. Recognizing this responsibility expands the focus of teaching from merely the transformation of information to what is being received as well."* The point about *The Taxonomy,* as Stice (1976) made clear, is that it is a powerful tool for analyzing one's own curriculum in respect of the cognitive skill that one is trying to develop. This point applies equally to the affective domain and the use of its taxonomy.

Irrespective of history, and language usage, it seems that "outcomes" have won the day, and in the sense of this discussion they are performance outcomes of the students as opposed to program outcomes, as, for example, those required by ABET 2000.

The term is also related to bench marking and standards in the United Kingdom where the Engineering professors Council has produced Engineering Graduate Output Standards. They are a set of generic statements that articulate the output standard of engineering graduates that are acceptable to government industry, professional institutions, university departments, and the graduates themselves, and they can be used when it is necessary for these different groups to communicate with one another on the subject of output standards. They are statements of the ability that a graduate is expected to demonstrate on graduation. That is *"The graduate has*

---

[4] See for example Gubbins list of critical thinking skills cited by Sternberg, (1985) and reprinted in Heywood (1989a). See also the profile of the critical thinker in the arts and humanities in Cromwell (1986), reprinted in Heywood (2000).

[5] The ABET criteria are not without influence outside of the United States. The civil engineering department at the University of Delft in The Netherlands have described in detail how they have applied them to their curriculum (Massie, 2002).

demonstrated the ability to do X in the context of Y or its equivalent. [X is the body of the ability and Y is the discipline specific engineering system with a level of complexity, in terms of the required skill, knowledge and understanding that is widely understood within the discipline]."[6]

A. Knowledge	
Knowledge of Specifics. Terminology. Specific facts. Ways and means of dealing with specifics. Conventions. Trends and sequences. Classification of categories. Criteria. Methodology. Universals and abstractions in a field. Principles and generalizations. Theories and structures.	Memorizing facts.
B. Intellectual abilities and skills	
Comprehension Translation. Interpretation Extrapolation	E.g Understanding that electrons flow in wires, and resistors impede the flow of electrons, causing energy dissipation. Ohm's law can be applied to a single resistor.
Application	Applying Ohm's law to solve a circuit as a Kirchoff's law mesh system for a double loop.
Analysis Of elements. Of relationships. Of organizational principles.	Using Kirchoff's law to solve multiple (more than two) mesh equations WITHOUT previous examples by the instructor.
Synthesis	
Production of a unique communication. Production of a plan, or proposed set of operations. Derivation of a set of abstract relations.	Being able to derive a generalized solution method, such as Node Voltage Analysis method, without help of instructor.
Evaluation	
Judgments in terms of internal evidence Judgments based on external criteria.	Deciding which of several alternative methods. Provides the most effective problem solution. This may also include qualitative value judgments based upon other design considerations including economic and social impact.

Exhibit 2.1. The Taxonomy of Educational Objectives. An outline of the major categories in the cognitive domain. The examples on the right relate to basic electrical circuits and are taken from Apple et al, (2002).

Nevertheless the idea of objectives has been influential among engineering teachers and the advantages and disadvantages of outcomes are unlikely to be different to those of objectives. In his article Stice (1976) reported the findings of a colleague[7] who had consulted faculty members about the value of objectives. She listed the disadvantages as follows:

- *Discourages creativity on the part of the teacher and learner.*
- *Takes the 'challenge out' of studying.*
- *Is not worth the amount of time and effort required*
- *Leads to concentration on the specific details of a subject, 'while the big picture' is missed by students.*
- Insults the students' intelligence. Seems mechanistic and dehumanizing.

But this need not be the case. The success of programs written by objectives will depend on the significance of the objectives chosen, and the way they are used for learning.

Engineering programs must demonstrate that their graduates have:
(a) An ability to apply knowledge of mathematics, science and engineering.
(b) An ability to design and conduct experiment, as well as to analyze and interpret data;
(c) An ability to design a system, component, or process to meet desired needs;
(d) An ability to function in multi-disciplinary teams;
(e) An ability to identify, formulate, and solve engineering problems;
(f) An understanding of professional and ethical responsibility
(g) An ability to communicate effectively;
(h) The broad education necessary to understand the impact of engineering solutions in a global/societal context;
(i) A recognition of the need for and an ability to engage in life-long learning;
(j) A knowledge of contemporary issues; and,
(k) An ability to use the techniques, skills, and modern engineering tools necessary for engineering practice.

Exhibit 2.2. The List of Program Outcomes in Section II of Engineering Criteria 2000. The Accreditation Board for Engineering and Technology (ABET)

To take the issue of the "big picture," Stice (1976) wrote, *"When I wrote my first set of instructional objectives it was for a course I had taught eight or ten times by the lecture method. It took considerably longer than I had expected, and I spent two days of concentrated effort going through the textbook to decide what topics were of paramount importance and what topics were 'nice to know' but not essential. When I finished, I was not very well satisfied with the results and laid them aside. About a week later I hauled them out again and worked on them some more. Finally obtaining a list of objectives I thought I could live with, I was a little surprised at the results.*

Several topics were omitted that I had always spent time on before, but which were not prerequisite information for the following course in the sequence...the omission of 'nice to know' material and the irrelevant yarns yielded about three weeks of extra time, which I was able to use in covering material that was important and prerequisite for the following course, but which I had never had time to cover in the past."

The advantages of using objectives were found to be:
- *"Forces an instructor to critically evaluate the relative importance of topics and the allocation of instructional time.*

[6] From documents on the EPC Engineering Graduate Standard. Engineering Professors Council, UK.

[7] Susan Hereford, Associate Director of the Texas Measurement Centre.

- *Can contribute to more open and candid classroom atmosphere, and more positive and honest teacher and student relationships.*
- *Focuses the students' attention on learning tasks rather than on 'psyching out' the instructor.*
- *May promote rather than discourage creativity through the reduction of anxiety about tests and grades.*
- *Causes the teacher to appreciate and make good use of individual differences in teaching and learning styles. It specifies the product and allows intelligent choice of the process by which an individual teacher or learner progresses toward the goal."*

Apply appropriate theoretical and practical methods to the analysis and solution of engineering problems

This includes the ability to
- Identify the complexities of the problem.
- Define theoretical and practical methods appropriate to the model
- Define the strategy for the solution of problems
  Synthesise appropriate options for design development, realisation and continuous improvement
- Make choices, taking cognisance of engineering, environmental commercial constraints and conflicts,
- Implement and evaluate outcomes.

Exhibit 2.3. Extracted from Standards and Routes to Registration as a Chartered Engineer, 1996. (Engineering Council, 1996.)

Some engineering educators continued to be persuaded of the value of *The Taxonomy*. For example, the objectives of a range of short modules designed to meet ABETs criteria were defined in terms of the Bloom categories.[8]   Pimmel (2003), who described the evaluation of the modules using self assessment pointed out that students had to be helped to achieve the ABET domains through effective teaching. Ketchum (1981) at the University of Notre Dame published a matrix of *The Taxonomy* domains against content. But, a later statement of objectives took into account both the affective and psychomotor domains. It was used by the Synthesis Coalition to test the credibility and dependability of students' written responses to a scenario assignment (McMartin, McKenna and Youssefi, 1999). At the Rose Hulman Institute of Technology it was used to design a competency matrix assessment for first year curricula in science, engineering, and mathematics (Anderson et al, 1996; Froyd, 1997), but it only covered the first four levels of *The Taxonomy).*

Nevertheless, with respect to student learning, Eisner (1979), an educationalist with special interests in art and design, reminded us that as well as intended outcomes (or whatever term is used), all classroom activities and all courses have unintended outcomes. Sometimes they may enhance learning and at other times

they may impede learning. Thus, in evaluating whether or not the objectives have been obtained the teacher needs to know what was actually learned and whether it was worthwhile. Indeed the evaluation may lead the teacher to change her/his objectives in a future lecture (seminar, etc.) or course.

2.2. Expressive Outcomes

Unlike the authors of *The Taxonomy* Eisner also made a distinction between behavioral objectives and problem solving. The authors of *The Taxonomy* believed that problem solving was involved in each of the categories described (see Anderson and Sosniak, 1994, or Bloom et al, 1956). Eisner conceded that it was an objective, but when he used it he did so to distinguish between pre-formulated goals and what actually happened. He argued that while there was a case for pre-formulated goals, there were many teaching activities for which we did not pre-formulate specific goals. We undertook them in anticipation that something would happen, even though we could not specify what (as, for example in business games and case studies). We do not think much beyond the data, even though we could predict from the ample criteria at our disposal. What we do is to evaluate retrospectively what happened against these criteria. From this he deduced that teachers should be able to plan activities that do not have any specific objectives. This led him to express the view of many educators, who would say with him that,

"Expressive activities precede rather than follow expressive outcomes. The tack to be taken with respect to the generation of expressive outcomes is to create activities which are seminal; what one is seeking is to have the students engage in activities that are sufficiently rich to allow for a wide, productive range of valuable outcomes. If behavioral objectives constitute the algorithms of the curriculum, expressive activities and outcomes constitute their heuristics" (Eisner, 1979).

There seem to be two difficulties with this view. The first, you might argue, is a quibble. It is, that even to establish a strategy that will allow things to emerge, is to formulate a goal in the expressive domain in which the cognitive and affective are merged. This will happen, for example, if cooperative learning is introduced for the purpose of developing social skills. The second objection is that all too often such statements can be used as an excuse for not planning teaching. A great deal of research has been done that shows that students rate many lectures poorly (Bligh, 1999). Often this weakness is related to poor planning and a lack of understanding of student learning. To follow Eisner properly demands both an understanding of how students learn, and how to plan classroom activities.

Nevertheless, Eisner was right to remind us of the expressive in education. All teaching and therefore all attempts to achieve objectives are informed by our affective dispositions, a point that has been taken up in discussions of the teaching of ethics to engineering students.

---

[8] The modules were of three 50 minute class periods, and designed for upper engineering classes. The self-assessments showed gains from pre- to post module assessments. This method (which is open to the criticism that it is not sufficiently objective) showed that these short modules *"are effective for traditional and non-traditional skills and for all levels of learning in Bloom's taxonomy".*

2.3. *The Taxonomy* and Its Influence in Engineering Education.

As previously indicated, some engineering teachers have found *The Taxonomy* in its original form to be of value. In the United States, Lindenlaub and Russell (1980) considered that it could be used for the improvement of instruction, and Felder (1985) used it to stimulate creativity in a course on chemical reactor design.

"For the third quiz of the semester I gave a five-week take-home exercise that asked students to make up and solve a final examination for the course. They were told that if they produced a straightforward, "Given this and this, calculate that" quiz with no mistakes they would receive a minimum passing grade; to receive more credit would require asking the hypothetical exam-takers to demonstrate the three higher level thinking skills of Bloom's Taxonomy: analysis (determination of mechanisms, decomposition of systems, and derivation of relations beyond what could be found in texts or courses notes); synthesis (application of techniques from other disciplines to reaction engineering problems in other disciplines); and evaluation (assessing the value of a design or product or system, rather than simply its technical correctness, and examination of environmental, safety, social, and ethical considerations in the content of process design analysis" (Felder, 1987, see also Chapter 11).

In their representation of *The Taxonomy,* Besterfield-Sacre et al, accompany the categories with a list of action verbs that describe the commands of the particular category of *The Taxonomy*, along with the type of question associated with each category (see Exhibit 2.5). The description of the comprehension category in *The Taxonomy* is shown in Exhibit 2.5. Batanov, Dimmitt and Chookittiktul (2000) have shown how it can be used in a Q & A (question and answer) teaching learning model to develop educational software. Ellis, Hafner and Mitropoulos (2004) used *The Taxonomy* as the basis for their automated instructional design program for those who want to design on-line courses.

More significantly, a framework based on *The Taxonomy* has been developed for better specifying the outcomes of the new ABET Criteria (2000) for accreditation in both the cognitive and affective domains (Besterfield-Sacre et al, 2000). A literature search and other data led to a tabulation of outcomes versus definition and reference. Two of these descriptions are shown in Exhibit 2.6. The other categories in their list are: an ability to apply knowledge of mathematics, science and engineering; an ability to design a system, component, or process to meet desired needs; an ability to function in multi disciplinary teams; an understanding of professional and ethical responsibility; an ability to communicate effectively; and the broad education necessary to understand the impact of engineering solutions in a global and societal context.

Gorman (2002) tackled the problem of the ABET criteria in a somewhat different way. He described a heuristic for framing a program's educational objectives to meet the requirements of criterion 3. First, it is necessary to identify the characteristics of the type of engineer a program wishes to graduate. His examples of heroes and heroines demonstrate the complexity of trying to achieve the objectives of criterion 3. In order to understand how these types of heroes and heroines achieve success it is necessary to understand the categories of knowledge used by them. Thus it is necessary to distinguish between tacit knowledge and what might be called formal knowledge. This formal knowledge comprises four categories. They are information (what), skills (how), judgement (when), and Wisdom (when). There is also the distributed knowledge that is possessed by a team. He discusses how each type of knowledge contributes (or not) to the objectives of criterion 3. Following Besterfield-Sacre et al, he suggested and showed that these categories could be related to those of the Bloom taxonomy. Approaching the task from this angle would seem to reduce the confusion described by Yokomoto and Bostwick.

In the United Kingdom the school examination boards were greatly influenced by *The Taxonomy*. Soon after its publication in England in 1964 subject examiners in the Advanced Level of the General Certificate of Education of the Joint Matriculation Board were required to specify the aims and objectives of their subjects and to show how marks were allocated against the chosen categories. Some used the categories more or less as they were while others took the idea and adapted it to their own needs. The authors of *The Taxonomy* had made it clear that the categories would not necessarily be suitable for every subject. The examiners of Geometrical and Engineering Drawing found this to be the case. They found it necessary to include categories for technique and visualization (see Exhibit 2.7). The more interesting case is, however, of Engineering Science. It is one of a few subjects whose system of assessment was the subject of continuous evaluation that has also been publicly documented (Carter, Heywood, and Kelly, 1986).

This examination is of interest since it was the forerunner of the model of the 'A' level examination in physics that is shown in the report of the US National research Council (Pellegrino et al, 2001). It differs from the original idea in that the designers took the view that for each domain objective a particular type of assessment would be appropriate. Hence, it was originally called a multiple objective examination. Later it was described as a multiple strategy approach to the assessment of student learning. It is an example of an assessment led curriculum.[9]

---

[9] The examination was established to demonstrate that engineers had different ways of thinking to other scientists because of the nature of the problems they had to solve. At the same time the student had to have a firm grounding in physics if the examination was to be taken as the equivalent to physics by university admissions officers. It was the subject of evaluation over a period of eighteen years. It then became, for "political" reasons Physics B. The practical aspects of the examination were retained. In this text the original design is described together with the evaluations of that design

It had been agreed that a multiple strategy examination would be set, and that this would incorporate assessed coursework. Both steps marked a considerable departure from tradition. The overall examination would, in addition to the coursework, include a test of knowledge (following the Bloom sub-categories), a comprehension test, a project planning and design test, and two tests of the applications of science to engineering problems including their social and economic context where possible. The examination would be set at the end of 2 years of continuous study at which time the marks for coursework would be incorporated into the final grade.

The test of knowledge would use objective items. The use of objective items in the English system of examinations was new at the time. Equally the replacement of a formal practical examination by coursework was new. The problem was that for this assessment to be acceptable to university selectors, the coursework assessment had to be shown to be reliable and valid, and for this reason the examiners decided on a semi-criterion referenced approach. This required the determination of objectives so that the rubrics for assessment and instructional procedures could be designed.

Although the inspiration for the objectives came from *The Taxonomy,* it was found that the principal categories did not express what was required. In the practical work, "technique" was required, and it was also expected that students would be able to demonstrate creativity. Thus, as with Engineering Drawing, a category for *technique* was introduced and, after much discussion was centered on McDonald's (1968) definitions of creativity and originality a category of *originality* was included (see Exhibit 2.8). This enabled the expression of behavioral objectives in this domain.

A major influence on this decision was an article by Ball (cited in Carter, Heywood, and Kelly, 1986), who was a lecturer in engineering design at the University of Liverpool (a more or less unique appointment in the United Kingdom in the late 1960s). In that article in which he expressed a design philosophy for engineering he distinguished between analysis and synthesis as follows:

"Before a designer can apply scientific principles to solve a particular problem he must first understand the scientific principles themselves. At this point the first educational problem arises. The student understands scientific principles by treating them in an analytical way: this treatment unavoidably suppresses his ability to handle problems in engineering design, in which the approach is dominated by synthesis.

A typical undergraduate problem illustrates the difference between the analytic and synthetic approaches. Figure 2.1 shows an idealised theoretical model of a simple bridge, represented by a thin weightless rod resting on two supports which is subjected to a vertical load. From this information the student can calculate the bending moment distributions across the span. By adding an additional piece of information derived from the thickness and width of the beam forming the span, he can determine the working stresses and compare them to the failure stresses, to predict whether such a bridge could carry the applied load satisfactorily. This approach to structures is analytical in nature since is presupposes that the span, position of loading, type of support, geometric properties of the beam, and the material from which the beam is made are all known factors.

In contrast the design problem which had to be solved before the analysis is possible is solved in a very different manner (Figure 2.2). In the case of the bridge the only known factors are the load which the bridge must carry and the distance or span, over which the load is to travel. Having introduced a solution before the problem was stated the reader will have already been conditioned to the obvious solution of Figure 2.1 whilst looking at Figure 2.2. However, the essence of the real problem is synthesis rather than analysis.

Synthesis, or engineering design in this case is concerned with the creation of a system which will meet a specified need under conditions where the end product cannot necessarily be foreseen ... .the essential difference between an analytical approach to a problem and a synthesised solution. In practice, the engineering of a product must proceed by synthesis of creative thinking. This is achieved by a mixture of scientifically based assumptions and estimates concerning a particular part, or sub-system or overall system, coupled with an analytic investigation into the behavior of the sub-system as the factors controlling it change. The analytical method can then be applied to the sub-system more accurately than before. The procedure is repeated for each sub-system until eventually the understanding of the various sub-systems leads to an understanding of the overall system."[10]

It will be noticed that in the engineering science categories, there is no statement of the knowledge required for coursework, but inspection of the demands of the categories shows that the Bloom sub categories meet these requirements. It will also be noticed that there are some statements that are specific to the subject as, for example, *design and evaluate.* The examiners found that the categories were not hierarchically ordered, and also that some of the sub categories were placed in categories other than the ones for which they were originally intended. There was considerable overlap between the domains.

The names of the categories were chosen because they expressed what the examiners believed engineering activity to be about, and the sub categories were chosen to describe the components of those activities. It will be noticed that although these objectives were for practical work, the authors felt there was no need to include a category for application. It was easily established that several approaches to practical work would be required. These are shown in Exhibit 2.9.

In the general introduction to the subject it was stated that *"A course in Engineering Science should be*

---

[10] This text appeared in an article in *Discover,y* which is a journal that is no longer published.

concerned with physical skills: the co-ordination of hand and eye." The skills specific to this are specified as making observations, estimating errors, handling equipment, maintaining concise and accurate records, and sketching quickly and meaningfully (JMB, 1967).

The controlled experiments are traditional experiments typical of the kind used in universities and schools at the time. They were also typical of the kind that would have been set in a formal examination prior to this development. The experimental investigations are a form of discovery learning (Heywood, 1976). These call for different skills to the controlled assignments. Projects are substantial exercises that also call for the deployment of other skills not used in either of the other two laboratory techniques.

British universities and schools had considerable experience of project work. In schools, *Project Technology*, a national curriculum project designed to generate interest in technological subjects and problems at school, tried to encourage interest in engineering through design and make projects. Gregory (1972), who wrote about Project Technology and its relation to engineering, said that *"central to this work in schools is a distinction between an individual's own creativity (at this stage poorly defined but perhaps indicating a general ability to generate ideas) and that of others, between concurrent and consecutive education (i.e. between learning while doing and learning first), between design activity and that of science, and between disciplined creativity and random work. Technology in this context is seen as a general process of using resources to achieve human purposes."*

One of the things that this work showed was how the definition of objectives in behavioral terms leads easily to the design of assessment rubrics. For completeness, summaries of the assessment rubrics for the experimental investigations and the project are shown in Exhibits 2.10 and 2.11. They also show the relationship with the objectives listed in Exhibits 2.8 and 2.9. These student assessment outcomes demonstrate the achievement of many of the outcomes required by the accrediting agencies as was demonstrated at the first Rose Hulman conference on assessment (Heywood, 1996). Recently in the United States Dempsey et al 2003 have demonstrated that the assessment of student performance on mini-projects can also be used to meet many of the outcomes of ABET 2000, and as a consequence it led to continuous improvement as did the assessments made with engineering science. A similar demonstration of the use of the subject-specific results from the Fundamentals of Engineering test conducted by the National Council of Examiners for Engineers and Surveyors as a means of assessing outcomes and helping with curriculum improvement was given by Nirmalakhandian, Daniel, and White (2004).

In the written examinations, for which 80% of the marks were given, the knowledge and comprehension sections clearly relate to the Bloom categories. However, as indicated above, one of the examination papers had two sub sections that were devoted to the applications of the principles of science to the solution of practical problems. The question might be asked, 'Would not it have been better to have called them 'application?" The answer to this question has to be "no" because the student would also have been using the other higher-order skills. The most appropriate title is probably 'problem-solving' because it involves all these skills in complex mental configurations. They are not hierarchically ordered as is proposed in *The Taxonomy*. But, it is a matter of personal choice because the questions were clearly designed to meet most of the criteria listed by Felder for his generic quiz (see above). So while there is no category of creativity in *The Taxonomy*, and irrespective of the earlier discussion, Felder used the higher-order categories to stimulate creativity as he defined it.

The examiners' approach to the design of the engineering science curriculum is described by Carter and Jordan (1990) as *"coordinated and global"* following the model proposed by Tyler (1949) and also discussed by Dressel (1954). They noted that, *"it was rehearsed more recently"* by another Carter (1984) for an undergraduate engineering course. That particular Carter (1985) subsequently published an article called the *"Taxonomy of Objectives for Professional Education"* (Carter, 1985). It proved to be very useful to three engineering educators who used it to test the *"feasibility of describing a degree in terms of its learning outcomes"* (Otter, 1992). It caused them to state very detailed prescriptions that they had drafted within a broader framework (see below).

In order to derive a curriculum in Industrial Engineering at Eindhoven Technological University, Meuwese (1968) used the categories of *The Taxonomy* to derive 300 statements from his colleagues in the Department of Industrial Engineering The same teachers then rated and classified them, after which they were factor, and cluster-analyzed. The factorial analysis yielded six main factors. These contained objectives related to:

Factor 1.   The social system components of industrial engineering.
Factor 2.   Machine shop technology.
Factor 3.   Systems analysis.
Factor 4.   Critical analysis and synthesis in industrial situations.
Factor 5.   Organization and planning.
Factor 6.   The management of mechanical systems.

At the same time, the ratings were subjected to hierarchical cluster analysis. Some of the clusters in what might be described as the area of communication are shown in Figure 2.3.

This methodology was used to design a first-year course in mechanical engineering in the Keller style (Meuwese, 1971).

Each of the course units contained the stated objectives, a list of references to specific pages in books which could be used, supplementary texts, a series of study questions, answers to these questions, and six diagnostic multiple-choice tests of approximately 12 items each.[11]

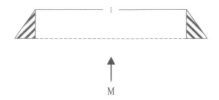

Figure 2.1. Simple Idealized Model of a Bridge.

Figure 2.2. Typical problem in design.

To conclude, a substantial case may be made for declaring behavioral as well as non behavioral objectives at both the level of classroom teaching, and the curriculum (course or program) provided they are limited in number and focus on well defined cognitive skill domains. However, the. designers of Engineering Science at the 'A' level, along with the results of Meuwese's research, suggest that the organization, planning, and management of mechanical systems are key skill areas that need to be accommodated within a engineering curriculum. Thus while the *Taxonomy* is based on the concept of cognitive skill areas (domains), its domains are by no means comprehensive. The task of the curriculum designer is to select a limited number of domains on which to focus in the knowledge that not only will it be impossible to obtain complete coverage but, also there will be many unintended outcomes.

The latter suggested that skill in interpersonal relations was important.. This view was supported by another evaluation of the job descriptions in adverts for professional people to work in industry and commerce. That investigation found domains in the areas of problem solving, managing and organising, communication, and team work. The investigators suggested how the curriculum might be designed to cater for their development. In the search for aims (and objectives) the curriculum designer will want to be sure that there is a match between what is done in the curriculum and what graduates will need for work and life. In the next part a task analysis of what engineers did in a particular organization is described, and this is followed by consideration of the value of alumni studies.

Part 2: *Summary*

There are many sources of objectives. One of the criticisms of those who used taxonomies to design the curriculum was that they were intent on creating a curriculum that would replicate themselves-that is, produce engineers who would do research and become academics.

Moreover, they were based on hypothetical models of what engineers actually did. An enquiry is described that sought to remedy this defect through a task analysis of engineers at work. It took into account the attitudes to the job and themselves that these engineers had. It revealed coherent domains in the areas of communication, diagnosis, and management (direction and control).

Studies of alumni may be a fruitful source of aims. Whereas, this Chapter is primarily concerned with learning objectives (including content areas), alumni studies may indicate whether or not program objectives are being achieved, such as the effectiveness of counseling, or whether the educational environment is conducive to learning. Practice and problems in the administration of alumni surveys are considered and some results reported.

A separate section is included on the transition from college to the workplace. It reinforces the arguments in the previous section for the development of generic skills. It is evident that the skills derived in this section encompass both cognitive and affective behaviors. This part ends with a brief note on some other approaches to the classification and derivation of objectives.

2.4. What do Engineers Actually Do?

One criticism of the taxonomies is that they were derived by persons intent on creating a curriculum that would replicate themselves-that is, produce engineers who would do research or become academic. A major employer in England criticized descriptions of what engineers did in the reports of the Engineering Industries Training Board (EITB, 1968a,b), the Council of Engineering Institutions (CEI, 1968a,b), and the Joint Matriculation Board's Engineering Science at the Advanced Level. He argued that they were based on hypothetical models of what engineers do. While this is. not an unreasonable approach, and while these models can lead to what are sometimes called "process" objectives as the diagrams in Figure 2.4 show, it is not an unreasonable complaint. A study of what engineers do at work would show the relevance or otherwise of university education to the world of engineering work.

---

[11] For a discussion of the differences between The Keller approach (PSI) and the Bloom approach, see Stice (1979) (see Chapter 14). In this case according to Meuwese (1971), *"After an introduction to inform the students about the system and to ask their cooperation in evaluation procedures, all students were given their first unit. The test for the unit was randomly chosen for each student from the six tests for that unit. If the score was below the norm, advice was given about the material to be studies again.. This advice was strictly on the basis of item responses, and was given by a graduate assistant who selected adequate advisory statements from a list of possible statements, following a specific description. After a period of study the student could do a second test and the procedure was repeated. If the results at the third try were still below the norm, then the student was tutored by the professor. Two afternoons a week were available for testing. For each group of 15 students an assistant was available, who scored tests, monitored the advice procedure and distributed materials".*

Taxonomy Category	Command Words and Question Type.
Knowledge	Arrange, define, describe, match, order, memorize, name, note, order, repeat. Who? What? When? Where? Questions
Comprehension.	Alter, change, classify define in your own words, discuss, explain, extend. Give examples, translate.
Application	Apply, calculate, compute, construct, operate, practice. How many? Which? Write an example question.
Analysis	Analyze, appraise, categorize, compare, conclude, contrast, criticize, diagnose, differentiate, etc. Why? Questions.
Synthesis	Assemble, compile, compose, create, improve synthesize. What if? How can we improve? What would happen if? How can we solve? Questions.
Evaluation	Appraise, argue, choose, certify, criticize, decide, deduce, defend, discriminate, estimate, evaluate, recommend, etc.

Exhibit 2.4. The categories of *The Taxonomy of Educational Objectives* showing the command words that begin questions. After Besterfield Sacre,- Shuman, L. J. Wolfe, H., Atman, C. J., McGourty, J., Miller, R. L., Olds, B. M., and G. M. Rogers (2000). (McBeath ,R (1992). Instruction and Evaluation in Higher Education: A Guide Book for Planning, Learning Outcomes. Education Technology (Reproduced by kind permission of *IEEE/)*.

Definition of the Comprehension Category

This category represents the lowest level of understanding, where the pupil knows and can make use of the material communicated without necessarily relating it to other material or seeing in it all its implications. It includes the ability to recognize freshly presented pieces of information as illustrations of particular generalizations, the ability to recognize the essential elements of information presented, to relate them to one another, and to obtain some total ordered view of the information as a whole. Comprehension behaviors can be subdivided into three types that are hierarchical in nature.

(a)   **Translation**: which requires the individual to transform a communication into another language, into other terms, or into another form of communication.

(b)   **Interpretation:** the ability to sift the important factors from the less important ones i.e. that is to show judgement.

(c)   **Extrapolation**: the ability to perceive the underlying relationship governing a relationship

Exhibit 2.5. More detailed explanation of Comprehension in the *Taxonomy* (Youngman et al, 1978).

Outcome	Definition
An ability to design and conduct experiments as well as to interpret data.	Comprises four straightforward elements: (1) designing, (2) conducting experiments, (3) analyzing data, (4) interpreting data. Statistically designed experiments, laboratory-based experiments, and field experiments were considered. Each element was further broken down into descriptors that encompass the larger element for example, designing experiments, determining the proper modes to use, considering the variables and constraints, using laboratory protocols, and considering ethical issues that arise.
An ability to identify, formulate, and solve engineering problems.	Is based on the problem solving process that has been well documented in engineering texts. The elements of the process include problem or opportunity identification, problem statement or system definition, problem formulation and abstraction, information and data collection, model translation, validation, experimental design, solution development or experimentation, interpretation, implementation, and documentation. Finally as most engineers eventually learn, the problem-solving process is never complete. Therefore a final element has been included: feedback and improvement.

Exhibit 2.6. Definition/Perspective used for defining the EC-2000 Outcomes 3A, K by Besterfield-Sacre et al (2000) in *IEEE Transactions on Education*, 43 (2), 100–110. (Reproduced with permission of *IEEE Transactions on Education*.)

At the time, in the United Kingdom, there had been only one investigation of what technologists did at work. This had been undertaken to determine the theoretical

---

The Objectives of the examination

This statement is intended to provide a general indication of the abilities which the examination will be designed to test in relation to the items listed in the syllabus. It is not suggested that such clear distinctions can always be applied in constructing examination questions, and a particular question may test more than one skill.

Knowledge and skills to be tested

1. **Knowledge**. The recall of terminology, conventions, basic constructions and engineering components. (Example:.Ability to distinguish the characteristics of multiplanar axonometric and oblique methods of projection.)

2. **Technique**. The ways and means of using drawing instruments to achieve good draughtsmanship, well-proportioned sketches as well as constructional accuracy. (Example. Ability to construct an accurate funicular polygon.)

3. **Visualization and interpretation**. The demonstration of basic form and function from verbal or graphical information; translation of written information into drawings and vice-versa; recognition of functional and dimensional requirements. (Examples. (a) Ability to construct a cam profile from a descriptive specification. (b) Ability to explain the functioning of a valve from its assembly drawing.)

4. **Application**. The thorough understanding of specified geometric and mechanical concepts, or components, within new practical situations. (Example. Ability to recall the graphical method ensuring constant velocity ratio for gear teeth and to apply it to construct a conjugate profile to a given arbitrary curve.).

5. **Analysis**. The breakdown of given material; into constituent parts in order to determine their effect and relationship within the whole. This process demands the recognition of elements essential for the application of analytical methods. (Example. Ability to analyze a mechanism to find the output force and displacement, given their input values.)

6. **Synthesis**. The putting together of geometric concepts and mechanical elements in such a way as constitute a new whole. (Example. The ability to propose locking devices and suitable bearings to make up a gear shaft of known function and geometrical proportions.)

Exhibit 2.7. Abilities to be tested in Geometrical and Engineering Drawing at the Advanced level of the General Certificate of Education. (Cited by Heywood, 1984, with permission of the Joint Matriculation Board.)

requirements for students of high polymer-technology (Langton, 1961). The United Kingdom Department of Employment decided to sponsor a more general investigation into the training objectives for technologists and technicians by means of an analysis of the work done by engineers in the highly innovative organization in the aircraft industry (Youngman et al, 1978).

The investigators argued that the operations derived by Meuwese (and a similar set derived by E. Matchet, unpublished) were too broad. It was necessary to be even more precise. To obtain this degree of precision, they interviewed a sample of persons in engineering functions in the company, to obtain their views about the jobs that they did. Apart from the fact that the interviews were.long (and recorded), the novel feature of the interview technique was its modification of the repertory grid technique developed by G. A. Kelly for

his theory of personal constructs (Bannister and Mair, 1968).

Kelly was not concerned with any ideal way of anticipating events but with the ways in which individuals actually choose (construct) and anticipate the events of which they are aware. Different people may anticipate different events and formulate different modes for anticipating similar events. For this reason the investigators thought it necessary to obtain information about attitudes to job and self as well as data about the structure of the organization, for the resulting behavior of the individual is a result of the interaction between the individual and the organization. They sought to find out how the engineers interviewed anticipated their work by asking them to indicate the differences and similarities in their jobs over time and with the people with whom they were associated both horizontally and vertically in the organizational structure.

Analysis of the interviews (39 in all) yielded 434 operations. These were then formed into a checklist that was distributed to all those in engineering functions in the firm. They were asked to rate those operations that applied to their jobs. The data were then subjected to cluster analysis and 14 segments were revealed as shown in Figure 2.5. These represented the engineering activities undertaken by this group of persons in engineering functions. After the respondents had completed the checklist they were interviewed. During the interview they were asked to comment on the first results from the check list analysis and to complete two instruments using a semantic differential technique (Osgood, Suci, and Tannenbaum, 1962) which sought to explore their attitudes to themselves and their jobs. The data obtained were factor-analyzed together with data giving their opinions of industrial training. This was also obtained during the interview. A profile of an engineer against the items of the semantic differential is shown in Figure 2.6. Fifty bipolar scales were included in the instruments.

Seven factors were identified in relation to job perceptions and these differentiated among engineers doing different types of work. The titles given to the factors were: subjective job evaluation; variety; satisfaction; objective job evaluation; responsibility and authority; stress, job involvement; and complexity.

Two examples from the factorial analysis of the semantic differential and training attitude survey showed its power in relation to the derivation of staff-development programs. First, the analysis indicated differences between the perception of the technicians in the sample and those in the remainder of the sample. The technicians did not think much of their jobs, for they consistently gave high ratings to individual semantic items such as "tedious", "involves little responsibility," and "requires little intelligence." These responses related to the debate about status in the professional institutions in the United Kingdom that was going on at the time. They felt that their opportunities for promotion were limited. The second, and perhaps most important point, was that with respect to attitudes to job, age and job level were more significant variables than educational qualifications.

Other cluster analyses were undertaken with respect to the tasks undertaken by particular groups of engineers (task and job level). It was also demonstrated that studies of this kind can show up inconsistencies in organizational structure.[12] However, the question to be put in this context is whether it is worthwhile turning these operations into a behavioral taxonomy.

1.	Technique.	(a)	the development of the facility for making accurate observations, and the ability to make reasonable estimates of errors incurred in making such observations.
		(b)	Familiarisation with and facility in the use of scientific apparatus and equipment.
2.	Originality.		The development of the ability to
		(c)	formulate hypotheses from given sets of observations.
		(d)	formulate experiments to test hypotheses.
		(e)	devise and improve upon experimental procedures
		(f)	appreciate the relative importance of errors in differing situations
3.	Analysis		The development of the ability to:
		(g)	discriminate between possible alternatives.
		(h)	formulate problems in a form appropriate for investigation
		(i)	recognize assumptions made and assess their importance.
		(j)	extrapolate.
4.	Synthesis		The development of the ability to:
		(k)	produce a unique communication.
		(l)	produce a plan or proposed set of abstract relations.
		(m)	derive a set of abstract relations.
		(n)	design and evaluate.

Exhibit 2.8. The objectives of coursework in Engineering Science at the Advanced level of the General Certificate of Education(JMB, 1967) (Reproduced with permission in Heywood, 1984)

If there is an advantage it would seem to lie in the perception it gives of skill categories, even though the titles are arbitrarily chosen. One of the engineering activities shown in Figure 2.5 is reclassified in Exhibit 2.12. While it shows some relation to *The Taxonomy* the categories are not the same.It is not (nor can it be) hierarchically ordered. It also shows the possibility of other important categories for taxonomy of engineering. For example, diagnosis is an important skill in other professions such as medicine.

There are those who would object to Management as a category, for it is more often than not associated with age and function rather than with a behavioral category. If we ask ourselves the question "What is management?" we find that the *Shorter Oxford English Dictionary* defines a manager as *'one who has direction and control."*

Thus those operations that indicated direction and control were placed in the management category. Those statements generally began with such terms as Initiate, Observe, Advise, Request, Decide, etc. In my submission the development of the behavioral classification from the ability groups illuminates the education and training needs in that particular enterprise. It also throws some light on more general needs, for all accept or acquire tasks which we have to decide how to do, how to implement, and how to evaluate, That is, we all direct and control. This study questions whether management can be construed as a separable elitist function or range of functions rather than a common human experience. Comparison of the Meuwese and Youngman lists of operations or abilities as they would now be called highlights the differences between the knowledge approach required by academics and the skills required by industry. One of the reasons for the industrial period in sandwich (cooperative) courses is that it should bring the two together or integrate them. It can do this through focused learning in which this integral relationship is to the fore. Learning, like management, is an activity that requires direction and control, but it is also an activity that requires motivation. Satisfaction in learning (not necessarily success) is a measure of the extent to which individual needs for direction and control are satisfied. Thus, it is not possible to ignore the affective and other relationships that depend on personality when considering the evaluation of attainments in the cognitive domain.

In Israel, Doron and Marco (1999) created a list of topics related to the training of B. Tech and Practical engineers working in 13 biotechnology organisations. These were given to directors and engineers who would be able to see the implications of the survey for future needs. They were asked to rate each item on a scale of relative importance. The findings suggested areas in which changes could be made to the syllabus. Practical engineers required skills in running and maintaining equipment; conducting experiments; and technical skill and precision. This requires that engineering departments acquire data from B.Tech engineers required capacity for originality and initiative; comprehension; precision; oral and written skill; and the ability to work in teams.

---

[12] Although it was not set up for the purpose of deriving training objectives, a study of the effectiveness of two different organizational structures in the electronics industry by Barnes (1960) of the Harvard Business School has a bearing on the derivation of objectives for training. As is the case in the above study it showed that organizational structures can impede the objectives of training. An equivalent study, but from a sociological perspective, in the United Kingdom by Burns and Stalker (1961) would lead to the same conclusion. Similarly, the organization of learning within universities could impede the achievement of objectives (Heywood, 2000).

Controlled assignments

These are of short duration and normally accomplished within a two-hour period: they are intimately connected with the subject matter. Students may work singly or in groups. Such assignments will:

a.   Reinforce and illuminate lesson material.
b.   Familiarize students with the use of scientific equipment.
c.   Develop a reliable habit of faithful observation, confirmation and immediate record in a journal style.
d.   Introduce techniques of review, analysis, deduction, and evaluation.
e.   Promote good style and presentation in the formal technical report.

Experimental investigations

These pose an engineering or a scientific problem and involve the student in an analysis of the situation and an appropriate selection of procedure and techniques for solution. The end point of the particular investigation may or may not be known, but the means for its assessment are comparatively discretionary.

The time needed for an investigation of this type should normally lie in the range 6 to 12 hours, and the record of the investigation should normally include:

a.   A clear account of the analysis of the problem.
b.   A brief report and comments on the work as the experiment proceeded.
c.   A comment on the results.
d.   An appraisal of what has been achieved.

Project investigations (projects)

These are major undertakings for which it is suggested that 50 hours of laboratory time would be suitable. The student will be required to design a device or design and conduct an investigation to fulfil a specification and to evaluate the degree of fulfilment achieved. Projects can call for mental connective abilities rather than for craft skills, and the time spent on construction or practical investigation should be kept to a minimum, the emphasis being on the design and formulation of problems, literature search in its widest sense, and evaluation. The report of the project should contain:

a.   A clear description of the project and the formulation of the practical problems arising from it.
b.   A work plan.
c.   A survey of the sources of information including literature, advice from staff, industry etc.
d.   A critical evaluation showing why the alternatives were rejected.
e.   A brief report of the practical methods pursued.
f.   An appraisal of what has been achieved.
g.   Acknowledgements.

Exhibit 2.9. The types of coursework used in Engineering Science at the Advanced level of the General Certificate of Education (JMB 1967; Carter, Heywood, and Kelly, 1986).

The student will show mastery in relation to

1.   Safe use of apparatus (6.b, 7b).
2.   Accuracy of observations (6a,7c).
3.   Presentation of Observations (6a, 7c,7e).
4.   Consistency of findings with observations (6a,7c,7d).
5.   Completeness of final report (6,7).

Performance relative to the semi-criteria below (see example of scale below in italics)

1.   Theoretical understanding (6,2; 6:3, 6;4; 7,2a,7,.3a).
2.   Planning the investigation(s) (6,2; 7,2a).
3.   Use of procedures and equipment (6a, 6b, 7, .2b) (see scale in italics below).
4.   Understanding and accounting for errors (6a, 7b),
5.   Critical review of performance and outcomes(6,4; 7, 2 c and d).
6.   Independence of contribution (from teacher and significant others (in particular in relation to the higher order skills (7,2; 7,3; 7,4).

Presentation of reports (style, etc)

1.   Organization of the reports, comprising selection of the material, logical presentation, use of   subheadings, cross referencing, general layout (7,.1e; 7, 2a,b).
2.   Style of presentation of the reports comprising use of language, ease of reading, freedom from repetition, neatness and accuracy in tables and graphs, diagrams, and of illustrations ((7, 1e:, 7, 1c; 7, 2b)

Example of one of the scales
In selecting the experimental procedures and equipment to be used the
candidate made a reasoned assessment of the alternatives available and came to a

well argued conclusion	Score 3
Lacked depth in considering the final choice	Score 2
Made some attempt at alternative approaches	Score 1
Unthinkingly adopted standard procedures or relied entirely on teachers advice	Score 0

Exhibit 2.10: Summary of the rubric for the assessment of experimental investigations in the coursework of Engineering Science at A Level. (Joint Matriculation Board, Manchester) (N.B. All candidates reports were first assessed by the teacher and then subject to external moderation (Carter, Heywood, and Kelly, 1986). The numbers in brackets relate to those in Exhibits 2.6 and 2.7 and show the relation of the objectives to the assessment rubric.

The student will demonstrate mastery in relation to

1. Production of work (7, 3).
2. Use of work plan (7, 3b).
3. Consistency of work (7.3 by teacher assessment and moderator assessment of report).
4. Use of information sources (7,3c).
5. Completeness of the final report (7,3).

Performance relative to the semi-criteria below (scales similar to those used for the experimental investigations. See Exhibit 11.)

6. Planning (6, .2; 7, ,3a, b, c).
7. Execution of the activity (6,.3, 7,.3d).
8. Level of design activity (6, 2e, 6, 4n, 7, 3).
9. Use of resources (7.3e).
10. Critical review of performance and outcomes (6, 4; 7,3d,e,f).
11. Independence of contribution.

Presentation of reports

Same as for the investigations. (see Exhibit 9).

Exhibit 2.11. Summary of the rubric for the assessment of the project in Engineering Science at the Advanced Level (Joint Matriculation Board Manchester). As with the experimental investigations-Exhibit 2.10, the reports were first assessed by the teacher and then externally moderate (Carter, Heywood, and Kelly, 1986)

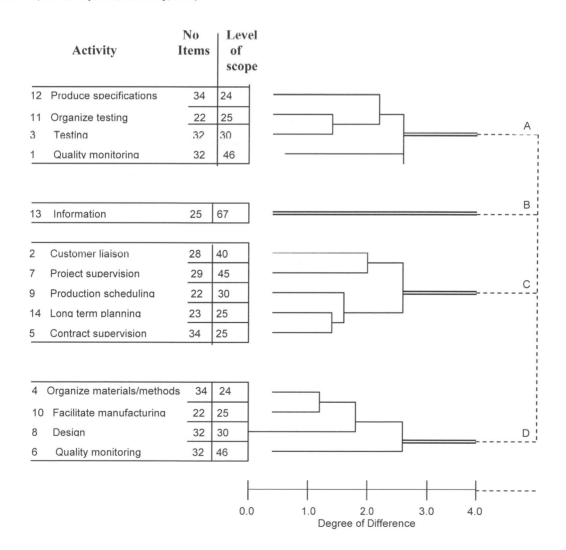

Figure 2.3. Part of the hierarchical analysis of a semantic structure from Meuwese's study of the objectives of industrial engineering (Cited by Youngman, et al, 1978).

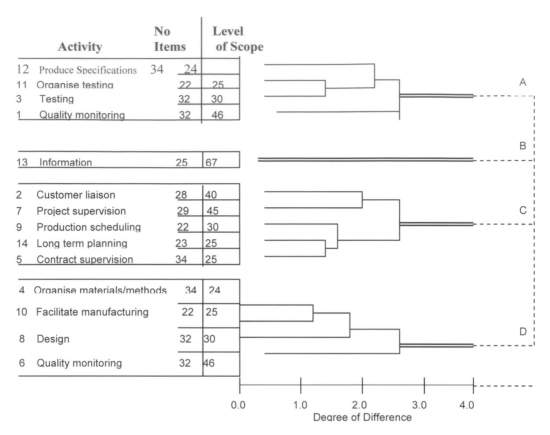

Activity	No Items	Level of Scope
12 Produce Specifications	34 24	
11 Organise testing	22	25
3 Testing	32	30
1 Quality monitoring	32	46
13 Information	25	67
2 Customer liaison	28	40
7 Project supervision	29	45
9 Production scheduling	22	30
14 Long term planning	23	25
5 Contract supervision	34	25
4 Organise materials/methods	34	24
10 Facilitate manufacturing	22	25
8 Design	32	30
6 Quality monitoring	32	46

Degree of Difference

Figure 2.4 The 14 engineering activities. These are ordered so that adjacent activities are relatively similar whereas a large separation is indicative of dissimilarity. The four sub sets are clearly shown.

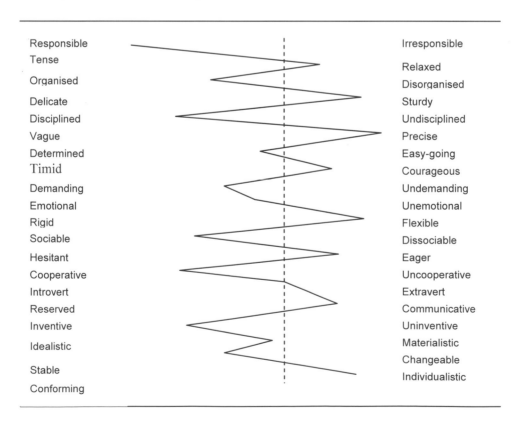

Responsible	Irresponsible
Tense	Relaxed
Organised	Disorganised
Delicate	Sturdy
Disciplined	Undisciplined
Vague	Precise
Determined	Easy-going
Timid	Courageous
Demanding	Undemanding
Emotional	Unemotional
Rigid	Flexible
Sociable	Dissociable
Hesitant	Eager
Cooperative	Uncooperative
Introvert	Extravert
Reserved	Communicative
Inventive	Uninventive
Idealistic	Materialistic
	Changeable
Stable	Individualistic
Conforming	

Figure 2.5. Examples of items from the semantic differential used to rate engineer's attitudes. to 'themselves' and their 'jobs'

2.5. Alumni and Other Similar Studies

Some institutions have obtained the views of their alumni about the experience of their higher education, andquality assurance agencies consider such studies to be relatively important in the evaluation of quality (Scales, Owen, and Leonard, 1998). ABET their constituents on an on going basis as part of continuous improvement, and surveys of alumni are being used for this purpose (Scales et al, 1998). The results of some of these surveys have been reported (e.g. Evans et al, 1993; McGourty et al, 1999).

More generally, in relation to alumni studies, in Canada, Donald and Denison (1996) explored the role of broad indicators in the evaluation of undergraduate education by alumni. They were particularly concerned with the level of satisfaction experienced by former students. Citing Astin (1993), they noted that student satisfaction is frequently overlooked in contemporary discussions of higher education outcomes. They made the point that satisfaction may well change in the first two or three years after graduation because during this period the graduates will be testing the value of their qualifications in the labour market.

Referring to Clarke et al, (1986a and 1986b), Donald and Denison drew attention to the fact that during this period graduates are likely to acquire insights into the effects of their educational experience. Consequently they will be able to highlight its strengths and weaknesses (Graham and Cockriel, 1990).

To pursue their investigation of broad indicators, Donald and Denison designeda simple questionnaire that asked for responses to a limited number of Likert-type scale items. Two open-ended items were included. These were *"(1) What features of your education at X would you have judged to have been most meaningful to your subsequent graduation? And (2) What advice would you care to offer the university based on your subsequent experience?"*

The items distinguished between broad indicators at the level of the institution and program. Their survey was conducted among graduates from five major programs. Although the response rate was small (12% = 356), which makes the validity questionable, they deemed it satisfactory for their purposes. Although they had much to say about the methodological issues surrounding their study, it is the result of the indicators relating to the quality of teaching and its value in preparing them for employment that are of great concern here. About half the sample reported that the quality of teaching was "high". Only 12% thought that it was "low". A greater proportion of the most recent graduates thought that the quality of teaching was "low". Do graduates become more sanguine about their education with age?

Institutional pressures were blamed for poor teaching.

"The inherent reward system for the professors leans heavily towards research and grants. The unfortunate result is a steady decline in the quality of classroom lectures and teaching in general. It would be useful to review the criteria for evaluating professor performance and increasingly emphasize teaching skills".

As Donald and Denison pointed out, it is unlikely that insights of this kind could be obtained from undergraduate ratings. The respondents' remarks also highlighted the difference between academic and professional needs with suggestions for more provision in the areas of communication skill, interpersonal skill and knowledge of business

In response to the first of the open-ended questions Donald and Denison found that the most frequently mentioned feature was the "ability to think". They suggested that this finding highlighted a discrepancy between the frames of reference of graduates and those of university decision-makers. *"Where the latter focused on administrative decisions between teaching, program and student life, alumni focused more on learning and developmental outcomes".* These graduates blurred the distinction between formal class and informal out-of-class learning. This illustrates the complexity of the higher education process and the need to take the kind of systems approaches to its study advocated by Pascarrela and Terenzini (1991).[13]

At Marquette University 85% of the 1980 cohort recommended that the emphasis on the humanities and social sciences should remain the same. However, only 61% said this in the 1992 cohort. Also 24% compared with 5% in the 1980 cohort recommended a decrease in these studies (Schneider and Niederjohn, 1995). In relation to this point a rather unusual survey of students was carried out at the Georgia Institute of Technology which asked them to state the relative emphasis that they would place on the 11 criteria of ABET 2000. It was found that the students did not appreciate the reasoning behind some of the criteria. They did not see the importance of the engineer's role in society. They felt this should not be the responsibility of the educational system but that of the individual. Perhaps this view will change once they have had some years at work. But, they were also as confused over the purpose of some of the criteria as were committee members responsible for devising the new curriculum (Peters, 1998).

Regan and Schmidt (1999) evaluated a series of skills, habits and knowledge areas by comparing the degree of importance to success in engineering alumni's evaluation of their current level of competence in the same areas. They found there was a high convergence between the results from alumni one year after their graduation and those from alumni five years after graduation.

The value of alumni surveys for small engineering departments in liberal arts colleges was discussed by Puerzer and Rooney (2002) of Hofstra

---

[13] Systems studies are particularly well illustrated by the longitudinal studies undertaken by Astin (1997), and on a small scale at Alverno College (Mentkowski and associates, 2000).

University. In part of their survey they listed the 12 published ABET criteria and asked the alumni to rate them on 5-point Likert type scales for both importance and preparation. The perceived importance was found to be similar to that found in other surveys (e.g., McGourty et al, see next paragraph). Among the many interesting findings was the fact that when the responses of those with and without graduate school experience were compared it was the importance and not the preparation that was perceived differently.

One of the hypotheses generated by the study which requires further examination is that students with low GPA's might perceive themselves to have been under prepared. Not withstanding the problems of self-report inventories, or the problems posed by intervening variables, (as for example, forgetfulness after a laps of time), McGourty et al (1999) of Columbia University, took the view that a well designed alumni survey could be of value in the assessment process. Therefore, they undertook the development of survey instruments with colleagues at the University of Pittsburgh. The two surveys differed in that the Columbia survey sought data on the undergraduate experience, further education, employment history, alumni association events, and the Centre for Career Services whereas the Pittsburgh survey concentrated on the educational processes which students experienced during their college life.[14]

It presupposed that these processes are directly related to the learning outcomes, and that is the basis of the work of those who investigate more generally the effectiveness of liberal arts programs in the United States (e.g. Astin, 1997, Pascarella and Terenzeni, 1991). Another difference between the two schools was that the Columbia instrument was designed with the help of alumni whereas the Pittsburgh instrument was not, on the ground that it could compromise the design and validity of the questionnaire. The Pittsburgh questionnaire distinguished between primary and secondary processes. The primary processes are core processes that are essential for the student's engineering education. The secondary processes are those that enable an individual to attend university and/or enhance their educational experience. These domains are very similar to those used by Yorke (1996), Yorke et al, (1998) in his development of a fine brush questionnaire for students to rate their educational experience [see Heywood (2000) for a summary].

The data were analyzed and related to the ABET criteria. The paper gave some examples of the data in order to illustrate the power of this method. Thus, at Columbia the majority of alumni felt that communication skills were of considerable importance to their careers but only 21% felt they were very well prepared in this domain. The conclusion was that the school needed to improve in this area. In the Pittsburgh survey that compared the alumni from two departments, the alumni had a relatively poor opinion of advising and counselling.

In regard to preparation for industry, 33% and 26% thought the experience was either "poor" or "fair."

McGourty et al believed they had demonstrated the value of such surveys but they caution that *"it is important to design the survey so that a department can solicit information regarding specific program objectives and outcomes. A 'one size fits all approach' will provide only limited information of program effectiveness."*

Regan and Schmidt (1999) also reported their findings back to departments. They found that: *"the value is variable depending on the response rate in each department"*. Some departments decided to supplement the survey with instruments of their own. This reinforces McGourty's point. However, of more significance is the Regan and Schmidt's disclosure of a concern expressed by their accrediting association, that there was little evidence to show that academic programs were organized around comprehensive goals and objectives for student learning.

Application
Use test reports from other firms.
Use test reports on earlier components.
Use Pert Chart**
Prepare rig for testing**
Simulate normal working conditions for a component**

Communication
Discuss testing requirements with technician.
Consult regarding cause of service fault.
Pass report to another engineer.
Notify designer regarding existence of a fault.
Advise production department concerning faults.

Diagnosis
Identify deviations from specifications.
Interpret performance graphs***
Interpret test reports supplied by technicians***
Confirm existence of fault by appropriate checks.
Monitor investigations into fault diagnosis.

Evaluation
Assess whether existing component meets customer specifications.
Assess success of fault removal attempt.
Examine reports supplied.
Assess validity of continuous budgets.**
Assess customer's real timing requirements.**

Management (Direction and Control)
Initiate diagnosis of fault.[2]
Suggest modifications to testing specifications.
Give advice to technicians on test results.
Observe dismantling of part- failure in service.
Decide measures to eliminate fault(s).

Exhibit 2.12. A subjective analysis (partial) of activity '1' in terms of operations contributing to skills of application, communication, diagnosis, evaluation and management (direction and control). In activity 1 there were 32 operations in all*. * These were assigned as follows: Application – 2; Communication – 5; Diagnosis – 11; Evaluation – 3; Management (Direction and Control) – 8.** Operations taken from other derived 'activities' tro make up groups of 5 operations.*** Illustrations overlap between the behavioral groups in the Exhibit arising from the subjective nature of the method of assignment. (Youngman et al, 1978).

---

[14] Copies of the Colombia and Pittsburgh surveys can be obtained from the authors.

For surveys to have meaning, departments must be clear about the objectives they wish to achieve and must design the items to evaluate whether those objectives have been achieved, while not avoiding the possibility that some objectives should be ditched and new ones entertained. In this respect, some departments have indicated that alumni studies have led to changes in their curriculum (e.g., Soldan, 1997)

Other organizations have obtained information from employers (e.g. Boyd et al, 1991). Just such an enquiry was part of a battery of surveys sponsored by the Quebec Ministry of Higher Education in which the views of College Teachers and Graduate technologists were also sought. They commented on the results in the light of learning theory and its application in the classroom. One recommendation was to use experiential learning models such as Kolb (1984) together with Boyd's (1982) cybersystemic theory in order to develop new instructional designs for electro-technology laboratory units.

They also suggested that Gagné and Merrill's learning theory could be used to completely redesign the electro-technology curriculum.

However, a university can have more general objectives with respect to learning, and at Brigham Young University alumni and students were surveyed to try and determine the key facilitators of learning. The results showed a small shift in factors between students and alumni. For example among the factors that enhance learning group work it was found to be relatively significant for students but not so for alumni. Lack of resources was among the factors that impeded learning for the students but it did not worry alumni so much. Alumni, however, felt there had been insufficient counselling. Both groups rated a poor professor along with tests and grades as the most significant impedance to effective learning (Hawks, 1996).[15]

In a second phase survey students reported lack of time as the most important factor impeding learning. In 1998 a survey that focused on lifelong learning reported that some alumni had experienced difficulty in adapting to change, and that the ability to work with other people required attention (Hawks, 1998).[16] In Britain there has been very little concern with alumni studies although independent researchers have attempted to evaluate the experience that graduates had of higher education. In the 1960's a number of surveys were made of the graduates in the engineering profession. These focused on specific subjects and the samples were drawn from graduate members of the professional institutions who may not all have come from universities.[17] (e.g., Chemical Engineering, Edgeworth Johnstone, 1961; Mechanical Engineering, Hutton and Gerstl, 1964; 1966; Lee, 1969; Monk, 1972; Moon, 1968: Metallurgists, Hopkins, 1967; Hornsby Smith, 1967). There were also two reports of surveys that had focused specifically on the mathematical needs of electrical engineers and metallurgists respectively (Clarke, 1967; Scott et al, 1966). There has been a continuing debate about how much mathematics engineers require (Chapter 7). Of these surveys the most influential was due to Hutton and Gerstl. They showed, among other things, the need for design to be incorporated in engineering courses. Monk's survey showed that because the terms' *design* and *designer* were used to describe work undertaken in the drawing office that mechanical engineering graduates sought jobs in management. This meant that they could arrive in senior positions without any skill in design. He argued that the publications of the Council of Engineering Institutions and the Engineering Industries Board on the jobs of designers and managers affirmed the perceived low status of design. This was further confirmed in the Youngman et al study reported above of whom Monk was a member of the team. Moon's survey focused on the ethical attitudes of engineers and is discussed in Chapter 3.

In Israel, questionnaires to engineers have been used to determine the education and training needs of industry for communications systems engineers by the Department of Education in Israel (Waks and Frank, 2000). In North Carolina, Graduates, employers and instructors were questioned about the importance of topics and levels of proficiency for two-year electro-technology programs. A variety of topics and levels of proficiency were required, and it was suggested that flexibility could be provided by modularized courses that were broken down into units.

Lee's (1969) study is of interest because in some respects it provides a cautionary tale in the interpretation of survey data. He seems to have been the first person to determine the objectives for practical work in engineering from the views of practising chartered mechanical engineers. He related these to the JMB classification of coursework described above.

One aspect of Lee's work that is seldom discussed is the finding (contrary to both our opinions) that engineers liked traditional laboratory work. It seems that they did not criticize it because they believed that it

---

[15] The technique used is of interest. In the first phase students were asked to list three things that promoted learning and three things that impeded learning in an open ended format. This produced a survey of the top 16 to 20 items arranged in random order. The commentary above refers primarily to the first phase except where stated. In this survey there is little focus on grades. There also appears to be no great worry about available resources

[16] Yet another enquiry undertaken many years ago at Brigham Young University sought to find out how employers differentiated between engineers and technologists (Smoot and King, 1981) which was a problem in the UK (e.g. Heywood, 1969).

[17] The professional institutions in Britain have Royal Charters that empower them to set qualifying examinations at Graduate level. This provided a major route for engineers who were undertaking part-time study in technical colleges. This part-time route was the major source of supply of mechanical and production engineers until the nineteen-seventies (Payne, 1960) when the regulations were changed, and the only way to become a chartered engineer was to take a full-time degree program at a university or college recognized by the appropriate professional institution. The general regulations of the institutions are similar to the ABET requirements. The specific regulations related to their examinations and were detailed syllabi.

was the one part of their course where they felt they were experiencing what they believed "real engineering" to be.

At the time the courses were focused heavily on engineering science, and the value of "real engineering" in courses continues to be discussed in the literature. This particular survey illustrates the value of supplementing questionnaires with in-depth interviews after an inquiry especially when a survey has contradicted forecast results. In regard to Lee's finding, there have been several papers of recent origin that report the welcome students give to "real engineering" experiences in their courses from year 1 and throughout (e.g. Marra and Palmer, 1999; see also Chapter 12).

In some respects these surveys covered the industrial stakeholders, but they were not specifically set up to do this as was a survey by McMartin and McGourty (1999). They asked industrialists to describe their involvement in several assessment activities. These were: defining student learning outcomes; defining program objectives; selecting and developing assessment tools; using assessment results for academic decisions; assessing student abilities in the classroom; assessing student performance outside of the classroom; evaluating academic programs and curricula; and evaluating assessment program. The results were compared with the views of engineering faculty and administrators.

Fifteen schools were involved. The interview technique was used with structured open-ended questions. A moderate involvement was defined as attendance at meetings 1 to 2 times/term, and intense was defined as 6 to 8 times/year. Half of the twelve industrialists interviewed played a moderate role in defining student learning outcomes. They were frequently asked only to react to a set of definitions. Otherwise they felt they had very little involvement in the other activities, and as the authors said: *"industry has been kept to the periphery of the planning process"*. They suggested that a major factor for this state of affairs was lack of trust on the part of the faculty. At the same time faculty do not understand their potential value. But they noted that great strides had been taken in involving industrialists in the direct assessment of student learning especially in design projects and capstone courses. They are involved in grading and provide professional feedback.

In England, in the 1960's, one investigator used a systems approach to evaluate the effectiveness of technology (engineering, maths and applied sciences) sandwich (cooperative) courses.[18] Information was also obtained not only from graduates but from employers, accrediting agencies, and external examiners. Simultaneously, information was collected from students and teachers in the courses, and pupils and their teachers in schools, about the perceptions they had of these courses (Heywood, 1969; Heywood, Pollitt and Mash,

1966). Most industrialists believed that their responsibility was the provision of training places. What went on in the academic period was a matter for the colleges. But, there were one or two industrialists who complained about the content of the curriculum (see below).

A similar approach was adopted at the University of Arizona where a task force was established to review the appropriateness of the undergraduate curricula to meet the needs of the engineering curricula in the decade ahead (Evans et al, 1993). They sampled students, alumni, industry representatives, and faculty. The rankings from the industrialists were obtained from a one-day special workshop. Each group was asked to rate ten attributes for their importance. They found that all groups rated problem recognition and solution first. But the investigators commented that: *"What is clear from this survey is that: (a) The engineering education literature, which in recent years has been urging a broader education, is validated by graduates who find their broad background generally as valuable as subjects in their major, (b) that insufficient development of communication skills remains a chronic problem that must be addressed."*

Evans et al, (1993) of the State University of Arizona also argued that, "engineering education may now need a bottom up approach that first establishes curriculum purpose and emphasis (i.e. specifications) based on discussions and consensus agreements among employers of engineers, alumni, students, and faculty-the customers of the educational system. Designing to meet these specifications should yield better curricula."

This was in similar vein to a follow up of the earlier British systems study (Heywood et al, 1966). Some senior industrialists complained about the courses not meeting the needs of industry during the survey. The Chairman of a Government Committee on the education and training of engineers for the electrical and manufacturing industries was severely critical of university education in a published paper (Bosworth, 1963, 1966). Accordingly the Vice-Chancellor of the University of Lancaster who wanted to establish an engineering department brought together a small group of engineering educators and industrialists who used a modified delphi technique to derive a curriculum. The participants met first as a group to produce an outline course. Each of them was then interviewed by the coordinator who on completion of the interviews circulated a draft text. There were then further meetings with the participants. On one occasion they met with a much larger group. The paper was drafted and redrafted until a consensus was reached. In producing the drafts the coordinator reviewed research and fitted relevant material to the model as a justification of what was proposed. One item that was brought into the report in support of the proposals was the Bloom Taxonomy. Several persons not involved in the group, including George Bosworth, were consulted as the activity continued (Heywood et al, 1966). The curriculum that resulted was so novel as to be

---

[18] These were not technology programs in the American usage of the term but four year programs equivalent to a university degree but, at colleges in the public sector. See Heywood (1989a, p. 6), for a diagram of the system.

beyond the plausibility structure of the day[19] but it did enable the Vice-Chancellor [20]to propose an innovative curriculum that was acceptable to the University and the University Grants Committee.

Evans et al (1993) suggested that their results were "indicative of mounting evidence that employers, especially those that are joining or that have joined the quality revolution, are desperate for people who do not have to learn on the job how to fit into a team-centred culture where, communication, interpersonal skills, and professionalism, are as important as technical skills."

During the same period employers persuaded the British government that this was the case for all graduates irrespective of subject. One novel investigation also supported that view. About 10,000 job advertisements for graduates in the British quality newspapers were analyzed for the skills sought. Fifty nine percent contained explicit reference to the personal skills required for performance in the job. Of the remainder, a further 15% could be inferred to require such characteristics. Of the 32 significant characteristics that were isolated 20 were considered to be genuine transferable skills. They collated into the four generic categories of communication; teamwork; problem solving (creativity); and management and organizing shown in Figure 2.7 (Green, 1990). The reader may like to turn to Section 6.5 for a more detailed discussion of this model.

The effect of this kind of information (and pressure from industrialists) on the British Government was that they established a five year project, to develop the skills of what was called *enterprise learning* across the university curriculum. The majority of universities participated in the initiative. The Committee that advised the Employment Department (that was responsible for this Enterprise in Higher Education initiative) listed the areas that every student should experience. These are shown in Exhibit 2.13 (Heywood, 1994),[21] Exhibit 2.14 shows a chart of how the Sheffield skills might be incorporated in teaching. The common skills (or core skills as they are sometimes called), required by the Business and Technician Council and the National Council for Vocational Qualifications are shown in Exhibit 2.15 (cited by Doderidge, 1999). Subsequently, universities were asked to ensure their graduates possessed certain "key skills." [They are now called "core skills" (see Chapter 15 Section 4 for details of these in engineering)].

At the University of Technology in Sydney, generic skills of this kind were incorporated within a more general listing of attributes required by graduates that included professional formation; technical expertise; and personal and academic development (Lowe, Scott, and Bagia, 2000).

A key issue is the extent too which generic skills, especially those in the cognitive domain, are transferable. With one or two exceptions, this is an area of learning that has received little attention in the engineering literature (see, for example, Pudlowski, 1990).

Davies, Csete and Poon (1999) of Hong Kong Polytechnic University designed a questionnaire that was administered to recent graduates in construction. The purpose was to determine (a) what skills they had employed in their initial experience of industry they had learned during their university education, and (b) in what skills were they deficient. A similar questionnaire was given to their employers who *"were asked to rate the importance of the listed skills for any graduate and then to comment specifically on the ability of the graduate who had named them as their immediate supervisor who was familiar with their work."* They found that the gap between expectations and revealed practice was not as great as they imagined. Employers did not rate graduates differently on levels of achievement in each of 16 skills. Employers rated graduate achievement higher than the graduate listening skills, cooperative team working, and creativity. Both employers and graduates believed they required more development in general intellectual and analytical skills, specific skill areas (e.g. law, building contracts), and more practical hands-on training.

A recent survey of engineering graduates in New Zealand showed that the main activities that they were engaged in were design and consultancy. The graduates moved rapidly into management situations. It is not surprising that Deans (1999) should have found that the knowledge based topics that were thought to be important were those related to the professional and managerial aspects of engineering. The science topics thought to be most helpful were those that were considered to be most general (e.g., mechanics).

Cognitive knowledge and skills
1.   **Knowledge:**- Key concepts of enterprise learning (accounting, economics, organisational behavior, inter and intra-personal behavior
2.   **Skills:**-The ability to handle information, evaluate evidence, think critically, think systemically (in terms of systems), solve problems, argue rationally, and think creatively

Social Skills, as for example the ability to communicate, and to work with others in a variety of roles both as leader and team member

Managing one's self, as for example, to be able to take initiative, to act independently, to take reasoned risks, to want to achieve, to be willing to change, to be able to adapt, to be able to know one's self and one's values, and to be able to assess one's actions

Learning to learn. To understand how one learns and solves problems in different contexts and to be able to apply the styles learnt appropriately in the solution of problems

---

Exhibit 2.13. The four broad areas of learning together with the elements they comprise that are important for equipping students for their working lives, as defined by the REAL working group of the Employment Department (1991) (cited in Heywood, 1994).

---

[19] It required a project or problem based approach for much of the time.

[20] Sir Charles Carter.

[21] In respect of engineers in the oil and gas industry see Connolly and Middleton (1996).

In the United Kingdom, an analysis of the marks for those taking their second year examinations was compared with those awarded by industrialists during their professional training. There was virtually no correlation between the two. Marshall (1994), who reported this, suggested that since such marks are measures of quality, the perceptions of quality that academics and industrialists have are very different. In sum, retrospective evaluations that relate the undergraduate experience of alumni to their subsequent employment are of considerable value to those concerned with education but the value of task analyzes of engineers at work is important since the content of engineering activities is constantly changing.

The surveys and task analyzes did not take into account problems and practice in the transition from college to the workplace. When this is done, it reinforces the findings of task analyzes, alumni, and employer studies as the next section will show.

2.6. Transition from College to Workplace

Little attention has been paid to issues surrounding the transition from college to work although all transitions are discontinuities that may prove difficult for some people (Heywood, 2000).

A novel investigation at two New England Institutions obtained student perceptions of their future. In addition to a questionnaire students were asked to complete the *Thematic Apperception Test* which had been used to measure achievement (Atkinson, 1958).

They hoped it would capture achievement, affiliation and power motivation, and compatibility. The students were also asked to complete *The Draw a Person Test* (Goodenough, 1973) in order to uncover interpersonal perceptions about self and other (Lancor and Karanian, 1998). The results indicated that students were not so clear or confident of what would be expected of them, or how they would be evaluated in the workplace. Lancor and Karanian argued that there was an onus on educators to help student's transfer smoothly to the workforce. Perhaps software of the kind that is used at Drexel University for the self-improvement of software engineers might be developed for undergraduates. The Personal Software Process *"seems to be excellent for substantially increasing student's insights and understanding of software engineering"* (Hislop, 1989).

Christiano and Ramirez (1993) looked at this problem in some detail. They argued, that statements of skill areas required in the work place also express the company's values, and the same is true of universities, and they influence decision making in the particular environment. There is, therefore, a need to improve the match between what industry expects and what students are taught. *"This means that the "how" of education can be just as important as the "what." The SCANS classroom, developed in Fort Worth public schools, is one possible way to change the "how" of education ... .In the SCANS classroom, there is often more than one viable solution to problems, and students work with peers and teachers to negotiate classroom activities and solve problems. Students often assess themselves (self-calibration of goals) in addition to external review and lessons are interdisciplinary in nature. Listening and speaking are fundamental to the learning process"*. (A description of the SCANS curriculum is given in Chapter 7). This confirms what was said in the previous section about the need for personal skill development in the curriculum. There is concern for the development of generic skills both within engineering courses, and across the university curriculum. Newcomer (2001) illustrated this point, and he showed how the objectives to be achieved were related to student learning outcomes in applied engineering statics and strength of materials design projects.

His illustrations are of interest because of his approach to the definition of objectives, and also his awareness of the importance of finding time for these objectives to be achieved. He distinguished between primary, secondary and tertiary objectives. If one tries, in any one course, to achieve all the generic skills required the technical content of the course could be compromised. In his illustration (Exhibit 2.16) 11 of the 12 generic skills agreed by the Engineering Technology Department at his university were intended to be achieved by the two courses. The intended learning outcomes are shown in Exhibit 2.17. The achievement of these objectives and outcomes was to be through design projects that integrated material from the two courses. These helped integrate the students' knowledge and bridged the gap between theory and practice. In many cases in this classification *"the sole primary learning objective is the technical knowledge,"* although this was not always true. The primary objective is the primary focus, while the tertiary objectives use material that is already known.

It will have been noticed that the achievement of generic skills requires attention to both cognitive and affective domains of learning. Those who developed *The Taxonomy* for the cognitive domain also recognized the need for taxonomies in the affective and psychomotor domains. They achieved a *Taxonomy of the Affective* domain, but work on the psychomotor domain was left to others. These are considered in the next part.

Part 3: Summary

A brief summary of The Taxonomy of Educational Objectives in the Affective Domain is given. Although educators took very little notice of this domain and concentrated on the cognitive it is not possible to separate the two domains in this way. The affective domain is becoming increasingly important with the emphasis that is being placed on group and teamwork, and development of professional attitudes in the engineering curricula. This part begins with a brief résumé of some other approaches to the classification and derivation of objectives.

2.7. Other Approaches to the Classification and Derivation of Objectives.

Without wishing to draw causal or linear historical relationships, it is useful to note that some members of the critical thinking movement began to develop their own taxonomies. There is little doubt that they were strongly influenced by *The Taxonomy*. However, in addition to adding items, they apparently disagreed with its classes. A distinction came to be made between knowledge and comprehension and Higher Order Thinking Skills (HOTS). Imrie's (1995) RECAP model followed this pattern. He divided his taxonomy into two tiers. At the first level, objectives stated the minimum essentials which students should achieve. These objectives would be tested by short answer, and/or multiple-choice questions. Students can be tested for mastery. A second level comprised analysis, synthesis, and evaluation problem solving skills. These objectives focused on skills of problem solving.

They could be tested by essays, case study questions, and use of norm referenced assessments One problem with the problem solving skills category was that some cognitive development theorists held that problem-solving skills are Piagetian skills and not the highest level of reflective judgement that can be obtained. Crooks (1988) cited by Imrie also used the term critical thinking to encompass these skills.

The SOLO Taxonomy (Biggs and Collis, 1982) attempted to link forms of knowledge with development. There are five modes of learning that have many similarities with the Piagetian development stages. These are sensori-motor, iconic, concrete-symbolic, formal and post-formal. The forms of knowledge related to these are tacit, intuitive, declarative, theoretical, and meta-theoretical. There are five structural levels (hierarchically ordered) in a learning cycle that is repeated in each form. Both Gibbs (1982) and Ramsden (1992) have described these levels in terms of the type of answers a person might give to a question. Following Gibbs' description the levels are:

Objectives of Higher Education

1. Basic knowledge
2. Comprehension of subject discipline
3. Self directed learning
4. Communication skills
5. Application to new situations
6. Invention
7. Assessing quality

Exhibit 2.14. Collier's (1989) principal objectives for higher education

Prestructural. A stage of ignorance where the learner has no knowledge of the question.
Unistructural. Where the learner is able to give an answer that contains one correct feature.

Multistructural. Where the answer contains a check list of items.
Relational. The answer integrates the items into an integrated whole.
Extended abstract. The answer is related to the more general body of knowledge

The SOLO taxonomy is also of interest because there is a conceptual over lap with the deep and surface learning strategies discussed in Chapter 5. Level 3 may correspond to surface learning, and levels 4 and 5 correspond to deep learning.

To complete this section with a return to the problem of categories, Collier (1989) suggested the list of categories for theology shown in Exhibit 2.18. These could apply to almost any subject including engineering. His short text explained how they related to teaching methods, learning and assessment and is as good an introduction to teaching and learning as any.

2.8. The Affective Domain

Denton and McKinney (2004) pointed out that the top 10 characteristics required from college graduates by the computing industry require both affective and cognitive capabilities. They are communication skills, honesty/integrity, teamwork skills, interpersonal skills, motivation/initiative, strong work ethic, analytical skills, flexibility/adaptability, computer skills and organizational skills. This standard created by the National Association of Colleges and Employers (ACM/IEEE, 2001) is entirely consistent with the findings of various studies sponsored by the UK Enterprise in Education Initiative (see above). For this reason, attention to this domain is becoming increasingly important as engineering curricula begin to emphasize group and team work and the development of professional attitudes. *The Taxonomy of Educational Objectives in the Affective Domain* (Krathwohl et al, 1964) summarized in Exhibit 2.19 is not very explicit about what the affective domain is. In this context it is taken to mean not only the value dispositions we hold but, the behaviors we adopt, and especially those enacted in relation to other people. It is a domain that is about *feeling*. Kaplan (1978) showed how the affective domain applied to classrooms (Exhibit 2.20), and Rice (1977) has suggested how it might be assessed in engineering. An interview technique was used by Alsop and Watts (2000) to discover the feelings that high school students (years 11 and 12) had in the United Kingdom for physics. They argued that if more was known about these feelings something might be able to be done to arrest the decline in enrollment to physics departments.

For many years educators took very little notice of this domain and concentrated on the cognitive domain; however, it is not possible to separate the two in this way. The two domains depend on each other, a fact that has been demonstrated by Imrie (1995) in the case of law, and by Freeman and Byrne (1976) with respect to medical general practice and most recently for engineering by Denton and McKinney, (2004). Indeed as the studies of industrial attitudes to higher education

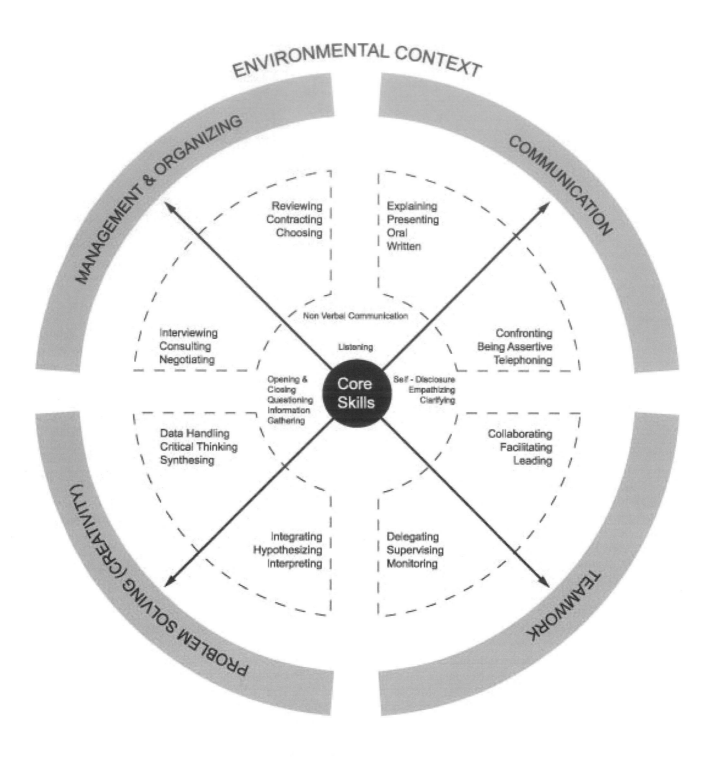

Figure 2.6. The personal transferable skills developmental model of the University of Sheffield's Personal Skills Unit (cited in Heywood, 1994, and reproduced with the permission of the Director).

show, industrialists are as interested, if not more interested, in the affective domain as they are in the cognitive. One industrialist (a Senior Training Officer with the British Steel Corporation) who took this view, analyzed the tasks of the managers he trained. He used *The Taxonomy* and against each activity in the cognitive domain he noted an activity in the affective domain that corresponded. One of his analyzes is shown in Exhibit - 2.21. A partial description of his attempt to construct a taxonomy for management is shown in Exhibit 2.22.

Neumann (1981) published a similar list for management skill teaching within a project course. His categories were Planning, Organizing, Directing, and Controlling. Besterfield-Sacre et al (2000) listed the categories of the affective domain for valuation and related it to the action verbs: *accept, challenge, defend, respect, question, support and enjoy.* Many statements of the goals of higher education would include *self awareness* and the ability to *self assess* (e.g., Alverno, 1994). These clearly belong to the affective domain.

Otter (1991) as previously mentioned (p. 53), described a statement of learning outcomes for engineering developed by a small group of engineers. They used the Carter (1985) taxonomy. as a checklist a within which they tried to identify the characteristics of a typical engineering graduate. Carter (1984) himself had applied it to engineering education. The categories in Carters' taxonomy depend as much on the affective domain as they do on the cognitive. They are

- Mental skills.
- Information skills.
- Action skills.
- Social skills.
- Mental quality.
- Attitudes and values.
- Personal characteristics
- Spiritual knowledge.
- Factual knowledge.
- Experiential knowledge.

Some examples from their statement of engineering outcomes are shown in Exhibit 2.23. Goals in this domain re unlikely to be achieved without some form of what has been called *Active Learning* (McGill and Beatty, 1992). Related to the idea of active or action learning is the concept of experiential learning, and Steinaker and Bell (1969) produced a taxonomy of experiential learning. This had categories for *exposure* (seeing, hearing, reacting, recognizing), *participation, identification* (classifying, explaining, experimenting, writing, drawing), *internalization* (generalising, comparing, contrasting, and transferring), and *dissemination.* In engineering cooperative learning is a learning method that is designed to achieve several important skills in the affective domain.

An attempt to relate teaching methods to the two domains, and a psychomotor domain was made by Weston and Cranton (1986). It is shown in Exhibit 2.24.

Denton and McKinney (2004) as a result of the evaluation of interventions to enhance affective development found that all affective factors, in their study, as measured by post-test scores showed significant correlations with course grade. But, they also found that during the course the affective factors decreased. If it is agreed that affective factors are important, and the evidence, particularly from motivation theory, suggests they are then, the curriculum needs to be designed to enhance affective development. Denton and McKinney made the following suggestions:

- Ensure meaningful student-faculty relationships.
- Encourage students to join learning communities through group work, supplemental programs, and peer mentoring.
- Encourage students to develop their own vision of success so as to justify their effort.
- Students should learn to set goals to direct their path to success.
- Tutors should provide well-designed assignments.
- Praise students when they excel.
- Connect the curriculum to the real world.
- Promote active learning.
- Break the routine and make learning fun.
- Challenge those who excel.
- Integrate affective objectives.
- Limit the size of introductory classes.

(See later Chapters for discussion of these and other relevant issues.)

- *Awareness* e.g., Listens to advice….recognizes own bias…..aware of feelings of others.
- *Willingness to receive.* e.g., seeks agreement from another…asks another to examine aesthetic value in the classroom…inquires how another feels about event or subject.
- *Responding,* e.g., complies with existing regulations….responds to a question….takes responsibility when offered.
- *Preference for a value,* e.g., seeks the value of another defends own value agrees with the value of another
- *Conceptualization of a value.* e.g., makes judgments (implies evaluation)….compares own value to that of another
- *Organization of a value system.*e.g. shows relationship of one value to another synthesizes two or more values into one value
- *Characterization by a value or value complex. Generalized set.*e.g., revises judgement based on evidence….makes judgements in light of situational context.
- *Characterization.* e.g. develops consistent mode of behaviour..Continually re-evaluates own mode of behaviour.

Exhibit 2.19. Summary of the Principal Categories of the Affective Domain of *The Taxonomy of Educational Objectives.* Vol. II *The Affective Domain* (Krathwohl et al, 1964).

	Communication (C)	Teamwork (T)	Problem-solving (P-S)	Managing and organizing (M)	Summary of profiles
Personal tutorial	Zone 1. All core skills. Zone 2 Explaining, presenting, written, confronting, being assertive		Zone 1 All core skills Zone 2 Critical thinking, synthesizing, interpreting, integrating, hypothesizing	Zone 1 All core skills Zone 2 Reviewing, contracting, negotiating	C = 4 T = 0 P-S = 6 M = 2
Seminar tutor-led.	Zone 1 All core skills. Zone 2. Explaining, confronting, being assertive		Zone 1 All core skills Zone 2 Critical thinking. synthesizing, interpreting	Zone 1 All core skills	C = 4 T = 0 P-S = 5 M = 0
Seminar Student-led *Individual*	Zone 1 All core skills Zone 2 Explaining, presenting oral and written, confronting, being assertive		Zone 1 All core skills Zone 2 Data handling, critical thinking, synthesizing, interpreting, integrating, hypothesizing	Zone 1 All core skills. Zone 2 Consulting	C = 5 T = 0 P-S = 6 M = 1
Seminar Student-led. *Team*	Zone 1 All core skills Zone 2 Explaining, presenting oral and written, confronting, being assertive	Zone 1 All core skills Zone 2 Collaborating, facilitating, leading, delegating.	Zone 1 All core skills Zone 2 Data handling, critical thinking, synthesizing, interpreting, integrating, hypothesizing	Zone 1 All core skills Zone 2 Reviewing, contracting, chairing, negotiating	C = 5 T = 4 P-S = 6 M = 4
Project theoretical eg ,library project, artifact study. *Individual*	Zone 1 All core skills Zone 2 Explaining, presenting oral and written, telephoning		Zone 1 All core skills Zone 2 Data handling, critical thinking, synthesizing, interpreting, integrating, hypothesizing	Zone 1 All core skills Zone 2 Reviewing, interviewing	C = 4 T = 0 P-S = 6 M = 6
Project- theoretical eg, artifact, survey, experimental practical, fieldwork. Team	Zone 1 All core skills Zone 2 Explaining, presenting oral and written, being assertive, telephoning	Zone 1 All core skills Zone 2 Collaborating, facilitating, leading, delegating	Zone 1 All core skills Zone 2 Data handling, critical thinking, synthesizing, interpreting, integrating, hypothesizing	Zone 1 All core skills Zone 2 Reviewing, contracting, chairing, interviewing, consulting negotiating	C = 5 T = 4 P-S = 6 M = 6
Project – 'live' work-based, clinical placement, company based *Team*	Zone 1 All core skills Zone 2 Explaining, presenting oral and written, confronting, being assertive telephoning	Zone 1 All core skills Zone 2 Collaborating, facilitating, leading, delegating, supervising	Zone 1 All core skills Zone 2 Data handling, critical thinking, synthesizing, interpreting, integrating, hypothesizing	Zone 1 All core skills Zone 2 Reviewing, contracting, chairing, interviewing, consulting negotiating	C = 6 T = 5 P-S = 6 M = 6
Student profile. Negotiated with tutor	Zone 1 All core skills Zone 2 Explaining, being assertive		Zone 1 All core skills Zone 2 Critical thinking, Synthesizing, interpreting, integrating	Zone 1 All core skills Zone 2 Reviewing	C = 2 T = 0 P-S = 4 M = 1

Exhibit 2.15. Active learning strategies to encourage development in the skill areas shown in Figure 2.6.

(a) BTEC Common Skills	(b) NCVQ Key Skills
Managing and developing self.	Application of number.
Working with and relating to others.	Communication.
Communicating.	Information technology.
Managing tasks and solving problems.	Improving own learning and performance.
Applying numeracy.	Working with others.
Applying design and creativity.	Problem solving.

Exhibit 2.16 Common skills for courses of the Business Technician Education Council (BTEC), and the National Council for Vocational Awards in the United Kingdom (after Doderidge, 1999) (reproduced with permission of *IEEE Proceedings Frontiers in Education Conference*).

Current learning objectives for applied engineering statics		Current learning objectives for Strength of materials.	
Primary	(a) Analytical	Primary	(a) Analytical
Secondary	(b)Project management (c) Teamwork. (d) Creative problem solving (e) Written communication.	Secondary	(b) Oral communication. (c) Teamwork. (d) Project management (e) Written communication
Tertiary	(f) Visual communication. (g)Ethics and professionalism	Tertiary	(f) Visual communication. (g) Business skills (h) Creative problem solving. (I) System thinking. (j) Self learning. (k)Ethics and professionalism.

Exhibit 2.17 Newcomer's (2001) distinction between primary, secondary, and tertiary levels of objectives. (reproduced with permission of *IEEE Proceedings Frontiers in Education Conference*).

Specific learning outcomes	Objective(s) Column (b) Exhibit 2.16
Determine internal force at any point in a structure	(a)
Determine deflection at any point in a structure	(a)
Determine stress at any point in a structure	(a)
Develop safe solution to an open-ended problem	(a)
Select appropriate materials to meet structural needs	(a), (h), (k).
Select appropriate materials to meet costs needs.	(a), (h), (I).
Estimate cost of manufacturing	(d), (h), (j).
Select realistic tolerances for needs.	(d), (h), (I).
Meet deadlines for project milestones	(c), (d).
Keep minutes of team meetings	(c), (d), (e).
Write project interim reports	(c), (d), (e).
Write a technical report to document work.	(c), (d), (e).
Create CAD documentation drawings.	(c), (f).
Assign team roles.	(c)
Listen effectively at meetings.	(c).
Show for team meetings.	(c), (d).
Complete individual tasks	(a), (c, (d).
Prepare and give professional design presentation.	(b), (c).

Exhibit 2. 18. Student learning outcomes for strength of materials (see Exhibit 2.17 (b).

Awareness
1. Listens to others
2. Receives others as co-workers
3. Listens to advice
4. Verbally pays attention to alternative points of view on a given issue
5. Refers to subgroup(s) (social, intellectual sex, race, etc.)
6. Acknowledges some aesthetic factor in the classroom(clothing, furniture, design, arrangement, art
7. Aware of feelings of others (introvert extravert, anxiety, hostility, sensitivity
8. Recognizes own bias as bias
9. Recognizes other bias as bias

Willingness to Receive
10. Seeks agreement from another
11. Seeks responsibility
12. Seeks information from another
13. Pursues another way of doing something
14. Seeks materials
15. Asks another to examine aesthetic factor in classroom
16. Inquiries how another feels about an event or subject

Responding
Acquiescence in Responding
17. Complies with existing regulations(rules.)
18. Complies to a suggestion or directive
19. Offers materials on request
20. Gives opinion when requested
21. Responds to a question
22. Takes responsibility when offered
23. Remains passive when a response is   indicated
24. Actively rejects direction(s) or suggestion(s).

Valuing
Preference for a value
25. Seeks the value of another
26. Defends value of another
27. Clearly expresses a value
28. Defends own value
29. Openly defends the right of another to possess value
30. Tries to convince another to accept a value
31. Agrees with value of another
32. Disagrees with the value of another

Organization
Conceptualization of a value
33. Makes deductions from abstractions
34. Makes judgments (implies evaluation.)
35. Compares own value to that of another
36. Attempts to identify the characteristics of a value or value system

Organizatiuon of value system
37. Compares and weighs alternatives
38. Shows relationship of one value to another
39. Ties a specific value into a system of values
40. Synthesizes two or more values into one value

Characterization by a value or value complex
Generalized set
41. Revises judgments based on evidence
42. Bases judgments on consideration of more than one proposal
43. Makes judgments in light of situational context

Exhibit 2.20. Kaplan's (1978) expansion of *The Taxonomy* of affective behavior for the classroom.

2.9. Concluding Remarks

Since the objectives movement got underway with the publication of *The Taxonomy of Educational Objectives,* criticisms of it have led to other categories, not necessarily hierarchically ordered. The language has also changed in favor of outcomes (learning/performance), although behavioral objectives and outcomes are concerned to say what ability a person should develop as a function of this or that instruction/learning. What matters is that teachers should be able to clearly state, whatever language they care to use, where they are going and what they intend students should be able to do as a result of their arrangements for instruction/learning.

There are many sources of aims and objectives. At the institutional level aims are likely to be broad and not necessarily related to objectives for learning. For example, the aim to increase the supply of qualified graduates in a particular subject is not immediately related to learning. If, however, a department has a large drop-out rate, then it is incumbent on the University to enquire into the reasons why this might be so. It may be found, for instance, that it is to do with the relationship between teaching and learning. Or, it may due to the level of entry qualification at which the students are admitted. it could, of course, be due to both. I would hold, while some would dispute, that the program objectives that relate specifically to the curriculum and learning objectives should be the same thing, and I would cite the case of engineering science in support of my case. To put it in another way the program objectives should for the most part be presented as domains with sub-abilities that clearly indicate the kind of assessment of learning that is required. More general program objectives should relate to the general experience of college that may or may not enhance learning, and thus to the achievement of the educational aims of the institution.

If my view is upheld, then those involved in the program need to work out which component parts are intended to achieve which learning objectives using.

	Knowledge	Comprehension	Application	Analysis	Synthesis	Evaluation	Affective behavior see Exhibit 2.20
1. Planning for and causing the required quantity of output to be maintained	Targets, tolerances, customer preferences,etc			Ability to recognize when a plan is not being met, skill in recognizing causes of disruption			Responding
2. Assigning employee to meet work schedules	Schedules, policies, methods, limits of authority	Skill in interpreting and translating policies and predicting outcomes	Skill in predicting probable effects of changes				Responding
3. Obtaining and/or checking the availability of the necessary materials, tools, machines and services in accordance with policies and procedures	Procedures, sources, policies	Skill in interpreting and translating policies and predicting outcomes	Skill in predicting probable effects of changes				Responding
4. The proper care and use of materials, tools machines and equipment within his /her unit	Familiarity with equipment				Ability to instruct in proper use and care of equipment		Valuing
5.Recommending and controlling overtime	Criteria, agreements, limits of authority	Skill in interpreting and translating agreements and predicting outcomes					Characterization by a value
6. Providing adequate materials and tools to meet the work program of the following shift.	Work program. Sources of tools and materials. Methods						Responding
7. Recording status of work and general conditions at the end of each shift.	Criteria	Skill in communicating					Awareness
	Criteria. Standards, Schedules	Skill in interpreting standards and schedules		Identifying causes of non-achievement	Ability to take corrective action		Valuing

Exhibit 2. 21. Extract from W. Humble's attempt to apply the *Taxonomy of Educational Objectives* to management in a steel works in the United Kingdom. Objective 4 "To plan and maintain work schedules to secure the required production of goods and services". (cited in Heywood, 1972). There were seven other objectives.

The ability to adapt and control

The ability to perceive the organizational structure and formal/informal relationships, value systems and languages, and, therefore, the needs of the organization.
Knowledge of the technical, human and financial aspects of the system or situation.
Understanding of the different thought processes in the solution of human or technological problems.
The ability to perceive one's own self (attitudes and needs).

The ability to control involves
Knowledge of
1. How the skills of those who have to be controlled should be used.
His or her requirements in relation to needs for communication, competence and excellence.
What people ought to be doing.
Whether or not they are doing it effectively.
How to create a climate in which jobs will be done effectively.
The ability to
1. Make things happen
2. Discriminate between relevant and irrelevant information, etc.

The ability to relate with people involves

(a) Knowledge of rights, responsibilities and obligations.
(b) Knowledge of ways of thinking (determinants of attitudes and values) of people in all parts of the organization.
(c) Ability to understand when action in the key environment is right and acceptable in those circumstances (i.e. to understand the effect of his behavior on the situation).
(d) Ability to predict the effects of his or her behavior and that of others on a situation.
(e) Ability to create the feeling that the job is important, etc
.

Exhibit 2.22. Partial derivation of a taxonomy of industrial objectives derived from works situations in which managers and workmen were in confrontation to some degree. (Due to W. Humble and cited in Heywood, 1989a.)

From the category of social skills
Take responsibility for the work of the group.
- Take the role of leader in group projects.
- Motivate the group and accept responsibility for activities

From the category of mental quality
Envisage solutions to engineering problems.
- List a number of alternative improvements that might be made to the layout of a gearbox.
- Devise combinational and sequential logic circuits.
- Devise mathematical models for engineering systems.
- Produce an original design to satisfy an engineering problem

From the category on attitudes and values
Assess individuals and take into account their views
- Demonstrate understanding of the role of a technical manager.
- Seek and respond to feedback from peers and superiors

From the category on personal characteristics
Perform under stress
- Make technical decisions regardless of other pressures.
- Confront criticism and respond accordingly

Category of the Spiritual
Take account of the social and moral dimension of engineering.
- Produce a design where environmental, economic and sociological factors are of prime importance.

Exhibit 2.23. learning outcomes in engineering in Otter (1991). The participants in the engineering study were R. Winterburn (City University), B. Munton (Nottingham Polytechnic), and C. Rees (Polytechnic of Wales). The other categories in the illustration come from the section headed personal qualities. (cited in Heywood, 1994.)

Domain and level.	Method.
Cognitive domain	
Knowledge	Lecture, CAI, drill and practice.
Comprehension	Lecture, modularized instruction, CAI.
Application.	Discussion, simulations and games CAI, modularized instruction, field experience, laboratory.
Analysis	Discussion, independent/group projects, simulations Field experience, role-playing, laboratory.
Synthesis	Independent/group projects, field experience, role-playing, laboratory.
Evaluation	Independent/group projects, field experience, laboratory.
Affective domain	
Receiving	Lecture, discussion, modularized instruction, field experience
Responding	Discussion, simulations, modularized instruction, role-playing, field experience.
Value	Discussion, independent/group projects, simulations, Role-playing, field experience.
Organization	Discussion, independent/group projects, field experience.
Characteriuzation by value	Independent projects, field experience
Psychomotor domain	
Perception	Demonstration (lecture), drill and practice.
Set	Demonstration (lecture), drill and practice.
Guided response	Peer teaching, games, role playing, field experience, Drill and practice.
Mechanism.	Games, role-playing, field experience, drill and practice.
Complex overt response	Games, field experience.
Adaptation	Independent projects, games, field experience.
Organization	Independent projects, games, field experience.

Exhibit 2.24. Matching objective, domain and level of learning to appropriate methods of instruction (from Weston and Cranton, 1986). CAI has been substituted for programd learning which appeared in the original. (cited in Heywood, 1989a and reproduced with the permission of the *Journal of Higher Education.*

which type of method If every tutor were teaching a decision making heuristic, or following the same learning styles approach at the same time then one has a recipe for disaster. The implication of an objectives approach is that it requires team planning while at the same time allowing individualteachers considerable freedom to develop their courses and lessons.

The second danger is that planners whether of programs, or courses or instructional periods, choose too many objectives, and overloading causes students to achieve none of them. The same applies to the selection of institutional and program aims. For this reason it is necessary to focus on a few significant aims and outcomes. To obtain this goal it is necessary to screen these lists using philosophy, sociology, and the psychology of learning. In so doing, new aims and objectives, or alternative approaches to the declaration of aims and objectives, may emerge. In this activity it will become clear whether or not a different curriculum model is required. At the same time, it brings together process and product, thereby giving rationality and coherence to the curriculum of the kind sought by Knight (2001). In the next four Chapters the role of philosophy, sociology, and the psychology of learning in screening and the development of the curriculum will be discussed

References

Adams, R. R., and R. E. Munsterman (1977). The impact of behavioral objectives on freshman engineering students. *Engineering Education,* 67, 391-394.

ACM/IEEE Computing Curricular, 2001. *Computer Science Volume, Chater 10. Professional practice* available at http://www.acm.org/sigcse/cc2001/cs-professionalpractice-html.

Alsop, S. and M. Watts (2000) Facts and feelings: exploring the affective domain in the learning of physics. *Physics Education ,* 35, (2), 132-138.

Alverno (1994). *Student Assessment as Learning at Alverno College.* Alverno College Institute, Milwakee, WI.

Anderson, C. W., et al, (1996). Competency matrix assessment in an integrated, first-year curriculum in science, engineering and mathematics. *Proceedings Frontiers in Education Conference,* 3, 1276-1280.

Anderson, L. W., and L. A. Sosniak (1994) (eds). *Bloom's Taxonomy. A Forty Year Retrospective.* National Society for the Study of Education. University of Chicago Press, Chicago.

Apple, D. K., Nygren, K. P., Williams, M. W. and D. M. Litynski (2002). Distinguishing and elevating levels of learning in engineering and technology instruction. *Proceedings Frontiers in Education Conference,*1, T4B-7 to 11.

Astin, A.W (1997). *What Matters in College. Four Critical Years Revisited.* Jossey Bass, San Francisco.(Paperback edition 1997).

Atkinson, J. W. (1958). *Motives in Fantasy, Action, in Society.* Van Nostrand, Princeton, NJ.

Bannister, D., and J. M. M. Mair (1968). *The Evaluation of Personal Constructs.* Academic Press, London.

Batanov, D. N., Dimmitt, N. J., and W. Chookittikul (2000) Q and A teaching/learning model as a new basis for developing educational software. *Proceedings Frontiers in Education Conference*, 1, F2B-12 to 17.

Besterfield-Sacre, M et al (2000). Defining the outcomes. A framework for EC 2000. *IEEE Transactions on Education.*,43, (2), 100-110.

Biggs, J. B. and K. F. Collis (1982). *Evaluating the Quality of Learning. The SOLO Taxonomy.* Academic Press, New York.

Bligh, D (1971, 1993,1999). *What's the Use of Lectures?* Penguin, Harmondsworth.

Bloom, B. S (1994). Reflections on the development and use of the taxonomy. In L. W. Anderson and L. A. Sosniak (eds.) *Bloom's Taxonomy. A Forty Year Retrospective.* 73rd Yearbook of the National Society for the Study of Education, University of Chicago Press, Chicago.

Bloom, B. S., et al (1956) (eds.) *The Taxonomy of Educational Objectives. 1 The Cognitive Domain.* David Mackay, New York.

Bobbitt, F. J (1924) *How to Make a Curriculum.* Houghton Mifflin, MA.

Borg, W. R (1972). The mini-course for changing teacher behavior. *Journal of Educational Psychology.* 63 (6) (LB 1051), A2 J 6.

Bosworth, G. S. (1963). Towards creative activity in engineering. *Universities Quarterly*, 17, 286.

Bosworth, G. S (1966) (Chairman of Committee). *The Education and Training Requirements for the Electrical and Mechanical Manufacturing Industries.* HMSO, London.

Bowyer, K (2000a). Goodearl and Aldred versus Hughes Aircraft: A Whistleblowing case study. *Proceedings Frontiers in Education Conference* 2, S2F- 2 to 7.

Boyd, G. M (1982). Essential elements of prescriptive models in educational cybernetics in *Progress in Cybernetics and Systems Research.* McGraw-Hill, London.

Boyd, G. M., Joos, G., Mulema, D. E., and I. E. Zielinska (1991). Enhancement needed for more viable electronics technologist education. *Proceedings Frontiers in Education Conference*, 742 – 747

Burns, T and G. Stalker (1961). *The Management of Innovation.* Tavistock, London.

Carter, G., Heywood, J., and D.T. Kelly (1986). *Case Study in Curriculum Assessment. GCE Engineering Science (Advanced).* Roundthorn Press, Manchester.

Carter, G., and T.A. Jordan (1990). Student Centred Learning in Engineering. Engineering Enhancement in Higher Education. Prospects and Problems. Monograph, University of Salford, Salford.

Carter, R. G (1984). Engineering Curriculum Design. *Institution of Electrical Engineers Proceedings*, 131, Part A, 678.

Carter, R. G (1985). Taxonomy of Objectives for Professional Education. *Studies in Higher Education,* 10, (2).

CEI (1963a). *Guidelines for Training Professional Engineers.* Council of Engineering Institutions, London.

CEI (1963b). Guidelines on Education and Ttraining for Management. Council of Engineering Institutions, London.

Christiano, S. J. E. and M. R. Ramirez (1993). Creativity in the classroom: special concerns and insights. *Proceedings Frontiers in Education Conference*, 209–212.

Clarke, R. J (1967). Mathematics and metallurgists. *Lancaster Studies in Higher Education*, 2, pp B1–B15.

Clarke, W., Lang, M., and E. Rechnitzer (1986a). *The class of 82. National survey of Graduates 1982.* Minister for Supply and Services, Ottawa.

Clarke, W., Lang, M., and E. Rechnitzer (1986b) The class of 82. *Report of the findings of the 1984 national survey of Graduates 1982.* Minister for Supply and services, Ottawa, Canada.

Cohen, L and L. Manion. (1977.) *A Guide to Teaching Practice.* 1st edition. Methuen, London.

Collier, G (1989). *A New Teaching. A New Learning.* SPCK, London.

Connelly, J. D., and J. C. R. Middleton (1996). Personal and professional skills for engineers': one perspective. *Engineering Science and Education Journal,* (June), pp 139-143.

Cromwell, L.S. (1986). *Teaching Critical Thinking in Arts and Humanities.* Alverno Productions, Milwaukee, WI.

Crooks, T. J. (1988). *Assessing Student Performance.* Green Guide 8. Higher Education Research and Development Society of Australasia, Sydney.

Davies, H. A., Csete, J., and L. K. Pon (1999). Employer's expectations of the performance of construction graduates. *International Journal of Engineering Education*, 15, (3), 191-198.

Deans, J (1999). The educational needs of graduate mechanical engineers in New Zealand. *European Journal of Engineering Education,* 24, (2), 151 – 162.

Dempsey, G. L., Aakwa, W. K. N.,, Higgins, B. D., and J. H. Irwin (2003). Electrical and computer engineering assessment via senior miniproject. *IEEE Transactions on Education,* 46, (3), 350 – 358.

Denton, L. F. and D. McKinney (2004). Affective factors and student achievement: a quantitative and qualitative study. *Proceedings Frontiers in Education Conference,* 1,TIG-6 to ll.

Doderidge, M (1999). Generic skill requirements for engineers in the 21st century. *Proceedings Frontiers in Education Conference,* 3,13a 9 to14.

Donald, J. G., and D. B. Denison (1996). Evaluating undergraduate education. The use of broad indicators. *Assessment and Evaluation in Higher Education,* 21, (1), 23-40/

Doron, R and S. Marco (1999). Syllabus evaluation by the job-analysis technique. *European Journal of Engineering Education,* 24, (2), 163-172.

Dressel, P. L. (1954). *Evaluation as in instruction.* Proceedings 1953 Conference on Test Problems. ETS, Princeton (cited by Carter and Jordan, 1990).

Edgeworth Johnstone, R (1961). A survey of chemical engineering education. *Transactions of the Institution of Chemical Engineers*, 39, 263.

EITB (1968a). *The Training of Engineers.* Engineering and Industrial Training Board, Watford.

EITB (1968b). *The Training of Managers.* Engineering and Industrial Training Board, Watford.

Eisner, E. W (1979). *The Educational Imagination. On the Design and Evaluation of School Programs.* MacMillan, New York.

Ellis, T. J., Hafner, W,, and F. Mitropoulos (2004). Automating instructional design with eCAD. *Proceedings Frontiers in Engineering Education,* I, TIH-1 to 6.

Evans, D. L., McNeill, B. W., and G. C. Beakley (1990) Design in engineering education: past views of future directions. *Engineering Education*, 80, (5), 517-522.

Evans, D. L. Beakley, G. C., Couch, P. E. and G. T. Yamaguchi (1993). Attributes of engineering graduates and their impact on curriculum design. *Journal of Engineering Education*, 82, (4), 203-211.

Felder, R. M (1985). The generic quiz: A device to stimulate creativity and higher level thinking skills. *Chemical Engineering Education.* Fall, p 176.

Felder, R. M (1987). On creating creative engineers. *Engineering Education*, 77, (4), 222-227.

Freeman, J., and P. Byrne (1976). *The Assessment of General Practice.* 2nd edition. Society for Research into Higher Education, London.

Froyd, J. E (1997). Competency matrix assessment for first-year curricula in science, engineering, and mathematics and ABET Criteria 2000. *Proceedings Frontiers in Education Conference*,3, 1190-1195.

Furst, E. J (1958). *The Construction of Evaluation Instruments.* David McKay, New York.

Furst, E. J (1994) Bloom's taxonomy: philosophical and educational issues. In L. W. Anderson and L. A. Sosniak (eds.) *Bloom's Taxonomy. A Forty-Year retrospective.* 73rd yearbook of the National Society for the Study of Education. University of Chicago Press, Chicago.

Gagné, R. M. and M. D. Merrill (1990). Reviewing the main points of David Merrill's learning theory. *Educational Technology*,30, (8), 36-41.

Gibbs, G. (1981). *Teaching students to learn. A student centred approach.* Open University Press, Milton Keynes.

Gibbs, G. (1992). Improving the quality of student learning through course design in R. Barnett (ed) *Learning to Effect.* Society for research into Higher Education, Open University Press, Buckingham.

Goodenough, F. (1973). Draw a Person in Di Leo's *Childrens Drawings as Diagnostic Aids.* Bruner/Mazel publishers, New York.

Gorman, M. E (2002) Turning students into professionals; types of knowledge and ABET engineering criteria. *Journal of Engineering Education,* 91, (3), 327–332.

Graham, S. W. and J. Cockriel (1990). An assessment of the perceived utility of various college majors. *NACADA Journal*,10, (1), 8–17.

Green, S (1990). Analysis of personal transferable skills requested by employees in graduate recruitment advertisements in June 1989. Sheffield Personal Skills Unit. University of Sheffield.

Gregory, S. A (1972) (ed.). *Creativity and Innovation in Engineering.* Butterworth, London.

Harrow, A. J (1972). A Taxonomy of the psychomotive domain. In *A Guide for developing Behavioral Objectives.* Mackay, New York.

Hawks, V (1996). Rediscovering learning: a survey of factors that affect student learning in engineering education. *Proceedings of the Frontiers in Education Conference,* 1, 314-317.

Hawks, V (1998). A perspective from industry on characteristics of life lonf learning. *Proceedings Frontiers in Education Conference,* 2,743-747.

Hereford, S. M (1979). The Keller Plan within a conventional academic environment: an empirical 'meta-analytic' study. *Engineering Education,* 70, (3), 250–260.

Heywood, J (1969). An Evaluation of certain post-war developments in Higher Technological Education. Thesis Volume 1. University of Lancaster Library, Lancaster.

Heywood, J (1976). Discovery methods in engineering science at 'A' level. *Bulletins of Mechanical Engineering Education.* 4,(2), 97-107.

Heywood, J (1984). *Considering the Curriculum during Student Teaching.* Kogan Page, London.

Heywood, J (1989a). *Assessment in Higher Education.* 2nd edition, Wiley, Chichester.

Heywood, J (1989b). Problems in the evaluation of focussing objectives and their implications for the design of systems models of the curriculum with special reference to comprehensive examinations. *Proceedings of the Frontiers in Education Conference.* 235-241.

Heywood, J (1994). *Enterprise Learning and its Assessment in Higher Education.* Technical Report No. 20. Employment Department, Sheffield.

Heywood, J (1996). The development of assessment and tests in a multiple strategy approach to examining a course in Engineering Science in the United Kingdom. Proceedings for Friday PM pp 37 43. Rose Hulman Institute of Terre Haute, Ind.

Heywood, J (2000). *Assessment in Higher Education. Student Learning, Teaching, Programs and Institutions.* Jessica Kingsley, London.

Heywood, J., Pollitt, J and V. Mash, (1966). The schools and technology. *Lancaster Studies in Higher Education* No 1. Pp 153 305.

Heywood, J., Lee, L. S., Monk, J. D., Row;ley, B. G. H., Turner, B. T. and J. Vogler (1966) The Education of professional Engineers for design and manufacture. *Lancaster Studies in Higher Education,* No. 1, pp 1 – 152.

Hislop, G. W (1999). Teaching process improvement in a graduate software engineering course. *Proceedings Frontiers in Education Conference,* 2. 12a 9-21

Hopkins, A. D (1967). The training of professional metallurgists. *Lancaster Studies in Higher Education,* 2, A1-A89.

Hornsby-Smith, M. P (1967). A study of three parallel degree-level courses in a department of metallurgy. *Lancaster Studies in Higher Education,* 2, C1–C65.

Hoyt, B. and M. Prince (2002). Helping students make the transition from novice to expert problem solvers. *Proceedings Frontiers in Education Conference,* F2A-7 to 11.

Hutton, S. P. and J. E. Girstl (1964). Engineering education and careers Proceedings of a symposium on education and careers. *Proceedings of the Institution of Mechanical Engineers,* 178, part 3F, 1964/1965.

Hutton, S. P. and J. E. Gerstl (1966). *The Anatomy of a Profession.* Tavistock, London.

Imrie, B. W (1995). Assessment for learning: quality and taxonomies. *Assessment and Evaluation in Higher Education,* 20, 2, 175-189.

Jackson, P. W (1992). Conceptions of the curriculum and curriculum specialists. In P. W. Jackson (ed.) *Handbook of Research on the Curriculum.* American Educational Research Association, Macmillan, New York.

JMB (1967). *Notes for the Guidance of Schools on Engineering Science at 'A' level.* No's 1 to 4. Joint Matriculation Board, Manchester.

Kaplan, L (1978). *Developing Objectives in the Affective Domain.* Collegiate Publishing, San Diego, CA.

Kashy, D. A., et al (2001). Individualized interactive exercises. A promising role for network technology. *Proceedings Frontiers in Education Conference,* FIC-8 to 13.

Ketchum, L. H. 1981). Teaching engineering design. *Engineering Education,* 71 (8) 797-801.

Knight, P. T (2001). Complexity and curriculum: a process approach to curriculum making. *Teaching in Higher Education,* 6, (3), 369-381.

Kolb. D. A (1984). *Experiential Learning: Experience as the Source of Learning and Development.* Prentice-Hall, Englewood Cliffs, NJ.

Krathwohl, D. R., Bloom, B and B. Masia (1964). *Taxonomy of Educational Objectives, II. The Affective Domain.* David Mackay, New York.

Lancor, L. B and B. A. Karanian (1998). College to work transitions: Students draw their futures. *Proceedings Frontiers in Education Conference,* 1, 657-662.

Langton, N (1961). *The Teaching of Theoretical Subjects to Students of High Polymer Technology.* Vol.1 and Reports to the Nuffield Foundation, London.

Lee, L. S (1969). Towards a classification of the objectives of undergraduate practical work in mechanical engineering. Thesis Library. University of Lancaster, Lancaster.

Lindenlaub, J. C., and J. D., Russell (1980). Getting started on improving instruction. *Engineering Education.* 70, (5), 413-417.

Lowe, D. B., Scott, C. A. and R. Bagia (2000). A skills development framework for learning computing tools in the context of engineering practice. *European Journal of Engineering Education,* 25, (1), 45–56.

McDonald, F (1968). *Educational Psychology.* Wadsworth, Belmont, CA.

McGill, I and L. Beatty (1992). *Action Learning. A Practitioners Guide.* Kogan Page, London.

McGourty, J., Besterfield-Sacre, M., Shuman, L. J., and H.. Wolfe (1999). Improving academic programs by capitalizing on Alumni's perceptions and experiences. *Proceedings Frontiers In Education Conference,* 3, 31a5-pp 9-15.

McMartin, F., and J. McGourty (1999). Involving industry in the assessment process: preliminary findings. *Proceedings Frontiers in Education Conference,* 3, 13a5 5 to 8.

McMartin, F., McKenna, A and K. Youssefi (1999) Establishing the trustworthiness of scenario assignments as assessment tools for undergraduate engineering education. *Proceedings Frontiers in Education Conference,* 3, 13c1-pp 7 to13.

Mager, R. F (1962). *Preparing Instructional Objectives.* Fearon Publishers.

Mansfield, G (1979). Designing your own min course. *Engineering Education,* 70, (2), 205–207.

Marra, R and B. Palmer (1999). Encouraging intellectual growth: Senior engineering profiles. *Proceedings Frontiers in Education Conference* 2, 12c1-1 to 6.

Marshall, P. (1994). Open exams: an experiment in student assessment. *Engineering Science and Education Journal, February,* 15-20.

Massie, W. W (2002). Curriculum revision in the light of ABET 2000 criteria. *Proceedings Frontiers in Education Conference,*1, T2B-9 to15.

Mentkowski, M and Associates (2000). *Learning that Lasts. Integrating Learning, Development, and Performance in College and Beyond.* Jossey Bass, San Francisco.

Meuwese, W (1968). Measurement of industrial engineering objectives. 16th International Congress of Applied Psychology, Amsterdam.

Meuwese, W (1971). *Construction and Evaluation of a Course in Technical Mechanics.* Committee for Higher Education (ccc/ESR(71)14). Committee for Higher Education, Council of Europe, Strasbourg.

Monk, J. D (1972). An investigation into the role of the design function in the education, training and career patterns of professional engineers. Thesis. University of Lancaster Library, Lancaster.

Moon, J (1968). The ethical attitudes of chartered mechanical engineers and their relationship to education. M.Litt. Thesis, University of Lancaster, Lancaster.

Neumann, E. S (1981). Teaching management skills in a comprehensive project course. *Engineering Education,* 71, (8), 790-794.

Newcomer, J. L (2001). Cross-course design projects for engineering technology students. *Proceedings Frontiers in Education Conference,* 2, F1G 1 to 6.

Nirmalakhandian, N., Daniel, D, and K. White (2004). Use of subject-specific FE exam results in outcomes assessment. *Journal of Engineering Education*, 93,(1), 73 – 78.

Ormell, C. P (1974). Bloom's taxonomy and the objectives of education. *Educational Research*,17,1, 3-15.

Osgood, C., Suci., G and P. Tanenbaum (1962). *The Measurement of Meaning*. University of Illinois Press, Urbana.

Otter, S (1991). *What Can Graduates Do ? A Consultative Document*. Unit for the Development of Continuing Adult Education (HMSO). Employment Department, Sheffield.

Otter, S (1992). *Learning Outcomes in Higher Education*. Unit for the Development of Adult Continuing Education (HMSO), Employment Department, Sheffield.

Pascarella, E. T., and P. T. Terenzini (1991). *How College Affects Students*. Jossey Bass, San Francisco.

Payne, G. L (1960). *Britain's Scientific and Technological Manpower*. Stanford University Press. Oxford.

Pellegrino, J. W., Chudowsky, N., and R. Glaser (2001) (eds.) *Knowing How Students Know. The Science and Design of Educational Assessment*. National Academy Press, Washington, DC.

Peters, D. W (1998). A students view of the ABET 2000 criteria. *Proceedings Frontiers in Education Conference*, 2, 872–874

Pimmel, R. L (2003). Student learning of criterion 3(a)–(k) outcomes with short instructional modules and the relationship to Bloom's Taxonomy. *Journal of Engineering Education* 92, (4), 351–359.

Prince, M and B. Hoyt (2002). Helping students make the transition from novice to expert problem solvers. *Proceedings Frontiers in Education Conference*, 2, F2A- 7 to 11.

Pudlowski, Z. J (1988). Visual communication via drawings and diagrams. *International Journal of Applied Engineering Education*, 4, (4),301-315.

Pudlowski, Z. J (1990). Transfer of knowledge in an analagous model. *International Journal of Engineering Education*, 6, (1), 23-36

Puerzer, R. J., and D. M. Rooney (2002). The alumni survey as an effective tool for small engineering programs. *Journal of Engineering Education*, 91, (1),109–116

Ramsden, P (1992). Learning and Teaching in Higher Education. Routledge, London.

Regan, T. M. and J. A. Schmidt (1999). Student learning outcomes: alumni, graduating senors and incoming freshmen. *Proceedings Frontiers in Education Conference*, 3,13a5 16 to 21.

Rhoads, T. R and R. J. Roedel (1999). The Wave Concept Inventory- A cognitive instrument based on Bloom's Taxonomy. *Proceedings Frontiers in Education Conference*, 13c1-14-18.

Rice, S. L. (1977). Techniques for evaluating objectives. *Engineering Education*, February, 395- 397.

Scales, K. C., Owen, S. S., and M. Leonard (1998). Preparing for program accreditation review under ABET engineering criteria 2000. Choosing outcome indicators. *Journal of Engineering Education*. 87, (3), 207–210.

Schneider, S. C., and R. J. Niederjohn (1995). Assessing Student learning outcomes using graduating senior exit surveys and alumni surveys. *Proceedings Frontiers in Education Conference*, 2c1-pp 1-5.

Scott, M. R. et al (1966). *The Use of Mathematics in the Electrical Industry*. Pitman, London.

Smoot, L. D and M. R. King. (1981). Engineering and technology: differences and similarities. *Engineering Education*, 71, (8), 757- 764.

Soldan, D.A., (1997). Alumni assessment in the ABET Environment. *Proceedings Frontiers in Education Conference*, 2, 1002-1005.

St. Clair, S., and N. Baker (2000). On line assistant for writing course objectives. *Proceedings Frontiers in Education Conference*, 2, F4F 3 to 8.

Steinaker, N., and M. R. Bell (1969). *An Experiential Taxonomy*. Academic Press, New York.

Stice, J. E (1976) A first step toward improved teaching. *Engineering Education*, 65, (5),394-398.

Stice, J. E (1979). PSI and Bloom's mastery model. A review and comparison. *Engineering Education*, 70, (2), 175-180.

Striegel, A and D. T. Rover (2002). Problem based learning in an introductory computer engineering course. *Proceedings Frontiers in Education Conference*, 2, F1G-7-13.

Svinicki, M. D (1976). The test: uses, construction and evaluation. *Engineering Education*, 66, (5), 408-411.

Tyler, R W (1949) *Basic Principles of Curriculum and Instruction*. University of Chicago Press, Chicago.

Waks, S and M. Frank (2000). Engineering curriculum versus industry needs- a case study. *IEEE Transactions on Education*, 43 (4), 349-352.

Waina, R. H. (1969). System design of the curriculum. *Engineering Education*, 60, (2), 97–99.

Weston, C.A. and P. A. Cranton (1986). Selecting instructional strategies. *Journal of Higher Education*, 57, (3), 259-288.

Wilhoyte, R (1965). Problems of meaning and reference in Bloom's Taxonomy. Cognitive Domain. Doctoral Thesis, Indiana University. Cited by Furst (1994).

Yokomoto, C. F., and W. D. Bostwick (1999). Modeling the process of writing measurable outcomes for Ec 2000. *Proceedings Frontiers in Education Conference*, 2, 11b1 18 to 22.

Yorke, M (1996). *Indicators of Program Quality*. Higher Education Quality Council. London.

Yorke, M. et al (1998). *Undergraduate non completion in Higher Education in England*. Higher Education Funding Council, Bristol.

Youngman, M.B., Oxtoby, R., Monk, J.D. and J. Heywood (1978). *Analysing Jobs*. Gower Press, Aldershot

CHAPTER 3: PHILOSOPHY AND SOCIOLOGY AND THE AIMS OF THE ENGINEERING CURRICULUM

Summary

The purpose of this Chapter is to illustrate the function of philosophy, and to a lesser degree sociology and social psychology, in screening aims and objectives (outcomes). A distinction is made between philosophy per se, and operational or working philosophy. By the latter is meant the value system that drives a particular curriculum, syllabus, course or training session. Many articles about new courses describe the philosophy that drives the program or course. Illustrations are given of such philosophies. The need to define a philosophy or rationale is an important drive in the development of new courses.

At a more fundamental level, engineering educators have sought to develop an understanding of the process of engineering from a philosophical base. Koen's (1987) design method has a profound epistemological base. However, there has been no agreement about the need for a philosophy of engineering, (in the same way that there has been about a philosophy of science, that can be applied to teaching in spite of attempts by several engineers to try to write such a philosophy. Is there a case for developing a history and philosophy of engineering that can be used in the teaching of engineering and technological literacy? Matthews (2000) recent study of the history and philosophy of the pendulum as a contribution to science literacy is cited as an analogue. It remains to be seen if Koen's development of his philosophy will firmly establish the case for a philosophy of engineering education (Koen, 2003).

At the heart of philosophy as it is applied in education is epistemology. The epistemology we have, even though we may be unaware that we have an epistemology, together with the values we hold are primary drives in the approaches we adopt to teaching and learning. This point is illustrated in some detail by contrasting constuctivism with realism. In the United States, and elsewhere, constructivism is dominating thinking about education in science in high schools. The origins of constructivism are discussed and an alternative position described.

Engineering education is also concerned with ethics. Much work undertaken by engineers has an ethical dimension. Discussion about ethics has centered on codes of conduct, on the one hand, and on questions about the nature of truth on the other. Consequently there is a brief repeat of the constructivist/realist debate as it applies in this context. Many papers have been written on whether or not ethics should be taught and, if it is to be taught, of what it should comprise. This discussion is reviewed.

The dimensions of sociology and social psychology considered are, supply and demand, minorities and women, the experience of college, organizational structure, and the humanities.

Organizational structure embraces the organization of courses.

The Chapter ends with a consideration of some of the implications for teaching that arise from this discussion, and it argues that engineers require a philosophical habit of mind if they are to develop a philosophy of engineering that can be applied to teaching.

The Chapter is presented in two parts. The first part deals with philosophical aspects and the second with some sociological dimensions. The end of the first part contains a summary of the recently published White Paper of the Liberal Education Division of the American Society for Engineering Education (Steneck, Olds, and Neeley, 2002).

Part 1. Philosophical Aspects

3. The Engineering Curriculum and Philosophy

An example of the use of theories of knowledge in the design of curriculum to meet criterion 3 of the ABET criteria by Gorman (2002) was briefly described in Chapter 2 (Section 2.4).

At a more general level, philosophical analysis is important in helping us to understand what it is we mean by some of the words we use to discuss student learning. For example, the differences if any, between knowledge and understanding often cause problems for teachers especially in their assessment role. Jinks (1996) wrote that: *"frequently it is the role of the teacher to set in place an assessment mechanism which directly tests the general subject knowledge while at the same time circuitously examining the student's real depth of understanding. It is the small but significant differences in individual responses to a set examination question or coursework problem that often separate knowledge from understanding."* He argued that knowledge precedes understanding, and he showed that while students can have good knowledge, they can have poor understanding. Using case studies, he showed how coursework in electronic engineering can be structured to bring about the discernment that is required. One of the case studies is of an examination structured in this way. (see Chapter 15).

More generally, Sherren and Long (1972) said that the "educator must consciously program those desirable 'engineering characteristic' behaviors having elements of influence, thought and action, which he will teach before he considers the creation or adoption of an instructional system."

In order to know which *"engineering characteristics"* he would like to teach, he must first examine his philosophy of engineering education to understand his goals and attitudes. Likewise an understanding of the relationship between the philosophies of the student and the teacher will, allow *him to choose a compatible educational theory which may be sensitive to the goals and attitudes of both."*

They went on to argue that if an educator has not examined his/her own philosophy, he/she could not be expected to examine the career goals of his/her students. Everyone, they said, teaches to his own philosophy and they listed four philosophies that teachers might choose to follow. These are realism, pragmatism, idealism and naturalism.[1] Some engineering educators would probably add empiricism in the form of constructivism to this list. Sherrin and Long's position was that conflict in philosophies could be detrimental to student learning. Written at a time of student idealism they said: *"The students of today are seeking professional skills in order to achieve the new idealism which we old pragmatists have not perceived. Students are now trying to save trees and wildlife"*....

More generally, and it is an important corrective in this discussion of the design of the curriculum, is the contention that educators should listen to students in order to understand the meaning that education has for them. This is not the same thing as saying that we should only do those things that have meaning for students, but that we should find ways of translating our meanings into meanings for them. This review of articles published in engineering journals makes it clear that for the most part the understanding of student learning has been that of a *tabula rasa* on which, by and large, information had to be written. It was an information-giving model (sometimes called the transmission model) that paid little attention to cognitive processing. It is argued here that engineering educators have to have a defensible epistemology on which to base their teaching. Koen's (1985) argument for the engineering method is supported by a substantial philosophical approach (Koen, 1987). Epistemology necessarily has a bearing on the design of the curriculum since the curriculum is the formal instrument for the engagement of the student in learning. Philosophy, as a special edition of the *International Journal of Technology and Design Education* shows, shapes the concepts of the curriculum (de Vries and Tamir, 1998).

Elms (1989) argued that the ability required to deal with complex and novel engineering problems was closely related to the concept of wisdom. He described how a course in civil engineering at the University of Kent at Canterbury attempted to achieve this goal by concentrating on developing total capability rather than knowledge alone.

Johnston et al, (1989) set out to answer the question as to why there should be a philosophy of engineering as opposed to a philosophy of science. They considered ontology, epistemology, and heuristics.[2] With respect to the latter they reviewed Koen's approach, and concluded that: *"engineering is a creative activity, as much as a science. The methodology of science would seem to be a necessary part, but only a part of engineering activity. A philosophy of engineering would seem to be possible, and to provide a basis for better training engineers and better understanding of the roles of engineers and engineering in our society. Both are key elements in making sure that advancing technology does contribute to social progress."*

Van Poolen (1989) subjected technological design to a philosophical analysis in which his frame of reference was the philosophy of Heidegger. The emphasis in Heidegger's philosophy is on wholeness and unity. A man cannot separate what one does from what a person is. Technology is, therefore, one of the person's ways of being. This has implications for design education. It leads Van Poolen to warn against technology for the sake of technology, a view that took him beyond a theory of knowledge.[3]

The position of two Portuguese researchers is very similar and is of some interest because although they do not make the point in so many words, their argument shows the centrality of engineering in a liberal education. This is because they consider that technology is the visible part of the culture and is the vehicle for "culture share" (Fernandes and Mendes, 2003). *"Technology is the main repository of social knowledge and culture and, as such, becomes the main tool for knowledge diffusion, accumulation, growth and socio-economic development: technology is the real proof of the existent society, knowledge and, as such, its main evidence. Consequently, it is also the most important instrument for teaching and learning and so it has the most important role in education, namely for engineers".*

Self (1997) considered the educational philosophies from which computer based learning derived. These were rational, pragmatic, critical, and radical. The last two come within the perspective of the sociology of knowledge. He concluded that many of the current trends in CBL design could be related to post-modern ideas about the role of technology in society.

As Ruthven (1978) wrote in an essay on mathematics, curricular prescriptions cannot be derived from a theory of knowledge alone because they have to take into account value positions. Nevertheless, many teachers are not aware of-or even if they are they cannot express it-the fact that their teaching is driven by a theory of knowledge which informs their theory of learning.

---

[1] Realism: the doctrine that universals (reality, knowledge, logic and values) exist outside the mind. Pragmatism; the doctrine that universals and their meaning are sought in functional practicality (see James, 1890); Idealism; the doctrine which affirms the central importance of the mind, or the spiritual ideal in the universals. Naturalism; the doctrine that personal thought, inclinations and action, are based on natural desires and instincts alone; denying the existence of any universals other than nature. Empiricism; experience is the raw material of knowledge claims. Knowledge is constructed (hence-constructivism), and knowledge of external reality is impossible. Flanagan (1991) considered it to be a branch of materialism or physicalism.

[2] A method for attempting to solve a problem. A method.e.g., as in studying.
[3] For another study of Heidegger's view of technology, see Walton (2000).

(This argument continues in the paragraphs that begin the next section.)

In a substantive contribution to the philosophy of science education Matthews (2000a), showed how the history and philosophy of the pendulum could contribute to both scientific literacy and the teaching of science. There is no equivalent in engineering, and in creating a philosophy of engineering, the engineer who does will find it necessary to critique the philosophies of technology that are being written, because of the thorough going confusion that there is in the public mind about engineering and technology. This is no small problem.

Sinclair and Tilston (1979), two engineers working in industry argued that the failure to achieve the goals of engineering education was due to the fact that it lacked a proper philosophical base that would provide the guidelines required. *"The engineer needs a philosophy to answer such questions as: 1. How does engineering relate to science? 2. What is the relationship of engineering to 'technology' (as interpreted by engineers, and as interpreted by social scientists)? 3. What is the proper field of activity for engineering technologists, as for example, as compared to that of engineers? 4. What degree of responsibility should engineers take in relation to the social impact of works of engineering? ...When the engineers lack a philosophical base for answering such questions as these, it is virtually impossible to formulate an adequate concept of what constitutes engineering. Without such a concept, the educator is severely handicapped in developing suitable curricula in engineering."* Sinclair and Tilston considered that a philosophy of engineering is largely a philosophy of the professions (see below).

Evidently, these issues still loom large, as is illustrated in a paper by Livshits and Sandler (1998) that considered contradictory tendencies in engineering education, as well as in another paper on whether cost engineering is an academic subject (Fong and Ip, 1999). But, all of the above assumes there is a common understanding about what an engineer is and, therefore, what an engineer does. That this is not the case is evidenced by the need engineers have to explain how they differ from scientists, a need that continues to be felt. Certainly in Britain the profession has long been engaged in a continuing search for identity, and it seems that this is now the case in the United States. Williams (2002/2003) of MIT wrote that *"as this professional identity dissipated in a process of expansive disintegration, engineering schools will have to evolve or else find another mission."*

The consequences of this view for the philosophical debate about what engineering is are profound, and they have equally profound consequences for the curriculum.

It has been argued that philosophy has an important role to play in determining the aims of the curriculum. It has also been shown that some engineering educators, in particular Koen, have grasped this issue.

However, the majority of teachers when they talk about *"the philosophy of a course"* are operationalizing the term. It is with the operational philosophies that curriculum designers have which is the next consideration of this review.

3.1. Operational or Working Philosophy

By operational or working philosophy is meant the value system that drives a particular curriculum, syllabus, course or teaching session. It is the personal motivation of individuals that sustains them or drives them to change. Many articles about new courses, irrespective of where in the world they were introduced, described the philosophy behind the program or course (e.g. Berg, 1992; Thompson and McChesney, 1999; Wild and Bradley, 1998). Sometimes the statement that emerges is so brief as to be meaningless; at other times it is substantive. The need to define a philosophy seems to felt when new courses are proposed and the new course needs to be justified. A basic need has been to establish what is distinctive about engineering education when compared with physics. Is engineering education simply the application of the principles of physics or is it something more?

Morant (1993) who wrote about electronics as an academic subject in the United Kingdom said that, "a clear course philosophy is also a good basis for determining strategic priorities. Higher education is responsible to students, industry and society in general to provide the best possible education with limited time resources and resources available. A logical basis is required for determining how to use resources for maximum efficiency." The underlying principles on which this philosophy should be based are that the objectives of higher education should be to:
"teach students how to think constructively in their subject...
For vocational courses to develop particular technical and personal skills needed to start a professional career...
To develop student's personality and 'world views' in a well rounded way."

In the United Kingdom, Harry Edels then Dean of the Faculty of Engineering Science at Liverpool University believed that one of the reasons that able high school students preferred physics to engineering was that they did not understand what engineering was about. He felt that in high school they should be exposed to the engineering habit of mind (Edels, 1968). To achieve this goal it would be necessary to replace the Physics A level entry requirement with an Engineering Science Examination at that level (discussed in Chapter 2). It would have to be seen to be the equivalent of physics, if university admissions officers were to select candidates with good grades in engineering science. At the same time, while being firmly based in science, it had to convey the essence of engineering. He had therefore to campaign among his colleagues and schoolteachers that the habit of mind was as important as the principles, but those principles would not be sacrificed if this approach was adopted. He was not very successful among his colleagues; had they given it their wholehearted support it might have remained as a subject for more than the 20 years that it did (Carter, Heywood, and Kelly, 1986). Yet the debate went on, and in 1989 a committee of the UK engineering professors felt the need to tabulate the differences between engineering and physics (Exhibit 3.1) (Sparkes, 1989). Subsequently, in order to define benchmarks in engineering the engineering professors defined the generic skills required by engineers (see Section 15.4).

As we have seen, in the opening paragraphs of this Chapter this debate about what engineering is has not be confined to the United Kingdom. In Canada Sinclair and Tilston (1979) considered that the failure to achieve the goals of engineering *can be attributed largely to the lack of a proper philosophical base which could provide the guidelines needed."*

Sinclair and Tilston, argued for a philosophy of the professions that would emphasize the creative decision making process that is common to all professions, and not the end-product. The problem that faculties face is to turn the engineering scientists they produce into professional engineers. They argued that this could only be achieved by coaching and not in the classroom.

Trybus (1990), who had held senior positions in academia, government and industry, in describing the attributes that educators should seek to engender in their students, said that there should be a *"minimal competence in the so-called engineering science."* He listed the levels of competence required as follows:

(1) *"The ability to understand what other people are talking about, which is attained by reading popular magazines (for instance most well read people are aware of the controversy surrounding cold-fusion experiments, though they probably could not critique such experiments)*

(2) *The ability to work a set problem, by a set technique, where only one answer is acceptable.*

(3) *The ability to discover a problem of a conventional kind without its being pointed out by anyone, though at this level the person still requires someone to gauge the appropriateness of the work.*

(4) *The ability to define a problem in an ill-defined situation and apply a complex combination of solution methods.*

(5) *The ability to define a new problem, previously unrecognised, and develop methods to solve it".*

In addition the student should have "the opportunity to design something that displays originality."

In the United States Koen (1985), as already indicated, derived an engineering method from an examination of different epistemological theories. At one level his work is at the fundamental level of philosophy while at another level it is a working philosophy since it clearly advocates a habit of mind based on thinking

heuristically that is, problem solving[4]. His ideas are supported, with some modification, by Andrews (1987), and Smith (1987). November (1991) applied Polya's heuristic as a general method for solving technical problems. But, they were not without their critics. Hazelrigg (1988), who would seem to have some sympathy with the tabulation suggested by Sparkes in Exhibit 3.1, ignored the philosophical underpinning of Koen's thesis. He argued that the strong connection between the physical sciences and engineering sometimes causes confusion about the distinctions between the two. He also argued that the kind of problem solving advocated by Koen and Andrews applied to the laws of nature but not to human processes. Thus, the problem solving they advocated is science. Their ideas appear to be more academic then practical. At the same time, Hazelrigg was critical of definitions about what engineers do, such as those produced by the National Research Council in *Engineering in Society*. They implied that *"an engineer is someone capable of doing engineering work, and engineering work is done by engineers."* In a masterpiece of understatement he wrote, that *"neither definition sheds light on the uniqueness of engineering."*

If one examines what senior engineers do when they are at work, then it is clear that the prowess and compensation of engineers depends on the extent to which they have responsibility for decision making. It clear, therefore, that the uniqueness of engineering when compared with pure science is that it is about decision making. He then discussed the nature of decision making and formulated a framework for the engineering process that could stand as syllabus structure. It would be non traditional and perhaps like that deduced by Heywood et al, (1966a), who were very concerned with what it is that engineers do (Youngman et al 1978)[5]. Hazelrigg suggested that engineers do not have a complete education, but his model seemed to pay little attention to the human dimensions of engineering. By contrast in the same edition of *Engineering Education*, Mark and Carver (1988) argued that few students want their world to be based on management and financial skills; therefore engineers must go back to school and have the opportunity to be exposed to a genuine liberal arts curriculum. Support for this view as well as for a fifth year to enable breadth is given by Wenk (1988), also in the same edition of *Engineering Education*.

There were, in the United Kingdom, conflicts between subject specialisms. For example the Institution of Mechanical Engineers opposed the award of a Royal Charter to the Institution of Production Engineers on the grounds that production engineering was part of the mechanical engineers work. Generally speaking, the institutions in the United Kingdom were founded because some engineers felt they were not adequately represented. The Institution of Mechanical Engineers itself was

---

[4] Koen has brought all his ideas together in a new book that is published by Oxford University Press (Koen, 2003).

[5] This writer's comment.

founded because some of its members felt the Institution of Civil Engineers did not support their particular branch of engineering. Whether or not cost engineering is a discipline was undertaken by Fong and Ip (1999). They evaluated it against 11 parameters suggested by King and Brownell which characterize an academic discipline. They found that cost engineering lacked an expression of human imagination, and a generalized syntactical and conceptual structure. It possessed all the other parameters which were a community of persons; a domain; a tradition; a specialized language or other system of symbols; a heritage of literature and a communications network; a valuative and affective stance; and, an instructive community.

At the University of Lancaster in the 1960's a department of Operational Research was established at the founding of the University. A few years later a Department of Engineering and a Department of Systems Engineering were established. The subject of systems engineering was a newly developing subject at that time and a journal was founded to meet its needs. In the first issue of that journal the philosophy of the Department at Lancaster was described by its head (chair), Gwilym Jenkins (1969). He argued that a piecemeal approach to the problems of firms and local and national government was no longer good enough if firms and nations are to compete. An overall approach was required, and this is what systems engineering supplied. This meant that systems engineers were generalists who always took an overall view of the situation. These remarks do less than justice to a very substantial paper that Jenkins gave on the topic.

Sometimes it is necessary to justify the inclusion of a new subject, especially if it is given department status [e.g. Knight, Prey, and Wulf, (1995) on the philosophy of a new curriculum in computer science.] An interesting analysis of *"described the basic philosophy underlying the systems approach to problem solving and has indicated how specialist techniques can be employed effectively at each stage."* He offered a history of the term systems engineering and endeavored to point out the differences between engineering and operational research. In his inaugural lecture at the University of Lancaster, Checkland, a colleague of Jenkins, in the same journal attempted to answer the question, *"Is systems engineering anti-human?"* This necessarily led him to a philosophical conclusion having argued in a different way the case for systems engineering as human study (Checkland, 1970).[6]

As we have seen in Britain in the 1960's, several official committees complained that engineering courses were not meeting the needs of industry (e.g. Bosworth, 1966; Feilden, 1963). The Chairman of one of them had written independently about the need to train creative engineers (Bosworth, 1963). In Britain, Hutton and Gerstl (1964; 1968) surveyed a representative sample of chartered mechanical engineers and concluded among other things that there was a need for mechanical engineers to be trained in design. Much the same debate about design took place in the United States (e.g., *Engineering Education,* No. 7 of Volume 58, 1968, is devoted to design education). Since then innumerable articles and papers have been published on the teaching of design. Among the questions that have been asked are Can it be taught? If it can, how should it be taught? Should it be integrated across the curriculum?…and so on. The very nature of what design is and how designers think has been the subject of much controversy. While these issues will be considered in more detail in Chapter 12, it is not surprising to find that those who would teach design have found it necessary to describe their philosophy of design education.

For example, Wheen (1978) of the Department of Civil Engineering of the University of Sydney contributed a paper in *Engineering Education* called *"The nurture of a design philosophy"*. In it, he wrote that *"as with most philosophies, a design philosophy is acquired by the designer over a period of time. It is usually described in retrospect to explain a course of action that has been developed by experience. Rarely, if ever, is the underlying philosophy first learned and then applied in subsequent action. In fact, many highly successful designers have probably never tried to look introspectively at their own behavior. Those who would teach, however, must seek to understand the motivation of successful practitioners in order to encourage similar development in their students. The more introspective among practising designers and the more design-oriented among teachers seem to be best fitted to guide would be designers through their formative years"*.

This led him to the view that *"student's awareness of an underlying philosophy can only come from experience of attempting real problems."* The implications for the curriculum are profound. Luegenbiehl and Dekker (1987) of the Rose Hulman Institute stressed the importance of values in design. They argued that teachers, whether they know it or not, convey values. Teachers need, therefore, to be able to identify the values they want to encourage in students. They proposed a technique by which teachers could work out the values that are important to them, curriculum leaders may find their 'design rap session' to be a valuable aid for curriculum improvement. The working out of values necessarily involves epistemology. In engineering two contrasting epistemologies govern current debates about teaching and learning. These are constructivism and realism.

3.2. Constructivism Versus Realism

Earlier it was said that some engineers would wish to include constructivism in Sherren and Long's (1972) list. An engineer once said to this writer that, *"we are all constructivists now."* But are we? What is clear, is that we have to answer this question to our own

---

[6] Volume 68 (8) of *Engineering Education* (1970) is primarily devoted to articles on systems engineering.

satisfaction. This is what is meant by the argument that a teacher should have a defensible epistemology.

Unfortunately there is no definition of constructivism in *The Cambridge Dictionary of Philosophy*. There are references to ethical constructivism and constructivism within the philosophy of mathematics. Also, there is no mention of the proponents of constructivism such as von Glasersfeld. Nevertheless it has become a driving force in science education. Matthews (1994) reported in 1987 that at the first international conference on the topic sixty papers were presented, at the second 1987, 160 were presented, and at the third 1993, 250 were presented (see McElwee, 1995).

SCIENCE (Goal: the pursuit of knowledge and understanding for its own sake)	ENGINEERING (Goal: the creation of successful artefacts and systems to meet people's wants and needs
Key scientific processes	**Corresponding engineering processes**
Discovery (mainly by controlled experimentation).	Invention, design, production
Analysis, generalization, and synthesis of hypotheses	Analysis and synthesis of design
Reductionism, involving the isolation and definition of distinct concepts	Holism, involving the integration of many competing demands, theories, and ideas
Making more or less value-free statements	Activities always value-laden
The search for, and theorizing about *causes* (e.g., gravity, electromagnetism)	The search for, and theorising about *processes* (eg control, information, networking)
Pursuit of accuracy in modeling	Pursuit of sufficient accuracy in modelling to achieve success
Drawing correct conclusions based on good theories and accurate data	Reaching good decisions based on incomplete date and approximate models
Experimental and logical skills	Design, construction, test, planning quality assurance, problem solving interpersonal, communication skills
Using predictions that turn out to be incorrect to falsify or improve the theories or data on which they were based	Trying to ensure, by subsequent action that even poor decisions turn out to be successful

Exhibit 3.1. Some differences between science and engineering (Engineering Professors Conference United Kingdom pamphlet).

Many of these were about the misperceptions that students of all age groups have of scientific concepts and principles and the difficulties of changing them.

Journals like *Research in Science and Technological Education* continue to publish such papers (e.g., Kim, Fisher and Barry, 1999).

Matthews quoted *"Fensham as a well placed observer, who remarked that the 'most conspicuous psychological influence on curriculum thinking in science since 1980 had been the constructivist view of learning"* (p. 137; Fensham, 1992, p. 801). Perhaps it is because of its association with psychology that it is not in the Cambridge Dictionary. Yet, as Matthews's, points out it is very much an epistemology in the empiricist tradition. (Sherren and Long might also be criticised for not putting empiricism in their list.) It is worth noting that in the year 1980, to which Fensham referred there appeared in *Engineering Education* a paper on the misperceptions that students have of principles in mechanics (Clement, 1981, see Chapter 4 on Concept Learning).

Constructivism is the most recent development in the long debate between realism and empiricism in science that extends back to Aristotle. It comes into the present curriculum debate in science via Piaget about whom there is an entry in the Dictionary.[7] During this period there was a corresponding development of social constructivism stemming from Durkheim (1972) and expressed powerfully by Berger and Luckman (1966). Together, these theories have had a profound influence on teaching in schools and both popular and academic books have been published on constructivism, teaching and the curriculum.[8]

Matthews' (1994) concern was with the role of the history and philosophy of science in science teaching. He argued that the history and philosophy of science should be a component in the training of those who are to teach science. *"Teachers, as professionals should have historical and philosophical knowledge of their subject matter quite independently of whether this knowledge is directly used in classrooms: teachers ought to know more about their subjects than what they are required to teach. Teachers have a professional responsibility to see beyond the school fence"* (p. 200). Matthews (in Australia) found support for this contention in the work of the Carnegie-funded National Teacher Assessment Project in the United States directed by Shulman (1986), which was concerned in part with the nature of teacher expertise and knowledge and how that knowledge is acquired.

---

[7] Piaget hypothesized, *"that our epistemic relations are constructed through the progressive organisation of increasingly behavioral interactions with physical objects. The cognitive system of the adult is neither learned in the Skinnerian sense nor genetically programd. Rather, it results from the organization of specific interactions whose character is shaped both by the features of objects interacted with (a process called accommodation) and by the current cognitive organization of the child (a process called assimilation). The tendency toward equilibrium results in a change in the nature of the interaction as well as the cognitive system"* R. Shiner, p 619, *Cambridge Dictionary of Philosophy*, Cambridge U. P., New York

[8] For a wide ranging text with contributions from some of the major players in the field see Steffe and Gale (1995). For a popular text see *Constructivist Classrooms* published by the Association for Supervision and Curriculum Development, Alexandria, VA. The book that set of the interest among science teachers in constructivism was by Driver (1983).

The problem for Matthews was that "a teacher's epistemology is (thus) largely picked up during his or her own science education: it is seldom consciously examined or refined. This is less desirable for the formation of something so influential in teaching practice, and so important in professional development." Thus, it is important that a professional science educator should be able to discuss in depth the realist-empiricist debate and the different positions taken up by such persons as Einstein, Leibniz, Mach, Newton, and Planck. It is contended here that the same dicta apply to engineering educators, and in particular curriculum leaders. In any case, since engineering educators receive the products of schooling, it is important they should know how and why they are being schooled.

Piaget held that there is a general cognitive faculty that governs the development of all aspects of human learning, and that concept development arises from the constructions made by the child. It is a process of *"personal, individual, intellectual construction arising from their activity in the world."* (Matthews, 1994, p. 138). From this position the core theses of psychological constructivism are:

1. *Knowledge is actively constructed by the cognizing subject, not passively received from the environment.*
2. *Coming to know is an adaptive process that organizes one's experiential world; it does not discover an independent,, pre-existing world outside the mind of the knower. (Lerman, 1989, cited by Matthews, 1994, p. 141).*

A more powerful statement about the principles of constructivism is made by von Glasersfeld (1993). Matthews (1994) described him as an idealist. He wrote, *"Facts are made by us and our way of experiencing,"* which is contrary to the realist position that facts exist independently of us. It has implications for teaching as Driver (1995) recognized.

"There is," she said (p. 387), *"an epistemological implication of this view of knowledge as constructed that has yet to be taken seriously by educators, and that is that to know something does not involve a correspondence between our conceptual schemes and what they represent 'out there;' we have no direct access to the real world. The emphasis on learning is not on correspondence with external reality, but the construction by the learners of schemes that are coherent and useful to them."* She went on to quote von Glasersfeld (1983) thus: [This view of knowledge] *"has serious consequences for our conceptualization of teaching and learning ... it will shift the emphasis from the student's correct replication of what the teacher does, to the student's successful organization of his or her own experiences."*

The implications of this for what is learned let alone for teaching are profound. The curriculum becomes a program of activities and not a body (syllabus) of knowledge. Is this what the engineer implied when he said, *"we are all constructivists now"?*

Driver and Bell (1986) summarised the constructivist view of learning as follows:

- *"Learning outcomes depend not only on the learning environment but also on the knowledge of the learner.*
- *Learning involves the construction of meanings. Meanings constructed by students from what they see or hear may not be those intended.*
- *The construction of meaning is a continuous and active process.*
- *Learners have the final responsibility for their learning.*

There are patterns in the types of meanings students construct due to shared experiences with the physical world and through natural language." (cited by Matthews, p. 144, 1994).

A similar summary of constructivism but applied to engineering education was made by Miller and Olds (1994). They described how it influenced a course in critical thinking at the Colorado School of Mines[9] They also provided a rare example of qualitative research in engineering education. In relation to a unit operation laboratory in chemical engineering Miller and Olds (2001) described their position as follows:

"As presently taught, the course relies heavily on a constructivist approach- that is, the cognitive theory suggesting that learners construct their own internal interpretation of objective knowledge based, in part on formal instruction, but also influenced by social and contextual aspects of the learning environment and previous life experiences (Teslow, Carlson and Miller, 1994). This view suggests that students "make their own meaning" of what they are learning by relying on mental models of the world, models that may be correct or may contain strongly held misconceptions (Atman and Nair, 1992). Rather than acting as acknowledged authorities transmitting objective knowledge to passive students, laboratory faculty use coaching and Socratic questioning techniques to help students understand complex technical phenomena by constructing mental models which perceive reality as perceived by acknowledged experts while minimising models containing significant misconceptions. Use of constructivist pedagogics creates an ideal context for assessing students' abilities to complete authentic engineering tasks rather than relying on artificial examinations which emphasize non-contextual recall of facts and closed-ended problem solving."

While Miller and Olds position is clear about what to do with students when they have a misperception this may not always be the case, particularly at school level. Matthews (1994) raised the issue of what does the teacher do when he or she finds there is a misconception? Is it accepted as an alternative framework? Does the

---

[9] See also Smith and Waller, (1997) who summarized this paradigm in relation to teaching engineering, and Crews (1997) who related it to the issue of intelligent learning environments to assist complex problem solving.

teacher try to change the child's understanding? He pointed out that while Driver and Oldham claimed that the curriculum is a program of activities from which knowledge and skills can be derived, it is still necessary to say what those knowledge and skills are.

Matthews also pointed out that the constructivist approach to teaching is not unique. Many teachers actively engage students in learning and do not require a particular epistemology to support their endeavors; and some would follow the steps or make similar steps to those described by Driver and Oldham (1986)[10]. The authors of engineering science at A level (see Chapter 2) would not have known about constructivism when they designed the procedures for coursework assessment and examination. They did, however, take a similar view of teaching as Miller and Olds, but at least one of them was known to be a moderate realist. The assessment scheme that Miller and Olds devised for their teams has many similarities with the rubrics designed for the assessment of coursework in engineering science (see Chapter 2, Carter, Heywood, and Kelly, 1986). The point is not so much to be critical of theory but to acknowledge that on the basis of a theory, good practice in teaching and assessment has been developed. There is no point in arguing that teachers should have a defensible theory of learning if it is to be judged by theory, and not by the practical outcomes it causes. Nor is it an excuse for discontinuing the debate.

Sociological constructivism, although in the same vein provides a different but complementary perspective. It is based on the view that reality is a social construct, and our construction of that reality depends on prior experience. Durkheim (1972-quoted by Matthews, 1994, p. 142) wrote, *"thought has its aim not the reproduction of a given reality but the construction of a future reality."* Berger and Luckmann (1966) elaborated this view, and it became interpreted, so far as science is concerned, and thus in engineering, that knowledge in these fields is socially constructed. Sociological constructivism is not concerned with what individuals believe but with how the social structure (environment) of those individuals determines what they believe, and it is clear from Berger and Luckman that science is not an exception.

In a theory of this kind knowledge is not absolute. It is relative. So far as the curriculum is concerned one of my teacher trainees wrote of the theory that:

"It is based on a phenomenological approach to the analysis of reality. In this view consciousness is subjective; when we perceive something we bestow

meaning on it, which will depend on our subjective consciousness, which has been determined by our past experiences. Thus, knowledge is not something to be brought into the classroom in neat fixed packages, but it is something which is determined in the classroom by the perceptions of the individuals therein" (quoted in Heywood, 1982b; p. 49).

In this respect it would seem to promote a curriculum that is similar to that described by Driver (see above). Teachers who adhere to this model of the curriculum will reject the traditional transmission model of the curriculum or the *received* paradigm as Eggleston (1977) calls it.[11] But many effective teachers who do not subscribe to these theories use such methods as they see appropriate. Similarly, there are equally valid reasons for changing a curriculum structure without resorting to theory. The value of the theories is that they bring important issues into relief.

One of the most interesting ideas to arise from this theory is that of curriculum negotiation: for a given, that the reality we have is a result of our environment, then, in these circumstances, the students with their teachers should design a curriculum that is real to them. In this sense the curriculum should be negotiable and worked out to meet the individual needs of students. Those who espouse this view believe, that the review of the curriculum which this perspective recommends, should be thoroughly critical (e.g., Young, 1971).

The degree of negotiation and its characteristics varies among teachers. For many there are considerable constraints imposed on them by the authorities responsible for the curriculum. In any case they all start from the premise that it gives the students ownership for, *"people tend to strive hardest for the things they wish to own, or to keep and enhance things they already own"* (Cook, 1992; p. 15). Cook contended that one of the reasons why the transmission model is maintained is that teachers believe that students are not capable of the ownership principle in practice. This view may be turned into a question that can be put to engineering educators, it is; Are engineering students capable of ownership of the curriculum? Cook gave an example of negotiation within the curriculum. If the teacher selects a topic the students should be made aware of why they have to study this topic. Negotiation with the students produces a design that will enable them to tackle the problem and such negotiation requires answers to these questions: *"What do we know already? What do we want to know and need to find out? How will we go about finding out? How will we*

---

[10] Driver and Oldham (1986) suggested that constructivist teaching takes place in steps. These are: elicitation (in which the students find out where they are at); restructuring ideas (in which students clarify meanings togteher); construct new ideas in the light of these discussions; evaluate these ideas by thinking them through, or by experiment; apply these ideas in different situations; and review them, i.e., reflect on them. They liken this last stage to learning how to learn or metacognition as understanding how we learn is now called.

---

[11] Eggleston (1977) calls the kind of curriculum that derives from sociological constructivism reflexive. Some sociologists consider that the received curriculum that incorporates the disciplines is a mechanism for those in power to exert control. The reflexive curriculum would put the power back with the teachers and students. The student quoted above wrote *"in this view the development of continued critical thinking skills would be a desirable one. The economic structure is as it is only because it has been defined by those in power. It is something which can be questioned and therefore changed and for this to happen critical evaluation will be necessary."*

know, and show, that we've found out when we've finished?"

Cook recognized that this is a common sense progression, and that it similar to the scientific method as commonly characterised. The questions in Wales and Stager's (1972) guided design method are similar. In this way, skills in engagement, exploration, and reflection are developed.

Boomer (1992) claimed that the negotiating teacher concept is constructivist. *"There can never be exact congruence between what a teacher or a textbook means to mean and what a learner makes of that meaning. The dance between teacher and taught represents a continuing negotiation of meaning"* (p. 279, see also Sheppard, Demsetz, and Clayton, 1999). If the aim is mutual understanding and communality of interpretation then this is (or should be) the goal of any teacher but it does not make him or her, a constructivist. While it may require a change in method, does it require a change in epistemology to one that is other than constructivist? To put it in another way can you negotiate even if you have the view of a modest realist? [12]

This discussion of constructivism has been simplified considerably. In the first place it gives no idea of the heterogeneity of the movement. Matthews (1994) listed fifteen varieties. In the second place it has not been contrasted with the claims of realism, and finally no attempt has been made to lend additional clarification to terms. For example Mathews (1994) considered that the terms "empiricist" and "realist" are often used interchangeably. Nevertheless, it is hoped that this discussion has demonstrated the value of philosophy in screening objectives and that teachers should have a defensible epistemological position. But this discussion is not meant to be the last word on the issue.[13]

However, before leaving this topic, it is of some importance to draw attention to a criticism of constructivism in science education by another Matthews (2000b), from Ireland. He challenged two of the basic premises of Piagetian theory. First, that there is a general cognitive facility that governs all aspects of human learning, and second that concept development is the result of progressive construction, initially out of the sensori-motor experience of the child. Matthews argued that research in the area of linguistics and cognitive science demonstrated that human cognition is a function of domain specific mechanisms in the brain and perceptual systems. (He drew on work, from among others, of diSessa, 1993 Fodor, 1983, Hatano and Inagaki, 1994, Resnick, 1994, and Spelke et al, 1994).[14]

Matthews suggested that one reason why children find science difficult to understand is the fact that innate modules filter the information from our senses and interpret it automatically. This is done in a mechanism that is not available to consciousness *"in a way that one can describe as naïve physics and biology."* If this is the case, then a lot of naïve science may not be learned, i.e., constructed. He went on to argue that it may not be possible to change these modules by learning, or to integrate them into a domain general aspect of cognitive functioning as suggested by Piaget. Moreover, many aspects of naïve physics and biology are likely to persist. Matthews (1997) wrote that if these naïve understandings are *"intuitive features of the world, then individuals will rarely feel them to be problematic and in need of explanation."*

He did not use recent advances in neuro psychology to advance the case for modularity although it would seem they do (e.g., Raichle, 1994). It would seem that to change ones naïve understandings, a high level of motivation would be required (Solomon, 1994).

In a later paper, Matthews (2000b) noted this point, and in order to arrive at a view of what all this means for teaching he used Anderson's (1992) theory of intelligence to describe the processing involved. Macintosh (1998) has pointed out that Anderson's theory of intelligence is a revised form of Spearman's (1927) two-factor theory. In Anderson's theory, intelligence consists of a basic processor. It is supplemented by a number of specific processors that act on particular types of information e.g., verbal information, visuo-spatial information. Limits are set on the specific processors by the action of the basic processor. Variations in the speed and efficiency of the basic processor cause variations in keeping with consequences for the actions of the specific processors[15]. Matthews adapted the theory in this way. Two routes are followed in which knowledge is created. One of these routes described knowledge acquired without conscious thought. He included modules for maths, science, language, and space. The other is knowledge acquired from conscious thought. He called

---

[12]Matthews (1994) suggests that modest realism contains the standard accepted realist theses: Theoretical terms in science attempt to refer to some reality; scientific theories are confirmable; scientific progress, in at least mature sciences, is due to their being increasingly true; the reality that science describes is largely independent of our thoughts and minds.

[13] For example, Shulman (1970), in an essay on the the relevance of psychology to mathematics education, discusses the epistemology of three educationalists- Gagné, Bruner, and Ausubel. Gagné's position can be traced back to Aristotle via the British empiricists. The child's mind is a *tabula rasa*. What is learned is the effect that experience makes on the blank slate. Bruner's epistemology, while influenced by the the gestalt psychologists and Piaget, can be traced back to Plato. Bruner advocates discovery learning because it elicits from the individual what the individual has always known but in a restructured form. Bruner is a rationalist and for him reason is the ultimate source of understanding not experience. Both Bruner and Gagné believe that the processes of knowledge getting and using are the key objectives of education. Ausubel whose position is a bit of both traditions sees the products of knowledge as the most important educational objective.

[14]Mathews (1997) cited the three components of naïve biology described by Hatano and Inagaki (1994, p. 173) As follows *knowledge enabling one to specify to which objects biology is applicable; a mode of inference which can produce consistent and reasonable predictions for attributes or behaviors of biological kinds; a non-intentional causal explanatory framework for behaviors needed for individual survival and bodily processes.*
[15] g = intelligence as traditionally defined.

these routes 1 and 2, respectively. Having set the scene he went on to consider the process of conceptual change.

"In many cases, conceptual change can be viewed as a process by which additional cognitive structures are built that, once firmly established can over-ride rather than merge with, the functioning of competing innate structures. In such cases, learners should acquire facility in the use of appropriate language, and establish the fundamentals of key concepts by rote learning. The expectation would be that once fundamental aspects of knowledge are established in the learner, there is a basis for by-passing competing innate structures."

To illustrate his point, he used as an example the fact that magnetic action violates one of the principles of naïve physics that says there is no action at a distance. Using his model of Anderson's theory of intelligence, he said:

"For an untutored person there is no path for explaining magnetic action through route 1, thus from the earliest ages humans recognise such events as discrepant. For an individual left without the guidance of someone acquainted with physics or magnets, a coherent explanation of magnetic action is hard to find. Howeve the fundamental difficulty facing the learner is not an understanding of magnets per se. Rather it is to accept that action at a distance occurs, and that science accounts for such events by invoking the notion of invisible forces. There is reason to doubt that learners will 'construct' this knowledge for themselves, or that such knowledge is best acquired through non-directive teaching techniques. In particular, if as suggested earlier, established cognitive structures can act as pseudo-modules for filtering information, it is desirable to promote the establishment of a routineised structure for forces acting at a distance. This may be achieved by using highly directive teaching techniques, including rote learning to help the learner adopt key concepts and associated linguistic terms ...."

This is the exact opposite of that proposed by the constructivists. Moreover, it is in keeping with the general idea of a received curriculum. Support for this view can be obtained from Schwartz and Bransford (1998), who found that in certain circumstances teaching by telling can work well (cited in Bransford, Brown and Cockney, 2000).[16] They do not however, take the view

that this demolishes constructivism. So Matthews, would not agree that this spells the end of constructivism, but he does argue that future research should be more critical of constructivist theorizing, and he finds support for this position from Solomon (1994).

Brown (2000), in a discussion of physiological parameters and learning in engineering, provides support for Matthew's thesis, but from the perspective of perceptual learning. He suggested that one of the reasons why there is so often a mismatch between teacher expectations and student performance is that teachers' may be trying to pump too much information down a band-limited channel in too short a period of time. He recorded that his own lecture notes contained 3000 bits per minute, whereas humans could only absorb about 12 bits per minute over (periods of many hours). This led him to advocate the use of "pictures'" in presentations because they are "worth a thousand hours." Citing Lemonick (1995), he pointed out that storage and recall mechanisms are very complex. For example, information presented through writing, speaking, and applying is stored in different parts of the brain. He also noted that since memory is dependent on the repetitive presentation and manipulation of information, it can be supported by rote learning. This is the point that Matthews made. Brown quoted Lemonick as follows: *"we think of learning and memory as separate functions; in fact they are not. Both are processes by which we acquire and store new data that makes them retrievable later on."*

Where then does this leave the curriculum leader in engineering? The answer to this question, in the absence of definitive conclusions, can only be approached pragmatically. It is clear, however, that there is confusion between epistemology and pedagogy, and it is misleading of the constructivists to attack realists on the ground of pedagogy. Even constructivists have to transmit knowledge because there are some things that cannot be discovered, at least in the time available or with the knowledge to hand. Such evidence as there is suggests that some teachers are *very directive* in their approach, and that others are *very non-directive*. The majority lie some where in between these extremes. Many teachers in both groups are considered to be effective by their students. It is also clear that some of the objectives of education may be better obtained by directive teaching methods while others will be better obtained by non-directive methods. An understanding of concepts and principles is required if there is to be an effective transfer of learning, and methods appropriate to acquiring this understanding should be used. In so far as the curriculum is concerned it is clear that it is never completely received. Teachers continually adapt and find alternative ways to teach as well as new ideas so the curriculum is continually restructured in small steps (Heywood, 1984).[17] At some stage the small steps taken by myriad teachers necessitate a curriculum review (see

---

[16] Bransford, Brown and Cockney write in Chapter 1 of *How People Learn* that: *"a common misconception regarding "constructivist" theories of knowledge (that existing knowledge is used to build nw knowledge) is that teachers should never tell students anything directly but, instead, should always allow them to construct knowledge for themselves. This confuses a theory of pedagogy (teaching) with a theory of knowing. Constructivists assume that all knowledge is constructed from previous knowledge, irrespective of how one is taught (Cobb, 1994) even listening to a lecture involves active attempts to construct new knowledge. Fish is Fish (Lionni, 1970), and attempts to teach children the earth is round (Vosniadou and Brewer, 1992) show why simply providing lectures does not work.*. See also Anderson, J. A., Reder, L. M., and H. A. Simon (1995). Applications and misapplications of cognitive psychology to mathematics education. http://www.psy.cmu.edu/-mm4b/misapplied.ntml.

---

[17] Restructuring is a term due to Eggleston, although Heywood (1984) gives it a slightly different meaning.

Chapter 1).

Within this context a particular issue of interest to engineering educators arises from the teaching of design. Designs are necessarily "constructed." Does constructivism mean that students need not be taught how to design? This was a major issue in the curriculum design for Engineering Science at A level that was discussed in Chapter 2.

Finally it may be argued that a legislated outcomes based curriculum is impossible in a strictly constructivist frame of reference since, the outcomes of knowledge creation cannot be anticipated unless the knowledge creator is directed to create knowledge in a particular area that can subsequently be judged true or false. In circumstances where students had agreed to pursue given outcomes it becomes possible, and in this eventuality the process becomes as important as product, and product becomes as important as process.

3.3. Ethics and Social Philosophy in the Engineering Curriculum

3.3.1. Arguing the Case for Ethics in Engineering Education

That social philosophy is having more and more of an impact on engineers is without doubt. Even so, Jackson (1989) found it necessary to make a plea for ethics in engineering education. More generally Luegenbiehl (1989), at the same conference, had to argue the value of liberal education in engineering courses. These pleas were made in spite of the fact that the teaching of ethics to engineers in the United States has a long history (Herkert, 2000). It should be noted that it is only recently that ethics has received the same kind of attention in Europe, where in the year 2000 a special number of the *European Journal of Engineering Education* was devoted to the issue (Volume 25, No 4, Zandvoort et al, eds.) A European handbook on engineering ethics is being prepared at the Ethics Centre of the Catholic University of Lille as part of the EU's Socrates program (Didier et al 2000). Much the same applies to Australia where the position has been summarized by Johnston, McGregor and Taylor (2000).

Engineers are increasingly undertaking technological work that creates ethical issues for the public, as for example in biomedical engineering (Brennan and Tooley, 2000). The environmental movement has had a considerable impact on the curriculum and has ensured that ethical considerations are in, for example, engineering case studies (Gunn and Vesilind, 1986; Vesilind, 1988). Catalano (1993), for example, described a course for developing an environmentally friendly engineering ethic that included both individual and societal values clarification. He showed the relevance of the ABET code of conduct[18] and

argued that the engineer ought to be able to use both right and left brain skills (see Chapters 4 and 5). Hersh (2000) considered the criteria for a code or other system of environmental ethics, and how best the engineering profession might be persuaded to adopt environmental ethics. However, at the University of Toronto a study of faculty attitudes to the contextual framework in which engineering takes place (i.e., human life, society and natural ecology) found that for engineering teachers to consider such issues is a luxury. By the time teachers obtain tenure their teaching and research is so embedded that they pay little attention to ethical issues (Vanderburg and Khan, 1994). The situation was no different in other Canadian universities. Anecdotal evidence suggested that it was the same in the United Kingdom where the move to broaden the engineering curriculum had been to include some form of management study. From a European perspective Van der Vorst (1998) considered that engineering education still emphasized the vocational technical education of students.

Haws (2001) reported a meta-study of 42 papers on ethics that had appeared between 1996 and 1999 in the Proceedings of the Annual Conference of the American Society for Engineering Education. He argued that these papers should be judged against two criteria.

The first of these was whether the course or activity promoted divergent thinking (p. 15). He argued that ethical behavior required, *"considering options and impacts beyond the narrow realm of engineering, engaging in unfettered discourse with non-engineers, and considering the ethical perspectives of virtue, rights, justice and care, as well as utility."* Engineers, he argued, are convergent thinkers, and *"without formal training in ethics to balance our natural tendency toward convergent thinking, the ethical implications of our work will not receive adequate consideration."*

The second criteria, which followed from the first is to enable students *"to formulate and defend their personal resolution to the kinds of ethical dilemmas encountered by engineers."* To achieve this goal students not only need to be encouraged to develop divergent thinking behaviors, but they need to be able to see the outcomes of engineering from the perspective of those who are not engineers. To facilitate such behavior they need to be able to articulate a common vocabulary, and this requires a theoretical grounding. Most of the papers he reviewed made no reference to the need for an ethical theory.

Pfatteicher (2001) suggested that the objectives for engineering ethics at the college level should be to *(1) "provide an understanding of the nature of engineering ethics, (2) provide students with an understanding of the value of engineering ethics, as opposed to the values of an ethical engineer, and (3) provide students with an understanding of the resolution of problems in engineering ethics".* She wanted students to be taught *"how to think about ethics rather than what to think about ethics".* Teachers have to provide students with a firm ground on which students can learn to make their

---

[18] ABET Engineering criteria require graduates to have "an understanding of professional and ethical responsibility" and "the broad education necessary to understand the impact of engineering solutions in a global context."

own decisions. In this respect, her view would seem to be little different from those of Haws.

In the following paragraphs, two dimensions of social philosophy are discussed. The first relates to the implementation of professional codes of conduct, and the second to the promotion of moral autonomy. Both are generally considered under the heading of ethics. They do not consider the general issue of training in moral enquiry as a normal part of university education.[19]

The approaches that have been developed toward the derivation and implementation of codes of conduct have been somewhat different in Great Britain and the United States. If anything, Great Britain appears to be a follower (Moon, 1992).

3.3.2. Codes of Conduct and Professional Responsibility

In Britain, Moon 1968, carried out a survey of graduate mechanical engineers. He found that a significant minority of members of the Institution of Mechanical Engineers were unaware that the Institution had a code of conduct. Since then the Institution has introduced rules of conduct. More significantly, however, the survey showed that the effect of their work on society or on operators or users of equipment *did not figure significantly in these judgements."..."A majority of engineers found no help in their education in forming ideas about professional behavior, and generally engineering tended to be treated amorally. The curriculum of the time suggested that the value system of engineering depended, almost solely, on its technical subjects"* (Moon, 1992). This finding was supported in part by another major study of mechanical engineers in Britain (Hutton and Gerstl, 1966)

Moon (1992) contrasted the acquisition of status by the medical profession and the failure to acquire status by engineers in Britain. He pointed out that when the medical profession was seen to be acting in the public interest, it gained the respect of the public. There is a continuous exposure to the public of the views of the British Medical Association on ethical matters and with every passing week such issues become more complex. There is a need to develop both expert and public capabilities for dealing with them.

In contrast the Institution of Mechanical Engineers had not taken ethical positions on public policy issues in which its members are involved. Since the public did not know if it had a view, it did not enhance the status of the profession

While the codes and rules were evolving (I.Mech.E. 1983) Moon drew attention to the possibility of conflicts of interest that can arise between engineers and their employers. In circumstances when there are potential conflicts, employees are more likely to go along with their employers than with rules set by the

professional institution which would require them to make public unethical activities (whistleblow).

The situation seems to be no different in the United States. Bella and Jenkins (1993) wrote: *"in an organizational setting where systematic distortion occurs, where the shared technological background emphasizes utility and productivity, and where the allure of the technological prize is extremely strong, it becomes quite easy for individuals to acquiesce in favor of being faithful agents and trustees and narrow their sense of responsibility to task assignments and roles."* Bella and Jenkins argued that engineers have to become responsible citizens, and *"our moral obligations must now include a willingness to engage others in the difficult work of defining what the crucial choices are that confront technological society and how to confront them."* But, look what happened to Berube at the microscopic level of work. He was a public service engineer who was sacked from his job shortly after President Reagan had recognised him for *"being one of the most persistent foes of waste, fraud and abuse."*

Berube, in an article in which he described the ethical conflicts an engineer is likely to meet, said: *"institutions that inculcate ethical beliefs grounded in personal responsibility and public accountability have done little to protect those (whistleblowers) who try to live up to the standards they have been taught"* (Berube, 1988). He thought that the Institutions had an obligation to protect members who found themselves in this situation. If they do not, then one might ask 'Why teach ethics?'

According to Bowyer (2000a), cases of whistle blowing are not rare occurrences. He documented a case involving the Hughes Aircraft Company in the United States, and suggested that it may be used as a case study. He also suggested that another way of using it was to assign it as a research paper. A good research paper would distinguish between criminal and civil trials, explain the role of the US False Claims Act, and discuss how the specifics of this case mesh with the IEEE Ethics Committee draft guidelines for engineers dissenting on ethical grounds.[20] In his paper, he noted that Principle 1.4 of the IEEE-CS/ACM Software Engineering Code of Ethics stated

"Disclose to appropriate persons or authorities any actual or potential danger to user, the public or the environment, that they reasonably believe to be associated with software or related documents."

This would require a professional to blow the whistle in certain circumstances irrespective of the cost to the professional (see Bowyer, 2000b). In the case study, two employees reported that faulty chips were knowingly being sent to military aircraft. Although both the United States Government and the whistleblowers received substantial damages, the whistleblowers lost their jobs,

---

[19]The objection to the teaching of applied ethics which is what the professions seem to do arises from the fact that mutually incompatible solutions may result, and the philosophical and professional rhetoric can hide the arbitrariness of the solution (see MacIntyre, 1990).

[20] IEEE Ethics Committee (2000). Draft Guidelines for Engineers dissenting on ethical grounds.
www.ieee.org/organizations/committee/ethics/eth.gui.html.

and the marriage of one of them broke up. Given the lack of knowledge among students about professional codes and the behavior such codes expect (Dyrud, 2000) it is not surprising that companies challenge whistleblowers. It is only when engineers as a group seek to implement their codes that this situation is likely to change. Davis (1998, cited by Dyrud) said, the codes help create a working environment amenable to ethical behavior. It is for this reason, in this day and age, that engineering students should participate in study of them (Ladd, 1991, cited by Dyrud, 2000).

3.3.3. Codes of Conduct and Moral Development

Haws (2001) was interested to establish if the codes of conduct contained elements of moral judgment. As defined by Rest, Thoma, and Edwards (1997) *"moral judgment is a psychological construct that characterises the process by which people determine that one course of action in a particular situation is morally right or wrong. Moral judgement involves defining what the moral issues are, how conflicts among parties are to be settled, and the rationale for deciding on a course of action."* Much of the work on moral judgment was inspired by a theory of moral development suggested by Kohlberg. Following Piaget based on the study of responses to moral dilemmas he suggested that there were six levels of development. At stage 1 an individual determines what is right and what is wrong according to its physical consequences. Thus being good equates to responding positively to the demands of others. Stage 2 is arrived at when right action is that which instrumentally satisfies a persons needs. These two stages were termed preconventional by Kohlberg. Stage 3 is characterized by good behavior which is designed to help or please others; in stage 4 it develops into behaviors related to doing one's duty, respect for authority and the maintenance of the social order. Kohlberg called stages 3 and 4 conventional. Stages 5 and 6 are post conventional. Stage 5 is a level where individuals define right action in terms of individual rights and standards that have been critically evaluated by society. The final stage of moral maturity occurs when right is defined by decision of one's conscience in accord with self selected ethical principles appealing to logical comprehensiveness, universality and consistency. These last stages correspond to the Piagetian level of formal operations and are to be seen in terms of justice reasoning. [21]

In 1990 Kohlberg discussed the possibility of a seventh stage because the highest stage of justice reasoning could not adequately answer the question "Why be moral?" Answers to this question required a cosmic perspective that could not be based solely on formal operational thought. "At the most mature level. Ethical life as whole is most equilibrated,: and there is a cognitive structure through which one experiences one's

own ideas about the right and the just as reflecting basic patterns of the cosmos, and experiences one's ethical actions as expressions of natural laws" (Kohlberg and Ryncarz, 1990). [22]

Most interest has however centered on the first 6 stages and ways of measuring them, and two tests have been developed for this purpose. the Defining Issues Test (DIT) and the *Moral Judgement Test* (MJT). The former has been widely used in the United States. Results among college students from the Defining Issues Test (DIT), suggest that among junior high students, only about 20% of the answers reflect positions at levels 5 and 6. But 50% of students who had graduated from professional school programs give responses that reflected levels 5 and 6 (Rest, Narvaez, and Thoma (1999).

Let's return to Haws analysis. He analyzed 42 papers and found that of the 12 that dealt with professional codes, most seemed to take an authoritarian (in the sense of dogma) stance. He pointed out that in terms of moral development of the type described by Kohlberg the codes function at the pre-conventional (authoritarian), or conventional (associational) levels of development. He argued that if this is taken to be the case then, *"it will restrict our students' ability to reason through their own values," and select ethically appropriate courses of action."* Instruction on the code itself does nothing to develop divergent thinking, or to see the ethical dilemmas created by engineering through the eyes of non-engineers. (In this respect one instructional approach might be to have students role-play an exercise in which consumer safety is involved; Cooley et al 1991). The need for moral judgement in computer ethics teaching has been made clear by Staehr and Byrne (2003). In a valuable review of Kohlberg's theory and the *Defining Issues Test* they also described an experiment in teaching within a computer ethics course that exposed the students to Kohlberg's theory. [23] The results suggested that the students that were exposed to this teaching showed gains in DIT scores taken before and after when compared with those in a control group. Unfortunately the samples were too small for any generalizations to be made. At the same time in the local classroom situation the result was significant and encouraging.

Haws also pointed out that only two of the papers made reference to the ethics of care that had been developed by feminist writers in response to Kohlberg's theoretical framework of development. Gilligan (1977) and Lyons (1983) had argued that women have a different view of social morality than do men. The primary concern of women is a systematic, lifelong concern for individuals. Thus in judging, an individual whose morality is based on justice will make judgements on *"how decisions are thought about and justified; or whether values, principles or standards are (were) maintained: especially fairness,* " whereas an individual whose morality is based on response and care will consider *"what happened/will happen, or how things worked out; or, whether relationships were/are maintained."* Haws felt this was a critical omission in a male profession that was trying to admit females to membership. It is of interest to note that in general , with the exception of the study mentioned above females do better on the DIT than males. Other more general criticisms of Kohlberg's theory can be made (see for example Crain, 1992).

In regard to teaching about conduct at a simple level, Passino (1998)[24] described how he linked unprofessional behavior in class such as coming late to class, doing homework in class, turning in someone else's name for the attendance question, and copying homework to similar behavior in industry (e.g., late for meetings at work, misrepresenting people's contributions to a group project, covering for somebody who is habitually late or a poor performer).

Similarly, cheating,[25] which is considered fairly regularly in engineering publications (e.g., Morgan and Foster, 1992; Harding, 2000; Carpenter et al, 2002), might be an anchor on which to build a component of an ethical program[26] Harding et al (2002) having compared the cheating policies in a number of institutions, concluded that universities with honor codes experienced a significantly lower level of self-reported cheating than colleges that did not. Discussion and development of honour codes by engineering students linked to consideration of professional codes might lead to a better understanding of the latter. But, as Pfatteicher (2001) has pointed out there are other college dilemmas that can be discussed. For example, *"The college has accepted your high school calculus course as counting toward your undergraduate degree, but you don't feel confident in your ability to do calculus"* or *"A fellow engineering student is binge drinking several times a week and is responsible for making final adjustments to the Future Car project you're on together."*

---

[24] Contains a useful list of references. The attendance question was a question set toward the end of class that was related to the next class.

[25] Cheating has become high tech. For example, tutors at Michigan State University that a former student had created a web site specifically for students on the courses that student had attended. The site. had proved successful in helping students to solve their homework and assessment problems. The tutors found that there were a group of students for whom plagiarism is acceptable (Masters et al, 2002). This has some similarity with the finding that there is a group of students for whom guessing in multiple choice questions is a normal activity.

[26] Cheating has become a major problem and is the subject of several investigations in engineering education. It has also become high tech. For example, tutors at Michigan State University found that a former student had created a Web site for students in their courses. It had proved successful in helping students to solve their homework and assessment problems. The tutors found that there were a group of students for whom plagiarism is acceptable Masters et al, 2002). This has some similarity with the finding that there is a group of students for "guessing" in multiple choice questions is a normal activity (Youngman and Heywood, 1979).

Angelo and Cross (1993) provided a structured approach to the use of dilemmas in the classroom. They argued that the pro's of this approach are: *"everyday ethical dilemmas allow students to try out various ethical positions, to practice their ethical reasoning skills on hypothetical but realistic problems, and to get feedback on their responses. These experiences can help them better prepare to face similar dilemmas late, when the stakes are much higher".* "When faculty learn what students' values are in relation to important ethical questions, they are better able to help students explore and rethink those issues and develop ethical reasoning skills."

"The cons of the approach are that "Some students resist and resent discussions of ethics and values in the classroom, or believe that no amount of discussion can change their own or their classmates' minds. For these students, Every Day Ethical Dilemmas may be an intrusion or simply a waste of time."

"Students' values may not be what the instructor hopes or expects them to be, as a result, the teacher may lose respect for interest in his or her students."

Maybe the problem of ethics courses is that they fail to provide the students with a *choc's des opinion,* because by the time students' reach college they had been taught ethics by the world around them. Thus, the problem in college was how to discuss in technical courses *"the consequences of making proper choices in their professional conduct based on the values they already hold."* How, asks Brown (1983), do we prepare them to cope with whistle blowing if they decide to take such action? It might be argued that it should be part of the task of the professional bodies to provide contracts that safeguard the stance an employee might take.

Some support for Brown's view can be obtained from research on the effect of engineering technology education on student ethics in Georgia (US) (Bannerman, 1989). He used a questionnaire that contained 20 scenarios. Each of these scenarios described a marginally ethical situation. Each situation was evaluated on a scale of 1 to 7. Data were collected from freshmen, parents, seniors, technology faculty, arts and science faculty, and business and industry leaders. He found that ethical orientation changed between the freshman year and the senior year, and that this change is in the direction of the faculty orientation. Moreover, there was a large difference between the ethical orientation of arts and science faculty, and industrial engineering technology faculty. He also found that that the parents' orientation was similar to that of the arts and science faculty.

These results led Bannerman to conclude that ethics courses do not contribute to a positive ethical orientation. "If it is deemed appropriate to modify student ethics, it appears that faculty role models will be more effective than ethics courses". This conclusion is supported by Hanson, McCarthy, and Paur (1993), who suggested that while many papers have been written on how to develop ethical decision making skills in engineering students, few have considered the ethical climate in which they study. It is not enough to provide lectures; it is also necessary provide an environment in which ethics are seen to be at work.

It is interesting to note that in a study at a north eastern university in the United States of the attitudes of electrical engineering students and students in an engineering technology degree program very similar results were obtained. The study was particularly concerned with the role of the IEEE in promoting its code through student professional activities. The ethical orientation of all electrical engineering students was goal- or consequence-based. Students had strong orientations toward ethical problems, but these changed with time. This indicated that students are open to all sorts of inputs that can radically change their overall ethical orientation. This in itself is a case for a course in moral reasoning (Nohmer, 1989). Clearly, courses, of themselves, do not necessarily cause changes in attitudes or behavior. But at the same time if ethical behavior is not to be governed by emotional responses to particular circumstances, a cognitive base is essential, and that is the argument for such courses.

Here, of course, I show some prejudice but students are often not persuaded of the value of much that is offered in engineering courses, and surveys might lead to a similar conclusion! In Britain students, in the Colleges of Advanced Technology taking engineering degree programs were very resistant to compulsory liberal studies. They did not see their relevance to engineering and wanted the time for engineering topics (Davies, 1965; Heywood, 1969). Fornaro, Heil and Jones (2000) said that *"students are resistant to focus on the more social aspects of problem solving,"* and they were reporting on the more immediate problem of the development of professional communication skills. Course designers can too easily give students what they want rather than provide them with what they need in some way that meets their motivational responses.

Moon (1992) hoped that ethics would be the catalyst for helping to change these relationships once it is accepted by both sides that, *"the essential purpose is the public benefit."* Moon considered that there has been much more support in the United States for the strengthening of professional ethics and accountability Moreover, it has been the subject of open discussion. He noted that an institute had been established to promote the study and understanding of engineering ethics, and text books had been produced on engineering ethics (e.g. Martin and Schinzinger, 1983). It became a growth industry. There have been some developments in the Engineering Council in the United Kingdom since Moon wrote.

In Australia, Johnston, McGregor and Taylor (2000) argued, that in order to practice engineering in a global context then a sophisticated understanding of the ways that ethical codes are constructed would be required. Community awareness will force engineers to question their decisions as they relate to the environment, and universities can encourage students to *"recognise,*

question, and challenge the assumptions underlying technical decision-making." (They cited Johnston, Gostelow and King, 2000). Their position is supported by van der Vorst (1998), who considered the question from a European perspective. He argued for the provision of philosophy and ethics courses alongside the engineering curriculum, as well as for their integration into its framework.

Dryud (2000) described an assignment on professional codes that she gave to mixed course of students including engineers. She argued that as a result of the assignment the students find a great degree of commonality between the professions. However, the exercise was more important because it helped students understand what *"being a professional means".* Haws would undoubtedly argue that such assignments have to be selected so as to give people outside of the profession a view of the profession. In this respect, one has to (a) analyze in some depth what the characteristics of a profession are and (b) look at the effects of restrictive practice on performance. For example, useful comparisons could be made between engineering, law, and medicine.

Bella and Jenkins (1993) argued that engineers have to become responsible citizens and *"our moral obligations must now include a willingness to engage others in the difficult work of defining what the crucial choices are that confront technological society and how to confront them."* In this way, given Moon's thesis, engineering would acquire status.

Moon (1992) argued that the prestige that accompanies status recognizes high levels of skill and knowledge that in turn require high moral standards and responsible conduct. The public confers status when it perceives that the professional role is to its benefit. At the moment it does not perceive this to be the case with engineers. Therefore, while an ethical code for engineers should be a safeguard for the public it has to be seen by the public to be of benefit. It has to have a moral purpose. It is from that starting point that ethical norms and procedures should be developed by the profession. Moon concluded that undergraduate education was well placed to provide programs about the principles guiding morality of professional behavior, and he found support for his argument from developments in the teaching of ethics in medicine in the United Kingdom (Pond, 1987).

3.3.4. Moral Purpose and Engineering Education

It follows from that argument that the purpose of ethics courses for engineers should be the understanding of moral purpose; and this is similar to the view taken by Martin and Schinzinger (1983), who argued that it should be about the promotion of moral autonomy. Nine of the papers that Haws (2001) reviewed referred to that particular text. However, Haws is critical of it on a number of grounds. He admitted that his criticism would become insignificant if there was sufficient classroom discussion and the students' had been given guided *"(thoughtful) supplemental reading."*[27]

Martin (1981) defined engineering ethics *"as the study of moral issues arising in engineering practice."* He argued that this involves three distinct but interrelated types of inquiry that he called normative or evaluative; conceptual, and descriptive. Martin said that the practical aim of normative ethics *"is to provide correct and correctly reasoned answers to concrete moral problems."* But, it also has a theoretical aim that is *"to identify and justify the general principles of basic obligation and moral ideals that ought to be affirmed by engineers and others involved in conducting engineering projects."* Conceptual inquiry is as the term implies about clarifying basic concepts, principles and arguments used in ethical issues and is necessarily interrelated with normative inquiry. Descriptive inquiry is to uncover the facts relating to particular situations. Martin argued that it should use the scientific method to explain. From this perspective, Martin argued for an interdisciplinary approach to the teaching of engineering ethics and gave examples of how it might work. In order to support moral autonomy, ethics courses should try to improve:

The ability to identify moral problems.
The ability to assess (evaluate) arguments.
The ability to form consistent and comprehensive viewpoints.
The ability to express these views orally and in writing.

The development of the last ability is more complicated than it seems for action in the real world embraces the whole of the affective domain, and is to some extent a function of personality. All of them have implications for teaching and assessment. As Martin (1981) said, it would be *"intolerable if grades be assigned on the basis of how closely students correspond to the teacher's moral outlook."* Writing about technology education, Rekus (1992) argued that technology teaching with a focus on moral education is not didactical (i.e., telling students) but a methodical (i.e., reflecting on experience) task.

In a different frame, Vesilind (1988) defined ethics for engineers *"as the study of systematic methodologies which when guided by individual moral values, can be useful in making value laden decisions."* As he said this definition has a clear engineering bias and he believed that this definition led to an ethical theory which could be reduced to a series of decision trees that could be applied to problems that require ethical reasoning. For him (following Morrill, 1980), morals are the value baggage that one carries along that activates the gates in ethical systems. He argued that many ethical problems or value-laden decisions could be reduced to the application of codes of ethics and the rules contained therein. They do not, however, cover every possible dilemma so it is necessary to select an ethical decision making system, although each system requires value-laden decisions. The *"moral values used in such decisions are the individual values which determine the outcome of specific questions within the ethical decision making process."* Morals cannot be taught but ethics that concentrates on methods of making personal decisions is value free and not concerned with right or wrong, or good or bad. In contrast, in the same issue of *Engineering Education* Shuldiner et al, (1988) suggested that the importance of human values should be taught. In his experience students who are attracted to engineering are not generally disposed to reflection and introspection; for this reason they should be exposed to the humanities.

3.3.5.   Teaching Ethics Through Case Studies and Role Plays

Haws (2001) found that 23 of the 42 papers he reviewed referred to the use of case studies. Haws considered that case studies could help the engineering student view engineering outcomes from the perspective of the non-engineer. However, while the written exercises and discussion that follow cases may help students' articulate personal feelings they do little to help them acquire the common language of ethics in engineering courses. There is no reason to believe that reading and behavior are causally linked. Didier (2000) suggested that this goal might be achieved by a modification of the case study method in which the students are presented with a real life study, and in which they role-played the various participants (workers, engineers, and mangers). Such an activity, she argued, brings them face to face with key questions about the role of the engineer, and about the abuses to which they can put their knowledge. For purposes of assessment the students selected situations that they had experienced in their training. In discussion groups they said why the case they chose has something to do with ethics. The final report that they presented had to contain:

"An introduction to justify the choice of topic: Why do you think this story deals with ethics? Which values and principles are dealt with? Why did you choose this topic?"

"A description of the individual and collective agents involved in the cases and analysis of the interests that are at stake: What is the topic underlying the decision? Who acts? Who undergoes the consequences of the decisions discussed? How are the decisions taken? Were all groups represented? What were the prevailing norms and laws? What is the main dilemma? Who has to cope with it?"

"A study of all the possible alternatives and a motivated decision: Are there alternatives? Are they realistic? Who could have suggested them? Who could have made them effective? What would you have done if you had had to decide? Why?"

---

[27](a) It does not mention the ethics of care.
(b) It lumps together the thinking of Ross and Rawls with Kant.
(c) It fails to make a strong enough link between utilitarianism and capitalism.
(d) It does not consider that differences in moral attitude could be a function of personality.

Heywood argued that the nearest a management course could come to teaching the "action" of management was through role-playing (FitzGibbon and Heywood, 1986). In a Master's degree course for experienced teachers, each participant was asked to write a role play based on their own experience. Each role-play was acted out by the participants with the writer of the role-play, acting as observer. At the end of the role- play each participant publicly stated what they had learnt. At the end of this reflection the writer explained what had actually happened, and the tutor then tried to place the proceedings and findings within a theoretical framework. The importance of debriefing cannot be overemphasized.

Some engineering schools have thought that service learning can bring reality to the teaching of professional responsibility. This was because work for the community requires heightened social awareness. Horenstein and Ruane (2002) described how the senior capstone design experience at Boston University provided situations in which social awareness was a prerequisite of success. Their three case studies showed situations that were all too familiar. In one case the students thought that all they had to do was to solve a technical problem. The consequence of this goal was that they designed a teaching aid for disabled people that were totally inappropriate. They had approached the problem as *"salesmen and not as developers."*

In another case they were disturbed to find young adults in a social needs setting. Many of them had not come into contact with severely handicapped students before, and they interacted more with the teaching staff, than with the handicapped students. These students also focused on the technical work. Some students had not behaved professionally because they had made off-hand remarks about these handicapped students. The authors did not say whether or not there was a substantial debriefing but the experience of the management role-plays suggests that if students are to benefit from such experiences de-briefing is necessary. Several of the papers that have been mentioned argued the case for ethics in engineering to be considered from environmental and global perspectives. There is, however, the equally important perspective of biomedical engineering. A few articles have been written on this dimension (e.g., Monzon, 1999).

There is a sense that in dealing with the "large issues" that the effects of science and engineering on the individual are overlooked. Indeed, they can be an escape from how we treat and are treated by our colleagues, those for whom we work, and those who work for us, and the ethical issues that are so often involved in such interaction. Luegenbiehl (1990), for example, was concerned that too often in the past, engineering ethics has been concerned with the analysis of large-scale disasters. He argued that this approach is not only unproductive but could be potentially destructive. Courses should focus on problems that are within the horizons of students. He cited as examples problems in the area of *"computer usage, conflicts of interest, secrecy,*

confidentiality, the rights of engineers, integrity, compensation, espionage, professionalism and bidding." Pearce (1997) used an algorithm, the steps of which paralleled the engineering design method in such a way that ethics could be used to teach the design method.

While Catalano (2004) agreed that the case study was a valuable teaching technique, he felt that it was not sufficient to meet the emphasis placed on ethics training by ABET and ASEE. The danger was that teaching codes of conduct and using case studies produced a very narrow view of ethics. It might be added that there is no guarantee whatever is done that it will effect student behavior once they have a working role in society. This has always been the dilemma of higher education irrespective of what subject(s) are learned. On the other hand, there is a strong argument for the view that unless the student is forced to study in depth that the chances of a transformation are not very high. Students should not be put in a situation where they surface learn for the sake of credits. Most teachers, if not all, will agree with that proposition.

Catalano gives one answer to the meaning of depth by arguing that when ethics is introduced into the curriculum, it has to be done at different levels of meaning. These he derives from the scheme that Dante used for his study of Exodus. In that scheme there were four levels of meaning. *These were "(a) literal, (b) analogical (c) moral, and (d) anagogical.(spiritual). At the first or literal level, integrating ethics may involve the use of case studies and reference codes from various professional societies. The questions posed to students might include: Are you aware of the various codes? And do such codes help in constructing answers to ethical dilemmas? At the second or analogical level integrating ethics may include challenges of students to identify; the analogy between proposed ethical dilemmas in an engineering context and a personal case in their own life.*

At the third or moral level, integrating ethics may involve a careful consideration of moral reasoning theories. For example, students may be asked to propose a solution to an ethical dilemma using a Utilitarian or a traditional rights based approach common to many western societies." (Given the current interest in the constructivist/realist debate they might be asked to establish their own position in the light of these different philosophies.) *"Lastly, at the highest or anagogical level, integration of ethics may involve reflection upon the modern age of technology and a consideration of entirely different view towards technology."*

He goes on to give a to brief explanation of how he has introduced the first three level into the freshman experience. He suggests that perhaps the most useful part of the course was a term design project that was introduced to provide a unifying element. One project that was used was the design of a chicken coop for a womens farm cooperative in Guatemala. The chicken coop had to be designed to *"result in increased egg and chicken production with minimum impact on local customs and societal practices as well as on the natural environment."* Catalano reports that the students began with some hostility. They did not think this was engineering. As the semester went on their attitudes changed and were replaced *"by a sense of accomplishment in making the world a little bit kinder, gentler place."*

This was not only the technique used. One that catches the imagination was called the *Compassion Practicum* in which the students had to propose and implement an activity that demonstrated a *"willingness to make a difference in a positive way in the world wherein action is the key, operative word."* This was found to have the most visible effect on students.

3.3.6.   Engineering Education and the Humanities

Even the term "humanities" is given different meanings by engineers. In one case that advocates the teaching of humanities to engineers the term is restricted to the study of the intellectual history of science and technology (Ben-Haim, 2000). More generally, Didier (2000) offered the reminder that in France the humanities have had an important role in engineering curricula. The two influences that brought this about were *"a secular one, with its 'meritocratic' ideal and the notion of the Polytechnician, whose vocation is to serve the state to the best of his ability and most loyally; and a Catholic one with its 'social engineer' ideal whose vocation is to be a moderator between the ruling and the working classes."* Perhaps, today we should talk about mediation between the political elite and the disenchanted voter.

A person who advocates liberal education might justly query the emphasis that these authorities place on the teaching of engineering ethics. Surely, they might argue, morality relates to one's personal principles, that is, the principles that one brings to college study or work. The authorities quoted, as we have seen, would probably agree with that, but the person concerned with a liberal education would argue that the stance a person takes stems from the epistemology he/she has, and in particular the notion he/she has of what 'truth' is. Many arguments arise between people because they have different notions of "truth", and this brings us back to constructivism because realists and constructivists differ in their notions of truth (Vardy and Grosch, 1994). In the earlier section on these topics, no case was put for teaching the students about the differences between these two epistemologies. Yet, a case can be made, for it is advocated by many, that students should learn the skills of learning to learn through meta-cognition in which they learn about their own learning behaviors. To be able to do this, they have to have access to this fundamental knowledge both of themselves and the ethical systems available to them. From the practical reality of learning concepts in engineering they can be connected with the practical reality of making decisions in value-laden circumstances where much depends on their notion of "truth."

A major problem for engineering educators is that study in the humanities can lead to curriculum overload. There is a serious problem in the balance of the curriculum especially when there is pressure to reduce the load-although this need not be the case as Swaim and Moretti (1991) have suggested. A curriculum leader might wish to evaluate the merits of an integrated curriculum in which the study of ethics *per se* derives from problems posed within the engineering and humanities subjects that are taught. For example, it should be possible to illustrate many ethical issues in courses on technology and society. Haws (2002) has suggested that web-based modules could be designed for tutors to use within their engineering courses. It is not an easy choice, for on the one hand engineering can pose the value laden issues with which it has to cope, but on the other hand, this might ignore the potential of some fundamental studies in the understanding of the epistemological basis (personal) of our decision making. It should be noted that there are very few studies of the attitudes of students either to the study of ethics or to the study of the humanities more generally.

Monk (1997), argued the case for the study of literature as the basis for the study of ethics. He pointed out that in the novel and in tragedy there are many examples of how people cope with ethical dilemmas. Literature shows that there is more to decision making in such dilemmas than scientific judgement, which would in any event be inappropriate. The emotions as much as cognition are involved in the action.

An introductory seminar that was based on paradoxes of the human condition at the Colorado School of Mines was apparently successful. The tutors reported that it affected the growing personal and professional attitudes of most students through its attempt to demonstrate dimensions of life that transcended money, success, and technical competence (Andrews, McBride, and Dendy Sloan, 1993).

The best way forward in these circumstances would seem to be to ensure that there is a theoretical grounding to underpin practical work with case studies and role playing in which the students are practically involved, divergent thinking encouraged, and affective qualities brought into play. But such study demands much reading and this is an activity that many engineering students are reluctant to undertake.

In this text there is little mention of the more general debate about the role of liberal education in the education of engineers yet in the United States there have been important reports as for example the ASEE Learning Report (ASEE, 1968), and most recently 2002 (Steneck, Olds, and Neeley, 2002). Separate consideration of the latter, given its importance, is provided in the next section. Thus far, following Newman, the view has been taken here that a philosophical frame of mind is at the heart of liberal education and that demands reading and discussion within and beyond the bounds of the subject.

3.3.7. An American White Paper on Liberal Education in Engineering

2002 saw the fruition of a study of liberal education undertaken by the Liberal Education Division of ASEE. At its Annual Conference, Steneck, Olds and Neeley (2002) presented a White Paper on recommendations for liberal education in engineering. It is evident that the thinking behind this paper was conditioned by a thorough knowledge of the arguments and investigations reported above. Their intention was to provide guidelines that would help engineering schools implement the ABET 2000 criteria that related to liberal education. They listed the following:

(1)   An ability to function on multidisciplinary teams.
(2)   An ability to identify, formulate, and solve engineering problems.
(3)   An understanding of professional and ethical responsibility.
(4)   An ability to communicate effectively.
(5)   The broad education necessary to understand the impact of engineering solutions in a global and societal context.
(6)   A recognition of the need for, and an ability to engage in, lifelong learning.
(7)   A knowledge of contemporary issues.

The authors noted that a liberal education is particularly useful for developing the ability to reflect on and think critically about the process of problem definition. The authors produced this White Paper because ABET did not specify how engineering schools should meet these criteria. They further argued that liberal education is not limited to these competencies, but is *"one aspect of a much larger educational enterprise whose goals have been debated for centuries and whose purposes go beyond those discussed here."* Later they say that, *"study in non-technical disciplines also gives students a better understanding of the society in which their technical products will be used"* and *"it helps students develop the character, understandings, and skills needed to formulate, analyze, and solve technological problems in a thoughtful, responsible way, within the context of a society's structures and mores."*

At the end of the paper the authors record that *"the approach outlined above blurs the boundaries between liberal education (also sometimes referred to as "general education" and engineering education in a way that we believe is beneficial. This beneficial blurring of boundaries, however, should not be allowed to obscure the distinctive value of liberal education for all students."*

In terms of integration as defined later in Chapter 8 the proposals are for a liberal education that is close to engineering (see Section 8.6). This is what happened in England when all the students in the Colleges of Advanced Technology (CAT) were required to take three hours per week of liberal studies. There was a drift toward subjects that were relevant to engineering, and the title "liberal studies" was dropped in favor of

complementary studies or general education (Davies, 1965). The comparative study of university and CAT students by Marris (1964) was accompanied by a profound discussion of the purpose of higher education and did not inspire an in-depth debate about such purposes. He alluded to the role that technological education could play in a liberal education but did not develop this theme. This element is missing from the White Paper. This, may be because it has taken the view that *'liberal education' sometimes connotes a withdrawal from the world..* However much it might be argued that this is a misinterpretation of what is meant by *"liberal education is an end in itself,"* it may be argued that the relevance of technological study to liberal education can only be understand within a broader understanding of the purposes of higher education.[28] One feature of the extensive debate and research in the United Kingdom at the time[29] was a differentiation that was made between technological students who were interested in close or tool/fringe subjects such as management, and those who were interest in cultural studies (Andrews and Mares, 1963).

The White Paper details the abilities required in four areas of competence. These are:

1.   Communication (including critical thinking skills, communication strategies, professional writing and presentation skills and fundamental speaking and presentation skills).
2.   Professional responsibility (including organization, professional codes of conduct, professional regulation, ethical reasoning, and personal values).
3.   Technology and culture (including history of science and technology, science technology and society studies, contemporary issues, and social ideals and values).
4.   Intellectual and cultural perspectives (including fundamental assumptions about the nature of reality and being, ways of knowing, and politics, society, and cultures).

The authors do not recommend any particular model of curriculum design but indicate that liberal education can be delivered through traditional courses in the humanities and social science, integrated courses taught by "experts in science/engineering disciplines, and interdisciplinary courses. Case studies and Projects also enable integrated study. Given the comments about the different types of student that Andrews and Mares found in Britain, it is of some interest to note that Mikic and Grasso (2002) recently reported that in a women's college the students were challenged to undertake socially relevant design projects. They had to design toys that would introduce children to the principles that underlie

---

[28] The judgment this writer would make would be as to whether the education provided produces a philosophical habit of mind since it is this that is the aim of liberal education.

[29] A review of publications (official and unofficial) will be found in Heywood (1972).

technology. Survey data revealed that students thought they had learned to work in teams and consider the impact of technology on society. Tests with the Myers Briggs Type Indicator (see Chapter 5) suggested that these students were particularly responsive to the ethic of social responsibility in engineering and that they were good communicators with a well-organized approach to practical problems solving.

Other approaches related to integrated and interdisciplinary course and project work are given further consideration in Chapters 8 and 9. The role of case studies is also considered in Chapter 14.

3.3.8.   Concluding Remark

There is no shortage of advice for aspirants in this field as to what they might do, as recent books and papers will testify (e.g., Hirsh, 1995; Latcha and Jordan, 1996; Martin and Huff, 1997; Fledderman, 1999; Herkert, 2000a,b; Stephan, 2000). It is important to be clear about what objectives are to be served. Perhaps the first step is to decide whether or not there is case for moral development. A substantial case has been made for this in the literature yet none of the authors quoted above (or in Haws meta-analysis) refer to it (see, for example, Kohlberg and Ryncarz, 1990, and Gilligan, Murphy, and Tappan, 1990). The answer that is given to this question has a considerable bearing on what might be done. Similarly, the Perry (1970) and King and Kitchener (1994) models have much to say about what might be done and when it should be done (see Chapter 6).

3.4. Other Aspects of Teaching in the Philosophical Areas

From the outset it is important that teachers recognizes the value systems they have. In systems where entry is relatively open to all comers, it is quite possible that the value systems of some of the students will be in conflict with those of the teacher. In these circumstances, cognitive dissonance may occur, and there is likely to be resistance to learning. This can be the case where students are only mildly critical of the teacher's viewpoint. When there is inconsistency the student can change his/her disposition toward the teacher from like to dislike when the messages sent by the teacher appear to be untenable. But Marshall (1980), who taught politics, showed that a teacher can cause learning through his/her teaching style, even if his/her rating with the students deteriorates during the course. It is possible that some of the students dropped out of engineering and science studies in the Seymour and Hewitt (1997) study because of dissonance. It will be appreciated that dissonance could create particular difficulties in ethics courses. However, as indicated above, there is a more general resistance among some engineering students to courses in liberal education that has to be overcome if the courses are to be successful, and this means imaginative teaching.

Angelo and Cross (1993) suggested that classroom opinion polls may be a valuable aid for the development of thinking in these subjects. These have as their goals that the student should:

- *Learn to understand perspectives and values of this subject.*
- *Develop an openness to new ideas.*
- *Develop and informed concern about contemporary social issues.*
- *Develop capacity to make informed ethical choices.*
- *Develop leadership skills.*
- *Develop a commitment to one's own values.*
- *Develop respect for others.*
- *Develop capacity to make wise decisions.*

They intend that the poll should be a simple device that can be easily tallied. Thus, a scale might be used that has as its poles strongly disagree and strongly agree. They gave the example of a professor who wanted to assess student views on nuclear energy before they began reading and discussion on this topic. He gave them the two questions shown in Exhibit 3.2. Angelo and Cross suggested that when students have had practice with the technique, they can be asked to explain and justify their opinions. They also pointed out that sharing the results shows students the diversity of views that can exist, and they hoped that it would enable them (the students) to learn to live and work with a range of opinions. For this reason such opinionnaires can be of value in teaching design. Students might be asked to conceive of a simple design and to share their views with their colleagues. This has the advantage of showing them that most design solutions do not have one right answer.

Angelo and Cross also suggested that double-entry journals could help students develop respect for others. These journals are completed in conjunction with required reading for the course. The left-hand column contains notes on the text. The right hand column *"explains the personal significance of the passage selected and responds to that passage. In this way, students engage in a dialogue with the text, exploring their reactions to the reading".* The purpose of this technique is to show students how to cope with the text. This is particularly important in general education programs for engineering students because, they are not exposed to textual study in their engineering courses. In the United Kingdom engineering students are not required to do a lot of reading, and texts in ethics might prove difficult for them. The information in a double-entry journal should help the teacher understand what is understood and plan accordingly.

As has already been discussed one of the best known techniques for dealing with issues in ethics is the ethical dilemma. A favourite dilemma that is cited by Angelo and Cross (1993) relates to cheating when student A tells student B that she is going to sit her boyfriends examination for him. This is presented to students who are then given ten minutes or so say that student B should do, if anything. Discussion of the comments should help students develop a capacity for making informed choices, and a respect for others, among other things. This example is also a reminder that this technique could be used in the teaching of engineering design where dilemmas in the are commonplace, but research by deBord (1993) reported in Section 6.5 suggests that dilemmas work best when they are subject specific.

Sindelar et al, (2003) pointed out that although the ABET criteria provided a stimulus for engineering graduates to act in an ethically responsible manner methods to asses how effective engineering educators were in preparing their students for this goal were "primitive at best." A collaboration between the Colorado School of Mines and the University of Pittsburgh set out to try and remedy this defect, and Sindelar and his colleagues reported on the first phase of this endeavor. This comprised the development of a rubric designed to classify levels of achievement in pre and post tests administered before and after a one semester course in engineering ethics with the intention of seeing if there were any "shifts" in ability as measured by the rubric. Each test asked the respondents to analyze two brief matched cases, the pre-test being given in class and the post-test as a homework exercise.

The five attributes identified for assessment were Recognition of dilemma (relevance); information (argumentation); analysis (complexity and depth); perspective (fairness); and resolution (argumentation). These were then assessed for four levels of achievement. For example, in respect of the second attribute (Information) *"at the lowest level (level i), respondents ignored pertinent facts or used misinformation. Moving higher on the scale, some students listed information without justifying relevance or applicability. At the high end of the scale, respondents were able to make, and justify, assumptions, sometimes bringing in information from their own experiences ".*

The investigators found that it was possible to develop a rubric that could produce internal consistency. This is consistent with the findings of other research on the use of rubrics[30] (e.g., Heywood, 2000 or other similar texts). The rubric also discriminated between the students, but there were some difficulties with the scenarios since the students' responses were found to be highly sensitive to them.

Support for the integration of humanities into the technical content of programs came from Shannon, LeMee and Stecher (1977). In their discussion of the philosophical background to the problem of the crisis of modern societies, they pointed out that it is a crisis of values. Therefore, any university study has to begin with the self because *"Man's greatest enemy is Man himself".* This means that a universal perspective has to be provided, and this goes beyond the perspective of a profession. It requires that the humanities and social science be thoroughly intermeshed into the technical content of programs, and they described a program that set to achieve that goal.

At the heart of the philosophical method is what is commonly called reflective practice in higher education. It has become a widely cited goal and is commonly coupled with self-assessment. In management and in-career short courses for teachers it is common practice to ask students either in a group or in response to a questionnaire to state their goals for the course. In this way the teacher can assess the extent of mismatch between his/her expectations and those of the course participants. Angelo and Cross consider the purposes of such activities are *"to learn to understand perspectives and values of this subject, develop ability to work productively with others, develop a commitment to personal achievement, Cultivate a sense of responsibility for one's own behavior, and develop a commitment to one's own values".* Related to this is the self-assessment of ways of learning (see Chapter 16). This would include the self-assessment of related skills and knowledge relevant to a particular course being studied. Information of this kind can be very helpful to teachers and enable them to better plan their lectures.

If I found a great house at a great price, close to work and near good schools, that was within five miles of a nuclear power plant, I would (circle only one);
a. be absolutely willing to consider buying it, and not worried about the plant.
b. be somewhat willing to consider buying, it but concerned about the plant.
c. be skeptical about buying it, and worried about the plant.
d. be absolutely unwilling to consider it because of the plant.
Assuming that I had a choice, if changes in my life-style would help make the construction of more nuclear power plants unnecessary I would (circle only one):
a. not be willing to use less electrical energy or par more for it.
b. be willing to use much less electrical energy but not pay more for it.
c. use the same amount of energy but be willing to pay a higher price for it
d. be willing to use much less electrical energy and pay a higher price for it.

Exhibit 3.2. Two questions put by a Professor to find out student views of nuclear energy. (cited by T. Angelo and P. K. Cross in *Classroom Assessment Techniques*, Jossey Bass, 1993).

In engineering skill, in self-assessment is extremely important in project work and design and should be part of a continuing process that informs planning and prediction, hence the importance of evaluating alternatives before a design is finally agreed. Engineers like all other students require both a philosophical habit of mind and a philosophy of engineering, and teachers should create a classroom and assessment environment in which it can be cultivated as Jinks (1996) has argued and demonstrated.

A major task is to find the time to get and persuade engineering students to read beyond the boundaries of technical problem solving. accompanied by a relative decline in interest in science and technology subjects.

---

[30] In this case the design was influenced by a scoring tool developed by Pinkus for assessing bioengineering students See also Pinkus 2000).

Part 2. Sociological Aspects

3.5. Screening with Sociology

In the screening of aims it is sometimes difficult to draw hard and fast lines between what is philosophy, sociology, and psychology. The discussion of epistemologies breached the line between philosophy and sociology with the discussion of the social constructivist model that originates in the realm of the sociology of knowledge. There is, therefore, no need to discuss it further. However, in the discussion of aims no reference was made to Barnett's work on the future of higher education that spans both philosophy and sociology (Barnett, 1990, see also MacIntyre, 1990). Barnett has been a prolific writer in this field, and his work should be of great interest to engineers since he sees technology as breaking down our traditional notions of what a university is.

Similarly, with "values," although the perspectives that philosophers and sociologists take differ considerably. In this respect sociology is much more directly connected to so-called "objective" measures. Values are related to the entering characteristics of students in the curriculum model; that is, they are part of the baggage that the student brings with them to learning (see Chapter. 1). Philosophically, as we have seen, values are related to what we think about our subject and how it should be taught. These remarks serve once again as a reminder of the complexity of the curriculum process that cannot be represented in the models. The sociological dimensions considered in this section relate to the supply and demand of students for engineering, the treatment of minorities and women in engineering curriculum, the experience of the curriculum, and organization and the curriculum. Problems relating to curriculum and institutional change are dealt with in other Chapters.

3.6. Supply and Demand: Entering Characteristics

At the macroscopic level, a variety of methods have been used to forecast the supply and demand for qualified manpower. They have not been particularly successful in understanding the shift in requirements that have taken place as a result of the interactions between technological development and social structure except in a very broad sense. Applicants for jobs are undoubtedly sensitive to employment prospects, and engineering employment is sensitive to the assumptions made in making forecasts (Kutscher, 1994).

Engineering schools are caught up in this web, and while they tend to be relatively closed systems they do have to take account of the supply side so as to ensure the number of students does not dwindle. In the United Kingdom there has been a continuing problem of ensuring that engineering schools get a reasonable share of the more able entrants. Unlike the situation in the United States, students in United Kingdom programs have found it extremely difficult to transfer from the program they enter to study in another field. To a greater or lesser degree, once they are in a program, the shape of their future career is determined. Engineering educators, therefore, watch what is happening in schools with considerable interest.

Up to 2001, students in England, Wales and Northern Ireland who had passed the public examinations for 16, year-olds had to choose three or four subjects to study in depth in high school for another two years.[31] At that time they took examinations (called A levels) in these subjects, the results of which were used for admission (and selection) to university courses. Up to about ten years ago, students split between the arts (including languages) and sciences. This suited the engineers very well. They would look for well-qualified students who had taken maths, physics, and chemistry or pure and applied maths and physics; the curriculum in university in engineering science began where these subjects left off. It was commonly argued that the public examination at the end of high school was equivalent to the end of first year in many university courses in other countries.

However, during the last twenty years there has been an enormous social change in respect of the supply of students. In the first place, the number of traditional students in schools who take a hybrid group of subjects (from arts and science or languages) has increased enormously. Secondly, there has been a massive demand for non traditional subjects (such as media studies) at university. Subjects such as logic, philosophy psychology and sociology have been introduced. These developments have been accompanied by a relative decline in interest in science and technology subjects. Thirdly, there has been a substantial rise in the number of non-traditional mature students (as defined by age). In some universities, their numbers match those of the traditional students. Many mature students will not have taken the public examinations at school, having left school at the age of 16. They will have obtained other qualifications and experience that universities and science departments are now prepared to accept.

One consequence of this has been that in some engineering departments', entry qualifications as measured by grades in public examinations have been lowered. This has caused a massive industry in local investigations, either at institution or department level, of

---

[31] In 2002 they were required to take five or more subjects called As levels in their first year. They then selected a limited number for more specialist study in their second year. These were called A2. Marks from As level were accumulated into the final A2 mark. The grading of students from this new system was criticised and led to an enquiry in September 2002. The grades of thousands of students had to be re-checked and some adjustments were made. This has led some commentators to argue for a system of examining like the International Baccalaureate. It seems to be accepted that this will happen in the next ten years. For the purposes of this text references are made to the traditional A level examination, and in particular to the well researched development in engineering science. It has also been argued that because the large number of non-traditional it would be better to use an aptitude test of the ACT/SAT type. Such a test, the Test of Academic Aptitude exists but was never recommended for use by the Committee of Vice-Chancellors and Principals.

the correlation between admission grade and grade awarded at final level to see if there has been a change in standards. Carter has pointed out the fallacies in this approach, and in particular noted that it does not account for the effects of the university process on performance. He also noted that the final grading system produced distortions in this relationship. He demonstrated his argument by data taken from a department of electrical engineering (Carter and Heywood, 1992). This paper is important since the model it describes has direct relevance to the measurement of quality and the problems of determining added value (Heywood, 2000). Longitudinal studies of the kind conducted by Felder (1995), Felder et al., (1993, 1994, 1995), adapted for cultural circumstances, can illuminate the points made by Carter and Heywood.

Science and Engineering departments found that they had to adapt to the new student intake. Thus some science and engineering departments began to offer foundation courses (UCAS, 1997), and some found it necessary to devise pre-program tests that would indicate what these potential students knew- and did not know. Preliminary years have also been introduced for traditional students who do not meet traditional entrance qualifications and are uncertain about their career choices. Such programs have necessitated changes in teaching practice. One of the problems is that such students often want to be involved in design, but what they understand by design is heavily influenced by the school curriculum in which they have engaged in "design and make" activities (called design and technology see Chapter 17). Such studies may be continued between 16 and 18 years). The net effect is that they have limited experience on which to make judgments with regard to their career realisation.

At Loughborough University, one approach to help them realize the nature of problem solving in mechanical engineering has been to use a structured problem solving methodology in which the preferred learning styles of students were matched to the course objectives. The learning outcomes were satisfied when the learner was able to generate design proposals on the basis of the concrete experience provided and personally constructed robust conceptual frameworks (Pace, 1999). In engineering, some departments have been concerned about the mathematical ability that students bring to their courses. Some now come with qualifications gained in technician courses and not the traditional A level. In one study where a diagnostic test was used it was found that the non traditional students required much more revision than the traditional students. In the final year examinations they performed as well as the traditional students with low grades at A level. Otherwise there was a direct correlation between grade obtained at A level and the mark awarded in the end of year examination. Those students who had attended a Maths Education Centre that had been established to help students revise through self-study material improved their performance. The chief problem seemed to be low algebraic understanding

(Lawson, 1995). Other academics have been interested to show how technology can enhance mathematical skills (e.g. Short, 1999,- see also Chapter 7).

Although the following is a digression it is interesting to note from a sociological perspective how things go full circle. The paper by Lawson is about students in a university that had graduated to that status from being a technical college. When the first steps were made in this direction in the 1960's, and 10 technical colleges were designated Colleges of Advanced Technology (CATs). One of their functions was to help technician students become graduates. They experienced exactly the same problems as are described by Lawson (Dickinson, 1964; Heywood, 1969). Evidently, institutional memories are short.

In the United States, Felder et al, (1994) showed that rural students did less well than urban students in engineering. It was suggested that one of the causes of this difference was that rural students did not come under family pressure to perform well.

More generally, in the United Kingdom there has also been interest in the prior knowledge of science that engineering students have. Clifford (1994) described in detail a diagnostic test that was given to mechanical engineering students. He compared their results with the expectations of staff and found considerable differences between the scores obtained by students (average 40.3%) and those expected by staff (expected score 80.7%). The knowledge that the students had fell well short of what was expected of them. One comment was that there might be inadequacies in 'A' level syllabuses. Whatever the cause, the consequences for teaching are considerable. Later the same tests were administered in two comparable university departments. Significant differences were found between the scores obtained in the two universities. These were attributed to different admissions strategies. The mean score expected by staff at the second university was more than twice the mean score obtained by the students, and there was an unusually clear relation between A level grade and performance (Adamson, Byrom, and Clifford, 1998).

At the University of Salford, some investigations suggested that a full psychometric profile would be of value, although no policy decision was ever taken on this issue (Heywood, Sharp, and Hides, 2001). In Mechanical Engineering some students were admitted for a two-year program after they had completed technician level courses in local technical colleges. Because the systems of teaching and assessment differed considerably, the university department found it had a major problem in bridging the gap between the two. It had to be planned, and this was a new experience. (Culver et al, 1994; Sharp and Culver, 1996). (This is, as is the paper by Pace, an example of curriculum improvement necessitated by circumstances. It was not the only the university to experience this problem with students at this level, and Anderson and Percival (1997) reported that they had received a grant to develop specific materials for such a program.

The supply problem that has continually exercised engineering academics throughout the last 50 years in the United Kingdom led to many surveys of the attitudes of school children to science and technology. The mid 1960's saw a profusion of such studies (Heywood, Mash, and Pollitt, 1996, Hutchings, 1963). As indicated previously, questions were asked about why more able students chose to do physics rather than engineering (Hutchings, 1963; Jones, 1963). The Institution of Mechanical Engineers established a committee to examine what contribution it could make to the school curriculum that would help change attitudes (Page, 1965).

In Holland a trust, The PATT Foundation, was established as a result of the success of the Pupils Attitude to Technology program (PATT). This has had a considerable influence on school technology. In addition to holding conferences, it has developed a scale to measure pupils attitudes to technology that has been used with and without modification in many countries including the United States (Raat, 1992; Bame and Dugger, 1992; Heywood, 1998; Householder and Bolin, 1993). One result is that there has been a continuing flow of papers on primary (elementary) and post-primary pupils' attitudes toward technology and toward this or that subject in science and technology since the early ones mentioned above.

In the long history of attitudinal surveys in the United Kingdom one is of special interest. In addition to surveying children in the age ranges 11 to 12 and 12 to 14, it also obtained information from industrialists in small, medium, and large companies about their perceptions of children's beliefs about industry. The pupils were asked to respond to Likert-like items about engineering and manufacturing. The industrialists also completed the same items with the instruction that they should indicate how they thought the pupils would respond to these items (Tonkinson and Gazey, 1997).

It was found that pupils' response to engineering and manufacturing was quite positive, but responses to 18 of the 34 statements differed from those that the industrialists expected them to be. These items were associated with controversial statements such as "engineering is boring." The majority of these children thought that engineering and manufacturing were interesting, but there was a high proportion who were unsure about these statements. Similarly, industrialists believed that children would not believe that engineering and manufacturing were creative. This was the opposite of what the pupils thought. But many children did not think that engineering and manufacturing provided exciting jobs, and in this respect they agreed with the industrialists. The industrialists thought the children would think engineering was unglamorous, and they did.

Tonkinson and Gazey pointed out that the image of the profession is a neglected factor and that some mechanism needed to be found to make it to be more glamorous. This was consistent with findings in the 1960's that pupils are well aware of prospects and potential in the variety of careers they assess. In general the industrialists conveyed a negative picture of industry. These results were in stark contrast with the respect that engineering is held in other European and Far-Eastern countries.[32] In this respect it could be of some import that the term technology as used by engineering educators in the United States has lower status than that of engineering, yet it is the status of design and technology that teachers are trying to raise in schools. It will, therefore, of interest to see what effect the new approach to technology in schools and the development of standards for this subject will have on attitudes toward engineering in the United States. Curriculum leaders may well find that studying the attitudes of students in their local schools could provide insights of some importance to the design of learning in higher education. They should note that understanding students begins in primary school and while there is an increasing literature on primary (elementary) children's approaches to technology, it has yet to be fitted into the pattern of human development (e.g. Constable, 1993). It has been suggested that gender attitudes to technology begin at this stage (Brown, 1993; Doornekamp, 1991). Nevertheless, it is clear that family, school, and society have a powerful influence on the expectations of the college experience that students bring with them to higher education.

The reader may like to turn to Chapter 17 where some of these issues are considered in more detail in relation to attrition and retention.

3.7. Minority Students (See also Section 17.1)

When this text was first written women and minorities were grouped together. But the point was made that they are different groups and sometimes require different treatment. Nevertheless, in the literature they are very often linked together. Throughout the last 30 or so years, there has been a small but persistent flow of papers about the education in engineering of minority groups particularly in the United States. It has concentrated on the failure of engineering to attract larger numbers from these groups[33] It has been argued that programs should address deficiencies in basic academic competencies in very bright latent achievers (Rogers, 1992). It has also been suggested that there should be pro-active mentoring by peers. At Clemson College this has had a profound effect on the retention of minority students (Lasser and Snelshire, 1995). It should be noted that mentors are paid for 10 hours per week.

At Purdue University, where minority groups were seriously underrepresented, a comprehensive program was introduced many years ago to remedy this

---

[32]   The authors cite Andersen Consulting (1995). *World-wide Manufacturing Competitiveness Survey.* Arthur Andersen, London.

[33]That it is a problem in the Western world generally is illustrated by, DeCeCchi, Timperon and Dececchi (1998), Canada,. Fontaine and Ohana (1999), France,. Kovaleva (1999),-Russia, Heywood, (1998),-England; Watt et al (1998), Scotland. These references are taken from *Abstracts of Research in Higher Education*, Carfax/Taylor and Francis.

defect. It comprised numerous activities including pre-college recruitment efforts, summer engineering workshops for 7th and 8th graders, pre-freshmen and cooperative education, minority introduction to engineering workshop etc. An evaluation after 20 years suggested that there were three missing links that were critical. These were an elementary outreach program, a parent involvement program, and a longitudinal follow-up evaluation program. Steps were taken to set up a Multicultural Engineering Comprehensive Career Academy. *Its purpose was to "instil confidence and an interest in preparing for college with technical, math, and science related to technical disciplines such as engineering"* (Budny, Blalock, and LeBold, 1991).

Many of the problems that minority groups have to face are also have to be faced by women, and many of the published papers focus on the problems of women.

3.8. Women in Engineering (See also Chapter 17)

It has also been a matter of policy to try to recruit more women into engineering. The small numbers of women in engineering is a general problem in the western world (e.g. Varcoe, 1990; UWA, 1996- in Australia;. see also Moxham and Roberts, 1995). In Australia and the United States access programs have been provided (Matheison and Corderoy, 1989; and Diggelman and Korta, 1992, and Newell et al, 2002, respectively), and in the United Kingdom there has been a Women into Science and Engineering Campaign (WISE)[34] with accompanying research (see Higgins et al, 1997; and SWAP, 1993). In Ghana girls have difficulties with maths concepts and are criticized for, and discouraged from taking an interest in engineering (Baryeh et al 2000). There is the possibility that some of these girls might have suffered from stereotype threat.

A specific example of stereotype threat, (which can apply to anyone irrespective of sex) is the poor performance of the females in difficult standardized tests in mathematics and engineering. Bell et al, (2003) who reported this finding in an earlier study ,described an experiment with a test selected from items in the practice tests for the Fundamentals of Engineering Examination. Samples of volunteer female and male students were randomly assigned to three test conditions. The difference between the conditions was in the information in the directions given at the beginning of each test. The instructions all began with a statement to the effect that the test had been shown to be "an excellent indicator of engineering aptitude and ability." In the first test it was noted that it had been particularly "effective at assessing people's engineering limitations in problem areas." In contrast, the directions in the second test were non-diagnostic. They simply explained why the students were asked to help develop the test. That was to check the items for future development. The directions for the third test concluded *"prior use of these problems has shown*

them to be gender fair that is men and women perform equally well on these problems. "

It was found that the performance of the women improved considerably in the condition of the third test. Both male and females had been chosen because they had high GPA's in engineering and had stated they were good at engineering and that it was important for them to be good at engineering. Although the samples were small, Bell and her colleagues pointed out, as the investigations reported below show, that classroom and department climates are important factors in female persistence in engineering. They believed their study added weight to these findings, and they countered the argument that the results showed that women were not tough enough for engineering by citing a study of white males, half of whom were told that Asians were better than whites at math. The students who were not given this information performed better than those who were given a difficult math examination (Aronson et al, 1999).

There is a continuous literature on the topic, and reports have ranged from studies of performance and retention (e.g., Chen et al., 1996, Anderson, Rowland and Urban, 2001, as retention is a function of housing and mentoring) to several indicating trends (e.g., Wadsworth, LeBold, and Daniels, 1991; Moskal, 2000). One consequence of this work has been the development of a number of K-12 initiatives (e.g., Koppel, Cano and Heyman, 2002; Wigal et al 2002- see Chapter 17). While there has been a considerable improvement in the standing of women, there is, according to Moskal (2000), still a long way to go. But this is not the same thing as changing women's attitudes toward the potential of studying engineering.

The attitudes of freshmen students are major determinants of persistence irrespective of how they might change in subsequent years. A large study of freshmen in 17 institutions in the United States found that as between pre and post-course attitudes and self-assessed confidence measures, women students were more comfortable than men with their study habits (Besterfield Sacre et al, 2001). However, the women continued to Exhibit lower self-confidence in their ability to succeed in engineering. Similar differences were found between Asian Pacific and Majority students. These results may be compared with a study that found that women alumnae rated self-confidence and good communication skills as the most important qualities for professional success (Robinson and Reilly, 1993).

In response to the view that electrical and mechanical devices intimidate women, a course was specially designed at the University of California Davis to introduce women students to physical devices and systems. Several articles had reported on the importance of female role models so in this course four female teaching assistants took responsibility for this task. The course was based on hands-on work in cooperative learning groups. The women had to become familiar with hand tools, and out-of-class assignments *"included*

---

[34] This term is also used in the United States.

reading articles on the climate for women in engineering and assignments in the text of David Macaulay's The Way Things Work." Case study methodology was used to evaluate the course. This included the analysis of research questions written by the students in their journals, focus groups, and interviews. Although the tutors felt that the course had achieved its objective of improving self-confidence, a number of questions needed to be answered. Among them was: *"Does an all-women class have pedagogical advantages, and if so how can this be implemented?"* (Henderson et al, 1994).

Comparison of the perceptions of females and males in a multimedia case study found that when compared with male students the females perceived *"better opportunities to learn from self to learn from others and to be challenged. These opportunities led to higher scores on the perceived higher level cognitive skill development for the female students ".* Mbarika, Sankar and Raju (2003) who conducted the study used the Crist Power Plant Case (Sankar and Raju, 2000. See also Section 14.1) noted that female students valued learner-driven constructs rather than more content-driven constructs when compared with the male students. While they were quick to acknowledge weaknesses in their approach and to suggest replication with larger samples, they offered the opinion that the presentation of information using Powerpoint might not be sufficient for females. They could be helped to *"develop an interest involving 'multi criteria' engineering and technical decisions effectively"* through multimedia activities that are challenging, and provide opportunities for learning by themselves and with others[35]

A study at Purdue by Thom, Pickering and Thompson (2002) of the perceptions of freshman students in aviation engineering to engineering and work revealed that the *"modern role model must display the characteristics women wish to see in a career, if the role model is to be successful. Just as the young women want to know that a technical career is supportive, has camaraderie, is challenging and is not de-feminizing, they also need for their role model to represent those factors."* The role model has to do this in a positive way and not focus on the past history of women at work otherwise the role model is unlikely to have the desired effect.

An interesting approach to this problem was taken at Pen State, Altoona where the women students in a course on computer repair and diagnosis were given the opportunity to become role models to each other (Shull

and Weiner, 2000). Opportunities were also given for the students to explore their own self perceptions and their relation to engineering and technology. The course (2 credits) was chosen because "computer technology is perceived as 'gender neutral'. That is, unlike most scientific fields, little or no social stigma is attached to computer expertise. If you are an expert in the computer field, you are a 'guru,' not a 'geek." An advantage of computer repair is that it is relatively easy and quick to gain a respectable level of expertise. Beginning with dismantling and reassembly of a nonworking computer, the students were taken through a series of exercises until they could diagnose and repair intentional bugs. In these exercises the women took the lead role of investigators. It was reported that the students gained in confidence, and during the six offerings from the class, 605 reported that they had worked on computer problems with others who has sought their advice. We are not told of its "transfer" effects to engineering laboratories, but it was an intention of the course that it would give women confidence to get involved in traditional laboratories.

It is not just at freshmen level that women experience difficulties. A small study at McGill University showed that women were significantly less likely than men to plan on graduate school (Baker, Tancred, and Whitesides, 2002). Among the factors that contributed to this were *"difficulties in obtaining reference letter, a low level of encouragement, and the discomfort of the engineering academic environment."* And, those who enter graduate school are also likely to experience discomfort. For example, Chesler and Chesler (2002) suggested that there was a need for organizational change that would support rather than try to assimilate women into the organization. For this to happen faculty had to value the qualities that women bring to the environment. They also argued that because of the variety of tasks which young graduates have to undertake, a system of multiple-mentoring should be provided including access to supportive senior women faculty. This is related to the point made by several authors that women continue to lack role models toward whom they can aspire. (See also Section 17.5).

A fairly large study across seven American institutions of higher education highlighted the need to distinguish between teacher and student contributions to classroom climate. When instructors were perceived to treat men and women in the same way, the more students were motivated to become engineers and to take responsibility for their learning. But, students were also found to be influenced by their peers, and if males were perceived to treat women differently, this had a negative impact on the women's development of skills for working in groups. Thus *"the chilly climate for women in engineering may be as much a factor of peer interaction as student–faculty interaction"* (Colbeck, Cabrera, and Terenzini, 1999).[36]

---

[35] The learner driven factor embraced learning interest, challenging learning, self reported learning, and learning from others. The context-driven factor measured the extrinsic value provided to the end user through multi-media instructional materials These constructs were quality (sufficient to enable the student to evaluate the case study); location (the ease with which data could be located, and understood and the assumptions made in its calculation); ease of use; and 'timeliness' the ability to complete tasks on time A higher order cognitive skill factor sought student perceptions of whether or not they believed their abilities to *"identify, integrate, evaluate, and interrelate concepts within the case study had improved.*

---

[36] The finding that males devalue females is corroborated in other studies, including Seymour and Hewitt (1997).

These investigators drew attention to the paradox that while team-based design projects can lead to increases in self-perceptions, they may also create a chilly climate for women and put them off wanting to join groups. Colbeck, Cabrera, and Terenzini suggested that some training on conflict resolution before group work began might be advantageous.

In Norway it was found that male students had a more positive attitude toward computer systems than did women. But, this study provided another reminder that attitudes, performance, and grade expectations are not the same thing. It was found that there was no noticeable difference between male and female grade expectations (HornÆs and Røyrvik, 2000)

On the downside, one reported that women were disadvantaged in laboratories and this caused a loss of self-confidence. But the differences were confined to the laboratory and not to understanding of course material (Cooney, 1991). At the same time a national study of women engineers in the workplace found that they had high levels of self-esteem. This was reported by Anderson (1993), who had already completed other studies in this field (e.g., Anderson, 1991). On the upside, Chen et al, (1996) reported that at North Carolina A & T State University female students, apart from one class, outperformed their male counterparts. They suggested three reasons for this outcome. First, pre-college studies better prepared them for the rigors of college in general and engineering studies specifically; the females had better high school grade point averages than males. Second, it was possible that the relatively high enrollment of females provide a female-friendly environment. Third, the females in this study did not suffer a loss of self-confidence.

Two studies reported at the 1997 Frontiers in Education Conference are of importance. Ambrose, Lazarus and Nair (1997) reported the analysis of the professional and personal histories of 88 women in engineering, computer science and science. Their conclusion was that, *"there is not a set of universal rules for women's attachment to and success in engineering, but one simple overriding conclusion: these women were encouraged or enabled to envision themselves as engineers"*. And this investigation was reinforced by a longitudinal study of students at the University of Washington. Brainard and Carlin (1997) reported that it was during the first and sophomore years that women were most likely to switch out of engineering. The reasons were loss of interest, academic difficulties and low grades. But even women who persisted felt that fear of losing interest, intimidation, lack of self-confidence, poor advising, and not being accepted by the department were barriers to their progress. It is not enough, therefore, to exhort women to persist. An environment in which they can persist has to be nurtured, and this seems to have occurred in the incorporation of professional and personal development activities in a program targeted at women and minorities at the Colorado School of Mines (Murphy and Martinez, 1997).

At the same school a study of male and female undergraduates in the EPICS program was initiated to evaluate the contributions that males and females made in their project teams. It was undertaken by observation using Eberhartd's (1987) method (Laeser et al., 2003, MacDonald, Laeser et al., 2001). Contrary to previous findings that women tended to use process-oriented skills while men tended to use task oriented skills, it was found that there were no differences between the males and females.[37] The investigators were not surprised by this outcome. Because the School was primarily an engineering school, it would attract a different population of women than other schools where the possibility of change to other courses is more easily accommodated. In regard to working in groups, although there were not statistically significant findings, there was an indication that the gender mix of the teams impacted on the functions of team members. *"An interesting question that emerges from this observation is whether males or females within the different team combinations that are more likely to display the functions of clarifying, encouraging and standard setting. In other words, does team composition impact the functions that males."* [38]

It would not be surprising to find that the "assigned role" is important. Therefore, it would seem that both males and females should have to play different *"assigned roles"* as part of their learning. (See Chapter 13 for a further discussion of this issue).

Stimulated by the literature that supported the view that women learn and behave in different ways to men, Gallaher and Pearson (2000) undertook a small study to examine in what ways this was the case. The climate of engineering technology programs was evaluated by obtaining the perceptions of female students to competition and challenge, faculty support, and inclusion. The women did *"not perceive a significant difference between the importance of competition and challenge to themselves and the degree to which it was emphasized in the program"*. However, the women believed that they required more support than was provided by faculty. They also believed that their abilities

---

[37] Eberhardt (1987) distinguished between five task functions (initiating, information seeking, information giving, clarifying, and summarizing),and five process functions (harmonizing; gatekeeping, encouraging, compromising, standard setting) that contribute to optimally functioning teams. The task functions are critical to product quality, and the process functions are critical to team satisfaction. The former relate to the implementation of tasks, and the latter relate to the efficient functioning of the team. These functions provide a framework for the analysis of team functioning. For another example of its use, see Laeser et al, (2002). They describe further work at the Colorado School of Mines.

[38] These investigators used a framework suggested by Eberhardt (1987) who distinguished between task functions (initiating, information seeking: information giving: clarifying: and, summarizing,), and five process functions (harmonizing: gatekeeping: encouraging: compromising,: standard setting) that contribute to optimally functioning teams. The task functions are critical to product quality, and the process functions are critical to team satisfaction. The former relate to the implementation of tasks, and the latter relate to the efficient functioning of the team.

were not accorded the recognition they would have liked. The level of peer support was less than one they would have liked. Gallaher and Pearson (2000) made the point, as others have done, that male faculty need to look at their biases, and involve women more in the learning process (see Chapter 17).

Design competitions were used at Tufts University in an introductory course in robotics. The competition required mixed groups of males and females to respond to robotic challenges. Pre-and post-course questionnaires (published in the paper) sought to determine prior knowledge and level of confidence; knowledge gained, change in confidence, and impressions of working in groups. The competencies included building and programming skills (Milto, Rogers, and Portsmore, 2002). In so far as the competitions were concerned the females liked them so long as they were not taken too seriously. By contrast the males liked them when they were cut-throat. Some females, it seemed, who lacked experience were less assertive in their groups than were males. Because confidence was gained during the course, it may have been due to the increase in experience. It was argued that in their secondary education, girls should be encouraged to use hands-on manipulatives. Unfortunately, the sample was too small to be able to generalize. Also, the inclusion of tests of spatial ability and convergent/divergent thinking might also yield valuable information (see Chapter 5).[39]

The Purdue University study referred to above found that young women regarded a supported environment as important. Within the concept of "support," they included courtesy and communication. Lack of courtesy was equated with workplace hostility and discrimination. Courtesy and communication were associated with professionalism. Nontechnical fields are seen as offering community and personal support. Young women want to maintain their female identity (Thom, Pickering, and Thompson, 2002).

Similar findings were reported in a study of students in science, engineering, and technology (SET) courses at Heriot-Watt University in Scotland.[40] (Cronin, Foster, and Lister, 1999). Thus, male teachers called on males more than females. They did not take women students seriously. This study also drew attention to the fact that male peers did not take women engineers seriously. Some of the male students evidently thought that physical attractiveness and intellectual ability are mutually exclusive. The sexism that existed did not deter the women from persisting in a predominantly male culture. This culture was reinforced by traditional approaches to teaching and assessment. The results were used in the design of two interventions in first and third year courses. These required changes in content, teaching

and learning in the third year course. This included the publication of course aims and the links that it had with other modules. The sequence of theory and practice was changed, and more demonstrations were included in lecture sessions. The teachers in the first-year course considered the changes to be about attracting more female students. The curriculum was changed and interactive lecturing techniques were introduced.

It was found that the changes in curriculum content, assessment techniques, and group work appealed to both male and female students. Thus, changes in the curriculum that are attractive are likely to be as attractive to many students. This finding supports the view that the curriculum for females described by Belenky et al, (1986) was one suited to most students, female and male. Nevertheless, their remaining concerns have to be addressed especially when women form a very small minority in a department. In any event, teachers will not change by edict. They have to be helped to change (see Chapter 17).

Hammond and Hammond (2002), in a theoretical analysis of the approaches to the study of women's performance in mathematics, argued that it is important to take into account "choice" along with other variables. If this is done it might indicate that women are absent from mathematics *"because: (a) they lack the autonomy to make independent choices; (b) they have the power to choose but they are alienated from mathematics because cultural taboos are still fresh in the mind; (c) their absence from math is an abstraction, i.e,. it is a statistical artefact."*

There is, therefore, a need for career preference inquiries whether or not the respondents have a high or low autonomy in making their choices. Thus, surveys should include items that evaluate *"individual preferences, aptitudes, needs and goals, family expectations, perception of autonomy in choice selection, satisfaction with choices made, and curricula performance."*

Summarizing the results of an international seminar on gender balance in engineering education method using ICT at Oulu Polytechnic in Finland, Alha and Gibson (2003) noted that there were few recorded criticisms of ICT courses because somehow ICT-based delivery courses become a "feminine way" of studying. *"The trend away from more traditional teaching methods toward a more holistic pedagogy involving extensive use of ICT provides flexibility in learning and facilitates wide support for individual communication and networking...that are particularly attractive to women."* Bissell et al (2003) of the Open University also suggest that a new generation of courses with changes in content, pedagogy and marking might have made technology courses more attractive for women.

---

[39] It is well established in the literature that women seem to be at a spatial disadvantage to men (see Section 5.4).

[40] Heriot-Watt University is a small college in Edinburgh that is primarily devoted to the teaching of science, engineering, and technological courses.

In sum, women need to acquire self-confidence in their ability to handle practical work. Role models can provide important encouragement, and ways of introducing role models into programs need to be found. Women need to be supported rather than assimilated, and teachers and male students have a major role to play in providing an effective culture in which women will feel at ease.

3.9. The Experience of College

In the United States there have been a number of studies that have tried to explain the nature of the experience undergone in higher education. Two that continue to have a bearing on the issue were due to Astin (1997) and Pascarella and Terenzini (1991). While they are inter related, their perspectives differ. Pascarella and Terenzini provided a large-scale analytical review of studies that had been done, and they described a number of models of retention that have been used to study the affects of college on the student experience. Most of these studies related to students in the liberal arts. They are of relevance to engineering since a study by Seymour and Hewitt (1997) suggested that science, mathematics and engineering departments not only lose academically poor students but, they also do not retain some academically able students. Seymour and Hewitt found that this did not worry educators in these schools because they were able to sublimate their responses. To put it in another way, they were able to blame other persons and/or policies for this state of affairs. They did not see that it was a problem they could solve. The relevance of the Astin and Pascarrela and Terenzini studies lies in the fact that the able students who left engineering went into the liberal arts. Therefore, the question arises, what is it that the liberal arts have to offer that engineering does not? Is engineering a liberal education? Do students entering engineering have an expectation of an education in engineering or a liberal education through engineering? and so on. The longitudinal studies of Felder et al, (1993, 1994, 1995) at North Carolina State University of engineering students are important contributions to the understanding of the student experience at these colleges that may be generalisable.[41] They highlight the need for effective teaching as does a paper by McDowell (1995).

More specifically, women have the opportunity to join disciplinary organizations such as ASEE, ASME, IEEE, AI Chem E, and or the generalist Society of Women Engineers (SWE). A study at Rowan University demonstrated the importance of membership of these organizations to women (Hartman and Hartman, 2003). It was found that membership of these organizations increased among students who were in the later stages of their education, and that membership of the SWE was particularly high although chemical engineering students were the most likely to be members, and that civil engineers are the most likely to be non-members. Those

in the electrical and mechanical disciplines were more likely to join discipline-specific organizations. No significant differences were found in pre-college backgrounds. Thus, the students began from similar starting points, but with time there were changes that appear to be a function of whether or not the student belonged to an organization.

Hartman and Hartman reported that the women who joined SWE and other organizations had higher GPA's than those who did not, from which they draw the conclusion that these women were not joining them because they needed more help than other women. Nevertheless there was an association with two dimensions of self confidence -that engineering is the right subject for them, and that they have the competencies for the study of engineering. It was found that women who had participated in student organizations started the year more confident in the view that engineering was the right subject for them. Whereas they were less confident in their competencies at the beginning of the year, by the end of the spring semester they were more confident in them than those who were not members of organizations. Evidently the SWE in particular "enhanced a sense of engineering efficacy through its support and help network, which in turn resulted in a greater commitment to the major and the profession." These organizations evidently supplied something that was value-added and its members are associated with higher academic achievement than 'those who did not belong to such organizations. The authors noted that these findings for a small institution are similar to those for the large public universities such as those by Astin (1997). They provide further support for Newman's (1852) view of the importance of peer group learning and halls of residence.

3.10. Organization

Related to the experience of college is the college's organization, and it seems that the problems are little different from the problems in industry.

At the beginning of the 1960s, two studies of firms in the electronic industries in Scotland and the United States highlighted the importance of organizational structure to innovation. The Scottish study drew a distinction between (a) firms that were organized along bureaucratic lines which they called mechanistic and (b) those that allowed more flexibility without lines of communication and instruction hierarchically ordered as in the former. They called this type of organization organistic and concluded that it was more open to innovation than mechanistic types of organization (Burns and Stalker, 1961). A similar type of study of the organization of Irish secondary schools came to the same conclusions with the caveat that the Principal could enhance or inhibit innovation (McMahon, 1974). Anecdotal evidence suggests this conclusion, and also applies to departmental chairpersons and Deans.

In an American study of two small departments engaged in aspects of electronics engineering, of around

---

[41] They are not discussed here because some of the findings are discussed at more appropriate places in the text.

30 persons in each, various dimensions of their organization were investigated. Following von Bertalanffy's (1950) theory of systems, the investigators found, in keeping with this theory, that the department which was relatively closed was less able to adapt than the department which was relatively open (Barnes, 1960). The department that was relatively closed was organized like the mechanistic model in the Scottish study, and the department that was relatively open like the organistic model. An important difference between the two studies was that the values of the participants as measured by the Allport, Vernon, and Lindzey, (1951) Scale of Values were measured in the American study. It was found that they had a bearing on the performance of the two departments. This was also the case in the study of engineers reported by Youngman et al, (1978) discussed in Chapter 2.

University departments tend to be relatively closed. They are made up of specialists who, by and large, do not see themselves as being generalists in any way. There is also some hierarchical ordering of status. This mechanistic model is reinforced by fairly rigorous structures for the provision of the curriculum (e.g., semesters, credits, modules, classrooms, time for a class). Many teachers are still unused to working in teams. In these circumstances it is particularly difficult to generate debate about the curriculum as a whole. For historic reasons, each of the subject specialisms will have been deemed to be necessary, so what is the purpose of a curriculum debate?

Faculty respond to curriculum drifts that are a function of changes in technology, and it is surprising to find some articles where those who teach mechanics claim to be fighting for its centrality in the curriculum. Nevertheless, a restricted notion of the curriculum prevails, so to propose, say for example, a problem-based learning approach to engineering that may require some reorganization of the curriculum and teamwork is perceived to be very difficult. Olds and Miller (1991) argued that if specialization is transferred to graduate work then the traditional concept of the department might have to be rethought. Marbury et al, (1991) lent some support to this view. They argued that a lead professor should work with a small group of students in most of their major courses during their junior, senior, and graduate years. *"This program would lean on regular courses and faculty to supply the technical content of some major courses and all minor courses. The intent is to have a dedicated and strongly interactive group that will overcome the distracting effects of today's "information explosion," "technology explosion", and "expanded curricula."* They liken the program to being a small "magnet school" within the school system or the Oxbridge tutorial system. At the University of Bremen there have been experiments with whole-day courses in which a range of teaching activities are devoted to the pursuit of a single topic (Ulrich and Bauchkhage, 1989)

The organization of classrooms can have a profound effect on learning. While lectures have their usefulness and may have profound effects in certain circumstances (Bligh, 1999, MacIntyre, 1990), there are modes of learning that may be more effective in the achievement of some objectives (outcomes) than other modes. This has been well demonstrated at school level, and studies of classroom organization in both the United Kingdom and the United States are very insightful (Cohen, Mannion, and Morrison, 1996; Good and Brophy, 2000). The work of Smith and others in cooperative education in higher education generally, and engineering education in particular, are testimony to this point (Johnson, Johnson, and Smith, 1991).

Unfortunately in Ireland and the United Kingdom very often the rooms and furniture are totally inappropriate for such activities. These buildings and classrooms were designed by architects whose notion of university teaching was that of information-giving to students organized in rows facing the lecturer. From time to time it becomes possible to reorganize teaching spaces and sometimes design new ones.

Whelchel (1991) was provoked by Koen's views on the differences between science and engineering to argue that there was too much specialization in engineering courses. In reality engineers should be generalists. The know-how component of engineering work was diminishing all the time. While technical know how was important, such problem solving should be independent of context [which is similar to Bruner's (1966) more general view of education in any subject]. The problem is how to get breadth. To achieve breadth, Whelchel proposed that undergraduates should attend many short courses. Depth would be achieved by a substantial design project and less time would be devoted to traditional problem solving.

Many of these issues are raised again in Chapter 7 in relation to curriculum change.

References

Adamson, J. Byrom, T., and H. Clifford (1998). Further comparative studies in the prior knowledge assessment of B.Eng (hons) course entrants. *International Journal of Mechanical Engineering Education*, 26, (3), 177–200.

Alha, K., and I. S. Gibson (2003), To improve gender balance in engineering education. *European Journal of Engineering Education*, 28, (2), 215–224.

Allport, G. W., Vernon, P. E., and G. Lindzey (1951). *Study of Values. Manual of Directions*. Houghton Mifflin, Boston.

Alha, K., and L.S. Gibson (2003). To improve gender balance in engineering education. *European Journal of Education*. 28, (2), 215-234.

Ambrose, S., Lazarus, B., and I, Nair (1997). No universal constants: journeys of women in engineering. *Proceedings Frontiers in Education Conference*, 1, 3–9.

Anderson, J. and F. Percival (1997). Developing HE staff to appreciate the needs of flexible learning for ACCESS students-developing flexible learning ACCESS students to appreciate needs in HE. In S. Armstrong, G. Thompson and S. Brown (eds.). *Facing Up to Radical Change in Universities and Colleges*. Kogan Page, London.

Anderson, M. (1992). *Intelligence and Development*. Blackwell, Oxford.

Anderson, M. R. (1991). Characterizations of the graduate: career change woman in engineering: recruitment and retention. *Proceedings Frontiers in Education Conference*, 248- 256.

Anderson, M. R (1993). Career change: Women engineers in the work place. *Proceedings Frontiers in Education Conference*, 86 – 90.

Anderson-Rowland, M. R., and J. E. Urban (2001). Evaluating freshmen retention efforts in engineering. *Proceedings Frontiers in Education Conference*, 1, T4g-1 Evaluating freshmen retention efforts in engineering housing.

Andrews, H., and C. Mares (1963) Liberal studies in advanced scientific and technological courses. Reported in NFER Occasional Publication No. 8. National Foundation for Educational Research, Slough.

Andrews, J. G (1987) In search of the engineering method. *Engineering Education*,78, (1), 29—30, 5557.

Andrews, J. K., McBride, G. T. and E. Dendy Sloan (1993). Humanities for engineers. A rich paradox. *Journal of Engineering Education,* 82, (3), 181—184.

Angelo, T., and P. K. Cross (1993). *Classroom Assessment Techniques*. Jossey Bass, San Francisco.

Aronson, J., Lustina, M. J., Good, C., and K. Keogh (1999). When white men can't do math: necessary and sufficient factors in stereotype threat. *Journal Experimental Social Psychology*, 35, 29–46.

Astin, A. W (1997). What Matters in College. Four Critical Years Revisited. Jossey Bass, San Francisco.

Atman, C. J., and I. Nair (1992). Constructivism: appropriate for engineering education. *Proceedings Annual Conference American Society for Engineering Education*, 1310—1312.

Baker, S., Tancred, P., and S. Whitesides (2002). Gender and graduate school: Engineering students confront life after the B. Eng. *Journal of Engineering Education*. 91, (1), 41—47.

Bame, A. E. and W. E. Dugger (1992). Pupils' attitudes towards technology. Executive summary of the PATT-USA study. In A.E. Bame and W.E. Dugger (eds.) *Technology Education. A Global Perspective*. Conference Proceedings. ITEA-PATT. International technology Association, Reston, VA.

Bannerman, J. W (1989). The effect of an engineering technology education on student ethics. *Proceedings World Conference on Engineering Education for Advancing Technology*. 2, 630—634.

Barnes, L. B. (1960) *Organizational Systems and Engineering Groups*. Harvard Graduate School of Business Administration, Boston.

Barnett, R. (1990). *The Idea of Higher Education*. Open University/SRHE. Buckingham.

Baryeh, E. A., Obu, R. Y., Lamptey, D. L., and N. Y. Baryeh (2000). Ghanaian women and the engineering profession. *International Journal of Mechanical Engineering Education*. 28, (4), 334—346.

Belenky, M. F., Clinchy, B. M., Goldberger, N. R., and J. M. Carule (1986). *Women's Ways of Knowing*. Basic Books, New York.

Bell, A. E., Spencer, S. J., Iserman, E., and C. E. R. Logel (2003). Sterotype threat and Womens Performance in Engineering. *Journal of Engineering Education*. 92,(4), 307—312.

Bella, D. A. and C. H. Jenkins (1993). The functionary, the citizen, and the engineer. *Journal of Engineering Education*, 82, (1) 38—42.

Ben-Haim, Y. (2000). Why the best engineers should study humanities. *International Journal of Mechanical Engineering Education*, 28 (2), 195—200.

Berg, C. A. (1992). On teaching design: Identifying the subject. *International Journal of Mechanical Engineering Education*, 20, (4), 235—240.

Berger, P. L. and T. Luckmann (1966) *The Social Construction of Reality*. Doubleday, New York.

Berube, B.G. (1988). A whistleblower's perspective of ethics in engineering. *Engineering Education*, 78,(5), 294—95.

Besterfield-Sacre, M., Moreno, M., Shuman, L. J. and C. J. Atman (2001) Gender and ethnicity differences in freshman engineering-student attitudes. A cross institutional study. *Journal of Engineering Education* 90,(4), 477—490.

Bissell, C., Chapman, D., Herman, C., and L. Robinson (2003). Still a gendered technology? Issues in teaching information and communication technologies at the UK Open University. *European Journal of Engineering Education*, 8,(1), 27—35.

Bligh, D. G. (1999). *What's the Use of Lectures?* Penguin, Harmondsworth.

Boomer, G (1992) Negotiating the curriculum in G. Boomer et al, (Eds.) *Negotiating the Curriculum. Educating for the 21st Century*. Falmer Press, London.

Bosworth, G. S (1966) (Chairman of Committee). The Education and Training Requirements for the Electrical and Mechanical Manufacturing Industries. HMSO, London.

Bosworth, G. S (1966). Toward creative activity in engineering. *Universities Quarterley*,17, 236.

Bowyer, K. W (2000). Goodearl and Aldred versus Hughes Aircraft: a whistle blowing case study. *Proceedings Frontier in Education Conference*, 3,SZF 2.

Bowyer, K (2000b). Ethics and Computing. IEEE Press, New York.

Bransford, J. D., Brown, A. L., and R. R. Cocking (2000) (eds.). *How People Learn. Brain, Mind, Experience and School*. National research Council, National Academy Press, Washington, DC

Brainard, S. G., and L. Carlin (1997). A longitudinal study of undergraduate women in engineering and science. *Proceedings Frontiers in Education Conference*,1,134—143.

Brennan, M. G., and M. A. Tooley (2000). Ethics and the biomedical engineer. *Engineering Science and Education Journal* (February),5-7.

Brown, C (1993). Bridging the gender gap in science and technology: how long will it take? *International Journal of Science and Technology Education*, 3,(2). 65–73.

Brown, F. K (1983). Technical ethics. *Engineering Education*, 73,(4), 298—300.

Brown, R.W (2000). Physiological parameters and learning. *Proceedings Frontiers in Education Conference*, 2,S2B-7–S2–B11.

Bruner, J (1966). *Toward a Theory of Instruction*. Norton, New York.

Budny, D., Blalock, M., and W. K. LeBold (1991). Supplying the missing link with Mecca-A. *Proceedings Frontier in Education Conference*, 332—333.

Burns, T and G. Stalker (1961). *The Management of Innovation*. Tavistock, London.

Carpenter, D. D., Harding, T. S., Montgomery, S. M., Steneck, N., and E. Dey (2002). Student perceptions of institutional and instructor based techniques for dealing with academic dishonesty. *Proceedings Frontiers in Education Conference*, 3,S1H 9 to14.

Carter, G. and J. Heywood (1992). The value added performance of electrical engineering students in a British University. *International Journal of Technology and Design Education,* 2,(1), 4–15.

Carter, G., Heywood, J. and D. T. Kelly (1986). *Case Study in Curriculum Assessment. GCE Engineering Science (Advanced)*. Roundthorn Press, Manchester.

Catalano, G. D (2004). Integrating ethics into the freshman year experience. *Proceedings Frontiers in Education Conference,*3, S3E-8–11

Catalano, G. D (1993). Developing an environmentally friendly engineering ethic: a course for undergraduate engineering students. *Journal of Engineering Education*,82, (1), 27–33.

Checkland, P (1970). *Journal of Systems Engineering* No 3. The University of Lancaster, Lancaster.

Chen, J. C., et al (1996). A study of female academic performance in mechanical engineering. *Proceedings Frontiers in Education Conference,* 1, 779—782.

Chesler, N. C. and M. A. Chesler (2002). Gender informed mentoring strategies for women engineering scholars: On establishing a caring community. *Journal of Engineering Education*, 91,(1),49–56.

Clement, J (1981). Solving problems with formulas: some limitations. *Engineering Education*, 150—162.

Clifford, H (1994). A comparison of expectations and achievement in a prior knowledge assessment of B.Eng (Hons) course entrants. *International Journal of Mechanical Engineering Education*, 22,(1),55–68.

Cobb, P (1994). Theories of mathematical learning and constructivism. A personal view. Paper presented at the Symposium on Trends and Perspectives in Mathematics Education, Institute for mathematics, University of Klagenfurt, Austria.

Cohen, L., Manion, L., and K. Morrison (1996). *A Guide to Teaching Practice*. 4th edition. Routledge, London.

Constable, H (1993). A note on the first technology assessment tasks at Key Stage 1. *International Journal of Technology and Design Education,* 3,(3),31—36.

Colbeck, C. L., Cabrera, A. F., and P. T. Terenzini, (1999). Learning Professional Competence and Confidence: The link between instructional practice and learning gains for female and male students. *Proceedings Frontiers in Education Conference.* 2,11a5 9 to14.

Cook, J (1992) Negotiating the Curriculum. Programming for Learning in G. Boomer et al, (eds.). *Negotiating the Curriculum. Educating for the 21ˢᵗ Century.* Falmer Press, London.

Cooley, W. L., Klinkhaechorn, P., McConnell, R. L., and N. T. Middleton (1991). Developing professionalism in the electrical engineering classroom. *IEEE Transactions on Education,* 34,(2) 149–154.

Cooney, E. M (1991). An investigation of geneder bias in EET laboratories. *Proceedings Frontiers in Education Conference,* 257–260.

Crain, W., (1992). *Theories of Development Concepts and Application.* 3ʳᵈ Edition, Prentice–Hall, Englewood Cliffs,NJ.

Crews, T (1997). Intelligent learning environments using educational technology to assist complex problem solving. *Proceedings frontier in Education Conference,* 2,911–916.

Cronin, C., Foster, M., and E. Lister (1999). SET for the future: Working towards inclusive science, engineering and technology curricula in higher education. *Studies in Higher Education,* 24,(2),165–181.

Culver, R. S., Cox, P., Sharp, J., and A. FitzGibbon (1994) Student learning profiles in two innovative honours degree engineering programs. *International Journal of Technology and Design Education,* 4, (3), 257,288.

Culver, R. S. and S. Fellows (1997). Using student created multimedia to teach design and communications. *Proceedings Frontiers in Education Conference,*

Cuthchins, M. A and S. C. McCrary (1970). Improving instruction through systems engineering. *Engineering Education,* 60,(8),823–826.

Davies, L (1965). *Liberal Studies and Technology.* Wales University Press, Cardiff.

Davis, M (1998). *Thinking Like an Engineer. Studies in the Ethics of a Profession.* Oxford University Press, New York.

Davis, M. (1993). Ethics across the curriculum: Teaching professional responsibility in technical courses. *Teaching Philosophy,* 16,205-235.

De Bord, (1993). Promoting Reflective Judgment in Causality Psychology Graduate Education. Thesis, The University of Missouri, Columbia. Cited by P. K. Wood.

DeCecchi, T., Timperon, M. E., and B. B. DeCecchi (1998). A study of women's engineering education. *Journal of Gender Studies.* 7, (1),21-38.

De Vries, M. J and A. Tamir (1998) (eds). Shaping concepts of technology: what concepts and how to shape them. *International Journal of Technology and Design Education,* 1997. All of issues 1 and 2 in one volume. 14 articles.

Dickenson, H (1964). Students in a CAT: Qualifications and success. *Universities Quarterly,* 18, 407.

Didier, C (2000). Engineering ethics at the Catholic University of Lille (France): research and teaching in a European context. *European Journal of Engineering Education,* 25, (4), 325-335.

Didier, C., Goujon, Ph., Hérirard Dubreuil, B and Ch Hogenhuis (2000) Introduction. *In Technology and Ethics. A European Quest for Socially Responsible Engineering.* Peeters, Leuven.

Diggleman., C., and L. Korta (1992). Introduction to engineering: developing a Coed course that is sensitive to the needs of women. *Proceedings Frontiers in Education Conference,* 284-287.

DiSessa, A (1993). Toward and epistemology of physics. *Cognition and Instruction,* 10, 105–225.

Doornekamp, B. G (1991). Gender differences in the acquisition of technical knowledge, skills and attitudes in Dutch primary education. *International Journal of Technology and Design Education,* 2,(1),37–47.

Driver, R (1983). *The Pupil as Scientist.* Open University Press, Milton Keynes.

Driver, R (1995). Constructivist approaches to teaching and learning in L.P. Steffe and J. Gale (eds.) *Constructivism in Education.* Lawrence Erlbaum, Hillsdale, NJ

Driver, R., and B. Bell (1986). Students' thinking and learning of science; a constructivist view. *School Science Review.* 67, 443-456.

Driver, R and V. Oldham (1986). A constructivist approach to curriculum development in science. *Studies in Science Education,* 13,105-122.

Durkheim, E (1972). *Selected Writings.* A. Giddens (ed). Cambridge University.Press. Cambridge.

Dyrud, M. A (2000). Right professional behavior: A classroom exercise using professional codes. *Proceedings Frontiers in Education Conference.* 2,S1F-1 to 4.

Eberhardt, L. Y (1987). *Working with Women's Groups.* Vol 1. Whole Person Association Inc., Duluth, Minnesota.

Edels, H. (1968). Technology in the sixth form. *Trends in Education,* No 10, April. Ministry of Education, London.

Eggleston, J (1977). *The Sociology of the School Curriculum.* Routledge, London.

Elms, D. G (1989). Wisdom engineering, *Proceedings World Conference on Engineering Education for Advancing Technology,* 574–578.

Feilden, G (1963) (Chairman of a Committee). *Engineering Design.* Department of Scientific and Industrial Research. HMSO, London.

Felder, R. M (1995) A longitudinal study of engineering student performance and retention. IV instructional methods and student responses to them. *Journal of Engineering Education,* 84,(4),361–367.

Felder, R. M., Forrest, K.D., Baker-Ward, L., Dietz, E.J. and P.H. Mohr (1993). A longitudinal study of engineering student performance and retention. I. Success and failure in the introductory course. *Journal of Engineering Education,* 82,(1),15–21.

Felder, R. M., Mohr, P.H., Dietz E.J. and L. Baker-Ward (1994). A longitudinal study of engineering student performance and attrition. II. Rural/Urban student difference. *Journal of Engineering Education* 83,(3),209–218.

Felder, R. M., Felder, G.N., Mauney, M., Hamrin, C.E. and E. J. Dietz (1995) A longitudinal study of engineering student performance and retention. III. Gender differences in student performance and attitudes. *Journal of Engineering Education,* 84,(2),151-164.

Fensham, P. J (1992). Science and technology. In P. W. Jackson (ed). *Handbook of Research on Curriculum.* Macmillan, New York.

Fernandes, A. S. C., and P. M. Mendes (2003). Technology as culture and embodied knowledge. *European Journal of Engineering Education.* 28, (2), 151-160.

FitzGibbon, A and J. Heywood (1986). The recognition of conjunctive and identity needs in teacher development. Their implications for planning of in-service training. *European Journal of Teacher Education,* 9, (3), 271-286

Flanagan, O (1991). *The Science of the Mind.* 2ⁿᵈ edition, 1995 printing. The MIT press, Cambridge, MA.

Fledderman, C.B (1999). *Engineering Ethics.* Prentice Hall, Englewood Cliffs, NJ.

Fleddermann, C. B (2000). Engineering ethics cases for electrical and computer engineering students. *IEEE Transactions on Education.* 43,(3),284.

Fletcher, S. L., Newell, D. C., Anderson-Rowland, M. R. and L. D. Newton (2001). The women in applied science, and engineering summer bridge programs: easing the transition for first-time female engineering students. *Proceedings Frontiers in Education Conference,* 3, S1F-5–9.

Fodor, J (1983). *The Modularity of Mind.* MIT Press, Cambridge, MA.

Fong, P. S., and D. K. Ip (1999). Cost engineering: a separate academic discipline. *European Journal of Engineering Education,* 24,(1),73–82.

Fontaine, J and D. Ohana (1999). Gender strategies and social representations: The choice of scientific post-baccalaurét streams in France. *European Journal of Education,* 34,(4),413-434.

Fornaro, R. J., Heil, M. R and V. E. Jones (2000). Cross-functional teams used in computer science senior design capstone projects. *Proceedings Frontiers in Education Conference,* 2, F4C-1 to 5.

Gallaher, J and F. Pearson (2000). Women's perceptions of climate in engineering technology programs. *Journal of Engineering Education.* 89,(3),309–314.

Gilligan, C., Murphy, J. M., and M B. Tappan (1990). Moral development beyond adolescence I.C.N. Alexander and E. J. Langer (eds). *Higher Stages of Human Development.* Oxford University Press, Oxford.

Gilligan, C (1977). In different Voice: women's conceptions of self and morals. *Harvard Educational Review*, 47, 481–517.

Gorman, M. E (2002) Turning students into professionals: types of knowledge and ABET engineering criteria. *Journal of Engineering Education* 91, (3),327-332

Good, T .L. and J. E. Brophy (2000). *Looking in Classrooms*, 8th edition. Harper and Row, New York.

Gunn, A. S. and P. A. Vesilind (1986). *Environmental Ethics for Engineers*. Lewis Publishers, Chelsea, Mich.

Hammond, T., and J. Hammond (2002). Gender-based under representation in computer science and related disciplines. *Proceedings Frontiers in Education Conference*, F3C- 5 to 10.

Hanson, A.T., McCarthy, W., and K. Paur (1993). Student/Professor ethics in engineering academia. *Journal of Engineering Education*, 82, (4), 216-222.

Harding, T. S (2000). Cheating: student attitudes and practical approaches to dealing with it. *Proceedings Frontiers in Education Conference*, 2, F3A21–F3A26.

Harding, T. S., Carpenter, D. D., Montogomery, S. M. and N. H. Steneck (2002). A comparison of the role of academic policies of several colleges on the cheating behavior of engineering and pre-engineering students. *Proceedings Frontiers in Education Conference*, 3,S1H-15– 20.

Hartman, H. and M. Hartman, (2003). Empowering Female Students: SWE vs Disciplinary Organization Participation. Proceedings Frontier in Education Conference. 2, FID 2 to 7

Hatano,G and K. Inagaki (1994). Young children's naïve theory of biology. *Cognition*, 50,171–188.

Haws, E. D. (2001) Ethics instruction in engineering education: a (mini) meta-analysis. *Journal of Engineering Education*. 90, (2), 223-231.

Haws, D. R (2002). Using the Web to integrate ethics in the engineering curriculum. *Proceedings Frontiers in Education Conference*, 3, S4F-7 to 12.

Hazelrigg, G. A., (1988). In Continuing Search of the Engineering Method. *Engineering Education*. 78,(10),118-121.

Henderson, J.M., Desroches, D.A.,McDonald, K.A., and M.M. Bland. (1944) Building the confidence of women engineering students with a new course to increase the understanding of physical services. *Journal of Engineering Education*. 83,(4),337–342.

Herkert, J. R (2000a). Ethical responsibility and societal context: integrating ethics and public policy considerations in the engineering curriculum. *Proceedings Frontiers in Education Conference*, 2,S1F-5.

Herkert, J. R (2000b). Engineering ethics education in the USA: content, pedagogy and the curriculum. *European Journal of Engineering Education*, 25,(4),303-313.

Herkert, J. R (2000c). Engineering ethics education in the USA: content, pedagogy and the curriculum. *European Journal of Engineering Education*, 25,(4),303-313.

Higgins, C., Watt, S., Evans, R., Cooper M., and A. Roger (1997). *Progression Guide: Women in in Science, Engineering and Technology in Higher Education*. Scottish Higher Education Funding Council, Edinburgh.

Higgins, C., Watt, S., Evans, R., Cooper, M., and A. Roger (1997). *Progression Guide: Women in Science, Engineering and Technology*. Scottish Higher Education Funding Council, Edinburgh.

Hersh, M. A (2000). Environmental ethics for engineers. *Engineering Science and Education Journal* (February),13-19.

Heywood, J (1969). An Evaluation of certain post-war developments in Higher Technological Education. Thesis Volume 1. University of Lancaster Library, Lancaster.

Heywood, J (1972) *Bibliography of British Technological Education and Training*. Hutchinson, London.

Heywood, J (1982). *Pitfalls and Planning in Student Teaching*. Kogan Page, London.

Heywood, J (1984). *Considering the Curriculum during Student Teaching*. Kogan Page, London.

Heywood, J (1998) Pupils attitudes to technology. A review of studies which have a bearing on the attitudes which freshmen bring to engineering. *Proceedings Frontiers in Education Conference*, 1,270–273

Heywood, J (1998). Pupils attitudes to technology. A review of studies which have a bearing on the attitudes which freshmen bring with them to engineering. *Proceedings Frontiers in Education Conference*, 1,270-273.

Heywood, J (2000). *Assessment in Higher Education. Student Learning, Teaching, Programmes and Institutions*. Jessica Kingsley, London.

Heywood, J., Lee, L. S., Monk, J. D., Rowley, B. G. H., Turner, B.T. and J. Vogler (1966). The Education of Professional Engineers for Design and manufacture. *Lancaster Studies in Higher Education*, No 1. P1-104.

Heywood, J. Mash, V., and J. Pollitt (1966) The Schools and Technology in *Lancaster Studies in Higher Education*. No 1.

Heywood, J. Sharp, J. M. and M. Hides (2001) (eds.). *Improving Teaching in Higher Education*. Salford University, Salford.

Hirsh, R. F (1995). Teaching about values and engineering. The American electric utility industry as a case study. *Proceedings Frontiers in Education Conference*, 3b4 9 to 13.

Hoit, M., and M. Ohland (1995). Institutionalizing curriculum change: a SUCCEED case history. *Proceedings Frontiers in Education Conference*, 3a 1-6 to 11.

Horenstein, M and M. Ruane (2002). Teaching social awareness through senior capstone design experience. *Proceedinga Froniters in Education Conference*, S3D- 7 to 12.

HornÆs, H. P., and O. Røyrvik (2000). Aptitudes, gender and computer algebra systems. *Journal of Engineering Education*, 89,(3),323–330.

Householder, D. L. and B. Bolin (1993). Technology; Its influence in the Secondary School in academic subjects and upon students' attitudes toward technology. *International Journal of Technology and Design Education*, 3,(2),5–18.

Hutchings, D. G. (1963). *The Schools and Technology*. Oxford University Department of Education, Oxford.

Hutton, S. P., and J. E. Gerstl (1964). Engineering Education and Careers. Proceeding of a Symposium on Education and Careers. *Proceedings Institution of Mechanical Engineers*, 178, Part 3F.

Hutton, S. P., and J. E. Gerstl (1966). *The Anatomy of a Profession*. Tavistock, London.

IEEE (2000). Draft Guide Lines for Engineers Dissenting on Ethical grounds. IEEE Ethics Committee, IEEE, Piscataway, NJ.

IMechE (1983). *Professional Code of Conduct*. PAB 2283A. Institution of Mechanical Engineers, London.

Jackson, M. W (1989). A plea for engineering ethics education. *Proceedings World Conference on Engineering Education for Advanced Technology*, 702–706.

James, W (1890). *The Principles of Psychology*. 3 Vols. Harvard University Press, Cambridge, MA. *Education*, 22,(3),279-293.

Jenkins, G. M (1969). The systems approach. *Journal of Systems Engineering*, 1, (1), 3-49.

Jinks, R. F (1996). Knowledge,.understanding (mind the gap). *Engineering Science and Education Journal*, (October),227-230.

Johnson, D. W., Johnson, R. T. and K. A. Smith (1991). *Active learning. Cooperation in the College Classroom*. Interaction Book Co. Edina, MN.

Johnston, S. F., Fourkis, R. E., Dietrich, H (1984). In search of a philosophy of engineering. *Proceedings of World Conference on Engineering Education for Advancing Technology*, 227–231.

Johnston, S. F., Gostelow, P., and J. King (2000). *Engineering and Society. Challenging Professional Practice*. Prentice–Hall, Englewood Cliffs, NJ.

Johnston, S., McGregor, H., and E. Taylor (2000). Practice-focused ethics in Australian engineering. *European Journal of Engineering Education*, 25, (4),315–324.

Jones, G. (1963). Why is there a shortage of engineers? *Engineering*, 13 September.

Kim, H., Fisher, D L. and J. Barry (1999). Assessment and investigation of constructivist science learning environments. *Research in Science and Technological Education*. 17,(2),239–250.

King, P. M. and K. S. Kitchener (1994). *Developing Reflective Practice*. Jossey Bass, San Francisco.

Knight, J. C., Prey, J. C., and W. A. Wulf (1997) A look back. Undergraduate computer science education: A new curriculum philosophy and overview. *Proceedings Frontiers in Education Conference*,2,722–727.

Koen, B. V (1985). *Definition of the Engineering Method.* Monograph. American Society for Engineering Education, Washington, DC.

Koen, B. V (1987). Generalization of the engineering method to the universal method. *Engineering Education,*77,(4),214-221

Koen, B.V (1994). Toward a strategy for teaching engineering design. *Journal of Engineering Education* 983,(3),193-201.

Koen, B. V (2003). *Discussion of the Method: Conducting the Engineers Approach to Problem Solving.* Oxford University Press, New York.

Kohlberg, L. and R. A. Ryncarz (1990) Beyond justice and reasoning: moral development and consideration of a seventh stage. In Alexander, C. N., and E. J. Langer. (eds.*). Higher Stages of Human Development.* Oxford University Press, Oxford.

Kohn, A (1993). *Punished by Rewards. The Trouble with Gold Stars, Incentive Plans, as, Praise, and other Bribe*s. Houghton Mifflin, Boston.

Koppel, N. B., Cano, R. M., and S. B. Heyman (2002). An attractive engineering option*. Proceedings Frontiers in Education Conference,* 2, F1C-3 to 7.

Kovaleva, N. (1999). Women and engineering training in Russia. *European Journal of Education.* 34,(4),425–435.

Kutscher, R. E. (1994). Projection of Employment of Engineers 1990–2005. *Journal of Engineering Education* 83,(3),203–208.

Laeser, M., Moskal, B. M., Knecht, R., and D. Lasich (2003). Engineering design: Examining the impact of gender and the team's gender composition. *Journal of Engineering Education,* 92,(1),49–56.

Lasser, S. J. S., and R. W. Snelshire (1996). The case for proactive mentoring for minorities in engineering. *Proceedings Frontiers in Education Conference,* 2,767-769.

Latcha, M., and W. Jordan (1996). To ship or not to ship. An engineering ethics case study. *Proceedings Frontiers in Education Conference,* 3, 1159–1163.

Lawson, D. A (1995). How well prepared are students for undergraduate engineering mathematics? *International Journal of Mechanical Engineering Education.* 23,(4),352–362.

Lemonick, M. D (1995). Glimpses of the mind. *Time,* July 31st. 52-60.. Macmillan, New York.

Lionni, L. (1970). *Fish is Fish.* Scholastic Press, New York.

Livshits, V., and B. Z. Sandler (199 8). Contradictory tendencies in engineeering education. *European Journal of Engineering Education,* 23, (1), 67–77.

Luegenbiehl, H. C (1989). The value of applied liberal education. *Proceedings of World Conference on Engineering Education for Advancing Technology,* 2, 626- 629.

Luegenbiehl, H. C (1990) Moving beyond disasters; ethical issues foe engineering students. *Proceedings Frontiers in Education Conference* (Vienna), 6-8.

Luegenbiehl, H. C. and D. L. Dekker (1987). The role of values in teaching design. *Engineering Education,* 77, (4), 243-246.

Lyons, N. P Two perspectives on self, relationships and morality. *Harvard Educational Review,* 53, (2), 125 – 145.

Mbarika, V. W., Sankar, C. S., and P. K. Raju, (2003). Identification Factors that Lead to Perceived Learning Improvements for Female Students. *IEEE Transactions on Education,* 46,(1),26–36.

Macdonnell-Laeser, M., Mascal, B. M., Knecht, R and D. Lasich (2001). The engineering process: examining male and female contributions. *Proceedings Frontiers in Education Conference,* 3, S1F 10 to 15.

Macintosh, N. J. (1997). *IQ and Human Intelligence.* Oxford University Press, Oxford.

MacIntyre, A (1990) Reconceiving the University as an institution and the lecture as genre in *Three Rival Versions of Moral Enquiry.* The 1988 Gifford Lectures. The University of Notre Dame Press, Notre Dame, In.

McDowell, L (1995). Effective teaching and learning on foundations and access courses in engineering, science and technology. *European Journal of Engineering Education,* 20,(4),417-425.

McElwee, P. G (1995) Personal to scientific understanding. 2 volumes. Doctoral thesis. University of Dublin Library, Dublin.

McMahon, J., (1974). Thesis for Master of Education. The Library. University of Dublin, Dublin.

Marbury, C. H., Barnes, F. S., Lawsine, L., and N. C. Nicholson (1991). A one room schoolhouse plan for engineering education. *IEEE Transactions on Education,* 34,(4),303–308.

Mark, H., and L. Carver (1988). The fourth revolution. Engineers for leadership. *Engineering Education,* 78,(10),104-108.

Marris, P. (1964). The *Experience of Higher Education,* Routledge, London.

Marshall, S., (1980). Cognitive-affective dissonance in the classroom. *Teaching Political Science,* 8,111–117.

Masters, S. J., Chen, K. C., Lee, K. H., and M. Najera (2002). The use of web-based technology in an introductory environmental engineering course. *Proceedings Frontiers in Education Conference,* 2, F1E-7 to-12.

Martin, C. D., and C. W. Huff (1997). A conceptual and pedagogical framework for teaching ethics and social impact in computer science. *Proceedings Frontiers in Education Conference,* 1, 479-483.

Martin, M. W (1981). Why should engineering ethics be taught? *Engineering Education,* 71, (4), 275–278.

Martin, M. W., and R. Schinzinger. (1983). *Ethics and Engineering.* McGraw Hill, New York.

Mathieson, W., and H. J. B. Corderoy (1989). Particpation of women in engineering. *Proceedings World Conference on Engineering Education for Advancing Technology,* 48-52.

Matthews, M. R. (1994). *Science Teaching. The Role of History and Philosophy of Science.* Routledge, London.

Matthews, M. R (2000). *Time for Science Education. How Teaching the History and Philosophy of Pendulum Motion can Contribute to Science Literacy.* Kluwer/Plenum, New York.

Matthews, P. S. C (1997). Problems with Piagetian constructivism. *Science and Education.* 6,105–119.

Matthews, P (2000). Learning Science: Education some insights from cognitive science. *Science and Education.* 9,.507–535.

Mikic, B., and D. Grasso (2002). Socially-relevant design. The TOYtech Project at Smith College. *Journal of Engineering Education,* 91,(3),319–326.

Miller, R. L. and B. M. Olds (1994). Encouraging critical thinking in an interactive chemical engineering laboratory environment. *Proceedings Frontiers in Education Conference,* 506–510.

Miller, R. L. and B. M. Olds (2001). Performance assessment of EC 2000 student outcomes in the unit operations laboratory. Proceedings Annual Conference ASEE. Session 3513.

Milto, E., Rogers, C., and M. Portsmore (2002). Gender differences in confidence levels, group interactions, and feelings about competition in an introductory robotics course. *Proceedings Frontiers in Education Conference,* F4C- 7 to 11.

Monk, J (1997). Good engineers. *European Journal of Engineering Education,* 22,(3),

Monzon, J. E (1999). Teaching ethical issues in biomedical engineering. *International Journal of Engineering Education,* 15,(4),276-281.

Moon, J (1968). The ethical attitudes of chartered mechanical engineers and their relationship to education. M.Litt. Thesis. University of Lancaster, Lancaster.

Moon, J (1992). The evolution of an ethical code for profcssional mechanical engineers. Doctoral thesis. University of Brighton, Brighton.

Morant, M. J (1993). Electronics as an academic subject. *International Journal of Electrical Engineering Education.*110-123.

Morgan, C. J. and W. Tad Foster (1992). Student cheating: An ethical dilemma. *Proceedings Frontiers in Education Conference,* 678 Morgan, C. J. and W. Tad Foster (1992). Student cheating: an ethical dilemma. *Proceedings Frontiers in Education Conference,* 678- 682.

Morrill, R. L (1980). *Teaching Values in College.* Jossey–Bass, San Francisco

Moskal, B. M. (2000). Looking to the future: women in science and engineering. *Proceedings Frontiers in Education Conference ,* 1, F1B pp 19 to 24.

Moxham, S., and P. Roberts (1995) *Gender in the Engineering Classroom.* Melbourne University, Swinburne University of Technology and University of Ballarat, Equal Opportunity Unit. Cited by Cronin et al , (1999).

Murphy, R. R., and J. Martinez (1997). Professional and persona;l development in research experiences for undergraduates. *Proceedings Frontiers in Education Conference,* 1378–1383.

Newell, D. C., Fletcher, S. L., and M. R. Anderson-Rowland (2002). The women in applied science and engineering (WISE) recruit programs: investing in the future. *Proceedings Frontiers in Education Conference*, F1C-15 to 18.

Newman, J. H (1852). *The Idea of a University*. Longmans Green, London.

Nohmer, F. J (1989). A comparative characteristic analysis of professional ethical values among electrical engineering students in an engineering and engineering technology cooperative educational program. Proceedings of the St Lawrence Section ASEE, Annual Meeting. 14D1,7–13.

November, G. S (1991). Introduction of a technical subject with a general problem solving methodology. *Proceedings Frontiers in Education Conference*, 388–393

Olds, B. M. and R. L. Miller (1991). Are departments obsolete? *Proceedings Frontiers in Education Conference*, 213–216.

Pace, S (1999). Teaching mechanical design principles on engineering foundation courses. *International Journal of Mechanical Engineering Education*, 28,(1),1–13.

Page, G. T (1965). *Engineering Among the Schools*. Institution of Mechanical Engineers, London.

Pascarella, E. T. and P. T. Terenzini (1991). *How College Affects Students*. Jossey Bass, San Fransisco.

Passino, K. M (1998). Teaching professional and ethical aspects of electrical engineering to a large class. *IEEE Transactions on Education*, 41,(4),273–285.

Pearce, J. A (1997). Using ethics to teach the design method. *Proceedings Frontiers in Education Conference*, 1,499-501.

Perry, W. B (1970). *Forms of Intellectual and Ethical Development in the College Years*. Holt, Riehart and Winston, New York.

Pfatteicher, S. K. A (2001). Teaching vs Preaching. Ec 2000 and the engineering ethics dilemma. *Journal of Engineering Education*. 90,(1),137-142.

Pinkus, R. T (2000). Ethics and Society II. Biomedical Engineering Summit Meeting. Whittaker Foundation. http://summit.whitaker.org/white/ethics.html.

Pond, D (1987). Report of a Working Party on the Teaching of Medical Ethics. Institute of Medical Ethics, London.. 5, 255– 266.

Raat, J (1992). A research project into pupils' attitudes towards technology in Bame, E. A. and W. E. Dugger (eds.). *Technology Education. A Global Perspective*. ITEA-PATT conference. International Technology Association, Reston, VA.

Raichle, M. E (1994). Visualizing the mind. *Scientific American*, April.

Rekus, J (1992). Teaching technology with a focus on moral education. *International Journal of Technology and Design Education*. 2,(2),41-46.

Resnick, L. B (1994). Situated rationalism: Biological and social preparation for learning in L. A. Hirschfeld and S. A. Gelman (eds.). *Mapping the Mind: Domain Specificity in Cognition and Culture*. Cambridge U.P., Cambridge.

Rest, J., Thoma, S., and L. Edwards, (2001). Designing and Validating a Measure of nioral judgment. Stage preference and stage consistency approaches. *Journal of Educational Psychology*, 89,5–28.

Robinson, D. A. G., and B. A. Reilly (1993). Women engineers: A study of educational preparation and professional success. *Journal of Engineering Education* 82, (2),78–82.

Rogers, D. B (1992). On the recruitment of minority and female engineering students: A long term talent development strategy. (1992). *Proceedings Frontiers in Education Conference*, 5i7- 5i21.

Ruthven, K (1978). The disciplines thesis and the curriculum: A case study. *British Journal of Educational Studies*,26,(2),163-176.

Sankar, C. S., and P. K. Raju, (2000). *Crist Power Plant Case Study*. Taverner Publishers, Anderson, Sc.

Schwartz, D. L and J. D. Bransford (1998). A time for telling. *Cognition and Instruction*,16,(4),475-522.

Self, J (1997). From constructionism to deconstructionism. Anticipating trends in educational styles. *European Journal Engineering Education*,22,(3),295-306

Sendaula, M. H. and S. J, Biswas (2004). Curriculum deceleration and on-line communities for working students, *Proceedings Frontiers in education Conference*. 1, T1E, 8-12.

Seymour, E. and N. M. Hewitt. (1997). *Talking About Leaving. Why Undergraduates Leave the Science*. Westview Press, Boulder, Co.

Shannon, T. A., LeMee, J. M., and M. Stecher (1977). A liberal professional education. A proposal for a holistic approach to the engineering curriculum. *Proceedings Frontiers in Education Conference*,261-267.

Sharp, J and R. Culver (1996). Cooperative learning in a manufacturing management course. *Proceedings Frontiers in Education Conference*, 161-171.

Sheppard, S., Demsetz, L., and J. Hayton (1999). Engineering Practice and textbook design. *Proceedings Frontiers in Education Conference*, 13b-7 to 11.

Sherren, D. C. and T. R. Long (1972). The educator's dilemma: What makes Clyde want to learn? *Engineering Education*, 63,(3),188-190. Product development: A case study. *IEEE Transactions on Education*, 43,(3),343–347.

Short, L (1999). Engineering mathematics teaching via the T1-92. Part I enhancing basic skills. *International Journal of Mechanical Engineering Education*, 27,(1),13.

Shuldiner, P.W. Carpenter, S. R. Cambel, A.B. and S.A. Schuh (1988) Value systems in conflict: a sampling of view points. *Engineering Education*, 78,(5),296-298. (Each presents a separate note).

Shull, P. J and P. D. Weiner (2000). "Thinking inside/outside the box". Retention of women in engineering. *Proceedings Frontiers in Education*, 2 ,F2F-13–F2F-16.

Shulman, L. S (1970). Psychology and mathematics education in E. G. Begle (ed.). *Mathematics Education*. 69th Yearbook of the Society for the Study of Education. University of Chicago Press, Chicago, Ill.

Shulman, L.S (1986). Those who understand. Knowledge growth in teaching. *Educational Researcher*. 15, 92).15,(2),4-14.

Sinclair, G., and W. Tilston (1979). Improved goals for engineering education. *Proceedings Frontiers in Education Conference, 252–258*.

Sindelar, M., et al (2003). Assessing Engineering Students Abilities to Resolve Ethical Dilemmas. *Proceedings Frontiers in Education Conference*. 3,52A-25–52A-31.

Smith, K. A (1987). Educational engineering. Heuristics for improving learning effectiveness and efficiency. *Engineering Education*, 77,(5),274-279.

Smith, K. A., and A. A. Waller (1997). Afterword: *New Paradigms for College Teaching*. In W. E. Campbell and K. A. Smith, (eds.). New Paradigms for College Teaching. Interaction Book Co. Edina, Mn.

Solomon, J (1994). The rise and fall of constructivism. *Studies in Science Education*, 23,1-19.

Sorby, S. A. and B. J. Baartmans (2000). The development and assessment of a course for enhancing the 3-D spatial visualization skills of first year engineering students. *Journal of Engineering Education*, 89,(3),301-307.

Sparkes, J. J (1989). *Quality in Engineering Education*. Engineering Professors' Conference, No 1, July.

Spearman, C (19270. *The Abilities of Man*. MacMillan, London.

Spelke, E. S., Katz, G., Purcell, S. E., Ehrlich, S. M., and K. Breinlinger (1994). Early knowledge of object motion, continuity and inertia. *Cognition*, 51,131-176.

Staehr, L. J., and G. J. Byrne (2003). Using Defining Issues Test for Evaluating Computer Ethics Teaching. *IEEE Transactions in Education*, 46,(2),229–234

Steffe, L. D. and J. Gale (1995) (eds.). *Constructivism in Education*. Lawrence Erlbaum, Hillsdale, NJ.

Steneck, N. H., Olds, B. M. and K. A. Neeley (2002) Recommendations for Liberal Education in Engineering: A Whitep Paper from the Liberal Education Division of the American Society for Engineering education. *Proceedings ASEE Annual Conference*. Session 1963.

Stephan, K. D., (2000). Engineering ethics education in the US. Where it is and where it should go. *Proceedings Frontiers in Education Conference*, 2, S1E-7.

Swaim, M and P. M. Moretti (1991). The case for the 120 hr B.S. *Engineering Education*, 81,(5),463–465.

SWAP (1993). Widening Access: Women into Engineering. Scottish Wider Access Program., Edinburgh.

Teslow, J. L., Carlson, L. E., and R. L. Miller (1994). Constructivism in Colorado: Applications of recent trends in cognitive science. *Proceedings Annual Conference, ASEE*, 136–144.

Thom, M., Pickering, M., and R. E. Thompson (2002). Understanding the barroiers to recruiting women in engineering and technology programs. *Proceedings Frontiers in Education Conference*, 2, F4C 1 to 6.

Thompson, G and C.R. McChesney (1999). The Royal Academy of Engineering Summer School for new teachers of engineering design. *International Journal of Mechanical Engineering Education*, 27,(2),164-172.

Tonkinson, J. and B. Gazey (1997). School children's and industrialists attitudes towards engineering and manufacturing engineering. *Engineering Science and Education Journal, February*, 31–36.

Trybus, M (1990) Afterthoughts from a found(er)ing father. *Engineering Education*. 80,(5),523-525.

Ulrich, J and K. Bauchkhage (1989). Whole day course. A new organizational unit in teaching engineering education. *Proceedings World Conference on Engineering Education for Advancing technology.* 1,321-324.

UWA (1996). *Do male and female students differ in their preferred style of learning*? University of Western Australia. Institutional Research Unit.

Vanderburg, W. H., and N. Khan (1994). How well is engineering education incorporating societal issues? *Journal of Engineering Education*, 83,(4),357-362.

van der Vorst, R (1998). Engineering ethics and professionalism. *European Journal of Engineering Education*, 23,(2),171-179.

van Poolen, L. J (1989). A philosophical perspective on design. *International Journal of Applied Engineering Education*, 5,(3),319–329.

Varcoe, J. M (1990), Women in engineeing. A graduate's view of the realities. Australian Association for Engineering Education. 2nd Annual Convention and Conference 1, 295–299.

Vardy, P., and P.Grosch (1994). *The Puzzle of Ethics*. Fount (Harper Collins), London.

Vesilind, P. A (1988). Rules, ethics and morals in engineering education. *Engineering Education*, 78, (5),289–293.

Von Bertalanffy, L (1950) The theory of open systems in physics and biology. *Science*, 111,(2872),23–29.

von Glasersfeld, E (1983). Learning as a constructive activity. In J. G. Bergeron and N. Herscovics (eds.). *Proceedings of the Fifth Annual Meeting of PME-NA*. Monteal, Canada. Vol 1, 41-69.

von Glasersfeld, E (1995). A constructivist approach to teaching in L. P. Steffe and J. Gale (eds.) *Constructivism in Education*. Lawrence Erlbaum; Hillsdale, NJ.

Vosniadov, S., and W. F. Brewer, (1989). The Concept of Earth's Shape: A study of conceptual change in children. Unpublished paper. Center for the Study of Reading. University of Illinois, Champagne.

Wadsworth, E. M., LeBold, W. K., and J. Z. Daniels (1991),Trends in women engineering programs and degrees. Harmony or discord? *Proceedings Frontiers in Education Conference*, 233–238.

Wales, C. E., and R. A. Stager (1972). The design of an educational system. *Engineering Education*, 62, (5),456-459.

Walton, R. (2000). Heidegger in the hands-on science and technology center: philosphical refelections on learning in informal settings. *Journal of Technology Education*, 12,(1),49-60.

Watt, S. M., Higgins, C., Roger, A., Cooper, M., Cronin, C., and J. Duffield (1998). Redressing the gender imbalance in science, engineering and technology within higher education. *Journal of Further and Higher Education*, 22,(1),85-100.

Wenk, E. (1988). Social economic and political change: portents for reform in engineering curricula. *Engineering Education*, 78,(10), 99-102.

Wheen, R. J. (1978). The nurture of a design philosphy. *Engineering Education* 69,(2),201-206

Whelchel, R. J. (1991). Engineering as a generalist profession. Implications for engineering. *Proceedings Frontiers in Education Conference*, 151-154

Wheway, R. T. (1989). Professional orientation- A subject dealing with ethics and professional behavior for final year engineering students *Proceedings World Conference on Engineering Education for Advancing Technology*, 2,62-625.

Wigal, C. M., Alp, N., McCullough, C., Smullen, S., and K. Winters (2002). ACES: Introducing girls to and building interest in engineering and computer science careers. *Proceedings Frontiers in Education Conference*, 2, F1C-8 to 13.

Wild, P. M., and C. Bradley (1998). Employing the concurrent design philosophy in developing and engineering design science program. *International Journal of Mechanical Engineering Education*. 26,(1),51-64.

Williams, R (2002). Retooling. *A Historian Confronts Technological Change*. MIT Press, Cambridge, MA.

Wong, Y. K., Chan, S. P. and S. K. Chgeung (1989). Application of learning theory to a computer assisted instruction package. *International Journal of Electrical Engineering Education*, 27, 237–246.

Wood, P. K., (1997). A secondary analysis of claims regarding the reflective judgment interview: Internal consistency, sequentiality and intro-individual differences in ill-structured problem solving. In J. Smart (ed.). *Higher Education, Handbook of Theory and Research*, Agathon Press, New York.

Young, M. F. D (1971) (ed). *Knowledge and Control*. Collier-Macmillan, London.

Young, P. M (1997). An integrated systems and control laboratory. *Proceedings Frontiers in Education Conference* 659-665.

Youngman, M. B., Oxtoby, R., Monk, J. D. and J. Heywood (1978). *Analysing Jobs*. Gower Press, Aldershot.

Zandvoort, H., van der Poel, I., and M. Brumsen (2000). Ethics in the engineering curricula: topics, trends and challenges for the future. *European Journal of Engineering Education*, 25, (4), 291–302.

Chapters 4, 5, and 6: Psychology and the screening of aims

Like philosophy and sociology, psychology is a many dimensional subject and some of its subject-matter overlaps with those subjects, as will be already evident. Clearly, the problems arising from the interaction of individuals with organizational structure briefly alluded to in the last Section are the province of social psychology in so far as they depend on knowledge of both sociology and psychology. The topic of the next three chapters is the application of various dimensions of learning and development to the curriculum, teaching, and learning. The reader may benefit from reading parallel papers by Wales and Stager (1972), Eder (1994), and Felder and Brent (2003), which cover similar ground but in much less detail.

A number of engineers have suggested how learning theories might be applied to engineering. For example, Edgerton (1989), who, among other things, saw a need for learning interventions of the kind advocated by Feuerstein et al, (1980) and Buriak, McNurlen, and Harper (1995), described a systems model of learning; and Eder (1994), and Wales and Stager (1972), integrated design theory with learning theory. Eftekhar and Strong (1998) suggested a theory of types of learners. Others have applied specific learning theories to the curriculum—as for example, the learning processes of children in natural settings (Mourtos, 1996), Skinner's behavioral theory (Wong, Chan and Cheung, 1989, Koen, 2003),and Skinner, and Gagné, and Ausubel (Stubbs and Watkins, 1996)—to the design of CAI and CBL. Greenberg, Smith, and Newman (2003) designed a module in Fourier Spectral Analysis on the basis of the National Science Foundation's report on *How People Learn* (Bransford, Brown and Cocking, 2000). Mazur's (1995), users manual on peer instruction, originally prepared for physics students has proved of interest to engineering educators. Sheppard, Demsetz, and Hayton (1999) have drawn attention to the relevance of learning theories for textbook design.

The Chapters that follow, however, will concentrate on the learning of concepts and principles (Chapter 4), learning strategies and styles (Chapter 5), and human development in relation to learning, including brief discussions of emotional intelligence and motivation (Chapter 6).

Plates 4, 5 and 6: Psychology and the screening of ...

CHAPTER 4: CONCEPTS AND PRINCIPLES

Summary and Introduction

For the purpose of this discussion a concept is defined as a class of stimuli which have common characteristics. It is not a stimulus but the classification of certain stimuli (de Cecco and Crawford, 1974; Gunter, Estes, and Schwab, 1999; Heywood, 1997; McDonald, 1968). Concepts are of varying degrees of abstraction, and some are more open to misinterpretation than others, as for example, "democracy." Such concepts are sometimes called "fuzzy" (Dunleavy, 1986; Howard, 1987). Concepts are the building blocks of knowledge. In engineering, concepts such as acceleration and velocity are often misperceived, as the research by Clement (1981, 1982) and many others shows.

The development of conceptual knowledge and procedural knowledge go hand in hand; that is abstract knowledge of concepts informs doing and knowledge obtained from doing informs conceptual understanding. The two function together in intricate ways (McCormick, 1997). Understanding concepts is the basis of metacognition.

The transfer of knowledge is not possible without an understanding of the concepts involved. The way that schema are constructed by individuals distinguishes the "expert" from the "novice". This has consequences for teaching and learning.

Principles or rules derive from relationships between concepts. A model of learning applied to teaching is used to illustrate this point (Gagné, 1967, 1984).

The usual way of teaching concepts is through examples. Even this is fraught with difficulty, and the way in which examples and non-examples are sequenced can influence learning (Heywood, 1997). Other methods of teaching concepts include analogies and metaphors (Gunter, Estes, and Schwab, 1999; Howard, 1987)

The knowledge required for a particular field of study may be described as an integrated framework of "key concepts." Such maps as these frameworks are sometimes called express and contain the essential knowledge required for the curriculum in that field. Their attainment is, therefore, an objective, hence the inclusion of key concepts among the aims and objectives in the models of the curriculum process (see Figures 1.4 and 1.5). But they may also help teachers understand how students learn, in addition, tests can indicate the misperceptions that students have of particular concepts.

Teachers may discover students' misperceptions by using concept inventories and protocols. Concept mapping may also be used for this purpose. Such maps are not only helpful in the design of the curriculum (using key concepts), but also can help the teacher understand (a) how students learn, and (b) the different stages they move through from being a novice to becoming an expert.

The importance of concept learning in engineering is underlined by the special panel that discussed the problem at the 2002 Frontiers in Education Conference."[1]

4. Concepts and Principles (Rules)

Concepts are classifications of stimuli that have common characteristics. They are constructions we make to help us understand the world, and often, as in science and engineering, they are simplifications of the world or extremely fuzzy. Nevertheless, from this perspective they are building blocks of knowledge.

Engineers are likely to be attracted to Gagné's models of learning since they use a language that is akin to scientific language. The earliest model (1967), in particular, shows the importance of concept learning for principle learning and problem solving. It is hierarchically ordered, and the understanding of concepts precedes that of the understanding of principles, and understanding of principles precedes the solving of problems (see Figure 4.1). In this theory a principle is the linking together of two concepts. The example he gave was, *"birds fly."* Unfortunately, it is somewhat more complex than this because some concepts embrace principles and they become fuzzy when there is debate about the principles that contribute to their structure. Again the concept of 'democracy' serves to illustrate the point.

In Gagné's model, irrespective of this complexity, problem solving can only be accomplished when the principles have been learned and understood. In later work Gagné said, *"learners have acquired a defined concept when they use a definition to put something they have not previously encountered or put some things into classes..."* Using the term rule rather than principle, learners have understood the rule *"when they can demonstrate its application to previously unencumbered instances."* This is what is meant by "transfer of learning." Principles or rules derive from relationships between concepts. *"Higher order rules"* as Gagné now calls problem solving, *"are obtained when two or three more previously learned rules are used to answer a question about an unfamiliar situation."* (Gagné, 1967, 1984, Gagné, Briggs and Wager, 1992; Petry, Mouton, and Reigeluth, 1987).

The transfer of knowledge is not possible without an understanding of the concepts involved. The way these schema are constructed by individuals distinguishes the "expert" from the "novice." This has consequences for teaching and learning.

Another way of looking at the problem is to distinguish between basic conceptual-level knowledge and strategic level knowledge. For example, in computer programming, the first level aims to help the student understand the principles that govern the actions executed by the program and to create a mental model of the

---

[1] Evans, D. L., et al, (2002) *Proceedings Frontiers in Education Conference*, 1, F2B-1.

system. These are the skills required for program design. At a second or higher level, there is a strategic level of knowledge. This is the level where meta-cognition comes into play. These are those involved in flexible problem solving and critical reflective thought. They are the skills required for solving novel problems and in programming debug logic errors. Staats et al, (2003), from whom the programming examples came, argued, that introductory courses in computer science and do not sufficiently emphasize the basic concepts or the strategic skills (and cited other papers in support),.

Gagné's approach as set out in the model (Figure 4.1) may be taught by either expository or guided discovery methods. There is some evidence that guided discovery approaches have a more dynamic effect on student motivation, and that students are more likely to have a better understanding of the concept or principle involved. In either case, teachers need to be cognizant of (a) the difficulties that students have in learning concepts and (b) the alternatives available, as for example, the exploration of student understanding of concepts through verbal protocols and specifically designed tests.

4.1. Misperceptions in Learning Engineering Concepts. Strategies for Their Detection.

It stands to reason that if concepts are misperceived so too will be principles and rules, and much of the difficulty that students have in learning in the science is with the understanding of the fundamental concepts that make up the knowledge structure of a particular science. Success in engineering depends on the ability to apply correctly understood principles. Unfortunately, as Clement has shown, this is often not the case. Moreover, it seems that many teachers do not appreciate the problems students (at all levels of education) have in learning concepts. One important consequence of such misunderstandings is that it might lead to bad teaching in schools. For example, Trumper and Gorsky (1996) reported that in Israel many physics students in pre-service training *"failed to affirm that the forces acting on an object are balanced during uniform motion, and thought that a net force acts in the direction of the motion. Moreover, most of them were not able to distinguish between uniform and changing motion"*. The test they used in this study is likely to be of interest to teachers of freshman mechanics.

Clement (1981, 1982) used protocols (Ericsson and Simon, 1993; Cowan, 1983; Larkin, 1979) in which students thought aloud about how they solved problems to try and understand their misperceptions. Many teachers do this when they are helping students to solve problems. The research protocol is a formal and systematic device that enables the collection of more detailed data and its analysis. (See also Chapter 12.)

Clement (1981) gave detailed accounts of two such interviews. The first related to the concept of acceleration. As explained by him, it seemed that Jim the student had demonstrated an understanding of the concept because he had successfully obtained the acceleration of an object as a function of time. However, when Jim was asked to draw a qualitative graph for the acceleration of a bicycle going through a valley between two hills he confounded the concept of acceleration with concepts of speed and distance. It appeared, wrote Clement, that while *"Jim can use a symbol manipulation algorithm, his understanding of the underlying concept of acceleration is weak. The student has a procedure for getting the right answer in special cases but demonstrates little understanding of the concept when asked to apply it in the practical situation. We may describe such a student as having a 'formula centred view of the concept."* (see Figure 4.2.)

This would appear to be a general problem. In the United Kingdom, Price in a letter to this writer (Heywood, 1974), wrote of a student taking A level Engineering Science as follows:

"You will recall that I asked one boy at this school to try out a diode valve experiment that we discussed and you read. As a matter of interest I asked him to design an experiment to verify a hypothesis (which he was to formulate) regarding water discharge through an orifice. He had not met this topic before. The result surprised me. He suggested that the velocity of discharge would increase more rapidly than the P.D. Why? Because 'it seems reasonable.' What form of increase? It is, 'that the velocity of transference from one pressure to another lower pressure is proportional to the square of the pressure difference'-again 'because it seems reasonable.' Note that the mathematical formulation is wrong in terms of the physics (see Figure 4.3). His graph agrees with the maths, not with the physics and includes both positive and negative flows. "

A similar problem was found in the Signals and Systems course at MIT. This is a course that is *"in large part detached from daily experience and significantly embedded in abstract mathematical modelling."* An analysis using clinical interview techniques showed that *"even though students Exhibit proficiency in performing mathematical algorithms in their analysis of physical systems, they may fail to see the mathematical-physical correspondence"* (Nasr, Hall, and Garik, 2003). The investigators believed that the data from the clinical interviews could be used to adjust and develop instruction and the active learning material they provided. [2]

In similar vein, Tuttle (2000) of the University of Queensland found that many students did not properly understand the difference between the static and stagnation *"conditions in fluid flow. Tuttle reported that an increase of understanding occurred when the students actually had to measure these quantities."*

Duncan-Hewitt et al. (2001) reported similar experiences with high school students in a work camp. "When asked to define "power" they confused it with "work" and "strength". Campers dutifully undertook the calculations and made the plots, but derived no understanding from this work".

---

[2] This paper provides a useful introduction to other studies of this problem, in particular those of diSessa (1983), and Chi and Slotta (1993) on whom their understanding is based.

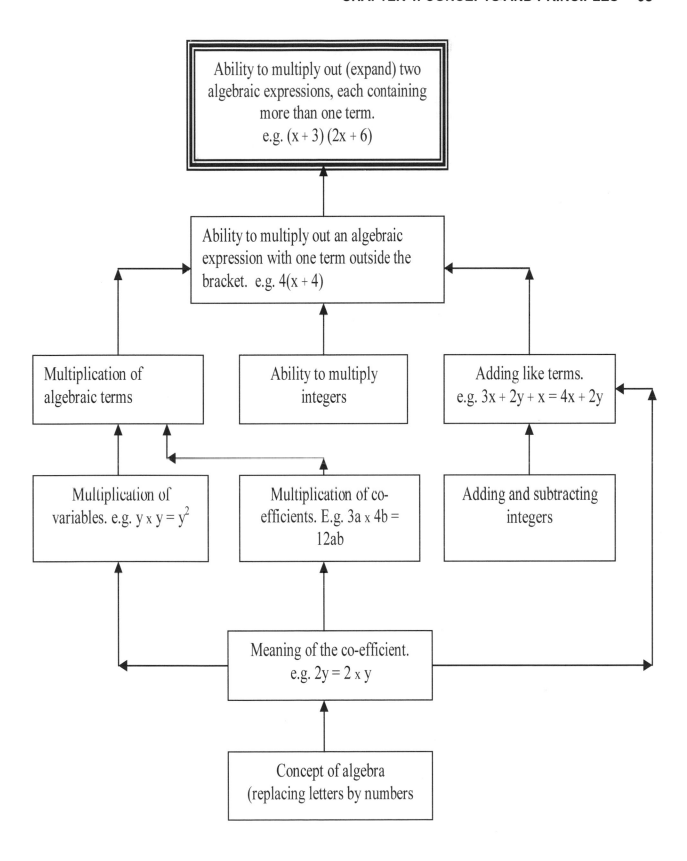

Figure 4.1. A model of Gagné's early approach to learning prepared by a student teacher (Algebra for 12-year-olds).

Clement (1981), in another study set an experimental test to 24 students before their final examination. Seventeen (71%) chose an inappropriate equation. He suggested that teachers should have more awareness of this situation and that they could acquire such information by asking students to draw qualitative maps and give more coherent explanations of what they have done. Fifteen years later, Atman and Nair (1992) made a similar recommendation after they found that freshmen students thought that ozone depletion and global warming were the same thing.

It has been pointed out that teachers are often unaware of how easy it is to be fooled into believing that only when they are asked "to apply" their knowledge, it becomes clear they have not understood. As Duncan-Hewitt et al, (2001) pointed out, this can be a particular problem with beginning students.

Students can also use computer tools to mask their understanding. To cope with this problem, Wheeler and McDonald (1998) suggested that students should be asked to write about the concept studied. They cited the example of *"convolution"*, which students could rely on the computer to perform, irrespective of whether or not they understood the concept. If they are asked, however, to write about the concept, the tutor can soon learn whether or not the student understands the concept.

Cowan (1998) also found that engineering students handled qualitative analysis ineffectively. He used protocols to help him understand what was happening. It led him to develop a style of tutorial question which *"literally demanded qualitative understanding, and offered no return for quantitative understanding- in other words, I introduced problems where a solution could not be obtained merely by applying formulae and carrying out, but called instead for the application of deep conceptual understanding."* He went on to say *"these problems, incidentally, often proved insuperable for conventional lecturers, accustomed to following algorithms rather than thinking."* Quantitative understanding that is the result of routine calculations does not necessarily require a sound grasp of the concept whereas qualitative understanding does.

A major problem faced by Clement was that he found that the perceptions that students had were relatively stable, and highly resistant to change. They retained these *"conceptual primitives."*

McElwee (1993) examined the misconceptions that college students of Home Economics had of changes in the state that occurs when water is boiled and found that these misconceptions persisted even when cognitive conflict had been introduced to try and change them.

Working with engineering students building, operating and exploring connections between heat flow, temperature differences, material thermal properties and material geometry, Ball and Patrick (1999) found that students' unscientific theories of heat transfer were quickly revealed. They claimed that the virtual experiment helped students gain a better grasp of important concepts. But this experiment was in a pilot study, and there was no follow-up test of retention [3] There are numerous examples of misconceptions in science. Two of the most recent studies in this area of research are related misconceptions of basic astronomy concepts (Trumper, 2000) and misunderstandings of quantum theory (Ireson, 2000).

As Driver (1983) and others have noted these misconceptions are already present in very young children. McElwee (1991), who had studied children's misconceptions in science in Ireland and the United States found there were few differences in the misconceptions held among average and high achieving students in both countries. He found that very few students (grade 8) adopted and integrated a new cognitive structure, although many more integrated specific concepts as a result of introducing cognitive conflict into the teaching strategy to try and change misconceptions[4]. Streveler and Miller, (2001) used a new method of analysis to examine student understanding of concepts at the Colorado School of Mines. The instructor identified 32 concepts (or terms) which the students were asked to cluster. This exercise was repeated again during the last week of instruction. In this way, changes resulting from the course could be evaluated and areas of difficulty discovered. Four clusters relating to economic analysis, energy transfer, analysis of processes, and heuristics were revealed. Some of the terms were scattered around the clusters. The post-test found some reshuffling. The four clusters remained but there were some additions to the third cluster. The heuristic terms became more closely structured; however, the terms are not, in practice, related in any fundamental way. This finding led the investigators, to suggest that the students might not have a deep understanding of these terms. Similarly, the term *"life cycle analysis"* did not seem to be understood, and it seemed that students might not have an understanding of how trouble shooting related to process design and analysis. This evaluation led to changes in course structure.

Hasan, Bagayoko and Kelley (2000) pointed out that it is important to distinguish between lack of knowledge and misconceptions. They borrowed the idea of the Certainty of Response Index from social sciences. The respondent is asked to give the degree (scaled) of certainty he/she has in his/her own ability to select and utilize knowledge. Low scores suggest guessing, and high scores suggest confidence in choice of answer. If the answer was wrong, when the certainty was high, then the student probably had a misconception.[5]

One simple way of testing prior knowledge is simply to ask students to demonstrate their understanding of a concept before instruction. Hein and Irvine (1999)

---

[3] The paper gives valuable descriptions of the misconceptions.

[4] See discussion of constructivism and realism in Chapter 3.

[5] They applied this index to a test developed for classical mechanics by Halloun and Hestenes (1985).

did this in an introductory physics laboratory and found that with respect to momentum, the students confused the mass of the vehicle and the magnitude of the impact force on collision. Subsequently the students were asked to complete another exercise after the laboratory instruction on momentum. While this yielded a considerable improvement, some misperceptions remained, which once again illustrates the difficulty of teaching concepts.[6]

Diagrams are powerful aids in learning about students' misunderstandings, as the work of Clement (above), research on concept mapping (below), and Steif (2004) have more recently shown.

Motivation has been found to be important for the understanding of concepts in one study. *With respect to the teaching of mechanics of materials,* Vable (2003) concluded that the incorporation of design into the course was a powerful motivator and enhanced the understanding of generalized mechanics of materials concepts (see Section 7.6).

In a tantalizing short note on work in progress Santi and Santi (2003) have suggested that techniques from psychotherapy can be used to help students learn to ask questions. At the center of unblocking, a misperception is the need for the student to be able to ask questions, and many students are more likely to learn the art of questioning in an environment that is free and safe from risk.

Teachers need to know what misperceptions students have and for this reason several inventories have been developed to reveal misconceptions in physics. The best known is due to Hestenes and his co-workers. (Hestenes, Wells, and Swackhamer, 1992). This inventory is widely used and has been credited with influencing developments in physics education in schools. It has also been used with engineering students (Evans and Hestenes, 2001); Hake, (1998) has stimulated similar test developments in signals and systems concepts, strength of materials, thermodynamics, and waves (Wage and Buck, 2001; Richardson, Morgan and Evans, 2001; Midkiff, Litzinger and Evans, 2001; Roedel et al, 1998). Tests of concepts of this kind are very important aids to understanding students learning (see, for example, Rhoads and Roedel,[7] 1999; Trumper, 2000).

But, as Miller et al, (2004) and his colleagues point out, there is a need to determine the relative difficulty and importance of concepts in a particular field of engineering. They had conducted delphi studies to determine what teachers thought were the difficult concepts in the fields of heat transfer, thermodynamics, and fluid mechanics; statics, dynamics and strength of materials, and circuits in electrical engineering. That this is a difficult and important task was illustrated by three groups of engineering educators who examined the delphi lists in an interactive session at the Frontiers in Education Conference.[8] It became clear that there are, as in the humanities, some concepts in engineering that are fuzzy. That is, they do not have clear boundaries or clear cut defining features. See Section 4.2 below).

Apart from the assumption that understanding concepts helps the student memorize when rote learning does not (Valentine, 1960: Novak, 1998), concept inventories assume that students will not be able to solve problems unless these concepts are understood. Consequently, there ought to be a good correlation between high scores on the test and good problem solving. That this may not be the case has been illustrated by Steif (2003) of Carnegie Mellon University. In a paper that gives illustrations of the misperceptions that students have in Statics, he described how a group of students were given two multifaceted problems to solve in homework on their own at the beginning of a course in the Mechanics of Materials. They had previously completed a course in Statics. The results were analyzed in detail to discover the frequency of misperception. Some weeks later the Statics Concept Inventory, which was under the process of development, was administered. It was found that for nearly all the concepts, there were a substantial number of students who erred in some way. Significant positive correlations were found between the grade obtained in Statics and performance on the multifaceted problems. Those who obtained correct answers also scored significantly higher on the concept inventory. However, he was *"unable to find correlations between good performance on inventory questions addressing a specific concept and the ability to use that concept in the context of multifaceted problems."* While he thought that should be the goal of a good concept inventory, he cautioned that *"problem solving often relies on recognizing the relevance of a concept, applying that concept correctly in context, and expressing the concept in symbol so as to lead to a correct qualification."*

To put it in another way, the concept inventories are not indicators of metacognitive skill. For this purpose a group of investigators have developed a *Metacognitive Skills Inventory* (MSI) for studies with computer science students (Miles et al, 2003). This has two subscales: Confidence and Decomposition. The decomposition subscale was important because it had been found that good programmers begin by decomposing the larger problem into several smaller sub-problems.

---

[6] I have cast this in a somewhat more negative sense than the authors. Detailed examples of student work in the written exercises are given.

[7] Sample questions from the paper were given by Roedel et al (1998). The inventory is based on the Bloom Taxonomy (Rhoads and Roedel, 1999).

---

[8] For details contact R. Miller at the Colorado School of Mines.

In order to track their way through the problem, they have to impose structure on the problem[9]. These investigators drew attention to (a) research that showed if a person does not set appropriate goals or sub-goals they very often use inadequate trial-and-error methods (Reif, 1990), and (b) other research that suggested that if students were notified of the need to plan ahead, they did (Berardi-Colletta, et al., 1995). Active questioning begins *"With what will you need to begin this task? And that surely is a question that should be asked in any topic area irrespective of computer science.*

In their evaluation these investigators also used a test of math anxiety and spatial ability. The MSI was found to correlate positively with grades in the computer science courses and to account for more of the variability in these grades than the math anxiety test. The two scales of the MSI were shown to tap different dimensions of metacognition, and the investigators concluded that if used with other more traditional measures, it was a useful tool in measuring computer expertise. They felt that there were indications that students with minimal metacognitive skills were those that opted out or dropped out of computer science barriers in their education.

One might expect that other investigators will begin to design inventories for testing metacognition in other areas. In this respect work undertaken by Kuhn et al, (1995) at Columbia University to develop metacognition among middle school students is of interest, and the same investigators have developed Kuhn's exercises for use in their evaluations. They showed again that "systematic decomposition of *problem structure is a crucial component of computer science skill*" (Staats et al, 2003).[10] Space does not permit description of the exercises which are recommended reading because the evidence suggests that problems can be set that test dimensions of *metacognition.*

4.2. Strategies for Teaching Concepts

Apart from cognitive conflict, one of the strategies that has been recommended to cope with this problem is discovery learning. Hunt and Minstrell (1994), who used this approach, showed that discovery learning would not allow the students to complete the coverage of the high school course in Physics within the allotted period of a year. However, they argued that it was more important to provide a firm rather than a fuzzy foundation in physics, which discovery learning did. They appreciated that this had implications for the design of the curriculum. Other studies support the view that teachers in higher education do not allow sufficient time students to learn. Student teachers have found that teaching examples, as the literature suggests, can be more time-consuming within the confines of a single classroom lesson than they supposed (Heywood, 1997).[11] Heywood (1992) also found that when students were given a prior-notice question for an examination that required the transfer of skill from a problem they had already been set to the formulation of a similar problem by themselves, that only one third were able to undertake a fairly complex task satisfactorily. However, when the group that followed were shown sample answers, the number of students completing the task satisfactorily increased by about one-third. It is fairly easy to replicate the kind of research that has been done on concept learning in engineering classrooms. Examples are important because as Cowan (1998) wrote, conceptual understanding usually begins with examples. He had been convinced that this was the case by Skemp (1971) a specialist in mathematics education. Skemp believed *"that it is essential that a concept is first encountered in the form of examples which establish the beginning of understanding. And he maintained that it is only when an initial understanding has been acquired, through the use and consideration of examples, that any abstract generalization or refinement of definition is possible or meaningful. For only at that point, he asserted has the learner developed sufficient understanding of the underlying concept on which to build theories and understanding which use and consolidate the concept."* (Cowan, 1998, p 2).

Cowan went on to describe how he had seen an elegant demonstration of this technique at an international conference in a keynote address on the acquisition of concepts. The lecturer *"taught her audience as she had taught her research subjects, the grammatical concept of the morpheme. First, she provided an assortment of examples, all of which were undoubtedly morphemes- and so this concept was established in the minds of her listeners- including me, who had not hitherto encountered it. Then she quickly tabled a set of examples, all of which were not morphemes- although I might have a little earlier have so classified them, while I was still uncertain about what a morpheme is. Thus the concept was yet*

---

[9]These investigators distinguish between standard composition and problem decomposition *"Standard decomposition includes such steps as algorithm development, the conversion of algorithm into some sort of flow chart or some sort of pseudo representation, the coding of that representation into a specific programming language, and the execution and debugging of the code (Volet and Lund, 1994). Problem decomposition in the object centred paradigm is approached somewhat differently. The focus of design then, is upon what rather than how. While this type of decomposition process should be inherently more natural than the decomposition required in traditional data processing approaches, research shows that without some inducement, people often ignore this step"* (Miles et al, 2003).

[10]In addition to the MSI,, they used a *Metacognitive Computer Skills Scale* (MCSS), and the Shipley Institute of Living Scale. The latter is a measure of cognitive ability. The MSI determines (a) the confidence that individuals have in their confidence to solve problems and (b) their awareness of their planning and evaluation processes during problem solving (decomposition). The MCSS assesses strategies of problem solving and awareness of these strategies.

[11]The main reports on the sequencing of examples are due to Brayley (1963); Huttenlocher (1962); Olsen (1963); Smoke (1933); and Yudin and Kates (1963). For a procedure similar to that described by Cowan (above) see Tennyson and Cochiarella (1986). For teaching concepts see Howard (1987). The students in this study were provided with the relevant summaries of these papers in De Cecco and Crawford (1974), and McDonald (1968). For a recent study that distinguishes between concept attainment and concept development, see Gunter, Estes, and Schwab (1999).

The Concept of Acceleration
I = Interviewer
J = Jim

1) I: Here's an expression for the speed of an object travelling on a straight line (Writes: $S_m = St^2 + 2t$) can you write an explanation for its acceleration?
2) J: That would be 10t plus 2.
3) I: And how did you get 10t plus 2?
4) J: Acceleration is the derivative of velocity.
5) I: What would acceleration be after 2 seconds?
6) J: (Writes: a = 10t + 2) 22 ft per second – I think these are the units
7) I: You substituted 2 for the t?
8) J: Yeah.
9) I: Lets do a graph of acceleration
10) J: (Jim constructs the graph shown in figure 2 piece by piece, as described below). That would be zero from here to here (Draws segment A-B in figure 2)

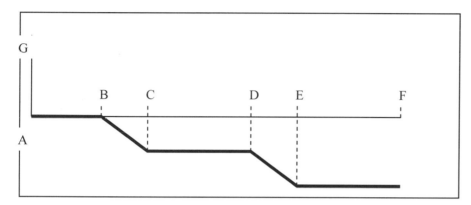

Figure 2: Students graph of cyclists acceleration

11) I: Why?
12) J: Because, there was no change in your acceleration, it was constant.
13) Would you label that B?
14) J: O.K. So acceleration is a change in velocity – so that's zero, because there's no change- the change here (b to c in the original picture) was negative-velocity was negative- so that would go down (draws line under B- C in graph) and acceleration zero (points to c-d in original picture. He draws C-D below axis).
15) I: So what's happening here (c-d) to acceleration?
16) J: Its constant
17) I: O.K. – now what
18) J: The I get stuck –uhm- velocity's negative (referring to d-e in picture) so acceleration has to be negative, so I don't know what to do – I guess I'll go down (draws the line under D-E in graph).
19) I: O.K.
20) J: And then its constant again like that (draws line under E-F)

Figure 4.2 Students misperceptions in mechanics illustrated by Clements (1981). (Reproduced with the permission of the author)

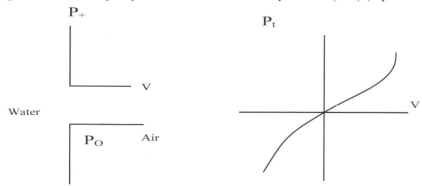

Water

Air

Figure 4.3. Problems in the transfer of learning between mathematical technique and physical explanation (G. Price, cited by Heywood, 1989a).

more firmly concreted in the minds of the learners like me in the audience, as it had been in her research study. As her next step, and in refinement of our understanding, she gave us some borderline examples of morphemes and no more; and, finally, other borderline examples which were marginally not morphemes. By this point we had well and truly mastered the concept of the morpheme from examples." (Cowan, 1998, p 2).

This point is laboured because it seems that very few teachers in higher education have any knowledge about the research that has been done on the use of examples in the teaching of concepts. If they had they might pay more attention to the design of lectures.

This early research led to the view that most, but not all students profit from a mix of examples and non-examples (McDonald, 1968). De Cecco and Crawford (1974) recommended that examples and non-examples should be presented simultaneously using appropriate aids. The potential for this approach in computer assisted learning will be obvious, and a similar approach to the teaching of concepts using an adaptive CAI system was described by Davidovic, Warren, and Trichima (2003). The screen of their generic computer-based instruction system showed a table of contents, an introduction box that introduced and defined new concepts to be learned, an explanation, and a box in which the concepts were explained in greater detail. The main feature was the provision of two boxes side-by-side for presentation of two examples that could be compared. The purpose was to provide multiple examples and through them enable the student to gain a deeper understanding that would lead to better, or more deep concept maps (see below). Below the two boxes were two other boxes for student work. An initial evaluation with 117 students in a one-hour tutorial suggested that the rate and extent of learning was significantly greater than when the features were used alone or both were absent.

The early research also poses problems about the meaning of "reality" in student learning. MacDonald (1968) described an investigation by a Soviet scientist Boguslavsky. He used real flowers on the one hand, and used diagrams of flowers on the other hand; those students who learned by diagrams learned the parts of the flower more accurately and easily. They were also able to transfer their knowledge to real flowers better than the group taught by real flowers. Evidently the real thing drowned out the essentials. It created "noise." Experiments such as this have implications for the design of computer assisted learning that uses animation and visuals.[12]   In this respect, although Clark and Wiebe (1999) do not cite Boguslavsky's research by implication, they confirmed his findings. Clearly, computer-assisted learning can contribute powerful tools for the visualization of concepts (e.g. Saad and Zaghloul, 2002). Nevertheless there is a problem with the meaning of "reality." Do all students have the same perception of

reality? Many engineering educators have argued for realism in teaching but do all students respond in the same way to teacher created reality. This problem will be considered again in Chapter 14, but in the meantime consider Edward's (1997)[13] comparison of a simulation of a schematic centrifugal pump with a realistic gas turbine. In so far as his students were concerned, both approaches had strengths as well as weaknesses. The schematic approach was favored for its ease of operation. The realistic approach allowed students to explore regions of instability even to the extent of an explosion, and the students appreciated this freedom. He came down in favor of the realistic option. However, the students were not tested and a plant is a far different thing to a pump. Caution in the interpretation of these results is required because the type of presentation may also depend on the objectives to be achieved.

Approaches based on "reality" are consistent with several theories of learning and development. For example, in Chapter 5 Kolb's learning theory is discussed. In his model, the process of learning begins in the concrete. But it is also linked to developmental theories of the kind discussed in Chapter 6. In Piagetian terms, many of the students in beginning engineering classes may not be, or have only just reached, the stage of formal operations. Consequently, some concepts may be too abstract for them to understand (Duncan-Hewitt et al, 2001). The realistic approach is also supported by work at Stanford University.   Brereton, Sheppard, and Leifer (1995) video taped third-and fourth-year engineering students in laboratories and dormitories with a view to understanding how students used the concepts taught. They observed that *"students rarely begin with stating their assumptions. First, they need to get involved in the context of the problem. Definitions help them begin linking theory. Then if they persist in exploring a topic, they begin to clarify such assumptions as "what is your system?"* We observe that, *"students need to actively connect theory to real tasks so that they learn to sort out key parameters and assumptions from the problem context."* These teachers found that discussion helped students to achieve this goal, but they also found that interest in learning theoretical concepts is enhanced when these concepts are related to hardware. In other studies, Sheppard and Leifer have shown how the dissection (dismantling) of artifacts helps students understand good and bad design (see Chapter 12). It would be interesting to know how the understanding of concepts is influenced by such dissections. In order to develop mental models of mathematical concepts, students have from an early age been given physical materials to manipulate, and it has been found that this can improve achievement and attitudes toward mathematics. Bucci et al, (2000) pointed out that this applies equally in higher education where they had used stacking cups and Lego to help students

---

[12] For developments with interactive web pages for distance learning using macromedia flash animation see Ferré et al (2002).

[13] Robert Gordon University in Aberdeen.

develop mathematical concepts in their computer science classes.

As indicated above some concepts are complex and fuzzy. Howard (1987), suggests that a complex domain may be studied by the use of prototype concepts. He gives the example of a psychiatric taxonomy that was criticized because there were unclear cases and no clear-cut defining features shared by exemplars of some categories. He drew attention to a comment by Cantor et al (1982) who pointed out that the dilemma could have been caused by the assumption that the domain could be *"usefully divided up into clear-cut classical-view concepts. Looking at the system as a set of prototype concepts gives a better basis for dealing with a diversity of mental disorders."* In any event, complex concepts will more than likely require additional strategies as they are analyzed, as for example, concept mapping and the use of analogies (Rothkop, 1995). Nersessian (1992) showed the importance of what Clerk Maxwell called physical analogies in scientific thinking. *"According to Nersessian,"* wrote Carey and Spelke (1994), *"a physical analogy exploits a set of mathematical relationships as they are embodied in a source domain about which there is only partial knowledge. In Maxwell's case the source domain was fluid mechanics as an embodiment of the mathematics of continuum mechanics, and the target domain was electromagnetism. By constructing the analog between these two areas of physics, Maxwell was able ultimately to construct an effective theory of electromagnetism."*

Carey and Spelke (1994) described this activity as mapping across the domains. *"Scientists who effect a translation from physics to mathematics are using their innately given system of knowledge of number to shed light on phenomena in the domain of their innately given system of knowledge of physics. Scientists do this by devising and using systems of measurement to create mappings between objects in the first system (numbers) and those in the second (bodies). Once mapping is created, the scientists can use conceptions of number to reason about physical objects."*[14] It is this capability that distinguishes the expert from the novice. This is of course what psychologists term the transfer of learning.[15]

At a less erudite level, relatively simple analogies can be used in engineering design. Woodson (1966) presented a list of engineering devices and their respective analogies in nature (Exhibit 4.1). Angelo and Cross (1993) described an approximate analogies assessment technique in which students are required to

complete the second half of an analogy. One of the examples they give is, *"voltage is to wattage as……..is to……,"* they suggest that the teaching goals of this technique are to:

- *"Develop ability to synthesize and integrate information and ideas.*
- *Develop ability to think creatively.*
- *Improve memory skills.*
- *Learn concepts and theories.*
- *Develop an openness to new ideas.*
- *Develop capacity to think for ones self."*

4.2.1. Teaching with Concept Cartoons

Concept cartoons have proved to be a popular approach to teaching and learning in physics. Their characteristics as described by Keogh, Naylor, and Wilson (1998) are,

- *"Minimal amounts of text, so that it is accessible and inviting to learners with limited literacy skills.*
- *Scientific ideas are applied in situations, so that learners are challenged to make connections between the scientific and the everyday.*
- *The alternative ideas put forward are based on research that identifies common areas of misunderstanding,*
- *so that learners are likely to see many alternatives as credible.*
- *the scientifically acceptable viewpoint(s) will be included among the alternatives.*

The alternatives put forward all appear to be of equal status, so that learners cannot work out which alternative is correct from the context."

4.2.2. Teaching with Animation

Computers have made possible animations and other types of elegant presentation. However, a word of caution about their use seems necessary. For example, Crynes, Greene and Dillon (2000) reported that *"too much animation can be distracting."* They reported that there was too much "flash." Their work gives some support to the view that the same rules that govern the learning of concepts in traditional situations apply in computer assisted environments. One of the governing principles is simplicity. However, Khaliq (2000) has pointed out that where the behavior of a physical phenomenon changes with changes in the parameters animation is an ideal way of learning the concept. He described how in a course on integrated circuit fabrication multimedia modules were used to show the fabrication of the device. Since they were a complement to classroom lectures, they could be viewed at any time.

Ball and Patrick (1999) of the RMIT University in Melbourne showed how animations could be used to help students discover their misconceptions and *"to make their puzzlement available for discussion and*

---

[14] It will be noticed that it was a domain specific knowledge theory that P. Matthews (1997) used to critique constructivism (see Chapter 3) This view takes the position that many cognitive abilities as a result of evolution, are arranged to deal with specific (specialized) information. A reader that summarizes and considers the issues in this field has been edited by Hirschfield and Gelman, and Carey and Spelke's article is included in that reader.

[15] Pudlowski (1990) has discussed the transfer of knowledge within electrical engineering, and more especially as it relates to the use of analogies in understanding the operation of electrical circuits.

investigation." The evidence suggested that the learner's personal theories of heat were poorly aligned with scientific theories. Therefore, they designed a simulated laboratory setting that enabled the students to specify and test their own expectations of heat transfer in an experimental situation. At the same time it enabled the teachers to better understand the students' difficulties. *"We wanted the students to predict what they expected to see, so that they would attend with more interest to their observations and hopefully identify and puzzle over any discrepancies. To facilitate this, we asked the students to work in pairs so that they could discuss their ideas as they evolved. The 'explain' phase of the task required students to reflect on the surprises they have encountered and to develop and refine hypotheses, rather than restate a theoretical position which they had already been taught.[16]"*

From the substantial evidence presented by the authors, this approach evidently worked well. It was found that the students had more difficulty with unsteady-state conditions than with steady-state ones. They were often surprised by what they found. For example, *"[we] expected temperature at steady state to take a parabolic form, flux to have a constant gradient"*. This turned out to be incorrect. *"We were not thinking". [we] expected to find that flux and temperature showed a linear curve at steady state. [we were surprised] to find that flux was constant.[17]"* Other examples were given, and often the students demonstrated what Ball and Patrick called the *"Oh I see"* phenomenon.[18]

Segall (2002) developed a new freshmen level course that illustrated basic engineering concepts and principles by means of science fiction films and literature. *"Central to the course delivery is 'poking' fun at the disobedience of the laws of nature and the misuse of engineering while at the same time teaching the correct behaviors"*. Part of the assessment required the students in to describe and explain at least five events where they believed the laws of physics were observed/and or violated. They were also asked to discuss any technology/society/ethical issues raised by the story. Feedback from the students suggested that the course was capable of teaching a wide range of students.

4.3. Concept Learning and Curriculum Design

From the perspective of curriculum design, it is important for the curriculum designer to have a view on the problems of concept learning. If he or she agrees that it is better to spend more time ensuring that students understand some concepts well, then he/she is faced with the substantial task of convincing colleagues that this

should be the case, and this will necessarily involve some curriculum re-design. Support for his/her case might be found if he/she were to devise a test to check (a) the misperceptions of his/her students and (b) their implications for the "learning" that her/his colleagues insist on "covering." What does one do about it if this hypothesis is established? How does one find more time for understanding?

The screening of aims from the psychological perspective of learning concepts has implications for the design of the curriculum in general and the design of classroom teaching in particular. Consider first its implications for the design of the curriculum. If it is correct that more time is required for learning, then the syllabus (content) has to be reduced. This means that the design team has to clarify what is essential, and this might be done through consideration of the 'key concepts' of the program or course (see Section 4.4 below). Second, consider how the performance of students in integrated programs might be affected by the perceptions that students have of the program. Third, what implications do the perceptions that students have of a course have for its design? The last two issues will be considered in Chapters 7 and 8 with respect to studies by McKenna et al, (2001), and Streveler and Miller (2001).

4.4. Key Concepts

The idea of key concepts comes from an American Hilda Taba (Taba and Freeman, 1964). They are procedural devices to help teachers in the selection and organization of course content. A group of key concepts is shown in Exhibit 4.2. They are of interest because they can be used in technological courses to analyze the effects of technology on society and vice versa. They also provide an example of how ethical considerations can be integrated into a technical course. Equally, they may be used to design a straightforward program in engineering. If an integrated approach is wanted then it would be necessary to list the key concepts of the engineering subject matter. Woodson (1966) published an array of laws and effects that is essentially a matrix of the concepts that were required for a curriculum in engineering design, at that time (Exhibit 4.3).

It will be noted that a concepts and skills list of the kind shown in Exhibit 4.2 can be applied at any level of education. It may come as a surprise to find that these came from a middle schools curriculum project in the United Kingdom that integrated history, geography and the social sciences. Course designers have to specify the level at which they operate and provide examples of the standards at that level. Lelouche and Morin (1998) have shown how the introduction of key concepts into an intelligent tutoring system can aid the teaching of the economic components in cost engineering. They distinguished between basic (i.e. Investment, interest, investment duration, and future investment value) and derived (i.e., compounding, compounding period, number of periods, interest rate, and effective rate) concepts. They pointed out that these concepts are bound together

---

[16]They cited a paper by Goldberg and Dykstra in Duit, Goldberg, and Niedderer (1992),. who had used a similar approach in optics and electricity.

[17]The three experiments required them to set up the conduction bench with a steam heater at one end set at 120°C and a cooler at the other end set at 20°C. The materials used were successively slabs of stainless steel; steel and brick; and steel, brick, and steel.

[18]See discussion of eureka and marker events in Chapter 6.

Engineering	Nature	Engineering (continued)	Nature (continued)
Tubular structural members	Reeds, bamboo, bones	Retractable landing gear, flying	Birds' legs
Levers, fulcrums	Muscle attachment to bone	Anti-wetting agents	Ducks' feather oil
Doors and hinges	Trap-door-spiders' nests	Camouflage	Animal colorings
Lock bolt	Trigger fish fins	Infra red homing devises	Rattle snake nasal "pits".
Traps and triggers	Venus fly-trap	Sonar-radar	Bat and dolphin navigation
Toggle	Knee	Electric pulse generator	Heart pacer; electric eel
Safe packaging	Cranium	Ultrasonic communication	Bat and dog hearing
Great wind resistance	Radial fibers on seed carrier	Illumination.	Firefly: phosphorescent fish
Lubrication	Joints between bones	Heat Insulation	Hair covering
Cooling and control	Skin surface evaporation	Level control	Inner ear canal
Squeeze pump	Heart	Jet Propulsion	Squid siphon
Roller pump	Intestinal peristalsis	Optimum plumbing	Veins of circulation system
Strainer	Whale-bone baleen	Regenerated tools	Beaver teeth
Improved zipper	Brambles and heather webs	Extruded products	Insect webs
Automatic clasping device	Chicken leg and claws	Light-sensitive motion	Morning-glory flower
Streamlining	Fish; birds		

Exhibit 4. 1 Woodson's (1966) list of engineering analogies with nature. (Reproduced from *An Introduction to Engineering Design* with permission of McGraw Hill)

1. **Communication**	The significant movement of individuals, groups, or resources , or the transmission of significant information.
2. **Power**	The purposive exercises of power over individuals and society's resources.
3. **Values and Beliefs**	The conscious or unconscious systems by which individuals and societies organize their response to natural social and supernatural disorders.
4. **Conflict/Consensus**	The ways in which individuals and groups adjust their behavior to natural and social circumstances.
5. **Similarity/Difference**	Classification of phenomena according to relevant criteria.
6. **Continuity/Change**	Distinction of phenomena along this essentially historical dimension. The notion that change in a state of affairs can be contributed to the phenomena preceding.
7. **Causes and consequences**	

Exhibit 4.2 A list of key concepts relevant to the study of the interaction between technology and society (Blyth et al, 1973).

[cited in Heywood (1989a) and reproduced with permission of W. A. L. Blyth]

Outputs/ Inputs	Acceleration	Current	Displacement	Electro-magnetic radiation	Force	Frequency	Nuclear radiation	Pressure	Temperature	Velocity	Voltage
Acceleration		Piezo-electric effect	Newton's laws		Newton's laws					Newton's laws	Resistance/ dimension
Current			Ampere's law Magneto-striction	Luminescence	Ampere's law	Ampere's law		Boyle's law	Joule's law	Ampere's law	Ohm's law
Displacement				Diffraction	Hooke's law	Organ pipe resonance		Radiation pressure			Piezo electric effect
Electro-magnetic radiation		Piezo-electric effect	Doppler effect	Luminescence		Diffraction		Ideal gas law			Photo electric effects
Force	Newton's laws	Ohm's law		X-rays Gamma rays				Ampere's law	Friction effects	Newton's laws;	Piezo electric effect
Frequency											Impedance /frequency
Nuclear radiation											
Pressure		Piezo-electric effect	Boyle's law	Geiger effect				Charle's law.	Charles' Law		Piezo electric effect
Temperature		Thermo-electric effect	Ideal gas law	Stefan-Boltzman law		Wein's displacement law		Bernoulli' theorem			Pyroel ectric effect
Velocity			Bernoulli's theorem		Ampere's law	Doppler effect			Joules law.		Electro-kinetic
Voltage		Ohm's law	Electro-capillarity		Stoke' law						

Exhibit 4.3 An array of laws and effects in engineering education due to T. T. Woodson (1966) in *An Introduction to Engineering Design* and reproduced by with permission by the publishers McGraw Hill)

by relations of various types. *"For example the binary relation 'kind of' binds each concept to the type of unit used to measure it."* There are also higher order relationships. Splitting relationships by the introduction, say, of a formula leads to the concept of a "factor".

Key concepts do not resolve fundamental issues surrounding general approaches to the curriculum, as for example the approach to be used in teaching computer science As Fincher (1999) pointed out in computer science there is the view that students must be taught the practice of programming before they can do anything else. But there are also other views as to how the subject might be approached. Each of these would lead to a different arrangement of the key concepts.[19].

Related to the idea of key concepts is the idea of concept clusters. Steif (2004) has shown how the articulation of concept clusters and skills required for the understanding of Statics can be of value if it helps organize both assessment and instruction, to which we should add learning. He acknowledges that it is difficult to test the validity of his approach but that it works for him. That surely is the essence of the relationship between the curriculum and the instructor. He distinguishes between (a) skills that are actions that can be mastered by rote practice and (b) concepts that demand much more careful explanation and deeper understanding. He argues that some errors may stem from inadequate skills rather than conceptual misunderstandings.

"Specifically, the inability to visualize and parse the system being analyzed, in the sense of discerning its separate parts and how they are connected." As several studies have shown this is the skill that 'experts' possess. He conceives of Statics as having four basic concept clusters for which four skills are needed for the solution of problems in these areas. The concept clusters are

1. *"Forces acting between bodies.*
2. *Combinations and/or distributions of forces acting on a body are statically to a force and a couple.*
3. *Conditions of contact between bodies or types of bodies imply simplification of forces.*
4. *Equilibrium conditions are imposed on a body.*

The skills needed for implementing concepts of statics are

1. *Discern separate parts of an assembly and where each connects with the others.*
2. *Discern the surfaces of contact between connected parts, and/or the relative motions that are permitted between two connected parts.*
3. *Group separate parts of an assembly in various ways and discern external parts that contacts a chosen group.*
4. Translate the forces and couples which could be exerted as a connection (e.g. there is only a force in a known direction) into the variables, constants, and vectors that represent them. "

4.5. Concept Mapping

The importance of concept mapping in expert learning has already been explained. Novak, Godwin, and Johnson (1983) defined a concept map as a frame of reference that organizes essential information into a visual framework that displays the attributes and values of the concept to be learned. Sims-Knight et al, (2004) describe concept maps as *"network diagrams in which concepts (nouns) are nodes and the relationships between concepts (verbs) are links."* Arrows on such maps indicate that the links are directional. Such maps are closed in the sense that *"the propositions are clearly analogous to the subject-verb-object structure of sentences,"* which give the right view. Mappings of processes such as the design process are open and related to the acquisition of procedural knowledge. They may not be of the tree structure that is common in engineering (see Section 5.2 for an expansion of their thinking).[20] As indicated, concept maps come in all shapes and sizes (e.g., Mayon-White, 1990). Hyerle (1996) distinguished between eight types of thinking map. A circle map helps define words or things in context and presents points of view. Bubble maps describe emotional, sensory and logical qualities. For example, at their center in a circle might be a heroic person, and from the center other circles describe the characteristics of the hero. Tree maps show relationships between main ideas and supporting details. Block schematic diagrams are examples of flow diagrams, as, for example, the London tube or the Washington (DC) metro. Engineers often use such maps to show causes and effects as well as to predict outcomes. Maps may also be used to form analogies or metaphors and these are often used to try and explain fuzzy concepts. Sometimes they look like the main support of a spider's web. Danserau and Newbern (1997) called bubble maps 'node' maps. The nodes contain the central ideas. The links go to other nodes surrounding the central node and show relationships between the nodes. The nodes are linked together via the central node and lead to a key concept. They argued that concept maps should provide easy illustrations of complex relationships, less work clutter, be easy to remember, and easy to navigate. Other illustrations of block schematics have been described by Sims-Knight et al (2004). They are "Branching," "Cats cradle," "Web" and "Linear." But, McAleese and Cowan warned that concept maps are only useful to the learner, if they are constructed by the learner

---

[19]Four different approaches are discussed in her paper.

[20]See Parkin (1993). Declarative knowledge is about "knowing that", procedural knowledge is about "knowing how to do things". Cohen (1984) says 'procedural knowledge is involved when experience serves to influence the organization of processes that guide performance without access to the knowledge that underlies the performance. Declarative knowledge is represented in a system... in which information... first processed or encoded, then stored in some explicitly accessible form for later use, and ultimately retrieved upon demand".(Cited by Eysenck and Keane, 1995).

(Cowan, private communication). It is a view that is beginning to be taken up by the engineering community, and systems are being developed in which student-constructed maps become the navigation tool that allows them to explore relevant content and expand their maps (McClellan et al, 2004).

4.5.1. Concept Maps at the General Level

Key concepts may be mapped at both general and specific levels. The general level is illustrated by Turns, Atman, and Adams (2000), who drew the concept map for engineering shown in Figure 4.4. The key concepts listed in Exhibit 4.2 would belong in the area labeled impact in Figure 4.4. They are more specific. Concept maps may also be drawn for courses and programs-as for example, in digital logic and computer organization concepts (Saad and Zaghloul, 2002), and as a road map to understanding the global curriculum (Jones, 2000) for electromagnetic formulae (Glover and Sengupta, 1996) and for helping students to obtain a high-level view of the materials in the Chapters of a textbook (McClellan et al, 2004).

They can be used to see if program objectives are being achieved (Gerchak et al, 2003). Danserau (1987) provided a map of an overview of a learning strategy system, and Donald (1982) showed a concept map for a physics course that was built around the concept of "wave shapes" (Figure 4.5). The branches in the physics tree go from the more important to the less important concepts.

Eder (1994) used quite complex maps to illustrate the relationships between learning theory, design theory, and science. Eder's map could be used as an aid to screening. Many articles in the engineering education journals contain concept maps, generally of the tree or spider type.

Key concept maps can come in many forms and are used to show the interrelationships within an idea framework. For example, they may be used to refocus the curriculum as Culver and Hackos (1982) did with the outline of a tree (Figure 4.6; see Section below). In another configuration they showed the structure of a course design to meet the needs of the Perry model of student development (see Chapter 6).

It will be seen that the expression of key concepts at this level is part, but only part of the expression of content, but in a different way to the traditional syllabus. It is for this reason they are placed alongside aims and objectives in Figure 1.4. But learning requires skills, and the outcomes of learning are a combination of knowledge, skill in both cognitive and affective domains, and value dispositions sometimes called attitudes. The curriculum designers who stated the key concepts in Exhibit 4.2 distinguished between intellectual, social and physical skills. These are shown in Exhibit 4.4. Wherever the term ability is used, it is describing a behavior that will be expected of the student at the end of the course. A major component of their program attended to the environment, and they hoped it

would be possible to enhance or develop, or even perhaps change, attitudes. Thus, they hoped they would be able to discriminate along the dimensions shown in Exhibit 4.5 (At Alverno College the demands of the generic abilities necessarily involve assessment of dispositions in the values domain (Alverno, 1994): Mentkowski and Associates, 2000).

So much for key concepts at the general level. At the level of the lecture theater the structure of key concepts is unpacked and the conceptual frameworks that lead to that structure are explained. As indicated above, it is necessary that students understand individual concepts if they are to grasp the structure.

4.5.2. Concept Maps at Specific Levels

Angelo and Cross (1993) considered that the teaching goals of concept mapping are to develop the ability to:

- *"draw reasonable inferences from observations.*
- *synthesize and integrate information and ideas.*
- *think holistically: to see the whole as well as the parts.*
- *learn concepts and theories in the subject.*
- *understand the perspectives and values of the subject.*
- *acquire an openness to new ideas.*
- *think for oneself."* [21]

It follows that if concept maps can be used to establish meaningful learning that they can be used to evaluate the knowledge students had of a field of study. Gerchak et al, (2003), who reported this study plan to convert the holistic score into a rubric and validate it with other expert assessors. In the meantime other approaches to the analysis of concept maps as well as the assessment of student learning continue to be reported (e.g., Sims-Knight et al, 2004).

Wheeler and Rogers (1999) reminded us that the mind makes mental models or representations and these models may be analogical or representational.[22] Their research was to determine if there was a need to improve UNIX skill acquisition for beginning computer science students. In order to establish if this was the case, they extracted their mental models from a sample of students for the purpose of developing ways of improving them. Although the technique for establishing the mental models is of interest, it is the results that are of concern here. They found that the mental models were text

---

[21]Concept maps may be used at all levels of schooling including the evaluation of primary (elementary) school technology (Thomson, 1997).

[22]Analogy and reminding strategies are key processes in memory but the use of analogies is not automatic and depends on the participant intentionally searching for an analogical solution (Eysenck and Keane, 1995). Schank (1982) suggested that at the highest level of abstraction. Thematic Organization Packages that link otherwise disparate ideas may be useful. Creative and analogical skills seem to rely on the ability to recognize and exploit common patterns and situations that differ markedly in content (Hampson and Morris, 1996).

descriptions and/or tree diagrams. But they also identified a model in which the subjects seemed to think that part of the process was going *"in and out of structures in order to move around, store items, and retrieve items."* They called this the "container" model.[23]

In a second stage they looked in more detail at two problem areas. These were the usage of commands and the container model. They concluded that while students learned with a tree model, they did not use it *"or did not know how to make it useful."* They observed that an experienced user of UNIX appeared to use the two models at different times; *"while describing the directory structure he seemed to be using the tree model, but while actually navigating through, he referred to container concept. They concluded that both types of model should be used together to increase the productivity and efficiency of the UNIX environment. These models are, in effect, concept maps, and the ability to use a variety of maps or schema characterizes the expert. They are our prior knowledge and they enable us to acquire knowledge in order to make the inferences necessary for solving problems[24] (see opening paragraph of Section 4.4). As Moreira (1985) pointed out, they might also be useful in establishing the prior knowledge that students have. They can also help identify gaps in student's knowledge. One study used them to identify gaps in the physics knowledge of trainee teachers. The authors suggested that this was a particularly useful method for those who have to teach science outside their specialism (Adamczk and Wilson, 1996). It is evident that maps of this kind are similar to mind maps and graphic organizers. Moreira (1985) also gave examples in English and Physics, and argued that they could be used to study the misconceptions that students have.*

Concept maps may be used by a teacher to structure a lecture, but they can also be used to understand how students learn; and students can use them as an aid to study (Landay, 1999, Darmofat, Soderholm, and Brodeur, 2002). For this purpose, Saad and Zaghloul (2002) have developed a visualization tool that enables students to build concept maps incrementally as the concepts are being discussed in class. They can be used at all levels of schooling including the evaluation of primary (elementary) school technology (Thomson, 1997). Danserau used maps as a guide to lectures by means of either a handout or overhead transparency. Once students are trained, they can generate their own maps, and if they wish, they can replace conventional notes with such maps (Landay, 1999; McCagg and Danserau, 1990). Czuckry,

Danserau, and Newburn (1997) argued that a team mapping project could replace a traditional term paper. In their study of students, who had completed a team mapping exercise in an introductory psychology and memory cognition course, they found that when asked to compare the mapping exercise with their perceptions of traditional writing assignments, the students said they learned more from the mapping exercise and found it more interesting. Sharp, Harb, and Terry (1997) indicated the value of concept maps in helping students to plan writing in engineering courses. A word of caution is required because it is clear that concept mapping may not be a panacea learning strategy for all students.

Recently, Sims-Knight et al, (2004) have required their students to use concept maps to describe the design process. They hoped that this would encourage them to understand that the design process was not a simple series of phases but instead a complex process that involved iteration and understanding of the inter-relationships between concepts.

Given their definition of a concept map (see above) it is of interest to note the nouns and verbs used in the construction of an expert map. The nouns were *"customer, design, feasibility, need, product, requirements, tentative design, testing, tradeoffs, and user. The verbs are: drives, design, evaluates, has, includes, influences and yields. The students task was to use some or all of the verbs provided to link with arrows the ten nodes, which could be placed anywhere on the page. "*

They designed an instructional package to help the students understand concept mapping as a device for understanding procedural knowledge. The students were able to complete a concept map about the structure of role playing games. Feedback was given and there was a post mortem. The task was then given and the resulting patterns were analyzed.

Five patterns were identified and the frequency of use was found to vary as between the major studied. In this case the majors were Computer and Information Science and Electrical and Computer Engineering. Close inspection of the subpatterns showed, for example, *"that no one in the class understood the relationship between feasibility, on the one hand, and requirements and tentative design, on the other hand. In fact fewer than 20 percent got any part of the pattern and 38 percent linked feasibility with design, which is much too late in the design process. This result tells the instructor that she or he needs to redesign instruction to promote understanding of how and why feasibility should be addressed when developing requirements and tentative design. "*Another example was given.

It is beyond the scope of this discussion to consider other details because the analysis is dependent on the diagrams with which it is accompanied. The reader is referred to the paper especially for the method of analysis.

---

[23]This model emerges quite clearly from the drawing shown in their paper.

[24]For example, reading depends on a wealth of prior knowledge. Many of the things that we read involve us in making inferences in order for us to understand the statement. Schank and Abelson (1997) suggested that in order to make these inferences, we have to have predictive schemata. They called them *scripts*. They are structures that contain stereotypical sequences of actions commonly undertaken in everyday settings Within these schemata there are *role-sets*-descriptions of other players in action-and *headings* of sub-schemata.

There is still much research to do. For example, do students with high levels of spatial ability do better with concept mapping than those with low levels? Do students with particular learning styles do better than those with other styles? Unfortunately, Hadwin and Winne (1996) had difficulty in finding more than four evaluation studies of concept mapping that met their criteria for rigorous research.

They offered the tentative conclusion that concept mapping could help students to study but that its success would be affected by the context in which the students were studying. When a course required deep as opposed to surface learning concept mapping was likely to be successful. The benefits of concept mapping emerge as students persist. The more students persist, the more likely they are to benefit. And, as is the case with so many strategies, students with low content knowledge might feel insecure when asked to map concepts. Such students are likely to have less confidence than other students, as a study by Fordyce (1992) suggests (see below). For students to learn any study strategy, it needs to be blended into the course, and training must be given. Okebukola (1992) showed that Nigerian students (pre-degree) who had experienced cooperative and individualistic experiences of concept mapping over a six-month period were significantly more successful in solving biological problems than a control group.

4.6. Learning About Learning from Mapping in Engineering

Fordyce (1992), in a small pilot study explored student understanding of mechanical stress and related it to the understanding of one of his colleagues. In this comparative sense his study was in the tradition of the expert/novice investigations undertaken by Simon and his colleagues, although it followed from the naïve conceptions investigated by Champagne, Gunstone, and Klopfer (1983). However, his starting point was with Ausubel's view that *"the most important single factor influencing learning is what the learner already knows....and teach him accordingly"* (Ausubel, Novak, and Hanesian, 1978).

Prior knowledge was found to be important in learning by Chi, Glaser and Rees (1982) who studied how novices and experts solved problems in physics.

The knowledge that experts have in physics is through schema that link the problem to principles. Eysenck and Keane (1995) summarized the result of the first study by Chi and his colleagues as follows: Novices and experts sort problems into related groups, but *"the two groups classified problems differently.[25] Novices tended to group together problems that had the same surface features: they grouped two problems together if they used trolleys or ramps. Novices were led by the key words and the objects in the problem. However, experts classified problems in terms of their deep structure. That is, they grouped together problems that could be solved by the same principles, even though these problems had different surface features."* In another investigation, Chi et al, (1981) reported that experts took more time to analyze problems than novices, who might be said to have charged in and applied equations immediately. As Seagull and Erdos (1990) put it when summarizing research in this area, from a teaching point of view poor problem solvers lack the motivation to persist. They skip steps and do not reason properly. Clearly the prior knowledge possessed by novices and experts is of considerable importance for them in the way they solve problems, and the development of schema is the task of the educator. Thus, if the educator has an understanding. of how these schema develop he/she is in a position to help/his/her student learn, and the importance of Fordyce's study is that it demonstrates this point. He wanted to find out how the undergraduate concept maps differed from those of an expert. Thus, he obtained a concept map from an expert colleague and compared it with those obtained from the students. The maps produced by the expert and the students were nothing like traditional concept maps. The left-hand side of the expert's map (Figure 4.7) showed the use of stress: On the right-hand side the relationship between stress and strain was described. The link between stress and strain was not simple. I draw attention to this observation because a student's misconception might be to think that this link is simple. The mapping and accompanying audio recording took the expert 25 minutes. A preliminary workshop was given to all students to exemplify what Fordyce was looking for. Then, during the first part of the term as the students became familiar with the mechanisms; they became their own researchers.

The questions they had to answer in this process of discovery were:

1) What are the features of the theme for you?
2) How do you hold the features (as an equation, as a picture of an equation, as a voice, as some *form of graphical representation, or as a real situation?).*
3) *What is the meaning of the feature for you? How do you interpret what you have justified?*
4) *What is the nature of the link between the features for you, if any?*

Of the several findings one is of particular interest. As the map was constructed, an element which Fordyce called the 'core' emerged. This was the area of the map the respondent felt most confident about. For first-year students this related to work they had done before entry to the undergraduate program, for example, in stress and strain the expressions for stress and strain formed the core (Figure 4.8). *"Where new material was*

---

[25] Eysenck and Keane (1995) liken the problems to be solved to the following, *"A block of mass M is dropped from a height x onto a spring of force of constant K. Neglecting friction, what is the maximum distance the spring will be compressed?"* The importance of these experiments to our understanding of how people learn, and its relation to teaching, especially in schools, is documented in *"How People Learn"* (Bransford et al, 2000).

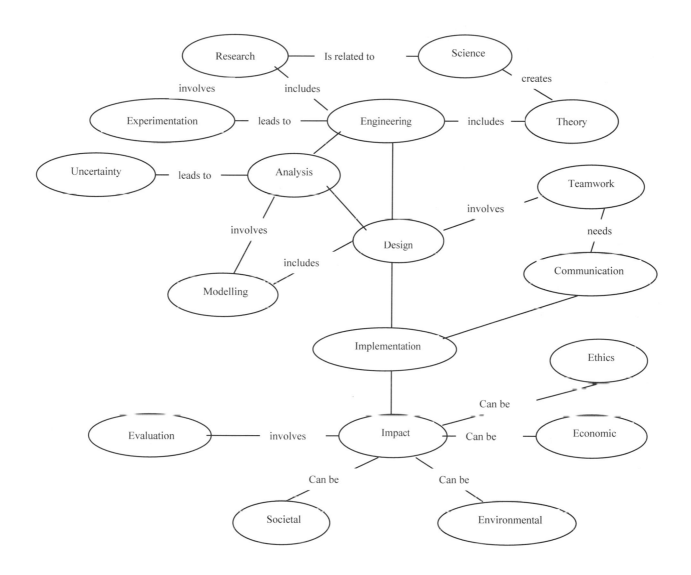

Figure 4.4 Concept map for engineering (Turns, Atman and Adams, 2000). (reproduced by kind permission of *IEEE Transactions on Education*).

defined this did not form the core in terms of confidence; the aspects or features of the map were known about and memorised but they had not been accommodated in the core." At this stage, in today's parlance, they had not been *"internalised"* and were not owned.

As well as eliciting data about the levels of confidence possessed by the students, the exercise also illuminated their difficulties and showed the teacher where they had to go. The *"novice"* engineers' maps had recognizable components of the *"experts"* map, but not their experience. Figure 4.9 shows a student who had a *"need to relate ideas to reality, to get the feel of the situation. Physical reality in terms of personal feelings is*

important for this student. Although no datum values are yet defined for him he is seeking their equivalent in his interpretation of a situation (strength being assessed by the amount of deflection occurring under a beam when it is stood on.". Figure 4.10 shows the maps produced by a third-year student.

Because the level of confidence was found to be important, this study highlighted the importance of the affective component in cognitive thinking. This dimension is a neglected aspect of teaching in the sciences, yet it seems that it is personal justification which provides the feeling of confidence in a topic area.

Related to this investigation is a study by Besterfield-Sacre et al, (1998) who reported on the level of confidence of freshman students at two American universities. They had found that the initial poor perception that they had of one's abilities was a significant factor in student attrition (Besterfield-Sacre, Atman, and Shuman, 1997). That study, which was concerned with gender differences, did not come up with conclusive findings, although it indicated trends. They found, (among other things) that at one university both genders increased their confidence in communication skills, and in basic engineering knowledge and skills, whereas at the other university both genders experienced significant decreases in their confidence with chemistry, engineering knowledge, and their belief in their ability to succeed in engineering. In general they thought that gender differences might be institution-specific.

Another study of concept mapping in the domain of biomedical engineering by Walker and King (2003) also showed that when experts and novices were asked to illustrate the relationships between the 10–20 most important concepts in biomedical engineering, the experts maps were much more dense than those of the students. A second study that obtained concept maps at different times in the course also showed that later maps contained a more precise vocabulary and more concepts and had greater validity. The maps in both studies, were unlike those offered by Fordyce's students of the more traditional type. The students considered that concept mapping helped their intellectual growth and helped them to *"hook things up."* How students trained in this way would perform in comparison with a traditional group of students had yet to be determined, but Walker and King believed they would do better in their examinations. Walker and King warned that because of the variability in experts maps, assessments should not be made by comparing student work with expert maps. They thought that questions that had a much greater focus could lead to maps that could be used in summative assessment.

Fordyce's study confirmed the view put forward previously that knowledge structures require time and experience to develop. Students cannot be hassled. Further, it supports the contention that teaching should be governed by an understanding of student learning. Teachers should avoid imposing their structures on those of beginning students. In so far as first-year students are concerned, Fordyce felt that *"it would be reasonable to expect only simple first level models in relation to confident 'unified scientific outcome' where it exists."*

Walker and King (2003) envisaged *"instructors giving students a brief orientation to the technique, and then asking them to construct maps (either individually or in pairs) at multiple time points during the semester. Students could then critique one another's and the instructor's concept maps. Used in such a way concept mapping provides substantial benefits to students, in terms of motivation and critical thinking skills, while exacting minimal cost from the instructor in terms of time and materials."*

4.7. Quantitative and Qualitative Understanding.

In 1983 Cowan issued a challenge to the readers of *Engineering Education.* He invited them to attempt to solve four engineering problems that he presented in diagrammatic form. He suggested that it should be possible to solve them within a period of eight minutes. In any event, they should stop work at the end of that period. While they were solving the problem they were to talk out their thoughts quietly to themselves.

He introduced this idea in the middle of an article which he had begun with an explanation of some investigations into student problem solving in structures that he done with the aid of audio protocols and written notes. In his approach the subject was involved in supplementing and partially analyzing his/her own account of his/her problem solving since they had to play back the tape to themselves.

He found that there were three types of problem solver. There were those *"who use forces as their starting points, and so I called them force-based problem solvers. For others the starting point is to predict the deflected shape of the structure, I called them movers. There are also a few who use abstract approaches of a purely theoretical nature and express entire problems in algebraic formulae; I described them as mathematicians."*

The reader will appreciate that with a sufficient number of protocols a problem-solving style instrument could have been devised that would have been relevant to his courses. Be that as it may, he found that no problem solver that he studied belonged exclusively to any one style. He asked his readers to say what kind of a problem solver they were whe n they solved one of the problems. He found that most of his subjects had difficulty in articulating what they were doing so the next problem for his readers was for them to take another example, and then recall and examine the phrases they used when they tried to solve that problem. Because most of his subjects became so interested in the research it had a tutorial effect on them. He then suggested to his readers that they tackle four or five sets of similar problems and discuss them with their peers. *"You might have a similar experience"* to the students.

He found that most undergraduates, when faced with such problems nearly always use quantitative analysis to try and solve them. Some may develop one really qualitative strategy *"to elicit the order of bending behavior in a structure (the commonest example is probably the sketching of an exaggerated deflected form. But few demonstrate intelligent reliance on an accumulated library of past experience, and very few manipulate these with any facility."* Cowan considered that numberless versions of a quantitative approach are prone to error, and do not describe what he means by qualitative understanding. There are a number of strategies that can be used, and a good engineer will

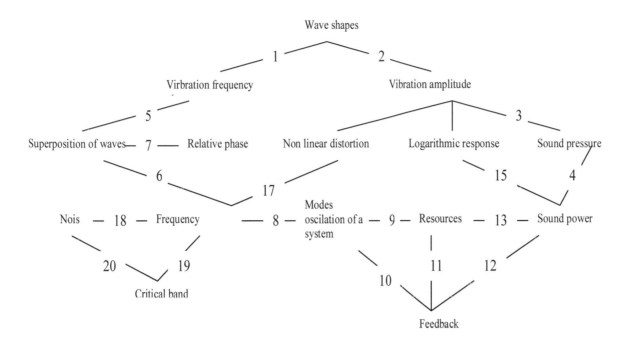

Figure 4.5. Concept map for a curriculum based on waves (Donald, 1986). (Cited by Heywood (1989) with the permission of the *Journal of Higher Education*)

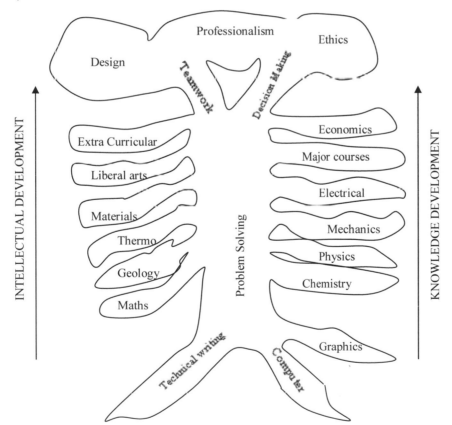

Figure 4.6. An alternative model of technical education that takes into account theories of intellectual development. due to Culver and Hackos (1982) and reproduced with permission of R. S. Culver.

Intellectual	Social	Physical
1. The ability to find information from a variety of sources	The ability to participate in small groups	The ability to manipulate equipment
2. The ability to communicate findings through an appropriate medium.	An awareness of significant groups within the community and the wider society.	The ability to manipulate equipment: to find and communicate information.
3. The ability to interpret pictures charts, graphs, maps etc	A developing understanding of how individuals relate to such groups.	The ability to explore the expressive powers of the human body to
4. The ability to evaluate information.	A willingness to consider participating constructively in the activities associated with these groups.	communicate ideas and feelings. The ability to plan and execute expressive activities to communicate
5. The ability to organize information through concepts and generalizations	The ability to exercise empathy (i.e. the capacity to imagine accurately what it might be like to be someone else).	ideas and feelings.
6 The ability to formulate hypotheses and generalizations		

Exhibit 4.4 The skills developed in association with the key concepts in Exhibit 4.2 (Blyth et al 1973). [Cited in Heywood (1989a) with the permission of W. A. L. Blyth.]

The student

1. Who responds willingly to a study of the environment.
2. Who shows awareness of the variety of ways of studying the environment and of testing ideas and hypotheses.
3. Who shows awareness of the variety of ways of communicating the findings of his or her enquiries.
4. Who is wary of over commitment to one framework of explanation and is alert to possible distortion of facts and omission of evidence.
5. Who is willing to identify with particular attitudes and values about the environment and relates these to other people.
6. Who has a characteristic set of attitudes and values but remains open to change.

Exhibit 4.5 Attitudes and values that Blyth et al (1973) felt they would be able to discriminate between for purposes of evaluation. [Cited in Heywood (1989) with the permission of W. A. L. Blyth.]

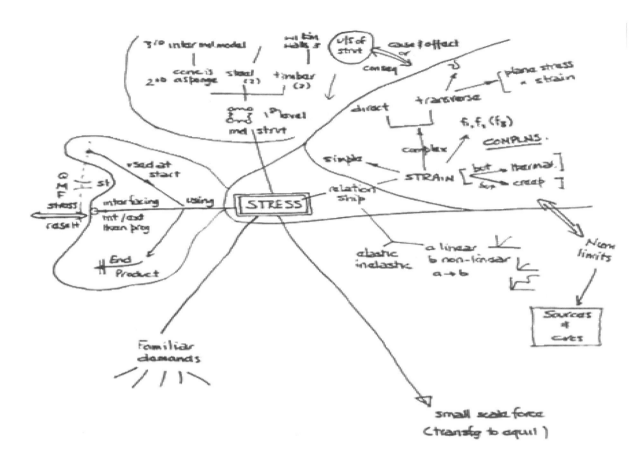

Figure 4.7. The Expert's Map [Fordyce, 1992, and also figures 4.8 4.9 and 4.10. All reproduced with permission of the author and the. *International Journal of Technology and Design Education*, Kluwer Academic Press].

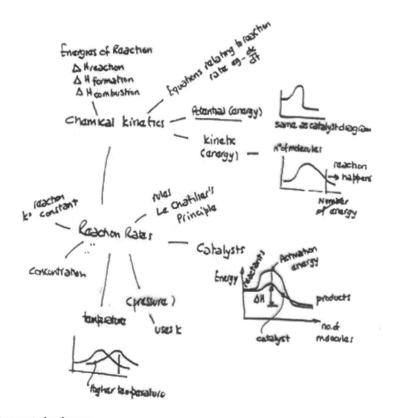

Figure 4,8. (a) A first year student's map

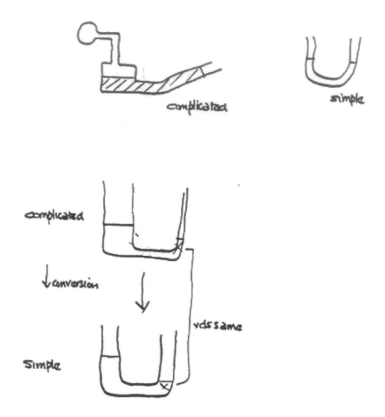

Figures 4.8 (b). A first year student's map.

Figure 4.8. Are maps of (a0 an area of chemistry and (b) of a simple system drawn by a first year student. Fordyce wrote that (a) *"represents a map of an area of chemistry where there was expressed confidence. Confidence is based here on the fact that two diagrams can be used to personally justify and explain features".* (b) *shows the desire to define a simple system or limited number of simple systems to explain all variations of a situation. .The use of another mechanism equivalent to some model of reality… has yet to be discovered. No feeling for situations exists in terms of datum values".*

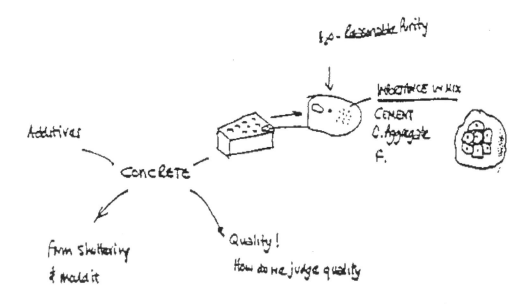

Figure 4.9 (a)

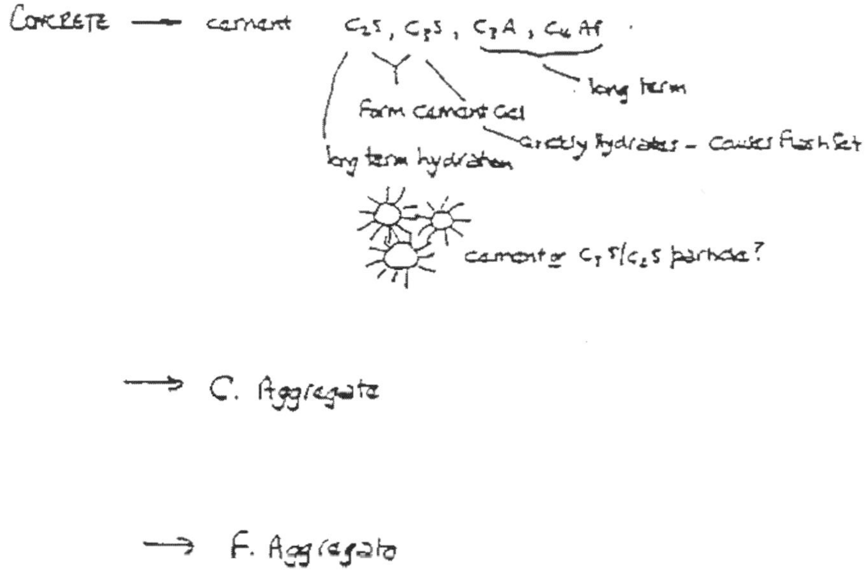

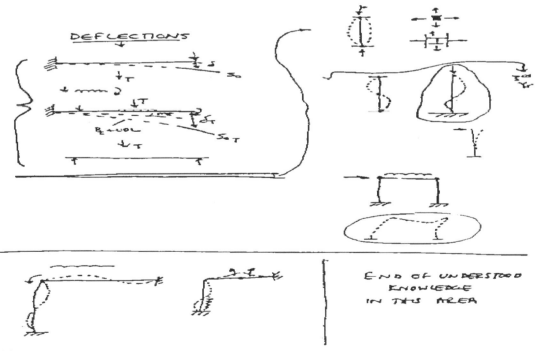

Figure 4.9 (b).

Figures 4.9 (a) and 4.9 (b). are illustrations of a student who has a need to relate ideas to reality to get the feel of the situation. Fordyce wrote, *Physical reality in terms of personal feelings is important to this individual....Although no datum values are yet defined for him he is seeking their equivalent in his interpretation of a situation (strength being assessed by the amount of deflection occurring under a beam when it is stood on)...In figure 4.9. (b) a later stage map of the same area, a "first level" but scientifically accepted model of the nature of cement has now replaced the simple version in figure 4.9 (a)".*

Figure 4.10 (a)

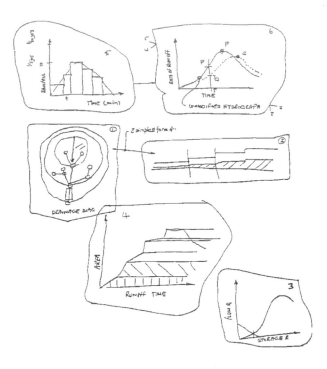

Figure 4.10 (b)

Figure 4. 10 A third year students map relating to (a) deflection of beams, and (b) a drainage system. Fordyce wrote in respect of (a) that while equations were used there was no personal meaning of the equations had been developed. And later…*"Outcome values could be judged as being reasonable but the nature of the deflective form was not there, so the confidence was note there."* **In respect of b, Zone 2 shows a single pipeline of increasing diameter, Zones 3, 4, 5, and 6 are mathematical descriptions of what is happening in the drainage system.** *"They could be justified from, in this case, real experiences and datum values".* **Real situations and real values are used to build confidence**

classify all structures into sub-groups and have a preferred strategy for dealing with that group.

A much more recent paper by Howard (1999) described a laboratory investigation based on a real-life problem. He argued that *"implicit problems involving practical application of engineering techniques and concepts can help students who have little experience with the physical world learn the significance of numbers."* If students are allowed to explore more, they will understand more of the physical and practical details of engineering. This is similar in intent to the experimental investigations in engineering science described earlier. However, they were not specified in the detail given by Howard, but they were meant to encourage a voyage of discovery

Unfortunately it is not possible to reprint Howard's paper even though it is short. But, the question might be asked, "Would the students understanding have improved if they had used protocols in conjunction with their peers?" (See also Howard, 1994).

Brereton, Sheppard and Leifer (1995) explored how students related fundamental concepts learned in analysis classes to experiences with hardware when the concepts are applied in design. This was done by video taping in situ not only in their laboratories but in their dormitories, as they worked in groups on a design project (Sheppard, 1992). [In the jargon of the social sciences

this procedure is known as ethnography,(e.g., Ashworth and Lucas,2000; Bogdan and Biklen,1998.[26]] For analysis they used a video interaction technique due to Jordan and Henderson (1992).

Their paper gives detailed descriptions of the conversations between the students that are reminiscent of the types of conversation reported by Cowan over the years.

Three of their comments are of interest. First, they found that students had difficulty in relating variables. They believed this was due in part to the fact that for the students, *"physical world realities like friction, uneven surfaces and irregular objects cast doubt on the nature of the relationships between the variables"*.(see Collinge,1994, in next Chapter and the suggestion about field independence-dependence). And then, in a statement that supports Cowan's thesis, *"students seemed to have little experience in qualitative reasoning about what should vary and what should noIn typical analysis problem sets they are used to being told what the independent variable is."* Finally, in what is one of the few papers among those that I have read on engineering education in America is the recognition, long accepted in the educational literature, that assessment drives learning (e.g., Marton, Hounsell, and Entwistle,

---

[26] See Chapter 15 for a resumé of qualitative research in the social sciences.

1984. Heywood, 1977, 1989).Thus, the assessment methods they used were *"reflective explorations in log books that linked group projects, fundamental concepts and observations outside the classroom, participation in discussion, and an individual project that explored a concept in the context of hardware."*

It has been argued in this Chapter that the learning of concepts is an extremely complex matter and requires that teachers carefully plan for their understanding. In the next Chapter the question of the influence of learning strategies and styles is considered.

References

Adamczyk, P., and M. Wilson (1996). Using concept maps with trainee physics teachers. *Physics Education*. 374-381.

Alverno (1994) *Student Assessment-As-Learning at Alverno College*. Alverno College Institute, Milwaukee, WI

Angelo, T., and P. K. Cross (1993). *Classroom Assessment Techniques*. Jossey Bass, San Francisco.

Ashworth, P., and U. Lucas (2000). Achieving empathy and engagement: A practical approach to the design an reporting of phenomenographic research. *Studies in Higher Education*, 25, (3), 295 – 307.

Atman, C. J., and I. Nair (1992). Constructivism: appropriate for engineering education. *Proceedings Annual Conference American Society for Engineering Education*, 1310–1312.

Ausubel, D. P., Novak, J. S., and H. Hanesian (1978). *Educational Psychology: A Cognitive View*. Holt, Rinehart and Winston, New York.

Ball. J., and K. Patrick (1999). Learning about heat transfer–"oh I see" experiences. *Proceedings Frontiers in Education Conference*, 2, 12e5 1 to 6

Berardi-Coletta, B., Buyer, L. S., Dominowski, R. L., and E. R. Rellinger (1995). Metacognition and problem solving; a process-oriented approach. *Journal of Experimental Psychology: Learning, Memory, and Cognition*, Vol 21.

Besterfield-Sacre, M., Atman, C. J. and L. J. Shuman (1997). Characteristics of freshman engineering students: models for determing student attrition and success in engineering. *Journal of Engineering Education*, 86, (2), 139 – 149.

Besterfield-Sacre, M., Amaya, N., Shuman, L., Atman, C., and R. Porter (1998). Understanding student confidence as it relates to first year achievement. *Proceedings Frontiers in Education Conference*, 1, 258-263.

Blyth, W.A.L., Derricott, R., Elliot, G.F. Sumner, H.M., and A. Waplington (1973).*History, Geography and Social Science 8–13*. An Interim Report. Liverpool Schools Council Project. University of Liverpool, Liverpool.

Bogdan, R. C. and S. K. Biklen (1998). *Qualitative Research for Education. An Introduction to Theory and Practice*. 3rd edition. Allyn and Bacon, Boston.

Booth, K. M., and B. W. James (2001). Interactive Learning in a higher education level 1 mechanics module. *International Journal of Science Education*, 23, (9), 955-967.

Bransford, J. D., Brown, A. L., and R. R. Cocking (2000) (eds.). *How People Learn*. Brain, Mind, Experience and School. National research Council, National Academy Press, Washington, DC.

Brayley, L (1963). Strategy selection and negative instances in concept learning. *Journal of Educational Psychology*.54, 154–159.

Brereton, M. Sheppard, S and L. Leifer (1995). How students connect engineering fundamentals to hardware design. International Conference on Engineering Design. August PRAHA.

Brereton, B., Sheppard, S., and L. Leifer (1995). Students connecting engineering fundamentals and hardware design: Observations and implications for the design of the curriculum. *Proceedings Frontiers in Education Conference*, 4d3 1 to 7.

Bucci, P, Long, T.J., Weide, B. W., and J. Hollingsworth (2000). Toys are us: presenting mathematical concepts in CS1/CS2. *Proceedings Frontiers in Education Conference*, 2, F4B-1 to 6.

Buriak, P., McNurlen, B., and J. Harper (1995). Systems model for learning. *Proceedings Frontiers in Education Conference*. 2a3, 1 to 7.

Cantor, N., Mischel, W., and J. C. Schwartz (1982) A prototype analysis of psychological situations. *Cogniitive Psychology*, 14, 45 -77.

Champagne, A. N., Gunstone, R. F. and l. E. Klopfer (1983). Naïve knowledge and science learning. *Research in Science and Technological Education*, 1, (2), 173–183

Carey, S. and E. Spelke (1994). Domain specific knowledge and conceptual change in L. A. Hirschfield and S. A. Gelman (eds). *Mapping the Mind*. Cambridge University Press, Cambridge, UK.

Chi, M., Feltovich, P. and R. Glaser (1981). Categorization and representation of physics problems by experts and Novices. *Cognitive Science*, 5, 121–152.

Chi, M., Glaser, R., and M. Farr (1988) (eds.). *The Nature of Expertise*. Lawrence Erlbaum, Hillsdale, NJ.

Chi, M, Glaser, R., and E. Rees (1982). Expertise in problem solving in R. J. Sternberg (ed.). *Advances in the Psychology of Human Intelligence*. Lawrence Erlbaum, Hillsdale, NJ.

Chi, M., and J. D. Slotta (1993). The ontological coherence of intuitive physics. *Cognition and Instruction*. 10, 249–260.

Clark, A. C., and E. N. Wiebe (1999). Scientific visualization for secondary and post secondary schools. *Journal of Technology Studies*. 24–32.

Clement. J (1981). Solving problems with formulas: some limitations. *Engineering Education*, 25, 150–162.

Clement, J (1982) Student preconeptions of introductory physics. *American Journal of Physics*,50, (1), 66–67.

Cohen, N. J (1984) Preserved learning capacity. Evidence for multiple memory systems. In L. R. Squire and N. Butters (eds.) *Neuropsychology of Memory*. Guilford Press, New York.

Collinge, J. N (1994). Some fundamental questions about scientific thinking. *Research in Science and Technological Education*, 12, (2), 161–174.

Cowan, J (1983).How engineers understand: an experiment for author and reader. *Engineering Education*, ??, (3), 301-304.

Cowan, J (1998). *One Becoming an Innovative University Teacher. Reflection in Action*. SRHE/Open University Press, Buckingham

Culver, R. S. and J. T. Hackos (1982). Perry's model of intellectual development. *Engineering Education*. 73, (2), 221–226.

Czuckry, M. and D.F. Danserau (1998). Node linking mapping as an alternative to traditional writing assignments in undergraduate psychology. Teaching Psychology cited by Danserau., and Newbern, (1997).

Crynes, B., Greene, B., and C. Dillon (2000). Lectrons or Lectures-which is the best for whom. *Proceedings Frontiers in Education Conference*. 3, S2D-21 to 24.

Danserau, D. F (1987) Technical learning strategies. *Engineering Education*, 77, (5), 280–284.

Danserau, D. F., and D..Newbern.. (1997). Using knowledge maps to enhance excellence in W.E. Campbell and K.A. Smith (eds) *New Paradigms for College Teaching*, Interaction Book Co, Edina, MI.

Darmofat, D. L., Soderhol, D. H., and D. R. Brodeur (2002). Using concept maps and concept questions to enhance conceptual understanding. *Proceedings Frontiers in Education Conference*, 1, T3A-1 to 5.

Davidovic, A., Warren, J., and E. Trichina (2003). Learning benefits of structural example-based adaptive tutoring systems. *IEEE Transactions on Education*, 46,(92), 241–251.

De Cecco, J .P., and W. R. Crawford (1974). *The Psychology of Learning and Instruction*. Prentice Hall, Englewood Cliffs, NJ.

DiSessa, A. A (1983). Evoluion of intuition in D. Gentner and A. Stevens (eds). *Mental Models*. Lawrence Erlbaum Associates, Hillsdale, NJ.

Donald, J.G (1982) Knowledge structures; methods for exploring course content. *Journal of Higher Education*, 54, (1), 31–41.

Driver, R (1983). *The Pupil as Scientist*. Open University Press, Milton Keynes.

Duit, R., Goldberg, F, and H. Niedderer (1992). (eds.) Research in Physics Learning: Theoretical issues and empirical studies. Proceedings International Workshop at the University of Bremer, Kiel, Germany. Institut für die Pädagogik de Naturwissenschaften an der Universität.

Duncan-Hewitt, W. C. et al (2001). Using developmental principles to plan design experiences for beginning engineering students. *Proceedings Frontiers in Education Conference*, 1, T3E-17 to 22.

Dunleavy, P (1986) *Studying for a Degree in the Humanities and Social Sciences*. Macmillan, London.

Eder, E (1994). Comparisons—Learning theories, design theory, science. *Journal of Engineering Education*, 83, (2), 111−119.

Edward, N. S (1997) An evaluation of student perceptions of screen presentations in computer based laboratory simulations. *European Journal of Engineering Education*. 22, (2), 142−151

Edgerton, R. H (1989). Cognitive science and engineering education. *Proceedings of World Conference on Engineering Education to for Advancing Technology*, 1, 382−384.

Eftekhar, N and R. D. Strong (1998). Toward dynamic modelling of a teaching/learning system Part 2: A new theory on types of learners. *International Journal of Engineering Education*, 16,(6), 368−406.

Ericsson, K. A., and H. Simon (1993). *Protocol Analysis: Verbal Reports as Data*. The MIT press, Cambridge MA.

Evans, D. L., and D. Hestenes (2001). The concept of the concept inventory assessment instrument. *Proceedings Frontiers in Education Conference*, 2, F2A-1.

Eysenck, M. W. and M. T. Keane (1995). *Cognitive Psychology. A Student's Handbook,*. 3rd edition. Erlbaum, Taylor Francis, Hove.

Felder, R. M and R. Brent (2003). Designing and teaching courses to satisfy the ABET criteria. *Journal of Engineering Education*, 92, (1), 7−24.

Ferré, E et al (2002). Flash animation in introductory Electrical Engineering Courses. *Proceedings Frontiers in Education Conference*, 1, T1F-1.

Feuerstein, R., Rand, V., Hoffman, M. B., and R. Miller (1980). *Instrumental Enrichment. An Intervention for Cognitive Modifiability*. University Park Press, Baltimore, MD.

Fincher, S (1999). What are we doing when we teach programming?.*Proceedings Frontiers in Education Conference,*12a4 −1−12e4 to 5.

Fordyce, D. (1992). The nature of student learning in engineering education. *International Journal of Technology and Design Education*, 2, (3), 22-40.

Gagné, R. M. (1967, 1984). *The Conditions of Learning* (4th Ed.). Holt, Rienhart and Winston, New York.

Gagné, R. M., Briggs, L. J., and W.W. Wager (1992.. *Principles of Instructional Design* (4th ed.). Harcourt, Brace, Jovanovich, Fort Worth.

Gerchak, J., Besterfield-Sacre, M., Shuman, L. J., and H. Wolfe (2003). Using concept maps for evaluating program objectives. *Proceedings Frontiers in Education Conference*, 1, T3B, 20 to 25.

Glover, T. A., and N. Sengupta (1996). A Map of Electromagnetic Formulae. *International Journal of Electrical Engineering Education*. 33, 8-10.

Greenberg, J. E., Smith, N. T., and J. Newman (2003). Instructional module in Fourier Spectral Analysis, based on the principles of "How people learn". *Journal of Engineering Education*, 92, (2), 155−166.

Gunter, M. A., Estes, T. H., and J. Schwab (1999). *Instruction. A Models Approach*. Alleyn and Bacon, Boston MA.

Hadwin, A. F., and P. M. Winne (1996). Study strategies have meagre support. A review with recommendations for implementation. *Journal of Higher Education* 67, (6), 692−715.

Hake, R (1998). Interactive-engagement vs traditional methods: a six thousand-student survey of mechanics test data for introductory physics courses. *American Journal of Physics*, 66, 64

Halloun, I. A. and D. Hestenes (1985). The initial knowledge state of college physics students. *American Journal of Physics*, 53, 1043−1048.

Hampson, P. J. and P. E. Morris (1996). *Understanding Cognition*. Blackwell, Oxford.

Hasan, S., Bagayoko, D., and E. L. Kelley (2000). Misconceptions and the Certainty of response Index. *Physics Education*, 34, (5), 294−299.

Hein, T. L and S. E. Irvine (Assessment of technology-based learning tools in an introductory physics laboratory. *Proceedings Frontiers in Education Conference*, 13c3−1 to 6.

Henderson,. Hestenes, D., Wells, M., and G. Swackhamer,(1992). Force Concept Inventory. *The Physics Teacher*, 30, 141.

Hestenes, D., Wells, M., and G. Swackhammer (1992). Force concept inventory. *The Physics Teacher*. 30,141.

Heywood, J (1974) *Assessment in History. Twelve to Fifteen*. Report No 1. Public Examinations Evaluation Project. School of Education, University of Dublin.

Heywood, J (1977). *Assessment in Higher Education*. First edition. Wiley, Chichester

Heywood, J (1989). *Assessment in Higher Education*, 2nd edition, Wiley, Chichester.

Heywood, J (1992) Student teachers of instruction in the classroom. in J. H. C. Vonk and H. J. van Helden (eds.) *New Prospects for Teacher Education in Europe. Association of Teacher Educators in Europe*, Brussels.

Heywood, J (1997). On the value of replicating forgotten research on the teaching of concepts during graduate student teaching. Association of Teacher Educators Conference, St Louis. ERIC ED 406 332.

Hirschfield, L. A. and S. A. Gelman (1994). *Mapping the Mind. Domain Specificity in Cognition and Culture*. Cambridge University Press, Cambridge, UK.

Howard, R. W (1987). Concepts *and Schemata: An Introduction*. Cassell, London.

Howard, B. (1994). Why don't they understand what they know? What to do about it! *Proceedings Frontiers in Education Conference* 573−578.

Howard, B (1999) Enough of this science and mathematics, lets do some engineering. *Proceedings Frontiers in Education Conference*, 2, 13d2-8−13d2-10

Hunt, E and J. Minstrell (1994). A cognitive approach to teaching physics in K. McGilly (ed.) *Classroom Lessons. Integrating Cognitive Theory in the Classroom*. MIT Press, Cambridge, MA.

Huttenlocher, J (1962). Some effects of negative instances on the formation of concepts. *Psychological Reports*. 11, 35-42.

Hyerle, D. (!996). Thinking maps; seeing and understanding. *Educational Leadership*, 53, (4), 85−89.

Hyman, W. and G. Miller (1989). Undergraduate bioengineering student design projects applied to real world problems for the handicapped. *International Journal of Applied Engineering Education*, 5 (4) 45−456.

Ireson, G. (2000) The quantum understanding of pre-university physics students. *Physics Education*, 35 (1) 15−21.

Jones, J. D (2000) Concept maps and competence charts: a roadmap to understanding the global curriculum. *Proceedings Frontiers in Education Conference*, 2, T2F−10.

Jordan, B and A. Henderson (1992). *Interaction analysis: Foundations and Practice*. Institute for Research on Learning, Palo Alto, CA.

Keogh, B., Naylor, S., and C. Wilson (1998). Concept cartoons. A new perspective on physics education. *Physics Education*. 33, (4), 219-225.

Khaliq, M. A (2001) Interactive multimedia courseware for integrated circuit fabrication courses. *Proceedings Frontiers in Education Conference*, 3, S1C-1 to 4.

Koen, B. V. (2000). *Discussion of the Method The Engineering Approach to Problem Solving*. Oxford University Press, New York.

Kuhn, D., Garcia-Mila, M., Zohar, A., and C. Anderson (1995). Strategies of Knowledge Acquisition. *Monographs of the Society for research in Child Development*. Vol. 60.

Landay, J. A. (1999). Using note-taking appliances for student collaboration. *Proceedings Frontiers in Education Conference*, 2, 12c4 15 to 20.

Larkin, J. H (1979). Processing information for effective problem solving. *Engineering Education*, 70 (3) 285–288.

LeLouche, R and J F. Morin (1998) Introduction of pedagogical concepts in domain modelling for an intelligent tutoring system. *European Journal of Engineering Education*, 23 (2) 255–271.

McCagg, J.G and D.F. Danserau (1990). A Convergent Paradigm for Examining Knowledge as a Learning Strategy. Annual meeting of the American Educational research Association, Boston, MA.

Macdonald, F (1968). *Educational Psychology*. Wadsworth, Belmont, CA.

McCormick, R (1997). Conceptual and procedural knowledge. *International Journal of Technology and Design Education*. 7, 141–159.

McClellan, J. H., Harvel, L. D., Velmurugan, R., Borkar, M and C. Scheibe (2004). CNT: Concept-map based navigation and discovery in a repositiory of learning content. *Proceedings Frontiers in Education Conference*, F1F- 13–F1F-18

McElwee, P. G (1991). Transition from personal to scientific understanding. *Research in Science and Technological Education*, 9, 139–155.

McElwee, P. G (1993). The conceptual understanding of scientific principles. *Home Economics*, 3, 5-17.

McKenna, A., McMartin, F., Terada, Y., Sirivedhin, V., and A, Agognino (2001). *Proceedings Annual Conference ASEE. Session* 1330.

Marton, F., Hounsell, D., and N.J. Entwistle (1984) eds. *The Experience of Learning*. Scottish Academic Press, Edinburgh.

Matthews, P.S.C (1997). Problems with Piagetian constructivism. *Science and Education*. 6, 105-119.

Matthew, R. G. S and D. C. Hughes (1994). Getting at deep learning: A problem-based approach. *Engineering Science and Education Journal*, October, 1, 234–240.

Mayon-White, B (1990). *Study Skills for Managers*. Paul Chapman, London.

Mazur, E (1995). *Peer Instruction: A User's Manual*. E. Mazur. Harvard University.

Mentkowski, M., and Associates (2000). *Learning that Lasts. Integrating Learning, Development, and Performance in College and Beyond*. Jossey Bass, San Francisco.

Midkiff, K. C., Litzinger, T. A., and D. L. Evans (2001). Development of engineering thermodynamics concept inventory instruments. *Proceedings Frontiers in Education Conference* 2, F2A 3.

Miles, D., Blum, T., Staats, W. J., and D. Dean (2003). Experiences with metacognitive skills inventory. *Proceedings Frontiers in Education Conference*, 1, T3B 8 to 13.

Miller, R. L., Streveler, R. A., Olds, B. M and M. A. Nelson (2004). Concept based engineering education: designing instruction to facilitate student understanding of difficult concepts in science and engineering. *Proceedings Frontiers in Education Conference*,SlA1-1 to 2.

Moreira, M. A (1985). Concept mapping an alternative strategy for evaluation. *Assessment and Evaluation in Higher Education*, 10, (2), 159–168.

Mourtos, N. J (1996). The nuts and bolts of cooperative learning in engineering. *Proceedings Frontiers in Education*, 624–627.

Mourtos, N. J. (1996). A model of learning as it applies to engineering. *Proceedings Frontiers in Education Conference*, 3, 1299–1302.

Nasr, R., Hall, S. R., and P. Garik (2003). Student misconceptions in signals and systems and their origins. *Proceedings Frontiers in Education Conference*, 1, T2E-23–T2E-28.

Nersessian, N. J (1992). How do scientists think? Capturing the dynamics of conceptual change in science. In R. N. Giere (ed.). *Cognitive Models of Science*. Minnesota Studies in the Philosophy of Science. 15, 3-44. University of Minnesota Press, Minneapolis.

Neumann, E. S (1981). Teaching management skills in a comprehensive project course. *Engineering Education*, 71, (8), 790–794.

Novak, J (1998). *Learning, Creating and Using Knowledge*. Lawrence Erlbaum Associates, Hillsdale, NJ.

Novak, J. D., Godwin, D.J., and G. Johnson (1983).The use of concept mapping in knowledge via mapping with junior high schools students. *Science Education*, 67, 625-645.

Okebukola, P. A (1992). Can good concept mappers be good problem solvers in science? *Research in Science and Technological Education*, 10, (2), 153–170.

Olsen, L. A (1963) Concept attainment of high school sophomores. *Journal of Educational Psychology*, 54, 213–216.

Parkin, A. T (1993). Memory Phenomena, Experiment and Theory. Blackwell, Oxford.

Petry, B, Mouton, H and C. M. Reigeluth (1987). A lesson based on the Gagné-Briggs theory of instruction. In C. M. Reigeluth (ed.). *Instructional Theories in Action*. Lawrence Erlbaum. Hillsdale, NJ.

Pudlowski, Z. J (1990). Transfer of knowledge in an analagous model. *International Journal of Engineering Education*, 6, (1), 23–36.

Reif, F (1990) Transcending prevailing approaches to science education. In M. Gardener (ed) *Toward a Scientific Practice of Science Education*. Lawrence Erlbaum, Hillsdale, NJ.

Reigiluth, C. M (1987). *Instructional Theories in Action. Lessons Illustrating Selected Theories and Models*. Lawrence Erlbaum, Hillsdale, NJ.

Rhoads, T. R. and R. J. Roedel (1999). The wave Concept Inventory- A cognitive instrument based on Bloom's Taxonomy. *Proceedings Frontiers in Education Conference*, 3, 13c-14 to 18.

Richardson, J., Morgan, J., and D. Evans (2001). Development of an engineering strength of material concept inventory assessment instrument. *Proceedings Frontiers in Education Conference*, 2, F2A-4.

Roedel, R. J. et al (1997). Projects that integrate engineering, physics, calculus and English in the Arizona State Foundation Coalition freshman program. *Proceedings Frontiers in Education Conference*, 38– 42.

Rothkopf, E. M (1995). Teaching for understanding- analogies for learning in electrical technology. *Proceedings Frontiers in Education,* 2b4-9–2b4-13.

Saad, A and A.-R.M. Zaghloul (2002). A knowledge visualization tool for teaching and learning computer engineering knowledge, concepts and skills. *Proceedings Frontiers in Education Conference*, 1, T2F–7 to 10.

Santi, P and M. M. Santi (2003). Using Psychptherapy techniques to reveal misconceptions and improve learning. *Proceedings Frontiers in Education Conference*, 1, T4A-1.

Schank, R. C (1982). *Dynamic Memory*. Cambridge University Press, New York.

Segall,, A. E (2002) Science fiction in the engineering classroom to help teach basic concepts and promote the profession. *Journal of Engineering Education*, 91, (4), 419–424.

Seagull, B., and G. Erdos (1990). Teaching problem-solving skills to adult developmental students. In K. J. Gilhooly, M. Keane, R. H. Logie, and G. Erdos (eds.). *Lines of Thinking: Reflections on the Psychology of Thought*. Vol 2. Wiley, Chichester.

Sharp, J. E, Harb., J.N., and R. E. Terry (1997). Combining Kolb learning styles and writing to learn in engineering classes. *Journal of Engineering Education*, 82, (2), 93-101.

Sheppard, S (1992). Mechanical disSection: an experience of how things work. Engineering Foundation Conference on Engineering Education. Curriculum Innovation. Jan 5 – 10. Santa Barbara.

Sheppard, S., Demetz, L., and J. Hayton. (1999). Engineering practice and textbook design. *Proceedings Frontiers in Education Conference*. 2,13b 7 to 11.

Skemp, R.R. (1971). *The Psychology of Learning Mathematics*. Penguin,Harmondsworth.

Sims-Knight, J., Upchurch, R. L., Pendergrass, N., Meressi, T., Fortier, P., Tchimev, P., VonderHeide, R., and M. Page (2004) Using concept maps to assess design process knowledge. *Proceedings Frontiers in Education Conference*, F1G-6 to 10.

Smoke, K. L (1933). Negative instances in concept learning. *Journal of Experimental Psychology*. 16, 583–588.

Staats, W. J., Dean, D., Blum, T., S-Y Lu (2003) Developing techniques for measuring and enhancing student's cognitive and meta-cognitive skills. *Proceedings Frontiers in Education Conference*. 1,T3B-2 to 7.

Steif, P. S (2003). Comparison between performance on a concept inventory and soving multifaceted problems. *Proceedings Frontiers in Education Conference*, 1, T3D- 17 to 22.

Steif, P (2004) An articulation of the concepts and skills which underlie engineering statics. *Proceedings Frontiers in Education Conference*, FIF-5 to 10.

Streveler, R. A., and R. L. Miller (2001). Investigating student misconceptions in the design process using multidimensional scaling. *Proceedings Annual Conference of the American Society for Engineering Education*. Paper 2630.

Stubbs, G., and M. Watkins (1996). Re-engineering CBL development. *Proceedings Frontiers in Education Conference*, 3, 1387–1390

Taba, H., and F. Freeman (1964). Teaching strategies and thought processes. *Teachers College Record*, 65, 524-534.

Tennyson, R. D., and M. J. Cocchiarella (1986). An empirically based instructional design theory for teaching concepts. *Review of Educational Research.* 56, 40-71.

Thomson, C. J (1997). Concept mapping as a means of evaluating primary school technology programs. *International Journal of Technology and Design Education*, 77, (1-2), 97–110.

Trumper, R (2000). University students' conceptions of basic astronomy concepts. *Physics Education.* 35, (1), 9- 15.

Trumper, R and P. Gorsky (1996). A Cross-college age study about physics students' conceptions of force in pre-service training for high school teachers. *Physics Education.* 31, (4), 227-236.

Tuttle, S. L (2000). An experiment for teaching hypersonic aerodynamics to undergraduate mechanical engineering students. *International Journal of Mechanical Engineering Education*, 28, (2), 151–162.

Turns, J., Atman, C and R. Adams (2000). Concept maps for engineering education: a cognitively motivated tool supporting varied assessment functions. *IEEE Transactions on Education*, 43, (2), 164–173.

Vable, M (2003). Enhancing understanding of concepts in mechanics of materials using design. *Proceedings Frontiers in Education Conference*, 3, S3B- 13 to 17.

Valentine, C. W. (1960). *Psychology and its Bearing on Education.* Methuen, London.

Volet, S. E., and C. P. Lund (1994). Metacognitive instruction in introductory computer programming. A Better explanatory construct for performance than traditional factors. *Journal of Educational Computing*, 10.(Cited by Miles et al, 2003)

Wage, K. E. and J. R. Buck (2001). Development of the Signals and Systems Concept Inventory (SSCI) assessment instrument *Proceedings Frontiers in Education Conference*. 2, F2A-2.

Wales, C. E., and R. A. Stager (1972). The design of an educational system. *Engineering Education*, 62, (5), 456–459.

Walker, J. M. T and P. H. King (2003). Concept mapping as a form of student assessment and instruction in the domain of bioengineering. *Journal of Engineering Education*, 92, (2), 167–180.

Webb, J. M (1994) The effects of feedback timing on learning facts: The role of response confidence. *Contemporary Educational Psychology.* 19, 251-256.

Wheeler, E and R. L. McDonald (1999). Writing in engineering courses. *Journal of Engineering Education.* 89, (4), 481-486.

Wheeler, E., and R. L. McDonald (1998). Using writing to enhance collaborative learning in engineering courses. *Proceedings Frontiers in Education Conference*, 1, 236–241.

Wheeler, J. J., and E. Rogers (1999). Mental models for introductory CSC concepts. *Proceedings Frontiers in Education Conference*, 3, 13A9-19 to 24.

Wong, Y. K., Chan, S. P., and S-K Cheung (1989). Application of learning theory to a computer assisted instruction package. *International Journal of Electrical Engineering Education*, 27, 237–246.

Woodson, T. T (1966). *An Introduction to Engineering Design.* McGraw Hill, New York.

Yudkin, L., and S. L. Kates (1963). Concept attainment and adolescent development. *Journal of Educational Psychology*, 54, 177–182.

Chapter 5: LEARNING STRATEGIES AND LEARNING STYLES

Summary and Introduction

The reader who approaches this topic for the first time may be confused by the usage of the terms "cognitive style" and "learning style." Snow, Corno, and Jackson (1996), under the heading "personal styles", write that "no category we have covered contains a more voluminous, complex and controversy-laced literature than that of personal styles.. They classified the kinds of constructs that have been studied under six headings. These are:

"Cognitive styles" involved in perception and thinking (e.g. field independence versus dependence, reflection versus impulsivity. "Learning styles" involved in approaches to learning and studying (e.g.. deep versus surface processing, comprehension learning versus operation learning). "Expressive styles," involved in verbal or nonverbal communication (e.g. tempo, constricted versus expansive). "Response styles" involved in self-perception and self-report (e.g., acquiescence, deception). "Defensive styles" involved in accommodating anxiety and conflict (e.g. obsessive-compulsive, hysterical), "Cognitive controls" a subset of style like but function–specific and unipolar controls on attention and behavior (e.g. constricted versus flexible control)" (p. 281).

Riding and Rayner (1998) argued that learning styles are a subset of cognitive styles, and in this they agreed with Sternberg and Grigorenko (1997), who also reviewed the literature on this concept. Sternberg and Grigorenko classified styles as cognition centered, personality centered, or activity centered. Those that are cognition centered have a relationship with ability and measures of intelligence, The MBTI personality measure that has been much used among engineering students is as its focus implies personality centered. The other instrument that has appealed to engineers, The Learning Styles Inventory (Kolb) is activity-centered.

It is a consolation to this writer that Snow, Corno and Jackson (1996) decided not to make any sharp distinction between learning styles and cognitive styles, or between styles and approaches. Nevertheless, I have made some distinctions and begin with a discussion of learning strategies.[1]

Learning strategies are devices that we use to cope with the learning environments we find ourselves in. Learning styles are dispositions we have to learning. They are preferred ways of organizing what we see and think. The Chapter begins with a discussion of strategies, and in particular deep and surface approaches to learning. It has been shown that learning environments and, in particular, the assessments used can have a harmful or less than positive effect on learning, as, for example, if they cause surface learning. For this reason the effects of an outcomes-based approach to assessment needs to be evaluated in terms of its effects on learning. From the perspective of engineering it has been shown that engineers require a variety of learning styles when they are engaged in projects. They need, for example, to be both convergent and divergent thinkers. The case for this view is presented. A brief discussion of field-independent and field-dependent styles of thinking follows. Although spatial ability is not strictly speaking a style, it is important in engineering design. Engineers need to be able to visualize, and consequently they need a highly developed spatial ability.

Therefore, since we have predispositions to learn, the style that we have may be in conflict with the style of teaching to which we are exposed, a major question is whether teaching and learning styles should be matched. Given that engineers need a variety of styles, it is incumbent on teachers to foster their development, and that suggests teachers may have to change their teaching styles. Engineers have used a number of instruments to determine the learning styles of their students. These include Kolb's Learning Styles Inventory and a summary of work that has been done to use it as a scheme for the design of instruction is given. Variations of the Kolb model are summarized in particular the 4 MAT scheme and Honey and Mumford model.

Felder and Silverman identified 32 learning styles and developed an inventory to test for these among engineering students. This is discussed. Style and personality are related and influence the way we learn in particular environments. Engineers have been particularly interested in the Myers Briggs Personality Indicator, and much is known about the personality profiles of engineering students from this test. The investigations among engineering students are summarized. Temperament evidently influences performance but to some extent as a function of the culture of the learning environment.

Other sections of the Chapter discuss cognitive styles analysis, the relationship between course structure and learning styles and learning strategies, learning styles and individualised environments. The review supports a point made by Hein and Budny (1999) that the learning style assessment tool used is not as critical as the assessment of learning styles. It illustrates the complexity of the learning process that teachers have to face when they guide the learning of a diverse group of students. Overall the reported research supports the need for variety in teaching and learning not only for the sake of learning but for preparation for work in industry. It also supports the case for multiple strategy approaches to the assessment of student learning.

5. Learning Strategies

Much attention has been paid in higher education to learning strategies although it seems that in

---

[1] It is of some interest to note that in the much cited "How People Learn" (Bransford, 2000) there is no mention of cognitive or learning styles.

engineering education more attention has been focused on learning styles. However, in relation to the learning of concepts, strategies are very important, and the strategies that students employ may be strongly influenced by the instructional method and assessment procedures used (Heywood, 2000). For this reason, new approaches to engineering education that adopt an outcomes approach need to establish the effects they have on learning, and in particular, whether they encourage deep or surface approaches to learning.

In Australia, the United Kingdom, and Scandinavia much attention has been paid to the *deep* and *surface* learning strategies identified by Marton and Säljö (Marton and Säljö, 1984, Marton, Hounsell and Entwistle, 1984, see also Entwistle, Hanley, and Ratcliffe, 1979). In the United Kingdom another type of student approach to learning was identified. It was defined as a *strategic* approach, and it described the type of student who tried to manipulate the assessment procedures to her/his own advantage by careful marrying her/his efforts to the reward system as they see it. This approach is related to extrinsic and achievement motivation. It seems to be similar to the academic orientation identified by Bey (1961) in the United States. Cassidy (1999) found that the strategic learning approach was associated with belief in one's capabilities and actual academic performance. Kneale (1997) suggested that there was a "worrying" increase in strategically motivated students in British universities. To return to the initial concept of deep and surface learning, Marton suggested that the strategies that are adopted are indicative of the different perceptions of what students believe is wanted from them by their teachers in order to measure their performance. That is, what knowledge, and the view they take of how this knowledge is to be used in the assessments devised (Wilson, 1981). It means not only that the ways in which students perceive instructions is important, but that what the student brings to learning is equally important. Marton found that *"for some* (students) *learning is through discourse and for others learning is discourse"*. Those who adopt the former strategy get involved in the activity while those who take the latter view allow learning *to happen to them*. It is this second group who are *surface* learners, who pay only superficial attention to the text, who are passive, who do not reflect, and who do not appreciate that understanding involves effort.

What this appears to be is the traditional distinction between active and passive learning that is understood by many academics when they talk about study in depth. What they do not seem to understand, and this applies in engineering in spite of literature stretching back over 40 years, is that the way they teach can cause learners to be active or passive. Therefore, the teaching and assessment strategies used can influence the orientation that students take to *deep* and *surface* learning. Clearly, if students are to overcome the misconceptions they have about concepts, then a *deep* learning approach will have to be encouraged. In this situation a traditional lecture approach, however good the

lecturer, may not be adequate (see Chapter 13). Often traditional approaches encourage the coverage of too much material in the time allowed and cause surface learning.

In engineering, Yokomoto (2000) conducted a preliminary experiment to see how his students could be encouraged to improve their problem-solving abilities and at the same time help their deep learning potential. He changed the traditional format of the 10-point quiz problem by adding a preliminary exercise. In arguing the case for this change, he noted that the traditional quiz can tell who can do the problem and who cannot, but it does not give any information about what is in the knowledge base of each student. Therefore, the preliminary question should be concerned with determining what that knowledge base is. He considered that the preliminary question should require a brainstorming quiz, as for example:

"Write, using words, equations, circuits, and graphs, all that you know about the self-bias method of biasing an n-channel JFET. Time limit four minutes. Maximum score four points."

Since the competencies which will be demonstrated in the second part of the quiz are quite different from those required for the first, a different style of question is required. His example followed the preliminary question as follows: *"Compute the gate-to-source voltage self bias circuit using a 2N3823 n-channel JFET with a 2kohm resistor in the source branch. Time limit: 6 minutes. Maximum score 6 points."*
The first question's score was based on the number of valid items written by the student, and the second question was marked traditionally. He expected that there would be a strong correlation between the scores for the two parts because he believed that students would not be able to solve the problem without a rich knowledge base. His initial data did not show this to be true except in the case of particular quizzes. The correlation obtained was 0.21. The range of correlations for the particular quizzes (0.07 to 0.53) suggested that part of the problem might lie in the design of the question. Heywood (2000) has pointed out that the ability to design good questions is seriously under rated. The findings as summarized by Yokomoto were:

- *30% of the students were above the mean on both components of the quiz.*
- *30% of the students were below the mean on both components of the quiz.*
- *20% of the students were above the mean on the knowledge base component but below the mean on the problem-solving component.*
- *20% of the students were below the mean on the knowledge base component but above the mean on the problem-solving component.*

Yokomoto (2000) also found that the correlation between the knowledge component and the students' examinations was 0.41. But this increased to 0.68 with the second question. This was statistically significant, whereas the former was not. The correlation between the exam averages and the composite score of the experimental test was 0.72, which was also significant. He agreed that the sample was too small and that the study must be repeated with larger numbers. Nevertheless, it did show the importance of question design, and it may have demonstrated the need for a different kind of knowledge test. Because students might not be able to express their knowledge base very well, such a test might be based on the concept maps described by Turns et al, (2000). In a previous study, Rosati and Yokomoto, (1993), had found that first–year students wanted to acquire the basics, whereas fourth–year students had wanted to learn problem-solving techniques. This, Yokomoto suggested, might explain why these students were able to solve problems without too much attention to the knowledge base. He had little to say about deep learning, but it would have been of considerable interest if he had had data from an inventory that assessed deep and surface learning.

Teachers will want to know if the inventories that have been developed to indicate study orientations will be of value to them. Entwistle and Ramsden (1983) developed the *Approaches to Study Inventory* that yielded four factors. The first factor was called *meaning orientation*. It had high loadings on the deep approach, and it was associated with comprehension learning and intrinsic motivation. By contrast the second factor, called the *reproducing orientation*, was highly loaded on the surface approach, operation learning, and improvidence. These were associated with fear and extrinsic motivation. This point was illustrated by Kember et al (1995), who, using the Biggs Study Process Questionnaire, found that surface approaches correlated with high attendance in class and long hours of study time. The former was accounted for by a need to have the lecturers explain the course,: the latter by the inefficiency of the surface approach that led to poor grades. The other factors in the Entwistle and Ramsden study related to *non-academic orientation* and *achieving orientation*.

A major problem for teachers is the extent to which these orientations are more or less permanent dispositions of the students or not. If they are permanent, then how does a teacher cope with these different types of orientations in the same group? If not, then, what are the implications for teaching and examining (assessment of learning), and the design of instruction for intellectual growth, if a deep approach is required?

Ramsden (1988) considered that the evidence for student consistency in approach over time is persuasive. However, he argued that consistency is not the same as "fixity of" and that orientations to study may be changed in response to teaching, assessment, and curriculum. University departments can, therefore, have a profound effect on the way students learn. Ramsden subsequently developed a (Course Experience Questionnaire) (CEQ) as part of a study on performance indicators for the Australian Vice-Chancellors Committee. Some doubts about the CEQ's use as a performance indicator were expressed by Mangin at a conference of Australian engineers. He felt that some of the scales (e.g., workload/difficulty) might unfairly penalize some courses. While he thought some good could come from the questionnaire, if used as a performance indicator, he thought that it may not get at the actual quality of the experience received. Subsequently the CEQ contained some extremely interesting comparative data (e.g., Wilson, Lizzio, and Ramsden, 1997).[2]

The next question is whether or not it is of value to use inventories that reveal the study habits and orientations of students (e.g., Richardson, 1994; 1995; Tait and Entwistle, 1996). Richards (2001) of The University of Virginia reported that the Estes–Richards Inventory of Study Habits, while it had proven to be a reliable tool, had results that were not strongly related to academic performance. The Australian and British experience is that such inventories may be helpful in identifying students at risk, provided that they are used with care (Richardson, 1994). They can show teachers what to expect of a particular class group, and they can help teachers explain what it is they expect deep learning to be.

Landis (1995), in a student guide for studying engineering, presented a number of strategies for academic success, including a simple skills inventory. In 1997 he described a procedure for comparing your students with those of successful students.[3] August et al. (2002) described a study survey inventory that they used at North Eastern University among computer science and mechanical engineering students. The 14 items were grouped as follows, reading the textbook and the published notes (4 items); solving homework problems (5 items); and problem solving exams (5 items). Each item had four options. Two instructors selected the option they thought represented best practice. A complete analysis was not given, but of the items in each group, only about 50% of the students reported behaviors that were consistent with best practice. *"We found that 25% of the respondents do not read the textbook or printed class notes at all. 44% do not have homework done in time for class when the homework is not collected. 22% take exams without having solved all the homework problems. 71% would rather have speed exams than thinking exams, and a little more than half of the students do not try to solve extra problems."* Unfortunately this information is not correlated with examination performance. Interpretation of such data also needs to take into account the culture in which the data was obtained. The authors argued that students could be coached in best practice, but that such coaching had to be geared to the needs of the particular student, for which reason they suggested that it is useful to know the

---

[2] For a recent discussion of this and British equivalent questionnaires see Heywood (2000).

[3] Cited by August et al (2002). Landis R. B. (1997). Enhancing engineering student success. A pedagogy for changing behaviors. ASEE Annual Conference, Milwaukee, WI, United Kingdomee, WI. They also cited Mack, G. E., et al. (2000). Fast track to achievement. Promoting achievement behaviors in engineering education. ASEE Annual Conference, St. Louis. Mo.

learning styles of the students. Landis (1995) also takes this position but suggests that students should find out their own learning styles for themselves because this will help them with their studies.

More generally, Pask and Scott (1972) argued that they are made aware of their (the students) learning strategies, and then provided with the materials designed to help them use that strategy. Pask and Scott were writing about the holist/serialist strategies that they had discovered, but their reasoning is generally applicable to other styles.[4]

The question also arises as to whether there is a relation between personality and approaches to study. Abouserie (1995) thought her results suggested that the personality in general, and self-esteem in particular, influence study dispositions. She had used a shortened version of Entwistle's inventory with an American Inventory [*Inventory of Learning Processes*, (Schmeck, 1993)], scales for Self–Esteem and achievement motivation.

Engineers, particularly in the United States have found the more general MBTI measure of personality to be of interest especially because it purports to measure learning styles (see below).

Finally, no mention has been made of the conceptions that students have of learning and the way that those conceptions influence their approaches to learning. Nor has any mention been made of the possibility that culture may influence these conceptions. In a phenomenographic study Marshall, Summers, and Woolnogh (1999) described an investigation with a small number of students in a foundation course at a British University. Their purpose was to investigate the conceptions of learning these students had.[5] Five conceptions of learning were identified among the group. They were:

1. Learning as memorizing definitions, equations and procedures.
2. Learning as applying equations and procedures.
3. Learning as making sense of physical concepts and procedures.
4. Learning as seeing phenomena in the world in a new way.
5. Learning as change of person.

The investigators pointed out that conceptions 1 and 2 have similarities with earlier hierarchies (Marton et al. 1993) from which the study was developed. These were learning as memorizing and reproducing, and learning as applying. The first conception in the earlier study was learning and increasing one's knowledge. The

fourth, fifth, and sixth conceptions were, learning as understanding, learning as seeing something in a different way, and learning as changing a person. These seem to correspond to 3, 4, and 5 in this study. Marshall et al. argued that in spite of the similarities, there are some fine-structure variations that could only be revealed by a phenomenographic study. It was found that the ways the outcomes of learning were judged by those students who held conceptions 1 and 2 was different to those who held conceptions 3 and 4. In 1 and 2 *"the learning outcome is judged in terms of external factors such as getting the right answer to set problems"*. In 3 and 4, *"learning is experienced in terms of awareness, and the outcome of learning is evaluated in terms of inner sense of coherence or integration."*

The authors also noted that there is a skill dimension to learning in the higher-order conceptions. It should be noted that only two students experienced the fourth type of learning, and both were mature students. The same was true of conception 5. The authors drew attention to differences in findings of this study and earlier investigations. They did not find this to be surprising since the context in which learning takes place can alter the conceptions that students have of learning, and they cited examples of epistemological differences between subjects (i.e., as between social science students, and science and engineering students) in support of their case. Their results have implications for the design of the curriculum if higher level conceptions of learning are to be encouraged. The dimensions associated with the transformation of learning required are *"students' reflection on their own learning, the 'skill' of transferring their knowledge and analytical approaches to situations beyond the learning context to phenomena in the world; and informal peer discussion."* This is a picture that has striking similarities with the findings of studies that looked at the relative capabilities of novices and experts that was described in Chapter 4.

These studies serve to underline the complexity of the learning process that teachers face when they have to guide learning among a diverse group of students. How then do they relate to learning styles?[6]

5.1. Learning Styles

We all have preferred ways of organizing what we see and think about or different styles of conceptualization and patterning activities (Messick and Associates, 1976), and these may be the most important characteristics of an individual with respect of learning (Tyler, 1978). Although numerous learning styles have been proposed (Grasha, 1984), only a few can be considered here. They have been selected because engineering educators have shown an interest in them, since it seems that an understanding of learning styles by teachers and students can enhance learning.

Indeed, at the 1999; Frontiers in Education Conference, a roundtable discussion on improving the

---

[4] *"Holists prefer global predicates and relations of topics. Serialists prefer not to use such relations and learn step-by-step. The holist learner is irredundant, eschewing redundant data (often known as enrichment data0 and apt to use such data. The redundant holist learns lessx rapidly but has faster although less accurate recall of tutorial material. The irredundant holist is more selective about teaching material"* (Pask, 1988). For a discussion of the application of this theory in engineering see Daniel (1975).

[5] Other details of the study that was more extensive than that reported in their paper are being published elsewhere.

[6] For another study using multiple measures see Booth and James (2001) in Chapter 15 on evaluation.

classroom environment considered that teaching for learning styles in engineering classes was of paramount importance, and that teachers should learn about their own learning styles (Klinger, Finelli, and Budny, 1999, or Finelli, Klinger and Budny, 2001). Felder and his colleagues have made important contributions to both theory and practice in the application of learning styles within the engineering curriculum. (e.g., Felder and Silverman, 1988: Felder, 1993), and their work has been taken up by others (e.g., Carrizosa and Sheppard, 2000).

Based on the view that no one theory embraces everything, Grasha took an eclectic view and considered that all theories should be examined for their potential in teaching, and this is the approach taken here. Among them he thought that Bandura's (1971) information processing approach to imitation learning, Kanfer's (1977) conceptions of self-control and self-regulation, and Janis (1982) and Mann's (1977) approaches to decision making and problem solving were of interest. His three articles provided a good introduction to the issues. In the first Grasha considered the problems of designing instruments to assess learning styles. The second is a critique of pencil and paper learning style tests, and a consideration of other ways of extracting data, such as interviews, although he did not mention protocols *per se* (Grasha, 1990). In the third article he considered teaching styles, although he did not consider in any detail the issue of matching teaching styles to learning styles (Grasha, 1994). Should they or should they not be matched? It seems to this writer that teachers who try to answer this question through experiments with their students are likely to gain considerable insight into the teaching-learning process because it affects them irrespective of the psychometric properties of the instrument.

In answer to the question- *"What learning style characteristics are most likely to prove useful for educators designing instructional processes?"* Grasha listed the following typology of characteristics of learning–style instruments that might be useful. He thought learning–style inventories should be able to:

- *Demonstrate internal consistency and test-retest reliability.*
- *Exhibit construct and predictive validity.*
- *Produce data that can be translated into instructional practices.*
- *Produce high degrees of satisfaction among learners placed in environments designed on the basis of the information it provided*
- *Help facilitate the learners' ability to acquire content and to demonstrate their ability to use content and*
- *Perform its magic in ways that are clearly superior to those possible without it.*

He did not know whether any of the existing instruments met these criteria. It is clear, however, that many engineering educators have been enthused about the Kolb theory and instrument as well as the MBTI instrument and Dunn and Dunn's approach (e.g. Dunn, Dunn and Perrin, 1994)[7]. Hein and Budny argued that *"the learning style assessment tool used is not as critical as the actual assessment of learning styles"*.

At the same time there are other theories and instruments that curriculum leaders should consider.

5.2. Convergent and Divergent Styles

Probably the best-known cognitive styles are those described on the continuum of convergent-divergent thinking. Divergent thinkers are commonly described as creative. These descriptions originated with Guilford's (1954) study of the intellect. The Guilford model assumed that creativity and intelligence are different things and that creativity is as important as intelligence. Convergent thinkers tend to concentrate on test questions that require a single answer, whereas divergent thinkers do not like the confines of conventional tests; they are more at home when generating many solutions. It is said that they perform well in activities like brainstorming. Divergence is associated with creativity, which for some teachers is contentious.

Hudson (1966), used tests for convergent and divergent thinking in the United Kingdom, and found that those who were studied arts (humanities) subjects were much more creative than those who studied science. One of the problems with the tests used by Hudson was that they were of the pencil and paper variety, and it was argued that scientific creativity was difficult to measure with such tests. (See Chapter 11 for a detailed discussion of creativity.) (Hudson's report led to a furor at the 'political level' because lack of divergence among scientists might have been a contributory factor to Britain's poor performance. It caused an investigation into the problem by the Council of Engineering Institutions (Gregory, 1972)).

Guilford considered that effective thinking resulted from the sequential use of convergent and divergent process a point that was illustrated for engineering by Whitfield (1975) (see Figure 5.1). Freeman, McComiskey and Buttle (1968) found that balance between convergence and divergence was an important predictor of academic performance among students of electrical engineering in the United Kingdom. In general, it is held that there has to be a balance between convergent and divergent thinking. This point is reinforced by a study at the University of Salford that also showed a clear relationship between performance on a test of engineering ability and aptitude and convergence and divergence. As Figure 5.2 showed, the best predictor of performance was not the level of the test score but the balance between convergence and divergence. The figure shows that there is a marked tendency for the best

---

[7]The Dunn and Dunn model was described by Hein and Budny (1999), and in their paper they also included a description of the Productivity Environmental Preference Survey (PEPS), which is a derivative of the Dunn and Dunn model. In (1998) Ingham, Meza, and Price (1998) reported a comparison of Mexican and American undergraduate students that used PEPS and the Tel-Aviv Activities and Accomplishments Survey to measure creativity.

performers to record central scores on both coordinates. The poorer students tended to perform high on one coordinate and low on the other [Carter and Jordan (1986) citing Freeman, Carter, and Jordan, (1979)].

Hartley and Greggs (1997) and Hartley (1998) divided students into four subject categories. These categories were those taking arts, arts and social sciences, social sciences, and the sciences. The students completed four tests with the purpose of replicating Hudson's study with university students. Taken as a continuum, they found only weak support for the view that divergent capability would decline in the direction of science. However, when the four categories were collapsed into two, there was a significant difference between those studying the arts and those studying science.

5.3. Field Dependence and Field Independence

Many factors come together to influence our perception. Thus, cognitive or learning style may also be described as a particular mode of perception that an individual brings to the understanding of his or her world. In the United States, Witkin (1976, Witkin and Goodenough, 1981) suggested that individual dispositions toward the perception of their environment lie on a continuum, the polar ends of which he called field-dependent and field-independent. Those who are field-dependent look at the world in a global way, while those who are field-independent see it analytically. The reaction of the field-dependent person to people, places and events is undifferentiated and complex. In contrast the events (objects) in the environment are not associated with the background of that environment by a person who is field-independent.[8] Macfarlane Smith (1964) suggested that the distinction between field-dependent and field-independent persons is similar to the distinction that has been found between individuals having high verbal and high spatial abilities, respectively.

The *Embedded Figures Test* (GEFT) that was developed to test for these dimensions is the only inventory for learning styles that does not depend on verbal statements.[9] The field-dependence-independence-dimension has been slightly related to verbal ability but unrelated to overall academic achievement (Witkin et al 1971). Several investigators have claimed that an individual's location on the continuum between the two poles contributes to academic choice, success and vocational preference (Witkin, 1976). Field-dependent persons require their learning to have more structure, direction and feedback than field-independent ones who tend for instance, to dislike collaborative learning. This would explain the everyday experience of teachers who find that some students who do not like group work are nevertheless good at analytical academic work. It means that in any event, programs should be designed with a variety of learning styles in order to cater for the students of different dispositions likely to be found in particular courses. Tyler (1978) has pointed out that the same may apply to teachers in higher education, and this would account for the preference that some teachers have for lectures and others for group discussion. This suggests that teachers should be aware of their learning styles.

At the University of Knoxville, Tennessee, the College of Engineering had developed a new integrated freshman program that improved the second year retention rate by 15% (Weber et al. 2000). It was designed in a variety of formats to address different learning styles. It was found that there was a group of students who, while performing well in the team project and computer tools component, performed badly in math and science. This was evident from low math scores in the ACT. A "Success Performance Indicator" (SPI) had been in use since 1994. This multiplied the high school GPA (on a four-point scale) by ten and added the math ACT score. It was found that students with scores of below 50 had a less than 1% chance of survival. In order to try and understand the difficulties that some students have with engineering problem solving, the Group Embedded Figures Test was used to explore the relationship between (a) the ability to disembed and (b) satisfactory performance in the mathematics and science component of the program (Clark, Seat, and Weber, 2000). The relationship between the entering students SPI and GEFT was also examined. The reason for choosing the test was that as indicated a field-independent person is likely to be a superior problem solver to a field-dependent person. Field-independent persons can 'pull-out' specific data from a given background.

Because the norms for the GEFT were obtained from liberal arts students, 53 liberal arts students were included in the test,. 157 second-semester freshmen engineering students were tested. All were volunteers.[10] It was found that all the hypotheses were supported by the data. Those who scored higher in the math and science component of the program also scored significantly higher on the GEFT. Similarly, there was a significant relationship between the text and the SPI score. The engineering students significantly identified more items than the liberal arts students.

---

[8] Field-independence is also known as psychological differentiation. *"In perception, when a stimulus array changes from perceived homogeneity so that the various aspects of the array become distinguished. Here one speaks of learning to differentiate between stimulus conditions"* (Reber, 1995). Hakstian and Cattell, quoted by Kline (2000), found a primary ability, called flexibility of closure which involves disregarding irrelevant stimuli in a field to find stimulus figures. The *Embedded Figures Test* loads on flexibility of closure. It is also related to the personality factor of independence.

[9] Pearson (1991) proposed that the GEFT could be improved if a geometrical progression from one type of complex figure to another was made. In the GEFT, geometrically complex and corresponding simple figures that can be located within complex figures are the basis of the test. In the test the complex and relevant simple figure are printed alongside of each other. The testee has to locate the two and pencil the simple figure in the complex figure. Pearson also proposed that field dependence/independence could be measured in a verbal way and he developed tests for this purpose.

---

[10] The paper described the procedure and ethics for obtaining the sample, along with the administrative procedures. Of the engineers 25% were female and 75% male. 87% were Caucasian; 8% African-American; 2.5% Asian, and 1.5% Hispanic. No comment is made on the differences between these groups.

Although there was significant positive correlation between the GEFT and student grades, it was only moderate. There is, it seems, some factor that prevents a high correlation. The authors suggested that this might be due to low motivation to succeed in the program. Some students who have the skills may not have the necessary drive to persist, and low-scoring students may no longer want to become engineers. They suggested that some inventory like the Strong Interest Inventory might also be used.[11] This study pointed to the need for a battery of instruments if the underlying processes of student learning are to be understood. Collinge (1994), in a study of scientific thinking, argued that the field-dependent-independent dimension would indicate who was and who was not capable of isolating significant variables. Subjects who were field-dependent would be unable to do such tasks. Of the two possibilities open to Collinge to counter this difficulty-which were (a) training in the perceptual dimension of field independence and (b) cognitive restructuring-he chose the latter because perceptual training had not been found to be successful. He argued and demonstrated that cognitive restructuring was a prerequisite to being able to perceive and manipulate variables in science. Field-independence helps to develop skills in *'careful comparison, reorganising and restructuring information, isolation of the particular form of the general, and disembedding of confounding and overlapping information.'*

Seventeen activities designed to promote cognitive restructuring were developed and administered to an experimental group. The Group Embedded Figures test was used with a science reasoning task, and significant increase in field independence and science skills were recorded. Field-Independence was found to be a factor in the application of formal operations, and cognitive restructuring was found to increase skill. Collinge concluded that *"Any activity that develops this type of careful observation is developing scientific thinking."*[12]

One study has gone so far as to suggest that the Embedded Figures Test measures cognitive ability rather than cognitive style (Highouse and Doverspike, 1987). Related to the field-independent dimension is the capacity to perceive spatial relations.

5.4. Visualization and Spatial Ability

MacFarlane Smith (1964) was the first to alert engineers in Britain to the importance of spatial ability. In a controversial thesis, he argued that the shortage of qualified engineers and scientists in Britain was due to the fact that the grammar schools (11–18 years) of the time did not emphasize teaching in subjects which would help develop the spatial and mechanical abilities essential for performance in technology. These would be subjects like woodwork, metalwork and technical drawing.[13] He also argued that mathematical ability was different from numerical ability. It depended on spatial ability. A variety of test data were adduced to support this argument, and he was one of the first persons to use the biographical data of distinguished scientists and mathematicians to support his case. The relevance of spatial ability and visualization to design should be self-evident. Indeed the changes that have been wrought in the graphics curriculum has ensured a continuing flow of articles on how to encourage visualization (e.g., Beaumont and Jackson, 1997; Edgerton and Upton, 1989; Myers, 1958, Newcomer et al. 1999; Wiley, 1991). But visualization and spatial ability are different things. Clearly, possession of the latter should facilitate the latter. (See p. 188 for further discussion of this point.) It also needs to be understood that there are different kinds of spatial reasoning capabilities.

With the aid of data on brain operations from the United States, MacFarlane Smith assumed that verbal/numerical abilities (which were associated with analogical reasoning) depended on the left hemisphere and that the capacity for relational thinking depended on the right. Here we have the origins of what has recently been called brain based learning in schools. The argument being that the curriculum has to cater to the whole brain (Caine and Caine, 1991; Jensen, 1998)

It is now known that hemispheric asymmetry is somewhat more complicated than this, and as yet no comprehensive model is available (Hellige, 1993; Jensen, 1998). At the same time Hellige argued from the data that hemispheric asymmetries do exist and influence behavior. Moreover, in the rather simplistic terms of an educator, there is no reason not to take the view that the curriculum encourages some mechanisms of the brain and under utilizes others.

It is now understood that the right hemisphere is dominant for processing global aspects of visual stimuli and the left hemisphere is dominant for processing local detail (Hellige, 1993). Visual–spatial processing is important for work in several professions including engineering, medicine, and science. Thus, tests of spatial ability are likely to be of use to tutors who have to select and deal with freshmen students. For example, Rochford (1989) reported a study at the University of Capetown which found that one of the reasons for underachievement in freshman courses in engineering drawing, astronomy, and chemistry was that the students were handicapped by lack of skill in three-dimensional learning. Over a four-year period it was found that one-sixth of students entering engineering had spatial

---

[11] The *Strong Vocational Interest Blank* was first developed in 1927. It has been regularly revised ever since. It measures 57 female and 67 male occupational groups. It contains six general occupational scales that were derived from the work of Holland. These are realistic, investigative, artistic, social, enterprising and conventional. There are 23 basic interest scales. It is based on American groups. Kline (2000) is of the opinion that the scales lack psychological meaning although he agrees that it might be used as a basis for discussion in vocational guidance or counselling. His view is that Holland's *Vocational Preference Inventory* is probably the best interest test available.

[12] The study was conducted with schoolchildren in the United Kingdom

---

[13] Engineering educators almost without exception did not accept 'A' levels in these subjects as qualifying for entry to a university course. The exception was the University of Leicester.

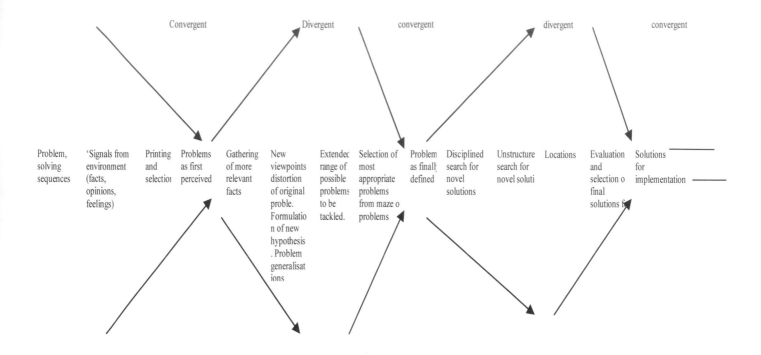

Figure 5.1. Part of Whitfield's (1975) illustration of the innovative (problem-solving) process (abbreviated). In the original diagram the phases were paralleled with sections for desirable personality characteristics, supporting techniques, and personal development methods.

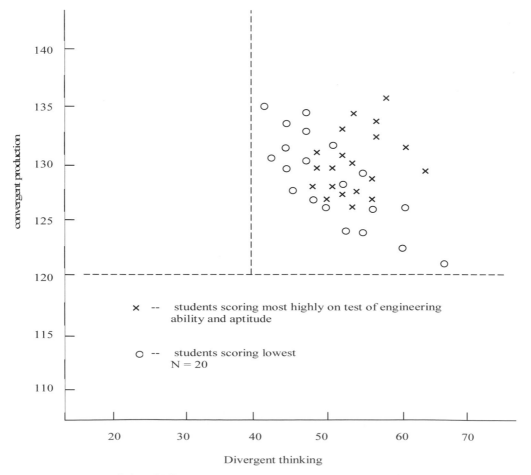

Figure 5.2. Reproduced with permission of J. Freeman from Freeman , Carter ,and Jordan (1986).

deficiencies that were associated with significant underachievement. For example, in chemistry, students.perceived depth and distance differently in photographs and equivalent line diagrams of molecular structures From the perspective of examinations it was concluded that: *"some students may be partially or temporarily disadvantaged by visual presentation in textbooks, or examination papers, of pictures of molecules either in photographic form alone or through the medium line drawings alone."* This finding has implications for the design of computer-assisted learning as Freeman and Thomas (2001 see below) have shown for biology. Rochford argued that because spatial skills could be acquired within an appropriately designed course, such tests should not be used for selection on their own. He reported experiments in training in geometric spatial programs that had improved scores in organic chemistry in support of this view (Lord, 1985).

Agogino and His (1995) of Berkeley found that the spatial skills and experiences of incoming engineering students were varied. There was also an indication of gender differences. Moreover, one of the causes of drop out was teaching to a single learning style. Exercises were devised in the synthesis coalition to determine the spatial capabilities of students in an introductory engineering course (N = 500). It was found that males had more experience of orthographic drawing and had better problem solving capability than females. Women also found it more difficult to generate isometric views. The effect of a spatial reasoning intervention was to remove gender differences, and in keeping with other research, women did better on traditional test items when they had more experience.

Peters, Chisholm, and Laeng (1995) of the University of Guelph cautioned against sweeping generalizations about females with respect to spatial ability. They administered the *Mental Rotation Test* (MRT) and the *Paper Folding Test* (PFT) to a group of 51 male and 52 female, first-year engineering students. The tests were repeated after an interval of three months. No significant differences between the two groups were found on the PFT instrument, but sex differences accounted for 17% of the variance in the MRT. They did not consider the differences to be robust and they were unable to say whether they were due to the difficulty of the test or whether it was due to the particular characteristics of the test. In a second investigation, they improved the experimental design. Two forms of the MRT were given and the PFT was not used. When the repeat test was given with the second form of the MRT, a large practice effect was shown. There were no sex differences among the group that had seen MRT before. With the group that had not seen the MRT before, there were significant differences, but the group performed at the same level as the students who had seen the test before when they first did that test. In as far academic performance was concerned, there were no significant differences in grades as between the sexes. Because, on the whole, these engineering students performed the mental rotation task better than BA students, Peters,

Chisholm, and Laeng thought this was evidence of self-selection by females into engineering. These findings were for very small samples, but they do support the view that specific attention should be paid to spatial development in engineering courses irrespective of gender.

In this respect, Agogino and His (1995) believed that specific attention should be given to spatial reasoning in engineering problem solving. For example, a course in scientific and technical visualization was developed for pre-engineering students in scientific visualization by a small consortium centered on North Carolina State University (Clark and Wiebe, 1999).

A major evaluation of the effects of a course for enhancing the spatial visualization skills of first year engineering students was reported by Sorby and Baartmans (2000). They pre and post tested this course with several tests of spatial qualities. They found that as a result of each course, (six were evaluated), there were significant gains that were independent of practice effects. Unfortunately they did note separate the sexes in their statistical summary. However, they did analyze the outcomes in terms of transcripts, performance in engineering graphics, retention rates, and choice of major. The results of those in the experimental group were compared with those who had initially failed The *Purdue Spatial Visualization Test*: Rotations, and did not take the visualization course. The evidence showed that of those who subsequently took a graphics course, those who had been in the experimental group did better that those in the control group. Eighty percent of the students who struggled with graphics did not continue in engineering. It was also found that the retention rate among women was higher in the experimental group.

Budny (1993), in what must be a seminal description of a level 1 classroom research showed the importance of visualization in learning calculus. This was demonstrated by the improved performance of his classes using a plotting calculator, and this result serves to reinforce MacFarlane Smith's point that mathematical understanding requires spatial and visual skills.

Hsi, Lin, and Bell (1997) studied engineers who used spatial reasoning in industry. Having identified the strategies used by engineers at work, they designed a specific program of instruction that was integrated into an engineering graphics course that had a high failure rate. New strategies enabled students to make significant progress in spatial reasoning. Spatial reasoning, as might be expected, was a significant predictor of course grade. The intervention also reduced gender differences, but at an insignificant level by the time of the post-tests.

There is considerable evidence that students in the biological sciences have difficulty in perceiving the 3D structure of a molecular configuration. This is evident in high schools when relatively advanced-level students are required to visualize how the diagrams should change to represent the effects of a rotating structure (Shubbar, 1990). Not surprisingly it is found that third-level students had similar difficulties (Freeman and Thomas, 2001). Clearly, computer associated-training may help the development of this type of capability. For example, Crown (2001) demonstrated how JavaScript Web, based games could improve the visualization skills of engineering graphics students. Crown reported that using these games the students learned and applied new concepts simultaneously. He also reported improved performance in examinations.

Freeman and Thomas warned, that in as far as problem solving in biology was concerned, that the student must use divergent thinking and heuristic approaches as well as convergent thinking dictated by algorithmic processes. If a program demands too much convergent thinking, then it may inhibit the development of strategies required for 3D literacy. This has implications for the method of assessment used in computer modeling courses. Similarly, those who advocate teaching solely by algorithms or heuristics would need to take this finding into account.

Richards (1995) pointed out that developments in computing have enabled the elimination of traditional engineering graphics courses. The basic ideas of visualization can be presented in CAD. While he did not give a formal evaluation he reported that his students were excited by their work with interactive solid modeling. Perhaps engineering students have better capability for 3D rotations than other students. Similarly, Waks and Verner (1997) claimed that spatial vision development might be aided through the manipulation of robot movements. In a similar vein Ross (1989) pointed out that engineering graphics concentrated on psychomotor skills rather than visual perception, and that interactive solid modeling should remove the barrier between 2D and 3D geometry.

There is a danger that designers of computer graphics courses become sanguine about their potential. Freeman and Thomas's investigation is clearly a warning against the assumption that learning in 3D is easy. If it is objected that their work was with biologists and that engineers have different aptitudes, then Pudlowski's studies in Sydney showed that this caution applies equally to engineering students (Pudlowski, 1988). He showed that the design of programs together with the design of equipment could enhance or impede the quality of perception of the exposed picture. He cited Kosslyn (1983) in support of this view. The process of reading advanced drawings; as for example, an electronic integrated circuit in process-and problems of presentation on a computer screen are no different from those on the page of a book. As indicated in Chapter 4 on concept learning, much more research is required in this area.

Graphics can be helpful aids in learning problem solving, and flow charts or pseudo-code are used to help students learn algorithms. Studies of how students comprehend algorithms had produced ambiguous results until Scanlan (1988) undertook a large- scale study to try and resolve the problem. The learners in 36 data structure classes at three universities were exposed to algorithms equally in flow charts and pseudo-code. Questionnaires were completed toward the end of the course. Nine questions tested the hypotheses, and four asked for gender, age, experience of computer programming, and reasons for preference. The theoretical position from which the hypotheses were drawn was that algorithmic techniques like pseudo-code and programming languages tap the left hemisphere whereas flow charts that contain considerable spatial information also have sequential, verbal, and logical stimuli that tap the right hemisphere. It was found that the students showed a strong preference for flow charts, from which it may be deduced that learning algorithms is easier when both hemispheres are involved. Another factor analytic study by Scanlan had revealed that the preference for flow charts was associated with ability to use spatial information.

Among the other findings were (1) The older the person, the greater the preference for flow charts. (2) The higher the student's GPA in computer science courses the more the student prefers flow charts for comprehending algorithms, and (3) Females tend to prefer flow charts more than males. Clearly the solution of many types of engineering problem requires equal facility with both hemispheres.

A number of problems have been posed in the literature but have not been investigated. For example, Yingli et al. (1998) described visualization and interactive experimental methods for teaching Chinese students about some electromagnetic problems in electrical engineering. This arose from their view that Chinese students, while being good at analytic thought, were not capable of intuitive thinking. For this reason they believed that it was necessary to get away from the traditional ways of teaching. They cited the example of the production of the rotating magnetic motive force in three-phase AC windings of electrical machines. Because the traditional method took so long (4 hours), it was difficult for the students to grasp the concept as a whole. Therefore, they produced simple models together with a program that enabled the students to simulate what was happening. Unfortunately, their evaluation was extremely limited, although they reported that the time taken for understanding to occur was reduced by 40%. Clearly, this is an area for major research.

Related to this problem is the substitution of real models for models on a screen using CAL. Edward (1997) evaluated two modes of computer presentation. One was of a turbine that was presented in realistic form, and the other was the schematic of a pump. Although they are not strictly comparable, he reported the results of a cluster analysis of the reported perceptions of the group of students who responded to these modes of instruction. He found that they divided into two groups. The first group strongly preferred the pump for ease of use, control, and clarity of readings. The second group took a neutral stance on these factors. The first group only slightly preferred visual appeal and practical application of the turbine. They rated both packages just below the midpoint. The second group learned little from the pump but a lot from the turbine. The schematic was favored for ease of operation, whereas visual appeal and practical appreciation of realistic presentation outweighed all other factors. Some students found its' more elaborate display confusing. Students, on the whole, learned more from this approach. These findings suggested that realism is more suited to one type of student than another. Clearly they are related to learning styles. Once again, it is important to undertake further investigations of this kind.

MacFarlane Smith (1964) drew attention to the need to distinguish between spatial ability and visual imagery. Sometimes the terms are used interchangeably. He quoted Myers (1958) as follows: *It does seem fairly clear that "'visualization' test items are usually more complicated and difficult than 'space' test items and there is some indication that they are likely to be more valid for predicting success in such criteria as grades in engineering drawing course".* Herrera (1998) reported that it was expected that the use of CAD systems would greatly reduce the time taken to teach a basic course in engineering drawing. In the initial run it was found that fewer students passed than in the traditional course, and that the time reduction was smaller than anticipated. They were making alterations to the course that would further reduce the time to develop visualization skills required to solve problems involving 3D objects. Herrera, himself, posed the key research question which is: *"How much and to what depth should CAD systems be taught, so that students' attention stays focused on training their minds to improve their visualization skills, and on applying graphical solutions to engineering problems?"* Unfortunately, this is only a summary of a very detailed study that left a number of questions unanswered.

Clearly engineering design graphics will have a considerable impact on future approaches to design. Barr and Juricic (1994), who believe that design is a learned behavior, envisaged that in the future the designer will create a single model for design representation that will span all aspects of design, analysis, production and maintenance.[14] They argued that in the ideation phase of a design freehand sketches are important, and students should be given the opportunity to do creative sketching. They found support for their argument in McKim's (1980) model of visualization. Support for the view that freehand drawing helps visualization is also to be found in a report of a course by Newcomer et al. (1999). They quoted two student responses to their course as follows: *"without visualizing the product in 3D you can't draw it and without drawing no one will understand your idea or concept....I struggled with computer graphics in high school and junior high. Those hand drawings really helped me bridge the art with graphics. I feel that I gained from every exercise."* It raises the question as to whether technology programs in schools should support creative sketching.

The answer to this question is complex. For example, it would seem that the introduction of courses that utilize virtual and distributed virtual reality may not facilitate the learning of all students, and particularly those with low visualization scores. As Sulbaran and Baker (2000) indicated, attention will have to be paid to the design of the program. Their limited experience suggested that virtual environments can support engineering teaching but the knowledge to be transferred will have to be chosen with care. It would have been interesting had they obtained (a) data of the kind provided by the *Group Embedded Figures Test*, and (b) learning styles inventories of the kind developed by Felder (1993; see below). As we have seen, Brown (2000) gave quite a different perspective on the need for students to have visualization skills. Pictorial presentation was one of the ways of reducing overload, in his view. But there is research on the school curriculum that throws some light on the problem that may also be of relevance to engineering education.

Welch, Barlex, and Lim (2000) found that irrespective of whether or not seventh graders were taught sketching skills, they did not use them as a mechanism for developing a proposal.[15] They used three-dimensional materials to develop their mental images. Welch and his colleagues suggested that compared with a designer these children had limited skills, but they argued that this should not be allowed to prevent them from generating and communicating design ideas. This was a follow-up study to an earlier study with a small group of grade 7 students in Canada which investigated the modeling processes they went through as they pursued a design task (Welch, 1998). The task was video-recorded, and protocol analysis was used to establish the strategies used. When he compared his findings with theories of modeling as described in the literature, he found five important differences. First, and perhaps most surprising, was the fact that three-dimensional modeling replaced two-dimensional modeling. They did not use sketching as a way to generate, develop, and communicate design proposals. This finding questions the generally understood purposes of sketching. Second, the subjects developed solutions serially rather than producing several solutions at the outset. This finding, for example, would of necessity have challenged the model used by the designers of engineering science in 1972 when they required students to consider alternative solutions in the planning of their projects although the students were much older (Carter, Heywood, and Kelly, 1986). The inclusion of this requirement was based on the evidence available at the time. This is an example of the need for continuous evaluation on the basis of new evidence: It is not necessarily an argument for change but rather an openness to change if proved wrong. Third, three-dimensional modeling was found to "fuel new ideas," and at the same time, (fourth), it helped refine ideas. Finally, the students evaluated their work throughout the process.

Welch was led to ask the following questions as a result of the study. "What are the most appropriate skills to teach students in order to facilitate their ability to externalize ideas? At what stage in their development as designers can and should students be taught three-

---

[14] This raises questions about the learning styles that students should have to cope with such integration

[15] This paper contains a good introduction to the use that design professionals make of sketching.

dimensional modeling skills? How are these skills best taught? Which materials best support students' learning of modeling techniques? And, perhaps most importantly, what cognitive development occurs as a result of a student's engagement in the design process skill modeling?"[16]

These questions were asked about young persons' attempts to design in schools. By implication they raised an important question about how engineering departments should respond to students who have been trained in this way. For example, in England it has been traditional to seek out entrants who have 'A' level examination passes in maths and physics. How should admissions officers prize the study of technology? Another question is what expectations, if any, does a course in technology create for engineering? Finally, what does research with these kinds of results have to say about design as a learned and teachable activity?

5.5. Kolb's Learning Theory and the Learning Styles Inventory

Kolb's (1984) experiential theory of learning is illustrated in Figure 5.3. It proposed that the learning of concepts is undertaken in cycles which involve four processes. First, there comes a specific experience that causes the learner to want to know more about that experience. For that to happen, the learner has to reflect on that experience from as many different points of view as possible. From this reflection the learner draws conclusions and uses them finally to influence decision-making or take action. A different style of learning is required for each activity. It will be apparent, for example, that the cycle draws the learner into a form of reflective practice (Cowan, 1998). The axes represent the available information or abstraction contained in the experience (Y-axes) and the processing of information through reflection or action on the conclusions drawn (X-axes). At the center the student is a receiver but as the student moves between the stages on the perimeter of the cycle, he/she is an actor (Svinicki and Dixon, 1987). In the previous sections the value of understanding both the spatial qualities and learning styles possessed by students has been shown. Among the learning styles that engineering educators have found of interest are those described by Kolb in his theory of learning.

Kolb's theory holds that we have a predisposition to think in a style associated with one of these activities. Thus, in any group of people one is likely to find persons with different learning dispositions or styles. He further argued, on the basis of research, that occupation and style are related. Learning is most effective when students move through each of the styles in the cycle. The implications of this theory for teaching and learning are quite profound. Kolb devised a *Learning Styles Inventory* (LSI) to evaluate an individual's learning disposition.

It is argued that different types of learner require

different treatments. Thus, in any event, if a teacher wishes to teach a concept or a principle he/she should teach it in four different ways since each class is likely to be made up of different kinds of learner (i.e., with respect to style). Todd (1991) adapted Svinicki and Dixon's (1987) model that illustrated the teaching strategies involved in each stage of the cycle for an introductory course in manufacturing engineering. His interpretation of the model is shown in Figure 5.4. The questions come from an adaptation of the Kolb model by McCarthy (1986), who called her method the 4MAT system. She also developed a Learning Type Measure (McCarthy and St. Germain, 1993). The learning styles were called types. Type 1-the divergers ask "Why" questions. Type 2-the assimilators ask "What" questions. Type 3-the convergers ask "How" questions, and Type 4-the accommodators ask, "what if" questions. It follows from this theory that students' need to be able to ask all four types of question. In Todd's course the different components of the cycle are catered for by the 10–15 minute presentations on manufacturing processes that they have researched. The students also undertook laboratory studies and team projects, and received instruction in the Kolb cycle to help them as they prepared for their presentations. Sharp, Harb and Terry (1997) have given examples of lesson plans in engineering based on the 4MAT model. Following FitzGibbon (1987) and Sharp (1998), both of whom summarized the McCarthy system and other research on Kolb with respect to engineering, the four styles are:

Convergers: Covergence relates to that part of problem solving which is related to the selection of a solution and the evaluation of the consequences of the solution. The dominant styles of convergers are abstract conceptualization and active experimentation. It is the mode of learning that has often been associated with the classroom and encouraged by traditional assessment. People with this style do best in tests where the problems require single solutions. Not very emotional, they tend to prefer things to people. In relation to engineering, convergers value usefulness and hands on-experience. They want to know how things work, but they want to find it out for themselves and preferably not in a group. They like to apply their knowledge in practice and may do so on the basis of inadequate data. They like to work to targets, and want their teacher to be a coach (Sharp, 1998).

Divergers. Divergence relates to that part of the problem-solving process that identifies differences (problems) and compares goals with reality. Divergers are the opposite to convergers.

Both terms (convergent and divergent) come from the early work on creativity, and Kolb cited Hudson's study in particular (see above). Divergers are best in the situation of concrete experience and reflective observation. They like to "imagine" and generate ideas. They are emotional and relate well to people, but do not perform well in tests that demand single solutions.

In relation to engineering they see many perspectives and imagine the implications of ambiguous situations. They like teaching strategies such as brainstorming and group work. Such strategies give them additional insight. They like sharing ideas (Sharp, 1998, see Chapters 11 and 12).

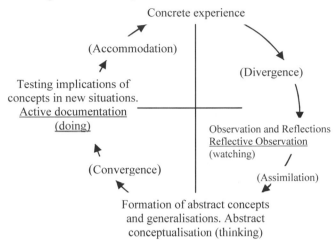

Figure 5.3. An adaptation of Kolb's experiential learning model based on Fitzgibbon (1987) and Stice (1987).

Assimilators: Assimilation relates to the solution of problems and the considerations of alternative solutions to the problem-solving process. The assimilator's dominant learning skills are abstract conceptualization and reflective observation. They are not so much concerned with people as with abstract concepts. They are interested in the precise and logical development of theory rather than its application. Kolb described them as pure rather than applied scientists.

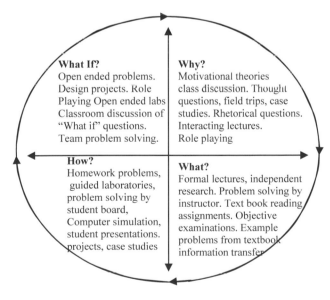

Figure 5.4. Todd's (1991) adaptation of Svinicki and Dixon's (1987) application of the Kolb model to teaching, showing the 4-MAT questions.

In relation to engineering teaching, they want the instructor to have authority, they are detail-oriented and methodical but like creating theories, and sometimes they can be impractical (Sharp, 1998). Thus, in a Purdue University course designed for learning styles, there is a weekly lecture when the teacher acts as an expert (Hein and Budny, 1999).

Accommodators: Accommodation relates to the choice of goal(s) and the execution of solutions in problem solving. Accommodators are the opposite of assimilators. Their dominant strengths are concrete experience and active experimentation. They like doing things and want to devise and implement experiments. Such individuals take more risks than those with other learning styles. Kolb said *"we have labelled this style accommodator because he tends to excel in those situations where he must adapt himself to specific immediate circumstances."* Such individuals are at ease with people, although they are relatively impatient. In regard to engineering, accommodators learn by trial and error rather than by logic. They are creative problem solvers but rely on others for the technical analysis. They don't want to follow structured procedures and can get involved in trivial activities. Their plans may not always be practical. They prefer a teacher who provides resources and evaluation (Sharp, 1998). To be most effective the instructor should stay out of the way, while simultaneously maximizing the opportunities for students to discover things for themselves (Hein and Budny, 1999).

Kolb believed that undergraduate education had a profound influence on style although he acknowledged that his results might have been due to the process of academic selection. As indicated there is some evidence to support the view that styles can change in response to task in higher education settings (see Section 5.6.3). Even if this were not the case many of the tasks of engineering and management require different styles as Whitfield has demonstrated (see below). It also seems that teachers are likely to teach methods that suit their own style of teaching, and it would require some effort from them to adapt to this style of teaching (Heywood, 1997).

In Australia, Holt and Solomon (1996, cited by Ayre and Nafalski, 2000) found that engineering education with its heavy emphasis on problem solving and engineering science relied on assimilators and convergers. This, they said, deflects attention from (a) design and invention, where divergent thinking is required and (b) business management which require accommodative thinking. In these circumstances students would have to adapt from a convergent style to a more divergent style. Hook (1990) suggested that more emphasis should be placed on group work designed to foster affective and behavioral competencies.

5.6. Learning Styles and Gender

In another study cited by Ayre and Nafalski (2000), Kraemer-Koehler, Tooney, and Beke (1995) at Purdue University found that only 16% of their first-year students possessed a typical engineering personality profile. It is important to be reminded that there may be differences in findings between different cultures and higher education structures, especially where there are differences in the degree of selectivity in admission procedures. With this in mind, it should be noted that Kraemer-Koehler, Tooney, and Beke found significant gender differences. Women were more likely to be extraverts than introverts, and strangely *"more theoretical than results oriented"*. (UWA, 1996). (The relationship between temperament and the curriculum is explored in more detail in the next section.)

Severiens and Ten Dam (1994) evaluated 26 Kolb studies for gender differences and found that men were more likely to prefer abstract conceptualization than women, which also seems to fit the picture of women's ways of knowing described by Belenky et al. (1986).

The working party of the University of Western Australia that reported this result (UWA, 1996) concluded that the literature provided substantial evidence that female and male learning styles differed, and also that learning styles could affect achievement. Ayre and Nafalski (2000) summarized the findings of this study as follows:

"Women prefer to participate verbally: and to be more self-disclosing than males,: they prefer collaboration to competition,: and for all these reasons they prefer to work in groups. They like to see the context of their learning. They tend to be less confident than men (especially with technical and mechanical aspects of their studies) and to seek more support than men do." This finding is in similar vein to that much publicized in, "Women's Ways of Knowing" (Belenky et al. 1986), but there is, as Ayre and Nafalski pointed out, a danger of stereotyping. Thus, in a revision of an "Electricity and Electronics" core subject, a variety of teaching methods were used so that most learning styles could be accommodated, and the experience of students extended through different modes of communication. Learning was contextualized within a problem-based learning system (McDermott, Nafalski, and Göl, 2000).

5.7. Variety at Work and Variety in Teaching

All four styles are required in problem solving. This is clear from the 4 MAT modification (see Figure 5.3) and Whitfield's (1975) study of creativity in industry (see Figure 5.1). There is, however, a difficulty with this thesis, for if a person selects a field which is consistent with his/her natural learning style he/she may try to mould their subsequent work to fit that style rather than allow a job to force them to learn other styles. For example, Plovnick (1971) found that the major style in physics classes was convergent. Ten years later, studies at Rutgers University by Enyeart, Baker and VanHarlingen (1990) found that deductive logical ability contributed more to achievement in an introductory college physics course than inductive logical ability. Plovnick predicted that those undergraduates who were divergers would be uncertain of physics with a career, and this was found to be true. The assumption here is that graduates entering careers in physics will find that jobs in physics require convergence. However, if Whitfield is correct, they will have to function at some time or another in all four modes of learning.

Using the Learning Styles Inventory together with an outcomes measure, Nulty and Barrett (1996) found that during the first third of their studies, student respondents in Australia adopted learning styles that were similar to each other irrespective of the main discipline studied. However, in the third year the learning styles appeared to be related to the discipline that was the principal focus of their study. Notwithstanding difficulties with the representativeness of their sample, the data led Nulty and Barrett to suggest that the problems faced by teachers of first-year students may be qualitatively different from those found by teachers of more senior students. *"In each discipline, teachers may need to adopt behaviors which accommodate the nature of students' learning styles. In addition teachers (and students) may benefit by doing this in such a way the students learn to converge on the learning style which more closely reflects the epistemological concerns of whichever discipline is in question."*

There is a danger that such a requirement would be at the expense of the everyday generic requirement that individuals should be able to adapt style to task.

An interesting feature of research in problem solving is the fact reported by several authorities that, once taught a method of problem solving, students use the same technique to solve all other problems. This "problem set," as Luchins (1942) called it, is extremely limiting and can prevent effective transfer. Experience can, therefore, both inhibit and enhance learning (Hesseling, 1966; Heywood, 1989). The same may be true of learning styles (Thomas and Bain, 1982). Cowan found, what would appear to be this effect, among the students whose problem solving techniques he studied (private communication).

Svinicki and Dixon (1987) agreed with Kolb that there are fundamental differences between the disciplines. And, because of these differences the discipline itself can circumscribe an instructor's choice of learning activities. They demonstrated how the application of the model might work in a number of different disciplines including architecture and engineering. (See above; Stice, 1987; and Sharp, Harb and Terry, 1997). More generally the model may be used for the design of courses in the area of computer science as Danchak (2000) has shown.

Ng, Tan, and Jong (1995) with students in Singapore used the Kolb model to develop a laboratory course that would give students experience of a real life situation In this case, the project was the design, and construction of a low-noise pre-amplifier. They found that, by giving the students the design, it hindered participation. It would have been better had they given the students a skeleton design and left them to work out the value of the components, etc. Learning styles have also been used as the basis of a curriculum renovation at the University of Tennessee (Gilliam et al., 1998). (see Chapter 14).

At Bucknell University, students (particularly non traditional students) who indicated they wished to attend graduate school and possibly pursue a career in academia were invited to participate in teams to pursue a project during the summer. This involved them in the design of courseware modules in which they had to cater for the Kolb learning styles. At the same time, they had to design formative and summative evaluation plans to determine the effectiveness of their modules. They were able to assess one of the modules in which the topic was taught in two sections. One section was taught through traditional lectures, and the other section with the multimedia software. It was found that biggest impediment that the students had was their limited experience of the instructional process and with the design itself. There was evidence that the student-produced courseware motivated their peers. The authors hoped that this approach would encourage non-traditional students to enter academia (Hoyt et al., 1998).

The importance of designing CAD so that there is not a mismatch between the learner and the program has been emphasized by Cross (1989). He argued that designers prefer a holistic strategy that is solution focused (right-brain) whereas the style of the computer is left-brain. That is, it is analytic and problem focussed. Designers will need CAD that is solution focused rather than problem focused. *"For example, the emphasis should be on the generation of solutions, and this should be possible before the problem is fully 'understood'. In design, understanding of the problem and of the 'solution' develops in parallel."* (Note the comments by Freeman and Thomas on the design of programs in the previous section. See also Boles et al, 1999, Section 5.10).

Kolb modified the first edition of his inventory because of evaluation research that proved non-supportive. The second instrument has also been criticized for lack of reliability and stability (Sims et al 1986). Highouse and Doverspike (1987) have tested its construct validity by correlating it with field-independence, field-dependence and the *Vocational Preference Inventory* (Holland, 1978). They concluded that it measured preferences rather more than style. Nevertheless, as studies by Loacker (2000), FitzGibbon (1987), and Heywood (1997) showed this inventory could be used by teachers to better understand their students and to design their courses. In Heywood's studies, not withstanding the problems of validity and language, teachers tested their students (age range 13–18) with the *Learning Styles Inventory*. The words were explained when requested by the students. It was found that the dispositions revealed helped the student-teachers' better understand their classes, and the results gave them insight into the needs of students with other dispositions than their own. To put this in another way, they came to see the need for variety in their teaching. In that particular study those trainee teachers were faced with a major task. First they had to change their teaching style in each quadrant. Second, in order to get some sense of the validity or otherwise of Kolb's theory, they could not teach the concept in four different ways, otherwise, there would be no means of assessing the learning that took place in each quadrant. Rather, they had to move the content forward so that there was a change of both style and content in each quadrant. They were then in a

position to write test items for each quadrant and see if those students in quadrant A did best in the questions set for quadrant A, and so on. The difficulties of providing content that will give test questions that have the same difficulty level will be readily appreciated. Thus, the model helped as much in lesson design as it did in the evaluation of the theory. Therefore, without administering the *Learning Styles Inventory*, teachers of engineering can design lessons that take a whole group through each phase of the cycle. The distribution of test results from a test designed to assess learning in each quadrant should give them some insight into class learning and their own performance.

In regard to test design, Sharp, Harb and Terry (1997) in their "writing across the curriculum program for engineers," suggested that assimilators might be comfortable with (a) free writing for comprehension and analysis, and (b) micro-themes that are small amounts of writing preceded by large amounts of thinking. Convergers will respond to short answers to problems so that the sheets can be used for further study. Accommodators like answering "what if" problems. Divergers like to express their views to others, so peer reviews of papers may be helpful. However, as Cowan (private communication) points out, a balance has to be achieved between shaping assessment to the learner and validly testing learning priorities, all of which supports the need for multiple-strategy assessments within courses. Sharp et al., (1997) showed how this might be achieved.

One exercise that Heywood's student-teachers' did was to describe what style they thought their students had after some weeks of teaching them in their class. They were then asked to use their descriptions as the basis for their evaluation. This saved the expense of having to purchase the inventory and also helped them obtain a better understanding of their students. Some general lessons were learned from this exercise. First, the student teachers thought that their students would become bored if they were always taught with this method. Second, they thought that the phases could be distributed across a number of class sessions. Some used two sessions while others used four. Third, the model was a useful guide to the planning of classroom sessions. Fourth, they appreciated that while the Inventory lacked reliability and to some extent validity, because some of the terms had to be explained, that it was worthwhile administering because it gave them insight into their students and promoted student interest. The student teachers learnt that some students did not respond to their teaching because of the pupils' approaches to learning, and therefore they found there was a need to provide variety in their teaching. Unfortunately, like all novelties that promote interest, it is difficult in the run-of-the-mill every-day teaching situation to continually create novelty, therefore, the object should be, with older students in particular, to show them how they can use the information gained to their own advantage.

With respect to engineering Felder and Silverman (1988), who identified a large number of learning styles, suggested that the idea is *"not to use all the techniques in every class but rather to pick several that look feasible and try them."* More, fundamentally the trick is to choose the instructional/learning strategy that is most likely to achieve the objectives to be obtained while taking into account the learning characteristics of the students.

A few student-teachers did not enter (begin the lesson) the cycle at the top. However, Cowan et al (1994) thought that it might not always be desirable to enter the Kolb cycle at the top (concrete experience). If you are going to test out a theory then you begin with the theory and *"prepare to test it out in your own situation, carry that through into the reality of everyday experience, and then reflect on what that tells you about the relevance and usefulness of the theory, and how you might modify it to suit your own needs and constraints."* Cowan (1998) used this premise to describe a model which overcame that criticism of the Kolb model made by the student-teachers that life would become very boring if learning became a series of Kolb cycles. His model rotated through experience, reflection, generalization, testing and back to experience. He pointed out that we should beware of the assumption of linear progress round the cycle. *"I have found that learners may take one particular experience, and hence assemble a fragment of a generalisation. They may then return to another particular experience, reflecting and again partially generalising. And, so they go on, oscillating between the two perhaps four or five times, before eventually being ready (or being prompted) to move on to the next stage."*

It may be argued, however, that Cowan's learners are at a reasonably high level of development. As Duncan-Hewitt et al (2001) and others have pointed out many beginning students are barely at the stage of formal operations (see Chapter 6) and for them beginning in their reality as the Kolb cycle does is probably the best approach for them to learn concepts (see examples in Section 4.1).

One advantage of a carefully designed program where variety is included partially in response to different styles is- that it forces both the teacher and the learner to adapt. It can, therefore, help promote learner adaptability, and that is currently held to be an important goal of higher education (Hayes and Allinson, 1996). Learning style theory was used to identify instructional delivery via media that were perceived by graduate student engineers to be effective. The inventory used was based on Kolb (1984) and Geiger et al, (1993, and was the first part of a questionnaire sent to students and instructors. The other two parts of the survey were designed to elicit attitudes to different instructional methods. The results showed that there were a number of strategies that were not sensitive to learning styles. Among the techniques suitable for media forms of delivery were demonstration lectures, homework problems, open-ended case studies, small group discussions, and video presentations. The authors considered that the challenge for teachers is to extend their repertoire of teaching methods to match the possibilities of the new technology (Rafe and Manley, 1997).

5.8. The Honey and Mumford Inventory

In the United Kingdom, Honey and Mumford (1992) developed a model that has many similarities with that of Kolb. They called their styles Activists, Reflectors, Theorists, and Pragmatists. Here is their description of the activist:

"Activists involve themselves and without bias in new experiences. They enjoy the here and now and are happy to be dominated by immediate experiences. They are open-minded, not sceptical, and this tends to make them enthusiasts about anything new. Their philosophy is: 'I'll try anything once'. Their days are filled with activity. They tackle problems by brainstorming. As soon as the excitement from one activity has died down they are busy looking for the next. They tend to thrive on the challenge of new experiences but are bored with implementation and longer-term consolidation. They are gregarious people constantly involving themselves with others but, in doing so, they seek to centre all activities round themselves."

Honey and Mumford developed an inventory for classifying persons into these styles which, unlike the other inventories previously mentioned, is cheap to obtain and easy to administer. Nor is there a professional requirement for training.

In the United Kingdom, a comparative study of the Felder and Soloman Index and the Honey and Mumford Inventory yielded somewhat disappointing psychometric data from a sample of engineering and business students (undergraduate, post graduate, and post-experience (Van Zwanenberg, Wilkinson, and Anderson, 2000). Neither instrument yielded internal consistencies of the order defined by Kline (1993). Neither instrument predicted academic performance. However, this result should be treated with caution when American data on the Felder and Soloman Index is being considered because the systems of assessment and teaching differ considerably to those in the United Kingdom. At the same time these investigators did not dissent from the view that it should assist students, especially those in engineering, find out about their preferences for learning.[17]

Looked at in terms of Riding's cognitive styles, the Felder and Soloman Index contains a mix of both cognitive and learning styles. The wholist/analytic and verbal/imagery of Riding and Rayner's (1998, see Section 5.10) framework correspond broadly to the sequential-global and visual-verbal scales in the Felder and Soloman Index. The analysis gave some support to another investigation that suggested that the Honey and Mumford Inventory only measures three scales.
Both inventories yield an activist style, but the other pole is not clearly defined. Van Zwanenberg, Wilkinson and

---

[17]One European program is developing customized learner-centred educational packages. Courses are designed with the four types of learner described by Honey and Mumford in mind. The students will respond to the inventory, and while they may be advised to take a module designed for a particular proposal, they can also try others. The scheme remains to be evaluated

Anderson (2000) proposed that learning styles might be explained as a circumplex. In such a model the strongest positive associations are adjacent. Thus, there are strong positive relationships between Reflection and between Theorizing, and Pragmatism and theorizing. Action and Reflection are opposites as are intuiting and sensing. But there is a slight relationship between Action and Sensing and between Action and Theorizing. Pragmatism seems to be unconnected with action as are sequential or global perception and visual or verbal. This study showed how the different models, at one and the same time, give partial insights into learning as well as demonstrating its complexity.

This section ends with a cautionary note. Outside of engineering an American study of biology students has challenged the validity of the Kolb theory. In that study students were exposed to two instructional methods on the basis that the theory predicts that "thinkers" would do better in an expository situation, and "feelers" would do better in an inquiry mode of instruction. In a one-semester biology course, eight lab sections were taught by one method, while eight were taught by the other. A common final examination (not seen by the instructors) was administered at the end of the course. It was found that the thinkers did better than the feelers under both methods (Lawson and Johnson, 2002).[18] But this does not null the idea that we have predispositions toward learning and that instructional design should not take this into account. It does mean that because we have done this, we should not expect every person in the class necessarily to perform equally well. It is evident that some engineering educators have found the Kolb model to be of value. But there are other models which engineering educators have also found to be of use (see below).

5.9. Industry and Behavioral and Learning Styles

Pisarski et al. (2000) and his colleagues at the University of Pittsburgh drew attention to the fact that industry not only wanted their employees to perform a specific function but they also wanted them to effectively perform in teams. This required the teaching of interpersonal skills that were not commonly taught in the curriculum. As we have seen in Chapter 2 the goals of the Enterprise in Higher Education Initiative in the United Kingdom were to ensure that every graduate leaving higher education possessed such skills.

The particular contribution of Pisarski et al, (2000) is to have distinguished between behavioral (personality) styles and to have linked them together with

learning styles in a matrix. The behavioral styles instrument was designed by one of the authors (Martinazzi). His categories as shown in Exhibit 5.1 are relator, socializer, thinker, and director. Learning styles were measured by an adaptation of the Kolb inventory with the following categories, innovative, analytical, common sense, and dynamic (Huck, Myers, and Wilson, 1989).

They administered these instruments on two occasions to 151 students in civil, electrical, and mechanical engineering technology spread across the four years of the program. They predicted that many of the students would be "common sense" learners," and in the behavioral categories, this would be "thinkers" and "directors." In fact, 70% of the students were found to be relators or socializers. They described these categories as follows:

"Relators are motivated to create a stable organized environment; tend to be patient and good listeners; and participate in a group rather than directing it, and listen more than talk. Socializers are motivated to persuade and influence others; tend to be open; verbalise thoughts and feelings, and prefer to work with people rather than alone."

This result showed why these students liked open classrooms and laboratory experiences.

The authors argued that while cooperative learning would be very beneficial, there were few directors in the group. In these circumstances, professors have to step in to provide leadership. But this again raised the question as to how stable these styles are, and whether or not they can be changed. Would it not be possible to train students to direct, and indeed, given the needs of industry, should there not be an obligation to provide such training in college? The authors acknowledged that these issues needed to be taken into account in the design of a curriculum or course.

Category	Descriptors
Relator	Loyal, cooperative, friendly casual, relaxed, informal, easy going, quiet, dependable, warm, sensitive, patient, supportive, caring.
Socializer	Spontaneous, animated, talkative, impulsive, risk-taker, emotional, enthusiastic, dreamer, creative, action, fun, playful, imaginative, optimistic, outgoing.
Thinker	Logical, conservative, businesslike, punctual, organized, careful, methodical, deliberate, formal, precise, reserved, accurate, cautious, calculating, analytic.
Director	Forceful, assertive, competitive, challenging, task-oriented, overbearing, dominant, efficient, fast-moving, decision maker, controlling, authoritative, results, independent, direct.

Exhibit 5.1. Categories and descriptors used to identify personality and behavioral styles by Pisarski et al (2000). (reproduced with permission of IEEE, *Proceedings Frontiers in Education Conference*.)

---

[18]This study also included a comparison with the neo-Piagetian development level of the students obtained by two items one of which was based on Karplus and Karplus (1970). This theory predicts that thinkers will outperform feelers in all modes of instruction, and that a positive correlation should exist between the Kolb thinking/feeling dimension and developmental level. They cited similar findings by Harasym et al, (1995). This work is in the tradition of work begun in England into Piagetian levels of reasoning by Shayer and Adey (1981). See Chapter 6.

More specifically, it is of interest to note that in electrical engineering technology the seniors had the largest number of relators, while the sophomores had the largest number of directors, and that that class had the most students with high-end SAT scores. If this were a significant and not an accidental relationship, it would have implications for course design.

Although the common sense learners did not form a majority (just over 40%), the least proportion was among the mechanical engineering technology students (28%). This group also had the highest number of analytic thinkers (49%). The investigators suggested that because the mechanical engineering technology students have fewer laboratory classes than the other groups this might force them to become *"analytically astute."*

It may also suggest that there is some instability in styles. While this is a small and local study, the results of which are not generalizable, it did show how, with relatively simple non-standardized instruments, departments may be led to reflect on what they are doing in their programs and courses, and so be led to change. This is the lesson, or point, of all the work that has been done on learning styles and learning strategies.

5.10.   Temperament and Learning Styles.

In a seminal paper on the psychologist and the university published in 1962, Furneaux (1962) demonstrated the importance of temperament in examination performance among a group of relatively high-achieving mechanical engineering students. The grades from the separate subject examinations of these students were averaged into a single grade for the purpose of the final degree award.[19] The students were not given the grades in individual subjects as a profile. In style, except for engineering drawing, all the examinations required the students to undertake substantial problem solving exercises. The investigation sought to answer the question, were those who were tense, excitable, and highly-strung likely to perform better than those who were phlegmatic, relaxed, and apparently well adjusted? Or, to put the question in another way, does the level of neuroticism influence performance?
It might be predicted that extraverts would not do as well as introverts, for, apart from anything else, introverts tend to be bookish, and, moreover, academic studies have as their goal the development of bookish traits. Introverts work hard to be reliable and accurate, but in the extreme they take so much time at the task that they might do badly in examinations. In contrast, extraverts might do an examination quickly, but this is likely to be at the expense of reliability.

Furneaux categorized the students into four groups; stable-extraverts, neurotic-extraverts, stable-introverts, and neurotic-introverts. The groups most likely to fail university examinations were found to be the stable-extraverts followed by (but at some distance

numerically) the neurotic-extraverts. In this particular study the neurotic-introverts did best.

Another simple test was administered to these students to measure intellectual speed, and it was found that among the stable-extraverts, those who were slowest tended to obtain low examination marks. In most American studies of test anxiety a negative relationship has been found with intelligence, but it has been suggested that this could have been due to the particular tests used, since under pressure of time their stress-inducing effects might contaminate the outcomes.

Furneaux explained the performance of these students in terms of the Yerkes-Dodson principle which was derived from studies of the behavior of rats. It was shown that rats who were hungry would make their way through a maze to find food more quickly than when they were replete. However, it was also found that if the drive that the rats exhibited reached too high a level, performance would decline. There is an optimal drive level for each task to be performed. Above this, performance falls off. The Yerkes−Dodson principle states that the optimal drive level is high for simple tasks but is reduced as the complexity of the task is increased. This means that high drive can soon go over the optimum level for complex tasks.

Given that individuals who easily enter into states of high drive are likely to obtain high neuroticism scores, then, Furneaux argued, it is this group which is likely to obtain high examination scores. Similarly, persons who have an extraverted disposition and at the same time have a low drive level will do badly in examinations. If these tendencies are related to the intellectual qualities of the examinees, then an introvert with high drive will be able to compensate for relatively poor intellectual qualities whereas, in contrast, good intellectual qualities may not compensate for extraversion and low drive.

Furneaux found that the more neurotic students did badly in the engineering drawing paper. Those who were stable did better. This, he argued, was because the task was so complex that optimum drive occurred at a low level. He found that the most common cause of failure was poor-quality drawing, which was of a kind that might be due to disturbing influences. Discussion with the examiner led Furneaux to the view that supra-optimal drive might have occurred, because there was some evidence of excessive sweating, lack of coordination, and faulty judgment.
The lessons for teachers from this study are that they should be clear about what are the most appropriate objectives to be achieved. Moreover, those objectives should take into account the temperament of the students. Furneaux showed that when the examination in engineering drawing changed, so did performance- for the better. The grade that had depended on the quality of the drawing presented was changed to respond to assessment of the ability to interpret and convey information using graphical methods. It is likely, (although we are not told), that the students were more interested in this than they were in perfectionist drawing.

---

[19] See Chapter 15 for other descriptions of the types of examination set in the United Kingdom.

Moreover, the skill performances required would correspond more to the skill requirements of the written examination. It was also observed that the students in the less stable groups improved their performance.

In the United States, Evans, McNeill, and Beakley (1990) also argued that engineering schools have emphasized learning that encourages introversion. By this they meant the teaching of the principles of engineering science. There is a need to allow students to be challenged by the problems of the unpredictable world and so encourage extraversion. The relationship with convergent and divergent thinking in real-world engineering should be apparent (see Figure 5.1). More recent papers at Frontiers in Education Conferences have echoed these points.

Since Furneaux's study there has been continuing interest in the relationship between individual differences and learning. In the United Kingdom, the Eysenck Personality Test, which is a successor to the instrument used by Furneaux, is commonly used to evaluate personality (Kline, 1993). It is likely to be used with other instruments such as a test of high-grade intelligence, as for example, AH6 (Heim, 1970; Kline, 1993).

A few years later, in the United States, Elton and Rose (1966) using the *Omnibus Personality Inventory*, found a significant difference between engineering students on the dimension of intellectual disposition. Strangely, an absence of high intellectual interest was found among the persisters. These results led them to suggest that the faculty might consider a second experimental program with the objective of developing new avenues of professional competence for the 25% who withdraw. In another report they argued that student-leaving is a result of maladjustment and directed hostility. In 1974 they suggested that the difference between those students who persist and those who do not might be due to personality.

This interest in Jung's extravert and introvert typology was shared in America by Briggs and Myers, who designed a questionnaire to elicit the preferences that individuals have for all the psychological types described by Jung. The Myers Briggs Type Indicator (MBTI) is intended as a measure of both personality and style. It has been promoted in engineering by McCaulley (1976, McCaulley at al, 1983, 1990); McCaulley at al, and by Smith, Irey, and McCaulley, (1973). One of the reasons for its popularity is that training courses for those who wish to administer the instrument are readily available. It is based on Jungian typology and describes 16 personality categories (types) into which individuals are said to fall. The MBTI has been criticized because it is difficult to obtain factor-analytic data which will show that it has validity (i.e., that individual's fall into these types) because the types are theoretical constructs. In the first edition of his now standard work, Kline considered that it merited an entry in his handbook on psychological testing because it was widely used in personnel testing. It has the disadvantage that we can all too readily see ourselves and others in the descriptions like those suggested by Kiersey

and Bates (1984), and we can all too easily begin to uncritically type each other with the letters assigned to the test parameters (see below). As Kline said, *"the critical question is whether the MBTI does classify individuals into these types or not. If it does we might still ask to what extent these types resemble those suggested by Jung. Even if they did not, however, it might still be the case that the typology is valuable for selection or vocational guidance."*

Subsequently, Kline (2000) searched for these types psychometrically.[20] For the moment, and at the very least, the MBTI can serve as an indicator of individual differences in a classroom even if they are not strictly the types proposed. Moreover, the literature that it has spawned can help teachers reflect on their dispositions to teaching as well as doing the same for students and their learning. Like the Learning Styles Inventory, it can be a valuable aid in the development of reflective practice (e.g. Kiersey and Bates, 1984; Silver and Hanson, 1995). Jung called the total personality the psyche. It is a complex network of interacting systems. The primary ones are the ego, the personal unconscious, and the collective unconscious. There are two primary attitudes and four basic functions. Together they constitute separate but related parts of the psyche. It is from these that the typologies referred to above derive. The basic dispositions are introversion and extraversion. According to Jung the conscious introvert is an extravert in his/her unconscious and vice versa (Engler, 1979).

The four basic functions are ways of orienting experience and perceiving the world. To quote Jung, *"These four functional types correspond to the obvious means by which consciousness obtains its orientation and experience".* (Engler, 1979). Thus *sensation* results from our sensing of the world through our senses to see what exists. *Feeling* is the activity of valuing and judging the world and tells us whether it is agreeable. *Intuition* is perception about the world via the unconscious, and our *thinking* gives meaning and understanding to the world we inhabit and tells us what it is. *Sensing and intuition* involve our immediate experiences, and are, almost contrary to everyday usage of *feeling*, because *feeling* and *thinking* were defined by Jung as rational functions since they require acts of judgement. At the same time the functions are grouped in opposite pairs (i.e.,

---

[20] Kline (2000) summarized work that he did with Saggino (Saggino and Kline, 1995, 1996) that attempted to assess the factor structure and the psychological meaning of the factors of MBTI, but in an Italian version of the test. They found that the first four factors resembled the four scale factors of MBTI and their work confirmed the four scale factors in the MBTI manual. Factor 1 resembled openness, Factor 2 extraversion, Factor 3 agreeableness, and Factor 4 conscientiousness. They then attempted to locate these MBTI factors in factor space by factoring them with the 16PF and EPQ personality inventories. With respect to the MBTI five factors, Factor 1 loaded with the MBTI factor 2 (extraversion), Factor 2 was P and loaded with MBTI factors 4 and 1, Factor 3 was most similar to N or anxietyand loaded with Factor 3. Factor 4 was difficult to identify but loaded on some of the anxiety primaries in 16PF and N of EPQ and MBTI factor 3. Factor 5 which loaded with MBTI factor 5 was intelligence. These findings do not bear out the typological claims of MBTI which are original aspects of the instrument.

thinking/feeling and *sensing/intuition*) and one function is dominant in each pair. According to Jung, as previously indicated, *"these four functional types correspond to the obvious by which consciousness obtains its orientation"*. Thus, a person who is dominant in *thinking* may have submerged the *feeling* function. One who is dominant in *sensing* may have submerged the *intuition function*. Those functions that are underdeveloped have the power to influence life, and it is from them that strange moods and symptoms emerge. The actualized self requires a synthesis of these four functions. Clearly, individuals have to reconcile many contradictions within their personality. Neurosis occurs when the reconciliation of these contradictions becomes difficult.

The Myers-Briggs Type Indicator pairs the perception and thinking functions for the purpose of assessing personality and produces four types as follows:

Sensing + Thinking   ST
Sensing + Feeling   SF
Intuition + Feeling   NF
Intuition + Thinking   NT

One of the reasons why it appeals to personnel selectors is that each of the above types is said to indicate career preferences e.g.

ST-applied science, business etc.

SF-patient care, community service etc.

NF-behavioral science, literature and art etc.

NT-physical science, research and management etc.

Yokomoto and his colleagues offered some words of caution to those who are new to personality theory and the MBTI in particular. *"[ ] the model is not as factual as it may seem. Like the preference for being right handed or left handed, each of the four scales describes opposing preferences. They do not identify traits as some may infer. Each person uses all eight preferences but generally four are preferred. To understand that people perceive and judge differently is to understand that people learn, make decisions, and assign values differently from one another"* (Yokomoto, Buchanan, and Ware, 1993).

Of course professional persons are likely to have all four types in them and teaching is no exception. As has been argued, we will want to learn according to our preferred type. Silver and Hanson (1995) have shown how teaching and learning might be classified against these psychological types. For example, teachers who are empathizers are SF, instructional managers are ST, theoreticians are NT, and facilitators are NF, friendly learners are SF; practical learners are ST; intellectual learners are NT and imaginative learners are NF. Similarly, one may classify the type of learning environment (e.g. organization and competition v discovery as ST v NT. The emphasis on instructional strategies (e.g., research vs self-expression) is NT v NF; teaching strategies (e.g.,. group investigations vs programmed instruction) is SF v ST; and evaluation and assessment procedures (e.g.,. objective tests v essay) is ST vs NT.

Whatever the validity of their instrument, the theory (when applied to educational practice) shows just how complex teaching and learning is and just how far removed it is from the stereotype of teaching as 'chalk and talk.' Teachers have to live with and design for diversity in learning. This point is no better illustrated than by McCaulley's (1990) finding that among 3,784 students from eight engineering schools, 53% preferred *sensing*. This trend was similar for both male and female students. This means that there were a large number of students in these American Engineering schools who were *intuitives*. McCaulley et al, (1983) reported an experiment by Yokomoto who, on the ground, that *sensing* types learn best when the material is based on experience and proceeds step-by-step with examples and hands on activities, taught his *sensing* students to master specific examples and then look for connections and patterns. In contrast, he taught *intuitive* students to master the mechanics in order to solve problems quickly rather than being brought to a halt when they had grasped the patterns.

McCaulley (1990) drew attention to the fact that the contributors to the July 1990 issue of *Engineering Education* (mainly on learning styles) favored courses that taught practical skills (S), creativity and Synthesis (N), and logical analysis (T), but rarely mentioned *feeling*. People skills are undervalued. She did not find this surprising since *"thinking is the more powerful tool for inanimate materials with which engineering is immediately concerned."* At the same time she found that thinking types are in the majority among engineering students. McCaulley had estimated that in the general population about two-thirds of males prefer *thinking* and two thirds of females preferred *feeling*. In the engineering population 75% males and 64% females preferred thinking She asked the question *"Are engineering schools preparing their students adequately for the 'people complexities' of the profession?"* She would not have been surprised to learn that at around the same time the Employment Department in the United Kingdom launched its *Enterprise in Higher Education Initiative*, which had as one of its objectives the rectification of this deficit among higher education students irrespective of the discipline studied (Heywood, 1994).

In 1993 Yokomoto, Buchanan, and Ware undertook a comparative study of lower division electrical and mechanical engineering majors and electrical engineering technology majors to determine if personality contributed to attitudes toward design and innovation. For this purpose they used a ten-question forced-choice inventory and the MBTI. The ten items in the inventory related to what the students perceived jobs would reward them for, what they would allow them to do, disposition toward risk-taking; how a person should be judged; and what type of engineering work they preferred to do.

Only three of the items showed any significant differences between the groups. First, the engineering majors indicated a preference for rewards for using conventional methods in clever innovative ways. This was in contrast to the technology majors who preferred to use new methods and technologies to solve conventional problems. However, when the engineering majors were classified by personality, the introverts took up the first position while the extraverts take up the latter.

Secondly the engineering majors preferred to be guided by the lessons of the past whereas the technology majors preferred to be alert to new possibilities and opportunities. Third, the electrical engineering majors preferred working on the development and design of new products, whereas the technology majors preferred working and testing new products. It might be argued, in the absence of information about course objectives, that having adopted a particular program the students prefer the "style" of that program. In Britain sandwich course students said they were more practical than university students, whereas university students saw themselves as potential managers. Students may have to justify to themselves the merits of the course they are on, and this is a matter of culture and identity (Heywood, 1969). This is not to say that personality and interest are unimportant but it is to recognize that ability and the micro culture of the institution may also be important. To an extent this is acknowledged in related findings and the conclusions that Yokomoto and his colleagues drew from them about teaching. For example, the engineering majors who were judgment types divided equally between (a) a preference for working on the design of new products, and (b) the assembly and testing of prototypes of new products. The perception types all chose the former.

The number of items in the questionnaire (four out of ten) that were influenced by type was low. Nevertheless, Yokomoto and his colleagues argued that while personality type was not a limiting factor in the selection of students into design and innovation there was a need for different approaches to teaching in those areas. They suggested that such teaching should be in the coaching mode rather than in the instructional mode.

The MBTI has also been used in the evaluation of innovative courses. At the University of Salford the MBTI was used as a diagnostic instrument in a bridging course (i.e. from technician courses to degree level work). Its intention was to help non-traditional university students gain an understanding of their natural learning styles and to develop more effective learning strategies. Compared with traditional entry students, it was found that the non-traditional students in this innovative course had higher levels of extraversion and feeling. Another test showed that they tended to converge on the problem rather than explore other possibilities (Culver et al, 1994).

Soulsby (1999) reported how the MBTI was used in an orientation course for engineers at the University of Connecticut. He wrote, *"the key here is to make the students aware that each is different, each has preferred learning modes, that instructors may or may not teach to their preferred mode, and to be aware of this possible mismatch."* Clearly, information of the kind yielded by the MBTI and other instruments is of value to those planning and implementing courses. The Salford study also illustrated the influence of prior knowledge and other experiences on learning, as do American studies by Blumner and Richards (1997) and by Richards,

Richards and Sheridan (1999), who used different instruments. Tutors need to know what these knowledge, skills and values are, as well as what the meta-cognitive awareness of the learners is (see also Moran, 1991).

In the United States a longitudinal investigation of students in a chemical engineering course taught in an innovative way compared the profiles on the course with performance. The MBTI showed that in the freshmen year of the course the *intuitors* earned higher grades than the *sensors,* and the *thinkers* outperformed the *feelers,* and the *judgers* outperformed the *perceivers.* The *introverts* had a slightly better GPA than the *extraverts,* but the *extraverts* subsequently turned in a better performance than the *introverts.* More *sensors* than *intuitors* rated the experimental course that emphasized applications over theory as more instructive than other more traditional courses they had attended. While it was not possible statistically to demonstrate whether the students in the more experimental group obtained greater mastery of curriculum content, the authors concluded that an instructor who integrates theory with practice can expect positive results (Felder, 1995; Felder, Felder and Dietz, 1997). Rosati (1997), from a seven-year longitudinal study of Canadian engineering students, found that success for the weaker students in their first year was more probable if they were type ITJ, and that graduation within four years was correlated with INTJ types. The findings of both the United Kingdom and United States studies support the concept of multiple strategy approaches to assessment and instruction. The point is that apart from achieving different objectives, they would cater for different learning approaches and personalities (Ryle, 1969). From the perspective of curriculum studies, and taking into account the findings of McKenna, Mongia, and Agogino (1998), these studies illustrate the value of within-department longitudinal studies using a variety of instruments because they can contribute to an understanding of how value might be added to a course.

Some students and faculty find that the Kolb inventory is too laden with jargon. Because of this view among her students, Montgomery (1995) used Soloman's (1992)[21] Inventory of Learning Styles. This was administered together with the MBTI. The categories of the instruments are processing (active/reflective); Perception (sensing/intuitive); input (visual/verbal); and understanding (sequential/global). The results were related to learning in multi-media program, and they showed that all the styles were catered for by the design. For example, a movie was included, and active learners felt that this movie was more useful than the reflective learners. Global learners learnt best when the technical material was presented in a larger context (see also Rafe and Manley 1997 above).

---

[21] Felder worked with Soloman to produce the Felder and Soloman index of learning styles. See Felder (1996), Felder and Siverman (1988), Soloman (1992) and Rosati (1999). Felder inventory at (URL)http://www2.ncsu.edu/unity/lockers/users/f/felder/public/IL.Spage.html.

There are situations in which MBTI may not yield the information required. For example, McKenna, Mongia, and Agogino (1998) used several different methods to triangulate, compare, and evaluate student performance in a multimedia engineering design class. The methods used were a web-based discussion tool and observations of students so that a triangulation could be obtained between what they said and what they did. All of the students took the MBTI. It was found that the information obtained by one method sometimes contradicted the information obtained by another method so the authors prescribed caution when interpreting performance from just one point of view. They were concerned to create diverse teams but found that the MBTI had limited potential for helping them create such teams. *"The personality profiles, when compared with other data sources, may not really be indicative of one's actions or behaviors"* (see Chapter 13). Once again, support is given to the need for a multiple strategy approach to assessment and evaluation.

It is appropriate at this time also to caution personality test users in countries other than the United States that American tests can distort perceptions about the suitability of a person for a particular profession. Wood and Butterworth (1997) pointed out that Britons and Americans answer questions differently. While the British are more emotionally controlled, they are less dominant, achievement-oriented, and flexible. Thus, Wood and Butterworth said that a person with a moderately high leadership score on an American test might in fact be too autocratic for a British organisation. Also, as between Britain and the USA larger gender differences than expected have been found with the MBTI among older and less well educated groups (Cook, 1997).

Yokomoto (private communication) pointed out that Learning Styles Inventories and personality measures are of great value for coaching and counseling. Learning Style Inventories give information about how one learns, while personality inventories have something to say about who you are. He finds the MBTI more helpful because it discloses how a person functions.

5.11. The Felder-Soloman Learning Styles Inventory.

In a paper that has now become seminal in engineering education, Felder and Silverman (1988) identified 32 learning styles and made recommendations about teaching techniques that would address all learning styles. Additionally they drew attention to the possible disparities that could exist between student learning styles and engineering teaching styles, some of which have already been mentioned. They listed five questions, the answers to which would define a student's learning style, and five questions that would define a teacher's learning style. This is somewhat different from asking teachers to respond to the Kolb *Learning Style Inventory* (see above). It will be seen that the questions shown in Exhibit 5.2 are greatly influenced by the Kolb, MBTI and Witkin theories.

The Felder-Soloman *Learning Styles Index*, which was developed from this analysis categorizes individuals on a 12 point scale along four dimensions. These are, active/reflective; sensing/intuitive; visual/verbal, and sequential/global.[22]

North American studies with this index yield fairly consistent results. For example studies at Ryerson University (Zywno and Waalen, 2001), Western University (Rosati, 1999), and Michigan (Montgomery et al,1995) showed the following proportions of learning preferences. active learners, 53, 69, and 67%: sensing learners, 66, 59, and 57%: visual learners, 86, 80, and 69%: and sequential learners, 72, 67, 71%, respectively.

Four reports of its use in somewhat different circumstances are of interest. In the first, 319 electrical and mechanical engineering students at St Jose State University were examined for their preferred learning style. These inventories were taken in classrooms with large immigrant and first-generation American populations. In addition to English, 28 different languages were spoken in one class of 70 students. We are not told when they were tested except that the results showed remarkable consistency over several years. Sixty percent of the students showed strong preferences for visual learning, 5% showed a strong preference for the sensing style, while only 4% had a strong preference for the intuiting style. Allen and Mourtos (2000), who conducted the study, pointed out that these results were consistent with the previous findings of Felder (e.g., 1993). They also noted that finding out the learning styles of such a diverse group of students *"forces faculty to acknowledge that relying solely on the traditional chalk-and-talk approach is not as effective as other more interactive methods."* Discussion of learning styles has become part of faculty development on that campus, and that has caused the adoption of a wide range of alternative teaching strategies. One of the authors (EA) tried to engage both the sensors and the reflectors through the use of "blue-sheet" activities in which students worked out problems using recently taught concepts with practical examples. The other writer (NM) used multimedia and web-based presentations to engage the visual learner, and through hands-on demonstrations the active learner. Unfortunately no data are provided about success rates; and that is, incidentally, a weakness in many reports.

Rosati (1996) used the Index of Learning Styles on groups of first-and fourth-year engineering students and faculty. He found that although faculty taught in a verbal style, they had a higher visualization orientation than the students. The students gave greater preference for active learning and sensing than faculty. The faculty were, however, more reflective and intuitive. In another report, Rosati (1999) said that significantly different

---

[22] It is usual to analyze the data in a bimodal format. Crynes, Greene, and Dillon (2000) argued that it was better to evaluate the index on a continuous scale-in their case 1–6 because this represents what students actually do and use.

Questions the answers to which help to define student learning and teaching styles.

Questions to students.	Questions to teachers.
1.What type of information does the student preferentially perceive: sensory (external)-sights, sounds, physical -possibilities, insights, hunches?	1. What type of information is emphasized by the instructor: concrete -factual, or abstract-conceptual, sensations, or intuitive (internal) theoretical?
2.Through which sensory channel is external information most effectively perceived: visual-pictures, diagrams graphs, demonstrations, or auditory -words sounds?	2. What mode of presentation is stressed: visual-pictures, diagrams, films, demonstrations, or verbal- lectures, readings, discussions?
3. With which organization of information is the student most comfortable: inductive-facts and observations are given, underlying principles are inferred, or deductive -principles are given, consequences and applications are deduced?	3. How is the presentation organized: Inductively- phenomena leading to principles, or deductively-principles leading to phenomena?
4. How does the student prefer to process information: actively through engagement in physical activity or discussion, or reflectively- through introspection?	4. What mode of student participation is facilitated by the presentation: active -students talk, move, reflect or passive- Students watch and listen?
5. How does the student progress toward understanding: sequentially in continual steps, or globally – in large jumps (holistically)?	5.What type of perspective is provided on the information presented: sequential-step-by-step- progression (the trees), or global-context and relevance (the forest)

Exhibit 5.2. Felder and Silverman's (1988) questions about learning styles and teaching styles. (Reproduced with the permission of R. M. Felder)

preferences were found for sub-groups such as male/female; first year/fourth year; and extraversion/introversion. The learning preferences of most students were active, sensing, visual, and sensual. Rosati concluded from both studies that faculty should cater for all learning styles in their presentation, which is yet another affirmation of this axiom. [e.g., Heywood, 1999; Kramer-Koehler, Tooney and Beke, 1995; see Rafe and Manley, 1997, and Montgomery, 1995, (above) in relation to learning through media]. A new digital processing laboratory was designed and built at Kettering University. It was based on the Felder-Silverman model. The teaching techniques to be used are shown in Exhibit 5.3 (Melton et al, 1999). (See also Chapter 14 sections on laboratory work).

In an altogether different investigation among a group of 33 assistant professors in a summer workshop at Stanford University, Carrizosa and Sheppard (2000) sought to establish if, *"given knowledge of how an individual prefers to receive information, can anything be known about how they will present information."* The investigation was concerned with effectiveness of communication between members of engineering design teams. The importance of this question to the oxymoron of matching teaching styles to learning styles will be evident. If those who are successful in engineering have learning styles that do not match those of their teachers, and if the teachers come from this group of students, then why is it that they, the teachers, adopt strategies that are different from those with which they were successful. And do they now learn in a different way? (See previous

discussion, and Beasley et al, (1995) below, who show that in one course those students who benefited most had the same style as their teachers.)

In the project (Carrizosa and Sheppard, 2000) it was hypothesized that teams composed of individuals with similar preferences would exhibit communication styles to match those preferences. A second goal was to examine the effect of having/or not having a hardware building kit during the conceptual phase of the design. It was argued that in the presence of a kit the engineers would neglect to generate alternative solutions and jump for the first conceived solution. This hypothesis is very similar to the description of the engineers' approach to the design of aircraft components reported by Youngman et al, (1978).

To validate their theory, Carrizosa and Sheppard divided the group into teams. Each team was matched for gender, and each team included two mechanical engineering assistant professors because the teams would be required to construct a device with mechanisms with which mechanical engineers would be familiar. The overall selection was made on the basis of performance on the information/reception (visual/oral) dimension of Felder's Learning Styles Inventory. The teams were chosen to have the following characteristics:

Team 1. On the average, strongly preferred to receive information visually.

Team 2. Had a moderate preference for learning visually.

Teams 3 and 4. Had a mild preference to receive information visually.

Data were collected from videotapes made during the first part of the exercise and working notes and drawings made by each team. A composite score based on aesthetics, accuracy, and measurement time was assigned to each device. The audio from teams 2 and 3 was found not to be usable. For the other teams, time was stamped for each new speaker and the length of each statement determined. Atman's scheme for the analysis of the engineering design process was adapted for video analysis to determine how the teams were engaged in conceptual design.

The analysis of the video recordings led to the view that much more was happening visually than communication by drawing. In addition to using drawing (i.e., the construction of a visual picture to explain an idea), there was *"communicative gesturing"*-for example, *"sketching or tracing with the hand."* There was also "using hardware" to illustrate some aspect of the design being worked on, and *"referencing hardware"* where a team member verbally references an artefact *"with a distinctive geometry to lever other team members visual representations of that artefact.* The investigators' pointed out that these modes were not mutually exclusive.

The analysis showed[23] that the participants did not engage in drawing during the exercise. This was in spite of the fact that they preferred to receive information visually, However, once the definition was expanded to take into account the other dimensions quoted above, it took up 21% of design time. A much richer picture of visual communication was obtained. However, there did not seem to be a relationship between preferences for reception and presentation. Team 1, which had the highest preference for receiving visual information, recorded the next lowest amount of visual information. In contrast, team 4 which had a mild preference for the presentation of visual communication used the most visual communication. The authors said the effectiveness of each of these modes should be addressed in a future study. As to the second hypothesis, it was found that the first idea selected by both teams was worked on, but this could have been due to the time constraint on completing the device. Thus, in future experiments the authors suggested that there should be no time constraints. It might also be suggested that while the Learning Style Inventory served the purpose of identifying the needs of individuals, additional tests of personality and performance might have given a more comprehensive profile of the individuals and teams.

Finally, as the media become important it is of considerable interest to know how the media and learning styles interact. A study at Ryerson University in Canada investigated the effect of hypermedia instruction on the achievement of students with different learning styles (Zywno and Waalen, 2001, see Zwyno and Kennedy, 2000, for details of the course). The investigators hypothesized that low achievers would benefit more from hypermedia instruction than from conventional instruction. They also hypothesized that differences

between learning styles would be minimized in the experimental group, but would remain unchanged in the control group.

In this study the students were randomly assigned to laboratory sections. Two instructors taught the course and they addressed the problem inherent in studies of this kind, as, for example, differences in instructional design and the treatment of students, the prior experience of the students, and the sample size. Thus, *"The learning environment for both groups was based on the experiential, project-based instructional design, and included the same level of use of advanced computer simulation tools, and of e mail."*

Learning style.	Laboratory Teaching Techniques for Addressing Style.
Sensing	Laboratory experiments expose students to material ranging from mathematics to software and hardware DSP implementation. Each lab is oriented toward physical, realist application.
Intuitive	Each laboratory is closely coupled with classroom lectures. Students can review the theory by accessing hyperlinks in web based laboratory procedure.
Visual	The laboratory procedures are presented as a block diagram or flowchart, showing (in pictures) experiment milestones and key point at which to record information
Verbal	The laboratory procedures are presented verbally and written form, describing both the laboratory procedure and the expected experimental results.
Inductive	Each laboratory experiment includes several mini-lab exercises that collectively emphasize an overall concept presented in class.
Deductive	Students are asked to extrapolate results of each mini-lab exercise to subsequent one. Students also write about the use of the concept in new or similar situations.
Active	Each laboratory has a group component requiring members to adopt specific responsibilities. The responsibilities vary throughout the term.
Reflective	Each laboratory has a component that is completed individually during open lab time. Students may work at an individual pace.
Sequential	The mini-lab exercises are organized in sequential fashion, building from simple ideas to more sophisticated implementation.
Global	The overall concept is repeatedly reinforced through the experiment by executing mini-lab exercises.

Exhibit 5.3 Learning styles and DSP laboratory teaching techniques used to address different styles by Melton, Finelli, and Rust (1999). (Reproduced with permission of *IEEE, Proceedings Frontiers in Education Conference.*)

---

[23] Presented for teams 1 and 4 only.

The benchmark instrument against which the hypotheses were tested was a prior academic performance measure as proposed by Wiezel (1998). They also calculated the effect size following APA (1994) and Thompson (1996). As indicated above the learning styles of their students were very similar to those reported in other North American studies.

It was found that the average grades of all course components were consistently higher in the experimental group. An average student in the experimental group performed 0.42 standard deviations higher than a student in the control group. Thus, the experimental procedures improved the performance of the low achievers. Fifty percent of the low achievers obtained marks above the class median, suggesting that the performance of the experimental group was not strongly related to prior performance. The prior performance of the control group was strongly correlated with their course grade. When the learning styles were related to performance, it was found that active, global, and sensing learners were over represented among the low achievers (defined as below the median). Apart from those with a verbal orientation the experimental group showed improvements in all styles with most above average improvements among the active, global, and visual learners.

No improvements were found in the control group with the least improvement being among the active, visual, and global learners. The authors drew attention to the fact that 75% of the students thought that technology should supplement and not replace student instructor applications. But, the authors reported that hypermedia instruction enhanced the quality of student-teacher interaction, and *"it reached all types of student helping them to catch up."*

In a similar vein, Carver, Howard, and Lane (1999) have argued that the Felder model is the most appropriate for hypermedia courseware, and by demonstration they showed that hypermedia could be tailored to meet the needs of all learning styles. But, their first approach provided the students with a "plethora" of tools. *"This confused some students because they were uncomfortable making active choices of what course material would be most conducive to their learning."* Their second approach tailored the course material more to the individual's learning style.

5.12. Cognitive Styles Analysis

Riding and Cheema (1991) reviewed the background to cognitive styles research and came to the conclusion that there were two basic dimensions of cognitive style. These were *"the holistic-analytic style of whether an individual tends to process information in wholes or parts, and the verbal-imagery style of whether an individual is inclined to represent information during thinking verbally or in images"*. They developed a computer-presented schedule to assess both ends of these two dimensions. This assessment is called Cognitive Style Analysis. Riding and Staley (1998) were interested in the self-perception that the students had of themselves as learners in relation to cognitive style and performance.

They argued that students have to develop a self-awareness of their style so that they can understand its appropriateness for the particular subject they are studying. They will then be in a position to view a mismatch as a challenge to find alternative strategies. They gave the example of *verbalizers* who could change pictorial information in a book to words, and *imagers* who could change words into illustrations (Riding, 1996). Clearly, the intention of those who use Kolb or 4MAT is that students should experience and be able to function in each dimension. The point that students should view mismatches arising from differences in subject matter as a challenge would not seem, however, to have been made as forcefully as it might have been.[24] In any case these studies are a reminder, as are the investigations with Felder's model, that there are dimensions to learning styles other than those defined by the Kolb model, and that they have to be taken into account in the planning of learning and its implementations. While there is some attention to the cognitive and affective domains it cannot be said to have been of any great import (see below).

5.13. Course Structure, Learning Strategies and Learning Styles

Ayre and Nafalski (2000) distinguished between learning strategies (that they confusingly call learning concepts) and learning styles. They argued, as is the intention of this review, that both are important perceptions in the context of teaching. On the one hand, there are those that believe learning styles are innate and biologically determined (e.g., Dunn, Dunn and Perrin, 1994; Klinger, Finelli, and Budny, 2000). On the other hand, there are those who believe that teachers, and in particular their assessment procedures, will determine the style (strategy) which students will adopt. This model, they argued, takes insufficient cognizance of personality. Ayre and Nafalski suggested that formal education becomes increasingly influential as the student moves through programs, and, therefore, it is at the beginning of programs that a student is likely to experience a mismatch between their learning style and teaching style. This means that they will not engage with their courses effectively unless teachers devise methods to accommodate individual needs. This proposition merits more investigation but it also illustrates the value of teachers ascertaining their learning styles.

In what for some will be a very contentious paper, Beasley et al. (1995) considered the implications of cognitive style for the design of the curriculum. They argued that although faculty search for diversity among students they often take measures that disproportionately disadvantage students who possess particular cognitive and perceptual characteristics. Moreover, these measures are said to enforce standards. Their effect is to produce a homogenized student cohort. They pointed out that while the curriculum at entry, with its weighting toward

---

[24] A research carried out in England used Cognitive Styles Analysis to try and understand what mental processes are involved in design and to ask if some styles were better than others for design (Lawler, 1996).

science, rewards those who can be classified as problem solvers, later activities shift to the advantage of other groups. One effect of this is that those students who are discouraged early leave the course because it no longer caters for their needs. They wrote, *"Instructors in senior design courses often complain about the student's inability to 'put it all together'. They note with dismay the 'good' students who flop when they get to real engineering'. Perhaps the apparent magnitude of the problem stems from the absence of students who would excel at integrative thinking, but who can now be found in the business school because they were weaker at pre-structured problem solving and dis-aggregative analysis."* Beasley et al. argued that the solution is to design a curriculum that will enable students to grow, not sequentially but in parallel. It should challenge students in their weak area and help them to blossom in their strong area. Thus, the mechanical engineering department at Clemson University undertook a cognitive styles analysis using Gordon's cognitive style typology (see Wilkes, 1992).

This typology is of four types. These are integrator; problem finder; problem solver; and implementer. It distinguishes between those who have a propensity for problem finding and those who are problem solvers. These styles are established from two measures: remote association and differentiation. *"Remote association is a mental quality that enables some to rapidly conceive of numerous novel possibilities and to almost instantly see that some are superior to others and that one is a solution to the problem...."* Differentiation is "related to the ability to discern subtle differences and make fine distinctions on the basis of relatively nebulous criteria, including subjective standards [   ]." This type is not bound by preconceived notions. Because there is a low correlation between the two, it is possible to distinguish between high and low performance on each of the dimensions and to correlate them with each of the learning styles.

Beasley and his colleagues found one surprising result in their pilot study. They expected the High (Differentiation)-Low (remote association) group to excel in the Senior thermal systems design course. The majority of C's were awarded to the high-low problem finders. Instead the Low-High group, most nearly matched by faculty, achieved the highest percentage of A's and B's. They suggested that the grades seem to reflect on the ability of students to follow conventional wisdom. To be in remote association was an advantage on this course. Their theory was upheld in that the initially dominant type drops as a proportion of the total with increasing time on the course. It was the cognitive types who were the same style as the majority of the faculty that benefited from the course!

5.14. Learning Styles and Individualised Environments.

Kolb's learning theory has been applied to the design of on-line instruction by Buch and Sena (2001). They developed a 40-page HTML website to deliver four lessons on the *"Process of Evolution"*. Each lesson was designed to match one of Kolb's learning styles. For example, the lesson designed to match the preferences of assimilators *"began with a theoretical tutorial on evolution. Because assimilators do not enjoy easy participation, pages were kept to an interactive minimum; the only required interaction was the pressing of a page-forward button. Names of the scientists and researchers were used to appeal to the assimilators appreciation of expert opinion. Because assimilators prefer to process information through reflective observation, the exercise was followed by a visual review of the concepts presented in the exercise. No written responses or any generation of ideas was required because answers to the problems were integrated in the review."*

Sixty-one psychology students participated in the exercise. They completed the LSI and were assigned a code based on their learning style. They went on-line and the code determined the lesson they received. About half received the lesson that matched their learning style. The others received a lesson that responded to the style most unlike their own. After the lesson they completed a short test on the material presented, and they responded to a questionnaire designed to measure perceptions of their learning experience. It was found that students who received lessons that matched their learning styles enjoyed the lesson and felt they had learned more. But the significance level of this result was only obtained after the analysis was controlled for prior experience on the internet. However, overall the results showed that students differ in their approaches to on-line learning, just as they do in ordinary classroom learning, and, moreover, that it is possible to design on-line learning that matches different learning styles.

Another approach with similar assumptions, but with different instruments, was used by Boles, Pillay, and Raj (1999) at Queensland University of Technology. They followed the analysis of cognitive styles suggested by Riding (see Section 5.9) In that analysis he distinguished between two principal styles-Wholist-Analytic (WA), and Verbal-Imagery (VI), and used his software for determining style.[25] Their teaching program was linear and designed to meet the needs of persons with these different styles. They found that there was a case for research on personalized CBI material.[26]

---

[25] Riding and Mathias (1991).

[26] They affirm the need to take into account cognitive processes in the design of CBI (see Kozma, 1994). They argued that in order to respond to perceptual learning needs each CBI screen should reflect the cognitive style being catered for. The designer should take into account the ratio of text to graphics, nature of the text information, and content of the information. For example, very vivid narrative text suits imagers, whereas a list of points suits verbalizers. Conceptual knowledge may require information from multiple sources. Based on work by Satterly and Telfer they suggested that although the needs of wholists and analysts are in contrast carefully designed advanced organizers may help them process information. But the student teachers with whom I worked evidently found it difficult to design advance organizers. Often they simply provided an introduction to a lesson.

A similar procedure to that adopted by Buch and Sena was used, and four groups of students representing WI, WV, AI, and AV were presented with either matched or mismatched instructional material. The students were assessed for cognitive style using the Cognitive Style Assessment courseware developed by Riding. The 134 undergraduates were in a digital communications class. The assessment tasks were for recall, labeling, explanation, and problem solving. Although the results were by no means conclusive, some support was found for Riding and Douglas's (1992) view that certain cognitive styles have an affinity with particular types of subject matter. There was also some support for Riding and Calvey's (1981) view that the effect of cognitive style on performance is a function of the task, although, it should be noted, that this point was derived from studies with 11-year old children.

Overall, these findings lend support to Buch and Sena's view that materials can be designed for on-line learning for individuals with different styles. So far the discussion has mainly centered on traditional learners and traditional learning environments. However, lifelong learning is becoming a reality. As such learning is often likely to be accomplished through the interactive World Wide Web; attention is now beginning to focus on the environment of the lone learner, as well as the characteristics he/she brings to that environment (e.g. Bamber 2000; Freeman, Sharp, and Bamber, 2000). Martinez and Bunderson, (2000) have shown the importance of emotions and intentions on learning in these situations. Their research was in the tradition of aptitude treatment interaction studies proposed by Cronbach (1957). He argued that the great challenge in education was to find the most appropriate treatment to which an individual could most easily adapt. (For an example of an aptitude treatment study, see Jackson, 1985).

Martinez and Bunderson described an intentional learning theory. This theory argued *"that the depth of an individual's emotions and intentions about why, when and how to use learning and how it can accomplish personal goals or change events is fundamental to understanding how successfully an individual learns, interacts with an environment, commits to learning, performs, and experiences learning and change."*

They used the theory to develop four learner difference profiles, called learner orientations. These are, in effect, learning styles. The four styles are Transforming Learners, Performing Learners, Conforming Learners, and Resistant Learners. Their purpose is to describe a learner's *"proclivity to take control, set goals, attain standards, manage resources, solve problems, and take risks to learn."* The theory proposed that learners are situated on a continuum of learning orientations along which they can move. Movement upwards requires *"greater effort, learning autonomy, and intentions, feelings, beliefs about learning than a downward range movement.t"* At one end of the continuum are transforming learners. They are deeply influenced by *"an awareness of the psychological*

aspects that motivate them. They place great importance on personal strengths, intrinsic resources, ability, committed, persistent, assertive effort, sophisticated learning, performance, and problem solving strategies, and positive expectations to self-manage long-range learning successfully...." At the other end of the continuum are resistant learners who *"doubt that (a) they can learn or enjoy achieving any goals set by others (b) compulsory academic learning and achievement can help them achieve personal goals or initiate desired changes, and (c) their personal values, interests, and goals can benefit from academic objectives."*

In many respects, these orientations are reminiscent of Bey's (1961) social theory of academic development and there are many similarities with the learning strategies and styles discussed in the previous section. The important difference is the apparent emphasis on the cognitive and the affective in learning that, perhaps, does not come across as well as it might have done in the previous discussion. By cognitive is meant the mental processes providing the drive to action (conation). These include intent, determination, deliberateness, desire, striving, etc.

Martinez and Bunderson developed a questionnaire to assess these orientations and used it to evaluate three Web-based learning environments. The questionnaire was designed for three factors. These were cognitive and affective learning focus; learning independence; and committed strategic planning and learning effort. Group interactions were found to be important because they helped support learner attitudes, learning efficacy, and intentional learning performance. The results suggested that those environments that supported individual learning orientation led to greater achievement in learning than those environments that conflicted with learning orientation. The authors argued that using learning orientation enables teachers to examine what specifically works for learners in different learning environments over time.

In similar vein, Larkin-Hein (2001), and Larkin-Hein and Budny (2001), have used the Productivity Preference Survey.[27] This is an inventory for the identification of individual adult preferences in a working or learning environment (Price, Dunn and Dunn, 1990). (Dunn and Dunn take the view that teaching styles should be matched to learning styles.)

The students in Larkin-Hein's course were studying an introduction to physics. One of the instructional techniques involved the students in on-line discussion. The provisional analysis suggested that

---

[27] Larkin, Feldgen and Chia (2002) have provided a detailed description of Dunn and Dunn's theory and the Personal Preference Survey. This paper describes how the Dunn and Dunn model has contributed to the design of an introductory physics course that is used at the American University and the University Buenos Aires. Writing assignments were one of the activities that were introduced. For example, one of the assignments asks the students to explain a concept that was highlighted in a class session. Another was to create sample examination questions (see Chapter 4). No details of assessment and performance are given but it is stated that the students found the writing activities useful, and that in sum they catered for a variety of learning styles.

students who participated in these discussions had a tendency to prefer to work alone. Larkin-Hein posited that such students might prefer this format to those who prefer to work with a peer or an authority figure. At the time of publication Larkin-Hein was not able to say whether this format suited a particular group of students.

It is interesting to note that the student participant comments in a questionnaire yielded objectives for (a) the on-line activity that are akin to those expected of students working to meet assignments, and (b) the provision of the liberal education of collegiate universities (Newman, 1851, 1949; see also Astin, 1997).

5.15. Learning Styles and the Design of Textbooks

Authors and publishers make assumptions about the make-up and presentation of their books in relation to the way in which individuals' learn. For the most part it is assumed that all individuals learn in the same way. Given the volume of evidence that supports the argument that individuals differ in their approaches to learning this cannot be the case. In response to this need Felder and Rousseau (2000) together with their publisher John Wiley produced a CD to accompany their textbook on chemical processes. The CD included the Index of Learning Styles, along with suggestions on how to use the book based on the reader's learning style.

Irwin (2002), also in a book published by John Wiley, incorporated a Learning Styles Inventory at the beginning of his text on circuit analysis. This thirteen-item inventory determines four styles. These are called visual; aural; reading/writing; and kinaesthetic.
The inventory does not anticipate that only a single style may emerge. There may be two. The reader is asked to determine his/her style(s) and then to consult the advice given them on how to read the book and from this to work out an optimum approach to reading the book. Charts are provided for each style. Each chart has information under the following headings:
1. Intake: to take in information.
2. To make a study package.
3. Text features that may help you the most.
4. Output: to do well in examinations.

Learning goals are stated at the beginning of the Chapters, and boxed "learning hints" and 'learning by doing' exercises appear throughout the Chapters. Wiley's are now producing books in other subjects using this formula.

Given that the internet is now being used by publishers to produce books (e.g., Larson, 2001), there is no reason to suppose that the same principles of pedagogy should not apply to them. We all have to learn concepts, and we variously bring different dispositions to our learning as the work reported by Martinez and Bunderson in the last section, and this Chapter generally, shows. The study of learning orientations in relation to performance related to the study of books should enable authors and teachers to establish what works over time.

5.16. Concluding Remarks.

This Chapter began with a reference to Snow, Corno, and Jackson (1996), who remarked that the literature on personal styles was voluminous and laced with controversy. In this spirit, this review is completed by another theory from two engineers. Eftekhar and Strong (1998) in Canada reviewed four learning style models (MBTI, Kolb, Felder, and Silverman, and the Herrmann Brain dominance model). From this review they conceptualized a model for two types of learners. These they called Type I and Type II.

"Type I learners might be known as Form-type learners who possess form-oriented minds. Form oriented learner's view learning tasks as their forms and outside appearances. In general, they see things in the way they look and not in the way they work. They are primarily memory-type learners and are oriented to what and how many type questions. Their minds hang on all types of in-going information (things, relationships and procedures) onto to hooks without active thought. In other words, in a Form mind, things relationships, and procedures once defined, all become forms. Form learners employ procedures to use the relationships and things on the hooks or episodes of information. In their worldview, a knowledgeable student is someone with a good store of memorized information and ready recall system."

"Type II learners might be known as Function-type learners who possess Function-oriented minds. Function-oriented students are primarily relationship-type students and are oriented to why and how type questions. They view learning tasks in their functions and in their reasons for being used. In general, they look at things in the way they work and not in the way they appear. Function-oriented students see learning experiments as methods and procedures that determine relationships that, subsequently determine parts (or things). Their minds create methods and procedures as possible on a continuing basis. In their worldview, a knowledgeable student is someone with insight and the means to solve new problems". The authors regarded these as two extreme types with "numberless variations in between *and any one learner would have some combination of Form and Function Learning abilities."*

In a lengthy paper the authors described some experiments with students they did to validate the theory, and described in a detail that is beyond the scope of this review to rehearse, its implications for teaching and the design of inventories to discriminate between learners along these dimensions.

Early in this Chapter, it was suggested that teachers would want to take up a point made by Hein and Budny (1999). This was to the effect that the learning style assessment tool used is not as critical as the actual assessment of learning styles because of the impact that it can have on teaching. This review of learning style research and development in engineering supports that view, and it is certainly supported by my work with student teachers (Heywood, 1999). My findings, that linked style to learning gains, suggested that these gains that were in a positive direction. Since this work was done in a school system that is dominated by examinations, the student teachers would not have commented favorably on the exercise had they not noticed such an improvement. (Heywood, 1992).

The Chapter illustrated the complexity of learning and points out the fact that different learning environments such as the disciplines or those deriving from the culture can influence the conceptions that we have of learning. The effects of culture should not be underestimated (see for example Pratt, Kelly, and Wong, 1999). Each of the styles and strategies offers some insight into learning. Overall, the reported research supports the need for variety in teaching and learning not only for the sake of learning, but for preparation for work in industry. It also supports the case for multiple strategy approaches to the assessment of student learning.

References

Abouscric, R (1995). Self-esteem and achievement motivation as determinants of students' approaches to studying. *Studies in Higher Education*, 20, (1), 19-26.

Agogino, A. M., and S. His (1995). Learning style based innovations to improve retention of female engineering students in the synthesis coalition. *Proceedings Frontiers in Education Conference*, 4a2-1 to 4.

APA (1994). *American Psychological Association Publication Manual*. 4th edition. American Psychological Association, Washington DC.

Astin, A. W. (1997). *What Matters in College. Four Critical years Revisited*. Jossey Bass, San Francisco.

Allen, E., and N. Mourtos (2000). Using learning styles preferences dat to inform classroom teaching and assessment activities. *Proceedings Frontiers in Education Conference*, 3, S2B- 6

August, R. J., Lopez, G. W., Yokomoto, C. F., and W. W. Buchanan (2002). Heuristic beliefs about problem solving in technology courses and their impact on problems solving exams. *Proceedings Frontiers in Education Conference*, 3, S2H-3-S2H-8

Ayre, M. and A. Nafalski (2000). Recognizing diverse learning styles in teaching and assessment of electronic engineering. *Proceedings Frontiers in Education Conference*, 1, T2B-18-T2B-23.

Bamber, D (2000). The Impact of constructs within learning styles on performance and other aspects. ADAPT/IDIEL Project. University of Salford, Salford, United Kingdom. Revised edition.

Bandura, A (1971). *Social Learning Theory*. General Learning Press, New York.

Barr, R. E. and D. Juricic (1994). From drafting to modern design representation: the evolution of engineering design graphics. *Journal of Engineering Education*, 83, (3), 263-270.

Beasley, D. E., Huey, C. O., Wilkes, J. M., and K. McCormick (1995). Cognitive styles and implications for the engineering curriculum. *Proceedings Frontiers in Education Conference*, 4d3-8 to 11.

Beaumont, M and D. Jackson (1997). Visualization as an aid to low-level programming. *Proceedings Frontiers in Education Conference*, 2, 1158-1163.

Belenky, M. F., Clinchy, B. M., Goldberger, N. R., and J. M. Carule (1986). *Women's Ways of Knowing*. Basic Books, New York.

Bey, C (1961). A social theory of intellectual development in N. Sanford (ed). *The American College*. Wiley, New York.

Blumner, H.N. and H.C. Richards (1997). Study habits and academic achievement of Engineering students. *Journal of Engineering Education*. 86, (2), 125-132.

Boles, W. W., Pillay, H., and L. Raj (1999). Matching cognitive styles to computer based instruction: an approach for enhanced learning in electrical engineering. *European Journal of Engineering Education*, 24, (4) 371-383.

Bransford, J. D. et al (2000). (eds.) *How People Learn*. National Academy Press, Washington, DC.

Brown, R.W (2000). Physiological parameters and learning. *Proceedings Frontiers in Education Conference*, 2, S2B-7 to 11.

Buch, K. and C. Sena (2001). Accommodating diverse learning styles in the design and delivery of on-line learning experiences. *International Journal of Engineering Education*, 17, (1), 93-98.

Budny, D (1993). Plotting calculators in group teaching. *Proceedings Frontiers in Education Conference*, 122–124.

Caine, R. N. and G. Caine (1991). *Making Connections. Teaching and the Human Brain*. Association for Supervision and Curriculum Development, Alexandria, VA.

Carrizosa, K and S. Sheppard (2000). The importance of learning styles in group design work. *Proceedings Frontiers in Education Conference*, 1, T2B-12 to 17.

Carter, G., Heywood, J and D.T. Kelly (1986). *Case Study in Curriculum Assessment. GCE Engineering Science (Advanced)*. Roundthorn Press, Manchester.

Carter, G., and T. A. Jordan (1986). *Student Centered Learning in Engineering. Engineering Enhancement in Higher Education: Prospects and Problems*. University of Salford, Salford, United Kingdom.

Carver, C. A., Howard, A. A. and W. D. Lane (1999). *IEEE Transactions on Education* 42, (1), 33 –38.

Cassidy, S (1999). Using self-report measure of student efficiency to evaluate teaching and learning in higher education. University of Salford Teaching and Learning Committee. Salford.

Clark, S, Seat, E and F. Weber (2000). The performance of engineering students on the group embedded figures test. *Proceedings Frontiers in Education Conference*, 1, T3A- 1 to 4

Clark, A. C., and E. N. Wiebe (1999). Scientific visualization for secondary and post-secondary schools. *The Journal of Technology Studies*. 24–32

Collinge, J. N (1994). Some fundamental questions about scientific thinking. *Research in Science and Technological Education*, 12, (2), 161–174.

Cook, M (1997). Gender differences in the CPI. *Occupational Psychology Conference Book of Proceedings*, 77–83.

Cowan, J (1998) *One Becoming an Innovative University Teacher. Reflection in Action*. SRHE/Open University Press, Buckingham

Cowan, J., Pottinger, I., Weedon, E., and H. Wood (1994). Development through researching your own practice. Mimeo. Open University in Scotland, Edinburgh.

Cronbach, L (1957). The two disciplines of scientific psychology. *American Psychologist*, 671–684.

Cross, N (1989). Learning, designing and computing: the relevance of cognitive styles to computer aided design education. *Proceedings of World Conference on Engineering Education for Advancing Technology*, 1, 556–559.

Crown, S. W. (2001). Journal of Engineering Education. 90,(3), 347-356.

Crynes, B., Greene, B., and C. Dillon (2000). Lectrons or lectures-which is the best for whom. *Proceedings Frontiers in Education Conference*, 3, S2D- 21 to 24.

Culver, R. S., Cox, P., Sharp, J., and A. FitzGibbon (1994) Student learning profiles in two innovative honours degree engineering programs. *International Journal of Technology and Design Education*, 4, (3), 257–288.

Danchak, M. M. (2000). Designing collaborative learning in large introductory courses. *Proceedings Frontiers in Education Conference*, I, T1B-7 to 10.

Daniel, J.S. (1975). Conversations, individuals and knowables: toward a theory of learning. *Engineering Education*, 65, (5), 415–420.:

Duncan-Hewitt , W. C. et al (2001). Using developmental principles to plan design experiences for beginning engineering students. *Proceedings Frontiers in Education Conference*, 1, T3E- 17 to 22.

Dunn, R., Dunn, K., and J. Perrin (1994). *Teaching Young Children through Their Individual Learning Styles*. Allyn and Bacon, Boston.

Edgerton, R. H. and K. Y. Upton (1989). A Case for visual thinking in engineering education. *Proceedings World Conference on Engineering Education for Advancing Technology*, 424–429.

Edward, N. S (1997). An evaluation of student perceptions of screen presentations in computer-based laboratory simulations. *European Journal of Engineering Education*, 22, (2), 142–151.

Eftekhar, N. and R. D. Strong (1998). Toward dynamic modeling of a teaching/learning system Part 2: a new theory on types of learners. *International Journal of Engineering Education*, 16, (6), 368–406.

Elton, C .F., and H. A. Rose (1966). Within university transfer. Its relation to personality characteristics. *Journal of Applied Psychology*, 50, (6), 539

Elton, C. F., and H. A. Rose (1974). Students who leave engineering. *Engineering Education*, 62, (1), 30-32.

Engler, B (1979). *Personality Theories. An Introduction.* Houghton Mifflin, MA.

Entwistle, N. J., Hanley, M., and G. Ratcliffe (1979). Approaches to learning and levels of understanding. *British Educational Research Journal*, 5, 99–114.

Entwistle, N.. J and P. Ramsden (1983). *Understanding Student Learning.* Croom Helm, London.

Entwistle , N. J., and S. Waterston (1987). Approaches to studying and levels of cognitive processing. *International Conference on Cognitive Processes in Student learning.* University of Lancaster, Lancaster.

Enyeart, M.A., Baker, D. and D. VanHarlingen (1990) Correlation of inductive and deductive and logical reasoning to college physics achievement. *Journal of Research in Science and Technology*, 17, (3), 263–267.

Evans, D. L., McNeill, B. W. and G. C. Beakley (1990) Design in engineering education: past views of future directions. *Engineering Education*, 80, (5), 517–522.

Felder, R. M (1993). Reaching the second tier: learning and teaching styles in college science education. *College Science Teaching*, 23, (5), 286–290.

Felder, R.. M (1995) A longitudinal study of engineering student performance and retention. IV instructional methods and student responses to them. *Journal of Engineering Education*, 84, (4), 361–367.

Felder, R. M , Felder, G.M and E.J. Dietz (1997). A longitudinal study of alternative approaches to engineering education: survey assessment of results. *Proceedings Frontiers in Education Conference* 3, 11284–11289. ASEE/IEEE, New York.

Felder, R. M and L. K. Silverman (1988). Learning and teaching styles in engineering education. *Engineering Education*, 78, 674–681.

Felder, R. M and R. W. Rousseau (2000). *Elementary Principles of Chemical Processes.* 3rd edition. Wiley, New York

Felder, R. M. (1996). Matters of style. *ASEE Prism,* December, 18 – 23.

Finelli, C. J., Klinger, A., and D. D. Budny (2001). Strategies for improving classroom environment. *Journal of Engineering Education.* 90, (4), 491–498.

FitzGibbon, A (1987). Kolb's experiential learning model as a model for supervision of classroom teaching for student teachers. *European Journal of Teacher Education*, 10, (2), 163–178.

Foley, B (1996). Using visualization tools to improve undergraduates' understanding of crystal structure. *Proceedings Frontiers in Education Conference* 2, 1079–1083.

Freeman, J., Carter, G., and T. A. Jordan (1978). Cognitive styles, personality factors, problem-solving skills and teaching approach in electrical engineering. *Assessment in Higher Education*, 3, 86.

Freeman, J., McComiskey, J.G. and D. Buttle (1968). Research into divergent and convergent thinking. *International Journal of Electrical Engineering Education*, 6, 99–108.

Freeman, J. Sharp, J. and D. Bamber (2000). A pre-course psychometric assessment of a group of learners.ADAPT/IDIEL Project. University of Salford, Salford, United Kingdom.

Freeman, J and E. Thomas (2001). Computer literacy in Biological science in J. Heywood, J., J. Sharp and M. Hides (eds) Improving *Teaching in Higher Education.* Teaching and learning Committee, University of Salford, Salford.

Furneaux, W.D (1962). The Psychologist and the university. *Universities Quarterly*, 17, 33.

Geiger, M. A., et al (1993). An examination of ipsative and normative versions of Kolb's learning style inventory. *Educational and Psychological Measurement*, 53, 717–726.

Gilliam, F. T. et al (1998). The Engage Program: Renovating the first year experience at the University of Tennessee. *Proceedings Frontiers in Education Conference*, 2, 814–819.

Grasha, A. F (1984) Learning styles: the journey from Greenwich Observatory (1796) to the college classroom (1984). *Improving College and University Teaching.* 32, (1), 46-53.

Grasha, A. F (1990). The naturalistic approach to learning styles. *College Teaching*, 38, (3), 106-113.

Grasha, A. F (1994). A matter of Style: The teacher, the expert, formal authority, personal model, facilitator, and delegator. *College Teaching*. 42, (4),142–149.

Gregory, S. A (1972) ch 1 of Gregory, S.A. (ed). *Creativity in Engineering.* Butterworths, London.

Guilford, J. (1954). *Psychometric Methods.* McGraw Hill, New York.

Hackstian, A. R. and R. B. Cattell (1974) The checking of primary ability structure on a broader basis of performance. British *Journal of Educational Psychology*, 44 – 154.

Harasym, P. H., Leong, E. J., Juschka, B. B., Lucier, G. E and F. L. Lorscheider (1995). Myers-Briggs psychological type and achievement in anatomy and physiology. *Advances in Physiology Education*, 13, 61–65.

Hartley, J. (1998). *Learning and Studying. A Research Perspective.* Routledge, London.

Hartley, J and M. A. Greggs (1997). Divergent thinking in arts and science students; contrary imaginations at Keele revisited. *Studies in Higher Education*, 22, (1), 93–97.

Hayes, J and C. Allinson (1996) The implications of learning styles for training and development: A discussion of the matching hypothesis. *British Journal of Management*, 7, 63–73.

Heim, A. (1970). *Intelligence and Personality. Their Assessment and Relationship.* Penguin, Harmondsworth

Hein, T. L., and D. D. Budny (1999). Teaching to student's learning styles: approaches that work. *Proceedings Frontiers in Education Conference*, 2, 12c1-7 to 14.

Hellige, J. B (1993). *Hemispheric Asymmetry; What's Right and what's Left.* Harvard University Press, Cambridge, MA.

Herrera, R (1998). Problems encountered when substituting the traditional drawing tools for CADF systems in engineering graphics courses. *Proceedings Frontiers in Education Conference*, 2, 677.

Hesseling, P (1966). *A Strategy for Evaluation, Research.* Van Gorcum. Aassen

Heywood, J (1969). An Evaluation of certain post-war developments in Higher Technological Education. Thesis, Volume 1. University of Lancaster Library, Lancaster.

Heywood, J (1989). *Learning, Adaptability and Change.* Paul Chapman, London.

Heywood, J (1992). Student teachers as researcher of instruction in the classroom. In J. H. C. Vonk, and H. J. Van Helden (eds.) *New Projects for Teacher Education in Europe. Association for Teacher Education in Europe,* Brussels.

Heywood, J (1994). *The Assessment of Enterprise Learning in Higher Education.* Employment Department. Technical Report No. 20. Sheffield.

Heywood, J (1997). An evaluation of Kolb's learning style theory by graduate student teachers during their teaching practice. Association of Teacher Educators conference, Washington, DC ERIC ED 406 333.

Heywood, J (1999) Linking theory to practice in pre-service training through classroom research . An evaluation of a course in a higher diploma program. Appendix pp. 23–42 of a Submission to the expert Advisory group on the content and duration of teacher education programs for post primary Teachers of the Department of Education and Science, Dublin.

Heywood, J (2000). *Assessment in Higher Education Student Learning, Teaching, Programmes and Institutions.* Jessica Kingsley, London.

Highouse, S and D. Doverspike (1987) The validity of the Learning Style Inventory 1985 as a predictor of cognitive style and occupational preference. *Educational and Psychological Measurement*, 47, (3), 749-753.

Holland, J. L (1978). *Manual for the Vocational Preference Inventory.* Consulting Psychologists Press, Palo Alto, CA

Holt, J., and F. Solomon (2000) Engineering Education- the way ahead. *Australasian Journal of Engineering Education*, 7 (1)

Honey, P., and A. Mumford (1992). *The Manual of Learning Styles.* Peter Honey Publisher, Maidenhead, United Kingdom

Hook, M. H (1990). Learning styles. Mismatching for a balanced profile. *Proceedings Australian Conference on Engineering Education.* 1, 251-256.

Hoyt, B., Mastascusa, E. J., Hanyak, M. E., Snyder, W. J. and T. P. Rich (1998) Using courseware authoring to mentor faculty of the future. *Proceedings Frontiers in Education Conference.* 1, 111-114.

Hsi, S., Linn, M. HC., and J.E. Bell (1997). The role of spatial reasoning in engineering and the design of spatial instruction. *Journal of Engineering Education*, 86, (2), 151−158.

Huck, R, Myers, R., and J. Wilson (1989). ADAPT: A developmental activity program for teachers. Allegheny Intermediate Unit, Pittsburgh.

Hudson, L (1962). Intelligence, divergence and potential quality. *Nature*, 196, 601.

Hudson, L. (1966). *Contrary Imaginations*. Methuen, London.

Ingham, J., Meza, R. M. P., and, G, Price (1998). A comparison of the learning style and creative talents of Mexican and American undergraduate students. *Proceedings Frontiers in Education Conference*, 1, 605−610.

Irwin, J. D (2002). *Basic Engineering Circuit Analysis*. 1st Edition, Wiley, New York.

Jackson, I (1985) On detecting aptitude effects in undergraduate academic achievement scores. *Assessment and Evaluation in Higher Education*. 10, (1) 71-88.

Janis, I. L (1982). *Stress, Attitudes and Decisions: Selected Papers*. Praeger, New York

Jensen, E (1998). *Teaching with the Brain in Mind*. Association for Supervision and Curriculum Development. Alexandria, VA.

Kanfer, F. H (1977). The many faces of self-control or behavior modification changes its focus in R. B. Stuart (ed.). *Behavioral Management. Strategies, Technique and Outcome*. Brunner/Mazel, New York.

Karplus, R and E. Karplus (1970). Intellectual development beyond elementary school, deductive logic. *School Science and Mathematics*, 70, 398−406.

Kember, D., Jamieson, Q., Pomfret, M., and E. T. T. Wong. (1995).Learning approaches, study time and academic performance. *Higher Education*, 29, (3), 329−343.

Kiersey, D., and M. Bates (1984). *Please Understand Me: An Essay in Temperament Styles*. Oxford Psychologists Press, Oxford.

Kline, P (1993). *The Handbook of Psychological Testing*. Routledge, London.

Kline, P (2000) *The Handbook of Psychological Testing, 2nd Edition*, Routledge, London.

Klinger, A., Finelli, C.J. and D.D. Budny (2000). Improving the classroom environment. *Proceedings Frontiers in Education Conference*, 1, T1B-1−T1b-6.

Kneale, P (1997). The rise of the 'strategic student'. How can we adapt to cope? In S. Armstrong, G. Thompson and S. Brown (eds.). *Facing Up to Radical Change in Universities and Colleges*. Kogan Page, London.

Kolb, D. A (1984). *Experiential Learning: Experience as the Source of Learning and Development*. Prentice-Hall, Englewood Cliffs, NJ.

Kosslyn, S. M. (1978). Imagery and cognitive development. A teleological approach. In R. Siegler (ed.). *Children's Thinking. What develops?* Lawrence Erlbaum, Hillsdale, NJ

Kosslyn, S. M (1983). *Ghosts in the Mind's Machine. Creating and using Images in the Brain*. Norton, New York.

Kozma, R. B (1994). Will media influence learning? Reframing the debate. *Educational Technology, Research and Development*. 42, 7 −19.

Kraemer-Koehler, P., Tooney, N.M., and D.P. Beke (1995). The use of learning style innovations to improve retention. *Proceedings Frontiers in Education Conference*, 1, 4a2-5 to 8.

Landis, R. B (1995). *Studying Engineering. A Road Map to a Rewarding Career*. Discovery Press/Legal Book Distributing, Los Angeles.

Larkin-Hein, T (2001). On-line discussions: A key to enhancing student motivation and understanding. *Proceedings Frontiers in Education Conference*, 2, F2G-6 to 12.

Larkin-Hein, T and D. D. Budny (2001). Research on learning style: applications in the physics and engineering classrooms. *IEEE Transactions on Education*, 44, (3), 276−281.

Larkin, T. L., Feldgen, M., and O. Chia (2002). A global approach to learning styles. *Proceedings Frontiers in Education Conference*, F1F- 9 to 14.

Larson, T. R (2001). Developing a participating textbook for the internet. *Journal of Engineering Education*, 90, (1), 49−54.

Lawler, T (1996). The use of cognitive style analysis and the APU design and technology assessment strategy as a means of clarifying and describing student design work. *Journal of Design and Technology Education*, 1, (1), 4−11.

Lawson, A. E. and M. Johnson (2002). The validity of Kolb learning styles and neo-Piagetian developmental levels in college biology. *Studies in Higher Education*, 27, (1), 79−88.

Loacker, G (1984); (2000) (ed). *Self-Assessment at Alverno College*. Alverno College, Milwaukee, WI

Lord, T. R (1985). Enhancing the visual-spatial aptitude of students. *Journal of Research in Science Teaching*, 22, 395−405.

Luchins, A. S (1942). Mechanisation in problem solving. The effect of Einstellung. *Psychological Monographs*, 248.

Mann, R, Ringwald, B. E., Arnold, S., Binder, J., Cytrynbaum, S., and J. W. Roswein (1970). *Conflict and Style in the College Classroom*. Wiley, New York.

Marton, F., Dall'Alba, G., and E. Beaty (1993). Conceptions of Learning. *International Journal of Education*, 19, (3), 277-299.

McCarthy, B (1986). *The 4MAT System: Teaching to Learning Styles with Right-Left Mode Techniques*. Excel inc. Barrington, Ill.

McCarthy, B., and C. St Germain (1993) *The Learning Type Measure*. Excel Inc., Barrington, Ill.

MacFarlane Smith, I (1964). *Spatial Ability*. University of London Press, London.

McCaulley, M. H (1976). Psychological types in engineering. Implications for teaching. *Engineering Education*, 66, (7), 729−736.

McCaulley, M et al (1983). Applications of psychological type in engineering. *Engineering Education*. 73, (5), 394−400.

McCaulley, M. H (1990). The MBTI and individual pathways in engineering design. *Engineering Education*. 80, (5), 535−542.

McDermott, K. J., Nafalski, A and O. Göl (2000) Active learning in the University of South Australia. *Proceedings Frontiers in Education Conference*, T1B-11 to 15.

McDermott, K. J., Göl, O and A. Nafalski (2000). Cooperative learning in South Australia. *Proceedings Frontiers in Education Conference*, 3, 31B−1 to 5.

McKenna, A., McMartin, F., Terada, Y., Sirivedhin, V., and A, Agonino (2001). *Proceedings Annual Conference ASEE*. Session 1330.

McKim, R.H (1968). Visual thinking and the design process. *Engineering Education*, 58, (7), 795−799.

McKenna, A, Mongia, L and A. Agognino (1998). Engineering design class. *Proceedings Frontiers in Education Conference*, 1, 264 − 269.

McKim, R. H. (1980). *Experiences in Visual Thinking*. 2nd edition. PWS Engineering, Boston, MA.

Magin, D. J (1990). The use of student course ratings as a performance indicator: A bias against engineering? *Proceedings Australian Engineers Conference* 313–318.

Magin, D. J and A. E. Churches 91995). Peer tutoring in engineering design: A case study. *Studies in Higher Education*, 20, (1), 73−85.

Marshall, D., Summers, M and B. Woolnough (1999). Students' conceptions of learning in an engineering context. *Higher Education*. 38, 291−309.

Martinez, M. and C. V. Bunderson (2000). Building interactive world wide web (Web) learning environments to match and support individual differences. *Journal of Interactive Learning Research*,11, (2), 163−195.

Marton, F., Hounsell, D., and N.J. Entwistle (1984) (eds.) *The Experience of Learning*. Scottish Academic Press, Edinburgh.

Marton, F and R. Säljö (1984). Approaches to Learning in F. Marton, D. Hounsell and N.J. Entwistle (eds). *The Experience of Learning*. Scottish Academic Press, Edinburgh.

Mentkowski, M and Associates (2000). Learning that Lasts. Integrating Learning, Development, and Performance in College and Beyond. Jossey-Bass, San Fransisco.

Melton, D. E., Finelli, C. J. and L. M. Rust (1999) A digital processing laboratory with style. *Proceedings Frontiers in Education Conference*, 2, 12b6 pp 14 to 19.

Messick, S. and associates (1976). *Individuality in Learning. Implications of Cognitive styles and Creativity for Human Development*. Jossey-Bass, San Francisco.

Montgomery, S. M (1995). Addressing diverse learning styles through use of multi-media. *Proceedings Frontiers in Education Conference*, 3a2 13t o 21.

Moran, A. (1991). What can learning styles research learn from cognitive psychology? *Educational Psychology*, 11, (3/4),239−245.

Myers, C. T (1958) *Some observations of problem solving in spatial relations tests. Research Memorandum* 58-16. Educational Testing Service, Princeton, NJ.

Myers, C. T (1958). The effects of training in mechanical drawing on spatial relation test scores as predictors of engineering drawing grades. R and D. report No. 58-4. Educational Testing Service, NJ.

Newcomer, J. L., Raudebaugh, R. A., McKell, E. K., and D.S. Kelley (1999). Visualization, Freehand drawing, solid modelling, and design in introductory engineering graphics. *Proceedings Frontiers in Education Conference* 2, 12d2-1 to 6.

Newman, J. H. (1851/2, 1949). *The Idea of a University. Defined and Illustrated.* Longmans Green, London.

Ng, L. S., Tan, O. I., and C. C. Jong (1995) Motivating engineering undergraduates with practical problems. International *Journal of Electrical Engineering Education*, 32, 201–213.

Nulty, D. D., and M. A. Barrett (1996) Transitions in students learning styles. *Studies in Higher Education*, 32, 201–213.

Pask, G (1988). Learning strategies, teaching strategies and conceptual learning or style in R.R. Schmeck (ed.) *Learning Strategies and Learning Styles.* Plenum Press, New York.

Pask, G and GCE. Scott (1972). Learning strategies and individual competence. *International Journal of Man-Machines Studies,* 4, 217

Pearson, F (1991). Cognitive style related to the design process. *International Journal of Technology and Design Education*, 1, (3), 152-158.

Peters, M., Chisolm, P and B. Laeng (1995). Spatial ability, student gender, and academic performance. *Journal of Engineering Education*, 84, (1), 69-73.

Pisarski, S., Martinazzi, R., Samples, J., and R. Youchak (2000). Analysis of the behavioral styles of engineering technology students and the inherent implications of this knowledge. *Proceedings Frontiers in Education Conference*, 2, S2E-6 to 9.

Plovnick, M.A (1971). A *Cognitive Theory of Occupational Role.* Sloan School of Management. Working paper 524–571. MIT, Cambridge, MA

Pratt, D. P., Kelly, M., and W. S. S. Wong (1999). Chinese conceptions of 'effective teaching' in Hong Kong: towards culturally sensitive evaluation of teaching. *International Journal of Lifelong Education*, 18, (4), 241–258.

Price, B., Dunn, R., and K. Dunn (1990). *Productivity Preference Survey; An Inventory for the Identification of Individual Adult Preferences in a Working Environment.* Price, Lawrence, KS.

Pudlowski, Z. J (1988). Visual communication via drawings and diagrams. *International Journal of Applied Engineering Education*, 4, (4), 301–315.

Rafe, G and H. H. Manley (1997). Learning style and instructional methods in a graduate level engineering program delivered by video teleconferencing technology. *Proceedings Frontiers in Education Conference*, 3, 1607–1612.

Ramsden, P (1988). Context and Strategy in R.R. Schmeck (ed). *Learning Strategies and Learning Styles.* Plenum Press, New York.

Reber, A. S (1995). *The Penguin Dictionary of Psychology*, Penguin, Harmondsworth.

Riding, R. J., and I. Cheema (1991). Cognitive tsyles-an overview and integration. *Educational Psychology.* 11, 193-215.

Riding, R. J., and G. Douglas (1993). The Effect of Cognitive Style and Mode of Presentation and Learning, *British Jopurnal of Educational Psychology.* 63, 297-307.

Richards, G (1995). Incorporating 3D modelling and visualization in the first year engineering curriculum. *Proceedings Frontiers in Education Conference*, 3C5- 15 to 20.

Richards, L. G. (2001). Further studies of study habits and study skills. *Proceedings Frontiers in Education Conference*, 3, S3D-13

Richards, L.G., Richards. H. C., and D. C. Sheridan (1999). Predicting success in a first year engineering course. The role of study habits. *Proceedings Frontiers in Education Conference*, 1, 11a7-5.

Richardson, J. T. E (1994). Using questionnaires to evaluate student learning. Some health warnings. In G. Gibbs (ed). *Improving Student Learning. Theory and Practice. Centre for Staff Development.* Oxford Brooks University, Oxford.

Richardson, J. T. E (1995). Mature students in higher education. An investigation into approaches to studying and academic performance. *Studies in Higher Education*, 20, (1), 5–17.

Riding, R. J (1996). *Learning Styles and Technology Based Training.* Employment Department, Sheffield.

Riding, R. J and S. G. Rayner (1998). *Cognitive Style and Learning Strategies.* David Fulton, London.

Riding, R. J and D. Mathias (1991). Cognitive styles and preferred learning mode. Reading attainment and cognitive ability in 11 yr old children. *Educational Psychology* 11, 383 – 393.

Riding, R. J and A. Staley. (1998). Self-perception as learner, cogntive style and business studies students' course performance. *Assessment and Evaluation in Higher Education.* 23, (1), 43–58.

Rochford, K (1989). Visual Learning Disabilities and Under-Achievement among Engineering Students. *Proceedings.Conference on Engineering Education for Advanced Technology.* Sydney, Australia.

Rosati, P (1996). Comparisons of learning preferences in an engineering program. *Proceedings Frontiers in Education Conference*, 3, 1441–1444.

Rosati, P (1997). Students psychological type and success in engineering programs. *Proceedings Frontiers in Education Conference,* 2, 781–784.

Rosati, P (1999). Specific differences and similarities in the learning preferences of engineering students. *Proceedings Frontiers in Education Conference*, 2, 12c1-17–12c- 22.

Rosati, P. and C. F. Yokomoto (1993). Student attitudes towards learning: by seniority and type. *Proceedings 1993 ASEE Annual Conference,* Urbana, Il pp 2038–2043.

Ross, W. A (1989). Enhancing Visualization of object geometry with interactive solids modelling. *International Journal of Applied Engineering Education.* 5, (ES), 571–574.

Ryle, A (1969). *Student Casualties.* Penguin Press, Allen Lane, London.

Saggino, A.. and P. Kline (1995). Item factor analysis of the Italian version of the Myers-Briggs Type Indicator. *Personality and Individual Differences*, 19, 243–249.

Saggino, A. and P. Kline (1996a). Item factor analysis of the seventy-one experimental items of the Italian version of the Myers-Briggs Type Indicator. *Personality and Individual Differences*, 21, 441–444.

Saggino, A. and P. Kline (1996b). The location of the Myers-Briggs Type Indicator in personality factor space. *Personality and Individual Differences*, 21, 592–597.

Scanlan, D (1988). Structured flow charts vs pseudo-code. The preference for learning algorithmics with a graphic method. *Engineering Education*, 78, (11), 173.

Shayer, M and P. S. Adey (1981). *Towards a Science of Science Teaching.* Heinemann, London.

Schmeck, R. R (1993) Learning styles of college students in R. Dillon and R.R. Schmeck. *Individual Differences in Cognition* Vol. 1. Academic Press, New York.

Severiens, S. G. and G. T. M. Ten Dam (1994). Gender differences in learning styles: a narrative review and quantitative meta-analysis. *Higher Education.* 27, (4), 487–501.

Sharp, J. E (1998). Learning styles and technical communication: improving communication and teamwork skills. *Proceedings Frontiers in Education Conference*, 1, 513–517.

Sharp, J. E, Harb, J. N., and R. E. Terry (1997) Combining Kolb learning styles and writing to learn in engineering classes. *Journal of Engineering Education*, 82, (2), 93-101

Shayer, M and P. Adey (1981). *Towards a Science of Science Teaching. Cognitive Development and Curriculum Demand.* Heinemann, London.

Shubbar, K. E (1990). Learning the visualization of rotations in diagrams of three dimensional structures. *Research in Science and Technological Education*, 8, (2), 145–154.

Silver, H. F., and R. J. Hanson (1995).*Learning Styles and Strategies.* Thoughtful Education Press, Princeton, NJ.

Sims, R., Veres, J. G., Watson, P., and K. E. Buckner (1986). The reliability and classification stability of the Learning Style Inventory, *Educational and Psychological Measurement.* 46, (3), 743-760.

Smith, A.B., Irey, R.K., and M.H. McCaulley (1973). Sel-paced instruction and college students' personalities. *Engineering Education* 63, (6), 435–440.

Snow, R. E., Corno, L., and D. Jackson (1996). Individual differences in affective and conative functions. In D. C. Berliner and R. C. Calfe (eds.). *Handbook of Educational Psychology*. American Psychological Association. Macmillan, New York.

Soloman, B. S (1992). *Inventory of Learning Styles*. North Carolina University.

Sorby, S. A., and B. J. Baartmans (2000). The development and assessment of a course for enhancing the 3-D spatial visualization skills of first year engineering students. *Journal of Engineering Education*, 89, (3), 301-307.

Soulsby, E. P (1999). University learning skills. A first year experience orientation course for engineers. *Proceedings Frontiers in Education Conference*, 1, 11a7-6 to 11.

Sternberg, R. J., and E. L. Grigorenko (1997). Are cognitive styles still in style? *American Psychologist*, 52, 700–712.

Stice, J. E. (1987). Using Kolb's cycle to improve student learning. *Engineering Education*. 77, (5), 291–296.

Sulbaran, T and N.C. Baker (2000). Enhancing engineering education through distributed virtual reality. *Proceedings Frontiers in Education Conference*, 2, S1D-13 to 18.

Svinicki, M. D and N. M. Dixon (1987). The Kolb Model modified for classroom activities. *College Teaching*, 35, (4), 141–146.

Tait, H., and N. J. Entwistle (1996). Identifying students at risk through ineffective study habits. *Higher Education*, 31, (1), 97–116.

Thomas, P. R., and J. D. Bain. (1982). Consistency in learning strategies. *Higher Education*, 11, (3), 249–259.

Todd, R. H. (1991). Teaching an introductory course in manufacturing processes. *Engineering Education*, 81, (5), 484–485.

Thompson, B (1996). AERA editorial policies regarding statistical significance testing. Three suggested reforms. *Educational Researcher*, 25, (2), 26–30.

Turns, J., Atman, C. and R. Adams (2000). Concept maps for engineering education: a cognitively motivated tool supporting varied assessment functions. *IEEE Transactions on Education*, 43, (2), 164 173.

Tyler, L.E (1978). *Individuality: Human Possibilities and Personal Choice in the Psychological Development of Men and Women*. Jossey-Bass, San Francisco.

UWA (1996). Do male and female students differ in their preferred style of learning? University of Western Australia, Institutional Research Unit.

van Zwanenberg, N., Wilkinson, L. J., and A. Anderson (2000). Felder and Silverman's Index of Learning Styles and Honey and Mumford's Learning Styles Questionnaire: how do they compare and do they predict academic performance. *Educational Psychologist*, 20, (3), 365–380.

Waks, J and I. M. Verner (1997). Spatial vision development through manipulating robot movements. *European Journal of Engineering Education* 22, (1), 35–43.

Weber, F. E., et al. (2000). The engage program: results from the first experience at the University of Tennessee. *Proceedings Frontiers in Education Conference*, 2, S2G-24 to 27.

Welch, M (1998). Students' use of three-dimensional modelling while designing and making a solution to a technological problem. *International Journal of Technology and Design Education* 8, (3), 241–260.

Welch, M. Barlex, D and H. S. Lim (2000). Sketching: friend or foe to the novice designer. *International Journal of Technology and Design Education*, 10, 125–148

Whitfield, P. R (1975).*Creativity in Industry*. Penguin, Harmondsworth.

Wiezel, A (1998). Measuring the success of virtual Tutoring. *Proceedings Frontiers in Education Conference* Session S1A.

Wiley, S. E (1991). Learning models for developing visualization in engineering graphics. *Proceedings Frontiers in Education Conference*, 552–555.

Wilkes, J (1992). An overview of Gordon's cognitive style typology. Paper distributed with presentation at South eastern regional Conference of the Association for Psychological Type. September.

Wilson, J. D (1981). *Student Learning in Higher Education*. Croom Helm, Beckenham.

Wilson, K. L., Lizzio, A., and P. Ramsden (1997). The development validation and application of the course experience questionnaire. *Studies in Higher Education*, 22, (1), 33–53.

Witkin, H. A (1976). Cognitive styles in academic performance and in teacher student relations in S. Messick et al (eds.) *Individuality in Learning*. Jossey-Bass, San Francisco.

Witkin, H. A., and D. R. Goodenough (1981) *Cognitive Styles*. International Universities Press, New York.

Witkin, H. A., Goodenough, D. R., and P. K. Oltman (1977) Role of the field dependent and field independent cognitive styles in academic evolution. A longtudinal study. *Journal of Educational Psychology*, 69, 197–211.

Witkin, H. A., Oltman, D. R., Raskin, E., and S. A. Karp (1971). *A Manual for Embedded Figures Test*. Consulting Psychologists Press, Palo Alto, CA.

Wood, R. and A. Butterworth (1997). Fair use of psychometrics in guidance. *Journal of Education and Work*, 10, (3), 281–292.

Yingli, L et al (1998). Visualization and interactive experiment of some electromagnetic problems considering cognitive features of Chinese students. *Proceedings Frontiers in Education Conference*, 2, 600-604.

Yokomoto, C. F. (2000). Promoting depth of knowledge through a new quiz format to improve problem-solving abilities. *Proceedings Frontiers in Education Conference*, 1, F2B-8 to 11.

Yokomoto, C. F., Buchanan, W. W., and R. Ware (1993). Assessing student attitudes toward design and innovation. *Proceedings Frontiers in Education Conference* 382–385

Youngman, M.B., Oxtoby, R., Monk, J.D. and J. Heywood (1978) *Analysing Jobs*. Gower Press, Aldershot.

Zywno, M. S., and D. C. Kennedy (2000). Integrating the internet, multimedia components, and hands on experimentation in problem-based control education. *Proceedings Frontiers in Education Conference*, T2D-5 to 10.

Zywno, M. S., and J. K. Waalen (2001). The effect of hypermedia instruction on achievement and attitudes of students with different learning styles. *Proceedings Annual Conference ASEE*.

CHAPTER 6: HUMAN DEVELOPMENT

Summary

Given the importance of human development after adolescence, it is perhaps surprising that little attention has been paid to this aspect in design for learning in higher education. It may be equally surprising that among the few exceptions that prove the rule are schools in engineering. The Colorado School of Mines and those responsible for the problem-solving course at McMaster University have taken particular notice of the Perry model of student development in college (Perry, 1970). This model was derived from studies of students at Harvard University. This theory is in the same vein as a theory that Piaget proposed for development from birth to adolescence. It proposes that college students go through a series of stages until they are able to cope with the world of relativism they find about them while at the same time maintaining commitment to a developed point of view. When students arrive at university the students seek black and white answers from teachers who are seen as the authority figures. Much teaching reinforces this mode of thinking and does not help students break away from this world into one where they can think for themselves. For one reason and another it seems that many students do not go beyond the middle step of this developmental process, at least in so far as it is observed in college. The models proposed by those who use this scheme to design curricula expose students to a variety of learning procedures in which the students can move from a dependence on teachers to using them as consultants. Gains have been reported in student development in those schools running models based on this or other programs where such development is thought to be important.

Perry argued that growth occurred in spurts and Culver and Sackman (1988) described these growth experiences as marker events. They argued that learning activities that have a high level of marker potential will involve the learner in activity based learning. If one wants to be an engineer, one has to behave as engineer and opportunities have to be provided for this to happen. Others have come to the same conclusion. Problems in the evaluation of curriculum designed on the basis of this model are discussed.

A similar approach to Perry's theory has been developed by King and Kitchener (1994). Some have argued that their model does not differ from Perry's. While acknowledging their debt to Perry they take a different view. It seems that there is difference between the two models in the final stages. In the King and Kitchener model growth is centerd on the development of reflective judgment hence, reflective practice. Irrespective of its validity, their work is particularly attractive to teachers because it relates the stages to instructional goals that can easily be translated into outcomes that would receive the assent of teachers.

While there is now a considerable body of research on adult human development, there has also been a substantial body of research on adult learning that is relevant to engineering education. This is discussed. It is pointed out that in order to make use of these theories many teachers will have to change their beliefs about teaching and learning. That is, from transmitters of information to facilitators or managers of learning.

Recently, engineering educators have begun to take notice of emotional (social) intelligence. They have argued that given its importance in the workplace, engineering schools have an obligation to provide for its development. A problem with the concept is that it embraces a multitude of dimensions. It is not a single unitary concept. Nevertheless, a considerable case may be made for training in these dimensions in engineering schools.

A considerable report could be made on motivation. However, this Chapter ends with a section on this topic that is confined to the little substance that has been written on the subject in the engineering education literature.

6. Post-Formal Reasoning: Perry

Perry's (1970) theory is post-Piagetian, hence the title of the section. It is argued that development does not end with a capability in formal reasoning around the age of 16, but continues into adulthood. Broadly speaking, according to Perry's theory, the attitudes we hold and the concepts and values with which they are associated depend on the stage of development we are at. There are nine stages (see Exhibit 6.1). They relate to curriculum and instruction in so far as together they either reinforce the stage we are at or help us to move forward to another stage. Perry argued that much teaching tends to reinforce the earlier stages.

In the first stages the students come to the university expecting to be told the truth, that is, what is right and what is wrong. Subject-based knowledge is absolute. Things are right or wrong, or true or false. Thus, in stage 1 all problems are seen to have right answers and authority must be followed. For this group, those whom they rate as the best teachers provide the right answers. By stage 3 it is apparent that authority is *"seeking the right answers"* and only in the future will we know the right answer. Perry calls these first three stages 'dualism.' From dualism the student moves into a phase of scepticism, for now it is clear that not only does the authority not have the right answers but everyone, including the student, has the right to hold his or her own opinions, and some of these can be supported by evidence. Thus, by stage 5, some answers are found to be better than others, and knowledge has to be considered in its context. It is a stage of relativism. Marra and Palmer (1999) pointed out that the move from stage 4 to stage 5 is a significant transition because the students now *accept "knowledge as, for the most part, transient and contextual"*... *"Students now accept themselves as one among many legitimate sources of knowledge and often forego their former view of instructors as absolute authorities."* The student begins to perceive that good choices are possible and that commitments have to be entered into. By stage 9 (acting on commitment) decisions are made with relative ease, a sense of identity and a personal style is obtained, and one is now able to take responsibility for one's own actions.

Positions 1 and 2: Dualism
All knowledge is known, and it is a collection of information. Right and wrong answers exist for everything. Teachers are responsible for giving information, students are responsible for producing it
Position 3: Early multiplicity
Knowledge includes methods for solving problems. There may be more than one right answer. Teachers help students learn how to learn, students are responsible for understanding and applying knowledge
Position 4: Late multiplicity
Uncertainty with respect to knowledge and diversity of opinion become legitimate. Teachers require evidence to support opinions and design choices, students learn how to think and analyze
Position 5. Relativism
All knowledge must be viewed in context. Teachers are consultants, students can synthesize and evaluate perspectives from different contexts
Positions 6 – 9. Commitment within Relativism
For life to have meaning, commitments must be made, taking into account that the world is a changing, relativistic place

---

Exhibit 6.1. The Perry positions or stages after Culver, Woods, and Fitch (1990). (Reproduced with the permission of R. S. Culver).

A problem for some people with this scheme is that in this process of development some students are faced with finding out for the first time that much knowledge is relative, and for some of them this may cause considerable dissonance. To others, from the outside looking in, it seems, as one former student at the Colorado School of Mines put it, that *"they, Culver, Woods and Fitch,* [see below]*, state that to become intellectually mature, you need to believe in a relativistic world and that if you believe in absolute authority, you are intellectually immature. These statements say a great deal about their own world views and nothing about the intellectual maturity of students"* (Jordan, 1990). Philosophically they have a case to defend because as Jordan argued, *"many engineering students are philosophically unsophisticated, this amounts to an indoctrination of students by faculty."* Not withstanding the distinguished British philosopher of education G. H. Bantock who argued that all education is indoctrination, the point is whether or not Perry meant to imply that all knowledge is relative. It may be argued that he did not, since in the final stage, a student makes a commitment within a relativistic world, and whether we like it or not, that is how we find the world. An alternative explanation is that there are very few absolutes and that as the range of knowledge increases so we have to adapt in the world. As any one with strongly held religious beliefs will affirm, this does not mean that those beliefs are renounced.

Indeed, it might be argued that they may have been only weak, and at the level of notional assent

(Newman, 1870).[1] Jordan would probably be satisfied with the Reflective Judgment Model, which seems to get over his difficulty (see below).

Apart from that there is a major issue that relates to the evaluation of programs. Academics suppose that students develop in higher education, but they make no special arrangements for this development. It is assumed that somehow year 2, courses are a development of year 1 courses, and year 3 on year 2, and so on. But they have no built-in guarantees that this is the case. The effect of one teacher in a year 2 course might be such that it is equivalent to year 1. Conversely, a year 1 course may be taught at a level that is equivalent to year 2.[2] The Perry model has the possibility of determining the developmental level of a course (Heywood, 1994).

One of the earliest attempts to apply the Perry model to the curriculum was by Knefflekamp, who adapted it for English. His schema is shown in Figure 6.1 Culver, Woods, and Fitch (1990), who also developed a curriculum based on the Perry model, argued that most students enter college at stage 2 or 3, although I have doubts about this, especially in relation to some students who enter my courses at the age of 17. However, their search for the correct answers may be due to their experience of the high school public examination system that encourages memory learning, and unique single answers. They may have been conditioned to expect the same thing in college.

Perry whose study was mainly of Harvard undergraduates,[3] found that growth occurred in spurts that were followed by periods of stabilization. This would seem to indicate equilibrium in the Piagetian sense. Culver and Sackman (1988) called growth experiences *"marker events".* (See also Culver, 1987) A marker event has the following characteristics.

- It is a significant even which influences an individual's development.
- It results in a change or expansion of the personal belief system.
- It provides new insight and, frequently, a change in priorities.
- It serves as an anchor for new learning and long-term memory recall.
- It can be positive or negative.
- It cannot be forced, but can be programmed.

Culver and Sackman evidently thought that a marker event began in the practical, and that it was a reflection on what happens that leads to abstraction or formal reasoning. (Insofar as positive learning is concerned, the story of Archimedes' experiment made such a profound impression on me when I was young, that I have always called such occasions "Eureka" events). More seriously, marker events seem to illustrate

---

[1] Newman (1870) distinguishes between real and notional assent. In this text I intend notional to mean surface without depth, without real understanding
[2] In the United Kingdom curriculum courses are distinguished by levels that approximate to the year of study.
[3] It also included a number of students from Radcliffe College.

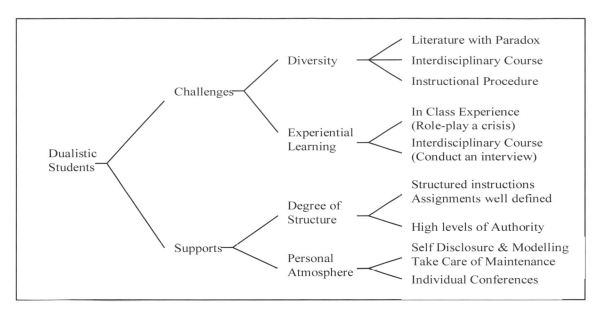

Figure 6.1. A representation of Knefflekamp's (1979) model of course design as described by Culver and Hackos (1982). (Reproduced with permission of R. S. Cilver).

a point made by the Scottish philosopher MacMurray. This was to the effect that our theories are developed from practical problems rather than the other way around.[4] These descriptions are also consistent with Lonergan's philosophy of insight.[5] Marker events come as a result of mental activity and may not come when an instructor desires. Indeed they may come when the course is over. Such is the nature of reflective thinking.

Culver and Sackman argued that learning activities that have high levels of marker potential will involve the learner in activity based learning. This is consistent with the views of such distinguished scholars as Bruner and James in the United States, and Mascall[6] in the United Kingdom, who believed the learner (novice) has to try to experiment with what it is like to become an expert. If one wants to be an engineer, one has to behave as an engineer.[7] Therefore, Culver would argue that

teachers have to provide opportunities for students to behave as engineers. Yokomoto, Voltmer, and Ware (1993), reached a similar conclusion independently of Culver. They borrowed an idea from Carl Sagan. The "aha" phenomenon describes a *"significant event which has a lasting impact on the learner, for in addition to solving the puzzle, he/she develops a feeling for empowerment and gains confidence that it can happen again. It becomes more significant if the person develops an enjoyment of the experience[...]"* Drawing on the work of Sternberg and Davidson (1982) they relate "aha" events to insight and "eureka". They believed that there were different levels of significant events. They wrote:

"At the lowest level, a student has an "Aha" experience, when he/she is shown how to solve a difficult problem, saying." Aha I know how to solve that problem." At the next level, the student says, "Aha I now see what I needed to know in order to solve that problem". At the next level the student says, "Aha I now see an interpretation of the principle in question that would have helped me solve the problem without assistance [...]. At still higher levels, the student may say, "Aha, I now see the relationship between the solution to a differential equation and the physical behavior of a dynamic system", "Aha I see the relationship between the Fast Fourier Transform and the Discrete Fourier Transform", or "Aha I now see how mathematical models can be used in mathematical design."

The "Aha" events would seem to be similar to the "Oh I See" experiences described by Ball and Patrick (1999) (see Section 4.2). They would seem to be somewhat less significant than the great events that give vent to "Eureka." Nevertheless, they are important in learning and might be regarded as the critical incidents of learning. Clearly, they do not mark a transition from one stage to another but describe the process of reaching a

---

[4] *"We know how large a part of our thinking is concerned with the solution of practical issues. In such cases it is obvious to everyone that the reference is to practical behavior, and that conclusions which have no bearing on the solution of our practical problems are without significance. The theoretical question is posed by the practical situation; for that very reason the significance and verification of the theoretical result, if it is meaningful at all, is the solution of a practical problem".* P22 MacMurray (1956)

[5] *"Insight is the source not only of theoretical knowledge but also of its practical applications and, indeed of all intelligent activity"* (from the Preface, Lonergan 1958). The 'Eureka' event or marker event is the insight that one has into insight.)

[6] The late E. L. Mascall was a renowned British theologian.

[7] Bruner wrote, *"A body of knowledge enshrined in a university faculty and embodied in a series of authoritative volumes, is the result of much prior intellectual activity. To instruct someone in these disciplines is not a matter of getting him to commit results to mind. Rather it is to teach him to participate in the process that makes possible the establishment of knowledge. We teach a subject not to produce little living libraries on that subject, but rather to get a student to think mathematically for himself, to consider matters as a historian does, to take part in the process of knowledge getting"* (Bruner, 1966).

stage. It is these kinds of incident that should be the focus of a student journal if it is to be used to encourage reflective practice.

As indicated above, Culver and his colleagues at the Colorado School of Mines used the Perry model as the basis for several course designs that help students grow to intellectual maturity (Culver and Hackos, 1982; Culver and Fitch, 1990, Culver and Olds, 1986; Pavelich, 1996: Pavelich and Moore, 1996). Culver and Hackos criticized the engineering curriculum because it did not encourage open-ended problem solving similar to that undertaken by engineers in the real world. They appreciated that the introduction of open-ended problem solving could make the students unsure of themselves because of the loss of structure Therefore, they proposed that the traditional subjects should be the tools for problem-solving while the 'trunk' of the course should be for traditional problem solving activities designed to bring the students along the stages of Perry's model (see Figure 4.6). Culver and Hackos felt that some of the problems arising from the dissonance that such courses create could be overcome if behavioral objectives are specified so as to show that complexity lies in the subject matter rather than the organization of the course.

Applied to design, which was the purpose of the Culver, Woods, and Fitch (1990) paper, it meant arriving at the stage where a student is prepared to accept responsibility for the engineering they propose and do. It also meant that they could cope with ambiguous situations. They argued that *"most college programs, while successfully teaching facts and procedures do not help students grow toward intellectual maturity."* Culver also argued, in a personal communication, that students' at lower levels of the scheme, while able to do problems that require highly structured analytical techniques, cannot cope with synthesis. This meant that students at low levels of intellectual maturity can pass examinations that emphasize analysis. He found support for this assertion in the work of Rokeach (1960). With regard to the philosophical issue and the liberal education of engineers, it suggests that they should have the opportunity to study the conflict between realism and constructivism in engineering courses that have a philosophical dimension (e.g. ethics).

Marra and Palmer (1999) considered the relationship of the stages with the ABET criteria for 2000. They argued, on the basis of various graduate profiles including one from Boeing, that graduating seniors' who have achieved position 5 or beyond are those who are required in the world of work. *"Graduates at Perry positions 5-9 should be able to sort through the multiple perspectives of team projects, argue for a view point or design proposal, and consider not only the technical aspects but the ethical and social aspects of their choices.* This writer would contest that to be able to do this they should be exposed, at a minimum, to some work like Vardy's on ethics.[8]

Pavelich and Moore (1996) explained how at the Colorado School of Mines most undergraduates completed project courses in six of their eight semesters, beginning in the first semester of their freshman year. In these courses the students worked in teams to solve an open-ended problem provided by a government or industrial agency. Pavelich and Moore pointed out that college educators have difficulty in teaching open-ended problem solving for the reason that freshmen, sophomores, and many seniors do not understand these problems as a professional does. Many freshmen, for example, do not understand why evidence has to be used to justify a decision. Sophomores and seniors see no need to devise alternative solutions.

In order to test Perry's theory, they chose to interview rather than use either of the two instruments that had been developed for this purpose (Moore, 1988). They were aware that there was only a moderate correlation between interviews and the schedules (Baxter-Magolda, 1987; Culver et al., 1994). Interviews generally gave higher ratings.

The interviewer's focus was placed on the thinking processes that lead to a conclusion and the ways students justified their points of view. The interviews were video taped, and independent raters evaluated them for Perry positions. Over 40 students were interviewed in each of the freshmen and senior years, and nearly that number in the sophomore year. The statistical data showed significant differences between the freshmen and late sophomores, and these differences increase when compared with the late seniors. On the Perry positions, the freshmen average position on a continuum was 3.27, the sophomores' rating was 3.71 and the seniors' rating was 4.28. Over one-quarter of the seniors tested above 5[9]. From the school's point of view, these students were in an excellent position to enter the profession. But, what of the students who were rated below position on the scale, for some of these were found to struggle with decision making related to their profession? Some of them *"acknowledged a multitude of possible answers to an open-ended problem in their profession, but see themselves as having no responsibility for a legitimate input, into deciding the direction of the problem's solution."* Their answer to the question as to how one operates when there are multiple demands on a design is *"You tell me what to optimize and I will optimize it for you."* They really see themselves as technicians awaiting the decisions of others.

A number of questions arise from the fact that it was a cross-sectional study. Such studies assume that what happens in each of the years is constant. They also assume the maturation observed is a function of the course. Some factor needs to be allowed for that part of maturation that is not influenced by college. This applies

---

[8] See also Marra, (1996) for origins of the project including costings.

[9] Woods et al, (1997), reported gains in intellectual development for seniors in the McMaster problem-solving program from about 3.5 (on average) in the third year to about 4.6 in the final year (see Chapter 9). This compared with levels found among college seniors that ranged from 2.8 to 3.1, reported by Fitch and Culver (1984).

particularly to longitudinal scores. It is not safe to assume that changed scores are reliable, and it is necessary to make allowance for that fact in their interpretation. Pascarella. and Terenzini (1991) who drew attention to this problem, also noted that *"change"* and *"development"* have different meanings. A change from time A to time B simply implies two different conditions that are not necessarily predictable. Development implies ordered, predictable and hierarchical shifts in behavior. Observed changes do not necessarily imply ordered growth.

Quite clearly Pavelich and Moore had as their aim the development of professionalism. From the perspective of curriculum leadership it is important, therefore, to know how this relates to the aptitude, age and achievements of the students.[10]

Much action research suffers from such weaknesses and the question that arises for curriculum leaders is whether the results should be used for curriculum decisions. In this case, the faculty at the Colorado School of Mines considered that, rather than change the curriculum, they should refine their teaching methods and balance challenge with support. While exposing students to the vagaries of knowledge and requiring them to deal with them, faculty would help the students deal with the discontinuities between the students' perceptions and those of their teachers. The faculty would have been aware of Baxter-Magolda's studies in which she showed that students operating at high levels of the Perry position preferred a working relationship with faculty akin to that of colleagues, whereas those at the lowest levels preferred a more distant, yet positive, relationship.

Since then, in order to reduce the time taken for measurement, they have begun to develop an interactive technology that would allow a computer to measure intellectual development (Miller, Olds, and Pavelich, 1998).

In another study at Penn State University, Marra and Palmer (1999; see also Marra, Palmer and Litzinger, 2000) tracked the intellectual growth of around 200 first-year and senior students. They found that among one sub sample of 27 seniors, seven had ratings of five or higher. They found that two students among this group had grade point averages of 2.26 and 3.36, respectively, and were interested to know why this should be so. In their paper they present a qualitative analysis of semistructured interviews with these seven students.[11] Of the seven two were women. The ages ranged from 21 to 23. The average math SAT score was 669, and the average verbal SAT score was 565. The average GPA was 3.05. By traditional norms these students would not be considered to be the best and brightest. Yet the interviews showed that they could deal with conflicting and ambiguous data and deal satisfactorily with the selection of alternatives. It is not possible to say, without some input measure, what the effects of the curriculum were on these students' intellectual development. Clearly it was not retroactive, and their experience of college affected them in both positive and negative ways, as for example, when working in group projects.

In a later comment on the study, Palmer and her colleagues summarized the findings of their longitudinal study (three spaced interviews) (Wise et al., 2000). They found that when the sample was reduced to 21 (as required by the longitudinal framework), the effect of the design course was not significant although it had a positive effect on the non-computer majors.

Of more importance was the finding that approximately two years later, the thought processes of these students were predominantly dualistic. The mean had risen from 3.27 to 3.33. But, the investigators suggested that there was an "opening" to position 4. It was found that high-scoring students who dropped out between the first and second interviews were unlikely to return. The effect of the design course was apparently not maintained, and this was also the case with those who attended the final interview eight months later. However, the mean rating of the final interviewees had moved upwards to 4.19 with one student on 5.0. In sum, significant group mean differences were found between first-and-fourth year and between third-and-fourth year groups, but not between first-and-third year groups.

Wise and his colleagues accounted for this lack of change in cognitive growth between the first and third year by the fact that most of the required courses were in the traditional lecture format. *"Little cognitive load between rote memorization and application of formulae is placed on the student, and the amount of information allows little time for reflection."* Given this hypothesis, they argued that the jump in cognitive growth between third and fourth year might be due to the changed learning environment (projects, team activities) that the students experience. At the same time, the investigators appeared

---

[10] One study that did correct for aptitude, prior achievement and age was at Alverno College. That investigation comprised both cross-sectional and longitudinal studies. One measure designed to measure development on the Perry continuum was used. To study how effective students were at considering all aspects of a controversial issue they used an *Analysis of Argument* test developed by Stewart (1977), see also Winter, McClelland and Stewart, 1981). *The Measure of Intellectual Development* developed by Kneffelkamp (1974) for determining the Perry continuum requires the respondent to write three short essays. The scoring is based on (a) the nature and origin of knowledge displayed, and (b) the responsibility taken for decision making. Somewhat less positive results were reported than in other studies. In the cross-sectional analysis seniors were found to be higher than freshmen on two of the essays; however in the longitudinal study while there was an increase in one of the essays, there was a decrease in one of the others. In the *Analysis of Argument* instrument the respondents have to attack and defend a complex issue. Separate scores are given for the arguments for and the arguments against. In the Alverno study of seniors, in the cross-sectional study it was found that there were statistically significant differences in scores were obtained on the defence score but not on the attack, although there were changes in the right direction (Mentkowski and Associates, 2000).

---

[11] An expert from the Center for the Study of Intellectual development, which is directed by Moore, rated the interviews. See Moore (1989) for a description of the Learning Environment Preference Schedules, and see Stonewater, Stonewater, and Hadley (1986) for an evaluation of two assessment instruments.

to be disappointed that ways had not been found to achieve higher levels of development with the majority of students.

A weakness of the study is that the changes reported above were based on post-test data alone. In the future it would be necessary to both pre-and post-test to see if curricular changes in the first and second years could raise the level of cognitive growth.

These findings are a warning to those who create change in the first year that, unless they arrange for subsequent years to follow up the achievements of the first, a lot of good work may be undone. This suggests that design should be the subject of development following a Bruner-type spiral curriculum.[12]

In conclusion, it is worth returning to the original report and to note the high value that these students placed on "real engineering," and the ability of the teacher to provide that reality, hence the importance of design in first year. We might leave this study with its comments of one of the male students: *"I learned that there's no right way to design an aeroplane. You can design 30 different airplanes and each one's going to have its benefits and there's going to be problems with each one…you have to decide at an early stage- well how we're going to do this, at least as a starting point for everything …. So you have to just use your best idea of what the final situation is going to be …. I think that's helpful as far as decision making because that's a completely ambiguous situation. And we had four groups each given exactly the same goals, the same specifications we had to meet for the plane, and all the groups came up with something just completely different, just ridiculously different, and all of them vaguely valid …."(Marra and Palmer, 1999).*

6.1. King and Kitchener's Reflective Judgment Model

Although this model has not been used with engineers, it is attractive, and it has been well researched. In many respects it is similar to the Perry scheme. Like Perry, it assumes that as individuals develop, so they become more able to evaluate the claims of knowledge, and both models advocate and support their points of view about controversial issues. *"The ability to make reflective judgments is the ultimate outcome of this progression."* To arrive at this destination the learner passes through seven stages, each of which has its own assumptions and logic in the reflective judgment model. The stages develop from the relatively simple to the relatively complex, each with a different strategy for solving ill-structured problems. Thus each stage has its own view of knowledge and concept justification. Reflective thinking takes place in stages 6 and 7. *"True reflective thinking pre-supposes that individuals hold epistemic assumptions that allow them to understand and*

accept real uncertainty". It is only when they engage in ill-structured or novel problems that they engage in reflective thinking as defined by King and Kitchener (1994). The outline of the stages is shown in Exhibit 6.2. King an Kitchener found that their model complemented another model due to Fischer (Fischer, Kenny and Pipp, 1990).[13]

Stage	Description
Stage 1	Knowing is limited to single concrete observations. What a person observes is true.
Stage 2.	Two categories for knowing; right answers and wrong answers. Good authorities have knowledge; bad authorities lack knowledge.
Stage 3.	In some areas, knowledge is certain and authorities that have that knowledge. In other areas, knowledge is temporarily uncertain. Only personal beliefs can be known.
Stage 4.	Concept that knowledge is unknown in several specific cases leads to the abstract generalization that knowledge is uncertain.
Stage 5.	Knowledge is uncertain and must be understood within a context; thus justification is context specific.
Stage 6.	Knowledge is uncertain but constructed by comparing evidence and opinion of different sides of an issue or across contexts.
Stage 7.	Knowledge is the outcome of a process of reasonable inquiry. This view is equivalent to a general principle that is consistent across domains.

Exhibit 6.2. Stages of the King and Kitchener (1994) Reflective Judgment Model (adapted).

Individuals will only operate at their optimal levels when they practice skills in familiar domains and receive environmental support for high level performance. Following Yokomoto et al (see above), there will be lots of "Ahas!" en-route. Unlike stage theory, which holds that all children pass through the

---

[12] At the University of Reading (United Kingdom) in the 1960's the Engineering Department arranged for projects of increasing demand to be done in each of the three years of the program (private communication from M. Deere).

[13] Fischer's skill theory is an attempt to resolve the paradox where most investigations show that most adults cannot perform complex tasks, yet common experience suggests they can think in sophisticated ways about abstract concepts. Fischer argued that these contradictory findings may be explained by a theory that considers cognitive development to be a function of the collaboration that a person has with his/her environment. Fischer calls this collaborative framework "skill theory." The contradictory findings of research are explained by the systematic variations in an individual's levels of performance. Individuals routinely function below their highest capacity in ordinary environmental conditions, but in environments that optimize performance they demonstrate high levels of performance (Fischer, Kenny, and Pipp, 1990). New levels of competence which enable adolescents and young adults to understand abstract concepts are acquired yet most of their behavior does not suggest they have made cognitive advances. One criterion that suggests a change in cognitive developmental level is a sudden alteration in performance during a limited age period. Fischer calls this a "spurt." The change from one cognitive level to another is characterised by a cluster of "spurts" in performance. The spurts do not occur at exactly the same age, nor do they take exactly the same form. Adolescents do not suddenly metamorphose on their fifteenth birthday. Instead, the change is relatively rapid, occupying a small interval of time.

same stages of development skill theory argues that the steps which individuals take to attain a skill vary considerably as between one individual and the next, as a function of the environment and the individual. Because of these variations, it will be difficult to find any two children who spontaneously follow the same steps in any domain. At the same time, the theory states that irrespective of the path taken, all skills pass through the same developmental levels. All skill acquisitions involve the same group of transformation rules. The position taken by Fischer et al. is similar to that taken by information-processing theorists namely that the *"same fundamental acquisition processes occur in development, learning and problem solving at all ages."* Instruction and assessment should, therefore, be designed to take account of these different needs. This theory has considerable implications for the design of modular curriculum systems and the pacing of assessment and learning within them.

In the Reflective Judgment model a spurt marks the emergence of a new stage. The skill levels in the Fischer model correspond directly to the stages of the Reflective Judgment Model. According to Pascarella and Terenzeni (1991), Rodgers (1989) considered that the first three stages coincided with Perry's but differences appeared in the framework at position 4. However, he was not able to conclude whether they were distinct theories or simply a clarification of Perry by King and Kitchener. King and Kitchener did not respond to Rodgers except by inference. They argued that the decisions students make when they are in relativistic frames of reference should reflect a level of cognitive development beyond relativism. In the Perry model, the student remains within the relativistic frame and has to make an act of faith in reaching a commitment. The purpose of the Reflective Judgment model is to deal with the form and nature of judgments made in the relativistic framework. Individuals, it is believed, hold epistemological positions beyond relativism. Whatever else one may say; such a position would seem to be more satisfying than Perry. King and Kitchener had much to say about teaching in higher education, and they take a broad of view of who may be a teacher and what teaching is. According to the Reflective Judgment Interview, first year students in the United States lie in the range stage 3 to stage 4. Seniors were found to be around stage 5. They argue that many seniors are at a loss when they are asked to defend their answers to ill-structured problems. Therefore, if reflective thinking is to be developed, teachers should:

- Show respect for students regardless of the developmental levels they may exhibit.
- Understand that students differ in the assumptions they make about knowledge.
- Familiarize students with ill-structured problems within the teacher's area of expertise.
- Create multiple opportunities for students to examine different points of view.

- Informally assess (i.e., from student journals, assignments etc.) assumptions about knowledge and how beliefs may be justified.
- Acknowledge that students work within a developmental range of stages and set expectations accordingly; and challenge students to engage in new ways of thinking while providing them with support; and recognize that students differ both in their perceptions of ill-structured problems and their responses to particular learning environments.
- Share with one another what they do and what they expect to achieve.
- They do not, however, believe there is one best way of teaching reflective thinking.

The differences between stage 3 and stage 6 from a teaching perspective are shown in Exhibit 6.3.

Stage 3.
Characteristic assumptions of stage 3. Reasoning.
Knowledge is absolutely certain in some areas and temporarily uncertain in other areas.
Beliefs are justified according to the word of an authority in areas of certainty and according to what "feels right" in areas of uncertainty.
Evidence can neither be evaluated nor used to reason to conclusions.
Opinions and beliefs cannot be distinguished from factual evidence.

Instructional goals for students.
Learn to use evidence in reasoning to a point of view.
Learn to view their own experience as one potential source of information but not as the only valid source of information.

Stage 6.
Promoting reflective thinking

Characteristic assumptions of Stage 6. reasoning.
Knowledge is uncertain and must be understood in relationship to context and evidence.
Some points of view may be tentatively judged as better than others.
Evidence on different points of view can be compared and evaluated as a basis for justification.

Instructional goals for students.
Learn to construct one's own point of view and to see that point of view as open to re-evaluation and revision in the light of new evidence.
Learn that though knowledge must be constructed, strong conclusions are epistemologically justified.

Exhibit 6.3. Promoting reflective thinking in the King and Kitchener model–stages 3 and 6. Reasoning.(Adapted from King and Kitchener, 1994. In their description (pp250-254) they also give for each stage a list of difficult tasks from the perspective of the particular stage, a sample of developmental assignments, and suggestions for developmental support for instructional goals)

1. It will be appreciated that since these descriptions could apply at any level of education, they would have to be developed to describe the requirements of a particular level [e.g., year on course, course level, *The Reflective Judgment Interview* (RJI)], which is the instrument used to detect the stage at which a student is, has been found to have high inter-rater reliability in specific subject domains. The interview is structured with standard probe questions, each with a specific purpose. Thus, two questions, that

will clearly elicit a level of development that are of direct relevance to today's media governed society are
1. How is it possible that people have such different views about this subject?"
2. "How is it possible that experts in the field disagree about this subject?" (King and Kitchener, 1994).

In a longitudinal study, a group of individuals who did not attend college were compared for reflective judgment with a group who did attend college. Although both groups showed an increase in reflective judgment, the group who attended college showed significant gains (King and Kitchener, 1994). Wood (1997) has carried out a major secondary analysis of claims regarding the *Reflective Judgment Interview*. He reported that while many of the conclusions about the instrument were consistent across the studies, there were some conflicting patterns in the conclusions because researchers had failed to *"consider plausible alternative explanations that a reasonable sceptic might raise."* He criticized researchers for not investigating the statistical procedures used in terms of what may and may not be concluded before beginning an investigation. There is nothing new in this criticism of replicatory research, but it needs to be restated.

Although smaller more selective colleges appear to do better on reflective judgment than public institutions this may be due to selectivity in admissions in the smaller institutions. Insofar as performance and expertise is concerned, it seems that differences between graduate student samples as a function of area of study are more pronounced at lower levels of study. Wood drew attention to an unpublished study by De Bord (1993), which found that graduate students in psychology scored significantly higher on RJI when topics dealt with ill-structured psychological dilemmas as opposed to the usual dilemma topics. There was a need to investigate whether the lower scores obtained by natural science/mathematics graduate students on the RJI would be improved if ill-structured topics in these subjects were included in the interview. Wood suggested that sampling of more general cognitive outcomes should be within a definite content area in order to control for discipline and intra-individual differences.

These findings clearly have relevance for those who intend to investigate the effects of the curriculum on the development of generic skills that are thought to be independent of content in such higher education systems as the United Kingdom.

Wood found that the psychometric properties of the RJI were promising, However, he thought that the design of college outcome measures using the instrument should take into account general verbal ability, educational attainment, and area of study. Astin (1997) would surely argue that account has to be taken of the whole process. Wood suggested that the next step is to design a more efficient and easily scored measure to assess reflective judgment. Wood's analysis found that differences between the samples were more pronounced at lower levels of educational attainment than at the higher levels. He noted that this is consistent with the

view that performance on the RJI is dependent on verbal ability (which is a necessary, but not sufficient condition for high scores).

Pascarella and Terenzini (1991), in their evaluation of within-college effects, drew attention to the fact that the magnitude of instructional and curricular effects on general cognitive skills tends to be smaller than the overall effects of college experience for liberal arts students. This, they suggested, may be due to the fact that development follows the gradual spurt cycles of the kind suggested by Fischer and by King and Kitchener. In an earlier paper, Kitchener (1993) had pointed out that no single instructional or curricular experience over a limited period is likely to have an impact on development that a carefully constructed set of cumulative experiences over a long period of time is likely to have. Clearly that was the view taken at the Colorado School of Mines in the design of their program (Pavelich and Moore, 1996). King and Kitchener (1994) assumed *"that teaching students to think reflectively is an institutional goal that is best met when it is built into the whole curriculum- and co-curriculum of the college."* The implication for engineering teachers is that in planning the curriculum they have to work as a team and share with one another what they do and what they expect to achieve. King and Kitchener did not, however, believe there was one best way of teaching reflective thinking.[14]

At the very least, the model, irrespective of the RJI, provides criteria against which teachers can design and evaluate their courses. For example, the interview may provide ideas for question design. Olds, in a private communication to Tsang (2002), described the Reflection Rubric that is shown in Exhibit 6.4. Its purpose is to document the stages of development of a student according to the reflective judgment model. Thus in the diagram, in evaluative thinking the progress of a student from reliance on authority to being able to evaluate the information presented is shown. It will be noticed that there can be confusion between what has in the past been considered to be evaluation and what now is called reflection. At issue is whether reflection is something more than evaluation, a question that derives from the reflection that borders on meditation which is undertaken by monks in both eastern and western traditions.

In Britain, little attention has been given to the detail of reflective judgment yet reflective judgment has become a major aim of higher education and needs to be thought about in some detail. King and Kitchener's work could serve as a major resource for constructive debate. In this respect it is strange to find that while Schön's ideas on reflective practice have been widely debated world wide, King and Kitchener (1994) have nothing to say about his work when surely there is some relationship. One of the most outstanding examples of reflective practice in action (if that is not a contradiction) is to be found in the work of a British engineering educator, John Cowan (1998).

---

[14]They provided a list of resources ranging across the arts and sciences (King, 1992).

6.2. The Crux Developmental Model

A short paper in the 2001 Frontiers in Education Conference introduced the Crux Developmental Model, the brainchild of Crux Consulting (Duncan-Hewitt, et al, 2001). Although short on psychometric detail, it was high on illustrations of the use of the developmental approach to engineering educators. Its inventors claim that its novelty lies in the pragmatic marriage of theory and practice, along with the fact that it can be used with a diverse range of populations beginning with the late adolescent, or beginning, engineering students. The circumstances of its illustration were three annual Science and Engineering Camps for high school students at the University of Idaho. The model derives from existing theories, in particular those of Perry, Belenky, and Fischer. It describes six levels of cognitive complexity for *"which there are defined, qualitative differences in self-concept, thought and value structure, and behaviors. More complex levels incorporate and transcend lower ones. Moreover, each level is, in effect a "crux." As in climbing, one needs determination and adequate support and protection provided by a mentor if one is even going to try to surmount it. One capable of operating at a higher level of intellectual complexity does not consistently operate at that level. One of the functions of higher complexity is the ability to discriminate between tasks which require a higher order and those tasks for which lower orders are more efficient." The "crux" would appear to have some similarities with "marker events" but it seems to owe more to Fischer's "spurts."* [15]

Duncan-Hewitt et al., were concerned to illustrate the problems of teaching at level 2 in order to bring about movement to level three. The Level 2 learner *"is capable of conceiving entities that one would characterize as "concrete" things have magnitude, persistence and properties that are distinct from one's perceptions. If you ask L2 for an abstraction, s/he will tend to give an example not the abstraction itself [ ] etc"* However, the L3 learner *"understands the abstractions, such as the idea of "relationship", and ideals exist, even if a concrete example cannot be articulated. L3's think logically, hypothetically, and strategically but decision quality varies because they still do not consider every option: they cannot construct a generalized regulatory system ...."*

With respect to the social dimension the L2 does not understand how the ideas of others should (could) impact on his own whereas the L3 understands that relationships exist to have meaning. S/He can reflect on these meanings whereas the L2 cannot, but that reflection stops when it generate *"what seems to the reflector-to be a logical or chronological sequence of behaviors,"* because meaning is related to conformity and harmony within the immediate culture.

To enable students to move from level 2 to level 3 teachers are advised to affirm level 2 while pushing the students toward level three. Thus, the teacher should provide the correct information with an authoritative style and by giving the student more responsibilities, move into a position where s/he is a guide and motivator. *"In the process, s/he expects to deal with emotions that arise when L'2s alternately feel constrained and controlled when facing mutual responsibilities and expectations, and then "out of self-control" when they do not meet expectations to master their impulses."*

Thus, a teacher will put them in teams to help develop interpersonal skills, and affirm their individual identity through continuing individual assessment. This assessment can be made relatively exciting in camp based activities if the students are asked to apply their knowledge during the activities or explain it. In this way the tutors learnt of the difficulties that high school students have in understanding concepts. (See also Chapter 4). They also learned of the value of moving from the concrete to the abstract, but they learned this from the application of the Crux model to the analysis of what happened, and not by reference to the Kolb cycle of learning (Chapter 5). Thus, the L2 learner is competent at abstractions to the extent they can be referred directly to the concrete.

By applying their model to a fluid mechanics activity [16] that seemed not to have been received very well, they were able to suggest modifications that might make it more suitable. The model indicated that the "procedural failure" of the activity was due to:

- *Lengthy periods of uninterrupted lecture to "explain" the abstractions but less feedback.*
- *Lacked assessment of understanding of concepts of intermediate complexity (e.g., viscosity) before using them to calculate even more abstract concepts.*
- *A more tenuous link between experiment (concrete), the calculations (complex abstract), and the topics of the critical thinking questions (completely abstract).*
- *The closure period was used to plot calculations, but not to probe campers' understanding.*

They suggested that in the future they should [17]:

- *Engage students' interest with concrete situations.*
- *Pose questions which the students might ask of themselves given these situations.*
- *Require "deep" active thinking by asking and requiring answers to critical thinking questions that force them to abstract from the concrete.*
- *Encourage group accountability by insisting upon validation of answers using checking algorithms (such as unit analysis).*
- *Require individual accountability by calling on group members at random (rather than a group spokesperson), forcing them to ensure that all members understand.*

---

[15] See footnote 9

[16] The fluid mechanics activity provided an *"introduction to the concepts of fluid mechanics, including viscous and inertial forces. Reynold's number, and drag coefficient by asking the campers to measure the terminal velocities of spheres of different materials in different fluids."*

[17] The quotation is slightly different from the original in that the first word of each item was a present participle.

EVALUATIVE THINKING	Unable to evaluate information presented: relies primarily on unexamined prior beliefs.	Presents information to support previously held beliefs; superficial understanding of information; acknowledges need to gather more information.	Uses information to establish well-supported argument for achieving goals; indicates need to gather more information to further support assertions.	Uses information to establish well supported argument for achieving goals; suggests viable strategies for addressing self-identified limitations.	
DIVERGENT THINKING	Does not make connections among relevant information.	Presents holistic self-assessment; limited breakdown and focus on achievement of individual goals.	Organizes available information into viable framework for exploring complexities of achieving goals.	Organizes and prioritizes available information appropriate for the task of sel-assessing achievement	
CONVERGENT THINKING	Presents information but does not attempt to interpret or analyze.	Provides limited interpretation or analysis of how well goals were met.	Presents interpretation and analysis from multiple perspectives of how well goals were met.	Presents interpretation and analysis from multiple perspectives of how well goals were met; also includes analysis of how to continue to attempt to achieve goals.	
COGNITIVE MEMORY	Asserts that goals were met; relies on external authority (moderators) for evaluations.	Uses limited information but acknowledges at least the possibility of uncertainty.	Uses range of carefully evaluated relevant information during self-assessment.	Uses range of carefully evaluated relevant information during self-assessment; suggests viable strategies for obtaining new information to address limitations.	

Exhibit 6.4. Barbara Old's, Reflective Rubric based on the Reflective Judgment Model as cited in Tsang (2002). The critical thinking skills are based on the Blosser Taxonomy. (Reproduced with the permission of *IEEE, Proceedings Frontiers in Education Conference.*)

- *Simplifying or eliminating higher-level concepts.*
- *Collecting answers in a large group session after working at a team level and then exploring correctness and meaning before proceeding with plotting step.*

6.3. Reflection in Practice

The idea that reflective practice is easily accomplished in the educational environment is not supported by the evidence. Students do not automatically or naturally think reflectively. It is a skill that has to be developed. An example of such development in software engineering has been given by Upchurch and Sims-Knight (1999). Using Turn's (1997) idea of learning essays, they began their project-based course with a request for a description of student's expectations of the course.[18] As might have been expected, the essays that

were returned showed little evidence of thought, and were very short. Thus, students required practice in essays that demanded reflection, and during the course they had to be supplied with scaffolding to help them develop this skill. The final activity required an essay in which the students compared the development of their behaviors prior to the course with those at the end. (In between times the students had to complete a post mortem and a team review.) The final essay was intended to be a legacy in which management lessons learned on the project were discussed.[19] It was found that students learned to correct their strategies with potential improvement strategies, and *"to articulate the influence between the way they worked with effort and quality."*

It is clear that developmental models pose a considerable challenge to education. For example, as mentioned above, in modular courses set at two different levels, one supposedly higher than the other, it is

[18.]Turns wrote " *In a learning essay, a student is generally supposed to document observations about their design experience, explore the implications of these observations, and articulate the lessons they have learnt through this thought process. When done in a manner consistent with this description, learning essays are an externalization of a student's attempt to explain the lessons contained in the experience. In particular, the research suggests that it would be particularly valuable for students to explain the relationships between what they did in the assigned project activities and (1) the goals of the class, (2) the goals of the assignment, (3) their prior understandings of the topic, and (4) their*

anticipated activity". Turn's described how this activity was given a web based support system, and gives examples of student essays together with a commentary. (See also Chapter 16)

[19] This is a simplified description of the structure of the course. Learning essays are intended to help students think through their cognitive processes and make plans on how to improve that process in relation to current learning ability. In this respect the paper contains a useful summary of cognitive science literature

conceivable that the design of instruction is such that both assume the same level of development and, in consequence, little development takes place. If it is correct that the development of reflective thinking skills should take place in subjects, does the compression of subjects into a 12 to 15 week period instead of the 24 to 30 weeks, which used to be the case for most universities in Britain, inhibit curriculum designs for growth? The Pavelich and Moore (1996) study indicated that they need not, but it demanded an integrated course over four years in which there were radical departures from traditional methods of teaching. Similar questions apply to the conduct and method of assessment.

There are, of course, other approaches to the development of reflective practice. These models suggest that all is not what it should be, and they challenge engineering departments to examine their approaches to the attainment of this goal among their students.

6.4. Lifelong Learning and Adult Learning

Much attention is being paid to lifelong learning or permanent education as it used to be called.[20] It is argued that in a knowledge-based society everyone has to be a lifelong learner. Taken together with the rapid advances in the applications of computer technology to distance learning, theorists and practitioners are arguing that the shape of universities is likely to change radically during the next 50 years.. There has, of course, been much discussion about continuing education in engineering worldwide [e.g., Australia (Muspratt, 1989); Canada (Heinke and Weihs,1989)], and recently Marra, Camplese, and Litzinger (1999) reviewed the literature in the light of the ABET requirements for 2000. They also compared engineering education with medical education where there is a strong tradition of continuing education (e.g., Davis and Fox, 1994). Insofar as engineering is concerned they argued that so long *as we as educators see our main task as "covering" the material we will never pause long enough to help our students learn to learn on their own",* and that such education begins in childhood.

Account needs to be taken of the warnings that have been made that distance learning and electronic media are not the panaceas some think them to be (Simonson, 1996; Schlosser, 1996; Smaldino, 1996). For example, a review of research in this area by Schlosser came to the conclusion that learning at a distance is not what students want, rather they want to be in the presence of a learning group. Simonson drew attention to a seminal paper by Clark (1983) in the *Review of Educational Research* who wrote that, *"the best current evidence is that media are mere vehicles that deliver instruction but do not influence student achievement any more than the truck that delivers groceries causes change in nutrition only the content of the vehicle can influence achievement."* Simonson considered that the same still

holds but pointed to a paradox that while students do not really want to learn at a distance, at the same time they are increasingly demanding to be allowed to learn at a distance. *"This is because there are many other considerations than personal preferences that motivate learners, especially about where and when they learn."* Given that this is the case then the educational community is faced with a major problem in the allocation of resources, and Simonson argued that institutions have to provide distance learning that is equivalent, or at least nearly equivalent to the learning experiences of local learners. Those institutions that cannot do this have no place in the field of distance learning. Schlosser in the same symposium concluded that the key question is not whether one medium works better than another, but *"What methods of instruction work?"* To which might be added the questions, What type and for what level?[21] (See Chapter 14 for further discussion on the new technologies and learning.)

Accompanying this debate about the future of learning in higher education is an increase in attention to adult learning. At the same time, much work is being done on higher stages of human development that has a bearing on such learning (e.g., Alexander and Langer, 1990). References to the literature in this field are to be found in papers written about engineering education, and one of the leaders in the field has contributed to engineering education (Knowles, 1975, 1990). It has to be said that some of the techniques that are advocated are already in use in school education, as for example, discovery learning (cited by Belbin and Belbin, 1972). And, with respect to engineering education more generally Crynes and Crynes (1997) pointed out from visits that they had made to lower primary (elementary) classes that what they had seen-that is the general attributes as opposed to the specific-had direct application to the engineering curriculum.

Razani (1991) (citing Tough, 1974) listed the principal characteristics of adult learners. They are (in abbreviated form):

1. When adults see a benefit in learning, they will invest considerable effort in it.
2. Adults have a self-concept of being responsible for their own lives.
3. Adults bring with them a quality of experience that is different to that brought by young persons to learning.
4. Adults become ready to learn those things they need to know. In relation to Perry, (or stage theories in general), Razani says that an *"especially rich source of readiness to learn is the developmental tasks associated with moving from one developmental stage to the next."*
5. Adults are task-centered or problem-centered in their approach to learning whereas young people have a subject-centered approach to learning

---

[20]Candy (1991) defines the aims of lifelong learning as being to equip people with skills and competencies necessary to continue with their own *"self-education,"* see Candy (1997).

[21]As if in answer to the question, Smaldino in the same symposium began to provide an answer.

6.   Adults are motivated by both extrinsic and intrinsic incentives, although they prefer the latter.

Razani made a useful division of engineering course content when he distinguished between vocabulary, concept, and recipe. He wrote:

"The goal of teaching in engineering courses is mainly to increase students' problem solving abilities using concepts and recipes. Vocabulary is needed in communicating ideas and for the understanding of the concepts and recipes. By concepts here we mean a basic principle or law, understanding of which is required to analyze an engineering system. By recipe it is meant a procedure, an algorithm, or a model to solve a particular problem. Concepts convey a general principle and idea while recipe refers to a specific application."[22]

From this description it would seem to be a moot point as to whether this allows for synthesis and creativity. However, the more general point is that it is simply a different way of looking at some of the points made earlier in Chapter 4 on concept learning. Razani, said that most engineering courses are either concept and vocabulary-oriented (e.g., thermodynamics), or recipe and vocabulary-oriented. He argued that adult learners who have plenty of experience often know the recipes, but are not sure of the validity of their application. He argued that if students understood these distinctions they could analyze the sources of their confusions. His experience was that nontraditional students respond to teaching that presents the concept and the vocabulary very early on and follows it up by recipes.

Beston, Fellows, and Culver (2000), investigated how adult learning helped develop self-directed learning and applied this to young university students. Their argument for doing this is that universities do not help students prepare for lifelong learning, but have an obligation so to do. It may be argued that it should begin in school and that part of the problem is the failure to appreciate that higher education is part of a continuum. This point is made by Wright (1993), who proposed a model of technology for schools that drew attention to the SCANS proposals, and the report on *Science for All Americans.*[23] Both Bruner (1960) and Heywood (1961) have argued that it is possible for young children to cope with concepts that we regard as difficult in a language that is appropriate to them. This argument is supported by the success of the philosophy for young children movement (Matthews, 1980). It is also supported by the fact that some writers have attempted to write books on complex issues for children. Particular mention should be

made of Stannard's series on Einstein.[24] At the 1999 Frontiers in Education conference, Pappas showed how Boolean logic could be used with grade 3 children. While this may sound both good and plausible, there is a need for a theoretical model of the curriculum that takes such requirements into account. They should not be "add-ons", or *ad hoc*. Appropriate models are likely to be found in Bruner's spiral curriculum and Whitehead's (1932) rhythm in education (see Chapter 7, and also Heywood's (1991) attempt to apply Whitehead's theory to School Technology). Wilson and Chizeck (2000), have described an outreach program that relates cognitive development to all stages of the school program. At the time they published their paper they were only able to report evidence of an anecdotal kind on the work they had completed with K-3.

Beston, Fellows and Culver, argued that the curriculum in engineering is loaded against the development of skills that will help students become lifelong learners. Much of the evidence in the preceding Chapters supports this assertion. Since students have expectations of just such a curriculum, any change, and it could be substantial change, requires that they should be persuaded of the value of interventions which may help them become self-directed learners. Eighteen-year-old students have to be weaned away from instructor-led learning, and information receiving.

To overcome this limitation Beston, Fellows and Culver applied Grow's model of self-directed learning to the design of instruction in a DteC course at Binghamton University, and an engineering science course at Broome Community College that was firmly grounded in Perry principles. The model is shown in Exhibit 6.5, and given the previous discussion of the Perry model should be self-explanatory. It is based on the concept of "readiness"[25] It is argued that teaching should be matched to the readiness of the student for learning, but of sufficient intellectual challenge to motivate the student to want to move forward. They used Grow's illustration of how this can be done, and go on to explain in detail how they have fitted the model to the two courses. As might be expected the program involved projects, portfolios, and journals (see also Culver and Fellows, 1997).

In an extension of this paper, Beston, Fellows and Culver (2000) made the point that, *"One of the immediate concerns of self-directed learning instruction is the effort that it takes to maintain the motivational levels of students. Students are initially motivated because they are in charge of seeking the content and methodology of their writing projects. The challenge to*

---

[22] See Chapter 4 on concept learning.
[23] The SCANS proposals are in a report from the US Department of Labor. The Secretary's Commission on Achieving Necessary Skills (SCANS). *What Work Requires of Schools*. US Department of Labour, Washington, DC. *Science for All Americans*. American Association for the Advancement of Science, Washington, DC.(See Chapter 7).

[24] Professor Stannard is from the Open University(e.g., Black Holes and Uncle Albert (1991). Faber and Faber, London). The present writer also attempted such a book in 1963 with a children's book on Albert Einstein published by Muller.
[25] Readiness is a Piagetian term and is related to the idea that children would not read until they were ready to read (reading readiness). It was applied to the readiness of university institutions to change by Heywood (1969). Grow derived his understanding of it from Hersey and Blanchard's (1988) situational leadership model.

the instructor is maintaining the motivation to get the job done."

"Students begin enthusiastically, but when they discover it is not as easy as they first imagined, they begin to give up. It is essential that either the teacher or the course assistant intervene to bring them back on track. This can be done as a whole class or with individual students."

In some respects this situation is similar to the experience of teachers responsible for the teaching of engineering science at A level in England.

Stage	Student	Teacher	Examples
1.	**Dependent**	**Authority, coach**	**Coaching with immediate feedback. Informational lecture.**
2	**Interested**	**Motivator, guide**	**Overcoming deficiencies and resistance.**
3	**Involved**	**Facilitator**	**Inspiring lecture plus guided discussion. Goal setting and learning strategies.**
			Discussion facilitated by teacher who participates as an equal. Seminar. Group project.
4	**Self-directed**	**Consultant**	**Internship, dissertation, individual work.**

Exhibit 6.5. The Staged Self-Directed Learning Model as described by Beston, Fellows, and Culver (2000*) (Reproduced with permission of IEEE, Proceedings Frontiers in Education Conference).*

The students were in the age range 16 to 18 and in their second year they undertook a substantial engineering project (see Chapter 2). They were also from the high-achieving end of the performance spectrum with expectations of study at university. The projects were chosen by the students, but the problem that teachers had was to constrain many students from going beyond the 50-hour laboratory time limit for their completion. Many students did their work home and this could have interfered with the other studies that they had to do. At the same time, there were some students who found it difficult to choose a suitable project, and as might be expected, the teachers also encountered problems with these students (Carter, Heywood, and Kelly, 1986). It is important to note that, when schools do undertake non traditional methods of teaching that motivate students, this can lead to disappointment with university studies that are traditional. The same thing can happen between primary (elementary: 5–12) and secondary education (12–18). For example, The Tipperary Leader Group sponsored an enterprise project among primary school in Tipperary. Children in 19 schools undertook to design,

manufacture, and sell products based on market research. They set up their own companies. There is nothing unusual about such mini-company activity in schools, but in this case the sponsors attempted to get teachers to place responsibility for the choice of product and its pursuit on the children. In several cases they were more than successful, and the pupils from one school were disappointed when in their secondary school the teachers of business studies would not allow them to undertake a similar project. Some of them complained to their primary school teacher and she suggested that they undertake a project from home, and this they did. It is significant, that the "skill" that these children believed they learned most, was to be able to work in teams! (Heywood, 2002). The experience of these two studies serves to illustrate the importance of a spiral approach to the curriculum.

Beston, Fellows, and Culver have not, as yet, provided a full evaluation of their program although they have described some of the difficulties experienced by tutors. One of these, the ready access to a file that contains detail of each student's progress, is being dealt with at this time. They also reported that teachers require a change in disposition if they are not used to working in a relatively loosely structured teaching environment, and they might argue, given other studies they have done, that this a function of a teacher's emotional intelligence.

6.5. Emotional, Practical, and Social Intelligence

Studies of the effect of temperament on learning and performance have a long history (see Section 5.8). It is clear that the emotions influence our response to learning and intelligence in the same way they influence our response to others. We have also learnt that we need to be able to govern (control) our emotions, and the ability to do this is sometimes called emotional (or social) intelligence. Goleman's (1995) published a book on emotional intelligence was an immediate best seller. In it he asked, *"What factors are at play, for example, when people of high IQ flounder and those of modest IQ do surprisingly well?"* He went on to argue, *"that the difference quite often lies in the abilities called here emotional intelligence, which include self-control, zeal and persistence, and the ability to motivate oneself. And these skills [...] can be taught to children giving them a better chance to use whatever intellectual potential the genetic lottery may have given them."*

The subjects of emotional and social intelligence have been studied during most of the last century, irrespective of whether they are the same construct or different constructs. Taken together, they may be considered as ways of *"understanding individual personality and social behavior"* (Zirkel, 2000). There are non traditional intelligences,' such as *"practical intelligence,"* that seem to overlap with them, and part of Sternberg's recent work has been to consider whether they are distinct or overlapping constructs (Hedlund and Sternberg, 2000). Bar-On and Parker (2000) have recently brought together the body of American literature on this topic in a Handbook that reviewed the controversies the concept, and they evaluated methods that attempted to assess social intelligence, as for example Bar-On's (2000) Emotional Quotient Inventory. Emotional Intelligence has been seen as both a personality construct and a mental ability (Mayer, Salovey, and Caruso, 2000). It is for this reason that much that has, for example, been done in Britain and elsewhere has been developed within the framework of traditional thinking about personality and intelligence and about the cognitive and affective domains of educational thinking.

Notwithstanding the debate about whether the traits that comprise emotional intelligence are personality traits or mental abilities for which adequate measures already exist it is quite clear that engineers need to possess "emotional intelligence" in their dealings with people. They need to behave competently. Indeed the philosophy of the Enterprise in Higher Education Initiative in the United Kingdom was based on the view that all graduates require skill in dealing with people (Heywood, 1994). The ability-based curriculum offered by Alverno College would claim to help students develop in this area.

Culver (1998) argued that promoting emotional intelligence would be necessary if a successful engineering program is to be achieved. To support his contention, Culver quoted a list of the components that make up emotional intelligence from the "self-science" curriculum used by Nueva School in California (Stone and Dillehunt, 1978). This list, which has been adapted, is:

Self-awareness: Observing yourself and recognizing your feelings with a view to action or trying to change action in specified circumstances. This can include mode of study, reactions to people, etc.

Personal decision-making: Examining one's actions and predicting the consequences. Knowing the basis of the decision, i.e., cognition or feeling. This covers the gamut of small and large decisions that relate to everyday actions.

Managing Feelings: Requires self-awareness in order to be able to handle anxieties, anger, insults, put-downs, and sadness.

Handling stress: Use of imagery and other methods of evaluation.

Empathy: Understanding how people feel and appreciating that in the learning situation students can become stressed, and that such stress can be reduced by the mode of instruction (e.g., the use of imagery, Heywood, 1996).

Communications: Becoming a good listener and question-asker; distinguishing between what someone does or says and your own reactions about it; sending "I" messages instead of blame.

Self-disclosure: Building trust in relationships and knowing when one can be open.

Insight: This is different from cognitive insight referred to previously. It is about understanding one's emotional life and being able to recognise similar patterns in others so as to better handle relationships.

Self-acceptance: Being able to acknowledge strengths and weaknesses, and being able to adapt where necessary.

Personal responsibility: Being able to take responsibility for one's own actions. This relates to personal decision making. Learning not to try and pass the buck when the buck really rests with one's self.

Assertiveness: The ability to be able to take a controlled stand, i.e., with neither anger nor meekness. Particularly important in decisions involving moral issues in engineering on which the professional ethic demands that a stand should be made.

Behavior in groups. Knowing when to participate, lead, and follow.

Conflict resolution: Using the win/win model to negotiate compromise. This is particularly important in industrial relations, and it applies to both partners in managerial conflicts.

In the Nueva list *behavior in groups* is called group dynamics, but this is in some respects misleading because group dynamics is the interaction between the various members of the group or the study of these interactions.

Cherniss (2000) pointed out that while the term emotional intelligence has not been used in industry, there is a long history of training and development in industry that has focused on the skills embraced by emotional intelligence. In Great Britain the management competencies described by the Management Charter Initiative clearly embrace the areas of emotional intelligence. On both sides of the Atlantic, there has been concern with the development of communication and empathy skills among physicians, and scales that overlap both the cognitive and affective domains have been developed for the assessment of trainee general practitioners (Freeman and Byrne, 1976). To this writer's knowledge, no attempt has been made to assess these skills among engineers as part of their professional certification.

Also, in the United Kingdom, a substantial program for the development of personal skills in relevant areas of the elementary and secondary school curriculum was designed (Hopson and Scally, 1981). There is vast popular literature on acquiring these skills, and there is a specialized literature in management.

Of interest to this review is the work of The Personal Development Project at Sheffield University that was described in Chapter 2. It was set up to advize and specify the personal skills with which graduates should be equipped, and to identify methods by which these skills may be inculcated as an integral part of teaching. The skills' model developed by the unit has already been described above in relation to industry's requirements of university graduates (Figure 2.7). It will be seen that more than 30 skills are involved. These are: Being assertive; Chairing; Clarifying; Closing; Collaborating; Confronting; Consulting; Contracting; Critical thinking; Data-handling; Decentering; Delegating; Empathizing; Explaining; Facilitating Hypothesizing; Information gathering; Integrating; Interpreting; Interviewing; Leading; Listening; Mentoring; Negotiating:

Communicating non-verbally; Opening; Presenting Questioning; Reflecting back; reviewing; Self-disclosure; Supervising; Synthesizing; and Telephoning. This list is a more broadly based than the Nueva list. Clearly both the affective and cognitive domains are embraced. The unit provided training in these areas within the contexts of specific subjects. It is argued by many authorities in Britain that these skills are generic and transferable-hence the title Personal Transferable Skills.

With respect to self-reflection, the unit reported that students showed marked individual differences in their ability to do this, and there were variations relating to the discipline studied. Thus, students in the health sciences were quite happy talking about their feelings whereas engineers were not. *"They were not used to talking in terms of feelings, nor could they see the relevance of such reflection to learning about engineering problems."*

It is of interest to note that a concept map was used to alert staff to these issues, and that the factors are classified in response to the questions Why? (Why not?), What? How? Who?

During the three-year period of the project the unit was able to set up opportunities for the acquisition of core and group skills in the four generic areas of communication, teamwork, problem-solving and managing and organizing in ten academic departments including engineering. Four active learning situations were compared for the opportunities they afforded for skill development. These were personal tutorials, seminars, project work, and student profile. The analysis was shown in Exhibit 2.14, and it relates to the diagram shown in Figure 2.7. A profile is provided on the right hand side of the matrix. Unit staff helped to promote these skills in the learning situations specified in the cells. Workshops and training sessions were also provided. For example, in General Practice (Medicine) tutors identified the skills they were inculcated during small group tutorial work, and they reviewed the extent to which these were made explicit to their students as valuable learning outcomes of the course. In this analysis (Exhibit 2.14) it is clear that student-led seminars and team projects offer greater scope for skill development than those situations where students work individually with a tutor.

There might be some debate as to whether these skills, taken as a whole, are representative of emotional intelligence as perceived by Culver. Equally it might be objected that the Nueva skills are not a distinct social or emotional intelligence but rather a set of personality traits, in which case, they are better called personal transferable skills. One way of looking at emotional intelligence is to consider it to be the interplay between the cognitive and the affective domains in the conduct of living, if you accept that living is problem-solving, which embraces critical thinking. But, as Hedlund and Sternberg (2000) pointed out, the competencies required to solve a problem will be a function of the type of problem faced.

With respect to Higher Education, Heywood (1994) argued that while the higher education curriculum neglected these skills, they were the same skills that authorities such as Newman (1851,-1949), much cited in support of liberal education believed to be essential if a liberal education was to be achieved. Heywood noted that academic intelligence had to go alongside the kind of practical intelligence defined by Sternberg, and he drew attention to Sternberg's study of lay people's views of intelligence that showed them to value the social and practical aspects of intelligence.

Sternberg and his colleagues included within the domain of practical intelligence practical problem solving, pragmatic intelligence, and everyday intelligence.

"Practical Intelligence involves a number of skills as applied to shaping of and selection of environments [Which is what Sternberg argued intelligent people do]. *These skills include among others, (1) recognizing problems, (2) defining problems, (3) allocating resources to solving problems, (4) mentally representing problems, (5) formulating strategies for solving problems, (6) monitoring solution of problems, and (7) evaluating solutions of problems"* (Sternberg and Grigorenko, 2000).

Hedlund and Sternberg (2000) considered that what differentiates emotional from social and practical intelligence is "tacit knowledge." That is, the knowledge that it not taught, but acquired as part of everyday living. The idea is vividly captured in Yorkshire dialect by the term "nouse!" The categories of tacit knowledge are managing self, managing others, and managing tasks. It will be understood that management education is about trying to influence these three types of knowledge. Such knowledge is procedural in the sense that it is associated with particular situations, and is transferred to similar situations and this is why the content of knowledge and the type of problem solved differentiate between the three constructs.

"The ability to acquire knowledge, whether it pertains to managing oneself, managing others, or managing tasks, can be characterized appropriately as an aspect of intelligence. It requires cognitive processes such as encoding essential information from the environment and recognizing associations between new information and existing knowledge. The decision to call this aspect of intelligence social, emotional, or practical intelligence will depend on one's perspective and one's purpose."

6.6. A Note on Testing for Emotional Intelligence.

Based on the evidence available at the time, which was relatively scant, Macintosh (1998) found that tests had not identified a general dimension of social intelligence. One battery of tests of social skills did correlate with measures of academic intelligence, and tests of social skills. This might suggest that they are related to more general aspects of intelligence. At the same time tests of social competence are found to be relatively independent of each other. Macintosh pointed out that this is hardly surprising given the *"wide variety of rather different skills used to cope with the very wide range of demands that social life imposes."[26]*

Since Macintosh discussed this issue, Dulewicz and Higgs (1999) of the Henley Management College have reported on a test of emotional intelligence (EI) that they have developed. It is a self-report instrument and the items were obtained from a survey of the literature and piloted on 201 senior managers. Eleven percent were from Europe and 25% were from the rest of the world. It has seven sub scales. These are: self-awareness, emotional resilience, motivation, interpersonal sensitivity, influence, decisiveness, and conscientiousness and integrity. For each of these a profile for high and low scorers is provided. Correlations between the tests, except those between interpersonal sensitivity and decisiveness, are relatively high and statistically significant. As the authors suggested, they appear to be measuring slightly different aspects of the same thing. They only found one significant correlation when biographical data were taken into account, and that was between age and sensitivity. Older people tended to be more sensitive. However, the overall score for EI was found to be independent of gender, sector, nationality, and responsibility. All of the scale scores were found to be reliable except that decisiveness and conscientiousness and integrity only just attained acceptable levels.

The construct validity of the instrument was evaluated on two occasions against well known tests of personality. In the second study the 16 PF Inventory, the *Belbin Team Roles Questionnaire* (which is a derivative of the 16 PF), and the Myers Briggs indicator were used with respect to the MBTI, which has been widely used among engineers, the investigators hypothesized negative correlations between introversion, motivation and influence and also, between feeling and decisiveness. Thinking and feeling types correlated with the EI factor self-awareness No correlations were found between extraversion and any of the EI scales. Support was also found for content and predictive validity. Dulewicz and Higgs argued that their data supported the view that emotional intelligence plays an important role in individual success. However, the research does not answer the questions posed by Macintosh about the construct itself and what is being measured. No standard intelligence test was administered, and the construct validity with personality measures suggested that one could equally well be looking at personality traits.

It is fairly clear, on the basis of past experience with learning styles and personality profiles, that engineering educators, once they are alerted to the problem, will want to experiment with tests like the one discussed or the *Emotional Competence Inventory* (Boyatzis, Goleman and Rhee, 2000) or the Emotional Quotient Inventory (Bar-On, 2000). It is important that they should familiarize themselves with the problems of interpretation with these tests. These are dealt with comprehensively in the Bar-On and Parker (2000) Handbook.

Irrespective of this theoretical discussion, it is evident from the forgoing that engineers need to acquire personal transferable skills, or the skills that Culver has listed which are said to construe emotional intelligence, if they are to perform satisfactorily in the workplace.

6.7. Beyond Testing

Koort and Reilly (2002) of the media lab at MIT argued that the ability to be able to identify a learner's cognitive-emotive state should enable teachers to provide more efficient and pleasurable learning experiences. They believed that teachers could do this by observing facial expressions, gross body language, and the tone and content of speech. Some teachers make such judgments automatically, but others are insensitive to such situations. Those who are sensitive to them may not know what to do about them in classroom situations. For this reason, and for the purpose of training, Kort and Reilly offered a four-quadrant model that related learning to the emotions. It is shown in Figure 6.2. "Similarities" with the Kolb model of learning styles will be apparent.

Koort and Reilly (2002) called the vertical axis the "learning axis". Knowledge is constructed in an upward direction and misconceptions are discarded in the downward direction. The intention is, on the one hand to show that learning in science, engineering and math is naturally cyclic, and on the other hand, to demonstrate that when students find themselves in the negative half that that this is inevitable. Thus, the teacher has to help students to keep orbiting the loop and *"to propel themselves, especially after a set-back."* The model suggests intervention strategies that the teacher might use in each quadrant.

6.8. Motivation

Linked to personality and emotional intelligence is the concept of motivation. In spite of a large literature on this topic, the number of papers in the engineering literature with motivation in the title is insignificant. Those who have done research in the area of deep and surface learning have pointed out that intrinsic motivation is important to deep learning (Ames and Ames 1989). Flammer (1972), in *Engineering Education* argued that *"Motivation is the single greatest factor behind achievement in any endeavour, including academic studies."* He pointed out that at university the student is "swamped" with content, and university education for that student becomes a fight for survival. Like so many others, he found that if students were allowed to choose their own research projects, they got really involved or, in the jargon, intrinsically motivated. He argued that students should be allowed to participate in setting their own goals. In so doing they could contract for the grade they wished to receive, define problems as well as solution procedures, and choose the areas they want to pursue in the applications part of the course. This happens in the few courses of independent study that are

---

[26]For a more recent discussion of these issues, especially in the United States, see Bar-On and Parker (2000).

offered in the United Kingdom. That it should happen in engineering is revolutionary. A more satisfactory approach to the reconciliation of learning and assessment objectives is probably by means of an assessment-led curriculum of the kind offered by Alverno College (Mentkowski and Associates, 2000).

A recent American study demonstrated a relationship between expectations and performance that is commonly stated in textbooks for student teachers (e.g., Bellon, Bellon and Blank, 1992). Students rose to the level of their teacher's expectations-in this case, teaching assistants. Among 750 students in the laboratory sections of an engineering graphics course, those who were taught by teaching assistants who set high standards performed better than those in laboratory sections where the grading standards were not as high. The investigators concluded that there were *"modest shifts in the level of subject material mastery"* (Mountain and Pleck, 2000).

Many courses are driven in the belief that motivation will be enhanced if courses are made more relevant even though how students perceive relevance has not been studied. Clearly, what is real to one student may not be real to another, and the advent of virtual systems changes our understanding of reality in learning.

The need for relevance is a reason for the use of project work, service learning (i.e. projects in the community e.g., Fleischmann, 2001), and so forth. In Sweden a multidisciplinary course has been built around real work situations in order to combine social and technical skills, more especially communication. The four components of the course are ethics, cognitive psychology, social psychology, and language and language interaction. Key concepts help the students relate theory to practice (Danielo et al., 2001). An interesting contribution from Yoder, McClellan and Schafer (1998) reminded their readers that 50 years ago students wanted to know how circuits worked, and to do this they were willing to build them. *"Now our students are more likely to have tinkered with a computer than have built a crystal radio."* They suggested that Digital Signal Processing should be the first engineering course that students take. The issue of relevance is taken up again in Chapter 14.

Elton (1996) related student learning to Maslow's hierarchy of needs. He considered the motivation of students who have high and low intrinsic commitment to study. A subject-oriented student is likely to have high intrinsic commitment, whereas an achievement-oriented student who is wholly examination oriented will have low intrinsic motivation. The latter group is likely to be quite large because their degree courses will not be related to the jobs they do. For this group, teachers need to concentrate on examination preparation so as to enhance the possibility of high achievement. Only when this need, which is at a lower level in the Maslow hierarchy, has been met should teachers try to increase the subject interest factor. Elton considered that examination preparation is the ability to make *"students feel more confident that they will be able to pass the examination."* He did not consider the possibility of enhancing the process by redesigning the examination.[27]

Stimulated by Herzberg's theory of motivation, Lee and Shih (2001) undertook a small case study to evaluate the motivation and hygiene factors at work in on-line learning. The key factors were found to be style of instruction, content of materials, and encouragement.

Flammer (1972) was of the opinion that the self-paced proctorial system of instruction was a good way of fostering motivation. He advocated the use of case studies because they could give the students a flavor of the reality of engineering. The ability to "master" a topic is a major source of motivation. He wrote: *"As long as we are obsessed with content we will never meet the more basic foundation requirements necessary for high level professional performance after graduation. We just don't have the time to get the student into higher forms of learning activities which would be such effective motivators. And yet I am intrigued with the idea that once we overcome a student's cumulative ignorance by mastery level performance and that once he is "turned on" he can absorb more content and with real understanding".* Would he say the same about today's programs?

In the Lee and Shih (2001) enquiry the student at the focus of the investigation said, "that on-learning tests let her feel more comfortable because she could get her grade immediately without asking an instructor."

An investigation of Israeli engineering students' creative thinking by Waks and Merdler (2003) began with the view that since creativity is the search for ne wand effective ideas, it requires sensitivity to gaps in knowledge together with the ability to evoke new ideas about the problem(s) to be solved. Such knowledge may be extrinsic or it may be intrinsic. For example, in a design team the project leader may require ideas to be followed up. In the classroom the instructor is often the source of extrinsic motivation, but in either case, how the leader achieves extrinsic motivation is of some importance. Waks and Merdler concluded from their study that creativity could be obtained either by (a) high intrinsic motivation and some supportive non-censorious extrinsic intervention by the instructor, or (b) evoking different points and perspectives on the project's issues. For example, "why is it' or, and not' and?"[28]

Culver and Yokomoto (1999) continuing the debate about emotional intelligence, gave a good example of intrinsic motivation. It reads: *"I was stuck on a boundary value conduction heat transfer problem in my*

---

[27]Elton's paper is of considerable interest since it relates to Herzberg's theory of motivation to student learning. He takes into account weaknesses and modifications to the theory by Cryer (1988) and Nias (1981). The categorization of student motivation into extrinsic, intrinsic, achievement-oriented, and social is due to Entwistle and Waterston (1987).

[28]Waks and Merdler (2003) followed other work by Csikszentmihalyi (1990), which suggested that a combination of low extrinsic motivation and high intrinsic motivation is the optimal influence of motivation on creative performance. They also used Amabile's (1996) distinction between suppressive and supportive extrinsic motivation. (See also Chapter 11)

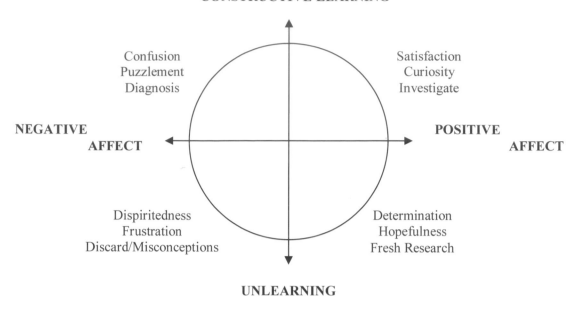

Figure 6.2. Motivation. Relating learning to the emotions (Kort and Reilly, 2002) (Reproduced with permission of IEEE, *Proceedings Frontiers in Education Conference*).

graduate studies. I had searched several reference texts and found a solution similar to the problem I wanted to solve, but was not sure where to go next. I was referred to a professor of applied math. I presented him with the problem with the assumption that he would suggest a procedure for starting the solution. Instead he pulled out a piece of paper and laid the problem out carefully. After thinking for a minute, he started writing. For the next twenty minutes, I sat silently as he methodically went about solving the problem. He was totally absorbed. I now know that he had entered the state of flow in which optimum performance occurs."

It is also, indirectly, an example of deep learning. The concept of "flow" comes from the work of Csikszentmihalyi (1990). Culver and Yokomoto (1999) considered the relation of optimum academicerformance to emotional intelligence in engineeringeducation. Csikszentmihalyi and Nakamura (1989) write that: *"Flow is what people feel when they enjoy what they are doing, when they would not want to do anything else. What makes flow so intrinsically motivating? The evidence suggests a simple answer: in flow, the human organism is functioning at its fullest capacity. When this happens, the experience is its own reward."* In many ways this is similar to the humanist psychologists' concept of self-actualization.

The reality is that most people believe that the experience of flow is a rare event, and this is probably true of self-actualization but as Culver and Yokomoto argue flow is what engineering teachers want their students to experience. For flow to be realized, the challenges and skills have to be equal. If they are-not, as for example, in a test where the skills required are more

than the challenge of the test-then the candidate may become bored. If the situation is the other way around and the skills are at a lower level than those required by the test, then the candidate is likely to experience anxiety. As Jaques (1970) has pointed out, the same is true of the workplace. If management want, to get rid of a worker, they can either make the job too hard or make it piffling. In the first case the person cannot do the job, so he/she is open to being fired. In the second case if boredom extends over a long period of time, he/she may seek a job elsewhere. Csikszentmihalyi and Namura consider that the possession of certain meta-skills enables a person not merely to respond to an environment but to control it. *"We hypothesize that it is largely because of such capacities that some people derive a great deal of enjoyment from their daily lives and spend relatively little time feeling apathetic, anxious or bored."* These capacities or meta-kills include the ability to continually adjust the balance between challenges and skills. This can be done by using anxiety and boredom as information, and also by identifying new challenges. This means that a person has to have the ability to cope with anxiety producing situations. Csikszentmihalyi and Namura also suggest that the ability to delay gratification is an important skill in this respect.

Culver and Yokomoto (1999) pointed out that the literature on self-directed learning relates to flow, and as Flammer (1972) argued projects provide a vehicle for this capacity to be developed. Culver and Yokomoto hoped they would be able to use the concept of flow to design training modules to promote self-directed learning in lower division engineering courses. And, also in relation to mastery, Culver and Yokomoto said of "experts" that *"After study and practice, he eventually reaches a point where he can perform the desired task without thinking about it. It is at this highest level of unconscious competence that flow is most likely to occur."* This does not necessarily mean a PSI system of learning but it does mean that the teacher's task is to facilitate mastery, and it is unlikely that that this will happen in a lecture series. It also has implications for the way examinations and tests are designed, as well as for the environments' where students live and work. Culver and Yokomoto used the example of mentoring in the EPICS course at the Colorado School of Mines to point out that feedback plays an important role in continuing the student's engagement with the program.

Culver and Yokomoto (1999) said that *"By designing our courses to provide an appropriate level of challenge, with multiple paths to learn material and continual feedback to monitor performance, we can assist students in achieving optimum academic performance."* This echoes a finding of Baillie and Fitzgerald (2000) about students who had dropped out from engineering courses at Imperial College (London). It was to the effect that students who could have persisted became demotivated because they did not see the challenge in engineering and perceive it as dull. Similarly, they do not know how to make the most of tutorials, and when they are no longer top of the class as they might have been at school, they feel isolated. As Baillie and Fitzgerald pointed out, there are remedies for this and some had been taken at the college? However, re-engineering of courses will depend on the teacher's perception of how a learner learns (or is motivated). If the teacher has a theory X-like model in which human behavior is explained mechanistically, and concepts and principles have to be explained in mechanistic terms, then the lecture method will be believed to create the conditions of learning. On the other hand, if the teacher perceives that students want to learn and will learn by themselves if-allowed, that is, the theory-Y type model-then the teacher will create learning conditions that may lead to flow and optimal academic performance.

Yokomoto (private communication), pointed out that if Furneaux's interpretation of his findings in terms of the Yerkes-Dodson principle is correct, and students' optimum level of performance varies as a function of personality, then teachers should take this into account when they interpret variations in examination performance among their students. This was also implicit in what Furneaux wrote.

It will be appreciated that the concept of intrinsic motivation brings its own problems of conceptualization, and this is a point of which Csikszentmihalyi and Nakumura are well aware. Kohn (1993) has discussed this matter in an appendix to his book *Punished by Rewards* in the same tenor as Culver and Yokomoto who have championed their work. Kohn argued that appropriate challenges have to be put before students, so challenges have to be put to teachers who

doubt these matters. One such challenge is to read Kohn's (1993) book,[29] even though it has a different focus.

References

Alexander, C. N and E. J. Langer (1990) (eds). *Higher Stages of Human Development*. Oxford University Press, New York.

Amabile, T. M (1996). *Creativity in Context. Update to Social Psychology of Creativity*. Westview Press, Boulder, CO.

Ames, C., and R. Ames (1989) *Research on Motivation in Education Vol 3. Goals and Cognitions*. Academic Press, San Diego, CA.

Assiter, K. V., and B. A. Karanian (2004). Work in progress- Cognitive, Affective and Social factors contributing to undergraduate computer science and engineering education. *Proceedings Frontiers in Education Conference*, 1, TIF-9 to 11.

Astin, A.W (1997). *What Matters in College. Four Critical years Revisited*. Jossey-Bass, San Francisco.

Baillie, C. and G. Fitzgerald (2000). Motivation and attrition in engineering education. *European Journal of Engineering Education*, 25.-(2), 145–145.

Ball, J., and K. Patrick (1999). Learning about heat transfer. "Oh I See" experiences. *Proceedings Frontiers in Education Conference* 2, 12c-5 to 6.

Barnett, R (1998). Rethinking the University. In *New Look, Old Values*. 16-18, Congress of University Convocations and Alumni Associations. Sheffield Hallam University, Marketing and Development, Sheffield.

Bar-On, R (2000). Emotional and social intelligence: insights from the Emotional Quotient inventory in R. Bar-On and J. D. A. Parker (eds.). *The Handbook of Emotional Intelligence*. Jossey-Bass, San Francisco.

Bar- On, R., and J. D. A. Parker (eds.) (2000). *The Handbook of Emotional Intelligence*. Jossey-Bass, San Francisco.

Baxter-Magdola, M. B (1987). Comparing open-ended interview and standardised measures of intelligence. *Journal of College Student Personnel*, 28, 443–448.

Belbin, E., and R. M. Belbin (1972). *Problems in Adult Retraining*. Heinemann, London.

Bellon, J. J., Bellon, E. C., and M. A. Blank (1992). *Teaching from a Research Knowledge Base. A Development and Renewal Process*. Merrill, New York

Berman, L. M (1984). Educating Children for Life Long Learning and a Life Long Learning Society. *Childhood Education*. 61, 99-106.

Beston, W., Fellows, S and R Culver (2000). Self directed learning in an ASL course. *Proceedings Frontiers in Education*, 1, T3G-1 to 6.

Bey, C (1961). A social theory of intellectual development in N. Sanford (ed.) *The American College*. Wiley, New York.

Biggs, J (1999) *Teaching for Quality Learning at University*. SRHE/Open University Press, London

Boyatzis, R. E., Goleman, D., and K. S. Rhee (2000). Clustering competence in emotional intelligence: insights from the Emotional Competence Inventory. Ch 16 in R. Bar-On and J. D. E. Parker eds *The Handbook of Emotional Intelligence*. Jossey-Bass, San Fransisco.

Bruner, J (1960). *The Process of Education*. Vintage, New York.

Bruner, J (1966). *Toward a Theory of Instruction*. Norton, New York.

Candy, P. C (1997). Some issues impacting on university teaching and learning. Implications for academic developers. In S. Armstrong, G. Thompson and S. Brown (eds.). *Facing up to Radical change in Universities and Colleges*. Kogan Page, London.

Carter, G., Heywood, J., and D.T. Kelly (1986). *Case Study in Curriculum Assessment. GCE Engineering Science (Advanced)*. Roundthorn Press, Manchester.

Cherniss, C (2000). Social and emotional competence in the workplace. Ch 20 in R. Bar-On and J. D. E. Parker eds. *The Handbook of Emotional Intelligence*. Jossey-Bass, San Francisco.

Clark, R (1983). Reconsidering research on learning from media. *Review of Educational Research*, 53.-(4), 445-459.

Coleman, D (1995). *Emotional Intelligence, Why it can matter more than IQ*. Bantam Books, New York.

---

[29] A general reader on motivation related to higher education is edited by M. Theall (1999). Unfortunately it is based solely on North American literature. A useful balance is provided by Elton (1996) some of whose views were mentioned in this Chapter

Cowan, J (1998). *One Becoming an Innovative University Teacher. Reflection in Action*. SRHE/Open University Press, Buckingham.

Cryer, P (1988). Insights into participants' behavior in educational games, simulations, and workshops: A catastrophe theory application to motivation. *Simulation/Games for Learning*, 18, 161-176.

Crynes, B. L and D. A. Crynes (1997) They already do it: Common practices in primary education that engineering education should use. *Proceedings Frontiers in Education Conference* 3, 12-19.

Csikszentmihalyi, M (1990). The domain of creativity in M. A. Runco and R. S. Albert (eds.). *Theories of Creativity*. Sage, Newbury Park, CA.

Csikszentmihalyi, M (1993). *The Evolving Self*. Harper Collins, New York.

Cskszentmahlyi, M., and J. Nakamura (1989) Dynamics of intrinsic motivation in C. Ames and R. Ames (eds.) *Research on Motivation in Education*. Vol 3. Goals and Cognitions. Academic Press, New York.

Culver, R. S (1987). Whose in charge here? Stimulating self-managed learning. *Engineering Education* February, 297–301.

Culver, R. S (1998) A review of emotional intelligence by Daniel Goldman. Implications for technical education. *Proceedings Frontiers in Education Conference* 855–860.

Culver, R. S., Cox, P., Sharp, J., and A. FitzGibbon (1994) Student learning profiles in two innovative honours degree engineering programs. *International Journal of Technology and Design Education*, 4-(3), 257-288.

Culver, R. S., and S. Fellows (1997). Using student created multimedia to teach design and communications. *Proceedings Frontiers in Education Conference*, 348–349.

Culver, R. S., and P. Fitch (1990) Design of an engineering course based on developmental instruction. *Proceedings Frontiers in Education Conference (Vienna)*.628-630.

Culver, R.S., and J.T. Hackos (1982). Perry's model of intellectual development. *Engineering Education*. 73, (2), 221-226.

Culver, R. S., and B. Olds (1986) EPICS: an integrated program for the first two years. *Proceedings ASEE St Lawrence Section Conference*, Troy, New York.

Culver, R. S., and N. Sackman. (1988) Learning with meaning through marker events. *Proceedings Frontiers in Education Conference*.

Culver, R. S., and C. Yokomoto.(1999) Optimum academic performance and its relation to emotional intelligence. *Proceedings Frontiers in Education Conference*. 13b7-26 to 29.

Culver, R.S., Woods, D., and P. Fitch (1990). Gaining professional expertise through design activities. *Engineering Education*, 80, (5), 533-536.

Davis, D. A., and R. D. Fox (1994). *The Physician as Learner. Linking Research to Practice*. American Medical Association, Chicago.

De Bord (1993). *Promoting reflective judgment in counselling psychology graduate education*. Thesis. University of Missouri, Columbia, cited by L. P. K. Wood.

Denton, L. F., Doran, M. V., and D. McKinney (2002). Integrated use of Bloom and Maslow for instructional success in technical and scientific fields. *Proceedings ASEE Annual Conference, Montreal*. http://www.asee.org/conferences/document2/2002.675.paper.pdf.

Denton, L. F and D. McKinney (2004). Affective factors and student achievement: A quantitative and qualitative study. *Proceedings Frontiers in Education Conference*, 1, TIG 6 to 11.

Dulewicz, V and M. Higgs (1999). *Can Emotional Intelligence be Measured and Developed?* Working Paper Series. Henley Management College, Henley-on Thames.

Duncan-Hewitt, W. C. et al (2001) Using developmental principles to plan design experiences for beginning engineering students. *Proceedings Frontiers in Education Conference*, 1, T3E-17 to 22.

Elton, L. R. B (1996). Strategies to enhance student motivation: a conceptual analysis. *Studies in Higher Education*, 21-(91), 57-68.

Entwistle, N.J and P. Ramsden (1983). *Understanding Student Learning*. Croom Helm, London.

Entwistle , N. J., and S. Waterston (1987). Approaches to studying and levels of cognitive processing. *International Conference on Cognitive Processes in Student Learning*. University of Lancaster, Lancaster.

Fischer, K. W., Kenny, S. L., and S. L. Pipp (1990). Hoe cognitive processes and environmental conditions organize discontinuities in the development of abstractions in C. N. Alexander and E. J. Langer (eds.). *Higher Stages of Human Development*. Oxford University Press, Oxford.

Fitch, P., and R. S. Culver (1984). Educational activities to stimulate intellectual development in Perry's Scheme. *Proceedings Annual Conference of ASEE*. 712-717.

Flammer, G. H. (1972). Applied motivation. A missing role in teaching. *Engineering Education*, 62, (6), 519-522.

Fleischmann, S (2001). Needed a few good knights for the information age-competence, courage, and compassion in the engineering curriculum. *Proceedings Frontiers in Education Conference*. 3,S1B-8 to 13.

Freeman, J and P. Byrne (1976). *The Assessment of General Practice*, 2nd edition. Society for Research into Higher Education, London.

Furneaux, W. D. (1962). The Psychologist and the university. *Universities Quarterly*, 17, 33.

Goleman, D (1994). *Emotional Intelligence. Why it Matters more than IQ*. Bantam Books, New York.

Grow, G. O Teaching learners to be self-directed. *Adult Education Quarterly*, 41, (3) 125–149.

Hedlund, J., and R. J. Sternberg (2000). Too many intelligences? Integrating social, emotional and practical intelligence. Ch 7. In R. Bar-On and J. D. E. Parker (eds.) *The Handbook of Emotional Intelligence*. Jossey-Bass, San Francisco.

Heinke, G. W., and H. H. Weihs. (1989). Continuing education for engineers in Canada. *Proceedings World Conference on Engineering Education for Advancing Technology* (Sydney), 1-545-548.

Hersey, P., and K, Blanchard (1988). *Management of Organizational Behavior. Managing Human Resources*. 5th edition, Prentice Hall, Englewood Cliffs, NJ

Heywood, J (1961). Research by sixth form boys, *Nature*, 191, 860–861.

Heywood, J (1969). An Evaluation of certain post-war developments in Higher Technological Education. Thesis, Vol 1. University of Lancaster Library, Lancaster. pp. 235-241.

Heywood, J (1991) Theory and practice of technology education: implications for the senior cycle of secondary education in M. Kussman and H. Steffen (eds.) *Aktuelle Themen de Technischen Bildung in Europa*. Europaishe Geselschaft fur Technische Bildung. Dusseldorf.

Heywood, J (1994). *Enterprise Learning and its Assessment in Higher Education*. Technical Report No. 20. Employment Department, Sheffield.

Heywood, J (1996). Theory into practice through the replication of research in student teaching practice. Paper presented at the Annual Association of Teacher Evaluators Conference. St. Louis, Mo.

Heywood, J (2002) SCOOPE and other primary (elementary) school projects with a challenge for engineering education *Proceedings Frontiers in Education Conference*. 2, F2C-6 to10.

Hopson, B., and M. Scally (1981). *Lifeskills Teaching*. McGraw Hill, London.

Huang, D. W., Diefes-Dux, H., Imbrie, P. K., Daku, B., and J. G. Kalliman (2004). Learning motivation evaluation for a computer-based instructional tutorial using ARCS model of motivational design. *Proceedings Frontiers in Education Conference*, 1, TIE-30-TIE-36.

Jaques, E (1970). *Work, Creativity, and Social Justice*. Heinemann, London.

Jordan,W. M (1990). Letter. *Engineering Education* 80, (April), 359-360.

Keller, J. M (1987). Strategies for stimulating the motivation to learn. *Performance and Instruction Journal*, 26-(8), 1-7

Keller, J. M (1987). The systematic process of motivational design. *Performance and Instruction Journal*. 26, (9-10), 1-8.

Keller, J. M (1998). Use of ARCS motivation model in courseware design. In *Instructional Designs for Microcomputer Courseware*. Erlbaum, Hillsdale, NJ

King, P. M. and K. S. Kitchener (1994). *Developing Reflective Practice*. Jossey-Bass, San Francisco.

King, P. M. and K. S. Kitchener (1992). (ed.) Special Issue on Reflective Judgment. *Liberal Education*. 88, (1).

Kitchener, K. S (1993). Cognition, meta-cognition and epistemic cognition. A three-level model of cognitive processing. *Human Development*, 4, 222-232

Kneffelkamp, L. L (1974*)*. Developmental instruction: Fostering intellectual and personal growth of college students. Unpublished Doctoral dissertation. University of Minnesota.

Knowles, M (1975). *Self Directed Learning. A Guide for Learners and Teachers.* Association Press, New York

Knowles, M (1990). *The Adult Learner. A Neglected Species.* Gulf Publishing, Houston, Tx.

Kohn, A (1993). *Punished by Rewards. The Trouble with Gold Stars, Incentive Planes, as, Praise, and other Bribes.* Houghton Mifflin, Boston.

Koort, B., and R. Reilly (2002). A Pedagogical model for teaching scientific domain knowledge. *Proceedings Frontiers in Education Conference*, 1, T3A-13 to 17.

Lee, W-I and B-Y, Shih (2001). A case study of motivation theory on the web-based learning. *Proceedings Frontiers in Education Conference*, 2, F3C-23 to 27

Lonergan, N. B (1958). *Insight.* Darlon, Longman and Todd. London

Macintosh, N.J (1998). *IQ and Human Intelligence.* Oxford University Press, Oxford.

MacMurray, J (1956). *The Self as Agent.* Faber and Faber, London.

Marra, R. M (1996). Developing a longitudinal evaluation program for a leadership minor. *Proceedings Frontiers in Education Conference*, 2, 895-904

Marra, R., and B. Palmer (1999) Encouraging intellectual growth: senior engineering profiles. *Proceedings Frontiers in Education Conference* 2, 12c1-1 to 6.

Marra, R. M., Palmer., B., and T. A. Litzinger (2000). The effects of a first year design course on student intellectual development as measured by the Perry Scheme. *Journal of Engineering Education.* 89, (1), 39-45.

Marra, R., Camplese, K. Z., and T. A. Litzinger (1999). Lifelong learning: a preliminary look at the literature in view of EC 2000. *Proceeding Frontiers In Education Conference* 1, 11a1-7 to 12.

Marra, R. M., and T. Wheeler (2000). The impact of an authentic student-centerd engineering project on student motivation. *Proceedings Frontiers in Education Conference*, F2C-8 to 13.

Mayer, J. D., Salovey, P., and D. R. Caruso (2000*)* Emotional intelligence as zeitgeist, as personality and as mental ability. In Ch 5 of R. Bar-On and J. D. E. Parker (eds.) *The Handbook of Emotional Intelligence.* Jossey-Bass, San Francisco.

Mentkowski, M. and Associates. (2000). *Learning that Lasts. Integrating Learning, Development, and Performance in College and Beyond.* Jossey-Bass, San Francisco.

Miller, R. L., Olds, B. M., and M. J. Pavelich (1998). Using intelligent computer technology to measure the intellectual development of engineering students *Proceedings Frontiers in Education Conference*, 2, 767-771.

Miller, R. L., and B. M. Olds (1994). Encouraging critical thinking in an interactive chemical engineering laboratory environment. *Proceedings Frontiers in Education Conference*, 506-510.

Moore, W. S (1988). *The Learning Environment. Preferences and Instruction Manual.* CSID, Olympia, W.A.

Moore, W. S (1989) The Learning Environment Preferences: Exploring the construct validity of an objective measure of the Perry scheme of intellectual development. *Journal of College Student Development*, 30, 504-514.

Mountain, J. R., and M. H. Pleck (2000). The role of expectations in the determination of educational outcomes. *Proceedings Frontiers in Education Conference*, 3, S2B-17 to 21

Muspratt, M (1989). Continuing education. *Proceedings of World Conference on Engineering Education for Advancing Technology (Sydney)*, 1, 487

Newman, J H (1870). *The Idea of a University.* Longmans Green, London.

Newman, J. H (1870). An Essay in Aid of a Grammar of Assent. Longmans Green, London.

Nias, J (1981). Teacher satisfaction and dissatisfaction. Herzberg's two factor hypothesis revisited. *British Journal of Sociology of Education*, 2, 235-246.

Pascarella, E. T., and P. T. Terenzini (1991). *How College Affects Students.* Jossey-Bass, San Francisco.

Pavelich, M. J (1996). Helping students develop higher-level thinking: Use of the Perry model. *Proceedings Frontiers in Education Conference*, 1, 163-167.

Pavelich, M. J. and W. S. Moore (1996). Measuring the effect of experiential education using the Perry model. *Journal of Engineering Education*, 85, 287-292

Perry, W. B (1970).*Forms of Intellectual and Ethical Development in the College Years.* Holt, Rienhart and Winston, New York.

Razani, A (1991). A Vocabulary, concept and recipe (VCR) approach in teaching engineering courses to adults, *Proceedings Frontiers in Education Conference*, 569.

Rodgers, R (1989). Student development in U. Delworth and S. Komies (eds). *Student Services. A Handbook for the Profession.* Jossey-Bass, San Francisco.

Rokeach, M (1960). The *Open and Closed Mind.* Basic Books, New York

Schlosser, C (1996): Distance education: what the literature says works. *Proceedings Frontiers in Education Conference.* 553- 555.

Simonson, M (1996). Distance Education: Trends and redefinition. *Proceedings Frontiers in Education Conference*, 549- 552

Smaldino, S. E (1996). Effective techniques for distance education instruction. *Proceedings Frontiers in Education Conference*, 556-559.

Stamouli, I., Doyle, E., and M. Huggard (2004). Establishing structured support for programming students. *Proceedings Frontiers in Education Conference*, 2, F2G-5 to 9.

Steanberg, R. S., and E. L. Grigorenko (2000). Practical intelligence and its development. In Chapter 10., R. Bar-On and J. D. E. Parker. (eds.) *The Handbook of Emotional Intelligence.* Jossey-Bass, San Francisco.

Sternberg, R. J., and J. E. Davidson. (1982). The mind of the puzzler. *Psychology Today*, 16, June, 37–44.

Stewart, A (1977). *Analysis of Argument. An Empirically Derived Measure of Intellectual Flexibility.* McBer and Co., Boston.

Stone , K. F., and H. Q. Dillehunt (1978). *Self Science the Subject in Me.* Goodyear Publications, Santa Monica.

Stonewater, B., Stonewater, J. K., and T. D. Hadley (1986). Intellectual development using the Perry scheme: an exploratory comparison of two instruments. *Journal of College Student Personnel*, 27, 542-547.

Tsang, E (2002). Use assessment to develop service learning reflection courses materials. *Proceedings Frontiers in Education Conference*, 2, F2A-15 to 19.

Theall, M (1999) (ed.) *Motivation from Within. Approaches for Encouraging Faculty and Students to Excel.* New Directions for Teaching and Learning. No. 78. Jossey-Bass, San Francisco.

Tough, A (1974). *The Adult Learning Project.* Ontario Institute for Studies in Education, Toronto.

Turns, J (1997). Learning essays and the reflective learner: supporting assessment in engineering design education. *Proceedings Frontiers in Education Conference*, 681–688.

Upchurch, L and J. E. Sims –Knight (1999) Reflective essays in software engineering. *Proceedings Frontiers in Education Conference*, 3, 13a6-15-13 to 18.

Waks, S., and M. Merdler (2003). Creative thinking of practical engineering students during a design project. *Research in Science and Technological Education.* 21-(1), 101–120.

Whitehead, A. N (1932). The Aims of Education. Benn, London.

Wilson, D. M. and H. Chizeck (2000). Aligning outreach with cognitive development: K-12 initiatives in electrical engineering at the University of Washington. *Proceedings Frontiers in Education Conference*, 1, T1E-12 to 17

Winter, D., McClelland, D. C., and A. Stewart (1981). *A New Case for Liberal Learning: Assessing Institutional Goals and Student Learning.* Jossey-Bass, San Francisco

Wise, J., Lee, Sang Ha., Litzinger, T. A., Marra, R. M., and B. Palmer (2001). Measuring cognitive growth in engineering undergraduates-a longitudinal study. *Proceedings Annual Conference, AEEE.*

Wood, P. K (1997). A secondary analysis of claims regarding the reflective judgment interview. Internal consistency, sequentiality and intra-individual differences in ill-structured problem solving. In J. Smart (ed.) *Higher Education. Handbook of Theory and Research.* Agathon Press, New York.

Woods, D. R et al (1997). Developing problem solving skills: The McMaster Problem Solving program. *Journal of Engineering Education*, 86, (2) 75-92.

Wright, R. T (1993). Engineering education starts early. *Proceedings Frontiers in Education Conference.* 523-527.

Yoder, M. A,. McClellan, J. H and R. W. Schafer (1998). Crystal radios or DSP first? *Proceedings Frontiers in Education Conference*, 695-698.

Yokomoto, C.F (2000). Promoting depth of knowledge through a new quiz format to improve problem-solving abilities. *Proceedings Frontiers in Education Conference*, 1, F2B-8 to 11.

Yokomoto, C. F., Voltmer, D. R., and R. Ware (1993). Incorporating the 'Aha!' experience into the classroom laboratory. *Proceedings of the Frontiers in Education Conference* 200–203.

Zirkel, S (2000). Social intelligence: the development and maintenance of purposive behavior. In Chapter 1, R. Bar-On and J. D. E. Parker (eds.) *The Handbook of Emotional Intelligence.* Jossey-Bass, San Francisco.

PART II: THE CURRICULUM AND ITS PARADIGMS IN PRACTICE

CHAPTER 7: CURRICULUM CHANGE AND CHANGING THE CURRICULUM

Summary

   This Chapter is primarily concerned with the factors that enhance and impede curriculum change. Curricula are the product of the culture and values of the society in which they are embedded. For this reason there are differences in approaches to engineering education across the world. In spite of the generality of engineering it is found that the transplantation of curriculum ideas from one country to another is difficult. Nevertheless, there are principles that provide a generalized understanding of the factors that impede and enhance change.

   This Chapter begins with a brief discussion of the distinguishing features of the formal, informal and hidden curricula. The discussion of change is constructed around three paradigms. They are termed "received," "reflexive," and "restructuring" after Eggleston (1977).

   The received paradigm describes a curriculum organization designed to meet the belief that there is a received body of understanding which is "given," even ascribed. It is predominantly non-negotiable. Most engineering curricula are primarily of this kind, although some negotiation may be allowed, and to this extent they are reflexive.

   More often than not large change of a structural nature is generated by outside agencies, as for example, ABET or the British Engineering Institutions. Such impositions may not always have the desired effect. Nevertheless it is clear that the received curriculum is subject to continuing minor modification. The aggregate of these modifications sometimes shows that major change has taken place. This point is illustrated by the examples of mechanics in the United States and mathematics in the United Kingdom as they applied to engineering education.

   Major factors that undoubtedly induce change are changes in the market on both the supply and demand sides of the equation. The problem about the debate about the relationship between the curriculum and industry is that the curriculum is neither, considered in terms of lifelong learning, or derived from an adequate theory of curriculum that embraces lifelong learning. In this sense a spiral approach may be a partial answer, as might be frameworks of the kind suggested by Whitehead (1932).

   The spiral approach is described. It is followed by a discussion of the generalist versus specialist debate. Generalists take cognizance of the view that it is not possible to keep adding to the curriculum and, therefore, what is required is a sound education in engineering fundamentals. To meet the goals of lifelong learning the curriculum may have to be tempered with some reflexive components.

   A reflexive curriculum derives from a constructivist position that holds that all knowledge is relative, therefore, it may be negotiated. A typical example of limited reflexivity is where students are allowed to choose their own topic for a project.

   A "restructured" curriculum, as defined here, results from an interaction between received and reflexive elements.

   An example of the startup of a new degree is described. It is left to the reader to decide if the curriculum developers would have been helped had they approached the problem from the perspective presented in this chapter.

   The remainder of the chapter is concerned with how change might be brought about and the kind of leadership that is required. The principles of change are derived from reports in the engineering literature that also relate to the literature on innovation. It is concluded that change is dependent on individuals who are dependent for its continuance on effective management, and trust. Of such is curriculum leadership.

7.   A Caveat Regarding the Examples that Follow

   During the last 30 or so years there have been many published descriptions of engineering curricula, and the chapters that follow are dependent on illustrations from that literature. Some of them describe intention rather than actuality. Unfortunately, little is known about what happened to these intentions because there has been so little evaluation. The same is true of the many descriptions of particular practices. Often the person describing a particular practice is the sole author of that practice, and if they stop doing that practice, even though it has been shown to have value, it ceases to be practiced when its author stops doing it. In such circumstances the question arises as to whether the practicalities of the curriculum can ever be discussed, except in the abstract. For such reasons, what happened to some of the activities described in the papers reviewed is not known. They are included because the ideas in them seem to be of value, or, fortunately, because they have been partially evaluated.

7.1. National Cultures and Change

   Curricula are a product of the culture and the values of the culture in which they are embedded. It is for this reason that it is difficult to transplant the educational practices of one country to another, and this applies as much to the countries within the European Union as it does to any other grouping of countries. For example, while the German "dual" system of education and training is admired by some experts in Britain and Ireland, it would not be possible to transport that system to those countries, even if it were deemed desirable because of the attitudes of industry toward training. At a more fundamental level although there may not seem to be many differences between the ABET (US) and SARTOR (UK) regulations (see Chapter 2), in practice their interpretation leads to different understandings of what the curriculum should be.

It is not surprising, therefore, that attendance at conferences of both engineering and teacher educators suggests that it is very difficult to transfer educational ideas, apart from those concerned with "nuts and bolts," across national boundaries. Like institutions within a particular culture, who when required to respond to government decisions adapt the requirement to suit their own security, so it is with nations. A case in point is the adoption of semesters and modules by many universities in the United Kingdom. They attempted to fit this framework to the traditional three-term year rather than follow the American pattern. Many university teachers felt that they got the worst of both worlds. Of course, institutions in a particular country carry a long baggage of history. Some of those that were born in the British Empire like Australia have carried this same baggage as Page and Murphy (1989) made clear, and this baggage carries with it, its own "language." Thus, while it might seem that it is easy to understand another system, it is more often than not, much more difficult than it seems.

Nowhere is it more difficult than in the area of assessment, especially when it is being discussed from American and British perspectives. Very different understandings of assessment exist on either side of the Atlantic. An inclination to discard the views of what happens elsewhere must be a loss to subject teachers who would not regard engineering as being bound by local boundaries. Consequently there are only a few comparative studies of engineering curricula, and some of them are not in sufficient depth to enhance the understanding of what happens elsewhere.

Nevertheless, Parnaby (1998), an industrialist and former President of the Institution of Electrical Engineers considered that much of the continuing debate in the United Kingdom about the education of engineer's was conducted from a very narrow viewpoint. It did not benefit from international comparisons as it should. He was equally critical of the role of industry with respect to both training in a learning society and employment potential.

Parnaby argued that it is very difficult in Britain *"to achieve consensus and committed national teamwork across, academia, government and industry and this results in a lack of consistency and too much fragmentation .... There are far too many initiatives and too much variety of provision"*. When this writer investigated the structure and function of sandwich courses (cooperative courses) he found over 20 different arrangements over the one that had been recommended. This was the four-year arrangement in which 6 months in industry was followed by six months in college for each of the four years. Parnaby lamented the failure of industry to support sandwich schemes and reported that only 5% of engineering students were on such courses. He also drew attention to the proliferation of degree courses with different titles, structures, and syllabuses. But is this different from other countries and in particular the United States? He argued that there was a need to define a core degree *"with some limited flexibility in the degree of specialism."* His thinking seems to have been influenced

by the 1996 recommendations of the Society of German Engineers.. They were, he wrote, to *"reduce specialisation and increase context level relating to technical, interdisciplinary and integrated systems matters: use project work and problem-oriented teaching to provide a focus and, all engineering courses to use a similar first year to give a broad foundation and facilitate cross-discipline transfer."* As will be shown in this and the next chapter, many American courses have moved in this direction during the freshman and sophomore years. In the absence of evaluation to the contrary, there seem to be many ways of achieving these goals, hence the need to consider what educational research has to say about best practice in achieving those goals. But first it is necessary to consider the nature of the curriculum in order to see if there are general principles that will provide some general understanding of the factors that enhance and impede change. First, it is necessary to define the curriculum.

7.2. The Curriculum: Formal, Informal and Hidden

The formal curriculum is the mechanism by which educational goals are delivered. It is normally associated with the subjects or subject areas that are prescribed for students to learn. Associated with it is an informal curriculum that an institution provides, as for example, debating societies, sporting activities, and community life in university halls of residence. The value placed on the contribution that halls of residence could make to a general education is made clear by Newman (1851), (see Chapter 17).

"When a multitude of young men, keen, open-hearted, sympathetic and observant, as young men are, come together and freely mix with each other, they are sure to learn from one another, even if there be no one to teach them; the conversation of all is a series of lectures to each and they gain for themselves new ideas and views, fresh matters of thought, and distinct principles for judging and acting, day by day." (From *The Idea of a University*, 1949; p 146. See also Culler, 1955.)

This informal education may make a significant contribution to the mission of the institution.

The achievement of these goals is in no small way a function of what has been called the hidden curriculum. It embraces all the learning that takes place independently of the formal learning in the classroom, within the institution, and more generally in society at large. To a large extent it governs the attitudes and values that shape our responses to formal learning. Lin (1979) has shown how it can effect learning in the engineering classroom.[1] Van Schalkwyk, Weyers and van Oostrum (1993) showed how the cultural milieu in which third world students of engineering grow up has a powerful influence on their learning and, as a result, on the problems they face in higher education.

The organization of the curricula will be a function of its goals. Therefore, the determination of

---

[1] The idea of the hidden curriculum comes from P. W. Jackson (1963). *Life in Classrooms*. Holt, Rinehart and Winston, New York.

goals is the first task of curriculum design. Fundamental to the determination of those goals are beliefs about the purposes of education and, because it is generally accepted that education is about learning, beliefs about how it is individuals learn. Statements about what should be and how it should be learned are consequences of these beliefs. Therefore, the curriculum designer will require a defensible philosophy that, on the one hand, has an epistemological base and, on the other hand, has a value position. This argument was set out in Chapter 3.

It is important to distinguish between epistemology and pedagogy (see Chapter 3). While the two are intimately related, they are different dimensions of knowledge and learning and understanding. Given the broadly stated and commonly quoted aim of education that "education is about developing the whole person," then the exploration of what this means in practice will necessarily involve those parts of psychology that concern themselves with human development, and the way individuals learn. Therefore, curriculum leaders and teachers should possess defensible theories of learning and human development (see Chapters 4–6).

Because formal education is a social artifact, and governments, in theory, organize it on behalf of society, Governments may also determine the goals of the curriculum. Very often the interpretation of the curriculum by governments can be at odds with what philosophers, psychologists, sociologists and teachers consider the aims of education to be. In engineering, the substitute for government is the profession, and just as in the case of schooling, it is possible to disagree with the profession about what it thinks the curriculum should be. That things are not cut and dried can be seen from the approaches to engineering education adopted in different countries.

7.3. The Nature of the Curriculum: The Received Paradigm

At school level the curriculum is likely to be organized around what are believed to be the disciplines of knowledge, and justification for this arrangement can be found in the philosophical work of Hirst (1975) in the United Kingdom, and Phenix (1964) in the United States. It can also be found in the work of the psychologist Bruner (1960; 1966). Such a curriculum is of a traditional kind. Eggleston (1977) suggested that they belonged to a *"received paradigm"* of curriculum organization because those responsible for the curriculum accept that there is a *"received body of understanding that is 'given,' even ascribed, and is predominantly non-negotiable."*

Although the epistemologies of Hirst, Phenix, and Bruner differ considerably, Eggleston had no difficulty in grouping them together within the received paradigm. These educators believed *"that there are established and knowable structures of knowledge that exist independently of teachers or indeed of any other individuals;" (they are not necessarily the subjects of the curriculum as we understand them), that these patterns may be discovered, clarified and comprehended, and that adherence to them is either necessary or at least highly*

desirable if curriculum is to be meaningful and learning experience successful."

Eggleston's received paradigm would seem to include the traditional and discipline approaches described by Posner (1992). Perhaps this is because the former has looked at the curriculum from an English perspective whereas the latter considered it from the American experience. In Posner's view the traditional approach is about the transmission of cultural heritage of western civilization, and this applies to the liberal education offered in higher education as Bloom (1987) made clear. Perhaps the best-known exponent of this view, through his book on *"Cultural Literacy"* is E. D. Hirsch Jr. Posner illustrated the philosophy as follows: *"The basic goal of education in a human community is acculturation, the transmission to children of the specific information shared by adults of the group or polis"* (Hirsch, 1987).

In explaining the origins of this movement in the work of William Harris, Posner drew attention to the fact that Harris had said that he believed that *"the teacher, using the lecture-recitation method, would be the driving force in the process and would be responsible for getting students to think about what they read. Examinations would monitor and classify the students as they progressed through a graded educational system" (p. 48).*

In Britain many would agree with this view, but they would also hold that this goal is achieved by the disciplines which they would associate with the traditional subjects of the curriculum. This view is reinforced by many governments in the western world who believe that education also has economic goals, and as such there are basic skills in literacy and numeracy that need to be developed in schools. Therefore, they specify the curriculum in these areas which the teachers are expected to transmit. There are also major debates about what should be in the history curriculum and, in English speaking countries, about the content and purpose of English.

In engineering a "communication" model seems to prevail. A message is transmitted on a particular channel and received, and hopefully it is subjected to feedback. Van Schalkwyk, Weyers and van Oostrum (1993), described the process as follows. *The teachers' function as the 'transmitters' of knowledge, of which they are the authorities. Students function as the 'receivers' of knowledge, which they store, recall and apply when required. Traditionally, much attention is paid to the receiving of the message; compulsory class attendance is an example. Little, if any, attention is paid to the processes by which student's store, recall, and apply knowledge. If they are considered at all, they are assumed to be skills that the student has already mastered in some previous context. What is not considered is the possibility that these skills may be unique to each domain of knowledge, including engineering. The 'channels' of communication are generally limited to lectures and prescribed texts.*

'Feedback' is generally limited to tests, examinations, and some assignments. 'Noise' factors in the physical, social, and psychological environment are mostly dealt with on an ad hoc basis. *"The 'message' in the process is assumed to be knowledge of the relevant subject."*

Many of the articles in the journals devoted to engineering education seem to be based on this model, and curriculum innovation is undertaken to produce learning that 'has' to be learned. Nevertheless, in the past 10 years there has been a substantial increase in the number of papers with ideas, practices, and evaluations of this model. For example, of the 165 contributions in the 1991 Frontiers in Education Conference Proceedings, 33 (20%) were rated as suitable for use in a hypothetical post-graduate training course for teachers in higher education. In 2000 the percentage had risen 36% (88 out of 243). While this suggests a considerable increase in interest in education, it is very small in terms of the worldwide context of engineering education.[2]

However, even in the received paradigm the content of the particular subjects of the curriculum does change over time even if only in small increments (Heywood, 1984). At school level there has, for example, been a worldwide interest in the introduction of technology (not information technology) into the school curriculum. In the United States, Standards for Technological Literacy have been declared (ITEA, 2000). In England, Design Technology is a subject in the national curriculum. In the United States there is no better illustration of this argument than the changes that have taken place in the mechanics curriculum, and in the United Kingdom mathematics education provides a similar illustration (see below).

Occasionally, external pressures cause changes in the structure of the curriculum, and these may be due to legislative action, or an authoritative intervention by, for example, ABET, or to changes in the market on either the supply or demand side or both. Sometimes there are major debates within academia such as that relating to generalist of specialist courses. These issues are dealt with in the sections that follow, the first of which considers some general changes that have taken place.

7.4. Changes in Traditional Approaches to the Engineering Curriculum

Evidence that the received curriculum is not immutable is to be found in the many changes that have taken place in its content since the end of the Second-World War. These have been of two main kinds. First, there have been changes within the subject structure of degree programs. Second, there has been the development of new degree programs, as for example, in biomedical engineering and nuclear engineering. Often, as in the case of these examples, new programs are caused by substantial changes in technology. But this is not always the case. For example, in England, where traditionally, degree programs were of three years' duration, the study period of courses for Chartered Engineer Status have been lengthened to four years. Originally it was argued that a four-year program was necessary if they were to have truly professional status. Part of the argument was based on (a) the high status of engineers in Germany and (b) the length of course that would be required to obtain that status. As a first step, they were able to persuade the government to fund four-year courses in a limited number of colleges to "enhance" the existing programs in those institutions (Carter and Jordan, 1990). Nowadays the norm for courses leading to the chartered engineer qualification is four years: admissions and output requirements are stated for each level of engineering attainment in the Engineers Register (Brown, 1998; SARTOR, 1997). While it may be argued that longer programs are necessary to meet the requirements of technology there is no doubt that the search for status for engineers strongly influenced this change (Heywood, 1969; Jordan, 1992). There have also been bridging courses to enable students in Colleges of Further Education who pursued technician courses to transfer to programs in universities offering programs that provided courses that would get them chartered status (Anderson and Percival, 1997; McDowell, 1995; Sharp and Culver, 2000; Sharp and White, 1991). The push to accept such students may be as much due to a shortage of recruits for engineering as it is for anything else.

In the United Kingdom many universities have both modularized and semesterized their courses. This has had an impact on both teaching assessment and, therefore, by definition, the curriculum. It was not accomplished without a ferocious debate, and many teachers regretted the change. The point is that these changes were implemented for pragmatic reasons, and no account was taken of how students develop, or of the work that had been done in the psychology of learning that was relevant to the issue (Heywood, 1994).

Many universities in England and Wales, particularly those that were created from Polytechnics in 1992, as well as some of the others, are experiencing substantial changes in the entering characteristics of their students. In terms of physics and math they have not achieved as well as past cohorts of students. Consequently adjustments have to be made to the curriculum, and some universities offer foundation courses to remedy these deficiencies in knowledge.[3] As the characteristics of the intake change, the system begins to emulate the American. That it is changing in this way seems to have been little perceived, and that such changes demand a positive rather than a reactive response from the higher education system also seems to be little understood.[4]

---

[2]Other commentators might arrive at different percentages depending on the criteria used. I allowed for reported research and substantial evaluations but also included papers that contained ideas that I regarded as important.

[3]As opposed to Foundation degrees. Foundation degrees have some similarities with associate degrees in the United States.

[4]Hence, there is considerable resistance to the idea that some universities should only be teaching institutions.

In the United States, student choice is a significant determinant in the numbers of students that a department has, and the ability of its programs to attract uncommitted but interested students is of considerable importance. A failure to attract students may well, lead to curriculum change. However, the regulations of a state may act as a constraint on what can be done. For example, engineering colleges in the University of California or the California State system are required to accept transfers from Community Colleges to the junior level. This places restrictions on what can be done in the lower division of engineering education (Soderstrand, 1994).

Quite clearly, the time available to do all the things a department would like to do has bothered departments, and there are a number of papers that illustrate how departments have compromised in order to make space in their programs. Clearly the received curriculum is flexible within certain limits.

It has also to be remembered that changes have consequences, not all of which will be foreseen. Unfortunately, many of the published articles have little to say about these effects of change. In order to illustrate this point, the next section looks at the effects of changing curricula on the take up of mechanics in the United States over a 20 year time frame, and the debate about engineering mathematics in the United Kingdom. Thereafter, the sections illustrate some of the changes that have taken place in curricula that would be classified as belonging to the received paradigm.

7.5. The Effect of Changes Within Programs to Subject Areas

Any substantial change in a program must of necessity affect other parts of the program. If something new is introduced then something has to be lost. Changes in technology have created new demands on programs with the consequence that the role and purpose of established courses in the curriculum has to be reconsidered. A good example of this is provided by Hansen and Fisher (1986) who studied changes in the role of mechanics education in engineering courses in the United States over a 25 year period. Their study followed up similar surveys in over 200 colleges and universities teaching engineering that had been undertaken in 1965 and 1975 to ascertain the status of mechanics education.

The results are difficult to summarize because of the many variations that were found. Nevertheless, it was found that mechanics was a separate field of study primarily at the graduate level, but that in universities without a clearly identifiable mechanics department there were programs within civil and mechanical engineering departments which closely paralleled an accredited bachelor's degree in mechanics. In the United Kingdom mechanics would be taught in these departments, but at the time of the survey there would have been an expectation that students would have done a substantial amount of mechanics in their high school science and mathematics courses. There were no separate departments of mechanics as in the United States.

At the time of the enquiry, ABET required that every accredited program must include at least one year of engineering science to *"provide a bridge between mathematics, basic sciences, and engineering practice."*

The survey showed that there had been a continuing decline in the number of mechanics departments over the 20 period. Basic mechanics remained a strong engineering science topic for civil and mechanical engineering. However, there was a decline in the number of courses offered in chemical and electrical engineering requiring statics, and over half the programs in these subjects did not require a course in the strength of materials.

The investigators found that these mechanics subjects were covered more than they had been at the time of the earlier surveys. The use of computers had increased substantially, as had the use of vector mechanics in strength of materials courses, but the respondents considered that the abilities of students had deteriorated in all areas but particularly in trigonometry, geometry, and graphics. An interesting finding related to the use of textbooks showed that only two textbooks accounted for 70% of the market in statics and dynamics.

Among the reasons advanced by the authors for these changes were *"a heavy emphasis on design at the expense of engineering science courses,"* and *"inadequate control by ABET to ensure broad engineering science coverage irrespective of engineering coverage."* The authors asked the question, *"Is there a value in mechanics as a common language of understanding for all engineers?"*

The debate about the reform of mechanics education continues, and a special issue of the *International Journal of Engineering Education* was devoted to teaching trends in mechanics education (Volume 16, Issue 5, 2000). Vable (2003) reported that whereas in the past dynamics, statics and the mechanics of materials were taught in separate courses, there were trends toward the integration of these subjects.[5] This was apparently a return to the organization of these subjects at the beginning of the twentieth century. However, an alternative to integration discussed by Vable is to generalize the concepts taught so that they can apply to a greater range of applications. Unfortunately, this inevitably involves more abstraction and some students will find this difficult. As indicated in Chapter 4, Vable suggested that this problem could be overcome by appropriate design problems, examples of which he gave.

Much the same can be said about mathematics, which was also the subject of a special issue of the *International Journal of Engineering Education* (Volume 15, issue 6, 1999). In the United Kingdom, debate about the mathematical needs of engineers and technologists dates back to at least the middle of the last century. For example, in 1964 Clarke (1967) sent a questionnaire to 500 Associates of the Institution of Metallurgists in the

---

[5] He cited discussions of this issue by Brinson et al., (1997), and Carroll (1997).

United Kingdom to find answers to the questions- Why teach mathematics to undergraduate metallurgists? What mathematics should be taught? And, how should mathematics be taught? Much the same questions were asked about engineering. Electrical engineers were surveyed for their views (Scott et al., 1966), and many distinguished scientists and managers contributed to the debate (e.g., Bondi, 1966; Lawrence, 1964).

Scott and his colleagues found that engineers experienced two kinds of difficulty in the use of mathematics. Firstly, although the mathematical knowledge was adequate, the formulation of a problem in mathematics was a stumbling block. To mitigate such difficulties, it was suggested that more emphasis on problem formulation should be given in undergraduate courses, and this should be accompanied by detailed analysis and discussion of real-life problems. The second difficulty was that engineers required topics that were then not on the undergraduate syllabus. In most cases they had to learn the topics for themselves.[6] Apart from making sure that suitable books were available, Scott felt that undergraduates could be prepared for this situation by the inclusion of independent study alongside traditional methods. Changes in the system of examining and assessment were also recommended. This kind of thinking has led to changes in courses but sometimes, some would say, to the detriment of mathematics (see below).

In the United States, Ruud et al., (1992) reported on a short course designed to illustrate the principles of science, mathematics, and engineering through manufacturing for teachers in Community Colleges and small four-year institutions. The areas selected were casting, circuit board manufacturing, and machining. The argument for this course was that in the first two years of college, the science and mathematics that were taught were by abstract models that were perceived by students to be irrelevant to engineering. Therefore, one has to draw the principles from the problem, and not the other way around as was more usually the case. There is philosophical support for this approach from the Scottish philosopher MacMurray (1956), who argued that theories arise from our need to solve practical problems. While the scientific principles were demonstrated, some readers might judge that it was not very successful with the mathematics.[7] Others might argue that the key to such programs lies in assessment in which the students' ability to apply the principles to other situations is demonstrated.

Larcombe (1998), who considered that mathematics teaching was in crisis, in a brief but comprehensive exercise reviewed developments during the preceding 20 years. Among them was the development of engineering mathematics as a field of study, especially at Loughborough University (Bajpai and James, 1985). Larcombe drew attention to several problems, three of which are of interest. The first was the change in aptitude in mathematics of persons entering engineering departments. He considered, and found support from, important mathematical organizations such as The London Mathematical Society, that the Standards of the Advanced (A) level examinations had declined. This meant that students come to University poorly prepared for university study. *"Many changes have been founded on misguided good intention rather than on tried and tested principles"* (citing Gardiner, 1994). This lack of preparation caused the Engineering Council and others to issue a report with recommendations on the teaching of mathematics in schools. It was particularly concerned with primary (elementary) school mathematics and the wide variation in mathematical standards that had occurred because of the variety of courses on offer in junior high school.

Neither they or Larcombe compared the English 3-year system of University Education with either the Scottish or Irish 4-year systems that start from a lower base in mathematics. His second point was that much of the general debate about mathematics in engineering is about the role of mathematics in modeling. He argued that the 'cookbook' approach with aesthetics suppressed has tended to become the norm in engineering departments. Related to this were the different perceptions that mathematicians and engineers have of the subject. *"It is the opposing default philosophies- termed 'rigour versus technique'- which assumes the pre-eminent position. In relation to modelling, the engineer might well contend that the object of mathematical study for the student in engineering is the acquisition of a certain body of factual knowledge and techniques in usually the most efficient manner possible. The mathematician, however, is more likely to insist that the standards of completeness and rigour in the treatment of mathematics be maintained so that a full mathematical appreciation of underlying concepts and structures can be reached in the context of modelling. [8] Both for different reasons have students' best interests at heart. These didactic stances display a level of mutual exclusivity, and the classroom experience-possibly dictated by the personal feelings of the lecturer-can have a huge effect on the opinions of emerging engineering graduates with regard to the role of mathematics in the profession."* [9]

If students perceive that what they require is "technique," then they are likely to react against teaching for "rigor." And, student attitudes to mathematics have caused a debate about who should teach mathematics to engineers.

A third point made by Larcombe was that computers have now become so powerful that they

---

[6] This continues to be the case. Bringslid (cited by McClelland, 2001) considers that engineers need training in logical abstraction and to be able to use mathematics in other fields.

[7] On the more general issue of relevance, Nahvi (1998) pointed out that in a typical freshman year a student of electrical engineering does not attend any courses in electrical engineering. He discussed the primary functions of a course in electrical engineering in the freshman year, and he proposed a sequence of integrated courses and laboratories that would provide a freshman experience of electrical engineering.

[8] He cited Clements (1985).

[9] A good example of the hidden curriculum at work.

relegate mathematics, because they can provide shortcuts to the solution of so many problems *"that are intrinsically mathematical."* There is, therefore, the problem of how best to integrate computers into the curriculum so that mathematical understanding is not diminished.[10] Interestingly enough computer scientists in the United States are anxious that their students are well trained in mathematics. They assume that this will make their students better software engineers because they will be able to transfer this knowledge in practice. But as Upchurch and Sims-Knight (1997) pointed out, research in cognitive science has shown that *"the probability that one will be able to apply what one has learned to new situations is quite low. Rather, one needs to be taught explicitly when and how to apply a solution. This requires explicit, often extensive, instruction which is typically absent from the computer science curriculum."* One suspects there is a lack of awareness of this research among engineering educators generally (see Anderson, 1987).

At the same time, it appears that the information technologies have improved the quality of statistics teaching in engineering courses (Acosta, 2000, cited by McClelland, 2001).

This appears to be true of the mathematics required for the B. Tech. Ed program at the University of Glasgow that trains students to teach technology in schools and also provides a route toward the status of incorporated engineer. Pollock (2004) reported on the effects of a move from traditional mathematics teaching to computer-assisted learning and computer-assisted assessment over a 12-year period. These changes had the purpose of increasing the recruitment and retention of non-traditional students. During this period the intake changed from students with relatively high-level qualifications in engineering and mathematics to students coming directly from high school with some mathematics and students from craft backgrounds with no mathematics. Also in this period, the time allowed for mathematics changed. At first it was taught to small groups over a period of three years, but this changed when the course provider withdrew; the response was to put the students in the same course as the first year engineering students. For various reasons, both the technology and the engineering students found this course difficult. So computer assisted learning was introduced to deliver the course in the hope that the course team would not be substantially overloaded. This program was evaluated by a United Kingdom national project to ensure that students were not being disadvantaged by CAL over

the lecture method. In fact there was a considerable improvement. The initial pass rate after the conventional examination was 38%,; but in the following year when CAL was introduced, it rose to 76%. Modifications to the system following discussions with the students led to 100% pass rates for two years. For the last four years, computer-aided assessment has been used. This led to what is in effect a course of individualized instruction.

"It would appear, therefore, that using CAL, for course delivery has all the benefits of small group teaching without the drawbacks of staff effort, and using CAA (Pollock, 2002) can force students to cover all topics whilst reducing staff time on assessment" (Pollock, 2004).

Unfortunately, Pollock does not consider some of the more profound issues raised in the preceding paragraphs. Questions about the syllabus and the purpose of teaching mathematics to such students are of considerable interest.

Clearly, market forces and changing technology do influence the attitudes of engineering schools to what should be taught, and to some extent the responses have been governed by cultural factors in responding student, employer and professional demands.

7.6. Changes in Response to the Student Market

One of the differences between engineering education in the United States and other countries like the United Kingdom is the way in which students are recruited. In the United States students during their freshman studies (first year) can try out subjects. This is not possible in the United Kingdom.[11] In the United Kingdom and similar countries traditional students choose to do engineering before they enter university. When they arrive at university they go straight into the engineering department. Nontraditional students in engineering are likely to have taken a technician (technology in the United States) education for whom bridging will be required. In either case students in these countries do not take any general education courses. It is very difficult for them to change to other studies, although not impossible. There has been some evidence over the years that dropouts find there way into other courses in the area of engineering.[12]

Parnaby (1998) argued that high school education in England in the years 10 through 12, because of its specialization, caused the shortage of engineering applicants. This specialist curriculum prevents the students from keeping their career options open. He compared the three to four subjects taken in England with the four to six in Scotland, the six for the *abitur* in Germany, and the broad high school education in the United States. What he does not say is that the broad education in Ireland, Scotland, and the United States

---

[10] It is interesting to compare Larcombe's approach to a commentary by Ruthven (1978) on maths as a discipline. Ruthven argued that common sense and social conceptions of the disciplines are in conflict with logical conceptions. *"It is a contingent social fact, rather than logical necessity that has led to the tradition of enquiry commonly known as mathematics"*. Ruthven's perspective is cultural. The reinterpretation of mathematics in strictly logical terms is to ignore the plausibility of the socio-historical context in which it has been taught and developed. The essential question for curriculum design is *"How can we reinterpret mathematics so that it will contribute to the development of a rational perspective on the lives and affairs of men?"*

[11] Although it was possible in the foundation year program that was offered by the University of Keele. That university did not have an engineering department. The effect of the foundation year was to cause a drift away from science (Iliffe, 1969).

[12] At technician levels.

necessitates a four-year degree program, and four or five years in Germany depending on the type of institution. Because the qualification for Chartered Engineers has been extended to four years (SARTOR, 1997), the perceived educational loss at 'A' level could lead to demand for 5-year programs. While a broader education in school and university may be desirable, there is no evidence that in the English cultural climate the leaving of career options open to later will cause more students to opt for engineering. If anything, the drift might be in the other direction.[13] Recent career reports suggest that students opt for studies that *appear* to have status, as, for example, media studies, which had the largest rate per annum growth, or law and accountancy. It was argued long ago that students are much more aware of the employment market than we think they are (Heywood, Pollitt, and Mash, 1966).

This is in marked contrast to the United States, where many students who have no specific commitment to engineering, and who are also very able, try out engineering, find it wanting, and decide not to persevere (Seymour and Hewitt, 1997).

When a student has other serious interests such as music or literature that they cannot pursue because of the loading of an engineering program, they may decide to take a liberal arts major. Since many students in the United States are still trying to find out where their interests lie, it is difficult for them to take engineering if they wish to explore other subjects. If their other interests are strong and they find engineering programs difficult or motivationally inadequate, they may give up engineering.

Reasoning from assumptions such as these, a "liberal engineering program" was designed at the University of Colorado at Boulder for the purpose of reducing the load while at the same time retaining a "sufficient core of principles" (Wachtel, Barnes, and Ravenal, 1994). It was intended to enable students to study other subjects that would give them breadth and diversity even though they would not have the breadth or depth of a traditionally qualified engineering student.

The authors answer to the question, "What key ideas and concepts of engineering should be included in the program?" was the following:

1. *The concepts associated with waves and EM fields: the notions of variations in time and space and how boundary conditions control the amplitude and phase of these waves.*
2. *The concepts associated with linear systems and the ability to build simple models of complex devices and systems; the ability to generate mathematical models for physical and information systems; the notions of feedback and its importance in stabilizing systems against parameter variations.*
3. *The concepts of information and noise, which require introducing ideas from, probability theory and the notion of random process and measurement of errors.*

4. *The basic ideas from logic and digital design, the structure of computer languages and computer architecture.*
5. *The concept of gain and the ability of electronic components to realize the functions needed to transmit and process information.*

They intended to meet these objectives in a five component core course. The five components were:

1. *Logic circuits and computing.*
2. *Electric circuits and power systems.*
3. *Electronics.*
4. *Electromagnetic fields.*
5. *Linear systems and communications.*

These courses would differ from those currently taught in that there would be more application in order to motivate the students. The *"new first course...will contain substantial amounts of descriptive material on how common electrical systems, such as CD's, TV, radio and power systems, work as well as an introduction to circuit theory."* The object of the course is to give a broad conceptual understanding of some areas of application in electrical engineering. While the problem of motivation was understood, the curriculum is still framed within a received paradigm and traditional assumptions about how students learn seem to have been made.

More generally, the National Science Foundation recognized the need for change and established coalitions to trial and evaluate new curriculum initiatives, especially in the junior years. They have revolutionised the curriculum as some of the innovations described in later Chapters show.

7.7. Changes in Response to the Employment Market

Industry has, as we have seen in earlier chapters (especially 2.5 and 2.6), made its views known. Dissatisfaction with engineering curricula have been voiced by industrialists throughout the period since the end of the Second-World War (Heywood, 1969), and will doubtless continue to be voiced. In the late 1970's the IEEE Educational Activities Board asked a committee of five managers, each from a large employer of electrical engineers, to set down their view of a curriculum for engineering education.

This committee believed that any effort to develop a model curriculum was doomed to failure *"because it would have to satisfy so many diverse parties"* (Baldwin et al., 1979). Of interest here is the procedure that the committee adopted.

Each member was asked to develop a model curriculum. No restrictions were prescribed and accreditation guidelines did not have to be met. However, each member was asked to recommend courses in eight categories that augmented the accreditation categories. These were:

- Communication skills.
- Basic sciences.
- Mathematics.
- Political and economic science.

- Humanities and social sciences.
- Interdisciplinary engineering science.
- Electrical engineering core.
- Technical electives.

"Some committee members formed sub-committees within their companies. Others simply sampled narrowly or broadly. Some started with reviews of existing college curricula. Others started from scratch. There was no communication between members during this first phase of the project" (Baldwin et al., 1979).

There was considerable diversity among the resulting models so the committee met to work out a compromise. The point was made that each of the models was also the result of a compromise.

"One illustration of compromise is especially noteworthy. Two members required a senior design project in their model curricula to provide an aspect of real-world engineering in contrast to the analysis of most courses. The compromise does not contain such a course because the majority felt that industry can more efficiently perform this function." The committee did agree that industry wanted a broadly based engineer at this level.

However, once again while the syllabuses were given in detail there were no references to learning. It would be interesting to speculate what would have emerged if this committee had been required to develop the curriculum in terms of learning outcomes. Nevertheless, the lessons for those who follow the received curriculum paradigm are as relevant today as they were then, and they would seem to be generally applicable. They are,

"1. There really exists no unique industry point of view". (This was consistent with findings in the United Kingdom (Heywood, 1969; Roizen and Jepson, 1985).

"2. The compromise curriculum reflects a current and not necessarily lasting point of view." This seems to be the case with any curriculum development.

"3. The model is not a radical departure, especially in the EE field. The high demand for graduates suggests that the educational sector must be doing generally a good job." A point of view like this is seldom put. The issue was whether education could do a better job. The assertion of this study was that it could. This view also supports the contention that curriculum change takes place in small increments but is relatively continuous.

"4. Various industrial employers seek more emphasis related to business problems [...] political economic and legal."

"5. Interpersonal relations as a factor in career success merits more consideration in college." This point continues to be made world wide.

"6. The college should especially concentrate on the things they do best: offer contact with highly competent teachers who turn their students on."

There is little evidence that a highly traditional approach without some reflexive element will achieve this goal.

The comments in 4 and 5 raise the issue (again) of how much a college should be responsible for direct preparation for industry, in the sense that a student is immediately ready for work. Many answer this question with the view that industrial expertise and experience of industry have a role to play in the curriculum. For example, in one of the developing nations, Nigeria, a trend was established at the Federal University of Technology to derive a high percentage of the academic and laboratory content from local industry (Achi, 1988). Some companies play a major role in project work and problem-based learning (see later Chapters for other examples).

In 1997, The US Society for Manufacturing Engineers reported that engineering graduates lacked the following qualities/skills: communication ability; teamwork, professionalism-interpersonal skills, and attributes; project management skills; business and industry appreciation; change management; commitment to lifelong learning (cited by Parnaby, 1998). At the risk of repetition, these are some of the qualities/skills that the Enterprise in Higher Education Initiative in UK believed every graduate should have (Heywood, 1994).[14] Specifically this American Society said that engineering graduates should have knowledge of ergonomics; quality systems design; product and process reliability engineering; general manufacturing processes for a variety of industries, statistics, and probability; and materials science and engineering (cited by Parnaby, 1998).

Ray and Farris (2000) took up the complaint that is sometimes made by industrialists that graduates are not capable of producing realizable results based on their conceptual designs. This view is very similar to much earlier findings by Burns and Stalker (1961) that resulted from a study of the Scottish electrical industry. In that culture, research engineers had difficulty in communicating with those responsible for manufacturing. This was a different industrial culture to the industry that Ray and Farris were considering, but the Burns and Stalker study highlighted the fact that special (colloquial) languages are developed within the sub systems of companies and that there is insufficient recognition of this in education. Writing nearly 40 years later of the situation in the United Kingdom, Parnaby (1998) said that engineering is multidisciplinary. *"The engineer has to understand the language of other functions and professional disciplines in order to communicate effectively, win budgets and develop his/her career into general management through his job rotation assignments."*

Ray and Farris argued that one of the reasons for the inexperience of young graduates was the fact that they were not able to understand the interrelationships between design and manufacturing processes until they undertook a senior capstone project. They, therefore,

---

[14]The use of the term "skill" is highly confused in the literature (see Chapter 2). Some "things" identified as "skills" would seem to be "qualities."

introduced a course in the freshman year that aimed to confront students with the problem of integration through a series of assigned design projects. They reported that the students were highly motivated by the course. Issues surrounding the development of integrated programs are discussed in the next chapter.

The problem with much of this debate about the relationship between curriculum and industry is that the problem is neither considered in terms of lifelong learning nor, considered in an adequate theory of curriculum that embraces lifelong learning. In this sense a spiral curriculum can only be a partial answer to the problem. Other frameworks-as, for example that proposed by Whitehead (1932)-are likely to be as helpful. The spiral concept is essentially a mechanism for dealing with increasing abstraction. Such a curriculum is important if it is argued that a general education is to be preferred to a specialist education. In the two sections that follow, the spiral model of the curriculum is described first, and the generalist versus specialist debate is second. It will be seen that the fourth generalist model described by Morant is somewhat akin to a spiral curriculum, and that the learning of a set of core engineering fundamentals as advocated by Rugarcia and his colleagues would benefit from a spiral approach to the design of the curriculum. So what is a spiral curriculum, and has it been tried in engineering?

7.8. The Received Curriculum as a Spiral.

The fact that the received curriculum changes, and nowhere is this more evident than in engineering, is supportive of Bruner's notion of a curriculum that is dynamic and evolving (Bruner, 1960). Many papers from engineering journals across the world testify to this fact and may be classified under the disciplines approach (e.g., Coll, 1994; Lipski, 1989; Morant, 1993; Patterson, 1994; Soderstrand, 1994). However, that is the limit of these papers. They do not, except with rare exception, show how the student should develop an inquiring mind within the syllabuses that have to be covered. Bruner's notions of the inquiring mind and an evolving curriculum led to a metaphor of *"the student as neophyte scientist."* In a course based on this principle the curriculum evolves through a process of discovery *learning*: It is reinforced by a spiral curriculum in which basic concepts are discussed at increasing levels of depth in different contexts, and in which there is feedback between the levels.

For example, at Worcester Polytechnic, where a traditional first-and second-year curriculum had worked well for many years, change was perceived to be necessary in order to better motivate students, improve the pedagogy, and create a better match between content and teaching technology, consequently a new course was developed that was based on the *"spiral approach in which concepts are introduced at an applications oriented level, and then repeatedly revisited with greater levels of sophistication"* in the classrooms and

laboratories of first-year students (Cyganski, Nicoletti, and Orr, 1994).[15]

This view only fits the notion of a received curriculum that is structured by disciplines and for which there is an accepted body of knowledge that has to be taught. It does not, however, fit the notion that a received curriculum is only to be delivered through "traditional" methods of teaching. Indeed, Eggleston included Bruner, the promoter of discovery learning, among those whose curriculum approach modeled this paradigm. He was anxious to demonstrate that the received label did not describe a range of reactionary or even traditional orientations of the curriculum and teaching. The traditional engineering curriculum is, however, a set of syllabuses taught by traditional laboratory and lecture methods.

It should not be thought that a spiral curriculum is easy to design. In studies of the differences in achievement levels of American and Japanese children Miwa (1992) found that Japanese children followed a concentrated approach in which the content is taught all at once in a particular grade. In contrast, in the United States, the concept may be covered over two or three grades, and in this way it resembles a "spiral." This meant repeated exercises in successive grades. There may have been too much repetition at the expense of moving forward. However, Miwa suggested that an important area of research was to establish if some topics are best taught through a spiral, and others by a concentrated approach. Usiskin (1993) argued that American students proceeded more slowly through the concepts, and when they get to a concept the tasks related to it are too simple. One effect of this is that American students come to concepts at a later stage than other countries. But, it should be noted that the ordering of subjects varies from mathematics curricula to curricula across the world (Howson, 1991). Furthermore, American teachers have to deal with ethnically heterogeneous groups of students whereas Japanese teachers teach ethnically homogenous groups, and classroom culture is profoundly influenced by the cultural mores.

Insofar as engineering is concerned, Woods (2000) of Sheffield University, in an editorial for the *Engineering Science and Education Journal*, warned of the dangers of throwing the baby out with the bath water when the syllabus is simplified. He suggested that, *"one possibility is to conceptualise the course in a way that encapsulates its timeless elements whilst discarding the superfluities and ephemera. As an example I wrote a paper in which I demonstrated that the elementary concepts of quantum mechanics could all be taught very simply....Technically, this method avoids discussion of Schrödinger's equation instead deriving as much as possible from the de Broglie relation, which is a far more primitive concept ... Often, the detailed results of the simplified rules are not the same as those given by the full calculation, and so the full calculation may still need*

---

[15]Based on survey data the investigators suggested that the change in the course had led to encouraging results.

to be covered later by a more advanced course,- (as Schrödinger's equation would need to be if my simplified introduction to quantum mechanics were presented initially). I believe that a teacher should try to ensure that, as far as possible, whatever simplified approach is used does contain as many as possible of the essential concepts of the more complex approach, and that it is these (rather than the actual simplified results) that are emphasised to students this might take the form of pointing out, for example, the dependence (or not) of the results on particular parameters introduced in the calculation ..." He has also demonstrated this approach in relation to Fermi energy (Woods, 1999).

7.9. Specialist Versus Generalist Approaches Within Programs.

In the United Kingdom there has often been a debate about the merits of specialist versus generalist courses, that is, the case for engineering science versus the specialisms of electrical and mechanical engineering. The tendency in the United Kingdom has been to specialize although the University of Durham has always taken a generalist view. Morant (1993) of that university discussed the case for electronics as a subject, and in so doing considered four approaches to the design of broad based courses. The University of Durham is one of a few universities to offer an undergraduate degree in engineering science.[16]

At the time, the beginning of the 1990's, there were no broad-based courses with the title electronics offered in those institutions that became the so-called 1992 universities. Many of the courses offered in those institutions were intended to produce graduates with a good understanding of one branch of electronics practice. Morant cited digital systems as an example. Even the graduates of such courses, he argued, would have a lot to learn. Broad-based courses outweigh the benefits of short-term specialization. *"The course must therefore, give a good understanding of the fundamentals that are likely to be of lasting value, and experience of applying them in unusual situations."* This view derived from the philosophy with which he opened his paper which was: *"to teach students how to think constructively in their subject. This requires a good understanding of fundamental principles and the development of a critical knowledge that is essential for innovations. Students should learn how to teach themselves and be encouraged to develop independence of mind."* Morant also believed that higher education should develop the student's personality and worldview in a well-rounded way. In this context it should be noted that the culture in which he operated was that of a university that had a similar collegiate structure to Oxford and Cambridge.

One of the problems with a broad-based approach is that a large number of abstract concepts have to be included, and this makes the course difficult. A program of this kind has to balance fundamentals, technology and systems, and students who are motivated

by the products of electronics who must not lose this motivation by *"over-concentration on fundamentals."* Because students like practical work, their capabilities in this area can be helped if some vocational skills are taught in the university. Engineering applications can broaden the student's perception of the subject. With this general philosophy in mind, Morant discussed four types of course structure that might be used. These derive from the structure of electronics, as perceived at the time.

The first structure was called linear subject. The objection to this approach is that students would not meet systems applications in each year of the course, and would not, therefore, be able to see where they were going. The second structure, termed parallel linear themes, required several themes to run in parallel over two or three years because of the hierarchical nature of such themes (e.g., waves). Morant considered that it had the same problem as the linear structure because there was a need to present some topics in depth early on.

The third structure, termed inverted, had been discussed in relation to IT courses. The idea was to develop the syllabus both upwards and downwards beginning with simple systems applications. Morant thought that its disadvantage was the postponement of more abstract concepts until the later years of the courses. Moreover, textbooks were generally designed for a bottom-up approach, which is a reminder of the power of the textbook in curriculum design.

The fourth structure (recursive) seems to be akin to Bruner's spiral curriculum. In the first year a descriptive overview of the subject is given. Each theme is developed in detail in later years. Morant argued that while the need for synchronization in later years was minimized, the disadvantage was the time-reducing repetition that was inherent in this structure. At the same time *"the recursive structure has a lot to recommend it on educational grounds. It requires four course ...a general survey of the entire subject of electronics in the first year could well run in parallel with remedial teaching in maths and physics, which could be an excellent way of preparing for the following years."* Thus, at Durham the course, at that time, began with a preparatory year, and in the remaining three years followed 12 themes.

These structures are clearly examples of the received curriculum. It will be noticed that although the general aims of the course require the use of skill in the transfer of learning, the overall approach pays no attention to the way students learn. Nor does it consider the influence of course structures on that learning apart from some elementary assumptions about what motivates students.

This is more or less true of the liberal engineering program discussed in the previous section in electrical and computer engineering at the University of Colorado Boulder (Wachtel, Barnes, and Ravenal, 1994). The view was taken that the best use of a four-year period was similar to that at Durham, but it expanded on what it called the "engineering outlook", and as such its

---

[16] The University of Lancaster is another.

philosophy is considerably different from that on which the Durham approach is based.

"*The program must focus on developing a sound knowledge of the fundamental concepts of electrical and computer engineering and, equally importantly, inculcating the 'engineering outlook'-the mix of physical insight, modelling skill, engineering judgement, and design ingenuity which characterizes the engineer- as well as reasoned appreciation of the social and engineering context in which engineering must be practised.*"

It was argued that students must develop skills of self-learning, and as we saw above the fourth year course seemed to be half-way in the direction of total independent study, and consequently it was more reflexive than the Durham program. The educators also proposed that the amount of time in the laboratory should be increased to develop skill in design and the evaluation of design. A core program served both courses, and the first year program had as its goal the transition from the math and science style of teaching in schools to an engineering approach. A design element was included in the first year course.

In the United States, Rugarcia et al., (2000) argued that it is not possible to provide students with all the technical knowledge that they will require in the workplace. Therefore, there needs to be a move away from "*an ever increasing number of speciality areas to providing a core set of engineering fundamentals helping students to integrate knowledge across course and disciplines, and equipping them with lifelong learning skills.*" The latter was conditioned by the rate of change of knowledge and the need to be able to sort out the wood from the trees. Equipping students' with skills for lifelong learning may require the addition of a reflexive or negotiated component in the curriculum.

7.10. The Control and Value of Knowledge: a Reflexive Paradigm

When sociologists analyze the curriculum, they often do so from the perspective of the control of knowledge. In this context the curriculum is seen as preserving the *status quo* and it is not questioned. In Britain, sociologists such as Young (1971) asked such questions as why it was that a curriculum was provided that caused many students from the working class to fail the examinations at the end of schooling, or to 'drop out' mentally and/or physically before those examinations?. He, and sociologists like him, argued that the received curriculum of this kind perpetuated these problems "*through the day-to-day activities of teachers and even of pupils*" (Eggleston, 1977, p. 68). These questions apply at all levels to the education of minorities, and engineering is no exception.

For these sociologists the received curriculum was divisive. It separated the working class from the middle and upper classes because the working class had to take subjects that were regarded as low status because they found it difficult to do mathematics, science, and English, which were and are subjects that have high status. The working class were given practical subjects like woodwork and metalwork, and in England engineering became applied science in order to gain status. School technology (however much technological literacy is important), is a low-status subject.

The same was true of the industrial arts in the United States but to compound the confusion a technology degree in the United States is regarded as inferior to an engineering degree. As such, perceptions may be created, on the one hand in the minds of students that technology is a low-status subject and, on the other hand, in the minds of university engineering teachers that it is also a low-status subject. In the United Kingdom, Parnaby (1998) wrote that the "whole situation is confused by contemporary references to technology and technologists without any clear definitions of what these labels mean." Parnaby suggested the definitions in Exhibit 7.1. It should also be noted that in some enterprises in the United Kingdom the term engineer is used to denote a variety of roles, some of which would not be undertaken by an engineer of chartered status. (Youngman et al., 1978). Moreover, physicists often did and do the jobs that Chartered Engineers do without any qualifications whatsoever, all of which created huge problems for the status of the engineering profession that remain to this day (Harrison, 1992).

The English sociologists argued that the epistemology of the received curriculum was at fault. Knowledge was socially constructed and, therefore, relative. They made this case long before the constructivism associated with Piaget became influential in science teaching (see Chapter 3). But they found that the received curriculum persisted.

Science	Knowledge and understanding of the physical world and the underlying laws which govern it.
Engineering	Creative, practical, cost-effective semi-em,pirical synthesis process with application of science and technology to solve problems and meet needs
Technology	A tool or systematic selection of tools and methodologies, often base on custom and practice, together with the application of knowledge designed to manipulate the materials of the physical world and create potential products in a reproducible and transferable way, or to effect artefact purpose or change.
Critical generic technologies	Technologies that, at an early stage of development, are believed likely to produce a wide array of returns and to solve specific societal bottle-knecks, but which are not tied to single specific product applications.

Exhibit 7. 1 Definitions due to J. Parnaby. *Engineering Science and Education Journal*, **1998, p 183.**

As Eggleston pointed out (following Kuhn), it is very difficult to be deviant, and this applied to university teachers as it did to school teachers. *"For many teachers in universities the constraints are not ones of which they are sharply aware. Their internalization of the received perspective that surrounds their work is sufficient to ensure that they are only infrequently conscious of their constraints. And most teachers do not need reminding that their own authority and role also spring from the existing social order"* [i.e., their profession]; *"that to challenge the system is to challenge their own present position."* (p. 70). That is why change is so difficult, even when change is apparently simple, as for example the grouping of subjects into "threads" that extend throughout the course (Mullisen, 1999[17]). Nevertheless, change does take place but usually like the changes in the design of an automobile, in small increments (Heywood, 1984).Sometimes there are spurts and substantial changes occur, but more often than not these are due to external forces, as for example, government pressure in England for university teachers to be trained in teaching, and most notably ABET in engineering.

In South Africa the removal of apartheid created huge problems for engineering departments because the communication model was not sufficient for non-traditional students. New approaches to teaching were required (van Schalkwyk, Weyers, and van Oostrum, 1993: see Chapter 12). But change depends on ideas. They have to be developed, circulated, and re circulated until the time is ripe and they appeal. Even so, the idea that is adopted may not have all the characteristics of the original idea (Newman, 1845).

In this respect, two important ideas have emerged from the phenomenological approach of constructivism to the curriculum. The first is that of negotiation. As we have seen (Chapter 3), the reality of a social system is, in this theory, an artifact. Common-sense knowledge is socially constructed, and, therefore, relative. The participants in a classroom take part in defining the reality of the classroom (i.e., its culture). In this situation, teachers and students should define a curriculum which is real to them in a social context. In this sense the curriculum is negotiable, negotiation having the purpose of meeting the needs of individual students. It is a curriculum that Eggleston (1977) would classify as *reflexive* in contrast to *received*. The trouble is that negotiate and negotiable are open to several interpretations. Negotiation can be limited or all embracing.

Boomer (1992), an Australian, wrote *"negotiating the curriculum means deliberately planning to invite students to contribute to, and to modify, the educational program, so that they will have a real investment both in the learning journey and in the outcomes"*. But he added the caveat that, *"negotiation*

also means making explicit, and then confronting the constraints of the learning context and the non-negotiable requirements that apply." (p. 14). In the same text, Cook (1992) stated the motivational principle that served the theory when he wrote that: *"the key to negotiation, both in theory and in practice, lies in the ownership principle: people tend to strive hardest for the things they wish to own, or to keep and enhance things they already own. The inverse is just as true and observable all around us: people find it difficult to give commitment to the property and ideas of others"* (p. 14).

In engineering the idea of negotiation is present when students are given the facility to choose their own projects. They may have to negotiate the project with their tutor if only to make sure that the project can be completed in the appropriate time, that they have the appropriate resources available, and that the tutor perceives it to be within the competence of the student. The ownership of the idea is, nevertheless, that of the student. This is quite different from being told what project or what investigation to do, or even to select a project from a list of topics. While it is quite clear which approach is more likely to develop independence in learning and independence in design, the issue of who should choose a project causes much debate.

Related to the idea of choosing one's own project is the idea of independent study where the course and associated studies are chosen by the student, subject to the university's capability to advise and assess the student's performance. Clearly, this is not practical in engineering programs since there is a body of knowledge that has to be learned. Nevertheless, at the University of Toronto the only required course in the fourth year was a course equivalent thesis or design project. Otherwise within constraints of prerequisites and requirements for accreditation, the students were free to design their own program (Smith, 1994). This might be regarded as a half way house toward independent study. (See Chapter 9.)

In practice, in engineering there is a tendency for curricula to be in the received part of the spectrum with some reflexive components, but the demand that engineering students should be prepared for such practice is also a demand for a more reflexive component in the curriculum. But this cannot be achieved without a received body of knowledge. A major issue that is unlikely to be resolved will be the continuing debate about the essential principles of the curriculum, what should be in and what should be out, and how it should be taught?

7.11. Starting a New Degree.

Since the end of the Second-World War a number of new universities have been created throughout the world. Some of these have had the opportunity to create new degree programs from scratch. One of these at Northern Territory University in Darwin, Australia began the development of a new degree program in the electrical and electronic area. This university was the outcome of a merger between an Institute of Technology

---

[17]The curricular threads at California Polytechnic State University are engineering design, engineering science, engineering analysis, engineering support, hands-on-engineering, engineering communication, engineering social skills, and liberal arts.

and a University College. The Institute of Technology had been modeled on the concept of the American Community College although it had a strong technical component. Its charter had allowed it to offer Baccalaureate degrees where relevant.

Patterson (1994), who described the development of the new degree, spent a sabbatical in the United States teaching at the University of Alaska, Fairbanks, which he considered to be similar to the Northern Territories University in terms of remoteness and the population to be served. Supported by comments in the Finniston Report (United Kingdom) he drew attention to the fact that Australian University degrees in engineering had become increasingly specialized. At the Institute of Technology level it was argued that graduates should be produced who suited the needs of employers. But Patterson pointed out that this trend was markedly different from those in other countries particularly Japan and the United States. Employers in Japan wanted graduates who had a theoretical base. The employer would teach the specializations. He also found that in the United States, employers also wanted graduates with general problem solving skills. On the basis of these findings, he argued that to produce graduates who were immediately useful was to provide a short-term solution only. This argument is the same as that put forward by Morant in the previous section, and it was the justification for a small university to attempt a program in engineering. While it could not offer a range of specializations, it could offer a degree where the accent was on fundamentals. Thus, in the fourth year there would be no electives.

However, to be credible the degree had to meet the accreditation requirements of the Institution of Engineers of Australia. Thus, while there was freedom to innovate, the innovation had to be accomplished in such a way that it achieved respectability. Anything that was too radical would not have been received with favor. As was explained in Chapter 2, this was the experience of the University of Lancaster when a working group produced a degree program in engineering for the Vice-Chancellor. The Senate of the University, which had no members that were engineers, rejected the model as being too radical (Heywood et al., 1966). However, when eventually engineering was established, it was as a Department of Engineering Science with an design engineer as its head. The three-year degree included electronic and mechanical streams that shared common courses. Innovation wise, this seems to have made the later development of a four-year mechatronics degree plausible and possible (Dorey, Bradley, and Dawson, 1989).

In the case of the Northern Territories University, in order to be plausible within its constituencies, the first year was designed to cover engineering material that was common in certain other Australian universities that were chosen because their programs related to the perceived needs of Northern territories University.

Because of the view that engineers are unlikely to remain in one narrow area, engineering subjects other than the electrical specialisation were retained in the core (e.g., statics and dynamics, fluid dynamics, and thermodynamics). Patterson would have liked to have changed the mathematics curriculum and, in particular, to reduce the calculus that had little relevance to engineering, but it would not have been possible to make unilateral changes of this kind in the engineering culture that was then current in Australia. He would also have included general education courses like those in the United States had that been plausible.

Finally, he believed that the contact hours (26 per week) were too high. Respectability demanded this requirement, but he felt that a *"degree could be rather more than just running from one assignment and laboratory class to the next in order to keep up."* Of such is the impact of the cultural pressure of the received curriculum. The question of contact hours continues to be an issue throughout the world. The reader is left to consider whether or not Patterson would have been helped if he had approached the curriculum from the perspective that has been presented in these paragraphs.

7.12.   Bringing About Change: Curriculum Leadership.

When Don Evans read the first part of this study, he asked me why it was that when so much was known about the effectiveness of certain strategies of teaching, that the rate of adoption was so low. He felt that this could be only understood by looking at theories of the diffusion of innovation such as those posited by Everett M. Rogers (1995). The work of the Coalitions in the United States has given some importance to the study of the diffusion of innovation and its subsequent maintenance, and a few papers have now addressed this topic.

It is important to appreciate that the curriculum is subject to a series of continuing changes of a minor nature. It is not much different from product development. As previously indicated, there are two main causes of these changes. These are (1) the effects of external pressures of one kind or another and (2) teacher innovation. As teachers learn how to teach in their classroom, they learn new ways and methods. That this is the case is illustrated by the numerous "nuts and bolts" papers that appear in the journals associated with engineering education. Some of this work diffuses into the system and is institutionalized in syllabuses which then undergo a minor restructuring.

In the very long run the history of how engineering education developed in countries associated with Britain is of interest. Page and Murphy (1988) of the University of Queensland offered such a reminder. Engineering in Britain had its origins in the crafts, and the earliest education for engineering was in a master-apprentice relationship in which learning was largely personalized, active, and participatory. It was learning by observation and experience. In stark contrast, when schools of engineering were established, they were primarily schools of applied science. Learning became group (lecture)-oriented and passive. Knowledge was increased but at the expense of skills. There is a broadly similar structure today, and *"most problems considered by students are very narrow."* The analogy with industrial development arises from the fact that the knowledge explosion has not led to a substantial re-organization of material but to an increase in the number of courses. *"The traditional response to new technology has been increasing specialization."* Much more is expected in the same amount of time. Page and Murphy's suggestions foreshadowed the developments that were take place in the coalitions in the United States. Among them they argued the case for the development of general problem-solving skills and for the provision of a strong open-ended problem-solving component. The demand for relevance almost certainly ensures some form or another of integrated study (see Chapter 8).

Very often, however, change is not institutionalised. At the university level, classroom change, more often than not, is only sustained as long as the innovator teaches the course. Froyd, Penberthy, and Watson (2000) called this model *"current change."* They argued that such innovation is unlikely to promote widespread change. Among the reasons for this are, first, that skeptics can often challenge the scientific rigor of the change. Second, the motivation for change lies with an individual member of faculty, and often other faculty are not convinced of the need for change. Third, change is more likely to occur when innovations are supported by a coalition of faculty.

Rogers (1995) considered that the transfer of ideas more frequently took place between individuals who have similar beliefs, attitudes, and attributes. He called the degree to which this exists between members of a group homophily.[18] *"More effective communication occurs between two or more individuals are homophilous."* Its opposite is heterophily. It leads to poor communication. It would seem that a group of engineering educators ought to be homophilous. However, it can be the case that some individuals in a group have a greater technical knowledge than other individuals in the group, and this may cause heterophily. But, Roger's said that *"the very nature of diffusion demands that at least some degree of heterophily be present between two participants,"* thus, part of the educational leadership role is to reduce heterophily.

Fisher, Fairweather, and Amey (2001) pointed out that that often innovations are valued by funding agencies, peer institutions, and employers but not by the home department. They reported on a study for the National Science Foundation that found that many instructional and curriculum innovations had not been disseminated (Eiseman and Fairweather, 1996). They cited the case of a teacher who had improved achievement and motivation by introducing student centered methods of learning in place of a traditional lecture program. He had found the approach time-consuming but worthwhile. *"By all accounts the*

innovation was a success. Yet departmental faculty rejected a petition to revise the traditional course format permanently because of the extra time commitment and the belief that such an investment was not important in promotion and tenure decisions. Faculty members teaching the course next year returned to its traditional lecture format."[19] One of the problems is the autonomy given to academics. University teachers are unused to working in teams, neither do many of them feel any collective responsibility toward the department or its goals, and *"the aggregate set of accomplishments of individual members of the faculty seldom fulfils all collective curricular and instructional obligations of an academic unit."*

Fisher, Fairweather, and Amey argued that often change is introduced without taking into account the complex roles of faculty members and that this itself leads to resistance to change. The conflict between teaching and research is often cited in this respect. They argued that there are other tensions which need to be recognized by both faculty and administrators if a department is to satisfy its collective responsibilities. These are collective responsibility versus individual faculty rewards; collective responsibility versus the boundaries of academic freedom; collective responsibility versus the maximization of individual autonomy; and collective responsibility versus faculty collegiality. They suggested a model for the systemic reform of curricular that takes these tensions into account. It is hierarchical and included the external environment, the institution, departments, faculty work including motivation and socialization, and this hierarchy is completed by student learning.

The tension in faculty collegiality relates to the ownership of courses. If only one person teaches the course, his/her learning objectives and content are unlikely to be challenged, and this may not be in the best interest of the department. Therefore, faculty should collectively agree *"on the basic boundaries between collegiality and academic freedom and how interpreting these boundaries affect course quality, program quality, and department efficiencies."* They also suggested that departments should be told of the innovations that individual members make with a view to making best practices *"planned innovations"* that become part of *"the department's culture."*

Most of the changes that are suggested by educators require a change in culture in the organization, be it a department or an institution. For example, in order to implement an integrated course in calculus and mechanics together with engineering fundamentals and engineering laboratory, faculty were brought together each week to discuss the students' progress. *"This discussion helped get additional help for students who*

---

[18] The concepts of homophily and heterophily were first discussed by Lazarsfield and Merton (1964).

[19] The same thing happened to a course run by this writer when he retired. He had been able to sustain an innovation that was shown to meet the objectives of the course because he was a permanent head of department. It was at the cost of a substantial increase in work load which he regarded as a small price to pay for what was achieved.

were struggling. The faculty gathered at the end of the quarter after all tests had been given and before grades were assigned. There was discussion of the individuals and their progress before grades were assigned. The faculty took note of attitudes, daily performance, and improvement. The faculty were concerned about true understanding of course materials and about retention" (Demel et al., 1994).

Apart from focus groups and workshops, there are other techniques that can be used to facilitate change. The Nominal Group Technique has been shown to have value in the development of programs that would be considered interdisciplinary.[20]

At the level of the institution the Colorado School of Mines had already a substantial history of educational innovation when in the early 1990's it developed a graduate profile (Middleton, 1998). In the year that it was completed a number of committees evaluated the extent to which the curriculum led to the attributes required in the profile. A consensus emerged to the effect that there was a need for curriculum reform. Therefore, a curriculum reform committee was established to develop a framework for the new curriculum. Once the framework was agreed across the campus, sub committees were established to work on four segments of the framework. These sub-committees involved nearly half the faculty of the school. Middleton and Trefny (1998) found that this was not always a straightforward process. There were many iterations and debates during the weekly meetings and occasionally there had to be arbitration. They reported that there was some reticence among faculty sectors about the implementation of detail, and consequently a limited number of pilot programs were established. These courses were new aspects of the freshmen and sophomore core, and they found product champions among the faculty who played leading roles in the subcommittees. The changes required the upper division program to be adapted so as to mesh with the changed junior core. The School used the revision of the catalogue to describe and organize these changes.

Middleton and Trefny (1998) highlighted the need to foster communication across the campus and departments if reform is to be successful. They wrote: *"we have demonstrated that collaboration and trust among the varied constituencies, together with faculty ownership and participation, have been critical in achieving progress. Retrospectively, we have seen more of an evolution of an atmosphere of collaboration rather than a mode of explicit planning to create that atmosphere. A culture of reform has grown, and this is fortunate because modern expectations will demand the continuous review and adaptation of curriculum and learning."*

Changes of this kind cannot be implemented without a cost to the institution. It is this writer's experience that often the institution wants substantial change at no cost. Middleton and Trefny (1998) reported that the Colorado School of Mines allocated $100,000 per annum for this process. Evidently there is also a substantial cost in time. For example, Merton et al., (2001), from an analysis of curricular change in the Foundation Coalition, reported that support for curricular improvement within and beyond the College of Engineering required significantly more design and effort than the change leaders had anticipated.

It might be argued that the Colorado School of Mines was not starting from scratch. It had had more than a decade of curriculum innovation of one kind or another. Granted that not everyone had been involved and that school-wide reform requires a much wider participation, there was nevertheless a foundation (readiness) for reform that seems to have been secure. The problem for many institutions is how to build those foundations.

In the United States, by far the most important pressure for change comes from the accrediting agencies, and this is true of all the industrialized nations. In the United States the ABET EC2000 criteria have stimulated change, and the effectiveness with which they are adopted often requires a considerable change in the culture of departments. Hoey and Nault (2001) suggested that excellence in assessment is *"intermittent, dispersed, and inconsistent for many engineering programs."* That this is likely to be the case is supported by a survey of the attitudes of faculty in the SUCCEED Coalition of teaching practices and perceptions of institutional attitudes to teaching by Felder et al., (1998). The survey showed a moderate involvement of the respondents in attending teaching seminars and implementing non traditional teaching practices. It was thought that the respondents were not representative but were among those who placed a high priority on teaching in the eight engineering schools.

Hoey and Nault (2001) reported an attempt to assess and then change the culture of assessment at a large research institution. This was achieved through focus groups that included staff, faculty, and administrators. They found that *trust* was the most important factor that limited the use of assessment. In order to develop *trust* in the organization, large follow-up workshops were initiated, and from these a preliminary inventory of best practices to build trust in assessment emerged.

The objectives of the workshops were to:

- *"Increase awareness about the importance of assessment and the meaningful alternatives available to developing and using assessment results.*
- *Participate with disciplinary peers in problem-solving to improve the quality of assessment.*
- *Work in partnership with other faculty, staff, and administrators to identify and resolve assessment issues, thus facilitating new communications across disciplines.*

---

[20]Nominal Group Technique is a development of brainstorming that uses qualitative and quantitative methods and enables the rank ordering of ideas. It has been used to develop a teacher education degree in the UK. (O'Neil and Jackson, 1983). See Chapters 11 and 15.

- *Develop strategies for 'closing the loop', and*
- *Compile and distribute to the campus the collective intellectual capital produced and to facilitate the further development of meaningful assessment procedures."*

Both the Colorado School of Mines project and the Ohio State projects implemented pilot schemes. This is a common practice by those who follow the science model of innovation. However, a study of a pilot curriculum in the Foundation coalition suggested that while they can be a useful step toward college wide implementation, they offer no more benefits than accrue from the construction of a prototype in engineering. But, Merton et al., (2001) considered it to be unwise to treat the pilot in the same way as a prototype in engineering because curriculum change is a complex activity that is further complicated by the vagaries of human behavior. Without effective communication the pilot team can become isolated from the rest of the faculty, and they noted that pilot curricula that are designed for a limited audience do not necessarily show how the pilot curriculum would work when mainstreamed among a more diverse body of students. Another perspective on the role of pilot studies was given by Froyd, Penberthy and Watson (2000) in their study of the factors that enhanced and inhibited change in the Foundation Coalition. They considered that the *current change* model described above did not lead to sustained change. They pointed out that that this had led some educators to advocate the process model of scientific discovery, which they called the *espoused change model* This involved the piloting of a curriculum and evaluating its results. It is set up as a scientific experiment. They give five reasons why this model does not work. The first is that all change requires the participants to change their behavior, *"and possibly their values."* Second, it is insufficiently realized that a change in learning outcomes may not be accomplished without changing the learning environment. Related to this is the fact that an educational experiment cannot assess the value of intended outcomes. *"Educational research can inform the process of educational change, but ultimately, the individuals or community in question must establish intended outcomes as a matter of values clarification."* They went on to criticize this experimental approach to curriculum change. They argued that scientists seldom accept the result of a single experiment; also they did not necessarily support a faculty member who is motivated to change, but uninformed. They also argued that there were inherent difficulties in comparing the performance of two teachers and their students. It is important to note that this is not a criticism of the pilot technique *per se*. In their approach they used a pilot.

Pendergrass, Laoulache and Fortier (2000), reported that they had made a successful transfer from a pilot study to the mainstream because the pilot was built with rigorous outcome assessment. Also faculty members questions were treated seriously regardless of motivation, and key individuals had to be motivated *"to study and*

make timely decisions about the new program."* In order to do that, they needed the power to redesign it.

It is possible to counteract some of these arguments. First, experiments can be valuable if teachers in a faculty have been schooled in what educational research has to say about the art and science of pedagogy. In this respect Gage's (1981) monograph *Hard Gains in Soft Science. The case of Pedagogy* remains a classic document on this topic. Second, if teachers undertake classroom assessment and research as advocated by Angelo and Cross (1993) and Cross and Steadman (1996), they will sharpen the reflective capability that they bring to the evaluation of such experiments. Third, they will be helped in this reflective activity, if, following Gage, a process-product model is used that is accompanied by some kind of ethnographic approach (e.g., Heywood, and Montagu Pollock, 1995). In carrying out such activities, they are level curriculum leaders.

That said, however, there is no doubt that Froyd and his colleagues are correct when they argue that ignoring the element of human behavior in curriculum change is the reason why so much change fails. Their view, like that of Evans with which this section began, is that change has to take into account how individuals and organizations interact. Pendergrass, Laoulache, and Fortier (2000) gave a graphic illustration of how, in spite of their subsequent success, they completely underestimated the reaction of faculty to the mainstreaming of a pilot study. They were shocked at the reaction they received. For this reason they argued that the use organizational change models might lead to greater success rate in successfully implementing change.

Froyd and his colleagues described how they implemented a model of institutional change based on a model for business organization developed by Kotter (1996). It focused on *"changing people's attitudes toward ongoing curriculum change and equipping them to continually change."* The headings of the steps as listed by Froyd, Penberthy, and Watson are:

- *"Establish need and energy for curricular change.*
- *Gather a leadership team to design and promote the curricular change.*
- *Define and agree upon new learning objectives and a new learning environment.*
- *Discuss the new objectives and environment with the college and revise based on feedback.*
- *Implement new curriculum using a pilot, if necessary.*
- *Conduct a formative evaluation of the program, investigating strengths and weaknesses of the current implementation, and indicators of short-term gains.*
- *Decide how the new approach may be used for the entire college and prepare implementation plan.*
- *Prepare faculty and staff for the new implementation, implement, and follow up with improvements."*

They argued that time spent on stage one is more than worthwhile. Answers have to be provided to the question "Why Change?" Faculty who are skeptical are likely to convey their attitudes to students, and this may influence negatively any experiment they may conduct. Given the problems of the *espoused* model, unless faculty have been trained in educational research and are able to interpret results, they are unlikely to be persuaded by research alone. However, research can indicate what learning environments may be effective in achieving specified objectives (outcomes). Those who seek to implement change are acting as curriculum leaders at the third level.

In the United Kingdom, Mathias and Rutherford (1983) described how they used the development of a Course Evaluation Scheme at the University of Birmingham to evaluate an organizational model that that had been developed from two models of course innovation. These were in the United States (Lindquist (L), 1978) and Sweden (Berg and Ostergren (B& O), 1979). The combination gave six decisive factors. These were *linkage* (L), *openness* (L), *gain/loss*(B&O), *leadership*(L & B&O), *ownership* (L,& B&O), and *power* (B&O). Lindquist had the dimension of 'rewards' that is similar to *gain/loss* in that it is a measure of the advantages and disadvantages for groups and individuals. *Linkage* is the bringing of people together across the organisation in order to confront them with new ideas. *Openness* is to seek ideas beyond one's primary group. This would seem to be related to the concept of "readiness" in educational psychology. It has been argued that this concept can be applied to the process of institutional change. Institutions have to be ready to change (Heywood, 1969).

Leaders in the Lindquist model are those who initiate, guide, and involve. They are also influential. More recent literature refers to the need for product champions. None of the studies, referred to above considered the possible role of change agents or curriculum leaders in the innovation process (see Chapter 1), although it should be appreciated that consultants of this kind can create heterophily because they can so easily talk a different language. Clearly, a product champion should also be a curriculum leader. One of the problems is that the learning of the educational language may be a lot more difficult than it seems, as at least one engineering educator has testified (see example cited by Heywood, 1995).

Mathias and Rutherford (1983) argued that this model is a *"potent tool of analysis in the area of local and relatively unplanned change as it is in more large-scale planned innovations."* They suggested that attempts by Boud (1979) among engineers and Hewton (1979) could be analyzed in this way. Of all the factors, *power* seemed them to be the most important. Without *power*-that is, the authority of the institution-innovations have relatively low status and may only lead to marginal change. As Pendergrass, Laoulache, and Fortier (2000) reported (see above), key individuals had to have *power* to ensure that the pilot study was mainstreamed. But *power* requires knowledge, and this text is about the knowledge that is required for the informed management of change or curriculum leadership.

Academic institutions are made up of an administrative body and a body of academic teachers. They share power between them even though academic decision makers belong, for organizational purposes, to the administrative body. Where power is shared in this way, it is sometimes difficult for academic administration to make tough decisions. *"Thus, due to opportunities that both sides have with regard to 'trumping the other's brick', this balanced power system can lead to the development of political stalemates which may result in institutional paralysis"* (Tomovic, 1996).

How to break this stalemate is the challenge facing higher education institutions and, in particular, engineering. Those who undertake this task can benefit from knowledge of change theories (see above for example) as well as reported successes and failures of innovations. At Purdue University in the School of Technology the principles of Total Quality Management were applied to classroom and student-learning assessment (Tomovic, 1996). Tomovic described how the Dean implemented the change process with the aid of a model developed by Miller and de Vries (1985).

In that model the five stages are denial, defense, discarding, adaptation, and internalization. At Purdue it was expected that the academic staff would deny there was a need for TQM. As the process is introduced, it was expected that the teachers would defend their own territories. In the third stage it was expected that some teachers would begin to take a leadership role, and others would begin to discard some of their past ways. Adaptation required the staff to begin working collaboratively and through trial and error work out what was best for them. In the final stage the teachers would naturally carry out the new approaches. This approach was used in the training of teachers for new approaches to assessment in the public examination system in Ireland where it was found that a substantial amount of time was required for internalization of the new philosophy and techniques.

At Purdue there were both top-down and bottom-up activities. No attempt was made to force the change through by fiat. Rather, teachers were invited to participate in the improvement. There was a carrot in that Motorola was the University's partner in the TQM University Challenge Program, and Motorola paid for 25 faculty to attend a five-day off-campus training program. The challenge program set specific and immediate goals. These were *"to develop and administer a customer survey; to develop a plan for TQM curriculum integration; and to conduct an internal assessment based on the Malcolm Baldridge Award Criteria."* These became the bottom-up activities. The top-down activities were the TQM training, the establishment of a school wide TQM committee and curriculum development.

One result of the training was the establishment of a cross-disciplinary support group. Tomovic reported that relative to the assessment initiative some kind of centralized training would reduce confusion. Such sessions can also serve to develop camaraderie. It was clear that the *"hallmark of managing change is employee involvement, In the case of assessment the hallmark of good assessment is faculty involvement"* and this was why in the Irish experiment the teachers were trained so that they could be involved in the design new methods of assessment.

An Australian educator who had reviewed the literature on change and observed an Australian case suggested a 4-stage model of change. In the first stage (Establishment), a proposal emerged from a small group that was disseminated and refined in the second stage. It was then subject to design and development during which tasks were undertaken, supported, and monitored. Curriculum materials emerged from this activity to be implemented by teachers and evaluated. Each stage had interactive and evaluative elements. The teachers were given support and resources made available. Walkington (2002) who undertook that study, synthesized the principles of change as follows:

- *"Change is a journey, not a blue print. It is non-linear, loaded with uncertainty.*
- *Both individualism and collectivism have a place within the process.*
- *Both top-down and bottom-up strategies of organization are required.*
- *Every person involved is a change agent with a variety of contributions (*In terms of this text every one is a curriculum leader).
- *Curriculum changes require contextual change for them to be accepted and sustained.*
- *Evaluation is a necessary component of change."* (Walkington, 2002).

7.13. Discussion

The factors that contribute to curriculum change have been considered against the backdrop of three curriculum paradigms. The first of these, the received paradigm, describes a curriculum that is *"dependent on a received body of understanding that is 'given,' even ascribed, and is predominantly non-negotiable."* The engineering curriculum primarily belongs to this paradigm. This knowledge base may evolve through a process of discovery, reinforced by a spiral curriculum in which the basic concepts are discussed at increasing level of depth in different contexts, and in which there is feedback between the levels. In any event, changes in technology create new knowledge needs. Nevertheless, this paradigm is conservative and those who operate it are conservative: change is slow and characterized by a series of minor changes with the occasional upheaval. The factors that contribute to this change have been considered, and it was shown that factors external to the institution (department) are more likely to cause change than factors from within.

In contrast to the received paradigm is the reflexive paradigm against which the constructivist model in sociological and sociological dimensions may be matched. Knowledge is constructed and, therefore, relative. The idea of negotiated curriculum comes from this paradigm. There is a limited amount of negotiation in some engineering curricula as, for example, in the choice of projects and assessment procedures. Preparation for engineering demands a more reflexive approach, but that

cannot be achieved without a received body of knowledge. That body of knowledge is subject to alteration as the perception of what engineering "presently is" changes and the prevailing technology demands changes in the knowledge framework. This means that the curriculum is continually being restructured even if only in small ways (the third paradigm).

Typically, an innovation is initiated and maintained by an individual instructor. When he/she stops that innovation, for whatever reason, it also comes to an end. For change to be sustained, faculty have to act as a team and support that change. How departmental structures may be changed was considered, and attention was drawn to the importance of product change champions and change agents with recognized power and knowledge. Change is dependent on individuals who are dependent for its continuance on management that uses its *power* to create *trust*. Curriculum leaders require power if they are to introduce change, and trust if it is to become a permanent feature of the curriculum.

References

Achi, P. B. U (1988). Approaching tertiary curriculum design from industrial training perspective. *International Journal of Applied Engineering Education.* 4, (6), 507-510.

Acosta, F. M. A (2000) Hints for the improvement of quality teaching in introductory engineering statistics courses. *European Journal of Engineering Education*, 25, 266–267.

Anderson, J (1987). Skill acquisition: compilation of weak-method problem solutions. *Psychological Review*, 94, 192–210.

Anderson, J., and F. Percival (1997). Developing HE staff to appreciate the needs of flexible learning for ACCESS students-developing flexible learning ACCESS students to appreciate needs in HE. In S. Armstrong, G. Thompson and S. Brown (eds). *Facing Up to Radical Change in Universities and Colleges.* Kogan Page, London

Angelo, T., and P. K. Cross (1993). *Classroom Assessment Techniques.* Jossey Bass, San Francisco.

Arms, V. M. (1994). Personal and Professional Enrichment: Humanities in the Engineering Curriculum, *Journal of Engineering Education.* 83, (2), 141-146.

Bajpai, A. C., and D. G. James (1985). Matehmatical education for engineers- a future perspective. *European Journal of Engineering Education.* 10, 277–283.

Baldwin, C. J., Cahn, C. R., Forman, J. W., Lehmann, H., and C. R. Wischmeyer (1979). A model undergraduate electrical engineering education. *Proceedings Frontiers in Education Conference*, 91-96.

Berg, B and B, Ostergren (1979). Innovation processes in higher education. *Studies in Higher Education*, 4, 261-268. In G. Boomer, G et al., (Eds.) *Negotiating the Curriculum. Educating for the 21st Century.* Falmer Press, London.

Bloom, A. D (1987). *The Closing of the American Mind.* Simon and Schuster, New York.

Bondi, H (1966). Mathematics, the universities and social change. *Universities Quarterly*, 20, 407.

Boomer, G (1992) *Negotiating the Curriculum. Educating for the 21st Century.* Falmer Press, London.

Boud, D (1979). Engineering success: the progress and problems in higher education development. *Studies in Higher Education* 4, 55-66.

Bringslid, O (1999). Multimedia books in the mathematical education of engineers. *European Journal of Engineering Education*, 24, 189.

Brinson, L. C., Belytschko, T., Moran, B., and T. Black (1997). Design and computational methods in basic mechanics courses. *Journal of Engineering Education*, 86, 159–166.

Brown, K (1998). SARTOR 97. The background and the learning shake-out for university engineering departments. *Engineering Science and Education Journal*, 7, (1), 41–48.

Bruner, J (1960). *The Process of Education*. Vintage, New York.

B uner, J (1966). *Toward a Theory of Instruction*. Norton, New York

Burns, T., and G. Stalker. (1961). *The Management of Innovation*. Tavistock, London.

Carroll, D. R (1997). Integrating design into sophomore and junior level mechanics courses. *Journal Engineering Education*, 86, 227–230.

Carter, G., and T. A. Jordan (1990). *Student Centred Learning in Engineering. Engineering Enhancement in Higher Education*. Prospects and Problems. Monograp, University of Salford, Salford.

Clarke, R.J (1967). Mathematics and metallurgists. *Lancaster Studies in Higher Education*, 2, B-1 to 15.

Clements, R. R (1985). The curriculum in the 1990's a personal view. *International Journal of Mathematics Education, Science and Technology*. 16, 233-238.

Coll, D. C (1994). Communications engineering: a new discipline for the 21st Century. *IEEE Transactions on Education*, 37, (2), 151-156.

Cook, J (1992) Negotiating the Curriculum. Programming for Learning. In G. Boomer et al., (eds.). *Negotiating the Curriculum. Educating for the 21st Century*. Falmer Press, London.

Cross, K. P. and M. Steadman (1996). *Classroom Research*. Jossey-Bass, San Francisco

Culler, A. D (1995). *The Imperial Intellect. A Study of Newman's Educational Ideal*. Yale U. P. Newhaven, Conn.

Cyganski, D., Nicolleti, D., and J. A. Orr (1994). A new introductory electrical engineering curriculum for the first year student. *IEEE Transactions on Education*. 37, (2), 171-177.

Demel, J. T. et al (1994). Changing the core-changing the culture. *Proceedings Frontiers in Education Conference*, 656-659

Dorey, A. P., Bradley, D. A., and D. Dawson (1989). Mecatraonics-integration in engineering. Proceedings World *Conference on Engineering Education for Advanced Technology*. Sydney, Australia. 186-189.

Eggleston, J (1977). *The Sociology of the School Curriculum*. Routledge, London.

Engineering Council and Others (1996). *Mathematics Formation*. Engineering Council, London.

Eiseman, J. and J. Fairweather (1996). *Evaluation of the National Science Foundation's Undergraduate Course and Curriculum Development Program*. Final report. National Science Foundation, Washington, DC.

Felder, R. M., Brent, R., Miller, T. K., Brawner, C. E. and R. H. Allen (1998). Faculty teaching practices and perceptions of institutional attitudes toward teaching at eight engineering schools. *Proceedings Frontiers in Education Conference*, 101-105.

Fisher, P. D., Fairweather, J., and M. Amey (2001). Systemic reform in undergraduate engineering education; the role of collective responsibility. *Proceeding Frontiers in Education Conference*, 1, T1A–1 to 6.

Froyd, J. E., Penberthy, D., and K. Watson (2000). Good educational experiments are not necessarily good change processes. *Proceedings Frontiers in Education Conference*, 2, F1G –1 to 6.

Gage, N. L (1981). *Hard Gains in the Soft Science. The Case of Pedagogy*. Phi Delta Kappa. Bloomington, Indiana.

Gardiner, A. D (1994). The long road back from nowhere. *Times Educational Supplement* (Math Extra). 7th October p II

Hansen, J. G. R. and C. A. Fisher (1986). Curricular emphasis in mechanics: A national update. *Engineering Education*. (April) 664- 669.

Harrison, J (1992) Undergraduate education and the "force field" generated by external institutions. *Proceedings Frontiers in Education Conference* 141 – 142.

Hewton, E. (1979). A strategy for promoting curriculum development in higher education. *Studies in Higher Education*, 4, 67-76.

Heywood, J. (1969). *An Evaluation of certain post-war developments in Higher Technological Education*. Thesis, Volume 1. University of Lancaster Library, Lancaster.

Heywood, J. (1984). *Considering the Curriculum during Student Teaching*. Kogan Page, London.

Heywood, J (1994). *Enterprise Learning and its Assessment in Higher Education. Technical Report No. 20*. Employment Department, Sheffield.

Heywood, J and H. Montagu Pollock (1977). *Science for Arts Students. A Case Study in Curriculum Development*. Society for Research into Higher Education, London.

Heywood, J., Pollitt, J., and V. Mash (1966) The Schools and Technology in *Lancaster Studies in Higher Education*. No 1,154–300.

Heywood, J (1995) Toward the improvement of quality in engineering education. *Proceedings Frontiers in Education.Conference*. 1, 2a3 to 13.

Hirsch, E. D (1987). *Cultural Literacy*. Houghton Mifflin. Boston.

Hirst, P (1975). *Knowledge and the Curriculum*. Routledge, London.

Hoey, J. J. and E. W. Nault (2001). Trust: essential to effective assessment. *Proceedings Frontiers in Education Conference*, 1, T1A-13.

Howson, G (1991) *National Curricula in Mathematics*. The Mathematical Association, Leicester.

Iliffe, A. H (1969). *The Foundation Year in The University of Keele. A Report to the University of Keele, Staffordshire*.

ITEA (2000). Standards for Technological Literacy. *Centre for the Study of Technology. Executive Summary. International Technology Education Association. Reston, VA*.

Jackson, P. W (1963). *Life in Classrooms*. Holt, Reinhart and Winston, New York.

Jordan, G (1992). *Engineers and Professional Self-Regulation*. Clarendon Press, Oxford.

Kuhn, T. S (1920). *The Structure of Scientific Revolutions*. University of Chicago Press, Chicago, Il.

Kolar, R. L., and D. A. Sabatini (1996). Coupling team learning and computer technology in project-driven undergraduate engineering Education. *Proceedings Frontiers in Education Conference*. 1, 172–175.

Kotter, J (1996) *Leading Change*. Harvard Business School, Boston.

Larcombe, P. J (1998). Engineering mathematics. The crisis continues. *Engineering Science and Education Journal*. 7, (6), 273.

Lawrence, J. R (1964). An Engineer's approach to the tasks of management. In *Symposium on Education and Careers*. Institution of Mechanical Engineers, London

Lazarsfield, P. F., and R. K. Merton (1964). Friendship and social process: A substantive and methodological analysis. In Monroe berger et al., (eds.). *Freedom and Control in Modern Society*. Octagon, New York.

Lindquist, J (1978). *Strategies for Change*. Pacific Soundings Press, Berkeley, CA.

Lin, H. (1979). The hidden curriculum of the introductory physics curriculum. *Engineering Education*, 70, (3), 289-294.

Lipski, T (1989). Polish power electric engineering academic education system. *World Conference on Engineering Education*, 1, 36-40.

MacMurray, J (1956). *The Self as Agent*. Faber and Faber, London.

Mathias, N. and D. Rutherford (1983). Decisive factors affecting an innovation: A case study. *Studies in Higher Education*, 8, (1), 45-56.

Matthews, G. B (1980) *Philosophy and the Young Child*. Harvard University Press, Cambridge MA

Mentkowski, M. and Asociates. (2000). *Learning that Lasts*. Jossey-Bass, San Francisco.

Merton, R. K (1968). *Social Theory and Social Structure*. Free Press, New York.

Merton, P., Clark, C., Richardson, J., and J. Froyd (2001). Engineering curricular change across the Foundation Coalition: potential lessons from qualitative research. *Proceedings Frontiers in Education Conference*, 3, F4B 15 to 20.

McClelland, B (2000). Digital learning and teaching in Higher Education. *European Journal of Engineering Education*. 26, (2), 107-116.

McDowell, L (1995). Effective teaching and learning on foundation and ACCESS courses in engineering, science, and technology. *European Journal of Engineering Education*, 20, (4), 417-425.

Middleton, N. T (1998). The revised core curriculum for engineering and science programs at the Colorado School of Mines. *Proceedings Frontiers in Education Conference*. 567-572.

Middleton, N. T. and J. U. Trefny (1998). Managing the human processes in curriculum reform. *Proceedings Frontiers in Education Conference*, 106 –110.

Miller, D and K. de Vries (1985). *The Neurotic Organization*. Jossey Bass, San Francisco.

Miwa, T (1992). School mathematics in Japan and the US. Focussing on recent trends in elementary and lower secondary school. In I. Wirszup and R. Strait (eds). *Development in School Mathematics*. Education Around the World. National Council of Teachers of Mathematics, Reston, VA.l.

Morant, M. J (1993). Electronics as an academic subject. *International Journal of Electrical Engineering Education*. 110-123

Mullisen, R. S (1999). A mechanical engineering program categorized into curricular threads. *International Journal of mechanical Engineering Education*. 27, (3), 230-238.

Nahvi, M (1998). Developing freshman-year experience in electrical engineering: primary functions and possible feature. *Proceedings Frontiers in Education Conference*. 1056-1061.

Newman, J. H (1845) *An Essay on the Development of Christian Doctrine*. Longmans green, London.

Newman, J.H (1851). *The Idea of a University. Defined and Illustrated*. Longmans Green, London.

O'Neil, M. J., and L. Jackson (1983). Nominal Group Technique: a process for initiating curriculum development in higher education. *Studies in Higher Education*, 8, (2), 129-138.

Page, N. W. and D. N .P. Murphy (1989). Educating engineers for a dynamic professional environment. *World Conference on Engineering Education for Advancing Technology*. 645-649.

Parnaby, J (1998). The requirements for engineering degree courses and graduate engineers: an industrial viewpoint. *Engineering Science and Education Journal*. 7, (4), 181-187.

Patterson, D. J (1994). The development of a bachelor of engineering program at the Northern Territory University, Australia. *IEEE Transactions on Education*. 37, (2), 178-183.

Pendergrass, N. A., Laoulache, R. N., and P. J. Fortier (2000). Mainstreaming an innovative 31-credit curriculum for first year engineering majors. *Proceedings Frontiers in Education* 3, S2G-13 to 17.

Phenix, P (1964). *Realms of Meaning*. McGraw Hill, New York.

Pollock, M. J (2002). Introduction of CAA into a mathematics course for technology students to address change in curriculum requirements. *International Journal of Technology and Design Education*, 1, (12) 249-270.

Pollock, M. J. (2004). Using computers to deliver a mathematics course to increase recruitment and retention of non-traditional students and reduce staff work load. Proceedings *Frontiers in Education Conference*, 1, TIH- 7 to 11.

Posner, G. J (1992). *Analyzing the Curriculum*. McGraw-Hill, New York.

Ray, J and J. Farris (2000). Integration of design and manufacturing processes in first year engineering curriculums. *Proceedings Frontiers in Education* 3, S2G 7 to 11.

Rogers, E. M (1995). *Diffusion of Innovations*, 4th Edition. The Free Press, New York.

Roizen, J., and M. Jepson (1985). *Degrees to Jobs. Employer Expectations of Higher Education*. Society for Research into Higher Education, London.

Rugarcia, A., Felder, R. M.., Woods, D. R., and J. E. Stice (2000). The future of engineering education. I. A vision for a new century. *Chemical Engineering Education*, 34, (1), 16-25.

Ruthven, K (1978). The disciplines thesis and the curriculum: A case study. *British Journal of Educational Studies*, 26, (2), 163-176.

Ruud, C. O. et al (1992). The principlesof science and mathematics reflected in engineering. *Proceedings Frontiers in Education Conference*, 775–781.

SARTOR. (1997). *Standards and Routes to Registration for the Engineering Council*. Engineers Council, London.

Scott, M. R. et al., (1966). *The Use of Mathematics in the Electrical Industry*. Pitman, London.

Seymour, E. and N. M. Hewitt (1997). *Talking About Leaving. Why Undergraduates Leave the Science*. Westview Press, Boulder, Co.

Sharp, J and A. J. White (1991). Changing input standards. *Proceedings Conference on Innovative Teaching in Engineering* Sheffield. 520.

Smith, H. W (1994). University of Toronto Curricula in Electrical and Computer Engineering. *IEEE Transactions on Education*. 37, (2), 158-168.

Soderstrand, M. A (1994). The new electrical and computer engineering curricula at the University of California Davis. *IEEE Transactions on Education, 37, (2), 136-146*.

Tomovic,, C. L (1996). Managing resistance to classroom and student learning assessment: Lessons learned from the past. *Proceedings Frontiers in Education Conference*, 802 - 805

Upchurch, R. L., and J. E. Sims-Knight. (1999). Integrating software process in computer science curriculum. *Proceedings Frontiers in Education Conference*. 13a6-15-13 to 18.

Usiskin, Z. (1993). Lessons from the Chicago Mathematics Project. *Educational Leadership*, 50, (8), 14-18.

Vable, M. (2003). Enhancing understanding of concepts in mechanics of materials using design. *Proceedings Frontiers in Education Conference*, 3, S3B- 13 to 17.

van Schalkwyk, J. J. D., Weyers, T and L. van Oostrum (1993). Traing Engineers in the third world context: the hidden curriculum. *Proceedings Frontiers in Education Conference*, 670-674.

Wachtel, H., Barnes, E. S., and R. Ravenal (1994). A new degree program for students seeking a broader education in addition to engineering. *IEEE Transactions on Education*, 37, (2), 163-166.

Walkington, J (2002) Curriculum change in engineering education. *European Journal of Engineering Education*, 27, (2), 133–148.

Whitehead, A. N (1932). *The Aims of Education and other Essays*. Benn, Edinburgh.

Woods, R. C (1999). Introducing formulas for Fermi energy. *IEEE Transactions on Education* 42, 153-154.

Woods, R. C. (2000). Simplifying the syllabus: Can we avoid throwing out the baby? *Engineering Science and Education Journal*. February 2, 3.

Young, M.F.D (1971) (ed). *Knowledge and Control*. Collier-Macmillan, London.

Young, P. M (1997). An integrated systems and control laboratory. *Proceedings Frontiers in Education Conference* 659-6

Youngman, M. B., Oxoby, R., Monk, J.D., and J. Heywood (1978) *Analysing Jobs* . Gower, Aldershot.

CHAPTER 8: INTERDISCIPLINARY AND INTEGRATED STUDIES

Summary

Like most terms used in higher education, interdisciplinary, integration (integrated), and transdisciplinary invite interpretation. The Chapter begins, therefore, with a brief discussion of these terms and their origins in curriculum usage.

A distinction is made between subjects in which the mode of thinking is "close" to engineering, and those where it differs substantially or is "distant" from engineering. It is suggested that the integration of "distant" subjects might be more difficult than those that are close."

The chapter continues with a discussion of the origins and scope of integrated studies. Rapidly changing technology sometimes makes it necessary to create a curriculum response in which subject matter is integrated. One example is the development of courses in mechatronics. There are other examples of this need, and four approaches to the integration of mathematics into the engineering curriculum have been delineated. Few of the reports indicate the learning benefits that might accrue to students from integrated study. At least one shows the benefits to the curriculum designer of a comprehensive knowledge of psychology.

One way of coping with the explosion of knowledge so as to avoid curriculum overload is to attempt some form of integration It has been found that interdisciplinary freshman laboratory programs may enhance the retention rates of women and minority students. More generally (as is discussed in another Chapter) projects are considered to be a powerful strategy for the integration and the understanding of the conceptual linkages between subjects.

Insofar as women students are concerned, it is reported that motivation is enhanced when project work focuses on technologies likely to be of use to women and families in the future. It has also been shown that women can be helped through the development writing skills. One argument for writing across the curriculum is based on the view that "clear writing indicates clear thinking." Transactional writing has been shown to help women students in the study of mathematics. Communication skills have come to be valued and some illustrations of courses designed to develop these skills are given. In general, courses are task-oriented and directed toward engineering activities. A case may be made for a broader approach that includes creative writing.

The next section extends the discussion begun in Chapter 3 on the integration of the humanities into the engineering curriculum. The reaction of students to such programs is noted, and an attempt to produce a philosophical engineer in the Netherlands is described.

Attempts to design courses around a set of principles rather than subjects (thematic integration) are described. Excluding project work that may cause such integration such approaches seem to lie outside the plausibility of what an engineering curriculum should be.

A few attempts have been made to integrate high level thinking skills across the curriculum and attention is drawn to the SCANS model for high school education as an exemplar.

Many of the studies reported rely on student questionnaires for their evaluation. There is a need for a more sophisticated approach to evaluation, a point which is illustrated by one study that sought to establish the meaning that integration has for students. But, for successful evaluation and successful curriculum design there is a need for comprehensive and general theory of integration that is based on learning Finally, one study reported that integration is fairly easy with small groups of students but difficult with large groups. It was argued that universities and schools of engineering are generally not suitable vehicles for integration unless there are changes in their organization.

8. Introduction

In the 1960's a number of novel degree and organizational structures emerged in Europe. Of special interest to this text was the idea of interdisciplinary institutions that would function around a particular concept. For example, an institute was established for the sociology and politics of work: Its purpose was to establish a theory of work (Heywood, 1973a). The OECD[1] shematized this approach as follows:

- "A single complex, concrete problem
- Disciplines noteworthy for their view points.
  - The variety of their viewpoints.
  - The possibility that the fields overlap.
  - The fact that no single discipline covers the entire problem.
- Different solutions all of which are necessarily incomplete, depending on the viewpoint of each discipline.
  - A synthesis.
  - A single solution."

At the time, this writer described this approach as "transdisciplinary."' He described a course which he ran for undergraduate engineers which linked the behavioral sciences (including economics) and humanities in a common framework. Its purpose was to introduce engineering students to their role in industry and society (Heywood, 1973b). It differed from the OECD definition in that it was not problem-based. This course was broad and introductory. It was designed only to meet the first stage of Whitehead's cycle of rhythm in learning (Whitehead, 1932). The idea of transdisciplinarity has been resurrected by Ertas et al., (2003), who think it is the direction the engineering curriculum will take. Following Kozmetsky (1997), they

---

[1]Organization for Economic and Cultural Development, Paris-An international government organization.

defined transdisciplinary as *"the integrated use of [the] tools, techniques and methods from various disciplines. Such thinking forces one to think, across, beyond and through the academic disciplines to encompass all type of knowledge about an idea, issue, or subjects."* As their paper shows, it leads to structures of the kind illustrated in Section 8.7. They noted that neither textbooks nor university organization made the development of such courses easy. Heywood (1973b) had also found that students used to unitary discipline approaches had difficulty with this kind of study. He also found that publishers resisted publishing interdisciplinary books, because they were not related to specific courses of a traditional type, and it was not until 1989 that he was able to publish an updated version o0f his original notes. Even then he was obliged to omit some of the original content (Heywood, 1989). Dyer and Schmalzel (1998) also reported great difficulty in finding textbooks that were structured around a *just-in-time* approach that would be suitable for projects.

In this context, Squires (1975) remarked that he had *"always felt that there was something vaguely continental about the term interdisciplinarity itself, but it may hide what is a considerable difficulty for people in the Anglo-Saxon world, that such thinking may involve us in habits of thought and concepts which are perhaps more familiar in continental traditions, concepts like totality and unity, which you will find frequently used in the OECD book for example. These are kinds of concepts which, if I may generalise horribly, people here tend to shy away from."*

Twenty years later, an English scientist working at Harvard University, in a letter to *The Times* concerning the ability of Oxford University to change, drew attention to the failure of the university to promote interdisciplinary courses when they were very much part of the American scene.

There has, however, been a long-standing debate about the relationship between academic study and training in industry during the educational programs for engineers. The term integration was used, and the debate was and is about the extent to which academic study and training can be integrated (e.g., Cory and Frostick, 1989; Fink, 2001; Heywood, 1969). In the United Kingdom the debate was originally about the integration that was possible in sandwich (cooperative) courses.

In academic engineering it was argued by some educators that the separation of a program of study into separate subjects in which the applications of science are studied impedes students from solving real-life engineering problems. Such problems draw not only on many dimensions of engineering science but on social studies and the humanities as well. This is widely recognized, and there have been some attempts world-wide, but more so in the United States to develop *transdisciplinary* courses. They are generally referred to as '*integrated*' and are, more often than not, based on the project method. Curriculum models of this kind have been called '*nested*' because they take advantage of natural combinations of knowledge and skill, as for

example, in the study of systems (Fogarty, 1993). Such studies may require teachers to work in teams, as, for example, when the students study in parallel, and not in a sequence. In academia, teamwork is sometimes difficult because teachers are to all intent and purpose "closed systems."

The term *"incorporation"* is sometimes used, and it is not always clear whether this is meant to be integration, or "interdisciplinary" in the sense that two or more subjects are studied independently for the same degree.[2] For example, in a first-year course at West Virginia University, there was an incorporation of computers, math, and design. *"One day per week is devoted to math. Three days a week are project work. Projects are chosen not for their mathematical content, but stress mathematics within each project. The engineering instructor does not replace the mathematics faculty or tutors. Engineers act as experts on the uses of mathematics. Since we feel most successful engineering students study co-operatively we promote group study in mathematics"* (Venable, McConnell and Stiller, 1995). It is probably more appropriate to speak of the incorporation of multi-media (internet, etc.) into courses than integration (Zwyno and Kennedy, 2000). Integration more usually applies to the application of concepts across subject disciplines in the search of a solution to the problem.

In the Universities of Aalborg and Roskilde in Denmark that were created in the 1960s, 50% of the student's time is spent in project work which generates much of the content of the student's learning (see Chapter 9).

Such project work requires considerable skill among its teachers because not only do projects create "webs of knowledge," but such "webs of knowledge" can be created by teachers. Fogarty (1993) gave the example of how the study of invention leads to the study of simple machines in science, to reading and writing about invention, and to practical inventing, which, if done in teams, contributes to the development of social skills. He called this a *"threaded"* curriculum in which "thinking," "study," and "social" skills are interwoven in the different subjects. This type of approach has come to be called "problem-based learning," and it is widely used in medicine and some engineering schools.

Both interdisciplinarity and integration is possible to distinguish subjects (knowledge areas) that are "close" to the subject with which they are to be integrated. Some might argue that their modes of thinking are similar, as for example, in engineering, science and mathematics. Other topics might be "relatively close," as for example, technical writing, whereas other subject areas are "distant," as, for example, English Literature, Ethics, and History. It might also be supposed that from the point of

---

[2]In the United Kingdom it is fairly common practice to take two subjects in a degree program in the humanities. Degrees in science and technology tend to be specialist, thus a degree in which students could study mechanical, electrical and production engineering in the first year at Coventry Polytechnic (now University) was unusual (Tubman, 1988).

view of the students', the integration of "distant" subjects will be more difficult for them, because of their different modes of thought than subjects that are relatively "close."[3]   It seems that the authors of the ASEE White Paper on liberal education take this view since they sought to blur the boundaries between engineering and the subjects commonly classed as liberal (Steneck, Olds, and Neeley, 2002). There might, however, be a danger that students may not realize the differences in approach of two subjects if they are integrated, as for example in ethics when related to engineering design.[4] Such are the problems involved in the transfer of learning.

LaPlaca, Newstetter and Yognathan (2001) provided an excellent example of the problem of trying to reconcile two distant intellectual disciplines in biomedical engineering thus, students *"need the modelling and quantitative skills of traditional engineers, but they also need the systems understanding representative of a more biological approach. In short, they need to be conversant with two intellectual traditions that are in some ways at odds with one another. Engineering seeks to analyze the world in order to set constraints and design while the life sciences work from hypotheses towards explanatory accounts of phenomena. Reconciling these two disparate practices requires cognitive flexibility and true interdisciplinary thinking."*

Similarly, Doom et al., (2003) pointed out the difficulties inherent in programs for bioinformatics. Where students hold degrees in either biology or computer science, they are likely to be required to take remedial studies in the area in which they did not qualify before they can undertake post-graduate work in bioinformatics. This can extend their studies by at least two years. The overall preparation for a masters degree then becomes of the order eight years. As an alternative, Doom and his colleagues proposed that biology and computer science be integrated into a four-year undergraduate program so that students become prepared for immediate entry to a Masters program.[5] In similar vein, Pinciroli, Masseroli and Tognola (2003) discuss programs at diploma and degree level in Medical Informatics and Telemedicine at Milan Polytechnic. In the sections that follow, developments and practice in integration will be discussed.

8.1. The Origins and Scope of Integrated Studies

There is little doubt that developments in technology have been the imperative for changes in attitude to integration. Finniston, Duggan, and Bement

(1989) writing of the experience in the United Kingdom said that *"the term 'integrated engineering' is not new and usually refers to those aspects which are considered interdisciplinary."* The Engineering Council (1988) had illustrated proposals for an integrated degree program. Because of the advent of computers and all that has come with them traditional engineering courses have had to become *"more broad based and interdisciplinary."* The introduction *of mechatronics* is a case in point. New technology often requires substantial change in the curriculum that involves some form of integration.[6] For example, Pour (2000), reminds us that in a rapidly changing technology, software systems are no longer built from scratch. Now, reusable software components are used as the building blocks of new component-based enterprise software systems. The changeover to new systems meets obstructions commonly found in the introduction of innovation in industry, for this reason, software engineers need a new set of skills, and the curriculum needs to reflect these needs. This it could do by integrating component-based enterprise software engineering into the software and information engineering curriculum.

Golshani, Panchanathan, and Friesen (2000) have argued the case for a curriculum in information engineering because students are not exposed to *'the basics and the complete picture of this important field.'* Electrical engineers and computer scientists as well as persons in management only get exposed to the particular parts of the theory that their realm of study is focused on. For example, computer scientists consider data processing and electrical engineers look at information from the perspective of coding.[7]

At the University of Lancaster a four-year degree in mechatronics was implemented which had the objective of providing the student *"with the intellectual tools necessary for an integrated approach to the design of real systems."* The broad-based interdisciplinary foundation which is characteristic of the Lancaster engineering curriculum was followed in the third and fourth years by specialism in mechatronics. Within the course a series of design exercises of about half a term (5 weeks) in length had to be completed (Dorey, Bradley, and Dawson, 1989). Similarly, in the Synthesis Coalition in the United States an attempt has been made to infuse mechatronics material into all four years of engineering study (Auslander and Jenison, 1995). In the EXSEL coalition a primary objective is the integration of engineering design into the curriculum (Regan and Miderman, 1995). Some fields such as nanotechnology, it

---

[3]At the University of Lancaster humanities students were required to take a minor course in science for art students. This was called the distant minor.

[4] I appreciate that this is contentious particularly when questions of the kind put by Kitto (2001) in response to design projects on flashlights. Are considered. They were,. *"What are the ethical considerations involved in selling a disposal flashlight with batteries that should not be thrown in the waste stream? What are the ethical issues involved in producing a low cost flashlight that does not meet the design intent? What choices do designers have to consider when producing a flashlight for a specific target audience?"*

[5]Full details of the program are given in the text.

[6]For a recent description of an interdisciplinary course in mechatronics see Shooter and McNeil (2002). This course is taught via-team work, and the students worked in interdisciplinary groups. In addition to engaging in meaningful discussion, they also acted as teachers by preparing lectures and exercises in their topics for students in the other disciplines.

[7]This particular paper illustrated the value of concept mapping in curriculum design, as did a paper on integrating knowledge across the engineering curriculum by Atman, Turns, and Mannering (1999 see Chapter 4).

is argued, are inherently interdisciplinary (Hersam, Luna, and Light, 2004).

Apart from integration between traditional engineering subjects, there are reports of the integration of engineering subjects with, for example, economics (Thuessen et al., 1992); English (Roedel et al., 1995, 1997); environmental education (van Zeeland, Krol, and Greenfield, 1990); ethics (Acharya, David, and Weil, 1995; Kitto, 2001); humanities and social sciences (Schumacher, Gabrielle, and Newcomer, 1995; O'Neal and Riddle, 1995); mathematics (Demel et al., 1994); and writing and communication (Ludlow and Schulz,1994; Hendricks and Pappas, 1996; Walker, 2000).

In the United Kingdom, The Engineering Council in pursuit of a generalist engineer proposed an integrated degree program, and a number of pilot studies were initiated (Levy, 1990). In the engineering coalitions supported by the National Science Foundation in the United States, much attention has been paid to the restructuring of first-year curricula, and this has involved the design of integrated programs (Al-Holou et al., 1998[8]).

Fink et al., (2000) distinguished between four approaches to the integration of science and mathematics in the curriculum. The first might be termed the traditional mode where integration is by chance. It is taught within the disciplines with little regard to application. The other end of the spectrum is where students learn chemistry, physics, and math in super courses in the context of meaningful application. They pointed out that for such courses to be effective, the institution has to make a considerable investment in resources, and a considerable (they said *"tremendous"*) effort has to be made to sustain the effort. They advocated an *"in-between" model in which there is some bridging of courses through work on common projects."* Fink and his colleagues regarded this approach as a first step. They proposed that this model could, with the aid of IT, provide *just in time* modules so that when the students are in interdisciplinary projects and require certain knowledge and skills in mathematics and science, they can draw on a self-contained module that includes the appropriate theory and background. They noted that this has been done in some courses, and the cited work by Kolar and Sabatini (1996) and Tien (1992) [see also Dyer and Schmalzel, (1998); and Spasov (2000) for other examples]. It had not been done across the whole civil engineering curriculum as they intended, although Spasov's curriculum was clearly an exception to this rule.

Froyd and Rogers (1997) argued that an integrated knowledge base is necessary because *"chasms between the disciplines are caused by differences in notation, terminology and emphasis. These chasms encourage students to perceive topics as isolated compartments. As a result, they place new instances of the same concept in different boxes with different names. Increased effectiveness and efficiency in the learning and teaching processes require the faculty help students (1) bridge gaps between disciplines and (2) build an interdisciplinary mindset."*[9]

And recent publications take interdisciplinarity to be a *sine qua non* of course design in the future (Evans, Goodnick, and Roedel, 2003).

Few writers refer to the educational (learning) benefits of such courses in educational terms. However, Young (1997) pointed out, with respect to an integrated systems and control laboratory, that *"it enables students to be exposed to a wide variety of applications and forces them to apply their knowledge in different ways, learning to make use of the tools of different disciplines. Bloom's well known taxonomy of educational objectives suggests that we need to push students' understanding beyond simply learning and applying facts, to enable them to combine ideas and critical judgements. The ability to evaluate evidence and use it to make sound judgements is also viewed as a sign of maturity in the Perry model of intellectual development often used in engineering. One of our goals is to help develop this type of critical thinking, and many educators believe that active learning via a properly designed laboratory is an excellent vehicle for doing just that."* Cowan (1998), described how in the civil engineering program at Heriot Watt University, three hours per week were time tabled for first-year students to undertake Interdisciplinary Studies. He recorded that this course, *"set out unashamedly to develop abilities which really matter in studies in higher education, and in professional life. Roughly speaking, the first term of the three-term course concentrated mainly on communication in the broadest sense of that word, including the abilities of listening, empathizing with feeling, and so on. The second term concentrated mainly on problem solving, again in the most liberal sense of that title. And the third dwelt on the relevant aspects of interpersonal skills, since much of the first course program in my department depended on a wide range of group activities and project work"* (pp. 12 and 13).

"A powerful component in the learning and teaching situation which had been set up for this course was the weekly writing and submitting for comment of what we called "learning journals." The purpose of the journal was to require the students to carefully think about the answer to some such question as "What have I learned about learning or thought about thinking, as a result of these IDS activities, which should make me more effective next week than I was last week?" Students were encouraged, if they so wished, to rephrase that question, to define "effective" in their own terms, and to focus their reflective journal writing-all as they found most useful."

Cowan went on to give a powerful illustration of the effect that these journals could have in developing reflective thinking. This work was begun before either

---

[8]This is a substantial description that highlights the differences between approaches to integration. It contains an extensive bibliography. Most recently, Olds and Miller (2004) have reported on a first-year integrated curriculum at the Colorado School of Mines.

[9]This paper carries a substantial bibliography.

Schön or Kolb had published their ideas although in his book Cowan related it to their theories. Cowan was strongly influenced by the need to understand how we learn.

Similarly, Staats and Blum (1999) described a scheme that attempted to incorporate recent research from cognitive psychology into their engineering course. It had the intention of improving the rate of retention and to help students with their cognitive skill development in computer science. In the same way as Fordyce obtained schema from his students (Chapter 4), they argued that students should be trained to become aware of their own mental models and become aware of the potential for analogical transfer. These mental activities are commonly referred to as metacognition. The intention was to introduce all students to this concept in their freshman year through a University experience in which every student in the introductory computer science course would be enrolled. *"Within this course we will introduce the notions of metacognition and give the first assessment inventory*[10] *Students will be encouraged to 'log' their thinking processes as the semester progresses. These thinking logs will be directed by scripted lead-ins, designed to promote analysis, application, synthesis and evaluation."* In order to develop skill in analogical transfer, the students will be helped to map and to see the abstract principles rather than the procedural similarities that bind a problem together. There are many similarities between this paper and the work of Atman and her colleagues previously mentioned in Chapter 4 (Atman, Turns, and Mannering, 1999). Based on an understanding of how experts think, it seeks to show how certain types of intervention throughout an engineering course can lead to an integrated understanding of an engineering discipline.

This is not to say that engineering educators are not trying to get first-year students to think as engineers. Baillie (1998), who surveyed over 70 institutions in 12 countries, reported that they are. The *"most common approach is to develop a new first year introductory subject to aid orientation as well as to help students learn how to learn and think like an engineer."*[11] But few of the studies reported illustrate the comprehensive awareness of the contribution that psychology can make that Staats and Blum showed.

8.2. The Overloaded Curriculum and the Explosion of Knowledge

There is no doubt that the explosion of knowledge and the time restraint of the curriculum have been a major cause of change. Ever increasing demands are being made on the curricula's that, as we have seen, inevitably are to be developed from a new philosophy. Because the traditional curriculum could not be further stretched, Fromm and Quinn (1989) felt that an entirely new approach was needed. So they proposed to

experiment with a new type of curriculum and received a substantial grant for this work from the National Science Foundation. This curriculum became known as the E4 Drexel Curriculum. It focused on the lower division. Newdick (1994) described the aims of this curriculum as follows:

- *"To provide integrated synchronised and relevant engineering competencies and knowledge.*
- *To develop oral and written personal communication skills.*
- *To emphasis the importance of experimental methods.*
- *To emphasize the use of the computer as a flexible, powerful, professional and intellectual tool.*
- *To instil a culture for life long learning"*

These aims were translated into a new course structure comprising:
1) *"fundamentals of engineering.*
2) *the mathematical and scientific foundations of engineering.*
3) *the engineering laboratory.*
4) *the personal and professional enrichment program".*

These components integrated 25 separate courses that were in the traditional program.[12] A key feature of the program was the provision of three state-of-the-art engineering laboratories in which the students could satisfy their curiosity and *"have fun doing experiments, it also serves to introduce some basic principles common to all experimentation."* In the American context this brought engineering to the students from the beginning of the course, and as research in the United Kingdom has shown, students want to have the experience of being engineers, and often they have found this in laboratory work (e.g. Lee, 1969).

The program was evaluated over a six-year period. The E4 students were found to have, in general, higher grade point averages than the control group and to have better rates of progress and retention. And as if to confirm Lee (1969), *"perhaps most importantly, many indicated in their written commentaries that they had begun to sense that the practice of the engineering profession would be personally exciting, rewarding and enjoyable."* (Al-Holou et al., 1998).

New programs of this kind do not necessarily resolve the problem of overload. It is this writer's experience that curriculum-designers all too easily put too much in and have to back track as the evaluation results become known. At Ohio State, the School of engineering was greatly influenced by the E4 curriculum, but they found that the initial pace was found to be too fast. Like the Drexel students the students in this program felt that the hands-on laboratory and design experiences helped them to see the integration within the topics. At the time of writing most of the students had remained in engineering (Demel et al., 1994).

At Morgan State University the value of immersion in engineering right from the first semester

---

[10]This is given in the paper.
[11]This paper carries a substantial bibliography.

---

[12] The paper contains detailed course objectives and descriptions.

seems to have paid off. The grade point average of the pilot group was 0.7 higher than a control group drawn from the pool of students, and the retention rate was 90% after the first year (Oni et al., 1992). (More examples will be given in Chapter 12.)

If a new topic is to be put into the curriculum, something has to give or it has to be integrated in such a way that it does not cause overloading. For example, Daneshavar (1999) argued that optical engineering concepts should be introduced into the engineering curriculum and showed how they could be presented as an integral part of electrical engineering. This was done partly to ensure that new and separate requirements were not loaded into the course, and partly because it could enhance depth and understanding in both fields.[13]

8.3. Women and Minorities Together

Notwithstanding the caveat that women's needs may be different from those of minorities, several of the reported programs focus on minorities and women together ,although there are some reports that focus solely on women.

Reference has already been made to the problem of introducing South African blacks to higher education after the abandonment of Apartheid. This required a substantial change in attitudes of the teachers to the teaching of foundations that would enable students to pursue courses in engineering. Much better known are the problems that minorities and women have experienced in the United States. Within engineering there have been many endeavors to try and solve the problems of these groups, and these necessarily focus on admissions, preparation to study, and the first year (see also Chapter 17).

At the University of Florida (Gainesville), a member of the SUCCEED coalition introduced an interdisciplinary engineering freshman laboratory in order to increase retention among women and minority students. It replaced a lecture program and was intended to achieve these and other goals through *"hands on experience." "The class rotates 14 groups of 20 students each through weekly three hour laboratory sessions in eleven engineering disciplines"* (Hoit and Ohland, 1995). A variety of formats were used. One of these involved three different one-hour experiments in which 12 students worked together on each experiment. The 12 students were divided into four groups. Each group performed a different one to two-hour experiment. During the last hour each group gave a 15-minute presentation on the experiment and results. In another format, a session began with a 20-minute lecture on the theory that was followed by a 40-minute experiment- *"mostly demonstration."* With the aid of computers the students reduced the data and completed laboratory reports. This approach resulted in a substantial increase in the retention of women and minorities when compared with the traditional lecture courses. It was also found that the

course *"did a better job about informing students about the engineering professions different disciplines as well as proving that the course better helped students make career choices."* The course was also used for a summer institute for K-12 teachers.

8.3.1. Women Only

At a more general level the point has been made that major technology companies who produce artifacts for the home and family do not employ female technologists. Morgan and Martinez (2000) of Texas A and M University described an intervention in the Foundations of Engineering that supported an initiative by the Institute of Women in Technology. It had as its intention the realization of ideas generated by and for women industry through cooperative efforts between students and industries. The 1999 enrolment in this section of the course included 34 female students out of a total of 52. *"The biggest difference between this class and the standard freshman entering class are the class activities and projects which focus on ideas for technologies that will be useful to women and families in the future."* The course was supported by a specific classroom, which was developed with aid from industry.

The students were asked to complete a self-assessment schedule to show whether or not specific skills had improved. The results confirmed the axiom that team projects improve skills in teamwork. More generally it was possible to conclude that the theme of women, families and technology produced a high level of motivation. *"Eventually, the student teams are intended to collaborate with students from other courses, both technical and non-technical, and at all levels. The result of this multi-level interdisciplinary interaction will be the design or implementation of idea(s) generated by the (separate) workshop"* (Morgan and Martinez, 2000).

As we shall see in the next section women can also be helped through mathematics and writing courses.

8.4. Writing Across the Curriculum, and Communication

In the United States there is a continuous flow of papers about the teaching of writing to engineers.[14] This is in contrast to the United Kingdom where it is assumed that students who matriculate to university are capable of writing in spite of much evidence to the contrary (Hewitt, 1967) and a continual flow of anecdotal evidence.[15] In the United States there is still concern that many engineering teachers are resistant to this need, and the case for writing has to be put at regular intervals.

Wheeler and McDonald (2000) began their argument for the teaching of writing, not as is often the case, with the view that engineers have to learn to write reports for different audiences as that is part of their job. Rather, they came at it from the perspective that it is

---

[13]From the examples of analogies that were given, it seems clear that the analogies should reinforce concept learning.

[14] Ford and Riley (2003) have provided a brief review of trends in the United States.

[15]Hewitt suggested on the basis of a substantial investigation that many students in the science area would fail the O level examination English taken at the age of 16.

through writing that skill in reflective practice can be developed. Students should write to learn. Put in another way by chemical engineers at the University of North Dakota, *"clear writing indicates clear thinking"* (Ludlow and Schulz, 1994). A similar view was put forward by Newcomer, Kitto, and Sylvester (2003). They described how meaningful writing assignments within technical courses could help students better understand technical materials, in addition to helping them to become more critical, and develop their writing skills.[16] The American White paper on Liberal Education in Engineering makes clear that it believes liberal education can make a major contribution to the development of critical thought, and writing is considered to be an important component of that education (Steneck, Olds, and Neeley, 2002).

It has been argued in the United States where females do less well in mathematics in college than males, that this is primarily a function of behaviors, beliefs and attitudes in the classroom. This places an obligation on teachers to adopt attitudes that are more female friendly. One research at Florida Miami-Dade Community College cited by Austin and Edwards (2001) showed that female-friendly teaching methods helped students of both genders. Austin and Edwards (2001) went further and argued that females would be helped in mathematics if they undertook transactional writing in that subject. This method has many similarities with protocols. *"Students, through written language, record their understanding of mathematical concepts, processes and applications. It is the kind of writing used in summaries and note taking"* (Austin and Edwards, 2001). Transformational writing is intended to be read by the members of an audience. In contrast, in the mathematics classroom, it is usually the teacher too whom a communication is addressed, whereas it could also be directed to that person's peers. It is a commentary on the learning process, and *"invites the students to see themselves as mathematicians."*[17] According to Austin and Edwards (citing other research), females who learn in this way are less prone to "math anxiety." The strong student is given the chance to be creative, and any student can vent her/his frustration.

In a substantial study that endeavored to eliminate the Hawthorne effect that might arise from novelty, Austin and Edwards concluded that writing does help engender a positive attitude toward mathematics among both males and females, and that female writers performed significantly better than non-writing females. The results suggested that writing helps females, and first time students. Those who persisted continued to pass in mathematics. As important as the case is for using writing to learn, it is equally important that engineers are able to communicate both orally and in writing. In addition to the oft cited figure that engineers spend up to 50% of their time in written or oral communication, recruiters stipulate that graduates should have communication skills (Baren,

1993). One consequence is that the need to develop communication skills is now being taken more seriously by engineering educators. One substantial response to this problem has been the creation of an engineering minor in communication and performance at the University of Tennessee, Knoxville. The designers of this course began by identifying gaps in the competencies required by engineering graduates. Fourteen competencies were derived, and seven of these were performance skills. *"These skills allow them to use their technical abilities as part of a team, to understand conflict as a means for discussion instead of an angry confrontation, and to respect difference as a creative opportunity rather than an obstacle"* (Seat, Parsons, and Poppen, 1999). The authors made the point that it is important to understand the cognitive style of engineers. This is because it is their dispositions that make it difficult for them to work with people in situations where outcomes are not easy to predict. As problem-solvers they are used to predicting outcomes that are correct. They look for solutions with mathematics, and not with the balancing of human behavior in interpersonal situations. Furthermore, if they are highly competitive, as is often the case, this disposition is likely to impede their performance in teams. If they are to behave effectively in teams, they will have to learn both intrapersonal and interpersonal skills, as well as how individuals and organizations interact.

A similar philosophy backed the Enterprise in Higher Education Initiative in the United Kingdom (see Chapter 2). However, the organizers wanted personal transferable skill development to take place within subjects and not through bolt-on extras. A strong case was made against this view but it prevailed (Heywood, 1994). Had the alternative won, then courses similar to those being developed at Knoxville would probably have met the criterion. At Knoxville the students had to take five courses. They were

- Facilitation of technical teams
- Facilitation of technical performance.
- Capstone practicum (supervised social service or technical discipline practicum)
- Two theoretical courses from social psychology; organizational psychology; principles of supervision; communication and conflict, and organizational communication.

The emphasis in the reported studies is very much on technical writing. Some universities emphasize writing across the curriculum, and others emphasize real-world workplace communication (Walker, 2000). Walker, who briefly reviewed these developments, proposed that writing centers should be located in Colleges of Engineering or Engineering Departments. She described the work of one that was based in an electrical and computing science department. This center had as its objectives the preparation of students to write well in upper-level courses, and to provide foundational writing strategies that students could use in the workplace. Group and individual consultations were provided as well as specific courses.

---

[16]Examples are given for an introduction to materials course, fluid power, and manufacturing automation and robotics.

[17]Which is how Bruner sees the role of education.

The pedagogical approach was based on genre theory. It follows from genre theory that each piece of writing is situated in time with objectives that have to meet the needs of a specific audience. Thus, students have to become familiar with different genre, and more particularly those in use in the engineering workplace. Consequently a variety of strategies are used to help students write laboratory reports. One, in particular, is of interest because it helped instructors to assess student understanding. It is to ask students to write a report for students in the semester behind. As Walker pointed out this is quite a different exercise (and more difficult), than writing a report for the instructor. It requires that students establish the needs of the audience, and this entails understanding the knowledge base of the audience, as well as the level of detail required. It means that the students have to learn to ask appropriate questions.

The goal of preparing students for writing and communication pervades most papers, but the perspectives that drive programs differ widely. At Virginia Polytechnic Institute, Hendricks and Pappas (1996) took the view that resistance to English among engineering students was as much due to attitude as it was to anything else. In support of this argument they drew attention to the fact that engineering students had higher verbal scores on the SAT than other entering students to the university. Therefore, the first task was to convince students that they had to develop a *"professionl persona" "a conscious communicative, and ethical approach to everyday professional behavior and collegial relationships in the workplace".* Their concept of a *professional persona* incorporated all the concepts of engineering described by Davis (1992, 1993) and the SCANS Report (1992). In a detailed evaluation that included the use of both self-assessment, and a longitudinal study of writing portfolios, they recorded that *"our students are now convinced that their chance of having a successful and stimulating career are as much related to their ability to communicate the results of their work as to their ability to perform that same work."*

In general the writing required of students is task, oriented and directed toward engineering activities. Students are not introduced to creative writing in a more general sense. However, there are strong arguments for a broader approach because engineers are often accused of having a narrow outlook. Since there is a relation between effective and creative writing and breadth of reading, and therefore the aims of liberal education, consideration ought to be given to this issue. That might lead to a revision of the concept of *professional persona*. (The reader may like to read the first three paragraphs of Section 8.9 at this point).

8.5. Humanities Across the Curriculum

Two of the approaches to liberal education in engineering that were recommended in the American White Paper were through either integrated or interdisciplinary study (Steneck, Olds, and Neeley, 2002). In that paper the term humanities included ethics. As was shown in Chapter 3, most of the literature referred to

ethics. The occasional paper referred to the humanities, and there were also occasional papers on the history of technology. This suggests that engineering students are not encouraged to follow programs that truly mirror the humanities, although the White Paper makes clear that this should not be the case. Insofar as ethics is concerned, the direction in the United States as seen from the literature seems to be toward the integration of the ethical material within engineering programs although there remain separate courses in ethics.

In Britain during the 1950s and 1960s it was considered that engineering students in the universities, because they were in a university, received a liberal education. In contrast students in technical colleges pursuing roughly identical courses were thought to be in need of compulsory liberal studies. Consequently a wide variety of courses were offered to cover the three hour weekly period required for such studies (Davies, 1965).

In 1970 the Council of Engineering Institutions introduced a compulsory subject in their degree level examination for Chartered Engineers with the title the Engineer and Society (CEI, 1966a; 1966b). A number of universities offered, in US parlance, courses of two or three credits' in this area. At the University of Liverpool, for example, a course was offered by a Division of Industrial Studies in the Faculty of Engineering Science that was intended to gain exemption from the Engineer and Society requirement of the Institution. This course embraced studies that were close to and distant from engineering. Units included aspects of running a manufacturing enterprise, as well as aspects of the history of technology, industrial relations, personnel management, economics, and organizational behavior. At Imperial College the problems of developing nations were included in its program (Goodlad, 1970).

Among the books that were recommended one by Armytage, *"A Social History of Engineering,"* received high commendation.[18] Many distinguished engineers talked about the value of students learning the history of engineering. However, there is no doubt that many of them took a naïve view of technological history. Bissell and Bennett (1997) distinguished between two such naïve approaches. The first approach they call the 'internalist.' Bissell and Bennett wrote that it tends *"to present an over simplified 'master narrative' of historical development,"* [which] *"can only be counter productive to the student engineer who will need to deal with complex socio-technological relationships in later professional life."* It tends to be linear. The other approach is often "triumph list" in which *"the progress of technology from early times to its present magnificence is presented from the standpoint of the present omitting any*

---

[18] A list of books that were typically used in such courses will be found in Heywood, (1971, pp. 103-109). For details of research and debate in this area see *ibid* pp. 80-82. Much of the research was on student attitudes. For details of the role of the Council of Engineering Institutions and its examination see *ibid* pp. 33-35. The Engineer in Society examination would cover such topics as professional practice, structure, finance, and economics of industry, industrial administration, and sociology.

false starts, alternative traditions, or rich contexts." (Bissell and Bennett, 1997).

Understanding the complexity of the interaction between society and technology has the possibility of transfer to real situations that are likely to face the student as professional engineer, and this is a merit of teaching history in the engineering curriculum. Thus, Bissell and Bennett, following Kuhn (1970), argued that history could give the engineering student

- *"A view of new things in old places.*
- *An insight into the nature of technological change.*
- *Illustrations of the complex relationship between technology and society.*
- *Valuable novel perspective of the subject matter for both learner and teacher."*

A major issue is whether the history of technology should be taught as a separate course or integrated into engineering subjects *per se*. There are also questions about the age (level of assessment and course level) at which it should be taught. O'Neal and Riddle (1995), tried to integrate a modified course on the rise of modern science into a first physics course (mechanics). They were able to compare an experimental course with two sections from a course in the rise of modern physics taught by more traditional methods. One of these sections was taught by a lecturer who had also observed the experimental course. The other section was taught by a team of teachers. They suspected that the first teacher had caused his section to be integrated even though this was not one of the goals.

The results of the course questionnaire suggested that the degree of integration was found to be positively related to student commitment and interest. They also felt that because the teacher of the experimental group had received awards for good teaching that his attributes contributed to the success of the course. They suggested that in such courses the instructor should consider the integration of the material to be of paramount importance. This is consistent with other reports and, it seems, is a general principle of integration. They also concluded that while team teaching helped integrate the material it was expensive, and that a good teacher could have the same effect. Perhaps their most important comment was that, *"in order to sustain the integration in a humanities course, a change in the culture of the university is required. The incongruity within a university curriculum is a result of the organization of the faculty into separate departments of specialists. Such an organization promotes the depth, but not the breadth required for curriculum integration."*

A half-way approach to integrating the humanities was developed at Renesselaer Polytechnic Institute (Schumacher, Gabriele, and Newcomer, 1995). They invented the idea of a "companion course." This course ran in parallel with the engineering design course. The companion course picked up themes that arose in the design course on a day-to-day basis. At the beginning of the semester the students were provided with three articles. These considered the history of an everyday object. This activity might be described as a historical form of reverse engineering (see Chapter 12). Of a cup of coffee they wrote, *"we learned about how the coffee beans were grown in South America and who grew them. We learned about the materials of the ship that brought the beans to North America and who mined the metal ores. We learned about who pumped the oil for heating the offices of the executives who ran the coffee business."* In the context of the *WorldWatch* magazine, *"environmental concerns drove the reverse engineering, the question of social justice arose as well."* The engineering design course included a period for reverse engineering in one of the semesters. One of the artifacts considered in this phase was a Troy-Bilt mulching self-propelled lawn mower. The effect of the *WorldWatch* discussion was that *"in our search for alternative material for the lawn mower, it is possible to pick materials that are technically satisfactory as well as produced in a socially just way-hence, the socially just lawn mower?"*

Perhaps the most interesting effort to integrate the training of engineers with social science and philosophy has been at the University of Twente in the Netherlands. Founded in 1964, it had the specific objective of training engineers for a changing society. Jelsma and Woudstra (1997) charted the development of the program from its inception to 1997. For 30 years the university ran (and continues to run) a twin-core program (Ph and S) in engineering, social sciences, business and public administration, and applied education. A bridging component links these two core curricula which are provided by a School of Philosophy and Social Science. The bridging curriculum included linguistics, history, science and society, and ergonomics; 12.5% of the total time is devoted to study in the area of philosophy and social science throughout the four years of the course.

During the first year an 80-contact-hour introductory interdisciplinary course is provided. This is followed by a disciplinary course of 100-contact-hour duration. The third year includes a theme course, and one or two follow-up courses that extend into the fourth year.

From 1983, the School of Philosophy and Social Sciences began its own degree (PhSTS) in the philosophy of science, technology, and society. It aimed *"to integrate an engineering study on the one hand, and philosophy, technology dynamics, and the history of science on the other hand."* In this program the whole of the first year is devoted to engineering. During the next three years only 30% of the time is devoted to engineering. The program has as its aims:

- *Competence for systematic reflection about technological developments.*
- *Understanding of the relevant developments in society.*
- *Capability to communicate with technical experts on scientific, technological and societal developments.*

Jelsma and Woudstra (1997) wrote that: '*philosophical engineers*' as the products of this course are called, are *"expected to be employed in jobs that are at the crossroads of technology and society, that is, in places where engineers must communicate with social, juridical and other experts, like advisory or consultancy jobs on matters of safety, health, environment, automations etc. Other job opportunities are in interdisciplinary research, in product development teams of firms or policy-making"*

The Ph and S programs have been evaluated against a standard student questionnaire since 1991. There have also been evaluations of faculty, along with external evaluations. Among the findings were that while the Ph & S courses were found interesting they did not motivate students, *"they do not raise much goodwill and interest for Ph & S related questions and themes."* This applied especially to the attitudes of first-year students, and this was in spite of satisfactory ratings of teaching. However, the students rated the personal education received from these courses much higher than their contribution to their technical education. The students chose specific courses for their perceived interest and relevance to the technical courses. The university had witnessed a change in student attitudes from the idealism of the 1960s to a situation where there was a shrinking labour market and increasing demands by employers. So the students wanted these courses to improve their career chances.

The attitudes of these students would seem to be similar to those of engineering students in other countries. They do not seem to have a concept of liberal education. As described, the education provided by the University of Twente does not seem to have been very liberal.[19] While it might be argued that if engineers are to take a more active role in society, they need an education that is truly liberal, the expectations of students and staff (for different reasons[20]) are relatively technocratic in their outlook and hardly liberal. Those who are persuaded to assist engineering departments provide a liberal education are faced with an up-hill task (see Haws, 2001). The problems faced by those who advocate a liberal education of this kind seem to be very similar to the problems faced by mathematics educators servicing engineering courses.

The issues surrounding the teaching of ethics, whether in other departments or by teachers of engineering were summarized in Chapter 3. The reader was also referred to the mini-meta analysis of approaches to ethics instruction in engineering described by Haws (2001). However, there remain one or two points that should be developed. First, because of the demand for relevance by both faculty and students, there is support for the case study approach (e.g., Gorman et al., 2000). Such case studies tend to be of large-scale events or of distant events of a kind that are unlikely to involve newly graduating engineers in ethical decisions. Such case studies, while enabling students to review them in the abstract, do not challenge students at the micro-level of personal behavior. They have little relevance to that aim of high education that is to produce a philosophical habit of mind (Newman, 1852, 1949). The focus is on incorporating *"an understanding of how technology affects humane life, society and the biosphere into engineering theory and design in order to ensure a greater compatibility between technology and its contexts"* (Vanderburg and Khan, 1994). In the Drexel E4 approach, it is to *"highlight humanistic concerns about the impact of technology so that students recognize the engineers' obligation to the world we all share"* (Arms, 1994). While an important goal, it is nevertheless a limited goal when placed alongside the breadth of mind that a humanities education is held to give. To be fair, some teachers do use ethical dilemmas and some of these dilemmas relate directly to student behavior (e.g., Angelo and Cross, 1993; Pfatteicher, 2001; see Chapter 3). The same conflict arises as for mathematics. In this case the question is whether participation in ethical cases without some substantial education in ethics is sufficient. To put the matter in another way, should a person resolve an ethical dilemma without understanding the principles (and their justification) on which the decision is based? A program that seems to have gone beyond these parameters is one called "Paradoxes of the Human Condition," which was run at the Colorado School of Mines (Andrews, Mcbride, and Sloan, 1993). The goals of this program were:

1. *"To acquaint the student with several of the deepest riddles of mans' existence through serious and purposeful study of great writings each of which dramatically explores one or more paradoxes as a central theme.*

2. *To develop in the student an awareness of the continuing presence of the paradoxes in his personal and professional life, and an understanding of the imperative for each person to confront such ultimates in finding a modus vivendi for himself.*

3. *To implant the attitudes of reflection and detachment and to promote the development of self-knowledge.*

4. *To create pressure situations for accelerated skill development in analytical reading, written and oral communication, and time management."*

The course *"immerses students in 15 weeks of reading, writing, and dialogue on literary and philosophical classics in the Western tradition."* The course was taught by means of paradoxes, for example, life and death, and freedom and necessity. Although no mention is made of the *Paideia* proposal (Adler, 1983), it would seem to have been developed with the same kind of thinking in mind.

---

[19] The university was conscious of the problem of motivating these students and overcoming the problem of disciplinarity. It was attempting to achieve the latter through case studies, and it is interesting to note that one of them was the microwave oven and gender used in the Rennsaeler course.

[20] Jelsma and Woudstra (1997) described in some detail the vicissitudes of the School of Philosophy and Social Sciences and the conflicts with the engineering departments. Such stories are familiar in American and British education.

8.6. Thematic Integration and Transdisciplinarity

A thematic curriculum is constructed around a set of unifying principles rather than around subjects. Schneck's (2001) paradigm *"addresses the current void between product-oriented skills training,"* which is what he believed engineering education to be, and *"process-oriented holistic training."* His model, which is being evaluated in a prototype course at Virginia Polytechnic Institute and State University, aims to show how engineering education *"can be made more deductive, integrative and process oriented."* The course title is *"Omniology; Integrated approach to Everything."* It is a response to the knowledge explosion. Schneck believed that if engineers can be taught early enough to think generically and globally, then new understandings will be seen as special cases of general conditions. Moreover, the student will be led to understand *"why he or she is learning what in each course, and where, when and how to apply what he or she is learning to the creative expression and solution of problems."* The fundamental proposition on which his paradigm is based relates to the nature of reality. He argued that reality derives from disturbances to systems that are in equilibrium, and that a "feedback/forward" model can be used to describe all the laws of physics. It is based on seven axioms that have seven corresponding theorems. The input to the model is the source of all reality and is potential energy. Thus, *"the axiom of potential asserts that energy is the inherent property that endows anything with the ability to become realized; where, by "realized," we mean "capable of stimulating some anatomical sense organ, and/or, some technological transducer, i.e., made perceptible to some observer".* The corresponding theorem of potential *"declares that potential energy is a property of implicit reality:"capable of being". Correlated with each type of unbalanced disturbance to which an equilibrated state will respond is a corresponding non-measurable intensive potential-an inherent attribute of that equilibrated state that endows it with the ability to respond to that specific disturbance."*

The output of the model is kinetic energy. The observer experiences the output as signals that are dimensions of perception, e.g., time, length, mass, temperature, and electric charge. They are experienced on a continuous scale that ranges from the super-cosmic to the sub-nuclear. This scale allows Schneck to make the case that the specific laws of physics are special cases of the seven axioms and theorems. At the time of writing, Schneck had completed the course once and only qualitative student evaluations were available. Some of their comments are included in his paper. These comments suggested that the course had been well received by the students.

A similar approach is found in a proposal that originated with a distinguished British engineer G. S. Bosworth. He had been Chairman of a Committee that had inquired into the education and training needs of the electrical and mechanical manufacturing industry (Bosworth, 1966). That committee had expressed concern that university courses did not provide a bridge to manufacturing, he also believed that engineers were not sufficiently creative (Bosworth, 1963). His idea was that engineering education should not be a collection of applied science subjects but derived from the nature of what engineering was. In his view it was an activity that was characterized by resources on the one hand and operations on the other. Inspired by this conceptual framework a group of engineers and educators worked out the details of a matrix and demonstrated how case studies could be used to show how engineering problems were solved within the matrix (Heywood et al., 1966). The particular example that showed how the model could be applied was based on earlier work by one of the group on an aircraft ventilating system (Turner, 1958: Figure 8.1). The group claimed that the principles commonly taught in first-year courses could be demonstrated through carefully selected case studies and projects without overloading students, and at the same time ensuring development in the skill of synthesis. The group believed that assessment could be designed to test the skills in *The Taxonomy of Educational Objectives* (Cognitive Domain).

Skates (2003) described how interdisciplinary projects were used at Plymouth University in engineering, but Traylor, Heer, and Fiez (2003) argued that in these cases the students are adapted to the project. They are argeed that this will not necessarily help students integrate knowledge. However, integration will occur if the project is adapted by the students, and this might be achieved by a platform for learning. A platform for learning is defined as a "common unifying object or experience that weaves together the various classes of the curriculum. They argue that if this common platform is used in many classes *"the inter-relationships and interdependencies of the classes are clearly illustrated."* They prefer a learning platform that is hands-on and preferably uses a physical object. They accept that "hands-on" does not necessarily mean a physical relationship, but it is necessary that there is *"intensive interaction between the student and the platform so that the student forms feelings of personal ownership toward the platform."* In this and another paper they describe how a platform for learning based on the design and development of a robot can be developed throughout the four years of the curriculum.

Ertas et al., (2003) suggested that the universal aspects of design and process provide the basis for extracting the common aspects between disciplines, and their model has many similarities with the Heywood et al., matrix. It is not surprising that Ertas and his colleagues should see the project method as the basis for the achievement of interdisciplinarity.

Subsequently, Lewis, another chairman of a committee[21] that had considered aspects of technological education modified and improved the matrix by

---

[21] The East Anglian Regional Council for Further Education. He also took a prominent role in the Electrical and Electronics Manufacturers Joint Education Board (EEMJEB).

Operations/Resources	(a) Energy	(b) Space	© Force	(d) Material	(e) Men
1. Form and properties	Heat; CO2, Effective temperature				
2. Location and acquisition	In wings,.off main power				
3. Measurement			Compressor characteristic;. pressure/flow temperature		
4. Control		Pilots, passengers, stewards, compartments			
5. Transformation and Conversion.	Cooling: heat removal from fluid			Filters in order to remove dust etc.	Number of passengers and crew.
6. Transmission		Recirculated air for heat balance..	Method of regulation.	What has to be recirculated? What has to be lost?	

Figure 8.1 Turner's application of a matrix developed by G. S. Bosworth to the problem of aircraft ventilation (Turner, 1958). Detail is obtained by further expansion of the boxes. For example 3c can show a family tree of compressors. In this way the curriculum can be built up on the basis of problems that may or may not be projects. The insertions in the matrix are given as examples. One field of study will appear in several places. Students could be encouraged to build their own matrix at the beginning of a course and pursue the branches of knowledge into where it leads them.

Operations/Resources	Energy	Force	Space	Materials	Vegetation	Animals	Man/Energy	Man/Ideas
Form and properties	Solar Climactic	Gravity Electro-Magnetic Inertial	Geometry	Solids, gases, liquids, plasma	Tres. Plants.	Mammals, insects		Pholosphy. aesthetics. politics.
Availability (extraction)	Magneto Hydo dynamic			Land, Sea, Fuel,	Food	Extinction	Athletics	Education
Measurement		Units	Astronomy	Geology	Growth		Efficiency of man/machine	Psychology selection
Control (storage)	Hydraulic pump storage		Space research					Sociology management
Conversion	Atomic power			Manufacture	Silage	Cookery	Power-assisted controls	Thought
Transmission	Coal or electricity DC/AC			Transport				Communication language

Figure 8.2. Lewis's adaptation of Bosworth's matrix for determining the elements of an integrated curriculum for an educational institution- in this case for a Regional College (Polytechnic) in the United Kingdom. The original matrix is in Heywood et al., (1966).

expanding the ideas on man. Man becomes a bridging concept between engineering and philosophy and social science. His version for a total college curriculum is shown in Figure 8.2. (Lewis, 1966). He argued that all students entering college would follow a common first session based on considerations of this matrix. The purpose of the course would be to consider what resources there are available to man and the way that he can control and direct them to his benefit.

Matrices such as this may be designed to break down curriculum barriers but with the reduction in specialisation they pose important problems of content and method. Principles have to be stated in such a way that the student understands them and very often, as is the case with mathematics, "its elegance and logic." Heywood (1967), who used the matrix to demonstrate a possible integration of technology and social studies, argued, that insofar as the example was concerned, mathematics is a hidden bridge not merely between engineering and social studies but also with science. Such concepts as probability, uncertainty, correlation, and causality not only help distinguish the different thought structures between subjects but underline similarities.

He illustrated this point by an essay topic that was set for arts (humanities) students studying the principles of physics that stated[22]

"Distinguish between the terms, 'mistake', 'discrepancy', 'uncertainty', 'systematic error', and 'random error' as applied to the testing of a hypothesis. Compare the usefulness of the concept of error as used in physics with that of the errors occurring in the study of your major subject." (Heywood, Montagu Pollock, 1977).

If the integration that is brought about by project work is excluded from this discussion, then very few reports could be found that discussed thematic integration. This suggests that it is difficult to implement and for many would lie outside the bounds of plausibility of what an engineering curriculum is. As Ertas and his colleagues noted, such programs require different course materials and a significantly different relationship between faculty and students than those that pertain in traditional courses. It might be added that often these changes in role are likely to prove difficult for some if not many students. Engineering is still oriented toward the disciplines and total integration is often not perceived as desirable by either staff or students in some cultures, although major breaks with this tradition have been made in first year courses in the United States few are truly transdisciplinary.

8.7. Integrating Skills Across the Curriculum. Ability Led Curricula

During the last 20 years there has been mentioned several times already, a move to encourage institutions to help their students acquire broad generic skills, at times known as personal transferable skills and at other times known as competencies or abilities (see Chapters 1 and 2). It is argued that these skills are transferable and that they may be developed within any subject. It is also argued that if students are to grasp the nature of these skills and their transferability, they have to be shown how they transfer (Saupe, 1961). One way to do this is to integrate them across the curriculum. The best-known model for achieving this goal is probably the ability-led curriculum at Alverno College (Alverno College, 1985[23]). It has received worldwide attention. It is assessment-led in the sense that it stems from the view that assessment can have a major positive effect on learning. More often than not, teachers think of assessment as having a negative effect on student learning and development. The challenge is to devise assessments that cause students to grow intellectually. At Alverno, student assessment-as-learning is *"a process, integral to learning, that involves observation and judgement of each student's performance on the basis of explicit criteria, with resulting feedback to the student."*[24] Of necessity it will be on a continuous basis and involve the student in the development of high-order skill in self-assessment (Loacker, 2000). Of interest to this section is the structure of the curriculum.

It is appropriate here, although it is not a subject for this report, to draw attention to the fact that from time to time it has been advocated that engineering should be made available to nonengineering undergraduates. For example, Ettouney (1994) described how engineering was integrated into the liberal education of all undergraduates at his university. It is easy to imagine how this might be achieved in a curriculum like that offered at Alverno. Five of their intended outcome domains relate to areas that many engineering educators think are inadequately dealt with in the curriculum (see Chapter 17).

The college defines the goals of liberal education in terms of eight expected outcomes. These are:
1.   Communication
2.   Analysis
3.   Problem solving
4.   Valuing in Decision-making
5.   Social Interaction
6.   Global perspectives
7.   Effective Citizenship
8.   Aesthetic responsiveness

---

[22]He suggested a classical text that provided a bridge between the social science and science/engineering was J. Radcliffe-Brown's (1964). *A Natural Science of Society*, The Free Press Glenco. He did not believe that social studies should be restricted to the study of sociology but should use from among them that which was necessary for the study of man. He was unaware of Bruner's MACOS program at the time, and thus with the similarities in philosophy.

[23]The curriculum and how it works are described in Alverno College, (1985) and Loacker (2000). The story of the longitudinal research on this curriculum is in Mentkowski and Associates (2000). It does not contain details of the curriculum and its philosophy.

[24]*"To assess. This term in its origin literally means to sit down beside. In its development it has come to mean using careful judgement based on the kind of close observation that comes from 'sitting down beside'* (Alverno College, 1985).

Originally these were called competencies, but because of its connotation with tasks that are discretely accomplished in specific contexts (i.e. training) the college stopped using the term and instead now calls them abilities. Others have used the term "qualities." In the United Kingdom the term capability has been used to describe such skills, and a Higher Education for Capability Project sought to encourage practitioners and institution to develop such skills (Stephenson and Yorke, 1998). It had many similarities with the Enterprise in Higher Education Initiative. Stephenson (1998) wrote that *"capability can be observed when we see people with justified confidence in their ability to*

- *Take effective and appropriate action.*
- *Explain what they are about.*
- *Live and work effectively with others.*
- *Continue to learn from their experience as individuals and in association with others, in a diverse and changing society."*

These were as much the purposes of the Enterprise in Higher Education Initiative in the United Kingdom as they are of Alverno College. The college wrote that these eight abilities *"represent an integrated combination of multiple components including skills, behaviors knowledge, values, attitudes, motives or dispositions, and self perceptions. For example, to be able to speak effectively one must be able-among countless other things- to relate ideas, project one's voice, have knowledge of what one is talking about, value communication (or someone of something) enough to do a good job, incorporate attitudes, and perceive of oneself as being able to perform."*

Alverno College argued that the curriculum is about developing these abilities and that in order to develop themselves, students must be able to see where they are at in order to be able to progress. Therefore each one of the abilities is comprised of six sequentially organized levels. They are shown in Exhibit 8.1. The other two levels are advanced outcomes that are obtained when they take their major. They are also expressed in generic terms but in practice are worked out in specific contexts. *"For example, the second level of analysis is to make inferences. In an English course, students learn to infer the motivation of characters from careful observation of their behavior. In a psychology internship at a local clinic, they learn to infer the needs of clients in a group therapy situation. In a comprehensive general education assessment that simulates a school board committee, they demonstrate their ability to infer the attitudes of parents from letters that reach the board."*

While the generic abilities apply to all the disciplines, the faculty does not always assess each of the eight abilities in each course rather they try to match the ability and the discipline.[25] The program requires the

design of specific assessments to plot the progress of students along the sequence.

There is no reason why the Alverno model cannot be adapted for use by a college of engineering or a course as Kellar et al., (2000) have shown. Unfortunately, however, they further confuse the terminology of assessment by using the term meta-assessment. Their matrix distinguished between the four years of the curriculum and the performance benchmarks required for each of 5 skills. Their matrix for problem solving in an integrated course is shown in Exhibit 8.2.

The holistic curriculum in chemical engineering at West Virginia University has some of the features of the Alverno model (Shaeiwitz et al.,1994). It defined nine qualities desired of chemical engineering graduates. They believed that these qualities could be imparted by the kind of learning activities to which the students are exposed. Its designers argued that engineering science had to be taught through applications, and for this reason there is an emphasis on real processes and projects that cut across traditional course boundaries. While the curriculum philosophy is similar to Alverno's, it does not mirror the assessment of student outcomes, although there is recognition that student projects *"are also measures of student learning because they illustrate students' ability to use what they have learned in previous semesters as well as the current semester."* The SCANS model curriculum that has been proposed for high schools in the United States is also a good example of a competency-or-ability based assessment-led curriculum.

The SCANS Report (1992) was the work of a commission appointed by the US Secretary of Labor. Its starting position was that *"the time when a high school diploma was a sure ticket to a job is within the memory of workers who have not yet retired: yet in many places today a high school diploma is little more than a certificate of attendance. As a result, employees discount the value of all diplomas, and many students do not work hard in school."* When it wrote this, the Commission had already discovered to its satisfaction what skills and competencies were associated with high-wage jobs. These are shown in Exhibit 8.3. They argued that all Americans should be entitled to multiple opportunities to learn the SCANS know-how well enough to earn a decent living. They argued that every employer in America should create its own strategic vision around the principles of the high-performance workplace. They believed that this task would require *"the reinvention of elementary and secondary education."* The Commission believed that the competencies should be integrated into core subjects such as English and Mathematics, which, theoretically, leaves the integrity of the individual disciplines intact. The example of how the commission thought this might happen is shown in Exhibit 8.4.

The American College Testing Program (ACT) developed a test for assessing the competencies identified by SCANS. It is a test that is intimately related to the curriculum and not independent of it. It offers workplace assessments in reading for information; applied

---

[25] In Heywood, J., *Examining in Second Level Education* (1977) ASTI, Dublin there is a model that shows how the subjects of the school curriculum can contribute to the development of skills like those in The *Taxonomy of Educational Objectives.*

mathematics; listening and writing; teamwork; locating information; applied technology; motivation; observing; and speaking and learning. The assessments are offered at five levels and are criterion referenced. The idea is that jobs should be profiled. In this way the job profile can be compared with the individual's performance profile so that it may be used for selection and diagnosis at work. High schools can use job profiling in consultation with employers to establish the levels of competency that students should have in order for them to obtain jobs.

Individuals are provided with portfolios. The information provided may include self-assessments of the examinee's perspective of workplace skill attainment, and instructor-guided information including grades, project results, training evaluations, or curriculum-embedded activity. It may also include outside examiner data as for example the work keys scores and other pertinent test information. The work keys assessment tests are each of one hour's duration. The results that are sent to the candidate explain the scores obtained and give quite detailed instructions on how that individual might improve his/her scores. The adoption of a SCANS-like curriculum in schools would have implications for the design of third-level curricula both in terms of content and instruction.

8.8. Project Work as a Mechanism for Integration

As indicated, the students at Ohio State saw the project as a means of understanding conceptual linkages between topics. The same was true of the students at Morgan State; here the teachers referred to this method as phenomena-driven. *"A phenomenon here may be defined as an observable or conceptual fact, event, process or circumstance that seeks further analysis. It is frequently an outward sign of the implications of the laws of nature"* (Oni et al., 1992. In the first semester this phenomenon was an electric vehicle. Attempts were made to integrate Physics 1, Chemistry 1, Calculus I and English I around it. In this way engineering was incorporated into a traditional science and mathematics course. The theme of the second semester was designed around the building and construction of a bridge. To achieve these goals within the framework of a traditional course, a core team of six instructors operated in teams. They were grouped in combinations suited to the work to be undertaken by the team. It will be noticed that the integrated course included a general education course. They pointed out that engineering students are required to do what amounts to a double curriculum because of this general education course that was prescribed. Moreover, often students do not see the relevance of such courses to their engineering. They are seen as courses *"to be passed in order to move on to the next phase of a student's academic program"* (Oni, et al., 1992).

Projects in English and Engineering were also included in the integrated introductory course for freshmen developed at Arizona State University (Roedel et al., 1995, 1997). In this part of the course, students learned to organize and develop ideas for both technical and general audiences. Throughout the semester the students kept detailed journals that described (through directed journaling assignments) their reflections on the science and engineering concepts included in the other portions of the class. Written reports were submitted for all engineering projects, including the final examination project. The reports were graded for exposition, style, clarity, and grammar by instructors of English. In addition the students learned the use of rhetorical principles with readings from the philosophy of science, engineering case studies, and so on" (Roedel et al., 1995). Once again failure rates for the course were lower than those typically experienced.

The projects evidently excited the students who also found that they *"revealed the connections between the four areas"*. They found the report writing process challenging and interesting, *"all discovered some of the wonder and excitement that comes naturally from doing creative work"* (Roedel et al., 1997). It is a common experience that project work motivates students and sometimes to the detriment of other studies if such there be (Carter, Heywood, and Kelly, 1986; see section on motivation in Chapter 9). Some courses could not be accomplished without projects. Service learning is a case in point. At Purdue University in the Engineering Projects in Community Service course undergraduates earn academic credit for participation in long-term team projects. A team of eight to fifteen undergraduates worked with a community service agency(ies) and a faculty or industry advisor. *"Each team is vertically-integrated, consisting of a mix of freshmen, sophomores, juniors and seniors and constituted for several years-from initial project definition through final deployment-with students participating for several semesters"*(Oakes et al., 2000). Each student is required to attend a weekly two-hour meeting with the team and a common one-hour lecture.[26] There were 250 students in the program in 1999. Nearly 1000 students had responded to questionnaires issued at the end of each semester since 1996. The most valuable thing that the students considered they had learnt was how to work in teams. Communication skills produced the 2nd highest rating.

An interesting feature of this program is the participation of Liberal Arts students. The instructor's reported that the Liberal Arts students require different communication styles to students from engineering. These tended to be more descriptive whereas the latter tended to want quantitative measures and a *"clearly defined problem to solve"*. The instructors pointed out that these *"two stereotypes are roadblocks for team unity"*. One consequence was that a liberal arts student who joins a group of engineers might have felt, and perhaps be, isolated. While the liberal arts student might have been better at communicating with the customer they were often relegated to clerical positions. The same kind of problem existed in Scottish companies between

---

[26]Full details of work requirements, credits, etc., and details of the project process are given in the paper.

Ability level. Domain 1	**Develop communication ability (effectively send and respond to communications for varied audiences and purposes)**
	Identify one's own strengths and weaknesses as a communicator.
Level 1.	Show analytic approach to effective communicating.
Level 2.	Communicate effectively.
Level 3.	Communicate effectively making relationships out of explicit frameworks from at least three major areas of knowledge.
Level 4	Communicate effectively with application of communication theory.
Level 5	Communicate with habitual effectiveness and application of theory, through coordinated use of different media that represents contemporary technological advancement in the communication field.
Level 6.	**These to be developed in writing, speaking, listening, using media quantified data, and the computer.**
Domain 2.	**Develop analytical capabilities.**
Level 1.	Show observational skills.
Level 2.	Draw reasonable inferences from observations.
Level 3.	Perceive and make relationships.
Level 4.	Analyse structure and organization.
Level 5.	Establish ability to employ frameworks from area of concentration or support area discipline in order to analyse.
Level 6.	Master ability to employ independently the frameworks from area of concentration or support area discipline in order to analyze.
Domain 3	**Develop workable problem solving skill.**
Level 1.	Identify the process, assumptions and limitations in problem solving approaches.
Level 2.	Recognize, analyze, and state a problem to be solved.
Level 3.	Apply a problem solving process to a problem.
Level 4.	Compare processes and evaluate own approach in solving problems.
Level 5.	Design and implement a process for resolving a problem which requires collaboration with others.
Level 6.	Demonstrate facility in solving problems in a variety of situations.
Domain 4.	**Develop facility in making value judgments and independent decisions.**
Level 1.	Identify own values.
Level 2.	Infer and analyse values in artistic and humanistic works.
Level 3.	Relate values to scientific and technological developments.
Level 4.	Engage in valuing in decision making in multiple contexts.
Level 5.	Analyse and formulate the value foundation/ framework of a specific area of knowledge, in its theory and practice.
Level 6.	Apply own theory of value and the value foundation of an area of knowledge in a professional context.
Domain 5	**Develop facility for social interaction**
Level 1.	Identify own interaction behaviors utilized in a group problem solving situation.
Level 2.	Analyse behavior of others within two theoretical frameworks.
Level 3	Evaluate behavior of self within two theoretical frameworks.
Level 4.	Demonstrate effective social interaction behavior in a variety of situations and circumstance.
Level 5.	Demonstrate effective interpersonal and intergroup behaviors in cross-cultural interactions.
Level 6.	Facilitate effective interpersonal and intergroup relationships in one's professional situation.
Domain 6	**Develop responsibility for the environment.**
Level 1.	Perceive and describe the complex relationships within the environment.
Level 2.	Observe and explain how the behavior of individuals and groups have an impact on the environment.
Level 3.	Observe and explain how the environment has an impact on the behavior of individuals and groups.
Level 4.	Respond holistically to environmental issues and evaluate the responses of others.
Level 5.	Respond holistically to environmental problems and independently develop responsible alternative solutions.
Level 6.	Select and rigorously support a responsible solution to an environmental problem with an implementation strategy.
Domain 7	**Develop awareness and understanding of the world in which the individual lives.**
Level 1.	Demonstrate, awareness, perception, and knowledge of observable events in the contemporary world.
Level 2.	Analyze contemporary events in their historical context.
Level 3.	Analyze interrelationships of contemporary events and conditions.
Level 4.	Demonstrate understanding of the world as a global unit for analyzing the impact of events of one society upon another.
Level 5.	Demonstrate understanding of professional responsibility in the contemporary world.
Level 6.	Take personal position regarding implications of contemporary events.
Domain 8	**Develop aesthetic responsibility to the arts.**
Level 1.	Express response to selected arts in terms of their formal elements and personal background.
Level 2.	Distinguish among artistic form in terms of their elements and personal response to selected art works.
Level 3.	Relate artistic works to the contexts in which they emerge.
Level 4.	Make and defend judgments about the quality of selected artistic expressions.
Level 5.	Choose and discuss artistic works which reflect personal vision of what it means to be human.
Level 6.	Demonstrate the impact of the arts on your life to this point and project their role in your personal future.

Exhibit 8.1. The eight Alverno abilities and their sub-levels. (Reproduced with permission of Alverno College from Heywood 1989).

ABET Criteria 2000				
Behavioral objectives	Freshman	Sophomore	Junior	Senior
Problem definition	Given scenario identify general problem statement.	Open-ended scenario. To be able to identify problem statement.	Work with client to identify problem statement.	Work with client messy data to identify problem statement.
Identify constraints and alternatives	Identify some alternatives.	Identify complete set of alternative.	Identify alternatives and set of constraints.	Be able to qualify alternatives.
Data collection and analysis	Collect data and analyze given techniques	Select appropriate analysis methods for data.	Given problem collect data and analyze.	Determine appropriate methods for and collect and analyze data
Solution/evaluation	Identify a solution.	Identify several solutions.	Identify solutions and evaluate.	Qualify solutions by ethical and social impact.
Implementation	Build small design projects.	Paper implement for complex designs.	Implementation criteria for client.	Work with client to implement solution.

Exhibit 8.2. The performance rubric for ABET 2000 criteria- problem solving in an integrated course at the University of Pittsburgh (Kellar et al., 2000). (Reproduced with permission of *IEEE, Proceedings in Education Conference*.)

Work place Competencies	Effective workers can productively use the following:
1. Resources	They know how to allocate time, money, materials, space and staff.
2. Interpersonal skills	They can work in teams, teach others, serve customers, lead, negotiate and work well with people from culturally diverse backgrounds.
3. Information	They can acquire and evaluate data, organize and maintain files, interpret and communicate, and use computers to process information.
4. Systems	They understand social, organizational, and technological systems; they can monitor and correct performance, and they can design or improve systems.
5. Technology	They can select equipment and tools, apply technology to specific tasks and maintain and troubleshoot equipment.
Foundation Skills	**Competent workers in a high performance workplace need the following:**
1 Basic skills	Reading, writing, arithmetic and mathematics, speaking and listening.
2. Thinking skills	The ability to learn, to reason, to think creatively, to make decisions, and to solve problems.
3. Personal qualities	Individual responsibility, self-esteem and self-management, sociability and integrity.

Exhibit 8.3. The SCANS competencies.

Competency	English/Writing	Mathematics	Science	Social Studies/Geography	History
Resources	Write a proposal for an after-school career lecture series that schedules speakers, coordinates audio-visual aids, and estimates costs.	Develop a monthly family budget, taking into account family expenses and revenues using information from the budget plan. Schedule a vacation trip that stays within the resources	Plan the material and time requirements for a chemistry experiment to be performed over a two-day period that demonstrates a natural growth process in terms of resource needs.	Design a chart of resource needs for a community of African Zulus. Analyze why three major cities grew to their current size.	Study the Vietnam War researching and orally presenting findings on the timing and logistics of transporting materials and troops to Vietnam and on the impact of the war on the Federal budget.
Interpersonal	Discus the pros and cons of the argument that Shakespeare's *Merchant of Venice* is a 'racist' play and should be banned from the school curriculum.	Present the results of a survey to the class, and justify the use of specific statistics to analyze and represent the data.	Work in a group to design an experiment to analyze content in the schools water. Teach the results to an elementary class.	Debate the issue of withdrawing US military support from Japan in front of a peer panel. Engage in a mock urban planning exercise for Paris.	Study the American Constitution and role play the negotiation of the free states/slave states clause by different signers.
Information	Identify and abstract passages from a novel to support an assertion about the values of a key character.	Design and carry out a survey and analyze the data in a spread sheet using algebraic formulas. Develop a table and a graphic display to communicate results.	In an entrepreneurship project present statistical data pertaining to a high tech company's production and sales. Use a computer to develop statistical charts.	Using numerical data and charts, develop and present conclusions about the effects of economic conditions on the quality of life in several countries.	Research and present pares on the effect of the Industrial Revolution on the class structure in Britain, citing sources used to arrive at conclusions.
Systems	Develop a computer model that analyzes the motivation of Shakespeare's *Hamlet*. Plot the events that increase or decrease Hamlet's motivation to	Develop a system to monitor and correct the heating/cooling process in a computer laboratory using principles of statistical process control.	Build a model of human population growth that includes the impact of the amount of food available, on birth and death rates etc. Do the same for a growth model for insects.	Analyze the accumulation of capital in industrialized nations in systems terms (as a reinforcing process with stocks and flows).	Develop a model of the social forces that led to the American Revolution. The explore the fit between that model and other revolutions.
Technology	Write an article showing the relationship between technology and the environment. Use word processing to write and edit papers after receiving teacher feedback.	Read manuals for several data-processing programs and write a memo recommending the best programs to handle a series of mathematical situations.	Calibrate a scale to weight accurate proportions of chemicals for an experiment. Trace the development of this technology from earliest uses to today.	Research and report on the development and functions of the seismography and its role in earthquake prediction and detection.	Analyze the effects of war on technological development. Use computer graphics to plot the relationship of the country's economic growth to periods of peace and war.

Ehibit 8.4. Examples of assignments that integrate the SCANS competencies into the core curriculum areas.

research and development engineers and those concerned with production and manufacturing. They spoke different languages (Burns and Stalker, 1961). It is not a purely American problem but a problem of the culture of industry. Such teams should be of considerable value to both types of students, and mutual understanding might be helped by some exercises in perceptual understanding (see for example Heywood, 1989). This discussion of learning through projects is expanded in Chapter 9.

8.9. The Evaluation of Integrated Programs

Many of the programs reported in the literature rely solely on student questionnaires for their evaluation. But one can never be sure about such data because any "novel" course that students agree to attend is likely to be accompanied by a Hawthorne effect. There have been a few substantial evaluations, as for example, those by Hendricks and Pappas (1996) and Austin and Edwards (2001). This issue will be taken up again in Chapter 15. In the meantime this section will focus on a study undertaken at the University of California at Berkeley which sought to establish what integration meant to the student. This is an important question. Mention has been made of attitudes in the United Kingdom that are ill disposed to integration. One argument that was heard was based on the view that the principles of the subject are not well understood if the mind is concentrating on integration. Answers to assertions of this kind are, therefore, of some importance. To some extent these answers will depend on the distance between subjects. Are they close or at a distance?

In their introductory report the investigators at Berkeley described interviews with 70 students. In these interviews they tried to establish what integration of maths, physics and engineering meant to the engineering students, how integration took place in the curriculum, as well as in student understanding, and what factors promoted or hindered learning (McKenna et al., 2001). (The method of interviewing and data analysis is discussed in the Chapter on evaluation).

When analyzed to answer the broad question *"How do students talk about integration?"* the data revealed that while most curriculum reform is dependent on pedagogy for change, there are complementary epistemological issues that need to be considered. In the language of the investigators these describe what happens to the students and what is done or thought by them. By this is meant the beliefs that students have about the nature of learning and problem-solving, and in this case their perceptions of math, physics, and engineering. Students, they found, held strong beliefs about the nature of the disciplines and these interacted with the efforts to reform both the curriculum and pedagogy. The data supported the view expressed by Al-Holou et al., (1998) that integration *"helps students visualize and understand links among different disciplines. These links can help practising engineers synthesize multidisciplinary solutions."* For example, the data showed that students valued *"learning activities that allow students to link concepts across classes"*. As indicated in Chapter 4, this

is the basis for the acquisition of expert schema and the transfer of learning. At the same time the students wanted the concepts to be attached *"to something 'tangible' in order for them to understand and make sense of the theory and the analysis"*. By contrast, students believed that the maths was of little relevance and too abstract. Links were not being provided, nor was the relevance clear.

As indicated, this was a first report of a very substantial investigation. The surprising thing to a writer who has been immersed in assessment-led curricular is that little attention is paid to the design of academic tests that would evaluate the student understanding and competency in transfer. This is one of the very big cultural differences between the two sides of the Atlantic. This matter will be raised again in Chapters 15 and 16.

Notice should be taken of work by Kellar et al., (2000), who reported that the integration of numerous disciplines was relatively easy in a pilot project of 25 students. However, it was much more difficult when the number of students was increased to 250. They found that universities are not suitably structured for the implementation of an integrated curriculum. There were many logistical barriers that had to be overcome, and this required a coordinator who would have to devote half his time to coordination.

Olds and Miller (2004) reported a longitudinal study of a first-year integrated engineering curriculum at the Colorado School of Mines. They found that it was associated with an improvement in the five-year graduation rate of "average" students. They also found that mentoring and learning communities were important. Students felt that "interactions with faculty and peers were the single most positive aspect of their experience." This is likely to be true of any circumstance that demands changes in expectations. Given the problems with first-year attrition in engineering in general, it is a lesson that would seem to apply generally (see Chapter 17).

Finally, concerning the issue of evaluation, it is clear that a comprehensive theory of integration related to human development and learning is required. This view is supported by developments in integrated freshmen courses in design (see Chapter 12) that are followed by more traditional studies. One possible approach would be to develop Whitehead's (1932) theory of rhythm in education. This would ensure that the value of the romance and grammar of subjects are appropriately placed at all stages of the curriculum. It is clear that integrated project work relates to his romance and synthesis stages. The problem is how to develop the conceptual understanding provided by the grammar of the subject.[27]

References

Acharya, M., Davis, M., and V. Weil (1995). Integrating ethics into a research experience. *Journal of Engineering Education*, 84, (2), 129-132.
Adler, M (1983). *The Paideia Proposal.* Macmillan, New York.

---

[27]The present writer has attempted to do this for high school technology and design programs (Heywood, 1991)

Al-Holou, N. et al (1998). First-year integrated curricula across engineering education coalitions. *Proceedings Frontiers in Education Conference*, 1, 177-179

Alverno College (1985). *Student Assessment-as-Learning at Alverno College*. Alverno College, Milwuakee, WI.

Andrews, J. K., McBride, G. T. and E. D. Sloan (1993). Humanities for undergraduate engineers: A rich paradox. *Journal of Engineering Education*, 82, (3), 181-184.

Angelo, T. and P. K. Cross (1993). *Classroom Assessment Techniques*. Jossey Bass, San Francisco.

Arms, V. A (1994). Personal and professional enrichment. Humanities in the engineering curriculum.. *Journal of Engineering Education*. 83, (2), 141–146.

Atman, C. J., Turns, J., and F. Mannering (1999). Integrating knowledge across the engineering curriculum. *Proceedings Frontiers in Education Conference*, 13b7-20 to 25.

Auslander, D. M., and R. Jenison (1995). Institutionalization of mechatronics engineering curricular materials. *Proceedings Frontiers in Education Conference*, 3A1-1 to 5.

Austin, S. S., and B. K. Edwards (2001). Transactional writing: constructing knowledge and reshaping beliefs in mathematics. *International Journal of Engineering Education* 17, (1), 40-58.

Baillie, C (1998). Addressing first year issues in engineering education. *European Journal of Engineering Education*. 23, (4), 453-465.

Baren, R (1993). Teaching writing in required undergraduate courses. A materials course example. *Journal of Engineering Education*. 82, (1), 59-61.

Bissell, C., and S. Bennett (1997). The role of the history of technology in the engineering curriculum. *European Journal of Engineering Education*, 22, (3), 267-275.

Bosworth, G. S (1966).(Chairman of a Committee). *The Education and Training Requirements for the Electrical and Mechanical Manufacturing Industry*. Committee on manpower resources for Science and Technology. HMSO, London.

Burns, T., and G. Stalker (1961). *The Management of Innovation*. Tavistock, London.

Carter, G., Heywood, J., and D. T. Kelly (1986).*Case Study in Curriculum Assessment. GCE Engineering (Advanced)*. Roundthorn Press, Manchester.

CEI (1966a). The Councils Examination. Part 1. Syllabuses and Specimen Papers. Council of Engineering Institutions, London.

CEI (1966b). The Councils Examination. Part 2 Syllabuses. Council of Engineering Institutions, London.

Cory, B. J., and D. L. Frostick, (1989). The integrated formation of engineers. *World Conference on Engineering Education for Advancing Technology*, Sydney, Australia. 170-173.

Cowan, J (1998). *One Becoming an Innovative University Teacher. Reflection in Action*. SRHE/Open University Press, Buckingham.

Daneshavar, K (1999) Integrating optical and electronic engineering courses. *IEEE Transactions on Education*. 42, (2), 124-128.

Davies, L (1965). *Liberal Studies and Technology*. Wales University Press, Cardiff.

Davis, M (1992) Integrating ethics into technical courses: IIT's experiment in its second year. *Proceedings Frontiers in Education Conference*, 64–68

Davis, M (1993). Ethics across the curriculum: teaching professional responsibility in technical courses. *Teaching Philosophy*, 16, 205–235.

Demel, J. T. et al (1994). Changing the core-changing the culture. *Proceedings Frontiers in Education Conference*, 656-659

Doom, T., Rayner, M., Krane, D., and O. Garcia (2003). Crossing the interdisciplinary barrier: a baccalaureate computer science option in bioinformatics. *IEEE Transactions on Education*, 46, (3), 387–393.

Dorey, A. P., Bradley, D. A., and D. Dawson (1989). Mecatraonics-integration in engineering. *Proceedings World Conference on Engineering Education for Advanced Technology*. 186-189. Sydney, Australia.

Dyer, S and J. Schmalzel (1998). Macro-electronics. Building the perfect beast. *Proceedings Frontiers in Education Conference*, 73–78

Engineering Council. *The Generalist Engineer- A Broader Course for an Engineering Degree*. (Limited circulation paper by J. Levy.)

Engineering Council (1988). *An Integrated Engineering Degree Program*. Engineering Council, London.

Ertas, A., Maxwell, T., Rainey, V. P., and M. M. Tanik (2003). Transformation of higher education. The transdisciplinary approach in engineering. *IEEE Transactions on Education*, 46, (2), 289–295.

Ettouney, O. M (1994). A new model for integrating engineering into the liberal education of non-engineering undergraduate students. *Journal of Engineering Education*, 83, (4), 349–356.

Evans, D. L., Goodnick, S. M., and R. J. Roedel (2003). ECE curriculum in 2013 and beyond: vision for a metropolitan public research university. *IEEE Transactions on Education*, 46, (4), 420–428.

Fink, F. K (2001) Integration of work based learning in engineering education. *Proceedings Frontiers in Education Conference*, 2, F3E-10-F3E-15.

Fink, F. K. and F. Bejers (1999). Integration of engineering practice into curriculum. 25 years of experience with problem based learning. *Proceedings Frontiers in Education Conference*. 11a2-7 to 12

Fink, L. D. et al., (2000). Reengineering sooner civil engineering education. *Proceedings Frontiers in Education Conference*, 1, T1F 3 to 8.

Finniston, M., Duggan, T. V., and J. M. Bement (1989). Integrated engineering education for advanced technology. *Proceedings World Conference on Engineering Education for Advanced Technology*. 1, 418-423. Sydney, Australia.

Fogarty, R (1993). *Integrating the Curriculum. A Collection*. IRI/Skylight Publ. Pallatine, Ill

Ford, J. D., and L. A. Riley (2003). Integrating communication and engineering education: a look at curricula, courses, and support systems. *Journal of Engineering Education*, 92, (4), 325–328.

Fromm, E., and R. G. Quinn (1989). An experiment to enhance the educational experience of engineering students. *Engineering Education*. 79, (3), 424-429.

Froyd, J. E., and G. J. Rogers (1997). Evolution and evaluation of an integrated first year curriculum. *Proceedings Frontiers in Education Conference*, 1107-1113.

Golshani, F., Panchanathan, S., and O. Friesen (2000). Alogical foundation for an information engineering curriculum. *Proceedings Frontiers in Education Conference*, 1, T3E-8 to 12.

Goodlad, S (1970). Project work in developing countries: A British experiment in engineering education. *International Journal of Electrical Engineering Education*, 8, 135.

Gorman, M. et al (2000). Integrating ethics and engineering: a graduate option in systems engineering, ethics and technology studies. *Journal of Engineering Education*, 89, (4), 461-470.

Haws, D. R (2001). Ethics instruction in engineering education: A (mini) meta-analysis. *Journal of Engineering Education*, 90, (2), 223-230.

Heer, D., Traylor, R. L., Thompson, T., and T. S. Fiez (2003). Enhancing the freshman experience using a platform form for learning. *IEEE Transactions on Education*, 46, (4), 434–443.

Hendricks, R. W. and E. C. Pappas (1996). Advanced engineering communication: an integrated writing and materials program for engineers. *Journal of Engineering Education*, 85, (4), 343-352.

Hersam, M. C., Luna, M., and G. Light (2004). Implementation of interdisciplinary group learning and peer assessment in a nanotechnology engineering course. *Journal of Engineering Education*, 93, (1), 49-59.

Hewitt, E. A (1967). *The Reliability of the GCE 'O' level examination in English*. Joint Matriculation Board, Manchester.

Heywood, J (1967). Social studies and technology in the sixth form: some implications for the study of the curriculum. *Studies in Education and Craft*, 1, (1), 12-19.

Heywood, J (1969). *An Evaluation of certain post-war developments in Higher Technological Education*. Thesis, Volume 1. University of Lancaster Library, Lancaster.

Heywood, J (1971). *A Bibliography of British Technological Education and Training*. Hutchinson, London.

Heywood, J (1973a) American and English influences on the development of a transdisciplinary course on the technologist and society. *Collected Papers of the ERM Division. Annual Conference of the American Society for Engineering Education*.12-29.

Heywood, J (1973b) New Courses and Degree Structures. Committee for Higher Education. Council of Europe, Strasbourg.

Heywood, J (1977) *Assessment in Higher Education*. First edition. Wiley, Chichester.

Heywood, J (1989) *Learning, Adaptability and Change*. Paul Chapman Publishing, London.

Heywood, J (1989a) *Assessment in Higher Education*. Wiley, Chichester.

Heywood, J (1989b) *Learning, Adaptability and Change*. Paul Chapman, London.

Heywood, J (1991) Theory and practice of technology education – implications for the senior cycle of secondary education in M. Kussman and H. Steffen (eds). *Aktuelle Themen der Technischen Bildung in Europa*. Eurepaische Gesellschaft fur Technische Bildung, Dusseldorf. Pp 66 – 76.

Heywood, J (1994) *Enterprise Learning and its Assessment in Higher Education*. Technical Report No. 20. Employment Department, Sheffield

Heywood, J et al (1966) The education of professional engineers for design and manufacture. *Lancaster Studies in Higher Education*, No 1 pp 5 –100. (University of Lancaster).

Hoit, M., and M. Ohland (1995). Institutionalizing curriculum change: a SUCCEED case history. *Proceedings Frontiers in Education Conference*, 3a 1-6 to 11.

Jelsma, J., and E. Woudstra. (1997). Integrated training of engineers for a changing society. *European Journal of Engineering Education*, 22, (3), 279-293.

Kellar, J. J. et al (2000) A problem based learning approach for freshman engineering. *Proceedings Frontiers in Education Conference*, F2G 7 to 10.

Kitto, K. L (2001). Integrating creative design experiences and ethics into materials science. *Proceedings Frontiers in Education Conference*. T2C-8 to 12.

Kolar, R. L., and D. A. Sabatini (1996). Coupling team learning and computer technology in project-driven undergraduate engineering Education. *Proceedings Frontiers in Education Conference*. 1, 172-175.

Kozmetsky, G (1997). Generational road maps and commercialization science and technology. *Journal Integrated Design Process Science*, 1, (1), 4–8.

Kuhn, T. S (1970). *The Structure of Scientific Revolutions*, 2nd Edition. Chicago University Press, Chicago.

LaPlaca, M. C., Newstetter, W. C., and A. P. Yognathan (2001). Probelm-based learning in biomedical engineering curricula. *Proceedings Frontiers in Education Conference* 2, F3E.-16- F3E.-21.

Lee, L. S (1969). *Towards a classification of the objectives of undergraduate practical work in mechanical engineering*. Thesis, Library. University of Lancaster, Lancaster.

Levy, J (1990). The integrated engineering degree program in G. Parry (ed). *Engineering Futures. New Audiences and Arrangements for Engineering Higher Education*. Engineering Council, London.

Lewis, E. R. L (1966). *Higher Education and the National Need*. Report of the 1966 Annual Conference of the East Anglian Regional Advisory Board for Further Education.

Loacker, G (2000). (ed.). *Self-Assessment at Alverno College*. Alverno College, Milwaukee, WI

Ludlow, D. K., and K. H. Schulz (1994). Writing across the chemical engineering curriculum at the University of North Dakota. *Journal of Engineering Education*, 83, (2), 169–171.

McKenna, A., McMartin, F., Terada, Y., Sirivedhin, V., and A, Agonino (2001). *Proceedings Annual Conference ASEE*. Session 1330.

Mentkowski, M and associates (2000). *Learning that Lasts*. Jossey Bass, San Francisco

Morgan, J., and D. Martinez (2000). A women and technology program for freshman engineering students. *Proceedings Frontiers in Education Conference*. 2, F2F-1 to 4.

Newdick, R (1994). The Drexel Curriculum. *Engineering Science and Education Journal*.October, 223-228.

Newcomer, J. L., Kitto, K. L., and B. Sylvester (2003). Written communication in a technical context: meaningful writing assignments for engineering technology students. *Proceedings Frontiers in Education Conference*, 2, F3E- 8 to 13.

Newman, J. H (1852). The *Idea of a University. Defined and Illustrated*. Longmans Green, London.

Oakes, W. C. et al (2000). EPICS. Interdisciplinary service learning using engineering design projects. *Proceedings Frontiers in Education Conference*, 1, T2F 4 to 9.

Olds, B. M., and R. L. Miller (2004). The effect of a first-year integrated engineering curriculum on graduation rates and student satisfaction: a longitudinal study. *Journal of Engineering Education*, 93, (1), 23– 6.

O'Neal, J. B and J. Riddle (1995). Integrating humanities with engineering through a course in the rise of modern science. *Proceedings Frontiers in Education Conference* 3b4-1-3b4- 4.

Oni, A. A., et al (1992). Preliminary first year evaluation of a phenomena driven engineering curriculum. *Proceedings Frontiers in Education Conference*. pp. 1- 6.

Pfatteicher, S. K. A (2001). Teaching vs preaching: EC2000 and the engineering ethics dilemma. *Journal of Engineering Education*. 90, (1), 137-142.

Pinciroli, V., Masseroli, M., and G. Tognola (2003). The educational offer in medical informatics ans telemedicine at the engineering faculty of the Politecnico de Milano. *IEEE Transactions on Rducation*, 46, (3), 394–398.

Pour, G (2000). Integrating component based and re-use driven software engineering business into the software and information engineering curriculum. *Proceedings Frontiers in Education Conference* T2C-18 to 23.

Radcliffe-Brown, A. R (1964). *A Natural Science of Society*. Free Press, Glencoe, NY.

Regan, T. M. and P. A, Miderman (1995). Institutionalizing change. *Proceedings Frontiers in Education Conference*. 3a1-12 to 16.

Roedel, R. J, et al (1995). An integrated project based, introductory course in calculus, physics, English and engineering. *Proceedings Frontiers in Education Conference*. 3C1-1 to 6

Roedel, R. J. et al (1997). Projects that integrate engineering, physics, calculus and English in the Arizona State Foundation Coalition freshman program. *Proceedings Frontiers in Education Conference*, 38–42.

Saupe, J (1961). In P. Dressel (ed.). *Evaluation in Higher Education*. Houghton Mifflin, Boston.

SCANS (1992). *Teaching the SCANS Competencies*. A SCANS Report for America 2000. US Department of Labor, Washington, DC.

Schneck, D. J (2001). Integrated learning: paradigm for a unified approach. *Journal of Engineering Education*. 90, (2), 213-217.

Schumacher, J., Gabriele, G., and J. Newcomer (1995). Teaching engineering design with humanities and social sciences comparison courses. *Proceedings Frontiers in Education Conference*, 3a6-8 to 12.

Seat, E., Parsons, J. R. and W. A. Poppen (1999). Engineering communication and performance minor. *Proceedings Frontiers in Education Conference*, 13ab-22 to 27.

Shaeiwitz, J. A., Whiting, W. B., and Turton, R. and R. C. Bailie (1994). The holistic curriculum. *Journal of Engineering Education*, 83, (4), 343 –348.

Shooter, S., and M. McNeil (2002). Interdisciplinary collaborative learning in mechatronics at Bucknell University. *Journal of Engineering Education*, 91, (3), 339–344.

Skates, G. W. (2003). Interdisciplinary project working in engineering education. *European Journal of Engineering Education*. "8, (2), 187-201.

Spasov, P (2000). Look, no timetable. *Proceedings Frontiers in Education Conference*, 3, S1B 12 to 17.

Squires, G (1975) in *Interdisciplinarity*. Society for Research into Higher Education, London.

Staats, J. W., and T. Blum (1999). Enhancing an object oriented curriculum: metacognitive assessment and training. *Proceedings Frontiers in Education Conference*, 13B7 13 to 19.

Steneck, N. H., Olds, B. M. and K. A. Neeley (2002). Recommendations for Liberal Education in engineering. A White paper from the Liberal Education Division of the American society for

Engineering Education. Session 1963. *Proceedings of the American Society for Engineering Education's Annual Conference.*

Stephenson, J., and M. Yorke. (1998). *Capability and Quality in Higher Education.*Kogan Page, London.

Stephenson, J. (1998). Chapter 1, page 2. In Stephenson, J., and M. Yorke. (eds.) *Capability and Quality in Higher Education.* Kogan Page, London.

Tien, C. N (1992). Looking Ahead: Engineering education for the Twenty First Century. Woodruff Distinguished Lecture, Georgia Institute of Technology. Office of Publications. May 7, 92-276.

Thuessen, G. J., et al (1992). The integration of economic principles with design in the undergraduate curriculum. *Proceedings Frontiers in Education Conference* 373-378.

Traylor, R..L., Heer, D., and T. S. Fiez (2003). Using an integrated platform for learning to reinvent engineering education. *IEEE Transactions on Education*, 46, (4), 409–419.

Tubman, K. A (1988). Students' appraisal of a combined engineering course. *International Journal of Applied Engineering Education* 4, (5), 467-469.

Turner, B. T (1958). High altitude passenger flying with special reference to air treatment. *Journal of the Junior Institution of Engineers*, 68, 219.

Vanderburg, W. H. and N. Khan (1994). How well is engineering education incorporating societal issues? *Journal of Engineering Education.* 83, (4), 357-362.

Van Zealand, K., Krol, A., and P, Greenfield.(1990). Incorporating environmental education in engineering: The integrated approach of the University of Queensland. *Conference of the Australian Association of Engineers.* 1, 107-112.

Venable, W., McConnell, R., and A. Stiller (1995). Incorporating mathematics in a freshman engineering course. *Proceedings Frontiers in Education Conference*, 3C1- 23 to 27.

Walker, K (2000). Integrating writing instruction into engineering courses. A writing center model. *Journal of Engineering Education.* 89, (3), 369-378.

Wheeler, E and R. L. McDonald. Writing in engineering courses. *Journal of Engineering Education.* 89, (4), 481-486.

Whitehead, A. N. (1932). *The Aims of Education.* Benn, London.

Young, P. M (1997). An integrated systems and control laboratory. *Proceedings Frontiers in Education Conference* 659-665.

Zwyno, M. S. and D. C. Kennedy (2000). Integrating the internet, multimedia components, and hands-on experimentation into problem-based control education. *Proceedings Frontiers in Education Conference* 1, T2D- 5 to 10.

CHAPTER 9: FROM PROJECTS TO PROBLEM-BASED LEARNING

Summary

There has been a long history of project work in engineering education, and recent initiatives have been able to build on that work. The Chapter begins, therefore, with a brief historical review.

Not everyone was happy with project work, especially when it was done in the final year because it limited the work that could be done in the traditional discipline. Its merits had to be demonstrated. There is now a profession-wide acceptance of the value of such work, and as indicated in Chapter 8, projects are often used as a vehicle for integrating the disciplines. In the early days of project work in sandwich (cooperative) courses in Britain, projects were seen as a mechanism for integrating the academic with the practica,l particularly when they were done in industry. At the time, the 1950s there was little in the way of educational theory from which to build a theory of integration.

An important case for project work is that they cause students to develop skills that cannot be assessed in traditional written examinations yet are essential for work as an engineer. For example, planning, synthesis, and evaluation.

In the British system, in particular, there were problems with assessment in relation to the mechanisms for measurement (see also Chapter 2), and the proportion of marks to be awarded within the final grade. Various aspects of assessment are including the use of journals and independent tests. Many of the problems experienced in those years continue to arise, and these are considered. Related to them is the issue of whether or not design could be taught (see Chapter 12). Projects were seen as a method of achieving this goal.

Projects may achieve a variety of goals, and the question arises as to whether project activities should be in the final year, in the beginning year, or spread across the program. It is clear that project work can motivate students and since they can provide the flavor of engineering there is an advantage in using them in beginning years especially when retention is an issue.

Project work often implies a change in teacher-student relationships. In project and problem-based learning teachers become managers and facilitators of learning. It is argued that teachers may require specific training in the design and implementation of PBL.

There are various ways of classifying projects but none of them are entirely satisfactory. A section considers classification by scope, (ie, time allowed) and technique and develops some of the points made in Chapter 2. Projects may also be classified by who chooses the project-the student(s) or the teacher. The arguments for teacher driven and student-driven projects are summarized, and which is chosen will depend on the objectives to be achieved. Thus, projects may also be assigned by whether or not they are for group or individual work. It has also been suggested that projects may be classified on a matrix that relates who does the assessment against who structures the learning experience. This applies in particular to problem-based learning.

Many students have difficulty in planning and evaluating projects. Learning contracts between teachers and students have been introduced by some teachers to help their students develop the skill of planning. The importance of textbooks in helping students to understand project planning and implementation has been supported by research.

Projects involve the solution-specific problems, but it is also possible to base the curriculum on problems. This is called problem-based learning (PBL) Examples of the use of PBL in engineering education are given. Attention is drawn to the fact that students have to have adequate prior-knowledge to be able to embark on a problem-based course. The design of such courses has to take into account the need for just-in-time resources (information).

The new universities in Denmark were designed around project based curricula, and the program at Aalborg in engineering is summarized. It seems to be a mix of project based and problem based learning given the definitions used here.

PBL may create problems for students who have to adapt to new methods of learning and relationships with their teachers. They are likely to need help getting started, and examples of programs that do this are cited. Space needs to be provided to help students develop the skills necessary for minimally supported learning.

Reports on problem-based learning in engineering education, although few in number, provide sufficient evidence to throw a challenge to engineering educators.

9. Introduction

As indicated in Chapter 8, many recently reported developments in the United States use projects as a means of integration. There is a long history of project work in engineering education, and recent initiatives have been able to build on that experience. It is therefore appropriate to begin this commentary with reference to that work.

Project teaching is seen as a powerful method of helping students to integrate their learning. At the same time, it enables realism to be brought to the study of engineering, and some courses could not be accomplished without the aid of projects.

In the United States there were and continue to be capstone design projects (e.g., Farr et al., 2001). These necessarily integrate previous experiences of theory and practice even when students and teachers are not consciously seeking such integration. In Europe there is considerable interest in project work and a complete issue of the *European Journal of Engineering Education* (21-2), 1996) is devoted to descriptions of project activities in different countries.[1]

---

[1] Unfortunately, there are no evaluations of consequence.

As indicated in Chapter 8, in the 1950s the British Government sponsored an alternative route to an engineering degree by upgrading a number of colleges in the technical college sector so that they could award degrees. The purpose of this route was to provide graduates with an interest in industry and manufacturing because it was thought that the universities should provide engineers and scientists oriented toward science and research. A key difference between the two degrees would be that the industrially oriented degree would be pursued by six-month alternations between industry and college over a four-year period like the cooperative courses in America. As indicated in Chapter 8, it was believed that these sandwich courses would yield an integration of theory and practice. One of the other differences was to be the completion of a substantial project during the final year with or without assistance from industry. This proved to be a very popular innovation among both faculty and students. However, it was not a unique development, and by the middle of the 1960s most university engineering departments were using project work in their final year. From studies of the literature published at that time, it seemed that there was little difference in objectives, although there were no studies of outcomes except of opinions as to what they perceived the outcomes to be (Heywood, 1969). General aims were specified, but nothing like the Bloom *Taxonomy* emerged. (*The Taxonomy* was not published in the United Kingdom until 1964).

Professor J. P. Duncan wrote:

"Personally I think much can and should be done towards this end. A student's three years at university, all too short for any expanding technology, constitutes his time for acquiring working factual knowledge. If that is imparted by engineering lecturers with practical experience... .the limitations and compromise necessary in practice and the need for creative ideas in the achievement of practical objectives can be woven into the presentation of technical lectures with more telling effect than in formal treatment. If in addition, one gives the student a largely self-directed, though supervized, graduation project or design to be accompanied by a thesis, one finds that most students are by no means unaware at graduation that engineering extends beyond a scientific horizon, and that there is great scope for personal initiative and creative ideas in the practice of engineering" (Duncan, 1962).

Not everyone in the universities was happy with final-year project work. Warburton (1961) felt that if projects were undertaken for their educational purpose, then the time allocated to them could be reduced by 20%. He believed that engineering courses were primarily about analysis and that not enough time was available for the teaching of engineering science. Nevertheless, there was published support for project work from the Birmingham University (Hayes and Tobias, 1965), Imperial College (de Malherbe and Wistreich, 1964), and Reading University (Deere, 1967), and this support continues to this day (e.g., Fincher and Petre, 1998).

Duncan's statement of the aims of projects in universities may be compared with the somewhat more specific aims written by the Head of a Department of Mechanical Engineering in a College of Advanced Technology. Steed (1961) wrote that they were:

"(a) to develop the initiative of a student and increase his confidence in his ability to tackle problems new to him.
(b) to teach students to plan a piece of work and carry it to a successful conclusion under conditions which in some degree are similar to industrial conditions e.g., under limited supervision."

Steed went on to explain how these aims led to individual projects;

"It follows that projects are perhaps best organized so that each student undertakes an individual piece of work and has his or her own topic or problem."

Steed suggested there were at least four possible forms that a project could undertake. These were:

1. *"The investigation of a problem necessitating experiment (this may include the design of experimental apparatus).*
2. *The design of a piece of engineering apparatus, equipment, or machinery (a student may sometimes be asked in addition, to build the apparatus etc).*
3. *The planning and layout for a process or project.*
4. *An investigation within the field of management."*

Steed believed that it was desirable that the student should come to some conclusions, and that en route the student should read the background literature, undertake limited building of apparatus, experiment with it, and prepare a final report. Others clearly followed this approach (e.g., Pullman, 1965). Steed also remarked that

"In some cases there might be merit in a small group of students working on the same topic, but if this is done care should be taken to see that each member of the group is both-academically and by personality-able to participate more or less equally in the work."

This worry arose from the problem of assessment. Typically, a project would contribute 25% of the grade in the final examination and at that time the assessment of group work was considered to be very difficult. The idea of peer assessment had not yet been generated. Typically in a Diploma in Technology project the students were allocated 6 hours per week (or one day) for the whole of the six-month period in college (Whitehead and Glover, 1967).

It is of interest to note that the Institution of Chemical Engineers set a part 3 written examination that was based on a project. It was also unusual in that the candidate received the question on October 1st and had to return his/her answer 2 months later on December 1st. The Institution published examples of the question (Jeffreys, 1961), and others prepared articles on the design problem (Hopton, 1950; Norman, 1959). Candidates were expected to show that they could design a complete chemical plant.

Irrespective of assessment, the complaint from industry that new graduates are unable to work in teams is of comparatively recent origin. At that time there was no pressure from industry for such training, nor had the idea of cooperative learning emerged. Even so American approaches to group work that have been developed are not well known in engineering circles in the United Kingdom (see Chapter 13).

The problems that arose in the 1950s and 1960s seem to differ little from those that are experienced today. It was in that period that a debate began about whether or not design could be taught. One response was that design, which was associated with the skill of synthesis, could be learned through projects (see Exhibit 9.1 and Chapter 12), and related to this view was the idea that projects could stimulate creativity (Hayes and Tobias, 1965). At Birmingham University the final-year project depended on preparatory work done in the preceding years of the course, and at Reading the skills of project work were understood to require development, and for this reason project work was included in the second year (see Exhibit 9.2). In the United States the need for such development among freshman engineering students was recognized by Farrell, Hesketh, and Slater (1999), who provided a curriculum in which two progressive mini-design projects led to a single in depth reverse engineering project in the second semester.

At Brunel University in the Special Engineering Program, first-year students undertook what was called an artifact study. The student conducted tests on an artifact manufactured or used by the student's industrial sponsor to establish its performance. It has some similarities with the dissection approach to design and understanding adopted at Stanford by Sheppard (Sheppard, 1992). The purpose of the exercise was to introduce the students to project work. In the second year, and with some similarity to the Reading approach, the students undertook tasks that had a ten-day life cycle. *"Each student undertakes ten different assignments with a partner who will be different in each case. The design course makes use of larger student groups, and concentrates on the initial processes of design, namely creativity and formulation. The specifications are deliberately ill defined, and quite naturally this uncertainty is disliked by students"* (Stone and Green-Armytage, 1986). During the 2nd industrial training period, students identified a suitable project like a component or subsystem design for limited project work during the third year. In the fourth year, 90% of the projects originated in industry during the students third industrial period. The projects were conducted on an individual basis and were very substantial.[2]

The term integration, when used, as it often was, applied to integration between the academic and industrial experiences. A commentary on the projects

reported above suggested that it was *"evident that in each phase of the project the student linked previous experiences in such a way that new ideas were developed. Some of these linkages were conscious while some others unconscious. Integration arises when there is a continuous interchange between past and present experiences in the formulation of new ideas. To some extent all "present" situations were founded on the integration of one or more sets of experiences. For the most part they are unstructured since they are not perceived within an easily defined frame of reference. Thus, design and manufacturing projects provided a structured frame of reference"* (Heywood, 1969).

That investigator came to the conclusion that more could have been done to influence the integration by faculty. He admitted that faculty, at that time, had little understanding of learning, and that as yet, some of the important developments in the field of learning in higher education had not taken place. Nevertheless, most faculty came to appreciate the value of projects and in particular their power to motivate learning (e.g., Stone and Green-Armytage, 1986).

9.1. Motivation

One of the problems that engineering departments faced in the United Kingdom was the shortage of applicants from schools. They blamed schoolteachers for this state of affairs. One response was that the school curriculum should include engineering as a subject as this should give students a flavor of what engineering was about and, thereby, stimulate their interest in the pursuit of engineering as a career. Most engineering teachers objected to this since they wanted specialist study in mathematics and physics in high school. However, when the Schools Council proposed *Project Technology*, a program in which during minority hours in the curriculum, students could undertake technological design and make activities, many engineering Professors welcomed this scheme as the appropriate way of stimulating an interest in engineering. This scheme ran very successfully for a number of years, and some of the projects that were completed were equally as good as many final-year projects in universities. It is interesting to note that many of the projects were to do with the design and manufacture of aids for the handicapped, and that this remains a popular area for project work to this day (Culver and Scudder, 1995), as does the design of children's toys (Ivins, 1997).

In the United States, Dyer and Schmalzel (1998) said that one of the reasons why they introduced project work was because of the high level of motivation induced by projects. Several reports suggested that students learn more from project work than they do in traditional lectures. Brazier (2000) reported that students had told them they were more motivated to work on projects that they were interested in, and this raized the question as to who should choose the projects.

In a criticism of some project work Mountain (2000), inferred, allbeit indirectly, that in many project

---

[2] Unfortunately, the experience of sandwich courses seems to have been lost. Now only a few universities sponsor them (Parnaby, 1996). The paper by Stone and Green-Armytage (1986) provides a useful description of practice and problems in sandwich courses.[See also O'Connor, Ainscough, Rakowski, and March 1985, Ellis, and Rakowski, and March (1985) for specific details of parts of the Brunel course].

situations where class regulations are maintained, that the adversarial nature of staff-student relationships is maintained. This might de-motivate students, and he suggested an arrangement that was being tried at the University of Texas-Tyler whereby staff and students joined together in an extended project of their own choice.

The idea was stimulated by the many competitions that engineering schools can enter. At Tyler, this activity is called *"The Labor of Love Project"*. *Project Technology* in the UK secondary schools was an activity of this kind. Nevertheless, many of those who have been engaged in project work would argue that even within the restraints of classroom regulations that students are highly motivated by projects. One of the problems is to prevent students from doing too much on their projects that is at the expense of other necessary academic studies. In the Engineering Science 'A' level projects the problem for the external moderators was that some students spent an inordinate amount of time on their projects. It was sometimes far beyond the recommended time in the regulations. In these circumstances does the external moderator penalize the student who has otherwise produced an excellent result?

9.2. Types of Project. Classification by Scope and Technique

There are various ways of classifying projects, and no one is entirely satisfactory. Dekker (1996), for example, distinguishes between "open ended" projects and "design projects" that have a different purpose. This is a reminder that projects can be classified by the purpose thay are intended to fulfil. However in this section the classification of project work is based on the coursework categories for the engineering science course described in Chapter 2, and in particular in Exhibit 2.9. There are other definitions that are similar, but their authors use their own terminology and one result of this is that the terminology is confused. For example, sometimes project-based and problem-based learning mean the same thing, at other times they don't.

In the engineering science examination a distinction was made between controlled assignments or traditional laboratory experiments snd experimental investigation. Some reports would suggest that the work undertaken by some students under the heading of projects is what is in effect an experimental investigation, which is essentially an open ended or discovery mode of investigation. In the notes for guidance the experimental investigations were described as *"minor pieces of scientific or engineering research."* Published examples of such investigations included: *"Determine the nature and size of electrical components between the terminals of a closed box; Investigate the properties and behaviour of 3 cm radio waves: Investigate the way of reducing heat losses, including the lagging of pipes, double glazing and polishing: Determine the energy losses in a machine (engine)" (JMB, 1972).* Popular investigations included

the evaluation of different household detergents and automobile engine oils (Heywood, 1976).

While providing experience of scientific investigation or design, these investigations also had the function of preparing the student for the major project experience. In Deere's terminology (Exhibit 9.2) they could be regarded as phase 1 projects.

Synthesis

Whether one is a "designer" or not, as an engineer one is involved in a main stream which synthesises. The requirement, therefore, is for sympathy towards design. The engineer must be aware of the broad features of design, even if his personal creativity is minimal. The features are

a.   **Specification** of the need in detail

b.   Feasibility, **demanding the creation of several solutions, and the selection of one (or two) for further study. (A corollary is that the quality of analysis must match the quality of the required answer. The student must be able to spot cases where a quick sum will suffice for the moment, and those where greater detail is required)**

c.   **The value of** rigorous **methods in the overall design function**

d.   Optimization

e.   Implementation **of the chosen solution. The sub-features here are that this often involves large-scale management-leading to a knowledge of management techniques-and the reconciliation of material supply and production resources with the chosen solution in detail**

f.   **At all points in the process of synthesis the engineer of whatever "kind" must be prepared to specify** criteria **by which decisions-often several inter-dependent decisions-can be measured**

g.   **The decisions noted above (f) to a large extent also depend on** judgment **and** opinion

---

Exhibit 9.1. The features of engineering synthesis outlined by M. Deere (1968) in a submission to a working party on professional examinations of the Society for Research into Higher Education. At the end of (f) he wrote, " Surely, any university course must set out to cultivate judgment, quite overtly, whatever else it does?"

These investigations, unlike the controlled assignments, were not undertaken in parallel with the course and did not illustrate the principles being taught at the time. The students could also choose what investigations they wanted to do. In contrast, one of the goals of the project-based French school curriculum in *Technologie* was that the students should learn the theory as they did the projects (Murray, 1986). It was also the approach used for a senior-level mechanical engineering elective in control systems, as well as for a freshman course in computer engineering at the University of Pittsburgh. The courses were built around a laboratory-scale model of a gantry crane used to move heavy loads. Early in the course, which Clark and Hake (1997) described as project-based learning the students were presented with a set of tasks that had to be completed with the model.

"Before handing out the individual projects, we generally state, on the first day of class, the overall goal: to position the gantry crane quickly and accurately. We then describe heuristically how this is accomplished, by discussing the crane, sensors and actuator, and their interconnection, with the key element being the controller. We briefly describe the controller design process (system modelling and mathematical development of the control law), and then discuss how the students will implement the controller at the end of the course. At this point, the students have a general idea of what is to be done, but they do not have the necessary tools to complete the project. The idea is that as the course is completed, they will continuously try to relate the concepts learned in class to the gantry-crane controller, and with that physical grounding, students will better understand and be able to use the material."

Phase 1 Projects. These occupy the bulk of the first term of year 2 and do not involve much creative design. Their purpose is to introduce the students to group projects generally, and specifically to get them thinking critically about the needs of the situation, and about existing systems. The choice of topic, and supervision is made and done by the tutor. The key words are **investigation** and **assessment.**

Phase 2 Projects.
These occupy the second and third terms of year 2. The students work in groups of about 6, where possible containing mixed cybernetic and engineering science students, and the task is to provide an outline design. The key word is **feasibility**, and the students proceed to creative work, and the choice of the optimum solution. In selecting projects the aim is to provide a range of field, and a range of type of project. For instance we do not want a preponderance of "research projects" to the neglect of "design projects," and the design projects should cover "new design" as well as "modification and improvement design." Certain "research" type projects have a place here because they can involve a fair amount of creative design.

Phase 3 Projects. These occupy the whole of year 3. They build directly on the experience of phase 2, and as far as the student is concerned, and are extended so that the group not only has to design a solution, but also actually build it and present it working satisfactorily at the end of the year. The key word is **implementation**. The students work in larger teams.

In both phase 2 and 3 projects, supervision is provided by and members of staff assigned to, the various groups, and the tutor acts as coordinator.

Exhibit 9.2. The sequence of project activities in the department of Applied Physical Science as described by the tutor (Deere, 1967).

The students had to answer a series of specific questions, as for example, *"plot the open-loop step response for a 2-volt input (show both velocity and position plots)."* Then finally they are asked to, *"design controllers which will allow the crane to have 'good' transient response in each of the following two scenario's, (i) operate at a desired constant speed, or (ii) move to a desired position."*

It will be seen that, in contrast to the experimental investigation in engineering science, this approach is highly structured. The initial questions are in the guided discovery mode for which reason the approach is best described as guided project-based learning. In engineering science the structure is provided by the objectives to be achieved and the assessment procedure (see Exhibit 2.10). While the student was expected to have the requisite knowledge to conduct and evaluate the investigation, the focus of the student's work should be on the acquisition of skill in investigation.[3] Recent discussions have suggested that in investigations the student is experiencing the role of engineering scientist whereas in the large-scale project he/she experiences engineering as it is practiced in design, management, making and evaluation.

Within the project method as defined here the scale of the operation can vary considerably. In the engineering science project, it was considered that during the second (final) year of the course the student should be occupied in the laboratory for no more than 50 hours, but this did not take into account the time spent on the project at home. Brazier (2000), in contrast, was of the opinion that it was not possible to have a project that was of sufficiently large scale within a single semester. It would enable junior-level students to (1) appreciate the planning process and (2) understand the necessity of the early phases of the software engineering process. Such projects lead to the experiences being contrived. Therefore it was necessary to spread the project over two semesters or to revise the approach. In her case, new high-level tools had made it possible to *"move toward the spiral model and/or rapid prototyping, students are now able to spend most of the semester on planning, requirements, specification, and the preliminary and detailed design phases. Then making use of these high level tools, complete a rapid prototype to verify requirements and or complete a working project by the end of the semester."* Planning is an important skill and is discussed again below.

9.2.1. Classification by "Who Chooses the Project"

Ansell (1998) distinguished between professor-driven, student-driven, and client-driven projects. In the first, the professor-driven, the teacher assigns the project. In this writer's experience, not only is this the most common mode of authorization it is the one that students expect irrespective of the type of project. It fits in with the transmission model of learning. Such projects are valuable aids to class learning when they are chosen to reinforce what is learnt in class. These can be design or investigation problems. Similarly, a project can be chosen that allows the students to integrate what they have learned in several courses.

A student-driven project is one chosen by the student. Such projects are likely to stimulate motivation because the project is likely to be in an area of the student's interest. As such, it may raise the level of self-

---

[3]For examples in control engineering, see Beauchamp-Báez and Meléndez-González (1998).

confidence. However, if for some reason or another, and this may well be the case with less able students, the project fails, then the student may equally experience a loss of confidence. This was the case with the engineering science projects.

Ansell (1998) argued that when student motivation is strong, the student may be so committed to a course of action that he/she does not consider alternative solutions. However, as the engineering science projects showed, when the assessment requires consideration of alternatives, the students will try to consider realistic alternatives. It was found that the less able students found it more difficult to provide realistic alternatives. More recent work among experts suggests that their use or non-use of alternatives is more complex than linear models of the problem-solving process allow.

A characteristic of the less able student is that they will tend to select a project that is not very challenging, which, as Ansell pointed out, is not likely to be the case with a teacher-driven project. Similarly, some students may choose projects that are too difficult, and this can be the case with professor-driven projects. Ansell cited the case of teams of students who had to complete a three-week project on an elevator controller which was found to be too difficult. He felt that had the students been allowed to choose between projects of varying difficulty, the students who needed an easier project would have had the opportunity to choose one that was easier. This assumes that the students understand their ability and the demands of the project. Since this is not always the case, there may have to be teacher intervention.

Ansell argued that student-driven projects might be less subject to the pressures an engineer would experience in industry. It is possible to argue, however, that the motivation acquired from interest can put the student under strong pressure if too much time is devoted to the project, especially at home. Students have to learn how to manage their study time, and this is surely a transferable skill. If this is the case, then all that differs between the industrial and the collegiate situations is the context. In the collegiate situation the client is the student him/herself. True, in the client-driven project another person is let down if targets are not met.

He also argued that student-driven projects are unlikely to be as "real" in the occupational sense as projects that are chosen by the professor, or more especially the client. But the drive for reality in project work often ignores the fact that what is real for a student may be quite different to what a teacher perceives should be real for that student. Student choice of project enables the student to investigate what is real for him or her.

There is also a problem in tutor-driven projects of the choice of projects. Klein (1991) pointed out that some artifacts that are deceptively simple may provide a complex learning activity which gives the student a *chocs des opinions*. The bicycle is one such artifact, and such projects can change the pedagogical environment substantially. He wrote, *"(1) the bicycle is not a trivial device as vast multitudes might otherwise presume at first glance; (ii) block diagram representations and state representations are not universal and not all powerful model forms; and (iii) the bicycle makes an ideal specimen for student inquiry because it is so deceptive in appearing simple but being highly complex. The students' familiarity with the bicycle adds to the pedagogical humbling of students. Quite frankly it is hard to motivate any student to learn anything if the student believes (i) that the answer is known and/or is simple and needs only to be memorized; (ii) that the student can spend an "all-nighter" just prior to an exam or report date and "get their usual A"; and (iii) that they can dry lab or otherwise bluff their way to a grade based on the usual university propensity to give generous partial credit for even wrong answers. By use of the open ended bicycle project within an otherwise routine course, the pedagogical environment becomes dramatically altered."* Therefore an advantage, of the teacher choosing projects is that he/she can present students with artifacts which may not appear to be complex that they would not normally choose.

Carter at the University of Salford operated a scheme in which all staff initially provided, anonymously, project titles and outlines that were communicated to all students. The students were then expected to rank in order the first five titles that corresponded most closely to their interests, or, indeed their own project. A matching procedure was then undertaken, with built-in routines that disallowed major over or underloading of individual staff members. In this way, matching was achieved for the majority of students, A second iteration was undertaken to match the remaining students (Carter and Jordan, 1990).

Similarly, at Nanyang University in Singapore where there was an enrollment of more than 600 students, enrollment an effort was made to provide the students with some choice of project. Each member of staff submitted two to three projects that after evaluation and editing were mailed to all students before the semester began. An allocation algorithm was used to allocate projects so as to try and meet student preferences. (These preferences were made known in responses from the students that could be optically read) (Teo and Ho, 1998). Following in the footsteps of Teo and Ho, Anwar and Bahaj (2003) described the use of integer programming in allocating students to projects in the Department of Civil and Environmental Engineering at the University of Southampton. The purposes were to make the allocation of staff to individual student projects as uniform as possible, and to try and ensure that students were given their project of first choice. A model was also described for the allocation of group projects.

At the same time, client-driven projects clearly have advantages even if the choice of project is not necessarily that of the student. Ansell argued that client-driven projects are more likely to involve realistic constraints and pressures, and he cited other authorities in support of this view on industry based capstone design (e.g., Ruud and Delevaux, 1997). A client-driven project will almost certainly require work that cuts across subject boundaries.

The client does not necessarily have to be a company. Ansell gave an example from a laboratory course that accompanied an introductory circuits course. In this course, sophomore engineering students were asked to work with occupational therapy students on an assistive design project chosen by their team. In these projects the occupational therapy students represented the interests of the client(s).[4] Ansell pointed out that if a student has had a successful project, it might be possible to use it for a talking point in an interview for a job. Work of this kind might be collected in portfolios for this purpose (see Chapter 16).

In Great Britain there was a problem in the timing of the project selection process in traditionally structured courses. Often the project has been a final year activity, and the students have been introduced to their supervisors at the end of the preceding year. In some instances they could plan their project during the last term of that year. While this had many advantages for the able student, those who were weak and had to re-sit examinations at the beginning of the final year were disadvantaged because they were required to think about their project and study for their re-sit examinations at the same time during the vacation. Another disadvantage of having to choose projects early was that the student might think of a better project during the summer vacation. The way in which these early stages were conducted had a considerable impact on the design of assessment (Allison and Benson cited by Carter and Jordan, 1990).

Arguments may be made for both teacher and student-driven projects. The choice will ultimately depend on the objectives that have to be achieved. The development of team skills will in all probability involve the teacher in the selection of the project whereas if the goal is the development of so-called 'autonomous' learning, then selection is probably best made by the student. Thus, projects may also be classified according to whether they are for teams or the individual.

9.2.2.   Group or Individual Projects

Almost all of the recent reports on projects and problem-based learning are group-based. A major reason for this is that industry complains that graduates are often unable to work in teams. However, the type of organization is not always reported. Some authors make it clear that the group is organized as a company. *"Each student had a dual assignment as a design engineer and an additional corporate function"* (Dyer and Schmalzel, 1998). Depending on the type of project, and if they undertake several projects, the students can be given experience of a wide range of jobs. In this way they learn additional skills to those of teamwork. For example, Cawley described a problem-based-course at Imperial College that accommodated 12 groups of 4 students. There were three pairs of problems, *"and each group of students is required to solve one problem from each pair acting as consultants to a client group. The client group must prepare a brief critique of their consultants' solution and discuss it at the oral presentations. The roles are reversed for the other problems of the pair. The students in the client group must devise their own criteria for assessing the consultants' solutions and these criteria are often the subject of debate and oral presentations"* (Cawley, 1989; p. 180, 1991).

More detailed consideration of group work and team-work is given in Chapter 13 on cooperative learning.

9.2.3.   Classification by Assessment and Structure.

Leifer and Sheppard,[5] in a matrix that is reminiscent of the Blake-Mouton grid[6] that locates different management styles, suggested that types of problem-based learning types may be classified by who makes the assessment, (which they called judgment), and who structures the course-that is the learning experience[7]. The learning experience may be structured by an instructor, the student, or an outsider. The assessment of that learning may be by an outsider, the student, or an instructor. These possibilities produce nine types, and Leifer and Sheppard give examples of each. The types are:

1. *Structured and judged by the instructor.*
2. *Each student selects, formulates and implements final project. Instructor grades*
3. *Student presentations and documentation of design work on industrial sponsored. Evaluated by course instructor.*
4. *Individual artifact presentations assigned by instructor, peer evaluated.*
5. *Each student selects, formulates and implements final project, peers evaluate intermediate stages of project.*
6. *Student presentations and documentation of design work on industrial sponsored-project evaluated by teaching assistants.*

---

[4] Culver and Scudder (1995) have contributed an important paper on the use of adaptive devices in the teaching of design. Having had junior-and senior-year students undertake such projects, they were in a position to list the advantages and disadvantages of such projects in teaching design. Two are of immediate interest. 1. If a client is identified and the students meet the client expectations may be created that cannot, by the very nature of project learning, be met in the time available. This raises questions about (a) whose responsibility it is to deliver, and (b) the grading of the project. Is it fair to tie the grade in the course to the completion and delivery of the project? 2. How can the projects be protected from liability suits? Other projects for the disabled have been described by Miller and Hyman (1987).

---

[5] Reality brings excitement to engineering education. Undated report. Department of Mechanical Engineering, Stanford University.
[6] Blake, R. R. and J. S. Mouton (1969)
[7] The idea for this classification came from Bridges, E. M. and P. Hallinger (1995).

Notes for guidance on the preparation of a project outline-Engineering Science

Title. This should be a clear statement of the problem to be tackled. While the title should be brief, it must not be so vague or so general that it does not convey the essence of the project.

Analysis of the problem. The problem to be dealt with in the project should be analyzed as fully as possible. A general statement of the problem should be given and, where possible, quantities laid down together with the limitations under which you will be working, such as restraints of size, cost, use and availability of workshop facilities and assistance. For example, if an engine test bed is to be constructed, the nature of the engine test bed and associated equipment should be stated, the use to which the engine is to be put should be given and the parameters to be measured should be listed. If the project is of a more investigatory nature a similar analysis is required. For example, if it is concerned with an investigation into atmospheric pollution, the nature of the variables to be measured, the periods over which measurements are to be made, the factors likely to affect these periods over which measurements are to be made, the factors likely to affect these variables and the uses which might be made of the information gained should be stated.

Practical problems to be solved. Having considered the project outline you will be able to recognize the major practical problems which need to be overcome. These may be the design and manufacture of a piece of equipment or the design of experimental procedures, or both.

Possible solutions. It should be possible at this stage to see your way to solving these major practical problems in order that success can be achieved. It is therefore important that you should offer likely solutions to these problems. It may be that one solution is so obviously the best that lengthy consideration of alternative approaches is unnecessary. In most cases, however, a number of alternative solutions will occur to you or will arise as a result of consultation with your teacher or other people. The final choice of a solution will in most cases depend on further work and consultation with your teacher or other people. Your outline should give the main direction of your ideas at the time of submission.

Resources. The choice of the best solution will also depend upon the resources you have available. You should, therefore, list under the appropriate headings, equipment, manufacturing facilities, materials required, references, consultants, technical assistance available and the approximate cost involved. Such headings will not be equally important for all projects.

Timetable. You will now be in a position to draw up an approximate timetable of operation. It does not help to make wild guesses about the number of hours you will need; it is better to work in weeks available and then split the period into component parts. Do not forget to list the time necessary for writing the final report. In planning your time always assume that any task will take you much longer than you imagine on a first consideration. It is also important to allow a certain degree of flexibility; if you draw a time sequence diagram, allow a fair amount of time for variation.

References. In submitting your project outline, list the books and articles you have read in connection with the planning, and also individuals whose advice you have sought

Future work. You are strongly advised to read the appropriate sections of *Notes for Guidance of Schools* at all stages of the project, particularly during the planning period. When the moderators have studied your outlines they will forward their comments to your teacher. You are strongly advised to follow any recommendations made by your teacher or the moderator.

Exhibit 9.3. Extract from the advice given in the project outline booklet for projects in Engineering Science at A Level of The Joint Matriculation Board (1972), Manchester. (Reproduced with permission of The Joint Matriculation Board, Manchester)

7. *Instructor assembles course goals statement, faculty peer synthesizes statement and student interviews into feedback statement to instructor.*
8. *Student interviews form a major component for feedback by faculty peer to instructor.*
9. *Faculty peers setup and facilitate small group interviews of students for feedback to instructor."*

9.3. Planning, Specifying, and Evaluation: Learning contracts

In general the process of solving problems can be characterized by two broad steps. These are problem identification, formulation and problem solving (McDonald, 1968). These involve different modes of thinking and different skills. Problem identification can be no less difficult than problem solving. When students have to choose their own projects, they often have to bring broad ideas into sharp focus. Similarly, when a professor gives the topic, or for that matter a client, the student has to bring focus to the idea for its subsequent development. If the idea is perceived to be too difficult then the student will flounder. In the engineering science

course the common weaknesses found in the planning stage were the tendency to attempt the "grand problem" (e.g., optimize yacht hull design), and the tendency to underestimate the time and resources required (Carter, Heywood, and Kelly, 1986).

Brazier (2000) reported similarly about her software engineering projects. *"Students are always amazed at the amount of time it takes to do a good job on the pre-implementation phases of the project. This was reflected in the timelines and weights given by the students in the initial course contract and the subsequent revisions to time and weights they made at the end of the semester."*

In the engineering science projects, some students found it difficult to formulate an appropriate problem, and, in general, these were more likely to be weak students. But the investigators boldly reported that *"On the other hand the best project proposals (and outcomes) bear comparison with similar efforts by third-year university undergraduates."* Weakness could be predicted from the title hence the inclusion of a note on the title in the advice given on the project outline in Exhibit 9.3.

Today this outline would be called a learning contract. Its function was to prevent students undertaking work which was likely to prove of little value either experimentally and/or for the potential accreditation in the assessment process. The preparation of this outline was estimated to require ten hours of student thought and research. It was *"a minor essay in engineering and as such constituted a planned problem-solving exercise. The nature of the problem to be tackled is generally decided by the student in consultation with the teacher."* When this planning exercise was completed, it was submitted by the student to the teacher for validation, who then transmitted it to an external moderator for judgment. As will be seen from Exhibit 9.3, it required a specification and, therefore a prediction about final outcome to be evaluated. It was not uncommon for project outlines to be returned by the moderators for revision. The project outline activity contributed marks to the final grade.

At Monash University in a fourth-year computing elective, students also stated their expected outcomes in a project proposal. The approach differed to engineering science in that the students presented their proposals in a seminar held during the first three weeks of the semester. During the last two weeks of the semester, they presented their final report. Students were expected to find their own learning materials with some help from the tutor (Hadgraft, 1997).

In mechanical engineering at the University of Bath, *"a contract of initial expectation"* was agreed between the supervisor and the students. This, once a precise specification had been agreed, set out the phases and timing of events and the requirements to meet their goal (Black, 1975)

In Brazier's (2000), software engineering projects after the teams had been selected, they, *"then selected their project and submitted a formal proposal in the form of a course contract. This contract included the preliminary plan, which consisted of the project description, a breakdown of the relative weights given for the grading of each phase, and timelines for the completion of each phase. This contract was then improved by the instructor with the understanding that it could be revized once before the implementation phase of the project."*

In the engineering science program, planning and evaluation was included in this section because the examiners found that the most difficult parts of the project were the planning and evaluation. Its implementation was relatively easy. Today the process of evaluation is often called reflective practice. Many of the engineering science students had great difficulty in looking back over the production of a completed artifact in order to answer the question:, *"What could I have done that would have improved the outcome?"*

Related to the problems of planning and reflection is an issue raized by Brazier. He wrote *"despite class lectures and assigned textbook chapters on various testing strategies, students did not understand what should go into a test plan. They obviously had tested the code they had written, but were not convinced of the need for a formal plan. In fact most of the plans were created after implementation as a report of the testing that was done."* Brazier commented that more work needed to be done to emphasize the importance of this phase.

In contrast the engineering science students received no formal support to help them understand engineering design. A request by this writer that a short course should be introduced within the syllabus was turned down in favor of a recommendation in the *Notes for Guidance* (JMB, 1972) that students should familiarize themselves with books on the topic such as E. V. Krick's *Introduction to Engineering Design* (Wiley). This, as is clear from Brazier's experience, is no guarantee that they will be able to design. Nevertheless, it seems clear that students need to be helped to evaluate and reflect.

The idea that students should read a book on design has been vindicated by Atman and Bursic (1996). They reported that freshmen who had read *"a textbook about design have more complex design processes than those who did not read the text. Those students who read the text spent longer solving the problems, generated more alternatives, transitioned more frequently between design steps* [see Chapter 12], *and considered more design criteria than those who did not read the text"*

9.4. Problem (Project)-Based Learning

Projects are activities designed to solve a particular problem, and they are often a strategy within a curriculum that employs traditional strategies. It would be possible to design a curriculum in which all the knowledge requirements were covered by carefully chosen projects [see example in Chapter 8 due to Heywood et al., (1966), and the real example of Aalborg described in the next section)]. It is also possible to design a curriculum that is based on problems and this is called problem-based learning.

As with everything else in education, the terminology is confused. Whereas most authors use PBL to refer to problem-based learning, some authors also use it for project-based learning. Sometimes project is used instead of problem. At other times it is suggested that there is a difference between the two, and sometimes they are called student-directed learning (McDermott, Nafalski, and Göl, 2000). Sometimes, problem-based learning refers to a whole program. More often than not, in engineering it refers to a course.

There is a not inconsiderable literature on the topic of problem-based learning and there are some general texts including an introduction to its design by an engineer, Donald Woods (1994). (see also Boud and Feletti, 1991). Generally, project-based learning is concerned with the development of cognitive and practical skills, whereas problem-based learning is concerned with the acquisition of content and its application.

The modern approach to problem-based learning has its origins in medicine and in particular at McMaster University in Canada (Barrows and Tamblyn, 1980). There have been many evaluations of problem-based learning in the health care professions (e.g., Dukes et al., 1998; Nooman, Schmidt, and Ezzat, 1990; Patel and Kaufman, 1995; Schwartz et al., 1997).

Woods, who developed a problem-solving program that incorporated some problem-based learning, was and is based at McMaster (Woods et al., 1997). He began his explanation of problem-based learning with this illustration:

"Professor Case asks: 'Here is a toaster that isn't working, fix it! Or better still improve it'. Professor English begins: 'Today we're going to study the flow of electricity through metals, and then we'll look at ... .'"

Woods goes on to say:

"Both approaches use problems but for two completely different reasons. Case uses problems to drive learning. English uses problems to illustrate how to use knowledge after you have learned it."

One approach is student centered, the other is teacher-centered. The former approach places great responsibility on the student to undertake his/her own learning. In both cases there is teacher involvement, and in both cases a knowledge base is required. However, the subject-based approach of Professor English concentrates on building up the base using problems to illustrate principles, whereas the approach of Professor Case is to develop a knowledge base by solving a range of problems. It is argued that the advantage of the latter is that it helps the learner comprehend new material far better than subject-based learning. Put in another way, the learner can claim ownership of the learning more readily, and this is much more likely to be the case when the Professor gives a problem area and leaves the students to find and define problems.

For example, Striegel and Rover (2002) have shown how problem-based learning matches the levels of the Bloom Taxonomy. Investigation involves application that requires active learning, and involves analysis that requires problem solving; implementation involves synthesis that requires creative thinking, and evaluation that requires critical thinking. But, as was shown in Chapter 2, the Bloom Taxonomy is not always the best descriptor of what is required in engineering. The reason why Cawley, of Imperial College turned to problem-based learning was that in the examination of a final year option the students tended to avoid questions requiring the type of diagnostic and problem-solving skills essential in engineering practice. He was worried that the course stressed too much technical theory at the expense of application.

The major aims of this problem-solving course were to:

1. *"develop the student' skills of modelling, analysing and proposing practical solutions to vibration problems in engineering;.*

2. *develop the students' skill of criticizing proposed solutions to problems;*
3. *develop students' appreciation of how systems vibrate;*
4. *introduce several standard methods of analysis;*
5. *develop the students' independent study skills;*
6. *develop students' oral and written presentation skills."* (Cawley, 1991 (pp. 177-178).

LaPlaca, Newstetter, and Yoganathan (2001) described problem-based learning in bio-medical engineering as follows:

"...the PBL approach requires that students come to their own conclusions. The problem solving process is actual learning not merely application of knowledge. For example a senior design class might present a problem as: design and optimize bi-directional interfaces between excitable cells and electrodes. A design statement such as this might be divided among several teams in a competition format and is open-ended, in that, teams would likely generate different designs. A PBL problem that was formulated to have students get to the same design stage while learning the curricular components associated with it might be stated as: "You are a BME researcher for a private start-up company who had some initial success in the implantation of bi-directional electrodes in damaged neural tissue. The last three implantations have failed and the company president wants to know why". The problem stated this way encourages the students to learn curricular components (e.g., cell biology, physiology, bioelectronics, signal processing) and elements of design"[8].

In their approach the final learning outcome is sometimes presented as a concept map. Typically the classroom sequence was as follows; The first class was for the development of the hypotheses possibly using brainstorming. The second class continued this exercise in order to generate the questions for inquiry. Beginning with the second class and continuing through to the fourth class, the learning issues were researched, and in parallel the hypotheses were revisited and focused. During the fifth and sixth classes the students worked independently or together to produce the outcome. Assessment (or evaluation as some writers prefer) was undertaken in the self-mode, by peers and by the instructor. The *"responsibility of the facilitator is to ask questions that probe the students' knowledge until they know the next step or process. An experienced PBL team will do this on their own-peer to peer."*

McIntyre (2002) had the opportunity to design and evaluate a problem based learning capstone course in construction engineering at North Dakota State University. He concluded that this approach more accurately reflected design and construction practice, promoted teamwork, and assisted the development of communication skills. The students obtained insights into

---

[8]For descriptions of PBL in Mechanics of Solids (Freshmen), and mechanisms and machine dynamics (Junior) see Hadim and Esche (2002).

project management, and this could *"help to mitigate the perceived adversarial relationships that can often occur between engineers, construction managers, and contractors."* The performance measures were designed for continuous improvement of the course, as well as from the documentation to answer the questions:

- *What did we find out?*
- *Did we learn anything and what will be do differently next time?*
- *How will we modify our curricula practices, indicators, targets, and/or assessment schedules?*[9]

Some approaches to problem based learning are based on cases. *"Small groups of students and a facilitator meet to discuss a case. The students receive an initial scenario and then must question the facilitator to get additional case information. At several points in the case, the students pause to reflect on the data they have collected so far, to generate questions about the data, and to hypothesize about underlying causal mechanisms or solutions for the problems. The students must also identify issues that they do not understand and need to learn more about. After considering the case with their naïve knowledge, the students independently research the learning issues they have identified. They then share what they learned, reconsider their hypotheses and/or generate new hypotheses in light of their new learning. At the completion of the case, the students' intentionally reflect on what they have learned. In addition, they assess their own and other group members contribution to the group's learning and collaboration"* (Hmelo et al., 1995).

A major problem in the implementation of problem-based learning relates to the resources that should be available to the students. What should they have and what should be left out for them to find on their own? While students should experience difficulty in obtaining resources and data, it should not be made too difficult, otherwise valuable time will be wasted.

A major resource is prior knowledge, and sometimes projects are chosen where knowledge has to be acquired by the students at some cost to them and their tutor. For example, *"when students set out to perform cost estimations, they found they had to learn how to do much of the work. While this has increased student independence and confidence, it is accompanied by ill effects. One such effect of this background deficiency is that added student workload is created. The time spent providing the information support students need likewise is troublesome. On a positive note, this problem has had the unexpected affect of binding groups together as they have been seen helping each-other through areas of uncertainty"* (Cline and Powers, 1997).

Teachers have to be prepared to design programs where information and other resources are available just-in-time, and this may involve them in designing pre-course activities.

9.5. The Aalborg Experiment

In the late 1960s a number of European nations introduced new degree structures. One of them was Denmark, where at Aalborg University and Roskilde University problem-based curricula were introduced across the institutions. It is almost a misnomer to continue to call them an experiment since they have been running for more than 25 years. Descriptions of the approach have appeared in the engineering literature from time to time (e.g., Cowan, 1998; Fink, 2001; Fink and Bejers, 1999; Ostergraad, 1989), and a book was published by the University Press (Kjersdam and Enemark, 1994). Many of the ideas for problem-based learning have their source of inspiration in this program.

Fink and Bejers (1999), described the program thus: *"On each semester students must carry out a major project- approx 500 hours of workload per student. With groups of 5-6 students this means 2000-3000 men hours per project. This calls for a high degree of cooperation with industry to find real-life engineering problems to solve. Each problem based project work comprises problem analysis and problem definition in engineering terms, problem solving and documentation in terms of a report or a scientific paper and poster".* The program leads via a bachelors degree (3½ years) to a Masters degree (5 years). 90% of the students proceed to the higher level. It takes 10 semesters. Mandatory courses in mathematics, computer science and circuit theory of some 400 hours per semester must be taken in the electronic, electrical, and computer engineering degree program.

Each of the groups is assigned an 18-m² "office." This room is their base. *"Another important function of the project group is the learning process after each lecture of approximately two hours, where the students are expected to go to their group rooms to solve some problems, simulations etc. based on the content of the lecture. This takes another two hours while the lecturer walks from group to group to facilitate the process."*

Cowan (1998), who has been associated with developments in the freshman year, described the problem-based component in that year as follows:
"A project originates in a problem area. One such problem area, which was explored recently by a full-class group (ca. 100 students) was the matter of working conditions in Aalborg. Project groups (of five or six students) identified problems in that area. One group chose to concentrate on the noise levels in butcheries; another on the fact that EC regulations will shortly render mushroom growing, as practiced in Denmark, illegal-and hence will lead to the demise of the mushroom growing industry unless a way can be found to improve working conditions. Consequently the butchery group found that they needed study-unit courses on acoustics, while the mushroom growers required instruction in biology, and the effect of spores and the like on human beings." "The project is assessed under two headings. One is the success of the group in tackling the problem

---

[9]These are the basic questions of evaluation and TQM (see Courter Chapter 12).

which they formulated. The other begins from the group's review of their performance. They should present a realistic and analytical self-appraisal of the processes they followed, and a constructive identification of their learning needs and their aspirations for the project they will undertake, perhaps in different groups, in the second semester...."

An evaluation study compared the experience of graduates on the Aalborg program with that of graduates from a traditional university in Denmark. It was found that there were clear differences between the groups in favor of the Aalborg program in those areas that prepared graduates for their first job after graduation. These related to communication, the ability to define engineering problems, the ability to carry out a total project, and the ability to carry out technical development and research, to cooperate with people of varying backgrounds, and to take into account the social consequences of technological innovation.

Another comparative study found that 23% of the Aalborg graduates said that the workload was too high. The nominated workload at Aalborg is 45 hours per week to include 9 hours of homework. Also, 41% of Aalborg students spent more than 16 hours per week on homework, and that was more than graduates from the other university, who on average, worked less at home.

Fink (2001), in a more recent paper showed how Aalborg is beginning to look at the integration of work-based learning into academic education through problem-based experiences. This would require that university-based projects would have to be substituted by company-based projects, student teams would have to be substituted with company based teams, and the curriculum would have to be reduced (i.e., number of courses) and include work-based learning.

9.6. Student Adaptation and Motivation

It is predictable, and a matter of common experience, that students may have difficulty in adapting to modes of teaching and learning that are far removed from their experience. In moves from teacher-centered instruction to student-centered learning, old certainties are removed and new uncertainties created (McKenzie, 1995; Thompson, 1990; Woods, 1994). Woods used a model of bereavement to show how students can be helped to accommodate change.

At the University of South Australia *"students fresh from high school found the demands of PBL almost intolerable,"* and so did one of the lecturers. Those responsible for the course came to recognize *"that the scope was too ambitious for an initial experience of PBL".* Moreover, *"the failure to reinforce the experience in the second and third years tended to blunt the benefits of the experiment."* But the authors argued that in spite of the fact that there was little to show, the students had learned a lot about various aspects of engineering, and *"they had also begun the long process of developing emotional intelligence"* (McDermott, Nafalski, and Gől, 2000).

Studies of student perceptions of the learning-assessment environment in economics at Maastricht and education at the University of Leuven confirmed the view that prior and recent experiences influence the learning strategies that students use. These in turn affect the quality of their learning outcomes. The investigators argued that this was why the intended outcomes of problem-based learning were not always achieved (Segers and Dochy, 2001).

At La Trobe University in Australia the orthoptics program is varied over its three years. It proceeds from being a more teacher-directed course to being more student-centered. It is designed to foster the development of inquiry skills (McKenzie, 1995). This progression is intended to enable students to slip into problem-based learning and reduce the fears which students have of nonconventional approaches to teaching. Dukes et al., (1998), also at La Trobe, found that nursing students had unsophisticated conceptions of and approaches to learning that were not linked to professional practice outcomes. However, by the time they completed their last PBL they had come to recognize the *"link between participation in the process and the development of knowledge and skills for professional practice."*

In engineering at Sir Sandford Fleming College in Canada the curriculum is in four stages that are intended to move the student through dependence, interest, and involvement to self-directed learning. In this curriculum a full-time project is the driving force and involves interdisciplinary team-based problem solving. Seminars dealing with content are provided as required, and students learn "just in time" to solve a real-world problem (Spasov, 2000).

Many students have difficulty in understanding what it is they are supposed to do (Dyer and Schmalzel, 1998). In this respect it is interesting to note that some fourth-year students doing a computing elective in civil engineering at Monash University had difficulty getting started (Hadgraft, 1997). Waters and McCracken (1997), pointed out that the adjustment to problem-based learning for students used to teacher-centered classrooms is difficult and especially so in the requirements phase. They were unable to say whether or not the difficulty was inherent in the requirements phase,[10] or in the way they were implemented the problem-based process. Given the difficulties that students have with problem-formulation and planning it would not be surprising if it were the former.

Instructors should be prepared to allow time for clarification, and this may be of at least a lecture length and, in my experience, may require repetition. Where teams are involved, time has to be allowed for clarification of who does what, and in relation to assessment some specific rubrics may have to be written.

---

[10]This would seem to be akin to the problem-identification and formulation and planning stage. They had tried to demonstrate PBL and also used a textbook on the topic.

Students are likely to have problems throughout the project, and it may be necessary for the instructor to hold whole class updates based on the generality of the questions being asked. While the value of projects in helping students to acquire time-management skills has already been stated, it needs to be stressed that such learning is also a problem for students, particularly when time is running out.

Cline and Powers (1997), found that at Carnegie-Mellon University in Chemical Engineering, students required to develop confidence in oral presentation. One or two presentations were not enough. Therefore, they increased the number of presentations required. During the class a one-page evaluation and comment form was completed by each participant. The teams then summarized the class comments, discussed the fairness of the comments, and formulated an action plane to improve the next presentation.

It would seem from the foregoing that some preparation for problem-based learning is desirable. At the University of Bradford in civil engineering, students took two prior courses on communication skills. The first was concerned with oral presentation, report writing and IT. The other was concerned with group processes (Matthew and Hughes, 1994).

Most of the reports on PBL claim that it enhanced student motivation and that learning was enhanced when compared with traditional courses. Unfortunately, the reader is expected to accept this on trust because little data is given. One would expect a novel approach to teaching to carry with it, its own Hawthorne effect. At the same time, the evidence from the reports on projects, to the effect that projects motivate the students, seems to be sufficient to suggest that PBL would consistently motivate students. But where it is a component of a program that includes traditional courses students might be highly motivated, but find the work load considerable. For example, Dyer and Schmalzel (1998), who used a variety of techniques, also reported that students learned more in their PBL electronics course and were more motivated. *"Feed back from students was telling as one typical student comment indicates: 'while I feel that the project was an excellent learning experience, it and its application took up far too much time'."* Kellar et al., (2000) concluded that students can only realistically handle about two projects per semester. They enable them to maintain continuity; increasing the number of projects loses this continuity between course material and the different applications that they come across.

Support for these points of view comes from research on PBL in medical education. Norman and Schmidt (1992), who reviewed studies that had compared problem-based learning with conventional curricula, concluded that students taking problem-based learning courses found them more stimulating than students taking conventional courses. Such courses can foster self-directed learning, increase retention of knowledge, and create interest in clinical subject matter.

9.7. Student Learning in Problem Based Approaches

Insofar as learning is concerned, Schwartz et al., (1997), reporting on the experience of problem-based learning in medicine at the University of Kentucky, found that PBL students performed significantly better in examinations designed to test the clinical application of knowledge. They also learned important time management skills.

At the South Dakota School of Mines, a multiple strategy approach to assessment is being developed. An evaluation of the pilot stage of a PBL project in which two carefully selected groups of freshman students were compared found that the experimental group did better academically. They also had a higher retention rate and were more satisfied with the course than the students in the control group (Kellar et al., 2000).

It might be expected that if teaching and learning methods change, there might be a change in outcomes. This was the experience of instructors at the Norwegian University of Science and Technology. In a course on structures, 30 students were split into two equal groups. *"One group continued with classical teaching from the previous semester, while the other class formed PBL groups, quit lecturing and applied web technology as explained above. In this way, it was thought that the PBL class had a control class, and the knowledge acquired in the two classes could be compared at the final exam. This turned out to be a mistake. The first class became expert in accurate calculation of the load capacity of slabs of a building, how reinforcements should be bent, and placed in concrete, etc. The PBL class was most concerned with the function of the building, which in this case was a parking garage, traffic flow and optimum use of the slab area. It was less important to save 20 mm in slab thickness, while this might be a major point for the traditional class. Hence, according to traditional teaching the first class acquired correct knowledge and more competence than the PBL students, while some teachers, owners and users in the market-place saw a substantial added value in the teamwork, leading to a holistic approach and solution. The two classes could not have the same exam, so a direct comparison was impossible"* (Lenschow, 1998).

Given the attention that is being paid to integrated programs in the first year of study in the United States, the work of Patel and Kaufman (1995), who examined the role of basic science knowledge in the clinical curriculum is of interest. They examined how medical students used basic science in both conventional and problem-based learning. They found that although basic science and clinical knowledge are 'spontaneously' generated, the basic science *"is so tightly tied to the clinical experience that students appear to be unable to detach basic science even when the clinical situations demand it."* There was no transfer of learning between the two. They found that the elaborations that students made when they were called on to 'think' about problem features using basic science led to a fragmentation of knowledge structures. These elaborations led to factual errors which, as with Clement's engineering students (Chapter 4), persisted from first to fourth year. Patel and Kaufman argued that some core basic sciences should be taught at the beginning of the curriculum outside of problem-based learning because well-organized coherent information is easier to remember than disjointed facts and because the purpose of science is to make it possible to organize observations.

Matthew and Hughes (1994), of the University of Bradford, in response to the complaint that the technical content of problem-based courses in civil engineering is reduced, replied that the simple coverage of a syllabus by a teacher *"is not an indicator of even surface learning by the students."* They could have quoted evidence to suggest that surface learning was the most that could generally be expected from such courses. They went on to say *"if we are serious about developing life-long learners then, in the short term something has to give; in other words we need to create space in timetables to enable students to develop the necessary skills for minimally supported learning."*

If we are serious about developing lifelong learners, then account has to be taken of the contribution that schooling can make to its development. In this respect design and technology have a considerable role to play if the findings of Williams and Williams (1997) are anything to go by. They designed a problem based learning component for the fourth year of a B. Ed degree in design and technology education.[11] Their evaluation, which included an 18-item Likert scale inventory, led them to the conclusion that while the students appreciated the acquisition of cognitive skills in the project, they did not see this as satisfying their learning needs. The explanation offered for this by Williams and Williams was that these students had not had much experience with learning methods other than those that were didactic and teacher centred prior to the problem based approach. They also suggested from another analysis that the students while appreciating the learner centred approach did not realise that it required them to individually research new knowledge. *"This interpretation is reinforced by the negative responses to the item 'How often would you use a similar methodology in your teaching?" (Third lowest mean of all the items). The implication here is that students did not see problem based learning as a valuable method, and could not see its relevance to their future teaching and learning."*

At the same time open-ended items revealed that students liked having the opportunity to develop a technology that was new to them. There was also a positive response to having to work with others in a group who had complementary skills, although some complained about the difficulty of motivating all group members. One of the groups was entirely made up of females and their reaction was significantly more positive than for those of the other groups. They perceived

themselves to work well as a group, and this created a generally positive attitude to problem based learning. The technology was new to them as well.

In spite of what could be construed as a negative report Williams and Williams (1997) concluded that the PBL methodology is appropriate for use in technology education, and that if it is not included together with a wide range of methodologies the total discipline of technology cannot be represented appropriately.

It is evident that if teachers in schools, and especially those in a subject that is project based, do not see the relevance of problem based learning, particularly in high school, they are creating a hurdle for students who have to do problem based learning early in their university program. They are certainly not helping them develop skills of lifelong learning.

9.8. The Assessment of Projects and Problem-Based Learning.

The assessment of project and problem-based learning provoked new challenges and problems. For example, should the assessment take into account work undertaken in the planning stage as happened in the JMB engineering science examination. Carter and Jordan (1986) were of the opinion that project outlines were required by a significant number of university departments in the UK. They also reported that many departments required presentations at seminars to be assessed. Some approaches were rather mean. That is, they provided additional evidence rather than a specific mark in the grading system.

A major problem is the mechanism by which the assessment achieves reliability. In Britain a variety of approaches have been used to try and achieve reliability. These have included the use of independent and progress assessors in addition to the supervisor (see Adderley et al., 1975). Allison and Benson (1983), who surveyed departments of engineering, found that most of those in their survey used a second assessor. They argued for diversification of responsibility not only to include a second assessor, but to provide for interviewing by pairs of staff.

Project work of whatever kind taps skills that cannot ordinarily be measured by a written text. For this reason it has been necessary to design criterion referenced schedules. In the engineering science coursework assessment, the moderators used a dichotomous marking scheme. At first, they found that as the scheme developed the standard of work improved and it became increasingly difficult to distinguish between the generally capable and the very good student. It was necessary to make such distinctions because in the public examination system in the United Kingdom the results have to be pseudo-norm-referenced, i.e., distributed along part of the normal curve. Therefore, the examiners changed section B to a semi-criterion referenced scheme. Three items from this scheme are shown in Exhibit 9.4 (see also Chapter 2 Exhibits 2.10 and 2.11). The effect of this change was to elevate the distribution at the lower mark

---

[11] In Australia.

end of the scale and so recognize some competence on the part of weaker candidates. In Figure 9.1 the drawn curve shows the results of the dichotomous marking for the last group that experienced that scheme. The circles show the results for the group who in the following year experienced the semi-criterion-referenced scheme. Over the years minor adjustments to that scheme were made.

The scheme was found to discriminate well between the candidates, and the published marks of the moderators showed a high degree of consistency over a ten-year period as measured by means and standard deviations.

In this scheme the concern was with the development of practical skills using the knowledge base that the student had. It did not specify knowledge required, although that knowledge was taken into account in the moderating exercise. In the engineering science scheme the concern was with the development of practical skills using the knowledge that the student had. It did not specify the knowledge required, although it was not possible to arrive at a satisfactory moderation of the scripts without taking that knowledge into account. Data were presented that showed that the teacher assessors marked slightly higher on average than the moderators, although there was a remarkable degree of agreement between them. It is of some interest to note that by and large the students performed better on the projects than they did on the investigations. In the case of the investigations the students found the quantification and interpretation of errors difficult (see assessment question in Exhibit 9.4), and in the projects awards for design (assessment question 9, see Exhibit 9.4) were difficult to come by (Carter, Heywood, and Kelly, 1986). Americans who are used to standardized testing are wary of this kind of grading because of the variance but Waters and McCracken (1997) *"feel the use of the graded artifacts is an excellent means of assessment of PBL."*

Stephanchick and Karim (1999) described a scheme for the evaluation of a software design component where the knowledge base had to be taken into account because such projects are primarily knowledge-based. Within each domain the student had to demonstrate skill in a number of competencies, and each of these are graded on a five-point scale. In group problem-based learning there is also a requirement that knowledge should be learned as well. This is a consequence of the role of the project in interdisciplinary study and the acquisition of knowledge. It becomes difficult to measure this knowledge in group projects. For this reason, some practitioners of problem-based learning give an end of semester examination to test the *"grasp of principles of the subject... to eliminate performance inconsistencies which are not reflected in the group only grades"*(Maskell, 1997). Cawley (1989) is cited by Maskell thus: *"Cawley found that the spread of marks for group only assessment was very small, with both student and teacher perceptions indicating that some students were performing much better than others, and that some students were not putting in a team effort."*

Waters and McCracken (1997) used mid-term and final examinations, the purpose of which was to give the students small problems that they could solve independently. The examination was of the open-book type, and as with Maskell, the problems were set to test the student's grasp of important concepts in the course. The mid-term examination consisted of four problems, and the final examination was a take-home examination designed to cover all aspects of the course. *"One question was designed to measure for transfer and one was designed to generate student reflection and overall self-assessment."* The idea of a take-home examination would be incomprehensible to many teachers in the United Kingdom.

At the University of Bradford, Matthew and Hughes (1994) tried a variety of methods of assessment in civil engineering. The conventional written examination was set primarily to reassure colleagues that standards were being maintained. They also tried group reports, essays, and oral presentations, and they also developed what they called an interactive exam. *"This is really just another problem, but this time the problem is solved by individuals, not the group. The students are given an outline of the problem; they then implement the strategy they have been using on the course in that they identify specific information they require in order to solve the problem. This information is available from us but only if the students ask specific questions. For example they may require information in order to identify specific information about ground water chemistry; asking for an analysis of the ground water is not sufficiently well defined, they should ask for an analysis of the ground water for specific contaminants, ie pH, chloride content, sulphate content, and also specify from what depth the water should be extracted. This type of assessment has proved (to us) to be very useful in seeing whether or not students can transfer knowledge and skills learned from one problem to aid them in solving a new problem."*

A problem with this system and indeed any system where the final grade is composed of a mark for coursework and a mark for the examination is the relative weighting to be given to the two components. Often students do a huge amount of coursework for relatively little recompense. In the Engineering Science scheme they also had to undertake controlled assignments and experimental investigations. In the initial years they were awarded up to 12% of the total mark for coursework. Students and teachers rightly complained, and consequently, the amount of coursework had to be reduced and the percentage available for it increased to 20% (Carter, Heywood, and Kelly, 1986). Davenport (2000) at Bilkent University in Turkey experienced similar pressures from freshman students undertaking project work in a computer programming course. In Maskell's system the examination counted for 25%, and in Hadgraft's (2000) problem-based computing elective the marks were split as follows 15% for the seminars 35% for the report, and 50% for the final product.

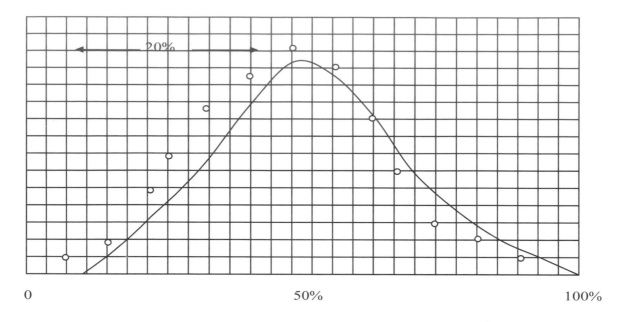

0   50%   100%

Coursework mark

Figure 9.1. Mark distributions year 1 vertical lines (dichotomous grading), and Year 2 circles (semi-criterion-referenced grading) (Carter, Heywood, and Kelly, 1986, p. 54).

Errors	
The report includes a statement of errors with estimates of	
Magnitudes and a discussion of their relative significance	3
A statement of errors and estimates of the magnitude of each error	2
A statement of errors (including the most important errors)	1
No explicit statement of errors	0
(a) the criteria relating to errors for the experimental investigations.	
Execution.	
In executing the plan the candidate gave thorough consideration to	
Realistic alternatives at every stage, and made a reasoned selection of the	
optimum solution in each case	3
Gave consideration to realistic alternative solutions with inadequate	
reasons for selection	2
Gave some attention to the consideration of alternative solutions	1
Paid little attention to this aspect of the work.	0
Design activity	
In relation to the design for all or part of the project with respect to the	
procedure or artifact the candidate produced a markedly significant	
And original contribution	3
An original contribution	2
A new device by applying a standard design technique	1
Little or no design activity during his work on the project.	
(b) Two of the criteria for the assessment of projects.	

Exhibit 9.4. Extracts from the rubrics for the experimental investigations and projects in Engineering Science. *Notes for the Guidance of Schools* No 4. **(JMB 1972).**

Because one of the students perceived the weighting of the components to be arbitrary, Hadgraft involved the students in the design of the assessment structure. *"This developed ownership of the assessment clearing one more hurdle which often stands in the way of effective learning."* The assessment of group projects faces staff with a considerable challenge. One of the major problems that had to be faced in group projects and problem-based learning is how to be fair to individual students when some of them may not have pulled their weight. Various solutions have been put forward to deal with this problem, and most of them involve an element of peer assessment. In order to account for individual contributions to the group effort, Maskell (1997)[12] used the peer performance index to adjust the lecturer determined group mark. This index varies according to the number of students in the group. In the case of small groups, it is derived by negotiation with the members of the group. In the case of large groups, it is derived from confidential peer ratings. The grade (G) is:

$$G = 0.5*GM + 0.5*GM*PI$$

where GM is the assessed group mark, and PI is the student-derived performance index (Maskell, 1997).

Ma (1996) of the City University of Hong Kong described a group decision support system for problem-based learning. The criteria for assessment were derived from consultation with the teachers, the students, and other faculty. The total mark for a project group is the sum of the weighted marks from the assessment form. Each group member is required to write down his or her percentage of contributions to the project, and the marks for an individual student are the product of his/her percentage contribution to the cumulated marks for the whole group.

There have been various reports that suggest that peer assessment can be reliable and valid. Quite naturally, students are likely to have concerns about it, and one way of allaying these fears is to negotiate the system with the students. Maskell, for example, gives students time to settle in (two or three weeks and no later) before he negotiates the procedure.

Another way of obtaining information about student contributions to group work is to require the final report to contain contributions from each individual in the group. At Sir Sandford Fleming College, in addition to this requirement, students submitted work in progress for questioning by their mentors. Eighty percent of the marks were awarded for individual performance in the project and individual tasks, oral and written communication skills, and technical skills. Twenty percent were awarded for teamwork in each of these areas as demonstrated in the team log and final report (Spasov, 2000).

Both project work and problem-based learning have promoted the use of journals and portfolios. The literature shows that a variety of approaches have been used (e.g., Cowan, 1989; Fink et al., 2000). Reports on projects are a form of journal or portfolio except that they

summarize what has been achieved. In the engineering science program students were expected to keep a log, and the final report was intended to be compiled from the log. The reports were more like a research paper, [JMB, (1972) gives examples]; and as we are reminded, research degrees are problem-based learning. Portfolios and Journals are discussed in more detail in Section 16.1. It cannot be said too often that if students are asked to keep a journal, the purposes have to be clear, and gains have to be perceived.

Finally, there should be no need to make the point that the assessment of student learning is an evaluation of the extent to which the goals have been achieved and that such evaluation is easily built into courses. The report on problem-based learning in sustainable technology (SDT) by Hmelo et al., (1995) may be used to illustrate this point. They used summative assessment to test student understanding of course content and transfer of learning. Two types of question were asked. There were those concerned with the definition of sustainable technology, as well as those concerned with comprehension and understanding. For the latter, the students were given a case study to read before answering the question, *"What are the sustainability issues in the case?"* Both questions were followed by subquestions relating to definitions, technical, ethical, environmental, and economic issues. Students were also asked to develop and present cases so that their understanding of the issues could be assessed.

The students were given pre- and post-tests, and in respect of the definitions there was a considerable improvement between the tests. However, the students did not show a significant improvement in their ability to identify SDT issues without any prompting. But when they were asked to identify particular types of issue, their performance improved.

The course had included students who weren't chemical engineers, so one hypothesis was to see if this group was the cause of the result. Analysis of variance found they were not. There were no significant differences between the two groups in this respect. It was also suggested that the students learned technical information that was specific to the case, and did not, or were unable to reflect on its use in other situations. The third possibility was that it related to the way in which the groups were organized. The student who had responsibility for research in each group may not have reported it adequately to the group. Clearly, if the transfer goal was still considered to be important, action needed to be taken. This discussion of assessment and evaluation is extended in Chapters 15 and 16.

9.9. The Role of Faculty

It seems that every alternative method of teaching to the traditional model involves the teacher in a change of role and/or more work. This is true of projects and problem-based learning, even when projects are instructor-driven. Dyer and Schmalzel (1998) wrote that: *"making the transition from a traditional lecture course to the project-*

---

[12] At James Cook University in Australia.

oriented approach is a natural extension of project engineering. Starting with a list of requirements, a sequence of project tasks must be defined and then implemented." This was certainly the view of those who designed the engineering science scheme, and it is reflected in its assessment rubric. They recognized that projects would change the role of teachers.

In project-based learning, teachers have to become managers of learning. They have to become more flexible (e.g., Hadim and Esche, 2002). The term facilitator has the same meaning. Reports of instructors on their roles show a variety of perceptions. For example, Hadgraft (1997) wrote that this means: "*providing students with adequate initial learning resources; providing a structured learning experience for those students who need it; providing a suitable physical environment where work and learning are possible; keeping student jobs on-track; helping to solve technical problems if necessary, and assessing student work.*" He pointed out that there are some students who fall behind, and this requires progress checks.

Hmelo et al., (1995), writing about a problem-based course in sustainable technology, said that: "*the role of the class instructor is to facilitate discussion around issues of technology, environment, economics and ethics (the dimensions of sustainable development), and to encourage the use of fundamental principles and tools to address these issues.*" Others simplify it to facilitate, guide and evaluate (Spasov, 2000). LaPlaca, Newstetter, and Yoganathan (2001) suggested that the facilitator should help students to build bridges between what they are doing and the more traditional courses that they have to follow.

Moust, De Grave, and Gijselaers (1990) pointed out that in medical problem-based learning, the instructor is generally a member of a team and the responsibility for the program belongs to the team with each member taking charge of a unit of subject matter.

Changes in attitude are required of both staff and students. The instructor has to adjust to student choice, and students have to learn to rely on their own problem solving capabilities rather than those of the instructor. They also have to learn to deal with their peers in different ways if they are working in groups. Dyer and Schmalzel (1998) wrote that: "*we are asking significantly more effort on the part of both the instructor and student. The instructor must be prepared to deliver JIT education on topics of immediate concern to students working on a particular phase of their project. However, many of the topics can be anticipated and planned for in advance.*" But such planning may involve them in more work than the preparation for traditional lectures. They go on to say that "*we are also asking more of our students. Not only must they master some number of traditional lecture/lab topics, but they must also develop effective skills in order to complete project work.*"

It would seem reasonable to suppose that just as students require some introduction (training) to problem-based learning, so do faculty. Such training would not only be on classroom management but would also be on the design of problems.

9.10.   Conclusions

The reports on problem-based learning, although relatively small in number, give sufficient evidence to throw a challenge to engineering educators. It cannot be dismissed as a luxury. The reports lead to the suggestion that because the skills developed are required by graduates in engineering practice, project work and/or problem-based learning should accompany more traditional approaches throughout the total curriculum, and not just in another phase (semester) of the overall program. In this way the needs of cognitive and affective development will be taken into account. The problems associated with assessment seem to be relatively easy to overcome. Project work requires changes in the roles of both students and teachers, and both groups would benefit from some training. In terms of the paradigms with which this part began (Chapter 7), the curriculum should have a greater reflexive component.

References

Adderley, K., et al (1975). *Project Methods in Higher Education.* Society for Research into Higher Education, London.

Allison, J., and F. A. Benson (1983). Undergraduate projects and their assessment. *IEE Proceedings*, 130, (Part A), 402.

Ansell, H. G (1998). Professor-driven, student-driven, and client-driven design projects. *Proceedings Frontiers in Education Conference*, 149–154.

Anwar, A. A., and A. S. Bahaj (2003). Swtudent project allocation using integer programming. *IEEE Transactions on Education* 46, (3), 359-367.

Atman, C. J., and K. M. Bursic (1996). Teaching engineering design. Can reading a textbook make a difference. *Research in Engineering Design.* 8, 240–250.

Barrows, H., and R. Tamblyn (1980). *Problem Based Learning: An Approach to Medical Education.* Springer, New York.

Beauchamp-Báez, G and L. V. Meléndez-González (1998). Design projects for digital and process control courses. *Proceedings Frontiers in Education Conference*, 69–72.

Black. J (1975). Allocation and assessment of project work in the final year of the engineering degree course at the University of Bath. *Assessment in Higher Education*, 1, (1), 35–53.

Blake, R. R., and J. S. Mouton (1964). *The Managerial Grid.* Gulf Publishing, Houston, TX

Boud, D and G. Feletti (eds) (1991). *The Challenge of Problem Based Learning.* Kogan Page.

Brazier, P (2000). Using high-level tools to implement software engineering projects. *Proceedings Frontiers in Education Conference*, 1, T2C-13 to18.

Bridges, E. M., and P. Hallinger. (1995). *Problem Based Learning in Leadership Development.* E. Clearinghouse on Education Management. Eugene, Oregon.

Carter, G., Heywood, J., and D.T. Kelly (1986). *Case Study in Curriculum Assessment. GCE Engineering Science (Advanced).* Roundthorn Press, Manchester.

Carter, G., and T. A. Jordan (1990). *Student Centred Learning in Engineering. Engineering Enhancement in Higher Education. Prospects and Problems.* Monograp, University of Salford, Salford.

Cawley, P (1989). The introduction of a problem-based option into a conventional engineering degree course. *Studies in Higher Education*, 14, 33–94.

Cawley, P (1991). A problem-based module in mechanical engineering in D. Boud and G. Feletti (eds.). *The Challenge of Problem-Based Learning.* Kogan Page, London.

Clark, W. W., and R. Hake. (1997). An example of project based learning using a laboratory gantry crane. *Proceedings of the Frontiers in Education Conference,* 1344−1348.

Cline, M., and G. J. Powers (1997). Problem based learning via open ended projects in Carnegie Mellon University's chemical engineering laboratory. *Proceedings Frontiers in Education Conference,* 350−354.

Cowan, J. (1998). *On Becoming an Innovative University Teacher. Reflection in Action.* SRHE/Open University Press, Buckingham.

Culver, R and D. Scudder (1995). Lessons learned on using adaptive devices for the disabled to teach design. *Proceedings Frontiers in Education Conference,* 2c£-12 to 15.

Davenport, D (2000) Experience using a project-based approach in an introductory programming course. *IEEE Transactions on Education.* 43, (4), 443-448.

Dekker, D. L (1996). The difference between "open ended projects" and "design projects." *Proceedings Frontiers in Education Conference.* 3, 1257-1259.

Deere, M (1967). Creative projects in university engineering. *New University,* 1, 30.

De Malherbe, M. C and J. G. Wistreich (1964). An experiment in education for design. *Chartered Mechanical Engineer,* 11, 149.

Dukes, M., Forbes, H., Hunter, S., and M. Prosser (1998) Problem based learning (PBL): conceptions and approaches of undergraduate students of nursing. *Advances in Health Science Education* 3, (1), 59−70.

Duncan, J. P (1962). The impact of professional engineering on the public. *Journal Junior Institution of Engineers,* 72, 139.

Dyer, S., and J. Schmalzel (1988). Macro-electronics. Building the perfect beast. *Proceedings Frontiers in Education Conference,* 73−78

Ellis, C. D., Rakowski, R. T., and P. T. C. March (1985). Design project case study: Capacitor design for high temperature applications. *International Journal of Applied Engineering Education.* 1, 349−53.

Farr, J. V., Lee, M. A., Metro, R. A. and J. P. Sutton (2001). Using systematic engineering design process to conduct undergraduate engineering management capstone projects. *Journal of Engineering Education,* 90, (2), 193−197.

Farrell, S., Hesketh, R. P., and C. Stewart Slater (1999). Investigation of the brewing process: an introduction to reverse process engineering in the freshman clinic at Rowan University. *Proceedings Frontiers in Education Conference,* 12b4-14 to18.

Fincher, S., and M. Petre (1998). Project-based learning practices in computer science education. *Proceedings Frontiers in Education* 3, 1185−1191.

Fink, F. K (2001) Integration of work based learning in engineering education. *Proceedings Frontiers in Education Conference,* 2, F3E-10 to15.

Fink, F. K. and F. Bejers (1999). Integration of engineering practice into curriculum. 25 years of experience with problem based learning. *Proceedings Frontiers in Education Conference.* 11a2-7 to 12

Fink, L. D. et al (2000). Reengineering sooner civil engineering education. *Proceedings Frontiers in Education Conference,* 1, T1F-3-T1F-8.

Hadgraft, R. (1997). Student reactions to a problem-based, fourth year computing elective in civil engineering. *European Journal of Engineering Education,* 22, (2), 115−123.

Hadim, H. A., and S. K. Esche (2002). Enhancing the engineering curriculum through project based learning. *Proceedings Frontiers in Education Conference,* 2, F3F-1 to 6.

Hayes, S. V. and S. A. Tobias (1965). The Project method of teaching creative mechanical engineering. *Proceedings of the Institution of Mechanical Engineers* (Special edition).

Hmelo, C. E., et al., (1995). A problem-based course in sustainable technology. *Proceedings Frontiers in Education Conference,* 4a3 1 to 5.

Heywood, J (1969). An evaluation of certain post-war developments in technological education. Thesis. University of Lancaster Library, Lancaster.

Heywood, J (1976). Discovery methods in engineering science at 'A' level. *International Journal of Mechanical Engineering Education.* 4, (2), 97-107.

Heywood, J (1989). *Learning, Adaptability and Change.* Paul Chapman Publishing, London.

Heywood, J., Lee, L. S., Monk, J. D., Moon, J., Rowley, B. G. H., Turner, B. T., and J. Vogler (1966). The Education of professional engineers for design and manufacture. (A model curriculum). *Lancaster Studies in Higher Education,* No 1, 2, 151.

Hopton, G. U (1950). *Transactions Institution of Chemical Engineers,* 28, 173.

Ivins, J. R (1997). Interdisciplinary project work: practice makes perfect. *IEEE Transactions on Education.* 40, (3), 179−183.

Jeffreys, G. V (1961). *The Manufacture of Acetic Anhydride.* Institution of Chemical Engineers, London.

JMB (1972). *Notes for the Guidance of Schools. Engineering Science at the Advanced Level.* Joint Matriculation Board, Manchester.

Kellar, J. J. et al (2000) A problem based learning approach for freshman engineering. *Proceedings Frontiers in Education Conference,* F2G − 7 to 10.

Kjersdam, F and S. Enemark (1994). *The Aalborg Experiment* Aalborg University Press, Aalborg, DK.

Klein, R. E. (1991). The bicycle project approach: A vehicle to relevancy and motivation. *Proceedings Frontiers in Education Conference,* 47−51.

LaPlaca, M. C., Newstetter, W. C., and A. P. Yoganathan (2001). Problem-based learning in biomedical engineering curricula. *Proceedings Frontiers in Education Conference* 2, F3E 16 to 21.

Leifer, L., and S. Sheppard (undated) Reality Brings Excitement to Engineering Education. Department of Mechanical Engineering, Stanford University, Stanford, CA

Lenschow, R. J (1998). From teaching to learning: A paradigm shift in engineering education and life long learning. *European Journal of Engineering Education,* 23, (2), 155−161.

Ma, J (1996). Group decision support system for assessment of problem-based learning. *IEEE Transactions in Education.* 39, (3), 388−393.

Maskell, D (1997). Problem-based design and assessment in a digital systems program. *Proceedings Frontiers in Education Conference,* 562−565.

Matthew, R. G. S and D. C. Hughes (1994). Getting at deep learning: a problem-based approach. *Engineering Science and Education Journal.* October 234−240.

McCracken, W. M., and R. Waters. (1997). Assessment and evaluation in problem based learning. *Proceedings Frontiers in Education Conference.* 689−693.

McIntyre, C (2002). Problem-based learning as applied to the construction and engineering capstone course at North Dakota State University. *Proceedings Frontiers in Education Conference,* F2D−1 to 6.

McDermott, K. J., Nafalski, A and O. Göl (2000) Active learning in the University of South Australia. *Proceedings Frontiers in Education Conference,* T1B−11 to 15.

McDonald, F (1968). *Educational Psychology.* Wadsworth, Belmont, CA.

McKenzie, L (1995). Teaching clinical reasoning to orthoptics students using problem-based learning . In J. Higgs and M. Jones (ed). *Clinical Reasoning in the Health Professions.* Butterworth; Oxford.

Miller, G., and W. Hyman (1987) Undergraduate bio-engineering projects applied to real world problems for the handicapped. *International Journal of Applied Engineering Education.* 5, (4), 45−1456.

Mountain, J. R. (2000). Extra-curriculum- the labor of love project. *Proceedings Frontiers in Education Conference,* S1B−11 to 17.

Moust, J. H. C., De Grave, W. S., and W. H. Gijselaers (1990). The tutor role: a neglected variable in the implementation of problem based learning in Z. M. Nooman et al., (eds). *Innovation in Medical Education. An Evaluation of its Present Status.* Springer, New York.

Murray, M (1986). Recent developments in the school curriculum in France in J. Heywood and P. Matthews (eds.). *Technology. Society and the School Curriculum: Practice and Theory in Europe*. Roundthorn Publishing, Manchester.

Nooman, Z. M., Schmidt, H. G., and E. S. Ezzat (1990) (eds.) *Innovations in Medical Education*. Springer, New York.

Norman, G. R. and H. G. Schmidt (1992). The psychological basis of problem-based learning: a review of evidence. *Academic Medicine*, 67, 557–568.

Norman, W. S (1959). The design problem. *Chemical Engineer*, 1, 50.

O'Connor, B., Ainscough, J., and Rakowski, R., and P. T. C. March (1985). The electrical tasks course in the special engineering program. *International Journal of Electrical Engineering Education*, 22, 197–204.

Ostergraad, J (1989). Experience with project organized problem centered engineering education. *Proceedings World Conference in Engineering Education for Advancing Technology*. 730–732. Sydney.

Parnaby, J (1998). The requirements for engineering degree courses and graduate engineers: an industrial viewpoint. *Engineering Science and Education Journal*. 7, (4), 181–187.

Patel, V. L., and D. R. Kaufman (1995). Clinical reasoning and biomedical knowledge: implications for teaching. In J. Higgs and M. Jones (eds.). *Clinical Reasoning in the Health Services*. Butterworth, Oxford.

Pullman, W. A (1964, 1965) Teaching design to sandwich course students. *Proceeding Institute of Mechanical Engineers*. Special Edition.

Ruud, C., and V. Delevaux (1997). Developing and conducting an industry based capstone design course. *Proceedings Frontiers in Education Conference*. 2, 644–647.

Schwartz, R. W., et al (1997). Problem based learning and performance based teaching: effective alternatives for undergraduate surgical education and assessment of student performance. *Medical Teacher*, 19, (1), 19–23.

Segers, M and F. Dochy (2001. New assessment forms in problem-based learning: the value-added of the students' perspective. *Studies in Higher Education*, 26, (3), 328–342.

Sheppard, S. D. (1992). Mechanical Dissection. An experience in how things work. Proceedings of the Engineering Education: Curriculum Innovation and Integration. Conference.Jan 6- 10. Santa Barbara,CA.

Spasov, P (2000). Look, no timetable. *Proceedings Frontiers in Education Conference*, 3, S1B –12 to 17.

Stephanchick, P and A. Karim (1999). Outcomes based program assessment: a practical approach. *Proceedings Frontiers in Education Conference*, 13d–2 to 6.

Steed, R. W (1961). Undergraduate project work. *Technical Education*, December.

Stone, C. R., and D. I. Green-Armytage (1986). A final year project case study. Engine combustion modelling. International *Journal of Applied Engineering. Education, 2*, (5/6), 283–288.

Striegel, A and D. T. Rover (2002). Problem based learning in an introductory computer engineering course. *Proceedings Frontiers in Education Conference*, 2, F1G–7 to 12.

Teo, C. Y. and D. J. Ho (1998). A systematic approach to the implementation of final year project in an electrical engineering undergraduate course. *IEEE Transactions on Education*. 41, (1), 25–29.

Thompson, D. G (1990). Reactions to the introduction of problem-based learning into a medical school: Faculty and student views. In Z. M. Nooman, K. H. Schmidt, and E. S. Ezzatt, (eds.) Innovation in Medical Education. Springer, New York.

Warburton, G. B (1961). Some effects of Recent Advances in Knowledge on the Education of Engineers. Inaugural Lecture, University of Nottingham, Nottingham.

Waters, R and W. M. McCracken (1997). Assessment and evaluation in problem based learning. *Proceedings Frontiers in Education Conference*, 689–693.

Whitehead, R. W. and K. J. Glover 91967). The influence of digital computers on the undergraduate course at Bradford Institute of technology. *International Journal of Electrical Engineering Education*, 5, 63

Williams, A., and P. J. Williams (1997). Problem based learning; an appropriate methodology for technology education. *Research in Science and Technological Education*. 15, (1), 91–103.

Woods, D. R (1994). *Problem-Based Learning: How to Gain the most from PBL*. McMaster University Bookshop; Hamilton, Ontario.

Woods, D. R. et al (1997). Developing problem solving skills: the McMaster problem solving program. *Journal of Engineering Education*. 86, (2), 75–-92

PART III: PROBLEM SOLVING, CREATIVITY, AND DESIGN

CHAPTER 10: PROBLEM SOLVING

Summary

Problem solving, creativity, and design are different dimensions of engineering that are at the heart of the activity itself. From the perspective of learning, there are many overlaps, yet not all problem solving is design and not all design is creative. For this reason, they are treated separately in the three chapters that follow, although common to them all is the issue as to whether or not they are discipline skills that can be developed through teaching for that purpose.

Woods (2000) takes the view that problem solving is a specific discipline, and this chapter includes a description of the McMaster Problem Solving Course that he inspired. Woods identified 150 heuristics or strategies for problem solving. As a result of this research, he and his colleagues changed the scheme and moved from a five-stage to a six-stage strategy. Their research does not support the view that the stages of a strategy should always be used serially. Prior to the discussion of the McMaster scheme, evidence from studies that have applied problem solving heuristics to the teaching of engineering is summarized. Particular attention is paid to the Polya model (and its adaptations), and to the Wales and Stager Guided design model. The evidence supports the hypothesis that not only can problem solving be taught, but also that it should be taught. Other evidence in support of this view is obtained from studies of the differences between novices and experts. Nevertheless, as the previous discussion of learning styles showed individuals approach problem solving in a variety of different ways, and this has implications for instruction.

Courses in problem solving cannot be one-off activities because the skills, [Woods and his colleagues (1997) identified 37 such skills], need to be developed and reinforced, practiced in the other subjects of the engineering curriculum.

An important ability in problem solving is to be able to think qualitatively as well as quantitatively, and many engineering students find this difficult. McCracken and Newstetter (2001) applied the concept of representational transformation (see Section 11.5d) to explain this concept. They argued that one reason why engineering students may find problem solving difficult is that each transformation uses different symbols and is, therefore, a different linguistic system. In this representation of engineering, engineers and engineering students require to learn a number of languages. These sections are preceded by a discussion of the role of testing (assessment of learning) on problem solving. The difficulty of designing adequate test questions should not be underestimated.

The chapter ends with a note on critical thinking and a discussion of the differences, (if any), between it and problem solving. Critical thinking as practised in the humanities is a different language. Apart from critical writing engineers can be introduced to critical thinking as practiced in the humanities in courses in ethics.

10. Introduction[1]

Many descriptions of what it is that engineers do emphasize that the primary activity of engineering is problem solving.[2] At the same time, over the years, there has been much criticism of engineering courses because they do not teach problem solving, at least in terms of the real problems that engineers are likely to face. It has been suggested that one reason for this state affairs is the overloaded curriculum, a consequence of which, is that teachers come to believe that memorization is the primary skill that students need to learn. The instruction given, supported by a transmission model of learning, aims to help students memorize even though teachers are aware of current understandings of how memory works.[3]

But there is also a view that there is no need to teach problem-solving skills. *"Many instructors cannot see it (problem solving) as an educational problem, feeling that students unable to work problems just do not understand the subject material"* (Red, 1981). Problem solving skills are apparently acquired from one's genes or developed through osmosis. However, like Red (1981), a number of engineering educators have accepted this criticism of their teaching and set out to teach problem solving skills (e.g., Lubkin, 1980). Such courses generally teach students to use heuristics.

Crudely speaking there have been three approaches to the development of problem solving skills. The first is to design assessments that test problem solving skills (e.g. Ruskin, 1967). The second is based on the use of heuristics. Koen (1985), for example, defined the engineering method as *"the use of heuristics to cause the best change in a poorly understood situation within the available resource"*. He took the term heuristic to mean *"anything that provides a plausible aid or direction in solving a problem but is in the final analysis unjustified, incapable of justification, and fallible"* (Koen, 1986). He suggested that the engineering concept of rule of thumb is a near-synonym. *The Oxford Dictionary* defines a heuristic as a rule or information used in the process of solving a problem.[4] Dekker

---

[1] For a general reader on problem solving, see Sterberg R. J., and E. J. Smith (eds). *Psychology of Human Thought*. Cambridge U. P. and in particular the chapter by A. Lesgold.

[2] Practice varies among authors concerning the use of a hyphen between problem and solving. In this text the term problem solving is used without the hyphen.

[3] For memory in relation to human intelligence see Mackintosh (1998) and Deary (2000), and for a general text see Parkin (1993).

[4] *The New Shorter Oxford Dictionary*, p 1228., 1993. In the sense of it being a rule. Wilcox (1990) has published a list of heuristics in electrical engineering. These include: Keep your designs simple; If you find a mistake, figure out why; when in doubt, don't guess, look it up and be sure.

(1995) looked on his stages as a *"road map"* or *"guide"* to follow. In The Oxford Dictionary sense the assessment schemes that have been developed for project work, like that for Engineering Science at A level, are heuristics.

A heuristic may be used in its original or a modified form (e.g., Red, 1981). An alternative has been to derive a heuristic from the literature on heuristics (e.g., Deek, Turoff, and McHugh, 1999). Others have generated a heuristic based on learning and how engineers apply their knowledge (e.g., Wales and Stager, 1972). Woods (2000), who prefers to use the term strategy, has listed 150 heuristics in an important review paper. The third approach is to try and understand how engineers learn. This approach is in the tradition of research on the differences between novices and experts in solving problems that has its origins in the work of H. A. Simon. An example of this approach by Fordyce was given in Chapter 4. Current work by Atman and her colleagues is in this vein (e.g., Atman and Nair, 1996).

Before examining these approaches the next section will outline the criticisms that have been made of engineering students and their problem-solving capabilities.

10.1. Problem Solving in Engineering Education

Over the years it has been argued that even if problem solving is taught to engineering students, it is taught in a way that is inimical to real life practice in engineering. Another interpretation of Furneaux's (1962) finding that the one major factor measured in engineering science examinations at a British University was more than likely related to the ability to pass examinations was that these examinations measured the ability to apply mathematics to problems in applied science (see Chapter 2). They required a single solution whereas real-life situations were often not amenable to problem-solving techniques that lead to a single solution. Even though Furneaux's work was completed 40 years ago, this complaint has continued to be echoed.

In 1986, Kahney (cited by Bolton and Ross, 1997) distinguished between well-defined and ill-structured problems. They also noted that others preferred to distinguish between open and closed problems but following Thompson (1987) they noted that these are but extreme ends of a spectrum. Closed problems that are amenable to a single correct solution are at one end of the spectrum, and open problems that are not amenable to such a solution are at the other end. They were writing of physics but then the examinations that Furneaux evaluated were, with the exception of engineering drawing, no more than applied physics (e.g. Aerodynamics, Acoustics, Electricity and Magnetism, Thermodynamics).[5] Engineering students were taught how to solve well-defined problems at the closed end of the spectrum. In many respects the details of this

spectrum can be seen in the taxonomy of problem solving described by Dean and Plants (1978).

It is summarized in Exhibit 10.1, and it shows a relationship between routines and higher-level skills of problem solving. At the same time, it illustrated the importance of routines in the development of open-ended problem-solving skills. For many students it represents levels of increasing difficulty. In this respect, Apple et al., (2002), suggested 5 levels of difficulty that occur in problem solving situations (Exhibit 10.2). Inspection of these levels suggests a crude relationship with the levels in *The Taxonomy of Educational Objectives*. A more specific relationship with the taxonomy has been made by Prince and Hoyt (2002), who distinguished between (a) introductory problem-solving in which knowledge, comprehension and application come into play, (b) intermediate problem solving involving analysis, and (c) advanced problem solving involving synthesis and evaluation. They made the point that traditional engineering courses relied heavily on textbook problems that did not require the problem solving skills that were relevant. They were exercises that tested the material in the chapter involved. *"That is not "problem solving" in any real sense."* They also pointed out that students who solved textbook problems might not be able to apply the concepts to real problems. It is well understood that transfer is very difficult (see Section 7.6).

One solution might be to change the style of problem that was taught and solved in lectures. This is what Prince and Hoyt did. They designed the curriculum and assessment to meet the requirements of *The Taxonomy* at each of the three phases they identified.

It was a view similar to that of Prince and Hoyt that led to a questioning of the validity of examinations in higher education as they were designed in the United Kingdom (Heywood, 1979).

Stages of problem solving sophistication
Routines
Operations which, once begun, afford no opportunity for decision, but proceed by simple or complex mathematical steps to a unique solution.

Diagnosis
Sorting out correct routines from incorrect routines for the solution of a particular problem.

Strategy
The choice of a particular routine for the solution of a problem which may be solved by several routines or variations of routines, all of which are known to the student.

Interpretation
The reduction of a real-world situation to data which can be used in a routine, and the expansion of a problem solution to determine its implications in the real world.

Generation
The development of routines which are new to the problem solver

Exhibit 10.1. Stages of problem solving sophistication described by Dean and Plants (1978; also Plants, Dean, Sears, and Venable, 1980) and summarized in this form by Red (1981). In the original text the authors described student activities and media for each of the levels. (Reproduced with permission of IEE, *Proceedings Frontiers in Education Conference*)

---

[5] The Engineering Drawing examination did produce a different factor but it was not of any great importance in the general structure of the terminal written examinations

Most recently Arvanitis and his colleagues at the University of Birmingham in the United Kingdom complained that in the education of computing and engineering professionals there was a discontinuity between software engineering and software.

"A typical introductory university programming course mainly focuses on the detailed understanding of the syntax and semantics of a language's constructs. This knowledge, however, does not translate directly into problem solving. The lack of effective problem solving skills becomes evident in later software engineering courses and eventually, when the student is employed in industry" (Arvenitis et al., 2001).[6] It may be surprising to read that Arvenitis and his colleagues reported that students possess knowledge that is too abstract. They are unable to apply problem solving techniques to programming or cope with frequent changes to project specifications. *"The graduate software engineering workforce is described by industrialists as 'very knowledgeable, but not a lot of use*[7,]" (Arvenitis et al., 2001).

In Scandinavia, Sutinen and Tarhio (2001)[8] pointed out that there was a need to train computer scientists in *"creative or innovative problem management"*. *"Because the term problem solving may cause misconceptions, we use the term 'problem management' to point out that the management of problems and potential solutions is a key issue in problem solving. The attributes creative and innovative emphasize the art of the problem management process: it has to be 'open' already at the problem definition phase. Also the process itself should be open to modifications of the initial problem.*

Level.	Description
1. Automatic	Performance of task without thinking.
2. Skill exercise	Consciously involved but minimal challenge using specific knowledge.
3 .Problem Solving	Challenging, but possible with current knowledge and skills through a strong problem solving approach.
4. Research	Requires additional knowledge that currently does not exist within a learning effort to effectively accomplish the task.
5. Overwhelming	Cannot be accomplished without a significant increase in capacity, most likely by bringing in additional expertise.

Exhibit 10.2. Levels of difficulty in problem solving situations due to Apple et al (2002). (Reproduced with permission of IEEE, *Proceedings Frontiers in Education Conference*)

On the other hand, the term management instead of solving stresses that a problem always undergoes a process. A solution of a problem is nothing more than one of the stages of this process: a potential end-product to be evaluated before finishing the more extensive process" (Sutinen and Tarhio, 2001).This view is in keeping with the axiom that a learner will be better able to learn to solve problems if the learner has a model of

the problem solving process in mind (Saupé, 1961). Today, our understanding of our processes of learning is called metacognition.

10.2.   Problem Solving and the Design of Assessment

If it is accepted that the mode of assessment, (where that assessment conditions grades) influences learning then on face validity grounds there is something in the view that assessment questions have not encouraged the development of ill-structured problem solving skills. The British have never been enamoured with objective tests. They have argued that multiple choice questions, which they associate with objective testing, encourage memorization and cannot develop higher-order skills such as problem solving. Such criticisms are made even when the contrary case is rigorously supported. This is not to say that such tests have not come in for criticism in the United States. Indeed it is criticisms of such tests in relation to the practical needs of students in everyday life that have led to the movement toward 'authentic' assessment. At the same time the British were open to similar criticism in that the long answer questions set in their examinations were at the closed end of the spectrum. Furneaux's findings led directly to the design of the examination structure for engineering science at A level, and that examination can lay claim to have been the first examination that was based on the principles of authentic assessment in the United Kingdom (Carter, Heywood, and Kelly, 1986). But, more of all this in Chapters 15 and 16. Here, it is sufficient to explore the meaning of open-ended and to enter caveats related to teaching for problem solving in schools and higher education. A study by Ruskin (1967) will be used for this purpose.

Ruskin taught an introductory sophomore course in materials science within the context of engineering design. In order to teach students how to select materials for new applications and to envision new materials for specific purposes, the students were provided with a series of problems that were accompanied by lectures. These were intended to help the students' understand the basic principles of materials science and be able to organize it in such a way that its application would be easy. Unusually, at that time, heavy dependence was placed on student access to the library because instead of a single text he gave references. By allowing the examination to be taken during a period of several days the conditions for dependence on the library were created. *"The problems expose(d) the student to the notion that sufficient and accurate data of the right type are always preferable to a theory but that usually the engineer lacks essential data so that he must use theoretical considerations to interpret available data for specific application. (The) problems stress(ed) interpolating and extrapolating (of) sketchy data or conflicting data with the aid of models to yield suitable answers. Whenever possible, compromises (were) required; through this ractice the students learn(t) to tolerate ambiguity, and*

---

[6]They cited Spohrer and Soloway (1986) in support of their argument.

[7]The internal quote is from Dawson, and Newsham (1997).Introducing software engineers to the real world, IEEE Software, 14, (6), 37 to 41.

[8]From universities in Finland and Sweden, respectively.

acquire(d) self-confidence, characteristics vital to successful design."

And in respect of the design of the question, examples of which were given, Ruskin wrote:

"Problem statements tend to be lengthy because they include more or less full descriptions of situations not previously familiar to the student. Student answers usually include both narratives and supporting calculations. Since there is usually no single preferred solution to the problems posed, they must be evaluated in detail, including the reasonableness of assumptions and value judgements made."

The difficulties of writing examination questions of this kind are illustrated by comments from the examiners on a type of question that was set in engineering science. In the first examination the following question was included in the paper.

"The figure represents some of the more important parts (A to E) of a single bar, 1 kw radiant electric fire. Discuss the purpose of these components and suggest a suitable material for each. (Base your discussion on the function each part has to fulfil and the requisite physical properties). Discuss the other factors that a manufacturer would consider in producing the components from particular materials. Describe and suggest materials for other parts which you believe will be necessary for satisfactory use of the fire, but which has not been indicated in the sketch."

The examiners' published comment on the answers was:

"This was the most popular question and the most badly done. Only one or two candidates calculated the resistance required for the element. Candidates tended not to answer the questions asked, e.g. they did not state the function of each of the parts of the fire and materials were often suggested without reasons. Candidates stated factors the manufacturer should consider, without discussion. The question was answered, on the whole, in too facile a manner".

Carter, Heywood, and Kelly (1986) wrote about this type of question:

"Although this type of question suffered from superficiality of response it was retained in similar form as a component of the examination for six years. However, significant attempts were made to direct candidates' answers into more detailed engineering analyses of the problems set, by requiring statements relevant, for example, to improved safety and efficiency, broadening the range of use or versatility of the device, and by specifying more closely, the parameters which were of most importance, e.g. electrical, mechanical, thermal or optical properties. Although this further guidance was given, the Examiners' reports continued to indicate that a significant proportion of the candidates' answers were superficial and that the necessary skills for attempting such questions were not being fully developed by the curriculum study as hoped. In the (seventh) year, therefore, this type of question was modified to consider not engineering devices, but engineering situations, and the methods of achieving solutions under a variety of constraints. Thus, in the next examination a question was set about the design of a technician's preparation room and the modifications to the design which would be necessary by the imposition of a 50% reduction in available finance after the first design stage. In this question the topic was deliberately chosen to lie within the familiarity and experience of the candidates; logical argument and judgement about possible alternative solutions were required from the candidate. The realities of life were introduced into the question through economic constraints and the skills of evaluation and judgement were tested. This type of question is, generally, most difficult to assess, but with experience the examiners are readily able to evaluate the cogent and relevant arguments and detect the simplistic and facile. Since the introduction of this type of question, there have been many excellent answers and there have been some signs of a general improvement in candidates' engineering reasoning, synthesis and evaluative ability"(Carter, Heywood, and Kelly, (1986). 40−41).

The experience of this examination leads to some caveats relating to instruction. The first seems to have been met by Ruskin; and it is that if students are to learn to answer such questions, they need to be trained to answer them. This is implicit in the engineering science study and it was certainly understood by the examiners. In support of this contention is a study of part of a school mathematics examination that teachers had designed to test problem solving. It was found that the students performed badly in this section. Further investigation revealed that while the teachers considered problem solving to be an important objective of the examination they made no attempt to teach it because the public examination made no demand for such skills (Heywood, McGuinness, and Murphy, 1980). Saupé (1961) made the point that transfer will only occur where there is a recognized similarity between the learning situation and the transfer situation. With respect to the design of examinations, transfer will only occur to the extent that students expect it to occur. This is why skill in analogical reasoning is important. The challenge for engineering education is to prepare students to look for the unexpected, and apply the rules in that situation.[9] In terms of the *Taxonomy of Educational Objectives* it is evident that these questions are aimed at what Prince and Hoyt (2002) termed intermediate and advanced problem solving (see above). It is probable that schools inadequately prepare their pupils to deal with questions that lie in the open or ill-structured end of the spectrum.

The second caveat relates to the validity of examinations (tests). Although questions may appear to have face-validity, as seems to be the case with Ruskin's examples, they may not be testing the skills desired. To evaluate if this is the case it would be necessary to include some other criterion measure. A tutor cannot claim to have improved problem solving skills unless

---

[9]Engineers in industry who often rely on past experience to help them through new situations sometimes find that experience is of no help (Youngman et al., 1978).

he/she has a measure of the student's problem solving abilities before instruction commences. Otherwise instructors will only be able to measure the learning that has been accomplished.

Ruskin's examples, as well as those of others, show that it is possible to design questions that depart from the traditional closed type of question. However, it should be remembered that tests within a course do not necessarily predict what a student will subsequently do in a novel situation. The case for-end-of year examinations that test for the transfer of learning rests on the ability to locate the examination at some time distant from course[10].

10.3. Learning Problem Solving with the Aid of Heuristics

The argument for teaching heuristics is based on the principle that if a learner knows the steps involved in problem solving, the learner's performance in problem solving will be improved. Saupé (1961) suggested the following steps:

1. Ability to recognize the existence of a problem.
2. Ability to define the problem.
3. Ability to select information pertinent to the problem.
4. Ability to recognize assumptions bearing on the problem.
5. Ability to make relevant hypotheses.
6. Ability to draw conclusions validly from assumptions, hypotheses and pertinent information.
7. Ability to judge the validity of the processes leading to the conclusion.
8. Ability to evaluate a conclusion in terms of its assessment.

Each of the steps in this model represents a different kind of ability, and help can be given to learners to develop these abilities.

Perhaps the best known heuristic is due to Polya. He wrote a book on its use in mathematics (Polya, 1957). The four stages of his model are: understand, plan, carry out, and look back. Fuller and Kardos (1980) have explained how maps, known as Polya Maps, can be used to define problems in engineering. Woods and his colleagues at McMaster modified Polya's heuristic for their problem-solving course at MacMaster (see Section 10.7). Red (1981) used Polya's heuristic when he began an experiment in an introductory course in engineering. He included lectures on the methodology of problem solving proposed by Polya. These were arranged to obtain a dynamic interaction between the lecturer (himself) and his students. They were supplemented by other lectures *"on assumptions/modelling, conditions and variables."*

This was to move the focus toward engineering problem solving. He found that: *"Students need considerable help in identifying the condition of the problem. The identification of the condition generally*

allows the equations for the solution to come forth. For example, isentropic and equilibrium statements identify conditions which often trigger the appropriate solution equations. This is an important transitional step for students, one which I spend considerable time discussing."

He shortened the content of the lectures so that the applications, followed by a modified version of Polya's heuristic, could be undertaken in class. The modified version is shown in Exhibit 10.3. It was adapted to include some of the necessary elements that engineers use in problem solving.

He presented grade data that showed a considerable improvement over and above courses not taught by this method. The average grade obtained by the students more than doubled. He also found that there was less "grumbling" about the severity of homework assignments. Students rated this problem solving module as their hardest course.

Red (1981) reported that colleagues who used the methodology found it difficult because *"many of the transitional steps an instructor uses to obtain the solution are performed unconsciously."* They have to learn how to teach such methodologies. One criticism of Polya's heuristic was that analysis using his model depended heavily on luck and good guessing.[11] Red said that in a sense this is right because the *"method only works sporadically unless students are given detailed instructions for each step of the strategy. For example, the 'condition' of the modified methodology required lectures on what we mean by systems, states and changes of state. We instructors sometimes expect students to recognize these concepts intuitively, but many do not. A problem-solving methodology is not, in itself, a panacea for student deficiencies.... For entering students who have minimal problem solving skills, the curriculum will continue to be hidden."*[12]

Red (1981), found support for teaching problem solving in the work of Woods (to be discussed later) and the Taxonomy (shown in exhibit 10.1) proposed by Dean and Plants (1978).

He argued that few students are beyond the routine stage when they enter university and he questioned whether many on graduation were proficient in interpretation and generation. Students struggle with these types of problems in their first two years, and this is a reason why some drop out of engineering.

Rosati (1987) used Polya's heuristic to design computer routines for problems in engineering statics. *"The routine forces the student to consider the limitations and simplifications involved in understanding the problem and then prompts him to formulate and sequence a plan for its solution. The student is cued in the appropriate construction of diagrams (and graphical constructions and allowed to choose both the position and direction of forces. The look back-stage forces a*

---

[10] In the United Kingdom many universities allowed a week to a fortnight between the end of tuition and the beginning of the examinations.

[11] He took this point from Greenfield (1978)

[12] He cited Lin's (1978) paper on the hidden curriculum in engineering.

review of the problem and an assimilation of the characteristics that can be applied to problems of similar type." (Diagrams of typical displays are given in the paper.)

Modified problem-solving methodology

Problem number and statement:
State the problem as presented or restate in a summarized form (be careful here, since restating might cause you to delete important information).

System diagram:
Draw the system diagram or a simplified version if one is present. Neatness is necessary, and the use of a straight-edge for drawing is recommended.

Given;
Briefly list the data and information necessary to solve the problem.

Find:
Briefly list the information to be found, i.e., *the unknowns*! List the unknowns in the order that will facilitate the solution, i.e., some of your unknowns must be found before others can be found.

Assumptions/conditions:
Briefly list the assumptions and conditions upon which your solution method (or plan) will be based. The assumptions enable you to approximate and simplify the system and system elements. The conditions identify the state or change in state of the system and its elements. Both together form the basis for making an understandable and realistic model of the system and its elements. It is in this stage that the important characteristics of the problem are identified and the unimportant neglected.

Modeling/variables:
Mathematical and/or graphical models of the system and its elements are identified based on the assumptions and conditions of the problem. Appropriate variables are defined to describe the characteristics of the system, its elements and the interactions with the environment. An example is the free-body diagram.

Plan:
Write down the equations from which the unknowns can be found using the given information. These equations are the connection between the given data and the unknowns.

Then:
1. Carry out the plan, i.e., apply the equations.
2. Check each step.
3. Underline or block in each answer so it is easily identified.
4. Make sure that each answer meets with common sense, i.e., *is it realistic?* Then make sure each answer satisfies the assumptions and conditions stated for the problem.

Exhibit 10.3 Red (1981) adaptation of Polya's heuristic.

Rosati found that the students liked the procedure although many would have liked more variety in the computer responses. For this reason the majority of students preferred the instructor presentation. The routines were helpful as a tutorial supplement rather than as a replacement for the instructors.

10.4.   Guided Design

In a series of papers in 1972[13] in which Wales and Stager (1972) discussed the relevance of educational

theory to engineering education they included a heuristic for teaching decision making. It was used initially with a course for freshmen engineering students called guided design. *"Guided design is part system, part attitude,"* and for this reason it is important to pay attention to the needs of students. In their theory they are perceived to be hierarchical and ordered as in Maslow's model.

The course *"is based on the conviction that the student who works through an ascending order of well designed problems, who is actively seeking solutions to problems rather than passively assimilating knowledge, will emerge not only better educated but far stronger intellectually"*. [From d'Amour and Wales (1977), who used the guided design approach to structure a course on the Nature of Evidence].

During the course the students *" work in small groups (and) attack open ended problems rather than masses of information"*. The course is structured so that each problem creates the need for subject matter that has to be learned independently by the student out of class time. Its purpose is to show that in decision making, knowledge of concepts, principles, and values is necessary. The teacher is a facilitator who in part listens and encourages the students to participate in the decision making process, in part, by asking them leading questions. They learn from the decision model with which they are presented. The problems are chosen to be relevant and interdisciplinary.

Wales, Nardi and Stager (1986) said their research into the decision making process led them to the view that experienced decision takers first defined the situation and then used four operations to arrive at a decision. It is this combination that forms the heuristic thus:
1.   Define the situation.
2.   State the goal.
3.   Generate ideas.
4.   Prepare a plan.
5.   Take action.
6.   Look back. Is the solution a good one?

Each of these three modes of thinking is combined with the operations of analysis, synthesis and evaluation. Thus, each step results in an action which these writers called evaluation: Ideas have to be selected after they have been generated, a plan has to be selected from the available options, and once action has been taken, the next action has to be selected. In their adaptation of the model, Eck and Wilhelm (1979) listed the steps of the model in this way 1) problem identification. 2) information gathering. 3) statement of objectives. 4) identification of constraints and assumptions. 5) generation of solutions. 6) analysis. 7) synthesis. and 8) evaluation of alternatives. They would seem to place analysis and synthesis as separate categories in a linear process, but that is hardly likely to be the case in complex processes.

In a particular set of publications, Wales, Nardi and Stager presented a series of Sherlock Holmes stories for solution. In these situations the decision-maker, (we might call him/her the detective) had to ask who is

---

[13]Wales C. E., and R. A. Stager (1972). In *Engineering Education*. 62, 5-6-7-8.

involved? (the actors). What things are involved? (the props). What happened? (actions). When did it happen (scene). Where did it happen? (scene). Why did it happen? (cause). How serious is its effect? (effect). These are of course questions that help the decision maker 'learn' about the situation, and in this sense this decision making model is also a model of learning. Thus, we might conclude that if students use such a model in problem solving they are likely to enhance their learning. Wales and his colleagues also claimed that the model is generalisable; that is, it can be used in any subject. They published examples in nursing, mathematics (Wales and Stager, 1990), research and practice (Wales, Nardi, and Stager, 1990), and the humanities supported by terminology appropriate to those subjects to argue their case (d'Amour and Wales, 1977).

Crews and Zeigler (1998), suggested that in order to design and write programs students need to follow steps in the software life cycle that are similar to the guided design heuristic. They are:
1. Analyze the problem.
2. Design a solution plan.
3. Construct an algorithm.
4. Implement the algorithm.
5. Test and debug algorithm.

Guided design has been widely use in the School of Engineering at West Virginia University. Eck and Wilhelm (1979) described its use in the laboratory portion of an undergraduate course in highway engineering (one three-hour session each week for a semester). In this case the subject matter was dealt with in lectures because of the lack of suitable material for self-study. The project involved a fictitious highway design team, and the material was designed to model the way that a 'transportation' engineering professional would plan and design a section of highway. The students' role played the projects and went through the stages of the decision heuristic as outlined above. They were provided with a handout that outlined the task and gave information about maintenance functions in small groups to help them with interpersonal relations. They also worked through a brief guided design so as to understand the rationale behind the project.

The approach also differed from the freshman courses in that there was no testing, although some testing took place in the lecture part of the course. Decisions about leadership were left to the group. As with all project work, the instructors found that it motivated the students and that there was greater cooperation among them. The use of a conference room for the reports created a more formal situation for the oral presentations, and this seemed to bring a positive response from the students in terms of the quality of the oral work. They found that students had difficulty with self-assessment. In response to a questionnaire the students felt that too much time was required for the project, but overall it seemed that the students felt that the emphasis on the design process and interpersonal relationships was worthwhile. The students wanted their instructors to produce a time schedule. But the instructors

felt that the experience is more valuable when the students take responsibility for their actions.

The tutors attempted to see if there was a relationship between interpersonal attitudes within groups and group performance. To do this they related the grade performance of groups to a group characteristic profile obtained from a questionnaire. It was designed to obtain information about the interpersonal relationships within the groups. The findings confirmed their view that interpersonal considerations are as important as technical considerations.

The Chemical Engineering Department at West Virginia University adopted the guided design approach in the freshman year and subsequently built study approaches that had an experiential emphasis into all the subsequent years. Evidence was presented which suggested that students who were graduates of the new program obtained better GPA's than those who graduated from the traditional program (Baillie and Wales, 1975).

Notwithstanding these reports, Staiger (1987) pointed out that there had only been two limited evaluative studies of guided design.[14] He believed that the guided design process method was a balanced learning process, and in order to evaluate this hypothesis view he used Jungian typology to evaluate a first semester introductory course in electrical engineering in which a guided design exercise was included. According to Jungian theory (see Chapter 5) a well-balanced course will meet the needs of a variety of student personalities, and in this respect he cited the types found in the Myers-Briggs Indicator (McCaulley et al., 1983). He obtained the perceptions of the students to a guided design exercise using a self-report inventory adapted from Kilmann and Taylor (1974).

The electrical engineering students were first given an exercise to introduce them to guided design. When this was completed, without mentioning Jungian typology, he asked the students if they would help him evaluate the method Having obtained their consent he ask them to go through another guided design exercise that comprised fourteen steps and to rate each step against the 8 experiential norms in the self-report inventory (see Exhibit 10.4).[15]

Notwithstanding difficulties with his method of analysis which he fully acknowledged, he concluded that in respect of this small group of students all of the functions were experienced in the combined group problem solving and self-study guided design. In type notation the students characterized the guided design project as E, S, N T, F P, J. This was consistent with his hypothesis, which was E S-P.[16]

Subsequently, Staiger (1989) repeated the exercise with two other groups using two other cases, and

[14]Miller, D (1981), Miller, D., Breyer, D., and M. Haucke (1983)
[15] The exercise is in Wales, Stager, and Long (1981)
[16]He calculated the average number of the students' selections for for each of the fourteen steps. E (extraversion) received approx. 13; S (sensation) 9; Thinking 7; and Perception 6. A full description of the course is given in Staiger (1985).

a good measure of agreement was found between them. He wrote that:

"The three guided design case studies show innate consistency with an imbalance towards interpersonal engaging (an essential ingredient for group dynamics) and a good balance of the other three bi-polar preferences, or experiential norms."

---

1. Being involved or connected with another person or persons (*interpersonal engaging*).
2. Working alone (*intrapersonal engaging*).
3. Asked to describe the details of a situation (*describing*).
4. Expected to make extrapolations or interpolations; the possibility for hunches, inferences, or suggestions that come from the situation (*associating*).
5. Developing or using concepts, classifications and/or theories to explain the situation; interpret the situation according to various concepts or theories (*conceptualizing*).
6. Placing values and emotional qualities on factors within the situation; responding according to what you like or dislike in the situation and how things affect you (*valuing*).
7. Paying attention to the sequence of events that produce phenomena (*processing*).
8. Generating some final solution or viewpoint, emphasis on results and the development of conclusions (*closuring*).

Exhibit 10.4. Staiger's Self-Report Inventory based on the experiential norms described by Kilmann and Taylor (1974). Their terms for these norms are shown in brackets. They were not used in the inventory. As a result of the evaluation, Staiger would add a 9th statement to take account the students interest in the guided design process. (Reproduced with permission of E. H. Staiger)

Finally, in a study that aimed to evaluate the value of decision-making characteristics in secondary education among 97 graduate student teachers, 33 of them used the Wales and Stager heuristic, others adapted the model, and 10 used the Polya model. They received some basic data about the Wales and Stager model. This included a newsletter that gave evidence in support for the model from learning theory and the Sherlock Holmes Cases.[17] In the lesson the student teachers were expected to take the students through a heuristic related to the subject material they were studying, and at a week distant to test the students on the knowledge of that class and their understanding of the heuristic. Most of the studies were done with students in the age range 12-14. Sixty of the students responded to a questionnaire. Before it began 27 were sceptical about the exercise but on completion this number had been reduced to eight. Thirty seven claimed that they were made aware of their own decision processes as a result of the exercise. In this particular year, only four said that the exercise demanded of them a considerable change in attitude whereas in two other years in which the experiment was conducted, around 30% said that it demanded change in their role as a teacher[18]. Over 90% in each of the three years said that the exercise was a valuable aid to their teaching. While it is not possible to say if the students' decision-making skills were improved as a result of the exercise, there was evidence of an improvement in average test performance, especially among average and weaker students. This is consistent with the view that some students will enhance their learning by using this or similar methods. It was reported that it gave structure to classes that weaker students, in particular, needed. The heuristic functioned in a wide range of subjects including languages and music, and this lent support to Wales and Stager's view that the model is generalizable. There was some evidence that some bright students did not like the heuristic and felt constrained, but this was not investigated (Heywood, 1996).

10.5.   Heuristics and the Engineering Method

Lydon, one of these student teachers whose project is described in the paper, pointed out that *"the knowledge they acquired is by no means permanently in their heads. Only by continued exposure to this type of exercise, or better still, this method of teaching will the pupils be able to become critical thinkers, or at the very least effective decision makers"*. This point is reinforced indirectly by another student teacher who reported that *"even though the students responded positively to the teaching of the decision making heuristic and were able to recall the various stages, when it came to attempting a second business game the heuristic was abandoned…. They didn't use the systematic approach, reverting instead to their basic instincts."* Such is the power of experience.

This seems to be the same problem that Arvanitis and his colleagues experienced. In their programming and software design course they wanted the students to adopt decomposition and abstraction problems to resolve complex problems. Their ethnographic study[19] was designed to see if second year students had learned these skills. They summarized the findings of their study as follows:

"Students tend to avoid attempting a conceptual design. Instead they begin to code immediately after they receive a laboratory exercise. This strategy appears to have developed from their first year "Introduction to Programming" course…."Once students rely on a build-and-fix strategy they have difficulties in applying a conceptual design method. This is shown even in complex problems where the strategy of build-and-fix is clearly inappropriate"…. Students' problem solving takes the form of compiler error message elimination." (Arvanitis

---

[17]The Sherlock Holmes Cases were kindly provided by Charles Wales. The Newsletter Wales, C. E. (ed.). *Center for Guided Design, Newsletter No 8*. West Virginia University, Morganstown, WV.

[18]In the paper, one of the reports by J. Lydon is described in detail (objectives, lesson plan and test) and the questionnaire data relates to his particular year group. However, the exercise was conducted in two other years and questionnaires were administered that produced roughly similar results.

[19]They cite Hammersley, M., and P. Atkinson (1995). Arvanitis et al write: *"60 students worked in small groups within a laboratory setting for four weeks. A team of teaching assistants worked with the students. One of the teaching assistants acted as the ethnographer. This allowed the researcher to be actively involved within the laboratory gathering data by observing the teams, analysing the laboratory books and administering individual, and unstructured interviews. The findings of the ethnographic researcher were systematically verified by the course leader and the authors of this paper."*

et al., 2001). This seems to be an example not only of prior-experience shaping the strategy, but of "set mechanization." That is the tendency always to use the same heuristic even though other approaches might be better (Luchins, 1942). It is not confined to programming, as Cowan (1983) made clear in respect of a course in structural mechanics. He found that *"some people use forces and equilibrium as their starting points and so I called them forced-based problem solvers. For others the starting point is to predict the deflected shape of the structure; I called them movers. There are also a few who use abstract approaches of a purely mathematical nature and express entire problems in terms of algebraic formulae; I described them as mathematicians"*.... *"No problem solver I studied belonged exclusively to any one of these groups. Almost everyone used each strategy at some time or other-but most had a preferred strategy they tended to favour, even for problems demonstrably more suited to a different approach."*

Inspection of the graduate student teachers' reports revealed that very few of them recognized the problem of "set" in problem solving and decision making. There is no reason to suppose that this does not apply with equal force to teachers in higher education. However, one student teacher of 16 year olds in a business studies class wrote that, *"the importance of set is that the teacher should try to design problems which have several different methods or solutions so that the student becomes aware that most complex problems and indeed the most simple ones can be solved in different ways. If they become familiar with this when facing new problems they will realise there may be more than one way to solve it"* (cited by Heywood, 1996). Some students incorporated an extra heuristic in their instruction. Commonly this was the additive model of decision making (Reed, 1988).

The findings that led to these remarks are in keeping with the view of Koen (1986), who argued *"Instead of a single heuristic used in isolation, a group of heuristics is usually required to solve most* (state of the art) *engineering design problem.... While in school students must learn that an engineering design is defined by its resources and, once in industry, be alert to the heuristics used in resource management in the corporation they ultimately join. They must also realize that engineering requires that decisions be made under uncertainty and look for the heuristics the practising engineer uses to control the risk resulting from this lack of knowledge."*

In the tradition of Einstein, Howard (1994) thought that the "thought experiments" referred to these heuristics as mental models. Students have to be helped to learn how to develop mental models, and this will sometimes mean reducing the level of abstraction because simple models are more easily assimilated than complex ones. *"Teaching should be done in a style that shows simple models, low order approximations, being developed and used. We can use physical approximations to help the student learn to build mental models."* His paper provided a useful set of examples in electrical and electronic engineering. An engineer requires a set of heuristics, and it needs to learn how to acquire them in industry. Of such is the importance of metacognition.

Deek, Turoff, and McHugh (1999) presented a case for a domain-specific problem solving model to help students learn programming. It illustrated Koen's point that groups of heuristics are required for engineering problem solving. They derived the model from a study of 12 heuristics including that by Wallas for creativity (see Chapter11). Each was analyzed under the headings of understanding and defining the problem, planning the solution, designing and implementing the solution, and verifying and presenting the results. They argued that since problem solving and program development is an interdependent process, an integrated methodology was required. Therefore, they synthesized the data from the 12 heuristics and produced a common model that was integrated into the development tasks. The stages of the model they derived are problem formulation, solution planning, solution design, solution translation, solution testing, and solution delivery. Inspection of the tasks and the knowledge and skills required for each stage showed that the completion of the cycle required the use of a number of heuristics. For example, in problem formulation the task was to create a problem description; use inquiry questions to refine problem description, and extract facts from refined problem description. Domain knowledge is required together with problem modeling and communications skills. This is in contrast with the solution delivery stage, the tasks of which are to document the solution, strategy, and results and to present the solution. This requires communication skills. This model and others make it clear that different skills are required throughout the process and, broadly speaking, that problem finding and problem solving require different skills (McDonald, 1968). This was found to be the case in Engineering Science, where problem formulation was difficult for some students and many found the final evaluation difficult.

10.6. Quantitative, Qualitative and Other Strategies in Problem Solving

However, the findings of Cowan (1983) and Larkin (1979) suggest that there is more to problem solving than the learning of a range of heuristics (see also p 122). They suggested that a major learning impediment is the inability of undergraduates, or novices as Larkin calls them, to use qualitative strategies in solving problems see Chapter 4). In their revisions of their program Arvanitis et al., (2001) took into account expert behavior.[20] Larkin (1979), in her study of novice and expert problem solving behaviors reported that *"in an expert's memory, physical principles are stored in chunks-groups of principles likely to be usefully applied together (see Chapter 4). Each chunk seems to be associated with a fundamental principle. When an expert accesses physical principles from memory to apply to a problem, he need not select from a large number of*

---

[20] They cited Linn and Clancy (1992).

individual relations, but instead selects one of a relatively small number of chunks."

After selecting a chunk, the expert applies some of the principles in it to generate a "qualitative analysis" of the problem. This qualitative analysis is concise, easily-remembered overview. It also seems to serve as a useful intermediate step between the original statement of the problem and the generation of quantitative relations". "In translating his qualitative analysis into quantitative relations the expert can access and apply quickly chunks of principles which are commonly used together. He need not go through the time-consuming and distracting process of independently selecting each individual principle."

Cowan listed the following qualitative strategies for the study of structures:

- *"Pushing" a roughly parabolic shape, according to a checklist.*
- *Using remembered solutions, with superposition.*
- *Breaking structures into substructures.*
- *Superimposing envelopes of moment.*
- *Releasing, then rejoining again.*
- *Rotating corners forcibly.*
- *Sketching deflections.*
- *Determining reaction directions."*

He then went on to issue this challenge:

"Only a surprisingly small proportion of graduate engineers classify the structures in sub-groups and have one preferred strategy for each sub-group. Few select a strategy deliberately, although they often associate one strategy with a type of problem. For example, one relatively able subject "pushes around" a basic parabolic shape in accordance with a personal checklist, when he tackles statically determinate beams. For a continuous beam, however, he superimposes familiar bending moment envelopes; and for a frame he identifies hinge rotations and works from there to a deflected form."

He then asked the engineering educator
"Which, if any, of these descriptions fit your style of problem solving?"

It seems to this writer that the answer to the question put by Arvanitis and his colleagues about how to train students begins with the tutor's understanding of his/her own learning processes particularly when they are faced with unusual problems. This should bring a realization that time needs to be spent on understanding how students learn and applying that knowledge to the design of learning. One example of how this might be done (by Fordyce), was described in Chapter 4. Larkin reported that when an experimental group of students were "acquainted" with processes for qualitative analysis and processes for chunking, their performance improved considerably over the control group. The role of inductive reasoning (i.e., the ability to induce rules) in such processes is important.[21] Cowan was led to develop a

series of self-study packages to help his students acquire these skills.

There should be little need to repeat the discussion in Chapter 5 that showed how different cognitive styles lead persons to approach problem solving in different ways, as for examples the contrasting approaches of convergers and divergers and serialists and wholists. Nevertheless, teachers need to take cognitive styles into account when they help students to acquire problem-solving skills.

McCracken and Newstetter (2001) drew attention to another dimension of problem solving and the ability to think both qualitatively and quantitatively. They called it *representational transformation* (see Section 11.6.4 on analogical thinking) Such transformations are *"built upon community-sanctioned practices often referred to as 'back of the envelope' calculations."* Engineers often do such calculations. They begin with a problem statement, which is then transformed into a diagrammatic account that shows the elements of the problem as they relate to each other and is then finally translated into a set of mathematical formulae. The diagrammatic account is qualitative. McCracken and Newstetter (2001) pointed out that the knowledge necessary to undertake these representational transformations is central to engineering practice. They argued that one of the reasons why students may find problem solving difficult is that since each of these representations uses different symbols, and is therefore a different linguistic system, engineering students are faced with having to learn three different languages. *"Multiple literacies are required to do engineering problem solving."* They found support for this argument in research that had been done in mathematics and science[22]. *"Unwittingly science and math education often asks students to learn more than one language at a time,"* and they suggested that the same is true of engineering. Indeed this might be the cause of the problem in student learning described by Price and recorded in Chapter 4. Additionally, ethics courses and issues in technology in society also embrace new languages, and this might be part of the reason why students either do not perceive them to be relevant or have difficulty with them.

McCraken and Newstetter have begun to investigate whether the different language (semiotic) systems used by engineers are taught in practice. Their initial study simply observed a professor while he was teaching to determine how his teaching related to three phases of problem-solving i.e., problem recognition, problem framing, and problem synthesis. They interviewed the teacher after the lecture to try and understand his perspective and how he knew how to solve problems. They concluded that whereas an engineering expert sees these three languages as one language, novices *"to*

---

[21] Inductive reasoning is the process of deducing a general rule from the observation and analysis of specific instances. Haverty et al (2000) investigated the role of inductive learning in mathematics and drew

attention to work by Zhu and Simon (1987). It showed that students learned and were able to transfer what they had learned when presented with worked-out examples from which they were able to induce how and when to apply each problem-solving method.

[22] They cited Lemke (1998) and O'Halloran (1998).

separate the languages of problem solving and as a result have difficulty making meaning of the relations and interactions between the semiotic systems that support engineering practice." The implications for practice are considerable.[23]

This would seem to be a promising line of research. What role could specific courses in problem solving play in developing the skill to handle different languages? The examples in this and the preceding sections self-evidently demonstrate both the need for, and the possibility of providing such specific training.

Another technique for helping students with problem solving requires the student problem solver to read the problem to another student. The problem solver must keep talking until the problem is solved. The student listener has to encourage the problem solver to keep talking. The listener is only allowed to point out errors. He/she must not indicate the correct solution (Whimbey and Lochhead, 1987). Lewis (1991) found that this method was very successful in a statics class, although it frustrated the good problem solvers because they had to slow down in order to describe their procedures. He also found that the poorer problem solvers read the problem and then stopped talking. In these cases the listeners were allowed to help a little. "When it was over, the poorer students would invariably say, *"I guess I really don't know the material."*

Yokomoto and Ware (1989) approached the issue of problem solving from the perspective of information processing and argued the case for coaching.[24] They suggested a problem solving paradigm based on information acquisition and reasoning. The paradigm is modelled by two bi-polar scales, and quantifies the dimensions in four quadrants giving four types of problem solver. The model was dynamic, domain specific and problem specific. Thus, a person could be in one problem solving domain in one quadrant for a specific problem, and in another domain for another type of problem in another quadrant. For many people this is an everyday experience and some might regard themselves as being better at solving problems in some specified domains than in other specified domains.

Type I problem solvers (Quadrant 1) are accomplished problem solvers who demonstrate they are proficient in the use of information acquisition processes and reasoning processes essential for solving problems in the particular domain being considered.

Type II problem solvers (Quadrant II) are those whose problem solving errors are due to the application of inferior reasoning processes to superior information for the domain in question.

Type III problem solvers (Quadrant III) are those whose errors are due to inferior information and inferior reasoning in the problem solving domain.

Type IV problem solvers (Quadrant IV) are those whose reasoning processes are superior but whose informational processes are inferior.

Yokomoto and Ware (1989) argued that students in each of these domains benefit from coaching. Thus, students of Type I will benefit from *"clearly written materials, clear lecture, sufficient examples and assignments, and clear feedback on their work."* Type II students benefit from a *"heightened awareness of formal reasoning, from a disclosure of the reasoning processes imbedded in the information* [metacognition], *and practice in reasoning."* Type III students require substantial coaching. Exercises need to be carefully prepared, the instructions need to be more detailed, and the instructor needs to be very patient. Type IV students benefit from *"instruction and practice in the processes that affect information acquisition they must be made to read for comprehension, to speed read, to listen for comprehension, to ask questions, to discuss, to make notes, to memorize, to scan notes, to draw pictures and visualize etc."*

But should training for problem solving be provided within courses or by a separate course in problem-solving? To put the issue in another way, Is problem-solving a subject-dependent skill or is it an independent discipline? The view taken by Woods and his colleagues at McMaster University is that it is a specific discipline. The design, implementation and evaluation over a period of 25 years, of a course designed to teach problem solving skills by Woods and his colleagues, is one of the most impressive studies, if not the most impressive, conducted in engineering education.

10.7. The McMaster University Course in Problem Solving

Circa 1973. *"We thought we did an excellent job of developing our students' ability to solve problems. We assigned many problems to be solved (in class and for homework). We worked many sample problems in class. We gave hints on what to do- sometimes we even listed the steps for certain types of problems. We chose textbooks that had a lot of worked examples. What else could we do?.... "We discovered that we had to do*

---

[23]They wrote, *"What we see in engineering classrooms is a reliance on eliminating the transformative moves from text to diagram, and thus the recognition and framing phases of problem solving. A reliance on synthesis with its associated symbolic representations dominates. There are many valid reasons for this. First, novices can easily become overwhelmed with too many representations. Also novices need to learn the manipulation of the mathematical representations first. Further novices need to see how multiple problems are solved prior to being exposed to ill-constrained problems. If we agree that these "fundamentals" must be taught first, when are the students taught to recognize and frame problems? How do they learn the languages of engineering problem solving and their relations to the phases of problem solving? When are they taught back of the envelope calculations? Our observations of the Biomedical Engineering graduate students lead us to believe students are not exposed to problem recognition and framing activities".*

[24]It is evident that problem solving may also be looked at as an information processing activity and this is in line with research on intelligence by Sternberg and his colleagues. Sternberg (1985), for example, found two meta components in a complex reasoning task. These were global and local planning. He found that more intelligent individuals tended to spend more time on global planning and less time on local planning than others. This is consistent with other findings by practicing teachers reported above. That work has much to offer teachers concerned with problem solving.

something else because our students were not as good as they should be at solving problems. Nor were students from other universities; nor were graduates working in industry" (Woods, 1979).

So Woods and his colleagues wrote to about a 1000 engineering departments around the world and obtained replies from about 20. They examined both psychological and popular literature on thinking, but nothing answered their needs. To try and supply this answer, Woods enrolled as a freshman in his own department's course in 1974. Each week he met with a volunteer group of students, a cross section in ability terms, and half male and half female. They showed him how they tried to solve their assignments. The skills needed to solve the problems were identified, and for each skill, materials were developed to help them perfect it within the context of their assignments. This process was continued into the junior and senior years. In 1978 Cameron Crowe, a colleague of Woods, repeated the experiment during part of the freshman year to ensure that Woods' group was not unique and that this class perceived the same difficulties. During this period these teachers attended workshops on problem solving, and observed groups in other universities. Woods listed a number of authorities from whom he and his colleagues had benefited.[25] As a result of this work they identified 18 learning objectives or competencies as they were sometimes called at that time.

Together with his colleagues Crowe, Hoffman, and Wright, he presented additional information about the development in another paper (Woods et al., 1979). That paper explains in more detail what happened in the four years with the volunteer students. It should be noted that in 1976 a group of these students had published a paper about their freshman experience (Leibold et al., 1976). The paper began with their view of the factors that contributed to problem solving. These were that:

1. There must be a problem or an awareness that a problem exists.
2. Six prerequisite skills and attitudes are essential. These are:
    (i)   The basic knowledge pertinent to the problem(s).
    (ii)   The learning skills necessary to obtain the information necessary to solve the problem.
    (iii) The motivation to want to solve the problem.
    (iv)   The memorized experience factors that provide order of magnitude "feelings" as to what assumptions can be made and how reasonable the answer is.
    (v)   The ability to communicate the answer; and perhaps,

    (vi)   Group skills if the problem must be solved by a group of people.[26]
3. An overall organized strategy is required.
4. For specific steps in the strategy, there are well-known alternatives.
5. A problem solver uses four abilities time and time again. These are, to create, analyze, generalize, and simplify.
6. Sets of "good hints" or "heuristics" have been developed about what to do next.

The importance of prerequisite knowledge is emphasized in a recent research among mathematics students at Carnegie Mellon University. Haverty et al (2000), in the tradition of research established by Simon at that institution, investigated the cognitive processes involved in inductive reasoning in mathematics. They identified data gathering, pattern finding, and hypothesis generation as the key areas of inductive activity, and they found that pattern finding played a critical role that had not been previously identified in the literature[27]. Moreover, the ability to detect patterns was *"directly related to participant's numerical knowledge and their speed of access to that knowledge"[28].* Woods et al., (1997) also recognized the importance of pattern recognition as a key skill.

The organizing strategy that was used by Woods was an extension of the Polya model based on protocols taken from experts. Woods and his colleagues assumed that students would want to solve the problem, so there was no need for the first stage of *motivation*-problem-sensing. They found that whereas Polya's *define* step involved analysis and creativity, it could be reduced to analysis only. This was because experts solved problems by the inclusion of a meditative step. That is, they thought about the problem first. In this step the problem is converted into a "real problem". Experts approach this step in a wide variety of ways. Like Cowan, and Larkin, Woods and his colleagues found this type of understanding to be qualitative. In contrast, they found that students charged into problems without taking the time to review and understand the problem statement. One of the reasons for this was that they were not aware of their own problem-solving processes. Today this has been widely represented in higher education as the need to develop a reflective capability or metacognition. This capability cannot, it seems, be developed without some

---

[25] Among them are; J. Lochhead, who had been associated with Clement (see Chapter 4), Larkin's work in general (see this chapter), Reif, who was associated with Larkin (Larkin and Brackett (1976), Sparks (1972): Marples, whose work is also reported in Lubkin (1980), and Black, Griffith, and Powell (1974). See also Lubkin, (1980), Whimbey and Lockhead, (1979).

[26] It will be noticed that apart from the sixth skill, quite independently, and during much of the same period those responsible for the JMB Engineering Science had made the same assumptions. Thus, while the assessment schedule focused on the skills of the chosen heuristic, the moderators of the project necessarily took into account the correctness of the available knowledge that the student had.

[27] This is somewhat unfair to Woods and his colleagues who had clearly identified pattern recognition as a key skill.

[28] Pattern recognition is used in the explore stage of the MacMaster model to determine if the issue is a problem or an exercise (Woods, 2000).

assistance.[29] *"The volunteer students emphasized how important it was for them to learn to slow down and analyze the problem statement carefully. Many discovered that in haste, they jumped in and solved the wrong problem. To slow the process down and to help them overcome the initial panic, we suggested that the problem statement be analyzed to ensure that that they knew the meaning of all the words, could identify the unknown, draw a diagram, isolate the system of interest, choose appropriate symbols, and identify the constraints and criteria. This we called the define step."*

Woods and his colleagues used the five-stage model for some years but as a result of the continuing evaluation, it was modified into six-steps. These were, (1) Engage, I want to learn. (2) Define the stated problem. (3) Explore. (4) Plan. (5) Do it. (6) Look back. like others had before and since it was found to be badly done, *"if it is done at all"* (Woods, 2000). It should be noted that they were fully aware that there were alternative strategies, and more importantly problem solvers do not use the strategy serially, and they devised tactics to prevent a *"linearity mindset"*. Woods and his colleagues did not list the traits that characterized the good problem solver (as defined by Whimbey in Whimbey and Lochhead, 1979), although they wished that they had. These were:

1. Good problem solvers persist. (Poor problem solvers lack motivation or attitude.)
2. Good problem solvers check and recheck their work. (Poor problem solvers lack accuracy.)
3. Good problem solvers can identify parts of the whole that are easier to grasp. Poor problem solvers cannot break problems into parts.)
4. Good problem solvers check methodically. (Poor problem solvers tend to guess when uncertain.)
5. Good problem solvers do more things. (Poor problem solvers are passive.)

Much of what they found either affirms or is affirmed by comments made in preceding sections. For example, they were surprised at the wide variety of personal preferences that sophomore students had. *"No single method worked for all."* They observed this as students came to handle the next steps in the strategy. They also found that when this group of students became stuck on what were thought to be easy problems, once the obstacle had been defined it could be overcome with an individual brainstorming session. They found that the junior year was one of consolidation, and the senior year was one of both consolidation and evaluation.

All in all these early experiences led them to believe that problem solving was a subject with its own terminology, learning objectives and preferred methods of teaching and learning. They had come to the conclusion, like those at Alverno College, that problem solving was a discipline in its own right, and they felt that taxonomies of problem solving of the kind developed by Plants et al., (1980) were of value. However, like the graduate student teachers found among their pupils,

Woods and his colleagues found that one single course in problem solving was inadequate without continual reinforcement and that such experience should be given as early in the curriculum as possible.[30] One of the challenges that had to be overcome was the pressure from other traditional courses.[31]

All of this led to the development of the McMaster Problem Solving Program (MPS) which is described in detail by Woods et al., (1997). In constructing this program they were influenced by other programs including those at Alverno College, Lipman's philosophy for young children, the Kempner-Tregoe decision-making program, and Wales and Stager's guided design to name but four. By now they had identified 37 separate skills. Four were related to self-management; fourteen related to problem solving skills for well-defined ordinary homework; five for solving ill-defined problems; seven for interpersonal and group skills; two skills for self-assessment; one for change management; and four lifelong learning skills. The skills are both cognitive and attitudinal and overlap.

To achieve development of these skills, they developed some 57 units, each ranging from 1-24 hours (e.g., what is problem solving? 1 hr; asking questions, 4-8 hours; coping with ambiguity, 10-15 hours). There were 18 units available for a second year 48 contact hour course to develop individual skill in solving traditional homework problems. Which units were selected depended on student needs. In the third year, a course in the first semester gives practice in applying these skills. In the second semester a course focuses on the development of interpersonal skills, lifelong learning, and teaching problem solving for open-ended systems and people. In the fourth year the focus continued in the same vein but for ill-defined and open-ended technical and interpersonal problems.

The program was established in 1982 and has been the subject of continuous evaluation ever since. The results are summarized in Woods et al., (1997). There is some indication that participation in the program improved the marks that students obtained in other courses. *The Course Perception Questionnaire* produced significantly higher ratings than those obtained from a control group in another engineering department. The program was found to increase the students' confidence in problem solving skills when compared with a control group.

In order to test students' skill in problem solving questions were devised that would enable students to display the processes they used to solve problems in chemical engineering. One of their examples is shown in Exhibit 10.5. It derived from the objectives listed in Exhibit 10.6. They also made evaluations of attitude and skill toward lifelong learning, alumni and recruiter response, and faculty and student acceptance. They

---

[29] See, for example, Cowan (1998) on reflective practice.

[30] In the student teacher as researcher exercise, they had to perform six different tasks similar to the one on teaching a heuristic described in this chapter.

[31] This was also found to be the case with the student teachers.

placed considerable importance on the development of skill in self–assessment, and they reported that performance against this criterion was better than that reported elsewhere.

"Our emphasis was on developing the skill through in-class "building" activities, then in-class and outside-class "bridging" the application of the skill to chemical engineering, and finally through "extending" the application to everyday life as documented through reflective journal writing." On the Perry measure [see Chapter 6] the level of students in the MPS program changed from about 3.5 in the third year to about 4.6 in the final year.

Clearly, for any course of this kind to be successful the opportunity to practice these skills and apply them in other subjects must be given. Thus, there would have to be a strong commitment by the department to such an endeavor. Nevertheless, the challenges that Woods et al., (1979) presented to engineering educators remain. Many, if not the majority, of engineering teachers continue to teach as they did before. If the magnitude of the literature is anything to go by, many remain to be persuaded that there is a problem, and this can only be due to the model of learning that governs their teaching. Woods has recently prepared a manual on "Preparing for PBL" that includes some of the papers that he and his colleagues have written on the topic (Woods, 2004).

For the troubleshooting problem given (in Figure 1, not reproduced here)

(a)   Brainstorm 50 possible causes and write these down in 10 minutes. (10 minutes)

(b)   Analyze your list, note the basis for classification, and divide your ideas into at least seven different categories (13 minutes).

(c)   Select four technically feasible ideas (2 minutes).

(d)   Select the 'craziest idea' and write about your thought processes as you use this idea as a trigger or a stepping stone to obtain a 'new' technically feasible idea (15 minutes).

Exhibit 10.5. Example of an assessment task in the McMaster Problem Solving Program in Engineering relating to Creativity, Classification and Awareness. (Woods et al., 1997). (Reproduced with the permission of D. R. Woods).

10.8.   A Note on Critical Thinking

Just as there has been a discussion about the merits or otherwise of exposing students to specific courses in problem solving, so there has been an argument, particularly in the non scientific domain, about the merits or otherwise of teaching critical thinking. Although exactly what the differences between the two modes of thinking are is a matter of debate. Similarly, there have been problems about its definition, and there have been attempts to define it by listing the skills that contribute to it. These discussions have been in the main confined to the liberal arts, but if psychology is considered to be a science then at least one book has been written on critical thinking in psychology (Halonen, 1986). In the liberal arts how to assess critical thinking is a major issue because most teachers of the humanities

consider the goal of a liberal arts education is to produce critical thinkers, just as engineers consider their goal is the production of effective problem solvers. It is equally an issue for minority engineering students (Fleming, Garcia, and Morning, (1995).

Similar debates to those in engineering about whether or not problem solving should be taught have raged[32]. Ennis (1992) distinguished between an infusion and an immersion approach to critical thinking. In respect of the former, he meant critical thinking instruction within subject matter teaching, in which the student is helped to think critically *"and in which general principles of critical thinking dispositions and abilities are made explicit."* Proponents of this approach include Glaser (1984), Resnick (1987), and Swartz (1987). In contrast, it is also held, that one learns to think critically if one becomes immersed in the subject. There is no need to make the principles of critical thinking explicit (McPeck, 1981). This is the 'osmosis' view and is typical of very many teachers in higher education, and as we have seen engineering.

The skills of critical thinking are sometimes called higher-order thinking skills. In this text the term reflective judgment has been used in Chapter 6, and the higher stages of this model and the Perry model with which it is associated involve critical thinking[33].

The case for training in reasoning and logic, with which critical thinking is associated, may be made from the common observation of 'ourselves' and 'others' when in argument. Outside our spheres of competence, none of us are very good at reasoning, or so it seems. And even in our areas of competence, we often appear to lose arguments because we have not thought things through (Perkins, 1995). Engineering employers in Australia apparently think that the capacity for independent and critical thinking is different from logical and orderly thinking and academic learning (Beder 2000, cited by Nelson, 2001). They believed that recent graduates were poor at problem solving, *"and particularly poor at critical thinking,"* although what is meant by critical thinking is not made clear by Nelson[34] For this reason analysis of the components of reasoning-that is, higher-order thinking-as a curriculum study would seem to make eminent sense.

---

[32]Summarized in Norris (1992) and *Theory into Practice* (1993).

[33]Before there was much discussion about the Perry model some research among undergraduates studying engineering and science in the United States had evaluated at the Piagetian level they were at, and had shown that many were at the *concrete operational* level and not the level of *formal operations* when they entered college (Renner, 1974). McKinnon (1976) reported that in Missouri /Oklahoma that many students from minority groups were only at the stage of concrete operations. He described a summer programme for pre freshman students of engineering designed to develop logical thinking. An interesting paper on how students move from novice to expert thinking that also seems to explain the difference (implicitly) between concrete and formal operations is given by Ma (1999). For a recent study of minority groups see Fleming, Garcia and Morning (1995; cited by Nelson, 2000).

[34]There is no reason why she should have done this within the context in which she was writing.

Curricula in engineering that attempt to bring students to high levels of cognitive development such as those at the Colorado School of Mines would appear to involve students in the development of critical thinking. The examples given of the King and Kitchener (1994) model show it to be based on an analysis of the components of reasoning listed by many other authorities.

There are other profiles such as the one for liberal arts that is shown in exhibit 10.7. It is fairly easy to make substitutions in this list, without endangering its integrity, that show that it applies to engineering. But is this the case for engineering in Exhibits 10.8 and 10.9? And, should it be? Engineers do not generally use the term critical thinking but instead use the term problem solving even though, it seems fairly clear, that the skills required for critical thinking, decision making, and problem solving are the same.[35] Some would use the term "logical thinking" (McKinnon, 1976). It would seem that they are differentiated by the cultural/subject context in which they are used, and thus the mode of thinking. Thus, for example, the constraints on thinking in the liberal arts are quite different to those in engineering. But the heritage of liberal arts students is that they think about critical thinking whereas the heritage of engineering students is to think about problem solving (see Chapter 3). Yet engineers would reject the criticism that they cannot think critically..

Given a term listed under 'concepts introduced, you should be able to give a word definition, list pertinent characteristics and cite an example. You will be able to describe d-lines, describe the limitations of short-term memory, and rationalize the processes used in brainstorming.

Given an object or a situation, as an individual you will be able to generate at least 50 uses, attributes, or ideas in 5 minutes.

Given an object or a situation, as an individual you will be able to generate at least 50 ideas in five minutes (or write about 50 ideas in ten minutes), and the ideas will belong to at least 7 different categories, and a group of three independent judges shall identify one idea that is 'unique.'

Given a crazy idea, you will be able to describe your mental processes used to convert that idea into a technically feasible idea by using the triggered idea as a 'stepping stone.'

You will be able to describe your preferred style of brainstorming and your preferred use of triggers..[36]

Exhibit 10.6. Five of the ten learning objectives for the McMaster Problem Solving Unit on Creativity as they relate to the assessment tasks shown in Exhibit 10.4(Woods et al, 1997). (Reproduced with the permission of D. R. Woods).

[35]Woods et al., (2000) use the term "Developing Critical Skills" as the subtitle of a publication on the future of engineering education. They do not refer to critical thinking in the paper, but only to skills and problem solving. The paper contains a useful summary of some of the areas mentioned in these paragraphs.
[36]"...we found that setting up a brainstorming atmosphere was often insufficient. Problem solvers need to develop 'triggers' that will keep the flow of ideas coming. Many have listed different triggers, what students need is extensive practice in using all the triggers and then time to develop those that fit their own style" (Woods et al., 1979).

Moreover, they could argue that emphasis on evaluation (self-assessment) and reflection in project work should be critical thinking

It may be argued that in courses in English, engineering students should acquire skills in critical thinking of the kind acquired by arts students, through composition of an appropriate kind. But technical writing, for example, is unlikely to achieve this because as Mathes (1979) argued, technical writing is a different genre, and it is much more likely to develop technical problem-solving skills than the skills of critical thinking being discussed here. It is self-evident that narrative writing will not achieve this goal.[37]

The most likely areas where skill in critical thinking might be developed are in the general area of engineering (technology) and society as it embraces ethics. This view was taken in the Department of Technology of California State University LA, where Nelson (2001) described a general education elective that was designed to meet the ABET criterion 3 outcome goals. The first objective was to focus on technology issues.

The students were, *"asked to think critically about the impact of technology on their lives and the lives of others"*. Therefore, the course reader contained readings on *"technology and education, technology and fear, technology and uncertainty, technology and capitalism, technology and work, technology and communication, technology and the body, technology and warfare etc"*. The purpose of these readings was to *"challenge the students' sense of social justice and fairness, and also to ask them to question the intentions of the authors"*. This was achieved by getting them to read conflicting readings in the areas listed. However, no evaluation, other than impressions, was presented. Even so, if one were presented, evaluations from tests might demonstrate that a person has the capacity to think critically but that is no guarantee of action based on such critical thought. At the same time, it is necessary to attempt a more comprehensive evaluation because if McCracken and Newstetter (2001) are correct, then students in such courses are being asked to learn a new language even though the focus is on relations between technology and society, and it is necessary to know how effective that language teaching is.

[37]Nevertheless, the importance of literacy in developing skill in critical or reflective thought cannot be underestimated. For example, Fleischmann (2001) in a very similar way to McCracken and Newstetter (2001) pointed out that in design various types of literacy are dominant during each phase. Thus, in the phase of problem identification the dominant literacy types are mechanical, conceptual, and cultural. In the modelling stage conceptual and mechanical types predominate. In the solution stage it is the conceptual and mechanical, while in the implementation phase it is the mechanical and cultural. Finally, in the presentation of solution, assumption of responsibility and credit the literacy styles are cultural, conceptual and mechanical. She argued that we typically spend most of our time on conceptual literacy and assume that the student will somehow gain mechanical and cultural literacy. In the Engineering service projects at Grand Valley State University there was simultaneous instruction in the steps of design and the types of literacy relevant to the phase. She did not, however, deal specifically with the issue of critical thinking.

10.9.   Conclusion and Discussion

Many engineering educators do not see that problem solving promotes difficulties for students. Consequently they do not believe that this merits specific attention. However, it has been shown that novices and experts are distinguished by their ability to think qualitatively. Novices find this difficult and need to be helped to acquire qualitative thinking skills. Prince and Hoyt (2002) have proposed that problem solving courses can contribute to the development of problem solving skills, and they suggest that these should be provided at the introductory, intermediate and advanced levels. At the same time, a small but growing group of engineers have demonstrated the value of paying attention to problem solving in their teaching.

A number of heuristics have proved to contribute to the development of problem solving skills and the enhancement of learning treatment in their courses.

Foundational Knowledge, abilities and attitudes
The critical thinker:
1. Asks significant and pertinent questions and states problems with specificity. Arrives at solutions through hypothesis, inquiry, analysis, and interpretations.
2. Assesses statements, insights, and arguments according to the knowledge and skills provided by formal and informal logic and by the principles of aesthetic judgement.
3. Derives meaning through an educated perception, whether propositional, systematic, or intuitive.
4. Formulates propositions or judgements in terms of clearly defined sets of criteria.
5. Strives to acquire knowledge of the various disciplines, knowing that such knowledge is a necessary, though not sufficient, condition for critical thinking.
6. Understands the different modes of thought appropriate to the various disciplines. Can apply these modes of thought to other disciplines and to life.
7. Is aware of the context or setting in which judgements are made, and of the practical consequences and values involved.
8. Thinks about the world through theories, assessing these theories and their contexts to determine the validity of their claims to knowledge of reality.
9. Seeks and expects to find different meanings simultaneously present in a work or event. Is intrigued and curious about phenomena others might avoid, disavow, or ignore.
10. Recognizes and accepts contradiction and ambiguity, understanding that they are an integral part of thought and creativity.
11. Constructs and interprets reality with a holistic and dialectical perspective. Sees the interconnectedness within a system and between systems.
12. Is aware of the problematical and ambiguous character of reality. Understands that language and knowledge are already interpretations of phenomena.
13. Tolerates ambiguity, yet can assume a committed position.
14. Is aware of the limitations of knowledge and exhibits epistemological humility.

Exhibit 10.7: Profile of the critical thinker in the arts and humanities. (Cromwell, 1986), (Reproduced with the permission of Cromwell, 1986.)

It can be learned by immersion (osmosis).A twenty five year programme of specific problem solving teaching, and its evaluation, not only shows the scope of the issue,

---

but demonstrates the case within engineering programs for treating problem solving as a specific discipline.

The critical thinker
1. Demonstrates capacity for continuing intellectual development and lifelong learning. Sees the development of critical thinking as an aim and as a process of self-assessment and correction.
2. Recognizes own intellectual potential and limitations in dealing with different tasks. Constantly evaluates the limitations and strives to develop the potential.
3. Extends the range of experience by educating the self in a variety of realms meaning
4. Recognizes the style of one's own thought in its creative potential as well as boundaries. Is willing to explore the style of others to augment one's own perception
5. Assumes responsibility for thought and action by being able and willing to explore their   meaning and consequences
6. Treats one's own thinking with dignity
7. Can apply insights from cultures other than one's own
8. Is self-directed, with the courage to criticize both society and self.
9. Demonstrates commitment to a specific world-view, while having the capacity to understand and accept others. Is open to the interchange of ideas and to the possibility of changing one's own views. Finds joy in the activity of thinking critically.

Exhibit 10.8. Knowledge, abilities and attitudes related to self-awareness. (Cromwell, 1986 reproduced with the permission of the author)

The critical thinker
1. Is aware of the development and production of knowledge and critical thinking as historical and social process of co-operation among human beings. Knows that thought and knowledge have relevance and meaning only in a social context.
2. Is aware that critical thinking is a social process, and so actively seeks critique from others to increase both self-awareness and understanding of society.
3. Enters willingly into the give and take of critical discussion. Is ready to be called upon to justify and defend thoughts and actions and is willing to call upon others to do the same.
4. Is sensitive to audience, taking seriously the task of communicating with others. Listens carefully and is able to express thoughts clearly, to argue cogently and appropriately, and to edit sensibly.
5. Examines the assumptions and validity of every communication. Is committed to reflection about the assumptions that guide our construction and interpretation reality.
6. Goes beyond own interests or own particular culture to understand other interests and points of view and to foster, when appropriate, synthesized ecumenical views.
7. Uses knowledge and skills to intervene and support critical and intelligent positions on controversial issues facing the community. Is specifically committed to defend or promote those individuals and social relations that will guarantee the possibility of continuous   development of critical thinking in any human being.

Exhibit 10.9. Knowledge, abilities, and attitudes related to the social dimension of critical thinking. (Cromwell, 1986, reproduced with the permission of the author)

References

Apple, D. K., Nygren, K. P., Williams, M. W., and D. M. Litynski (2002). Distinguishing and elevating levels of learning in engineering and technology instruction. *Proceedings Frontiers in Education Conference*, 1, T4B–7 to 11.

Arvanitis, T. N., Todd, M. J., Gibb, A. J., and E. Orihashi (2001). Understanding students' problem solving performance in the context o programming-in the-small: an ethnographic study. *Proceedings Frontiers in Education Conference* 1, F1D-20 to 24

Atman, C.J., and I. Nair (1996). Engineering in context: an empirical Study of freshman students' conceptual frameworks. *Journal of Engineering Education*, 85, (4), 317-326

Baillie, R. C., and C. E. Wales (1975). PRIDE: A new approach to experiential learning. *Engineering Education* 65, (5), 398-402.

Beder, S (2000). Valuable skills learnt from basket weaving. *Engineers Australia*, March p 46.

Black, P. J., Griffith, J. A. R. and W. B. Powell (1974). Skills sessions. *Physics Education* 9, 18 – 22.

Bolton, J., and S. Ross (1997). Developing students' physics problem solving skills. *Physics Education*, 32, (3), 176-185.

Carter, G., Heywood, J., and D. T. Kelly (1986). *A Case Study in Curriculum Assessment. GCE Engineering Science (Advanced).* Roundthorn, Manchester.

Cowan, J (1983). How engineers understand: an experiment for author and reader. *Engineering Education* (January), 301–304.

Cowan, J (1998). *On Becoming an Innovative University Teacher.* SRHE and Open University Press, Buckingham

Crews, T and U, Zeigler (1998). The flowchart interpreter for introducing programming courses. *Proceedings Frontiers in Education Conference* 307–312

Cromwell, L. S (1986). *Teaching Critical Thinking in the Arts and the Humanities.* Alverno Productions, Milwaukee, WI.

D'Amour, G., and C. E. Wales (1977). Improving problem solving skills through a course in Guided Design. *Engineering Education*, February 381–384.

Dawson, R. J., and R. W. Newsham (1997). Introducing software engineers to the real world. *IEEE Software* 14, (6), 37 41.

Dean, R. H., and H. L. Plants (1978). Divide and conquer or how to use the problem solving taxonomy to improve the teaching of problem solving. *Proceedings Frontiers in Education Conference*, 268–274.

Deary, I. J (2000). *Looking Down on Human Intelligence. From Psychometrics to the Brain.* Oxford University Press, Oxford.

Deek, F. P., Turoff, M , and J A McHugh (1999) A common model for problem solving and program development. *IEEE Transactions on Education* 42, (4), 331–336.

Dekker, D. L (1995). Engineering design processes, problem solving and creativity. *Proceedings Frontiers in Education Conference* 3. 3a5 16 to 19.

Eck, R. W., and W. J. Wilhelm (1979). Guided design: an approach to education for the practice of engineering. *Engineering Education*, November, 191–197.

Ennis, R. H. (1982). The degree to which critical thinking is subject to specific: Clarification and needed research in S. P. Norris (ed.) *The Generalizability of Critical Thinking.* St. Martins Press, New York.

Fleischmann, S. T (2001). Needed: A few good knights for the information age- competence, courage and compassion in the engineering curriculum. *Proceedings Frontiers in Education Conference* 3, S1B 8 to 13.

Fleming, J., Garcia, N., and C. Morning (1995). The critical thinking skills of minority engineering students. *Journal of Negro Education*, 64, (4), 43-453.

Fuller, M., and G. Kardos (1980). Structure and process in problem solving in J. Lubkin (ed.) *The Teaching of Problem Solving in Engineering and Related Fields.* ASEE, Washington, DC.

Furneaux, W. D (1962). The psychologist and the university. *Universities Quarterly*, 17, 33.

Glaser, R (1984). Learning and instruction: a letter for a time capsule in S. F. Chipman et al., (eds.) *Thinking and Learning Skills*, Erlbaum, Hillsdale, NJ.

Greenfield, L. B (1978) Student problem solving. *Engineering Education*, April 709–712.

Halonen, S. J (1986) (ed.). *Teaching Critical Thinking in Psychology.* Alverno Publications, Milwaukee, WI.

Hammersley, M., and P. Atkinson (1995). *Ethnography: Principles and Practice.* Routledge, London.

Haverty, L. A., Koedinger, K. R., Klahr, D and M. W. Alibali (2000). Solving inductive reasoning problems in mathematics: Not-so-trivial pursuit. *Cognitive Science*. 24, (2), 249-298.

Heywood, J (1979). *Assessment in Higher Education*. 1st edition. Wiley, Chichester.

Heywood, J (1996). An engineering approach to teaching decision making skills in schools using an engineering heuristic. *Proceedings Frontiers in Education Conference*, 1, 67 – 73

Heywood, J., McGuinness, S and D. E. Murphy (1980). *Final Report of the Public Examinations Evaluation Project.* School of Education, University of Dublin, Dublin.

Howard, B (1994). Why don't they understand what they know? What to do about it. *Proceedings Frontiers in Education Conference*. 573-578.

Kahney, H (1986). *Problem Solving. A Common Sense Approach*. Open University Press, Milton Keynes.

Kilmann, R., and V. Taylor (1974). A contingency approach to laboratory learning: psychological types versus experiential norms. *Human Relations*, 27, (9), 891–909.

King, P. M., and K. S. Kitchener (1974). *Developing Reflective Practice.* Jossey Bass, San Francisco.

Koen, B. V (1985). *Definition of the Engineering Method*. ASEE, Washington, DC.

Koen, B. V (1986). The engineering method and the State-of-the-Art. *Engineering Education*, April 670–674.

Larkin, J. H (1979). Processing information for effective problem solving. *Engineering Education*, 70, (3), 285–288.

Leibold, B. G., Moreland, J. L. C., Ross, D. C., and J. A. Butko (1976). Problem solving: A freshman experience. *Engineering Education*. 67, (2), 172–176.

Lenke, J (1998). Mutimedia literacy demands of the scientific curriculum. *Linguistics and Education*. 10, (3), 247-271.

Lewis, R. B. (1991). Creative teaching and learning in a statics class. *Engineering Education*, 81, (1), 15 17.

Lin, H. (1978). The hidden curriculum of the introductory physics classroom. *Engineering Education*. December. 289–294.

Linn, M. C., and M. J. Clancy. (1992). Can expert's explanations help students develop program design skills. *International Journal of Man Machine studies*. 36,511-551.

Lubkin, J. L (1980) (ed.). *The Teaching of Elementary Problem Solving in Engineering and Related Fields.* Monograph. ASEE, Washington, DC.

Luchins, A. S (1942). Mechanisation in problem solving: the effect of "Einstellung." *Psychological Monographs,* No 248.

Ma, J A case study in student reasoning about feedback control in a computer based learning environment. *Proceedings Frontiers in Education Conference*, 12d4 7 to 12.

McCaulley, M et al (1983). Applications of psychological type in engineering. *Engineering Education*. 73, (5), 394–400.

McCracken, W. M. and W. C. Newstetter (2001). Text to diagram to symbol: Representational transformations in problem solving. *Proceedings Frontiers in Education Conference*, F2G 13 to 17.

McDonald, F (1968). *Educational Psychology.* Wordsworth, Belmont, CA.

McKinnon, J. W (1976). Encouraging logical thinking in selected pre-engineering students. *Engineering Education* 66, (7), 740 –744.

Mackintosh, N. J (1998). *IQ and Human Intelligence*. Oxford University Press, Oxford.

McPeck, J. E (1981). *Critical Thinking and Education*. St. Martins Press, New York.

Mathes, J. C. (1979). Communication skills. Problem solving: The engineering in technical communication. *Proceedings Frontiers in Education Conference*. 109−112.

Miller, D (1981). Motivational factors in student preferences for lecture or guided design approaches to instruction. *Educational and Psychological Research,* 1, (1), 47–49

Miller, D., Bryer, D., and M. Haucke (1983). Performance satisfaction theory and attitudes about the guided design approach to instruction training. *Psychology*, 20, (1), 31-34

Nelson, S (2001). Impact of technology on individuals and society: a critical thinking and lifelong learning class for engineering students. *Proceedings Frontiers in Education Conference.* 3, S1B 14 to 18.

Norris, S. P (1992) (ed). *The Generalizability of Critical Thinking. Multiple Perspectives on an Educational Ideal.* St Martins Press, New York.

O'Halloran, K. L (1998). Classroom discourse in mathematics: a multisemiotic analysis. *Linguistics and Education.* 10, (3), 359–388.

Parkin, A J (1993). *Memory. Phenomena, Experiment, and Theory.* Blackwell, Oxford.

Perkins, D. N (1995) Outsmarting IQ. *The Emerging Science of Learnable Intelligence.* Free Press, New York.

Plants, H. L., Dean, R. K., Sears, J. T and W. S. Venable (1980). A Taxonomy of problem solving activities and its implications for teaching. In J. Lubkin (ed.) *The Teaching of Elementary Problem Solving in Engineering and Related Fields.* ASEE, Washington, DC.

Polya, G (1957). *How to Solve It,.* 2nd edition. Doubleday Anchor, Garden City

Prince, M., and B. Hoyt (2002). Helping students make the transition from novice to expert problem-solvers. *Proceedings Frontiers in Education Conference,* 2, F2A 7 to 11.

Red, W. E (1981). Problem solving and beginning engineering students. *Engineering Education.* 72, (2), 167–170.

Reed, S. K (1988). *Cognition. Theory and Applications.* 2nd edition. Brooks/Cole, Pacific Grove, CA.

Reif, F., Larkin, J. H., and G. C. Brackett (1976). Teaching general learning and problem solving skills. *American Journal of Physics,* 44, 212.

Renner, R. J (1974). Learning, motivation and Piaget. *Engineering Education.* 64, (6), 416

Resnick, L. B (1987). *Education and Learning to Think.* National Academy Press, Washington, DC.

Rosati, P. A (1987) Practising a problem-solving strategy with computer tutorials. *International Journal of Applied Engineering Education,* 3, (1), 49–53.

Ruskin, A. M (1967). Engineering problems for an introductory materials course. *Engineering Education,* 58, (3), 220–222.

Saupé, J (1961) Chapter 2 in P. Dressel (ed.). *Evaluation in Higher Education.* Houghton Mifflin, Boston.

Sparks, R. E (1972). Inventive Reasoning in D. M. Flourney (ed.). *The New Teachers.* Jossey Bass, San Francisco.

Spohrer, J., and E. Soloway (1986). Novice mistakes: are folk wisdoms correct. *Communications of the ACM,* 29, (7), 624–632.

Staiger, E. H (1985). A spiral sequenced guided design course in electronic communication systems. *IEEE Transactions on Education.* E-28, (2), 79-84.

Staiger, E. H (1987). A preliminary analysis of guided design using Jungian typology. *Engineering Education,* February 309–312.

Staiger, E. H (1989). Profiles of guided design case studies from Jungian typology. *International Journal of Applied Engineering Education.* 5, (1), 13–15.

Sternberg, R. J (1985). *Beyond IQ. A Triarchic Theory of Human Intelligence.* Cambridge University Press, Cambridge, UK.

Sternberg, R. J and E. J. Smith (eds.) (1988). *Psychology of Human Thought.* Cambridge University.Press, New York

Striegel, A and D. T. Rover (2002). Problem based learning in an introductory computer engineering course. *Proceedings Frontiers in Education Conference,* 2, F1G−7 −F1G−12.

Sutinen, E and J. Tarhio (2001). Teaching to identify problems in a creative way . *Proceedings Frontiers in Education Conference,* 1, T1D−8 to 13.

Swartz, R. J. (1987) Teaching for thinking: a developmental model for infusion of thinking skills into mainstream instruction in J. B. Baron and R. J. Sternberg (eds.). *Teaching Thinking Skills: Theory and Practice.* W. H. Freeman, New York.

Thompson, N (1987). *Thinking like a Physicist.* IOP Publishers, Bristol.

Wales, C. E., and R. A. Stager. (1986).Series of papers on Guided Design in issues 5, 6, 7 and 8 of Vol 62. *Engineering Education.*

Wales, C. E., Nardi, A. H and R. A. Stager (1986). *Professional Decision Making.* Center for Guided Design. West Virginia University, Morganstown, WV

Wales, C. E., Nardi, A. H., and R. A. Stager (1990). Research or practice. The debate goes on. *International Journal of Technology and Design Education,* 1, (1), 40–47.

Wales, C. E. and R. A. Stager (1990). *Thinking with Equations. Problem Solving in Math and Science.* Center for Guided Design, West Virginia University, Morganstown, WV.

Wales, C E., Stager, R. A., and T.Long (1981). *Guided Engineering Design. Project Book* (2nd Edition) West Publishing. St Paul. Minn.

Whimbey, R. E. and J. Lockhead (1979). *Problem Solving and Comprehension.* Franklin Institute Press, Philadelphia.

Wilcox, A. D (1990). *Engineering Design for Electrical Engineering Students.* Prentice Hall, Englewood Cliffs, NJ

Woods, D. R (2004). *Preparing for PBL.* D. R.Woods, McMaster University, Hamilton,ON.

Woods, D. R (1979). Teaching problem solving skills. *Proceedings Frontiers in Education Conference,* 293–297.

Woods, D. R (2000) An evidence based strategy for problem solving. *Journal of Engineering Education,* 89, (4), 443–460.

Woods, D. R., Crowe, C. M., Hoffman, T. W., and J. D. Wright (1979). Major challenges to teaching problem solving skills. *Engineering Education.* 70, (3), 277–284.

Woods, D. R., Felder, R. M., Rugarcia, A., and J. E. Stice (2000). The future of engineering education. III. developing Critical Skills. *Chemical Engineering Education,* 34, (2), 108–117.

Woods, D. R. et al (1997). Developing problem solving skills: the McMaster Problem solving program. *Journal of Engineering Education,* 86, (2), 75–91.

Yokomoto, C. F and R. Ware (1989) A view of common sense through a problem solving paradigm ASEE Annual Conference (Text supplied by the authors).

Youngman, M. B., Oxtoby, R., Monk, J. D and J. Heywood (1978). *Analysing Jobs.* Gower Press, Aldershot.

Zhu, X., and H. A. Simon (1987). Learning mathematics from examples by doing. *Cognition and Instruction,* 4, (3), 137–166.

CHAPTER 11: CREATIVITY

Summary

Creativity is a complex phenomenon. The first section of the Chapter is concerned with (a) the distinction between creativity and problem solving, and (b) the different behaviors exhibited by scientists and engineers in creative behavior. Although there has been much discussion about the meaning of creativity it is clear that creativity, is perceived to be something different to problem solving. The importance of creativity as a dimension of liberal education is considered, and it provides a rationale for the inclusion of engineering in programs of general education as has happened in schools in many countries.

A major issue is whether or not creativity can be taught. The view taken in this Chapter is that many problems associated with the fostering of creativity in formal education can be addressed in engineering education through modifications to teaching and assessment in traditional courses and projects. The difficulty of designing performance assessments is considered: Rubrics and questions are not easy to design. At the same time, there is a case for courses that focus on creativity, innovation, and inventions. Illustrations of such courses are given. Some suggestions for research in this area are given.

The chapter incorporates discussion of theories of creativity due to Amabile, Guilford and Dacey and Lennon. It is noted that some engine,ering educators have been influenced by Guilford's model with its concern with the fluency of ideas. Consequently strategies for helping students acquire fluency in idea generation such as brainstorming and lateral thinking have been found to be helpful. Guilford's theory also generated ideas about testing that some engineering educators have found useful.

Amabile's model and Csikzentmihalyi's concept of flow are briefly described, and their relevance to the understanding of the creative process examined. The sections on the theoretical dimension conclude with a brief resumé of Dacey and Lennon's comprehensive general theory of creativity that embraces features from several earlier theories including those of Amabile and Guilford.

Creativity involves a certain amount of risk, and engineers and engineering students have to be allowed sufficient discretion to take risk. This implies that their environment has to be protected, and this applies as much to the educational environment as it does to the educational. At the same time, to make the best use of such environments a strong knowledge base is required.

11   Creativity and Problem Solving

While creativity is clearly linked to problem solving and might have been considered in the last chapter it is considered here for convenience. It also overlaps with the following chapter on design and the earlier Chapter on projects and problem-based learning because many engineering teachers believe that creativity is best enhanced, or taught, through the project method.

It is not the purpose of this Chapter to raise creativity to a special status that has about it the magical or the mystical.[1] The development of creativity is related to all those things that govern problem solving, and as was shown in Chapter 10, these in turn relate to how we acquire schemata (see Chapter 4) and the workings of memory. They also relate to left-brain right-brain problems (see Chapter 5 and e.g.,, Williamson and Hudspeth, 1982).

Dekker presented a paper at the 1995 Frontiers in Education Conference that had the title *"Engineering Design Processes, Problem Solving and Creativity."* He wrote about this title in his abstract as follows:

"There is confusion as to what the terms in the title mean. None of them are clearly defined. "The engineering design processes" are often confused with open ended-problems. "Problem Solving" has many definitions. "Creativity" is much more than the prevalent "free thinking" view. The lack of a common definition leads to a confusion when people, faculty included, are discussing these topics."

One hopes that some clarification has emerged about the usage of terms like problem solving, problem based learning, and critical thinking, how they have been used, and by whom. Nevertheless, it is still possible to take another step, and make explicit one point of Dekker's that was left implicit in the last Chapter. That is, that the Polya model, in one of its forms or another, is a generalizable model that applies to all sizes and shapes of problems to be solved in the short or the long term and that range in depth from the trivial to the profound. We are all problem solvers, and we continually solve problems, big and small (i.e., as perceived by us) throughout the day (Heywood, 1989). We are also all critics of *"this and that"* even though the demands of logic are not often met. How effective we are depends on context and the way our personal traits interact with that framework. Given that reasoning, the same must be true of creativity. Indeed, as Waks and Merdler (2003) noted, Sternberg and Lubart (1995) considered that mental abilities are like those involved in the location of specific information, the comparison of new with old, and the sorting of data to give meaningful information and knowledge. All of these involve analysis and synthesis, as well as creative aptitudes. We all have the potential to solve problems, be critical and be creative. The problem for engineering educators is to develop that potential within the context of engineering, and this requires an understanding of the design process and how problems are creatively solved in that context.

---

[1]This is a rewording of an introduction to a brief discussion of creativity by Hampson and Morris (1996).

Dekker argued that there are three activities that separate the design process from problem solving. He called them conceptual design, embodiment design, and detail design. These relate to the generation of a concept, preliminary layout and configuration, and detail and specification.[2]

It is evident that some problems may be solved routinely while others require ingenuity for their solution. And, in everyday parlance, not every solution that is regarded as ingenious would be regarded as creative. Yet, engineers look for creative as well as ingenious solutions to problems.

Christiano and Ramirez (1993) argued that *"it is necessary to make a distinction between algorithmic tasks and heuristic or creative tasks. If the path to a problem solution is clear and straightforward from the beginning it is an algorithmic task. A creative task must be left open ended to some degree to allow the individual to search for different solution paths. This is the essence of individual creativity."*

Clearly creativity is perceived to be something different from problem solving. It is equally clear that lack of creativity among engineering students has bothered some educators from time to time, although Dekker was of the opinion that *"creativity is given a back seat in design education because it is poorly understood and difficult to teach."* A major problem considered by several engineering educators is the view that both students and teachers are averse to taking risks (Whitfield, 1972). McClelland (1969) has gone so far as to argue that the way engineers are socialized (training + professionalism) is inhibitive of innovation. However, Sternberg (1988) made the point that creative people have a sense of acceptable risk but *"they need to recognise that there are some projects, whatever the field that are too risky".*

In the United Kingdom engineers considered that one of the ways in which they differed from scientists was in the way they used creativity. For example, Gregory and Monk (1972) used the concept of fluency of ideas to distinguish between creativity in engineering and science, and that is as good as any point to start this discussion.

In a study of the scope of engineering, technical and social models, Gregory and Turner (1972) distinguished between science and design with the aid of the diagram shown in figure 11.1. They pointed out that inspection of all the models of the design activity led to the view that it was *"a sequential decision process, involving operations upon information with internal reconciliation, which proceeds from an ill-defined problem situation to a specification sufficient for relevant and effective action to be taken."[3]* For our purpose it is the utilisation of this diagram by Gregory and Monk (1972) to differentiate between creativity in science and

engineering in terms of fluency that is of interest. They argued that science was concerned with increasing insight into the behavior of the universe whereas, design is concerned with achieving a perceived need. The design activity is terminated by a complete specification. *"The only link between science and engineering is by way of a pool of knowledge. Engineers generally require a greater fluency in the production of ideas according to these models."* Therefore, engineers should be more creative than scientists.

Elsewhere, Court (1998) drew attention to work by Cross who had argued that there is a particular "designerly way" of thinking, and to Lawson who made the same distinction as Ball (see Chapter 2) between analysis and synthesis and concluded that engineering designers solve problems by synthesis. This discussion could continue, and no doubt will, but elsewhere. There has been an excellent debate about the role of creativity in design and technology education in elementary and secondary schools. A recent summary by Atkinson (2000) drew attention to a study by Lewis (1999), who *"suggested that technology education could provide appropriate situations for pupils to come to understand technology whilst engaging in acts of technological creation. He [Lewis] believed that technology was in essence the manifestation of human creativity".* Christiano and Ramirez (1993) argued that there are humanistic reasons for the promotion of creativity. These are:

"1. Creativity allows people the flexibility necessary to cope with constant social and scientific change. Traits associated with creativity such as originality and acceptance of new ideas are becoming more important as technology advances.

2. Creativity protects our human dignity-it is our unique creative ideas that set us apart from routine and programmable computers and machines.

3. Creativity promotes spiritual well-being- the ability to adjust to changing situations is vital mental health.[4]"

Thus, a case for engineering as component of liberal education can be made since it tackles problems for which particular kinds of creativity are required.

Just as with problem solving and critical thinking there has been a debate about whether or not creativity can be taught (e.g., Cooley, 1967; Hayes and Tobias, 1964; Kreith, 1967; McKinnon, 1961; Porcupile, 1969; Törnkvist, 1998), and it continues to this day (Richards, 1998). The view taken in this Chapter is that many problems associated with the fostering of creativity can be addressed in engineering education through modifications to teaching and assessment in traditional courses and projects, but that there is also a case for courses that focus on creativity, innovation and invention. Yet, all this predicates that we know what creativity is. So what is creativity?

11.1.   Creativity, Innovation and Originality.

We commonly try to define the characteristics of creative

---

[2]He cites Pahl, G., and W. Beitz (1988). In K. Wallace (editor) *Engineering Design: A Systematic Approach.* The Design Council. Springer-Verlag.

[3]   Concepts of design will be discussed in Chapter 12.

[4]They cited Cropley, McLeod (1989). in this respect.

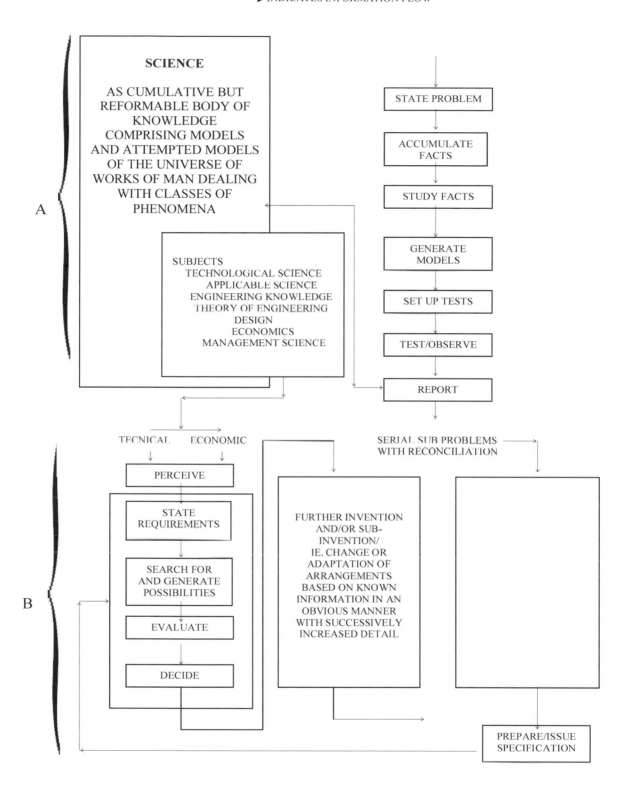

Figure 11.1. Gregory and Turner's (1972) distinction between science and design illustrated [on p. 39 of S. Gregory (ed.). *Creativity and Innovation in Engineering*., Butterworths]

people, and there is a vast literature on this topic.

Richards (1998) at the University of Virginia developed a survey instrument to evaluate mechanical engineering students' beliefs about creativity and intelligence. He found that the attributes most frequently associated with creativity included, novelty, fluency, open-mindedness, unconventionality, synthesis, insightfulness, and attitude. These are traits, and Hawlader and Poo (1989) drew attention to a definition by an engineering director of Rolls Royce, who defined creativity as *"an ability or aptitude, probably innate, which allows him to think of, dream up, visualize or imagine new or unusual solutions to problems."* (Conway, 1969).

There are many other definitions of creativity. They range from the short to the long. The simplest appears to be that it is the *"process of arriving at ingenious concepts not previously known by the individual"* (Ramirez, 1993). In another paper that writer relates it to artefacts thus, *"Creative artefacts arise when the resulting meaning is composed of novel components or in a novel combination or even novel meaning"* (Ramirez, 1994). Creativity is defined by the meaning that an object has for us. McDonald (1968) enabled us to distinguish between creativity and originality when he pointed out that *"creative is the label we apply to the products of another person's originality."* Thus, it is with improvements in originality defined as a behavior *"which occurs relatively infrequently, is uncommon under given conditions, and is relevant to those conditions"* (Maltzman, 1960) with which we should be concerned with in education.

From the perspective of originality, Pahl and Beitz (1988) cited by Court, 1998) distinguished between the following types of design,

1. *"Original design. This involves the elaboration of an original solution principle for a system, plant, machine or assembly, with the same, a similar or new task, e.g., the Dyson cyclonic vacuum cleaner.*
2. *Adaptive design. This involves adapting a known system (the solution principle remaining the same) to a changed task, e.g., the development of anti-lock brakes for automobiles, which had previously been used on aircraft for many years.*
3. *Variant design. This involves varying the size and/or the arrangement of certain aspects of a chosen system, the function and solution principle remaining unchanged e.g., an automobile manufacturer will make cars of various sizes within one range."*

As Court pointed out, while little bits of creativity will be required in both *adaptive* and *variant* design,, *new* creative products are *original*. Therefore, there is a minimum need for engineering students to be aware of methods of creative thinking and their application. The same may be deduced from the three higher levels of creativity suggested by Taylor that more precisely describe creativity in engineering. *"These include "technical" creativity, characterized by unusual skills or proficiency; "inventive" creativity in which known concepts are used in novel ways; and "emergent"*

creativity in which completely new ides are formulated and stated"[5] [cited by Christiano and Ramirez (1993)].

In relation to the work environment, Amabile (1996) distinguished between creativity and innovation. Creativity is defined as *"the production of novel and appropriate ideas by individuals or small groups of individuals or small groups of individuals working closely together,"* and innovation is *"the successful implementation of ideas by an organization"* (cited by Dacey and Lennon, 1998, page 244).

Rosenfeld and Servo (1990) differentiated between creativity and innovation by the equation

Innovation = Conception + Invention + Exploitation.

Creativity is the generation of novel ideas, and innovation is the task of making money with them. Engineers need both whether in the academic or industrial fields. The creative teacher is concerned with the exploitation of new ways of teaching and the industrialist is concerned with the exploitation of ideas in the market. It is for this reason that so much project work involves students in the task of "making" or exploiting their ideas, as for example, in a computer program. Rosenfeld and Servo wrote that *"the word invention applies to any novel idea that is transformed into reality; and the word exploitation refers to getting the most out of an invention"* (p. 252).

11.2.   Creativity in the Engineering Context

A brief introduction to the problem of creativity in engineering was made in the context of learning styles and traits in Chapter 5. There, it was mentioned that the idea of convergent and divergent learning styles in the Kolb theory of learning had first been given prominence by Guilford in his model of the intellect (Guilford, 1959; 1967). It was noted that an engineer, Whitfield, in his study of creativity, made clear that both convergent and divergent thinking were required in the engineering process, and his model of the process was shown see Figure 5.1). It was also noted that research by Hudson (1962; 1966) on creativity among highly able sixth formers (K10-K12) in the United Kingdom had upset many engineers and scientists. This was in spite of the fact that the tests used were open to substantial criticism.[6] The results led to the view that in schools in England, those who were pursuing studies in the arts (humanities) were likely to be more creative than those who pursued the sciences. They tended to diverge whereas the science oriented students tended to converge. This was according to the pencil and paper tests used in this study. In any event during that period there was a substantial debate about creativity in engineering and a working party of the Council of Engineering Institutions and the Design Research Society organized a conference on the topic, the

---

[5]These were given in Cropley and McLeod (1989). See also C. W. Taylor (1972). Can organizations be creative too? In C. W. Taylor (ed.). *Climate for Creativity.* Pergamon Press., New York.

[6]On the grounds that the particular scale used and the method of scoring made it impossible for science students to be other than convergers (Christie, 1968).

papers of which were subsequently published (Gregory, 1972). [7]

Prior to the 1972 symposium, there had been a National Conference on Creative Engineering Education at Woods Hole in the United States in 1965. Whitfield (1972) noted that it recommended that engineering schools should positively promote creative engineering problem solving and that students should undertake projects that brought them into contact with a whole range of industrial activities associated with innovation and invention. Several important papers were also published during the 1960s (e.g., Brogden and Sprecher, 1964; Hollander, 1965; Owens, 1961; Owens et al, 1957; Sprecher, 1959). [8] By far the largest amount of work was done on creativity among scientists (e.g., Mooney, 1963; Pelz and Andrews, 1966; Taylor and Barron, 1963). It seems that since then, in a period of thirty years or so, very few papers have been published on creativity and engineering if the comments by Christiano and Ramirez (1993), Mitchell (1998), and Richards (1998) can be taken as representative. Since then, at sporadic intervals, a few papers published in the engineering education journals have directly addressed this topic, and in 1998 one issue of *the European Journal of Engineering Education* was primarily devoted to creativity. [9] An interesting question is whether the papers in the *European Journal* differ very much except in specifics from those that went long before. [10] However, several of the papers in the *European Journal* considered the role of assessment and examinations in developing creativity which had not been the case in the previous literature.

In 1996 the Australian Institute of Engineers called for no less than a cultural change in engineering education. Mitchell (1998), who cited this report, noted that creativity and innovation did not rate a mention in the list of graduate attributes even though they were mentioned in the report. Mitchell's review led her to the belief that in order to get a comprehensive idea of creativity in engineering education, we will have to get beyond the divergent or lateral thinking component that has dominated much discussion.

Guilford's theory of the intellect as it related to creativity has been misinterpreted by some writers and teachers who considered creativity to be no more and no less than an expression of divergent thinking. At the same time it is, nevertheless, correct to say that among teachers the idea that they encouraged convergent thinking rather than divergent thinking to the detriment of learning did create an important discussion about teaching (e.g., Sternberg and Lubart, 1995; Torrance 1975; Vernon, 1972). Torrance (1975, 1995), argued that one of the reasons why there was a shortage of teachers who could encourage creativity was that they were not prepared to

take the risk of losing control. In the same vein, Sternberg and Lubart (1995) argued that students are made risk-averse because schools discourage failure. And these views were reflected in the engineering debate. Insofar as engineering is concerned, this issue has not gone away; engineering educators need to take note of Torrance's conclusion that teachers need to be trained to cultivate creativity. They argued that analysis and synthesis were key skills in creative thinking and that activities such as the location of specific information and the re-ordering of apparently unrelated data into a meaningful patter required creative aptitudes. They argued that creativity was generated by six interacting factors, namely, intelligence, cognitive style, personality, motivation, and intelligence.

Guilford believed that, taken together, the ability to see that a problem exists (problem sensitivity), flexibility in the way problems are approached and solved, and the fluency with which ideas (especially novel ideas) are generated characterize the creative thinker. In the context of convergent and divergent thinking, convergers were less likely to produce ideas fluently and would be less flexible in their approaches to solving problems. His idea of the creative process is described in the next section.

Ramirez (1993) argued that each quadrant in the Kolb has a role to play in creative thinking. He described the 4Mat model as follows: *"The Why? quadrant provides the motivation for learning, which although important for learning in general, is especially critical for creative thought to take place. The entire premise of creativity in the pursuit of innovation is to be unconventional. Without suitable motivation there is no reason to try something new if the conventional route will do. The "What? quadrant provides the knowledge which is necessary for creative processes to occur."* Hence the importance of prior knowledge and the mechanisms for its retrieval (i.e., memory). [11] *"Knowledge can exist as structure so the manner in which it is presented (context and sequence) plays a role in the way it is to be used and/or modified or built upon later. The How? Quadrant provides the stage for emulation of expert problem solving to occur. The application of the material in a well controlled environment is necessary to further reinforce the decision to take risks first introduced in the Why? Quadrant.... The last quadrant, the What if? Quadrant is one of the most important for engineering students, as it is here that most of their engineering judgement is developed. Engineering judgement is extremely vital to creativity since it allows us to make simplifications of complex situations."*

This has some similarity with the view that creativity could be obtained in more than one way, as for example, the provision of different points of view on problems raised by a project. *"Why is it, or and not and?* (Waks and Merdler, 2003).

[7] It should be noted that this was a collection of papers by and for engineers. The authors, however, had taken much note of psychological and organizational research to that date.

[8] See Gregory (1972) for an overview.

[9] This was also a collection of papers by and for engineers.

[10] It is this writer's contention that the 1972 work is more instructive, and that for the time being, at least, it has seminal value.

[11] There is relatively little written on the memory in the engineering literature.

Guilford's model of the intellect was also important because it provided an alternative theory of intelligence in which creativity was considered to be separate to and as important as intelligence.[12] Waks and Merdler (2003) noted that some authorities take the view that while high intelligence is essential it is not a sufficient condition for creativity. But they ask, how high is high? And, what are the effects of context on content on the outcome? Similarly with knowledge, *"Can it be that the amount of knowledge alone has impact on creative performance? What about the ways in which knowledge is obtained?"*[13] Low correlations have been found between grade performance and originality among engineering students (Taylor and Barron, 1963). Christiano and Ramirez (1993) reported a study of engineers which showed that high performance depended on characteristics that were associated with creativity.[14] Nevertheless, it has been suggested that an IQ of 115 and above is necessary for creative activity in engineering (Gregory, 1972). Sternberg (1985), made the point that intelligence was a necessary but not sufficient condition for creativity. Gregory argued that for *"creativity to be shown, a high level of functioning in the knowledge acquisition components would seem to be necessary."*

Guilford's research also generated ideas for testing that are of interest to engineers. These tests were developed by the research group that defined the concepts, and as might have been expected, they load on the factor they called fluency (Kline, 2000).[15] Guilford's work belongs to the category of study which considers antecedents to be important. Thus, there have been studies of the effect of leadership on performance. Others have considered the need for feedback and recognition, the need for discretion, the effect of positive feelings, personality, and the impact of the environment (organisational structure) on creative performance (West

and Farr, 1990). There has also been interest in the process of creativity and some of the research that is categorized as antecedent spills over to work on the creative process.

11.3.   The Creative Process

In 1926 Wallas suggested a model of creative thinking that has had a lasting influence on thinking about creativity. As interpreted by Kreith (1967) as the basis for undergraduate research in engineering, the four stages are:

1. *Preparation, involving a thorough investigation of the problem by reading, experiment, and discussion.*
2. *Incubation, involving a conscious mental digestion and assimilation of all pertinent information acquired; this state is often followed by a period of withdrawal from the problem if the tension and frustration involved in seeking a solution become too severe.*
3. *Illumination, involving the appearance of a creative idea, the intuitive flash of insight.*
4. *Verification, involving experimental testing of the idea.*

Very often when tutors are introducing students to the research process, they will outline similar stages. One of the reasons for introducing projects into undergraduate education is to encourage the creative process, but there is no research to indicate whether individual projects are more likely to stimulate creativity among individuals than group projects. As indicated in Chapter 10, there has been no serious attempt to evaluate the relative merits of individual and group projects.

Most investigators believe that the stages are too rigid, and there is a debate about whether or not there is unconscious incubation in creative thinking; although as West and Farr (1990) pointed out, the model does not say that incubation always occurs unconsciously. One of the terms introduced in this particular debate was that of *"creative worrying."* (Olton, 1979, cited by West and Farr, 1990).

A model that was used for the purpose of designing training for creativity in organizations was developed by Basadur et al (1982). Unlike the Wallas model that only considered thought processes this model also considered the cognitive behaviors that were involved. It had three stages that are very similar to those described in Chapter 10 for problem solving. They are problem finding, problem solving, and solution implementation. However, each stage is a two-step process in which ideas are generated uncritically (ideation) and then evaluated for the best (evaluation).[16]

Another model that has been much discussed is due to Amabile (1983). She suggested a five-stage model. The stages are:

1. Task presentation.
2. Preparation.
3. Idea generation.
4. Idea validation.
5. Outcome assessment.

---

[12]Although Guilford's structure of the intellect model has been shown to be psychometrically unsound (Gustafsson and Undheim, 1996; Mackintosh, 1998) there is little doubt that the ideas that came from the model concerning creativity were important. In other work, he showed that various temperament factors influenced the maintenance of cognitive activity (Snow, Corno and Jackson, 1996), and the idea of decomposing the intellect into a number of factors caused other questions to be raised that would lead to answers to questions about the performance of women in science (Linn, Songer, and Eylon, 1996).

[13]Waks and Merdler drew attention to Perkins (1990) 'tension theory' that argues that *"there is a need for optimal knowledge, enough to generate creative thinking, but not to bring about stiffness."* They also noted that Weisberg's (1999) foundation theory suggested a monotonic positive relation between knowledge and creativity. The statement is one of two explanations to the question *"Does originality stem exclusively from the cognitive trait of observing problems from different points of view, or from a sound and well intrinsically motivated basis?*

[14]Reported in Cropley, A. J. and J. McLeod. (1989).*Fostering Academic Excellence* (1989). Pergammon Press, New York.

[15]These tests are:- (1) "Consequences". It is intended to measure ideational fluency, originality and flexibility. Subjects are required to write out the consequences of unusual situations; there are five items in each of the two forms. (2) "Fluency." It is intended to measure word fluency, expressional fluency, ideational fluency, and flexibility and originality. (3) Alternate uses. It is intended to measure flexibility but may also measure originality and fluency. Kline (2000) concludes that these tests measure a second order factor as set out in Cattell, R. B. (1971), *Personality and Learning Theory,* Springer, New York..

[16] This description is based on that in West and Farr (2000).

In the preparation stage the individual has to acquire information and recall information already existent in the memory. The final stage is a decision about whether or not the problem can be solved. The process is terminated or returned to stage 1.

To some extent, these stages are reminiscent not only of the Wallas model but of some of the problem-solving models discussed earlier. Very often we are presented with tasks which we have to complete. Amabile argued that individual's are more likely to solve a problem if their intrinsic motivation is high. In this respect it is to some extent in the tradition of Herzberg (as well as Theory X and Theory Y), because the *hygiene* factors are extrinsic factors (Theory X), and the *satisfiers* are primarily intrinsic (Theory Y). According to Amabile intrinsic motivation also facilitates idea generation. It is a stage of divergence whereas idea validation is a stage of convergence.

Subsequently, Amabile accepted that certain types of extrinsic motivation might enhance creativity. In a revision of her theory in 1996, she proposed that creative performance required domain relevant skills, creativity-relevant processes, and task motivation. One has to have a good knowledge of the domain if one is to be creative in that domain-in this case, a dimension of engineering. Of the strategies that a person uses to generate the creative process task motivation is the most important component. The level of domain-relevant skills and creativity relevant processes determine what a person "can do." But what a person "will do," is determined by the domain-related skills, creative processes, and intrinsic motivation. Engineers need to have a strong knowledge base while being deliberately open to the problem situation (Freeman, Butcher, and Christie, 1979; Ramirez, 1994).

King (1990) considered that Amabile's earlier model was useful because it showed *"how-and where-the skills of the individual affect the progress of the process."* It thus had implications for the design of the curriculum and project work.

It should not be surprising that Amabile found that discretion-that is, the freedom to do something or not-is an important antecedent to creative work, although 'complete' freedom on how to spend one's time may not be as successful at stimulating creative behavior as 'some' freedom.

As indicated in Chapter 6, Amabile distinguished between supportive and suppressive extrinsic motivation in the generation of creativity. Amabile claims that her model leads to a social psychology of creativity, but King (1990) argued that social factors have only an indirect effect on the process described. However, Heywood (1972) reported that management could inhibit or enhance creativity, and Amabile (1996) considered that the manager's role is the most important environmental factor. For example, eight engineers in a study by Klukken, Parsons, and Columbus (1997) were subject to social and environmental constraints. Their study revealed four clusters of attributes that contributed to creative endeavor. These were motivation, environment and work conditions, tools, and mental processes. These engineers were aware of their intrinsic motivation and wanted opportunities that would enable them *"to express themselves in novel solutions."* This is related to their attitude, which Klukken and his colleagues called engrossment and connection. It relates to the feeling of exhilaration that comes from doing what you want to do. Clearly, management can have a substantial influence on the working environment The combination of engrossment and connection would seem to be related to Csikzentmihalyi's (1993) concept of *flow*. He described flow as follows:

"If a tennis player is asked how it feels when a game is going well, she will describe a state of mind that is very similar to the description a chess player will give of a good tournament. So will be a description of how it feels to be absorbed in painting, or playing a difficult piece of music. Watching a good play or reading a stimulating book also seems to produce the same mental state. I called it 'flow' because this was the metaphor several respondents used for how it felt when their experience was most enjoyable-it was like being carried away by a current, everything moving smoothly without effort.... Contrary to expectation, "flow" usually happens not during relaxing moments of leisure and entertainment, but rather when we are actively involved in a difficult enterprise, in a task that stretches our physical or mental abilities . It turns out that when challenges are high and personal skills are used to the utmost, we experience this rare state of consciousness...even a usually boring job, once the challenges are brought into balance with the person's skills and the goals clarified, can be exciting and involving" [pxiii].[17]

Many engineers will have experienced flow. It would seem that the processes of creativity are carried along with the flow (Mitchell, 1998). Therefore, engineering education has to enable students to experience flow, and this requires an appropriate educational environment. The abstract of a paper by Holmes (1998) puts it more strongly. It simply reads *"Creativity is not an optional extra. It is the essence of life."*

These engineers wanted a secure environment and this is consistent with other studies conducted over a period of thirty years (e.g., Whitfield, 1972). They needed to be totally engaged on the task and protected from excessive managerial interference. The same is true of students (Baillie and Walker, 1998). They need to be protected from their teachers. Thus, Lovelace (1986) argued that it is the responsibility of the manager to manipulate the environment, and clearly Baillie and Walker and others who engaged in creativity teaching believed this to be the case for educational environments.

---

[17]This quotation is not taken from his book on *Flow; The Psychology of Optimal Experience*.(1990) Harper and Row, New York. It comes from *The Evolving Self* (1993). Harper, New York.

Finally, engineers need to have a strong knowledge base while being deliberately open to the problem situation (Freeman, Butcher, and Christie, 1979; Ramirez, 1994).

11.4. Dacey and Lennon's General Theory of Creativity

In 1998 Dacey and Lennon contributed a substantive review of research into creativity. It included biological, psychological, and social factors. These were integrated into a comprehensive bio-psychosocial explanation of how creativity works. Uniquely, they linked it to Guilford's Creative Problem-Solving Model. Guilford's model is a multiple trait approach to the intellect. It has three components. These are called *operations*, *products*, and *contents*. The operations are cognition, memory, divergent production, convergent production, and evaluation. The products are units, classes, relations, systems, transformations, and implications. The contents are figural, symbolic, semantic, and behavioral. As we have seen, among engineers interest seems to have centered mainly on convergent, and divergent thinking which Guilford thought was important in creativity, but not totally so. Other dimensions of the intellect had a role to play. Gregory's (1972) adaptation of Guilford's model is shown in Figure 11.2. Dacey and Lennon also produced a diagram. The differences between the two are primarily of presentation. The diagram shows that we receive inputs of specific information that we filter. The filtering process simply allows us to reject that information and make no further move, or to continue with the problem. The first input might be unconscious, and an individual may be unwilling to let this information surface. Dacey and Lennon pointed out that the ego defense mechanisms of regression and repression function at a high level in this stage, as will the collective unconscious and bipolar activity. In the second stage of cognition the problem is sensed and structured. At the second exit, an individual will quit because of a conscious reason for not pursuing the problem, as, for example, if it is not worth the time to solve that problem. If, however, the problem is thought to be worth solving, then answers are generated. This is the stage that involves convergent and divergent thinking. Dacey and Lennon pointed out that this is the stage where most people give up and use exit III. However, if they decide to persevere, then new information is obtained, and new answers are generated. There is an exit at all stages and there are filters in each of the two cognition stages Every stage is subject to evaluation, and all stages are related to the contents in the way shown in the diagram. A person who arrives at the fifth stage is likely to be creative. As indicated above, Dacey and Lennon reviewed all the research on creativity in the biological, social, and psychological domains. They distinguished between cognitive and personality factors in the psychological domain. Their analysis revealed a number of factors in each group-for example, convergent and divergent thinking in the cognitive category, and a number of ego defense mechanisms in the personality category. They suggested that the factors in each of the categories function at a high, medium or low (or inactive) level in each of the stages of the Guilford model. For example, divergent thinking is inactive in stage I (the first filter), is high in stage II, the first stage of cognition, moderate in stages II and III, and is low in the V stage. All of the cognitive factors (see below) except convergent and divergent thinking are high in stage V. Similarly, all of the personality factors with are high in stage V, but the biological factor of repression is inactive, and the social factor of a positive innovative educational environment is only moderate. Apart from that all, social factors are high in stage V but they have low effects in the first three stages. Dacey and Lennon's list of factors is as follows:

Biological. ACTH[18]; bipolar activity; CREB's[19]; interhemispheric coordination and microneuronal development,

Personality. Collective unconscious; delay gratification; ego strength; flexibility; functional freedom; gender role stereotyping; perseverance; preference for disorder; regression; repression; risk taking; self-control; stimulus freedom; sublimation and tolerance of ambiguity.

Cognitive. Collective unconscious; cognitive mobility; convergent thinking; divergent thinking; ego control; ego resilience; field independence; lateral thinking; remote associates; use of metaphor.

Social. Being late born, positive effects; high family socio economic factors; innovative educational environment, negative effects; supportive political climate, positive effects.

Dacey and Lennon (1998) suggested that it is possible to make the following generalizations about the way creativity works:

"Being creative is not simply a case of having high intelligence. Although having above-average intelligence is necessary being an intellectual genius is not. In

---

[18]ACTH is a hormone. Dacey and Lennon (1998) wrote: *"at high levels of brain stimulation, a higher level of ACTH is secreted which stimulates communication between the hemispheres of the brain. Specifically ACTH neuropeptides act to facilitate communication between neurons, which results in higher levels of cognition and significantly greater productivity. When an individual is in the filtering stage, there is no need for high communication between the hemispheres because the person is functioning unconsciously. As the person's stimulation increases throughout the next four stages of creativity, the levels of cognition and production reflect the amount of ACTH that is secreted. When interhemispheric communication is most needed- in the Production II stage- ACTH secretion is at its highest"* (p. 228). Dacey and Lennon apply this to the second and third stages of the Wallas model. ACTH is produced when the hypothalamus stimulates the pituitary gland. A interesting discussion of the role of the hypothalamus in the emotions will be found in LeDoux (1998, p. 240).

[19]CREB is a protein that influences what will and will not be remembered (see LeDoux, 1998). Dacey and Lennon wrote: *"Creative persons have superior memory functions. They have not only a high-level ability to remember but also the capacity to recognize what is worth remembering and what to avoid storing in the first place. This ability functions at low to moderate level, albeit without awareness, in Stage I and at a moderate level at both production stages. CREBs main contribution comes at cognition stages, particularly Cognition II. In this stage, the greater the breadth of previously stored information contributes to an excellent organization of problem parameters, which in turn enhances the superior production of solutions"* (p. 229)

addition to mental ability, creativity depends on certain physical, personality and motivational variables, as well as on certain environmental circumstances. All people are born with the ability to be creative at some level, although whether this ability exists on a continuum or whether it is qualitatively different at the highest levels is still a matter of debate. The "nature versus nurture" debate is over. There is now little doubt that three factors- biological, psychological and social-play a role in the creative act. Creativity tends to follow developmental trends over the life span and may be most readily cultivated during peak periods of life. There is no longer any doubt that creative ability can be purposely enhanced. This is true not only of individuals but also of groups such as industrial unit and task forces." (Dacey and Lennon, 1998. pp. 225 and 226).

One of the problems with generalizations of this kind is that often they smooth out things that are important. Thus, in the comments on intelligence they do not point out the importance of memory. To be fair, Dacey and Lennon (1998) do suggest a need for research on memory, and it might be added training. This, of course brings the issue back to concept learning (Chapter 4).

Dacey and Lennon's theory re-introduced some variables that had been neglected in creativity research, and it made clear that what makes creativity work is complex. who design education and training programs for creativity It is not possible to make simplistic statements to the effect that *"this causes that."*

These theories do not solve the differences between scientific and engineering creativity because of problems inherent in the definitions of what scientists and engineers are. They are, nevertheless, important to those engaged in such debates because they are about the identity of these professions. They also inform those who design education and training programs for creativity.

11.5.   Creativity Education and Training.

One of the earliest attempts in the United Kingdom to address the problem of creativity within an engineering program was due to Monk (1972). His program is shown in Exhibit 11.1. It owed much to the ideas of de Bono (see below) and Guilford, and much attention was paid to the generation and evaluation of ideas.

There have been several reported attempts to provide creativity training in industry. The problem with all short courses is that unless they can be followed up, and unless managers utilize the skills learned by their personnel, this learning is often wasted. These courses necessarily change attitudes and managers often found it difficult to cope with such change. In short, it was found that in the in-company courses evaluated by this writer, the aims were sometimes confused, and often there were more than could be met in the time available. Very often the training officers did not take an instructional role but brought in outsiders to give key note talks. This meant that the course became a series of discontinuities (Heywood, 1972).

As indicated earlier, Basadur, Green, and Green (1982) devised a model for creativity training. West and Farr (1990), who cited this study reported that while it led to increased practice and performance of ideation it did not do so in the problem finding stage. The investigators wrote that, *"It may be that one is able to get participants to do problem finding (cognitive and behavioral) yet still not like problem Finding (attitudinal)."* This is consistent with Heywood's findings reported in a previous paragraph.

At college level a number of courses that have the intention of developing creativity among their goals have been reported. The starting point for three case studies evaluated by Baillie and Walker (1998) at the University of Sydney was to provide conditions for learning in which the students had freedom that allowed for creativity. They also had to provide the conditions for motivation that would generate student autonomy in learning. The tutors did not want to add something new to the curriculum, but tried *"to see creativity as inherent to the learning process and to extend the application of this creativity to other matters."* Consistent with this approach is the use of the project method, now generally regarded as part of the engineering curriculum, as vehicles for developing creativity (e.g., Acar, 1998; Blicblau and Steiner, 1998; Matthews and Jahanian, 1999).

The first case study reported by Baillie and Walker is about the first year of the mechanical engineering program in which there was a course on professional engineering. It was established to foster *"the students ability to think for themselves, both to find (ask questions about) and to solve (discover answers to the problems facing today's society."*

The students were divided into three groups, and three person teaching teams, (the members of whom came from different teaching backgrounds), rotated among the groups. This arrangement allowed a number of different teaching strategies to be used. These included group work, interviews, discussions, and communications exercises. Learning how to learn exercises were also included little detail of the strategies is given in the paper. For assessment the students had to select one or more topics from the course and then submit for approval a paragraph on that they would like to explore in their report. They were told to express their opinions in their reports, but only so long as they could back up their views. Baillie and Walker commented that the flexibility allowed in the reports was necessary to allow the students to be more creative. It *"extended originality in their ways of expressing ideas as well as in their choice of projects."*

The Biggs and Collis SOLO Taxonomy was used to analyse the reports (see Chapter 2). The taxonomy enabled the assessors to look for a hierarchy of expressions of learning. These ranged as follows: (1) no relevant information; (2) one relevant aspect focused on; (3) several aspects focused on in isolation; to (4) several

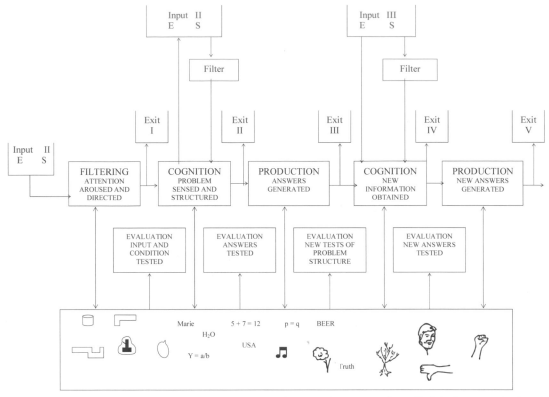

Figure 11.2. Gregory's (1972) adaptation of Guilford's model of the creative process.(On p 73 of S. Gregory (ed.) *Creativity and Innovation in Engineering.* **Butterworths, London)**

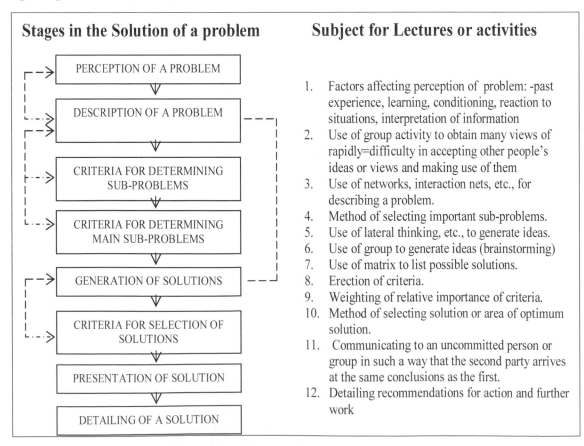

Stages in the Solution of a problem

- PERCEPTION OF A PROBLEM
- DESCRIPTION OF A PROBLEM
- CRITERIA FOR DETERMINING SUB-PROBLEMS
- CRITERIA FOR DETERMINING MAIN SUB-PROBLEMS
- GENERATION OF SOLUTIONS
- CRITERIA FOR SELECTION OF SOLUTIONS
- PRESENTATION OF SOLUTION
- DETAILING OF A SOLUTION

Subject for Lectures or activities

1. Factors affecting perception of problem: -past experience, learning, conditioning, reaction to situations, interpretation of information
2. Use of group activity to obtain many views of rapidly=difficulty in accepting other people's ideas or views and making use of them
3. Use of networks, interaction nets, etc., for describing a problem.
4. Method of selecting important sub-problems.
5. Use of lateral thinking, etc., to generate ideas.
6. Use of group to generate ideas (brainstorming)
7. Use of matrix to list possible solutions.
8. Erection of criteria.
9. Weighting of relative importance of criteria.
10. Method of selecting solution or area of optimum solution.
11. Communicating to an uncommitted person or group in such a way that the second party arrives at the same conclusions as the first.
12. Detailing recommendations for action and further work

Exhibit 11.1. Outline scheme for teaching problem solving and creativity (Monk, 1972). From the Course description of the Engineering Problem Solving Seminar at Enfield College of Technology subsequently published by J. D. Monk (1972) together with a complete description of one problem.

factors considered and related to each other.[20]

Several teaching techniques were used at Imperial College, London, in an interdepartmental project that had as its aim the development of creativity. The students were introduced to a number of creative thinking techniques.

"In particular, 'brainstorming' was adopted as the encompassing title, and during the group sessions many aspects of the other techniques were used as a standard means of searching for new ideas...From the outset, each student within the group is required to develop and propose an 'idea' which is capable of solving the problem. Typically, this is in the form of a sketch and it should clearly show how the design is expected to function .... Emphasis was firmly placed on the creative methods used, rather than a discussion of the technical issues, and focusing on the strategies processes involved. The technical aspects were dealt with once the conceptual arrangement was selected and evaluated against the initial specification" (Court, 1998).

In a second project at the University of Sydney, a core course in materials for mechanical, mechatronic, and aeronautical engineering changed its teaching and examining techniques with a view to fostering creativity. The changes required a move from traditional type teaching techniques (i.e., lectures) to interactive methods involving small groups. The change in examination was sought because the traditional exam (i.e., a timed test without books) produced varying amounts of information but little evidence of deep learning. Also interviews with the students showed that *"however interesting they had found the course, the intentions were being undermined by the assessment, in particular the final examination"..."and their learning would be focused on memorizing facts"* (Baillie and Walker, 1998).

A complete change was made in the assessment strategy, and a power test was introduced.[21] Interviews and nominal group techniques were used to evaluate the course. Now students thought that the examination *"tested two things-your understanding and your ability to explain what you understand".* But, *"open book examinations are a lot harder".* However, when the examination questions were analyzed by the SOLO Taxonomy, it was found, that as in previous years the style of question had not produced high level answers. The power test, however, produced answers that ranged from *"multi-structural as a pass to extended abstract for high distinction"*

Baillie and Walker found, as this writer had found, that descriptive questions can encourage memorization. *"A question needs some element of open endedness if it is to inspire creative thought."* In

examination systems of the kind that function in Australia, Europe and the United Kingdom it is very difficult for teachers to break out of the Constraints of traditional teaching and take the risks required by 'new' techniques-for example, to ask students to write and answer their own question!

A pilot study at the Universities of Uppsala and Växjö in Sweden reported by Berglund et al (1998), also started from the perspective that examinations have to be redesigned if students' creativity is to be increased. They reminded the reader that in Sweden *"Examination is normally a final exam requiring also that all assignments and labs have been carried out satisfactorily. The way to examine a course is, however, to a great extent up to the teacher."* This was the case for me throughout my teaching career, but subject to the influence of external examiners. In Sweden there is local freedom to create programs and content. Nevertheless, conventions and culture constrain educational systems. These cause teachers to be conservative and somewhat resistant to change. Berglund et al., following in the tradition of Marton (see Chapter 5), wanted to encourage deep learning. To accomplish this they replaced the final traditional exam in Computer Architecture with public seminars on programming projects. *"During the seminars* [each of 15 minutes duration] *two groups of students were at the blackboard in front of the class. One of the groups was defending its project (defendants), while the other group acted as opponents and asked questions about the project. The public were asked to participate in the discussion as well."* The structure of the seminars was as follows:

1. *"The opponents presented the project to the defendants as well as to the public. In this way, the defendants could see that the opponents had really understood their project, and the public got a presentation of data structures, algorithms, etc.*
2. *The opponents and the audience asked questions of the defendants. The opponents were clearly instructed to put emphasis on the issues where the defendants had found good solutions. In this way, the public were presented with a variety of good examples.*
3. *The defendants gave their judgements on the project. Again, they were instructed to put their emphasis on the strong points".*

At Växjö each work group of students gave an oral presentation for 25 minutes which was judged by assessors who were not the instructors.

In addition, in both universities the continuous assessment of small tasks was undertaken in addition to written final exams. The results for the first course in Algebra at Växjö showed an almost 100% improvement in the number of students who passed the examination. Despite all that has been written about teacher and student workloads, the workload of the teachers at Växjö was found to be too high, and this was exacerbated by the fact that some of the problems set were too difficult, and

---

[20] This structure is similar in some respects to items in the schedule shown in Exhibit 2. 10.

[21] See Chapter on assessment. A power test is an untimed examination that allows students to tackle substantial problems without being subject to unrealistic time constraints. Baillie and Tookey (1997) provided a detailed analysis of performance in this type of examination.

these demanded extra tutoring. The new plan also placed a heavy load on the students. The instructors also learned that it required more resources than they had envisaged. At Uppsala, the students complained that the workload was too high but they did not want to return to classical methods of teaching and examination. Both institutions considered that the pilot program had been successful, and they intended to continue in the direction set by these pilot studies.

The third case study at the University of Sydney was a Physics seminar which used a 'quasi-Socratic' dialogue. The teacher acted as a facilitator. It was hoped that provocation would challenge students to think about their approaches to learning. *"For example, the group of students attending the seminar were asked to identify what they find difficult in learning physics, and the individual answers to this are recorded on the board as a list. When the list is looked at as whole, a pattern emerges which points to underlying conceptions of learning."* They wanted the students to come to view learning as *"an inherently creative process"* (Baillie and Walker, 1998).

The seminar was evaluated by questionnaire immediately after its completion. Interviews some months after the seminar showed that the students were *"still very mindful of the major issues raised in the seminar and had since developed specific practices regarding their learning that were more consistent with a deep and creative approach."*

Waks and Merdler (2003) set out to identify the pattern of the engagement in creative thinking during a final project that took more than a year to complete. They also examined the role of self-perception toward creative performance and examined the instructors' involvement in the process. The 120 engineering students who contributed to the study were engaged in the fields of electronics, software, architecture, marketing, and industrial design. The students and their instructors defined six generic project stages. These were: (1) forming an idea; (2) market and requirements survey; (3) organizing and analysing information; (4) preliminary design; (5) detailed design; and (6) evaluating-refining product.

Three tests of creative thinking were administered to determine fluency, flexibility, and originality. These were administered together with a general questionnaire on three occasions during the project and a SAM (Something About Myself) questionnaire was administered during the first project stage.[22]

It is of interest to note that they were not able to establish the validity of the fluency test among the software students because 30% refused to state previous ideas as well as the chosen one, for fear that their ideas would be stolen!

Nevertheless, the findings that emerged showed some differences between the groups. When compared with the first and fifth stages, the electronics students showed highest originality in the third stage (organizing and analyzing information). Moreover, their originality positively correlated with their fluency.

The software students depended on fluency to generate flexibility and were most fluent and flexible in the first stage (forming an idea). But like the electronics students, they did not focus on the second stage (market requirements survey).

The architectural students became more creative as the project became more advanced: This is very similar to the marketing students, who became more able to generate original ideas as the project progressed. It is strange that they should have demonstrated less creative thinking in the second stage (market and requirements survey).

While particular project stages seemed to influence the industrial design students, they did not influence the industrial design students who were found to be the most creative of the groups. It was found that among these students, interest was the dominant factor in evoking flexibility and originality. Among the other groups, notwithstanding the points made above, there were no significant differences between them on the three measures of creativity.

Students of architecture and industrial design attributed higher creative behavior to themselves. Whatever the field, this investigation showed the importance of flexibility and creativity. It also showed the importance of the instructor and the relationship between student and instructor. Negative attitudes by the instructor could suppress the motivation to be creative, particularly during the idea formation stage, but the negative influences of extrinsic motivation were dominant in most stages.

Perhaps the most interesting finding was that some students skipped stages. The industrial design students skipped the organizing and analyzing stage, and the marketing students started designing by details. The software and electronics students did not inspect the market and requirements. Waks and Merdler suggested that because the students did not approach the project in a linear, algorithmic, and vertical manner their flexibility and originality was reduced. They arrived at this "tentative assumption" by comparison with the architecture students. Those architectural students who engaged in creative activities thought of themselves as creative persons even though they had not manifested higher originality in the first stage. But the architectural students creative thinking was shown to be related to specific instructions. Following Crutchfield (1962), who had argued that creative people are neither conformist nor non-conformist but simply are not concerned with conformity, Waks and Merdler suggested that *"if the instructor represents conformity, as to the way the*

---

[22]These were the Torrance Test of Creative Thinking (Torrance, 1974).

students should be advised during the project, then no wonder that attitudes to the instructor have no impact on originality."

In contrast to the "within course" developments described above, some institutions have introduced specific engineering courses to foster creativity. For example, Richards (1998) of the University of Virginia (Charlottsville) gave brief descriptions of several courses that had been introduced specifically to foster creativity. In the first year, there was a course in Engineering Concepts and Design in which the design component was project-based. Each instructor assigned up to five design projects in the semester. A graduate-level computer-aided engineering and design course required students to include an original design as part of the students' work. Shared courses between faculty from Engineering and Commerce were offered in the Technology and Product Development Life Style courses and Creativity and New Product Development courses. In the former, team-based projects were intended to stimulate creative thinking. In the latter there was an emphasis on innovation in the commercial sector. Finally, they offered a unique course in Invention and Design that was open to students from any school in the University. In this course, teams of students invent and design in each of three domains that spanned the range of innovation activities. Richards (1998) wrote that *"All of these courses are non-traditional and somewhat subversive. They undermine the idea that there is one right answer to every problem and it can only be found through analysis."* Richards listed six principles that had emerged from his experience of teaching creativity. Taken together with thinking on assessment, they provide a frame of reference for the design of courses in creativity and innovation. Richards's six principles, with some comments, are:

1. We must help students to broaden their perspectives.
2. We must require innovation.

    "If creativity is expected of them students will Exhibit it. As they experience being creative, they will seek further opportunities to do so. This requires that we expand the types of problems we assign, and the types of solutions we accept and encourage...." Farr (1990) assumed that given the right circumstances most if not all individuals are capable of being innovative. Moreover, they are capable of increasing the level of motivation in their work roles.

3. We must promote product orientation.
4. We must make students aware of the nature and conditions for creativity.

    "We can enhance creativity in our students by helping them understand the social and psychological processes involved. In our classes we explicitly discuss the theory and practice of creativity. To realize their creative potential, students must develop certain attitudes, behaviors and habits, as well as domain knowledge and

thinking skills. They should study what is known about creativity, design, invention, innovation, and especially entrepreneurship". This is an example of learning how to learn within context, but this understanding is also the understanding required by managers who want to encourage creativity (see Section 11.2 above), and it should, therefore, contribute to the acquisition of a management skill. Students might also be asked to undertake some of the creativity tests described in the previous section.

5. We must provide the tools for creativity both physical and cognitive.
6. Our ultimate goal is to require original creative work as part of every engineering course.

    As indicated in earlier paragraphs, much attention has been paid to strategies for the development of creativity and in particular those for the generation of an evaluation of ideas. These are considered next.

11.6. Generating Ideas

Past experience is a powerful inhibitor of change. While we learn by experience, it is necessary to keep an open mind and avoid the temptation to allow a "set" to determine our thinking strategies (Heywood, 1989; Baillie and Walker, 1998). Court (1998) linked this idea to the creative person who is expected to be someone, *"who is characterized by open-mindedness, self motivation, cooperative ability, and possibly artistic vision."*

It is interesting to note that in Gregory and Turner's definition of design the activity ends with specification. Some other engineering activity is required to produce the artefact. In the design projects that have become popular in engineering education the process is often taken through to implementation and evaluation. The point to be made here is that it may be necessary in this continuation phase to resort to the generation of ideas and their evaluation with respect to particular problems that occur in implementation and/or manufacture. The techniques used to generate ideas apply in any problem-solving situation, and the overall activity of engineering can be defined as a sequence of problems that have to be solved-some big, some small; some easy, some difficult.

The need for both convergent and divergent thinking in the engineering activity is clear from both Figure 11.2 and Whitfield's model (Figure 5.1). Divergent thinking is required for the generation of ideas. Brainstorming, synectics, and lateral thinking have been used for this purpose. As Monk made clear it is important that these are group activities because there has to be general acquiescence to the idea chosen, and some members of the group may have found it difficult to accept the idea in the first instance. Prior-experience, as we have seen (Chapter 4) can create perceptual blocks, and in Monk's course a technique described by Rokeach (1960) in *The Open and Closed Mind* was used to illustrate this effect. It is easy to fall into "set mechanization".

An information-processing model of the creative process due to L. Jones and described by King (1990) identified four barriers or blocks to creative thinking. I have added a fifth. These were:

1. strategic Blocks. These relate to the skills of creative problem solving.
2. value Blocks. They are a form of dissonance and arise from the beliefs that managers (teachers) have regarding how individuals (work) learn. King (1990) gives the example of a manager who has a Theory X view of motivation. This would inhibit him from looking at an environment in which creative workers have to work from a different perspective. This, as Baillie and Walker (1998) reported, can be difficult for teachers who want to introduce innovative practices in engineering education to develop creativity. Related to this are the effects of past experience.(See 5 below.)
3. perceptual bocks cause managers to overlook opportunities or anticipate threats.
4. Self-image blocks arise from a lack of confidence in opposing resistance to change.
5. Past experience is a very powerful inhibitor of change because of the tendency to ask "how did we do this before?"

Clearly these are not mutually exclusive. Several approaches for the generation of ideas discussed below have been used in educational programs and industry.

11.6.1. Brainstorming and Its Variants

Many papers in engineering education have reported that students use brainstorming to develop ideas. The evaluation of these ideas may be supplemented by other techniques. Thus, in a freshman creative engineering course at Prairie View A and M University, in the stage of obtaining preliminary ideas,

"Each member presents his or her ideas during the group meeting. Three and two-dimensional pictorials are sketched to develop the brainstorming ideas. Students develop research methods for obtaining relevant information about their design project. Survey methods such as personal interviews, and questionnaire are also used to gather opinions and reaction to preliminary ideas. Students are encouraged to develop as many ideas as possible" (Warsame, Biney, and Morgan, 1995).

Woods (1994) suggested that the principles of brainstorming are to *"defer criticism and judgement of ideas, to encourage the building on the ideas of others, to express ideas succinctly so that no elaboration is required as to how something might work."*

Weisberg (1986), cited by Farr (1990), listed the following rules for brainstorming:

1. *"Judgements about ideas are withheld until all ideas have been generated; in particular, criticism is not allowed during the idea generation stage.*

2. *'Freewheeling' is encouraged; that is, members of the group are told that the more the idea deviates from existing practice, the better.*
3. *Quantity of possible solutions is stated as the goal of the idea generation stage.*
4. *Combination of ideas already expressed is encouraged as well as the extension or modification of others', solutions."*

Typically the leader, who may be a student, writes down the information on a flipchart[23] Woods (1994) added that repetition of ideas is okay, and that triggers to restart the flow of ideas should be used when necessary. He also provided a checklist for monitoring brainstorming.

Yukhl (1994) cited research to the effect that brainstorming is only partially successful because, while it improved idea generation when compared with other groups that interacted regularly, it was not a guarantee that all inhibition was reduced. It is fairly evident that individual members of the group are likely to be affected differently by the process to other members in the group. Other work on groups suggests that personality is likely to be important. For example, Farr (1990) cited research that suggested that those individuals who could tolerate ambiguity and were low in communication apprehension produced more ideas. To overcome the problem of inhibition, more structured techniques have been developed and both Yukhl (1994) and Farr (1990) cited research that suggests that such techniques are superior to brainstorming.

The first of these, the nominal group technique, was developed specifically to reduce inhibition.[24] It is suggested that there is an advantage to be had if the leader and nominal group members have had experience of brainstorming. In a nominal group, members write their ideas on a slip of paper. Discussion is forbidden. The time allowed for this phase will vary, but should not be longer than about 15 minutes. In the next stage, each member, suggests one idea which the leader writes on a flip chart. This part of the activity is also completed without discussion. During the round-robin the members are asked to build on each others' ideas, and when it is completed, the leader reviews the list in order to seek clarification of statements and obtain assenting and dissenting views about their relevance to the problem. George and Cowan (1999) summarized the stages of the nominal group technique as follows: question-setting; reflection; pooling; clarification; evaluation; review.

According to Farr (1990), nominal groups produced more ideas than brainstorming groups, and they had an even greater advantage if the size of the group was increased. Farr (1990) also reported research by Dunette which found that the solutions produced by a nominal

---

[23.]The reader will find a cartoon illustration in Carter et al., (1984).

[24.]See also Chapter 16 for discussion of the nominal group technique in evaluation.

group were as good as or better in quality than those produced by a traditional brainstorming group. One of the problems with brainstorming is that often the groups discard quality solutions prematurely (Osborn 1963).

Synectics is another technique that has been used to overcome inhibitions in perceiving, and thinking. It makes use of fantasy and analogy. The stages of the technique are:

1. The leader states the problem.
2. Each member of the group is then asked to restate the problem in writing. They are asked to use fantasy (imagery) in arriving at the problem re-statement, irrespective of how unrealistic the ideas are.
3. The problem re-statements are posted on a board.
4. The group study the statements.
5. The leader chooses one on which to focus.
6. Members are asked to put the problem out of their mind temporarily. At the same time they are asked to use imagery about other subjects. In one type of "excursion" (as this activity is called) *the leader asks for images from some field of natural science and selects promising examples for the group to discuss*" (p. 426, Yukhl, 1994). Another approach, by way of analogy, is to ask members to discuss what it would feel like to be
7. The metaphorical images so developed are applied to the problem re statement. The "fit" may or may not be successful. If it is not, then the members of the group are taken through another "excursion." This is repeated until a solution is found.

11.6.2. Lateral Thinking

At company level, de Bono's idea of lateral thinking has proved to be of interest, and many short courses have been given by him in organizations that had the purpose of encouraging this and other equally important types of thinking. It has also been introduced into undergraduate courses in engineering. The idea is in the same genre as divergent thinking. de Bono (1978) explains its origins as follows, "*Creativity is a value word and represents a value judgement no one ever calls creative something new which he dislikes. Creativity also has too many artistic connotations to describe the process of changing concepts and perceptions. Many artists have valuable concepts and perceptions but are not especially good at changing them. So it was necessary to create the neutral label 'lateral thinking' to describe the change from one way of thinking to another*" (p. 8). It is, therefore, something more than style. Convergence and divergence are contrasting styles but they do not necessarily imply an ability to look at problems in other ways, yet it is evident from Whitfield (Chapter 4) that there is a need to be able to do both. de Bono is also at pains to add that even though he is known for his textbook on lateral thinking, lateral thinking is only one of six sections of his course on thinking. His courses on thinking raises again the question of the value

of specific courses on thinking (problem solving, decision making, critical thinking, learning how to learn) within engineering programs.

To be able to think laterally, we have to be prepared to think in another mode. We have to be open to new ways of looking at things. We have to want to do this. Lateral thinking does not take place without a disposition to want to think laterally. For this reason, as we have seen, courses in engineering problem solving may include components that have the intention of helping us to learn how perception influences and prejudices[25] our thinking (Monk, 1972).[26] Lateral thinking is intended to shift the patterns created by set mechanization in order to create new and possibly better patterns. For this reason it welcomes irrelevant information. It is not linear and does not necessarily follow a step-by-step process. To think laterally, we have often to remove rigidities in our thinking, and this can often be painful. There are several methods that we can use to achieve this change, and these include random stimulation, humor, challenges, and brainstorming. All are aimed at providing us with a different perspective. de Bono lays great store on humor because it generally involves switching from one pattern to another. The double meaning of words can be used to drive the learner's thinking into a side-track.

Al-Jayyousi (1999) described how, in the Department of Civil Engineering at the Applied Science University in Amman, case studies were used to develop lateral thinking. In his arrangement students were grouped together in three's or five's. He described the approach as follows:

1. "*The instructor only presents a background and an overview about each case study. Each case study is decomposed into different elements, such as, 'users', 'needs', and constraints. The instructors' role in all the steps is as facilitator. He does not need to provide significant input to help the students generate solutions.*
2. *Through brainstorming, all possible 'patterned' or 'vertical solutions' are sorted out. Specifically, the students are asked to develop a list of possible solutions which are typical within each discipline. For example, if we have traffic congestion at a highway, civil engineers are likely to give standard solutions. These include; (1) change traffic signal, (2) choose a different route, (3) add more lanes or build an interchange. An attempt to develop a comprehensive list of 'vertical solutions' is made in this step.*
3. *The instructor utilises random simulation and provocation to urge students to 'escape' and challenge the pattern and to develop a list of possible lateral solutions for each case study.*

---

[25] The term bias is sometimes used as an alternative to prejudice.

[26] See Abercrombie (1960); Hesseling (1966); and Heywood (1989).

4. *Analysis of the various lateral solutions are presented and evaluated. Specific reference is made to each solution and how it escaped the pattern*
5. *This is achieved by utilising the decomposed elements (in step 1) to construct simple forms of cognitive mapping."*

Al-Jayyousi illustrated this approach by three case studies. Two points of interest emerged from his evaluation. First, he noted that in the search for lateral solutions, students cross the boundary lines of subject disciplines. For example, in finding the solution to a highway problem, they had to use information technology and communication engineering. Second, in solving a water supply and demand problem the students' considered structural problems. They wanted to build, construct, and drill. These intending civil engineers viewed their future role as 'builders,' and they proposed solutions that were "likely to be structural with a focus on the supply side of the problem." Al-Jayyousi (1999) was not surprised by this finding, because this engineering course focused on the design and construction of structures. It was not accompanied by any program in systems engineering. Lateral thinking during the case study caused the students to shift their focus from the 'supply' side to the 'demand' side. This shift in thinking produced a wide variety of solutions to the water problem in arid conditions. This investigation not only illustrates how our perceptions of role influence our approach to solving problems, but also has more general implications for the role of systems concepts in framing that perception.[27]

Ideas have to be evaluated and Hawlader and Poo (1989) drew attention to several checklists that are to be found in Le Bouef (1986). While they focused on industrial issues they do have relevance to project work in engineering education. The first checklist was due to Osborn (1957). The questions were:
1. Is the idea effective?
2. Is it an efficient idea?
3. Is it compatible with human nature?
4. Is it compatible with goals?
5. Is the time of introduction right?
6. Is it a feasible idea?
7. Is the idea simple?

At one time in the 1960s and 1970s the technique of value analysis was popular in industry (Buck and Butler, 1970). The questions it asked were:
1. What is it?
2. What does it do?
3. What does it cost?
4. What else will do the job?
5. What does that cost?

And finally a checklist used by the United States Navy was:
1. Will it increase production or improve quality?

2. Is it a more efficient use of manpower?
3. Does it improve method of operation, maintenance or construction?
4. Is it an improvement over present tools and machinery?
5. Does it improve safety?
6. Does it prevent waste or conserve materials?
7. Does it eliminate unnecessary work/
8. Does it reduce cost?
9. Does it improve present method?
10. Will it improve present condition?

11.6.3. Morphological Analysis

In morphological analysis a problem is broken down into its elements (i.e. components, of a system, process), and each component or phase is subjected to an analysis of all the ways in which it can achieve its objective. West and Farr (1990) pointed out that this could produce an unworkable number of solutions, although it ensured that no possibility went unnoticed. Turner and Dunn (1972) suggested that the number of possibilities could be contained if they were displayed as a family tree. They described a process for achieving a solution. It began *"by recognising that the solution to the design problem as a whole will be a system which can be described by a set of properties (its behavior), a set of constituents (essential parts) and a unique relationship between the constituents (the morphology)."* Solution generation proceeds in five stages that are:
1. Identification of class. *"What does not yet exist can be considered strange; it helps if it can be made familiar by locating it among known artefacts."* This can be done by analogy (see below).
2. Naming the parts. The purpose of this is to identify and name the elements of the system possibly using analogies.
3. Morphology. Putting together associations between the parts.
4. Substitution. List the elements and other elements that have the same attributes. The listing is done in sets.
5. Synthesis. Selections from the sets are associated with the system morphology. The development will be halted once there is a substantial objection to a variant.

11.6.4. Analogical Thinking

Cognitive psychologists distinguish between analogical and propositional symbolic mental representations. They define a representation *as "any notation or sign or set of symbols that 'represents' something to us"* (Eysenck and Keane, 1995, p. 203). *"Analogical representations tend to be images that may be either visual, auditory, olfactory, tactile, or kinetic. Propositional representations are language like representations that capture the ideational content of the*

---

[27]The ability to shift from one perspective (point of view) to another is at the heart of Sternberg's approach to creativity.

mind, irrespective of the original modality in which that information was encountered" (p. 206).

Eysenck and Keane reminded us, as do several of the authors of engineering papers, that Einstein's thought experiments were based on analogy, and analogy plays a major role in art and literature (Koestler, 1964) and theology (e.g., Brümmer, 1981; Williams, 2000). In engineering Woodson (see Chapter 4) has demonstrated the value of analogies from nature to engineering design, as has Laithwaite (1996). Keane (1988) showed the contribution that analogical reasoning can make to creative thinking.[28] In such thinking, one set of ideas is mapped into another. He gave the example of how Rutherford used the concept of the solar system to understand and explain the atom. This is a process of analogical mapping, but while mapping can be used to generate hypotheses, it does not provide a full account of the process of scientific discovery.

The use of analogy depends on the ability to retrieve analogous stories from the memory. Keane found that individuals were more likely to retrieve close analogues than distant analogues. This suggested that during training, the possibility of distant analogues has to be pointed out if they are to be retrieved. In Keane's study it was found that a story that was mid-way between the two extremes produced intermediate rates of retrieval. Eysenck and Keane (1995) drew attention to other research that suggested that individuals tend to retrieve analogues that share only superficial features. *"One reason why acts of creativity, involving remote analogies, are fairly rare is that most people have difficulty retrieving potentially relevant experiences from memory"* (p. 397). But they also cited research which suggested that deeply held analogues can be retrieved once they are separated from competing analogues.[29] From the practical point of view, Turner and Dunn (1972) pointed out that it is possible to take analogical thinking to extremes, where, for example, it is thought that *"not only are there electrical solutions to all problems but they are preferable."*

11.7.   Assessment, Evaluation, and Teaching

Just as with problem solving, the promotion of creativity requires a considerable change of attitudes toward both teaching and assessment on the part of faculty, collectively and individually. If faculty simply support a particular instructor's endeavor to teach creativity, but do not allow the value of creativity to pervade the program, then students will do that which the program requires. If the tests require convergent behavior, then the students will provide that behavior, at least those who have a strategic orientation toward study. (See below for a partial example of this effect).

The teacher has to become a facilitator, a manager of learning who provides the right resources at the right time. *"The fundamental guideline is that the instructor does not teach creativity s/he acts as a catalyst for what lies in each student. Acting as a sherpa who has traversed the same knowledge terrain many times before, on many different paths, s/he must guide them to where experience dictates it is likely that they will be most fulfilled. But when the students wish to move in a new and unknown direction that they see as more fulfilling, s/he must be willing to lead them even if there is no predetermined guarantee of success. This entails an adjustment in the risk-aversiveness of the teacher as the lessons may not follow exactly the lesson plan. Instead it will follow a path(s) towards fulfilment of the course objectives"* (Ramirez, 1993). Clearly, this has implications for the course objectives in that more attention has to be paid to those in the expressive domain.

The same point has been made by Törnkvist (1998), who added that all engineering instructors' should be conversant with and able to use modern educational theory. He argued that engineering education was unduly geared towards science and that this caused some students who would make engineers to be ruled out. This emphasis on science was the result of an inferiority complex which was an impediment to the development of creative thinking. Engineering Departments should be prepared to encourage experienced teachers who find it difficult to do research.

Clearly, teachers have to learn new skills in questioning if they are to be able to offer Guidance to students. Felder (1985, 1987), in much quoted papers on creativity in engineering education, described how he had tried to encourage problem solving and creativity through different approaches to assessment. His ideas for questioning apply as much to the classroom as they do to tests. He suggested:

1. *"Questions that call for ideational fluency (where what counts is the quantity of possible solutions, not their quality), flexibility (variety of solutions), and originality.*
2. *Questions that are poorly defined and convergent.*
3. *Questions that require a synthesis of material that transcends course or disciplinary boundaries.*
4. *Questions that require evaluation, in which technical decisions must be tempered with social ethical considerations.*
5. *Questions that call for problem finding and definition in addition to, or instead of, problem solving."*

As indicated in Chapter 2, Felder (1987) described his first excursion with a new style of quiz. *"For the third quiz of the semester I gave a five-week take-home exercise that asked students to make up and solve a final examination for the course. They were told that if they produced straightforward 'Given this, calculate that' quiz with no mistakes, they would receive a minimum passing grade; to receive more credit would require*

---

[28]Cited in Eysenck and Keane (1995).

[29]Recommended for further reading, Eysenck and Keane (1995) Gilhooly, K. J. (1995). *Thinking: Directed, Undirected and Creative*. 3rd edition. Academic Press, London.

asking hypothetical exam-takers to demonstrate the three higher-level thinking skills of Bloom's Taxonomy: analysis (determination of mechanisms, decomposition of systems, and derivation of relations beyond what could be found in texts and notes): synthesis (application of techniques from other disciplines to reaction engineering problems, application of reaction engineering techniques to problems in other disciplines): and evaluation (assessing the value of a design or product or system, rather than simply its technical correctness, and examination of environmental, safety, social, and ethical considerations in the context of process design and analysis)." Felder called this test a *"Generic quiz."* He reported that the students found the test very difficult, instructive, and enjoyable.

For many examiners a creativity question would be too great a risk to take if they thought the answers would to be too difficult and unreliable to mark. Thus, assessment that comprehends creativity presents a major challenge to the educational system as Baillie and Walker (1998) made clear. (See above).

Tests of creativity cannot achieve this goal, although they can help in the evaluation of courses. For example, at Rensselaer Polytechnic Institute, Carlson et al., (1995) used *Guilford's Alternate Uses* test[30] as part of a multi-dimensional evaluation of a new course-Introduction to Engineering Electronics for freshman students. The primary intention of this course was to demonstrate *"to students that engineering work is relevant, rewarding, and even fun."* It was concerned primarily with objectives in the affective domain, and two projects were included in the latter part of the course to stimulate creativity.

The Alternate Uses Test asks respondents to give alternative uses for six common items, with the answers to be given in a period of eight minutes. Carlson and his colleagues used two forms of the test, one for pre-test and the other for post-test. They also set the test to a control group of a matched sample of students not in the course. The mean score of the control group was 14.88 compared with the experimental group's 21.27. The pretest score of the experimental group was 17.9, and the difference between pre-test and post-test was statistically significant. Unfortunately, the numbers in the groups were small, which meant that the data had to be interpreted with caution. However, at the level of the school, and taking into account the realities of local evaluation, and the purposes for which it is done, then the authors will have been well pleased with their findings. Psychometricians might have suggested that other tests could have produced different findings. An interesting comparison of American and Mexican engineering students that used the Tel-Aviv *Activities and Accomplishments Inventory* (TAAI) was reported by Ingham, Meza, and Price (1998). The comparison also included the Dunn, Dunn, and Price

(1998)[31] *Productivity Preference Survey* for measuring learning styles. The TAAI developed by Milgram (1994) is a self-report biographical questionnaire that assesses extracurricular interests, activities, and accomplishments in 10 domains on the basis of the frequency with which they are reported. Both groups of students showed *"an affinity for the creative domain of science, and simultaneously possessed similar preferences for learning tactually (hands on) and needing mobility (need to move when learning)."* These were the findings that were relevant to the curriculum and they supported trends to innovate in the engineering curriculum.

There can be a problem with written tests because there could be a tendency for the student to think in the analytic mode. The problem in traditional examinations is that no formula has been found whereby students can be given space for the totally 'free' expression of ideas or, for using their own methods to solve problems[32]. This brings us full circle to the role of assessment and its power to influence learning behavior especially in public examination systems.

For example, in the United Kingdom where the assessment of performance was traditionally obtained from written examinations the introduction of project work created problems for examiners since they were required to incorporate the marks for projects and coursework within the final grade which had to be pseudo-norm referenced (that is, marked to the curve).[33] The response by many examiners, as was shown in Chapter 2 in respect to engineering science, was to create semi-criterion referenced rubrics that covered key domains of what was considered to be the thought processes undergone in engineering activities.

One of the criticisms of these rubrics was that they could fall into the same trap as the written examination in that those who assiduously followed the rubrics were more likely to produce a higher performance than those who did not. That much is self-evident. But, and this was the catch, if the rubrics did not value *originality,* then they probably inhibited *originality* among those who were capable of such thinking but were not very good at exam taking. This point may be illustrated by a recent investigation among fifty 15-16-year-olds' taking the public examination for that age level in Design and Technology (Atkinson, 1994). Within this examination the subactivities of design are assessed by means of a simple linear model of the process.

Atkinson, who had already argued that this model stifled creativity, investigated the relationship between the development of higher-order thinking such as creative and problem-solving skills and the demand for

---

[30]Guilford, J. P. et al., *Alternate Uses*. Sheridan Psychological Services, Orange, CA.

[31]See also Chapter 5.

[32]Matthews and Jahanian (1999) at Temple University claimed to have examined the theoretical aspects of creativity through a specially designed test but no details were given, nor are we told if the students received specific instruction for this, and what the content of that instruction might have been.

[33] See Chapters 10, 15 and 16.

high performance in examinations (Atkinson, 2000). For this purpose he adapted De Carlo's (1983) *Psychological Games* to measure creativity. He also used a Goal Orientation Index designed by Atman (1986). This particular index evaluates behavioral characteristics associated with the accomplishment of certain personal goals. Pupils' perceptions of their ability and enjoyment to design were obtained prior to the course, and motivation was rated during an on-going process of observation so both quantitative and qualitative data were obtained. Notwithstanding the small sample the study raised a number of issues that are pertinent not only to secondary education but to engineering education as well.

First, it was found that the highly structured model helped some students achieve high examination performance. This is consistent with Heywood's (1996) finding that many students benefited from the Wales and Stager heuristic. However, when the data are correlated with the results of the creativity test (assuming it was a suitable measure), then, *"forty percent of those who achieved poor marks for their design projects were highly creative...and, thirty percent of the pupils who achieved high marks had been categorised as 'not creative."* It seems as Furneaux (1962) argued that the assessment was testing examination passing ability and the teachers ability to train them in that skill (see Chapter 2).

Atkinson argued that the examiners tended *"to reward 'thin' evidence that is well presented rather rewarding the use of higher order skills, in particular creative thinking and appropriate design processes."* It should be noticed that this was not the case with the engineering science examination, and considerable feedback from the examiners to the schools ensured that this was not so. It is a fair criticism of that examination, however, that because much attention was paid to the assessment of the high level skills of analysis, synthesis, and evaluation, not as many marks were awarded for originality as there might have been.

In sum, assessment may enhance or inhibit creativity, but those strategies that enhance creativity are difficult to design; moreover, teachers have to make a considerable change in their attitudes to assessment if creativity is to be evaluated successfully.

11.8.   Conclusions and Discussion

It is evident that there is a need for a much greater research into creativity in engineering education. For example, given the extensive use of design projects, and the argument that these stimulate creativity, it is important to encourage research that examines the creativity dimension of such learning. It is also important to examine the influence of both formative and summative assessment on creativity.

At the same time, evidence has to been found to support the contention that many of the problems associated with the fostering of creativity can be addressed through modifications to teaching and assessment in traditional courses and projects. Such approaches require the instructor to take the view that creativity is an inherent component of the learning process in engineering education. Those parts of a program or course that focus on learning how to learn should incorporate creativity and demonstrate how it can be used to develop autonomy and freedom in learning.

A substantial case can also be made for courses that focus specifically on creativity, innovation, and invention. Such courses should be designed with the principles of creativity learning in mind, and not be delivered in traditional modes. That would be self-defeating.

References

Abercrombie, M. L. J (1960). *The Anatomy of Judgement*. Penguin, Harmondsworth.

Acar, B. S (1998). Releasing creativity in interdisciplinary systems engineering course. *European Journal of Engineering Education, 23*, (2), 133–141.

Al-Jayyousi, O (1999). Introduction to lateral thinking to civil and environmental education. *International Journal of Engineering Education*, 15, (3), 1999–205.

Amabile, T. M (1983). *The Social Psychology of Creativity*. Springer-Verlag, New York.

Amabile, T. M (1996). *Creativity in Context*. Westview Press, Boulder, CO.

Atkinson, E. S (1994). Key factors which affect pupils performance in technology project work. IIn J. S. Smith (ed.). *IDATER 94. Design and Technology*. Loughborough University, Loughborough.

Atkinson, E. S (2000). Does the need for high levels of performance curtail the development of creativity in design technology and project work? *International Journal of Technology and Design Education*, 10, (3), 255 281.

Atman, K. S (1986). *Goal Orientation Index* Curriculum Innovators and Implementors, Pittsburgh.

Baillie, C., and S. Tookey (1997). The "power test": its impact on student learning in a materials science course for engineering students. *Assessment and Evaluation in Higher Education*, 22, (1), 33–38.

Baillie, C., and P. Walker.(1998). Fostering creative thinking in student engineers. *European Journal of Engineering Education* 23, (1), 35–44.

Basadur, M., Green, G. B., and G. Green (1982). Training in creative problem solving: effects on ideation and problem finding and solving in an industrial research organization. *Human Performance*, 30, 41-70

Ben-Arroyo, A. F (1979). Creative design education. *Proceedings Frontiers of Education Conference*, 414–417.

Berglund, A., Daniels, M., Hedenborg, A., and A. Tengstrand (1998). Fostering creativity through projects. *European Journal of Engineering Education* 23, (1), 45–54.

Blicblau, A. S., and J. M. Steiner (1998). Fostering creativity through engineering projects. *European Journal of Engineering Education*. 23, (1), 55–65.

Brogden, H. E., and T. B. Sprecher (1964). *Criteria of Creativity and Potential*. McGraw Hill, New York.

Brümmer, V (1981). *Theological and Philosophical Inquiry. An Introduction*. Macmillan, London.

Buck, C. H., and D. Butler (1970). *Economic Product Design*. Collins, London.

Carlson, B., Schock, P., Kalsher, M., and B. Raciot (1995). Evaluating a motivational freshman course. *Proceedings Frontiers in Education Conference*. 2a6 14 to 18.

Carter R., Martin, J., Mayblin, B., and M. Munday (1984). *Systems Management and Change*. A Graphic Guide. Paul Chapman, London.

Caltell, R. B. (1971). *Personality and Learning Theory*, Springer, New York.

Christiano, S. J. E.., and M. R. Ramirez. (1993). Creativity in the classroom: special concerns and insights. *Proceedings Frontiers in Education Conference*, 209–212.

Christie, T. (1968). The sixth form in H. J. Butcher (ed). *Educational Research in Britain*. University of London Press, London.

Conway, H. G (1969). Creativity and Innovation in Engineering. The Betts Brown Memorial Lecture. Heriot-Watt University. Edinburgh.

Cooley, P (1967). Creative design- can it be taught? *Chartered Mechanical Engineer*, 14, 228

Court, A. W (1998). Improving creativity in engineering design education. *European Journal of Engineering Education*, 23, (2), 141–154.

Cropley, A. J., and J. McLeod (1989). *Fostering Academic Excellence.* Pergamon, New York.

Crutchfield, R (1962). Conformity and creative thinking, In H. Gruber, G. Terrell, and M. Westheimer (eds.) *Contemporary Approaches to Creative Thinking.* Atherton, New York.

Csikszentmihalyi. M (1993). *The Evolving Self.* Harper Collins, New York.

Dacey, J. S., and K. H. Lennon (1998). *Understanding Creativity. The Interplay of Biological, Psychological and Social Factors.* Jossey Bass, San Francisco.

de Bono, E (1970). *Lateral Thinking.* Pelican/Penguin. Harmondsworth, Middx

de Bono, E (1978). *Teaching Thinking.* Pelican/Penguin. Harmondsworth, Middx.

De Carlo, N. A (1983). *Psychological Games.* Guild Publishing, London.

Dekker, D. L (1995). Engineering design processes, problem solving and creativity. *Proceedings Frontiers in Education Conference* 3. 3a5-16-3a-5 to 19.

Dekker,D. L (1996). The difference between "open ended projects" and "design projects". *Proceedings Frontiers in Education Conference,* 1257–1259.

Dunn, R., Dunn, K., and G. E. Price (1993). *Productivity Environmental Preference Survey.* Price Systems, Lawrence, KS.

Eysenck, M. W., and M. T. Keane (1995). *Cognitive Psychology. A Student's Handbook.* 3rd edition. Erlbaum, Taylor Francis, Hove.

Farr, J. L (1990). Facilitating individual role innovation. In West M.A., and J. L. Farr (1990) *Innovation and Creativity at Work. Pyschological and Organizational Strategies.* Wiley, Chichester.

Felder, R. M (1985). The generic quiz. A device to stimulate creativity and higher level thinking skills. *Chemical Engineering.* Fall p 176

Felder, R. M (1987). On creating creative engineers. *Engineering Education.* 77, (4), 222–227.

Freeman, J., Butcher, H. J., and T. Christie. (1979). *Creativity: A Selective Review of Research.* 2nd edition. Society for Research into Higher Education, London.

Furneaux, W. D (1962). The psychologist and the University. *Universities Quarterly,* 17, 33.

George, J., and J. Cowan (1999). *A Handbook of Techniques for Formative Evaluation.* Kogan Page, London.

Gilhooly, K. J (1995) *Thinking: Directed, Undirected and Creative.* 3rd Edition. Academic Press, London.

Gregory, S. A (1972) (ed.). *Creativity and Innovation in Engineering.* Butterworths, London.

Gregory, S. A., and J. D. Monk. (1972.. Creativity: definitions and models. In S. A. Gregory (ed.) *Creativity and Innovation in Engineering.* Butterworths, London.

Gregory, S. A and B. T. Turner. (1972). The scope of engineering including social and technical models In S. A Gregory (ed.) *Creativity and Innovation in Engineering*, Butterworths, London.

Guilford, J. P (1959). Traits of creativity in H. H. Anderson (ed.). *Creativity and its Cultivation.* Harper, New York.

Guilford, J. P (1967). *The Nature of Human Intelligence.* McGraw-Hill, New York.

Guilford, J. P (1975). Creativity: a quarter century of progress. In I. A. Taylor and J. W. Getzels (eds.). *Perspectives in Creativity.* Aldine de Gruter, Hawthorne, NY.

Gustafsson, J. E., and J. O. Undheim. (1996). Individual differences in cognitive functions in D. C. Berliner and R. C. Calfee (eds.). *Handbook of Educational Psychology.* American Psychological Association, Macmillan, New York.

Hampson, P. J. and P. E. Morris (1996). *Understanding Cognition.* Blackwell, Oxford.

Hawlader, M. N. A. and A. N. Poo (1989). Development of creative and innovative talents of students. *International Journal of Applied Engineering Education.* 5, (3), 331–339.

Hayes, S. V. and S. A. Tobias (1964). The project method of teaching creative mechanical engineering. *Proceedings Institution of Mechanical Engineers*, V. 179 (special issue).

Herzberg, F., Mausner, B., and B. Synderman (1959). *The Motivation to Work.* Wiley, New York.

Hesseling, P (1966). *A Strategy for Evaluation Research.* Van Gorcum, Aassen

Heywood, J (1972). Short courses in the development of originality. In S. A. Gregory (ed.) *Creativity and Innovation in Engineering.* Butterworth, London.

Heywood, J (1989). *Learning, Adaptability and Change.* Paul Chapman, London.

Heywood, J (1996). An engineering approach to teaching decision making skills in schools using an engineering heuristic. *Proceedings Frontiers in Education Conference,* 1, 67–73

Hollander, S (1965). *The Sources of Increased Efficiency: A Case Study of Du Pont Rayon Manufacturing Plants.* MIT Press, Cambridge, MA.

Holmes, S (1998) There must be more to life than this. *European Journal of Engineering Education,* 23, (2), 191–198.

Hudson, L (1962). Intelligence, divergence and potential quality. *Nature,* 196, 601.

Hudson, L (1966). *Contrary Imaginations.* Methuen, London.

Ingham, J., Meza, R. M. P., and G. Price (1998). Comparison of the learning style and creative talents of Mexican and American undergraduate engineering students. *Proceedings Frontiers in Education Conference,* 605-610

Keane, M. T (1988). *Analogical Problem Solving.* Wiley, Chichester.

King, N (1990). Innovation at work: the research literature. In M. A West and J. L. Farr (eds.). *Innovation and Creativity at Work.* Wiley, Chichester.

Kline, P (2000) *Handbook of Psychological Testing.* 2nd edition. Routledge, London.

Klukken, P. G., Parsons, J. R., and P. J. Columbus (1997). Creative experience in engineering practice: implications for engineering education. *Journal of Engineering Education,* 86, (2), 133–138.

Koestler, A (1964). *The Act of Creation.* Dell, New York.

Kreith, F (1967) Developing creative thought through undergraduate research. *Engineering Education.* 57, (7), 504–506.

Laithwaite, E. R (1996). Invention before Adam and Eve. *Engineering Science and Education Journal,* 5, (2), 57–62.

Le Boeuf, M (1986). *Imagineering.* Berkeley Book, New York.

LeDoux, J (1998) The *Emotional Brain.* Weidenfeld and Nicolson, London.

Lewis, T (1999). Research in technology education. Some areas of need. *Journal of Technology Education.* 10, (2), 41–56.

Linn, M. C., Songer, N. B., and B-S, Eylon (1996). Shifts and convergences in science learning and instruction in D. C. Berliner and R. C. Calfee (eds.). *Handbook of Educational Psychology.* American Psychological Association. Macmillan, New York.

Lovelace, R. F (1986). Stimulating creativity through managerial intervention. *R and D Management,* 16, 161–174.

McClelland, D. C (1969). The role of achievement motivation in the transfer of technology. In W. H. Gruber and D. G. Marquis (eds). *Factors in the Transfer of Technology.* MIT Press, Cambridge, MA.

McDonald, F (1968). *Educational Psychology.* Wadsworth, Belmont, CA.

Mackintosh, N. J (1998). *IQ and Human Intelligence.* Oxford University Press, Oxford.

McKinnon, D. W (1961). Fostering creativity in students of engineering. *Engineering Education,* 52, 129

Maltzmann, I. M (1960). On the training of originality. *Psychological Review,* 67, 229-242

Matthews, J. M., and S. Jahanian (1999) A pedagogical strategy for gradual enhancement of creative performance of the students. *European Journal of Engineering Education,* 24, (1), 49–58.

Milgram, R. M (1994). *Tel-Aviv Activities and Accomplishments Inventory.* School of Education, Tel Aviv University, Israel.

Mitchell, C. A (1998) Creativity is about being free.... *European Journal of Engineering Education*, 23, (1), 23–34.

Monk, J. D (1972). Creativity in higher education. In S. A. Gregory (ed.) *Creativity and Innovation in Engineering*. Butterworths, London.

Mooney, R. L (1963). A conceptual model for integrating four approaches to the identification of basic talent. In C. W. Taylor and F. W. Barron (eds.) *Scientific Creativity: its Recognition and Development*. Wiley, New York.

Olton, R. M (1979). Experimental studies of incubations. Searching for the elusive. *Journal of Creative Behavior*, 13, 9–22.

Osborn, A. F (1957/1963). *Applied Imagination*. Scribner, New York.

Owens, W. A (1961). Cognitive, non-cognitive and environmental correlates of mechanical ingenuity Report, Purdue University.

Owens, W. A., Schumacher, C. F., and J. B. Clarke (1957). The measurement of creativity in machine design. *Journal of Applied Psychology*. 41, 297.

Pahl, G., and W. Beitz. (1988). In K. Wallace (ed.). *Engineering Design. A Systematic Approach*. The Design Council. Springer Verlag.

Pekz, D. C (1963). Relationships between measures of scientific performance and other variables. In C. W. Taylor and F. W. Barron (eds) *Scientific Creativity: Its Recognition and Development*. Wiley, New York

Pelz, D. C., and F. M. Andrews (1966). *Scientists in Organizations: Production Climates for Research and Development*. Wiley, New York.

Perkins, N. D (1990). The nature and nurture of creativity in B. F. Jones and L. Idol (eds). *Dimensions of Thinking and Cognitive Instruction*. Lawrence Erlbaum, Hillsdale, NJ.

Porcupile, J. C (1969). An inductive approach to teaching creativity. *Bulletin of Mechanical Engineering Education*, 8, 327.

Ramirez, M. R (1993). The influence of learning styles on creativity. *Proceedings ASEE Centennial Meeting*. Session 2225. American Society for Engineering Education.

Ramirez, M. R. (1994). A meaningful theory of creativity: Design as knowledge: implications for engineering design. *Proceedings Frontiers in Education Conference*, 594-597

Richards, L. G (1998). Stimulating creativity: Teaching engineers to be innovators. *Proceedings Frontiers in Education Conference*, 1034–1039.

Rokeach, M (1960). *The Open and Closed Mind*. Basic Books, New York

Rosenfeld, R., and J. C. Servo. (1990). Facilitating innovation in large organizations. In M. A. West and J. L. Farr (eds.). *Innovation and Creativity at Work* Wiley, Chichester.

Snow, R., Corno, L., and D. Jackson III. (1996). Individual differences. In affective and conative functions in D. C. Berliner and R. C. Calfee (eds.). *Handbook of Educational Psychology*. American Psychological Association. MacMillan, New York.

Sprecher, T. B (1959). A study of engineers criteria for creativity. *Journal of Applied Psychology*, 43, (2), 141

Sternberg, R. J (1985). *Beyond IQ. A Triarchic Theory of Human Intelligence*. Cambridge University Press, Cambridge, UK.

Sternberg R. J (1988). A three facet model of creativity. In R. J. Sternberg (ed.). *The Nature of Creativity*. Cambridge University Press, Cambridge, UK.

Sternberg, R. J (1991). An investment theory of creativity and its development. *Human Development* 34, 1–31.

Sternberg, R. J., and T. Lubart (1995). *Defying the Crowd. Cultivating Creativity in a Culture of Conformity*. Free Press, New York.

Sternberg, R. J and T. I. Lubart (1996). Investing in creativity. *American Psychologist*, 51, 677–688.

Taylor, C. W (1972). Can organizations be creative too? In C. W. Taylor (ed.). *Climate for Creativity*. Pergamon Press., New York.

Taylor, C. W., and F. W. Barron. (1963) (eds.). *Scientific Creativity: Recognition and Development*. Wiley, New York.

Törnkvist, S (1998). Creativity. Can it be taught? The case of engineering education. *European Journal of Engineering Education*, 23, (1), 5–12.

Torrance, E. P (1975). Creativity research in education; still alive. In I. A. Taylor and J. W. Getzels (eds.). *Perspectives in Creativity*. Aldine de Gruyter, Hawthorne, NY.

Torrance, E. P (1995). *Why Fly? A Philosophy of Creativity*. Ablex. Norwood, NJ.

Turner B. T. and S. C. Dunn (1972). The range of procedures and strategies. Part 2. In S. A. Gregory (ed.). *Creativity and Innovation in Engineering*. Butterworth, London.

Vernon, P. E (1972) (ed.). *Creativity*. Penguin, Harmondsworth.

Waks, S., and M. Merdler (2003). Creative thinking of practical engineering students during a design project. *Research in Science and Technological Education*, 21, (1), 101–120.

Wallas, G (1926). The Art of Thought. Harcourt Brace, Orlando, Fl

Warsame, A., Biney, P. O., and J. O. Morgan (1995). Innovations in teaching creative engineering at freshman level. *Proceedings Frontiers in Education Conference*. 2C4- 21 to 24.

Weisberg, R. W (1986). *Creativity, Genius and Other Myths*. W. H. Freeman, New York.

Weisberg, R. W (1999). Creativity and knowledge: a challenge to theories. In R. J. Sternberg (ed.) *Handbook of Creativity*. Cambridge University Press, Cambridge.

West, M. A., and J. L. Farr (1990). Innovation at work. In M. A. West and J. L. Farr (eds.) *Innovation and Creativity at Work. Psychological and Organizational* Strategies. Wiley, Chichester.

Whitfield, P. R (1972). Environment and Engineering. In S. A. Gregory (ed.). *Creativity and Innovation in Engineering*. Butterworth, London.

Williams, R (2000). *On Christian Theology*. Oxford University Press, Oxford.

Williamson, K. J., and R. J. Hudspeth (1982). Teaching holistic thought through engineering design. *Engineering Education*. 72, (7), 698–703.

Woods, D. R (1994). *Problem Based Learning. How to gain the most from PBL*. McMaster University Bookshop, Hamilton, Ontario.

Woodson, T. T (1966). *An Introduction to Engineering Design*. McGraw Hill, New York.

Yukhl, G (1994). *Leadership in Organizations*. 3rd edition. Prentice Hall, Englewood Cliffs, NJ.

CHAPTER 12: DESIGN

Summary and Introduction

Since design is at the heart of so much engineering activity, it might be thought that its inclusion in the engineering curriculum would be a sine qua non. Not so! The issue of whether or not to teach design has been hotly debated. The responses to this debate, which is described in the first section of this Chapter, have differed as a function of the particular culture in which it has taken place. And this, in spite of the fact that the pressures have often been more or less identical, as for example the retention and attraction of students to engineering, and the views of industry.

As an example of the differences between cultures, the American response at the freshman level is as much due to the need to retain students who are testing the waters of engineering as it is to anything else. In contrast, students entering courses modeled on the British approach have already made up their minds to become engineers. Moreover, the courses they pursued in high school have had a bearing on the design of engineering studies; and in the past, great use was made of the physics and maths taught. Although there is a shortage of students for engineering courses, university teachers in England look to the secondary schools to persuade students to take on engineering as a career. One consequence is that, by and large, they do not look at their own curricula and whether or not it needs to be changed. There is, for example, the odd example of a department rejecting an innovative course that had proved to be attractive to both nontraditional students and employers.

Underlying this debate, and irrespective of culture, is the issue of how much "hard" science should underpin engineering, and whether or not "soft" design is best left to industry. One response of those who promote engineering design has been to argue that it is a discipline, and they have sought a theoretical framework on which to base their arguments. They have argued that it differs fundamentally from engineering science in that it is concerned with "wicked" problems, and that it is not so much "learning product" based as focused on the "learning process," which, itself, is the process of design. Others have attempted to develop a formal structure within which design issues can be systematically considered. At the same time, taking design to be a cognitive activity, serious attempts have been made to systematically study the problem-solving behaviors of novice and expert designers with methods that have not been traditionally used in engineering education. These studies, which are described in Section (12.8), should make a considerable contribution to the debate about what the design curriculum should be, and how it should be taught.

Projects are widely used as a mechanism for teaching design, and what has been learned from the general use of projects as summarized in Chapter 9 applies equally to design projects. Nevertheless, it is important to distinguish between engineering problem-solving projects and engineering design projects. This is done in the second section. Similarly, there is a demand for engineers to be creative, and this extends to creativity in the design, and in some ways this Chapter on design is an extension of or a development of the previous Chapter (Chapter 11) on creativity. Blicblau and Steiner (1998) held that because projects relate basic principles and concepts to real problems, student's creativity is improved.

Unfortunately, as with all discussions of practice in any subject of the curriculum, matters are complex. Linear expositions are of their nature reductionist, and the Chapters in Parts II and III that are about the curriculum have focused on particular issues that have been much discussed. Yet they have to borrow conceptual elements from each other if a comprehensive understanding is to be obtained. Thus, in the case of design, a comprehensive approach to its curriculum and teaching is thought by some to require an interdisciplinary and integrated approach to knowledge as discussed in Chapter 8. Even in simple design projects, students often need to use knowledge from different subject areas. There is, therefore, necessarily some overlapping with items in previous Chapters.

Following MacMurray's[1] dictum that all out theoretical activities have their origins in our practical requirements, the first sections of this Chapter are devoted to practice and some of the principal goals that courses have tried to achieve. For example, it is widely held that if students are to be motivated by projects, they should be "real," although it is clear that many teachers have different views as to what constitutes reality (see also Chapter 9). It is argued by some educators that if students are to be prepared for industry then, "reality" is best achieved through industrially sponsored projects which may or may not be completed in industry. In any event since industrial projects are usually undertaken in teams many teachers consider that educational projects in design should be conducted in teams. Discussion of teamwork is postponed to the next Chapter (Chapter 13), which also considers cooperative learning practices in engineering education. However, a case for individual design projects is also presented in this Chapter on the grounds that there are some learning skills that might be best learned through such projects (see also Chapter 9).

Particular attention is paid to the question of motivation. Do these courses motivate students and do

---

[1] Scottish philosopher quoted by the British Prime Minister Tony Blair. This dictum is in the *Self as Agent* (1957).

they retain them in courses? The answer in both cases seems to be an unequivocal "yes."

There has also been some debate about where the design process begins and ends. Some engineering design courses end when the specification is achieved. Others, if not most, are designed to go right through to the manufacture and evaluation of an artefact[2] In this way a balance between the learning process and learning product can be achieved, and students can be given an introductory preparation to manufacturing. The rationale behind much project work is "learning (designing)-by-doing." Design is often described as a linear process, and there are many linear models. The same objection to these models is the same as those that apply to models of problem solving (see Chapter 9). It is that they over-simplify what is a complex process, They also assume that design is accomplished by rational behaviors without any influence of the extra rational. The implications of this controversy for the curriculum are considered. Attention is drawn to the lessons that can be learned from studies that are being undertaken of elementary school children learning technology and to design (Sections 12.5, 12.6 and 12.7).

The outcome of the debate about whether or not to teach design has been increasing attention to design within the curriculum especially in the United States. New courses have been developed, and more attention has been paid to design in existing courses. Attention seems have focussed mainly on first-year and final-year programs. There are one or two instances of carefully designed activities that are sequentially arranged throughout all the years of the curriculum (see also Chapter 9). The second section (12.2) of this Chapter outlines some of these changes and makes use of a model developed by Sheppard that summarizes the types of change that have taken place in freshmen courses in the United States.

As we saw, teaching problem solving and creativity also affects the role of the teacher (Chapters, 9, 10, and 11). The same is true of the teaching of design, and some aspects of this dimension are further developed. Just as the role of teachers changes, so too does the role of students, and this often requires much adjustment on their part.

As indicated, the development of design studies has been accompanied by searches for a theoretical basis for design courses. The possibility that Perkins general theory of Knowledge as Design can contribute to this framework is examined. It has shown that several courses conform to elements listed in his outcomes for teaching. Within engineering Koen's general theory of the engineering method that necessarily embraces design is discussed.

There is a paucity of research and evaluation in this area. However a concerted attempt to establish a methodology that can analyze design problem solving behavior has been made by Atman and her colleagues. The results of these studies are likely to have a

considerable bearing on our understanding of learning in design courses and, therefore, on the design of instruction. In the meantime, Sheppard's conclusion that students need to experience several different approaches to design can be supported from learning theory (see Chapter 5) and merits further investigation.

12. To Teach or Not to Teach Design

There has been a long-standing debate about whether design can or cannot be taught, and whether it should or should not be taught. As Evans, McNeill, and Beakley (1990)[3] wrote, *"The subject seems to occupy the top drawer of a Pandora's box of controversial curricular matters, a box often opened only as accreditation time approaches."* Underlying this view are issues about what is design? And, what should the curriculum of design be? By that time the National Science Foundation was sponsoring curriculum development projects that provided undergraduates with a design experience (Ernst and Lohmann, 1990). These included projects that involved engineering college-wide curriculum-integration, design within disciplines, contextually sensitive design curricula (e.g., within a multi-disciplinary social context), and curriculum enhancement through modern design technology (e.g., using computers).

The history of this debate, as charted by Evans, McNeill, and Beakley, showed that as early as 1955 the Grinter Committee recommended an *"integrated study of engineering analysis, design, and engineering systems for professional background, planned and carried out to stimulate creative and imaginative thinking, and making full use of the basic and engineering sciences."* The committee wanted the equivalent of one year of engineering analysis and design in the accreditation criteria.

Much of the debate, and it occurred elsewhere in the world, can be described as a battle between the hard (engineering science) and the soft (design) aspects of engineering, or the science and art of engineering. Muster and Mistree (1989) took the view that the fundamental differences as to what constitutes truth for practitioners in the sciences and arts has inhibited the creation of a science of design. In Ireland and the United Kingdom degrees in industrial and product design were often taught in Art Colleges, and attempts were made in these countries to distinguish between engineering and industrial design (Ewing, 1987).[4] Recently, attempts have been made to define a taxonomy of AI for designers (McCardle, 2002). Since 1955 the case for teaching design has continued to be made.

---

[2]An artefact may be "mechanical," or a software product in this context.

[3]This article is in an issue of *Engineering Education* devoted to Engineering Design that was also edited by these authors.

[4]Ewing (1987) wrote *"The engineering designer uses skills aimed primarily at a technical solution; 'fitness for purpose' means a primary concern with function, or at most, reliability at least costs. The industrial designer works on an altogether broader canvas of integrated activity embracing performance, ergonomics, materials and manufacture, and of course aesthetics* (p. 3)

In Australia, Page (1989) pointed out that engineering education had two origins. There was, on the one hand, a set of subjects spawned by university physics departments in the areas of mechanics and electrics, and, on the other hand, practical training for tradesman and technicians provided by technical education institutions. Page did not mention that the products of these institutions were often called engineers by the public, and in the United Kingdom and the countries of the British Commonwealth, this has had major consequences for the profession which has been bedeviled by discussions about its relative status in the community. He did, however, say that in order *"to establish an academic respectability, the engineering departments adopted the scientific philosophy of physics, as it then was, and the same criterion for measurement of excellence."* This was a philosophy of reductionism in which it was argued that the whole curriculum had to be broken down into its constituent parts if you wanted to understand the whole.[5] He argued that this created difficulties for industry because, for example, in the case of aircraft design, engineers who were narrowly trained specialists could not perceive it as a system. He went on to argue that *"As the major manufacturing nations saw their products poorly rated against relative newcomers despite their academic dominance of the sub-disciplines, programs were introduced to incorporate design and manufacturing studies within degree programs."*

In Britain this was made difficult because the engineering drawing programs that accompanied engineering courses were not held in any degree of respect. The difficulty was compounded by the fact that the design office in many companies was often a drawing office that dealt with historical realities. That is, it produced operational drawings of realities that had been created elsewhere. It was not creative; moreover, those working in these offices may well have been trained in technical education institutions.

Monk (1972) surveyed corporate and noncorporate members of the Institution of Mechanical Engineers. Among the questions he asked were some about the mobility and lack of engineering designers, the effectiveness of their education vis-à-vis the engineering design function, and the function of management in the engineering profession when compared with the function of engineering design.[6] He found that while his

respondents highlighted the importance of the design office by ranking it first, few of the respondents were actually employed in such offices. Moreover, they had no intention of returning to the design department. The engineering design office had a low currency value due to the lack of responsibility afforded to the design engineer and the corresponding lack of opportunity it gave the engineer to acquire the skills of the management function (Monk and Heywood, 1977). These writers pointed out that the booklets on the education and training of engineers published by the Council of Engineering Institutions and the Engineering Industries Training Board reinforced a "management" stereotype of the successful engineer to the detriment of the design function.

Page (1989), in his study of developments in engineering education, argued that where design studies were introduced, they often lacked rigor and produced designs (products) that were unrealistic. There was now a move away from this situation to the teaching of engineering design that has as one of its purposes the overview of the role of science in the manufacture of engineering artifacts.

Among the major objections that design has had to overcome, and some teachers continue to take these views, is that design does not lend itself to objective assessment and that there is no theoretical basis for design education. The latter is used to argue that it is not a discipline in its own right, but that is to tie the meaning of theory narrowly to the idea that theory is for prediction. Opposed to this is the view that theories of design lie in the understanding of the process, not the product. It is this view that has led to a theory of knowledge (Perkins, 1986). Indeed, design meets one dictionary definition of a theory which states that a theory is *"A mental scheme of something to be done, or a way of doing something; a systematic statement of rules or principles to be followed...the systematic conception of something"* (*The New Shorter Oxford English Dictionary*, 1993, p. 3274).

Page, pointed out that intellectual effort in the universities was rewarded by scientific papers in learned journals that are regarded more highly than efforts at design. This is not to say that it was not taught in British Universities. Indeed Cambridge prided itself on its design teaching (Wallace, 1981), and the first professor (chair) at the University of Lancaster was a design engineer from that department. Another big objection that has had to be overcome is that design cannot be taught at an early stage because students do not have sufficient knowledge of analysis. For example, Hoole (1991) objected to senior design projects being done for industry on two grounds. The first was that projects were all to variable in the quality of learning they induced. The second, and more important, argument from his point of view was that they took time away from the enhancement of the theoretical

---

[5] In this case the constituent parts are the subjects of the engineering curriculum.

[6] *The engineering design function was defined as. (a) the act or supervision of procedures leading to the solution of technological or engineering problems requiring in general considerable background knowledge of processes and methods of one or more of the recognized engineering disciplines and with the application where necessary of the axioms and mathematical models which form the basis of the applied sciences, and (b) that the major part of such an activity should be direct involvement in the interpretation or production of technical engineering drawings of three dimensional artifacts. The management function is defined as (a) In global terms the implementation of a company's economic, contractual and sales policies. The direction and control of the company's resources consisting of money, material and manpower. And, (b) In day to day terms an advisory role in problem-solving:*

---

arbitration in the erection of criteria and final responsibility for making judgements on issues for which the authority has been quite clearly delegated" (Monk and Heywood, 1977).

knowledge that students should have. It was only with a substantial theoretical base that students could fully appreciate what they learned in industry. Universities do not provide the equivalent of industrial projects in such circumstances and they should, therefore, content themselves by concentrating on engineering design theory.[7] This is very similar to the view of objectives of project work discussed in Chapter 10. But, as Warner (1989) from the University of Adelaide indicated, research showed that this argument did not stand up to scrutiny.[8] He went on to say that *the history of engineering development gives any number of real examples of how design practice usually precedes theory, and how it is not necessary to undertake accurate analysis in order to achieve a successful design. Prototype testing and model testing are time-honoured alternatives to rigorous analysis as a basis for design in many fields of civil engineering. For example, reinforced concrete slabs were successfully designed and constructed and were in common use at the turn of the century (nineteenth), long before proper methods of analysis were introduced. The classic paper explaining the statics of slabs was only published in 1914, and in fact a full understanding of slab behavior at service load and at collapse is only now emerging for what is the most common form of floor construction throughout the world.*"

Warner went on to describe a course in engineering that included a strong element of creative design and problem solving. He noted that in Australia, creative design was beginning to be emphasized at a much earlier stage (Holt and Radcliffe, 1984), and this has since become a pattern in many engineering courses in the United States (Sheppard, 2002). Lyons and Messick (1993) of the Indiana Institute of Technology wrote that *our experience in both academic and industrial worlds has led us to concur with E. S. Furguson who states that "necessary as the analytical tools of science and mathematics most certainly are, more important is the development in students and neophyte engineers of sound judgement and an intuitive sense of fitness and adequacy, and that 'unquantifiable judgement and choices are the elements that determine the way a design experience comes together'.*"

The arguments about whether or not design could be taught go back to at least the 1960s and the conferences on creativity described in the last Chapter. They continued to be repeated at regular intervals. In 1980 in a short paper *Yes, Design Can Be Taught,*

Henderson of the University of California at Davis caught the essence of the case through an extensive quotation from a graduate student who attended his course on design. In that course he required the students to write a personal statement about their projects. It is clear that this was an example of reflective practice (although at the time this term had not come into use in education). Part of one statement is shown in Exhibit 12.1. It suggests that the experience was helping that neophyte engineer to develop *"sound judgement and an intuitive sense of fitness and adequacy."*

"..........*Design is the test that doesn't work and the parts that malfunction when the whole department has come down to observe. It is seeing the simple and obvious solution just as the machine shop delivers your original design to you. It is discovering that your tests did not control a critical parameter and that your results are invalid. It is the search for equipment and instruments necessary to conduct your tests but lost or hidden somewhere on the campus by a former graduate student. It is finally finding this equipment only to discover that it is broken or not exactly what you needed*"

"*Design is discovering that there is no such thing as a controlled experiment and that every test and modification affects your system in more ways than are realized. Design is bewilderment and the feeling that you have absolutely no explanation for the results of the last test*".

"*But most important is the realization of what design is not. It is not an individual process. If you consider all the books read and all the meetings, discussions and conversations with colleagues with supervisors, professors, colleagues, acquaintances and your friends that relate in some way to your design and if you trace these sources back to their origin, you realize that design is a group effort. It is the summation of all human expertise, which when combined, acts much like a computer program randomly incrementing. In this case perhaps a more accurate term is 'muddling towards a solution'.*"

Exhibit 12. 1. Henderson (1980) required his graduates to include a personal statement about their experience of the project in their thesis. He gave the complete statement due to Jeff Canclini. The above are the last few paragraphs of that statement as printed in *Engineering Education,* January, 1980). (Reproduced with permission of the author)

It might be argued that developments to teach design in America were helped by the need to attract and retain students. Too much analysis in mathematics and science in the first year can de-motivate students, particularly if the teaching is uninspiring (Seymour and Hewitt, 1997). Such courses, others argued, did not show students what engineering was about. Warner (1989) argued that in such courses, students obtained a problem set that could impair their ability to develop design skills. They did not acquire skill in tackling open-ended problems ("wicked" problems as they have been called), and he noted that often engineering problems were often not solved by engineers! Engineering designers have to learn to tolerate ambiguity, and education in engineering design should have as one of its goals that of helping students become comfortable with ambiguity (Leifer, 1995; cited in Sheppard, 2002). The problems that designers have to solve are the antithesis of those solved by scientists in their search for truth.

---

[7]Lest an injustice be done to Hoole, it is important to note that he acknowledges the importance of design. He distinguished between the discrete options and continuous options that designers have to make. Discrete options involve common sense as well as social and economic considerations. Common sense cannot be taught in the university. Such decisions are fallible and can be made less fallible by knowledge-based expert system technology that could be taught in the university. The continuous spectrum of options depends on choices between different methods of modeling that can be taught in engineering analysis.

[8]He cited de Simone (1968) and Taylor and Barron (1963) in support of his case.

In the United States, integrated courses were proposed to *"address the lack of connectivity between the topics in basic science and introductory engineering courses"* (Lyons and Messick, 1993). Key features of courses that set out to achieve this goal were the integrated design project, and attempts to *"provide undergraduates with the opportunity to work on "real world projects,"* and sometimes to work with *"engineers from industry and gain valuable experience that would not otherwise be possible"* (Sutton, 1995). To achieve this goal, new skills would be required especially in teamwork, communication, time management and open-ended problem solving. So it was that the teaching of design began to evolve around such skills, and some teachers began to recognise that design is not only a social activity but has social consequences.

McCaulley (1990), who applied the MBTI personality test to engineering students, suggested that a major factor in the resistance to design among faculty and students was that they did not have the personality characteristics that would give them an enthusiasm for design. She pointed out that those students who would be enthusiastic about design would require a supportive environment. *"This means being sure to appreciate good contributions and toning down some tough analytical criticism-so natural to thinking types-when criticism will decrease participation without increasing productivity."*

A recent report of an evaluation of a re-engineering approach to engineering design showed that in a group where there were sensing (S) types, (who preferred to process information through their senses) and intuitive (N) types (who preferred to process information internally), it was necessary to provide for both hands-on and abstractness components in each and every segment of the course material (Wood et al., 2001).

So what has happened in practice?

12.1.   Developments in Practice

12.1.1. Introduction

There was a large positive response to the question, "Can design be taught?" Numerous approaches to the teaching of design have been reported (Sheppard, 2002; Wankat and Oreovicz, 1993; Wood et al., 2001). These developments were most manifest in the United States, but important ideas and course developments, although not on such a grand scale, took place in other parts of the world. Most of these courses are trying to achieve more than one objective, and also deliberately seek sub-objectives, or see them met as a function of what happens in courses. There are very few significant evaluations. At the same time traditional approaches to evaluation have had some influence at local levels in determining the future of courses. Most of the developments involve projects and/or case studies. As Dekker (1996) pointed out, engineering design projects are different from engineering projects (see Chapter 10). *The "engineering design project must also have some conceptual design, some embodiment design, and some detail design, or it*

will not be a design project"... (engineering projects are open-ended).

"Engineers will do many of both kinds of project during their careers. It is important that we, as faculty, recognize the difference when we structure learning experiences for our students."[9]

Some teachers took a linear approach to the teaching of design and followed models like that proposed by Krick (1966). At the Catholic University Louvain, Wright's (1989) simplified six phase model was used (Denayer et al., 2003).

Many of the developments in the US took place in freshmen courses. Sheppard and Jennison (1997, a, b) and Sheppard (2002), proposed a matrix for the evaluation of these programs. It is shown in Figure 12.1. The two dimensions are *"what is taught and learned" and "how what is taught."* The former is a skill dimension, the latter a pedagogical dimension. The "what" dimension ranges from 100% specific knowledge and content to 100% key design qualities. The "how" dimension ranges from 100% individual based activities to 100% team based activities. The skill knowledge dimension ranges from traditional courses with conventional examinations, and instructional type teaching, with standard textbooks, to the other extreme where there *"are courses that include open-ended problem solving, achievement of goals is rarely measurable with conventional exams (and may require observational methods such as ethnography or video interaction analysis, longitudinal snapshots such as portfolios, or reflective methods such as journaling), subject matter is not consistent from year to year, course is process/method oriented, teaching method is experiential in nature. It is difficult to take pulse of class in a quantitative manner to see if the students are "getting it", and a textbook is generally not available"* (Sheppard, 2000).

The pedagogical dimension *"encompasses the relationship between the students, the overall classroom environment and atmosphere, whether homework assignments are collective or individual responsibility, whether work is assessed on an individual or group basis, and the extent to which that classroom time is used for lecturing or group work. This dimension reflects whether a student sees him or her-self as an individual learning a body of knowledge and/or gaining competency that is collectively responsible for learning, sharing and utilizing knowledge"* (Sheppard, 2000).

Courses are classified by their location on the matrix, and this is determined by the qualities met by the course on the rating scale shown in Exhibit 12.2. Each quality is comprised of a competency and an attitude.

---

[9]He cited Pahl and Beitz (1988), who defined the design process as 1. Clarify the task. 2. Conceptual design. 3. Embodiment design. 4. Detail design.

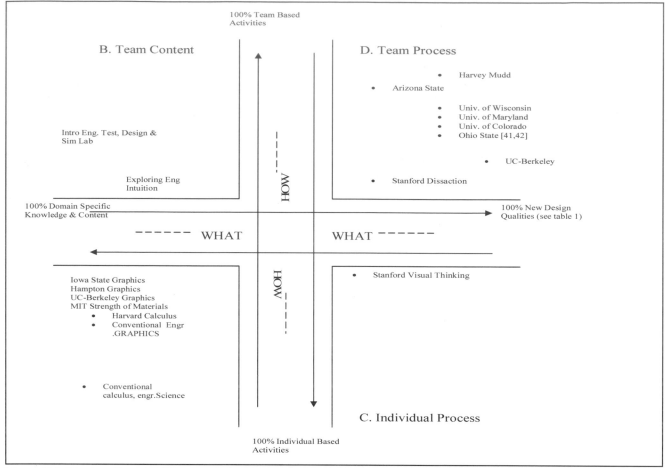

Figure 12.1. The two dimensional-framework for viewing freshmen design courses, including placement of illustrative courses due to Sheppard, S and R. Jenison.(1997) Examples of Freshman Design Education. *International Journal of Engineering Education.* 13, (4), 248-261. [Reproduced with permission of the S.D. Sheppard]

Its purpose is to specify the qualities that a design engineer needs to have to be effective in that role[10].

A recent review of the studio course at Harvey Mudd College, whose course is at one extreme, is summarized in brief below in Section 12.1.2.

One of the problems with first-year design courses in the United States was the fact that students had very little knowledge of engineering course work and could not do the calculations associated with design. McCreanor et al., (2002) reported that this left the students with the idea that engineering design and engineering analysis were unrelated and completely separate processes. To overcome this difficulty, they modified their introduction engineering design course to include an introduction to basic technical concepts. Motivation was maintained through the use of design competitions in which the students were provided with kits with which to complete specified projects. During the course the students undertook a relatively simple project which was followed by a complex and more open-ended

project.[11]. The teachers who assigned the project acted as clients rather than instructors. They were told not to solve the problem but to give guidance. The students were only to be given a basic specification so that they were forced to ask questions. The specification did not cover all the eventualities that would arise.[12]. The modified course included seminars the intention of which was to provide the students with engineering tools and quantitative methods for analyzing their designs prior to construction. The eight technical seminars dealt with the following conceptual areas:

- *"Potential energy, kinetic energy and mechanical energy storage.*
- *Trusses and structures.*
- *Static and dynamic forces.*
- *Electricity: DC fundamentals and electric motors.*
- *Springs: theory, design and construction.*
- *Moments, Gears and gearing.*
- *Buoyancy and stability."*

[10]Details of the courses shown in the matrix are given in the paper by Sheppard and Jenison.

[11]A complete description is given of one project. The teams followed a typical design process which is outlined.

[12]A rule book was provided and changes to specifications had to be agreed by the course coordinator because of the competitive element.

It was found from a simple student evaluation that just over one-half of the students thought the seminars were useful in the design of the vehicle. Sixty percent found they were applicable in other parts of the curriculum. Many of the comments were on the content and timing of the seminars. Some students wanted them to be regularly scheduled and others wanted them to be related more directly to the projects. The teachers remained convinced that the seminars added value to the course.

In the traditional British system, teachers would have expected their students to have "covered" the content of those seminars in high school. As the system changes, that may not always be the case. But with more mature students entering college, it might be expected that some remedial action would be necessary. This was always the case with those universities that took students from both high school and technical colleges (i.e., technician training). This meant, to put it crudely, that technical college students required topping up in mathematics and science while the high school students required an introduction to engineering. Subsequently, the rules of the profession were changed so as to ensure the intake had relatively common standards but as indicated elsewhere, this can no longer be guaranteed. In the earlier situation, high school students benefited if they had been in industry and experienced workshop practice prior to beginning college (see I. Mech., E. 1962). But sandwich (cooperative) courses are no longer in vogue.

12.1.2. Sequential and Other Approaches to Teaching Design

Although some of these developments in the United States relate either to the junior or to the senior years, the literature is primarily concerned to the junior years. However, there have been courses that use the project method across the curriculum. In the United Kingdom for example, the Department of Engineering Design and Manufacture at the University of Hull (UK) projects were used throughout the four-year degree in Engineering Design and Manufacture. In the first year, students undertook a design, make, and test project activity which was run as a competition between groups of students. *"The main benefit of this exercise is perhaps not evident until the second year when formal design methodology is presented to the students with a retrospective look at the unstructured design decisions made during the first year exercise"* (Hurst, James, and Raines, 1993). In the second year the design module was integrated with a workshop experience. Students undertook an individual project in which they designed, made, and kept an artifact of their own choosing. Prototypes were completed in a period of about 50 hours. A design report was completed. It included costings. A bill of materials was produced and assessed after which the students manufactured their artifacts. A final report was submitted that covered the manufacturing together with an evaluation of what had been learned. At the end

of this stage, Hurst, James, and Raines suggested that students had had first-hand experience of the consequences of design decisions and the constraints imposed by manufacturing. In the third year the students carried out industrially linked projects. The students also spent three weeks working as project teams in local companies. *"These projects have many aims, including exposing the students to industrial circumstances within which they must employ their engineering knowledge and design process skills whilst encouraging effective planning and working within groups."* In their final year the students have to complete *"two substantial individual project... the work provides excellent training in project planning in terms of definition of objectives, utilization of available time and resources, and preparation of reports to a professional standard."* This scheme is reminiscent of the scheme used at the University of Reading in the 1960s (see Chapter 9; Deere, 1967). Unfortunately, the authors did not provide an evaluation. The same is true of a report of a novel development at Rhode Island University (Viets, 1990).

The engineer or engineering student should be able to

1. Communicate, negotiate, and persuade.
2. Work effectively in a team.
3. Engage in self-evaluation and reflection.
4. Utilize graphical and visual representations and thinking.
5. Exercise creative and intuitive instincts.
6. Find information and use a variety of sources (i.e., resourcefulness).
7. Identify critical technology and approaches; stay abreast of change in professional practice.
8. Use of analysis in support of synthesis.
9. Appropriately model the physical world with mathematics
10. Consider economic, social and environmental aspects of a problem.
11. Think with a systems orientation, considering the the integration and needs of various facets of the problem.
12. Define and formulate an open-ended and/or under defined problem including specifications.
13. Generate and evaluate alternative solutions
14. Use systematic, modern step-by-step problem-solving approach. Recognize the need for and implement iteration.
15. Build-up real hardware to prototype ideas
16. Trouble shoot and test hardware

Exhibit 12.2. Qualities expected in a design engineer, and that engineering courses should be helping engineering students to develop. [Due to Sheppard (2002). Reproduced with the permission of the Author]

Viets (1990) described a course that was being tested in which design was incorporated into required engineering courses throughout the curriculum. *"As freshmen or sophomores these students begin a design project that they will complete in their senior year. In various courses, they work on and complete the portion of the project that relates to a particular course, building their design piece by piece over the years"*. He gave details of the Mechanical Engineering Department's jet aircraft project, and how each course contributed to the whole. For example, in the statics course the trusses that support the wing structures were designed, and in kinematics the landing gear and wing flap mechanisms were designed. The program culminated in a comprehensive design in which all the parts were *"pulled together."* The Product and Manufacturing System Design Project (PAMS) at the University of Birmingham had some similarities with the approach described by Viets. In order to integrate the diverse material covered in manufacturing engineering, a team project was undertaken over the three years of the degree program by teams of between 6 and 10 students.

"The students start with a scenario of a small fictitious company in which they are the engineering team. In the first year the team has to establish the need for a product, starting from a completely blank sheet of paper. In the second year a product has to be designed to meet this perceived need. In the third year a manufacturing system has to be designed to meet this perceived need. In the third year a manufacturing system has to be designed that can make the product commercially and in sufficient quantity" (Jarvis and Quick, 1995). In addition to the objective of integration it was expected that students would experience 'total design.' It was also expected that a number of personal transferable skills would be learned. A covert objective was that the students would learn something about what engineers actually did in industry. A unique feature of this project was the need to keep the teams together over a very long period.

It would seem that teachers who work in manufacturing consider that total design for manufacturing has of necessity to be an integrated activity (see Chapter 8) Tomovic and Eigenbrod (1993) of Purdue University argued that the total design activity could be described 6 core phases. These were: market investigation; specification; conceptual design; detail design; manufacturing; and sales. These could only be taught through an integrated approach. As previously indicated above (and in Chapter 8), many possibilities for the integration of design with other subjects exist, as, for example, ethics (Kitto, 2001), but more especially in terms of the social function of design, a factor which is increasingly recognized.

Schumacher and Gabriele (1999) reported a survey of industrial and product design programs and found that they fell into two categories: *"one stresses technical or engineering expertise (housed in an engineering school), and the second stresses aesthetics or arts expertise (housed in an arts and/or architecture school). Since, there is little if any overlap, they fail to integrate the insights and expertise of each other. Moreover, neither incorporates into the curriculum an adequate expertise in how products shape social and cultural relationships and how in turn these relationships shape products."*

In order to balance traditional approaches to Industrial design and engineering design with the approaches of science and technology studies, a course was developed at Rensselaer Polytechnic in which: *"Students will develop a general engineering knowledge*

through meeting the degree requirements for Engineering Science and a set of analytical skills for understanding society and culture through meeting the degree requirements of Science and Technology Studies" (Schumacher and Gabriele, 1999). During each semester the students would participate in a design studio that had as its objective the integration of the technical, aesthetic and social dimensions of engineering design. During these studios, students would be expected to complete a portfolio of their design experiences.

The idea of the studio in engineering education had been summarized by Little and Cardenas (2001) of Harvey Mudd College. They suggested *"that one could construct a spectrum ranging from one extreme consisting of courses in which "studio" is little more than a room full of computers in which students work in a self-taught mode with guided computer exercises to the other extreme in which students work on open ended design projects under a mentor who encourages and comments on ongoing work, and guides students to engage in visual creative application of principles."* Little and Cardenas considered that the studio as used in architecture is appropriate for engineering education and they described the recent development of a course based on this model at Harvey Mudd College. Particular attention was paid to the physical space because it was likely to affect the way students respond to active learning.[13] The Harvey Mudd syllabus reads, *"students will work alone or in teams on particular design exercises which allow the students to learn by doing, to learn by observing the results of others, and to learn from one another while trying out new ideas."* The general principles of the pedagogy were based on Kuhn (1998). They were that there should be frequent critiques of work in progress by peers, instructors, and visitors that should be both formal and informal in nature. Within these conversations, it was expected that heterogeneous issues would arise. Precedents would be gained from the study of previous work that would enable students to think about the big picture. Perhaps a better way to think about the studio and its objectives is to think of students in an art studio where their work is one-to-one inspection by everyone in the class and where the teacher is a coach or a mentor.

Clearly, and especially when a studio course is taught in the first year, many students will have to be helped to re-orient. Although Little and Cardenas could not say what the effects of the studio *per se* were on learning because it overlapped with other forms of active learning, they did, however, argue that it was a viable form of learning for engineering design.[14]

Wild and Bradley (1998), of the University of Victoria argued that it was important to propose alternative courses so that if the window of opportunity occurred, the ideas would be available for use. They argued that

---

[13]Some evidence in support of this view will be found in Grulke, Beert, and Lane (2001).

[14]See Dym (1993) for the origins of the approach to computing in the studio, and Dym (1994b) for the origins of the program at Harvey Mudd.

engineering educators should emulate more the practices of industry when the time comes to develop or modify programs. Their 'new' idea was to use a concurrent engineering paradigm to present a challenge to engineering educators. They began with the oft-repeated view that current engineering programs concentrated on analysis at the expense of the fundamentals of mechanical engineering design, and where a sequential approach to design through design, manufacturing and marketing was undertaken there was often little or no communication between the departments. They cited Chisholm's stringent criticisms of design in British engineering education, and used Eder (1988) in support of their views. But as this chapter shows, much is being done to offset these criticisms. The interest in their paper lies in the model of curriculum they proposed. It is shown in Figure 12.2. It is based on the applications of concurrent engineering to curriculum design. They argued that the philosophy of design embraced by concurrent engineering meant that the tasks in the design process that were normally conceived of as progressing linearly would now be executed in parallel, or concurrently. Their intention was that engineering fundamentals would be approached by methods that helped students to self-learn.

In a three-university collaboration, Kumar et al., (2000) used design projects to train students to work co-operatively within a concurrent engineering framework. *"More importantly, the students were sensitized to the concept of remote real-time manufacturing and to the potential of computer integrated information technology."* However, this was not a total curriculum change of the kind suggested by Wild and Bradley.

12.1.3. Fostering Motivation through Design and Project Work

Because of the concern to retain students especially at the end of first-year programs there have been attempts to create teaching and learning environments that motivate students (Sheppard, 2000). There was particular concern for the retention of minority and women students.[15] Some curriculum designers look at the issue from the "glass is half-full" perspective in that they use such courses to attract students to engineering (e.g., Ahlgren, 2001). It was argued, as in other courses, that there would be a relationship between engineering design and retention because the ability to undertake hands on real world activities would create an interest in engineering that was sufficient to motivate the students to remain in their courses.

Courter (1996) of the University of Wisconsin-Madison, in one of the few thorough evaluations of a new first year course in engineering pointed out that the course had many characteristics in common with Total Quality Management (TQM). Her evaluation, which involved triangulation of interviews with students,

student focus groups, and survey groups, combined with observation of classes was set against the following characteristics:

1. *Outcomes (customer) focus.*
2. *Teamwork process.*
3. *Continuous improvement culture.*
4. *Data based decision process.*
5. *Authentic real-world product.*
6. *Supportive resources.*
7. *Systems approach.*

Thus, the questions that Courter's investigation sought to answer were:
*"1. What are the effects of a TQM curriculum innovation, namely, the first year design course on faculty and student teaching and learning experiences? And,
2. What are the major student and faculty outcomes?"*

The course comprised one lecture per week, one three-hour lab per week, and the completion of a project. Homework was given; journals and notes were kept. The students gave two presentations. They also undertook peer and self-assessment.

Given that this course was a volunteer course (in that it did not fulfil any program requirement, although it carried credit), and given that it was expected to provide the motivation that would encourage students to pursue an engineering program, in its totality, this was perhaps a bold, if not rash, innovation. The evaluation showed that both male and female students were concerned that the course should fit the curriculum. It needed to count It needed to be 'sold' to the faculty. Courter summarized the retention rates for the students who attended the first course. It was 96%, and after four semesters 89.5%. This compared with a low average first-year retention rate for pre-engineering cohorts of between 50% and 70%. 18 of the 20 women remained in the program. Courter, Millar and Lyons (1998) entered the caveat that a single course cannot hope to solve all the problems of retention. The students still had to deal with traditional "weed out" courses such as calculus. Yet this is what courses of this kind apparently achieve. Since the Madison experience is not an isolated event, it is appropriate to relate it to the experience of other universities experience of motivation, self-confidence, reality, and teacher role. This is done in the paragraphs that follow.[16]

It remains surprising that students will undertake courses that offer little or no credit. In one collaborative project between three universities, 75 students from across the disciplines including non-engineers and across the semesters designed built and tested a payload (scientific experiment) for a rocket that was actually launched. The program took place over a period of two years and involved a 1-credit course. As Marra and Wheeler (2000) who reported the project, wrote, *"we were struck by the enthusiasm with which the students participated in the project. Why would a busy student*

[15]Courter makes specific reference to the courses at Rose Holman, North Eastern University, University of North Dakota, University of Maryland, Iowa State University, and Stanford University. The course was one semester long. Courter evaluated the first two semesters with the focus being on the first

[16]The Madison course continues to run and there is an excess of applicants over available places.

spend roughly ten hours per week on a project and a course that offered only one credit."[17]

It may be argued that this was likely to be an attractive project since it was at the frontiers of science and technology. Yet the projects described by Courter (1996), which some may say by contrast were dull, also motivated the students. In the first semester at Madison the students had focused on *"access for wheel chair users for historic buildings at Old World Wisconsin. Wheel chair access to an additional building on the. engineering campus was also involved."* But, reported Courter, they were undertaking these projects for real-world customers, and *"the students' concern for society appears to be genuine."*

The types of design project that respond to student needs and the type that students would choose given the chance is an area that merits further investigation

Angelov, Freedman and Renshaw (1999) argued the case for toy design as follows: *"Toy design has proved to be the perfect subject for a first-year design course. It familiarizes the student with general techniques and methodology, and simulates a professional work environment Methodologies for design of washing machines, jet fighters, and screwdrivers have much in common with toy design. However, unlike more traditional design subjects toy design appeals to a multidisciplinary audience with little or no technical knowledge and even attracts students with no interest in the engineering profession. Virtually all students are toy experts having had at least 17 years of experience with toys of varying levels and complexities. Finally, designing concepts for toys distils design and creative thinking by eliminating concern for practical implementation."*

Among children's activities that have been successful had been the design of playground swings and see-saws. The latter were built by women high school students during a summer engineering program at the University of Maryland-College Park. Because of the success of the engineering design course that included these projects, when the curriculum was revised, the engineering design course became a program requirement (Zhang, 1999). The success of the course as measured by change in enrollments showed a rise in enrolments of 350 students from 1994 to 1998 (i.e., from 500 to 850)[18].

Lego and other similar kits are commonly used in first year engineering courses Thus in the mechanical engineering department of the University of Nevada at Reno students who worked in pairs completed ten Lego based assignments of increasing difficulty. Some of these were competitive. Performance based grading was used. *"The course culminates with a robot battle, which requires programming a fully autonomous mobile robot.*

Creative solutions, on the verge of cheating, are both highly encouraged and highly rewarded." Several papers have reported the value of robotics in providing engineering design-oriented experiences. Both in the United Kingdom and the United States students have found the design of assistive devices for various kinds of disability to be of value (Culver and Scudder, 1995; Kumar et al.,, 2000; Miller and Hyman, 1989). Others have also described the value of competitions in motivating students, and these include entry in national competitions (e.g., Ahlgren, 2001,[19] Verner and Ahlgren, 2002: DeVault, 1998), and internationally West and Shimizu (1992).   Some teachers fear that grading schemes that intend to foster collaboration among teams may have the opposite effect because of the effects of competition.[20]

The report by Marra and Wheeler (2000) is distinguished from other studies by the fact that these investigators attempted to measure changes in intrinsic motivation and to observe the effects of extrinsic motivation. For this purpose they used *The Motivated Strategies for Learning Questionnaire*[21]. The four scales that they selected from the instrument were

1. *Intrinsic Goal Orientation Scale.*
2. *Extrinsic Goal Orientation Scale.*
3. *Task Value. (Interest, importance, or usefulness to student).*
4. *Control of Learning beliefs. (Whether students believe their efforts to learn will have positive results).*

The students were asked to rate the SPIRIT program, as the artificial earth satellite payload project was called, and the lower division students were also asked to rate a general education course on the grounds that such classes were generally delivered to large numbers in the lecture format.

The investigators found that the lower division students *"reported statistically significant differences between SPIRIT and the comparison course for three of the four items comprising the extrinsic motivation scale."* They also, as a result of another analysis, reported that on eight of the eighteen items of the inventory that were used, lower division students rated the *"SPIRIT experience and their comparison courses significantly different (at the 0.05 level) than those students who were already in their major."* On a seven point scale the lower division students rated their comparison course 3.6 and the SPIRIT course 6.7 respectively, and the upper division students gave their comparison course 5.79 and the SPIRIT course 5.1.

---

[17] Another component of the course was a publicity campaign that the authors thought was attractive to the students who participated from other faculties. There were also several component test events, and a K-12 outreach program.

[18] The paper in which this work was summarized is devoted to the problem of resource management of such a large class.

---

[19] National robotics competition sponsored by Trinity College. The author described a team-based engineering design experience to develop an autonomous competitive fire fighting mobile robot in a first year engineering course in a primarily liberal arts college.

[20] Wang (2001) does not put it as strongly as this, but it seems evident from what he wrote.

[21] See Pintrich and Johnson (1990)

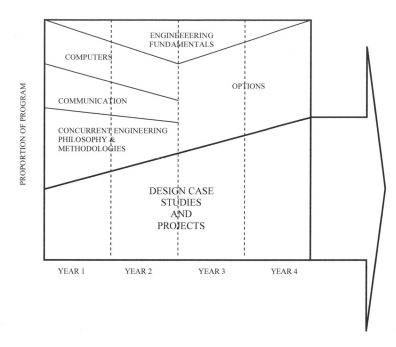

PROPORTION OF PROGRAM

ENGINEEERING FUNDAMENTALS

COMPUTERS

OPTIONS

COMMUNICATION

CONCURRENT ENGINEERING PHILOSOPHY & METHODOLOGIES

DESIGN CASE STUDIES AND PROJECTS

YEAR 1   YEAR 2   YEAR 3   YEAR 4

Figure 12.2. Concurrent engineering education program layout due to P. M. Wild and C. Bradley (1998). "Employing the concurrent design philosophy in developing an engineering design science program". *International Journal of Mechanical Engineering Education,* **26, (1) 51 -64. (Reproduced with permission of the authors and the** *International Journal of Engineering Education***)**

.

The authors pointed out that the comparison course chosen by seniors was not from the general education program but from engineering that was related to their careers. Taking all the results together, Marra and Wheeler asserted that this type of project is of great value in universities like Penn State where the majority of students enrol in general education courses mostly outside their major. They drew attention to the fact that the hands-on activity, the teamwork, and the student run nature of the course contribute to retention.

These illustrations confirm that design and project activities can be instrumental in the fostering of intrinsic motivation.

12.1.4. Self-Confidence and Learning on One's Own.

Related to motivation is the acquisition of self-confidence and the ability to learn on ones own. Bailey and Hill (1998) of the University of Southampton cited from a much-quoted work by Cross (1989) that *"in order to cope with the uncertainty of ill defined problems, the designer has to have the self-confidence to define, redefine, and change the problem as given, in the light of solutions that emerge in the very process of designing."* This implies that designers have to learn to learn on their own and projects are ideal for this purpose as Wang (2001). But as was pointed out in Chapter 11, this involves risk; by and large, engineering teachers and their students are not risk takers. Bailey and Hill cited French (1991), who argued that if technical confidence is to be acquired it is necessary for teaching to be design-

oriented. The Lego type of approach in which a number of small projects are completed is supported by Mickelburgh and Wareham (1994), who argued that repeated exposure to such problems enhances self-confidence. Projects of one kind or another are seen as the solution to the development of self-confidence.

Bailey and Smith's response was to incorporate computer-based hypermedia into a first-year mechanical engineering design course in order to *"mimic the way in which a professional engineer would create a set of specifications and complete a design on the basis of those specifications."* Groups of three students each had to solve a paper-based problem. Each team was given a specification relating to a wheel mount for a racing car. The teachers felt that the students should have the opportunity to create their own specifications rather than have them given. Student responses to the exercise were obtained from a five-point scale inventory and a confidence log. It was found that students had difficulty in understanding the problem. They also felt the exercise was too long, so, in the following year, deadlines for different parts of the exercise were given, and a more detailed introduction was provided. It should be said that difficulties of this kind are to be found in other reports of project work. (See Chapter 9).

The confidence log included 4 scaled questions on the confidence with which the students dealt with certain issues. Pre-and post-confidence logs were obtained, and these showed that there had been a movement up the scale of confidence to a position where almost all of the students were within the "very confident" or "some confidence" bands. Those students without previous industrial experience gained confidence *"more concerning their ability to use CAD software and to use it to create accurate technical drawings."* The fact that a few students showed little confidence in the items shows the value of such logs in isolating students who may be in need of help. All too often satisfaction with a generally good result leads teachers to neglect the one or two who may need help. It is possible to design courses that appear to be attractive that can have the opposite effect if they are too demanding for some students.

It is argued that the reason why many women are not attracted to engineering is that they lack self-confidence in practical work. As Zang (see above) remarked, projects may go some way to resolving this problem. This has been found to be true of mature women on a technology access course (Tizard, 1993). In Bailey and Hill's exercise, there were 5 female students. The results suggested that *"either the female students got more out of their use of the application, or that their confidence in their skills increased more than that of the male students."* Overall both the male and female students found the exercises difficult, although all of those who attempted the exercise completed it.

The female students in the University of Wisconsin-Madison freshmen engineering design course are reported to have developed confidence and to have had a positive introduction to a field they regarded as traditionally male (Courter, Millar, and Lyons, 1998). Finelli (1999) found no differences between male and female students in her experiment with freshmen design students, she suggested, as Anderson-Rowland (1998) had done, that women and minority students *"may be better retained in engineering if they are exposed in their first semester to teamwork and projects."*

Moore and Berry (1999) recorded that recruiters had said that as a result of the new approach to the teaching of design with industrially sponsored projects, that seniors were *"very self confident and proactive in indicating their strengths, their experience in working in teams, and other project related capabilities."* (Some students had joined their sponsor after graduation while others had said that they would not like to work for the sponsor.)

Given an appropriate instructional environment, design projects can foster self-confidence and the ability to learn on one'' own among both sexes.

12.1.5. The Quest for Industrial Realism

The purpose of those projects that required the design of children's toys or used children's toys like Lego was to enable students to get some idea of the design process. Other instructors have tried to create reality through simulations of the organization of a company. Collier et al., (1995) of Northern Arizona University described how, in an experimental course, the teachers and students organised into a company. Six members of the faculty played the roles of company president, 4 division managers, and a quality manager. Each of these had to wear two hats, i.e. division manager

(line) and chief engineer (staff). An industrial adviser acted as the client. The campus Safety Officer acted as the Environmental Protection Agency. The four divisions were made up of two sophomore groups and two junior groups. The divisions were subdivided into sections. Each junior section was linked to a sophomore section. Because students from all the engineering majors were involved, a wide range of learning opportunities had to be provided. These are shown in Exhibit 12.3.

The project *"involved a scenario structured around a hazardous waste processing site located in a decommissioned underground ICBM complex in southern California A drum of toxic chemicals was being transported through an underground tunnel on its way to the incineration chamber when an earthquake occurred, the drum was abandoned when the crew escaped from the tunnel. The facility operator contacted our engineering firm, On-Line Disaster Response Action Teams (ODRAT) to develop a special purpose computer controlled robotic devise to negotiate the tunnel, locate and retrieve the drum, and deposit it safely outside the tunnel entrance."*

One of the problems they experienced was the strong influence of the engineering disciplines on the interests of the students. The students did not readily cross discipline boundaries. The project involved 5 faculty, 128 students, 4 classrooms, 4 laboratories, class schedules, and project materials. As such, it presented a considerable "coordination" challenge for faculty. They were not put off by the experiment, and they described changes that would be made for the next project. Although an interdisciplinary project was created, the opportunity to get students to reflect on organizational structures does not seem to have been taken. A summary of Barnes (1960) classic study of engineers and organizational groups might have led to a very revealing reflection by the students.

Also in Arizona but at Tucson, Gerhard (1999) described how he had set up a pseudo-corporation in a junior electronics design class with himself as the manager of engineering. The teaching assistants (TA's) became staff engineers and the students were called "program participants." The TA's acted as mentors and the intention of this arrangement was to change the culture of the classroom. His philosophy was drawn from Koen (1994), and he set out to systematically modify student behavior by carefully graded exercises that began with short open-ended design experiences followed by several larger design problems.

His evaluation was obtained from student rating forms that included additional comment spaces and discussions with students. He was of the opinion that the course had been successful. However, there were still problems because some students *"either by choice or because of deficiencies in understanding learning skills, do not appreciably alter their behavior practices."* He explained what happened with some students as follows:

"... many of the needs for greater assistance and extended laboratory time result from a lack of an intuitive understanding of the material, especially from the rerequisite electronics course. The original behavior they had adopted to learn electronics circuits often was the memorization of equations.... A number of students willing to change felt they learn a great deal from the course....Those who can't or will not change are often frustrated ...."

Gerhard noted that the projects could be changed from course to course so as to avoid plagiarism. He also took the view that behavior modification should begin earlier in the program. This view is supported by Courter (1996), who found that freshmen students *demonstrated a systematic, creative team approach to problem solving. Their approach was systematic in the sense that they followed a step-by-step design process. It engendered creativity because both faculty and students, separately, together, and alone (among their peers) used brainstorming techniques, were open to one another's ideas, and were not limited by their individual capacities. Finally relying primarily on their peers and secondarily on senior assistants and instructors to generate multiple approaches to problems, they used the team approach to create a better product."*

Of course in teamwork, tutors have to be satisfied that all students are changing their behaviors. It is easy to go out of sight in teams. Courter suggested that the students were open to one another's ideas and not limited by their individual capacities. It was recognized that assessment would have to change. In addition to peer assessment the students were asked to write journals, and complete an end-of-semester essay, all of which should have given some insight into their understanding.

Gerhard's study raised the question as to whether a key component in any design course should be learning about learning. Those who are persuaded by Perkins (1986) theory of knowledge as design are equally likely to be persuaded that student understanding of how they learn is likely to be beneficial.

It is not uncommon to find projects in which students are assigned company roles. It is, however, uncommon to find examples of faculty changing their roles in this way, but there is a consensus to be found in many reports that academic faculty have to change their roles and that this more often than not requires a change in the culture of the department.(See Sections 12.3 and 9.12).

Another approach to providing reality is for the projects to be industrially sponsored (e.g.,Carnahan, Thurston, and Ruhl, 1992; Coleman and Shelnutt, 1995; Moore and Berry, 1999; Nicol, 1989; Olds, Pavelich, and Yeats, 1990; Sutton, 1995).There is a long tradition in 'cooperative' ('sandwich' in the United Kingdom) courses of students undertaking project work, as well as in practical skill training in industry (see Chapter 8). However, Yung and Leung (1997) argued that these dimensions should be emphasized in all engineering

attempted to continue this behavior despite a number of cautions that failure to modify would, and did, result in great difficulty in meeting program expectations. Some would not even record node voltages if the circuit did not work at their first attempt, but randomly changed component values[ ] Those students who are able and programs irrespective of their structure because such goals could be achieved by simulation. They described how this goal was being met at the City University of Hong Kong, and in so doing they illustrated the importance of culture on curriculum. *"A significant portion of time in each course is put aside for an integrated training program on product design. Through the program, a student may acquire sufficient and relevant practical skills."*

- Mechanical structure and mechanisms
- Electrical sensors and actuators
- Computer control and status displays
- Environmental concerns
- Physical site characteristics such as soil types, drainage patterns, topography, access etc
- Engineering economics
- Numerical analysis
- Statistics
- Material selection
- Safety
- Regulations and legal issues
- Ethics and professionalism
- Computer design
- Computer presentation tools
- Term interaction and leadership
- Verbal, written and computer communications
- Proposals
- Specifications
- Schedules
- Budgets
- Reports
- Presentation
- Customer interaction

Exhibit 12.3: The learning opportunities that had to be provided in the company simulated project at North Arizona University (Collier et al., 1995). (Reproduced with permission of IEEE, *Proceedings Frontiers in Education Conference*)

Yung and Leung noted that students were weak on entry in handling tools and instruments when they entered the program so they had to take a 42-hour (1hr lecture 2hour lab) course in electrical and electronic measurement in the electronic engineering (honours) degree program. This course is terminated by a practical exam in which each student is asked to design an experimental set-up for a given assignment. Some coursework exercises are also assessed. In the two summers there were ten 44-hour weeks (each) devoted to practical activities. In the first year this work was undertaken in a workshop that simulated a manufacturing environment. In the second year it was undertaken in an industrial grade workshop facility. During that period the students converted a prototype, prepared in the second year (second semester) in a course on electronic product design, into a product that was saleable on the world market. In the first semester of the second year the students' lectures included value analysis, production planning, cost inventory management, quality control and productivity management, demand forecasting, pricing, and product promotion. In year 1 the students were taught in small groups, to design a simple electronic apparatus. The authors argued that this arrangement was more efficient than the traditional sandwich course.

12.2.   The Role of the Teacher.

Courter (1996) observed that the introduction of the new course in design at UCW-Madison (see above) demanded a paradigm shift on the part of the teachers if the principles of TQM were to be adopted.

Such shifts were required

1.   *From faculty-driven to customer-driven course design.*
2.   *From after-the-fact faculty evaluation of student's performance to real time feedback.*
3.   *From individual to team focus.*
4.   *From content mastery to learner mastery.*
5.   *From faculty as lecturer to faculty as facilitator of learning* (Fraser et al., 1994).

Thompson and McChesney (1999) who organized a summer school for new teachers of engineering design on behalf of the Royal Academy of Engineering (United Kingdom) argued that *"the role of the teacher is to provide an atmosphere in which individual and team work can flouris…. It involves close interaction between students and teachers."* It must enable students to develop self-confidence. As Hurst, James, and Raines (1993) pointed out, this is no small task in the British system where the Research Assessment (quality assurance) Exercises put considerable pressure on staff, particularly in innovative programs that are staff intensive. They reported that that they had kept their research going and suggested that this was due to the ethos of the department that encouraged enthusiasm.[22]

The role of the teacher in design studies that involve projects has been variously described as coach or manager and facilitator. In projects that have clients (simulated or otherwise), tutors sometimes act as liaison between the students in thc clients. One effect of tutors becoming managers is that they are not required nor expected to have a detailed knowledge of content. At the Colorado School of Mines the faculty were required to act as coaches, and this was a new role for them. They had to constrain their *"urge to over-teach."* They had to learn not to interfere, and to cope with not being needed, and with the frustrations of things not going as planned (Olds, Pavelich, and Yeats, 1990).

Thompson (1993) of the University of Manchester Institute of Science and Technology, wrote that, *"One attractive approach to teaching is for teachers to become immersed in their students' work. The teaching concept is to work constructively from within the student activity. If projects are set to which the teacher does not know a good solution, the teacher effectively works with each student team when problems arise".* (This approach would be familiar to many schoolteachers[23]). *"Obviously, the teacher should be capable of setting work which should be within the abilities of the class. The important point is that the teacher shares the design experience and helps the students find their solutions. The temptation to direct the group to the teacher's solution must be avoided."* In the British system this has implications for assessment.[24]

Courter (1996) found that both the faculty and the individual project teams developed into learning communities and that within the student teams the prime source of affirmation were the students' peers. Senior engineering students (senior assistants) were primary sources of advice, and the students' did not mind approaching them, and most students *"were comfortable communicating with their faculty person."*

The demand for facilitators to help improve teamwork skills among engineering upperclassmen led the University of Tennessee at Knoxville to implement a training program jointly with the College of Education. Knight et al., (1999) described its evaluation. It was implemented as a class during the fall and spring semesters and was in three phases. It had the dual function of training the upperclassmen in team work skills in order to support freshmen who were working in their first design team. In the first phase, teaching methods such as video[25] and role playing exercises are used to develop the basic skills of teamwork. In the second phase the students, now facilitators, practice the skills learned with design teams of freshmen who are completing simple projects. In the third phase the facilitators met with an instructor to evaluate their experience of working with the design teams for the purpose of solving problems related to that experience. The scale of the exercise may be judged from the fact that in the second year 21 facilitators worked with 150 freshmen divided into 30 teams. Five of the facilitators

---

[22] For a report of an American workshop see Dym, Sheppard, and Wesner (2001).

[23] That is, of this writer's knowledge.

[24] Thompson wrote that in the United Kingdom there was a view that every question in written questions should contain a design element. But he argued that that *"many examination questions which are claimed to be of a design type simply involve a reversal of an established process. An example would be: 'Determine the thickness required for a thin cylinder under an internal pressure of x is the stress level should not exceed…' Such questions are said to be preferred to the case where a complete component and loading is specified and then the maximum stress asked for. Really this is the same question".* An example of a three-hour written paper in design for final year students is given in his paper. But given that this paper was found to be difficult (low results compared with those in engineering science examinations), he asked whether the examination material is the problem?. Is the design course failing to teach students how to design? He thought that the problem was that in a three hour period, students were unable to develop their ideas.

[25] The paper does not say whether or not this is micro-teaching in which students observe how they behave in role playing exercises. It is a technique used extensively in teacher education. Lectures were also given.

were female. All were Caucasian. The evaluation included both qualitative and quantitative data. The MBTI (see Chapter 5) was administered as a pre-test. *The Facilitator Behavior Inventory* was administered as a post-test. This inventory is a 33-item inventory designed for this study to measure the application of facilitation skills in a team. They also used two scales from the SYMLOG instrument[26] designed to measure task orientation and team orientation. The qualitative data relied on phenomenological interviewing. Thus,

"Following the initial question, 'What has been your experience of the facilitation class?' the facilitators (of the interview) were instructed to talk about whatever stood out to them about their experience. The interviewer asked follow up questions to clarify and broaden the description of the experience. When the facilitator felt as if he/she had covered everything, the interview was over". The interviews each of about 30 minutes duration were taped and analyzed for themes (patterns) in the experience.[27]

Since *The Facilitator Behavior Inventory* was still being developed, the investigators said that caution should be exercised in interpreting the results, although some of the evidence suggested it was valid. Overall, insofar as the facilitators were concerned, the program seemed to have a positive effect on their teamwork and social skills. In its turn it seemed to have had a positive impact on the freshmen teams, and it seemed to provide an outlet for those engineering students who had a tendency to extraversion. *"The application of facilitation skills and the generally extraverted personality characteristics of the facilitators appear to have ensured a more cooperative, positive, and generally team-oriented attitude in the freshmen groups."*

The authors commented that engineering students seemed to need help in making the transitions from an engineering frame of mind to the kind of thinking required in the social sciences. This is consistent with the experience of instructors in post-graduate courses which prepare science graduates for teaching in secondary schools in Ireland. Given the personality make-up of engineers, their interests, and their methods of solving problems, this is not surprising (see also Chapter 13). But it is also to learn yet another language (see Section 10.7). The same applies to faculty who agree to become facilitators of teamwork. Che and Zhang (1999) reported on the use of workshops for this purpose, and showed the relevance of work that has been done in management development and training for this purpose.

Courter's study threw a different light on this issue. Her evaluation showed that over a two-year period in making the paradigm shift required for the new approach to teaching and learning, the faculty themselves went through a learning process. Consistent with the philosophy of learning by doing, they themselves learned some profound lessons. For example, at the most basic level they learned they had to change their goals. In the fall semester these were

- *Work constructively in a team*
- *Learn some engineering principles and engineering language.*
- *Seek out, digest, and use information from diverse sources.*
- *Learn from and teach your colleagues.*
- *Get to know your customers: wheelchair users and building staff.*
- *Communicate your designs effectively.*
- *Understand the design environment (business, legal, social).*
- *Keep a personal record of your design process and your learning.*

By the second semester the philosophy of "Introduction to Engineering" had changed to

- *Allow students to learn how to form and work in teams (team dynamics)*
- *Provide the opportunity for a sequence of successful experience for the student.*
- *Have students acquire a feeling (hands-on) of what engineering entails and might encompass.*
- *Develop design process skills on a "real" design project with "real" customers.*
- *Develop skills for hardware and software usage in the projects on an as-needed basis.*
- *Develop context for engineering curriculum, so students see connections among math, science, and technology classes.*
- *Develop confidence in engineering as a career, particularly for students with little prior knowledge or experience in engineering-type activities.*

This is a quite remarkable change, but there were other changes. The faculty began to focus on student needs which helped increase student motivation. Learner mastery came to be more important than content mastery, and the curriculum moved from being faculty centered to student centered. They changed their roles to *"that of "guides-on-the side" and mentors rather than a source of knowledge. Furthermore they began to recognise that process was as important as the product and to question the value of standard assessment strategies to improve student learning".* It goes without saying that they learned to work as a team. There was considerable learning on their part but the question remains: "Would they have benefited from some formal training in learning?"

For the effective teaching of design through project activities, both teachers and students have to learn to change their role. There is some evidence that training can help them make this adaptation.

[26]Bales, R. F. Cohens, S. P., and S. A. Williamson (undated) *SYMLOG: A System for the multiple Level Observation of Groups.* Free Press, New York. As cited by Knight et al., (1999).

[27]Knight et al.,(1999) used as their source Polkinghorne D. E (1989). For other references see, Cresswell (1998), and see Easterby-Smith, (1994) for interviewing in the evaluation of training.

12.3.   Mentors and Mentoring

Faculty mentors have been assigned to students and student teams in some project work. At Rose Hulman their purpose is to serve as an observer for team performance. They are not meant to be resource agents or to participate *"directly (or ideally indirectly) in various team projects/assignments."* This allowed the teams to take ownership of their work. Their function is to *"observe the teaming process and act as a resource for the team when directly involved in the project solution"* (Moore and Berry, 1999).[28]

Elger, Beyerlein, and Budwig (2000) claimed to have facilitated a "mentoring culture" by using cooperative learning activities and coaching to encourage students to believe that they could design. For this reason they allowed students to fail and to move on to their next design. No specific methods of design were prescribed, but the students were required to regularly reflect on their design. They reported a dramatic improvement in reflective thinking.

Sometimes the mentors have been teaching assistants, and at other times they have been students from previous years. In the case of the first year engineering courses described by Ahlgren (2001), the teams were assigned mentors who had been students from a previous year. Four of the five teams regarded their mentors favorably, and a number of students indicated that they would be interested in becoming mentors. The intention was that the mentors should be concerned with the non technical aspects of teamwork and give general support. However, it was found that the teams relied on the mentors for important technical help, and this meant that they had to be selected for their technical skills.

Evidently there is a role for mentors in student design teams. If they are students, it is important to ensure that they are able to offer the technical help that student are likely to seek. Such "tuition" has been found to be valuable, and this finding lends further support to the view that design can be taught.

12.4.   Knowledge as Design

12.4.1. Defining Design

Answers to the question "Can design be taught?" have of necessity created a debate about the nature of design, what it is, whether there is a theory of design education, and the methods by which it should be taught. Some of the most interesting discussions of these issues have been provided by those who have evaluated Design and Technology curricula in schools. First, therefore, to arrive at theory of design education, it is necessary to have a view of what design is. Unfortunately, there are several views and none is universally acceptable.

Herbert Simon, the Nobel Laureate who published work on expert behavior and the methods used to study such behavior suggested a general definition of design that Dym (1993) considered to be close to engineering concerns. It was to the effect that design is intended to produce a *" description of an artifice in terms of its organization and functioning-its interface between inner and outer environments"* (cited by Dym, 1993). Although Dym went on to give his own definition of design as *"the systematic, intelligent generation and evaluation of specifications for artifacts whose form and function achieve stated objectives and satisfy specified constraints,"* he used Simon's view in support of his view that representation was the key issue in design. *"It is not that problem solving and evaluation are less important: they are as important, but they too must be expressed and implemented at an appropriate level of abstraction. Thus, they are also inextricably bound up with concepts of representation." .*He went on to argue that, *"Appropriate representations or hierarchies of representations can be found for both form and function, and they do interact. Further, the statement of a design problem, including it objectives and any applicable constraints, can be cast in terms of these representations. There are problem-solving techniques that exploit these representations for the generation and enumeration of design alternatives. Design alternatives can be translated from representation hierarchy into a set of specifications for fabrication."*

Dym argued that modeling by engineering science and operations research limited design potential because of their reliance on numerical methods. AI research based on the idea of symbolic representation could provide a new vocabulary that would be of help in the study of design knowledge. He illustrated this point by reference to the knowledge-based system PRIDE, which was used to design paper transports in copiers. He also gave an example of an expert system that automatically checked a building for compliance with Fire Protection Codes. These examples showed how symbolic representation could be used to describe and analyze complex configurations. Developing skill in symbolic representation was to develop skill in a new language (see Section 10.7). Modern programming environments would make it possible for students to explore design within the context of design and analysis courses.

In contrast, Muster and Mistree (1989) believed that Simon and others were attempting to incorporate design as an art into a science of design (i.e., within the natural sciences). But they believed this could not be done because the *"central role of experience–based intuition in design makes the science of design uniquely different from the natural sciences."*

---

[28]The focus of this paper is on a four-quarter course sequence starting in the spring of the junior year that is industrially sponsored.

12.4.2. Perkins Theory of Knowledge as Design

It would have been interesting to know how they would have reacted to Perkins general theory of knowledge as design. In his philosophy, knowledge is created as a result of design; it is also understood as design. Perkins argued that *"one might say that a design is a structure adapted to a purpose. Sometimes a single person conceives that structure and its purpose-Benjamin Franklin as the inventor of the lightning rod. Sometimes a structure gets shaped to a structure gradually over time, through the ingenuity of many individuals–the ballpoint pen as a remote descendant of the quill pen. Sometimes a structure gets adapted by a relatively blind process of social evolution, as with customs and languages that reflect human psychological and cultural needs. But notice that in this book we do not use another sense of design: regular pattern that serves no particular purpose as in ripples on sand dunes."*

Perkins went on to make a distinction between knowledge as information and knowledge as design. In the majority of engineering courses, knowledge is being conveyed as information. That knowledge is adapted so that it can be transferred to other situations. An important ability in the designer's repertoire is to be able break away from experience or, as Perkins put it, *"familiar frames of reference."* Perkins suggested that if we view the pieces of knowledge that we have as structures, this will enable us to do just that. For example, *"You know the layout of your town or city-so you can get to work, to your home, to the airport, wherever you want to go. Again your knowledge is well adapted: if you have lived in a place a while, you probably have a rather comprehensive "mental map" of the area that you can apply not only in finding places you normally go to but in navigating to new locations in the same area. Similar points can be made about knowing the rules of chess or your favourite foods. For these examples of every day practical knowledge, knowledge as design does make sense."*

He argued that a theory of understanding is required that reflects the theme of design. Therefore, one has to understand the nature of design, and this is obtained from answers to the following four questions:

1. What is its purpose(s)?
2. What is its structure?
3. What are the model cases of it?
4. What are the arguments that explain and evaluate it?

These questions are the link with engineering design because they are familiar to designers. Consider them in relation to the many heuristics for problem solving described in Chapters 3 and 10. These questions are asked when students try to answer the question, *"How did others solve a particular problem?"* And, when they ask the question, *"How would I solve a particular problem?"* Sheppard (1992) argued that answering such questions by dissecting artifacts prior to participation in design mechanics courses makes such courses more

meaningful. For this reason she developed at Stanford a course on *"mechanical dissection"* which also sought to help students acquire skill in answering these questions, and those that asked, *"Why does the solution work?"* And, *"What problems am I interested in solving?"* The goals of the course are shown in Exhibit 12.4.[29]

Smith (1998) reported a successful attempt to teach design for Assembly (DFA) by the dissection method. His paper is of particular interest, because of the grading methods used (see Chapter 16). Reverse engineering is a similar process of dissection. At Rowan University in a freshman clinic the students analyzed the brewing process. This took place in the second semester after the students had experienced a series of hands-on engineering projects. These included the dissection of cheap commercial products. The purpose of the brewing project was to introduce students to engineering fundamentals. The students began with an evaluation of commercial beers and worked backwards to the design and improvement of the commercial equipment required for their production (Farrell, Hesketh and Slater, 1999)[30].

Answering his own questions led Perkins to a general theory of understanding entrenched in the theme of design. This means that structures such as governments, theorems, experiments, and short stories are designs, and this broadens the whole concept of what we perceive to be design. Knowledge of design is active: It is purposive.

Perkins explained in detail how this applied to learning, dealing with such aspects as problem finding, modeling, and intrinsic motivation. Of interest here, however, are his views about schooling and teaching. He argued that schooling is held back by four tacitly held hypotheses that have no foundation. These are:

1   That knowledge is information.
2.   This leads to the view that you cannot think or do science unless you know a lot of science. (He gives other illustrations, as for example, you cannot understand modern society without studying the details of American and European history.) People only learn skills through practice, e.g., no one can teach you how to
3.   Understand something that is hard to understand. *"Teachers can only give you lots of exercises relevant to such accomplishments."*
4.   Standard problems and exercises capture the skills of a discipline. For example, it is assumed that *"when you solve a textbook chemistry problem, you are doing a large part of what being a chemist involves, albeit at an elementary level"* (pp. 212, 213).

---

[29] The artifacts dissected were an HP printer; a fishing reel preceded by a fishing trip so that the students would have an awareness of what was involved; a ten speed bicycle; and an artifact of each student's choosing. For an evaluation see Lind, Roschelle, and Stevens (1994).
[30] New courses in reverse engineering have also been developed at the University of Texas- Austin, MIT and US Airforce Academy (Wood et al., 2001).

Those who advocate the teaching of design encounter resistance to their work because these views are deeply embedded in the 'unconscious' of the system, and they are reinforced in the knowledge that they are simple to deliver and, at least from a superficial point of view, appear to work. This does not mean that they cannot be changed. The introduction of design in many institutions suggests they can. Perkins view of knowledge of design also led him to views about what teachers and schools should do. Among other things, he suggested that the theory of knowledge should be made *"plain to students"* (i.e., as appropriate to their level). *"Even first-graders can have a basic appreciation of the sense behind the designs of tricycles and pencils and how the design questions abet understanding those designs"* (p. 214).

This point is no better illustrated by research into design and technology teaching in primary (elementary) schools in Britain and Canada. A British study of primary (elementary)-age children suggested that there are similarities in the approaches of children and professional designers when they work with professional designers. Davies (1996), during a period of four months, engaged his 9-10-year-old children in the formation of an opera company as part of a design and technology course. They wrote, composed, designed, produced, and performed their own piece of musical theatre. The children were given advice by a freelance designer whose job was to design sets and costumes for the theatre. This designer treated the children as apprentices. Davies gave the details of an interview of the designer's reaction to working with children.

Davies observed that his study had demonstrated the importance of play in learning. In this respect he was affirming the work of Jerome Bruner (Bruner, Jolly, and Sylver, 1976). Thus, *"children's interactions with objects"* [while they play] *"also helps them to become familiar with their properties and functions in an intimate way, which can give them particular insight into what materials can and cannot do...making links between an object helps children to think of new ways of using it"*... as, for example, refuse sacks.

Davies reminded us that when children see the purpose of a task they are capable of seeing it through the eyes of others, and he cited Donaldson (1978) and his own observations in support of this view. *"In other words, as long as the context makes sense to a child, the very act of playing with something concrete in a design situation can help him to develop abstract thought."* Citing the work of Kosslyn (1978) on mental imaging, he found that there was evidence that children scanned their mental images, but if Kosslyn is correct thinking visually and scanning became less important as children learned to process and hold information in other forms.

To give mechanical engineering students *an understanding of mechanical artifacts* through hands-on dissection experiences and exposure to the vocabulary of mechanical design systems, thinking visually and scanning became less important as children learned to process and hold information in other forms.

The jump that Davies asked us to make is that *"the thought processes of children and designers may be closer than we have realised"* because *"successful designers are those who have kept hold of their imaging abilities, and developed them in parallel with other mental attributes"* He concluded that *",my experience of working with children and designer together is that they are able to talk the same language, and build on the approaches they hold in common. Because the aspects of designing activity described above are entirely natural to children, they respond instinctively to the apprenticeship model of education offered by the designer in the classroom, rather than to more rigid, curriculum-led attempts to teach children design."*[31]

1. To develop an *awareness of Design Process* through hands-on design exercises/assignments that highlight the importance of functional specifications in design and how they map into specific functions, and the non-unique mapping between functional specifications and the final design solution (ie., multiple solutions).
2. To make students aware of the *power of clear, concise communications* (oral, written, and graphical) by having them present descriptions of mechanical artifacts and critique each others work.
3. To develop *resourcefulness and problem solving skills* through labs that require students to reason about function of three-dimensional objects.

Exhibit 12.4. The objectives of Sheppard's Course on Mechanical Dissection (Cited from Sheppard, 1992. See also Brereton, Sheppard, and Leifer, 1995). (Reproduced with the permission of the Author)

The question is, "What happens to that language in post-primary education, and why does it have to be restored in engineering education?" In effect, Sheppard (1992) is restoring that language when she asks her students to dissect artifacts, for that is precisely what children do so often in their play. We might ask, Is the best use of this made in their formal elementary schooling?

"Design and Technology" is also taught in schools in Canada. Roth (1996) evaluated a course for grade 4 children called "Engineering for Children:" Its purposes were to introduce science concepts, provide ill-defined problem-solving contexts, and foster positive attitudes to science and technology. The children were pre and post-tested, and audio and video-tapes were made. The technique of analysis was similar in some respects to the protocol analyzes described by Atman and her colleagues in recent papers on novice designers (see below).

Because talking, negotiating, and communicating design are considered to be the main activities of design engineers, the course unit was developed *"To let students develop their skills in and through the same kind of activities. Whole class discussions provided many opportunities for*

---

[31] For the sake of brevity I have left Davies at this point. However, his paper deals with the "big idea", the role of narrative language in design activity, drawing and modeling, and personal knowledge in designing

developing an engineering related design discourse. In particular the verbal and visual presentations served as occasions to stimulate interactions ...." Roth went on to describe the different kinds of discourse that the children undertook. All of it is very reminiscent of what is to be found among groups of novices pursuing engineering design in a college context.

He found that prior to instruction the students had scant knowledge of engineering and engineering-related techniques. By the end of the course, however they had acquired *"a competent engineering-related language that allowed them to articulate their experiences. This discourse was striking in its variations and allowed students to integrate their personal meanings."* It had come about not through the imposition of textbook definitions but through discourse in their groups. The language they learned was not the result of memory or teacher given definitions. It was *"rich engineering design language to talk over and about design artifacts and the activity of designing."*

It seems from these activities in primary (elementary) schools that there is evidence to support the theory that there is a natural language of design. Moreover, they would seem to present powerful illustrations of Perkins theory of knowledge as design. The pupils were asking Perkins four questions that help the understanding of any design that is, What is its purpose (or purposes)? What is its structure? What are model cases of it?), What are the arguments that explain or evaluate it? Perkins other suggestions were:

1. *Present knowledge from the perspective of design.* By this he meant that the design questions should be used to convey knowledge. Implicit in this view is the idea that at times the barriers between the knowledge areas (disciplines) get broken down whether the teacher likes it or not. Those who advocate the teaching of design in engineering argue that the solution of most engineering problems requires knowledge from several disciplines, and that for the purpose of education, knowledge is integrated by the project method, in addition to appropriately structured scaffolds in their associated curriculum. In the United Kingdom, at least, there is a marked reluctance to allow interdisciplinary study in secondary education. The curriculum is discipline oriented. Yet, some of the goals of education at the primary level in England cannot be achieved without some form of interdisciplinary work (Blyth et al., 1973, 1993)

2. *Treat knowledge as functional.* By this he meant that knowledge has to be put to work. *"We have to keep the learner doing something with the knowledge gained."* Again those who teach engineering design accept the idea of learning by doing as axiomatic. Moreover, it can be done with simple models built and tested by the students (e.g Ben-Arryoyo, 1979). The MIT sophomore Introduction to Engineering

Design course in mechanical engineering was based on the principle of learning by doing (West, Flowers, and Gilmore, 1990). In this respect it was no different in objective to the design and make projects encouraged in school education. This model has consequences for what is regarded as design because in the MIT scheme it results in a manufactured product whereas in other schemes the design ends with a specification, and whether that justifies the description hands-on is a moot point.[32] The value of hands-on experience, according to West, Flowers, and Gilmore, is that it *"reveals that simple analytical tools can enable you to make design decisions without time consuming experimentation. It also shows their limitations because the real world frequently does not conform to the idealizations to which analysis applies."* They also argued that students need experience of fabrication. *"In just a few hours, it is possible to teach students some important engineering principles that determine the application of different fabrication and manufacturing processes and to introduce the vocabulary of basic machine elements."*

It has been shown in Ireland that in a short concentrated course (two weeks' duration), high school students can be introduced to fabrication with these principles in mind (Owen and Heywood, 1990). Manufacturing is a different language, and failure to appreciate its vocabulary creates the kind of communications gap that Burns and Stalker (1961) found in their study of innovation in the Scottish electronics industry.

There has been some debate about the levels of mathematics that should be used. For example, Elger, Beyerlein and Budwig (2000) considered that their Design Build and Test (DBT) project for engineering students was *"unusual because of the extensive use of science and math to guide design efforts prior to construction."*
Another way of viewing Perkins theory of knowledge as design that comes from this third principle of learning by doing is to view the learner as designer. Impelluso and Metoyer (2000) reported that an introductory mechanical engineering course at San Diego State University was being remodeled around this strategy. They found support for this approach in that others had researched and implemented this strategy. The variation they introduced was the concept of the student as "instructional designer." In support of this approach, they cited the view proffered by Palthepu, Greer, and McCalla (1991) that *"knowledge seems to reinforced and internalized when the learner is put in the place of the teacher."* Impelluso and Metoyer argued that instructional design is a sub-set of design that is consistent with Perkins theory. They therefore set up an

---

[32] It is, equally, an important point in the study of learning and merits research.

experiment in which two groups of students were asked to complete a project in virtual reality, after they had received 13 weeks of instruction in the design, manufacturing, and analysis of structures. The instructions to the two groups are shown in Exhibit 12.5. The experimental group had to design a tutorial. It was predicted that the students in this group would show more positive affective development, as measured by level of confidence, and more positive conceptual knowledge than students in a control group. In a study that must be regarded as exploratory because of the small numbers involved, it was found that the experimental group gained significantly in their conceptual understanding when compared with the control group. However, this was not the case in the affective domain. The investigators suggested that one explanation for this was that the experimental group had time to reflect on their weaknesses and misperceptions. This would naturally lead to less confidence, but this was compensated by the substantial increase in conceptual understanding and the reflective thinking that went with it.

With respect to the dvMockup and animation, the control group experienced a significant increase in confidence whereas the experimental group did not. The investigators suggested that this might have been due to the fact that it occurred after the design of instruction, and since this was the challenging part of the exercise the experimental group might not have had as much time as they needed to put into this component of the exercise. A little more detail, including illustrations, is given in a later paper (Impelluso and Metoyer-Guidry, 2001). In that paper they made the point, well understood in teacher education that projects/assignments need to be well organized and instructions and expectations clearly stated. They also suggested that students should receive some instruction and guidance on how to design educational artifacts. The exercise showed that the concept of the student as instructional designer is worth pursuing. It also lent support to Perkins theory.

3. *Target performances, not target information.* This led Perkins to advocate an objectives or, as it is now called, an outcomes approach to education.

4. *Add strategic knowledge.* He argued that the four design questions are strategic knowledge. They lead to an understanding of principles. For example, when you are stuck think of a model case that you can examine from all angles. Learn to summarize the strategic content that you are considering. He argued specifically that thinking skills should be taught and students led to an understanding of metacognition (Nickersen, Perkins and Smith, 1985; see also Heywood, 1996; Wales and Stager, 1990). There is certainly some awareness of this among those who teach engineering design, but whether or not they would go so far as to integrate the design process more formally with substantial instruction on learning how to learn is a different matter.

5. *Products rather than short answers.* Perkins wrote that *"a focus on design naturally favors products rather than short answers as the outcome of student activities"* (p. 217). This has implications for assessment. More generally, those who teach engineering design would accept this principle as axiomatic. Perkins made the important point that teaching needs to be "closed loop." That is to say, students need to get fairly immediate feedback about their work. This is particularly important where a premium is placed on learning by doing because one can often be led to faulty conclusions and these can become part of the repertoire of experience. Moreover, as has been argued, embedded experience may be inhibitive of innovation.

A.   Control group assignment.
design a wrench in proEngineer.
Once the design is complete, stress test the wrench using the finite element code, Macr/Mentat.
Next produce the wrench (brass and aluminium) using proManufacture.
Last, animate and advertise the wrench using dv/Mockup (a sharedmulti-user world).

B.   Experimental group assignment.
1..Design wrench in proEngineer.
2. Once the design is complete, stress test the wrench using the finite element code, Marc/Mentat.In addition design a tutorial for upper level students who wanted to learn how to use Marc/Mentat.
3. Produce the wrench (brass and aluminum) using proManufacture*.
4.Last, animate and advertise the wrench using dvMockup.

*the students were helped in this activity by upper-level students.

Exhibit 12.5. The work assigned to the experimental and control groups in the learner as instructional designer experiment at San Diego State University (Impelluso and Metoyer, 2000). (Reproduced with permission of IEEE, *Proceedings Frontiers in Education Conference.*)

Perkins philosophy applied to engineering design is a theory of knowledge developed by a psychologist interested in learning that lends much support to what is already being accomplished in engineering design. Moreover, for those who teach design and who want to substantiate it with a theory, then that theory is likely to be grounded in an epistemology, and this would seem to be the underlying principle behind Koen's engineering method. The consolation is that any attempt at an epistemology is bound to be controversial!

12.5.   Koen's Behavioral Approach to the Teaching of Design.

Koen (1985, 1994) like Venable (1988), was among those who in the 1970s took a substantial interest in individualized instruction and was influenced by the work of Keller (see Chapter 14). The psychology of learning that they advocated was that of behaviorism, and they applied it to design.

Koen (1994) presented a development of his heuristic-based engineering method that began with the view that *"design is doing something, it is behaviour."* In this very broad sense it is a process, and that usage of the word is probably acceptable to most. If it is narrowly interpreted, as some people believe Skinner does, then for many teachers it will not be acceptable because it leads to a very confined approach to instruction and numerous statements of outcomes. But to begin at the beginning, Koen, argued that design is a *"repertoire of behaviours that are interdependent and interconnected in complex ways"*. For example, *"Complex behaviors control the amount of risk the engineer is willing to take. An engineering design is always dependent on the amount of resources available and this implies a complex set of trade-offs to determine the appropriate behaviors to allocate these resources. Finally, engineers typically solve problems of interest to humans and must find the correct desires of the client."*

Koen argued that the collection of behaviors that engineers have differs fundamentally from one engineer to the next and from one country to the next. He cited differences between American and Japanese approaches to the solution of problems. Differences between the United Kingdom and the United States in approaches to design education are evident in the literature and can be accounted for by the historical/cultural context in which they were developed. It seems fairly clear that these behaviors are both cognitive and affective (i.e., attitudinal). Koen went on to argue that the set of behaviors that a student has are different from those that a professional has. The engineer's approach to design is fundamentally different to that of the student. This is of course similar to the understanding that has emerged from the research on experts and novices, and this is why the work by Atman and her associates on student approaches to design is so important. Koen argued that because this is the case, the purpose of teaching engineering design is to *"develop a strategy for changing the repertoire of design behaviors of the student to that of an acceptable professional engineer,"* to which he added, *"using behavior modification."* He then attempted to demonstrate the relationship between design and behavioral analysis with the aid of three concepts.

His starting point was Thorndike's law of effect that states that *"behavior is modified by its consequences."* It is very similar to Pavlov's dogs. If we like something as a result of a particular 'behavior,' we are likely to repeat that behavior. If we don't like the outcome, we won't repeat it. Koen pointed out that in teaching engineering design, instructors are lax in their response to deadlines, yet in engineering it is important to meet deadlines, and this is an appropriate behavior that should be reinforced in teaching. *"A good design engineer should have a fallback position in case of an emergency. A good design engineer should not delay work on the project until the last minute when failure can spell disaster."* Underlying this issue is the problem of how much of attitudes acquired in school and college do we take with us into employment. It may be more than we care to admit. Koen suggested that the student group *"that is able to anticipate problems, and complete the project in spite of set-backs should receive higher grades."*

Koen examined the conditions for reinforcement. There are a number of basic schedules. *Continuous* describes the schedule when the behavior is rewarded every time it is used. A *fixed ratio schedule* will reward the performance after the behavior has been observed for a fixed number of times. When this number is varied systematically or randomly, it is said to be a variable ratio schedule. A fixed interval schedule is when the reward is given after specified period of time. Koen cited the case of examinations. These are set at a fixed time, and one consequence of this is cramming. He also gave the example of a personalized system of instruction that showed how students speeded up their work as the appointed time for completion neared. Neither of these instances produces effective learning. He went on to apply this concept to the 'capstone' design course. *"We could plot some measure of student effort throughout the course, we would find that initially student behavior was low increasingly rapidly to culminate in an "all niter" near the end of the semester."* The likelihood is that given another project the students would repeat the same behavior. His experience of industry led him to believe that this 'scallop' could not wholly be removed but it could be lessened, and he suggested that design teams should be required to meet regularly each afternoon without any formal distractions. *"Theory predicts that since a good grade is contingent on the behavior of "working on the project," this behavior should quickly dominate the behavior of doing nothing during the hourly meeting."*

He also criticized design courses because they did not build up the complex repertoire of behavior of successive approximations (known as *shaping* or *differentiation*) required by designers. A one-off project did not do this. For example, students do not learn how to *"allocate resources to the parts of the project that need most work, but instead they allocate those resources to those parts of the project that are the most fun, the easiest and so forth"*. This can only be overcome by training for which reason the *"student must pass through the design process repeatedly with more and more complex problems"*.

Koen suggested the following heuristics for teaching design.[33] *Always give the best answer within available resources.*
1. *Attack the weak link.*
2. *Make small changes in the state-of-the-art.*

---

[33] They are detailed in his monograph on the engineering method (Koen, 1985).

3. *Use an engineering morphology as an heuristic to get started.*
4. *Keep up with current literature.*
5. Use science where appropriate.

Develop a solution by successive approximations. Koen appreciated that there were other theories of learning and *"that the future will bring a successful effort to apply them to engineering."* The emerging literature suggests that this is beginning to happen. It is a pity that the word 'behavior' creates such emotions because education is about changing 'people' behavior in the cognitive and affective domain. In the case of design, all that has been said leads the reader to the view that both students and teachers are being asked to change the ways they learn and teach. It is appropriate, therefore, to leave this section with one view of the behavioral changes required of students that was stimulated by the ideas of Koen and others. It is shown in Exhibit 12.6.

Original Behavior	Desired Behavior
"Formula grabbing"	Intuitive understanding
Compartmentalization of knowledge	Better vertical and horizontal integration and associative skills
Crisis mode time management (responsibility)(excuses for late work)	Time use planning
Expectations of "Textbook" problems with unique solutions (analytic formula-based approach)	Ability to deal with open ended problems/solutions - (synthesis/approach)
"Trial and error" approach to design	Methodical design process
Student as "student"	Student as preprofessional
Write a few notes now, decipher later	Organized lab notebook
Avoidance of information technology	Active use of same
Working as a lone individual	Working as an active member of a team

Exhibit 12..6. Targeted student behaviors and desired modification in an engineering design course due to G. C. Gerhard (1999). (Reproduced by kind permission of *IEEE Transactions on Education*)

12.6.   Models of the Engineering Design Process

The teaching of design is of necessity influenced by what teachers think the design process is. For example, Woodson (1966) in his *"Introduction to Engineering Design"* wrote that *"The engineer must hence maintain an organized approach to his work. The logical development of a task far surpasses a haphazard, intuitive one, because of the crucial importance of countless items of detail in the final success"* (p. 21, 1966).[34]

He went on to say that "problem solving" is the name given to procedures suggested for organizing the smaller units of engineering work. He called the larger units of engineering work "projects," and he went on to give a list of procedures for solving problems. One of these was the design process according to Asimow (1962). It comprised phases of analysis, synthesis, evaluation, decision, optimization, revision and implementation. Within his list he included one for law. It comprised phases of reject irrelevant material, translate and restate, and state legal issues (Ballantine, 1949). Surprisingly, Woodson (1966) included the Wallas (1926) model of the creative act (preparation, incubation, illumination, and elaboration). Other models cited included one used by the General Electric Corporation and another used by the Royal Military Academy.

In the same year Krick in his *"Introduction to Engineering and Engineering Design"* considered that problem solving was an integral part of the problem solving process. Krick argued that the design process was a five-phase procedure. These phases were *"problem formulation- the problem at hand is defined in a broad-detail free manner. Problem analysis- now it is defined in detail. The search, Alternative solutions are accumulated through inquiry, invention, research etc. Decision- the alternatives are evaluated, compared, and screened until the best solution evolves. Specification- the chosen solution is documented in detail"*[35].

It was this book that was recommended to teachers and students who took the JMB Engineering Science examination in the 1970s. As we saw in Chapters 9 and 10, many other models have been described including Wales and Stager's guided design method for problem solving and decision making.

However, such models are open to the criticism that they are not based on the analysis of actual design behavior. Such criticisms have come from both those working in engineering education and teachers of design and technology in primary (elementary) and high schools. The latter are particularly concerned because they lead to simple linear models that are used as the basis of assessment. Nevertheless, the models highlight important skills that are required in design, and research indicates the importance of such skills. The two approaches also highlight different aspects of the design process to which consideration must be given. In the paragraphs that follow, the debate that has been conducted about the assessment of design and technology programs in schools will be used to focus on these issues. Objections to assessment based on simple linear models are based on the view that design is more complex than the models

---

[34] He added *"every connected relay, switch, vacuum tube, and wire must be operating for a telephone call to go through; and very microscopic leak must be avoided in order to keep a refrigeration*

system in service." It is an easy task to update these examples to account for changes in teaching.

[35] His text included chapters on each of these phases. An interesting chapter is included on optimization of "your problem solving and decision making." Other chapters were included on modeling and computation.

suggest. Moreover, it involves extra rational processes. These views are supported by the studies of design problem behavior that have been and are being conducted in engineering education by Atman and her colleagues.

The development of design and technology curricula in schools encouraged the development of other models to those listed by Woodson. Johnsey (1995) identified seventeen such models, only one of which related generally to how designers think (i.e., Lawson, 1980). It is of interest to note that these particular models were developed in relation to Design and Technology curricula in England.

Johnsey classified these models by the process skills they sought to develop. He considered that those involved in design were: identifying, clarifying, specifying, researching, generating, selecting, modeling, planning, making, testing, modifying, and evaluating.

It is possible to criticize all these lists. Within the school curriculum in design and technology, the design process incorporates manufacturing, and this is the case with many projects in engineering education. Thus, in this respect they differ little from real-life situations to be found in industry. From an engineering perspective the inclusion of optimization in Johnsey's list might have been considered.

One of the most interesting models from the perspective of this text is due to the Engineering Council (1985). The Council recommended for problem solving in science and technology in primary (elementary) schools the following process; identifying and specifying market need; research and development; selection of the optimum solution from a number of options; more detailed design and material selection; manufacturing process defined; manufacturing processes implemented; trials; evaluations; and sale and use. It was not the only model to include selling. The *Technologie* curriculum in France required market research, manufacture, and sale. In that curriculum an attempt is made to integrate theory with practice (Murray, 1986). But the link with the consumer was tenuous in that it was based on custom designed questionnaires. Denton and McDonagh (2002) have shown how focus groups can be used in school and university to obtain a better user/designer interface (see Section 15.4).

Johnsey offered his own definitions of terms as follows: *"A **process** can be taken as a way of going about achieving an end and the separate parts of a process can be defined as **process skills**. If the 'end' is the solution to a practical, open-ended problem then, in a broad sense, it can be called the problem-solving process. If the 'end' is the fulfilment of a need or a designed product then the **design process** has been used. Clearly there are many circumstances in which design and problem-solving are the same thing".* He like other writers used these terms interchangeably. It is also evident that there is confusion about the creative process and the design process. His objective was to explore the way teachers think children go about designing and making. (This is different from finding out how children think they go about designing and making, which is the subject of the next section.)

He pointed out that most models tend to be linear. This is not surprising given Woodson's description of the design process. But Johnsey notes that there are one or two departures, as, for example, the cyclical model due to Kelly et al., (1987), and a loop model due to the Department of Education in England (DES, 1987). In practice as we saw in Chapters 10 and 11 experts, do not necessarily follow a linear approach.

The Assessment of Performance Unit (APU), a government organization, argued for an interactive model between theory and practice-practice being made. It was "described *as 'the interaction between thought and action"* (Kelly et al., 1987), and later as the interaction between head and hand" (Johnsey, 1995). Design and make are not separated but integrated functions. *"The model depicts a constant to-ing and fro-ing between thinking and doing. It is a theoretical model which would be almost impossible to observe in reality without knowing what pupils were thinking at all times. It does, however, provide a powerful view of what might happen when pupils design and make. It gives a new standpoint from which to take stock of the design process. It also provides a powerful argument for making assessments of the whole process of designing and making rather than just the parts of it which might easily be recorded in a written paper. This would almost certainly have been a strong motivating factor behind the creation of such a model by a body charged with developing assessment procedures in design and technology"* (Johnsey, 1995).

Johnsey argued that the model is "essentially linear." It separates some skills that, perhaps, should not be separated (i.e., drawing and the modeling of solids), and others seem to be out of the sequence described in Johnsey's model. But is it linear? To answer that question we have to know what the student is thinking. Is there a logical progression of thought in their thinking?

12.7.   The Complexity of Design and Extra Rational Behavior

In England, Jeffery (1991) argued that while these linear methodological approaches worked, they implied a *"a logical progression of thought which does not necessarily parallel the pattern of human thinking."* Puk (1995) would later argue that "thinking" implied an understanding of the irrational processes that contributed to design.

One danger is that some teachers might treat such models as a ritual and not an intellectual exercise. The problem is further complicated by the fact that teachers' have differing views of what design is, and may be influenced by assessment systems that are dominated by the need for product outcomes (McCormick and Davidson, 1996). Mittell and Penny (1997) also reported disfunctions between policy and practice, with teacher concentration being on product output.

Jeffery argued that one of the problems these models had was that they caused reports of design which were to be used for assessment purposes to conform to the model rather then to display what actually happened. Jeffery recorded that the Lawson (1980) model based on a scientific and operations research approach was used as a model for the development of design and technology syllabuses in the early years. However, Lawson had found that *"science students tended to start by trying to understand the problem, whereas the design students examined possible solutions."* This is analogous with the view that the problems of science and engineering design differ because they have to achieve different purposes (Powell, 1987), and in solving such problems, students have to tolerate ambiguity (Leifer, 1995). The approach to design in architecture is often cited in support of this case.

Given that students have differing dispositions to the way in which they wish to tackle problems and that some may behave as scientists and others as designers, then difficulties are created for the teacher of design, and especially for its assessment.

Citing Darke (1979) generation conjecture analysis model Jeffery argued that approaches to design education derived from this model were at odds with the approaches derived from linear-rational models. Darke's model *"indicates that pre-structuring-suggesting approximate solutions and the use of known solution types is an essential aspect of designing. The strength of his model lies firstly in the way in which a large number of possible solutions are reduced and made manageable; and secondly in the way in which it enables a start to be made in those situations where decisions can only be made once the principle of a solution is known."* Jeffery argued that it would have been helpful if examiners had attached more importance to the initial stages of design and made them more meaningful, and at the same time showed that evaluation was an integral part of the activity. It may be argued that the project planning assessments in JMB Engineering Science, taken together with the written paper requiring a design specification, met this requirement, as well as the requirement for evaluation sought by Jeffery (Carter, Heywood, and Kelly, 1986). Heywood has argued it could have been done better if formal teaching in design had been offered. However, Jeffery argued that designers did not begin by preparing a full list of all the factors to be considered. *"Instead, they reduced the number of possible solutions by fixing on a particular objective at the outset."* This finding does have implications for the way in which assessment procedures seek to assess capability in judging alternatives as part of the process, and not at the beginning of the process. The engineering science scheme attempted to do both. It also attempted, as Jeffery wanted, to assess the project as a whole and identify evidence of design thinking where it took place in a project. Jeffery looked for a way of recording *"the on-going interaction or 'dialogue' between ideas, modelled proposals, and critical evaluations."*

The value of recording or journaling in engineering design education has been highlighted by Cowan (1998). He demonstrated that this led students to an understanding of the "process" of engineering design. He showed that awareness of process improved the design of effective model structures: *"it is potentially creative to construct, in a particular situation, something of a dialogue between the description of the process and the reality of the process"* (p. 58, Cowan, 1998). Cowan reported that it had been necessary for the teachers to intervene especially when the description of the process did not conform with what the teacher observed them doing. *"If that proved to be so, the students had to stop their designing and fabricating activity, and had to rewrite a more accurate statement of the process in which they were now engaged in order to satisfy the tutor"* (p. 57, Cowan). Cowan pointed out that the students were being trained to reflect-in-action, but he also argued the case for "reflection for action" and this seems to be what Jeffery was seeking when he asked examiners to pay more attention to the initial part of the project. It would also seem that the approach adopted by Cowan would assist students to become more comfortable in dealing with ambiguity.

In Canada, Puk (1995) also criticized the linear–rational models. First they simplified what was a complex process, Second, they did not take into account the extra-rational element in design. In effect he was asking teachers to define what it is they mean by "thinking." He argued that an analogy with quantum theory best described "the true nature of designing." Following the Heisenberg principle Puk argued that it is not possible to know ahead of time what path the designer will follow (through his model). *"No two episodes of designing will ever be identical"*. As in quantum theory *"observation by a second party (e.g., the teacher or a peer) will have a significant effect on the path of the designer...."* His model is shown in Figure 12.3. It is presented in quantum analogical terms. The inner ring *"contains the central framework with which generalized rational processes (middle ring) and extra rational processes (outer ring) interact."*

The central framework is clearly a derivative from other models including Wallas (1926). It proposed that the design process *"moves through stages of dissonance, developing structure, finding resolution and generalizing to other situations."* Associated with each of these are specific skills (abilities). Puk noted that in the first stage the designer has to "decide" what it is he/she has to do in order to resolve the dissonance in the mind. Citing Wales, Nardi, and Stager (1990), he said that decision making is at the heart of the design process, and students would, therefore, need skill in recognizing opportunities for design in a given situation, being able to surface thoughts and feelings, developing a personal narrative, and defining problems. He recognized that there were many other sub-skills that could be chosen but these *"appeared to be the most important without over-taxing the working memory of the student."*

Dissonance is resolved by creating a structure or an "initial image." As the structure evolves, so the image may undergo change. Teaching and assessment strategies are required that facilitate that development. Again specific skills are required to accomplish this task. Puk considered them to be the ability to establish an image, to locate and obtain resources, to assess the adequacy of the resources and information (evaluation), and to record the data and continually refine the initial image.

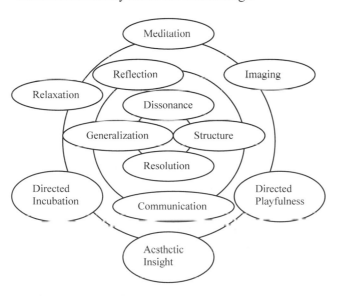

Figure 12.3. A Quantum design scheme due to T. PUK. In Creating a quantum design schema: Integrating extra-rational and rational learning process. (Reproduced with the permission of the *International Journal of Design and Technology Education, and Kluwer Academic Press.* 5, 255-266.)

Although creating structure involves resolution, Puk argued that it is a distinctive phase since it leads to the final resolution, and the process of evaluation is key. *"At some point of resolution, the designer will come to a suitable conclusion by developing a final sketch, drawing, 3D model, computer model etc. However, there will be a continuous process of evaluating that conclusion i.e. assessing the solution, predicting the viability and revising and refining where necessary. The student must then plan the production and actually make the final product."*

Puk did not consider that this is the end of the process because the product has to be evaluated if the overall experience is to lead to its use (transfer of learning) to other situations. Hence the term "generalization."

Clearly, these processes are influenced by other kinds of mental activity, more especially reflection. Puk distinguished between Schön's "reflection on practice" and "reflection in practice." However, as Jeffery pointed out, the stage of dissonance is part of the beginning and beginnings involve "reflection for action," as indeed

would any iterative process that involves evaluation. This would occur in all the phases of Puk's central framework. Thus, the middle ring requires the ability to reflect and communicate results.

The third ring *"consists of a number of processes which are thought to occur at the unconscious and pre-conscious levels of the mind"* (i.e., at the level of the extra-rational). It is these that provide a link to models of creativity such as those provided by Wallas (1926). Thus, before each design activity, all thoughts should be blocked out to create *"a quietness of the mind."* The student might then create images and models in the head. Imagery exercises might be used in this activity of meditation. No one, wrote Puk, *"can predict which extra-rational skill needs to be integrated with which rational skill."* Playfulness is important because it allows the students to make risk-free explorations." *The designer might playfully re-arrange the parts of the initial schema, through a kind of 'doodling' in order to create new associations. While this is going on, the designer must use his aesthetic insight to determine when the new associations feel right."*

There are times when the designer should do other things (relaxation) like listening to music, engaging in exercise, and so forth. It should help unconscious and conscious levels make their natural connections.

It might be suggested that such activities are the common experience of those who engage in creative work, as, for example, in writing. Puk's argument is that the importance of the extra-rational in design is seriously underestimated. There are several implications for teaching at school level that might apply in higher education, but of particular importance is the point that extra-rational processes of insight and intuition cannot be pressed into the limited periods of the traditional timetable. Similarly, not all these skills are likely to be developed when working in teams; therefore, there is an important place for individual projects in the curriculum because of this need (see also Chapter 10). Like other teachers he argued that ambiguity should be purposely sequenced into the curriculum. Puk's theory merits attention.

12.8.   Toward an Understanding of Design Problem Behavior

The investigations to be described in this section were undertaken at the Universities of Pittsburgh and Washington-Seattle during the last ten years. They had as their general objective the evaluation of teaching strategies in the light of information about student design behavior. They had as their specific objectives the identification of competencies that contributed to expert performance in design and the evaluation of the effectiveness of design courses in developing such courses. They took the view that iteration was an integral part of the design process. *"Iteration can be a goal-directed, non-linear process that utilizes heuristic reasoning processes and strategies to gather and filter information about the problem, and to inform the revision of possible solutions. A cyclical iterative design procedure is believed to be a natural feature of the designer's competency (Bucciarelli, 1996) and lead to better quality solutions (Hybs and Gero, 1990) Iteration can be a process of converting an ill-structured problem into a well-structured solution–a process which is often hidden in the final artifact"* (Adams and Atman, 1999).

An example of the iterative processes of interpretation, selection, and planning in design is given by Adams and Atman. They wrote, *"First the student accesses information to identify a stated design objective. Then, the student utilizes monitor and search strategies to identify alternatives. Next, the student organizes and examines these alternatives, integrating problem definition with alternative, selection, to specify and select a solution that best meets the design objective. Finally the student monitors the implementation of these solutions to verify that they will meet design objectives."*[36]

In the design model proposed by Adams and Atman the inputs are the information processing activities of accessing information; clarifying; monitoring progress and evaluating. These are used *"to justify decisions for implementing change to the design state"* i.e., the output in terms of process, problem representation, and solution. In arriving at the final design decision, a number of interim steps are taken each of which involves a decision and these steps are called *"Transition Behaviors."*[37] They are reasoning processes that guide output decisions on the basis of the knowledge inputs. Because they are reasoning processes, *"they can be classified as either diagnostic or transformative processes."* Adams and Atman made the point that design decisions may not always be based on that information.

Diagnostic processes can help with analysis and evaluation, and transformative processes with synthesis and the generation of new knowledge, as, for example, *"the generation of new alternatives based on a revised understanding of the problem."* Transition behaviors are important in design and the number of transitions used may distinguish between expert and novice designers. Atman and her colleagues have used verbal protocols to analyze the behavior of students in engineering design courses, and the paper by Adams and Atman (1999) had as its purpose the establishment of codes for the evaluation of transition behaviors. Examples from these codes are given in Exhibit 12.7.

Previously, Atman and Bursic (1998) and others[38] had shown how the protocol approach used by Ericcson and Simon (1993) and others suggested *"that experts tend to use decomposition (solving small portions of the problem) and opportunistic behavior (interspersing concept generation and information seeking) while developing their designs. They tend to begin with a concept from previous experience, and then decompose and adapt this potential solution until it satisfies the current problem specifications. Hence, experienced designers may accept less than the best possible solution. Also, they typically do not develop many alternatives while designing. Instead they tend to refine their original conceptual idea. While experts utilize decomposition they do not lose sight of the larger problem. Novice designers tend to spend little time gathering information and thinking about the problem in order to develop a "good" initial concept."*

However, Mullins, Atman and Shuman (1999) argued that relatively little had been learned from the earlier studies that would enable the question, *"Has the early introduction of engineering design improved students' capabilities?"* to be answered. This, they argued, was due to the *"inadequacy of traditional measures such as student attitudes and content knowledge to assess performance of a process skill like design."*

Therefore, Mullins, Atman, and Shuman (1999) undertook a study to evaluate the design behavior of freshmen students using verbal protocols and a written study. Seventy-six freshmen students participated in the study. Sixteen participated in a pre-semester protocol study in parallel with twenty students who completed the written study. Similar numbers contributed to the post semester study.[39] The subjects in the written study solved the same two problems as those in the protocol study but they did not speak aloud. While the protocol study was used to analyze the process and the quality of the solutions with time, a coding scheme for the analysis of the segments of the protocol was developed from a content analysis of seven engineering design texts, and this gave the steps in the design process shown in Exhibit 12.8. An expert panel validated lists of design criteria for each problem. One point was given for each criteria even if it was only mentioned. In addition, points were awarded for communications, explicit assumptions made, and technical accuracy.

"The quality of each student's final design was assessed for both problems. A master list of all subjects' solutions and physical features of each solution was developed for each problem. An expert panel then evaluated features of each alternative problem.... The experts' input was also used to develop weights to score the subjects' solutions

---

[36] This example is based on verbal protocol data that are given in the last part of the paper.

[37] They write, *"Transition behaviors capture the processes of making interim design decisions between steps of the design process in terms of information processing activities and decision activities. As reasoning processes that utilize information processing activities. As reasoning processes, transition behaviors can be classified as either diagnostic or transformative processes."*

[38] They cited Ennis and Gyeszly (1991); Ullman, Dietrich and Stauffer, (1988); Guidon, (1990); Christiaans and Dorst, (1992); Sutcliffe and Maiden.

[39] The study was not, therefore, a direct measure of gain.

relative to the features included. The experts made pairwise comparisons between all possible pairs of design solutions, dividing 100 points between the pairs for each comparison. The constant sum algorithm was then applied to these judgements in order to arrive at a set of relative weights.[40] *Subjects then received a score based on the sum of the weights of the "necessary" features they included in the final solution."*

The differences between the two protocol groups were assessed by word counts, the number of transitions between design steps, and the quality of the process scores. If the number of words is taken as a measure of the amount of effort, then the post-semester group contributed more effort to the solution of the problems. Similarly, post-semester students used a more iterative design process than the pre-semester students.

Mullins, Atman and Shuman (1999) illustrated the time lines for one of the problems. Pre-semester students followed the sequence Define the problem, generate alternatives, and analyzes whereas, post-semester students Defined the problem, generated alternatives, defined the problem again, generated alternatives again and analyzed. *"The most typical strategy used by pre-semester subjects (six of sixteen) was to complete only one transition, from problem definition to generate alternatives. The most typical strategy used by post-semester subjects (five of the fifteen) was three transitions. Also the maximum number of transitions for a pre-semester subject was eight compared to 18 for a post-semester subject."*

Overall the investigators concluded that after one semester the students were better unstructured problem solvers. Insofar as the "quality of the product" was concerned, no significant differences were found between the pre- and post-semester students in either the protocol or the written study. However, there was a significant difference between the protocol and written students quality in favor of the written students. The investigators considered that this was probably due to the fact that those engaged in the written study produced more detailed diagrams than those who contributed to the protocols.

A third question was set to evaluate skill in defining the problem. It read, *"Over the summer the Midwest experienced massive flooding of the Mississipi River. What factors would you take into account in designing a retaining wall system for the Mississipi?"* More design criteria were mentioned by post than pre-semester students in both the protocol and written studies. While the semester had a developmental effect on student outcomes, it did not affect the quality of the solutions. The investigators thought that there were four possible explanations for these results. First, the course may not have contained content that was sufficient for the students to develop better solutions. Second, the evaluation measures may not have been sufficiently sensitive to detect differences. Third, more time might have been required for the production of better solutions. Fourth, the type of problem set may not have produced effects that could be documented.

To counter the argument, that the other courses that the students took in calculus, chemistry, physics and the humanities might have contributed to the observed effects, the authors drew attention to the Atman and Bursic study (see above). This had shown that measurable effects on the student design process occurred after students had read a short text on engineering design. In their study of the effects of textbooks on learning, Atman and Bursic (1996) had also used verbal protocol analysis. They found that those students who read textbooks exhibited more complex design processes than those who had not. *"They spent longer solving the problems, generated more alternatives, transitioned more frequently between design steps, and considered more criteria than those who did not respond to the text."*[41]

Example of a transition behavior for information processing
Clarifying strategies.
Clarify. Requests for information to understand the problem.
Organize. Arrange information into categories or map objectives to possible solutions.
Examine. Analyze accuracy, quality, or completeness of a solution.
Example of a transition behavior for decision activities.
Changes to problem definition.
Identify. Identify or describe constraints, objectives, and violations.
Redefine. Alter initial representation by changing or elaborating constraints and objectives.

Exhibit 12.7. Examples of transition behaviors for information processing and decision activities. The other information processing activities were Monitoring strategies (Monitor and Reflect); Accessing strategies (Access, Search); Evaluating Strategies (Evaluate, Verify). The other transition behavior activities were Changes to process (Plan); Changes to solution (Modify, Improve, Integrate); Selection of solution (Capture, Select, Specify). From Adams and Atman (1999) (Reproduced with permission of *IEEE, Proceedings Frontiers in Education Conference*).

Define the problem: goals and objectives of the problem are determined, assumptions are made and requirements and constraints are noted.
Generate alternative solutions: the brainstorming of ideas and developing these ideas into broad solutions to the problem.
Analysis: comparison of alternatives based on economic, social and safety considerations and checking the solution against requirements and constraints.
Selection: considering the tradeoffs involved in the choice of one alternative over another.

Exhibit 12.8 Steps in the design process identified by Mullins, Atman and Shuman (1999) that were used for the protocol analysis. Because the student's completed the problems in a single session in the laboratory, the design steps of information gathering, communication and implementation were not included in the analysis. *IEEE, Transactions on Education*, 42, (4), p 282). (Reproduced with permission of *IEEE Transactions on Education*)

---

[40] See Guilford (1954).

[41] As quoted by Mullins, Atman and Shuman, 1999.

Using the Missisipi problem, Bogusch, Turns and Atman (2000) quantified differences between freshmen and seniors in solving design problems. They wished to examine the breadth that freshmen and seniors brought to the solving of problems ("problem scoping" as they call it). They were particularly concerned to develop and evaluate a coding scheme and this paper presented the preliminary analysis only. In this case the students were given an unlimited amount of time to solve the problem while thinking aloud. The coding scheme used for the analysis embraced two dimensions. These were codes for physical location (i.e., wall, water, bank, and shore) and four frames of reference (i.e., technical, logistical, natural, and social). The latter dimension was included to discover whether senior students identified more technical factors than freshmen. A preliminary analysis was undertaken. Fifteen freshmen at the beginning of their first semester, and 10 mechanical engineering seniors who had not taken part in earlier studies participated.[42] The preliminary analysis revealed that the range in the number of statements was 11 to 75 for the senior's and 4 to 22 for the freshmen. The number of subject statements varied more for the seniors than it did for the freshmen. The average number of coded statements by the students who would consider in designing a retaining wall for physical location was 34 by the seniors and 11 by the freshmen. For technical statements the average number made was 15 by the seniors and 4 by the freshmen. *"A difference between the two groups was seen, however, as more seniors considered design factors relating to the bank and the shore, and more seniors considered logistical and social issues."*

Technically, they found that the evaluation of whether one statement is an exact repetition of another statement can promote difficulties. Youngman et al., (1978) had the same problem in their study of engineers at work, in which they used statements from interviews to design a work study instrument for evaluation by cluster analysis (see Chapter 2). The intention of Atman and her colleagues was to further the evaluation of the quality of the statements, to establish the number of unique statements made by each respondents, and to analyze the specific design factors identified.

Another approach to understanding how students design was described by Brockman (1996). There are some similarities with his study and the work undertaken by Atman and her colleagues. He wanted to establish how sophomore students spent their time during design projects in a course on computer programming. Using surveys in an unusual way, he found that there was a strong negative correlation between design time and the number of heuristics used, and that the more successful programmers produced stronger conceptual designs for their programs before implementation. However, the survey was limited by the fact that it was undertaken after the project was completed. Moreover, it was difficult to accurately determine the distribution of time among the tasks. The survey had little to say about the effects of iteration and repetition. To overcome these difficulties, Brockman developed a model for software development in which student tasks (duration of) and transitions could be calibrated against those used by a designer directly from a computer analysis of what the student was doing while designing the program. The results of an experiment to validate the model suggested a correlation between the amount of time spent on conceptual design and the likelihood of iteration. When he wrote that paper, he had not found a way of effectively transferring that knowledge to the students so that they became more effective designers.

It is evident that Atman and her colleagues, as well as others, are developing powerful tools for the analysis of student behavior in design work, and that this should lead to a better understanding of the instructional processes best suited for developing student design competencies.

12.9.   In Conclusion

There has been continuing debate about whether or not design should be taught and, indeed, whether or not it can be taught within the engineering curriculum. Those who have argued the case for design are on the ascendancy, at least in the United States. It is important to remember that those developments that have taken place in other countries have done so as a particular function of their engineering cultural history. Thus the reasons for, and contents of, new courses in design, or the inclusion of design within existing courses, differ from country to country. Nevertheless, there are some features that are common to many of these courses irrespective of the cultural imperative. There is, for example, the pressure from industry to produce engineers who are to work, with little extra training, on real-world "wicked" problems and to bring a capability for work in teams. Thus, team project-design work became a feature of many design courses. However, in the absence of evidence to the contrary, there remains a case for individual projects to help with the development of skill in reflective thinking.

In the United States the need to retain able students for engineering after the freshmen year led to the introduction design courses in that year. By involving students in the solution of real-life problems it was hoped they would integrate knowledge learned in other courses and see its relevance to engineering. Thus they were, encouraged to find an identity with engineering and engineers. Such evaluations as have been published suggest that they have been successful in achieving these aims. They also show, as do many anecdotes, that

---

[42] The freshmen were chosen because previous work (research by Mullins, Atman and Shuman, 1999) *had shown them most likely to have the "worst" performance. The mechanical engineering seniors were selected because previous work* (Bursic and Atman, 1997) *had shown that this group out performs other groups at the information gathering stage of solving design problems, and therefore are most likely to have the "best" performance."*

participation in such courses, irrespective of level, demands a considerable change in the role and attitudes of both students and teachers. Teachers become guides and students discoverers, and there is as much attention to process as there is to product.

At the same time, some engineering educators have engaged in the search for a theoretical basis for the discipline of design. Several models have been proposed. Research on the thinking processes of experts and novices is likely to make a significant contribution to this debate. There is evidence that suggests that engineering educators would benefit from research on the teaching (and learning) of design and technology in schools. The application of linear models of the design process in school studies has thrown up a number of questions about the role of such models in the curriculum. Non linear models that take into account the extra-rational in design have been developed.

Another common feature is the enormous variety in the approaches that have been adopted for the teaching of design within different cultures irrespective of level. As with engineering project work, there are one or two cases where the department concerned has designed the whole program so that project activities are included in each year with objectives appropriate to that year. Inspection of Sheppard's model that locates the type of freshmen courses in four quadrants has many similarities with the Kolb learning styles. While projects are likely to cater for all learning styles, it is of some import to know exactly how they do this and if there are tendencies to favor some styles at the expense of others. Sheppard (2002) argued that students should experience activities in each of the four quadrants of her model during the four years of their programs.[43] Her argument would be reinforced if the chosen projects could be related to the stages of student development, as, for example, those described by King and Kitchener (1994) or Perry (1970)

References

Adams, R. S., and C. J. Atman (1999). Cognitive processes in iterative design behavior. *Proceedings Frontiers in Education Conference*, 11a6-13-11 to 18.

Ahlgren, D. J (2001). Fire-fighting robots and first year engineering design: Trinity College experience. *Proceedings Frontiers in Education Conference*, 3, S2E- 1 to 6.

Anderson-Rowland, M. I (1998). The effect of course sequence on the retention of freshmen engineering students: When should the introductory engeering course be offered? *Proceedings Frontiers in Education Conference*. 252-257.

Angelov, M. A., Friedman, M. B., and A. A. Renshaw (1999). Introducing engineering design into the first year curriculum. *Proceedings Frontiers in Education Conference*, 12 a6- 7 to 11.

Asimow, M (1962). *Introduction to Design*. Prentice Hall, Englewood Cliffs.NJ

Atman, C. J., and K. M. Bursic (1996). Teaching engineering design. Can reading a textbook make a difference. *Research in Engineering Design*, 8, 240–250.

Atman, C. J., Chimka, J. R., Bursic, K. M. and H. L. Nachtman (1999). A comparison of freshmen and senior engineering design processes. *Design Studies*, 20, (2), 131–152.

Bailey, J. D., and M. Hill (1998). The use of a hypermedia system to develop confidence in engineering design. *International Journal of Mechanical Engineering Education*. 26, (2), 111-125.

Ballantine, H. W (1949). *Ballantine's Problems in Law*. 3rd Ed. West Publishing, St. Paul, Minnesota.

Barnes, L. B (1960). *Engineers and Organizational Groups*. Harvard University, School of Business Administration.

Ben-Arroyo, A. F (1979). Creative design education. *Proceedings Frontiers of Education Conference*, 414–417.

Blyth, W. A. L (1993). Subsidiarity in education: the example of British primary humanities. *The Curriculum Journal*. 4, (2),283–294

Blyth, W. A. L., Derricott, R., Elliott, G. F., Summer, H. M., and A. Waplington. (1973). *History, Geography, and Social Science, 8-13, An Interim Statement*. Schools Council Project. University of Liverpool.

Blicblau, A. S., and J. M. Steiner (1998). Fostering Creativity through engineering projects. *European Journal of Engineering education*.

Bogusch, L. I., Turns, J., and C. J. Atman (2000). Engineering design factors: how broadly do students define problems. *Proceedings Frontiers in Education Conference*, 3, S3A-7 to 12.

Brereton, M., Sheppard, S., and L. Leifer (1995). Students connecting engineering fundamentals and hardware design: observations and implications for the design of curriculum and assessment methods. *Proceedings Frontiers in Education Conference*. 4d3-1-4d3-7.

Brockham, J. B (1996). Evaluation of student design procedures. *Proceedings Frontiers in Education Conference*, 189-193.

Bruner, J., Jolly, A., and K. Sylver (eds.) (1976). *Play: its role in Development and Evolution*. Harmonsdworth, Penguin.

Bucciarelli, L. L (1996). *Designing Engineers*. MIT Press. Cambridge, MA

Burns, T and G. Stalker (1961). *The Management of Innovation*. Tavistock, London.

Bursic, K. M., and C. J. Atman (1997). Information Gathering: A critical step for quality in the design process. *Quality Management Journal*. 4, (4), 60-75.

Carnahan, J. V., Thurston, D. L., and R. L. Ruhl (1992). Experiences with an industrially sponsored project course. *Proceedings Frontiers in Education Conference*, 219–223.

Carter, G., Heywood, J.,, and D. T. Kelly (1986). *A Case Study in Curriculum Assessment. GCE Engineering Science (Advanced)*. Roundthorn, Manchester.

Che, X., and G. Zhang (1999) Development of an on-line teaching portfolio for freshman design. *Proceedings Frontiers in Education Conference*. 13b1-26 to 30.

Christiaans, H. H. C. M., and K. H. Dorst (1992). Cognitive models in industrial design engineering. A protocol study. *Design Theory and Methodology*. 42, 131–140.

Coleman, R. J. and J. W. Shelnutt (1995). Fostering university/university partnerships. *Proceedings Frontiers of Education Conference*, 2a1-8 to 11.

Collier, K et al., (1995). Corporate structure in the classroom: a model for teaching engineering design. *Proceedings Frontiers in Education Conference* 2a2.-5 to 9.

Courter, S. L. S (1996). A grounded theory of the positive attributes of a TQM curriculum innovation. A multi-case study of a cross-disciplinary course in engineering. Doctoral dissertation. University of Wisconsin – Madison.

Courter, S. L. S., Millar, S. B., and L. Lyons (1998). From the student's point of view: experiences in a freshman engineering design course. *Journal of Engineering Education*, 87, (3), 283–288.

Cowan, J (1983). How engineers understand: an experiment for author and reader. *Engineering Education* (January), 301 – 304.

Cowan, J (1998). On becoming an Innovative University Teacher. *Reflection in Action*, SRHE/Open University Press, Buckingham.

Cresswell, J. W (1998). *Qualitative Inquiry and Research Design. Choosing Among Five Traditions*. Sage, Thousand Oaks, CA.

Cross, J (1989). *Engineering Design Methods*. Wiley, Chichester.

Culver, R. S., and D. Scudder (1995). Lessons learned on using adaptive devices for the disabled to teach design. *Proceedings Frontiers in Education Conference*, 2c3-12 to 15.

Darke, J (1999). The primary generator and the design process. *Design Studies*. 1, (1), 38.

Davies, D (1996). Professional design and primary children. *International Journal of Technology and Design Education*, 6, 45–59.

---

[43] She illustrated this point with reference to a proposal for a mechanical engineering curriculum at Stanford University.

Dekker, D. L (1996). The difference between "open-ended projects" and "design projects". *Proceedings Frontiers in Education Conference,* 3, 1257-1259.

Deere, M (1967). Creative projects in university engineering. *New University*, 1, 30.

Denton, H., and D. McDonagh (2003). Using focus group methods to improve students' designproject research inschools drawing parallels from action research at undergraduate level. *International Journal of Technology and Design Education.* 13, 129-144.

Denayer, I., Thaels, K., Vander Sloten, J., and R. Gobin (2003). Teaching a structured approach to the design process for undergraduate engineering students by problem-based education. *European Journal of Engineering Education*, 28, (2), 203- 214.

de Simone, D. V (ed.) (1968). *Education for Innovation.* Pergamon, Oxford.

Dekker, L. D (1996). The difference between "open ended projects" and "design projects". *Proceedings Frontiers in Education Conference*, 1257–1259.

DES (1987). *Craft Design and Technology 5 to 16.* HMSO, London.

Donaldson, M (1978). *Children's Minds.* Fontana Press, Glasgow.

De Vault, J. E (1998) A competition: Motivated interdisciplinary design experience. *Proceedings Frontiers in Education Conference.* 460-465.

Dym, C. L (1993). The role of symbolic representation in engineering design education. *IEEE Transactions on Education.* 36, (1), 187 – 183.

Dym, C. L (1994a). *Engineering Design. A Synthesis of Views.* Cambridge University Press., New York.

Dym, C. L (1994b). Teaching design to freshmen: style and content. *Journal of Engineering Education*, 83, (4), 303–310.

Dym, C. L., Sheppard, S. D., and J. W. Wesner (2001). Dsigning design education for the 21 at century. *Journal of Engineering Education*, 90, (3), 291–294.

Easterby-Smith, M (1994) *Evaluating management Development, Training and Eduction.* 2nd Edition, Gower, Aldershot.

Eder, W. E (1988) Education for engineering design- application of design science. *International Journal of Applied Engineering Education.* Special issue on Engineering design 167–184.

Elger, F., Beyerlein, S. W., and R. S. Budwig (2000) Using design, build and test projects to teach engineering. *Proceedings Frontiers in Education Conference*, 2, F£C-9 to 13.

Engineering Council, Standing Conference on Schools Science and Technology (1985*). Problem Solving: Science and technology in primary Schools.* The Design Council, London.

Ennis, C. W., and S. W. Gyeszly (1991). Protocol analysis of the engineering systems design process. *Research in Engineering Design*, 3, (1), 15–22.

Ericsson, K. A., and H. A. Simon (1993). *Protocol Analysis: Verbal Reports as Data.* MIT Press, Cambridge, MA.

Ernst, E. W., and J. R. Lohmann (1990). Designing undergraduate design curricula. *Engineering Education*, 80, (5), 543–547.

Evans, D. L., McNeill, B. W., and G. C. Beakley (1990). Design in engineering education: past views of future directions. *Engineering Education.* 80, (5), 517–522.

Ewing, P. D (1987). *Curriculum Development Report on Industrial Design Engineering.* The Design Council, United Kingdom.

Farrell, S., Hesketh, R. P., and C. S. Slater (1999). Investigation of the brewing process. An introduction to reverse process engineering and design in the freshman clinic at Rowan University. *Proceedings Frontiers in Education Conference*, 12b4–14 to 18.

Finelli, C. J (1999). A team-oriented, project based freshmen problem solving course: benefits of an early exposure. *Proceedings Frontiers in Education Conference,* 11a2–26-11a2–30.

French, M (1991). Design insight and technical confidence in R. A. Smith (ed.). *Innovative Teaching in Engineering.* Ellis Horwood, Chichester.

Gerhard, G. C (1999). Teaching design with behavior modification techniques in a pseudo-corporate environment. *IEEE Transactions on Education*, 42, (4), 255–261.

Grinter Committee (1955) Final report on the Evaluation of Engineering Education. *Engineering Education* 46, 25

Grulke, E. A., Beert, D. C., and D. R. Lane (2001). The effects of physical environment on engineering team performance: A case study. *Journal of Engineering Education,* 90, (3), 319-330.

Guilford, J (1954). *Psychometric Methods.* McGraw Hill, New York.

Guindon, R (1990) Designing the design process: exploring opportunistic thoughts. *Human-Computer Interaction* 5, 305–344.

Henderson, J. M (1980). Yes, design can be taught. *Engineering Education.* 71, (4), 302.

Heywood, J (1996). An engineering approach to teaching decision making skills in schools using an engineering heuristic. *Proceedings Frontiers in Education Conference,* 1, 67–73.

Holt, J. E., and D. F. Radcliffe (1984). The mechanical design course at the University of Queensland- philosophy and practice. *International Journal of Mechanical Engineering Education*, 13, (2), 275-280.

Hoole, S. R. H (1991). Engineering education, design, and senior projects. *IEEE Transactions on Education.* 34, (2), 193–197.

Hurst, K. S., and James, R. D., and M. Raines (199?). The progressive use of projects in an engineering design course. *International Journal of Mechanical Engineering Education*, 21, 94), 371–379.

Hybs, I., and J. S. Gero (1992). An evolutionary process model of design. *Design Studies*, 13, (3), 273.

I. Mech. E (1962). *Experiments in Graduate Training.* Institution of Mechanical Engineers, London.

Impelluso, T., and T. Metoyer (2000) Virtual reality and learning by design: tools for integrating mechanical engineering projects. *Proceedings Frontiers in Education Conference*, 2, F3C-14 to 19.

Impelluso, T., and T. Metoyer-Guidry (2001). Virtual reality and learning by design. Tools for integrating mechanical engineering concepts. *Journal of Engineering Education.* 90, (4), 527–534.

Jarvis, N., and N. Quick (1995). Innovation in engineering education: The 'PAMS' project. *Studies in Higher Education.* 20, (2), 173-185.

Jeffery, J. R (1991). An investigation of systematic design methods in craft, design and technology (CDT). *International Journal of Technology and Design Education.* 1, (3), 141–151.

Johnsey, R (1995). The design process- does riot exist? A critical review of published models for the design process in England and Wales. *International Journal of Technology and Design Education*, 5, 199–217.

Kelly, A. V et al (1987). *Design and Technological Activity- A Framework for Assessment.* APU/HMSO, London.

King, P. M., and K. S. Kitchener (1974). *Developing Reflective Practice.* Jossey Bass, San Francisco.

Kitto, K. L 2001). Integrating creative design experiences and ethics into materials science. *Proceedings Frontiers in Education Conference*, T2C-8 to 12.

Knight, D. et al (1999). An evaluation of a design team facilitator training program for engineering upper classes*. Proceedings Frontiers in Education Conference*, 13b2-6 to 11.

Koen, B. V (1985). *Definition of the Engineering Method.* ASEE, Washington. DC

Koen, B. V (1994). Toward a strategy for teaching design. *Journal of Engineering Education,* 83, (3), 193–202.

Kosslyn, S. M (1978). Imagery and cognitive development. A teleological approach in R. Siegler, (ed.). *Children's Thinking. What develops?* Lawrence Erlbaum, Hillsdale, NJ

Krick, E. V (1966). *An Introduction to Engineering and Engineering Design.* Wiley, New York.

Kuhn, S (1998). The software design studio. An Explanation. *IEEE Software* 15, (2), 65–71.

Kumar, V., Kinzel, G., Wei, S., Bengu, G., and J. Zhou (2000). Multi-university design projects. *Journal of Engineering Education.* 89, (3), 353–360.

Lawson, B. R (1980). *How Designers Think.* Architectural Press, London.

Leifer, L (1995). Remarks made at the International Workshop on project Basec Learning. Aug 7–10. Stanford University.

Linde, C., Roschelle, J., and R. Stevens (1994). Innovative assessment for innovative engineering education. Video based interaction analysis.

A method for assessment and improvement of the synthesis curriculum. Report to the NSF Synthesis Coalition. Institute for research on Learning. Palo Alto, CA.

Little, P., and M, Cardenas (2001). The use of "studio" methods in the introductory engineering design curriculum. *Journal of Engineering Education*. 90, (3), 309-318.

Lyons, H. I., And G. A. Messick (1993). Science and engineering design: integrating the freshman experience. *Proceedings Frontiers in Education Conference*, 61 – 64.

McCardle, J. R (2002). The challenge of integrating AI and smart technology in design education. *International Journal of Technology and Design Education*. 12, (1), 59–76.

McCaulley, M. H (1990). The MBTI and individual pathways in engineering design. *Engineering Education*. 80, (5), 537–542.

McCormick, R., and M. Davidson (1996) Problem solving and the tyranny of product outcomes. *Journal of Design and Technology Education*. 1, (3), 230–241.

McCreanor, P. J. et al (2002). Introducing fundamental design concepts in a freshman design course. *Proceedings Frontiers in Education Conference*, 3, S1D-10 to 15.

MacMurray, J (1957). *The Self as Agent*. Faber and Faber, London.

Marra, R. M., and T. Wheeler (2000). The impact of an authentic student-centred engineering project on student motivation. *Proceedings Frontiers in Education Conference*, F2C-8 to 13.

Mickelburgh, N. C., and D. G. Wareham (1994). Teaching engineering to increase motivation. *Journal of Professional Issues in Engineering Education and Practice*, 120, 29–35.

Miller, G., and W. Hyman (1989) Undergraduate bio-engineering projects applied to real world problems for the handicapped. *International Journal of Applied Engineering Education*. 5, (4), 451–456.

Mittell, I., and A. Penny (1997). Teacher perceptions of design and technology. A study of disjunction between policy and practice. *International Journal of Technology and Design Education*. 7, 279–293.

Monk, J. D (1972) An investigation into the role of the design function in the education and training and career patterns of professional mechanical engineers. Thesis. University of Lancaster Library, Lancaster.

Monk, J. D., and J. Heywood (1977) The education and career patterns of professional mechanical engineers in design and management. *The Vocational Aspect of Education*, 29, (72), 5-16.

Moore, D and F. Berry (1999). Industrial sponsored design projects addressed by student design teams. *Proceedings Frontiers in Education Conference*, 11b2–15 to 20.

Moore, P et al (1999). A comparison of freshman and seniors engineering design processes. *Design Studies*. 20, (2), 131-152

Mullins, C. A., Atman, C. J., and L. J. Shuman (1999) Freshman engineers' performance when solving design problems. *IEEE Transactions on Education* 42, (4), 281–287.

Murray, M (1986). Recent developments in the school curriculum in France in J. Heywood and P. Matthews (eds.). *Technology, Society, and the School Curriculum. Practice and Theory in Europe*. Roundthron, Manchester.

Muster, D., and F. Mistree (1989). Engineering design as it moves from an art to a science. Its import on the education process. *Proceedings World Conference on Engineering Education for Advancing Technology* (Sydney), 751–755.

Nickerson, R., Perkins, D.W., and E. Smith (1985). *The Teaching of Thinking*. Lawrence Erlbaum Associates, Hillsdale, NJ

Nicol, R. W. (1989). Managing industry sponsored undergraduate design projects. *Proceedins World Conference on Engineering Education for Advancing Technology*. Sydney 756.

Olds, B. M., Pavelich, M. J., and F. R. Yeats (1990). Teaching the design process to freshmen and sophomores. *Engineering Education*, 80, (5), 554–560.

Owen, S., and J. Heywood (1990). Transition technology in Ireland: An experimental course. *International Journal of Technology and Design Education*, 1, (1), 21–32.

Page, D. R (1989). Design studies as a technological integrator. *Prodeedings World Conference on Engineering Education for Advancing Technology* (Sydney) 579–581.

Pahl, G., and W. Beitz (1988) in K. Wallace (ed). *Engineering Design. A Systematic Approach*. The Design Council. Springer Verlag.

Palthepu, S., Greer, G., and G. McCalla (1991). Learning by teaching in L. Birnbaum (ed). *Proceedings of International Conference on Learning Systems*. ERIC document reproduction service – ED 343 560 p. 357.

Perkins, D. N (1986). *Knowledge as Design*. Lawrence Erlbaum, Hillsdale, NJ

Perry, W (1970). *Forms of Intellectual and Ethical Development in the College Years: A Scheme*. Holt Rinehart and Winston, Troy, MO.

Polkinghorne, D. G (1989). Phenomological Research Methods. In R.S. Valle and S. Halling, (Eds.) *Existential-Phenomological Perspective in Psychology*. Plenum Press.

Powell, J. A (1987). Is architectural design a trivial pursuit? *Design Studies*, 8, (4), 191.

Puk, T (1995). Creating a quantum design schema: integrating extrarational and rational learning processes. *International Journal of Technology and Design Education*. 5, 255–266.

Roth, W. M. (1996). Learning to talk engineering design: results from an interpretive study in a Grade 4/5 classroom. *International Journal of Technology of Technology and Design Education*, 6, 107–135.

Schön, D (1983). *The Reflective Practitioner*. Basic Books, New York.

Schumacher, J., and G. A. Gabriele (1999). Product design and innovation: a new curriculum combining the humanities and engineering. *Proceedings Frontiers in Education Conference* 11a6–19-11a6–24.

Seymour, E and N. M. Hewitt (1997). *Talking About Leaving. Why Undergraduates Leave the Sciences*. Westview Press, Boulder, CO.

Sheppard, S (1992). Mechanical dissection: an experience of how things work. *Engineering Foundation Conference on Engineering Education. Curriculum Innovation*. Jan 5–10. Santa Barbara.

Sheppard, S (2002). Thoughts on Freshman Engineering Design Experiences. Stanford University (Mechanical Engineering)

Sheppard, S. D., and R. Jenlson (1997a). Freshmen engineering design experiences: an organizational framework. *International Journal of Engineering Education* 13, (3), 190-197.

Sheppard, S., and R. Jenison et al., (1997b). Examples of Freshmen design education. *International Journal of Engineering Education* 13, (4) 248-261.

Smith, R. P (1998). Teaching design for assembly using product disassembly. *IEEE Transactions on Education* 41, (1), 50–52.

Sutcliffe, A. G., and N. A. M. Maiden (1992). Analyzing the novice analysts. Cognitive methods in soft ware engineering. *International Journal of Man-Machine Studies*, 36, 719 – 740

Sutton, J. C (1995). A successful undergraduate design centre. *Proceedings Frontiers in Education Conference*. 3a5 –9 to 12.

Taylor, C. W., and F. W. Barron (1963) (eds). *Scientific Creativity: Recognition and Development*. Wiley, New York.

Tizard, J (1993) Curriculum design for technology access. *International Journal of Electrical Engineering Education*, 30, 42–43.

Thompson, G (1993). On the assessment of student design ability. *International Journal of Mechanical Engineering Education*, 21, (1), 72–80.

Thompson, G., and C. R. McChesney (1999) The Royal Academy of Engineering summer school for new teachers of engineering design. *International Journal of Mechanical Engineering Education*. 27, (2), 164–173.

Tomovic, M. M., and L. K. Eigenbrod (1993). Preparing technology students for design in the 21st century. *Proceeding Frontiers in Education Conference*, 221–225.

Ullman, D. G., Dietrich, T. G., and L. A. Stauffer (1988). A model of the mechanical design process based on empirical data. AI-EDAM 2, (1), 33–52

Venable, W. S (1988). Developing a behavioral approach to teaching design. *International Journal of Applied Engineering Education*. 4, (3), 237–242

Verner, I. M., and D. J. Ahlgren (2002). Fire fighting robot contest: interdisciplinary design curricula in college and high school. *Journal of Engineering Education*, 91, (3), 355 –360.

Viets, H. (1990). Designing across the curriculum. *Engineering Education.* 80, (5), 567.

Wales, C. E., Nardi, A. H., and R. A. Stager (1990). Research or practice. The debate goes on. *International Journal of Technology and Design Education*, 1, (1), 40–47.

Wales, C. E., and R. A. Stager (1990). *Thinking with Equations. Problem Solving in Math and Science.* Center for Guided Design, West Virginia University, Morganstown, WV.

Wallace, K. M (1981). Mechanical engineering design teaching- The Cambridge experience in *Education for Tomorrow's Engineering Designers,* pp. 63–72. Institution of Mechanical Engineers, London.

Wallas, G (1926). *The Art of Thought.* Harcourt Brace, Orlando, FL.

Wang, E (2001). Teaching fresmen design , creativity and programming with Legos and Labview. *Proceedings Frontiers in Education Conference* 2, F3G- 11 to 15.

Wankat, P. C. and F. S. Oreovicz (1993). *Teaching Engineering.* McGraw Hill, New York.

Warner, R. F (1989). Introduction of planning, design and problem solving into first year oif engineering design. *Proceedings World Conference on Engineering Education for Advancing Technology* (Sydney). 582 – 585.

West, H., Flowers, W., and D. Gilmore (1990) Hands-on design in engineering education: learning by doing what? *Engineering Education*, 80, (5), 560 – 555.

West, H., and M. Shimuzu (1992). Mit-ti Tech joint educational project in design. *Proceedings Frontiers in Education Conference.* 693-697.

Wild, P. M and C. Bradley (1998) Employing the concurrent design philosophy in developing an engineering design science program. *International Journal of Mechanical Engineering Edu*cation. 26, (1), 51 – 64.

Wood, K. L., Jensen, D., Belder, J., and K. N. Otto (2001). Engineering and redsesign. Courses incrementally and systematically teach design. *Journal of Engineering Education,* 90, (3), 363–374.

Wood, K. L. Jensen, D., Bezdek, J., and K.N. Otto (2001). Reverse engineering and redesign: courses to incrementally and systematically teach design. *Journal of Engineering Education*, 90, (3), 363 – 374

Woodson, T. T (1966). *An Introduction to Engineering Design.* McGraw Hill, New York.

Youngman, M. B., Oxtoby, R., Monk, J. D and J. Heywood (1978). *Analysing Jobs*. Gower Press, Aldershot.

Yung, E. K. N. and S. W. Leung (1997). Integrated training program on product design in an undergraduate course. *IEEE Transactions on Education,* 40, (1), 46–51.

Zhang, G (1999). A support structure of teaching engineering design to freshmen students. *Proceedings Frontiers in Education Conference*, 12a6–1 to 8.

Part IV

COOPERATIVE LEARNING AND TEAMWORK; OTHER INSTRUCTIONAL PRACTICES AND THE NEW TECHNOLOGIES, ASSESSMENT AND EVALUATION; THE FORMAL ASSESSMENT OF STUDENT LEARNING: ALTERNATIVE ASSESSMENT; ATTRITION AND RETENTION; EPILOGUE

INTRODUCTION TO CHAPTERS 13 AND 14.
THE LECTURE

Throughout this text there have been references to innovations that have required changes from what have commonly been called traditional methods to non-traditional methods of teaching. For many engineering educators, good teaching is synonymous with good lecturing and all that that entails. For many engineering teachers the idea that the lecture is a monologue in which students may or may not be allowed to ask questions prevails (van Dijk, van den Berg, and van Keulen, 2001). They believe that it is not possible to get participation in large classes, and they also believe that without this method they would not be able "cover" the material (content) required by the syllabus. In this behavior they are often supported by the rules of the professional associations which validate their qualifications (Manley, cited by Rowe and Harris, 2000). Underlying these perceptions is a particular view of teaching and learning. The teacher is an information giver, the student is a receiver, and such feedback as there is from tests may or may not produce data which will affect teacher or learner behavior. During the last thirty years there has been a slow but powerful recognition of the value of formative assessment in helping teachers and students change their learning behaviors. Within the same period but especially within the last half, there has been a move to active learning on the ground that the passive learning that takes place in a lecture is very inefficient. This has required teachers to change their perception of teaching and the role of the teacher to a model of teaching as the facilitation or management of learning. The same kind of change has also been taken place in the management of the tutorial that is used to support lecture courses especially as it becomes an aid in computer assisted learning (e.g., Merino and Abel, 2003).

The primary focus of Chapters 13 and 14 is on active learning. The demand for teamwork in industry has supported a considerable development in cooperative learning and group work, and the literature available merits a Chapter on this topic. Chapter 14 considers some other interventions and, via discussion of the role of simulation in laboratory work, concludes with a more general discussion of practice and problems with the new technologies. It is not exhaustive. To set the scene, this extended introduction considers the role of the lecture. Some experiments in the role of tutorials that accompany lecture programs are described in Section 14.3.5 on peer tutoring.

For many teachers the transition from one mode of instruction to another is difficult because apart from anything else it requires considerable changes in attitude to adapt to the new relationship that is required between teacher and student. It means letting go of the total control of learning through continuous instruction (recitation) in order to allow the student to have a much greater say in that control and how he/she should control her/his learning. At its simplest, such change means a move away from the lecture method to other methods of learning and, in particular, group work.

The first edition of Donald Bligh's *"What's the Use of Lectures?"* (1971) received, and recent editions continue to receive, much attention. Although it was very critical of the lecture method, it recognized that lectures had a place in the curriculum, and that they could be improved. Bligh's book encouraged some engineering educators to try to improve their lecturing (Engin and Engin, 1977).[1] Bassey (1994) demonstrated that Bligh's data could be interpreted to put lectures in a more favorable light.[2] To be fair Bligh indicated ways in which the traditional lecture could be made more effective. Among his suggestions was the idea that lectures should be broken up with such activities as group work and buzz groups[3]. (See also Section 14.5 for a discussion of the use in lectures and web-based technology. While the lecture continues to valued, as for example, at Imperial College it is as Melville (2003) reported supported by other forms of contact in the best institutions and the findings of experience and research suggest that that it is the most proficient way for learning.

For example, Byerley (2001), at the United States Air force Academy, changed his typically traditional approach to the lecture to introduce a number of active learning techniques in his introductory thermodynamics class. His new lectures were structured as follows:

- *"5 minutes of lesson introduction-using multimedia presentation.*
- *20 minutes of active presentation-using combination of multimedia and blackboard.*
- *20 minutes of active learning in individual and small group activities.*
- *5 minutes of lesson recap using game show or two minutes written and oral presentation.*

While his final examination produced a lower performance than that of the previous course there was a considerable improvement in the scores for the design project.

He thought that the reason for this result was that the test was in multiple choice format and tested memory[4].[5] The

---

[1] There were other works in the same period that were equally critical of the lecture method. e.g., Cooper and Foy (1967) and McLeish (1968).

[2] Bassey (1994) wrote *"I suggest he (Bligh) should have expressed his results as a closed generalisation, perhaps like this- In 68 studies carried out up to 1971 it was found in over half that the lecture is no more and no less effective than other methods for transmitting information. However in just under a quarter of these studies the lecture was found to be more effective and in a similar number it was found to be less effective."*

[3] In which students in pairs are invited to discuss among themselves a problem (issue) set by the lecturer. This may lead to contributions from the floor.

[4] See, also Lewis (1991), who changed his teaching of problem solving to a more student-centered activity he retained about 20 minutes of his classroom time for lecture type input.

[5] Another example of participation is that of a dynamics course at the University of Queensland. Asokanthan (1997) involved students in demonstrations that required their participation in simulations, and

results might have been different had it tested higher order skills.

It is a common experience that the research strategies don't yield the differences that might be expected between control and experimental groups because of poor test design.

At Vanderbilt University, Shiavi and Broderson (2002) evaluated the use of different modes of instruction in an introductory course in computing in engineering. One mode was a *"combined structure in which 40 students met with their instructor in a classroom twice a week for 50 minutes, and in groups of 20 met with the instructor and his teaching assistant in the instructional computing laboratory for 75 minutes. The other mode was the laboratory structure. All 40 students meet with their instructor and teaching assistant twice a week for 110 minutes each meeting was in the instructional computing laboratory. A minimal amount of lecturing was done in the beginning of the laboratory periods."* The students were assigned to the two modalities randomly and they received the same course. This was demonstrated by the fact that there were no significant differences between the two groups in respect of their performance at the different levels of difficulty presented by the topics. The justification for the continuation of one mode as opposed to the other would, in these circumstances, have to be made on grounds other than performance, as, for example, the effects of the strategy on motivation.

At MIT a module on Fourier Spectral Analysis designed on the basis of the "How People Learn" Report from the National Science Foundation (Bransford, Brown, and Cocking, 1999) augmented traditional instruction with a web-based tutorial, group discussion ,and an interactive demonstration (Greenberg, Smith, and Newman, 2003). Rubrics were developed to assess understanding of concepts. In this investigation, instructors from the Harvard-MIT Division of Health Science and Technology taught the course by traditional methods in one year, and in the following year they used the module. Unfortunately, the basic characteristics of the students in each group are not given. But since this is the 'live' experience of all college courses the finding that the experimental course produced better understanding of the concepts is what mattered to the teachers, although it provides a challenge to those who teach by traditional methods alone as do the other activities reported here.

For example, another investigation at the University of Cincinnati of a course in statics compared traditional methods of instruction with four different methods of technology enhancement. These were interactive video originating; interactive video receiving, web-assisted presentation, and, streaming media presentation. The students' who volunteered, were randomly assigned to five sections each of which was taught by an instructor with considerable teaching experience and interested in the particular mode in which the section was taught. The best results were obtained from the web-based class whereas the worst results came from the traditional class. The web-based and streaming media sections required more time on task than the traditional course, and the investigators considered this to be an important contributory factor. But apart from the web-based format the students did not think that anyone of the other formats was more effective than the traditional mode. While the technology assisted courses encouraged greater interest, the teachers noted that a great deal of attention needs to be paid to the design of production (Rutz et al., 2003). Many papers about technology-enhanced instruction demonstrate that such instruction is not cheap, and that its value lies in the learning enhancement it gives.

Very often, resistance to change comes from students. They expect and want traditional lectures. van Dijk and his colleagues at Delft University of Technology in The Netherlands demonstrated that it was possible to activate students in lectures even when they did not expect to be activated (van Dijk, 1988). He and his colleagues suggested that peer instruction and voting systems were possible ways of interactive teaching, and in this they were following in the footsteps of Liebman (1996) and Mazur (1997).

In another study, van Dijk and his colleagues compared the lecture as a monologue in which the students were allowed to ask questions, with a group that used interactive voting during the lecture and another group that used a combination of peer instruction and interactive voting. The interactive voting system is an electronic system that allows the presenter to keep in touch with her/his audience. In the experimental lecture the teacher was allowed to ask six questions. While the answers are anonymous, the teacher can display the results on a screen for the class to see, and for the teacher to give feedback. Peer instruction can also be given during the lecture.

They found that in the "voting" lecture the students were rather passive, and they deduced that this was due to their unfamiliarity with this mode of teaching. This led them to suggest that lecturers should explain to students what is expected of them in lectures. Interactive teaching does not automatically result in students who are more activated compared with students in a traditional lecture. At the same time, students learned as much in the interactive lecture as they did in the traditional lecture. Therefore, they argued, that a traditional lecture is not a prerequisite for learning in engineering. Citing Kyriacou and Marshall (1989), they pointed out that since one cannot know what is happening to a student in a lecture, it is necessary to distinguish between students' activities and students' cognitive experiences. *"Hence, it is possible that interactive teaching will not result in active cognitive experiences. A student may, for example, choose not to think deeply about the questions the lecturer asks. Similarly, traditional lecturing behavior*

---

physical models and videos were introduced. These were group activities and the students who had to prepare them could also contribute to the mode of presentation. Several programming languages were available to them, including MECHANICA. Others are engaged in developing hybrid programs that introduce some form of electronic learning in classrooms and positive responses have been obtained from the students.

will not automatically result in passive students who are accepting information offered without thinking critically about it. The results do not imply that activation is superfluous. Even though it is possible for students to be mentally active during lectures while listening to teacher's exposition, the chances are that more students will be more mentally engaged when involved in learning activities like reading, writing, discussing and problem solving."

The distinguished philosopher Alisdair MacIntyre linked his discussion of the lecture method to the purpose of university education. He considered that university education was in disarray because it lacked the coherence that it had when moral philosophy was the cornerstone of the curriculum. He believed that in order for the university to once again become a place of *"constrained disagreement,."* the lecture approach might have to be reconceived. It should be a place of controversy,[6] and thus *"the lecture will perhaps be transformed into, perhaps abandoned in exchange for, a theater of the intelligence, a theater in turn requiring critical commentary from both its adherents and its opponents. And among the purposes to be served by both theater and genealogical commentary will be the undermining of all traditional forms of authority, including the authority of the lecturer."*

While this is an important consideration in the humanities part of the engineering curriculum (indeed MacIntyre is highly critical of the applied ethics encouraged by the professions), it runs counter to the concept of the received curriculum in engineering.

The argument here is that the lecture which is concerned with "technique" is by no means the best way of obtaining understanding of the concepts and principles involved, and a battery of evidence has been assembled to support this view. Nevertheless, the lecture still has a role to play, but this depends on the objectives to be achieved.

For many teachers a change in style from lecturer to facilitator or leader of learning is not accomplished without difficulty. They may find it helpful in the design of their instruction if they were to produce a matrix of objectives versus instructional strategies of the kind undertaken more generally by Weston and Cranton (see Exhibit 2.23). More than that, as Fincher (1999) has pointed out they will require evaluation and evidences of

the success of any given approach. Her problem, which related to the three approaches used to teach computer programming, was that there was little evaluative work in the literature *"and much less which is comparable across institutions and diverse student populations."* There is certainly a problem with "transfer" of ideas across cultural boundaries. But in the long run, if I think from classroom assessment that my work needs improvement, the question is surely "Does this particular study interest/satisfy me enough to take a risk and do something similar?"

Many of the strategies discussed in Chapters 13 and 14 require teachers to take a risk. In its turn, risk taking requires careful planning. There is no scope for 'winging' it. Some of the principles and problems of changing from teacher to student-centered teaching will have become apparent in the preceding Chapters. Following Catalano and Catalano (1997), the requirements for a teacher in student-centered instruction are:

1. To be able to model thinking (processing skills).
2. To be able to define where you want your students to be cognitively.
3. To be able to design questions which facilitate student exploration/growth.
4. o be able to use visual tools to assist students in "seeing" how information can be connected and to be able to help them to use these tools.
5. To be able to provide group learning settings.
6. To be able to use analogies and metaphors.
7. To be able to provide a non-threatening "no risk" mechanism for indirect dialogue between teacher and students.[7] In Chapter 13 group work, cooperative learning, and teamwork are considered.

---

[6] "For what I have imagined is after all in some ways nothing other than a twentieth-century version of the thirteenth-century university, especially the University of Paris, the university in which Augustinians and Aristotelians each conducted their own systematic enquiries while at the same time engaging in systematic controversy. What such controversy now requires is not only a restoration of the link between the lecture and the disputation *but also a recognition that the lecturer speaks not with the voice of a single acknowledged authoritative reason, but as one committed to some particular partisan standpoint. The lecture, as we have inherited it from the late nineteenth century, is a genre in which characteristically the lecturer invites the assent of his or her audience to his or her propositions or arguments. But in a university thus reconceived a central task of the lecturer when concerned in any way with issues of justification —most obviously in moral and theological enquiry, but also elsewhere- will be both to elicit the dissent of at least some large part of his or her audience and to explain to them why they will be bound to dissent and what it is in their condition which ensures this".*

[7] This paper is accompanied with a useful bibliography. For a more recent and more detailed study see Felder and Brent (2003).

CHAPTER 13: COOPERATIVE LEARNING AND TEAMWORK

13. Introduction: The Case for Cooperative Learning

It has been argued for some fifty years and more that group work of one kind or another is a more effective way of learning the material of academic subjects than that provided by the lecture method.

Astin (1997) summarized the results of his large-scale longitudinal studies of students in American liberal arts programs and reported that: *"classroom research has consistently shown that cooperative learning approaches (as they have come to be known) produce positive outcomes that are superior to those obtained through traditional competitive approaches"* (p. 427, e.g., Bruffee, 1993). The success of cooperative learning arises from powerful influence of the peer group on the student, a fact recognized by Newman as long ago as 1852. In the United Kingdom it is not surprizing to find that since the end of the Second World War there has been continuing advocacy of small group teaching (e.g., Abercrombie, 1978; Collier, 1983; 1989; Jaques, 1991). McDermott, Göl, and Nafaklski (2000) have described developments in cooperative learning in Australia, Devi (2001) in India, Kreijns and Kirschener (2001) in the Netherlands, and Dimitriadis et al., (2001) and Marques, Navarro, and Daradoumis (2001) in Spain.

Pavelich, in a review paper at the 2002 ASEE annual conference, cited a meta-study by Springer, Stanne, and Dovan (1999) of 39 studies with useful evaluations of cooperative learning. It showed a 0.51 average improvement in learning with a move from the 50th to the 70th percentile on standardized examination results.[8] At the University of Puerto Rico and associated institutions, evidence was adduced that suggested[9] that when minority students were exposed to cooperative learning, the rate of attrition was reduced (Morrell et al., 2001). But there have been criticisms of the research that has been done because much of it has not been properly controlled (Druckman and Bjork, cited in Anderson, Reder, and Simon, 1996). More generally, Prince (2004), who reviewed research across the spectrum of active learning strategies, concluded that there was broad support for the elements that he had studied.

Specifically, with respect to engineering design, the Center for the Study of Higher Education at Pennsylvania State University developed a *Classroom Activities Outcome Survey* for the purpose of evaluating cooperative learning within the ECSEL coalition. This instrument gathered information in three areas. These were, " *1) Students' personal and academic backgrounds, and demographic characteristics; 2) the instructional characteristics of the course in which they were enrolled when completing the questionnaire, and 3) the extent to which students believed they had made progress in a variety of learning and skill development areas as a result of taking that particular course"* (Terenzini et al., 2001).

The course characteristics related to collaborative learning, problem solving activities, feedback, and interaction with faculty/peers. Factorial analysis revealed course-related gains in the domains of design skills, problem solving skills, communication skills, and group skills. There was also a group of unscaled items in which gains were shown.

The instrument was administered to students enrolled in 17 ECSEL active learning or collaborative learning courses/sections and 6 non-ECSEL traditional courses /sections at six engineering schools. Tutors were asked to select them because they had common goals in the achievement of skill in engineering design. The courses were spread across the years of the program providing a nonrandom sample of nearly 500 students in 23 courses.

Terenzini et al., (2001) calculated an effect size to show the differences between the ECSEL and non-ECSEL groups. The data revealed considerable differences between the groups and showed that what happened in the two courses was significantly different. Similarly, there were statistically significant differences between the groups with the exception of problem solving in the factorially derived scales. The gains were in favor of the collaborative learning group. The most gain was in the 'group skill' domain. The differences were relatively large, and the gains were found to persist after analyses that took into account the entering characteristics of the students.

The investigators argued that since self-reports had been found to correlate with achievement test scores *"to the extent that self-report measures reflect the content of learning under consideration,"* they are valid measures of the effect of the course on learning.[10] Terenzini and his colleagues also argued that while they could not be sure that the ECSEL and non-ECSEL courses had the same educational objective of teaching design skills, the learning outcomes evaluated were those identified by ABET to be important. They also noted that while no account was taken of the instructor's skills the effect size was so great that controlling for instructor skills, would not have reduced the magnitude.

But as Hilz and Benbunan-Fich (1997) pointed out, the measures used by Terenzini and his colleagues are subjective. In their investigation of asynchronous learning networks, they showed that while there was a significant interaction effect between teamwork and technology, the groups on-line had slightly better perceptions of learning than individuals on-line. The latter reported the worst conditions for learning. However, there were no significant differences between the groups on the scores for the relevant part of the final

---

[8] Notes provided by M. Pavelich. Colorado School of Mines.

[9] Many of the studies reported in engineering would not meet these criteria. Nevertheless, they do satisfy the instructors involved.

[10] They cited Anaya (1999) and Pike (1995).

examination. However, they pointed out that each measure of learning is different and that the observed measure of the examination assumes it is a valid measure of actual learning. Once again the point needs to be made that examinations are often not very valid. In any case the subjective factors may indicate a very small to price to pay, especially if they can be linked to a reduction in attrition.

For example, at the University of Salford, Booth and James (2001) thought that first-year students would be encouraged to undertake deep learning if they learned level 1 mechanics in cooperative learning groups. Conceptual questions were put to the groups. Booth and James were unable to demonstrate an improvement in deep learning or conceptual understanding. They suggested that because more than half the students had a learning style that coped well with traditional lectures, the changes made might not have been sufficiently challenging when coupled with the short time scale of the course. However, comments in the focus group and responses in a questionnaire showed that the students were entirely positive about the course and wanted to know why this method of teaching was not employed in other courses.[11] It would seem that there was a motivational element that was important.

One objection too much of the research that has been reported is that it is North American based and, therefore, may be culturally biased. Such research aggregates outcomes. It does not tell us about the internal dynamics of groups, and it leads to the suppositions that all persons learn equally and that there is no isolation within teams. But isolation in a group can be hidden, and it is for this reason that the study of the dynamics of such groups is important (see Section 13.4 and Haller et al., 2000). Nevertheless, these aggregates tell a positive story about learning in cooperative groups, and engineering educators, by and large, have as yet to take up the challenge. Taken together, all the research suggests that there is a positive role for collaborative/action learning in engineering programs but *"that it is not the panacea that always provides outcomes superior or equivalent to those of individual training"* (Anderson, Reder, and Simon, 1996). Ultimately, what matters is that instructional strategies should be chosen for the objectives they best achieve, and what the individual instructor is able to achieve with them; and that is often a matter of inclination and personality.[12] These objectives might be

as much to do with the affective domain as they are with the cognitive.

It is likely that more than one strategy will benefit learning. For example, Pimmel (2001) described how among the strategies used, mini-lectures were interspersed with cooperative activities in a taught program in design methodology, project management, engineering communications, and professional ethics at the University of Alabama.[13] When tested for their preferences, most students favored the laboratory mode over the lecture mode. Comparable with this was the desire to learn for oneself. The investigators found that a major reason for these dispositions was the fact that the students had learned some of the material in high school and were motivated to learn on their own. Also on complex topics such as MATLAB the students could get immediate answers to their questions. As between year 1 and year 2 there was a change from learning about 3 D modeling and Excel in the laboratory to learning by oneself. One reason for this was that members of the year-two group were found to be more introverted than the year one group and were better able to reflect on the mathematical concepts when learning by themselves. Overall, they concluded that in courses where there is a high level of computer usage, a laboratory/studio approach that is prefaced with a short lecture was the most appropriate mode of instruction.[14] More generally, "The real question, I suppose (wrote Astin), is whether we and our faculty colleagues are willing to consider the possibility that the student's 'general education' consists of something more than the content of what is taught and the particular form in which this content is packaged" (p. 408).

The view is taken that group work has two purposes. The first is the enhancement of learning, and the second is the learning of teamwork skills that will enable students to perform in projects, because as Smith (2004) has so admirably demonstrated, project work and the management of projects are at the heart of the engineering activity. It is also assumed that any group activity where several persons work together is or may be converted to a team activity (Pimmel, 2003). The primary purpose of this Chapter is to discuss the claims that have been made for various kinds of group work in engineering education.

13.1. Group Work , Syndicates, Base Groups and Formal Cooperative Learning.

The generic term used to describe the involvement of students in their own learning is active

---

[11] Concepts were measured by the *Force Concept Inventory*; The Kolb Learning Styles Inventory was used together with a reduced version of Tait and Entwistle's (1996) ASSIST questionnaire by James and Turner, (1998).

[12] A study among student teachers at the University of Florida supported this view. It compared lecture, cooperative learning and programd instruction methods of instruction and found no differences in achievemen across the three treatments. *"The purpose of instruction is important to the selection of method. The purpose of instruction in this study was for college students to acquire basic concepts and make simple application of these concepts.... Had other purposes been identified such as development of higher order thinking skills or development of interpersonal skills in problem solving, then perhaps a*

significant difference would have been found" (Kromrey and Purdom, 1995).

[13] It accompanied the capstone design project Their paper is very comprehensive and describes the various exercises in detail.

[14] They were also able to compare students who used laptop computers with those who did not. They found that the laptop users were uncomfortable with them at the beginning of the semester but were equally comfortable with them at the end. This represented a considerable gain for the novice users. Those who used laptops preferred to learn by lecture. This was thought to be because they were inexperienced or that there were more visual learners among them.

learning. It is to be contrasted with the passive listening done in a lecture. Any form of collaboration is active learning. Group work is, therefore, a subset of active learning. It may be undertaken on the Web through chat rooms, etc.

Groups can last for one class[15] or they can last for a long period. Project based learning is likely require a group to remain together for some time. Smith reported that cooperative learning groups are generally made up of two or four persons but there are examples in the engineering literature of larger groups especially when they are being used to simulate an industrial organization.

As indicated in Chapter 10 problem-based learning in teams is a form of cooperative learning. *"The intellectual activity of building models to solve problems-an explicit activity of constructing or creating the qualitative or quantitative relationships-helps students understand, explain predict etc."* (Smith and Starfield, 1993; Starfield, Smith, and Blaloch, 1994). Smith argued that *"the process of building models in face-to-face interpersonal interaction results in learning that is difficult to achieve in any other way."*

Cooperative learning is based on the premise that working together to accomplish shared goals enhances learning. It may take place in lectures (Smith and Waller, 1997), or mini lectures may be used to support it. This learning may be in both the cognitive and affective domains, and sometimes the purpose of the group is to enhance the so-called affective skills of interpersonal behavior, as, for example, those required for working in teams. The four levels of group skills that are encouraged in cooperative learning are *forming, functioning, formulating and fermenting.* In the first, participants learn how to structure a group. In the second they learn how to maintain it through sharing ideas and clarifying the task. In the third they learn how to understand and retain what is learned, thus they learn to summarize and reason verbally with accuracy. Finally, they exercise the higher-order thinking skills, and these include the ability to handle conflict. Many of the published contributions on group work reviewed take the cognitive dimension for granted and focus on the other objectives of group work, or the problems of group work and its grading.

In North America the recent stimulus to undertake group work in engineering education has been the form known as cooperative learning (Johnson, Johnson, and Smith, 1991a,b). It is sometimes called collaborative learning. In the UK the terms small group learning and syndicate teaching cover a range of similar activities. At its simplest the buzz group described by Bligh (1993) takes place in a lecture when the instructor requests students to discuss within the period of a minute or so an important aspect of his/her lecture. It is a relatively informal activity. Many teachers believe that simply to assign students to work in a group will benefit learning. They take no account of the fact that students may not want to work together, and do so only because

grades might be involved. Smith (1995) called such groups *pseudo learning groups.* A slightly better approach is when students accept that they must work together. They expect to be rewarded as individuals and the assignments are so structured that they can work individually. Smith called this a traditional classroom learning group. *"In such groups helping and sharing is minimised. Some students loaf, seeking a free ride on the efforts of their more conscientious group mates."*

The essence of cooperative learning is active discussion by group members committed to perform an assigned task. Smith (1995) distinguished between formal and informal cooperative learning groups. An informal group might last for only a few minutes or at most a class period. He wrote, *"they are often organized so that students engage in focused discussions before and after a lecture and interspersing turn-to–your partner discussions."* (i.e., buzz groups), *"throughout the lecture."* Such activity enables the student to better embrace the content of the lecture through an engagement with her/himself on that content. One form of this approach is what Collier (1989) termed Associative Group Discussion.

In Associative Group Discussion (AGD) the instructor provides the students with a short task. *"...the students are given a brief passage to analyse individually or they inspect a slide or a chart, or watch a short video tape or read a report of a student project or field study"* Collier, 1989, p89). The instructor then asks one or two questions of a *"probing or controversial kind"* in order to set the scene for a debate. Collier pointed out that this will only work if the tutors and students had learned new roles. As has been shown in the case of problem based learning and other changes, the climate of an institution or a department can foster such change.

Collier (1989) promoted a syndicate approach for achieving the higher-order skills in his list of objectives (see Exhibit 2. 24). Syndicates are cooperative groups in which a class is divided up into groups of five to carry out assignments that form the major body of the work that has to be achieved. The tutor is available as a consultant and conducts plenary sessions. *"The heart of the technique is the intensive debate within syndicates, which ... should not inhibit individuals from developing their own distinctive opinions."* (p. 104). In so doing it will help them develop higher skills. Students will be *"expressing ideas cogently (objective 4); applying what they have learned to new settings (objective 5); analysing and argument (objective 6); devising new schemes (objective 7); and assessing the quality of argument (objective 8)"*(p. 104). Collier made the point that it encouraged students to be more critical in their approach to reading, and this relates to Atman and Bursic's (1996) finding that reading about design improved the quality of learning design. Although Collier's remarks were made in the language of the humanities, it is easy to translate it to the language of engineering as Williams and Beaujean (1993) showed (see below).

This syndicate method is very similar to the project approach in engineering design adopted by

[15]See Blackwell (1991).

Gerhard (1999) and described in Chapter 12. It clearly contains the essential elements of cooperative learning, although the authors do not explain in any detail what went on in the process of continuous monitoring, for which reason a comparison with group processing is not possible.

Cooperative learning as developed by Johnson and Johnson at the University of Minnesota , and Slavin at The Johns Hopkins University, *"is the instructional use of small groups so that students work together to maximize their own and each others' learning"* (Smith, 1995). It has been pioneered in higher education particularly by Johnson and Johnson, and in engineering especially by Smith (Johnson, Johnson, and Smith, 1991a, b, Smith, undated).

"Carefully structured cooperative learning involves people working in teams to accomplish a common goal, under conditions that involve both positive interdependence (all members must cooperate to complete the task) and individual and group accountability (each member is accountable for the complete final outcome)" (Smith, 1995).

In cooperative learning, *Base* groups are long term stable heterogeneous groups that last for the whole of a course. Their purpose *"is to provide each student the support, encouragement, and assistance he or she needs to make academic progress.... When students have successes, insights, questions or concerns they wish to discuss; they can contact other members of their base group. Base groups typically manage the daily paperwork of the course through the use of group folders"* (Smith, 1995).

Such groups are very similar to quality circles except that they do not come together voluntarily, although there is no reason why they should not. As Courter (1996), and Null (1997), have pointed out, cooperative learning can be designed to meet the principle of TQM. In Null's courses, quality circles were used for the TQM principles of *"focusing on understanding, improving process, and performing continuous improvement."* Thus, peers reviewed programming assignments. In so doing they were exposed to different approaches to solving the problem. They were also asked to think about how they could improve the algorithms and the code. In this way they obtained a better understanding of the programming language in use. If they can see better ways of doing things, they can do benchmarking. *"During these quality circles, student groups are required to write evaluation comments on the code they are reviewing. For every negative comment, they must find at least one positive one. The groups then redo certain projects based on peer reviews. This helps shift the focus from the grade on the project to the expected outcome."* Null also made the point that *"helping students to work in groups in academia when the stakes are relatively small, allows them to make mistakes and learn how to correct them, without worrying about the more serious consequences (such as losing their jobs)."*

As Trytten (2001) explained, cooperative learning occurs when the group has common goals, mutual rewards, shared resources, and complementary roles. For the reason that students complained about having to work in groups and used clandestine means to conceal the lack of group interaction, she decided to change to cooperative learning.[16] She found that cooperative learning was much better. It worked well when in-class assignments were created which were designed to have the same problem, specific choice, and simultaneous reports.[17] She described the procedure as follows, *"For each major topic, a multiple choice quiz was created which required that students meet high level learning objectives to answer correctly. These quizzes typically had six to eight problems. Students first took the quiz as individuals. Then the students took the same quiz as a group. The individual and group quizzes made up 40% of the grade each. The remaining 20% of the grade came from peer evaluation After the quizzes are finished, the class discusses the correct answers collectively, when time permits (timing the multiple choice quizzes has been a problem since they always take substantially more time than it seems they should). This exercise takes an entire class period... and has been very effective in generating intense intragroup discussion, as well as productive group discussions."*

During the course of the program Trytten changed the test style from closed to open book and notes. Because the tests were designed to assess high level learning, she argued that the answers could not readily be gained from the text. The advantage was that it improved the discussion.

Clearly, such tests would have to be set at a level that will involve the more able students (Haller et al., 2000). Trytten reported that individuals working on their own averaged 4/8 questions while the small groups averaged 7/8 questions, but she did not comment on the effect of the individuals taking the test first. Students consistently reported in informal feedback that they could not pass the class without the group quizzes. They had caused lots of out of class discussion.

Typically, members in cooperative groups are given roles. Although the roles' shown in Exhibit 13.1, appeared in an article on engineering education (Tylavsky, 1999), the same kind of organization can be found in primary (elementary) schools (Kirk, 1997). An attempt is made to compare the two in Exhibit 13.1. In Kirk's study, which was about learning mathematics, the checker was also charged with encouraging participation. There was no equivalent of the leader. In spelling the roles of "asker" and "speller" were introduced. Often the roles parallel a typical engineering group. For example, in a civil engineering freshman team the reader who ensured that the team understood the problem and understood their role in solving it was called the project manager. The chief engineer was the *encourager*, the engineer was

---

[16]Computer graphics course.

[17]She followed a procedure recommended by Michaelson, Fink, and Knight (1997).

the *checker*, and the client representative was the *summarizer* responsible for presenting the final report (Hart and Groccia, 1994; see Section 13.3 for other examples). Williams and Beaujean (1993) in their syndicate groups at the University of Glamorgan, *"employed"* nine students in key positions in a company (.e.g., senior applications engineer; senior design engineers for circuits and software and for hardware. Senior engineers for assembly, test, production quality and component quality; repair and rework manager, and plant engineer).

Role	Responsibility
Leader	Makes decisions when the team is deadlocked, reports out answers when teams are poled, insures that scribe is the only person holding a pencil. (Kirk- no exact equivalent but explainer of ideas.
Scribe	Writes the team's ideas analysis, designs, solutions etc on paper (Kirk-reader as well as recorder).
Checker	Checks that everyone understands the evolving solution and that everyone provides input into the process (Kirk-encourager of participation).
Devil's advocate	Challenges the suggestions and understanding made by the team. Forces all team members to support their suggestions.

Exhibit 13.1. Team roles and responsibilities in cooperative learning as presented by D. J. Tylavsky (1999) of Arizona State University and compared with those from an elementary school (Kirk, 1997). (Reproduced with permission of *IEEE, Proceeding Frontiers in Education Conference*)

The syndicate reports to a member of the academic staff who takes the role of a senior company executive. In this syndicate the members could request lectures on any topic relevant to the pursuit of the topic i.e. engineering or managerial. It is a form of just-in-time learning, as the material is made available at the point of need. Williams and Beaujean (1993) found that the choice of subject area for the syndicate was critical. It had to be chosen for adequate coverage to meet the needs of the target group. They found, like others before them, that the involvement of the group promoted great interest. Provided that the students were motivated, they were *"able to retain and apply far more information than students taught using conventional courses."* No statistical detail was provided in support of this statement. One or two contributions focused on the transfer of learning to new problems and tasks, and the "affinity groups" described by Gates and her colleagues (2000) have this as an objective, particularly as it applies to transfer to workplace situations. They listed some generally accepted axioms from learning theory. The essential difference between their list and a set of principles published by Saupé (1961) related to the inclusion of dialogue. Saupe's principles applied to the individual learner. Merging the two lists produced the following axioms:

1. The tasks share common elements (e.g., knowledge structures and learning contexts). Learning will be more effective when it possesses meaning, organization, and structure. This requires that the learners recognize the existence of the problem, in order to be able to define it (Saupé, 1961).
2. It follows that learners should seek and see relationships or patterns in what they learn
3. The learner goes beyond what is directly taught by elaborating it and developing self-explanations).
4. The learners monitor their understanding as they work and are aware of what they know and how they come to know.
5. The strategies are learned to a high level of fluency in the context of the expected application. Transfer will occur if there is a recognized similarity between the learning and the transfer situations, and it will occur to the extent that it is expected to occur (Saupé, 1961).
6. The learners see themselves as in charge of learning rather than being directed by another. Learners learn only what they themselves do (Saupé, 1961).
7. Meaning is developed through dialog in which both (all) parties establish what the other knows and adjust their communication to the partner's knowledge.
8. Learning contexts make use of scaffolding in which other people, tools or guidance systems carry some of the performance load.
9. Learning is practised in social communities where elaboration and adjusting interpretations are regularly practised.

There are one or two examples of the use of cooperative learning to overcome the misconceptions that first-year students have of mechanics and thermodynamics, respectively, from universities in Australia (see Chapter 4; Hessami and Sillitoes, 1990; Mills et al., 1999). Insofar as engineering design is concerned there are a different set of cognitive skills to be learned about the design process (see Chapter 12), project. At Michigan State University the computer-engineering capstone design course required the students to collaborate in teams to develop and evaluate a product that contained an embedded computer. To achieve this goal the teams, who worked together for a semester, nominated members to "skill teams" to acquire skills essential for the completion of the project (e.g., design tools software, how to use powerpoint) (Rover and Fisher, 1997). A subsequent evaluation showed student satisfaction with the course was very high (Rover, 2000).

One means of structuring cooperative learning is through writing. Wheeler and McDonald (1998) described how writing was integrated into a senior capstone design course. *"There was real interdependence in the project as it was too large for any individual- the work had to be split among team members. The group had to succeed for any individual to succeed. The team leader decided how each member could most effectively contribute to the overall group success. An integral part of this effort was the writing required throughout the project. The group members often communicated by e mail, and the frequent progress reports to their faculty advisors and industrial clients often required them to work and write frequently together. The writing component in this course, especially, may have been the most important factor in ensuring effective collaboration. Each student had to write in order to inform the others on the team of their progress, and the overall team progress had to be reported to their advisors and industrial client."*

Trytten (2001) took an opposite view with respect to computer programming. She distinguished between sequential, stratification, and horizontal communication models in which communication was sparse. She considered that the best model is between two people who create the composition; it did not generalize to large groups.

The problems that arise in cooperative learning relate to the achievement of these goals, and in the academic setting, issues arise as to how teamwork can be evaluated and its assessments used for grading. Problems arise, for example, when not every member chooses to participate (hitchhiking as it is sometimes called), or when leaders prevent members from participating. Thus, a major problem relates to the selection of members of the group. Issues related to these problems will be discussed in later sections.

In sum, five parameters characterize cooperative learning groups. These are as follows:

1) Motivation derives from the common objective of enhancing each member's learning. The evidence that group work motivates students is extensive. Doubtless this is in part because *"students bring something of themselves to the exercise and share with each other"* (De Vault, 1998).

2) Each member of the group is accountable to the group and holds the other members of the group accountable for achieving the task.

3) *"Group members work face-to-face to produce joint work-products. They do real work together. Students promote each other's success through helping, sharing, assisting explaining, and encouraging. They provide both academic and personal support based on a commitment and caring about each other".* Positive independence can be achieved by making each member of the group an expert in a specific area on the basis of his/her past experience. If, in addition, each person is given a specifically defined task, role interdependence is created (e.g., Gates, Delgado, and Mondragon, 2000,-and the sections below).

4) Each member of the group learns teamwork skills that they are expected to deploy in the group.

5) Groups emphasize continuing evaluation of their work and their team performance. This is called group processing. *"At the end of their working period the groups process their functioning by answering two questions: (1) What is something that each member did to the group that was helpful for the group and (2) What is something each member could do to make the group even better tomorrow?"* (Smith and Waller, 1997).

13.2.   The Selection and Structuring of Groups

Various approaches have been used for the selection of group members. These range from students selecting their own groups to faculty selecting the members. Wheeler and McDonald (1998), for example, drew numbers from a hat to designate teams of 3 students each. Schultz (1998) reported that self-selection was *"disastrous. Like grouped with like".* The very worst group that he selected *"was a group of very high-performing serious students with good grades. They were very individualistic and were never willing to trust ideas from other members- before the idea was even fully expressed, other members would interrupt with what they thought were better ideas. They could not pull together and were unwilling to risk leaving any of their "points" to someone else's performance".* In contrast, *"there was a group that described themselves as the "left-overs" that performed moderately well. Their claim to fame was that they never argued. They were not the best students, but they seemed willing to work and their group actually performed better than groups with higher-grade students."*

At Rose-Hulman Institute of Technology where senior students participated in externally sponsored projects, the students were given summaries of the projects available. They then had to submit a project assignment application. In this application the students had to indicate the three projects that interested them most, and to suggest non-standard courses or experiences that might be required for the project. Together with an understanding of the student's capabilities, the application was used by course faculty to allocate the student to one of the teams to try and ensure group cohesiveness. (Moore and Farbrother, 2000, Moore and Berry, 2001).

Because the selection of students for the groups at the University of Pretoria in South Africa was contentious, it was agreed that the lecturer should select the groups. The objection to students selecting their own groups was that groups could become polarized in such a way that higher or lower performance resulted. Teamwork might be defeated because of the hierarchies existing among peer groups, and group composition could be made along ethnic and gender lines. It will be appreciated that this was a particularly sensitive issue in South Africa. To accomplish selection, the students were categorized into 5 groups. The first of these included those students who were strong in practical skills but weak in theory. The mark difference between the two was 30%. The second group was made up of all those students who fell in the top 10%. Three other categories were also sorted by marks.

One student from each category was included in each group. Gender and ethnic selection was left to the students. It was reported that this procedure worked well

(Craig and van Waveren, 1997).[18]

The topics chosen for the projects related to the coefficient of thermal expansion, noise levels in passenger cars, and a speed awareness campaign. The projects lasted for two weeks. Tasks were assigned to the students who were encouraged to "take responsibility for the task but not necessarily the workload." To achieve this, some team-work skills were required. The five tasks were:

1. *Experimental resources. Procurement of materials and instrumentation. Logistics.*
2. *Data acquisition. Quality, format, recording, processing and documentation of data.*
3. *Presenter. Presentation on second Wednesday, preparation of transparencies. Selling of project.*
4. *Report writing. Writing of total report, ordering of sections, quality and style of report, binding.*
5. *Planning. Time management: scheduling of students, lecturers and instrumentation. Management of equipment, facilities and manpower.*

Schultz (1998) of Purdue University-West Lafayette), whose experience of self-selection was recorded above, set semester long projects in Electrical Engineering Technology. These required a microcontroller and software. He found that getting a good mix of skills in each group was the most difficult part of the management process. The first part of his selection process was to ensure that that in each group there was a microcontroller "expert." This was done by inspection of the grades of those who had completed a microcontroller course. Sometimes these were students who had been graded C but with a strong interest in the area. Once these "experts" had been assigned to the group, the remainder of the students were selected by the MBTI in order to get a good mix of potential leaders, organizers, innovators, people who follow through, and peace-makers. Unfortunately, most technology students belonged to one of the two types NT and Nf, so the tutor's task was to avoid groups that were all leaders or followers. Thus, he distributed the rare personality types first, and then he combined the others almost "randomly." This procedure did not realize perfection, but Schultz argued that almost any method is better than self-selection. It may be that heavy course loads or personal problems might interfere with what seemed to be good predictions. He found assignment guidelines that clearly stated the rules for both the course and the groups reduced the number of complaints.

Ramírez et al., (1998), of the University of Puerto Rico-Mayagüez, thought that too much cohesion in groups could lead to over-conformity in group thinking. Some organizations need mavericks to rock the boat occasionally, and less mutual admiration. [Cowan {private communication} wrote that one of the problems

with mavericks is that a group can spend so much time controlling the maverick that the essential task is lost]. Nevertheless, Ramírez highlighted the value of heterogeneity in the membership of groups. Their technology-based entrepreneurship courses included students from technical and non technical disciplines. They were grouped heterogeneously as they might be in industry, but on the basis of their academic background only. This meant that in formulating the problem the students had to learn to communicate the knowledge of their own subject specialities in order to arrive at a common goal. Ramírez and his colleagues believed that an agreed goal rather than a leader per se should direct the team.

However, in order to build leadership, as the semester developed and the design management unfolded, students undertook the leadership role, as the occasion demanded. *"For example, an electrical engineering student may be asked to solve a technical problem related to power consumption and battery selection on a proposed product. At that time he/she is the leader of the group and assigns tasks to other members. He/she becomes the authority to whom team members come with questions or problems they may face in carrying out their assignments. Later when a marketing strategy needs to be developed to sell the company's product, a marketing student will become the leader and assign the necessary tasks."* In this way it is anticipated that the students would come to understand the way in which their discipline fits into a corporate activity. They should also gain respect for those who bring knowledge from different fields. To develop teamwork, competition was encouraged between the teams, and they found that the teams wanted to be the best.

In a course in software engineering at the University of Texas- El Paso, the class was divided into multiple teams of five members each. The "affinity" groups were mentioned above. The students had to apply for a position and provide a resumé. The course professor selected the students in order to ensure that the teams comprised a diversity of experience. Students obtained experience of leadership when they were assigned the lead role for a particular job. Group work was based on the Johnson and Johnson model of cooperative learning (Gates, Delgado, and Mondragon, 2000).

These attempts to simulate industrial reality go someway to offsetting the criticism that industrial reality can never be simulated at the undergraduate level because it can never replicate the hierarchies and motivations present in the industrial environment (Aller, 1993). They at least provide for hierarchy and heterogeneity. In this respect, multi-level approaches may overcome this difficulty, and several have been reported. The affinity group approach described by Gates and her colleagues mixed students from a wide variety of educational and family backgrounds and at different levels in their

---

[18]A similar approach was adopted in a semi-conductor processing course at San Jose State University. The teams were selected on the basis of high/low GPA, work experience, and major. Graduate students who also took the course were dispersed throughout the teams (Allen, Muscat, and Green, 1996).

educational careers (i.e., undergraduates and graduates) in long-term endeavors. In the first instance, each project is a semester long. New entrants come as others graduate. Each student has a faculty mentor. An orientation course is provided at the beginning of each year and has the purposes of (a) preparing new entrants in the philosophy of the course, group work, and (b) restoring the commitment of those already in the group this orientation course is conducted as a group activity (Gates et al., 1999).

The technical purpose of the groups is to enable the students to contribute to research projects. At the beginning of each semester, each student is required to prepare a specification of research and personal goals and to declare targets that have to be met en-route. At the weekly meetings, in order to develop reflective thinking, they are required to answer three questions. These are: *"What have you learned or accomplished this week? What needs to be done? What obstacles have you encountered?"* This type of questioning is often used for the completion of student journals. An example of the use of such questions in a computer science course was described by Teller and Gates (2000).

Clayton, Martin and Martin (2000), reported on a vertically integrated materials science and engineering course that included mixed sophomore, junior, and senior teams. It was assumed, but not required, that the senior members would take charge of the project and delegate work to the juniors and sophomores. Apart from this being a more realistic simulation of industrial situations, they were anxious to foster peer learning. *"Perhaps the most fundamental goal of the course was to transfer responsibility for learning from the faculty to the student."*

The students who had participated in teams were asked to respond to a questionnaire before the course began and at the end of the course. The reception was mixed, although the positive ratings outweighed the negative. Most of the problems were typical of all teams, but the authors indicated that they would give more attention to the sophomore contribution in order to make better use of their experience.

At Purdue University a service learning program the *"Engineering Projects in Community Service"* undertook *"real"* projects for the community, some of which lasted several years (Oakes et al., 2000). The teams of between eight to fifteen undergraduates were vertically integrated and included non-engineers and liberal arts students. It was found that planning and communication were essential for their success. From 898 students who completed evaluations it was found that for both engineers and non-engineers teamwork was the most valuable quality learned.

Writing of the liberal arts students in the program the industrial adviser reported that *"Liberal Arts students, being more descriptive are very good at communication with customers and sort out their requirements from long descriptions of their problems. After the problems are defined, Liberal Arts students are usually dismissed and are directed to handle clerical tasks. The team seems to have this strong division between the two groups of students and fails to realize that no task can be done properly without knowledge of the others."* The adviser from the Liberal Arts Faculty welcomed the project but echoed some words of warning. While it was an asset for the Liberal Arts students to have learned some of the language of engineering, they must not be consigned to secretarial roles. Ways had to be found to integrate them more into the process. *"The struggle between the Liberal Arts and Engineering students is not that different from the problems faced by real companies. Sales and marketing are often ignored or belittled by engineers. Accounting is degraded to non-creative bean counters. For teams that consist of both engineering and non-engineering students efforts should be made to integrate all members of the teams. This is an excellent learning experience for their later careers"* (Oakes et al., 2000).

In a postgraduate course on marine technology at the University of Strathclyde, students worked in groups in the workshops for a period of 6 months on a project that was related to current off-shore research. An interesting dimension of the project, which added to its reality, was that students were required to prepare a hypothetical case for the funding of a development of their research (Kuo and Sayer, 1986). It was found that when the class as a whole chose the type of system to be examined and each group was given particular responsibilities for areas such as construction, installation, motion characteristics, etc., this led to greater depth of study in pure engineering areas. Previously, the groups had been assigned to a particular type of system. This had led to excessive competition between the groups that had been at the expense of the detail that was required. The teachers found that the weakest aspect of the work was the research proposal, which tended to be too ambitious. The instructors believed this to be due to the student's inexperience as much as to anything else. They argued that this group work would be helpful to the students in their future careers. We might ask, What would have happened to their learning if these graduate students had been part of a multi-level team in which they had to mentor undergraduates?

At the United States Military Academy, where the Department of Electrical Engineering and Computer Science provided a five course sequence in electrical engineering focused on electronic design for students in other fields (life sciences, modern languages, engineering management, engineering physics), it was possible to create interdisciplinary design teams. Lane and Sayles (1995), who described the rather complex process for selecting the projects and the teams, reported that teams solely composed of electrical engineering majors did not perform as well as the interdisciplinary teams. They offered no explanation as to why this may have been. The best performances were from those teams that were heavily interdisciplinary. Could it be that an interdisciplinary team causes more lateral thinking in those phases of a project that require such thinking? They also reported that there was a strong correlation between personality as measured by the MBTI and team performance. No data were given. They intended to evaluate the data in order to see if personality should be taken into account in assignment of the students to groups.

At the United States Airforce Academy, Brickell, et al., (1994) compared five methods of assigning groups to design projects. They distinguished between heterogeneous and homogeneous GPA and heterogeneous and homogeneous interest in order to assign the groups. Thus, the groups were (1) heterogeneous GPA and interest, (2) heterogeneous GPA and homogeneous interest, (3) heterogeneous interest and homogeneous GPA, (4) homogeneous GPA and homogeneous interest, and (5) self-select. The fifth group was used as a control. The students completed an inventory against a 9 point Likert type scale that ranged from "strongly agree" to "strongly disagree." The categories of the inventory were, **Criteria** (including questions items like *"I believe this course will be relevant to my future," "This course stimulated me to think about the material outside of class"*); **Instructor, Projects** *(e.g., "projects, exercises and labs helped me think more deeply about the material")*; **Classmates** *(e.g., "my classmates helped me increase my subject knowledge");* and **Course** *(e.g., "this course helped me develop my thinking skills")*. Each group had both technical and nontechnical majors. In methods 3 and 4 the members of the group had similar GPA's. Most groups comprised 4 persons.

As between all the groups and the control group, no statistically significant differences were found between them when they were compared with the grades determined for individual effort. The same was found to be true of overall total grades. However, when the group grades were inspected, they were found to be significantly higher for methods 2 and 3 than for the control group. Method 2 had the lowest variance among the grades. There was no significant difference between groups 1 and 4 and the control. Overall group selection had only slight effects on group performance. Taking into account an analysis of attitudes, the authors concluded that *"appointed groups with a mixture of homogeneity and heterogeneity perform better (earn higher grades) when compared with self selected groups."* The Self-selection group had the poorest attitudes. The investigators suggested that the results might have been dependent on the nature/type of group tasks.[19] They were not surprised to find that the students took a little longer to complete the first project than the second because

those appointed to a group have to learn to work together and time has to be allowed for this to happen (Courter, Millar and Lyons, 1998). A case study, reported at the end of the next section, raised questions about the gender mix of groups (Haller et al., 2000). While the investigators suggested that more research needed to be done they pointed out that single females in a group could be strongly disadvantaged and might not fully participate in the work of the group. All female groups might be better. They cited Tonso (1996) and Rosser (1997) in support of this argument. (See also Chapter 17).

Overall it seems that in the absence of behavioral data to the contrary, heterogeneity which takes into account the problem of gender mix is to be preferred.[20] There is some evidence that the type of task may influence group behavior.

13.3. Personality, Performance, and the Dynamics of Groups

Reference has already been made in Chapter 5 to the findings of McKenna, Mongia and Agogino (1998). They had found that personality profiles did not really help in the selection of teams, although Trytten (2001) had used the extravert and introvert dimensions of the MBTI (see Chapter 5) to help assign students to groups (Chapter 5). Nevertheless, it is easy to see why there should be interest in selecting groups by means of personality measures, and others have been found to be profitable. For example, Exhibit 13.2 lists the behaviors (players) that Allen, Muscat, and Green (1996) found in their teams. They typed these players as (1) Bad Apple; (2) Know-it-All; (3) Passivity; (4) Obsessive; and (5) Infighting. (One might have called the fourth group fearful given that there is nothing like the fear of fear.[21]) It would almost seem to be self evident from this list that personality will play a role in team performance. In this case it was used to try and avoid negative behaviors in groups. But it also ought to be done by taking into account the contribution that individuals can make to particular roles such as those listed in Exhibit 13.1. The categorization in Exhibit 13.3 is due to Belbin (1981), who argued that each member of a group or team has both a functional and a team role. Thus, while presenting the functional aspect, the individual will do so within the framework of a predetermined disposition. In his theory the team roles are limited to the eight shown in the exhibit.

Wilde (1999), borrowed from Belbin's theory the idea of defining management team roles as they relate to the results of standardized psychological tests. He wanted to define roles that were more oriented to engineering design teams. He obtained data from a preference questionnaire based on the Myers-Briggs Type Indicator that had been administered to the Stanford

---

[19]This is a very convoluted summary of what was a complex study that took into account the method of assignment by the 8 instructors. Those teaching multiple sections of the courses were likely to have different methods of assignment. The assignment of all groups in a particular section was by the same method. 442 students took part in the exercise. The time taken to undertake the projects was taken into account Students in group 2 had the least amount of time invested in projects. All groups took a little longer to complete the first project than on the second. This might be expected as students learn about the project method as one of the goals of projects.

---

[20]A study by McAnear and Seat (2001) is not discussed here because the authors recognized that in their study of male and female perceptions of performance in groups, there was a pronounced halo in the ratings, and the number of females in the sample was small.)

[21]To use part of a dictum from Franklin D. Roosevelt.

design teams over a period of several years. This team role model ohuman personality. It gave coordinate systems that were slightly different to the MBTI. These are shown in Figure 13.1(a) and 13.1(b). The two domains derive from that part of Jung's theory that deals with attitude types (disposition) and functions. It will be recalled (Chapter 5) that in Jung's theory of personality the basic attitudes or dispositions are extraversion and introversion. They lie on a continuum and individuals demonstrate a degree of one or other of these attitudes as their dominant disposition. However, Jung asserted that within the unconscious the person is of the opposite type, i.e., a conscious introvert is an unconscious extravert. Equally important are the "functions" of which there are two pairs. They describe the ways in which we perceive and act on our environment and their influences on us. One pair is sensation and intuition, and the other pair is thinking and feeling. It is said that the latter are rational functions because they involve us in making judgements or decisions. Both pairs lie on a continuum. This was well illustrated by Engler (1979) when she wrote, *"a professor, for example, may have so cultivated his intellectual and cognitive powers that the feeling and intuitive aspects of his personality are submerged. While primitive and undeveloped, they may nevertheless invade his life in the form of strange moods, symptoms, or projections."* The actualized self is a synthesis of the four functions.

Description of behaviors

1. One or more of the members is not buying into the team concept. That student is actively disruptive of team progress by his/her attitude and behavior.

2. One team member dominates the team. The value of leadership by a strong student is perverted to the point that other team members are brow-beaten until they are not willing to participate in the group intellectually. This can be exacerbated by 'passivity' (described next).

3. Team members are uncertain in their own knowledge, and will therefore allow anyone who appears to know what they are doing determine their course of action. This is unhealthy in that the 'leader' may be frequently incorrect-simply possessed with greater self-confidence.

4. The team is incapacitated by fear of mistakes. No member is willing to take responsibility for moving the group along, so progress halts.

5. Team members disagree frequently and do not resolve disputes. One of more members is noticeably 'put out' that the team is not following their advice or is placing too much burden on them.

Exhibit 13.2. Negative team behaviors found by Allen, Muscat and Green (1996) in their study of interdisciplinary team learning in a semiconductor processing task. (Reproduced with permission of IEEE, Proceedings Frontiers in Education Conference).

Wilde asks us to imagine a collection of stimulus variables that form a perception domain and another set of response variables that make up a judgement domain. Each domain has two independent variables. One is the disposition continuum and describes whether the domain activity is external or internal to the

person, while the other relates to the functions that describe the process of how the person does the domain activity. Wilde represented this by *"a coordinate system on four opposing pairs of unit vectors, one pair for each variable. The members of each pair are complementary in that they point in the opposite directions corresponding to the two variable extremes."* These are shown in the diagrams in Figure13.2(a) and 13.2(b). They also show how the roles relate to the model. They are derived from Jung's explanation of the eight ways in which the mind is used (cognitive modes). Wilde argued that these bisect the four quadrants in each domain to form eight octants, and from descriptions of the octant it was possible to associate a team role with each of them. Hence, the sixteen roles.[22]

Wilde wanted to quantify both the Jung Model and the Myers-Briggs model so that he could indicate to a respondent to his questionnaire both his/her direction and distance along the axes. The listing in Exhibits 13.4(a) and 13.4(b) and the diagrams have been greatly simplified from those in the paper. It needs to be stressed that an individual may have interests in more than one role, and that the purpose of the website is to interpret and individual's preferences as moderate or clear in the roles shown.

Team roles	Concerns and attributes
1. Chairman	Concerned with the attainment of objectives. While dominant will not will not be assertive.
2. Shaper	A Synthesizer. Wants to bring everything together so that the project can be initiated and completed. Full of nervous energy and able to challenge and respond to challenge.
3. The plant	When the team is bogged down has the imagination to look for new ideas.
4. The monitor/evaluator	Brings dispassionate analysis to the problem. Tse (1985) Calls him a "cold fish". Is also highly intelligent.
5. The company worker.	Concerned with practical implementation. Is disciplined in his/her approach and requires plenty of character.
6. Resource investigator	Looks for outside ideas and brings them back to the group.
7. Team worker	Helps make the team work. Understands the emotional needs of the group.
8. Finisher	Wants to get things done properly. Is anxious and worries about detail.

Exhibit 13.3. Summary of Belbin's list of team roles showing their concerns and attributes.

---

[22]It is beyond the scope of this report to consider Wilde's theory in detail and, therefore, to give it due justice.

The stimulus to this work, as indicated, was the student design teams at Stanford that had been successful in winning many prizes. They had been selected on the basis of the adapted MBTI. This had enabled the selectors to create teams of different interests and so help the team cope with unforeseen circumstances. Because of the breadth of knowledge in the group this was found to be the case.

Information derived from this work contributed to the definition of the new roles. Its success provided a strong argument for the use of such tests in team building, or at a very minimum to enlighten students about their preferences so that they can understand the dynamics of teamwork.[23]

Another example of the use of MBTI to support teamwork has been described by Finelli (1999), whose study at Kettering University was mentioned in Chapter 9. She reported that in the sixth week of term The Myers Briggs Type Inventory of learning styles was explained to students in the project teams. The students were asked to respond to a version of the learning style inventory due to Hogan and Champagne (1980). Finelli's objective was to *"enlighten the students about their own personal preferences and the preferences of their team mates."* A team project for the course asked the *"teams to prepare a short essay describing the personality styles of their team and comparing and contrasting traits of each member of the team."* They were also asked to state four personality differences that could affect the working of the team, and to suggest ways in which these differences could be used to the team's advantage. Unfortunately, no detailed information is given about their responses other than that the students found the exercise rewarding and that the teachers expected the teams to work more effectively because of it. The inventory had found a diversity of styles among the groups.

Others have used the Kolbe index as a basis for team selection. Kolbe, (1989, 1993), Timmermann, Lingard, and Barnes (2001) of California State University-Northridge began their study from the position that one of the difficulties in persuading both staff and students in computer science to engage in active learning was the belief that students prefer to work alone rather than in a group. The finding that among a group of 300 or so students responding to the MBTI, 47% were found to be introverts and 37% extraverts, with 15% being evenly split, gave some credence to this position.

The Kolbe theory holds that team synergy contributes to group productivity: thus, groups should be selected to maximise synergy. Therefore, the Kolbe Index types persons for this purpose. A productive team will require the talent of each type but they have to be balanced by how individuals make use of these talents. These four striving instincts are expressed through operational zones that are described by 'initiative', 'respond', and 'prevent'. The Kolbe Index provides a score of the instinct against these zones and indicates how an individual is willing to act, and how an individual won't act (Lingard and Berry, 2002). According to this theory 25% of any of any group should be initiating, 50% responding, and 25% preventing.

Timmermann, Lingard and Barnes, (1989, 1993) used the Kolbe Index to assess their students' natural approaches to problem solving (conation). They found that most of them were fact finders.[24] The four action modes (striving instincts) identified by Kolbe were (1) Fact Finder, who is a person that collects data and establishes priorities; (2) Follow Thru, who is a person that seeks structure and makes schedules; (3) Quick Start, who is person that takes risks, improvises, and plays hunches;, and (4) Implementer, who innovates, takes risks, improvises, and plays hunches.

We each have these qualities to some degree but are most effective when we utulize those that are strongest. Timmerman and his colleagues found that 48% of their software students functioned naturally in the fact finder mode; 64% demonstrated this mode as either their first or second highest mode. Such persons want to be well prepared and are uncomfortable in impromptu discussions. They also found these modes among faculty, thus, they argued, one reason why teachers might not want to use active learning techniques was that they did not like learning in this mode. But, in their view, an instructor has, nevertheless, to select exercises that are suited to the learning styles of the students.

Fitzpatrick, Askin, and Goldberg (2001) also found a large number of fact finder's but no implementers in a Systems and Industrial Engineering course. They studied the performance of teams using software from the Kolbe Corporation, and found some groups that had been selected by GPA did not have adequate skill levels to enable the team to perform effectively, and students had to be reassigned. A subjective evaluation suggested that the Kolbe model was predictive. From their data, like Wilde, they developed a mathematical programming model for selecting effective teams.

Following the earlier study at Northridge, Lingard and Berry reexamined some of the earlier data to see if there was a relationship between group synergy and group performance. They found a significant correlation between synergy and project scores.

They also found that age (range 21.3 to 38 years) did not contribute to group performance. Older groups did no better than the younger. Given this finding, it is not surprising that there should be no relation between project scores and work experience. No relationship was found between the percentage of women in a team and the team score. Nor did the relative cultural diversities of the group, as measured by language, produce significant relationships with project scores. However, from a calculation of group participation a

---

[24]The four action modes correspond to four instinctive behaviors. These are probing, patterning, innovating and demonstrating. A more detailed discussion of this theory will be found in Fitzpatrick, Askin, and Goldberg (2001)

(a) The perception domain

Visionary.	Imagines various product forms and uses	Possibility process
Strategist.	Speculates on project and process failure.	Imagination mode
Inspector.	Detects and corrects errors prototypes.	Concentration attitude
Investigator.	Gets facts and knowhow	Knowledge mode
Prototyper.	Builds and tests models and prototypes	Facts process
Test pilot.	Pushes performance envelope.	Experiment mode
Entrepreneur.	Explores new products and methods	Exploration attitude
Innovator.	Synthesizes new products.	Synthesis mode

(b) The judgment domain.

Needfinder	Evaluates human factors and consumer issues	Feeling process.
Critiquer	Addresses aesthetic and moral issues	Evaluation mode.
Reviewer	Compares performance with goals and standards.	Appraisal attitude
Simulator	Analyzes performance and efficiency	Analysis mode
Methodologist	Sets deadlines, defines procedures and breaks Bottleknecks	Thinking process.
Coordinator	Focuses effort and saves time	Organization mode.
Diplomat	Harmonizes team, client and consumer	Control attitude.
Conciliator	Detects and resolves interpersonal issues	Teamwork mode.

Exhibit 13.4. (a) Roles in the perception domain. Simplified from Wilde (1999). Shows the relationship to attitude (disposition), function (process), and cognitive mode. In the original, each of these is accompanied by a descriptor, as, for example, the test pilot "senses the moment, tries things out, experiments with performance. (b) Roles in the judgment domain also simplified from role. As in (a), illustrations of the attitude, process, and mode were given, as, for example, thinking process- impersonal, logical orderly, fair minded, objective).

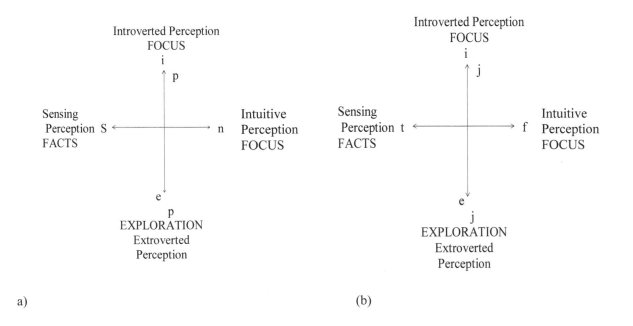

a)   (b)

Figure 13. 1. Wilde's basis for (a) the perception domain and (b) the judgment domain. (Reproduced with permission of the author)

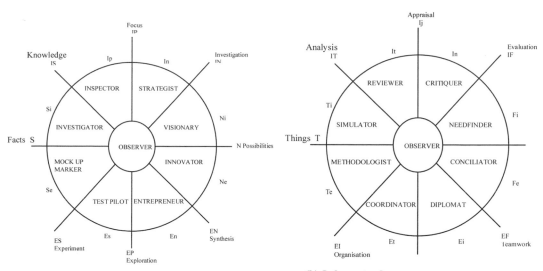

(a) Perception roles

(b) Judgment roles
Perception radial roles alternating with characteristics

Figure 13.2. .When a person has no clear or even moderate projections on any of a domains role vectors, the interest is said to be in a "central" role, justifying perhaps at least tentative association with any of the domain roles not covered by team mates. The preception central role is called "observer"; the judgment central role, "mediator"–both valid team functions. A central role interest is shown by shading the inner circle." (Wilde, 1999 Proceedings ASME Design Engineering Conference, Las Vegas). (Reproduced with the permission of the author)

significant relationship was found with project scores. This finding suggested that project success might be enhanced if there was better participation among the members of the group. It was also found that smaller teams did better. These findings led Lingard and Berry to advocate, as others had, training in the understanding of group processes in order for individuals to help them establish 'comfortable relationships'.

Another report at the same conference by a group at Georgia Tech who had evaluated a collaborative website (CoWeb) lent some support to this view (Guzdial et al., 2001). They had found that students in engineering mathematics had not seen collaboration as conducive to their success. Guzdial and his colleagues thought that faculty might be in agreement with the students. They suggested that this was because in engineering mathematics students have to solve problems that require single answers, classes tended to be competitive, and students resist collaboration. The found that the classes that had been successful with CoWeb had dealt with ill-structured problems where there were many correct answers. This led them to suggest that to overcome this resistance to group work students should be led into collaboration through having to deal with problems that have more than one solution. Similarly, in the first instance, collaboration should be limited to a low-level of commitment such as a single homework assignment. Confidence has to be built.

At Coventry University, Halstead and Martin (2002) used the Honey and Mumford Learning Style Inventory (see Chapter 5) with the purpose of *"encouraging the students to engage more fully with their own learning, and to take responsibility for it"* and to assign them to groups. The students were level 2 and level 3. It was found that all the students showed a strong reflective learning style, and that it persisted into level 3. This was worrying because it meant that there was still some dependence on the lecturer in the final stages of the program. (See Perry's theory of development in Chapter 6). In order to select students into groups, the students were given the option of either being selected on the basis of their learning styles, or of selecting the groups themselves. Equal numbers elected for each method. The performance results of the experimental groups were compared with those from a control group. It was found that within the groups the average score were almost identical. The activist scores of the self-selected groups produced a wider variance than that produced by the selected groups. Halstead and Martin thought that this might have had a negative effect on the groups if the students preferred noninteractive exercises. However, those who were selected by their learning styles, achieved much better results than the self-selected groups in the pilot study. This might well have been due to the personality profile of the self-selected groups as another British study might lead us to believe.

Like Halstead and Martin's study, it was conducted with small numbers at the University of Salford among students reading manufacturing technology. The results lent support to Smith's (1993) recommendations for cooperative learning. It also gave support to the view that personality plays an important part in the dynamics of the group (Freeman and Sharp, 2001).

1. In that study 32 students were divided into 5 groups on the basis of a range of psychometric measures for

2. *intelligence, personality, aptitude and interest.[25] The characteristics of the 5 Groups were*
3. *High convergent scores, low divergence scores plus low extraversion. (N = 6)*
4. *High convergent scores, low divergence scores plus high critical scores. (N = 6).*
5. *Balanced convergence/divergence scores plus high critical scores. (N = 7).*
6. *Balanced convergence/divergence scores plus high benevolence scores (N = 6).*
7. *High divergence scores, low convergence scores plus high extraversion. (N = 7).*

The learning process within the groups was identified by observation, as well as by written reports from the group members after the exercises had been completed. The observers were doctoral students who had been briefed in the use of the Flander's Interaction Analysis Technique (Amidon and House, 1976).[26]

The observers were asked to rate the groups according to content and quality of ideas produced; the number of new and original ideas produced; and group participation and interaction. There were two discussion sessions that lasted 45 minutes each. The groups were asked to elect a chairman and rapporteur. During the discussion the group had to complete a report. Of the five observers, one tended to be more critical, and one tended to be more lenient than the others. Their scores tended to become more discriminating as they went from discussion to discussion. The investigators changed the arrangements after the first discussion in order for each group to be observed by two observers.

After the discussions, each rapporteur read their summary of their groups discussion. The observers then gave ratings and general assessments. Questions were allowed and the progress of each group discussed. Freeman and Sharp discovered an interesting difference between the observers and the students. The observers were found to be hesitant and nervous. Their diction was

also poor. In contrast, the presentational skills of the students were extremely high. The need to make a presentation allowed *"the students to come into their own before the assembly and was clearly an aid to personality development."* Freeman and Sharp, however, observed that while the students were particularly skillful in their manipulation of abbreviations (e.g., CAL, GNP), they did not critically examine these terms in relation to the topics. [It should be noted that the average IQ of students in the different schools at Salford University is between 128 and 130 which is relatively high (Freeman and Thomas, 2001)[27]. In order to ensure a greater depth of discussion Freeman and Sharp considered that it would have been better to have initiated a goal directed exercise that would have required *"individual accountability, personal interaction, and promotive interaction"* (p. 136).[28] This would, it seems, require clearly defined roles. They might also have asked for group processing prior to the assembly.

With respect to the content and quality of ideas produced, the observers produced a similar pattern of scores, although the mean increased for the second discussion (from 3.2 to 4.2 on a five-point scale). However, group 5 was rated much higher than the other for its ability to generate new and original ideas. This was to be expected given the predominance of divergent thinking and extraversion in the group. At the same time, this group was rated below the other groups for participation and interaction. Group 2 obtained the lowest mean score for the generation of new and original ideas, and groups 3 and 4 obtained means of 3.5. However, they cohered much better in the first discussion, and apart from group 2 the other groups improved their coherence in the second session with groups 3 and 4 showing the greatest improvement. One of the problems observed in the fifth group was that whilst they generated new ideas they did not follow them up with a thorough evaluation. *"When a new idea arose this quickly displaced the idea under discussion giving an impression of erratic progress to the observer."* (p. 135). The convergers, groups 1 & 2, were found to lack leadership. *"There was a lack of enthusiasm which might have brought greater progress"* (p. 135). They also observed that on occasion there were two chairman, a self-appointed one taking over. Roles did not always persist. The groups reported as being most

---

[25]The AH6 (scientific) Group test of High Grade Intelligence. The Hypotheses test: a measure of divergent thinking. The Eysenck Personality Inventory. The Vocational Preference Inventory. The Controversial Statements Inventory. The Photographs Test- First impressions of personality. In tests of the latter type students are asked to judge attributes of the head and shoulders of individuals. In this case they were photographs of 38 students. The respondents were asked to judge if they were English or German students. They were also asked to give ratings of some personality traits on a three point scale. The test *"facilitates the development of a benevolent/critical continuum which is obtained by summating the bias (positive or negative) in the personality ratings. In the Photograph test- 'benevolents' were the individuals with the highest number of 'above average' ratings; 'criticals' were the individuals with the greatest number of 'below average' ratings. There has been an observed relationship between these variables and the extraversion/introversion continuum."*

[26] An observers assessment sheet required *"(1) Clear identification of the position of each student and identification of the Chairman and reporter on the assessment sheet. (2) showing the actual number of contributions made by each individual member (denoted by a simple count on the assessment sheet). (3) The approximate length of time taken for each individual's contribution (increment on a box) (4) The number of ideas generated by individuals [   ]. (5) the main communication highways i.e. who in particular were individuals talking to".*

[27]Sharp and Freeman were aware that highly intelligent respondents could skew test results because of their test sophistication. To overcome this, the photographs test was used to conceal the actual purpose of the investigation. Therefore, the students were told that the research workers were interested in the assessment of the personalities of university students, whereas they were really interested in systematic trends and tendencies in their judgement. Support for indirect assessment of this kind is to be found in the work of Argyle (1976).

[28]The first discussion topic was –"What knowledge, skills and level of understanding will be required by manufacturing managers of the future? The second topic was a discussion of a research paper on computer integrated management (CIM) in which the students were instructed as follows: the research report you have been given discusses CIM in the packaging industry. What does your group think will be the effects of CIM on manufacturing management in the 1990's with particular reference to organizational and personnel related issues?" (p. 133).

effective in terms of all round performance were those that were balanced between convergence and divergence (i.e., Groups 3 and 4). Freeman and Sharp pointed out that Guilford (1979) had argued that "balance" characterized the effective individual and that this study showed it to be true of group behavior as well. Analysis of the independent reports showed that the group discussions had stimulated the students to think independently.

At the same time there is a problem about how individual contributions are assessed. Not every one has the personality attribute that makes for strong oral contributions yet in the penultimate their understanding might contribute to the solution (findings). Freeman and Sharp pointed out that *"some students who had contributed little to the discussion had clearly been paying attention to everything that had gone on and had identified key aspects of the exercise. The exercise had clearly been an important learning experience for them and furthermore they had been able to identify the elements and factors in the learning process on which they had gained the greatest benefit".* Freeman and Sharp went on to say, *"This is clearly a function of personality."* They considered that this lent further support to the cooperative method proposed by Smith (1993) and Smith, Johnson, and Johnson (1992), because individuals have to take responsibility for their roles. There may still be problems for some students, and understanding the behaviors of the more introverted students would enable greater peer support. Such understanding, as Lingard and Berry (2002) found, is likely to require prior training.

Another Sharp (2001), argued that the Kolb learning style theory could be helpful in training students for teamwork skills. For example, they could relate the theory to their laboratory group interactions and thus analyze their group behaviors as a function of the styles that they bring to the group. She also suggested that the theory could be used to analyze and target the audience and enhance communication skills. Her work in these areas was at an exploratory stage.

Finelli (2001) showed that when students discussed learning styles in relation to teamwork, this impacted on their working together. During the class in which the learning styles were discussed, they also completed the Felder and Soloman inventory. For part of their homework they had to write a short essay describing the learning preferences of the students in their team, and the whole study involved them in tabulating the results of the learning style inventory and also comparing and contrasting the learning styles of each member of their team. Peer ratings and self-assessments suggested that the students exposed to this treatment increased their skills more than a group of students with much more experience of teamwork.

An alternative approach to the study of group behavior that has a long history and is much favored derives from anthropology and the qualitative techniques that have been developed in the social sciences (see Chapter 15). In education, such approaches, as, for example, those of illuminative evaluation, are the basis for action research (or evaluation) that is concerned with understanding for improvement[29]. It is not undertaken for the purpose of obtaining scientific generalizations although it may throw up issues that are of general purport (Bassey, 1994). One example of such a case study was described by Haller et al., (2000) who used a qualitative method known as conversation analysis to understand the internal dynamics among four volunteer student groups. They were taking a course in Chemical Process Principles at North Carolina State University[30].

From conversation analysis it is possible to establish how dialogue is used in workgroups, and from that to say something about the effectiveness of such groups. (The reader of the original paper will find similarities with protocol analysis).   In this study, transcripts of one problem solving session from each group were analyzed. It was found that the students engaged in two quite different kinds of conversation. Given that the purpose of cooperative grouping is to enhance learning, then necessarily there must be teaching. Thus, one form of conversation was the transfer of knowledge (TK). This happens when a student becomes a teacher and as such takes on the predominant role either with a member of the group or the group.[31] Haller and her colleagues showed that such conversations are dialogical and not monological. Within the dialogue the pupil gives feedback about his/her understanding of the problem and this may account for the enhancement of learning which persons in cooperative groups experience. Feedback is very often not given in lectures, and for that reason students consult each other after the lecture, hence the importance of jointly completed homework.

The other kind of dialogue that the students engaged in was "collective sequences"(CS). In such sequences the dialogue between the roles was mainly symmetrical. Knowledge is exchanged but there is no teacher present. Each role player participates. In such sequences there is much overlapping and simultaneous conversation, but the participants in Haller's groups did not perceive the overlaps as interruptions. Moreover, at any one time there could be several questions on the table; often more than one student responded at the same time to a question. We are all familiar with such conversations and it is not surprising to find that they were *"generally fragmented, tending to contain short and incomplete phrases and clauses rather than a full clear and explicitly expressed explanation".* But, said the investigators, *"students appeared to be working out the problem in situ rather than anyone having solved the*

---

[29]Published in cyclostyle format "Evaluation as Illumination" by M. Parlett and D. Hamilton (1972), University of Edinburgh caused a major stir in thinking about educational research. An illustration of the illuminative approach will be found in Heywood and Montagu Pollock (1976). See also, Bogdan and Biklen (1998), Stake (1995). See Chapter 15.

[30]The groups comprised 3 males: 4 females: 2 females and 1 male; 2 females and 2 males.

[31] On the basis of work by Keppler and Luckmann (1991) they expected to find this particular type of conversation.

problem in advance." Such sequences they argued provide *"good practice for the kind of group work students will do in engineering design settings, where there is no unequivocally right answer and an optimal solution to the problem must be worked out using the expertise of all group members"*These investigators found that 69% of the teaching sequences analyzed fell into the TK category and 37% into the CS category. The highest percentage of CS's came from the all-female group. One of the major problems observed was that one member of the group would continually initiate a teaching sequence. She/he was the perpetual student, and in the illustration given, the other two members of the group became frustrated because they were unable to obtain understanding from this student. That particular student only became the teacher once in fifteen sequences.

Haller and her colleagues also found that a group member could cause the group to dysfunction when that person made it difficult for others to contribute to the group effort. Once again the suggestion was made that some prior training, in this case in social dialogue, would have helped to make the groups more functional. They also noted, and again others have made this point, that the choice of assignment is important. It has to be sufficiently challenging to involve all members of the group otherwise able students will want to solve the problem on their own. The authors did not comment on the entering characteristics of the group in relation to this issue. However, they suggested that students pre-work the relatively straightforward parts of the assignment before the group meeting.

A recent study at the Colorado School of Mines suggested that the skill required for work in mixed gender teams might benefit from some training (Laeser et al., 2003). Typically, studies of mixed gender teams have shown that males are focused on the task functions while females are focused on the process functions described by Eberhardt (1987); see page 132). To put it in another way, females and males contribute different skills to the team. However, this was not found to be the case in this investigation: Less than 5% of the process functions were observed across the teams irrespective of gender mix.[32] Gender seemed to have little impact on the functions of individual members of the team. It was found that *"mixed gender teams displayed the lowest level of performance across all team compositions"* in the first design course in the sequence. It was for this reason that the authors felt that some training to help students work in mixed gender teams might be necessary. Cooperation might be required at a level greater than that for which first year students could function without help.

Laeser and her colleagues suggested that one implication of these findings was that classroom decisions relating to teamwork should not be based on the general research into teams because the engineering classroom might be a special case. For example, The Colorado School of Mines, in which the study was conducted, is primarily an engineering college and *"the commonalities between males and females are likely to be especially exaggerated."* Although not directly comparable, in this respect it is of some interest to compare these findings with the outcomes of investigations at Heriot-Watt University in Edinburgh (see Chapter 17) because it is a small college and is oriented to studies in science, engineering and technology.

In addition to observing team dynamics, this study also evaluated the final reports of the teams and a rubric that had been developed at the School was revised for this purpose (Moskal, Leydens, and Pavelich, 2002). In the first course of the sequence, it was found that majority male teams outperformed majority female teams. However, in the second course of the sequence the position was reversed. Majority female teams outperformed majority male teams. The investigators suggested that this was consistent with the view that females who have corrected any deficiencies they might have had in the first year became more able to demonstrate their engineering knowledge. Similarly, other research had noted that women in first year engineering courses lacked self-confidence (Felder, 1995), and the first year is used to gain confidence. Laeser and her colleagues also pointed out that a contributory reason for this reversal in female fortunes might have been due to overconfidence among the males.

Much of the research on teams in engineering education has been done with male students. It cannot be assumed that it applies to mixed gender groups. For this reason, there is need for more research on this issue. For example, in the case of the previously mentioned study, it would have been of interest had personality and learning style data been obtained.

13.4.   Group Working Across Universities[33]

Because distributed group working is increasingly evident in software engineering, the United Kingdom Universities of Durham and Keele, and the University of Manchester Institute of Science and Technology (UMIST) initiated a joint program wherein sub-projects would be carried out on a group basis. Three students, one from each of the universities, *"were required to specify, design, develop, test, and document a software application."* There were three sub-projects. Each sub-project had to be completed by two groups working independently of each other. Thus, eighteen students were involved (Brereton et al., 2000). Planning had to take account of the different course structures within the participating universities, the different technical backgrounds of the students who participated, and the different requirements for final year projects in

---

[32] The students participating in the study were divided into all male teams, teams with more males than females (majority male), more females than males in the teams (majority female), and teams comprising half females and half males. The teams were made up of between 4 and 6 students.

[33] Only one study is reported in this section. There are others, as for example, Orsak and Etter (1996).

each of the three universities. Prior to the project, students and instructors took part in a team building exercise during which the students were told about the aims of the exercise and the role of the sub-projects.

The first stage of the project was to provide a low-cost PC cooperative environment which would include video conferencing, shared drawing and shared repository facilities (Gumbley, 1997). In the second stage, distributed groups of students completed a series of case studies involving software-engineering tasks with synchronous group working tools. In the final stage the students participated in substantial subprojects that took several weeks to complete. These subprojects embraced both asynchronous and synchronous learning. The technology used video, audio, chat, white board, and shared repository.

Brereton et al., (2000) found that in spite of the fact that the students were self-selected problems associated with group learning emerged. For example, one student failed to contribute to his group's activities. Another did not turn up for the synchronous learning sessions. It also *"became clear during the second collaborative period that the individual goals of some of the students differed significantly from their fellow group members, particularly with respect to completing the implementation component of the subproject."* By and large, students found the projects beneficial. Brereton et al., (2000) reported that the lessons learned about the software engineering issues were:

- *"Students benefit from wider access to expertise, which is extremely valuable to small departments.*
- *Students learn about the problems of cooperating without a shared history.*
- *It was felt to be important that the chosen tasks span the whole software development life-cycle.*
- *Training in the use of the chosen technologies is needed."*

13.5. The Working Environment

It has long been understood in industrial social psychology that an organization is both a social and a technical system. Many years have passed since Rice related this theory to the university as an organization. Consequently, a number of myths have become established about the design of educational institutions based on naïve understandings of how people learn. Few articles in the literature reviewed for this book evaluated the learning environment in spite of the fact the technology is impacting on approaches to learning. The idea that underpins social technical systems theory is that an organization is both a technical and a social system, and that the motivation to work can only be understood by attention to both systems. In college terms a classroom is a form of socio-technical system. So to is a library. Although they did not mention this theory Grulke, Beert, and Lane (2001) gave an excellent demonstration of the principles of this approach in their evaluation of the effect of the environment on engineering team performance.

In their study they compared a group of three teams who worked in a more or less custom designed training classroom for technology with three teams who had to find any space that was available in the engineering complex.[34] Within the treatment classroom there were three different organizational arrangements. The control groups found spaces two of which approximated in many respects to the treatment room[35]. Grulke, Beert, and Lane (2001) were particularly interested in evaluating "environment competence." That is, how well students utilize available resources. The problem to be solved was chosen to challenge the teams and put them under pressure.[36]

Technical performance was measured by the quality of the teams' technical results and written communication as assessed by the references cited, and accuracy of the kinetic model deduced. A self-report instrument was administered at the end of the exercise. The treatment groups presented better quality reports with fewer technical errors, but one of the control group teams produced one of the best technical solutions. A team effectiveness instrument evaluated student perceptions of the team's performance. No significant differences between the groups were found with this measure of team effectiveness.

Two instruments were developed for students to (a) evaluate their experience of their performance in the environment in which they worked (*Team Environment Survey*), and (b) to rate their experience of eight design criteria thought to contribute the enhancement of collaborative learning in groups. It was also a measure of environmental satisfaction (*Small Group Environment Rating Form*). In the first schedule there were 24 semantic differential items. Taken together there were no significant differences, but on four items there were significant differences. The control teams were worried by the shared location for project materials. The treatment teams thought the environment created a sense of realism; they were more satisfied with the conditions of the scenario, and they were more certain that the environment helped them to work well together. With respect to the design the only statistically significant difference between the groups was ease of interaction. The activities were also observed.

---

[34]N = 36. Chemistry, materials engineering and chemical engineering majors. Groups determined by the number of chemists 1 being assigned to each group. The groups were selected so that approximately equivalent skills were in the treatment and control groups.

[35] The different systems were presented in plan and photographic form in the paper.

[36]The authors call the method used *"charette,"* but it is not explained. A footnote is given from which the reader is left to draw their own conclusions. The term *"alludes to a process that originated at the Ecole des Beaux-Arts Sschool of Architecture in 19th century Paris. Students, after a period of intense effort to meet their project deadline, would jump on the charette (little cart) used by the proctors to collect the projects. Riding along, they put finishing touches on their work in the final minutes before their presentations were due. This final intensity of creative effport epitomizes a charette. This problem solving approach generates a high degree of motivation on the part of participants."*

At first sight, it might appear that environment did not have the effect predicted by the investigators. But, as they pointed out, the study became problematic when the control groups with their local knowledge of the space that was available, sought spaces that approximated somewhat to the database conditions in the treatment classroom! However, the database search was completed by the treatment teams fifteen minutes in advance of the control groups. The configuration of the team space and the location of resources affected the sharing of technical articles. Although the development of the kinetic model created the most discussion two reports from control group teams contained many technical errors, and all of the control group teams took longer to complete and correct their work. Only one team (a treatment group team) allowed sufficient time to complete the report. There seems that there may have been a Hawthorne effect in that *"their performance contrasts markedly with team performance in similar term projects both in prior and subsequent years."*

On balance there was support for the view that the environment does matter. In the first place there were substantial differences in the technical performance of the two groups, and some would say that that is all that matters. The investigators also drew attention to the view that in experiential learning, realism is important, and the treatment group felt that this was the case in their environment. Moreover, the treatment groups were more satisfied, and the investigators noted that the environment enabled sustained concentration. The fact that the control group teams chose environments which nearly mirrored the treatment environment is of some significance. Do we inherently understand the environments that will help us learn? It would seem so because the *"control teams wanted their turn in room 72 to prove what they could do."*

13.6. Preparation (Training) for Group Work

It is evident from the foregoing that there is an acceptance among engineering educators who practice teamwork exercises that students can be prepared for teamwork. It is understood that team behaviors can be learned, and Smith (2004) has provided a basic text for such training. Since the success of cooperative learning depends on the confidence that the participants have, and since many participants are uncomfortable with group work, training can help develop confidence (DiBiasio and Groccia, 1995; Felder, 1995; Free et al., 1993). At the same time, small group work can be used to help students adjust to university life during their first year of study as has been found in the teaching of thermodynamics at Victoria University of Technology[37] (Hessami and Sillitoes, 1990). Grulke, Beert, and Lane (2001), argued that not only should students be given prior training on the principles and practice of self-directed teams, but that they should be prepared to know *"what to expect from the settings that are available."*

Similarly, at the University of Puerto Rico it was argued that attrition was reduced by the introduction of cooperative learning (see above). But its implementation required a considerable change in the academic culture, and this was achieved in no small measure by training faculty in cooperative learning procedures (Morrell et al., 2001). That such training has to be substantive was indicated by the fact that while *"60% of faculty members surveyed felt confident in their knowledge of CL theory and role assignment"*... they felt less confident in *"areas such as conflict resolution, grading activities and individual accountability"*. However, faculty members perceived *"more positive than negative changes in student attitudes."*

A variety of training strategies have been proposed that range from the relatively simple to the complete course. Ramírez et al., (1998) hoped that the skills would be learned as a consequence of the way the course is organized. [38]However, in the first week the students were given written material on team-building and a seminar on organizational behavior. They also participated *"in a number of hands-on activities to expose the newly formed teams to situations that accelerate team cohesiveness, build trust and require teamwork."*

Others think that more formal tuition should be provided. For example, Schultz (1998), whose work was described above, had provided for an introduction to group dynamics in the first week, but in the future they would come to the projects having completed a pre-requisite course that dealt with group interactions in the Communications Department. Clayton, Martin, and Martin (2000), whose work was also discussed above, provided instruction on working in teams in terms of member roles, the conduct of meetings, delegation and follow-up, but their evaluation led them to the view that much more time should be spent teaching teamwork skills, especially to seniors.

Blair (1993) of the University of Edinburgh described how in their fourth and fifth years, students in the Department of Electrical Engineering received a short intensive module on project management skills before undertaking a nine-month placement in industry. The module was structured around an introductory lecture.[39] This was followed up by team activities of two or more days that allowed the students to judge the validity of the theory presented in the lecture by practising some of the techniques that had been suggested. Although only a few students had taken the course, their views were consistent with those reported in other papers. They had learned that engineering design is necessarily a social process which is a reminder of an important point made by Bucciarelli (1988) and reinforced by West and Shimizu (1992) as a result of a comparative study of collaboration among American and Japanese students.

On the basis of field dependence/independence theory, Seat and Lord (1998) designed a six-module

---

[37]Footscray, Australia.

[38]They gave an example of *"building leadership"* to illustrate how this was accomplished.

[39]Described in full in the paper.

course for learning interaction skills.[40] The course is shown in Exhibit 13. 5. It is based on the premise that many engineers are field-independent and prefer to work by themselves and not in a group. They found that engineers and engineering students complained about role plays, *"because the training was not written down for them to study on their own."* To overcome this disposition, they needed to be coached in interaction skills. In the course described, there were two components. The first was about an applied soft-skill, and the second was a discussion on how people work. Each module was accompanied by an experiential learning exercise and an outside activity to encourage the extension of the skills learned into everyday life. Two of their findings related to the timing of such communication courses. First, they argued that such training is best started in the freshmen year. Second, although it had been taught in engineering classes with great success, it had failed when they had tried to introduce it into the capstone projects. *"Although students patiently sit through it, they never seem to gain new skills. In fact, they resent the interruption and devalue the effects of good interpersonal skills. Successful timing means that learning the modules is the student's task, not just another chore lumped on the technical task."* Seat and Lord pointed out the importance of debriefing the students on what worked and what did not work in a group situation. Debriefing was *"the mechanism for learning how to apply these skills in real situations"*. Often it took as much time as a class period.[41]

In another paper, Lord (2001) reported that student response to mandatory cooperative homework learning teams in a junior materials science course suggested that the students had found the teamwork helpful and that it had enhanced their learning.

At IUPUI[42] the Department of Organizational Leadership and Supervision, which is within the School of Engineering and Technology, offered a course on Human Behavior in Organizations. It was an introduction to experiential, self-directed learning teams.[43] Students

participated in a simulated work team. *"The primary purpose of class assignments is to provide the students with the opportunity to work in a team that is expected to make decisions, analyze problems and solve them. Within this context the teams analyze their own behavior in real time. Student team projects as well as the dynamics involved in the team process are thoroughly analyzed. Students experience theory in action, and learn together how to analyze their behavior. They can test out theories and practice behaviors unfamiliar and new to them. Students have the opportunity to immerse themselves in the study of how and why teams function..."* (Goodwin et al., 1999).

The authors reported that recent alumni surveys showed that graduates placed high value on teamwork skills, but that their own alumni *"gave less than a satisfactory rating to their team experiences within their major"* and this provided them with a substantial argument for stand-alone courses of they kind they offered.[44] Their program required that the course tutors(s) should be given in facilitation. In any event this should be an integral part of those courses that are being given to develop university teachers (as in the United Kingdom), and teaching assistants (as in the United States). Students complained that group work could be frustrating and added little to their experience. *"Their concerns include other student's work influencing their grades, finding adequate meeting time, and unequal distribution of work"* (David and Wellington, 1998).

One student, in another study, said that it is all very well working in hierarchies if you have the requisite knowledge. *"If I did not know some technical thing, probably no one else in the team did either. There wasn't enough experience to make the most of everybody's strong points"* (Cited by Aller, 1993). Lack of knowledge can curtail team interaction as Sutton and Thompson (1998) reported. They wanted to integrate teams of engineers, geologists and geophysicists and found that when students perceived a knowledge disparity (real or not), this could induce a feeling of inferiority and lead to lack of participation in the group. The solution to this problem *"was initiated through two cross-training periods. Subject areas from each discipline were assigned to each team. After a period of research a team member selected at random, would teach the entire class the appointed subject material. Once knowledge was shared, the questions were asked, the feelings of inadequacy began to diminish."*

These findings imply that projects have to be carefully chosen so that the range of expertise required reflects that available in the team. Alternatively, if individuals are assigned to be experts in a particular area,

[40]For an introductory paper see Seat et al., (1996). This was developed at the University of Tennessee-Knoxville and the University of San Diego.

[41]FitzGibbon and Heywood (1986/1989) have shown the importance of debriefing after role plays when training school principals.

[42]Indiana University-Purdue University Indianapolis

[43]The idea of self directed work groups (SDWG's) has been around for a long time. It stems from the principle that the more a person is involved in their work, the more they will be committed to the achievement of the organizations goals. They provide job enrichment and have been practised at all levels of organization. A good example is that of the Volvo engine plant in Sweden. In Europe they have been described by various terms e.g., Group technology; autonomous work groups; cellular organization. Theoretically they originate in the application of open systems theory to production lines, and are a form of job enrichment, aimed at producing self-actualisation. There are variations in the degree of responsibility and autonomy that such groups have. In the United States a useful summary of SDWG's is to be found in David and Wellington (1998) who applied the characteristics of SDWG's to classroom settings in two universities. They borrowed a definition from Thamhain (1996); *"groups of employees who have day*

to day responsibility for managing themselves and the work they perform with minimum supervision."
[44] In the United Kingdom, Heywood (1994) concluded, as a result of a study for the Enterprise Learning Initiative in Higher Education, that a substantial case could be made for stand-alone courses in the understanding of human behavior and the development of teamwork skills.

then provision has to be made for them to familiarize themselves with that area and ensure that they have expertise in it. But, prior to this as David and Wellington pointed out, it is important to discuss the concerns that students have about group work. In this way their expectations will be made clear to all members of the team, and their solutions as to how they can be resolved in the future will be taken on board. For this reason David and Wellington required their teams to draw up a code of conduct.

An interesting development in the preparation of students for group work has been described by Null (1997). Among the goals of the exercise were the development of critical thinking skills and the preparation of the syllabus. Null described her approach as follows: *"As the initial step in becoming part of a group, on the first day of the class I ask students to break into teams of their choice (about 3-4 students per group) and begin thinking about what they want to learn in class, (Why are you here? What do you want to learn?) As discussion warrants, I talk for short periods of time about certain topics that might be required for the course, topics that have been covered in the past and current topics (always an easy thing to do in computer science). Each group is charged with creating a list of topics it believes the course should cover. After a period of time (about 45 minutes) we work as a group to establish a reasonable list of topics."*

"To help students develop critical thinking skills they are asked to determine why certain topics are necessary. For their first homework assignment they are asked to verify the importance of each of the topics in the class list. The intent is to allow students to discover that the topics that are important in the field of computer science, and that they should learn for this reason and not because "the teacher says so". To perform this verification by themselves would be overwhelming. The students generally divide the list into pieces and each person is responsible for his/her sublist. They are given several days to complete this assignment.... Even if the instructor has to give the students a list of topics, it is a good motivational technique to ask the students to perform the verification process."

Next, the students were asked *"to help design the syllabus of their course. This assignment includes developing a class mission (being clear on purpose or beginning with the end in mind, developing class goals (which forces them to look at their needs and meet them), selecting appropriate topics for the course (based on verification); determining how the topics should be covered (lecture, projects, films, guest speakers, labs); analyzing to what depth the topics should be covered (where the levels of depth might include exposure, familiarity or mastery); and, perhaps more importantly, determining how students should be evaluated in the course (exams, quizzes, presentations, projects, homework), keeping in mind the syllabus should be designed as an outcome based tool, not a grade oriented one."*

In another course a "crisis design exercise" was used to help with team building in a course on Integrated Product Development at the University of Vermont-Burlington. The class included graduate and undergraduate students, as wel as students from colleges other than engineering (Shirland and Manock, 2000). The purposes of the "crisis design exercise" were:

- *"To explore rapid design methodology for solving real problems under time pressure.*
- *To explore the role of engineering and management tradeoffs in a proposed solution.*
- *To act as a benchmarking exercise to lay the foundation for later examination of blocks to creativity and successful problem solving within team problem solving processes."*

"The crisis design exercise is done at the second or third class meeting of the semester, just after the project teams have been assigned. A normal 75 minute lecture is begun by one of the participating professors when it is quickly interrupted by another faculty member rushing into the classroom with sketchy news of a developing crisis. Students are told that the 'authorities' need their help to recommend a workable solution, and that they are to immediately go to separate rooms to brainstorm possible solution ideas. In a previous class, they have been given suggestions as to how to begin problem solving as a group. They are told that they may send a representative back to the main classroom to ask clarifying questions and seek additional information."

Shirland and Manock (2000) gave examples of these exercises one of which was: *"A community boathouse with a class of first grade children and their teacher onboard has broken away from its dock and is drifting away from shore. It is leaking fuel and slowly sinking in storm-agitated waves. Students must decide how to rescue the children before the boathouse sinks."*

13.7.   Training for Leadership

At the Univeristat Rovira I Virgili in Spain, first year chemical engineering students were divided into teams to undertake a horizontally integrated design project. Each team was led by two fourth-year students. One of them acted as the team leader, and the other acted as the knowledge manager. They alternated the roles between the two semesters. The instructors regarded them as 'coaches'. In order for them to undertake these roles they had to acquire project leadership, team management, and facilitative skills. This was achieved by participation in a fourth year course on project management. They were then put to use in the Project Management in Practice Course (Witt et al., 2002). This course brought together the first year teams and the fourth year students for formal weekly team meetings. The fourth year students also met with the tutors in plenary sessions each week.

The role of the team leader entails:

- "[Development and application] *of a method to establish the composition of the teams.*
- Helping] *the team to set overall goal and specific objectives and to develop a project plan.*

Module 1. The Nature of Problem Solvers
Concepts learned. How the very qualities that make problem solvers successful tend to cause difficulties with interpersonal interactions. The abilities that created the successful problem solver are then used to learn successful communication skills.
Classroom principles: Field independence/dependence learning theory; learning a communications structure for the independent learner; a format for phrasing statements.
Experiential exercise: Carkhuff's laws of communication.
Outside practice. What's fun/What's worst exercise.

Module 2. Getting Information
Concepts learned: Problem solvers need to get information so that they can identify, understand, and then solve the problem.
Classroom principles. Why interview? Interviewing don'ts; interviewing do's; Under the surface,-getting to the real information; understanding dialogue.
Experiential exercise. Interviewing for Information Exercise.
Outside practice. Expert/novice Interview Question Preparation.

Module 3. Giving Advice
Concepts learned. Techniques for giving advice and presenting ideas so that they are heard. Principles of giving feedback for coaching each other.
Classroom principles. Whys of giving advice; why we do it, why we should do it, why it doesn't work; specific ways of giving advice; how to give feedback.
Experiential exercise. Giving Feedback exercise using Values Game, Values awareness exercise.
Outside practice. Expert/Novice interviews.

Module 4. Defending Yourself
Concepts learned. Techniques for self-defense against specific verbal attack and typical workplace manipulation of individuals. The concept of a personal right to clarification is developed. Principles of how behavior is controlled through norms is explored.
Classroom principles. The many forms of harassment: jargon, cliché, innuendo; personal attack; defending yourself; identifying harassment; the role of norms.
Experiential exercise; language exercise.
Outside practice. "What is your style?" exercise.

Module 5. Disagreeing Agreeably
Concepts learned. Using communication skills to effectively express opinions. Principles of socio-technical problem solving. Principles of preferences in team decision making.
Classroom principles. Interfering group interactions; helping group interactions; preferences in team decision making; socio-technical influences on advice giving and receiving.
Experiential exercise. Coached group discussion of a sensitive issue.
Outside practice: Observation of typical problem-solving team interaction.

Module 6. Case Studies
Concepts learned. Consideration of blind spots and assumptions we make on race, gender, and ethnicity. Principles of the differences in team preferences in decision making based on gender are explored.
Classroom principles: Getting a communication strategy; How our blindspots effect our strategies; how to accommodate differences.
Experiential exercise: Case study 1. Emotional encounters. Case study 2. Aggressive encounters.
Outside practice. Strategizing an interaction.

Exhibit 13.5 A Six Module Training Scheme for teaching Interaction Skills devised by Seat and Lord (1998). (Reproduced with permission of *IEEE, Proceedings Frontiers in Education Conference*)

- [Helping] *the team members to clarify their roles, responsibilities, quality standards for their job, norms and operational procedures.*
- [Managing] *the project and formal team meetings.*
- [Facilitating] *the development of the team.*
- Helping] *the team to manage conflict.*
- [Developing] *communication and decision making skills among the team members.*
- [Facilitating] *the integration of new students into the team.*
- [Evaluating] *regularly and providing a final grade on the development of team skills and the quality of the job done by the first year students."*

The responsibilities of the knowledge manager were to:
- *"Establish a liaison with first year instructors to clearly identify their needs and requirements on the project and to assure that the project scope is aligned with them.*
- *Identify first year student's knowledge gaps.*
- *Devise learning activities to help first year students to achieve by themselves the instructional objectives selected by the instructors.*
- *Ensure the first year students achieve the instructional objectives.*
- *Assist the team to connect with the project stakeholders to obtain materials and knowledge necessary to solve the project....*
- *To evaluate regularly and provide a final grade on the knowledge acquisition by final year students."*

In this system there is potential for role conflict between the instructors and the coaches. The students have to be able to perceive the coach's role and value it. This means that the instructors have to be seen to puttheir trust in the arrangement. In this way it is hoped that the students will assume responsibility for their own learning. While the paper described some of the things that happened and is suggestive of positive outcomes there was no formal evaluation. The Dow Chemical Company provided expertise in coaching and change management skills to help faculty adapt to their new roles

13.8. Peer Evaluation (see also Chapter 16)

Martinazzi (1998a),[45] found that on occasion, because members of his Student Learning Teams (SLT) sometimes lacked skill in conflict resolution, an SLT would break-up. He learned from his students that there was a need to provide a meaningful evaluation of each team member's performance. The results would also have to contribute to each member's grade, and to contribute to team cohesion, these results would also have to be given to the group. Martinazzi's students felt that the best way to accomplish such assessment was by means of peer evaluation.

Accordingly the students were asked to design an instrument for peer evaluation. They suggested 39 diverse questions for assessment. After discussion the students realized that it would be impossible to assess so many diverse areas. Therefore, each member was asked to rate each item for its relative importance. The highest score was given to *"shows up for team meetings."* The lowest score was for the items, *"asks appropriate questions during work sessions"*, and *"How comfortable are you working with team members?"* The ten questions that that received the top scores are shown in Exhibit 13.6. It will be noticed that five questions were ranked in tenth position.

Shows up for team meetings.

Attends class regularly.

Contributes to team's solution to examination problems.

Demonstrates respect for other team members.

Willing to help other team members in and out of class.

Is team member available for extra team study session for tests?

Level of contribution to the team.

Did team member participate in establishing team's missions and goals?

Has a positive attitude towards the team.

Participates in the teams out of class discussion.

  (a) How well does team member attempt to accomplish team's mission and goals?

  (b) Eagerly accepts and shares all term responsibilities.

  (c) Has a "sharing" attitude towards team members.

  (d) In this team members truly earning the grade they are receiving

---

Exhibit 13.6. Peer Evaluation Instrument (rank order of importance of items) (Martinazzi, 1998). (Reproduced with permission of *IEEE, Proceedings Frontiers in Education*).

Martinazzi reported an evaluation of this instrument with 23 students from the Student Learning Teams. The average scores of the teams tended to be high[46]. The highest score was for the item, *"has a 'sharing' attitude toward team members"*, and the next highest score was given to five items all of which related to *"accountability and contribution"*. Martinazzi wrote that, *"overall, these top five questions emphasize the "soft skills' associated with being on a team."*

Repeatedly in this review, attention has been drawn to the heavy workload faced by engineering students. The students in these learning teams were no exception, and Martinazzi considered that this was the reason why the lowest scores were for items that indicated students' unavailability for extra-work sessions. The evaluation was repeated at quarterly intervals during the semester (i.e., once every three or four weeks). Martinazzi reported that the evaluation that had the most impact on the students was the first one. *"Students unfamiliar with being on a team learned quickly what was valued by their peers. The instructors shared with the students the score they received from their peers. This served as a "wake up" call to those who may have needed it. The most important aspect of giving the results to the students focused on setting a very clear set of expectations for each member of the SLTs. Knowing exactly what was expected of them as it related to being an effective member of the SLT proved to be an invaluable learning experience for the students."*

One suggestion considered was that each member of the SLT should numerically rank in order the contribution of the team members and include him/herself in the ranking. There is some support from this approach to peer evaluation in the literature (e.g., Kane and Lawler, 1978)[47] For example, on the basis of a study of a relatively small and homogenous group of engineering students at the University of Tennessee-Knoxville,[48] McAnear, Seat, and Weber (2000) argued that ratings are relatively reliable. Their study is also a reminder that there are other important dimensions which can be rated, as, for example, decision-making. They assessed and evaluated individual contributions to team performance with the aid of the Team Developer Computer Based Peer Rating Survey (Dominick, Reilly and McGourty, 1997). This instrument enables the participants to compare their perceptions of any one of 50 team behaviors with the average perception of other team members. 1 "never" and 5 "always" type Likert scales measured these behaviors. The dimensions covered were communication, decision making, collaboration, and self-management. Inter-rater reliabilities have been found to range from 0.88 to 0.92 student ratings compared with faculty and teaching assistants have been found to be significant.[49]

---

[45]At the University of Pittsburgh-Johnstown. This work was carried out with student learning teams(SLT). The course required the integration of academic cooperative learning with an industrial based module used to develop corporate teams (Martinazzi, 1998b).

[46]The scale was 5-always/positive contributor to rarely/negative contributor.

[47]Cited by McNear, Seat, and Weber (2000).

[48] N=114. 88 males and 26 females. 83% Caucasian and 17% ethnic minorities. The sample was reduced to 87 because of a technology failure.

[49] The authors cite personal correspondence with J. McGourty for this information.

In view of the findings of Saavedra and Kwun (1993), McAnear and his colleagues wanted to establish if the raters would tend to produce ratings that would enhance their own standing i.e., their ratings would be higher for themselves than their peers. In order to take into account personality, they used the MBTI, which was administered during the first week of the course. They found no significant interaction between dimension and personality type. However, a significant difference was found between self- and team ratings. Self-ratings were consistently higher, but while this lent some support to the hypothesis the fact that the differences were consistent suggested that they provided *"a dependable assessment of individual behavior on the team."* Nor did these findings support the view put forward by Saavedra and Kwun that outstanding team contributors would provide more accurate ratings. However, they noted that in both cases their findings *"should not be considered as strong evidence that students provide more accurate ratings."* That is not, however, the same thing as saying that such ratings were not dependable. At the same time, research was still required to evaluate the validity of these ratings for grading purposes. They cautioned that their sample was small, and that a more diverse sample might have shown self-enhancement to be more significant. Also, whereas Saavedra and Kwun used peer ratings to define outstanding contributors, McAnear and his colleagues had used performance in a traditional examination.

13.9.   Self Assessment (see also Chapter 16).

If a person is to judge others then they should be able to judge themselves. A pre-requisite of self-assessment is self-awareness, and this can be developed among student engineers as Yokomoto and Ware (1994) have shown. MacKay, Wurst, and Barker (1996) built self-evaluation into to their team process, and each student was required to complete a self-evaluation as part of their project report. Within the student report, there was a discussion section that allowed the students to recount any issues concerning the conduct of the project they thought should be included. Many schedules that are directly relevant to the self-evaluation of teamwork have been developed, and one is shown in Exhibit 13.7. Smith (2004) includes a self-assessment schedules for handling conflict.

13.10.   The Assessment and Evaluation of Team Functioning

There is an obligation on instructors to evaluate what happens in their classes and group work is not an exception to this principle. Because students have to write reports, and assess themselves and their peers, there is a wealth of data open to instructors for such evaluation. For example, McKay, Wurst, and Barker (1996) of the University of Connecticut examined 46 reports to try and establish what teamwork aspects presented the most difficulty in the course. The projects were in the area of integrated product and process development. The reports were checked for the following:

1. Conducting and arranging effective team meetings.
2. Communicating design information between team mates.
3. Resolving interpersonal, technical, or leadership team conflicts.
4. Ensuring that all members shared responsibility for the project.
5. Partitioning the project among team members.
6. Designing the sub module of the project.
7. Interfacing the separate sub modules using formal interface specifications.
8. Testing the system during the integration process.
9. Implementing the team design using protoboards, wires, and integrated circuits.

The responses yielded three impediments to project work. These were (1) the experience that groups had in trying to arrange meetings due to conflicts created by their schedules, off campus jobs, and off campus housing, etc; (2) difficulties in defining the interface needed to connect the sub modules; and (3) arranging for all the members to have modules of equal complexity. Of course such information could have been obtained from a structured questionnaire, but sometimes the reports yielded insights that would not otherwise be obtained from questionnaires. Often structured questionnaires do not consider the technical aspects of the project, as, for example, those considered in items 6-9.

The term assessment in the title of this section has been used in the sense of Angelo and Cross (1993) to imply that instructors should be evaluating what is happening in their teams for the purpose of remediation. Haller et al., (2000), as the result of a case study, suggested nine axioms for addressing interactional problems. These were:

1. *"Help students to understand the interactional problems they might have already encountered or might encounter in the future.*
2. *Make students aware that some approaches to problem solving are more appropriate than others when doing group work.*
3. *Point out to students who feel slowed down by the group that the best way to learn something at a deep level is by teaching it to someone else.*
4. *Remind students that teacher-pupil roles are flexible in healthy groups, with students alternating between the roles.*
5. *When students complain about doing all the work suggest ways to encourage more widespread active participation.*
6. *When students complain about the blocking behavior of one of the group members, propose strategies for countering over dominance.*
7. *Involve the entire class in developing strategies for dealing with common interactional problems.*
8. *Use an active listening strategy for seriously dysfunctional groups."*

They developed the ninth point as follows: *"When all else has failed with a group, bring the group into your office. If there are two points of view regarding the issue in contention... ask the principal adherent of one of them to state his/her case, as calmly and objectively as possible. Then ask the opposition leader to restate that case, without changing it or responding to it. If the restatement is not completely accurate, the first student corrects the mistake and the second one restates the first one's position. When the restatement is satisfactory to the first student the second student has to restate it to the second student's satisfaction. By the end of this exercise, the group is generally half way or more to resolving the problem, and if asked, can often propose excellent strategies for resolving the problem and avoiding it in the future."*

Rowland (2001) suggested a set of hierarchical criteria for evaluating project selection, use of skill sets, team dynamics, project mentoring and project reporting. These criteria were used by students to rate teamwork at the University of Kansas. Exhibit 13.8(a) and (b) shows the rating levels for the use of skill sets and team dynamics. In the study with respect to "the use of skill sets, seven teams cited levels 3, 4, or 5 as appropriate for their team experiences, but four reported only level two activity. For team dynamics, eight teams chose level 4 and one level 5.

As in all teaching situations, it is necessary to evaluate learning independently of formal assessment. Null (1997), for example, gave her student teams 3 minute papers at the end of the class. As a team, they are asked to decide *"what one concept covered that day they felt was presented best and with what one concept they feel could have been presented differently, or they don't feel comfortable with... Letting them do this as a team makes them feel a little less uneasy about something they might initially view as criticizing the instructor. ... I have found that it even helps improve student's verbal and written communication skills as well as their awareness."*

13.11. Grading (see also Chapter 16)

Grading is problematic. Smith (1995) counseled that a criterion-referenced procedure should be used. This promotes difficulties in systems such as the British where grading is pseudo norm referenced, (or marked to the curve as this procedure is described in the United States). Semi-criterion referenced approaches have been used for projects (see Chapter 2) to overcome this difficulty. A variety of other approaches have been used as the examples that follow show.

Sometimes no attempt is made to assess an activity directly. For example, at the University of Aston a series of lectures intended to create an awareness of the impact of programmable electronic systems on society among first-year students was re-arranged into five 2 hour long seminars. The topic for discussion was presented in a period of about eighteen minutes. For the purposes of presentation and discussion the class was divided into five consortia each of four persons. In a seminar one group is charged with researching the topic and making a presentation, a second group began the discussion with an interrogation by asking questions or offering opinions), a third group had the task of summarising each speech, and the fourth group was required to comment on the presentation. Eighty percent of the students had a role to play in each seminar. While there was an extremely high level of attendance at the seminars, no attempt was made to assess the performance. This was accomplished by asking each student to complete a 2000 word assignment on a topic allied to the material in the seminar program (Carpenter, 1993).

Mourtos (1994), who, apart from suggesting an approach to grading that depended on positive interdependence, drew attention to the fact that sometimes cooperative teams benefited from substantial prior knowledge. Thus, in the first semester of his course on aircraft design individuals were asked to work out their own designs in order to prepare them for a more demanding team project in the second semester. He argued that while each individual should be held accountable for their own design, cooperation could be achieved if each member of the team took responsibility for editing the reports of the other members of the team and *"making suggestions for improvement, marking any technical errors, and noting strengths."* For three person teams he suggested that reward interdependence could be structured in one or more of the following ways

- *"Each individual's reports are graded as usual on a scale from 0–100 subtracting 3 points for every English error (spelling, punctuation, grammar, etc.) and 6 points for every technical error found by the Professor. But in addition, editors are penalized 1 and 2 points respectively for each type of error in their own scores (negative-reward interdependence).*

- *If all three individual reports score higher than 90% all scores are rounded up to 100 (positive reward interdependence).*

- *If all three individual reports score higher than 80% editors are given back the points they were penalized for errors they had missed in their team mates reports."*

Mortous reported that his students were tested for their knowledge of basic design issues by written tests during the semester. Because the teams were responsible for different parts of the design when the oral reports were made, each student was asked questions to ensure that they had knowledge of each part of the design process.

Just as there has been an effort to involve peers in the evaluation of their colleagues in teamwork, so to there have been efforts to involve peers in grading. Wheeler and McDonald (1998) of the Virginia Military Institute commented, with respect to the peer review of writing, that *"students seem more willing to submit shoddy work to their professor than to their peers."* Writing is a form of essay, and Wheeler and McDonald point out that when writing is integrated into the course instructors can see what student's understand and what they don't understand. In a course on solid-sate devices, where writing was used to enhance collaborative learning, writing portfolios were required. Bonus points were used in the grading system. For the writing portfolio's, quizzes and exams a 5% bonus was given to each team member of teams whose members scored above 75%, 6% bonus for a score above 80%, 7% for a score above 85%, and 8% for marks above 90%.

It is easily forgotten that group work can be part of everyday classroom work. For example, Blackwell (1991) described how group discussion was organized and rated during a four-week component of a course on cardiac devices.[50] The class was broken up into groups of four or five students. Each group selected four topic areas from a list of eight. Each member was given a packet of articles. These included an article related to the topic the group had chosen. The group was then given a list of questions relating to each topic. Each list had one "unique" question the answer to which would be found in only one of the articles. The questions were open-ended. The groups were told that 70% of the questions in the test would come from the question list.

(a) Use of skill sets

Level 1.   Only skills of one team member are used on the project. Others simply follow along.

Level 2   Some skills are used from more than one team member but not all.

Level 3.   Most skill sets of team members are used.

Level 4.   Each tem member works on a major component, explains it to other team members, and shows how it can be combined with other parts to form the overall system.

Level 5.   All team member skills are used, some feedback between team members being essential as the project progresses, problems evaluated and corrective action taken.

(b) Team dynamics

Level 1   Team members primarily work alone. Little or no team interaction occurs.

Level 2. A student leader takes charge, assigns tasks, and coordinates activity, leading to project completion.

Level 3. Team members learn how teaming experiences should be used and apply them to move projects ahead.

Level 4. Varying levels of team activity and interactions occur, including some discord but general agreement with compromise on team focus. Moderate dependence on team principles.

Level 5.   All team members meet together several times weekly, have strong team dynamics, set intermediate deadlines, and depend on each other to keep on schedule for project completion careful journaling keeps team on focus and on schedule. Team dynamics feature the use of skill sets.

Exhibit 13.8. Team rating scales for the use of skill sets and team dynamics used at the University of Kansas Department of Electrical Engineering and Computer Science (Rowland, 2001). (Reproduced with permission of *IEEE, Proceedings Frontiers in Education Conference*).

The "unique" question forced each member to read the articles in their packet. Serious discussion took place in normal class time because of the need to solve unknown aspects of the topic. This approach to testing was relatively rare in engineering education in the United States because it used a combination of essay and problem format.

"Essay tests are not common in a technical course, but the author felt that since each group could work on the test as a group, there needed to be a heavy demand on their thinking abilities, ideally with a series of questions which did not have 'one' correct answer, but were open-ended. That is the groups were forced to combine information out of several articles to answer each question, and were commonly required to make one or more assumptions on the way to their answer." It will be seen that Blackwell's assessment procedure was designed to force all the students to take part.

Null (1997) gave group lab quizzes that involved the application of new concepts, or the modification of a computer program that did not work. They were made difficult for one person to complete in the required time. Similarly, in order to encourage group work, the first project that had to be done was one which students would have difficulty in completing on their own.

It is a characteristic of academics that they design the most complicated systems of assessment, and it seems that this can be true of students. Schultz (1998) reported that when it was left to the teams, some groups *"had very complicated formulae that first gave equal shares but then pooled the "excess" points above the minimum for the grade and moved those points around to bring one member up to the next higher grade. It reflected good teamwork, but was quite complex to administer."* Their most recent approach *"was to take only the final project performance scores and apportion them by the ratings of the other group members. Assuming a group of four, each person rated the other three not themselves since they may be either greedy or overly humble. The normalized scores were summed for each individual, so rating everyone high was no better than rating everyone low it was the differential that counted. If the group did poorly but everyone contributed equally, they shared in a low score. If a group did well but all their ratings credited one individual with doing the most work, then the rest of the group got a little below the group average. Finally, if everyone in the group rated one individual last, that one got nothing and the rest got somewhat above the average for the group."*

Peer assessment in a second year project in digital systems at the University of Manchester was introduced to overcome the difficulty that student weaknesses could be covered up in groups. The students are told to imagine that a contractor, hiring the group, is so impressed with their work that a bonus of £2000 is offered for division among the group on the basis of individual merit as perceived by colleagues. Each person is therefore asked to submit what they believe to be a fair division of the £2000 among all group members. It is, however, pointed out that the self-allotted bonus will be omitted when computing overall bonuses, so as to avoid any distortion through self interest. If a member of the group refuses to participate, their bonus is set at zero. The bonus voting exercise is carried out in secret, but students can, by a majority agreement, disclose the outcome (Harrison and Jones, 1997). At the time, only 10% of the total marks were awarded for this exercise; but because

---

[50] Within a course on Biomedical Electronic Systems.

the students took it very seriously, they thought that in the future they might have to raise this level.

13.12. Toward a Science of Engineering Design Teams

Most of what has been written about training for teamwork in industry has assumed that the behavior of teams is well understood, and certainly there is a body of knowledge that would suggest that that is the case. But while much of it may well stand the test of time Mabogunje and others of the Stanford Center for Design Research considered that new techniques of evaluation may lead to a science of engineering design team selection. Their proposed approach may lead to understandings that reflect on the organization of training for teamwork in higher education

In their discussion paper, Mabogunje and his colleagues distinguished between the "physics" and the "chemistry" of teams. The domain of "physics" describes the knowledge structure of a team, whereas the "chemistry" describes the personalities of team members (i.e., their cognitive styles, temperaments, responses to stressful situations, and interpersonal characteristics).

By science of design teams they mean the ability to predict what a design team of given properties will do in a given situation. They want to account for "creep" in the design situation. That is, where there is a deviation such that over time the product that is designed does not meet the clients needs.

Mabogunje et al., (2001) proposed that a combination of multiple observation and simulation based analysis could be used analyze complex problem situations of this kind. The method they proposed is very similar to action research as practiced in education. It follows the heuristic "observe, analyze-intervene, and study the effects." The analysis would lead to the design of new tools and methods. The cycle could be repeated so as to gain further understanding of what has happened.

In previous work they had demonstrated the value of video recordings and learning styles inventories and had shown that most of the communication within groups had been mismatched with respect to the receivers (Carrizosa and Sheppard, 2000). They suggested that these techniques could be supplemented by interviews and questionnaires. (In educational research jargon, this is "triangulation.") By far the most interesting suggestion they made was that magnetic resonance imaging could be used to better understand design behavior. In support of this view, they cited studies at Darnstadt University, where Goker (1997) reported an investigation of novice and expert designers using electroencephalography. They also cited a study at Stanford where it was found that specific brain activities differentiated between visual experiences, or images, which were later well remembered, remembered less well, or forgotten (Brewer et al., 1998).[51] *"As an illustration, this latter finding can be adapted to the requirements of the creep problem by assuming the subjects are representatives of the*

marketing department. Consider therefore the situation in which we recorded brain activity of the subjects during the exercise, where they are generating and refining a space of images that describe a potential solution to the design problem, and a week later we have them describe this space of images to another set of participants representing the engineering department. Brewster et al.,'s work should potentially enable us to know the strength of memory of the images for each marketing representative. Conceptually then, this will enable us to predict which representatives will have a higher probability of relaying incorrect information."

In this approach computer simulation would be used to analyze the data and, thus to obtain a further understanding of both the interactions and the decisions that should be made about interventions. They argued that such a science would lead to the development of new strategies for managing design teams and the possible development of improved design environments. Clearly, such understanding would have implications for the management of learning teams in the university context.

13.13. Conclusions

From the foregoing, it will be seen that there is a substantial case for cooperative/collaborative action learning in engineering education. In the first place, industry requires graduates who are able to work in teams. Most studies report that they were with relatively small groups (two to four) although some investigations have been with relatively large groups. The evidence favors heterogeneous rather than homogeneous groups, but there is also some evidence which suggests that females can be disadvantaged in groups, particularly if they are the only female. More studies of the distribution of the sexes within groups are required, as are studies of methods of learning in computer-assisted collaborative learning environments. In regard to the latter, a step in this direction has been made by Kreijns and Kirschener (2001) of the Open University in the Netherlands, who have proposed a theory for developing group awareness in computer mediated communication.

There is some evidence which suggests that some combinations of personality types within groups can lead to dysfunctional groups. In such circumstances it has been suggested that tutors can take action to remove the factors that lead to dysfunction. The balance of thinking is in favor of the selection of groups by tutors rather than self-selection by students.

There are several illustrations of how the difficulties associated with group work (e.g., social loafing) can be overcome, and peer assessment has been used to contribute to this as well as to overcome the difficulty of assigning grades to students for group work.

Groups are used to develop skills in both the cognitive and affective domains, and many of the papers concentrate on the development of teamwork skills. There is no evidence to suggest that concentration on the affective is at the expense of the cognitive, and many studies report enhanced learning as a result of group

---

[51] Cognitive Neuroscience Laboratory, Stanford University.

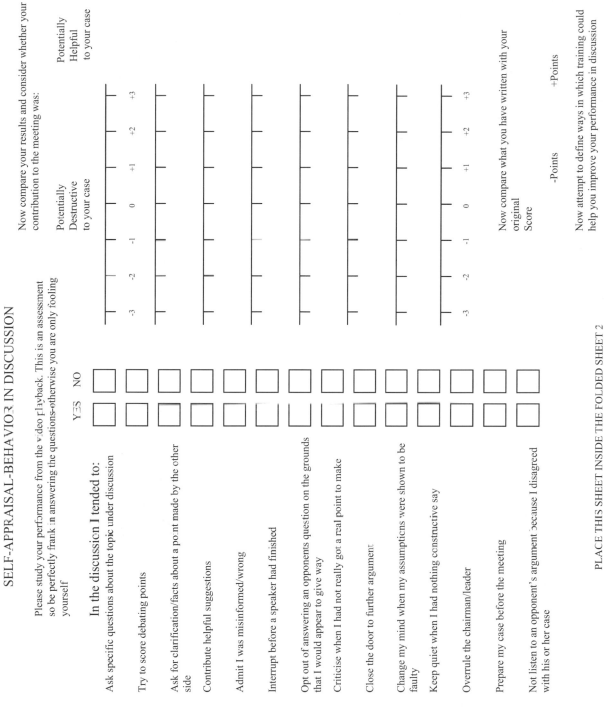

SELF-APPRAISAL-BEHAVIOR IN DISCUSSION

Please study your performance from the video playback. This is an assessment so be perfectly frank in answering the questions-otherwise you are only fooling yourself

Now compare your results and consider whether your contribution to the meeting was:

In the discussion I tended to:

YES   NO

	Potentially Destructive to your case						Potentially Helpful to your case
	-3	-2	-1	0	+1	+2	+3

Ask specific questions about the topic under discussion

Try to score debating points

Ask for clarification/facts about a point made by the other side

Contribute helpful suggestions

Admit I was misinformed/wrong

Interrupt before a speaker had finished

Opt out of answering an opponents question on the grounds that I would appear to give way

Criticise when I had not really got a real point to make

Close the door to further argument

Change my mind when my assumptions were shown to be faulty

Keep quiet when I had nothing constructive say

Overrule the chairman/leader

Prepare my case before the meeting

Not listen to an opponent's argument because I disagreed with his or her case

Now compare what you have written with your original Score

-Points   +Points

Now attempt to define ways in which training could help you improve your performance in discussion

PLACE THIS SHEET INSIDE THE FOLDED SHEET 2
AND FOLD OVER THE RIGHT HANDED EDGE SO THE ANSWERS
SHOW IN CUT-OUTS

Exhibit 13.7. Self-appraisal of performance in negotiating groups developed by J. Freeman and J. Heywood (Heywood, 1989b)

work. There is considerable agreement that skills in teamwork are enhanced if there is prior training. Thus, in situations where there is little or no change in the objective performance of students, instructors have to weigh subjective factors such as perceived motivation and perception of skill development in the balance. The evidence is that such judgments are more likely to be favorable than not.

The evidence supports the view that properly organized (planned) cooperative groups are much more effective than the creation of groups for the sake of having groups. Instructors are likely to find that such planning is time-consuming, but they will also find that such exercises motivate students to do more work than they would otherwise have done.

References

Abercrombie, M. L. J (1978). *Aims and Techniques of Group Discussion*, 4th Edition. Society for Research into Higher Education, London.

Allen, E. L., Muscat, A. J. and E .D. H. Green (1996). Interdisciplinary team learning in a semiconductor process in course. *Proceedings Frontiers in Education Conference* 31–34.

Aller, M (1993). "Just like they do in industry". Concerns about teamwork practices in engineering design courses. *Proceedings Frontiers in Education Conference*, 489–492.

Amidon, E. J., amd J. B. House (1976). *Interactive Analysis.* Addison Wesley, Reading, MA.

Anaya, G (1999). College impact on student learning: comparing the use of self reported gains, standardized test scores, and college grades. *Research in Higher Education* 40, 499–527.

Anderson, J. R., Reder, L. M., and H. A. Simon (1996). Situated learning in education. *Educational Researcher,* 25, (4), 5–11.

Angelo, T., and P. K. Cross (1993). *Classroom Assessment Techniques.* Jossey Bass, San Francisco.

Argyle, M (1976). *The Scientific Study of Social Behavior.* Methuen, London.

Asokanthan, S. F (1997). Active learning methods for teaching dynamics- development and implementation. *Proceedings Frontiers in Education Conference,* 3, 1349-1353.

Astin, A.W (1997). *What Matters in College. Four Critical years Revisited.* Jossey Bass, San Francisco.

Atman, C. J., and K. M. Bursic (1986). Teaching engineering design: Can reading a textbook make a difference. *Research in Engineering Design.* 8, 240-250.

Bassey, M (1994). *Creating Education Through Research.* British Educational Research Association. Kirklington Moor Press, Newark, UK

Belbin, R. M (1981). *Management Teams. Why They Succeed or Fail,* Heinemann, Oxford.

Black, J (1976).Project work in the final year of an engineering degree course in the University of Bath. *Assessment in Higher Education,* 1, 35.

Blackwell, G. R (1991). Group discussion techniques in a technical course. *Proceedings Frontiers in Education Conference,* 430–432.

Blair, G. M (1993). Laying the foundations for effective teamwork. *Engineering Science and Education Journal (February)* 15 – 19.

Bligh, D (1971, 1993, 1999). *What's the Use of Lectures?* Penguin, Harmondsworth.

Bogdan, R. C., and S. A. Biklen (1998). *Qualitative Research for Education. An Introduction to Theory and Methods.* 3rd ed. Allyn and Bacon, Boston.

Booth, M. K., and B. W. James (2001). Interactive learning in higher education level 1 – mechanics module. *International Journal of Science Education,* 23, (9), 955–967.

Bransford, J. D., Brown, A. L., and R. R. Cocking (eds.). *How people Learn: Brain, Mind, Experience and School.* National Academy Press, Washington, DC.

Brereton, O. P., Lees, S., Bedson, R., Boldyreff, C., Drummond, S., Layzell, P. J., Macaulay, L. A., and R. Young (2000). Student group working across universities. A case study in software engineering. *IEEE Transactions on Education* 43, (4), 394–399.

Brewer, J. B., Zhao, Z, Desmond, J. E., Glover, G. H and J. D. E Gabrieli (1998). Making memories. Brain activity that predicts how well visual experience will be remembered. *Science* 28, (5380), 1185.

Brickell, J. L., Porter, D. B., Reynolds, M. F., and R. D. Cosgrove (1994). Assigning students to groups for engineering design projects: a comparison of five methods. *Journal of Engineering Education,* 83, (3), 259–262.

Bruffee, K. A (1993). *Collaborative Learning. Higher Education, Interdependence, and the Authority of Knowledge.* The Johns Hopkins University Press, Baltimore.

Bucciarelli, L. L (1988). An ethnographic perspective on engineering design. *Design Studies,* 9, (8) 159 – 168.

Byerley, A, R (2001) Using multimedia and "active learning" techniques to "energize" an introductory engineering thermodynamics class. *Proceedings Frontiers in Education Conference,* 1, T3b-1- T3b-8.

Carpenter, G (1993) 'People and systems:' an exercise in student participation. *International Journal of Electrical Engineering Education,* 30, (2), 143–151.

Carrizosa, K., and S. Sheppard (200). The importance of learning styles in group design work. *Proceedings Frontiers in Education Conference,* 1, T2B-12 to 17.

Catalano, G. D. and K. C. Catalano (1997). Transformation from techer-centered to student centered engineering education. *Proceedings Frontiers in Education Conference,* 1, 95–100.

Clayton, J. Martin, D and S. W. Martin (2000). Multi-level design teams: a success story? *Proceedings Frontiers in Education* F2C– 2 to 7.

Collier, G (1993) (ed). *The Management of Peer Group Learning.* Society for Research into Higher Education, London.

Collier, G (1989). *A New teaching. A New Learning.* SPCK, London.

Cooper, B and J. M. Foy (1967) Evaluating the effectiveness of lecture. Universities *Quarterly,* 21, 182–185.

Courter, S. L. S (1996). *A grounded theory of the positive attributes of a TQM curriculum innovation. A multi-case study of a cross-disciplinary course in engineering. Doctoral dissertation. University of Wisconsin – Madison.*

Courter, S. L. S., Millar, S. B., and L.Lyons (1998). From the student's point of view: experiences in a freshman engineering design course. *Journal of Engineering Education,* 87, (3), 283–288.

Craig, K. J., and C. C. van Waveren (1997). Simulating the engineering project environment using cooperative learning: a second-year course case study. *International Journal of Mechanical Engineering Education,* 25, (4), 290–297.

David, J. S., and C. A. Wellington (1998). Using self-directed work group conspts for successful classroom group experiences. *Proceedings Frontiers in Education Conference,* 385-390.

De Vault, J. E (1998). A competition-motivated, interdisciplinary design experience. *Proceedings Frontiers in Education Conference,* 460–465

Devi, N. Rama (2001). Active and cooperative learning among BE. students. *Proceedings Frontiers in Education Conference,* 1, T1B-16 to 18.

Di biasio, D., and J. Groccia (1995). Active and cooperative learning in an introductory chemical engineering course. *Proceedings Frontiers in Education Conference,* 3C2- 19-3C2-22.

Dimitriadis, Y. A., Martinez, A., Rubia, B and M. J. Gallego (2001). Cooperative learning in computer architecture: an educational project and its network support. *Proceedings Frontiers in Education Conference,* 1, T4-13 to 18.

Dominick, P., Reilly, R and J. McGourty (1997). The effects of peer feedback on team behavior. *Group and Organizational Management,* 22, (2), 508–520

Druckman, D., and R. a. Bjork (eds.) (1994) *Learning , Remembering, Believing: Enhancing Team and Individual Performance.* National Academy Press, Washington, DC.

Eberhardt, L. Y (1987) *Working with Women's Groups.* Vol 1. Whole Person Association Inc. Duluth, Minnesota.

Engin, A. W., and A. E. Engin (1977). The Lecture: greater effectiveness for a familiar method. *Engineering Education.* February 358–362.

Engler, B (1979). *Personality Theories. An Introduction.* Houghton Mifflin, MA.

Felder, R .M (1995) A *longitudinal study of engineering student performance and retention. IV instructional methods and student responses to them. Journal of Engineering Education*, 84, (4), 361-367.

Felder, R. M., and R. Brent (2003). Designing and teaching courses to satisfy ABET criteria. *Journal of Engineering Education.* 92, (1), 7–24.

Fincher, S (1999). What are we doing when we teach programming? *Proceedings Frontiers in Education Conference*, 12a4-1 to 6.

Finelli, C. J (1999). A team-oriented, project based freshmen problem solving course: benefits of an early exposure. *Proceedings Frontiers in Education Conference*, 11a2–26 to 30.

Finelli, C. J. (2001) Assessing improvement in students' team skills and using a learning style inventory to increase it. *Proceedoings Frontiers in Education Conference,* S2C- 14 to 17.

FitzGibbon, A and J. Heywood (1986) Recognition of conjunctive and identity needs in teacher development: their implications for planning of in-service training. *European Journal of Teacher Education* 9, (3), 271–286.

FitzGibbon, A and J. Heywood (1989) L'autovaluatazione nella formazione (experience e richerche. *Dirigenti Scuola* 2, December, 31-33.

Fitzpatrick, F., Askin, R., and J. Goldberg (2001) Using student conative behaviors and technical skills to form effective project teams. *Proceedings Frontiers in Education Conference* 3, S2G- 8 to 13.

Free, J. C., Gygi, C. K., Todd, R. H., Sorensen, E. D and S. P. Magleby (1993). Strategies for developing teamsmanship in the context of design education for product development. A progress report. *Proceedings Frontiers in Education Conference,* 482 – 488.

Freeman, J and J. Sharp (2001). Group dynamics and the learning process. In J. Heywood, J. M. Sharp and M. Hides (eds). *Improving Teaching In Higher Education.* University of Salford, Salford, UK

Freeman, J and E. Thomas (2001). Computer literacy in Biological science in J. Heywood, J., J. Sharp and M. Hides (eds) *Improving Teaching in Higher Education. Teaching and learning Committee,* University of Salford, Salford.

Gates, A. O., Delgado, N., and O. Mondragon (2000) A structured approach for managing a practical soft ware engineering course. *Proceedings Frontiers in Education Conference*, 1, T1C, 21 to 26.

Gates, A. Q., Teller, P. T., Bernat, A., Cabrera, S., and C. K. Della-Piana (1999).A Cooperative Model for Orienting Students to Research Groups, *Proceedings Frontiers in..E.ducation,*13a4-6 to 12.

George, J and J. Cowan (1999). *A Handbook of Techniques for Formative Evaluation.* Kogan Page, London.

Gerhard, G. C (1999). Teaching design with behavior modification techniques in a pseudo-corporate environment. *IEEE Transactions on Education*, 42, (4), 255 – 261.

Goker, M. H (1997). The effects of experience during design problem solving. *Design Studies* 18, 405 – 426.

Goodwin, C., Hundley, S. P. Fox, P. L. and R. Wolter (1999). The design, facilitation, and assessment of team skills in engineering curricula: two delivery methods for an integrated curricula. *Proceedings Frontiers in Education Conference*, 13b2 – 21 to 23.

Greenberg, J. E., Smith, N. T and J. H. Newman (2003). Instructional module in Fourier Spectral Analysis, based on principles of "How People Learn". *Journal of Engineering Education*, 92, (2), 155 – 166.

Gulke, E. A., Beert, D. C., and D. R. Lane (2001). The effects of physical environment on engineering team performance: a case study. *Journal of Engineering Education*, 90, (3), 319 – 330.

Guilford, J (1979). *The Nature of the Intellect.* McGraw Hill, New York.

Gumbly, M (1997). *Procurement and set up of low cost video conferencing in a student environment.* Department of Computer Science, Keele University, Staffordshire (JTAP Project Report).

Haller, C. R., Gallagher, V. J., Weldon, T. L and R. M. Felder (2000) Dynamics of peer education in cooperative learning workshops. *Journal of Engineering Education.* 89, (3), 285 – 294.

Halstead, A and L. Martin (2002). Learning styles: a tool for selecting students for group work. International *Journal of Electrical Engineering Education*, 39, (3), 245- 252.

Harrison, C. G. and P. L. Jones (1997). A creative class project based on VHDL, synthesis and FPGA design. *International Journal of Electrical Engineering Education*, 341, 370 - 375

Hart, F. L. and J. Groccia (1994). Fundamentals in civil engineering and computers- a freshman design course. *Proceedings Frontiers in Engineering Education* 321 - 326

Hessami, M and F. Sillitoe (1990). Thermodynamicphobia: respite, reprise and recovery. *AAEE Conference* 2, 325 – 330.

Heywood, J (1989b). *Learning, Adaptability and Change.* Paul Chapman, London.

Heywood, J (1994). *Enterprise Learning and its Assessment in Higher Education.* Technical Report No. 20. Employment Department, Sheffield.

Heywood, J. and H. Montagu Pollock (1977). *Science for Arts Students. A Case Study in Curriculum Development.* Society for Research into Higher Education, London.

Hilz, S. R and R. Benbunan- Fich (1997) Evaluating the importance of collaborative learning in ALN's. *Proceedings Frontiers in Education Conference* 432 - 436

Hogan, R. C and D. W. Champagne (1980). *Annual Handbook of Group Facilitators.* Chapter on. Personal Style Inventory pp 89– 99. University Associates.

James, P and A. Turner (1998). *Measuring the Development of Deep Learning.* TLQIS. Final Report. Teaching and Learning Committee. University of Salford, Salford.

Jaques, D (1991). *Learning in Groups.* Kogan Page, London.

Johnson, D.W., Johnson, R.T. and K.A. Smith (1991a). *Active learning. Cooperation in the College Classroom.* Interaction Book Co. Edina, MN.

Johnson, D. W., Johnson, R. T. and K. A. Smith (1991b). *Cooperative Learning: Increasing College Faculty Instructional Productivity.* ASHE-ERIC. Report on Higher Education. The George Washington University, Washington, DC

Kane, J. S and E. E. Lawler (1978). Methods of peer assessment. *Psychological Bulletin*, 85, (3), 555–586.

Kepler, A and T. Luckmann (1991). Teaching conversational transmission of knowledge in I. Markova and K. Foppa (eds) *Asymmetrics in Dialogue.* Harvester Wheatsheaf, Herts.

Kirk, T. (1997). *The effectiveness of cooperative learning in a primary School in Ireland.* Ph. D. Thesis. Two volumes. University of Dublin.

Kolb. D. A (1984). *Experiential Learning: Experience as the Source of Learning and Development.* Prentice-Hall, Englewood Cliffs, NJ.

Kolbe, K (1989). *The Connative Connection.* Addison Wesley, New York.

Kolbe, K (1993). *Pure Instinct.* Random House, New York.

Kreijns, K. and P. A. Kirschener (2001). The social affordances of computer-supported collaborative learning environments. *Proceedings Frontieres in Education Conference*, 1, T1F- 12 to 17.

Kromrey, J. D and D. M. Purdom (1995). A comparison of lecture, cooperative learning and programd instruction at college level. *Studies in Higher Education*, 20, (3), 341–349.

Kuo, C and P. Sayer (1986). A group study approach to marine technology education. *International Journal of Applied Engineering Education* 2, (5/6), 311–317.

Kyriacou, C. H. and S. Marshall (1989). The nature of Active Learning. *Evaluation and Research in Education*, 3, 1-5.

Laeser, M., Moskal, B. M., Knecht, R., and D. Lasich (2003). Engineering design: examining the impact of gender and the team's gender composition. *Journal of Engineering Education*, 92, (1), 49 – 56.

Lane, W. D. and A. H. Sayles (1995). Integrated team design. *Proceedings Frontiers in Education Conference*, 2a2-1 to 4.

Lewis, R. B (1991). Creative teaching and learning in a statics class. *Engineering Education*, 81, (1), 15 – 18.

Liebman,, J. S (1996). Promoting active learning during lectures. *OR/MS, 2*

Lingard, R and E. Berry (2002). Teaching teamwork skills in software engineering based on understanding of factors affecting group performance. *Proceedings Frontiers in Education Conference,* S3G- 1 to 6.

Lord, S. M (2001). Student response to cooperative learning homework teams: mid course and final evaluations. *Proceedings Frontiers in Education Conference 1*, T3B- 14 to 18.

Mabogunje, A., Carrizosa, K., Sheppard, S., and L. Leifer (2001). Towards a science of engineering design teams. *International Conference on Engineering Design.* Glasgow, August, 2001.

McAnear, T. P. and E. Seat (2001). Perceptions of team performance: a comparison of male and female engineering students. *Proceedings Frontiers in Educsation Conference*, 3, S2A-10 to 14.

McAnear, T. P., Seat, E and F. Weber (2000). Predictors of student rating accuracy. *Proceedings Frontiers in Education Conference*, 3, S1A- 1 to 4.

McDermott, K. J., Nafalski, A and O. Göl (2000) Active learning in the University of South Australia. *Proceedings Frontiers in Education Conference*, T1B – 11 to 15.

McDermott, K. J., Göl, O and A. Nafalski (2000). Cooperative learning in South Australia. *Proceedings Frontiers in Education Conference*, 3, 31B – 1 to 5.

MacIntyre, A (1990) *Reconceiving the University as an institution and the lecture as genre in Three Rival Versions of Moral Enquiry.* The 1988 Gifford Lectures. The University of Notre Dame Press, Notre Dame, Indiana.

MacKay, B., Wurst, K., and K. Barker (1996). Teaching IPPD and teamwork in an engineering design course. *Proceedings Frontiers in Education Conference*, 703 – 706.

McKenna, A., McMartin, F., Terada, Y., Sirivedhin, V., and A, Aogonino (2001). *Proceedings Annual Conference ASEE.* Session 1330.

McLeish, J (1968). *The Lecture Method.* Cambridge Monographs on Teaching Methods, No 1. Cambridge Institute of Education, Cambridge.

McKenna, A., Mongia, L., and A. Agognino (1998). Engineering design Class. *Proceedings Frontiers in Education Conference,* 1, 264-269.

Martinazzi, R (1998a). Design and development of peer evaluation instrument for "student learning teams" *Proceedings Frontiers in Education Conference*, 2, 784 – 789

Mazur, E (1997). *Peer Instruction: Users manual.* Mazur Harvard University.

Martinazzi, R (1998b). Student learning teams in engineering economics. *Proceedings ASEE Annul Conference.* June.

Melville, P (2003). The renaissance engineer: Ideas from Physics. *European Journal of Engineering education,* 28, (2), 139-194.

Merino, D. N., and K. D. Abel (2003). Evaluating the effectiveness of computer tutorials versus traditional lecturing in accounting topics. *Journal of Engineering Education,* 92, (2), 189-193.

Michaelson, L. K., Fink, L. D. and A. Knight (1997). Designing effective group activities: lessons for classroom teaching and faculty development. *To Improve the Acadaemy.* 16, 373 – 398. New Forums Press and the Professional Development Network in Higher Education.

Mills, D., McKittrick, B., Mulhall, P., and S. Feteri (1999). CUP. Cooperative learning that works. *Physics Education* 34, (1), 10 – 16.

Moore, D and F. Berry (2001). Industrial sponsored design projects addressed by student design teams. *Journal of Engineering Education,* 90, (1), 69 – 74.

Moore, D. and B. Farbrother (2000). Pedagogical and organizational components and issues of externally sponsored senior design teams. *Proceedings Frontiers in Education Conference*, F1C- 6 to 11.

Morrell, L., Bueda, R., Orengo, M., and A. Sanchez (2001). After so much effort. Is faculty using cooperative in the classroom? *Journal of Engineering Education.* 90, (3), 357 – 362.

Moskal, B., Krecht, R., and M. Pavelich (2001). The design report rubric: assessing the impact of program design on the learning process. *Journal of the Art of Teaching. Assessment of Learning.* 8, (1), 18 – 33.

Moskal, B. M., Leydens, J. A., and M. J. Pavelich (2002). Validity, Reliability and the Assessment of Engineering Education. *Journal of Engineering Education,* 91, (3), 351-354.

Mourtos, N. J (1994). The nuts and bolts of cooperative learning in engineering. *Proceedings Frontiers in Education Conference*, 624 – 627.

Null, L (1997). TQM and collaborative learning: a perfect match. *Proceedings Frontiers in Education Conference*, 290 – 294.

Oakes, W. C., Krull, A., Coyle, E. J. Jamieson, L. H and M. Kong (2000). EPICS: Interdisciplinary service learning using engineering design projects. *Proceedings Frontiers in Education Conference*, 1, T2F- 4 to 9.

Orsak, G. C and D. M. Etter (1996). Connecting the engineer to the 21st Century through virtual teaming. *IEEE Transactions on Education 39*, 165 – 179.

Parlett, M and D. Hamilton (1972). Evaluation as Illumination. A New Approach to the Study of Innovatory Programs. Center for Research in Education Sciences. Cyclostyled pamphlet., Edinburgh University, Scotland.

Pike,G. R (1995). The relationship between self-reports of college experiences and achievement test scores. *Research in Higher Education* 36, 1–22.

Pimmel, R (2001) Cooperative learning instructional activities in a capstone design course. *Journal of Engineering Education*, 90, (3), 413– 422.

Pimmel, R (2003). A practical approach for converting group assignments to team projects. *IEEE Transactions on Education*, 46, (2), 273 – 282.

Prince, M (2004). Does active learning work? A review of research. *Journal of Engineering Education, 93, (3), 223 – 232.*

Ramirez L. M. de., Velez-Arocho, J. I., Zayas-Carbro, J. L. and M. A. Torres (1998). Developing and assessing teamwork skills in a multi-disciplinary course. *Proceedings Frontiers in Education Conference*, 1, 432–446.

Rosser, S. V (1997). *Re-Engineering Female-Friendly Science. Teachers* College Press, New York

Rover, D. T (2000) Perspectives on learning in a capstone design course. *Proceedings Frontiers in Education Conference*, F4C- 14 to 19

Rover, D. T. and P. D. Fisher (1997). Cross-functional teaming in a capstone engineering design course. *Proceedings Frontiers in Education Conference* 215 – 219

Rowland, J. R (2001). A fine-grid method for evaluating multi-disciplinary team experiences. *Proceedings Frontiers in Education Conference,* 1, T4A-5 to 8.

Rutz, E. et al (2003). Student performance and acceptance of instructional technology. Comparing technology enhanced and traditional instruction for a course of statics. *Journal of Engineering Education*, 92, (2), 133-140.

Saavedra, R., and S. K. Kwun (1993). Peer evaluation in self-managing work groups. *Journal of Applied Psychology* 78, (3), 450 – 462.

Saupé, J (1961). Learning in P. Dressel (ed) *Evaluation in Higher Education.* Houghton Mifflin, Boston.

Schultz, T. W (1998). Practical problems in organizing student groups. *Proceedings Frontiers in Education Conference* 1, 242 – 245.

Seat, J. E and S. Lord (1998). Enabling effective engineering teams. A program for teaching interaction skills. *Proceedings Frontiers in Education Conference,* 1, 246 – 251.

Seat, J. E., Poppen, W. A., Boone, K and J. R. Parsons (1996). Making design teams work. *Proceedings Frontiers in Education Conference* 1, 272 – 275.

Sharp, J. E (2001). Teaching teamwork communication with Kolb learning style theory. *Proceedings Frontiers in Education Conference* 2, F2C – 1 to 2.

Shiavi, R and A. Brodersen (2002). Study of instructional modalities for introductory computing. *Proceedings Frontiers in Education Conference.* 3, S1F–5 to 9.

Shirland, L. E and J. Manock (2000). Collaborative teaching of integrated product development: a case study. *IEEE Transactions on Education*, 43, (3), 343–347.

Smith, K. A (1992) *Cooperation in the College Classroom (with special reference to engineering).* Department of Civil and Mineral Engineering, University of Minnesota, Minneapolis, MN.

Smith, K. A (1995). Cooperative learning: effective teamwork in engineering classrooms. *Proceedings Frontiers in Education Conference* 2, 2b5. 13 to 18.

Smith, K. A (2004). *Teamwork and Project Management.* 2nd Edition. McGraw Hill, New York.

Smith, K. A and A. M. Starfield (1993). Building models to solve problems in J. H. Clarke and R. W. Biddle (eds). *Teaching Critical Thinking: Reports from across the Curriculum.* Prentice Hall, Englewood Cliffs, NJ.

Smith, K. A. and A. A. Waller (1997). Cooperative learning for new teachers in W. E. Campbell and K. A. Smith (eds) *New Paradigms for College Teaching*. Interaction Book Co. Edina, MN.

Springer, L., Stanne, M. E., and S. S. Donovan (1999). Effects of small group learning on undergraduates in science, mathematics, engineering technology: a meta-analysis. *Review of Educational Research*, 69, 21 – 51.

Stake, R. E (1995). *The Art of Case Study Research*. Sage, Thousand Oakes, CA

Starfield, A. M., Smith, K. A., and A. L. Blaloch (1994). *How to model it: Problem Solving for the Computer Age*. Burgers International Group Inc. Edina, MN.

Sutton, J., and R. Thompson (1998). Multidisciplinary integration. A decision methodology and procedure for instruction. *Proceedings Frontiers in Education Conference*, 1, 450–455

Tait, H and N. J. Entwistle (1996). Identifying students at risk through ineffective study strategies. *Higher Education*, 31, 99–118.

Teller, P. J. and A. Q. Gates (2000). Applying the affinity group research model to computer research projects. *Proceedings Frontiers in Education Conference*, 3, S1G–7 to 12.

Terenzini, P. T., Cabrera, A. F., Colbeck, C. L., Parente, J. M., and S. A. Bjorklund (2001). Collaborative learning vs lecture/discussion students' reported learning gains. *Journal of Engineering Education*, 90, (1), 123–130.

Thamhain, H. J (1996). Enhancing innovative performance of self-directed engineering teams. *Engineering Management Journal*, 8, (3) 31–39.

Timmerman, B., Lingard, R., and G. M. Barnes (2001). Active learning with upper division computer science students. *Proceedings Frontiers in Education Conference*, 1, T3B-19 to 23.

Tonso, K. L (1996). The impact of cultural norms on women. *Journal of Engineering Education*. 85, (3), 217–225.

Tse, K. K (1985). *Marks and Spencer. Anatomy of Britain's Most Efficiently Managed Company*. Pergamon, Oxford.

Trytten, D. A (2001). Progressing from small group work to cooperative learning: a case study from computer science. *Journal of Engineering Education* 90, (1), 85 – 92.

Tylavsky, D. J (1999). Active learning in a mediated classroom for a freshmen level course in digital systems design. *Proceedings Frontiers in Education Conference*, 13b2–13 to 18.

van Dijk, L. A., van den Berg, G. C., and H. van Keulen (1998). Experiencing activation in lectures: case studies into activating lecturing behavior and the students. 11th International Conference on the First Year Experience. Dublin, Ireland.

van Dijk, L. A., van den Berg, G. C. and H. van Keulen (2001). Interactive lectures in engineering education. *European Journal of Engineering Education*, 26, (1), 15–28.

Wheeler, E and R. L. McDonald (1998). Using writing to enhance collaborative learning in engineering courses. *Proceedings Frontiers in Education Conference*, 1, 236–241.

West, H and M. Shimizu (1992). MIT – TI Tech joint educational project in design. *Proceedings Frontiers in Education Conference*, 693–697

Weston, C. A., and P. A. Cranton (1986) Selecting Instructional Strategies. *Journal of Higher Education*. 57, (3), 259-288.

Wilde, D. J (1999). Design team roles. Proceedings 1999 ASME Design Engineering Conference. Sept. Las Vegas, Nevada (paper DTM- 99 003)

Williams, R. J and D. A. Beaujean (1993). Developing engineering competence through the median of syndicate studies. *Engineering Science and Education Journal* (February), 35 – 39.

Witt, H. J et al (2002) Development of coaching competencies in students through a project-based cooperative learning approach. *Proceedings Frontiers in Education Conference*, F2A-1 to 6.

Yokomoto, C. F. and R. Ware (1994).What pre-exam and post-exam quizzes can tell us about test construction. *Proceedings Frontiers in Education Conference*, 2c1- 6 to 8.

CHAPTER 14: OTHER INSTRUCTIONAL PRACTICES AND THE NEW TECHNOLOGIES

Summary and Introduction

In this Chapter a number of apparently disparate instructional practices are discussed. At a general level they are bound by the fact that how they function is very much a matter of the objectives their instructors wish them to achieve. All of them can be adapted for use with the new technologies.

The Chapter begins with a discussion of practice and problems with case studies, debates, and mock trials. It is argued that each of them can contribute to the development of intellectual skills that are unlikely to be developed in traditional lecture based courses. They each require changes in the traditional roles associated with teachers and students. The latter have to become actively engaged in learning while the former have to ensure that that engagement takes place. The students are placed in a position where they have to begin to responsibility for their own learning.

In addition to the development of intellectual skills these methods have the goal of better relating theory to practice. A variety of approaches are available for teachers who want to use case studies.

Nowhere are students expected to exercise self-discipline more than in systems of individualized instruction that allow students to work at their own pace. The Keller and Bloom approaches to mastery learning are compared, and variations in the Keller plan including semi-paced mastery are discussed. It is clear that computer assisted PSI courses are able to accommodate quite sophisticated approaches to the development of higher order cognitive skills. The issue of mastery grading is discussed, and a case is made for the training of proctors. It is concluded that PSI may take a step in the direction of helping students gain more control of the learning process and through that control a commitment to educational self-direction.

A discussion of laboratory work leads to consideration of the value of simulation, and also the meaning of "hands-on" and "real" in the simulated context. The section begins with some comments on the objectives of laboratory education, and it notes an urgent need to consider laboratory objectives within the context of distance education.

During the forty-year period covered by this review there has been a move away from teacher-controlled to student-centered laboratory learning. Inquiry (discovery)-based learning is found to experience the same problems that have been experienced in school education. Like all of the strategies discussed in this chapter it needs to be carefully planned. Its great asset is the motivation that it causes among students.

Integrated laboratories and integrated laboratory work have the potential to reflect industrial practice as well as to show the relationship between the disciplines that constitute engineering.

The hands-on versus simulation debate is considered. Simulations are here to stay, but some kind of hands-on work seems to be necessary. Hands-on experiments should be carefully chosen so as to challenge student perceptions of the engineering problems involved. They should not, therefore, be a simplified version designed to demonstrate scientific principles. A simulator, like a laboratory experiment should be regarded as a challenging textbook in action.

Discussion of laboratory work in distance learning leads into a more general discussion of the new technologies and learning. When compared with conventional learning, it is concluded that the principles of learning that apply in conventional instructional methodology apply equally to the design of instruction for use with new technologies. Poorly designed instruction using the new technologies can be as harmful to learning as poorly delivered conventional instruction.

14. Case Studies, Debates, and Mock Trials

A number of engineering schools use the case study method for teaching. How this method that is widely used in business schools and medicine, should be used has been explained by a group from the Harvard Business School. Their book is the standard work (Barnes, Christensen, and Hansen, 1994).

In the 1960s at least thirty engineering schools were using case methods for design education. Then it was reported by about half those engaged in such work that students could only benefit from case material if they learn how to use it first. A similar number of schools reported that it motivated students better than in traditional classes (Fuchs, 1968).

In the following year, Vesper and Adams (1969) reported the ratings of teaching objectives from professors and students who had been taught by the case method, and those from a larger sample of professors who had attended case method institutes. These ratings suggested that cases teach something that is complementary to what is taught in traditional courses. This finding continues to be supported in the literature.

There are national centers for case studies in the United Kingdom at the Cranfield Institute of Technology, as well as in the United States at the Center for Case Studies in Engineering at the Rose-Hulman Institute of Technology,[1] and the National Engineering Delivery System (NEEDS).[2] Books have also been written with cases (e.g.,, Fuchs and Steidel, 1973; Petroski, 1995; Vesper, 1975). More generally the American Association for Higher Education has presented evidence for case study approaches across the curriculum (Hutchings, 1993).

---

[1] http://www.civeng.carlton.ca/ECL/
[2] http://edr.stanford.educ/html/synthesis/synthesis.html
For addresses see *ASEE Prism*. March 1995, p. 19.

As might be expected, case study learning is being promoted on the web (Richards, Gorman, and Scherer, 1995).

Case studies and case problems may be designed by the individual teacher. This writer required his post-graduate students all of them mature students with experience of their work, to write studies based on their experience. They were instructed to leave them sufficiently incomplete for their classmates to role-play each case to a conclusion. This brought reality to the class and the instructor did not have to write an imaginary case study. An extension of this approach at the undergraduate level might involve the students in writing a case through library research, testing problems etc. Case studies can be small (1 page) and conducted within a very limited period of time, or they can be substantial. Alic (1977) for example reported case studies that were accompanied by 46 pages of written materials. A complete curriculum can be constructed around case studies (eg., Kulonda, 2001).

The basis of case teaching is discussion. The pedagogical principles as summarized by the Harvard group are:

"First ... teachers and students share as partners the responsibilities and privileges of learning. Second, ... a discussion class ... needs to become a learning community with shared goals, values, and operational responsibilities dedicated to collective as well as personal learning. Third, a discussion teacher needs to forge a primary alliance with students as well as subject matter. Subject matter defines the boundaries of the intellectual territory; student's intellects, learning styles, fears and aspirations shape their paths on inquiry" (Barnes, Christensen, and Hansen, 1994, p. 5).

Like cooperative learning, it requires changes in teaching technique and also in the way students approach their learning. Of course, case studies may be undertaken by cooperative learning groups.

Given that the basis of the method is discussion there can be many approaches. *"The idea of case studies encompasses a broad range of writings from reports that chronicle events and describe events[3] to those that are meant to teach. Common to all these types of case studies is that they offer a rich description which the reader can use to draw comparisons to other similar situations"* (Baker and Ma, 1999). The case study method in firmly embedded in educational thinking as a method of research (e.g., Stake, 1995: Cohen, Mannion and Morrison, 2000).[4]

The concern here is with case studies for teaching. Vesper and Adams (1969) distinguished two approaches to the use of the case study in engineering. They wrote:

"The case problem approach seeks to put the student into the position of an engineer faced with an unsolved problem by describing such a problem with him and leaving open the formulation of a solution. In contrast the case history approach (Fuchs, 1968) describes both the problem and the outcome, with the aim of letting the student learn from retrospection of the whole adventure."

Kardos (1978), a Canadian Professor, considered that the purpose of case studies was to develop skills rather than acquire knowledge. This assumed that students had an appropriate level of knowledge with which to cope with the case. *"In good discussions, the students seem to originate all the ideas, organize the discussion, establish priorities and cover the material in the allotted time without interference from the instructor. As students wrestle with the problems that arise in the case, they learn to think, to identify useful information, to recognize false leads and false constraints. They should develop the skill of coherent problem definition and the ability to formulate the best course of action, plus the skill of defending decisions."*

Richards distinguished between case studies that illustrated a principle or an approach to engineering, case problems that are open ended and leave the solutions to the students, and case histories that are primarily about mistakes in engineering.

14.1.   Purposes of Case Studies

Because case studies and case problems are based on real engineering problems that have occurred or relate to actual practice, they provide an introduction to engineering and simultaneously to the real world. Fitzgerald (1995) related the experience of Christopher Brown at Worcester Polytechnic Institute, who heard from one of his recent graduates that while he had learned a lot of theory in school and *"knew the academic side of machining, but not where in the machine the tool went. He had never even looked in the catalogue."* This led Brown to develop cases that dealt with such issues.[5] Thus case studies help relate theory to practice but more importantly they should show the value of theory.

Case problems and case studies can be designed to help students understand concepts. Anwar and Ford (2001)[6] described a case for electrical engineering technology students that enabled them to apply concepts to a real-life situation, and thereby better understand the concepts. Part of the text read as follows,

"The ACME BioTech Compnay owns several facilities in various geographical regions. At one of the facilities water is provided by a drilled well. A water pump, driven by an electric motor, pressurizes the system as illustrated below. The motor and wiring are shown in the figure. Three changes have to be made to the system.
1.   *The electric motor needs replacement.*
2.   *An emergency OFF switch is to be installed near the motor.*

---

[3] See for example Koen, and Schmidt (2001)..

[4] This was the focus of Baker and Ma's study in which they described a case study of student learning, and a case study of teaching practice.

[5] The student who went to work in a company that made ball valves out of castings had been required to select the tool insert for the machining operation as his first job.

[6] There are two papers about this course. Anwar,(2001) and Anwar and Ford (2001). They give different cases based on the ACME Bio Tech company. The former also deals with cases in Technical Writing.

3. *A mechanism to turn the motor ON should be installed near the water pump.*

The changes needed are for the following reasons.

*   *The electric motor has failed and must be replaced.*
*   *Following a routine inspection by ACME Bio Tech's insurance carrier, the inspector asked that an emergency OFF switch must be provided near the motor. Because of the non-standard nature of ACME Bio Tech's production, the various insurance policies needed to cover the company's operations are difficult to obtain. Therefore, the request from the insurance company's inspector is not subject to negotiation.*
*   *The pump and motor are always in operation and the automatic ON/OFF control of the system is through electrical contacts in the pressure switch. However, the system has occasionally failed in the past. It has been discovered that some means to override the automatic pressure switch and manually start the motor must be provided near the pump."*

The teams were then provided with a list of tasks to do. These included the use of catalogues, because the selection of equipment based on analyzes of the problems, necessarily required the understanding of concepts. They also had to write memos and make oral presentations.

In 1998 the Della CD-ROM won the Premier Award for Excellence in Engineering Education Courseware. It provided a case study of a power plant (Della) designed to show that *"good decisions require that managers become involved in understanding unfamiliar technologies and strike a balance between technical, financial and management issues"* (Raju et al., 2000). It was created for the reason that students become involved in real world problems have to understand the concepts of design. The full case was published elsewhere (Raju and Sankar, 1998).

"A problem in this case study was the heavy vibration when the 120,000 pound turbine-generator unit at Della Power Plant was taken up to a high speed during start up. The manufacturer's representative diagnosed the problem as due to possible breakage of some parts and recommended that at a cost of $0.9 million, the unit be disassembled and retainer rings inspected. The plant engineer diagnosed that the problem was due to an oil whip and recommended that the turbine unit be restarted immediately. The cost would be nil if the unit functioned properly and could be as high as $19.5 million if the unit failed during the restart. The plant manager had to make a difficult choice between restarting the turbine-generator unit or shutting it down for maintenance considering financial, technical and safety issues."

The authors thought that the understanding required of the students would be of the:

*   Non-technical forces that profoundly effect engineering decisions.
*   Technical forces that profoundly effect engineering decisions.

*   Importance of teamwork and communication in engineering practice.

At the same time students would be able to:

*   Identify criteria to solve problems in unstructured situations.
*   Analyze alternatives given multiple criteria.
*   Be actively involved in a learning situation.

The case was evaluated in two universities where it was favorably received by the students. It was found that the presentation was enhanced by multi-media (i.e.,, audio and video). The teachers learned that the case study enabled the students to tackle *"significant and challenging problems."* and that theory was integrated with practice.

In contrast to this large case, Henderson, Bellman, and Furman (1983) pointed out that quite simple cases may be given for homework. This would also apply to the development of problem solving skills. In this respect, one of the advantages of "real life" projects is that it is unlikely that there will be one solution. As Brown (Fitzgerald, 1995) pointed out, *"you can't look at what's right for engineering or what's right for manufacturing, you have to figure out what's best for the company. It has to be simultaneous-you have to work with design and manufacturing and business together."*

Alic (1977) argued that the principle of guided design could be applied to case studies. This principle was *"the carefully arranged sequence of instruction and feedback which does the guiding."* One reason for doing this was that the materials available for guided design were based on hypothetical situations. Such guided case studies would be provided with a written sequence of instructions and feedback, which would *"incorporate in some fashion most of all of the historical material found in conventional case studies."* Because of the constraints of historical fact the guidance given is less precise and authoritative and students have to read between the lines. Alic was of the opinion that the hybrid nature of the guided case study placed it between a guided design project and a case study. Since guided design projects seem to be more appropriate for elementary engineering courses, the introduction of guided case studies after guided design projects provided a sequential introduction to case studies and then to project work (see Section 14.3 for Alic's description of the approach).

More often than not, the solution to problems requires knowledge from more than one discipline, for this reason, some approaches to engineering case studies have involved non-engineering students. But such cases have to be designed with care; otherwise, one group or another may be disadvantaged. One case study that was used with both senior engineering and senior management students related to the maintenance of a power station (Raju et al.,., 1999). The students were shown a video in which the *"alternatives faced by the management and the criteria they considered were explained."* At the end of the video the plant manager assigned the case study. They were also shown a second video that showed how management arrived at a solution.

Each team was asked to defend an option. *"The assignment/questions given them were: (1) Defend each option. (2) Compare and contrast the alternatives using the project criteria. (3) What were the critical components of the unit and what was the possible outcome of failure of each component? (4) What other alternatives are possible?"*

The business studies students rated the exercise with lower scores, although they valued the activity. They also indicated that they felt out of touch with the technical dimension. Overall, both business and engineering students indicated that they had benefited from the activity. The instructors were encouraged by the evaluation.

As with group work, it is held that case study learning helps students develop workplace skills not merely because the case *"presents a scenario that practising engineers are likely to encounter in the work place"*[7] but because the method promotes discussion and, therefore, communication skills. Depending on how they are managed and written, they help with the development of interpersonal skills.

14.1.1. Approaches to Teaching with Engineering Cases

Alic (1977) described a modification of Vesper and Hays Hewlett Packard Co case study. The case study began with an introduction as follows:

"The following true story relates the activities of an engineer named Tony Badger during the course of one particular project. As you proceed through the guided case study you will be given much the same information, Tony had to work with at each step. This will be presented in the form of 'feedbacks.' The accompanying questions will allow you to work on many of the very problems Tony encountered."

"There follow several pages of descriptive material concluding with the first question to the student which is answered in feedback in Tony's own words as he describes how he attacked the problem. This is the basic procedure used: to cast the feedbacks in the form of quoted responses (which may be apocryphal as long as they describe the desired versimilitude) or samples of the work of the engineer-protagonist in whose place a student is asked to imagine himself. Then, as the student works through the sequence of questions and feedbacks, he or she is constantly aware that the guidance is that of historical truth [ ]Thus the student can feel free to disagree with the way the project was conducted without seeming to challenge an authority figure."

Vesper (1978) argued that there were easy and hard ways of teaching with cases. Instructors make life hard for themselves when they lecture about the case and fail to involve the students in the case. To do this, the teachers have to be thoroughly prepared, although Vesper felt that they could not immerse themselves in the way the participants had. Moreover, the case may have taken several months whereas the lecturer can give only limited time to preparation. Similarly, if the teacher guides discussion (in the normal sense and not in the sense of the guided case), that instructor will have to be thoroughly prepared if they are to be an effective referee. Vesper's view was that guiding a discussion is quite an arduous task. It is made the more difficult if the teacher has also to assess performance. Class led discussion is equally difficult for the teacher. Once again the teacher has to be thoroughly prepared and if he/she cannot extract some engineering lessons from the discourse the students will become frustrated because their discussion has not led anywhere. Vesper suggested that there was an easier way that did not involve the instructor in extensive preparation. The stages are,

1. Homework. Analyze and prepare solutions for individual presentation to the class.
2. Assign in advance a team of three or four students to prepare in advance an in depth analysis to be presented orally to the class.
3. At the beginning of the class select individual students to present their analyzes.
4. The team then presents its analysis.
5. The team receives questions and directs general discussion.

A course of between four and ten case studies can be pre-planned. The fact that the students do no know who will be called should encourage all them to participate.

Throughout this process the instructor observes both for purposes of feedback and grading. Peer assessment might be used. Vesper, for example, gave each student 100 points to divide between the members of the team excluding that of the assessor. The aggregates can be presented to the team and used as a component of grading. Assessment data can also be obtained from quizzes given before the class begins the case study and written assignments could follow.

Clancy, Quinn, and Miller (2001) of Worcester Polytechnic Institute reported an evaluation of the impact of case studies on ethical understanding among first year students. The approach that they used to the implementation of the case studies is of interest. The particular laboratory was of 3 hours duration. During this time the students, who were divided into groups of not more than eight, read discussed and recorded 4 case studies. These case studies had been selected so that they were suitable for freshmen students.[8] They were edited so that they were no longer than two paragraphs. Because one of the goals of the exercise was to encourage a debate on ethical choices they were also edited so as to avoid any *"obviously correct choice."*

In order to guide the discussions questions were provided with the intention of forcing the students to consider the points of view of conflicting characters.

A final question asked the students to list as many different courses of action that each character

---

[7]Quotation taken from Anwar and Ford (2000)

[8]These cases were selected from a search of the On Line Ethics center (http://www.onlinethics.org) and the national Institute for Engineering Ethics (http://www.niee.org).

might take to resolve the dilemma in the case.

Before the cases were discussed, an assessment was made which tested the number of resolving actions to a case that the students could list.[9] This demonstrated that there were likely to be several courses of action that could be taken. When this was completed the students had to read the IEEE code of ethics,[10] an exercise that could be accomplished in relatively short time.

The discussion and recording of each case took 20 minutes. When the discussions were finished, each group was asked to lead a discussion about one of the cases. They were given 10 minutes to choose a leader and organize the points to be made. Each discussion took ten minutes. The tutor helped to focus the discussion and to draw out facets that the students were missing. To conclude the activity, the instructor gave a summary and conclusions.

The evaluation with volunteer students consisted of three additional case studies that were selected and intended to be similar in complexity and ambiguity to the previous case studies. Instead of the discussion questions, the students were instructed to *"List as many different courses of action as you can think of that might be used to resolve the ethical issue/dilemma described in this case. You may list courses of action that may have been taken at any time before, during, or after the events given in the case description. If appropriate make a separate list for each character. Number your responses as '1', '2', '3'."* The second and third assessments were made one week and five weeks after the laboratory.

The analysis showed that there were no differences in the number of courses of action proposed as between the pre- and post-assessments. It is possible to argue that change might not be expected in a course of such a short duration. Apart from everything else, such courses require the learning of a new language and an attitudinal change to problem solving.[11] Clancy and her colleagues relied on the shortness argument and draw attention to a paper by Self and Ellison (1998), who reported measurable change over a semester. They suggested that such a laboratory course might encourage students to take a semester long course in ethics, contribute to progressive learning in this area, and convince students that ethics is likely to be important in their careers.[12]

At Arizona State University a traditional lecture-oriented case study capstone course in computer science was compared with an experimental team-oriented collaborative project (Neumann and Woodfill, 1998). The purpose was to see if the collaborative project would better respond to changes in engineering practice. In contrast with the two-or three-person teams that typically

worked on a capstone project, the collaborative project required more than 100 students from a variety of engineering departments as well as some from economics and marketing to work in a virtual company. The traditional capstone course incorporated three discipline specific instructional objectives. These were system level design optimization, real-time design constraints, and software reliability and accuracy. The instructional objectives for the collaborative project were team-oriented design teams, multidisciplinary design practices, and concurrent design practices. The prime aim as expressed in the ABET criteria was to *"enable the student with an opportunity to appreciate how the seemingly disparate aspects of their academic study work in concert to achieve engineering designs."*

The case study paradigm was based on a computer system that was specifically designed for the course. Students were *"required to interact with the system as a user, a technical reviewer of the design, and s a design engineer"* and, were supported by lecture and laboratory resources.

"When the students completed the assignment, they were provided with copies of the hardware design schematics and operating source code. In this way, the classroom discussions of laboratory assignments naturally transition into discussions concerning the manner in which the system carried out the programr's instructions ...." The instructors were able to arrange projects that took into account the experiences and interests of individual students."

The volunteer students in the collaborative project had to produce a functional prototype of an autonomous vehicle for marking athletic playing fields. Although the students had to complete the normal requirements for their senior design project, and they had no technical mentors with experience in the field, the vehicle was produced.

The prime management difficulty reported was the compartmentalization that is traditional in industrial organizations which had the effect of giving more opportunity for the team leaders to develop their communication skills than other members of the team. This meant there were inconsistencies in what individuals learned. This problem was compounded by the fact that academic departments retained key performance measures so that the relative importance of technical outcomes varied across faculty. It should be noted that the teams came mainly from a single academic discipline. However, Neumann and Woodfill, argued that the students as a group developed their communication skills.

"The benefits of this communication include: encouraging interdisciplinary cross training, developing presentation skills, enhancing awareness of other technical areas, and encouraging interest and participation in peer based design reviews. These benefits could be seen in our computer system engineering team's weekly project meetings as students presented a technical situation report, identified critical scheduling tasks,

---

[9] The paper is not very clear about this test.

[10] (http://www.ieee.org)

[11] See Freeman, Lynn and Baker, 2001.

[12] More often than not, ethics case studies relate to civil and mechanical engineering however, Fleddermann (2000) has provided four cases that relate to electrical and computer engineering.

solicited help from other project teams, and performed peer reviews for technical designs."

Although the collaborative approach was rejected, Neumann and Woodfill reported that observing these two approaches had led them to make changes in the case study design. They moved, as it were, to a more student-centered approach. The number of formal presentations required was increased as was the use of student led presentations of sections of the case study materials. They also incorporated peer-based review as part of the formal course evaluation.

The examples in this section show that case studies utilize a number of teaching methods. Both Agogino and Kulonda have pointed out that because of this variety, they can respond to student learning styles. Quoted by Fitzgerald (1995), Agogino said that *"with our user interface, each student can choose the type of presentation he she finds most appealing- navigating to pictures or text, spending time reading text or looking at videos, and so on. But all modules also require active learning; there are logic questions, open-ended questions and quizzes. There are places to stop for reflection, so it's not like watching MTV."* (See also Agogino and Evans, undated).

Kulonda, (2001) pointed out that in the case method the issues come via the concrete experience of the Kolb Cycle. The method itself forces reflective observation if students are to draw conclusions. If the students have to apply the concept to a new situation, then the other styles are used.

Newcomer (2004) has pointed out that more often than not, students read the same case and join in discussion about the case. In contrast, he has placed the responsibility on students to write or narrate a report on a case, the data of which was researched by them. The students undertake the work individually; and when in one course they present the results orally, the entire class gets to hear each other's work.

"In [the] manufacturing, Ergonomics, Safety and Health [course] the students write a short paper to highlight the avoidable errors in an industrial accident, and in Engineering and Society, a course that combines technical writing and ethics, students put together a presentation and a brief written summary on an engineering failure or near miss that highlight the ethical issues involved. In both assignments students research the cases and draw their own conclusions. In their narration students must argue a position that emphasizes what their classmates should learn from the case."

Newcomer argues that students learn from this approach to organize evidence and present a persuasive argument. He reported that the students found this approach interesting, and he was of the opinion that it engaged them in learning.

This section has shown that there are a variety of approaches available for those who want to use case studies. While some may be more easily managed than others, like most departures from the traditional, more work is involved. Kulonda (2001) reproduced a list due to Bonoma (1989) of the questions that a teacher has to ask during preparation. This is shown in Exhibit 14.1. Kulonda also detailed a complete course in operations engineering. It showed the relationship between performance objectives, educational objectives, topics, level of achievement required, and learning strategy.

14.2.   Debates and Mock Trials

Debates and mock trials have much in common with case studies. While debates are commonly used as a means of learning in the humanities there are a few reports of their use in engineering. Alford and Surdu (2002) reported on their use in computer science courses at the US Military Academy. They argued that debates could:

- help students organize and synthesize information (i.e., higher-order-thinking) and that the degree too which they do that, is similar to a *"thorough end of term study for an examination."*
- encourage students to learn on their own.
- increase students cooperative skills.
- improve verbal skills.

For a debate to be effective it requires a good topic. These may come from topics that have been discussed in depth in the course, topics discussed briefly during the course, and relevant topics not discussed in the semester. The first encourages analysis and synthesis; the second encourages the development of the students general knowledge; the third encourages the application of what has been learned on the course.

There are three possibilities for assigning the position that students should take in the debate. In the first the students have to prepare half the topic in that they are told which position they have to attend.

- What are the major issues which this case intended to illustrate?
- Where in the course (series of cases) does this case come? How can it be related to other cases so far analyzed or yet to come?
- What are the major "themes" with which my course deals? How can I reinforce those themes with today's case?
- In what order should the case issues be raised?
- How should the analytic information from the case be recorded on blackboards? What does my board plan look like?
- What errors, analytic blind alleys, traps and other "red herrings" does the case encourage from the students? What lessons can be learned by the students falling into them?
- Which of my students would learn the most, and from whom would the whole class learn the most, if he/she was allowed the first 10 – 20 minutes to "open" the case by presenting a detailed analysis? Is such an "opening" the right way to start this discussion?
- Have I done enough preparation, and do I have the confidence to abandon my plans and do some learning myself as new topics or angles that I have not thought about come up in class?
- Are summary comments appropriate at the end of this case? What would they be?

Exhibit 14. 1. Bonoma's (1989) Preparation checklist for a case study cited by Kulunda (2001) In the *Journal of Engineering Education*)

To ensure they learn both halves, they can be told to prepare for a debate without being told which position they have to take until much nearer the time of the debate (say a week). In this situation they are forced to evaluate arguments for and against. The roles may be assigned at the beginning of the debate but this requires substantial preparation. Some time has to be allowed at the beginning of the debate for the team to work out their strategy unless they are required to do this beforehand.

The United States Military Academy tried student versus student, student versus faculty and faculty versus faculty debates. The authors preferred the student versus faculty debate because this produced a high level of effort from the students.

While debates are most easily undertaken in small classes, they can be undertaken with larger audiences. The audience may be invited to submit questions or ask questions directly from the floor. Several teams can be prepared and switched after every round. Students can be required to submit a critique of the debates, and also to select the winning team.[13]

Each year at the Academy they have debated the issue, *"Should the goal of AI be the creation of a thinking machine?"* Another topic discussed by the authors was that *"ADA should replace JAVA as the standard language in undergraduate computer programs."*

Simulated debates in the history of engineering advances were used by Reynolds (1976) at the University of Wisconsin – Madison. He found that if the students were given the materials to reach their own decisions, most of them chose to defend the position that won. To get over this problem, the class was divided into two and those addicted to this "superiority by hindsight" were put in the side that lost.

"Students were asked to prepare a three to five page position paper to be handed in at the end of the debate. To lend more credibility to the simulation, and to make the task of preparation more interesting, they were usually presented with an imaginary set of circumstances as a backdrop for their performances. For the AC v DC controversy I asked the students to prepare the arguments as if they were engineers representing either Edison General Electric (DC) or Westinghouse Electric (AC) and attempting to sell their particular system to the Mayor and City Council of St Louis in late 1888."

Mock trials have many similarities with debates. At the University of Valparaiso (Indiana) senior civil engineering students joined with third-year law students to represent the plaintiffs, designer, and contractors in each of three trials. The engineers were to be the expert witnesses, and they had to explain in lay terms all the technical concepts involved in the case and also to give their opinion of the probable cause of failure. This involved them in several meetings with the law students who had to prepare the engineering students to act as expert witnesses. The cases were argued in front of a practicing judge.

Tarhini and Vandercoy (2000), who conducted these classes, reported that *"it forced students to completely understand the causes of structural collapse so they might clearly understand those causes, and it compelled collaboration with third year law students."* They also noted that it provided an introduction to professional responsibility through the application of the ASCE Code of Ethics to the behavior of expert witnesses. That is, to render opinions based on facts only.

Inevitably the engineering students had to learn a new language and the logic of argument used by lawyers.[14]

14.3. Personalized Instruction (PSI)

"My feeling is that engineering goes through cycles" said Larry Richards in response to a question by Fitzgerald (1995) that asked him why there was a renewed interest in case studies. The same might well be said about systems of personalized instruction because Koen, one of the pioneers of personalized instruction (PSI) in engineering (Koen, 1971; Koen et al., 1975), recently described work with PSI on web based learning courses (Crynes, Greene and Dillon, 2000; Koen and Schmidt, 2001). By the 1980s PSI had been facilitated by computers (Goodson, 1977; Shale and Cowper, 1982), and in 1992, Eaton had described the operation of computer-based, self-guided instruction in laboratory data acquisition and control (Eaton, 1992). But what started with great zest had fizzled out by the mid-1980s. Recently, however, Haws (1998) took a more dispassionate look at PSI and pointed out that it was a system that should encourage students to take more responsibility for their own learning. This, as was made clear in earlier Chapters had become one of the major goals of higher education. At the same time, students do need to be directed in professional courses, and there can be conflict between the search for autonomy and the need to follow a hierarchy of learning.

PSI has been used in engineering, science, and medical education (Kulik, Kulik and Cohen, 1979). It is a form of competency-based learning and instruction that requires mastery of content. It differs slightly from Bloom's approach to mastery learning, as will be shown (Bloom, 1976). It is commonly known by the name of its inventor as the Keller Plan (Keller, 1968).[15] The assessments are criterion-referenced. It was mainly used in the United States, and most of the literature referenced in the following paragraphs is American.[16] In engineering, it was particularly promoted at the University of Texas-Austin (Koen, 1971; Koen et al., 1975; Roth, 1973; Stice, 1979), and at Drexel University (Calkins and Thomas, 1979; Smiernow and Lawley, 1980). Very large numbers of students were involved.

---

[13] For detailed discussion of pedagogy of debates see Allen, Willmingon and Sprague (1991) Chapter 16.

[14] A good example of these two approaches compared is to be found in Woodson (1966)

[15] *Engineering Education* carried a retrospective article by F. S. Keller in 1985. Testimony of an Educational Reformer. 76, (3),144 – 148.

[16] In England a course in Physical geography has been described that contributed 15% to the final examination (Clark and Gregory, 1982). Another course in geography in Australia was described by Cho (1982)

The Keller scheme has the following features
1. The student proceeds at his or her own pace.
2. Complete mastery must be obtained.
3. Lectures are used as a means of motivation. (Students qualify for lectures that are used as a reward: the material in the lectures is not examined.)
4. Proctors are more senior students to whom the students bring their work.

A course is divided into units, and each unit takes about one week. On completion the student is given a 'readiness' test for the next unit by the proctor. If students fail this test, they repeat the unit and take another test (not the original). This process is repeated until they pass the unit. The proctor provides the tutoring, as did monitors in the British system of school education in the nineteenth century.

Keller's method originally relied on printed materials, but it is now understood that any type of material can be used. For example, audio-visual aids have been used with success (Pearson and Carswell, 1979). It is evident that the programd instruction of that period and now computer-assisted instruction can be used with PSI.

In contrast to Keller's scheme of individualized instruction Bloom's approach to mastery learning involves lectures, group discussion and reading assignments. At that time cooperative learning was barely in vogue but the relevance will be self-evident. Stice, (1979) of The University of Texas at Austin listed the similarities between the two approaches as follows[17]:

1. *"They define the level of learning required to achieve mastery.*
2. *They assume that nearly all students can learn and will learn if instruction is properly designed.*
3. *Course material is broken down into small learning units.*
4. *The units are sequenced so that material in later units builds upon that which came before.*
5. *They require careful specification of instructional objectives*
6. *They require careful design of tests that allow both student and teacher to evaluate the student's achievement of objectives.*
7. *They use a number of tests so that students get a great deal of feedback to enable them to "see how they are doing", and correct misconceptions early.*
8. *They provide some sort of prescriptive instruction for the student who does not achieve mastery.*
9. *Grading is on an absolute basis; students are graded against the mastery criterion and not against each other.*
10 *Course atmosphere is positive; everything is designed to help students achieve the objectives, and they are not punished for their mistakes."*

Of the differences, Stice drew particular attention to the definition of mastery. In the Keller plan, 100% mastery is required. Engineering educators often allow 80% or 90% marks, which is similar to the Bloom method. This was because of the familiar response to questions that showed the theoretical understanding and application to have been correct but the answer wrong because of a fault in the arithmetic. In these circumstances the tutors did not want the students to have to repeat the whole unit, so they allowed them to pass provided that they found the error and corrected it in a short time. Other differences between the two are:

1. PSI units are typically of one week's duration. Mastery learning units are generally of two weeks' duration.
2. PSI delivery relies on self-study. Mastery learning relies on whatever technique of group teaching the teacher uses. Lectures may be used.
3. PSI courses are self-paced. Mastery learning courses are teacher paced. In the former when the student feels ready to take a test, they take it. In the latter the students take the test at the same time. These are formative tests, and no record is kept of them. There is a Summative test at the end of the course.
4. PSI tests are substantive and use a variety of testing formats. Mastery tests are short and of the objective type. The PSI student takes between three and four times as many tests as the mastery student.
5. In PSI, as soon as the proctor grades the test, the student has the feedback. They may also provide tutorial assistance. *"Mastery learning courses are different in this regard. The teacher's initial assignments direct the student to particular readings and other learning materials, and the formative test determines the students' achievement of course objectives for a given unit. The answer sheet passed out after the test has been taken, however, gives not only the desired answer for the questions on the test, but also an alternate set of instructional correctives for each question. Bloom contends that if the instructional materials had been suited for a particular student, he or she would have learned adequately. If learning did not occur, restudying the same material is not effective for the student: better try a different instructional approach"* (Stice, 1979).
6. Grading is determined by the number of units covered in the PSI course, as well as by a Summative test in mastery courses.

In both cases, as with all departures from the traditional lecture approach, teachers have to do a great deal of planning but mastery approaches require less work than PSI courses. Stice was of the opinion that in engineering it would not be possible to test two weeks' work in fifteen minutes because the questions are mainly of a problem type. He thought that this objection might be overcome by the use of a take-home test. Gessner (1974) found that the students spent too much time on testing. After discussing the matter with his students he gave take-home tests that were set on the understanding that the closed folders would not be opened until the students were ready.

Gessner's (1974) approach to the design of self-paced instruction in engineering is shown in Figure 14.1. His paper is of particular interest because he showed

---

[17] Stice provides an extensive quotation on the design of the two approaches from Block, (1974).

graphically the cumulative test average over 30 periods. It was found that those students who could maintain the pace had consistently higher average scores than the students who lagged behind. *"The majority of the class were highly motivated in their work, and their test performance was consistently high, even on tests taken beyond the minimum required number."* He argued that this was due to the incentive offered; i.e.,, students had to complete a minimum of six tests, but they could elect to take additional tests on new Chapters with the condition that one low-test score would be omitted in the averaging.[18]

When Stice (1979) wrote, Kulik and Kulik (1975) had already reported a meta-study of PSI courses. They had found that out of 39 reported comparisons, 38 reported that the test performance was better in the PSI than in conventional courses, and that in 34 of these cases the difference was statistically significant. In a later analysis (61 studies), Kulik and his colleagues (1979) reported that in PSI courses the improvement in student performance is the same for low-aptitude as it is for high-aptitude students. Drop out rates appeared to be higher from PSI courses. Roth (1973), of the Electrical Engineering Department at The University of Texas, Austin reported on a course that had been run on four consecutive semesters. Faculty learned much during this period, and the course was subject to modification. While the students adapted readily to self-pacing, the time taken to complete the course varied widely. The fastest student completed all 20 units in less than four weeks while the slowest students took a whole semester to complete about half the course. For those students who completed it in one semester, the average time was 8 to 9 hours within the range 2 hours to 20 hours per week. Roth found that while most students were capable of self-pacing, many had difficulties with self-starting; thus class attendance was required until unit three was passed. On the fifth occasion that PSI was offered, a comparative study was made between the PSI sections and a concurrent lecture section. Students were assigned to sections according to time preferences. The material covered was identical, with the exception that the PSI students did not do the required homework for the lecture section. The PSI students obtained, on average, 9.6 points higher than the lecture students in a final examination. They also spent 1.4 hours per week more on the course, and poorer students tended to spend more time on the PSI course than they would have done on a lecture course.

Also at the University of Texas at Austin, a major evaluation that took into account dropout (and incompletion) was reported by Hereford (1979). She found the picture to be somewhat complex. First, she was able to have reasonably sized control group of students not taking PSI, and she found a statistically significant

difference between the two groups in the first semester. The dropout rate was greater in the PSI courses. However, she did not find any differences in the following two semesters, a result that was contrary to findings in the literature. She thought that this was due to a change in requirements of the university regulations. This required the implementation of end of semester deadlines. It had the effect of motivating students to complete and thus reduced the number of incompletes.

Hereford reported that the main reason given by students for not completing PSI was that *"they were too far behind."* In the control group the reason given for dropping out was that they were not doing well in the course or were failing. Only one PSI student who was interviewed gave that reason. Proctors, because of their continuous contact with students were, asked to say why they thought students dropped out. Sixty eight percent of the reasons given by them related to problems with self-pacing (or by implication). Twenty five percent suggested that some students dropped out because they were not suited to one or more aspects of the PSI method other than self-pacing. Interviews with those who had dropped out produced suggestions to improve PSI that *"were in direct conflict with the principles upon which Keller based the method."* However, the students reported that they liked the organized material, the high level of mastery required, the sense of accomplishment, and the access to proctors. The latter was mentioned most frequently. *"It is ironic that the source of many of the dropping students' difficulty-self pacing–was also one of the most appreciated elements of the PSI method mentioned in the interviews."*

Procrastination was defined (for purposes of the research) and investigated by Hereford. Procrastination is the perception that tutors have that some students progress through the course at a rate slower than average. She found that procrastination decreased with instructor experience. The two strategies that were most used to decrease procrastination were average progress lines and deadlines. The problem with these approaches is that the introduction of such strategies alters the self-pacing intentions of the Keller plan. Progress lines are a more subtle way of doing this than deadlines. Hereford thought that some element of pacing might have to be introduced to meet the constraints of the university calendar. Procrastination was not found to affect mastery, although it did affect course grades, there being more procrastinators among those who gained lower grades.

Most of the publications reviewed refer to the problem of procrastination, but few make clear the complexity of the issue as Calkins and Thomas (1979) did. They distinguished between procrastination that is not the responsibility of the student, as for example, illness, and procrastination that is the responsibility of the student, as, for example, the decision to spend more time on other courses. Among the latter group, there were those who progress too slowly through their course but at a rate that is commensurate with their ability and

---

[18]Haws (1998) has described in some detail his philosophy for wanting to introduce PSI and what happened when he did.

experience. They called these students slow self pacing students (SSP). They try. The real procrastinating student is the one that can but doesn't try. They called this group procrastinating self pacing students (PSP). The problem for them is one of intrinsic motivation, and unfortunately the Keller scheme is based on extrinsic motivation. They thought that SSP students might benefit from charts and deadlines but that PSP students' would benefit more from reinforcement from their coaches.

Calkins and Thomas (1979) analyzed data from the Drexel consortium that had some 5000 students take PSI courses. Their purpose was to draw up a profile of the successful student so as to be able to match them to appropriate courses, and from these data design a course that a PSP student might find favorable. The six components of this course were:

- Modified self-pacing with targets for completion of units.
- Decreased size of modules. Same course material to be broken down into smaller units.
- Smaller ratio of students to mentors, i.e., 2 or 3 to 1.
- Increased used of homework/problem-solving examples.
- Careful selection of mentors to ensure they have empathy with students.
- Some personal contact with the course instructor.

In a small analyzis of two courses, they found that those who had had one or more PSI courses tended to have higher final examination scores. They also took fewer weeks to complete the course. The higher overall grade point average was correlated with higher final course. They also took fewer weeks to complete and had a positive attitude to the course. The more outside work older students did, the more they procrastinated.

Much more recently, Crynes, Greene, and Dillon (2000)[19] at Oklahoma compared a CD-ROM-Web self-paced method with traditional lecturing. *"The traditional method included 3 lectures per week, three major examinations, a final examination, 23 quizzes and homework. The experimental method included one required meeting a week, two optimal meeting periods, modules, mastery tests, 10 quizzes, a final examination and little homework. The CD ROM contained the 10 modules over which the students were tested."* Students volunteered for two sections. Some of them selected the experimental course because they perceived it to give them greater freedom while some chose the traditional course because they were apprehensive about the new technologies. This suggests that some students should not be pressed into the new technologies without prior training.

A minimum rate was required from the PSI students in order for them to take the same final examination as the final class. A common pre-test was given to both groups. Information about learning style preferences, motives, preparation, and attitudes were obtained.[20] No significant differences were found between the groups.

Another study of students in a Master's degree program in Sweden also found that there was no strong evidence that students with different learning styles reacted differently to the computer. There was a weak tendency for "good students" to take greater advantage of their computers than "weak students" (Berglund and Daniels, 2000).[21]

In the Oklahoma study it was found that the experimental group felt they lacked confidence in their background knowledge, and the authors explained this by the fact that there were more "students at risk" in the experimental group. Otherwise the groups differed in the other dimensions of motivation that were measured. The experimental group read and re-read the material more than the traditional group. As the authors pointed out, the experimental group worked in a self-study mode and this result is not surprising.

The experimental group liked the flexibility that the CD-ROM gave them, and they found it more useful than the traditional group found their text. Given that both groups were statistically identical in achieving the learning objectives, was the CD-ROM SPI program worthwhile? Crynes, Greene, and Dillon felt it was because students had to assume responsibility for their learning, and the teacher is freed from lecturing for much of the time. In this way, more attention can be given to those who need help.

As reported in Chapter 7 (Section 7.5) Pollock (2004) described changes in instruction over a twelve-year period in mathematics. These went from small group teaching through large group to CAL and CAA. When the CAL was introduced, the students were given work sheets every week for different topics. When they were ready they completed a multiple-choice test. This improved the overall pass rate, and substantially more students obtained more than 60% in the exam. The students reported that they liked being tested in this way, that is, they liked to take the tests when they felt they were ready. So the tutors changed the assessment from class exams and degree exams to a set of ten tests. CAA was introduced to achieve this goal and the improvements in performance were maintained. A tutor was available to the students.

Pollock considered that the two main disadvantages were that some students took too long in preparing for their assessments. She alleviated this by changing the final test to cover all the topics in the course. From a tutorial perspective the CAA, because it requires only final answers, it does not help the tutor understand student learning difficulties unless they keep notes of all their work.

---

[19] University of Oklahoma

[20] Felder's learning style inventory was used.

[21] Study orientation was obtained from a modified version of Gibbs (1992) inventory. This inventory distinguished between "doers" who have an achieving orientation, and students with a meaning orientation. The latter, look for a deeper understanding whereas the doer's try to learn the text rather than the meaning.

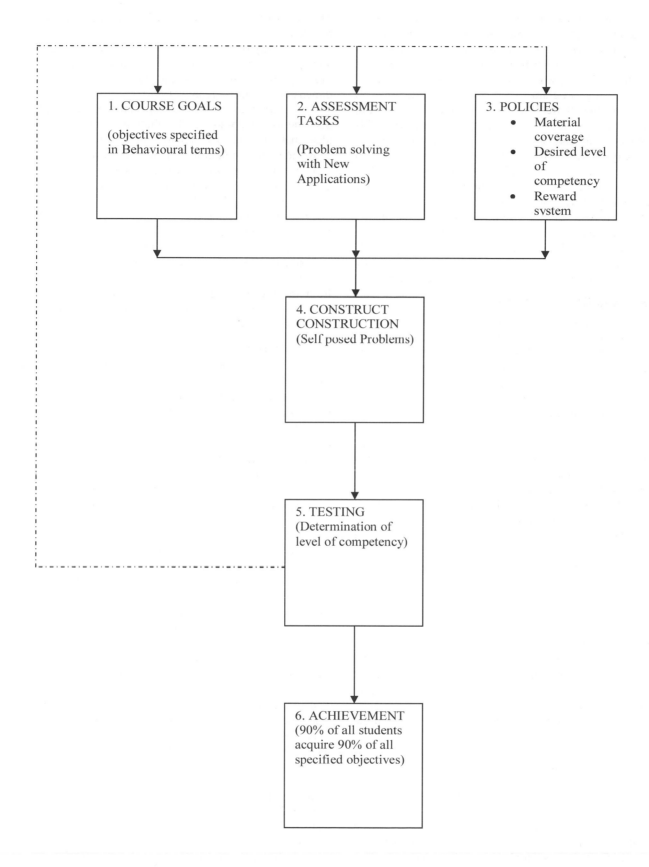

Figure 14.1. Gessner's (1974) approach to self-paced learning. (Cited in Heywood (1979) and Reproduced with permission of *ASEE/Journal of Engineering Education.*)

The views of administrators in engineering toward PSI at the University of Texas-Austin will be found in Koen et al., (1975). In this respect, a paper by Predeborn (1979) described how a specially designed instructional center was developed to administer a self-paced learning program. This overcame difficulties in relation to the clerical work that faculty experienced when they ran their own self-paced courses. This particular center ran two courses. It was open 7 hours a day, 5 days a week with two or three resource people on duty each hour. It was staffed by two teachers. They participated on a voluntary basis during each quarter. One faculty member was assigned to each course each quarter, but both teachers worked with both courses. They spent 8 hours each week in the center. The remainder of the time was staffed by selected student proctors. The paper is accompanied by design drawings of the center, faculty work-load distributions, timetables, and student usage.

14.3.1. Grading in PSI and Mastery

It is expected that students who have followed the Keller scheme will either perform well (A and B) or fail (F). Few C's or D's are expected, although the number of fails should not be high for those who complete the program. The grade is determined by the number of units taken together with the result of a comprehensive final examination. The ratio of marks may be of the order 75% to 25%.

In contrast, the grade obtained from a mastery learning program depends on the score obtained in a summative examination at the end of the course. The grading is determined by the mastery criterion set at the beginning of the course. If the mark is 85%, then all students with 85% and above get an A. It is intended that in the ideal situation, no one should fail and most should get an A.

Teachers more often than not adapt schemes such as these. Armacost and Pet-Armacost (2003) treated mastery grading as a form of assessment-led learning. They considered that each examination should be a little bit harder than the previous one. It should raise "slightly" expectations about the content and style, but students should understand what is required of them prior to the course. They also argued that re-examination should follow reasonably quickly after the failed examination. They applied mastery-based grading to that part of the course evaluation (operations research) that involved the term examinations.[22]

Armacost and Pet-Armacost found that *"test grades improved with each re-examination. The number of students decreased with each subsequent re-examination, but those who persisted found their grades continued to increase"*. They acknowledged that some of this improvement in performance was due to improved test-taking skills. Seventy-five per cent of the students who participated considered that they had learned better.

Thus the test came to be viewed as an assessment that helped learning.

Many of the reports on PSI indicate that the first attempts are a major learning experience for faculty and this applies as much to grading as it does to the other dimensions of course (Haws, 1998).

For many teachers, especially those used to marking to pseudo-normal distribution (or the curve), the idea that all students should pass is problematic. A substantial change in attitude is required from them. One approach that has been used in a system that awards grades against the curve is to require mastery for a basic pass level. This approach was used by the tutors of an informatics course at the University of Technology-Sydney. Achievement of mastery guaranteed a pass. Higher grades could be obtained by taking an advanced assessment although it seems that there was no compulsion to do so. The mastery grade was determined from module assessments, an oral, and a journal. The journal was regarded as an important component of the assessment (Lowe, Scott, and Bagin, 2000).

14.3.2. Variations in the Keller Plan

At Purdue University the Department of Electrical Engineering had offered introductory courses in both lecture and PSI format, and students were allowed to choose which one to take. It was felt that each method had its advantages. The teachers also felt that procrastination was the most serious disadvantage of PSI while in the lecture method student deficiencies could accumulate over time, and large lecture classes were more impersonal. The department therefore introduced a hybrid program that utilized the advantages of each.

Lindenlaub, Groff, and Nunke, (1981) described the hybrid system as follows:
"Students were required to attend scheduled lectures during the first week of the semester. A portion of these periods was used to explain the operation of the system, and students were given assignments requiring them to use the department's self study facilities. The remaining time was used to introduce basic concepts and work example problems. During the rest of the semester students spent only one hour a week in scheduled classroom activity, with other time devoted to self-study activities. The lecture session was divided into thirds, so that the professor typically met only a third of the students each day... Since the class was divided into thirds, three design problems were devised for each major."[23] Formative and Summative techniques of evaluation were used. A meaningful comparison group was found, and comparisons were made with three in-course examinations and a final examination. Insofar as the final examination was concerned, there was no statistical difference between the results of the two groups.

Student ratings suggested that the hybrid course instructor was perceived to be more effective than the

---

[22]The paper is of considerable interest because detailed examples of second and third re-examinations are given. It includes the request form for re-examination. It amounts to a contract.

[23]Full details of the syllabus and timetabling arrangements are given in the paper.

lecture section instructor. The course study aids were also perceived to be effective. They were able to make crude comparisons with those for an independent study section and, whereas the hybrid and lecture courses were perceived of being of equal value, they were thought to be less valuable than the independent study. As a consequence of this evaluation, the system was revised to *"emphasize a spectrum of instructional techniques rather than a more narrow focus on independent study techniques and design problems... the lectures were divided into three types of activities instead of three groups."* The evaluation showed that the students did not find value in the majority of study aids offered. Their comment on the use of video aids is of interest. These tapes were designed to show how the solutions unfolded and to be able repeat any part of the solution as many times as they would like. The students did not seem to use the tapes in that mode but rather to treat them as a lecture, which suggested that students might have to be trained in their use.

The Purdue University course was intended for large groups of students. In stark contrast, Fowler and Watkins (1977) described courses that were used with 16 students where the faster students became the proctors for the slower students. The instructor made the course materials available on an individual basis to three students, with not very encouraging results. With a fourth student a weekly meeting time was established which could either be postponed or changed at the request of the student.

Subsequently, five more students took the course and were successful, although one was a procrastinator. This time goals were set at the weekly meetings. Fowler and Watkins's were of the impression that the most important predictor of success was the student's self-discipline, and this was a forecast of things to come with distance learning and CAI. For this reason, it is worth quoting their view of the value of independent study courses such as these to the student. They wrote:

- *"Students must take a much more active role in the educational process. Letting material slide until just before a quiz won't work.*
- *The informal teacher-student relationship, combined with the lack of pressure on readiness tests, make learning much more product of his own efforts.*
- *The student feels a much greater sense of accomplishment because the learning is much more a product of his own efforts than those of a lecturer.*
- *The depth of understanding of course material attained is much greater.*
- *In a properly designed course of this type, a student ends the course with the confidence that he or she can pick up an unfamiliar book and learn from it without the aid of a teacher.*
- *The two way communication encouraged by the system of instruction made the acquisition of information an exciting process.*
- *This mode of instruction can build the overall self-confidence of students tremendously."*

Other variations of the Keller plan were reported. One, at Auburn University, was particularly concerned with student motivation (Renoll, 1976). Renoll had come to the conclusion that the problems posed by PSI were not so much due to the concept as to the day to day management of a course. He believed these could be overcome by modifying the concept of PSI. The course that he ran comprised a series of mini-course topics that varied in length from one to three weeks. A formal laboratory/lecture session took place once at which progress and problems were discussed. In an important departure from the strict Keller approach, he divided the class into groups of three or four at the beginning of the course. At the end of any mini topic, they could change groups if they wished. To motivate them, he shared with them an actual engineering problem that was related to the mini topic the students were about to begin. He also used 'attention getter's', not all of which were successful. One was a variation of the brick problem, namely: *"Each student is given a metal paper clip and asked to list as many non-conventional uses for it as possible in 3 minutes."*

In an approach similar to that used in cooperative learning, he required that each student in the group be responsible for obtaining a particular piece of information relevant to the design problem. His other, not inconsiderable departure from the Keller plan was in the system of grading. *"Two conventional quizzes are given, one at mid quarter and a final, each counting for 25 percent of the final grade. The remaining 50 percent comes from evaluating the engineering reports prepared by each group for the mini course topic. Each member of the group gets the same grade."* This procedure has many critics as studies of the evaluation of group work indicate.

14.3.3. Semi-Paced Teaching

Another writer who described his approach as a series of min-courses differed from the Keller plan in that he controlled the pacing (Cleaver, 1976). Hence, the term *"semi-paced teaching."* He described his system as follows:

"Conventional lectures are given three times weekly. After each lecture a 15 minute written quiz is given on the previous weeks work. Following each quiz, a solution sheet is handed out to provide students with immediate feedback. Graded quizzes are returned at the next class meeting."

"The first of the three quizzes on each unit is mandatory; the other two are optional. The student's highest grade on any of the three quizzes is the recorded grade for the unit. Thus, the student has a chance to learn the material in the usual way, and then two chances to learn by his mistakes. The term "semi-paced" is used because of this feature of the program. The student must, in general, go at the instructor' speed, but within each unit he may go at his own speed, achieving any level of perfection that he is willing to study for. Thus a course becomes a series of min-courses, and it is the philosophy of this teaching method that many relatively easy mini-

goals are easier to achieve than one difficult grand goal."

The final examination was of 150 minutes' duration and designed to test the retention of the concepts taught in the units.

He compared the results of two groups, one of which was taught the same material by conventional lecturing, and found that the semi-paced group achieved higher mean scores. It had a more limited range of marks than the control group in the final examination. The mean grade point average of the control group prior to the course was slightly higher than that of the experimental group, and from this finding he concluded that the success of the experimental group was due to the instructional method.

14.3.4. Immediate Feedback

Cleaver (1976) took from the Keller scheme the importance of immediate feedback. Another approach to the conduct of lessons so as to give immediate feedback that is useful to both the student and instructor was described by Belbin and Belbin (1972). They described a self-evaluation system used by the Center Universitaire de Co-operation Economique et Sociale at Nancy in France for training adult men and women in mathematics and science, developed by Bertrand Schwartz in 1964. This comprised evaluation sessions in the evenings. In the first part of the evening session a discourse was given for about 40 minutes. After a break, group work organized by an assistant involving discussion of the lecture or exercises in application to their daily work takes place for 40 minutes at the end of the session. During the break, 20 minutes were devoted to self-evaluation, after which questions are set. The answers were given when the test was completed. The students had to mark their own answers and record one of the following:

1. Failed to understand the text of the question
2. Made an error in the calculation.
3. Misused or used a wrong formula.
4. Forgot something. Made an error of reasoning.
5. Failed in some other way.

The assistant analyzed the papers (which were unnamed) and also made comments if necessary. The teacher was given an analysis so that he or she could judge the effectiveness of his teaching and decide whether to repeat parts of the course.

It is the self-assessment within the scheme that sets it apart from the mastery and PSI programs described above. The tests were not criterion referenced. However, self-assessment could be built into those programs. E-learning makes possible quick feedback.

14.3.5. Levels of Cognitive Skill Performance; Remediation

Cleaver (1976) used his final examination to test the retention of concepts. It is not clear which level of understanding it embraced, but a criticism of PSI approaches is that they do not test for the higher order skills of thinking. The constant testing might reinforce

memory skills at the expense of other skills. A review of work in mathematics in Australia and New Zealand suggested that mastery learning had limitations in university courses in the context of 'problem-solving'. Imrie, Blithe, and Johnston (1980) argued, therefore, that the assessment should be two tiered to incorporate both mastery and problem solving levels. In an evaluation of a mastery-learning package in microbiology, the students were distinguished by their performance on a test designed to meet the six levels of *The Taxonomy of Educational Objectives*. It was found that the attitudes toward the package of the students achieving high-level performances became more favorable whereas those of the students attaining low levels became less favorable between pre and post questionnaires. The attitudes of both groups to the test were unfavorable! (Whiting, 1982).

Experiments early in the period of this review with computer-assisted materials indicated that quite sophisticated problem-solving approaches could be accommodated in mastery and PSI packages. As with non-computerized approaches, it was found to be useful in remediation (Shale and Cowper, 1982; Mihkelson, 1985) and helpful in improving performance (Pazdernick and Walaszek, 1983).

14.3.6. A General Comment on Peer Tutoring, and the Selection and Training of Proctors

In regard to personalized instruction where peer involvement is a *sine qua non,* several papers refer to the need for proctors to be carefully, chosen. At Drexel University, student coaches were available on average for 18 hours per week in the Learning Center to administer and grade tests. *"All coaches take a concurrent seminar in engineering education, which introduces concepts in the psychology of learning. The head coach is a graduate student with overall responsibility for proctoring and book keeping."* Calkins and Thomas (1979), also of Drexel, drew attention (see above) to the need to select coaches who had empathy with students. Peer tutoring has been undertaken outside of PSI schemes and often students have undertaken the tutoring of less experienced students. For example, a well-publicised scheme at Imperial College involved engineering students tutoring students in secondary schools (Goodlad and Hirst, 1989; Goodlad et al., 1979). More recent peer instruction in crystallography at Imperial College has been reported by Baillie and Grimes (1999).

At the Nottingham Trent University, final year students have supervised first-year mechanical engineering project work. The purpose was to develop their communication skills for which they received 4% of the marks in their final degree award (Saunders, 1992). At the University of New South Wales the change over from traditional paper and pencil design subjects to computer graphics using a state-of-the-art package promoted a problem in that there were insufficient work stations to accommodate all the students. Therefore, only a quarter of the students, were given the computer graphics course. In the following year there were a sufficient number of work stations for all second year students to use the package. The solution was to use those who had learned how to use the package during the previous year to tutor those who had not during a four-week program.

Magin and Churches (1995) reported that this worked well. Student-to-student teaching of this kind was found to create a learning environment in which there was open communication and enquiry. Because the tutors had been recently exposed to the problem themselves, there was empathy between them and their tutees. However, Magin and Churches were concerned that the tutors did not gain as much as could have been gained from the exercise in terms of learning. To achieve that goal, their work would have to have been assessed, and for this to be accomplished specific learning goals would have to have been stated, as, for example, in the area of communication.

A more ambitious project in engineering at the University of Nevada-Reno was reported by Adams, Nash, and Leifer (2001). They described how two courses were team-taught by students. The experience of the first course led to changes in the second course that produced higher student ratings. Each student gave one lecture related to the Chapters in the book normally used to cover the course. A contract for grading was designed by the students at the beginning of the course. On the positive side it was found that students claimed to remember more with less work input. Students could recall 12 (SD = 3.6) out of 19 presentations. The students also looked forward to the class and paid better attention. They reported that they had a lot of fun. However, on the negative side, students mistrusted the accuracy of peer-presented material, and they thought the course could have been better organized. As might be expected, faculty raised concern about student qualifications for teaching. When the second course was planned, it was agreed to allow students to do a report instead of a lecture if they preferred written presentations. The students were also to be coached twice before the presentation of their reports. A significant difference between the ratings of the two courses was found in favor of the latter. As in the first case, student recall of content was positive.

Baillie and Grimes (1999), on the basis that it had been established that the tutees of trained tutors, did better than those of untrained tutors provided a weekend training course that was designed to help potential tutors understand how they might facilitate the learning process. They were given sessions on deep and surface learning, and on the management of groups, and they were *"helped to explore good group practice techniques, such as probing, brainstorming, recording group interactions in order to monitor group dynamics, developing listening and communication skills and closing techniques."* The scheme was run once per fortnight during the first year. Fifty percent of the students attended most of the tutorials. Both students and tutors noted that some groups were oversubscribed and some had poor attendance, but the students seem to have found the scheme beneficial.

The tutors understanding of crystallography was enhanced.

At Sheffield Hallam University a comparison between an experimental group in which there was peer assisted learning with a control group within a conventional tutorial[24] yielded a modest but statistically significant improvement in examination results. In the experimental groups the seating pattern was adjusted to approximate a horseshoe. The tutor's (teacher's) position was outside the horseshoe and out of direct eye contact. All sessions were student-led, and a structured approach was used. During the lead in direct questions to the tutor were allowed. "The structure used in the tutorial evolved around each individual student being encouraged to provide a model answer that they could describe to the class, thereby encouraging the peer-assisted learning activity. The model answer was in response to one of a series of tutorial problems set by the tutor and distributed by handout. Students were asked to work in pairs or triples and select one of the questions to deliver. A typical session would involve students presenting their model solutions in pairs, on the OHP or board to the group at the level demanded by the group. Simple questions justified a simple statement of the numeric solution; harder questions required a step-by-step approach. The group then dealt with the questions that the pairs had been unable to solve, with the tutor acting as facilitator." The tutors considered that there was an improvement in working and presentational skills.

The teachers suggested that a longitudinal study might elucidate whether meta-cognitive skills had improved as a result of such interactions. It might also be possible through an ethnographic approach to study such groups as a learning community.

14.3.7. Off-Campus PSI

Roberson and Crowe (1975), having had experience of PSI, were of the opinion that self-paced instruction had the advantage over traditional correspondence courses of instant feedback, but since they wrote, there have been major developments in distant learning and the use of PC's in that learning. Recently, Koen and Schmidt (2001) have described how a PSI course in engineering was developed for transmission over the Web. There will undoubtedly be more developments of this kind.

14.3.8. Some Concluding Remarks on PSI

PSI was not without its critics. Gessler (1974) argued that it encouraged mediocrity since the requirement that all students must master the knowledge meant that the material would be set at an intermediate level. He also argued that because students were able to take whatever time they liked this would induce in them the wrong attitudes in the practice of engineering. The lecture-type situation with its deadlines created a real

---

[24]Students work at problems and request help from the tutor if desired. In this case the students in the control group were selected on a random basis. Pre and post-tests were administered. Again there was a modest effect size in favor of the experimental group.

world situation. His final point was that PSI changes the meaning of grades because every entrant passes. They represent a statement that every student has acquired a minimum knowledge.

Leuba and Flammer (1976) criticized Gessler on the ground that he was unfamiliar with the approach. With respect to the lecture method they pointed out that PSI was learner-centered. In such a system the instructor *"feels a deep responsibility to help each student achieve the course objectives"* whereas in instructor-centered learning the teacher simply off-loads the material. Apart from the fact that it was perfectly permissible to require students to achieve certain goals within a specified time, PSI fostered excellence and self-confidence, and attitudes were as much a function of self confidence as anything else.

Roberson and Crowe (1975) suggested that no one should enter into PSI unless he/she could reasonably assume that he/she would be able to teach the course for several years. The literature reviewed here shows that faculty members have to go through a learning-process, and that often changes are made after the first year. Haws (1998) recent description of his own experience affirms this finding.

Just as care has to be taken with the initiation of teachers so too does care have to be taken with the initiation of students. The literature shows clearly that faculty members have to be prepared to change their attitudes toward teaching and especially assessment. They have to move from becoming purveyors of information to managers of learning. They become people who design the system and then keep it going. There are many similarities with cooperative learning.

PSI and its variants promote a fundamental challenge to educators. Assessment was probably the most difficult thing that teachers wanting to change had to face. It might well be that this was one of the reasons that PSI was not widely adopted. Whereas they are used to grading over spectrum, PSI is seeking to pass everybody. They can argue that mastery will lower standards. They can also argue that it leads to procrastination. But, don't students make the same choices in other courses? Other teachers argue that it is too behaviorist and that it does not help students learn to stand on their own feet, which is a major goal of higher education. Haws (1998) wrote:

"At first glance, there may seem to be a conflict between achieving learning readiness and enhancing self-directedness (one seems to require control while the other seems to require a relinquishment of control). However, PSI can accomplish both of these goals. PSI allows a student to stipulate both content and level of performance, while simultaneously giving our students more control over the learning process, helping them to develop commitment and moving them philosophically toward educational self-directedness. While PSI is not the whole journey, it can be a step in the right direction."

14.4.   Laboratory Work

Throughout the forty-year period covered by this review there has been a steady flow of papers on laboratory work. Some of them have been about new techniques for solving old problems, others have been in response to new technologies. Most of the new approaches that have been introduced have not been accompanied by evaluations other than that of the anecdotal responses of students to their experience. At the same time, there has been a fairly continuous debate about the purposes of laboratory work, and this has led to some changes in both content and laboratory design. This debate continues as laboratory work begins to adjust to web based learning. It is this debate that is the focus of this part of this Chapter. It seems that in the late 1960s in both the United Kingdom and the United States some teachers wanted to break away from what they called "cookbook" or "recipe" experiments (see Section 14.4.1). It also seems, as the quotations below show that conventional laboratory experiments of that kind continued to be required into the 1990s. Nevertheless, during the period there was a continuous flow or reports describing both small and large changes in laboratory work. In the middle nineteen nineties some papers from Australia and the United Kingdom expressed the fear that laboratory work was in decline and that there was a danger that the products of universities would be trained only in abstract engineering (Jinks, 1994). This raised the question of the value of "hands on" work and, with the possibility of computer simulation the meaning of terms like "hands on" and "reality."

Accompanying the desire for change in the 1960s was a movement among a few teachers in the United Kingdom and United States, stimulated in no small measure by The Taxonomy of Educational Objectives, to define the aims of laboratory work and to operationalize its objectives. In the United Kingdom engineering science at A level was the first engineering subject to attempt this task. Its aims and learning objectives were declared and methods of assessment derived to ascertain that those objectives had been obtained (see Chapter 2 Exhibits 2,8, 2.9, and 2.10). This marked an important step in public examining because concern shifted from the determination of reliability in the assessment of cookbook experiments to the evaluation of their validity. In its turn this led to the use of criterion and semi-criterion referenced measures of practical competence within a public examination that was pseudo-norm referenced. A brief account of these developments was given in Chapter 2 (Carter, Heywood, and Kelly, 1986).

As explained in Chapter 1 the objectives of Engineering Science took another important step in public examining in that a much debated declaration was made of the attitudes and interests that would be developed as a result of the study of the subject (see Exhibit 1.2). No provision was made for their assessment as such. It was believed that course work would make a significant contribution to their acquisition.

Project work was already in vogue in universities and it was fairly easy to operationalize objectives for the assessment of projects. The investigation of the purposes of laboratory work led to the view that many of its purposes could not be achieved with cookbook experiments (called controlled assignments), and that it would be necessary to include some form of discovery learning (called experimental investigations). This threefold categorization of laboratory work was used by Lee (1969) in his study of the attitudes of mechanical engineers to their laboratory education.

Carter wished to bring these ideas to university level engineering education, and with the help of Lee and others, he conducted a number of educational investigations at the University of Salford. With Jordan he summarized this work together with that of other studies that had been done in the United Kingdom in a monograph that was circulated to electrical engineering departments and the engineering professors (Carter and Jordan, 1986). Their purpose was to show the relevance of these researches to the recommendations of the Finniston Committee on engineering education that related to the theoretical and practical curriculum (Carter and Jordan, 1986). Included in the summaries are a list of aims for engineering courses published by the Institution of Mechanical Engineers (1984), a list of goals published by the Council for National Academic Awards (CNAA), and quotations from the Engineering Council on the features of an engineering. Of most interest was the list of 20 aims or non-behavioral objectives for undergraduate laboratory work derived from the work of Lee (1969, 1975) and Jordan (1981). In a separate table, Carter and Jordan gave examples of behavioral objectives related to those aims that were capable of being tested (see also Carter et al., 1980). This tabulation is shown in Exhibit 14.2. They were derived from a content analysis of 25 papers and cognizance of the data from the engineering science examination. While it does not relate these to specific methods of instruction, inspection shows that many would not be achieved with cookbook assignments. During this early period and also in the United Kingdom, Boud (1978)(see also Boud, Dunn, and Hegarty-Hazel 1989) developed a laboratory aims questionnaire the purpose of which was to help with course improvement. In the United States, Rice (1975) also developed a teaching objectives checklist. It comprised 37 non-behavioral statements that were grouped in four categories. These were (1) subject-matter content, (2) equipment and instrumentation, (3) student attitudes and habits, and (4) experimental method. The third category was like the engineering science list rather a mixed bag and included such items as *"practice in synthesis", "sense of responsibility and integrity."* They were also derived from a content analysis of numerous books and papers.

Rice had the intention of establishing the relative importance of objectives because general statements about the aims of mechanical engineering education were too vague. When asked which teaching objectives are most important and which are relatively unimportant. He invited the reader to answer these questions in respect of the example that follows: *(a) instruction in the function and use of specific pieces of equipment (what it is used for, when it is appropriate to use it), (b) instruction in the mechanics of specific equipment (how it works), or (c) instruction in the operating characteristics of specific equipment (e.g.,, volumetric efficiency, sensitivity at 400°F etc). Which of these teaching objectives is most important? Which, if any, is relatively unimportant?"* Apart from his key questions, his example also serves as a reminder of the difficulties experienced in writing objectives.

Rice developed a rating scale that asked teachers to indicate whether each objective should be emphasized and whether it was being emphasized in laboratory instruction. The ratings were made on a seven-point scale. The separation between these two rating perspectives provided an indication of whether or not a change in emphasis was required of a teaching objective.[25]

He found that in the first category, only one objective of six was found to be deserving of strong emphasis. This was *"relations between theoretical studies and experimental studies."* In the second category *"the function and use of specific instrumentation, and the operating characteristics of specific instrumentation"* required additional emphasis The student attitudes and habits category showed that a significant increase in emphasis was wanted *for "practice in synthesis," "engineering judgement,"* and *"an ability to recognize the relationship of specific cases to general principles and laws."* All of the teaching objectives in the experimental method category were highly rated, some more so than others.

As Rice recognized, these results were very much a product of the culture in which students and teachers functioned at the time. The interest was focused on technical methods and not on the personal and the interpersonal.

Nearly thirty years later, Feisel (who was a Vice-President of the IEEE) and Peterson (2002) argued that while the question of the goals of laboratory education had been addressed before, it had not been discussed *"extensively in the context of distance education or with regard to the massive computing power that enables highly sophisticated simulations."* Given that there is a clear trend to replace traditional laboratories with virtual laboratories, it was important that this issue should be discussed since the evaluation of these laboratories depends on the objectives they wish to achieve (Amigud et al., 2002).[26]

---

[25] The checklist was completed by 30 mechanical engineering professors at Stanford University, The University of Santa Clara and the University of California at Berkeley and Davis.

[26] This is based on a data base of 100 web-enabled laboratories. 30% were used to replace traditional laboratories. 12% offered passive simulation; 69% offered active simulation; 11% offered remote manipulation; and 8% were game-like. Most used Java programs.

Aim	Behavioral Objective Capable of being Tested and of being Observed.	Aim	Behavioral Objective Capable of being Tested and Observed.
1. To stimulate and maintain the students interest in engineering	Student likes working in the laboratory, is often seen there, arrives early, leaves late.	11. To provide each student with an opportunity to practice the role of a professional engineer so that he/she can learn to perform that role.	Student exhibits responsible, truthful and reliable attitude towards data use of time, care of equipment, etc
2 To illustrate, supplement and emphasize material taught in lecture	Student uses lecture material, in laboratory problems and vice-versa, and has knowledge of methods learned.	12. To provide the student with a valuable stimulant to independent thinking.	Student creates his/her own solution to problems, does not wait to be told what to do. In discussion, student puts his own point clearly.
3 To train student to keep a continuous record of laboratory work.	Student keeps well laid out notebook for this purpose rather than loose scraps of paper.	13. To show the use of practical work as a process of discovery.	
4. To train the student in a formal writing of experimental procedures, adopted in laboratory practicals and the writing ot technical reports.	Student hands in well written reports on time, discusses them with tutors, and attempts to improve them.	14. To demonstrate use of experimental work as an alternative to analytical methods of solving engineering problems.	
5. To teach the student how to plan an experiment so that he derives meaningful data.	Student comes to laboratory having read necessary references and with a prepared plan of operation.	15. To help students understand that small models of plant or processes can aid greatly in the understanding and improvement of such plant and processes.	
6 To give the student training in the processing and interpretation of experimental data.	Student uses graphs and tables intelligently, draws fair conclusions from them, and deals sensibly with errors.	16. To familiarize the student with the need to communicate technical concepts and situations; to inform and persuade management to certain courses of action to disseminate technical knowledge and expertise for the benefit of all.	Student can explain clearly what he has done and why using proper technical concepts, and using graphs, tables, sketches, etc., as seems most useful.
7. To train the student to use particular apparatus, test procedures or standard equipment.	Student shows competence in handling common laboratory equipment and learns to use new equipment quickly.	17. To help students bridge the gap between the unreality of the academic situation and industrial scene, with its associated social economic and other restraints which engineers encounter.	
8. To improve the learning/teaching process by improving the communication and rapport between staff and students.	Student talks with staff, initiating discussion on the experiment and other matters.	18. To teach the student how accurate measurements made with laboratory equipment can be; to teach him how to devise methods that are precise when precision is required.	Student can determine and report errors correctly, and can devise more accurate methods of measurement and demonstrate them. Student also guesses correctly when to ignore errors and when to "round off" numbers.
9. To strengthen the student's understanding of engineering design, by showing him/her that practical work and design work must be integrated to achieve viable solutions in design problems.		19.To teach the student what "scientific method is and how it is applied in the engineering laboratory.	
10. To develop the student's skill in problem solving in both single and multi-solution situations.	Student progresses from "dashing off in all directions" methods to planned attacks on problems.	20. To give the student confidence in his ability to imagine a concept or hypothesis, to test it, and to carry out that experiment and report its results to others.	Student acts confidently yet safely in the laboratory.

Exhibit 14. 2. Aims of Laboratory work and some behavioral objectives (Carter and Jordan, 1986). (Reproduced with permission of the G. Carter).

Objectives	Objectives
Objective 1. Instrumentation. Apply appropriate sensors, instrumentation, and/or software tools to make measurements of physical quantities.	**Objective 8. Psychomotor.** Demonstrate competence in selection, modification, and operation of appropriate engineering tools and resources.
Objective 2. Models. Identify the strengths and limitations of theoretical models as predictors of real world behaviors. This may include evaluating whether a theory adequately describes a physical event and establishing or validating a relationship between measured data and underlying physical principles.	**Objective 9. Safety.** Recognize health, safety, and environmental issues related to technological processes and activities, and deal with them responsibly. **Objective 10. Communications.** Communicate effectively about laboratory work with a specific audience, both orally and in writing, at levels ranging from executive summaries to comprehensive technical reports.
Objective 3. Experiment. Devise an experimental approach, specify appropriate equipment and procedures, implement those procedures and interpret the resulting data to characterize an engineering material, component, or system.	**Objective 11. Teamwork.** Work effectively in teams, including structure individual and joint accountability; assign roles, responsibilities, and tasks; monitor progress; meet deadlines; and integrate individual contributions into a final deliverable.
Objective 5. Design. Design, build, or assemble a part, product or system, including using specific methodologies, equipment, or materials; meeting client requirements; developing system specifications from requirements; and testing and debugging a prototype, system, or process using appropriate tools to satisfy requirements.	**Objective 12. Ethics in the lab.** Behave with highest ethical standards, including reporting, information objectively, and interacting with integrity. **Objective 13. Sensory awareness.** Use the human senses to gather information and to make sound engineering judgments in formulating conclusions about real world problems.
Objective 6. Learn from failure. Recognize unsuccessful outcomes due to faulty equipment, parts, code, construction, process, or design, and then re-engineer effective solutions.	
Objective 7. Creativity. Demonstrate appropriate levels of independent thought, creativity, and capability in real-world problem solving.	

Exhibit 14.3. Learning Objectives for Engineering Laboratories. Presented for discussion at the Frontiers in Education Conference, Boston, 2002.

Feisel and Peterson presented a list of objectives derived from colloquy for discussion at the 2002 Frontiers in Education Conference. This list is shown in Exhibit 14.3. In the sections that follow, some of the innovations that have been described in papers are discussed. The effectiveness with which such objectives will be achieved depends in no small way on the way in which the laboratory is designed. In this respect the work of Amigud and his colleagues in assessing the quality of such labs is to be welcomed. Their study led them to define ten quality factors that would lead to an effective laboratory. These were *"(1) clear goal statement, (2) VARK (learning style) support, (3) interactivity, (4) user guide, (5) quick to download, (6) website easy to navigate, (7) aesthetic appeal, (8) chat function, (9) links to helpful ancillary information, and (10) accomplishment of goal verified by student test results."* They argued that the absence of any one of these *"vital components"* meant that the laboratory did not meet today's student expectations. Their analysis may be criticized in that it did not obtain learning criteria (i.e., purpose in terms of conveyance of information, higher order learning etc). It did, however, take into account the extent to which the laboratory catered to learning preferences following the VARK model (Visual, Aural, Read/write, and Kinesthetic). They found that 56 laboratories supported 3 styles, and 7% supported all four

styles. *"Visual attributes contribute more than 50% of laboratory components"*[27].

14.4.1. From Teacher Focused to Student-Centered Laboratory Work

Complaints about laboratory methods have been variously illustrated as:

"'cook book' experiments, each made up of a set of instructions that the student is to follow by rote. Essentially the student learns only the structure of laboratory experimentation which involves standard experimental procedures" (Rosenthal, 1967).

"Cawley (1989) suggests that the content and organization of many such classes has changed little over the years despite long standing criticism of their educational value, a quarter of a century ago Martin and Lewis were complaining about tightly controlled, predictable experiments where students' critical faculties went largely untested" (Grant, 1994 [UK]).

"Laboratory protocols in elementary Physics and Chemistry have become rigid and prescriptive, allowing no room for experimentation" (Abel, 1995).

"Laboratory experiments have become cook book situations in which technology has obscured the

---

[27] The authors described in detail the laboratories that met these 10 criteria.

working of the basic principles and student has achieved little more than the recording of data or observing mysterious results" (Feldman and Hofinger, 1997).

In Australia *"the laboratory experience of students, especially in their first year, focuses on 'recipe' experiments which offer limited challenges"* (Kirkup et al., 1998).

This is not to say that cook book experiments do not have value. It may be *"satisfactory if the purpose is to develop psychomotor skills and the ability to use measuring instruments. These purposes become less important as easy-to-use digital instruments have replaced analog instruments which often required considerable expertise. However learning to use instruments or tools is still a legitimate purpose for the laboratory course. A cook book approach may be used when the purpose is to reinforce theory. Unfortunately, this does not tend to be extremely convincing, and a discovery approach is more effective"* (Wankat and Oreovicz , 1993, p. 180).

"Typically the equipment is set up before the students arrive. They follow a prescribed routine of making adjustments and taking readings. Analysis too is generally suggested in the handout. Pointers are generally offered by the supervision on the nature of the discussion" (Edward, 2002b [UK]).[28]

Such cook book experiments provide a limited learning environment and a major purpose of introducing inquiry learning was to create a learning environment that would encourage learning as opposed to rote performance and memory.

This was the view taken in 1967 by Rosenthal and the authors of the Engineering Science Curriculum discussed above. The so-called cook book experiments were called "controlled assignments," and the objectives showed the students what they were intended to achieve and students were expected to undertake about eight such experiments in the two years of the course (Exhibit 2.9). The results were to be recorded in a journal, which, although not assessed, could be inspected by the examiners. The experiments that were submitted for assessment were of a discovery kind. Initially, four were required, but this was reduced to two. It was intended that the student would present two, but not in the same areas of inquiry, for assessment. These would be the best that they had conducted during the two-year period of the course. These experimental investigations were in the discovery mode that was popular in elementary and middle schools in the United Kingdom.[29] The assessment criteria are set out in Exhibit 2.10.

Although there was a substantial history of project work in the Universities and Colleges of Advanced Technology in the United Kingdom there was little evidence of student centered laboratory work. The

examiners of engineering science were concerned that examination of traditional laboratory experiments in a three-hour period told them very little about the skills the student had. What they assessed was a written report, and a skilful student could easily contrive a good report irrespective of understanding. For this reason they introduced open-ended experimentation as a means of assessing that understanding.

The value of such an approach in university courses was demonstrated almost immediately by Carter and Lee (1975). With data collected from a nineteen item questionnaire of staff and students at the University of Salford, they concluded that, *"both faculty and students judge the major aims of laboratory work to be reinforcement of lecture material and stimulus to independent thinking, to acquire skills of experimental techniques and communication, but that students desire a more open-ended approach and greater relevance to engineering than faculty admit."*[30] The argument for a more open ended approach to laboratory work that continues to be made in the United Kingdom (Edward, 2002)[31]

By the mid 1990s articles began to appear that reported a decline in traditional laboratory teaching (e.g., Jinks, 1994). Grant (1994) of the University of Strathclyde went so far as to say that traditional laboratory teaching was under threat. *"The economic arguments for continuing decline are seductive. Computer software can now simulate a wide variety of experimental work, so there is the prospect of freeing dedicated laboratory space for other purposes, at the price of an increase in computational facilities. The latter is easy to defend as such facilities are by their nature multi-purpose and are heavily used. There is, however, a counter-argument, and in the present climate it must be expressed with some force. Engineering can be a brutal profession: the practitioner is continually faced with the consequences of his actions, in clear and often tangible form. Anything that distances him from reality carries with it a danger. Practical laboratory work is uniquely well placed to convey certain messages to the student, messages which are an essential part of his formation as an engineer. The fact that it has been used with so little imagination in the past should not blind us to its intrinsic value."* He went on to argue that experiments could be brief and informative: Experiments that went wrong were remembered. It followed that experiments should be designed to have unexpected results that could be

---

[28]Edward (2002) repeated that this was generally the case.

[29]The Nuffield Foundation sponsored curriculum developments in the school science curriculum in biology, chemistry and physics that had a strong discovery element to them. They followed in the wake of similar programs in the United States.

[30] Indeed, elsewhere in the paper they reported that staff believed *"that students were incapable of performing open-ended creativity experiments since they lacked basic knowledge".* But by this time Heywood and Kelly (1973) had published the first evaluation of engineering science and reported that pre-university entry students could undertake open-ended experiments.

[31]In the United States in one experiment it was found that students in an "Introduction to computers in engineering" course who had been randomly assigned to lecture/laboratory or laboratory only strategies preferred the all laboratory student-centered courses except for internet material. The students were also much more comfortable with computers. Working by oneself or in the laboratory for less intense computational topics were preferred equally (Shiavi et al., 2000).

discussed with the group. This implied that students should be able to make oral presentations to the group, and thereby, enhance their communication skills.[32]

The issue of hands-on versus simulation will be taken up again later, but in the sections that follow some ideas of teachers who have taken up the challenge to make laboratory work more stimulating will be discussed.

14.4.2. Inquiry-Based Learning.

Rosenthal (1967) outlined what a student had to do in guided discovery learning as follows:

1. *The student formulates a simple experiment based on ideas related to the laboratory course.*
2. *He writes a short proposal of his design, including what he wants to do, how he is planning to do it, and what results he expects.*
3. *The student gives a short presentation to teacher and class to acquaint them with his idea. This gives him the opportunity to discuss with his classmates the question of feasibility of the proposed experiment and to get their comments and suggestions.*
4. *He gives a list of equipment that he will need to the technician to ensure that it is available and will be set up at an appropriate time.*
5. *The student prepares a report of the experiment as far as he can before coming in to do the actual experimenting.*
6. *He then experiments and considers many modifications or redesigns. At the same time, the student keeps a log of the steps that he takes so that he can see the process by which he achieve his goal.*
7. *The technical report is completed.*
8. *The student gives a short demonstration to teacher and class of how his experiment works and what it shows.*

The general similarities with the engineering science approach as illustrated in Exhibit 2.10 will be apparent. The details differ. Some discovery approaches may occupy a single laboratory session. Investigations in the A level engineering science, as for example, the evaluation of different washing up liquids or engineering oils could occupy as much as eight hours of laboratory time.

Rosenthal's ideas were based on work that he had done at the City College of New York. At the time he had suggested but not completed an experiment to evaluate the merits of discovery versus conventional laboratory work. Although no reports of such experiments were found in the engineering literature, such comparisons have been made with middle and high school students and the findings are similar to those reported in subsequent papers (Heywood and Heywood, 1993).

At the University of Pennsylvania a Discovery-Oriented Labs course was designed for engineering students in their second semester. It had been developed from a summer institute with elementary school teachers and was designed to overcome the difficulty that students

"seem increasingly to be impoverished with respect to first hand knowledge about how virtually anything works" (Abel, 1995). Eight experiments were available for the course.

It was found that the students had very little practical knowledge. None of them had seen a single-pole double-throw switch before. *"None could explain why the steady pressure of a finger on a doorbell button and a DC current source could produce an oscillation".* Other examples were given, and evidence that this continues to be a widespread problem in the United States is to be found in a paper by Ross (2000)[33]. Abel (1995) reported that the student response was uniformly positive. However, the students felt that they lacked preparation or prior exposure to the concepts upon which the experiments were based. *"All of the students valued the specific knowledge they gained and many were torn between the positive aspects of having no predetermined protocol and the negative aspects of no knowing (being told) what to do. If this sounds like a classic adolescent dilemma, it should come as no surprise."* It is an example of the use of laboratory work to help students climb the steps of intellectual development (á la Perry) *and some courses have been reported that have this objective* (Young, 1997)

Like Abel (1995), Ross (2000) of the University of Detroit Mercy wanted to provide a hands-on experience through which the students would come to an understanding of concepts and principles. He also wanted the students to be able to distinguish observation from inference and to apply inductive forms of reasoning instead of only deductive forms. Twelve experiments in electricity and magnetism were devised for this introductory course. For example, in tracing light rays the *"students develop the concepts of light rays and practice drawing ray diagrams to locate the image of various objects. They investigate the properties of converging and diverging optical elements such as lenses and mirrors."*[34]

Ross claimed that these inquiry-based experiments (some are described in full in the text), helped develop higher-order thinking skills, as for example, the ability to be able to predict an outcome. They also helped students take responsibility for their learning and gave them the opportunity to experiment first hand. He did not, however, comment on the management of the class whereas Abel does. Abel pointed out that discovery learning, especially when principles are not given but have to be found, takes much longer. Consequently the breadth of coverage is reduced. This finding is consistent with the studies in secondary schools noted above. He felt that this was justified in the first year *because of its impact on attitudes toward laboratory work and the specific exposure to hands on activities that we took for granted a generation ago and*

---

[32]He gives examples and additional references.

---

[33] Who also cites McDermott and Schaffer (1992).

[34]In the United Kingdom until recently teachers would have expected work of this kind to have been done in secondary school physics.

rarely find it in entering students." He thought that more might be achieved with upperclassmen.[35]

One of the intentions of the experimental investigations in engineering science was that the students would design the experiment themselves. This is a form of discovery whose degree of guidance depends on how the question is set.

The engineering department at The Robert Gordon University (Aberdeen, Scotland) felt that investigative procedures of this kind would enable them to solve the problems of a modular course that brought together students from relatively different disciplines with varying degrees of competence in physics. The course, Technology 1, was intended to give an introduction to basic concepts, and it was decided that the appropriate way to teach basic thermodynamics concepts was through experimental investigation (Edward, 2002).

"The laboratory was conducted in groups of around six which the students themselves selected. Each group was given one or more kitchen electric heating or cooling device. Their broad objective-all the initial guidance they were given- was to investigate the device(s) in terms of thermodynamic principles and materials properties and selection. They were required to formulate specific objectives, an experimental plan indicating how they proposed to achieve these objectives and a hazard analysis and risk minimisation exercise. All of these had to be approved by a staff member before they were allowed to proceed. This was not quite the 'sink or swim' predicament it might sound. The five staff members present worked with the groups. Although they did not suggest any solutions they helped them to ask questions about what would be useful information to establish about the products, what data could be acquired from the appliances, what additional equipment they would need and how they might interpret results."

This activity had many similarities with the mechanical dissection approach advocated by Sheppard and her colleagues at Stanford University. The evaluation, which is discussed in the last section, was thought provoking.

Feldman and Hofinger (1997) of Purdue University, in an approach that had many similarities with Edward's involved the whole of sophomore students in the design of experiments in a materials laboratory. They described one of the experiments as follows:

"The second experiment was to empirically determine the characteristics of a compression spring. Each team was given a different spring, but the testing process was again determined by the whole class. A long bar was mounted in a pivot fixture on an existing static test frame. The spring was fastened approximately one-third of the bar length from the pivot with the weights at

the far end. As the weights were added, the deflection of the beam was recorded. Reduction of the data included consideration for non-perpendicular forces and the angle of the moment arm. Combining the load data with the initial material and diameter parameters, the operating characteristics were determined."

Feldman and Hofinger found support for this approach in Kolb's learning theory (Chapter 5). *"The lecture required the use of the students personal experience and at least some reflective observation. The addition of homework added the need for conceptualization. Assignment of the laboratory triggered a requirement for greater understanding which combined experience with more thinking before the interactive discussion with team members"* (reflective observation), and so on. They reported that the lab reports showed evidence of higher-order thinking and better understanding than before.

At San Jose State University a laboratory course for advanced thin-film processes has been developed that integrated the fabrication of thin films with design of experiment and statistical analysis of data. The authors argued that the general principles of this course could be applied in other areas of study (Gleixner, et al., 2002).But the extent to which involvement in the design of the experiment is adequate preparation for laboratory work as required by Johnstone, Watt and Zaman (1998)[36] is not clear. They argued that for meaningful learning to take place students have to be thoroughly prepared for laboratory work. *"The student has to be aware of what the lab is about, what the background theory is, what techniques are required, what kind of things to expect in the light of theory, so that the expected when it occurs will be evident."* It is in this context that they suggested that it *"helps if the student has some hand in planning the experiment, even in a modest way. Such pre-lab preparation is not optimal, but essential."*

Johnstone, Watt, and Zaman (1998) developed a pre lab program that has some affinity with Ausubel's advanced organizer (Ausubel, Novak, and Hanesian, 1978). The pre-lab sheet incorporated the following headings:

(a) What does it do?
(b) How does it work?
(c) What will it measure?
(d) What should I know before I begin?
(e) What do I do?[37]

These pre-lab sheets were issued a week before the lab and completion was required before the lab. A post-lab activity was provided to enable the students to explore what they had learned. The dimensions of the Kolb cycle are apparent. Using an attitude questionnaire one-week after each experiment, it was found that the pre-lab had fostered a positive attitude to the changes made in the laboratory. There was a considerable improvement in most post-lab work.

---

[35] At Mississipi State University, physics for engineering courses were supplemented with web-based content. This included just-in-time-teaching inquiry based learning through on-line tutorials. The example given in the paper focused on the understanding and interpretation of one-dimensional kinematics graphs. *"the aim of the tutorial is to get students to discover the meaning of different graph elements by allowing them to see the effect of their selection"* (Mzoughi, 2000).

[36] University of Glasgow, Scotland.

[37] A detailed example is given in the appendix of the paper.

An advanced organizer should cover the principles of what is to be learned in the main lab or lecture. Kostek (1991) gave an example of what would appear to be a perfect advanced organizer. He found that students had great difficulty in a computer-integrated manufacturing technology laboratory with the integration and coordination of relatively complex pieces of equipment. In particular, they had difficulty in visualizing the manufacturing task based solely on written instructions. The students suggested that a prior demonstration would be helpful. To accommodate this request, each lab assignment was video-taped so that it could be viewed prior to the assignment. As a result, it was found that students' gained more insight into the assignments, and the completion time was decreased.

Pre-requisites were encouraged in a level 1 course at Coventry University. Jinks (1994) gave an example of the one that follows:

- *"Identify, from a supplied list of common operational amplifier circuit configurations, each amplifier type/functions.*
- *Identify which of the amplifier types investigated would be most suitable for a particular task, e.g., coupling the output signal of a transducer to the input data acquisition system.*
- *Make calculations to determine values of circuit components for the chosen amplifier design.*
- *Draw a practical layout diagram for the chosen circuit."*

An approach that also seems to have the characteristics of an advanced organizer was used at the United States Military Academy. An automated workstation had been introduced into the laboratory exercises. The standard exercise began with the students having to design a circuit. Prior to this they had to build the circuit in a simulation program and make measurements to verify the correctness of the design. It is used as a "rehearsal". The teachers found that it *increased the students' confidence in the laboratory. "They came to the laboratory with an understanding of what was expected of the actual circuit and with an understanding of how to evaluate whether the desired results were achieved"* (Lane, Shaw, and Stice, 1992).

It is often said that if you want to learn anything try and teach it. This would ensure that these criteria are met. This idea was utilized at Miami University (Oxford, OH) when the laboratory program of a lower level course was re-designed to better prepare students for the capstone course (Schmahl, 1998). It had been found that the students tended to solve the problem immediately without taking time to work with their customers to properly define the problem and its objectives, or to evaluate alternative solutions. In the new course the students were divided into teams. Each team had to investigate an assigned topic and prepare a laboratory exercise for students in other teams to perform. Three weeks were allowed for this planning activity. Each team prepared a short paper that was presented to the class as a whole. The second phase (also three weeks) began with

the class as customers determining the objectives to be met by the project. *"Each team then develops laboratory exercise (the product) for their tool. The lab exercise should meet class objectives and be designed to provide a minimum level of competency with the tool as well as to reinforce theories/concepts learned in the class."* During the three weeks that follow the students perform each others labs. "Opportunities are then provided for improving the developed lab exercises based upon feedback from the performing teams." This process illustrates continuous quality improvement. In the last two weeks the exercise was revised and a report prepared that included information about the revision. The final version was also tested and evaluated.

In Australia, as in the United States, physics departments provide introductory physics courses for engineers. In these circumstances there is a problem of bringing into the physics curriculum engineering applications. This can be a quite fundamental issue for physicists because engineering is the reverse or opposite of physics in that science postulates theories and tests its predictions whereas engineering begins with practice and formulates models that are adequate for the prediction of performance (Edward, 2002a).

Notwithstanding this issue, a new laboratory program was introduced that contained experiments with an 'engineering' flavor at the University of Technology Sydney. The program was changed after an 18-month process of consultation that was assisted by an expert in educational development (Kirkup et al., 1998). The other program parameters were:

"compulsory pre-work accompanying each laboratory session, to orient students to information the upcoming experiment and provide useful background.-time for students to devise their own experimental procedures.-opportunities to describe their methods and results to the whole class in a semi-formal manner. Experiments linked to, and sequenced with material delivered in lectures. Larger units of work, each spanning more than one week.-all students performing the same experiment within the same week, replacing the old program's 'circus' of experiments."

This led to a program that began with a 1-week introductory session followed by the development of basic skills during a 4-week period. In its turn this was followed by 2 weeks on mechanics and 3 weeks on thermal aspects. Assessments were made at the end of each of three major components by means of a skills test, report, and poster. The purpose of the mechanics, Given the definitions was *"To design an experiment to study the factors that affect the efficiency of energy transfer in a system consisting of a bow and arrow and to study the relationship between force, displacement and energy."* Given the definition above, this would be classified as an experimental investigation.

The lectures were sequenced with the laboratory work and the students found that the relationship between lecture and laboratory was made clear. The team also considered that this was in no small measure due to the engineering flavor given to the experiments. There was an increase in the number of positive responses from students when compared with responses from students on the unreformed course. The great asset revealed by the reports on inquiry base learning is the motivation that it causes among students. To be successful it has to be carefully planned.

14.5. The Integration of theory with Practice, and other Dimensions of Integration.

One of the failings of curriculum design has been to provide for the integration of lecture topics with laboratory experimentation designed to illustrate and reinforce those principles. Little attention has been paid to the use of experiments as advanced organizers for theoretical understanding. Many of the studies reported here are conscious of this failing and have tried to remedy this defect, mostly in the direction of lecture followed by laboratory. One or two novel approaches have been reported. One of these, an integrated laboratory, was described by the Engineering Technology Faculty at State University College at Buffalo (Beasley, Culkowski, and Guffner, 1990). These laboratory facilities provided for the integration of lecture, laboratory, and office. They arose from the fact that many of the students were part-time and working in industry, who on graduation were expected to contribute immediately to corporate profitability. The engineering faculty believed that this required specialized teaching techniques that could best be provided by such integration.[38] They considered that the benefits of this approach were:

- *"Efficient presentation and demonstration of interconnected theoretical and applied concepts in a single facility.*
- *Increased information retention, owing to less time needed between faculty presentations and demonstration of concepts, and individual student investigations and applications.*
- *Ability to use full-scale test equipment for physical "proofs," as well as demonstrations of the sensitivity of theoretical principles to changes or errors in test procedures.*
- *Reduced tendency to "compartmentalise" instructional concepts into abstract theory and physical applications; students experience the subject as a connected body of information.*
- *Maximized student/faculty contact for instructional, advisory and remedial purposes which promotes the professional role of the faculty and helps immerse the student in a technological learning environment.*
- *Spontaneous demonstrations by faculty using readily accessible equipment."*

On the downside, these facilities limited the number of students (35 per facility) and increased faculty contact hours.

At the University of California-Sacramento two electronics laboratories were restructured so that one became a teaching laboratory and the other a project room.[39] The teaching laboratory was designed so that the lecture and laboratory experience could be blended in a "seamless web" (Matthews, 2002). The teachers noted that a frequent complaint of the students was that the bench tops were too small. This raises the question of the design of buildings for learning; but that is not a topic, for this review how ever worthy it might be.

The idea of integrated laboratories has special appeal for secondary schools and teacher training colleges that wish to develop programs in technology with limited resources. There have been experiments with such laboratories in Ireland (Murray and Donovan, 1986) and the United Kingdom (Heywood, 1986; Hill, 1986: Owen, 1986). In France the subject of technologie was deliberately set up on a project basis in which the theoretical learning would accompany the work done in laboratories and workshops. Classroom teaching could be undertaken within the same facility in some schools (Murray, 1986).

Integration may also take place around conceptual areas. For example, at Colorado State University a laboratory was designed for active learning that serviced all engineering departments in systems and control (Young, 1997). At Wilkes University a design course which served as an introduction to strength of materials and design also served to demonstrate the interrelatedness of various aspects of mechanical engineering and to develop concepts related to experimentation. To achieve the latter goal, students were required to decide the experimental procedures appropriate for their project, how they should be applied, and the purpose they were intended to serve (Sawyers and Mirman, 1998). The authors hoped that the lab would foster the higher stages of development in the Perry model.

At Coventry University, because experimental study had many features that were common to the different disciplines of engineering, a level 1 experimental module was introduced to service these disciplines. In the first phase, students were introduced to the concept of engineering experimentation through established procedures. *"The aim is to improve and correct experimental deficiencies in order to instil the necessary competence and confidence required for 'fledgling engineers'."* The second phase was subject specific and the experiments were chosen to relate directly to the courses studied by the students. The course was student-centered (Jinks, 1994).

14.5.1. Hands on Versus Simulation[40]

This section is written at a time when enormous changes are taking place in the technology of information giving and receiving. It is now possible to simulate the hitherto unseen. Instead of being at a laboratory bench

---

[38] The paper includes the designs of laboratories for materials science/testing and machine design, and the energy of mechanical systems. The latter was the most difficult to design.

[39] The designs are given in the paper.

[40] A short and good introduction to the debate about hands on versus simulation will be found in Magin and Kanapathipillai (2000), and Ogot, Elliott and Glumac (2003).

with real tools and apparatus, experiments can be animated and the student learns through interaction with a computer program. Engineering educators are making full use of the new tools available to them. The effectiveness of these tools as instruments of learning is now being widely investigated.

In the first place, there is a need to investigate student's perceptions of "hands-on" and "practical," now that so many experiments can be simulated. What, for example, is meant by reality and how does this relate to the perceptions that students have of themselves as engineers? It will be recalled that Lee (1969) found that mechanical engineers actually liked the experiments that they did in spite of the fact that they were of a traditional kind. It seemed that this was because it was the only time in their courses that they felt they were being engineer's (Chapter 2).

Views such as these continue to be recorded by graduates and students. In the United Kingdom Edward (2002a) reported that "they had found that engineering students see themselves as essentially practical. Laboratory work, is therefore, seen as an important component of their formation." Similarly, at the Department of Electrical Engineering at the University of Arkansas-Fayatville, it was found from interviews with graduating seniors over a number of years that the students did not think the program provided sufficient practical training. Employers were of a similar opinion. They believed, as the students did, that students "needed a greater exposure to a wider variety of experiments and equipment." Following a substantial curriculum evaluation and revision, the curriculum became laboratory intensive and the requirement of 2 semester credit hours was changed to a 9 semester credit hour requirement. While meeting the students' desired objectives, it increased faculty workloads. Because some faculty did not fully support the curriculum there was some doubt about the quality of some of the exercises (Martin and Brown, 1998).[41] However, the point here is that the curriculum, was changed to respond to the criticism that it was not sufficiently practical. But the situation is changing because Weisner and Lan (2004) draw attention to the fact that *"more and more, the engineer works from a control room or, at least, from behind a computer screen... an engineer spends less and less time out in the field manipulating production rates and other manufacturing variables by adjusting physical equipment. "* There is, they report, a serious disconnect between what universities provide in mechanical engineering and what industry needs (Sorby et al., 1999), which could only be met by simulations.

Even in distance learning, hands-on activities have been valued and home experiment kits have in the distant past been included in instructional packages (Dobney et al., 1979). In that program the teachers designed their learning packages to encourage the development of higher-order thinking skills following the approaches described by Gagné and Briggs (1974).

Hands-on work continues to be valued and in electrical subjects it can be relatively cheap. For example, Hof et al., (2001) described how in an introduction to data storage systems course for juniors and seniors three laboratory experiments were introduced to *"enrich the students' understanding of magnetic hysteresis, magnetic sensors, and storage systems."* The third experiment made use of a CTR-109 Radio Shack tape recorder adapted for purpose of the experiment.

It seems evident that there is a difference between "hands-on" and "making things." By hands-on seems to be meant the construction of "things" to understand their "working." Translated to the laboratory experience, this has meant the illustration of theory in practice. It has not meant designing, making, and evaluating performance against a specification. This would seem to be a function of project work, and perhaps this is sufficient to meet the identity needs of aspiring engineers; but as engineers become more remote from traditional practice in many fields (Weisner and Lan, 2004), the notion that what is practical is likely to change and with it the requirements for identity. Given that this is the case, laboratory work is about the verification of theory; in practice the next concern is with extent to which simulation can help to achieve this end.

14.5.2 Simulation

Following Heideberg (cited by Ball and Patrick, 1999), simulations may be defined as:

"Programs in which the computer acts as an exploratory tool, supporting a real world activity while facilitating user understanding of the processes involved in complex and dynamic systems which may be otherwise inaccessible. The interactivity inherent in many of the hypermedia based simulations currently being produced provide simulation models which not only enable the user to experience some otherwise inaccessible system, but to bring it back to life in the sense that the user may interact with, obtain immediate feedback from and perhaps alter the underlying model" (Ball and Patrick, 1999).

An example of an inaccessible system is that of heat transfer. *"Heat transfer cannot be directly observed, and is only known by its effect"* (Ball and Patrick, 1999). This creates a learning difficulty because students have to imagine what happens, and this may lead to the misconceptions that so often occur in physics (see Chapter 4). As Ball and Patrick showed, heat flow and temperature can be simulated and interactive arrangements can enable "learners" to "see" what is not normally visible.

Simulations are not necessarily done with computers. Lee, Gu, and Li (2002) argued that it is very difficult to observe and evaluate the performance of a *malfunctioning relay through computer simulation or* benchtop testing. They had described a simulated power system that was a very substantial piece of equipment that would enable students to understand protective relay system behavior in practice. It may be argued that case

---

[41] There were other problems that included (a) worry about the budgetary implications of high equipment usage, and (b) the loading on teaching assistants

studies like the Della Plant Study could resolve this problem. There is simply no evidence, one way or the other, to indicate how best to enable students to gain an operational understanding that will influence their behavior in a real life situation.

There are many other illustrations of real-life situations that can only be demonstrated in the laboratory by simulations either of a practical kind or with a computer, as, for example, the statics involved in the design of bridges. In chemical engineering it is hoped that process simulation will enable problems of large-scale plant to be better understood. Process simulation is already used in design, as it is in equilibrium stage operations primarily with respect to multi-component distillation. Savelski, Dahm, and Hesketh (2001) have argued the case for its use across the range of subjects in chemical engineering. They considered process simulation to be underutilized, and that it could be used as a pedagogical aid in lower-level courses such as thermodynamics.

Its purpose is to take away the drudgery of calculation by performing complex computations. Clough (2000), cited by Savelski et al pointed out that there is a danger that simulations of this kind can encourage surface learning. Care has to be taken to ensure that student understanding of the process being modeled is enhanced. It must not *provide a crutch to allow them to solve problems with only a surface understanding of the processes they are modelling.*

A major problem for teachers who consider process simulation as a possible aid is that at the present time it is very expensive and the cost benefits are not always clear. Moreover, it takes a long time to master. Insofar as chemical engineering is concerned, Savelski, Dahm, and Hesketh suggested that in thermodynamics, process simulation enabled a teacher to present the material inductively without resort to time consuming experiments.

A web based discussion[42] about the role of process simulation among a group of engineers, most of whom were not chemical engineers, led to the view that if simulation is to be used in the earlier years, the number of variables to be used should be kept to a minimum. As students develop so the number of variables should be increased. The curriculum could be organized in a spiral. The concepts would be introduced at a level appropriate to the students and then developed throughout the curriculum so that in the final stages the student is able to understand their complexity, and at the same time appreciate the real world options open to them.

As Baillie and Percoco (2000) reported of the situation in the United Kingdom and in particular Imperial College, many lecturers believe that their teaching is enhanced by the ability to use real-life simulations that help to motivate students and aid their understanding. This would seem to be the world-wide view.

14.5.3. Hands-On Plus Simulation

An investigation by Magin and Kanapathipillai (2000) of the University of New South Wales throws some light on the questions put earlier about student perceptions of "practical" and "real". They pointed out that very little was known about what students think the role of experimentation in engineering education is. How do they operationalize experimentation? To remedy this defect they conducted interviews with 32 third-year students enrolled in a two-semester laboratory course in laboratory experimentation. Seven group interviews were conducted at the end of the first semester. The focused discussion technique recommended by Gibbs (1982) was used. The questions were based on Grant's idea that students learn when there is a significant mismatch between experimental results and theoretical prediction (see above). The students were asked if they had experienced any such mismatch. Following extended discussion the students were then asked, *"whether their experience of conducting laboratory investigations had resulted in any basic change to their understanding of engineering as a discipline?"*

In discussion groups of this kind the interviewer cannot always be sure where the discussion will lead. In one group it led to a discussion on whether computer simulation or modelling could replace hands on experimentation. Two of the students in the group said that the laboratory could not achieve as much as a simulation whereas three did not.

Magin and Kanapathipillai found that all that was needed to promote an awareness of the value of experimentation in providing data that could not be obtained from analysis were one or two key experiments, but *"a substantial minority appeared to have little or no understanding of this."* Thus, it was unlikely that those students could make sound judgments about the merits or otherwise of laboratory-based approaches. They drew attention to research by Tawney (1976) at Imperial College, who suggested that extensive use of simulations could reinforce this kind of poor thinking.

The students described much of their laboratory as being concerned *"with demonstrating theory with developing techniques such as measurement and instrumentation."* Magin and Kanapathipillai concluded that hands-on experimentation needs to be retained in the first years of formative study. However, it should be designed so that students can test the limits of theory *"e.g., where boundary conditions are not well understood, and through this develop students' appreciation of the essential role of experimentation and empirical validation in such situations"*[43].

Experiments have been and are being initiated to compare the merits of simulations and other on-line

---

[42]Facilitated by Dr. Sandra Courter for a professional development program called "Knowing." Engineering Learning Center, University of Wisconsin-Madison.

[43]They accepted that some that some laboratory activities could be replaced with simulations and enhance learning and they cited Hazel and Baillie (1998) in this respect.

activities with traditional laboratories and teaching (see, for example, Corter et al., below). Weisner and Lan (2004) using control and test groups evaluated the impact of computer-simulated experiments upon student learning in a senior unit operations laboratory. The data included a comprehensive examination over the course, a questionnaire that asked the students how well they perceived their learning in respect of the ABET criteria (group 3), and what recommendations they would make in respect of their oral presentations. They found that the students were not adversely affected by computer-based experiments. These students would not have welcomed a totally computer-based laboratory but appreciated the value of a computerized component. Weisner and Lan concluded that student learning is enhanced when computer-based and physical experiments are designed to complement each other. *"With the physical portion of the lab, students obtain a feel for what the equipment looks and feels like as well as how it operates. With the computer-based portion, the students become familiar with the computer interfaces that are similar to industrial control rooms and learn to manipulate the equipment via those controls. They can also explore operating scenarios, which are not easily or economically investigated with physical equipment ...."*

To return to the issue of hands on versus simulation or remote laboratories there is clearly a need for further research. A model of a multiple strategy approach for evaluation that has been piloted has been proposed by Corter et al., (2004). It included measures of satisfaction, learning style, learning outcomes, and achievement. It was used with a small number of junior mechanical engineering majors in a course on machine dynamics and mechanisms and contrasted a remote laboratory with a traditional laboratory. The purpose of the lab course was to deepen understanding through the collection of data, its analysis, and the drawing of conclusions. Six laboratory sessions were allocated to the course. Three of these were conducted traditionally and three were remote.

There were no significant differences in the learning outcomes achieved from either strategy. The students rated the remote labs, as effective or more effective than the traditional labs, but no significant relationships were found between the characteristics of the students and the rated satisfaction. Some trends were present, as, for example, the lower-ability students gave slightly higher ratings to the remote labs when they were directly compared to the hands-on format. Corter and his colleagues plan to replicate the study with a broader range of topics and tested skills, and to more thoroughly investigate the role of spatial ability in preference for remote or hands on learning. In this respect another study that involved a comparison of on-line tutors with a text is of interest. It found that the students in this study preferred a text explanation to accompany graphic visualization, and they preferred tutors that give graphic visualization even if an explanation was not available (Kumar, 2004).

Clearly there is a need for much more research of this kind.

14.5.4. Laboratory Work in Distance Learning.

The big challenge has been to provide hands-on laboratory experiments in flexible and distance learning. A number of teachers are attempting to do just that. For example, Gillet et al., (2001) developed a distributed laboratory that enabled students in remote places to participate in hands-on sessions with real equipment at the learning base. The distance learners could observe through real-time video the effects of their instructions on an instrument, e.g., a servo-drive system. The experiments listed were concerned with the tracking of a specified trajectory using a model helicopter; the stabilization at a specified position of an inverted pendulum, and the control of temperature and pressure using an environmental chamber. This system had been used locally and across the Atlantic between Switzerland and the United States. The teachers found that satisfactory hands-on learning at a distance depended on the dynamic behavior being visually observable for maximum impact. Motion control is more visually dramatic than pressure of temperature control. *Also "the dynamic behavior has to be neither too fast or too slow. If it is too fast, changes will not be observable using the broadcast video given the restriction of achievable transfer rates of approximately 10 frames per second. If too slow, the pedagogical benefit of interactive operations will be lost."* At the same time, the physical system has to be easily revertible to its initial state so that it can be handed to the next user without the aid of a technician.

So far, there are very few evaluations of the effectiveness of remote controlled and in-person operated laboratories. One comparative study of laboratories designed to illustrate the fundamentals of compressible fluid mechanics did not find any significant difference between the students who performed in the in-person or remote environment Ogot, Elliott, and Glumac, 2003). These teachers followed the principles outlined by Gillet et al., (2001) and others. In particular, they held that simulations could not alone present all the problems that could be seen in the laboratory. Moreover, hands-on experience was necessary for effective learning.

In their study the Web group was split into two. The first group was given a prescribed hour to go through the pre lab individually while the second group went through the pre-lab at their convenience. It was found that there were significant differences in the scores of the two groups. The second group spent much less time reading *the pre* lab material than the first group. Therefore, the challenge is to develop methodologies that ensure students, if left to their own devices, go through the pre-lab exercises in depth. This finding is consistent with Johnstone's views outlined above, and the more general theory of advanced organization.

It was found that 87% of the in-person group "agreed somewhat" or "strongly agreed" that the data they had collected were accurate. This suggested to the faculty that the in-person group was significantly more confident in their data than the remote group even though both groups had obtained data that were within acceptable limits of uncertainty. As if in contradiction when asked to affirm the statement *"I was concerned about making mistakes when running the experiment"* fifty eight percent of the in-person group responded to the affirmative dimensions, whereas only 28% of the remote students "strongly agreed" or "agreed somewhat" with the statement. The teachers suggested that while the ability to have direct hands-on experience might increase confidence in the data, the fact that they had to operate the equipment manually might have led *"to increased anxiety when running the experiment as there [were] more things that could be set incorrectly."*

14.5.5. In Conclusion

It is clear that simulation is here to stay, and there are many examples of its use both in college and in distance learning. It is clear that it can demonstrate and simplify many things that cannot be demonstrated in the laboratory. It is also clear, as, for example in circuit design, that it can provide students with an array of circuits that can be handled speedily (e.g., Masson, 1999). This is not the case when students have to assemble and investigate the performance of a circuit in the laboratory. There is also evidence that some simulations can encourage deep learning. However, some teachers feel that students will benefit if, in addition to the simulation, they have to do one or two experiments in the laboratory. But it is argued that these experiments should be carefully chosen so as to challenge student perceptions of the engineering problems involved. They should not be a simplified version arranged to demonstrate the scientific principles. A simulator, just like a laboratory experiment, can be regarded as a challenging textbook in action.

14.6.   Technology and Learning

Throughout this review, references have been made to reports of interventions in learning with some form or another of technology. Since the era of programd instruction in the 1960s, technology has changed rapidly and learners can be more comfortable with computer approaches to programd instruction. At each stage, some engineering educators have implemented the new technologies and attempted to evaluate them. But the pace of change has been such as to make a review of *much that was done in the first years* covered by this review redundant. Since the primary purpose of this review has been to extract enduring principles, it was not thought necessary to review many of these papers although at the time they were important for the ideas they generated (e.g., Plants and Venable, 1985).

To begin where Chapters 13 and 14 began with the lecture, there is no doubt that modern technology has made possible major improvements in the techniques used in lectures, as for example, Powerpoint.

Meyer, Niessen, and Reuther (1997) described an experimental course in which the lecture material was video taped for access by the students at a work station that included a networked terminal plus a standard television receiver. The students could also access a course "lecture work book." The system could be e mailed to ask the teacher or course assistant questions about the course material. Meyer and his colleagues were able to analyze the use that was made of the "flexibility" offered. They found that the videos were used extensively to revise for examinations and to help with homework problems. It was also found that certain of the videos were more popular than others (Reuther and Meyer, 1997).[44]

In addition to the technology delivered lectures there was a weekly "recitation style" class in which the students had the opportunity to ask questions about the course material. A quiz was also administered. A major feature of the design was that the lectures were presented in logically unitized variable length segments and were not constrained by the traditional 50 or 60 minute format.

Compared with the results from previous courses run in a traditional way there was an increase in GPA. It might be argued that this was due to the novelty effect of the experiment. At the same time, a few students were "academically hurt" by their participation in this experiment. A questionnaire revealed that the most helpful feature of the format was the flexibility afforded for viewing lectures along with their unitized format.

But these techniques are subject to the same principles of learning that have been discussed in this review. Put simply, they can, as many lectures do, encourage surface learning or they can be used to encourage deep learning.

As long ago as the 1960s politicians were hoping that student numbers could be increased through the use of televised lectures. Some lessons were learned that continue to be relevant, and they are being learned as web-based instruction is introduced. For example, Dutton (1988), who taught an off-campus course with video-tape, in addition to visiting the external site on three occasions, also scheduled regular times when he *would* be available on the telephone. He found that only a few students availed themselves of this opportunity. Most *"spent far too much time puzzling over a certain point when a simple telephone call would have sufficed."* He found that the single most important factor that ensured the successful presentation of a video-taped course was the preparation of the class notes, a factor that applies to any educational activity.

Dutton did not find any differences in performance between distant and local based groups, and this seems to have been the case with other American studies reported around that time. On occasion the TV students were older than the university students. Teachers across the world recorded that the maturity that older students' brought to their studies was accompanied by higher levels of motivation.

---

[44] The two papers come together in *Proceedings of the Frontiers in Education Conference.* The description above has been simplified. There is a complete description of the development of the technology in the papers

At Virginia Commonwealth University the TV students gave lower ratings to "quality of textbook" and "reasonableness of course load" than the campus students (Wergin, Boland, and Haas, 1986). Over two-thirds of the TV students believed they were getting an equivalent education to the campus students. But some of the campus students found that the technology was intrusive and that it depersonalized the lecture. This can easily happen with the latest technology.[45] These investigators drew attention to the decreased opportunity for personal interaction. While that was to be expected, it was not expected that it would happen with the campus course. But as Wergin and his colleagues pointed out, the off-campus students could be helped with additional tutorials. At that time, computer assisted tutorials and e mail were beginning to come into their own (Karplus and Silvestri, 1983).

Web-based communication has made possible exchange tuition across international boundaries. Lectures at Carnegie Mellon University were recorded by digital video camera, and at the same time a set of powerpoint slides were made to accompany each lecture. These were transmitted to the Technology University at Delft in the Netherlands. The movies ran alongside the slides and were stopped (often) for the lecturers to discuss material as the movie progressed. Student groups met at the beginning of the course through a video-conference. Thereafter, they communicated by e mail, phone, and chat. It was found that students preferred short video clips to lecture length clips (Henden et al., 2002)[46].

Downing at al., (1988) reported that students preferred e-mail to supplement their interaction with faculty, and that it improved the quality of instruction[47]

Twelve years later, Sharp (2000) reported, on the basis of a student questionnaire, that few of the professors in her department communicated by e-mail. Her survey showed that students valued e-mail as a teaching and communications device.[48] In part this was due to its immediacy, which is something that class notes and materials do not have. The survey found that students preferred e-mail to web page use. Among her recommendations to teachers were:

- *"Keep e-mail messages relatively short without attachments.*
- *Avoid sending either too few or too many group messages.*
- *Note that students are concerned about e mail overload.*
- *Gauge how much time students need to receive messages about an assignment before due date."*

Sharp also argued that e-mail should be used to intervene in students work so as to promote learning, and she reported that students wanted the teachers to be efficient technical communicators.

One objection to on-line teaching is that it takes more time than traditional teaching. Hislop (2001) attempted to test this assumption with a few teachers who were paid to keep time logs. He found that although the on-line teaching took longer the actual difference was very small.[49] Hislop did not take into account the course design time. But Eriksson, Goler, and Muchin (2001) reported that in the design of a course on the "Planning and Design of Web Pages" at Chalmers University in Sweden much time was taken up and that such developments require project management. More generally, in using a web based approach within college Collis, Winnips, and Moonen (2000) showed that when the program was designed to give structured support the tutors work time soared (see below).

Eriksson and his colleagues compared the same course delivered on line with a more conventional class that met three hours each week for three hours of lectures and hand-on practice. It contained many of the elements of on-line teaching which make a true comparison suspect. Nevertheless, they reported that the on line students experienced greater satisfaction than the conventional students' during the course, even though they were less dissatisfied with online communication. They concluded that the online students adapted easily to learning in the digital environment. The great advantage of the course to the distance students was the asynchronous time and location dimension. They wrote about the two groups: *"We have a subjective personal reflection about our attitudes as teachers towards the students. When communicating online with students we made no differences in how we interacted with the students. They got the same online attention and equal feedback on assignments (usually we never considered if the students were online or conventional). But when recapitulating the courses, it is mostly the students we have met in person who we remember. It was much more difficult to remember the names of the distance education students. It was if they had never existed."*

Koen (2002) pointed out that "presence" is as important in web learning as it is in the lecture theater. *"Presence is defined as the difference in the relationship between the performance and the audience in a live play."* There is, wrote Koen, *"a sense of spontaneity, risk and improvisation."* He contrasted that situation with the taped drama that is used in televisions. It is characterized by *"professionalism, high production values, and sterility".*

These have their parallels on the one hand with the lecture and on the other hand with a web-based course. *"Presence concerns the feeling that a student is in a real classroom in real time with a real professor in*

---

[45] In a web based conference that allowed information to be typed in by the participants during their discussion, I found that the noise of my keyboard was picked up by the microphone and caused a disturbance.

[46] For details of the distance learning project between SUNY and the Istanbul Technical University in Turkey, see Kalkan and Shields (2002).

[47] The options were mail, phone call, remote talk back, and written note. The on-campus students gave face-to-face the highest rating

[48] Complete details of the survey instrument are given, and a list of techniques for teachers provided

---

[49] The categories analyzed were administration, discussion, e-mail, grading, lecture, materials, phone, talk and technology. There was an 'other' category.

control of learning." The problem in web-based learning is to provide "presence." Koen carried out an experiment to see if this could be done. Students responded favorably to a PSI courses into which a number of strategies had been introduced to create "presence." These included a splash page that showed other students learning at their computers. The intention of this was to incorporate the student into the learning situation. He also used Proctor and professor web cams, a glide camera, and pre-recorded segments. The most important of these was the Proctor cam. The proctor's behavior could be shaped as efficiently over the web as in the face-to-face situation. Koen was able to provide "presence" from Japan. He concluded that it did not matter where the professor was located.

His attempt to undertake a lecture course from a distance was not so successful. A number of technical difficulties were experienced, including the problem of the time delay between Texas and Japan where he was lecturing. He was led to conclude that in the comparative evaluation of live versus on-line lecture, one should first look at the teacher and what he/she is doing because in certain circumstances the teacher's presence may be inconsequential. We cannot necessarily conclude *"that the presence of a master teacher in the same situation would make no difference."* This suggests that something more than simple class ratings are required if on line learning is to be satisfactorily evaluated. It also implies that teachers might require training of the kind that could be derived from the work of Hailey and Hailey on genre in on-line communication.

This point is affirmed by work carried out by Hailey and his colleagues (Hailey, Grant, Davie, and Hult, 2001; Hailey and Hailey, 2002). In the first of these papers they found, contrary to many other studies, that internet-based education could be *"unpredictable and explosive. A few troublesome on-line students may stage vitriolic and embarrassing attacks that can sometimes threaten a teacher's career."* This remark arose from an analysis of some 400 on-line courses, and they concluded that teachers who develop on-line courses should not use *"naively designed heuristics."* They considered that the problems arose not from the technology but from the genres[50] they use. *"For example, interactive discussion in a traditional class is made up of a series of short conversations; interactive discussion in an on-line course is made up of a series of short essays. Although the essays and discussions are in some respects similar, they are also in many respects different, with measurably different affects on learning."*

They also spotted a serious weakness in the investigations that had been reported. Most of the articles they reviewed focused on the media and not on the genres relevant to education. Hailey and Hailey (2002) have argued that in order to convert traditional instruction in to full true digital instruction then the high bandwidths are required.[51]

But there is support for the view that information technology can enhance learning. Kadiyala and Crynes (1998) presented a substantive review of the literature on the effectiveness of information technology in education. This incorporated some 2180 studies since it embraced meta-analyzes that had been previously reported. It covered all sectors of education, including a large number of institutions from elementary, middle, and high schools.

They quoted from a meta-analysis of interactive video instruction to the effect that published journal articles reported a significantly higher mean size effect than dissertations, theses, and government reports. There were very few negative results. But they said, *"it seems hardly likely that all use of information technology results in improvements".* At the same time, and in spite of the fact that they did not comment on the quality of the research, they concluded that there was *"convincing evidence that information technologies enhance learning when the pedagogy is sound, and when there is a good match of technology techniques and objectives".* If Hailey and Hailey are correct then the role of genre will have to be taken into account in future evaluation studies.

14.6.1. Compared with Conventional Learning

Just as with conventional teaching, Christie, Jaun, and Jonsson (2002) of Chalmers University in Sweden warned that *"failure to plan. Deliver and assess ICT based courses on sound pedagogical grounds merely means that poor teaching and learning practices are disseminated more widely and more quickly."* They posed the following questions

- In relation to Pedagogy. "Will students learn better in ICT based courses?"
- In relation to ethics. *"Will the teaching and learning experience be fair and equitable and assist but students and teachers to become better people?"*
- In relation to organization. *"Will the organization better achieve its aims? These aims can be economic, political and social as well as pedagogical."*

When Baillie and Percoco (2000) wrote they suggested that there had been little research to support the claims of lecturers about the learning benefits of ICT. Since, then, if the *Proceedings of the Frontiers in Education Conference* are representative of developments, there has been an increasing amount of documented evidence ranging from unsophisticated evaluations to quite sophisticated attempts at judgment. Answers to the questions posed by Christie and his colleagues are being given in each of the areas listed, as is evident from the above discussion. It is possible to hazard a guess that there is now the data with which to develop an extensive matrix that relates objectives to instructional technique, materials, and method of assessment. In this final section some of the questions that have been raised will be considered.

---

[50]Style characterized by a particular form or purpose, e.g., chalk, talk, PowerPoint presentation, demonstration, talking head, and sermons may be classified as lectures.

[51]They discuss the technical possibilities and experiments they have done in the paper.

In regard to pedagogy the reports that are emerging suggest that many of the principles of learning that apply in conventional classrooms should also apply in electronic classrooms. This is not surprising since we can obtain from computer assisted learning *"drill and practice, lessons constructed for individual differences, example led learning, learning by analogy, discovery and hypothesis testing, spatial problem solving, learning from simulations"*, and in addition tutoring can be provided (Eberts, 1986). These are accompanied by sub-strategies similar to those used in the classroom such as providing hints, asking questions, providing parts of a solution etc (Collis, Winnips, and Moonen, 2000). We hope that our students learning will be improved and we also hope that it will motivate students. Much of what has been reported was based on studies reliant on small numbers, and often undertaken in conditions that do not meet rigorous experimental criteria. But, taken together they tell the story of a developing and exciting pedagogy.

At its simplest, Lu, Zhu, and Stokes (2000) reported a study of freshmen in a modern physics course at City University of Hong Kong that provided evidence of a significant improvement in learning with the use of the Web. But they also found that surfing irrelevant material impeded learning. This problem of defocusing exists in conventional environments. Is it likely to be worse in the Web environment?

Another report from Hong Kong's Technical College on interactive teaching in Electrical and Communication Engineering took the view that Web based teaching requires a high degree of maturity on the part of the student and was really only suitable for senior classes (Chu, 1999). Is there a relationship with cognitive development?

A small qualitative study at Loyola College, Baltimore, is very revealing. Keilson, King, and Sapnar (1999) wished to help students learn physics by doing it on the Web. For this purpose, they created a module (with submodules) on the pendulum. Students from a first year introduction to engineering class and a sophomore engineering mechanics class were asked to test the model. When they tested the model, they were observed by students from the Writing and Media Department. The observers were asked to complete a usability questionnaire that gave information about how the student tester navigated the module. This record included information about the difficulties and successes that the students had. The students were asked to complete a navigation questionnaire that more or less covered the same topics that the observers were asked to study. But they also had to complete a lab report, take a test of learning effectiveness, and complete a summary. The lab reports were guided exercises.

The best source of information was found to be the observers' reports. For example, *"At least one group did not understand and follow directions, which were clearly printed, namely to use simulations to do the third lab component, although none of this appeared in the survey information, it did become evident in the observer's notes and in the materials that the students*

handed in". The observers' reports contained summaries that could equally well apply to a conventional teaching situation. Some of the findings were:

- "Students often want to 'wing it' not spending time on reading text or instructions…. Many did not bother to thoroughly read the text or to follow directions carefully and so missed out on the insights they were supposed to achieve". Sulbaran and Nelson (2000) also found that when students were given the opportunity to interact with the virtual world they did not read the instructions. They concluded that: *"any attempt to provide text information has to be rigorously studied and weighted.*
- *Students generally preferred watching pictures/video to reading.*
- *Students aimlessly "played" with the simulations without developing insight or coherent explanation. They are not learning what you think they are learning, just the techniques to do the task at hand, but not larger concepts.*
- *Students don't come to class prepared.*
- *Even though it is preferred, video-on-line can be too long and boring."*

The teachers drew the conclusion that there was a problem of engagement with the discovery process. They agreed that the video was too long and thought that it should be reduced from 9 minutes to about 2. *"Bells and whistles do not necessarily enhance a Web page or learning."* This view was supported by other investigators (e.g., Lewis, 1986; Sulbaran and Baker, 2000) The analogy with the finding that young children more easily learn the parts of a flower from a line drawing than from a real flower will be apparent (see Chapter 4). Sulbaran and Baker found that *"the multimedia video of a lab experiment did not enhance student learning compared to a "low bandwidth" version with still pictures and textual explanations"*. This is very similar to a finding of Reamon and Sheppard (1998), who taught the DC motor to a group of mechanical engineering undergraduates but used two versions of the courseware that differed in the level of interactivity demanded. They found that there was no evidence to support the view that higher levels of interaction created deeper learning. They thought that the search for higher levels of interactivity could be inefficient and might be counterproductive. Once again, what might be called the *"law of simplicity of in learning"* was upheld.

Findings such as these have implications for costs in the preparation stage as well as for learning. Patton (1999), who designed courses for outreach courses, argued that it was essential to keep the information/preparation energy ratio high. For this reason he tended not to incorporate highly polished or production quality graphics. *"Scanned-in-hand diagrams provide the same information with much less preparation time."* He had found that in his classes live interactive experiences were not essential because most of the questions arose from homework problems and not during class. And again there is the need for guidance if enquiry based learning is to be effective is demonstrated by the Loyola study. *"Self-exploration without guidance usually results in limited discovery"* (Keilson, King, and Sapnar, 1999).

Another instructional theory that has been applied to the integration of software process into the computer science curriculum is the model of cognitive apprenticeship described by Collins, Brown, and Newman (Upchurch and Sims-Knight, 1997). This model of instruction promotes four types of knowledge i.e., domain knowledge, heuristic strategies, control strategies (guidelines to focus direction during the various activities), and learning strategies (knowledge about how to learn). There are six stages in the process: modeling, coaching, scaffolding, exploration, articulation, and reflection. The title of the theory derives from the principle that learning should begin with modeling. Just as in an ordinary apprenticeship, the master craftsman demonstrates to the learner how a task should be done, so students watch an expert and listen as the expert explains out aloud how he/she is going to solve a problem (how-to knowledge). The students then, in small groups, undertake a similar task under the supervision of the expert who now acts as coach. The support given by the expert is reduced as the students begin to demonstrate expert behavior. The students have to articulate their knowledge of the process, and in this way they are encouraged to reflect on the activity and consider alternative solutions.

The laboratory that was developed was designed to get over the difficulty of noncontributory participants in working groups. Everyone had to experience the process. *"Reviews were introduced to help students identify defects in development artefacts. The rationale is threefold: a) students need the opportunity to see how others think about different kinds of problems, b) they need to find strategies other than testing to identify problems, and c) they need to learn to read and evaluate code.... During requirements inspection the instructor (expert) provided the model of articulating and discussing the decision making process. During this activity, the students assumed the role of reviewers (apprentices), requesting clarification and asking questions."*

"The students then worked in review teams on their products. In this situation the instructor provided the scaffolding...encouraging questions and comments. Checklists, used during the preparation and conduct of the reviews, provided a focus for thought and action. Each student had the opportunity to work in each of three identified roles during the course".

Experience of this project led Upchurch and Sims-Knight to conclude that it supported the cognitive apprenticeship model because in this environment, how-to knowledge could be explicitly taught and subsequently engage the students in the development of the required skills. Since the modeling stage demonstrates the whole process, it is an advanced organizer.

Electronic learning can be highly controlled and tightly coupled to the learner as in traditional lectures or it can be loosely coupled to the learner. In the former the electronic system takes over the role of the instructor and answers questions. In the latter the system may simply be used to assist the instructor. The advent of multimedia has opened up the range of possibilities. For example, Daku and Jeffery (2000) described an interactive computer based tutorial for MATLAB. *"Students are engaged in learning new concepts and syntax with video, audio and interactive exercises. The interactive exercises, which are the distinguishing feature of the tutorial, use a specially designed exercise window which has a background software interface to MATLAB. The learner is challenged with problems in the exercise window immediately after covering new concepts. Hints, example solutions, multiple choice quizzes and test problems, requiring the use of proper MATLAB structure and syntax add to the learning experience."*

A student evaluation showed that for topics like this the students preferred this approach to the lecture assignment. But preference and performance are two different things, and no information is given about relative performance in the conventional and new setting.

A key issue that parallels the expository versus discovery mode of teaching debate is the extent to which a web-based environment in college should be supported. To what extent should the learner control the process? At the University of Twente in the Netherlands, students were asked to choose between structured-support and learner choice versions of the same course on the design and development of educational technology products and services and the new technologies. This was to enable the instructors to answer the questions:

"Will students' attitudes toward the course and course content be higher and will student transfer-type learning be higher if students are supported in a structured way and required to make use of a variety of study activities via WWW based tools and resources (participating in collaborative activities and discussions about the study materials supported by WWW-based tools, searching for supplementary examples via the WWW, using groupware tools for collaborative generation of summaries or readings selected by themselves as valuable for the course, receiving instructor feedback via the WWW on their on-going work and collaborative activities) than if they are not?" (Collis, Winnips, and Moonen, 2000).

Answers to this question were important because the faculty had adopted a philosophy of fewer lecturers and more personalized communication between instructors and students.

In seeking to answer this question they also summed the time spent by instructors and students in the two approaches and related this to student attitudes and performance. The structured support that was given was extensive.[52] The course was organized around three units each of two weeks duration. Within each unit there were

---

[52]Full details of the course are given in the paper.

6 topics. Each unit began with a lecture that gave an overview of the unit. A printed reader was provided together with an article for each of the 18 topics. A final examination of multiple choice items was intended to test for basic knowledge and also transfer. The learner-choice group was assigned an essay for each block that was considered to be equivalent to the amount of work required of the students in the structured support group. These essays could be handed in at any time before the final examination, and the students were free to submit draft comments. The structured students were required to work in groups of three, and each group was assigned one of the topics in the unit. *"During the week each of the three persons had to first read the instructor provided article for that topic and then find another article, on the WWW or in the library, that he or she felt would make an appropriate additional study selection for the topic. To do this each student had to probably read a number of possible articles and then make a choice.... The three members of the group [then] had to decide which of the three articles would be best for an assigned synopsis for the class. One prepared a report giving the full citation of each article and the reasons for selecting one and not selecting others. A draft synopsis of the selected article had to be prepared and the material from all the groups had to be submitted via the course website."* [53]

During the weekend the instructors evaluated the articles and gave "careful feedback" related to the choice of article and quality of the draft. This amounted to about two pages of text. The electronic system prevented the learner choice group from seeing them. The feedback was followed by a session in a classroom where the instructors were present. Each group discussed with its instructor the feedback received, and then had to revise its synopsis. The 6 synopses had to be posted by the end of the session so that the learner choice group would have a week to read the synopses. This activity was repeated for each block.

All of the structured support students participated. There was variation in the quality of the synopses, and half went beyond what was required in terms of length and detail. The level of completion was "exceptional" for courses in the faculty.

A large number of the learner-choice students did not submit their essays and did not sit the final examination. None of them chose to submit draft versions of their three essays. An average score of 7.55 (out of ten) was obtained and that compared with 8.25 for the supported group. In the Dutch system there is no requirement for students to attend lectures. The attendance at lectures of the supported group was much higher than that of the learner choice group. From a time keeping log, it was found that the structured support group spent twice as much time studying the instructor designed material as the learner choice group. The time spent by the structured-support groups in searching for books and journals averaged at 337 minutes per student whereas it was only 7 minutes for the learner-choice

group. In total the structured-support group said the worked for 46 hours and the learner choice group 31 hours. The course requirement was for 80 hours.

No significant differences were found between the examination results of the two groups, but there was a slight difference for those questions said to test for transfer. The structured support group did better on these items.

The teachers pointed out that these results could only be suggestive because the study was carried in a real setting and the characteristics of the students in the groups may correlate with the results rather than the results being a causal effect of the treatment. First, the structured-support group worked harder and more systematically than the learner-choice group. They also took part in a larger variety of learning experiences. But this effort neither showed in the examination or in more positive student attitudes. Both groups, however, were equally satisfied with what they received.

"Each of the three instructors spent between two and three times more time on the course than the structured-support students, and between four and six more times on the course than the learner-choice students."

The instructors concluded that their time would be reduced in further cycles of the course. They also thought that the test might not have been reliable or valid although the students perceived it to be valid. They considered that some students might need structured support but that it might not have to be as great as was given in this course. Also the nature of the assignment could be simplified. Other modifications were suggested.

Their final point was that some teachers with *"faith and conviction"* would want to develop such approaches because they *"believe that increased contact between students and instructors comprise good teaching."*

Related to this study, and almost its mirror, is the question of how the learners capacity for self-regulation is influenced by environment of the hypermedia with which he or she is faced.. Hypermedia environments are characterized by nonlinearity. There are degrees of non-linearity of presentation each of which defines the number of choices available to the learner.

McManus (2000) distinguished between four levels of nonlinearity. A fifth level, the linear, was characterized by a beginning, a middle, and an end, and could only be navigated from beginning to end. In the second level, the browsable it was possible to start, stop, review, go forward and backward, or skip to the end. The third level is called linked. There are no predefined beginnings and ends in this mode, and navigation is accomplished with a menu to select nodes, but each node is linear. The fourth level, the searchable, is navigated with a menu or through key word searches. The fifth level is similar to the fourth, but hyperlinks are added. It is illustrated by some computer help documents. Examples of level one are radio and TV; examples of level two are books, videotapes, and discs, examples of level three, are menu-based hypermedia, and examples of level four,

---

[53] Slightly edited from the original.

are multimedia encyclopaedias. At each level the learner has increasing control over the pacing of the presentation. Given the concern in higher education for autonomous or independent learning, it might be supposed that those learners who have a high level of self regulation would do well in situations where there is a high-level choice. McManus used a group of student teachers to test this theory. To some extent, the results were confirmed in that highly self-regulating learners responded badly at the lowest level of nonlinearity, while medium self-regulating learners responded badly in the highest non-linear situation. The low and medium self-regulating students obtained reasonably high scores in the low levels of nonlinearity where they responded well to the pre-organized presentation. At the same time, the high self-regulating learners did not do so well in the high non-linear environment. They did best in the medium environment. One explanation might be that they were offered too much choice as in the case of written essay examinations that offer choice, or as McManus suggested that it may be that either they were too inexperienced or the environment did not lend itself to self-regulation strategies.

This study underlined the value of design for individualized instruction and the need for the design to take into account the needs of the learner. The value of advanced organizers was also assessed in this investigation, and it was found that they were of relatively little use in nonlinear environments but that in highly nonlinear environments they might help learners activate prior knowledge which would help them better organize the information presented. But this would require an accurate assessment of learner attributes, and the self-report inventory that McManus used might not have been the best approach to measuring self-regulation.[54]

Of relevance to these investigations is the relation of learning styles to student performance, self regulation, and motivation. At Liverpool, John Moore's University learning styles were tested for a relationship with student opinions on web site enhancement of current teaching, the interest and challenge they felt was given by the module, and their views on the appropriateness of the way the module was taught. No associations were found (MacClelland, 2001). At the American University, Larkin-Hein (2001) reported that the students who engaged in on-line discussion in an introductory physics course tended to be those whom the learning style suggested preferred to work alone. She noted that the on-line discussion format was essentially an individual activity and would be attractive to that type of student. Her particular technique was also available at any time, and it might have attracted students who preferred to work in the evening.

It would seem from all of these examples that the principles of learning that apply in conventional instructional theory and design apply equally to the design of instruction using the new technologies. Moreover, investigation of learning in the new technologies is likely to throw up some important hypotheses for investigation in conventional instruction.

However, Ellis, Hafner, and Mitropoulos (2004) point out that while instructors are encouraged to offer on-line courses, little support is given to those who want to restructure courses. Teachers have to re-learn how to teach in their new environment. If they don't, mistakes will be perpetrated. Even an experienced teacher can miss the non-verbal cues that gauge a student's understanding, and the immediacy of the question-response-follow-up cycle can be lost. Thus, teachers have to become fluent with theories of instructional design. They describe how one particular theory was used to design a course in electronics. The system incorporated a course requirement brainstormer, learning outcome generator, assignment generator, schedule generator, and evaluation generator. For some teachers the approach might be too Skinnerian. However, other work that Ellis has done with his colleagues to determine what constitutes value in on-line teaching is likely to be of considerable interest. In their first paper Cohen and Ellis (2003) described how they had determined quality indicators for on-line work. Five factors were found. These were community of learners, instructor accessibility, class organization, "feel" of the class, and peer impact. The relevance of these to the eCAD is apparent. In a second study, they validated these criteria using a nominal group technique. This led to a more detailed view of what might be the internal structure of the factors. Of particular interest is the fact that the idea of community did not appear to be important to the doctoral students who participated in the investigation, nor was it clearly defined

It is clear that there is much to be learned about the on-line learning environment both about instructional design and the design of the learning environment. It is equally clear that teachers will require substantial support if they are to make an effective transition from traditional modes of teaching.

References:

Abel, J. M (1995). DOLFFEN: discovery oriented lab for first year engineers. *Proceedings Frontiers in Education Conference*, 2c4-1 to 4.

Adams, J., Nash, J., and L. Leifer (2001). Senior- level undergraduate team teaching of an entire engineering elective course. *Proceedings Frontiers in Education Conference*, 1, T4B-25 to 29.

Agogino, A., and J. G. Evan (undated). Multimedia Case Studies of Design in Industry. Unpublished Working paper. Engineering Systems Research Center. U. C. Berkley, Berkley, CA.

Alford, K. L., and J. R. Surdu (2002). Using in-class debates as teaching tool. *Proceedings Frontiers in Education Conference*, 3, S1F- 10 to 15.

Alic, J. A (1977). Adding guidance to case studies. *Engineering Education*, 67, 374-376

.Allen, R R., Willmington, S. C., and J. Sprague (1991). *Communication in the Secondary School. A Pedagogy*. 3rd edition. Gorsuch Scarisbrick Publishers, Scottsdale, Arizona.

Amigud, Y et al., (2002). Assessing the quality of web-enabled laboratories in undergraduate education. *Proceeding Frontiers in Education Conference* 2, F3E- 12 to 16

---

[54] He used a modified form of the MSLQ-Motivated Strategies for Learning Questionnaire (Pintrich and Garcia, 1991). This has five scales :control beliefs; elaboration; metacognitive self-regulation, organization, and self-efficacy.

Anderson, J. R., Reder, L. M., and H. A. Simon (1996). Situated learning in education. *Educational Researcher*, 25, (4), 5–11.

Anwar, S (2001). Use of engineering case studies to teach associate degree electrical engineering technology students. *Proceedings Frontiers in Education Conference*, S1G- 8 to 10

Anwar, S and P. Ford (20). Use of case study approach to teach engineering technology students. *International of Electrical Engineering Education*, 38, (1), 1–10.

Armacost, R. L and J. Pet-Armacost (2003). Using mastery-based grading to facilitate learning. *Proceedings Frontiers in Education Conference*, 1, T3A- 20 to 25.

Ausubel, D. P., Novak, J. D., and J. Hanesian (1978). *Educational Psychology. A Cognitive View*. Holt, Rinehart and Woinston, New York.

Baillie, C. A., and R. W. Grimes (1999). Pccr tutoring in crystallography. *European Journal of Engineering Education*, 24, (2), 173–181.

Baillie, C., and G. Percoco (2000). A study of present use and usefulness of computer-based learning in a technical university. *European Journal of Engineering Education*, 25, (1), 33–43.

Baker, J., and J. Ma (1999). Using case studies to evaluate learning technologies. *Proceedings Frontiers of Engineering Conference*, 13c3-12-13c3-17.

Ball, J., and K. Patrick (1999). Learning about heat transfer. "Oh I See" experiences. *Proceedings Frontiers in Education Conference*, 2, 12c5-1 to 6.

Barnes, L. B., Christensen, C. R., and A. J. Hansen (1994). *Teaching and the Case Method*. 3rd edition. Harvard Business School, Boston, MA.

Beasley, C. A., Culkowski, P. M. and G. E. Guffner (1990). Integration of lecture and laboratory in a technology program. *Engineering Education*, 80, (3), 433–435.

Belbin, E., and R. M. Belbin (1972). *Problems in Adult Retraining*. Heinemann, London.

Berglund, A and M. Daniels (2000). How do individual portable computers effect student's learning *Proceedings Frontiers in Education Conference*, 3, S3D- 7 to 10

Block, J. H (1974). *Schools, Society and Mastery Learning*. Holt, Rinehart and Winston, New York.

Bloom, B. S (1976). *Human Characteristics of School Learning*. Mackay, New York.

Bonoma, T. V (1989) *Learning with Cases*. Harvard Business School Publishing. Case 9–589–080, 1-10.

Boud, D. J (1978). The laboratory aims questionnaire. *Higher Education*, 2

Boud, D., Dunn, J., and E. Hegarty-Hazel (1989). *Teaching in Laboratories*. Open University Press, Milton Keynes.

Byerley, A. R (2001). Using multimedia and "active learning" techniques to "energize" an introductory engineering thermodynamics class. *Proceedings Frontiers in Education Conference*, 1, T3B- 1 to 8.

Calkins, J. L. and D. H. Thomas (1979). Characteristics of successful PSI student and prediction of performance on PSI courses. *Proceedings Frontiers in Education Conference*, 211–216.

Carter, G., Armour, D. G., Lee, L. S., and R. Sharples (1980). Assessment of undergraduate electrical engineering laboratory studies. *IEE Proceedings* 127, Part A, (7), 460.

Carter, G., and Heywood, J., and D. T. Kelly (1986). *A Case Study in Curriculum development. GCE Engineering Science (Advanced)*. Roundthorn, Manchester.

Carter, G. and T, A. Jordan 91986). *Student centered Learning in Engineering. Engineering Enhancement in Higher Education*. Monograph. University of Salford, Salford.

Carter, G and L. S. Lee (1975). A study of attitudes of first year undergraduate electrical engineering laboratory work at the University of Salford. *International Journal of Electrical Engineering education*, 12, (3), 278–289.

Cawley, P (1989) Is laboratory teaching effective? *International Journal of Mechanical Engineering Education* 17, 15–27.

Cho, C (1982). Experiences with a work book for spatial data analysis. *Journal of Geography in Higher Education*. 6, (2), 133–139.

Christie, M., Juan, A., and L. E. Jonsson (2002). Evaluating the use of ICT in engineering education. *European Journal of Engineering Education*, 27, (1), 13-20.

Chu, K. C (1999). The development of a web-base teaching system for engineering education. *Engineering Science and Education Journal*, June, 115–118.

Clancy, E. A., Quinn, P. M., and J. E. Miller (2001). Using case studies to increase awareness of, and improve resolution strategies for ethical issues in engineering. *Proceedings Frontiers in Education Conference* S1E- 20 to 25.

Clark, M. J. and K. J. Gregory (1982). Physical geography techniques: a self-paced university course. *Journal of Geography in Higher Education* 6, (2), 123–132.

Cleaver, T. G (1976). A controlled study of the semi-paced teaching method. *Engineering Education*, 66, (4), 323–325.

Clough, D. E (2000). Using process simulators with dynamics/control capabilities to teach unit and control strategies. Proc. A. I.Ch.E annual meeting cited by Savelski et al., (2001).

Cohen, L., Mannion, L., and K. Morrison (2000) *Research Methods in Education*. Fifth edition. Routledge, London.

Cohen, M. S., and T. J. Ellis (2004) Developing criteria set for an on-line learning environment from the student and faculty perspectives. *Journal of Engineering Education*.

Cohen, M. S., and T. J. Ellis (2004) validating a criteria set for an online learning environment. *Proceedings Frontiers in Education Conference*, 2, F1D- 23 to 27.

Cohen, M. S., and T. J. Ellis (2004) Integrated virtual learning system for programmable logic controller. *Proceedings Frontiers in Education Conference*, 93, (2),161-169.

Collins, A. J., Brown, S and S. E. Newman. Cognitive Apprenticeship: teaching the crafts of reading, writing and mathematics in L. B. Resnick (ed). *Knowing , Learning and Instruction. Essays in Honor of Robert Glaser*. Erlbaum, Hillsdale NJ.

Collis, B., Winnips, K.,, and J. Moonen (2000). Structured support versus learner choice via the World Wide Web: Where is the payoff? *Journal of Interactive Learning Research*, 11, (2), 131–162.

Corter, J. E., Nickerson, J. V., Esche, S. K., and C. Chassapis (2004). Remote versus hands-on labs: a comparative study *Proceedings Frontiers in Education Conference*, 2 F1G-17 to 21.

Crynes, B., Greene, B., and C. Dillon (2000). Lectrons or lectures-which is the best for whom? *Proceedings Frontiers in Education Conference*, 3, S2D- 21 to 24.

Daku, B. L. F., and K. Jeffery (2000). An interactive computer-based tutorial for MATLAB. *Proceedings Frontiers in Education Conference*, 2, F2D-2 to 7.

Dobney, P. T., Walker, R., Ledwidge, T. J. and G. N. Ramakrishnan (1979). Laboratory instruction in physics and instrumentation for external study courses in engineering. *Proceedings Frontiers in Education Conference* 200–207.

Downing, E., Schooley, L. C., Matz, E. M., Nelson, L. N., and R. Martinez (1988). Improving instructor/student interaction with electronic mail. *Engineering Education*, 78, (4), 247–250.

Dutton, J. C (1988). A comparison of live and video taped presentation of a graduate ME course. *Engineering Education*, 78, (4), 243–246.

Eaton, J. K (1992). Computer-based, self-guided instruction in laboratory data acquisition and control. *Proceedings Frontiers in Education Conference*, 809–813.

Eberts, R. E (1986). Learning Strategies and CAI design. *International Journal of Applied Engineering Education*, 2, (1), 51-59.

Edward, N. S (2002a). The role of laboratory work in engineering education: student and staff perceptions. *International Journal of Electrical Engineering Education*, 39, (1), 11–19.

Edward, N. S (2002b) Evaluation of a student-centered approach to first-year undergraduate engineering laboratories. *International Journal of Electrical Engineering Education*, 39, (4), 310–319.

Ellis, T. J., Hafner, W., and F. Mitropoulos (2004). Automating instructional design with eCAD. *Proceedings Frontiers in Education Conference*, 1, T1H-1 to 6.

Erikkson, T., Goler, A., and S. Murchin (2001) A comparison with on-line communication in distance education and in conventional education. *Proceedings Frontiers in Education Conference*, 1, T2F-20 to 25.

Feisel, L. D., and G. D. Peterson (2002) Learning objectives for engineering laboratories. *Proceedings Frontiers in Education Conference*. 2, F1D-1.

Feldman, L. J., and R. J. Hofinger (1997). Active participation by sophomore students in the design of experiments. *Proceedings Frontiers in Education Conference,* 3, 1526–1529.

Fitzgerald, N (1995). Teaching with cases. *ASEE Prism* (March). 16 – 20.

Fleddermann, C. B (2000) Engineering ethics cases for electriucal and computer engineering students. *IEEE Transactions on Education,* 43, (3), 284

Fowler, W. T. and R. D. Watkins (1977). A solution to small enrolments: PSI materials in independent studies. *Engineering Education* 67, 198–200

Freeman, J., Lynn, N., and R. Baker (2001). The evaluation of a program for the development of business and enterprise skills. In J. Heywood, J. M. Sharp and M. Hides (eds). *Improving Teaching in Higher Education.* University of Salford, Salford, UK.

Fuchs, H. O (1968). Case material for design education. *Engineering Education,* 58, 830–832.

Fuchs, H. O. and R. F. Steidel (eds).(1973) *Ten Cases in Engineering Design.* Longman, London.

Gagné, R. M. and L. J. Briggs (1974) *Principles of Instructional Design.* Holt, Rienhart and Winston, New York.

Gessler, J (1974). SPI: Goodbye education?. *Engineering Education,* 65, 3) 252–255.

Gessner, F. B (1974). An experiment in modified self-paced learning. *Engineering Education* 64, (4), 368

Gibbs, G (1982) *Eliciting Student Feedback from Structured Group Sessions.* Oxford Educational Development Unit, Oxford Polytechnic.

Gibbs, G (1992). *Improving the Quality of Student Learning.* Technical Educational Services, Bristol.

Gillet, D., Latchman, H. A., Salzmann, C., and O. D. Crisallew (2001). Hands on laboratory experiments in flexible and distance learning. *Journal of Engineering Education* 90, (2), 187–191.

Gleixner, S., et al (2002). Teaching design of experiments and statistical analysis of data through laboratory experiments. *Proceedings Frontiers in Education Conference* 1, T2D–1 to 5.

Goodlad, S., Abidi, A., Anscow, P., and J. Harris (1979). The Pimlico Connection: undergraduates as tutors in schools. *Studies in Higher Education,* 4, 191–201.

Goodlad, S and B. Hirst (1989). *Peer Tutoring: A Guide to Learning by Tutoring.* Kogan Page, London.

Goodson, C. E (1977). A self-paced computer-assisted instruction program in technical mathematics. *Engineering Education* (February) 367–371

Grant, A. D (1994). The effective use of laboratories in undergraduate courses. *International Journal of Mechanical Engineering Education,* 23, (2), 95–101.

Hadipriono, F., and R. E. Larew (1985). Simulation laboratory designed to prevent construction related failures. *Engineering Education.*70, (2), 168–170.

Hailey, D., Grant Davie, K., and C. Hult (2001). Online education horror stories worthy of Halloween. *Computers and Composition,* special issue. Winter, 387–397.

Hailey, D. E., and C. E. Hailey (2002). Genre theory, engineering education and circumventing internet bandwidth problems. *Proceedings Frontiers in Education Conference,* T3E-1 to-7.

Haws, D. R (1998). Personal refelctions on PSI in engineering mechanics. *Proceedings Frontiers in Education Conference,* 280–285.

Hazel, E and C. Baillie (1998). Improving Teaching and Learning in Laboratories. Gold Guide Series No 4. Higher Education Research and Development Society of Australasia, Canberra.

Henden, P. M. et al., (2002). The use of video-taped lectures and web-based communications in teaching; a distance teaching and cross-Atlantic collaboration. *European Journal of Engineering Education,* 27, (1), 29–48.

Henderson, J. M., Bellman, L. E., and B. J. Furman (1983). A Case for teaching engineering with cases. *Engineering Education,* 73, (4), 288-292.

Hereford, S. M (1979). The Keller plan within a conventional academic environment: an empirical meta-analytic study. *Engineering Education,* 70, (3), 250–260.

Heywood, J (1986). Curriculum innovation and socio-economic change. The case for technology. A personal recap. In J. Heywood and P.

Matthews (eds). *Technology, Society and the School Curriculum. Practice and Theory in Europe.* Roundthorn, Manchester.

Heywood, J (1977) *Assessment in Higher Education.* Wiley, Chichester.

Heywood, J., and S. Heywood (1993). The training of student teachers in discovery methods of teaching and learning in A-L, Leino et al., (eds). *Integration of Technology and Reflection in Teaching: A Challenge for European Teacher Education.* Association of Teacher Education in Europe, Brussels.

Heywood, J and D. T. Kelly (1973).The evaluation of coursework- a study of engineering science among schools in England and Wales. *Proceedings Frontiers in Education Conference,* 269 – 276.

Hill, G (1986) An electronics course established under the Technical and Vocational Education Initiative in J. Heywood and P. Matthews (eds.) *Technology, Society and the School Curriculum. Practice and theory in Europe.* Roundthorn, Manchester.

Hislop, G. W (2001). Does teaching on line take more time. *Proceedings Frontiers in Education Conference,* 1, T1F- 23 to 27.

Hof, J. P Van't, Bain, J. A., White, R. M and J-G, Zhu (2001). An undergraduate laboratory in magnetic recording fundamentals. *IEEE Transactions on Educattion,* 44, (3), 224–231.

Hutchings, P (1993). *Using Cases to Improve College Teaching. A Guide to more Reflective Practice.* American Association for Higher Education, Washington, DC.

Imrie, B. W., Blithe, T. M. and L. C. Johnston (1980) A review of Keller principles with reference to mathematics covering Australasia. *British Journal of Educational Technology,* 11, (2), 105–121.

Jinks, R (1994). Developing experimental skills in engineering undergraduates. *Engineering Science and Education Journal* december. 287–290.

Johnstone, A. H., Watt, A., and T. U. Zaman (1998). The students' attitude and cognition change to a physics laboratory. *Physics Education,* 33, (1), 22–29.

Jordan, T. A (1981) *An Evaluation of the Effectiveness of First Year Electronic Engineering Laboratory Studies.* Doctoral thesis. University of Salford, Salford.

Kadiyala, M., and B. Crynes (1998). Where's the proof? A review of literature on effectiveness of information technology in education. *Proceedings Frontiers in Education Conference,* 33–37.

Kalkan, M., and M. A. Shields (2002). Distance learning in ITU: pilot projects and their implications. *Proceedings Frontiers in Education Conference,* 2, F1-15 to 18.

Kardos. G (1978). Pointers on using engineering cases in class. *Engineering Education,* 68, (4), 347–349.

Karplus, A. K., and A. C. Silvestri (1983). Development of computer-assisted tutorial. *Engineering Education,* 73, (5), 379–381.

Keller, F. S (1968). "Goodbye Teacher." *Journal of Applied Behavior Analysis.* 1, 79–89.

Keller, F. S (1985) Testimony of an Educational Reformer, *Engineering Education,* 76, (3), 144-148.

Keilson, S., King, E., and M. Sapnar (1999). Learning science by doing science on the Web. *Proceedings Frontiers in Education Conference,* 13d4-7 to 12.

Kirkup, L., Johnson, S., Hazel, E., Cheary, A. W., Green, D. C., Swift, P., and W. Holliday (1998). Designing a new physics labarotory program for first year engineering students. *Physics Education,* 33, (4), 258–265.

Koen, B. V (1971). Self-paced instruction in engineering: a case study. *IEEE Transactions on Education,* E- 14:1 13–20.

Koen, B. V (2002). On the importance of "presence" in a web-based course. *Proceedings Frontiers in Education Conference,* 1, T3E- 21 to 26.

Koen, B. V. and K.. J. Schmidt (2001). The professor and the media laboratory: a case study in web-based course creation. *Proceedings Frontiers in Education Conference,* 2, F3F- 7 to 10.

Koen, B. V., Wissler, E. H., Lamb, J. P. and L. L. Hoberock. (1975). PSI Management: Down the administrative chain. *Engineering Education,* 66, (2), 165–168.

Kostek, T. E (1991). Video recording laboratory experiments for open laboratory environments. *Proceedings Frontiers in Education Conference,* 475–477.

Kulik, J. A., and C, Y, Kulik (1975). The effectiveness of personalized instruction. *Engineering Education*. 66, (3), 229–231.

Kulik, J. A., Kulik, C. L. C., and P. A. Cohen (1979) A meta-analysis of outcome studies of Keller's personalized system of instruction. *American Psychologist*, 307–318.

Kulonda, D. J (2001). Case learning methodology in operations engineering. *Journal of Engineering Education*, 90, (3), 299–303.

Kumar, A. N (2004) Using on-line tutors for learning- What do students think? *Proceedings Frontiers in Education Conference*, 1, T3F- 9 to 13.

Lane, W. D., Shaw, R and J. A. Stine (1993). A totally integrated laboratory experience. *Proceedings Frontiers in Education Conference*, 704–708.

Larkin-Hein, T (2001). On Line Discussions: a key to enhancing student motivation and understanding? *Proceedings Frontiers in Education Conference*, 2, FG-6 to 12.

Lee, L. S (1969). Toward a classification of the objectives of undergraduate practical work in mechanical engineering. M.Litt Thesis, University of Lancaster, Lancaster.

Lee, L. S (1975). *A study of First Year Undergraduate Electrical Engineering Laboratory Work*. Doctoral Thesis. University of Salford, Salford.

Lee, W-J, Gu, J-C., and R. J. Li (2002). A physical laboratory for protective relay education. *IEEE Transactions on Education*, 45, (2), 182-186

Leuba, R. J., and Flammer, G. H. (1976) Self-paced Instruction. Hello, Education. *Engineering Education*. 66, (2), 196-198.

Lewis, R. K (1986) Creative teaching and learning in a statics class. *Engineering Education* 15–18.

Lindenlaub, J. C., Groff, M. G., and S. Nunke (1981). A hybrid lecture/self-study system for large engineering classes. *Engineering Education*. 70, (3), 201–207.

Lowe, D. B., Scott, C. A., and R. Bagia (2000). A skills development framework for learning computing tools in the context of engineering practice. *European Journal of Engineering Education*, 25, (1), 45–56.

Lu, A. Y., Zhu, J. J. H., and M. Stokes (2000). The use and effects of Web-based instruction: evidence from a single source study. *Journal of Interactive Learning Research*, 11, (2), 197–218.

Magin, D. J., and A. E. Churches(1995). Peer tutoring in engineering design: a case study. *Studies in Higher Education*, 20, (1), 73–85.

Magin, D. J and S. Kanapathippillai (2000). Engineering students' understanding of the role of experiment. *European Journal of Engineering Education*, 25, (4), 351–358.

MacClelland, B (2001). Digital learning and teaching: evaluation of developments for students in higher education. *European Journal of Engineering Education*, 26, (2), 107 115.

McDermott, L. C., and P. C. Shaffer (1992). Research as a guide to curriculum development. An example from introductory electricity. Part 1 Investigation of student understanding. *American Journal of Physics*, 60, 11, 994.

McManus, T. F (2000). Individualizing instruction in a web-based hypermedia learning environment: nonlinearity, advance organizers, and self-regulated learners. *Journal of Interactive Learning Research*, 11, (3), 219–251.

Martin, D. G., and J. C. Lewis. (1968). Effective laboratory teaching. *Bulletin of Mechanical Engineering Education*, 7, 51-57.

Martin, T. W., and W. D. Brown (1998). Experience with laboratory-intensive curriculum in electrical engineering. *Proceedings Frontiers in Education Conference*, 1145–1148.

Masson, A. M (2000). Web-based simulations for computer- assisted learning in the higher education sector. *Engineering Science and Education Journal*. June. 9, 107–114.

Matthews, T. W (2002). Creation of an electronics teaching laboratory as part of an overall infrastructure upgrade. *Proceedings Frontiers in Education Conference*, 1, T1D- 17 to 21.

Meyer, D. G., Niessen, C., and A. Reuther (1997). Experiment multimedia –delivered course formats. *Proceedings Frontiers in Education Conference*, 1407–1410.

Mihkelson, A (1985). Computer assisted instruction in remedial teaching in first year chemistry. *Education in Chemistry* 22, (4), 117–118.

Murray, M (1986) recent developments in the school curriculum in France in J. Heywood and P. Matthews 9eds). *Technology, Society and the School Curriculum. Practice and Theory in Europe*. Roundthorn, Mancchester.

Murray, M and J. Donovan (1986). Resources and deficiencies in the voluntary sectorr of secondary education in Ireland. In J. Heywood and P. Matthews (eds). *Technology, Society and the School Curriculum. Practice and Theory in Europe*. Roundthorn, Manchester.

Mzoughi, T (2000). PERC – A collaboration between engineering and Arts and Science faculty to help ensure better student preparation. *Proceedings Frontiers in Education Conference*, F2B-1 to 6.

Neumann, W. T., and M. C. Woodfill (1998). A comparison of alternative approaches to the capstone experience: case studies versus collaborative projects. *Proceedings Frontiers in Education Conference*, 470–474.

Newcomer, J. L (2004). Work in progress- A fresh look at case studies. *Proceedings Frontiers in Education Conference*, 2, F2F-13 to 14.

Ogut, M., Elliott, G., and N. Glumac (2003), An assessment of in-person and remotely operated laboratories. *Journal of Engineering Education* 92, (1), 57-64.

Owen, S 1986). The introduction of technology in a tertiary college in J. heywood and P. Matthews (eds). *Technology, Society and the School Curriculum. Practice and Theory in Europe*. Roundthorn, Manchester.

Patton, J. B (1999). Instructional technology environments for engineering outreach. *Proceedings Frontiers in Education Conference*, 1, 12b2-3 to 8.

Pazdernik, T. L., and E. J. Walaszek (1983). A computer-assisted teaching system in pharmacology for the health profession. *Journal of Medical Education*. 58, (4), 341–348

Pearson, M., and D. J. Carswell (1979). Student evaluation of Utopia. *Education in Chemistry*, 15, (3), 84.

Petroski, N (1995). *Design Paradigms. Case Histories of Error and Judgement in Engineering*. Cambridge University Press, New York.

Pintrich, P. R., and T. Garcia (1991). Student goal orientation and self regulation in the college classroom. In M, Maehr and P. R. Pintrich (eds) *Advances in Motivation and Achievement. Goals and Self-regulatory Processes. V*ol 7. JAI Press, Greenwich, CT.

Plants, H. L., and W. S. Venable (1985). Programmed instruction is alive and well in West Virginia. *Engineering Education*, 75, (5), 277–279.

Pollock, M. J (2004) Using computers to deliver a mathematics course, to increase recruitment and retention rate of non traditional students and reduce staff workload. *Proceedings Frontiers in Education Conference*, 1, T1H-7 to 11.

Predebon, W. W (1979). An instructional center for self-paced program courses: an alternate for reluctant faculty. *Proceedings Frontiers in Education Conference*, 150

Raju, P. K., and C. S. Sankar (1998). "Della Steam Plant: should the turbine be shut off?" *Case Research Journal*, 18 (1 and 2), 133–150.

Raju, P. K., Sankar, C. S., Halpin, G., and Gl. Halpin (1999) Bringing theory and practice together in engineering schools. *Proceedings Frontiers in Education Conference*, 11a2 1 to 6.

Raju, P. K., Sankar, C. S., Halpin, G., Halpin, Gl and J. Good (2000). Evaluation of an engineering education courseware across different campuses. *Proceedings Frontiers in Education Conference* 1, T4B–11 to 15.

Reamon, D., and S. Sheppard (1998). Motor Workshop: The role of interactivity in promoting learning. *Proceedings Frontiers in Education Conference*,2, 672–676.

Renoll, E (1976). Motivating students in modified self-paced design course. *Engineering Education*, 66, (5), 405–407.

Reuther, A., and D. G. Meyer (1997). Analysis of daily student usage of an educational multi media system. *Proceedings Frontiers in Education Conference*, 1412–1417.

Reynolds, T. S (1976). Using simulated debate to teach history of engineering advances. *Engineering Education*, 67, (2), 184–187.

Rice, S. L (1975). Objectives for engineering laboratory instruction. *Engineering Education*, 65, (4), 285–288.

Richards, L. G., Gorman, M. E. and W. T. Scherer (1995). Case based education in the age of the internet. *Proceedings Frontiers in Education Conferrence*. 2c5- 9 to 12.

Ruchards, L. G., Gorman, M., Scherer, W. T and R. D. Landel (1995) Promoting active learning with cases and instructional models. *Journal of Engineering Education*. October issue.

Roberson, J. A., and C. T. Crowe (1975). Is self-paced instruction really worth it? Engineering Education, 66, April, 761–765.

Rosenthal, L (1967). Guided discovery teaching in the engineering laboratory. *Engineering Eucation*, 58, (3), 196–198.

Ross, R (2000). Inquiry-Based experiments in the introductory physics laboratory. *Proceedings Frontiers in Education Conference* 2, F1D-1 to 6.

Roth, C. H (1973). Continuing effectiveness of personalized self-paced instruction in digital systems engineering. *Engineering Education* 63, (6), 447–450.

Rowe, J. W. K. and R. G. Harris (2001). A theory-based modification of the engineering tutorial. *European Journal of Engineering Education*, 25, (3), 235 – 242.

Saunders, D (1992). Peer tutoring in higher education. *Studies in Higher Education*, 17, 211–218.

Savelski, M. J., Dahm, K., and R. P. Hesketh (2001). Is process simulation effectively utilized in chemical engineering course. ASEE Annual Conference, session 3513.

Sawyers, D. R., and C. R. Mirman (1998). Experimental concepts in a cross-disciplinary capstone course for mechanical engineers. *Proceedings Frontiers in Education Conference*, 405–410.

Schmahl, K. E (1998). Expanding the objectives of laboratory experience. *International Journal of Engineering Education*, 14, (6), 419–425.

Self, D. J., and E. M. Ellison (1998). Teaching engineering ethics. Assessment of its influence on moral reasoning skills. *Journal of Engineering Education*, January 29-34

Shale, D., and D. Cowper (1982) Computer basic support system for mastery instruction. *Assessment and Evaluation in Higher Education*. 7, (2), 167–180.

Sharp, J. E (2000). E-Teaching simply with e mail. *Proceedings Frontiers in Education Conference*, 3, S3B- 8 to 13.

Shiavi, R., Brodersen, A., Bourne, J., and A. Pingree (2000). Comparison of instructional modalities for a course "introduction to computing in engineering". *Proceedings Frontiers in Education Conference*, 1, T3G–14 to 16.

Smiernow, G. A. and A. Lawley (1980). Decentralised sequenced instruction (DSI) at Drexel. Engineering Education, 70, (5), 423-426.

Smith, A. B., Irey, P. K., and M. McCaulley (1973) *Engineering Education*, 63, (6), 435–440.

Sorby, S. A. et al (1999). Modernization of the Mechanical Engineering Curriculum and Guide-Lines for Computer-aided Engineering Instruction. *Computer Applications in Engineering Education*, 7, (4), 252-260.

Stake, R. E (1995). *The Art of Case Study Research*. Sage, Thousand Oakes, CA.

Stice, J.E. (1979). PSI and Bloom's mastery model. A review and comparison. *Engineering Education*, 70, (2), 175-180.

Sulbaran, T and N. C. Baker (2000). Enhancing engineering education through distributed virtual reality. *Proceedings Frontiers in Education Conference,* 3, S1D-13 to 18.

Tarhini, K. M., and D. E. Vandercoy (2000). Engineering students as expert witnesses in mock trials. *Proceedings Frontiers in Education Conference,* 1, T1F–1 to 2.

Tawney, D (1976). Simulation and modelling in science computer assisted learning. Technical Report no 11, National Development Program in Computer Assisted Learning. NDPCAL, London.

Upchurch, R. L., and J. E. Sims-Knight (1997). Integrating software process in computer science curriculum. *Proceedings Frontiers in Education Conference,* 867–871.

Vesper, K. H (1975). *Engineers at Work: A Case Book*. Houghton Mifflin, Boston.

Vesper, K. H (1978). An easier way to teach with engineering cases. *Engineering Education* 68, (4), 349–351

Vesper, K. H., and J. L. Adams. (1969). Evaluating learning from the case method. *Engineering Education*, 60, (2), 104–106.

Wankat, P. C., and F. S. Oreovicz (1993). *Teaching Engineering*. McGraw Hill, New York.

Wiesner, T. F., and W. Lan (2004). Comparison of student learning in physical and simulated unit operations experiments. *Journal of Engineering Education*, 93, (3), 195-204.

Wergin, J. F., Boland, D., and T. W. Haas (1986). Televising graduate engineering courses: results of an instructional experiment. *Engineering Education*, 77, (2), 109–112.

Whiting, J (1982). Cognitive assessment and student attitude. *Assessment and Evaluation in Higher Education*. 7, (1), 54–73.

Woodson, T. T (1966). *An Introduction to Engineering Design*. McGraw Hill, New York.

Young, M (1997). An integrated engineering systems and control laboratory. *Proceedings Frontiers in Education Conference*, 2, 659–665

CHAPTER 15: ASSESSMENT AND EVALUATION

Summary and Introduction

At this stage we come to the two remaining components of the curriculum process outlined in Chapter 1, assessment and evaluation. Like the processes of instruction and learning, they have to meet the same objectives, and they contribute as much to the determination of objectives as do instruction and learning. This is why in Chapter 2 detailed reference was made to some procedures for assessment in order to illustrate these relationships. It is also why in other Chapters it has been appropriate to deal with some aspects of assessment within them. For example, peer assessment is considered in both Chapter 9 on projects and problem based learning, and Chapter 13 on teamwork. Many brief examples of approaches to assessment within courses have been given.

Much has already been written about how instructors assess their courses, and in the course of these chapters it will have become clear that it is possible to make a distinction between traditional and non-traditional approaches to assessment. It may not have become clear, however, just how muddled the terminology of assessment has become. Therefore, this Chapter begins with a discussion of the uses to which it is put, to assist readers in accessing and understanding literature from a variety of sources. Although it often replaces "evaluation," this term has been retained in this Chapter in that some knowledge of the theory and practice of evaluation as it has been understood in the social sciences may be helpful.

The Chapter begins, therefore, with a brief discussion of the uses of the term assessment. Two uses of the term 'multiple strategy assessment' are discussed, and a distinction is made between program assessment and the assessment of student learning although in practice the two overlap. A brief account of the origins and development of evaluation theory and practice follows. Since some engineering studies have used external evaluators, a section on the role of the evaluator is included. The role of the evaluator was much debated in evaluation research. The high expectations of the scientific model were not met, and the reaction against it led to the development of qualitative research based on the anthropological paradigm.

Developments in evaluation research in higher education followed a roughly similar pattern. As might be expected, the scientific model has predominated in research in engineering education, but there is an emerging school of qualitative research that is throwing much light on some important issues.

The remainder of the chapter is concerned with program assessment. The differences between procedures in the United States and the United Kingdom (subject review) are discussed. The remainder of the Chapter summarizes the different techniques used for program assessment.

It is concluded that program evaluation has to be multiple strategy in approach and that "In order for a course or curriculum project to be successful, the evaluation process must also be successful. It must be carefully thought out at the very beginning of the project, implemented with the same enthusiasm as the actual content development and implementation, and executed continuously throughout the life of the project"(Prey, 1999).

15. Uses of the Term Assessment[1]

How the term assessment is used varies from country to country. In Britain, its original use was to describe the psychological needs of school children with behavioral and learning difficulties. However, in the 1960s when universities began to assess work done during a course, as for example an essay, as well as performance in terminal examinations taken at the end of the program, the terms "continuous assessment" and "coursework assessment" came into use. By 1969 the Committee of Vice-Chancellors and Principals was reporting on the Assessment of Academic Performance (CVCP, 1969).[2] This concern was with the assessment of student learning, and this continues to be its usage in the United Kingdom, as seems to be the case in many British ex-territories. For example, in Hong Kong the terms 'assessment elements' and 'assessment strategy' in a paper on quality assurance in project supervision referred to the selection of tutors, monitoring by internal examiners, monitoring by the course co-ordinator, and monitoring by external examiners (Chan, 1997).

In contrast, in America there was no need for the concept of coursework or continuous assessment, because that is what the Americans did. Consequently they had difficulty in understanding these terms. American marks were arrived at by a combination of marks from quizzes, tests, homework, and a final examination, and a number of papers in the engineering literature describe variations in the proportions of marks allowed for these different dimensions. The British view of coursework was a substantial exercise, as, for example, a 5000-word paper, or a project, or substantial laboratory work. Homework was never assessed if ever given.

Hartle (1986) drew attention to six commonly used meanings of assessment. The first and most common of these referred to state-mandated requirements

---

[1] For a detailed account and bibliography see Heywood (2000). For a recent review of the American approaches and experience, see the special issue of *The International Journal of Engineering Education* Vol. 18, No 2, 2002, edited by G. Rogers.

[2] In 1976 a conference was held at Hull University on The Teaching of Electronic Engineering in Degree Courses. The conference proceedings included a paper by M. J. Howes and D. V. Morgan that compared traditional terminal examination assessment with a continuous assessment scheme based on theoretical and experimental projects at Leeds University. The continuous assessment was favorably received in the department by staff and students. The same conference also recorded an attempt to introduce PSI at the University of Southampton by B. R. Wilkins and A. P. Dorey.

to evaluate academic programs for quality. In the United Kingdom the terms subject review and teaching quality assessment have both been associated with this kind of assessment, and a government agency has been established for this regulatory purpose, the Quality Assurance Agency (QAA). Related to this assurance activity was the development of performance indicators; this happened in the United States as well, which included audits of the use of testing for counseling and placement, admission into higher education and the mechanisms for this, attrition and retention, and the use of licensing examinations. In the United Kingdom particular attention has been paid to the relation between input and output qualifications and rates of retention. There are many more.

In 1986 The National Governors Association argued that a multiple strategy approach to assessment was required at this level, and this would embrace post-secondary testing (NGA, 1986). Such testing would provide other important indicators, and with them it might be possible to determine the value-added to a student by attendance at University. For example, currently in the United Kingdom it is being argued in very simplistic terms that because a graduate earns more over a lifetime than a nongraduate, undergraduates ought to be prepared to pay for their university education, this apart from the fact that the assumption is dangerously flawed. Policymakers tend to grab hold of simple figures without understanding them, as, for example, in the use to which they put studies of the comparative performance of students in different countries in especially mathematics.

Midway between the state and the college are the professional organizations. They, too, have objectives that must be achieved. While it has seemed unlikely that there would be a mismatch between their objectives and those of the legislators recently, in the United Kingdom, a conflict of interest has begun to emerge. Nevertheless, these associations will want to be in a position to influence the legislators to accept their program evaluations.[3] ABET has chosen to use the term "program assessment" instead of "evaluation," and "outcomes" instead of objectives (see Chapter 2). Multiple strategy approaches are being used to evaluate courses (Atman, Adams, and Turns (2000).

In Britain the concept of the assessment of student learning was focused on how best to test for different objectives, and is best illustrated by the example of the engineering science at A level examination described in Chapter 2. The experience of this examination led to a different concept of multiple strategy assessment, also published in 1986 (Carter, Heywood, and Kelly, 1986).[4]

Alverno College's much publicized curriculum also used a multiple strategy approach to assessment, but it went beyond the confines of designing appropriate measures to test student learning. The Office of Institutional Research also measured such things as student development to ensure that institutional aims were being met (Mentokowski et al., 2000). In the diagrams in Figures 1.3 and 1.4 (Chapter 1) measurements of this kind belong to the evaluation component because they have something to say about how the institution and the curriculum influence learning. They belong to the area of evaluation or program assessment as it is now called. Assessment in these illustrations relates directly to the formal assessment of academic learning, and, by implication, of teaching by some form of test or schedule. It may, for example, in addition to tests, include portfolios, project reports, and videos of performances. It would not include student ratings. Independently of grading, teachers make many simple tests of student learning. Fifty of these have been described by Angelo and Cross (1993) under the title of "classroom assessment." Parker et al., (2001) call this quality assessment, which they define as *the process of measuring performance, work product or a learning skill and giving feedback, which documents growth and provides directives to improve future performance."* In the United Kingdom that definition might comprehend continuous assessment if it allowed grading. Parker et al., then go on to define evaluation as *"a judgement or determination of the quality of a performance, product or use of a process against a standard"* which in the United Kingdom would be the final examination when designed for that purpose. The term evaluation would not necessarily be used to define that activity, partly because in the United Kingdom different definitions of the key terms have been used.

In the United States, a committee on assessment of the National Academy also decided not to use the term evaluation. It brought the dimensions of 'knowing what students know,' 'knowing how students know,' and 'knowing how students come to know' together under the heading of the assessment of student learning (Pellegrino, Chudowsky, and Glaser, 2001).

Evaluations may be undertaken at every level of institutional practice, that is, the course, the program, the college, and the institution. In this sense, measures for classroom assessment of the kind described by Angelo and Cross are evaluations taken by teachers for their own enlightenment.

There has also been a debate about the differences between self-assessment and self-evaluation. This is discussed in Chapter 16.

All in all, the situation is very messy because the

---

[3] In Great Britain the process of approving courses seeking degrees of the National Council for Academic Awards was called "Validation" (Church, 1988. Silver, 1990). Most of these colleges became universities in 1992. This gave them the right to validate their own degrees. The process of validation undoubtedly helped them acquire the standards appropriate for university work, and the influence of the CNAA remains. Validation did not imply that the degree was accredited by a professional body only that degree had validity in relation to generally accepted standards. A college required this validation in order to be able to awarded the degree. If it wanted accreditation then it might have had to take additional measures over and above those that were necessary for the degree.

---

[4] It was originally called multiple-objective, and this idea was recommended by the Committee on the Form and Function of the Inter mediate certificate examination in Ireland.

term assessment is favored and used to describe all these activities. It is very difficult to run against the tide. This has the disadvantage that some teachers may not be aware of the developments in evaluation theory and practice that have taken place since the 1960s, and the substantial literature that arose from these developments. Developments in evaluation in higher education followed a similar pattern and a brief inspection of this history is indicative of the attitudes that might be taken to program assessment.[5]

15.1.   Developments in Evaluation[6]

The early evaluators hoped that their work would lead to rational decision making by policymakers. This would be achieved by collecting objective information about the outcomes of programs (Weiss, 1972). In 1965, legislation in the United States for elementary and secondary education mandated evaluation.

The response of evaluators to this demand was to develop experimental and quasi-experimental research designs of a traditional kind. The Government had demanded rigorous scientific data, and the evaluators thought that policymaking should be viewed as social experimentation (Rivlin, 1971). This, they believed, would lead to social reform. Experimental designs required comparisons, and, if done in the early stages of the project, a factorial approach could be used to design the significant elements of the program, whose effects could then be evaluated.

Shapiro (1986) pointed out that the emphasis on the scientific approach was because education was to be used to alleviate poverty. Consequently those who were employed to do evaluation came from the fields of education and educational psychology in which the agricultural-botany model of research predominated. It is not surprising to find engineers using similar models for the evaluation of their interventions.

However, the scientific approach came to be criticized because it did not live up to the high expectations that it had generated. Guba (1969) argued that this failure was due to a series of lacks. *"Lack of an adequate definition of evaluation; lack of an adequate evaluation theory; lack of knowledge about decision processes; lack of criteria on which judgements might be based; lack of approaches; lack of mechanisms for organizing, processing and reporting evaluative information; and lack of trained personnel"* (Guba cited by Shapiro, 1986).

15.1.1. The Role of the Evaluator

The foregoing were the issues that educational evaluators had to face in England in the Schools Council Projects. The Schools Council was established in 1965. It was intended to have an oversight over the school curriculum. It initiated a number of curriculum projects with the requirement that they should be evaluated. (Interestingly enough the first initiative was to try to interest children in technology.) Usually, an evaluator was appointed to the project team. Broadly speaking the role of the evaluator was ill-defined, particularly with respect to the contractual relationships between the stakeholders, some of whom could be said to be in competing roles. At times it seemed to some evaluators that the team tolerated them because the policymakers desired them. Their problems gave rise to a substantial debate that paralleled an important debate about teacher accountability.

An American research concluded that political considerations, and the personal involvement of the evaluator, significantly influenced evaluation use (Patton et al., 1977). Given the need for accountability, it is possible that those who employed evaluators had a naïve concept of evaluation. More cynically, perhaps they simply wanted the evaluator to provide affirmation of what they were doing.

It is likely that in curriculum developments in engineering and technology education in the future, evaluations will be required. There was a major debate about whether or not evaluators should be internal, that is, part of the team (school/department), or external. The advantages of an external evaluator will be apparent. If an internal evaluator is appointed, it is essential that there be a contract with the stakeholders that states clearly what is wanted from the evaluator. Boud (1979), writing about his own experience as an evaluator of a program in higher education in Scotland, said *"anyone choosing to engage in work of this kind must ask himself whether he should best undertake a well-defined project which is sufficiently limited in scope to produce unambiguous results, but which may be peripheral to the real issues of undergraduate teaching and learning, or whether he should tackle the more important and more relevant problems which are not amenable to clear solutions which are subject to local political pressures and which are impossible to report without controversy... the second is infinitely more rewarding and offers the satisfaction of helping bring about the occasional real improvement in undergraduate curricula."* It is the *"difference between "telling it as it is" and "telling it as it would like to be."* It is no mean choice.[7]

Practice is still far from rigorous. For example, in a recent study, Mutharasan et al., (1997) of Drexel University reported a case study in which an external evaluator was used; they do not comment on their perception of the role of that person. While they reported the recommendations of that person, they did not say how many were taken on board.

Shapiro cited Feldman and March (1981), who argued that organizations were concerned with information gathering rather than analysis. *"The*

---

[5]Shapiro (1986) suggests that the formal field of evaluation began in 1965.

[6]Apart from the comments on developments in the United Kingdom this section is based mainly on a limited summary of a substantive review by Shapiro (1986).

[7]This writer had this choice to make with respect to the enquiry into the Colleges of Advanced Technology and sandwich courses that has been mentioned in this review. He chose to "tell it as it is."

organizational search for information is symbolic. They contended that organizations gather information to take on the appearance of rationality and competence in decision making, but the nature of organizations is such that options for behavior are limited" (Shapiro, 1986).

In these circumstances, woe betide an evaluator who provides an analysis. Whatever the analysis, it will put the organization on the defensive, particularly if the evaluation has political implications of which the evaluator may not be aware. *"The greater the political implications of the decision (who gets what, when and how), the greater the influence of these factors and correspondingly the less the influence of evaluation data"* (Shapiro, 1986).

This happens at all levels of the organization: for example between the department and the college (faculty, school); between the school and the university; and between the university and the managing funding agency.

15.1.2. Evaluation in Higher Education

According to Shapiro, when evaluation began in higher education in the United States, its purpose was nonpolitical. In the United States it functioned within the system in order to help internal decision-making. However, a decline in economic fortune led to the beginnings of public accountability. In Britain the universities did not experience the luxury of a non-political situation. They were at first forced to make internal decisions because of reductions in funding, and then they became subject to public accountability. The term evaluation was never used.

In Great Britain[8] the established universities, unlike the degree awarding polytechnics, had been relatively sheltered from the realities of life until in the early 1990s the government changed the arrangements for funding with the intention of bringing the old and new universities under the more or less direct control of the Department of Education.[9] The polytechnics became universities in 1992. This action more than doubled the number of universities. Economic circumstances continued to contribute to their difficulties because successive governments found it easy to squeeze them. Huge demands were placed on them to increase the

numbers in higher education. At the same time, all degree granting institutions now had to respond to academic audits[10] that examined their procedures, and they required the provision of extensive documentation which included data about a restricted range of performance indicators. In addition their funding came to depend in no small measure on the results of a five yearly research assessment exercise which rated departments for success or otherwise on a five point scale. The requirements of this exercise meant that staff had to plan what they would achieve for each five-year period in terms of publication output. Subsequently a five-yearly subject review was introduced and subjects (departments) were rated under six headings, each rated 1 to 4 commonly though misleadingly conflated (on a 24 point scale) especially by newspapers who published their own rankings of departments.[11] This process called for considerable documentation, and these data were inspected, as were teachers, during a five day period. It caused considerable controversy, and the demands were subsequently reduced.

After at least one full cycle, it was argued that the few inadequacies which had been identified had been eliminated, justifying a lighter touch audit which would assume that institutions now had in place their own systems to exercise oversight of their stewardship of standards and the quality of the learning experience.

Subject review corresponds to program assessment in the United States and is now based on self-assessment that is externally judged and confirmed. As in the United States, professional subjects had the problem of meeting the demands of this exercise as well as those of their professional organizations, and a problem was to reconcile these two demands. As in the United States, *"accountability became the external demand for documentation of program outcomes of higher education programs"* (Shapiro, 1986).

Astin (1974) in the United States proposed a "Taxonomy of Higher Education Objectives." He argued that the evaluation data that was collected was concerned with means not ends.[12] He felt they should be concerned with outcomes. He categorized student outcomes into cognitive and affective, and he categorized the outcomes of research into psychological and behavioral. Such outcomes included, knowledge, intelligence, critical thinking ability, basic skills, self-concept, attitudes and beliefs, educational and occupational attainment, career choice, mental health, and interpersonal relations.

In Great Britain there has been a longstanding controversy about the ability of the 'A' level entrance examinations to predict the level of subsequent success.

---

[8]Education in Britain is administered by the different countries that make up the United Kingdom, and in consequence there are some differences between them, and more especially between Scotland and the others.

[9] It was always possible to obtain a degree in the technical college sector in the United Kingdom. Government policy from 1956 was to upgrade a number of colleges to become degree awarding institutions. These colleges were first under the control of local government, and then they received their funds direct from government. This system was known as a binary system. A similar system functioned in Australia. The universities were, however, financed by a University Grants Committee which shielded them from the direct influence of government. When the Polytechnics became universities, they and the established universities were brought into a new funding mechanism. Higher Education Funding Councils were established for England and Wales, Northern Ireland, and Scotland. The situation in Scotland has always been and is somewhat different from that in England, also the requirements for quality assurance differ in some respects, although the general approach is similar.

---

[10]This was in addition to financial auditing

[11]The headings were 1,curriculum design, content and organization. 2, Teaching, learning and assessment 3, Student progression and achievement 4, Student support and guidance. 5, Learning resources. 6, Quality assurance and enhancement. The criteria for the four point scale were 1. Inadequate contribution to the attainment of objectives. 2. Acceptable contribution.

[12]These data came to be called performance indicators.

While they give a reasonable prediction of success, they are fairly poor at predicting the level of that success. Carter pointed out that a correlation between input and output performance, by its very nature, smoothes out many variables that contribute to success. He noted that the only place that a person with an 'A' grade can go is down if he/she does not stay at the same level. In contrast a person with a grade D at entry can go in one of three directions. They can go up or down or remain at the same level. A single score does not fully describe how the performance of a population varies.

Carter described a model which would explain how the 'A' level examination, the results of which are approximately normally distributed at input to higher education, is transformed into an approximately normal distribution at output. The model was tested on two cohorts of electrical engineering student graduating in successive years. The results showed that the overall trend is for the lower end of the input mark spectrum to be upward shifted in performance. The mid-range of the input mark spectrum is less shifted (perhaps even static with improved statistics), and the upper range of the input mark spectrum is downwardly shifted. In all cases, initial populations on any mark interval are broadened towards the output (Carter and Heywood, 1991). These results supported Marsh's contention that engineering students with a low input mark would have a considerable chance of success if they were given an appropriate educational experience (Marsh, 1988).

Another study of performance at two comparable universities in England largely confirmed this analysis. It questioned the validity of A level as a predictor and suggested that nonintellectual factors should be examined (Adamson and Clifford, 2002). To understand the relationships (if any), it is necessary to understand the educational process to which the students are subjected.

The literature of engineering education suggests that many of those writing about and conducting program assessment have taken many of these points on board. For example, Dabney et al., (2001) reported that one of the lessons learned in preparing for ABET Ec2000 accreditation was that the evaluation had to be collaborative and involve all the stakeholders if it was to be successful. They are also making judgments of worth and value; while this may not be the information that the institution requires, it is the information that the practitioners require. And it is the information, if utilized, that builds reputations among the student fraternity.

15.1.3. Reaction to the Scientific Approach in Evaluation, and the Practitioner

The reaction against the scientific approach that was based on outcomes was first noted during the late 1960s. Beginning with Stake (1967), evaluation theorists began to emphasize the importance of process because designs based on experimental results do not indicate directions for improvement. Thus, Stufflebeam (1969) proposed a model that looked at the context-input-process-product. It maintained a system level approach to

educational decision making. It brought together in a synthesis the different elements of the educational system. It was this kind of approach that was used in the evaluation of sandwich (cooperative) courses in the United Kingdom by Heywood (1969). Atman's protocol analyses of design behavior requiring the recording and judging of procedural events in the freshman year (Atman and Bursic, 1998), and Felder's longitudinal studies have some similarities with this model.

As Shapiro pointed out, the attention to process by these theorists implied a more descriptive approach because, in order to understand the process, descriptive information was required and this demanded a qualitative approach rather than a quantitative approach to evaluation.

[It is beyond the remit of this study to go into the origins and theories that have accompanied the development of qualitative research. It should be noted that the term "qualitative" is not easily defined because it comes from several research traditions and partly because of the use of a variety of terms that, if not quite identical in meaning, are closely related. The main traditions from which qualitative research comes are ethnographic. It is work carried out largely in cross-cultural contexts and case studies (used in cross cultural contexts but also found in medical and psychiatric work, particularly psychoanalysis) (Madaus and Kellaghan, 1992). These traditions are considered in detail in Denzil and Lincoln (1994). These paragraphs are based on the British tradition of case study work (and my experience of it) that the American R. E. Stake, who is often cited by engineering educators, acknowledges was the beginning of his own interest in such work (Hamilton et al., 1977). An engineering perspective from the United States that may be read in parallel with these comments is due to Leydens, Moskal, and Pavelich (2004)].

The experimental approach by itself was inadequate and needed to be supplemented by other approaches. Stake began and continues to advocate case study research. In Britain the implicit argument for a more qualitative approach to evaluation was explicated by Parlett and Hamilton (1976) in a Roneo printed documented from Edinburgh University that became seminal with the title "Illumination as Evaluation" (1972).[13]

Parlett and Hamilton regarded illuminative evaluation as a general research strategy: *"The choice of research tactics follows not from research doctrine but from decisions in each case as to the best available techniques: the problem defines the methods used not vice versa... there are three stages: investigators observe, inquire further, then seek to explain....Obviously the three stages overlap and functionally interrelate the transition from stage to stage, as the investigation unfold, and problem areas become progressively clarified and redefined. The course of study cannot be charted in*

[13]Illuminative is a term suggested by Martin Trow, an American sociologist with interests in comparative higher education. See Parlett and Hamilton, (1976) for a published version.

advance. Beginning with an extensive data base the researchers systematically reduce the breadth of their enquiry to give more concentrated attention to emerging issues. This 'progressive focusing' permits unique and unpredicted phenomena to be given due weight. It reduces the problem of data overload, and prevents the accumulation of a mass of unanalysed material. Within this three-stage framework, an information profile is assembled using data collected from five areas: observation; interviews; questionnaires and tests; documentary background sources; psychological, social environmental and educational factors...Its primary concern is with description and interpretation rather than measurement and prediction. It stands unambiguously within the alternative anthropological paradigm" (from the 1972 document).

An important feature of their approach is the wish to "understand" what is going on. If the early questions do not lead to such understanding and new issues emerge then the research design has to be changed. This Parlett and Hamilton called *"progressive focusing."*

From these beginnings the qualitative research movement in education in the United Kingdom began and it has been used to understand the processes of innovation in education[14]. Some of the activities suggested by Angelo and Cross are illuminative, and Lin's (1979) study of the hidden curriculum in engineering is in this vein. McKenna et al., (2001) in their evaluation of student perceptions of an integrated curriculum followed the spirit of illuminative evaluation when the questions that they asked in the interviews were *"rephrased, new more relevant questions were asked, and ineffective questions were deleted."* They followed Huberman and Miles (1994) model of data collection and analysis, and that meant that the *"analysis is on going and occurs during study design and planning, during data collection, and continues after data collection has been completed".* Again this is in the illuminative tradition even though inspired by American theories more especially that of Glaser and Strauss (1967).[15]

Some investigators wanted to promote a synthesis between the two approaches and argued that the two paradigms could be mixed and matched. Multiple data sources and methods should be used. They called this *"triangulation".* More recently qualitative investigators have used this term and it has come to mean the use of two or more approaches to collecting data about the same problem. Stake (1995) writing of case study methods said that triangulation is *"working to substantiate an interpretation or to clarify its different meanings."*

In the context of engineering education,[16]

Shuman et al., (2001) have used it to describe a synthesis between the two methods. They wrote, *"Portfolios are an excellent triangulation device- a qualitative way of validating such quantitative measures as transcript evaluation and student attitudinal surveys."*

In some circumstances the illuminative (ethnographic as it is sometimes called) approach will be more appropriate, in studies of the curriculum process among small numbers, as, for example, at Lancaster University on the evaluation of a course in Physics for students in the humanities. In that study, this writer acted first as an independent observer and then as a participant observer (Heywood and Montagu Pollock, 1977). Even then, illumination from discussions will often arise from questions which in effect tease out the effects of the process in producing outcomes. Ultimately they are input-output questions. The significance of the illuminative approach is in its focus on both the system and the process. Above all, it focuses on practice. Writing of the *syllabus,* Parlett and Hamilton said,

"In practice, objectives are commonly re-ordered, redefined, abandoned or forgotten. The original "ideal" formulation ceases to be accurate, or indeed of much relevance. Few in practice take catalogue descriptions and lists of objectives seriously, save it seems for the traditional evaluator. To switch from discussing the instructional system in abstract form to describing the details of its implementation – is to cross to another realm."

It is of considerable interest to note that some engineering educators are calling for and undertaking qualitative studies, so of what concern is this for the individual engineering educator? If assessment and evaluation are to become integrating activities in the process of educating engineers, then teachers must themselves have an 'illuminative attitude.' They must want to test their ideas and evaluate their courses. They might want to do this at the level 1 of leadership that is, with classroom assessment of the type suggested by Angelo and Cross (1993). Or, they might want to carry out level 2 classroom research in the qualitative mode as advocated by Cross and Steadman (1996), or of the more traditional kind advocated by Heywood (1992), and exemplified in many of the studies reported in this review. They might want to do it by themselves, or invite an independent observer into their classrooms, or use a consultant. Some efforts may be good, some may be bad. Action research, however crude, is surely better than blissful ignorance of the fact that we are not achieving what we want to achieve.[17]

George and Cowan (1999) took action research to be the conduct of investigations of a research nature that produce useful findings relevant to a particular situation, and the people and subject studies from which the findings were obtained. Defined in this way the classroom assessment activities described by Angelo and

---

[14]For a detailed account the theory and practice of qualitative research, see Denzin and Lincoln (1994). For an introduction to its use (and methodology of use) in technology education, see Hoepfl (1997).

[15]Called grounded theory.

[16]At the 2003 Frontiers in Education Conference workshops on qualitative research in education were given by Alisha Waller with Mark Urban Lurain and David DiBiasio

[17]Studies that have the intention of producing decisions for action are sometimes called 'action research,' and there is a literature on this topic (Zuber-Skeritt, 1992).

Cross (1993) are action research. Indeed as Peter Knight (private communication) has pointed out, all assessment is a form of research.

LeBold and Ward (1995) described how over a 25-year period, research in the Purdue engineering school moved from what they called *status quo* educational research to action-oriented research. They cited the women in engineering program as an example, and in this area Radziemski and Mitchell (2000) also conducted an action research.[18]

In a review paper Kember and McKay (1996) argued the case for action research as a means of faculty development.[19] They assumed that action research was done by the participants. They summarized the dimensions of action research as:

- *Is concerned with social practice.*
- *Is participative.*
- *Allows participants to decide topics.*
- *Aims toward improvement.*
- *Is a cyclical process.*
- *Involves systematic enquiry.*
- *Is a reflective process.*

Their vision of faculty development through action research was that:

1. *"Project teams are composed of small groups who share similar interest or concern,*
2. *The topic for the project is defined by the participants to fit within the broad aim of investigating and improving some aspect of their own teaching.*
3. *Project groups meet regularly to report observations and critique their own practices. This discourse provides for the possibility of perspective transformation.*
4. *Projects proceed through cycles of planning, action, observation, and reflection. At least two cycles are normally necessary to implement and refine any innovatory practices. The time scale for the cycles is consistent with the extended period necessary for perspective transformation.*
5. *Evidence of the effectiveness of teaching practices and their influence on student learning outcomes are gathered using interpretive methods.*
6. *The evidence gathered can be used to convince departmental colleagues not originally participating in the project that they too should change their practices and the curriculum.*
7. *Lessons learned from the projects can be disseminated to a wider audience through publications. Participants are therefore eligible for rewards through the traditional value system of universities".*

An excellent example of the approach of action research has been provided by Popov (2003) of Nottingham University. It focused on final-year projects in mechanical engineering, and its purpose was to evaluate the program. It found, among other things, that students need to be alerted to the care with which projects should be chosen, that group work required to be improved in order to obtain a better balance between individual and group tutorials, and that the program would benefit from an element of peer and self assessment.

There are many similarities with the approach of quality circles except that in that case, when the problem is solved the circle dissolves. There are also many similarities with the type of research advocated by Cross and Steadman (1996). George et al., (2003) of the University of Technology Jamaica reported on the ongoing use of the Kember model in industrial electronics and mechatronics to explore means of improving students analytical and communication skills. In that course, failure rates had been high. A student participated in the small action research group set up for this purpose.

Action research of this kind would require a product champion, and it is that kind of role that was envisaged for curriculum leaders at level 3 (see also paper by George et al., 2003).

15.2. Developments in Evaluation in Engineering.

In some respects, evaluation studies have followed the same pattern as in the social sciences. As happened in the social sciences, the trend of recent requirements in America (ABET Ec2000) has been to focus on validity.[20] In engineering, as might be expected, many of the investigations are of the scientific kind and approach evaluation with quasi-experimental models. Typically, pre- and post-tests have been given to experimental and control groups. The results are accompanied by tests of statistical significance of one kind or another (e.g., Steif, 2003). Occasionally, multivariate and discriminant analyses are made (e.g., Ingham, Meza, and Price, 1998; Sullivan, Daghestani and Parsaei, 1996; Thomas et al., 1996), and there have been factorial studies in the tradition of the agricultural botany model (e.g., Roney and Woods 2003; Terenzini et al., 2001). It has been argued that insufficient attention has been given by some authors to the statistical ramifications of their results when using multiple comparison techniques. Larpkiataworn et al., (2003) have illustrated this point with respect to Type I and Type II errors in classification tables, and they considered tree diagrams as an alternative to such tables. Others have been concerned with methodology, as, for example the determination of rater bias [Harris and Cox, (2003); see also Blake (2003), and Woods and Chan, (2003):]. In the United States this is likely to become a much discussed issue as the move to non-traditional methods of assessment grows as a functions of the need to assess skills that cannot be

---

[18]They cited Baskerville et al., (1996) on action research. For another example see Clear and Daniels (2000).
[19]Details of an action research project are given in full in the paper.
[20]The European reader who wants to have quick review of developments in accreditation in the United States should consult Schachterle (1999).

assessed by traditional objective tests [e.g. teamwork; see Powers, Upchurch, and Stokes, (2003) for work in progress].

Cluster analysis has also been used (Streveler and Miller, 2001, Youngman et al., 1978). Studies embracing one or more of these techniques have been reported in the other Chapters of this text. The number of studies reported of this kind is on the increase, and there is little need to discuss the techniques here. A few studies have been reported that are based on either ethnographic techniques or incorporate ethnographic techniques within them. The number of such studies is also on the increase.

It has been argued that insufficient attention has been given by some authors to the statistical ramifications of their results when using multiple comparison techniques. Larpkiataworn et al., (2003) have illustrated this point in repect of Type I and Type II errors in classification tables, and they considered tree diagrams as an alternative to such tables.

As has been indicated, several problems have been found with the traditional scientific model. First, and at the most elementary level, is the problem of fairness. This problem has, for example, become an issue in medical research where some have argued that it is not fair to give patients placebos in drug trials. In education, some have held that students in a control group are at a disadvantage to those who receive the experimental treatment. Of course the control group may not be at a disadvantage if the experiment fails- in which case it is the experimental group that has been treated unfairly. Therefore, in classroom research the tutor has an obligation to ensure that no one is at a disadvantage. One consequence of this is that there is now a literature on doing sensitive research, and it is a requirement in many courses of educational research that the topic be discussed (Lee, 1993).

One problem that is experienced, particularly when it is a course modification that is being evaluated, is that the control group will have to be a group of students who have completed the unrevised course. One method of handling this problem is to make the revised course of equal length to the unrevised course, and for the same lecturer to teach both courses. Comparable examinations would have to be used. All these points are noted in a report on an attempt to integrate economic principles with design (Thuessen et al., 1992).

A second problem relates to the amount of data that should be collected. In psychometric testing, it is held that a single test is not very revealing. Therefore, the student should be exposed to a range of tests that measure different qualities. The question arises in educational research as to how many instruments respondents should have to complete. In the engineering literature, while it is recognized that for comparative purposes groups should be of corresponding aptitude, other possible important parameters such as intelligence, learning style, personality, and spatial ability are not always taken into account.

Often the gains brought about by an experimental approach, when compared with the approach that has been changed, are not great. This creates a problem for those who wish to push ahead with the change, and it leads to statements such as *"we are convinced that the course has been improved by the additional enthusiasm of the students."*[21] This could have been avoided if some measure of motivation had been included. They argued that students would increase their efforts in order to get better grades. The other problem with motivation is the well-known Hawthorne effect. Students might well respond more positively to that which is novel and not built-in. Evidence has been presented in other chapters, which shows the value of using several instruments. Unfortunately the time is often not available for the administration of a comprehensive battery of tests, and compromises have to be made. It might be added that although a small gain may not be statistically significant, for individual candidates a small change in marks may make all the difference to the student's grade. At the same time such differences are likely to be within the standard error, and less attention to this dimension seems to be made among investigators than might be considered desirable.

A major problem relates to the validity of exit questionnaires that ask students to state whether or not their skills have changed as a result of the course. Surely the final examinations or some other independent criterion such as performance in a project should have been designed to give such information.[22] If change is to be sustained, it is important to show that students in experimental programs perform no less well. How this is to be done will influence the choice of instruments to be used.

Problems arise when the population is small because factors that are internal and external to a specific learning situation might pollute the results. With large inhomogenous populations, these can be minimized by random sampling and the use of control groups (Campbell and Stanley, 1966). But in classroom situations groups can be very small and control groups impossible. To overcome this difficulty in an evaluation of two approaches to laboratory work, Freeman, Carter and Jordan (1978) used the Solomon four group strategy that is shown in Figure 15.1. This was designed to measure the effects of two courses, and the major variable between the two was the style of laboratory work to which the students were exposed. For analysis the members of each course were divided into two subgroups. Course A was designed so that the students would move from a small number of rather formal experiments to more open ended problem solving practicals, and finally to a final design project.

Course B was designed so that the laboratory

---

[21] Taken from the Thuessen et al., study. They also argued that because new material had been introduced, there was an overall increase in the effectiveness of the course.

[22] In a follow up to the Thuessen program exit questionnaires were used to determine this point. See Callen et al., 1995.

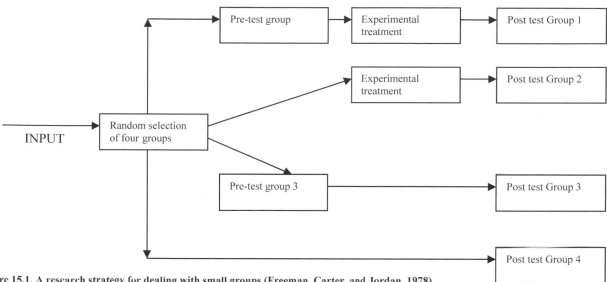

Figure 15.1. A research strategy for dealing with small groups (Freeman, Carter, and Jordan, 1978)

work kept in step with the lectures in order for reinforcement between them. Quite precise instruction sheets were given. This was in contrast to course A, where the information became progressively less complete. The material studied and the type and range of instrumentation was similar.

An agreed list of proficiencies that students should display was agreed, and eighteen practical tests were designed to measure these proficiencies. They imitated typical exam conditions commonly in use in the United Kingdom. While it was found that there were considerable gains between pre- and post-test scores, it was also found that the gains were greater for the students in course B, which confounded the original hypothesis that was based on what best practice was conceived to be at the time.

When the data were further analyzed it was found that few students had attempted more than two-thirds of the test. Students in course A performed better on components that were expected to possess a higher proportion of cognitive skill, whereas the students in course B performed better on components that exercised recall skills.

Without this more detailed study of the actual situation, incorrect curriculum decisions might have been made.

In engineering, in response to the limitations of quantitative research, some investigators have undertaken additional qualitative studies. And in certain circumstances it has been found that quantitative studies are necessary for the illumination of qualitative data. For example, at the University of Joensuu in Finland, where high school students studied a first-year university course in computer science and programming quantitative data was obtained from the analysis of logged actions, submitted exercises, web-based questionnaires, and end-of-course examinations. Qualitative data provided feedback during the course, on completion of the courses

feedback was provided by interviews and questionnaires (Meisalo, Sutinen, and Torvinen, 2003).

Quantitative data showed that "lack of time" was an important contributory factor in drop-out, but follow-up questions by e-mail yielded a greater depth of understanding and provided novel insights to their initial observations. It was found that these young high school students were unable to estimate the time required for university courses, and adaptations to the course were made to take not only this into account but also the fact that most drop-outs had only very limited skills. Methodologically, it was found that face-to-face questioning instead of e-mail obtained *"much better information on motivation and attitudes to distance learning and programming."*

Srinivasan et al., (2003) also used qualitative and quantitative methodologies to a evaluate a laboratory component in a four course sequence in communications systems that had been included to increase student learning. The quantitative study used the traditional scientific model with volunteer control and treatment groups. The qualitative study focused on the perceptions of students as expressed in electronic journals sent after each assignment, along with interviews. The interviews were analyzed for themes. When questioned the students were encouraged *"to express thought not directly related to the questions asked"*. Students from the control group did not participate in the qualitative study. The overarching question was, *"Does the signal and systems laboratory experience improve student understanding of the fundamental systems and communications concepts?"*

The quantitative data suggested, although it was not conclusive, that the laboratory experience did give students an advantage over those who had not received that experience. As in the previous study reported above, analyses of the data gave insights that would not have been found from quantitative data even though more questions were raised than were answered. Most of the students, while not believing the laboratory experience affected their performance, believed that it had helped to clarify their concepts and made the course more interesting. In part this was due to the fact that students liked translating theoretical concepts into "real" examples on the laboratory equipment. Of more interest was the emergence of a difference in perception *"between students and faculty as to what an electrical engineer actually does... some students perceived themselves to be technicians and gave more importance to the practical aspects involved in using the equipment over the theoretical concepts that were expected to be clarified by the equipment"*. But the most intriguing question that arose was that the interviewers did not learn where the student motivation was directed if it was not translated into a "motivation to achieve course objectives." And, that is yet another reminder of the complexity of the teaching/learning process and the need to treat simple measures with caution.

At its simplest and yet most difficult qualitative research involves observation and the observer may or may not be a participant. In the Science for Arts student case study that involved this writer, he began by being independent and ended up as a participant. The methods were not particularly sophisticated as the study was focused on the development of the curriculum and not on the development of social theory. Nevertheless, it was anthropological in its approach (Heywood and Montagu Pollock, 1977).

Reamon and Sheppard (1996) studied analytic problem solving in engineering by videotaping upper-level students while they performed an assignment in a mechanical design course[23]. They based their analysis on a definition of learning due to Greeno et al., (1993) that some might find problematic. It was to the effect that *"knowing is the ability to interact with things and other people in a situation, and learning is improvement in that ability."* Thus, the experiment involved the observation of persons working in pairs. In this theory the learner is an agent who brings abilities to the situation, and the resources in the environment are termed "affordances". In this environment the affordances included worktable, paper, pencils, handouts, Working Model mechanical simulation software, the analytical capability of that software, and a legotechnics building set. One group had

available to them all four affordances, another only one. The situations that the four groups had to face were all different, nevertheless *"they all learned about designing mechanisms because they interacted successfully in their situations."* The problem was to determine which situation was the most effective learning environment.

This was done by examining the videos for evidence of the completeness of the mental models developed by the pairs. *"Mental models feature cognitive objects which correspond to physical objects, situations, or relationships that can be used to simulate actions of events in other situations"* [transfer]. *"When a student is able to form a complete and functional mental model of a situation, we say he understands that subject."*[24] These models are built up from mental representations of either a physical kind or a mental kind, as, for example, symbolic expressions and prior mental models.[25] Within each learning environment, certain information, such as diagrams, equations, and Lego models served as the representations that could serve to help the pairs form their mental models. Reamon and Sheppard analyzed their observations in these terms and showed that the completeness of the mental models differed as between the pairs. They concluded that in the *"ideal environment, a rich situational experience builds a students intuition about the domain. This experience is followed by the development of abstractable symbolic relationships. When these two experiences are properly linked, the student completes a mental model which allows him to transfer his knowledge to other domains."* The importance to learning was that it was the quantity and type of resources available that determined the effectiveness of the learning domain.

Clearly, approaches of this kind are powerful techniques for understanding processes of learning and the factors in the environment that impede or enhance that learning.[26]
Other work at Stanford in this qualitative tradition also included the study of the social interactions in design teams. It was this work together with that of Atman and her colleagues (Atman and Bursic, 1998) on the protocol analysis of design behavior that influenced a curriculum innovation at The Cooper Union. There they developed an ethnographic approach for the purpose of the assessment of communication modes in the design teams at the Cooper Union. Del Cerro et al., (2001) gave the following definition of ethnomethodology as it applied to engineering; *"treating engineering communication as utterances by an alien culture to be objectively analyzed by the anthropologist for the purpose of improving the*

---

[23]In Europe the use of video recordings is classed as phenomenography and derives from work by Marton et al., (1976) in Sweden. It developed out of the study of students' experiences of learning and has extended to how lecturers experience their teaching. Despite the volume of work in this area, Ashworth and Lucas (2000) have argued that various aspects of its methodology need to be refined.. For example, there is the problem of how to engage with the student's lived experience. They set out guidelines, and discussed the need for 'bracketing', that is, the need for the research worker to set aside their own assumptions in order to faithfully register the student's point of view. Among other things, they suggest that the researcher's interviewing skills should be subject to ongoing review. Phenomonography differs from ethnography in that the ethnographer focuses on the group whereas the phenomenographer focuses on the individual. How the phenomenographer views learning influences the interpretations they give to the events being analysed. Some take the constructivist position that a person constructs their reality; others take the view that it is the context that in forms their thinking (Catherine Griffin, personal communication).

[24]The relevance of this to concept mapping, and in particular the differences between the expert and the novice in Fordyce's experiment described in Chapter 4 should be apparent. Similarly this is an expression of the conditions for transfer.
[25]These representations are in some circumstances similar to the basic schema (concepts) discussed in Chapter 4. In this paper they applied to the total situation.
[26]For an approach to the development of critical thinking in the laboratory that also used qualitative measures see Miller and Olds (1994).

culture, i.e., increasing engineering design Productivity."[27] In social psychology this is termed "account analysis."[28]

At the Cooper Union a study of the communication modes and content used by engineering students in a special projects course on Robotics for Theatre. The aim of the project was to provide a generic model of assessment (evaluation) that could be tailored for unique learning environments. Questionnaires were used, as were journals and student expressions of their views on the communication learning process. The assessor, an ethnographer, also participated in the project and the assessor's work developed in parallel with that of the team. It had as its objective the documentation of the interactions among the various members of the team in order to track the course, content, and type of information flow. Observation was *critical for a meaningful formulation of a situated assessment plan. Nevertheless, the assessment results presented in this report do not constitute so much an assessor's ethnography as an ethnography by the team itself, however guided by specific questions.* The key questions were,

"1. *We would like to know more about your innovation process?*

2. *What have you learned from your participation in this project?*

3. *What means of communication did you use most commonly?*

4. *Your robot was designed to be an actor in theatre. What did you have to learn from the field of theatre in order to successfully design your robot?*"

The investigation was guided by these questions, recorded communication flows and other relevant information including self-assessment. The final questionnaire was administered after the project had finished.

Each of the questions was followed by sub-questions related to the topic, which served to validate the assumptions on which the assessment plan was formulated. These were:

"(a) *Learning is a network-like process.*

(b) *Team projects foster innovations.*

(c) *Successful conceptual design may be a function of creativity*

(d) *Gathering data about members of the team helps to measure innovation and learning.*

(e) *Task clarification and product definition are critical in conceptual design.*

(f) *The current process of socio-economic and educational restructuring features a clear*

convergence of work methods, processes and objectives among R & D settings, industry and academia."

Validation of these objectives required an analysis of team dynamics and the measurement of motivation. The assessment protocol implementation matrix that resulted tabulated outcomes: strategies and actions: assessment methods: Feedback procedures-against- resource mobilization for creative problem-solving: interdisciplinarity: teamwork: communication skills: Tech-tools incorporation: Management/leadership.

For example, the protocol for outcomes for resource mobilization for creative problem solving read *"To identify sources of information and ideas used by students-to assess students' effectiveness in gathering information relevant to the project, and to improve students' research and documentation skills."* The feedback procedures for tech-tools incorporation were *"Instructor is responsible for fixing problems and adjusting the techtool support system based on students' feedback,-ongoing project diary review, ongoing review of internet resources available."*[29]

To achieve these goals, it was intended to create a web based portfolio that would track the progress of each student, and include a project profile where information utilization and student initiatives would be recorded. It would include interdisciplinary and communication sections. Leadership of the team would be rotated amongst the members so that each one had the opportunity to lead.

Another case study undertook an investigation of the experience of adult students in freshmen classes at the University of Tennessee. The adults in the enquiry were all over the age of 24, and they were either new entrants or re-entrants. They were placed in design teams with students who were straight out of high school (Tichon and Seat, 2002). These adults consented to audio taped interviews that were to be transcribed and analyzed. The idea was to obtain *"a first person description of some specified domain of experience with the course of the dialogue largely set by the respondent"*. To achieve this goal, the respondents were asked the question:

"Tell me in as much detail as you can, about your experience of being an older student placed on engineering project teams with traditional first-year students."

No other topics were introduced. The participants initiated every topic discussed while the interviewer sought clarification and expansion of the topic.

Once the protocols were transcribed, a group of persons trained in the analysis of protocols looked for common themes. This method of analysis does not eliminate but minimizes assessor bias, and it helps with error detection.

While this was a case study with only five participants, its findings are of relevance because of the

---

[27]They cited the work of G. Button and P. Dourish. Technomethodology: Paradoxes and possibilities. http//www.acm.org/sigs/sigchi/chi96/proceedings/papers/Button/jpd.txt.htm.

[28]Account analysis is *"the analysis of both social force and explanatory content of the speech produced by social actors as a guide to the structure of the cognitive resources required for the genesis of intelligible and warrantable social action by those actors"* [Harré, (1977) cited by Jones. (1998)].

---

[29]The complete matrix is given in the paper.

increasing number of adult students coming into higher education. The findings were:

1. *"Older students had a sense of helping younger team mates.*
2. *They believed they took charge of their teams.*
3. *They were apprehensive about being placed in a team of traditional students.*
4. *They felt academically behind their younger counterparts.*
5. *They received academic help from the younger students in the team."*

Care has to be taken with single questions. Very often when they are used for course evaluation, as, for example, the question "What was the value to you of your attendance at the course?" the respondents may use different criteria of value may to determine their answers. This was the case in a study of a management course evaluated by Burgoyne (1975), cited by Easterby Smith 1994). But such information can be very useful for the development of questionnaires (see below).

At the level of the curriculum, Merton et al., (2001) investigated the process of change in the curriculum initiatives of the Foundation Coalition (see also Chapter.7.12). Six case studies were initiated. About 25 key teachers and administrators in each of the participating institutions were interviewed. From each data base a draft report that identified critical events, salient issues, and lessons learned was sent to each institution for comment and factual correction. The investigators found that even in the same institution the accounts of change differed from one to another. The interviewees had focused on what was relevant to them. Put together, they provide a story of change, and such stories make sense of change. "Storytelling in organizations is the preferred sense making currency of human relationships among internal and external stakeholders" [Weick, (1995) cited by Merton et al.,(2001)].

The analyses of these stories show the complexity of the curriculum change process. It required careful planning and sustained effort to achieve success. What counted for success varied from institution to institution. Evaluation is very much about the collection (extraction) of individual and institutional stories.

15.3. Developments in Program Assessment (evaluation) in Engineering Education in the United Kingdom and United States

While both countries have a double focus, that on the profession and the educational institution in which the course is given, American literature is clearly focused on the outcomes that ABET requires for accreditation (see Exhibit 2.2). The EC2000 regulations have stimulated enormous interest in assessment, that is the assessment of whether these outcomes are met or not, and an annual conference on *Best assessment Practice* has been run by the Rose-Hulman College with support from NSF. The majority of the papers were on program assessment or how the ABET criteria might be evaluated.

"A distinction is made between program educational objectives- statements that describe the expected accomplishments of graduates during the first few years after graduation, and program outcomes-statements that describe what students are expected to know and be able to do by the time of graduation, the achievement of which indicates that the student is equipped to achieve the program educational objectives." (Avers, 1999).

ABET requires the institutions to say how the criteria are met, that is, measured. Thus for a particular course the criteria will be stated and tools of assessment determined that should measure against these criteria (see, for example, Carlson et al., 2000: Meyer, 1997: Steneck, 1999). Some of these will be the tools that are normally used to measure student learning. Others relate to the evaluation of the course by students, alumni, etc. Some are borrowed from management practices, as, for example, SWOT analysis which pin- points strengths and weaknesses in various curriculum structures (Wilkinson et al., 2000).

The contrast with Great Britain is considerable where there is no significant movement for formal assessments of this kind. In contrast, as indicated in Section 15.2.2, national initiatives have established a framework for Higher Educational Qualifications which specifies the type of demand expected of each undergraduate level and at the Master's level. This is linked to extensive subject benchmark statements. Regular program review, in which there is external appraisal of provision against the framework and the subject bench marks, is now the norm. The external examiners base their judgments on samples of student coursework, examinations, and dissertations.

The subject review was highly controversial, not least because of the additional and heavy work entailed. Professional subjects also had to meet the criteria of their own accrediting organizations and there were attempts to align the documentation so that the work- load could be reduced. Within each subject area, benchmarking exercises were undertaken, and the Engineering Professors Council designed an output standard model, that is, a set of generic statements that articulates the output standards of engineering graduates. The professors took the view that if such a model could be identified, a conventional peer group procedure would emerge that would determine acceptable levels of output standards[30] from the wide variety of engineering programs that are available (White, 2000). The graduate profile is described by a set of ability statements. A benchmark statement[31] was to be expressed in the following form: *"The graduate has demonstrated the ability to do X in the context of Y or its equivalent [Y is a discipline-specific*

---

[30] A standard = a framework or template containing a description of the level of attainment of a graduate ward. For example, in engineering the level of attainment recognised by the award of an M.Eng in Mechanical Engineering.

[31] Benchmark = a level descriptor. Benchmarks do not define a level, or scope, but illustrate it or imply it by example.

engineering system with a level of complexity, in terms of the required skill, knowledge and understanding, that is widely understood within the discipline]" (White, 2000).

The achievement of these statements depended on a view of what an engineer does. From this understanding, six ability statements were derived that related to the generic concept of engineering. These were:

- *To transform existing systems into conceptual models.*
- *To transform conceptual models into determinable models.*
- *To use determinable models to obtain system specification in terms of parametric values.*
- *To select optimum specifications and create physical models.*
- *To apply the results from physical models to create real target systems.*
- *To critically review real target systems and personal performance.*

From these it is possible to define the component sub-abilities that make up a generic ability.

In Chapter 2 it was explained that complaints from industry had led to the view that all graduates, irrespective of subject, required certain skills in which many at that time were judged to be deficient. These came to be called key skills. In engineering these are communication, IT, application of number, working with others, problem solving, and improving one's own learning and performance. IT is hardly a skill, the list illustrates the sloppy approach to definition that has characterized the thinking of policy makers in this area. The sub-abilities in each of the categories covered these levels implicitly.

Within the British system of higher education, the external examiners are increasingly being asked to play a major role. Since Warren Piper's (1994) report, they are required to (a) consider how the examinations, teaching strategies, and curriculum are integrated to meet the objectives of the curriculum and (b) to comment on standards. They now have the framework for higher education qualifications and subject benchmarks as a guide. Some universities are now providing on site introductions to the curriculum they are to examine, and Warren Piper's idea that they should be trained has already come about in many institutions. The examinations are therefore key indicators of quality.

Taken together, these developments have meant that the quality assessment of education is in the hands of the university and that professional development is in the hands of the professional institution (e.g., Institution of Civil Engineers).

The institutions have power because they are the qualifying authorities from whom the award of Chartered Engineer is gained. They have their own qualifications route and university degree programs seek exemptions from that route. Thus, the requirements of the Engineering Council that integrates the work of all the Engineering Institutions impinge on the universities. It was, for example, the requirements of the Council that led

to four year instead of three year programs. As was shown in Chapter 2, the competencies required for registration are very similar to those required by ABET (Exhibit 2.3). In practice, the institutions worry about entry requirements and syllabuses rather than about quality assurance. This has consequences for higher education institutions because they have to maintain those standards of entry. In one case a program was rejected because the university wished to allow for flexible entry. The university argued that provided the output standards were met, that was all that was necessary. Its task was to provide a process that would enable those standards to be met. But that was not acceptable to the professional body. Decisions of this kind have consequences for innovation, particularly when they are made to fly in the face of research on the relationship between input and output qualifications, of the kind reported above, that would have supported the decision that the university had made. This raises the question, "Who audits the auditors?" This is a question that is being considered in company law in both the United Kingdom and the United States at the present time. It also raises the question, What must research do to challenge effectively deeply held opinions? How can they be made to consider changes that would benefit the system? For example, a huge amount of time is spent on examining by teaching staff. Many years ago, Carter and Lee (1975) found that in first-year electrical engineering courses, most universities followed the same syllabus. They argued that a national standardised objective test could be used for this purpose. This proposal was never seriously discussed. It would only become possible if the institutions were to take a lead.

A consequence of this structure is that there is no national concern for the assessment of student learning because the educational dimension of quality is vested in the individual university and the professional dimension is vested in the professional institutions acting through the Engineering Council. This is not to say that changes are not being made in the curriculum and teaching, they are, as examples in this text show. But measurements of the kind suggested by Shuman et al., (2001) are not, except insofar as they are made by individuals, or departments, or as part of university policy (e.g., alumni surveys).

These differences explain the difficulties that the present writer had at the first Rose-Hulman conference in explaining how the engineering science examination met many of the ABET criteria because in the United Kingdom system examinations provide *prima facie* evidence for the quality assurance exercise. It was argued in the paper that they could be designed to assess that the program outcomes had been achieved.

15.4.   Program Assessment.

15.4.1. General

The revolution brought about by ABET 2000 has caused a deluge of papers and a lot of repetition. These relate to general approaches to preparation (Duerden and Garland, 1998; McGourty, 1998; Rogers and Sando, 1996;

Yokomoto et al., 1999; Yokomoto 2001); problems in making the work done effective; techniques, tools (Ahlgren and Palladino 2000), and documentation (e.g., Jamieson, Oakes, and Coyle, 2001). In this section a novel approach to preparation is first described. This is followed by comments on the implications of continuous quality improvement (CQI) for faculty.

First, in search of reality and inspired by other enquiries that had demonstrated the importance of team ownership,[32] students in a systems design class were asked to create an ABET 2000 program evaluation process at George Mason University. As part of the task, the students had to find out what other systems engineering departments had done in order to achieve the same goal, and they also had to study the material that their own department had submitted for its previous accreditation. The documentation in the paper shows that the task was successfully completed (Brouse, 1999).

Second, Sims-Knight and her colleagues (2000) drew attention to the fact that the ABET criteria are deliberately geared toward cognitive skill development or processes. These outcomes have to be assessed and such assessments should form the basis for improvement. Continuous quality improvement is required. They cited the example of a capstone course to illustrate the problem *"The students design projects are assessed either by an independent reading of the final reports or by grades in the course. The faculty must then use the outcome of that assessment to improve the program. The assessment by grade or by independent rubric gives only limited clues as to what knowledge or processes might be most effectively improved. Furthermore, it does not tell where in the program improvement is needed. Course-based process assessment embedded into a continuous improvement loop is needed to identify where and how to improve."* This particular statement enables a further explanation of the United Kingdom system, for part of the external examiners' role in assessing the examination scripts, projects and other coursework, to identify areas of improvement based on their experience of best practice. In coming to a view, the examiner will, more often than not, have interviewed a sample of students. The external examiner may also identify best practice(s) that can build on the repertoire of experience presently available to the teachers. The objection to this approach is that it is not as systematic as might be.

In the same vein as the arguments above, Sims-Knight and her colleagues took issue with the three traditional models of course assessment. That is, the instructional model that is informed by exams, reports, artifacts, and end-of-course teaching evaluations, the experimental models of the kind discussed above, and the value added model based on prior and post course tests. They argued that these are concerned with quantitative and summative judgements whereas the ABET criteria require attention to process, that is to the formative. Therefore, the goal of assessment in a continuous improvement model is to help faculty understand the

processes at work. In other words, it is formative evaluation.[33] Ethnographic studies of the kind described above also have this as their goal.

To achieve this goal in a program teachers have first, *"to create assessments that will reveal students' processes rather than evaluating students' products. Second, they have to evaluate those assessments not in terms of success or failure (theirs or the students') but rather as an identification of opportunities for improvement. Third, they must adopt an incremental attitude, that is, they must accept that improvement takes place over a number of iterations of the process."*

For many teachers the change in disposition required to achieve this goal is not accomplished without some difficulty; in recognition of this fact, Sims-Knight et al., provided workshops (supported by a website) that would help institutionalize these procedures. The workshops were intended to help teachers complete an 'assessment plan' that incorporated an extant assessment into a continuous assessment loop. A second plan was to create an assessment for an ABET a–k outcome or for a pedagogical innovation. Those that were submitted were analyzed and a summary was given in the paper. The teachers found it difficult to anticipate how they might change their courses on the basis of their evaluation.

The general conclusion was that the central problem was that of prior experience which is consistent with innovation theory. *"They all had pre-existing assessment models from their past experiences teaching and/or reading or doing educational research. We had to show them that course-based assessment was not about evaluating the adequacy of either students or instructors, that any data they collected could be kept to themselves (although we asked them to write reports), and that they needed to think through how to make assessments that would inform decision making about their courses."*

This kind of situation is a common experience of those who analyze innovation in industry (e.g., Youngman et al., (1978), or evaluate in-company or in career training courses (e.g., Hesseling, 1966). Those concerned with preparing managers for change in short courses have found that it is necessary to administer a *chocs des opinions* early in the course (Hesseling, 1966).

15.4.2. Methodologies for Program Assessment

Insofar as ABET 2000 is concerned, Shuman et al., (2001) identified twelve methodologies that could be used for program assessment.[34] They indicated in a matrix which ones could be used to assess the ABET outcome measures. The 12 methodologies are: authentic assessment, physical portfolios, electronic portfolios, student journals, competency measurements, intellectual development, concept maps, verbal protocols, student surveys, student interviews, focus groups, and alumni

---

[32]Marin, Armstrong, and Keys (1999) were cited.

[33]Many papers deal with formative evaluation but do not necessarily relate it to CQI. See Della-Piana and Bernat (1999) for one that does. In this case student self-assessment is important because CQI is focused on customer needs (Regan and Schmidt, 1999).

[34]Shuman et al., also list questions for research on the methodologies they listed that are particularly pertinent.

surveys (Chapter 2).[35] Several institutions have involved industry in the process of the assessment of programs and student learning (.e.g., McMartin and McGourty, 1999)[36]. Others have made site visits as part program assessment (Ramesh and Mattiuzzi, 2001). Some institutions appointed outside assessors to evaluate their evaluation processes. For example, McCreanor (2001) reported that an outside assessment process review team said of his engineering school's evaluation process that there was an over-reliance on surveys, and that student grades were an insufficient means of assessing the design and use of experimental techniques. Other institutions had appointed professionals to help with the process (Dabney et al., 2001).

In the United Kingdom George and Cowan (1999) also identified formative evaluation of the learning process either immediately after a learning experience or after a time elapse, repertory grid, interpersonal process recall, critical incidents, delphi, and a number of other techniques. Among these was the nominal group technique that was described in Section 11.7.

Clearly, some of these necessarily overlap with instruments that may be used for the formal assessment of learning. Other instruments have a role to play in formative evaluation. Other methodologies have been identified by Cowan and others in the United Kingdom. Some of them are considered below.

Authentic assessment is an umbrella term. According to Fischer and King (1995), it is an inclusive term for alternative assessment methods (i.e., to the traditional norm referenced tests) 'that examine student's ability to solve problems or perform tasks that closely resemble authentic situations.'. In engineering, 'authentic' implies 'real.' Since the drive in much engineering education has been to simulate 'real' life engineering, the assessments that have to be made are necessarily authentic. Thus, in engineering there is already substantial experience of authentic assessment because of the attempts to successfully validate project and laboratory work. Given a broad interpretation of the term 'real' to mean what is real to the student, authentic assessment would embrace portfolios and journals. Authentic assessment would also embrace competency/ability-based measures. Because these assessments can be used for grading they are discussed Chapter 16.

These particular authorities in their work on program assessment are following in the tradition of triangulation, which itself is in the tradition of psychometric testing. That is, the more you know about a person or process, the better the picture of that person or process. Thus, psychometric testers try, insofar as possible, to set a battery of tests. In engineering this can

be seen in the work of Freeman and his colleagues at Salford University (see Chapter 13). It is, therefore, surprising to find that in the above list there is no mention of psychometric tests, as for example, the MBTI, which has been widely used and valued in the United States. At Texas A & M University, the MBTI together with the *California Test of Critical Thinking*[37], the Hestenes' *Force Concept Inventory,* and *Mechanics Baseline Tests*[38] contributed to the program evaluation (Corleto, et al., 1996; see also Brown, Cross, and Selby, 1990).[39]

Seat, Parsons, and Poppen (1999) pointed out that the measurement of personal change is difficult and cannot be done by surveys, which will reveal cognitive responses to change rather than behavioral change.

Related to this is the intellectual development of learning. Much work has been done in one or two institutions in the United States to design courses on the basis of certain theories of intellectual development, as well as to implement and evaluate them. The importance of this dimension of learning and its implications both for teaching practice and curriculum design has yet to be understood by the academic community. It is by no means clear, for example, that the way in which teaching is conducted for curriculum levels in the United Kingdom corresponds to student levels of intellectual development, and the consequences that this may have for learning and performance.

As was noted in Chapter 4 concept maps, in addition to their use as vehicles for research and development, that is, in the understanding of student misperceptions and the design of the curriculum, may also be used for evaluation.

15.4.3. Student Attitudes, Experience, and Learning

15.4.3.1. Student Ratings and Surveys

Student ratings are the most researched dimension of teaching and learning in higher education. Of the more than 2000 papers that have been written on the subject, a few have come from engineering educators (e.g., Edwards, Favin and Teesdale, 1979). These ratings are considered to be of importance by legislators. There have also been attempts to develop standard questionnaires, as, for example, the Australian originated *Course Experience Questionnaire* (CEQ; Ramsden, 1991). This is a distinctly general instrument; in Australia it showed that there were statistically significant differences between institutions. It has also been used in the United Kingdom (Gibbs and Lucas, 1995). Yorke (1996), however, took a different view and thought that it would not apply in the United Kingdom. He developed an alternative instrument that had wider coverage than the CEQ.

---

[35]Volume 43, issue No. 2 of *IEEE Transactions on Education* is devoted to assessment and provides a good introduction for the non-American reader.

[36]In this respect the work of Alverno College, which trains and uses voluntary assessors for the assessment of student learning, is of interest (Mentkowski et al., 2000)

[37] Facione, P. A and N. C. Facione. *California Critical Thinking Test.* The California Academic Press: Millbrae, CA.

[38] Hestenes, D and M. Wells (1992).

[39] Unfortunately, no analysis is provided.

McBean (1991) undertook an evaluation of a 17-item teaching and course-rating scheme in the engineering school of the University of Waterloo. The items were evaluated on a five-point scale with the extremes being characterized by a statement appropriate to the questions asked. It was found that there was no correlation between averages of the six items on course evaluation and the global question (i.e.,, *What was your overall appraisal of this course?*). Because McBean found high correlations among the questions on teaching effectiveness, he argued that all that was necessary for the assessment of course effectiveness was the global question. McBean noted that the items needed to be uniformly graded, and at least one in his schedule required modification. Work among business students by Fox (2000) led to the conclusion that the less the rating scales and the more students could comment, the better. *"It is better to allow students to define their own appreciation of a course rather than impose an evaluation structure through detailed questions."*

An interesting approach to the evaluation of a course in mechatronics in Japan has been reported by Kaneda et al., (1999). They sought information about domains of cooperation, working, hardship, regret, pleasure, outcome for the student, and request. The concept of 'working' related to 'unfinished' because of dependency and shortage of time. 'Regret' related to unfinished project, tiredness, outcome to their study, and request for changes in aspects of the course (e.g., shorten lecture).[40]

Another technique that will involve the teacher in some reading and analysis is to ask the students to write a letter about the course to the next group of students. It should state what was attractive, what was unattractive, what was most important, and how best to study for the course (George and Cowan, 1999).

There may also be self-reports (i.e., perception measures) to enable teachers to see if students believe they have met the competencies required by the objectives of the course (Khan, 1999; see also Chapter 16). The need to demonstrate that ABET criteria are met forces this approach. Zhang (1998), for example, asked students in a senior engineering design course to read the EC 2000 criteria and then to write a learning essay on their experience of these criteria with the aid of an outcome assessment matrix. They were asked to rate themselves against the EC 2000 criterion 3 abilities on a five-point scale (substantial knowledge to very limited knowledge). The students indicated a rating for the first day in class, and they indicated another rating at some distant period when the evaluation took place. Others have used the same categories and used a graduated scale for understanding (e.g., Mourtos and Furman, 2002). Lickert or modified Lickert scales seem to be favourites in the engineering literature. A more simple approach is to asked the respondent to disagree or agree with a series of statements such as *"Engineers have lots of opportunities to be creative"* (Mourtos and Furman, 2002).

Attitudinal and self-assessment surveys are difficult to design, and they should be piloted, that is, tried out on an independent population. Sometimes, survey questionnaires contain questions that are biased. Minor changes in wording can lead to major changes in response. The ordering of questions can also influence the results. The context of the survey may also have profound effects. For example, evaluative judgments require representations of the object of judgment (target) and of a standard against which that judgment is evaluated. Both representations are context-dependent. In taking into account the effects of context, the investigator should remember *"that answers to survey questions are always problematic in meaning... there are several strategies that can help the investigator from being misled by response effects. One... is to use more than a single or small number of questions; to vary their format and wording in order to minimize, or at least be aware of a particular type of effect, and to look at the responses independently and not simply as interchangeable components in a scale"*(Schwartz, Groves, and Schuman, 1998).[41] One might, therefore, consider the inclusion of an (or a few) open-ended question(s).

A major problem relates to the length of the survey. Often they can be too long. Therefore, when designing a survey, it is important to be clear about the objectives that the investigator wishes to achieve. Each item can then, on a face validity basis prior to pilot testing, be judged against the likely reward it will produce in terms of those objectives.

For these reasons, institutions and their teachers may wish to use an inventory that has been established elsewhere that would seem to be contextually relevant. In engineering, a number of engineering schools have used the instrument developed at Pittsburgh for the study of student attitudes (Besterfield-Sacre, Atman, and Shuman, 1998). The same group also developed a questionnaire for (Besterfield-Sacre et al., 1997; McGourty et al., 1999). (See also Chapter 2 on alumni surveys). Texas A & M University are developing two questionnaires. One of these is intended to measure attitudes to competencies that are targeted in the freshman year. These are communication skills, integration of knowledge, life-long learning, technological skills, and teaming. The second inventory, *The Engineering Perception Test*, was designed for use as both a pre- and post-test. It measures pre-college experience. As a post-test, it was intended to measure student perceptions of their experience in the freshman year. It included scales for science/math preparation, self-appraisal, willingness to accept outside help, teaming perceptions and integration of knowledge (Graham and Caso, 2002). The measures are still in development.

---

[40]Unfortunately the text suffers from ambiguities in translation.

[41] There are many textbooks on educational and social research that deal with the design of attitudinal surveys. The short text by Schwarz, Groves, and Schuman provides an excellent introduction.

Shuman et al., (2001) noted that questionnaires were seldom used to track changes in student attitudes, and they argued for a development that could be used across institutions. There have, of course, been some major longitudinal studies in the United States (see below). It would be interesting to see if the Australian *Course Evaluation Questionnaire* (CEQ) is relevant in the American situation since it sets out to achieve that goal. Or do institutions have to develop their own instruments because of differences in cultures and objectives between institutions. Finally, Shuman et al., remind us that self-assessments of abilities are by no means reliable and such measures ought to be anchored in other perspectives. To put it in another way, course tests should be designed to assess the objectives of the course.

The lesson of Fox's (2000) work is that much can be learned from simple open-ended items. To some extent, this is supported by Gale et al., (2003), who used a 12 item course evaluation questionnaire among 181 course at the University of Colorado-Boulder found that the dominant item linked to instructor and course ratings was *"instructor accessibility"*. This item far outweighed items relating to course load and grade expectation. Similarly, Shuman et al., (2001) felt that open questions and structured interview together with focus groups might yield valuable information about the professional and ethical requirements of ABET 2000.

In the paragraphs that follow, non-survey techniques of eliciting information about learning are discussed.

15.4.4. Learning About Learning Difficulties Using Verbal Protocols

The verbal protocol work that Shuman et al., refer to is of a highly sophisticated nature; and because it requires a substantial amount of work it may be off-putting (Atman and Bursic, 1998). However, it is possible to reduce the workload very considerably when all that is required is a modest enquiry. George and Cowan (1999) included a description of an approach to the evaluation of CAL software. Three students were recruited on a voluntary basis, and it was made known to them that the findings would be anonymous.

"We began. I sat one student at the terminal, with the other two at her shoulder. I told her to go into the package after the last that she had used in the CAL lab. She should then work on just as she would usually do but talking out her thoughts and feelings aloud as she did so, rather as a police driver in training talks out observations and thoughts and actions to describe the task while driving through traffic. As an explanation, I quickly took the machine into the program that I began to follow illustrating what I was seeking as a style of commentary. I told her that she would work more slowly than usual, with this additional burden of providing a running commentary, but this was not to worry her."

"I asked the two other students to listen carefully, and try to understand what she was doing, and why. I asked them not to think about what they themselves would do, at any point in her progress; but to try to

understand her reasoning and priorities. In particular I charged the two observers to ask questions of the active student so that if she were to be called away to the telephone, one of the observers could sit down and carry on working with the materials just as she would have done.... I sat quietly in the background, and made note of anything that seemed significant."

"After 15–20 minutes, I got them to change places. Otherwise we followed the same procedure. I encouraged the second student to begin at the beginning and not to pick up where the first had left off. Then we changed for a third and last time, and did the same thing again."

Then, *"I reported that it had seemed to me that*

- *Certain points mattered strongly to at least one of you (and I listed examples, such as tediously repeated explanation, and a welcome feedback on inaccurate responses).*

- *There were points on which you disagreed, or worked or reacted in different ways [...]*

- *There were certain points or tasks or instructions that created problems for you, other than the difficulty of the material [...]*

- *These features of the program were the ones you praised or enthused about [...]"*[42]

The lists were discussed and, with the students' permission, passed anonymously to the course tutor; as a consequence, substantial changes in the style of the CAL materials were made. In subsequent enquiries of this type, Cowan (personal communication) summarized findings on a proforma which then went to the whole class, who quickly responded to each on a 4-point scale ranging from strongly agree to strongly disagree and then, in an open-ended response, added statements to describe significant features of their approach which had not been mentioned.

Studies of this kind could be paralleled with automatic monitoring of the kind described by Brockman (1996; see Chapter 12, Section 9). Rahkila and Karjalainen (1999) of Helsinki University of Technology have also described a system of logging. From the teachers point of view, the value of a logging system is that it can provide answers to the questions:

- *How much time would the students spend with it?*
- *How much material would they go through?*
- *In which order would the students study the topics?*
- *Are there pages/topics that students would spend a lot more time on than others?*
- *Are there pages/topics that students would skip?*
- *What is the average time students spend on the application or page?*
- *Would the students take the default path or would they use the possibility to study the topics in some other order?*

While answers to these questions give some insight into program design, they do not account for why?

---

[42]George and Cowan give some examples of what was found in the text.

An alternative is to observe the students testing a package.

At Loyola College, Baltimore, observers who were undertaking a class in various measurements in the social sciences were recruited to observe students testing a web-based package. The students also completed a navigation questionnaire, a conceptual test of learning effectiveness, and a lab report. The observers completed a usability survey and also provided a summary. The investigators found that the best source of information was the observers' reports. In both of these experiments it would have been interesting to see what additional information a verbal protocol would have provided.

15.4.5. Interpersonal Process Recall.

This is a technique that has its origins in the training of counselors. It has been used with first year students in The United Kingdom Open University. It can only be used with agreement of the tutor and students. It involves the videoing of a teacher giving a tutorial. The camera is focused on the tutor. At the end of the tutorial, some students are asked to spend about twenty minutes 'unpacking' their experience. The exercise begins with the student observing a replay of a part of the videotape. The tape is stopped every twenty seconds, or when the student's expression indicates that something interesting was happening. At each pause the interviewer asks the student what feelings or thoughts they were recalling. The interviewer tries to take notes. One could do this with more than one student, and this might require more than one interviewer.

George and Cowan (1999) described one such exercise. They described how the tutor chatted with the students as the class assembled. When the class was settled, the tutor gave a summary of the main points that had emerged in a 'warm-up' period. They focused on this summary because they thought it would be endorsed as effective practice. On the contrary; the summary had created frustration because it stimulated more ideas and questions. The interviewers found that the students would not have dreamt of telling the tutor this because they were appreciative of the effort that he put into the tutorial. This information caused the tutor to ask in later warm ups if there were further questions. These were dealt with before new topics were introduced.

15.4.6. The Repertory Grid Technique

The repertory grid technique is also useful in understanding student learning, and in deriving questionnaires. The technique is based on Kelly's personal construct psychology. This theory is based on the model of a person as scientist. A person's actions are determined by how they classify and interpret their environment; different people may anticipate different events and formulate different modes for anticipating similar events. The repertory grid is a technique that was devised to discover a person's perceptions of that environment. It has been widely used in organizations. Apart from its use in deriving questionnaires, it may be of considerable value in helping individuals to understand

their learning processes. It also has the capability to yield the unexpected because it can probe deeply into a person's experience (Easterby-Smith, 1994).

The features of the grid are:

1. A set of elements which are the things, people, or situations to be examined.
2. A set of constructs that are pairs of statements used by the respondent to compare and contrast the elements selected.
3. A linking mechanism, normally ticks or crosses or a series of rating scales which demonstrate how each of the elements are construed on each of the constructs obtained. In this way a grid is constructed.

Easterby-Smith gives the following example of the first two features. The activity is to consider three makes of motor vehicle. *"Ford, Volvo and Honda. These would constitute a set of three elements One of the most common ways of obtaining constructs is to derive them from three such elements (known as triading) by deciding in what way two of the elements are similar to each other, and yet different from the third. This should produce a word or phrase describing the similarity between the pair, and a contrasting word or phrase describing what it is that makes the third one distinct from the initial pair. Thus one person might look at these three elements and decide that Ford and Volvo are most alike in that they are European car manufacturers, whereas Honda is different in being a Japanese manufacturer of cars. Another person might consider the triad and decide that Ford and Honda were most alike in having lower prices, whereas Volvo has an image of being expensive."*

As explained in Chapter 2 (Section 2.5) Youngman et al., (1978) used a modification of this technique to derive a checklist from the way in which the engineers they analyzed anticipated their work. Each engineer was encouraged to isolate what to him were the significant parts of work and to describe them in terms of behavior, operations, or activities, and this he could do by contrasting his work with that done by others with whom he worked. As with the Tichon and Seat study, the engineers determined the content of the interview. The interviews ranged in time from thirty minutes to two hours. The list of operations was derived from the transcriptions of these interviews.

George and Cowan (1999) considered that the repertory grid had considerable potential in situations where *"students carry out their own analyses, and report, from snowball or pyramid groups, the range of constructs which they have identified."* In their book they give an account of its use by Weedon (1994), who wanted to discover reactions to the comments she added to submitted written work.[43]

15.4.7. Critical Incidents

A critical incident is something unusual (a discontinuity or exceptional circumstance), that is recorded in order to

---

[43]For a study of the role of confidence of teachers teaching design and technology to girls in England that uses the repertory grid method, see Davies (2000).

understand the reality of normal behavior. It can help to identify issues and events and provide illustrations of behavior but it can only use a very small sample of the total range of incidents. The technique was used in the Herzberg studies of motivation (Easterby-Smith, 1994). It has been widely used in industry for the study of unsafe acts (Sanders and McCormick, 1987), and, it has been used to study the work of Principals and Post holders in schools in Ireland.

It is also used as the basis for journals (see Chapter 16). They have been used in the evaluation of programs at the University of Texas-El Paso, as a method for answering evaluation questions. For example, the evaluation question *"What are the essential elements of good student-faculty mentor relationship in computer science?"* Is established by a critical incident questionnaire *"that asks students to describe when program activities worked well and when they did not"* (Della-Piana and Bernat, 1999).

Critical incidents may be obtained by questionnaires, and by observations of classroom activities.

15.4.8. Focus Groups.

Focus groups are used to discover opinions and feeling about a given question. Denton and McDonagh (2003) wrote that a *"focus group is an umbrella term. It centre on a gathering of target users brought together for relatively informal discussion on a specific topic or issue. A Chairperson (moderator) using a flexible schedule of questions (the moderator's draft), promotes discussion, while carefully ensuring not to direct, but guide the group through issues that emerge as important to them. A variety of techniques can be used to promote discussion."* In the case of product design *"an obvious technique is to have examples of products available for direct handling."* Focus groups can, for example, be used to evaluate student questionnaires during their design phase. George and Cowan suggested that they could be used to:

- *Identify and confirm issues.*
- *Develop emerging themes and concerns.*
- *Articulate concerns or generate hypotheses.*
- *Expand and illuminate quantitative feedback.*
- *Develop courses or student support in a learner directed way.*
- *Get feedback on interim interpretations of findings from other sources.*

Richards and Rogers (1996) reported their successful use in the evaluation of a new sophomore engineering program. The focus groups, yielded among other things, that the winter quarter of the course was heavily overloaded. At the same time they were *"very positive about the availability of the faculty."*

Denton and McDonagh (2003) reported a five-year action research project that explored two innovations.[44] These were:

---

[44]They followed the principles for focus groups suggested by Cohen, Mannion, and Morrison (2000).

"1. The training of student designers in the management of focus groups. The aim is to bring the user-focus into the design team and design process itself.
2. The Employment of focus group methodologies at several points within the design process rather than only at the beginning. This allows designers to explore the reaction to ideas at various stages within the development process."

Among the outcomes was the development of a protocol for focus group work that is published in full in their paper.

The first case study was based on protocols that had been established by market researchers with the purpose of enabling a designer to gather data suitable for future design work. In the second case study the same protocol was used by an undergraduate design student in a focus group of users in order to help with the generation of concepts and the development of a product. This approach was replicated in a third project with two recently graduated designers. *"Initially a focus was established to provide pre-design phase data. Subsequently the group was used to gain feedback on initial design concepts. In parallel, a new focus group was formed (i.e., members not sensitised to the project). The intention here was to examine how this group (cold users) responded in relation to the first group (not users). These groups met a total of four times throughout the project, to provide feedback at specific points in the project."*

Apart from the protocol that was developed, Denton and McDonagh concluded that focus groups could be used in the planning stage for pre-design concept generation/selection, concept development, and concept refinement.

They found that members of groups can become too interested in the outcomes of the project a consequence of which was that their feedback might be biased. If new members are introduced to the group new insights may be gained. In design terms this might mean an additional work cost. Experienced designers could benefit from such exposure.

Focus groups are not a panacea, but they can encourage user-centered design and designers may "broaden their own empathic horizons" as they bring designers into much closer contact with users than other methods. Similarly, in universities and schools, focus groups have the potential to improve design studies although if they are not handled wisely they can generate much superficial data. They may be particularly useful in helping students to understand topics that are poorly understood. But for focus groups to be both efficient and effective, moderators need to be trained. Samples have to be carefully chosen, and if volunteers are used the success of the group will depend on their good will.

15.4.9. The Delphi Technique

In Section 7.2, reference was made to a program in engineering that was designed for the Vice-Chancellor of the University of Lancaster by a group of educators and industrialists. In order to get agreement among a group who found it difficult to meet prior to and following a symposium on the topic, the lead writer drafted a model curriculum. This was circulated to each individual. It was then revised and circulated as before. When agreement was reached the curriculum was presented to the Vice-Chancellor (Heywood et al., 1966). This procedure is known as a delphi technique. (Linstone and Turoff, 1975).George and Cowan have suggested how this technique might be used to evaluate a course. Their approach involves an evaluator who is independent of the teaching team. Suppose that the course to be evaluated is part of a distance learning program. The evaluator would ask each student to send her the strengths and weaknesses of the course and to indicate suggestions for the next course. The responses are then collated and the summaries sent out for vetting. That is, agreement, corrections and omissions. The summary is then revised and circulated once more.

Strevelor et al., (2003) have described how they used the Delphi technique to reach a consensus among a group of experienced engineering faculty about the difficulty and importance of fundamental concepts in thermal and transport sciences.[45]

Although it is time consuming, it has the advantage of being anonymous and comprehensive.

15.4.10. T-Groups

T groups were popular in management training in the 1960s (Whitaker, 1965), and one or two engineering educators practiced them (Bartee, 1967; South, 1969). Argyris was a major proponent of them in his work on organizations (Argyris, 1999). They were developed as means for studying group dynamics and are in the tradition established by Kurt Lewin (1951).

Apart from the understanding of group behavior through the observation of behavior in an unstructured situation the T-Group, or at least an adaptation of the idea, can be used for evaluation. When it is used for training, it is unstructured so that the group members are free of authority and regulation, insofar as that is possible. Bartee (1967) took the view that the objective was learning how to learn. Thus, at the first meeting of the class, Bartee asked his students to *"conduct the course, complete it, and provide a grade for each student."* In the early sessions he refused to be either instructor or leader. As the sessions progressed, they became less tendentious. There were fewer chaotic periods of group conflict.   Bartee described the early sessions as follows: *"the individuals and the group initially experience great anxiety and conflict because of the relative absence of authority and regulation. The individuals experienced ambiguous relationships with other members of the group, because each of them had a different idea of what was appropriate. The result was that the students became anxious, even though they did not realize this or understand it. In one sense, the student was faced with an identity crisis or a problem of social*

survival as he tried conventional methods of group relationship that consistently failed. He found himself thrust into a leaderless, rule less situation that proved to be very strange and most frustrating."

"Some students responded to the situation by attempting to distribute the power or control that the instructor refused to assume. An individual would find out how much control he could gain and how much he had to give up. He often became tense and anxious when he could not maintain as much control as he felt that he needed. Each member of the group had different needs and different concepts of what the group goal should be. If the group moved in a direction or goal to which an individual did not wish to commit himself, he often withdrew or sabotaged the group."

As indicated, things got much better and the response from students was positive.

An adaptation of this approach was used to evaluate an in-company training course in the British Steel Corporation by Humble and this writer. Eleven persons who had attended a one-week course for managers were asked to participate in a one week evaluation at a residential university. These individuals were all in management posts but had a variety of qualifications and duties. The question for evaluation was whether such courses could meet the needs of such a diverse group of personnel. When the discussion began it seemed that there were few points of agreement. During the week, however, they began to try and define the objectives of the course and by the end of the week they had come to the conclusion that there was a common set of objectives that met their needs. In this process, they had moved from perceptions that were governed by their needs and experiences to a more objective view of what the company required and found that to a large extent it had met their needs (Heywood, 1970).

15.5.   Longitudinal Surveys

There have been a few longitudinal studies in the United States, the major lead, in this respect, coming from Felder et al., (1993, 1994) Felder, (1995a) Felder (1995b), and Felder, (1998), who compared alternative teaching programs. Following in this tradition, the Office of Institutional Research at Embery-Riddle Aeronautical University evaluated a new integrated curriculum in engineering. In addition to quantitative data about rates of retention etc., students were surveyed for their reactions (attitudes) to the program. Watret and Martin (2002) summarized data from that component of the research. The University had experienced very high failure rates in physics and calculus in the freshman year. Having studied other programs it decided to connect mathematics and physics and to incorporate a common technology into each course. The examinations would integrate maths and physics through the solution of engineering problems, and the students were encouraged to take responsibility for their learning through active learning and cooperation. The study reported followed a cohort through four years, and the student questionnaire was designed to see if the specific goals of the course had been met. Some

---

[45] They also cite Adler and Ziglio (1966) and Dalkey and Helmer, (1973).

comparative data are given for a class that started four years later. The data showed that, compared with a control group of students in traditional courses, the new course had higher retention rates, and a significantly higher number of students from the new course remained in aeronautical engineering.

Felder's longitudinal study included measures of psychological type. He and his colleagues were able to obtain responses from students who were in both traditional and nontraditional courses. While they were not able to verify the relative levels of mastery of content and high level skills, and while some of the positive effects that were observed among non-traditional students might have been due to the Hawthorne effect, they argued that: *"positive results can be expected if an instructor teaches in a way that integrates theory and practice rather than proceeding deductively from theory to practice, and if the students are required to work with, earn from, and teach one another rather then relying on the instructor as the sole source of information".* (Felder's studies are summarized in Felder et al., 1997).

The study would seem to support the view of studies in other sectors of education that students respond best in circumstances where there a variety of instructional strategies are used. Of such is the value of longitudinal studies. It has also been argued that good teaching should encourage a Hawthorne effect.

15.6.   Concluding Remarks

Most of the comments above have been concerned with methodologies for evaluating student learning. It is clear that single measures are often inadequate for many evaluation tasks and that multiple measures are likely to be more informative. Numerous measures are available, particularly at the level of the classroom. Many of them are qualitative. Depending on the type of qualitative research, there may be problems of objectivity, that is, the imposition of one's own assumptions on the interpretation of the data. It is also clear that formative evaluation is as important as Summative evaluation.

It is equally clear that institutions can influence change. Their structures and organization can have a benign effect on innovation or they can impede organization. Part of the task of the evaluator is to sort out the contradictions, *'competing stories'* as they have been called, that exist in the organization.

A brief mention was made of the work of the Foundation Coalition in trying to understand change. The investigators found that change is a complex process. It is important that evaluations of change continue in order that those who have to implement change can plan that change. Among the factors that enhance or impede change are the teachers that comprise the community in which change is sought. Therefore, measurements of teacher attitudes are as important as the measurement of student attitudes (Felder et al., 1998). Unless there is strong leadership, teacher values can lead to loss of support in areas that they see a peripheral, as, for example, ethics and professional responsibility. Steneck

(1999) thought that the support for his program in ethics could diminish because of competition with other parts of the program as the program was re-engineered.

It is appropriate to end this Chapter with a quotation from Prey (1999) of the University of Virginia who wrote; *"In order for a course or curriculum project to be successful, the evaluation process must also be successful. It must be carefully thought out at the very beginning of the project, implemented with the same enthusiasm as the actual content development and implementation, and executed continuously throughout the life of the project."*

References

Adamson, J., and H. Clifford (2002). A level university examination results for engineering undergraduates. *International Journal of Mechanical Engineering Education* 30, (3), 265–279.

Adler, M., and E. Ziglio (1966) (eds.) Gazing into the oracle: *The Delphi Method nd its Application to Social Policy and Public health.*

Ahlgren, D. J., and J. L. Palladino (2000). Developing assessment tools for ABET EC 2000. *Proceedings Frontiers in Education Conference*, 1 T1A-17 to-22.

Angelo, T., and K. P. Cross. (1993). *Classroom Assessment.* Jossey Bass, San Francisco.

Argyris, C. (1999) *On Organizational Learning.* Blackwell, Oxford.

Ashworth, P., and U. Lucas (2000) Achieving empathy and engagement: a practical approach to the design, conduct and reporting of phenomenographic research. *Studies in Higher Education,* 25, (3), 295–308.

Astin, A. W. (1974) Measuring the outcomes of Higher Education *in* H. R. Bowen (ed.) *Evaluating institutions for Accountability. New Directions for Institutional Research* Jossey Bass, San Francisco.

Atman, C. J., Adams, R. S., and J. Turns (2000). Using multiple methods to evaluate freshmen design course. *Proceedings Frontiers in Education Conference*, 1, S1A-6 to 13.

Atman, C. J., and K. M. Bursic (1998). Verbal protocol analysis as a method to document engineering student design. *Journal of Engineering Education*, 1–12. Special issue on Assessment.

Avers, C. D (1999) Criteria 2000: lessons learned. *The Interface* (IEEE/ASEE) No 2. August.

Bartee, E. M (1967). T- Group Methods in engineering education. *Engineering Education* 58, (2) 159–160.

Baskerville, R. L et al (1996) A critical perspective on action research as a method for information systems research. *Journal of Information Technology*, 11, 235–246.

Besterfield Sacre, N., Amaya, N. Y., Shuman, L. J., Atman, C. J., and R. L. Porter (1998). Understanding student confidence as it relates to first year achievement. *Proceedings Frontiers in Education Conference*, 1, 258–263.

Besterfield-Sacre, M. E., Atman, C. J., and L. J. Shuman (1998) Engineering student attitudes assessment . *Journal of Engineering Education*, 87, (2), 133-141.

Besterfield-Sacre, M. E., Atman, C. J., Shuman, L. J. and H. Wolfe (1997). Development of customer-based outcome measures for an engineering program. *Annual Conference Proceedings American Society for Engineering Education*, 16–18 (CD-ROM)

Blake, M. B (2003) Iterative processing algorithms to detect biases in assessments. *IEEE Transactions on Education.* 46, (1), 124-132.

Boud, D. (1979). Engineering success: the progress and problems of a higher education development project. *Studies in Higher Education,* 4, (1), 55–66.

Boyd, D. W (1978). A formula method for assigning letter grades. *Engineering Education*, 69, (2), 207–210.

Brockman, J. B (1996). Evaluation of student design processes. *Proceedings Frontiers in Education Conference*, 189–193.

Brouse, S (1999). Senior design project. ABET 2000 certification. *Proceedings Frontiers in Education Conference*, 11b2–1 to 6.

Brown, N., W., Cross, E. J., and G. V. Selby (1990). Personality of students persisting in engineering-comparisons and implications for instruction. *Proceedings Frontiers in Education Conference*, 165–167.

Brown, R (2001). Multi-choice versus descriptive examinations. *Proceedings Frontiers in Education Conference*, 1, T3A–13 to 18.

Burgoyne, J. G (1975). The judgement process in management students' evaluation of their learning experiences. *Human Relations*, 28, (6), 543–569.

Cllan, W. R. et al (1995) Statistical anaylsis of students' performance in new engineering science core courses with economic and design concepts. *Proceedings Frontiers in Education Conference*, 3c3–1 to 4.

Campbell, D. T., and J. C. Stanley (1966) *Experimental and Quasi Experimental Design for Research*, Rand McNally, Chicago.

Carlson, L. E., Yost, S. A., Krishnan, M., and S. Das (2000). Outcomes-based assessment for comprehensive curriculum development in mechatronics. *Proceedings Frontiers in Education Conference*, 1, T4A–1 to 5.

Carter, G., and J. Heywood (1992) The value-added performance of electrical engineering students in a British University. *International Journal of Technology and Design Education*, 2, 1, 4–14.

Carter, G., Heywood., J., and D. T. Kelly (1986) *A Case Study in Curriculum Assessment. GCE Engineering Science (Advanced)*. Roundthorn, Manchester.

Carter, G and L. S. Lee (1975). University first year electrical engineering examinations. *International Journal of Electrical Engineering Education*, 11, 149.

Chan, S. F (1997). Quality assurance in project supervision within tertiary distance education. *Engineering Science and Education Journal*, 6, 188–194.

Che, X (1999) Development of an on-line teaching portfolio for freshman design. *Proceedings Frontiers in Education Conference*, 13b1–26 to 30.

Church, C. H (1988). The qualities of validation. *Studies in Higher Education*, 13, (1), 27–44.

Clear, T., and M. Daniels (2000). Using groupware for international collaborative learning. *Proceedings Frontiers in Education Conference*, 2, F1C – 18 to 23.

Cohen, L., Manion, L., and K. Morrison (2000). *Research Methods in Education*. Routledge, London.

Corleto, C. R., Kimball, J. L., Tipton, A. R., and R. A. MacLauchlin (1996). Foundation coalition integrated engineering curriculum at Texas A & M University- Kingsville. Development, implementation and assessment. *Proceedings Frontiers in Education Conference*, 2, 1141–1145.

Cross, K. P., and M. Steadman (1996). *Classroom Research*. Jossey Bass, San Francisco.

CVCP (1969) *The Assessment of Undergraduate Performance*. Committee of Vice-Chancellors and Principals, London.

Dabney, S., Creighton, R. L., Johnson, J. P., and E. Ernst (2001).A comprehensive system for student program assessment: lessons learned. *International Journal of Engineering Education*, 17 (1), 81–87.

Dalkey, N., and O. Helmer (1963) An experimental application of the Delphi method to the use of experts, *Management Science*. 9, 458-467.

Davies, T (2000). Confidence! Its role in creative teaching and learning of design and technology. *Journal of Technology Education*, 12, (1), 18–31.

Del Cerro, G et al (2001). Assessing communication modes in design project teams. *Proceedings Frontiers in Education Conference*. 1, T2G–5 to 12.

Della-Piana, C. K and A. Bernat (1999). Evaluating the undergraduate research experience in computer science: developing a framework for gathering information about the effectiveness of impact. *Proceedings Frontiers in Education Conference*. 13c7 –6 to 10.

Denton, H., and D. McDonagh (2003). Using focus group methods to improve students' design project research in schools: drawing parallels from action research at undergraduate level. *International Journal of Technology and Design Education*, 13, 139–144.

Denzin, N. K., and Y. S. Lincoln (1994*). Handbook of Qualitative Research*. Sage, Thousand Oaks, CA.

Duerden, S et al (1997). Trendy technology or a learning tool? Using electronic journal on Webnotes TM for curriculum integration in the freshman program in engineering at ASU. *Proceedings Frontiers in Education Conference*, 3, 1549–1556.

Duerden, S., and J. Garland (1998) Goals, objectives, and performance criteria: A useful assessment tool for students and teachers. *Proceedings Frontiers in Education Conference* 2, 773–777.

Easterby-Smith, M (1994). *Evaluating Management Development, Training and Education*. 2nd Edition. Gower, Aldershot.

Edwards, P., Favin, S., and J. Teesdale (1979). Evaluation of educational programs: Why? How? By whom? *Proceedings Frontiers in Education Conference*, 323–329.

Felder, R. M (1995b) A longitudinal study of engineering student performance and retention. IV. Instructional methods and student responses to them. *Journal of Engineering Education* 84, (4), 361–367.

Felder, R. M., Felder, G. N., and E. J. Dietz (1997) A longitudinal study of alternative approaches to engineering education: survey of assessment results. *Proceedings Frontiers in Engineering Education*, 3, 1284–1289.

Felder, R. M et al (1993) A longitudinal study of engineering student performance and retention I. Success and failure in the introductory course. *Journal of Engineering Education*, 82, (1), 15 –21.

Felder, R. M., Mohr, P. H., Dietz, E. J., and L. Baker-Ward (1994) A longitudinal study of engineering student performance and retention. II Differences between students from urban and rural backgrounds. *Journal of Engineering Education* 83, (3), 209–217.

Felder, R. M et al (1995a). A longitudinal study of engineering student performance and retention. III Gender differences in student performance and attitudes. *Journal of Engineering Education* 4, (2), 151 – 174.

Felder, R. M. et al (1998). Faculty teaching practices and perceptions of institutional attitudes toward teaching at eight engineering schools. *Proceedings Frontiers in Education Conference*, 101–106.

Feldman, M. F and J. G. March (1981). Information in organizations as symbol and signal. *Administrative Science Quarterly*, 26, 171–186.

Fischer, C. F. and R. M. King (1995). *Authentic Assessment: A guide to Implementation*. Sage, Thousand Oaks, CA.

Fox, R (2000) From quantitative to qualitative assessment: evaluating student questionnaires of teaching effectiveness. In J. Heywood, J. Sharp and M. Hides (eds.) *Improving Teaching in Higher Education*. University of Salford, Salford.

Frair, L (1995). Student peer evaluations using the analytic hierarchy process method. *Proceedings Frontiers in Education Conference*, 4c3–1 to 5.

Freeman, J., and P. Byrne (1976) *Assessment of Post-Graduate Training in General Practice*. 2nd edition. Society for Research into Higher Education, London.

Freeman, J., Carter, G., and T. A. Jordan (1978). Cognitive styles, personality factors, problem solving skills and teaching approach in electrical engineering. *Assessment in Higher Education*, 3, 86.

Gale, K., Knight, D. W., Carlson, L. E. and J. F. Sullivan (2003). Making the grade with strudents: the case of accessibility. *Journal of Engineering Education*, 92, (4), 337–444.

George, J., and J. Cowan (1999). *A Handbook of Techniques for Formative Evaluation*. Kogan Page, London.

George, N., Craven, M., Williams-Myers, C., and P. Bonnick (2003). Using action research to enhance teaching and learning at the University of Technology Jamaica. *Assessment and Evaluation in Higher Education*, 28, (3), 239–250.

Gibbs, G. and L. Lucas (1995). Research to Improve Student Learning in large Classes. International Improving Student learning Symposium. Mimeo.

Glaser, B. G. and A. E. Strauss (1967*). The Discovery of Grounded Theory. Strategies for Qualitative Research*. Aldin, Chicago.

Graham, J. M and R. Caso (2002). Measuring engineering freshman attitudes and perceptions of their first year academic experience: the continuing development of two assessment instruments. *Proceedings Frontiers in Education Conference*, 2, F3B-6 to11.

Greeno, J, et al (1993). Transfer of situated learning in Detterman and Sternberg (eds). *Transfer on Trial*. Ablex Publishing, NJ.

Guba, E. G (1969). The failure of educational evaluation. *Educational Technology*, , 29–38.

Hamilton, D., Jenkins, D., King, C., Macdonald, B and M. Parlett (1977). (eds.). *Beyond the Numbers Game*. Macmillan, London.

Harré, R (1977)The ethogenic approach: theory and practice in L. Berkowitz (ed.). *Advances in Experimental Social Psychology*. Vol 10. Academic Press, New York.

Harris, R. H., and M. F. Cox (2003) Developing and observation system to capture instructional differences in engineering education. *Journal of Engineering Education*, 92, (4), 329-336.

Hartle, T, T. W (1986) The growing interest in measuring educational achievement of college students. In C. Adelman (ed). *Assessment in Higher Education*. US Department of Education, Washington, DC.

Helfers, C., Duerden, S., Garland, J., and D. Evans (1999). An effective peer revision method for engineering students in first-year English courses. *Proceedings Frontiers in Education Conference*, 3, 13a6–7 to 12.

Hesseling, P (1966). *A Strategy for Evaluation Research*. Van Gorcum. Aassen.

Hestenes, D., and M. Wells (1992) A mechanics baseline test. *The Physics Teacher*. 30, 159-162.

Heywood, J (1969) An Evaluation of certain Post-War developments in Higher technological Education. Thesis. 2 volumes. University of Lancaster, Lancaster.

Heywood, J (1970). Paper at Symposium on Creativity in Engineering. Council of Engineering Institutions and Aston University.

Heywood, J (1992).Student teachers as researchers of instruction in the classroom. In J. H. C. Vork and H. J. van Heleden..*New Prospects for Teachers* Association for Teachers Education in Europe, Brussels.

Heywood, J (2000). *Assessment in Higher Education. Student learning, Teaching, Programs and Institutions*. Jessica Kingsley, London.

Heywood, J. and H. Montagu Pollock (1977). *Science for Arts Students. A Case Study in Curriculum Development*. Society for Research into Higher Education, London.

Heywood, J et al (1966) The Education of Professional Engineers for Design and Manufacture: A model Curriculum. *Lancaster Studies in Higher Education*. 1, 5-152.

Hoepfl, M. C (1997). Choosing qualitative research: a primer for technology education researchers. *Journal of Technology Education*, 9, (1), 47–63.

Huberman, A .M., and M. B. Miles (1994). Data management and analysis methods in N K. Denzin and Y. S. Lincoln (eds). *Handbook of Qualitative Research*. Sage, Beverly Hills, CA.

Ingham, J., Meza, R. M. P., and G. Price (1998). A comparison of the learning style and creative talents of Mexican and American undergraduate engineering students. *Proceedings Frontiers in Education Conference*, 605–610.

Jamieson, L. H., Oakes, W. C., and E. J. Coyle (2001). EPICS: documenting service learning to meet EC 2000. *Proceedings Frontiers in Education Conference*, 1, T2A- 1 to 6.

Jones, E. E (1998). Major developments in five decades of social psychology. In Gilbert, D. T., Fiske, S. T. and G. Lindzey (eds). *Handbook of Social Psychology*. Vol. 1. 4th edition. McGraw Hill, New York.

Kaneda, T., Fujisawa, S., Yoshida, T, Yoshitani, Y, Nishi, T., and K. Hiroguchi (1999). Making music performance robots and their ensemble. *Proceedings Frontiers in Education Conference* 2, 12b4-1 to 6.

Khan, H (1999). Integration of robust 3D modelling software into the design curriculum. *Proceedings Frontiers in Education Conference*, 2, 12d2—24 to 29.

Kember, D., and I. McKay (1996). Action research into the quality of student learning. A paradigm for faculty development. *Journal of Higher Education*, 67, (5), 528–554.

Larpkiataworn, S et al (2003). Special considerations when using statistical analysis in engineering education assessment and evaluation. *Journal of Engineering Education*, 92, (3), 207–218.

LeBold, W. K. and S. K. Ward (1995). 25 years of frontiers educational research: the call for action-oriented research. *Proceedings Frontiers in Education Conference* 2b3–1 to 7

Lee, R. M (1993). *Doing Sensitive Research*. Sage, Thousand Oaks, CA.

Lewin, K (1951). *Field Theory in Social Sci*ence. Harper, New York.

Leydens, J. A., Moskal, B. M. and M. J. Pavelich (2004). Qualitative methods used in the asssessment of engineering education. *Journal of Engineering Education*, 93, (1), 65–72.

Lin, H (1979). The hidden curriculum of the introductory physics class. *Engineering Education*. 70, (3), 289-294

Linstone, H. A., and M. Turoff (1975) (eds.) *The Delphi Techniques and Applications*. Addison Wesley, Reading, MA.

Madaus, G, F., and T. Kellaghan (1992). Curriculum evaluation and assessment. In P. Jackson (ed.). *Handbook of Research on Curriculum*. AERA/Macmillan, New York.

Martin, J. A., Armstrong, J. E., and J. L. Keys (1999) Elements of an optimal capstone design experience. *Journal of Engineering Education*. (1), 19-22.

Marsh, H (1988) Accreditation in practice. Report of a seminar (April) at the Institution of Mechanical Engineers, London.

Marton, F et al (1976). On qualitative 1. Outcomes and Process 2. Outcomes as a function of Learners task. *British Journal of Educational Psychology*, 46.4-11 and 115-127.

Marton, F., and R Säljö (1976). On qualitative differences in learning. *British Journal of Educational Psychology*, 46.

McBean, E. A (1991). Analyses of teaching and course questionnaires: case study. *Engineering Education*, 81, (4), 439–442.

McCreanor, P. T (2001). Quantitatively assessing an outcome on designing and conducting experiments and analysing data for ABET 2000. *Proceedings Frontiers in Education Conference*, 1, t2A–12 to 16.

McGourty, J., Besterfield-Sacre, M., Shuman, L. J., and H. Wolfe (1999). Improving academic programs by capitalizing on alumni's perceptions and experiences. *Proceedings Frontiers in Education Conference*, 3, 13a5–9 t o 15.

McGourty, J., Sebastian, C., and W. Swart (1998) Development of a comprehensive assessment program in engineering education. *Journal of Engineering Education*, 87, (4), 355-361.

McKenna, A., MacMartin, F., Terada, Y., Sirivedhin, V and A. Agogino (2001). Paper 1330. Annual Conference Proceedings of the American Society for Engineering Education.

McMartin, F., and J. McGourty (1999). Involving Industry in the assessment process. Preliminary findings. *Proceedings Frontiers in Education Conference*, 3, 13a5 2 to 8.

Mentokowski et al (2000). *Learning that Lasts*. Jossey Bass, San Francisco.

Meisalo, V., Sutinen, E and S. Torvinen (2003). Choosing appropriate methods for evaluating and improving the learning process in distance programming courses. *Proceedings Frontiers in Education Conference*, 1, T2B–11 to 16.

Merton, P., Clark, C., Richardson, J., and J. Froyd (2001).Engineering curricular change across the foundation coalition: potenital lessons from qualitative research. *Proceedings Frontiers in Education Conference*, F4B–15 to 20.

Meyer, D. G (1997) A criteria based course and instructor evaluation system: recent experiences in development and utilization. *Proceedings Frontiers in Education Conference*, 18–5192

Miller, R. L.,and B. M. Olds (1994). Encouraging critical thinking in an interactive chemical engineering laboratory environment. *Proceedings Frontiers in Education Conference*, 506–510.

Mourtos, N. J (1997). Portfolio assessment in aerodynamics. *Proceedings Frontiers in Education Conference* 91–94.

Mourtos, N. J., and B. J. Furman (2002). Assessing the effectiveness of an introductory engineering courses for freshmen. *Proceedings Frontiers in Education Conference*, 2, F3B–12 to 16.

Mutharasan, R., Magee, W., Wheatley, M., and Y. Lee (1997). Multimedia assisted instruction in upper level engineering courses. *Proceedings Frontiers in Education Conference*, 2, 1175–1178.

NGA (1986). *The Governors 1991 Report on Education*. National Governors Association, Washington, DC.

Parker, P. E. et al (2001). Differentiating assessment from evaluation as continuous improvement tools. *Proceedings Frontiers in Education Conference*, 1, T3A–1 to 6.

Parlett, M and D. Hamilton (1976) *Evaluation as illumination. A new approach to the study of innovatory programs*. In G. V. Glass (ed) Evaluation Studies Review Annual Vol 1. Sage, Beverley Hills.

Patton, M. L. and associates (1977) In search of impact: an analysis of the utilization of federal health evaluation research. In C. H. Weiss (ed). *Using Social Science Research in Public Policy Making*. D. C. Heath, Lexington, MA.

Pellegrino, J. W., Chudowsky, N., and R. Glaser (2001) (eds). *Knowing What Students Know. The Science and Design of Educational Assessment.* National Academy Press. Washington, DC.

Popov, A (2003). Final undergraduate project in engineering: towards more efficient and effective tutorials. *European Journal of Engineering Education,* 28, (1), 17–26.

Powers, T. A., Upchurch, R and S. L. Stokes (2003). Work in Progress. Using Assessment to improve teams in engineering education. *Proceedings Frontiers in Education Conference,* 3, S4D-7.

Prey, J. C (1999) Evaluation: What did it tell us? A review of the evaluation process of a new curriculum. *Proceedings Frontiers in Education Conference,* 13c7−11to5.

Radzienski, C., and K. Mitchell (2000). Different is good: barriers to retention for women in software engineering. *Proceedings Frontiers in Education Conference,* 2, F2F- 21 to 24.

Rahkila, M., and M. Karjalainen (1999). Evaluation of learning in computer based education using log systems. *Proceedings Frontiers in Education Conference,* 2, 12a3−16 to 21.

Ramesh, S. K., and C. Mattiuzzi (2001). Closing the loop: industry site visits for program outcomes assessment. *Proceedings Frontiers in Education Conference,* 1, T2A-7 to 10.

Ramsden, P (1991). A performance indicator of teaching quality in higher education: the course experience questionnaire. *Studies in Higher Education,* 16, (2), 129–150.

Reamon, D., and S. Sheppard (1996). Analytic problem solving methodology. Analytic problem solving methodology. *Proceedings Frontiers in Education Conference,* 484–488.

Regan, T. M. and J. A. Schmidt (1999) Student learning outcomes. Alumni, graduating seniors and incoming freshmen. *Proceedings Frontiers in Education Conference,* 3, 13a5−16 to 21.

Rhoads, T. R., Duerden, S. J., and J. Garland (1998). Views about writing survey- a new writing attitudinal survey applied to engineering students. *Proceedings Frontiers in Education Conference,* 973–979.

Rhoads, T. R., and R. J. Roedel (1999). The Wave Concept Inventory- A cognitive instrument based on Bloom's Taxonomy. *Proceedings Frontiers in Education Conference,* 3, 13c−14 to 18.

Richards, D. E., and G. M. Rogers (1996). A new sophomore engineering curriculum- the first year experience. *Proceedings Frontiers in Education Conference,* 1281–1284.

Rivlin, A. M (1971) *Systematic Thinking for Social Action.* Brookings Institution, Washington, DC.

Roedel, R. J., El Ghazaly, S., Rhoads, T. E. and E. El-Sharawy (1998). Wave Concepts Inventory- An assessment tool for courses in electromagnetic engineering. *Proceedings Frontiers in Education Conference,* 647–656,

Rogers, G. M., and J. K. Sando (1996). *Stepping Ahead: An Assessment Plan Development Guide.* Rose-Hulman Institute, Terre Haute, Indiana.

Roney, S. D., and D. R. Woods (2003) Ideas to minimise examination anxiety. *Journal of Engineering Education.* 92, (3), 249-256.

Sackman, H (1975) Delphi critique: Expert Opinions, Forecasting and Group Process. D. C. Heath, Lexington, MA.

Sanders, M. S., and E. J. McCormick (1987). *Human Factors in Engineering and Design.* 6th edition. McGraw Hill, New York.

Schachterle, L. (1999). Outcomes assessment and accreditation in AS engineering formation. *European Journal of Engineering Education,* 24, (2), 121–131.

Schwartz, N., Groves, R. M., and H. Schuman (1998) Survey methods. Ch 4 in D. T. Gilbert, S. T. Fiske and G. Lindzey 9eds). *The Handbook of Social Psychology.* Volume 1 4th edition. McGraw Hill, New York.

Seat, E., Parsons, J. R., and W. A. Poppen (1999) Engineering communication and performance minor. *Proceedings in Frontiers in Education Conference,* 3, 13a6-22 to 27.

Segers, M., and P. Dochy (2001). New assessment forms in problem-based learning: the value added of the students' perspective. *Studies in Higher Education,* 26 (3), 327–343

Shapiro, J. Z (1986). Evaluation research and Educational Decision making. A Review of the Literature. In J. C. Smart (ed) *Higher Education: Handbook of Theory and Research.* Volume 2. Agathon Press, New York.

Shuman, L. et al (2001). Matching assessment methods to outcomes: definitions and research questions. ASEE Annual Conference Session 3530.

Silver, H (1990) *A Higher Education. The Council for National Academic Awards and British Higher Education 1964 –1989.* Falmer, London.

Sims-Knight, J. E., Fowler, E., Pendergrass, N., and R. L. Upchurch (2000) Course-based assessment: engaging faculty in reflective practice. *Proceedings Frontiers in Education Conference,* 1, T3A−11 to 15.

South, O (1969). Experiments with T-groups in manager education for engineers. *Engineering Education* 59, (8), 953–956.

Srinivasan, S., Pérez, L. C., Palmer, R. D., Anderson, M. F., and A. John Boye (2003). Assessing laboratory effectiveness in electrical engineering courses. *Proceedings Frontiers in Education Conference,* 1, T2E-−5 to 9.

Stake, R. E (1967). The countenance of educational evaluation. *Teachers College Record,* 68, 523–540.

Steneck, N. H (1999) Designing teaching and assessment tools for an integrated engineering ethics curriculum. *Proceedings Frontiers in Education Conference,* 2, 12d6−11 to 17.

Steif, P. S (2003) Comparison between performance on a concept inventory and solving multi faceted problems, *Proceedings Frontiers in Education Conference,*T3D-17 to 22.

Storms, B. A., Sheingold, K., Nuzez, A. M. and J. I. Heller (1998). *The Feasibility, Comparability and Value of Local Scorings of Performance Assessments.* Educational Testing Service, Princeton, NJ.

Streveler, R. A. and R. L. Miller (2001). Investigating student misconceptions in the design process using multidimensional scaling. Session 2630. *Proceedings Annual Conference of the American Society for Engineering Education.* Nashville, TN.

Streveler, R. A., Olds, B., Miller, R. L., and N. A Nelson (2003). Using a Delphi study ti identify the most difficult concepts for students to master in thermal and transport science. *Proceedings American Society for Engineering Education Annual Conference.* Nashville, TN.

Stufflebeam, D. L (1969) Evaluation as enlightenment for decision making. In W. A. Beatty (ed) *Improving Educational Assessment and an Inventory of Measures of Affective Behavior.* Association for Supervision and Curriculum Development, Washington, DC.

Sullivan, W. G., Daghestani, S. F and H. R. Parsaei (1996) Multivariate analysis of student performance in large engineering economy classes. *Proceedings Frontiers in Education Conference,* 1, 180–184.

Thomas, E. W et al (1996). Using discriminant analysis to identify students at risk. *Proceedings Frontiers in Education Conference* 185–188.

Terenzini, P. T., Cabrera, a. F., Colbeck, C. L., Bjorklund, S. A., and J. M. Parente (2001) Racial and ethic diversity: Does it promote learning? *Journal of Higher Education.* 72, (5), 509-531.

Thuessen, G. J. et al (1992). The integration of economic principles with design in the undergraduate curriculum. *Proceedings Frontiers in Education Conference,* 373–378.

Tichon, M. A and E. Seat (2002). In their own word: the experience of older undergraduate students placed on engineering project teams with traditional first-year students. *Proceedings Frontiers in Education Conference,* 3, S3C− 6 to12.

Warren Piper, D (1994). *Are Professors Professional. The Organisation of University Examinations.* Jessica Kingsley, London.

Watret, J. R., and C. J. Martin (2002). Longitudinal assessment of the integrated curriculum in engineering (ICE). *Proceedings Frontiers in Education Conference,* 3, S1A- 6 to 11.

Weedon, E. M (1994). *An Investigation into using Self-Administered Kelly Analysis.* Project Report 94/5. Open University in Scotland, Edinburgh.

Weick, K. A (1995). *Sensemaking in Organizations. Perspectives on Corporate Transformation.* Oxford University Press, New York.

Weiss, C. H (1972). *Evaluation Research.* Prentice Hall, Englewood Cliffs, NJ.

Whitaker, G (1965). *T-Group Training.* ATM Occasional Papers, No 2. Blackwell, Oxford.

White, J (2000). The EPC model of defining the output standard of an engineering graduate. *Engineering Science and Education Journal.* August, 155 − 160.

Wilkinson, K. R., Finelli, C. J., Hynes, E., and B. Alzzahabi (2000). University-wide curriculum reform: two processes to aid in decision making. *Proceedings Frontiers in Education Conference,* 1, TA4- 6 to 11.

Woods, R. C., and K. L. Chan (2003) Comparison of two qualitative methods of determining rate bias. *Journal of Engineering education.* 92, (4), 295-306.

Yokomoto, C. F (2001). Design your outcomes assessment process as an exercise in open ended problem solving. *Proceedings Frontiers in Education Conference*, 3, S2F−1 to 6.

Yokomoto, C. F., Goodwin, C., and D. Williamson. (1998) Development of a school wide assessment plan – questions answered and questions raised. *Proceedings Frontiers in Education Conference*, 1 123 – 128.

Yorke, M (1996) *Indicators of Program Quality*. Higher Education Quality Council, Bristol.

Youngman, M. B., Oxtoby, R., Monk, J. D., and J. Heywood (1978). *Analysing Jobs*. Gower, Aldershot.

Zhang, G (1998) Information based engineering design *Proceedings Frontiers in Education Conference,* 2, 884–889.

Zuber-Skeritt, O (1992). *Action Research in Higher Education. Examples and Reflections.* Kogan Page, London.

CHAPTER 16: THE FORMAL ASSESSMENT OF STUDENT LEARNING: ALTERNATIVE ASSESSMENT.

Summary and Introduction

Early in the report of the National Research Council's committee on assessment, it is written that "Most common kinds of educational tests do a reasonable job with certain functions of testing such as measuring knowledge of basic facts and procedures and producing overall estimates of proficiency for an area of the curriculum," but the question remains as to whether they "capture the kinds of complex knowledge and skills that are emphasized in contemporary standards and deemed essential for success in an information based economy" (Pellegrino, Chudowsky, and Glaser, 2000).

In recent years many engineering educators have taken a similar view, although their answers to the problem differed from those presented in the report, which is primarily concerned with school education. In America they have followed in the path of other educators in higher education, as, for example, Wiggins (1993) who advocated authentic assessment. The responses to the demand for alternative assessments have been different in other countries. Thus, in the 1960s in the United Kingdom continuous assessment was seen to be the answer to the problems inherent in the final examination.

Engineering is particularly suited to authentic assessment because of its desire to simulate the real world that students will meet when they exit from their courses. Project work has been introduced, laboratory methods have changed and continue to change because of technological advances, and over the forty-year period covered by this review, much experimentation has been done with new forms of assessment. These same advances have caused changes in curriculum content. The higher level cognitive skills required in the real world are not tested or predicted by the objective tests that are common in the United States or by the problem style exams set in England and many of the universities in countries of the Commonwealth. The major "alternatives" have been in the use of journals, portfolios, peer assessment and self-assessment. The primary purpose of this Chapter is to consider these nontraditional or alternative approaches to assessment. It should not be assumed, however, that authentic means superior.[1] There remains a lot of work to be done to determine the validity of many of the rubrics used. Face validity is an insufficient criterion for their evaluation. Traditional approaches to examining and testing remain important. What matters is that they too should be subject to continuing development.[2] For this reason, this Chapter concludes with some comments on conventional examining and testing. Whatever system of assessment is used a key art is question setting.

It is now understood, better than it ever has been that assessment is not an isolated activity. It exerts a powerful influence on learning and it must be aligned with the curriculum, teaching and learning. Because the curriculum has many objectives, assessment like teaching will be multiple-strategy, each method being chosen for the objective that it is most likely to achieve. For this reason, nontraditional (authentic) as well as traditional measures will be required if a person's performance is to be satisfactorily judged. There is growing experience of this pedagogy of assessment among engineering educators. Some have been prepared to take risks in the quest for greater validity with the type of tests they use. There is plenty of room for experimentation and innovation in the methodologies of assessment.

16. Learning Journals and Portfolios

16.1. Journals and Diaries

Learning journals come in all shapes and sizes and mean many things to many people (Moon, 1999). Yokomoto (1993a), for example, described how students in electrical engineering were given the opportunity to earn extra credit by keeping a journal that demonstrated their knowledge base. Its purposes were to:

- *"Help students assimilate information through writing.*
- *Demonstrate to students the complexity of information through a writing exercise that requires them to record and classify information according to their type, such as procedures, axiomatic equations, approximations etc[3].*
- *Have a coaching instrument at hand when the student says "I knew all the material, I just froze in the exam." A journal provides a concrete starting point."*

Because the journal was not compulsory, Yokomoto could not say if it enhanced performance. But he offered the opinion that *"superior students are extracting more information than I expected.... It has shown me how much better the information gathering processes of superior students are, including attention span and note taking skills."*

At Southampton Institute a laboratory logbook was introduced into a level 1, circuit theory course. A major purpose of this innovation was to cause regular attendance because this was seen to a contributing factor to poor attainment rates. Both full time and part time students took the course, and some of them did not have

---

[1] For a criticism of authentic assessment see Terwilliger (1997).

[2] It is worth noting the work of medical educators in the field of examining and testing, as, for example, the development of the modified essay question (e.g. Fabb and Marshall, 1983; Heywood, 2000).

[3] The instructions included notes on procedures, word definitions, operational definitions, axiomatic equations, developed equations, rules of thumb, approximations, circuit models of devices, equation models of devices, strategies, and conventions.

good time management skills or underestimated the commitment required for the successful completion of the course (Wellington and Collier, 2002).

During supervised sessions, students carried out a number of practical activities that they were required to document in the laboratory logbook. The format of the logbook was prescribed, and the entries were assessed against a standard set of criteria. The students also completed a tutorial workbook in which they attempted to solve example questions. All the example sheets were set in objective format, and this reduced the time taken to assess the tutorial workbooks. The tutorial workbook made a significant contribution (30%) to the student's final score, and it was assessed at regular intervals.

The effect was to significantly improve attendance rates. Seventy percent of the students passed the unit at the first attempt. This was a considerable improvement over the results of previous years.

The Learning Assessment Journal described by Carroll et al., (1996) was quite different. *"It comprised a semester's worth of forms for different roles in cooperative learning, reading logs, self-assessment forms, and instruments for team reporting. Each instrument provides hints to assist the student in synthesizing course concepts and in reflecting about individual as well as team performance."* The journal was intended to support endeavours to develop learning, thinking, problem solving, and communication and teamwork skills. The view was also taken that assessment was a process to be developed.

The teachers found that the journal gave ownership of learning, and that constructive interdependence was displayed. But they also found that the importance of reflection in technical courses was underscored: It should have been given a more appropriate weight.

Rover and Fisher (1998) were somewhat more upbeat about the value of journals in upper level courses in developing reflective thinking. But they also reported that the journals required more time by both the student and instructor. In their courses the journal was a key element in the development of self-assessment.

In the integrated freshman course at Arizona State University, electronic journaling was used to encourage integration.[4] The students had to explain math, physics or engineering concepts. The entries were completed in a word processing program, and that encouraged the students to check their mistakes and grammar. All of the faculty had access to the journal and responded to the students by e-mail. The students were set a variety of tasks, one of which was to rewrite a traditional fairy tale as if modern technology had been available. Another old favorite was the design of a launch-and-release mechanism that would allow them to drop an egg from 60 feet without breaking it. A student survey showed that the majority preferred the electronic journal to the traditional paper journal (Duerden, et al., 1997).

An evaluation of student journals in a statistics class did not reveal any significant difference between those whom used the journals and those who did not, in their final examinations. However, Rumpf and Mehra (1988), who reported this study, found that those who used journals were supportive and some of the students were enthusiastic about them. The students reported that it had helped them develop their written communication skills. The teachers reported that it had increased motivation and made the students more inquisitive.

As indicated above, journals can play a role in evaluation. An example of the use of journals in evaluation has been provided by Mutharasan et al., (1997). They were concerned with evaluation of a new upper level course in Engineering Biotechnology in which the students had to prepare a journal for discussion on a weekly basis with their tutors. Early on this revealed that the students had some difficulty with biological principles. They also lacked a textbook. The journals showed that as the course progressed the students learned that engineering could be used in "far-out-fields". The external evaluator of this program recommended that "the writing of weekly journals should become a part of learning by use of specific questions that allow for in-depth processing, reviewing as well as clarifying concepts."

The differences between design and research are often blurred, but it is evident that teachers can learn from journals about student learning. They can also be used for research as Sobeck II (2002) showed. He was interested to find out how and what representations students use when they solve design problems. He and two research assistants analyzed 21 journals of mechanical engineering students and found that in spite of the availability of computers, students relied on hand drawn representations to help them explore problem and solution spaces.[5]

In Sweden, Lundström and Booth (2000) introduced journals to complement a more traditional teaching approach. It comprised three reports relating theory to an application project. The goal was to obtain a more integrated understanding and thus demonstrate an understanding of each of the 5 subcourses. These reports contributed 6% of the final examination mark. These reports were sent to the tutor for comment via e-mail. The students could respond.

It was found that the applications provided a starting point for student led discussions in the lecture, and the tutor's view was that the students showed greater interest in theory and application. The students thought the journals worked well, and those who did well in the journals also did well in the examination.

Cowan (1998) began to experiment with what he called learning journals in the early 1980s. His freshman students in civil engineering had to take a course in interdisciplinary studies (IDS). Its purpose was to develop abilities that contributed to study in higher education and professional life. The students had to

---

[4] The journal used was WebNotes

[5] The technique of coding and analysis will be of interest to those contemplating a similar investigation.

undertake a weekly writing exercise. In this exercise, students had *"to think carefully about the answer to some such question as what have I learned about learning or thought about thinking, as a result of these IDS activities, which would make me more effective next week than I was last week?' Students were encouraged, if they so wished, to rephrase the question, to define 'effective' in their own terms and to focus their reflective journal writing- all as they found most useful."*

The students initially found great difficulty in meeting the demand for the weekly submissions. They were not assessed. The feedback comments from the tutors were not judgmental. *"We simply tried to understand and to identify with what was written. Where we didn't understand we asked a question- but it was not a threatening or critical question, simply a question genuinely suggesting the need to clarify. Where there seemed to be a break in the logic, we gently pointed it out, but without implying criticism or suggesting how the break might be repaired. Where it would have been helpful to test a confident statement against recent experience, we suggested how that might be done, without implying that it should be done. Where a success was reported, we enthused. We expected no response to come to us. There was seldom any feedback of that type."*

It was not until the second half of the second term that the students began to experience "Damascus Road" like experiences. Students have to learn to reflect and thus make the journal effective. They may have to be helped through the process.

It might be argued that these results are not surprising. The more learners know about reflective activity, the more they are likely to appreciate its complexity, and the more they will want time to develop their thought as they perceive themselves to be in a learning process that may appear to have components of extra-rationality (Puk, 1995). A pertinent question would have been to establish the extent to which they perceived the first period as a stressful learning experience. There is a danger that in the demand for reflection reflective practice becomes trivialized (see Chapter 12.7).

This course was self-assessed, with students claiming (with evidence) and rating the development of (a) higher-level cognitive and interpersonal abilities, and (b) metacognition that they ascribed directly to the course. Interviews by an independent investigator some six months later revealed strong endorsement of the experience and the self-assessing which had led to self-direction. Some 25% of students continued to keep such journals-unasked. Unfortunately, Cowan does not tell us 'who' these students were when compared with the others.

In teacher education, postgraduate-students were asked to keep a journal of their school experience. Their approach was superficial. They found it difficult to move from keeping a diary to recording critical incidents that affected their learning about teaching. These students were not the only ones to behave in this way. Many students in an on-line course in software design also produced descriptive diaries even though it was intended

that they should be used for reflection. Hamilton-Jones and Svane (2003) reported that those who had reflected analytically had begun to see the relevance of the component parts of the course.[6] It was evident that even though the students had received training in self-reflection, they found it difficult to self-reflect "on-command." Instructed reflection seemed to come more easily to students who had not received such training. Control students who received a blended-model of learning and two lecture sessions performed better than those in the traditional group in the college. The investigators felt that the experimental course might need more structure during the first weeks, because comments in the diaries suggested that the students had not fully grasped what was required of them. This study indicates the important contribution that diary work can make to tutor understanding of the processes at work in their courses (see Section 13.1 for other comments on this course).

Moon (1999) has summarized the difficulties that learners find difficult in writing journals. These are:

- They do not see the relevance of journal writing to what they are doing
- They might feel that reflection is overemphasized.
- They do not believe they will be able to produce what the teacher wants or they spend too much time trying to produce what they believe the teacher wants.
- They do not perceive the exercise to be of value and begrudge the time they have to give to it.
- The student's study habits may not accord with regular entries. Like examinations, they leave revision to the last moment.

Moon pointed out that while journal writing can be successful the writer can go stale, and teachers have to judge at some point whether it is worthwhile carrying on with the activity.

It could be argued that the collection of Cowan's students' weekly reflections is a portfolio. Thus, much of what is said about journals applies to portfolios.

George and Cowan (1999) also showed how reflective journals can be fitted into to the Kolb learning cycle. It might be suggested that students with experience of journal writing should be invited to examine their work in terms of the Kolb Cycle, and especially to use it to plan "active experimentation" of their generalizations.

16.1.2. Portfolios

In Great Britain the term portfolio has been used to describe components of public systems of assessment at

---

[6]This study investigated the reflective assessments made for a module- Current issues in Edutainment Software Design (ESD) given to seniors at Halmstead University, Sweden. This was compared with control groups of students in a senior level module in E-commerce designed for international students on exchange, and two groups of students taking a course in on-line learning at University College, Worcester. A VLE (basic system for cooperative working) was used in the course. The language used throughout was English.

the technician level (BTEC, 1992).[7] They are used as the basis for National Vocational Qualifications (NCVQs). In Canadian higher education the portfolio is often understood as a summary statement that fronts a collection of evidence. Slater (1996) distinguished between showcase portfolios, checklist portfolios and open-format portfolios in use in science education (see also Slater and Astwood, 1995). They also seem to serve a variety of purposes, and Wolf (1998) made the point that they might serve different purposes at the different levels of education. For example, it was thought by the British Employment Department that portfolios would record achievements that school leavers could show employers. Use of this idea was made in an advanced digital design course at Utah State University. The final examination of this course required the students to compile a portfolio of their best design experience in a format that could be shown to an employer. In the finals week they were told to bring this portfolio for an employment interview. *"By the time they came in for the interview they felt confident about what they had accomplished in digital design. They could show their design approach and talk about the details. They could also talk intelligently about how design is carried out in industry and the devices available for implementing designs"* (Wheeler, 1996). In Great Britain, Wright (1993) suggested that portfolios should be used in ratings of Continuing Professional Development.[8]

Portfolios are now one of the recommended tools for outcomes assessment in engineering (Olds, 1997).

Little is known about the advantages and disadvantages of portfolios in higher education, and most of the research on portfolios has been done in elementary and secondary schools.[9] Both of the major testing agencies in the United States have developed portfolio systems (ACT, Colton et al., 1997; ETS, Storms et al., 1998). In Sweden the idea of the portfolio has been borrowed from the school system to try and assess the engineering students capability in *fronesis* or political knowledge, *"that is the ability to understand and interpret the situation at hand and decide about appropriate actions"* (Lennartsson and Sundin, 2001). It was reported that the preliminary experience was encouraging.

The use of portfolios in engineering and school technology education is of comparatively recent origin. They are not, for example, mentioned in Wankat and Oreovicz (1993). A paper published in 1995 suggested that the portfolio with reflective assessment could provide for the continuous improvement of students and teachers and reconcile student needs with coursework (Cress and

McCullough-Cress, 1995). The authors argued that undergraduate courses had to be constructed as a learning organization of the kind described by Senge (1990) and Senge et al., (1994). Senge's five disciplines could be supported by portfolio work[10].

At the same time, it is clear that reports of projects which describe the process are portfolios. For example, the combination of reports of experimental investigations and projects presented for assessment in Engineering Science satisfy Sharp's definition that a portfolio is a collection of student work that tells a story of achievement and growth (Sharp, 1997). *"Crucially,"* wrote Baume and Yorke (2002) *"it usually also contains reflective commentary, in which the course participant shows how they have interrogated their experience and related to their practice and understandings to cognate evidence from the literature and elsewhere. It is typically expected that insights will go beyond a quotidian pragmatism to connect with relevant theoretical constructs. The assumption is that theory is an important component for the bridges being built between practice in different contexts."*[11]

In one engineering course in the United States, the tutor marked the one or two page reflective component that accompanied the portfolio and not the portfolio itself, which seems to be similar to the Canadian concept of a portfolio referred to above. Some students might regard this as an unfair practice unless they agree to such practice (reported in a conference discussion). Clearly the entry would have to demonstrate reflective practice and indicate where examples could be found in the portfolio. The trouble is that the assessment of large portfolios can be time consuming.[12] Mourtos (1997), who assessed student learning in an aerodynamics course, reported that it took him 30 to 45 minutes to review each portfolio provided that all the assignments had been previously marked. An interesting feature of the assignments was that after they were returned, the students had the opportunity to revise them and include them in the portfolio. In this way the instructor could see if there had been an improvement.

The last assignment, which had to be placed first in the portfolio, required the students to reflect on their entire learning experience, what they learned, how they learned, and what challenged them. Mourtos (1997) reported that many students found this reflective exercise. He wondered if one reason for this might have been that the students were not used to "reflecting."

As indicated above, Slater (1996) drew attention to the *"showcase portfolio,"* which is a limited portfolio in which might be asked *"to include items that represent (1) their best work; (2) their most interesting work; (3)*

---

[7]Equivalent to technology degrees in the United States at the higher levels called Higher National Certificates

[8]He suggested that procedures similar to those in use for National Vocational Qualifications could be used.

[9]The whole of volume 5, issue 3 of *Assessment in Education: Principles, Policy and Practice* is devoted to portfolios and records of achievement.

[10]The five disciplines are Systems thinking, personal mastery, shared vision, mental models and team learning.

[11]Baume and Yorke were writing about the use of portfolios to assess university teachers in the UK.

[12]The reports of classroom research that I marked took anything from 20 to 50 minutes each. 100 took around 30 hours to mark and this was done on 5 occasions in each year of the course.

their most improved work; and (4) their favourite work." This is in contrast to an open-format portfolio in which students may present anything that demonstrates mastery of a given list of learning objectives. A checklist portfolio gives the student a choice of a number of different assignment selections from the course syllabus.

In higher education, Renee Betz [13] (private communication) drew attention to the fact that the type of entry depended on the purpose of the portfolio. She distinguished between the *showcase* portfolio and a *developmental or growth* portfolio in English. With relation to self-assessment in the former she asks, *"How can one encourage students to decide what is their own best work, regardless of the outside evaluation? And, how can we know what criteria a major is using in deciding what is the best work?"* In contrast, the growth portfolio places the responsibility for the selection on the students and necessarily encourages self-assessment. In her approach to portfolios, Betz suggested that reflective pieces should form a major part of the contents.

At Rose-Hulman College, Williams (2002) traced the origins of portfolios in writing in order to demonstrate their use in engineering. They were introduced in the engineering curriculum via writing. It was found that the scope of the learning that the portfolio was to document should be limited. It was also found that rubrics had to be developed to accurately assess that learning. Other reports suggest that it is valuable to involve students in determining those criteria.

At Sheffield Hallam University an integrated degree course accredited by both the Institutions of Electrical and Mechanical Engineers required that *"25% of the final year mark would be allocated to the presentation of a portfolio demonstrating professional, personal and technical achievement as a potential engineer"* (Payne et al., 1993; Ashworth et al., 1996) The idea was borrowed from the Art and Design courses in the University, and it was believed that because a students actual work was put on "show," it was a much more rigorous means of the assessment of future performance than the use of examinations themselves. Such a display would at the same time show the development of the student and give further indication of that student's potential.

Throughout the four years of the course, the students were expected to involve themselves in a "Ghost" company (Bramhall et al., 1991). Payne and his colleagues reported that in the first year of the course, students did not understand the concept of the portfolio and consequently did not collect suitable materials for it. It was also found that although the "Ghost" company caused practice in certain professional skill areas, there needed to be a basic and remedial training in certain areas, especially those related to learning and studying. Therefore, it was decided to extend a new program in personal and professional development (PPD) to the first year of the course.

Not only did students have to be helped, but so did staff. The core team found that the introduction of portfolios was a continuing challenge. They had also to involve another 15 teachers in portfolio assessment. Many of these teachers, while enthusiastic, found they were required to change their roles to be more facilitative and to be explicitly concerned with professional development, which is, as has been shown, consistent with the experience of others who have departed from traditional procedures. Payne and his colleagues drew the conclusion that before anyone participated in a course of this kind, they would require intensive training.

The power of assessment to lead learning is also evident in the fact that students experienced the portfolio in different ways. *"For integrated students there is the certainty that they have to prepare and present a portfolio, and that it will count for 25% of their degree mark. They are thus likely to be more committed to the PPD program and to portfolio work in general. However, because no significant assessment takes place in early years, the less enthusiastic B. Eng. Integrated students have tended to miss a larger proportion of the PPD classes than other class sessions."* Payne and his colleagues were of the opinion that the students saw the PPD classes as less important than the academic subjects. This is consistent with earlier reports on the attitudes of Diploma in Technology students to complementary and liberal studies. When the portfolio was conceived, it was undertaken as an alternative to traditional assessment. However, the experience of portfolio assessment convinced staff that they had to be clear about what they were assessing, particularly because portfolios opened up the process to view. Thus, insofar as was possible, the portfolio was used to assess within *"a job or work related context the application of engineering knowledge and skills, and the professional functioning of a potential professional engineer."*

Ashworth et al., (1996) in a later evaluation reported that the portfolio encouraged self-reflection. From being a task to be fulfilled, the students gained a strong feeling of ownership and relevance and became emotionally committed to it.

Electronic learning has made possible electronic portfolios. [14] Upchurch and Sims-Knight (2002) considered that electronic portfolios could provide a longitudinal record of work, feedback from instructors and peers, and process postmortems. They used electronic portfolios in a software engineering course that required a team project.

The project teams were of 4 to 6 persons. The instructor chose one from each team to be the project manager. They had to choose who did what and justify their choice. Each team negotiated process roles among themselves and with the project manager, and each project team had a customer

---

[13] Sometime director of the AAHE assessment forum.

[14] A detailed description of the construction of a web-based portfolio will be found in Sander (2000). See also Schweiker, Moore and Voltmer (2002) for details of the work at Rose-Hulman Institute of Technology.

Reporting was done electronically. The instructor provided assignments, viewed student work, and gave feedback. The feedback became part of the portfolio. A survey of a small number of students yield relatively positive responses.

There are a number of intrinsic dilemmas in using portfolios for assessment that won't go away; for example, the tension between the personal nature of the portfolio and the need there were for teachers to apply impersonal assessment criteria. Ashworth and his colleagues argued that there were some difficulties in helping the development of personal and professional capabilities. They noted that because the technique is resource intensive, it works better with small groups of students. They believed that so long as formal examinations remain, there would not a large-scale implementation of portfolios in the United Kingdom. Nevertheless, as indicated, both testing agencies in the United States have developed portfolios for large-scale use.

Welch and Martinovich-Barhite (in Colton et al., 1997) concluded that the successful implementation of a portfolio assessment system must include a refined set of rubrics that have been field tested and piloted. The reliability of the results can be increased by the systematic exposure of the scoring rubric and assignments to participating teachers in a large scale system. The students must be able to understand the rubric and the tie between the example of work selected and the scoring process. This view was also taken by LeMahieu, Gitomer, and Eresh (1995), who evaluated the Pittsburgh Writing Scheme that used portfolios. They suggested that the shared understanding that is required to satisfy psychometric concerns could be achieved through a hermeneutic approach. This raises the question as to whether portfolios should be marked by a single assessor.

Slater (1996) suggested that each piece of work should be scored against the extent of evidence submitted. That is, no evidence would be given 0; weak evidence would receive 1 point; adequate evidence 2 points; and strong evidence 4 points. The latter would show that *"the evidence is presented accurately and clearly indicates understanding by integration across concepts. Opinions and positions are clearly supported by referenced facts."* But these marks have to be collated for grades and Slater suggested that, for example, a Grade A would be given for strong in 11 objectives and adequate in 3 for a portfolio that required demonstrations of mastery in 14 course objectives. Similarly, D+ would be given for adequate in at least 12.

In the United States the idea of teachers keeping a portfolio has been encouraged not only because of its pedagogical merit but also for its use in appraisal. In the United Kingdom the Staff Educational Development Association uses the portfolio for the accreditation of university teachers. The new Institute of Learning and Teaching in Higher Education is also using the portfolio for the same purpose, and many of the prescibed courses for the accreditation of new university teachers follow a similar approach.. The American Association for Higher

Education had a teaching initiative in this area (Anderson, 1993) The teachers of a freshman course on engineering design at The University of Maryland-College Park developed such a portfolio and found that it provided evidence *"of improving teaching/learning effectiveness."* The portfolio was constructed in four pages. These were teaching material, teamwork, support structure, and assessment. The components of the assessment section were program educational objectives, program outcomes and assessment, faculty, and facilities (Che, 1999). The individual teacher is responsible for that part of the portfolio that relates to their contributions to the course.

There are few studies of the reliability of portfolio assessment. Baume and Yorke (2002) in their evaluation of a course for university teachers summarized the results of the studies that have been done. Their own work led them to the conclusion that reliable portfolio assessment is not easy to achieve. The scheme that they evaluated required 75 judgments per portfolio. They found that at the level of the assessment of individual elements the reliabilities stood comparison with those found in the other studies, and they drew attention to work by Nystrand et al., (1993). They suggested that assessing one element at a time would increase reliability. Baume and Yorke did not consider the relation between holism and particularism in assessment, an issue that has been considered in engineering in respect of peer assessment (see below). Overall it is difficult to believe that given well understood criteria in professional subjects like engineering,[15] it should not be possible to achieve reliabilities that would compare with those obtained with project reports.

It should also be evident that both journals and portfolios can be used to evaluate the effectiveness with which a course is achieving the outcomes required by accrediting agencies and, therefore, for continuous curriculum improvement. (See, for example, Dempsey et al., 2003.)

16.2.   Peer Assessment and Self-Assessment

The idea that peer assessment and self-assessment is something unusual is without foundation. Much of our time is spent judging our peers or other people, we certainly spend time judging ourselves, and we worry about the judgments that people make about us. No wonder some of us are wary of peer assessment. Yet, reports of project and laboratory work have often required students to evaluate what is done either in teams or as individuals. These are forms of peer assessment and self-assessment.

Technically at issue is the validity and reliability of our judgments. The question is whether or not formal procedures for judging others, as well as ourselves, can be made more reliable and valid. But the other major question is whether peer assessment and self-assessment should be used for grading as well as an instructional technique. Boud (1989), one of the pioneers of peer

---

[15] One might expect that these criteria might be less subjective than those used to assess teacher performance.

assessment and self-assessment, thought not, because it might compromise their pedagogical promise. Others have argued that because they may not be reliable or valid, they might reduce the confidence we have in university standards; but recent debates about grade inflation and research on examiner reliability is not particularly awe inspiring. In contrast, Magin and Helmore (2001) argued that if peer assessments were used for summative purposes, they might *"promote greater seriousness and commitment on the part of the students."* In summative assessments of this kind, students are empowered to make decisions that count. On the other hand, *"If students are made aware that their assessments cannot be counted towards final grading, either because they are considered unable to make valid or reliable assessments, or because they cannot be trusted to do so, then we should not be surprised if it is difficult to convince them of the learning value of engaging in peer assessment"* (Magin and Helmore, 2001).

Peers are also used to review work. At Arizona State University peers are used in workshops to make suggestions about their reports and essays. They work in pairs and check that the assignment criteria are met. For this purpose the students were provided with a check list in the form of questions, such as the following: In the executive summary, does the writer begin by stating the problem and forecasting the discussion? It also included open-ended questions on the strength and weaknesses of the report (Helfers et al., 1999).[16]

The tutors could, if they wished use components of the work, as for, example, *"a sample thesis statement or introduction."* The tutors were of the opinion that the students grow in confidence as the course progressed. Nelson (2000) used a much less detailed assessment schedule. Both Halfers and Nelson took the view that what the students do meets the training needs for the peer review process. Nelson's approach was to get them to use the checklist for a few assignments and then to wean them from them. If the quality of the evaluations fell, he re-instated the checklists. He drew attention to comments by Riley (1999), who argued that peer review, while being valuable as an editorial check, was otherwise often superficial. Nelson responded by setting competitive collaborative exercises that were problem oriented and creative. These were not peer reviewed.

In neither case were the students involved in grading.

16.2.1. Peer Assessment

Boud (1986) pointed out that when the aim of assessment is feedback (formative), students themselves can provide each other with useful feedback and reinforcement. While this often happens in the laboratory, it does not do so universally, and Boud argued that peer assessment should be formalized in the laboratory. In this way, students will begin to take responsibility for their

own learning and gain insight into their own performance through having to judge the work of others. They are, therefore, a useful adjunct to assessment by teachers.

Web-based learning has made it possible for peer-peer evaluations to provide feedback to each other in a way that teachers cannot, and for it to be anonymous (Rada and Hu, 2002). Another reason for interest in peer assessment is that it is possibly the only satisfactory way of obtaining information about the contributions of the individuals within a team to the work of the team. That said there are many reported examples the peer assessment of teamwork in engineering programs.

A quite simple reason for support of peer assessment is that it can help a teacher who is overloaded. For this reason, Mafi (1989) helped his situation by arranging for homework to be marked by peers. He approached his students by marking the first two sets of problems in order to *"convey my standards on appropriate procedure, format, accuracy and neatness."* Thereafter, he took on a supervisory role as each student marked the assignment of a classmate. For this purpose the students were grouped in pairs and given the solutions. Instruction was given about grading and standards. The pairings were changed each week. The grading took place during the weekend. Mafi argued that students marked similarly because they had seen the teacher's standards marked twice. Some commentators would consider that to be a considerable act of faith. The majority of students did not object to marking their colleague's work, and they reported that it enhanced learning.

One complaint is that friendships may bias the results, but there is little evidence to suggest that this is the case. One study has found that racial prejudice may be found in peer evaluations, and for this reason it was suggested that groups should be homogeneous, but this defeats the rationale of group work.

Goldfinch and Raeside (1990) warned against peer assessments that are arrived at as a result of group discussion about the contribution that each member made to the activity. While it may be seen to be 'fairer,' it could lead to marks which reflect the personalities of the students, and not their actual contributions. In their study, the students privately rated the other members of the group. Marks were then calculated from these ratings by the tutors. The group project submission was given a group mark. A peer assessment factor was then calculated from the individual submissions. An individual's mark was the product of the peer assessment factor and the group mark. Students who contributed less than the average were given a relatively small percentage of the group mark, while those who contributed more were given larger percentages. They felt that this method achieved the aim of rewarding individual students according to the percentage of the group's success that they contributed. One of the problems of schemes like this is the large amount of subjectivity that is likely to be present in reporting.

Goldfinch and Raeside objected to traditional rating scales used for peer group assessment because the

---

[16]Members of this team also developed a comprehensive writing survey (Rhoads, Duerden and Garland (1998).

students found them difficult to complete. Students also found it difficult to remember what had happened so they designed a different schema like those used in primary trait analysis. This approach was used with a large class of 200 students working in groups of three four or five on a realistic problem.

Orsmond, Merry, and Reiling (1996) also drew attention to the difficulties that students had with traditional rating scales. They asked students to rate posters (the relevance to portfolio assessment in design will be apparent), against five criteria on a 0–4 scale. The categories which were further defined were self explanatory, clear purpose (hypothesis), clear and justified conclusions, visually effective and attractive, and helpful level of detail. They wanted to examine the marking of individual criteria because in the past, peer assessment studies had compared the mean tutor grade and that of the student for a given item of their work. Their overall findings were that the overall agreement between tutors and students was 18%, with 56% of the students overmarking and 26% undermarking. However, they found that these scores masked what was happening within the categories. A significant number of students undermarked 'clear and justified conclusion' whereas a significant number overmarked 'visually effective and helpful level of detail' when compared with the tutor. Various explanations for these differences were offered. One of them was that the students did not understand the meaning of the criteria? Was it a lack of ability or a failure to understand the criteria? Other studies had found that students did not understand the criteria. It is an open question as to whether the results would have changed had a primary trait scale been used. The students in the Orsmond study reported that they had benefited from the study: They said they had been challenged and had learned to be more critical, as well as to work in a more structured way. Orsmond and his colleagues noted that when the marking was against clear criteria, disagreements between tutor and student can easily be identified, and the tutor could be challenged. The tutor then allocated the marks on the basis of the project report *"in which the specific tasks that have been carried out are clearly identified by the students themselves, who have signed their own pieces of work."* The diaries are then used to confirm the tutor's own assessment. They were also a check against cheating. Because the project began with a detailed brief that included a time schedule another indicator is available of the work carried out by individual members of the group. The students were carefully briefed on the process. In the second part the student peer marking was carried out in a classroom situation under examination conditions. This was partly to underline the seriousness of the exercise, and partly to avoid 'mark fixing cartels.' It was found that the marks reflected the variation in contributions within a normal distribution.

Rafiq and Fullerton (1996) modified Goldfinch and Raeside's model for use in civil engineering. In the original model the students completed a two-part questionnaire. The first part related to skills involved in project tasks; the second part summarized a list of process skills related to group activities. When this was trialed, Rafiq and Fullerton found that the groups were reluctant to mark each other's work. The tutor monitoring the work also felt that bias crept into some of the assessments, and students had difficulty in remembering who did what. Rafiq and Fullerton, therefore, changed part one. Now the students were asked to keep a project diary. The tutor then allocated the marks on the basis of the project report *"in which specific tasks that had been carried out are clearly identified by the students themselves, who have assigned their own pieces of work."* The diaries were then used to confirm the tutor's own assessment. They were also a check against cheating. Because the project began with a detailed brief that included a time schedule, another indicator of the work carried out by individual members of the group was available. The students were carefully briefed about the process. In the second part the student peer marking was carried out in a classroom situation under examination conditions. This was partly to underline the seriousness of the exercise and partly to avoid *"mark-fixing cartels."* It was found that the marks reflected the variation in contributions within a normal distribution.

Butcher, Stefani, and Tariq (1995) were much more confident about the peer assessment performances of students in the biosciences. Their study is of interest, because it incorporated peer and self-assessment. It is also of interest because of the mark scheme that was used. They arranged for self (A) and peer (B) assessment of project work by other group members; self assessment (C) of a contribution to a poster; peer assessment (D) of contributions to the poster by other group members; peer assessment of posters by students from other groups (E); and staff assessment (F) of the posters. They found that the self-assessment marks were higher than those awarded by the peers. However, while these differences were not statistically significant the discrimination of students with different abilities was achieved. The strongest assessor driven variation was found among staff. Butcher and his colleagues argued that students *"could be assessed solely by one another to yield a useful complementary grade which might be used in conjunction with other forms of assessment in their courses."*

The marks derived from these projects contributed 10%. The formula they used to derive the individual's mark from the group mark was

¼ (mean of A and B) + ¼ (mean of C and D) + ½ (F) = The individual's mark.[17]

In another study of the relative validity of peer evaluation and self-evaluation in self directed interdependent teams at the Colorado School of Mines, Thompson (2001) found that the correlations between the criteria of (a) effort applied to task and (b) technical knowledge applied to task, in self-evaluation, were very

---

[17]See Lejk, Wyvill and Farrow (1996) for a survey of methods for deriving individual grades from group assessment. Also Topping (1998) for a more general review.

low. In contrast the same correlation for peer evaluation against the same criteria were relatively high (0.71 and 0.76 respectively) after the students had completed a first project. The correlations were slightly reduced after the students had completed a second project (0.61 and 0.66). This suggested that the validity of the peer evaluations was relatively high, and that they would be a good source of information for tutors wishing to improve teamwork. Self-evaluations, on the other hand, should not be used for assessing the truth of teamwork skills.

Thompson drew on self-enhancement theory to explain these differences. In this theory, people perceive themselves to be better than others, thus there is likely to be positive bias in their self-assessments when compared to the evaluations that they made of their peers. This was found to be the case with both criteria at the end of the 1st and 2nd projects. In support of this view, he cited work by John and Robins (1994), who had found that self-enhancement bias in ratings was strongly related to measures of narcissism.[18]

Magin and Helmore (2001) were of the opinion that while some situations contained many impediments that would prevent fair marking, other situations like the assessment of oral skills would have minimal impediments. In the oral presentation situation the audience are mostly peers, and consequently the presenter must be able to communicate with them. Their judgments must have face validity, and even if individuals have low reliability, the averaged scores of a number of raters increase the reliability.[19] They also pointed out that in previous studies, reliabilities had been calculated from the correlations of the average marks awarded by peers and their teachers; but this, as Magin and Helmore pointed out (citing Topping, 1998), is a measurement of validity. They did not compare peer assessments with other peer assessments, or with their own assessments over time.

To overcome these limitations, Magin and Helmore designed a study in which the communication skills of final year mechanical and manufacturing students at the University of New South Wales were rated by teams of students and teams of teachers. Analysis of variance was used to provide separate inter-rater reliability estimates for the two groups.

Each student was assessed by approximately five students and between three and seven teachers. Each student made a 15 minute presentation that was followed by 5 minutes of discussion. Prior to the exercise, the students were assessed on four preliminary tasks. These were:

1. The dispatch of a 50-word abstract of the thesis by e mail.
2. Revision of the abstract after consultation with other students.
3. A four-minute talk about the progress of the thesis.
4. A seven-minute talk on a topic of their choice.

Since feedback was given by a tutor and discussions on what constituted an effective technical presentation took place, this amounted to indirect training for the assessment task.

The assessment of these oral presentations was important because it was used for both formative and summative purposes. The performance was rated on eight dimensions, and a global summative mark was also recorded. Ratings were required to the questions *"did the speaker*

1. *Speak loudly enough?*
2. *Have clear diction?*
3. *Use the English language properly?*
4. *Use visual aids effectively?*
5. *Have adequate eye contact?*
6. *Inform you adequately of the thesis topic?*
7. *Present the information logically?*
8. *Handle the questions well?"*

At the end of the session the presenter received the mark sheets and thus obtained 'instant' feedback. The dimensions were rated on a 10 point scale calibrated from 0 to 100. Spaces were made available for comment. The raters also recorded a global summative mark expressed as a percentage. *"The global mark is specified as an overall assessment of the 'level of confidence and skill attained by the student in making an oral presentation using audio visual aids'. "*

In support of the global mark, they cited the work of Hodges et al., (1996) in medical education. They had reported that the inter-rater reliability of global ratings was superior to that achieved with detailed checklists and concluded that, for summative purposes, it was *"probably unnecessary to employ time consuming detailed versions of a checklist.*[20]

It was found that:
1. In all four years in which the study was replicated the peers over-marked, a finding that is at variance with other studies. On the other hand, the marks were more bunched than those of the teachers, a finding that

---

[18] It is not possible to repeat here the details of the research design which used generalizability theory.
[19] Magin and Helmore cite Houston et al., (1991) in support of this view.

[20] In the slightly difficult circumstances of single rater marking reports on the assessment of classroom research by student teachers are of interest. The assessment check list was categorized into seven domains. The students were given information about how the components of the domain contributed to the score of that domain. In addition the rater also gave a holistic score. The rater found that *"the spread of answers within each individual domain was made and the small number of marks available did not always do justice to this spread".* This was particularly true of two of the domains, and one of them had to be given more prominence in later schedules which meant adjusting the marks available to the other domains. *"Second, the summed marks did not always reflect the quality of the report. Some were over-marked and some were under-marked. In order to get over this difficulty an impression mark was given after the scoring had been completed. This became the real mark unless the student objected. Since there are problems with discretionary reconciliation, as Wiliam (1995) has pointed out, it was important to justify the mark and allow negotiation. Therefore, a written justification of the marks accompanied each schedule."* The rater's impression marks were independently evaluated over a seven year period, and the means and standard deviations were found to be consistent over that period (Heywood, 2000 p 296)

was consistent with those of other studies[21].

2. The reliabilities obtained from the one way analyzes of variance showed that teacher reliabilities were consistently high, and that the student reliabilities were much lower than those of the teachers. Put in another way, 2 peer ratings were equivalent to 1 teacher rating.

3. There was a trend to greater homogeneity of student marks over the four years that might have been due to more familiarity with audio-visual aids.

Taken together, it was found that students need to be persuaded to be more discriminating, but that the scores of a single teacher were unlikely to be better than the averaged scores of peers. For this reason, in summative assessments the two could be combined. Magin and Helmore were of the opinion that this could foster skills of professional judgment, and could invest oral assessment with greater reliability.

Unfortunately, Thompson (1992) gave no technical support for a conclusion that is in stark contrast with that presented by Magin and Helmore. It was to the effect that in an engineering program the ranking of peer assessments of oral presentations compared well with that of academic staff. Moreover, the peers were *generally more critical of their colleagues' work and give lower marks*". He took the view however, that *"a formal peer group assessment method is an abdication of responsibility. The concept of peer group moderation of an examiner's marks, in open discussion with the examiner, is quite acceptable provided that the examiner reflects on 'the evidence' and takes the final decisions."*

A novel approach to peer assessment of teams was described by Burkhardt and Turner (2001). They used a jigsaw approach in which the project was divided into subprojects. Project teams were then formed with members with areas of expertise that related to the sub-projects. Secondary expert teams were then formed for with members who had similar expertise. *"The project team maintains responsibility for completion of the project while the expert teams are responsible for mastering the designated areas as well as developing a strategy for teaching the members of their project team what they have learned"*. The students were asked to rate their peers first on a scale of 0–4, and also to distribute a mythical $1000 among the members of the team. They found that the student assessments were consistent with their observations of the final reports, but the distribution of grades among team members was found to be problematic.

Peer assessment and self-assessment introduced at the Universities of Leuven (Belgium) in the educational sciences and Maastricht (The Netherlands) in economics and business administration in student centered and problem based learning. The written

examination at Maastricht assessed the extent to which students could define, analyze and solve novel, authentic problems. Collaborative work at Leuven was judged by peer assessment on a weekly basis. Segers and Dochy (2001) evaluated the instructional, and criterion validity of these measures. In the Leuven case they found, as other studies had done, that in self-assessment the students either oversold or undersold themselves when compared with the tutor's mark. The students found it easier to criticize their peers critically than to critically evaluate themselves'. Therefore, students have to be helped to develop this skill, and this might be accomplished in part by engaging the students in the operationalization of the criteria of assessment. This is to engage the students in "hidden" training and raises the question of the formal value of training students to make such judgments.

At Maastricht, in spite of what was perceived to be an improved examination, the instructors reported that the students did badly. Student perceptions led to the view that this was in part due to tutorial groups that allowed insufficient time for discussion and critical reflection. In both cases the study of student perceptions had thrown up questions of validity in the sense of mismatches between the learning environment planned by the teachers and the environment experienced by the learners.

Rada and Hu (2002) of the University of Maryland have described a web based system that enabled quick feedback among students from which patterns of student commenting could be determined. The students were given an exercise, and students and the system notified students and teachers of 'troubled answers.' They found that a number of the exercise answers received no comments and that some students gave many comments whereas others gave few. This variation creates a problem for the management of student learning and the matching of students within the system. Rada and Hu reported that in their system the teacher provided rules about who should comment on whom, and the computer enforced these rules. Students are pragmatic in their approach to such systems. If grading is important, then students will tend to be discriminating, however, if grading does not matter, the students are unlikely to make a serious attempt to grade. The web based management system was able to warn a student if they gave an abnormally high or low score, thereby giving the student the chance to modify the score. *"In practice, students will take advantage of this opportunity to fix mistakes that they have made in grading."*

An endeavor to improve technical writing via web-based peer review of final reports was reported by Eschenbach (2001).[22] *"Students elect their own topics and work in teams over a 10-week period to prepare these large documents (Draft Environmental Impact Statement/Report). On the Monday of the last week of the*

---

[21] Frair (1995) who was beginning to experiment with cooperative learning as a team based activity in a course that emphasized the design of production, found that the students rated everyone equal. He designed an Analytic Hierarchy Process Method to overcome this difficulty, which is beyond the scope of this review to describe.

[22] The software is described in the paper. It allows for the peer review of documents.

semester, the student teams submit two copies of their documents. One document is put on reserve in the library, while the other is submitted to the instructor to be graded. Over the last week of class during finals week, each student is assigned to review 2 other student environmental impact assessment documents. These peer reviews require students to reflect on their peers' work and their own work. The reviews also represent an activity that the students may need to perform in the future as environmental impact assessment professionals. The reviewing also helped students prepare for the mock public meetings when the teams presented their reports.

Eschenbach reported that many of the evaluations were profound. She thought they showed a level of deep learning that it would not have been possible to assess in traditional examinations. Eschenbach found that when at the beginning of the course students had to review two professional environmental impact documents, they had difficulty in operating at Bloom's level of evaluation. They tended to summarize rather than critique. Although these skills had developed someway by the end of the semester, she wondered if their skill in evaluation related to their Perry level of development, had it increased or decreased.

16.2.2. Self Assessment Versus Self Evaluation

Earlier it was suggested that the term "assessment" has replaced the term "evaluation". Thus, it might be construed that self-assessment and self-evaluation are the same thing. Indeed, that was the way it was taken earlier. However, Klenowski (1995), an Australian research worker, took a different view. He argued that self-evaluation is somewhat broader because it is *the evaluation or judgment of the worth of one's performance and the identification of one's strengths and weaknesses with a view to improving ones learning outcomes.* One might argue that this would embrace self-report inventories of the kind that have been used to compare the levels of perceived confidence between males and females in engineering programs, although the term "learning dispositions" might be preferable to "learning outcomes." Klenowski considered that self-assessment was the assigning of grade which is a narrower mental activity than self-evaluation because *it refers to ascribing value to a learning experience: first in the identification of criteria used; second by what is considered meritorious: and third, by outlining the implications for future action.* Cowan (1998) takes a similar view to Klenowski, but it is not the view of Boud (1995) with whom Cowan took issue. Cowan argued that when Boud writes that self-assessment *has the self as agent and audience,* and is essentially formative and not absolute, although it can be used for summative purposes, he (Boud) is writing about self-evaluation. Cowan argued that evaluation *is a process in which judgments are made by comparing performance with criteria or standards.* He says that assessment is concerned with *outcomes* whereas evaluation is concerned with *process.*

But surely, by definition, any comparison against standards is a grading or assessment. Cowan responded (private communication), *"perhaps an evaluation of a process is qualitative, whereas grading is quantitative."*

A process is a complex flow of outcomes that lead to a solution or proposition. With respect to the 'A' level engineering science projects, the student was asked to engage in a critical review (Carter, Heywood, and Kelly, 1986). The instruction read:

"In comparing the final product with the original specification the candidate has produced a through and objective discussion in which consideration has been given to all major aspects of the work including suggestions for further development, and a critical appraisal of the conduct of projects with a clear indication of lessons learned, etc."

It was intended that this should have engaged the candidate in an evaluation of the processes that led to the final solution. The lessons learned should have inspired the growth in knowledge required for Newman's philosophical habit of mind which would seem to be very similar to what today is commonly called reflective practice.

This critical review had its origins in the category of evaluation in *The Taxonomy of Educational Objectives.*

"Evaluation is defined as the making of judgment about the value for some purpose, of ideas, works, solutions, methods, material, etc. It involves the use of criteria as well as standards for appraising the extent to which particulars are accurate, effective, economical, or satisfying. The judgments may be either quantitative or qualitative, and the criteria may be either those determined by the student or those which are given him...it is not necessarily the last step in thinking or problem solving. It is quite possible that the evaluative process will in some case be the prelude to the acquisition of new knowledge, a new attempt at comprehension or application, or a new analysis or synthesis" (Bloom, 1956).

Irrespective of the debate about terms, it is likely that self-assessment and self-evaluation will continue to be used interchangeably. It is clear, however, that students find formal self-assessment and self-evaluation difficult. Some treat it as a superficial exercise, others find it difficult to get beyond superficiality and may not recognize that what they present is superficial, and a few are able to function at a deeper level. Clearly the pedagogical aim should be the development of reflective practice. An investigation at Sheffield University showed that this is not likely to be accomplished without some difficulty because students vary in their ability to reflect. Engineering students found it most difficult. They were not used *to talking in terms of feelings, nor could they see the relevance of such reflection to learning about engineering problems!* This was in contrast to students taking health related courses who found it helped them understand the feelings of their patients (Allen, 1991).

There is probably not much point in pursuing Loacker of Alverno College (private communication) said, it is up to each writer to define the terms as they use them. So what about the practice of self-assessment/evaluation in engineering education?

16.2.3. Self Assessment in Practice

Boud, Churches, and Smith (1986)[23] pointed out that the rubrics for self-assessment should be made as explicit as possible and that students can be involved in this activity (Boyd and Cowan, 1986). Boud and his colleagues involved staff in the designation of criteria for an experimental self-assessment exercise in an introductory course in engineering design. It was undertaken in three consecutive years.

"The exercise provided a set of factors to be considered in judging a design exercise (criteria) and asked students to assess (judge) the extent to which they applied each factor in their design. They were asked to make a written statement about each factor and to award themselves a mark out of ten on each. Eleven factors were provided and students had the opportunity to add two more of their own and assess themselves with respect to them. In addition to the self assessment, the students were asked to complete a brief questionnaire which sought their views about self-assessment and the worth of the exercise. These were handed in anonymously at the same time as their self-assessment exercises, and guarantees were given that these would not be analyzed until all marking had finished."

This exercise was introduced after the course had been planned, which was a weakness that Boud and his colleagues recognized. Self-assessment needs to be introduced when other changes are being made, or the existing course needs to be rearranged so that it becomes and integral part of the learning process. Moreover, if the students are involved in planning the criteria, then the criteria become explicit to them. Nevertheless, the students *"did find the exercise useful in clarifying and identifying specific deficiencies"* that could be addressed later in the course. Because the activity was retrospective the students did not monitor their own progress throughout the project, nor did they discuss their work with their peers or teachers, which Boud and his colleagues thought would have been advantageous.

An interesting comment in the discussion related to the design of the questionnaire ((as well as to rubrics) was to the effect that students for whom English was their second language had difficulty in understanding some of the questions. *"For example, the question 'how good was the method (design procedure) you used in order to achieve your design? was sometimes interpreted to mean 'how effective (functional) would the device be, if built to your design?"*

At Worcester Polytechnic Institute a self-assessment survey was administered before and after a course in design in the Electrical and Computer Engineering Department. Its purpose was to see how well

this particular semantic discussion further. Therefore, as the course was meeting ABET requirements. Thus, the students were asked to rate their ability on a scale of 1–10 on parameters like develop specifications, synthesize design, and determine a design's manufacturability. Considerable gains were reported on each of dimensions (Polizzotto and Michalson, 2001).

Gentili et al., (1999) also reported on the use of self-assessment in design that involved teamwork. The students were asked to assess their change in performance in a specified period by deciding if they made significant progress, if they worked on a competency or if they did not work on the competency in that period. The competencies were information gathering, problem definition, idea generation, evaluation and decision making, implementation, teamwork, and communication. They reported that while first year students could recognize their growth, they were not able to accurately score their performance relative to specified targeted design capabilities.

Some authors call student ratings of their perception of their abilities self reports. An interesting use of self-reports has been demonstrated at Purdue University-West Lafayette. Here a Mathematics Science Inventory has been used to identify weak and strong beginning students who are then assigned to appropriate courses during the first year. It was hoped that this would increase achievement and retention. In this instrument students are asked to rate their knowledge of a particular concept or principle on the scale "ever heard of it/ heard of it/general knowledge/general and detailed knowledge/extensive knowledge" (LeBold, Budny, and Ward, 1998).

When it was post tested at the end of the first semester, similar results were recorded for two years. These showed that at entry there were significant differences in the math and chemistry backgrounds of the students, and that by the end of the first semester there had been significant gains. LeBold and his colleagues argued, that since it had been shown consistently that academic performance in the first year was the best predictor of engineering retention, self-report inventories of this kind could be used to place students in courses that were likely to optimize their academic performance.

Confidence in one's abilities undoubtedly helps with academic prowess. Thus, questions that ask students how confident they are in a particular area of study can be of use to instructors in the evaluation of the course. Very often, as Besterfield Sacre et al., (1998) found, inventories that seek to do this sometimes throw up more questions than are answered.

16.2.4. Grading, and Training for Peer Assessment and Self Assessment

As was shown earlier, self-assessments may be subject to positive bias, but there is a somewhat alternative view to that suggested by self-enhancement theory (see Thompson above). It is due to Rokeach (1960), who argued that we do desire to know the truth about ourselves. There is a tendency in human behavior to want

---

[23] see also Boud and Holmes (1981).

our judgments to be reliable and valid. Nevertheless, there is, as Dobson (1989) pointed out, a tendency among the majority of people to slightly distort these self-evaluations in order to maintain positive self-knowledge. Dobson said of job selection that *"it can be inferred that the probability of an inflated self-assessment increases when honesty is not valued; it is believed that an inflated self-assessment increases the probability of being selected (for a job); the job concerned is highly valued; or there are no alternative jobs available."* The converse applies in the case of accurate self-disclosure.

In relation to the validity and reliability of marking of self-assessments, educators have to take into account the potential conflict between the need for accurate self knowledge on the one hand and positive self-knowledge on the other, for the way in which learners resolve this conflict influences their motivation. Since the context of learning is also an influence on motivation, it will not be possible to divorce self-assessment from the context of learning (Boyd and Cowan, 1986). Claxton (1995) has argued that involvement in grading helps to develop critical faculties because the student has internalize the functions of correction and evaluation. *"This fosters the vital distinction between the "informative" and the "emotive" functions of evaluation. Being able to turn a critical eye on one's own product, while at the same time retaining equanimity towards self, is the vital factor in the development of resilience Peer nomination; peer ranking and peer rating."*

If self-assessment is to be used in grading, it has to be given a sufficient role to make it worthwhile; or if its overall contribution is very small, then the students have to value its pedagogical contribution (Penny and Grover, 1996).

Dobson (1989) distinguished between three methods of peer rating. In peer nomination, each member of the group is asked to nominate and place in rank order the members of the group as being high or low on some performance characteristic. If the group is large, they may be asked to nominate and rank a specified number. In peer ranking, each member of the group is asked to rank all the other members of the group with respect to some performance characteristic. In contrast, in peer rating, each member of the group is rated on a scale with respect to some performance characteristics. This is in essence the technique used to obtain peer grades in higher education. Dobson was writing from the perspective of management and personnel selection. His finding from an evaluation of 39 studies in that area led him to conclude that peer nominations and peer rankings were more valid than peer ratings.

Educators in peer and self-assessment have consistently reported the need for well-defined criteria. One might suppose that if the scheme used for self-assessment is criterion referenced, the greater the reliability and validity that it might have. It may also be supposed that self-assessments in the cognitive domain would be more accurate than those made of the personal domain, since so many other factors enter into the making of personal judgments. Falchikov (1986) pointed out that it was likely that criterion referenced schemes should lead to greater agreement between students and teachers.

Earl (1986) took an opposite view of the need to state criteria. In the context of peer assessment, the staff involved in her study questioned how explicit the criteria should be. They felt that the degree of explanation depended on what the staff wanted the peer assessment to do. So they agreed to minimize the instructor imposed criteria and opted for general guidelines. An alternative that might have gotten over this difficulty was to have allowed the students to work out their own criteria for negotiation with their teachers.

The reports suggest that students do not readily reflect on their experiences, and when they do they become more concerned with lower order criteria than with higher levels of conceptual understanding Penny and Grover, 1996). It may, therefore, be sensible to provide some form of training in peer assessment and self assessment. This is done, for example, in the McMaster Problem Solving program (Woods et al., 1988).

In the workshop

- *We introduce the reasons for self-assessment as being to motivate, to develop our confidence, to help us to see where we are, and to develop a skill that is needed throughout life to guide us in modifying our life and setting goals.*

- *We clarify that assessment is not something to be avoided and that it is not an evaluation of persona worth (the focus is on performance).*

- *The students pretest their awareness and skill and we clarify the overall objectives of the workshop.*

- *By role playing we demonstrate that assessment requires agreement about criteria, procedures and an 'observable' performance.*

- *The initial task is for the students to 'demonstrate that they can start a car' or 'open a door' or 'sharpen a pencil'. They start by dividing the overall task into subtasks. Then they are given definitions as to what is 'observable' and 'what is not observable'. (know versus list; be aware versus describe). Armed with these definitions, and some practice activities to develop their ability to identify and create 'observable objectives', they then critique their previous efforts about 'starting the car'. They correct their previous efforts.*

- *The term criterion is defined; they practice creating criteria for such tasks as 'selecting the fastest writer' or 'selecting the longest string'. This leads to concepts of identifying the 'given conditions' and using a 'measurable criterion'. Often the wording of the observable skill has to be revised until a cohesive set of observable objectives and measurable criteria is obtained. They return to the task of 'starting the car' and apply this skill.*

- *By now the students are familiar with the concepts of identifying sub-goals creating observable objectives, identifying criteria converting these to measurable criteria and revising the objectives-criteria until they are compatible. They then repeat this whole activity for the task of creating a job application.*

- *They then extend this to creating objectives and criteria for developing on one of the components of the 'problem-solving skill that they want to work on during the course.*

- *The students post-test their awareness and skill and as a group discover what they learned from each activity and where they might apply the skill to situations found in everyday work or university life. They review objectives for the Unit and check whether they can achieve each objective according to the criteria* (Woods, Haymark, and Marshall 1988).

Related to self-assessment is the motivation to check one's work. That should be a habit, and Petro (2001) argued that engineering teachers should help students develop this skill. In a small experiment he found that there was a positive correlation between good scores and cross checking. Quite simple errors could lead to a loss of marks. He hoped that by designing the questions in his quizzes in such a way that they would encourage cross-checking, the students would cross-check in the final comprehensive exam. They did not. He gave four reasons for this. First was overconfidence in what one had done. Second, was that some students just don't care whether their answers are correct. Third, poorer students may adopt the attitude that "ignorance is bliss". The fourth reason was lack of direct training. Students could be helped to resolve discrepancies that cross-checking reveals. Clearly one of the objectives of self assessment should be to encourage cross-checking, and in so doing help the student face up to weaknesses. Perhaps peer assessment is the way to encourage cross checking.[See also Roney and Woods (2003) Section 16.9].

16.3.   Collaborative or Negotiated Assessment

An outstanding example of collaborative assessment in engineering that has been published is due to Boyd (a student) and Cowan (her tutor). In a course in design in civil engineering, Cowan gave the students responsibility for their own assessment of learning according to their own choices of learning outcomes.. He established a contract with the class that they would set their goals week-by-week. He would not provide advice or direction.

"In lieu of examinations each learner would prepare self assessment in the form of a criteria list of her desired goals, a description of her actual learning and a reconciliation of these (in relation to agreed bench marks), leading to choice of mark. Each stage in this process of assessment would be open to questioning, and discussion; but the ultimate decision would remain completely within the jurisdiction of the learner."

Their short paper is about what happened (Boyd and Cowan, 1986). Boyd was shown the Perry model of intellectual development (Chapter 6) in order for her to gain understanding of the psychological roots of learning. She wrote of her third year experience with Cowan, when he had placed the responsibility for learning and assessment on the students, that:

"In accepting responsibility for setting my own criteria, I clearly made a commitment to my eventual choice. Hence my learning must be rated at one of the higher levels of Perry's scale. Surface processing, which is encouraged by cue consciousness, was absent-because I had chosen my aims and criteria and directed my learning accordingly. And deep processing was positively encouraged- because I was subject to no pressures other than those that were self imposed."

They met again after Boyd had completed four months of her final year, when both instruction and the assessment were conventional. Their comments on that later situation are in stark contrast for they concluded that:

"There was no commitment at the higher level on Perry's scale, except in part of the final year project, where she had opted to work on her own criteria, rather than those of her supervisor."

"Hard won habits of deep-processing and, in particular, of rigorously searching for key points and issues persisted to some extent in her private reading and even in attendance at lectures, although there was a marked regression compared with the working style in third year design."

"At the same time cue-seeking and cue-conscious activity were more frequent, more deliberate and more purposeful."

They continued,

"These highly subjective and presumably biased impressions prompt us to wonder if it is possible to generate higher level commitment without involving the learners in setting goals and criteria; and also if the habit of deep-processing, once developed is likely to persist to some extent, even when circumstances actively encourage surface processing."

It is evident that if students are to make the most of their experience, they must reflect on it both at the time and in retrospect. But, more than that, it should become a habit of mind. Such reflections should not be ad-hoc; for this reason, diaries, learning journals, and portfolios have an important role to play. Boyd and Cowan (1986) were led to question *"if it is possible to generate higher Perry level of commitment, without involving learners in setting their own goals and criteria"* which is why they argue self-assessment should replace examinations. If the goal of engineering education is the development of reflective practitioners, then the lesson for assessment would seem to be that it should be multi-strategy in its approach. Like the curriculum, it should be designed as a spiral, and in the final circle it should allow the student to take off on their own against agreed bench marks.

16.4. Contrasting Traditions in Assessment and Grading

The traditional stereotype of the American system of examining is one that is reliant on multiple choice questions (objective tests).[24] It contrasts with the traditional system that functions in many countries of the old British Empire and that is based on essays or their equivalent in problem solving exercises.[25] The criticism of objective tests is that they primarily test knowledge of recall, and that of essays that they are unreliable. American criticisms of the British approach are based on the concept of the standardised test. Thus, in the United States, while course grades are obtained from a variety of assessments, (e.g., quizzes, regular tests, homework, and a final course exam), entry to graduate school may depend on performance in a standardised graduate test.[26]

In both systems there have been major moves away from the stereotype that are illustrated by the moves toward more "authentic" learning and testing, as for example, in project work, and the use of portfolios, journals, peer assessment and self assessment. But the literature also shows that there have been many minor developments in traditional examinations. A few of these are described below.

16.4.1. Objective, Short Answer and Essay Tests

There is vast literature on objective testing, and there is hardly need to review it here. It is usually associated with multiple choice questions whereas the definition of an objective tests is one to which there is only one right answer. As indicated above, the view outside of America is that objective items can test only at the level of knowledge and comprehension. But it is clear from examples in the literature that objective items can test problem solving skills. Yet in the development of a computer assisted personalized approach that supported conceptual, numerical, and essay problems, Kashy et al., (2001) found that synthesis and judgment required essay questions. By using the applet format they were able to cause the students to undertake an experiment that required the accurate collection of data and to use the concepts learned to solve the problem. In this mastery learning situation, in which the number of attempts to solve a problem were measured, they found that the applet questions were the most difficult. It was also found that the students who did well in their homework tended to do well in the final examination, and the correlation was slightly higher for the applet problems.

Canelos and Catchen (1989) have provided a good discussion of this issue from an American perspective. Nevertheless, a criticism might be made of American engineering educators to the effect that they

appear not to have considered recent developments testing such as the application of latent trait theory to item banking.[27]

Part of the misunderstanding arises from the fact that such items have to be completed quickly. For example, if skill in diagnosis in electrical circuits is to be tested by asking the student to identify faulty (v correct) circuits, the reading of the circuits might take some time. Computer assisted design of tests should enable a variety of approaches to be made to the design of items that allow a variety of approaches to the selection of the answer than the simple format of multiple choice questions as Zaina, Bressan, and Ruggiero (2002).[28]

Recent developments in computer assisted instruction may lead to a change of attitude toward objective tests. For example, Hwang (2003) of Nan University Taiwan has summarized recent work in this field prior to describing a test-sheet-generating algorithm for multiple assessment requirements.[29] He pointed out that the quality of test items relates not only to the item bank but also to the way the test sheet is constructed to take into account multiple test requirements. These would be the degree of difficulty, average discriminations, length of test time, number of test items, and specified distribution of test weights. In Hwang's model, fuzzy logic theory is used to determine the difficulty levels according to the learning status and personal features of each student. Items can be clustered into groups with the same properties, and with dynamic programming a test sheet can be constructed. He compared his approach with two other test-sheet generating methods against objective criteria and found his techniques to be better. The model would be able to embrace item response or latent trait models.

Another major criticism of objective items is that is not possible to observe the process that the student goes through when they answer the question. When this is possible, partial credit may be given for correct process but wrong answer (Posey, 1965). The value of objective tests in a multiple strategy approach to examining and assessment has still to be sold as a paper by Brown (2001) of the RMIT University in Australia shows. Brown made the point that objective items are not easy to design.

Objective tests are being used in the United Kingdom (Wellington and Collier, 2002)[30]; but as the

---

[24]In 1988 Canelos and Catchen (1989) reported a survey of testing practices in American engineering departments.

[25]See Thompson (1992) for a description of fixed length written examinations in Great Britain, especially as they relate to the testing of design.

[26]For example, the Fundamentals of Engineering examination set by the National Council of Examiners for Engineering and Surveying.

[27]Latent trait theory is sometimes called item-response theory. A trait level is the equivalent of the true score which is derived from the candidates performance. The candidate's ability is assumed to be constant: it is the error that varies and causes the responses to vary about the true ability or trait level. The models (curves) attempt to describe the relationship between the observed responses and the latent trait level as a function of the characteristics of the test items. The models consider items not test scores. The ability of an individual's responses to the items can be predicted. See Chapter 4 of Pellegrino, Chudowsky, and Glaser (2000).

[28]University of São Paulo.

[29] Among other papers cited by Hwang were Feldman and Jones (1997), Hwang (1998) and Lira, Bronfam and Ezaguirre (1990)

[30] Southampton Institute.

intake to universities, and engineering courses in that attention will be given to inventories like those that have been developed at Arizona State University following the work by Hestenes, Wells, and Swackhamer (1992) on the *Force Concept Inventory*. Papers on the *Wave Concepts Inventory* give illustrations of the objective items and show their relation to the Bloom Taxonomy (Roedel et al., 1998: Rhoads and Roedel, 1999). In the 1980s many articles in *Engineering Education* were of instructional. That is, they assumed the reader did not know about the topic. In the case of objective tests, and the possibility of machine scoring them, three articles in the November 1986 issue illustrated the basic principles. As such, they are seminal (Leuba, 1986a, 1986b; Nelson, Hughes, and Virgo, 1986). A much earlier article argued the case for improving innovative teaching with computer-generated exams (Lubkin, 1975).

One of the criticisms of objective tests is that the answers to items can easily be guessed. To compensate for guessing, a correction formula is sometimes applied. There have also been attempts to compensate for guessing by awarding negatives marks. Excell (2000) argued that the toleration of random answering breached the principle that students should not be awarded marks for work they had not done. Also, even though the marks awarded might be small, they could be differences in larger overall aggregates. He suggested that one way around this problem was to include a distracter that was patently "stupid." Those candidates who selected the stupid answer would be penalized by a mark of -1. This scheme was tried at the University of Bradford, and the average score was only slightly higher than those obtained in other subjects assessed by traditional methods. Hwang (2003) drew attention to a knowledge based computer assisted instruction system reported in New Zealand that could change the numeric component of the items while the test was in progress, which, it was held, prevented the student from guessing (Fan, Tina, and Shue, 1996).

Although a well-designed test may be reliable, it may not necessarily be valid. This appeared to be the case with a 30-item test that was used in a pre/post test arrangement to evaluate the effectiveness of an active component of the dynamics section of a course. No differences were found between the interactive and traditional sections of the course, and the investigators thought that this might be due to the fact that the test did not tap into the types and activities and skills used in the interactive component. They were, therefore, developing a test with open-ended applied problems similar to those encountered by the students in the interactive component (Yaeger et al., 1999).

In a study in South Africa, a move toward the use of short answer questions within a traditional paper was described by Hanrahan (1992). While he agreed that *"skilfully-set problems can test fundamental knowledge, the student's ability, proficiency in standard procedures and his ability to judge whether his attempt is correct,"* he pointed out that they took a significant amount of time

particular, changes in the United Kingdom, it is likely to mark. He proposed, therefore, to include short answer questions. In these questions *"The given information comprises one of: a short statement, a diagram, a table, a graph, an oscilloscope screen display or equation or an equation. The required quantity is stated in the find box as a concise sentence or a mathematical expression"* the questions had to have an unequivocal answer, but the degree of complexity and, therefore, difficulty was limited. He marked the answers on a right or wrong basis. He described several different formats. He said that a 1 hour paper might include one 20 to 30 minute full problem and 10 short answers of about 3 minutes duration each. A 3-hour paper would include six full problems and these would account for 75% of the marks. This is somewhat different from the short questions in the JMB Engineering Science paper, which were of 10-15 minutes' duration. In the comprehension exercise the questions required very short answers. Hanrahan found that the correlation between students' answers on short questions and problem questions was *"meaningful."*

Short answer questions are commonly used in quizzes in the United States. Yokomoto and Ware (1995) wanted to test the hypothesis that short problems were as effective as long problems because they had found that the correlation between the post exam quiz and the formal exam was very high. It could be that up to 815 of the factors contributing to the formal exam also contributed to the post-exam quiz. Therefore, he gave a pre-exam quiz and a post-exam quiz in the class period after the exam. Short problems for the pre-exam quizzes were selected solely on the basis of testing basic principles. In the post-exam quiz the problems were selected to test the concepts covered by the exam. The time allowed problem was the same in both pre-tests and post-tests. Two courses were examined in this way. From correlation and regression analyzes they found that the post-exam test was superior to the pre-exam test and that 72% of the factors associated with the formal examination were contained in the post examination. While accepting the small-scale limitation of the investigation, Yokomoto and Ware argued that short problems must be carefully written if they are to emulate long problem questions. In a subsequent paper, Yokomoto (2000) described how the classroom quiz might be modified to explore the knowledge base that the student has. The quiz had two components, the first of which was essentially brainstorming. He asked:

"Write, using words, equations, circuits, and graphs, all that you know about the self-bias method of biasing an n-channel JFET. Time limit; four minutes. Maximum score four points."

To score this he counted the number of valid responses and assigned a grade from one to four. The student did not have to write a fixed number of items to get the four points; rather, it depended on the overall performance of the class. To his surprise the correlation between the two components of the test was small. He made various suggestions as to why this might be. Overall he thought that there was need for a larger study in to the nature of knowledge base and the way it might be examined.

At the University of Sydney an experiment with 'power test' was used in a materials science course (Baillie and Toohey, 1997). This is a variation of a partly tailored exam (Bedard, 1974). In this examination, students are allowed to take as long as they like, within limits. They are also allowed to consult notes and reference sources and confer with their peers.

Baillie and Toohey said that, *"it is important to design the questions so that students are required to synthesize information from a variety of sources, apply their knowledge to specific contexts and justify their choices. If not well planned the open book exam may simply become an exercise in looking up the 'right answer."* They gave two examples, one of which was,

"You are contracted to design a metal platform as a base for a company's research unit in the Antarctic. Write a report for the company supporting your choice of metal/metals with which to build the platform."

Comparisons were made with the results from students who took the same examination but with closed books in the previous year. It was found that more students adopted deeper approaches to learning [They had classified the answers against the SOLO Taxonomy (Biggs and Collis, 1982).] However, some students were not happy with the new approach and may have continued to surface learn. Baillie and Toohey pointed out that great care had to be taken in introducing innovations of this kind if all the students were to be relatively happy with the new procedure. One of things they did was involve students in the determination of some of the objectives. Their evaluation included nominal group discussion, group discussion and interviews. In the nominal group, discussion took place on a voluntary basis during the final tutorial class. The questions that Baillie and Toohey asked were:

"What did you like about the course? What did you think about the open book assessment before the trial exam? What are you feeling right now about the exam? Can you give some idea of how you study for this course and how that might be different from how you study for this course -what do you actually do? What is the learning on this course?"

The questions were asked in the final tutorial. Students attended on a voluntary basis.

In the United Kingdom, Marshall (1994) used what he called *open exams* in a course on Power Conversion at the University of Surrey. In educational practice they are better known as 'prior-notice questions.' (Gibbs et al., 1986). In the way they were used by Marshall, the question that would be asked in the final examination would be given to the students at the beginning of the course. The numerical data were changed. In his case the course was of one year duration. Gibbs and his colleagues defined the paper by the amount of time required for completion; i.e., they had to be handed in at a specific time. Thus, a 168-hour paper was handed out one week before the answer had to be submitted. This might get over the difficulty pointed out by Thompson (1992), who thought that 3 hour written papers on design did not allow the student sufficient time to develop their ideas (see Section 12.3).

Marshall found that he could examine every principle that had been taught in the course. The question was divided into sections. A section obtained full marks if the solution was correct and supported by a complete working solution. No credit was given for partly correct solutions. There was no choice of questions. He claimed that in contrast with traditional examinations, this approach ensured that students covered the whole of the syllabus and that it motivated the students toward a target. He found that it did not discriminate among the most able students, but it distinguished between the competent and the incompetent. The greatest improvement was among the middle ranking students judged by comparison with results obtained from traditional examinations.

He felt that this type of examination reduced student stress, and he calculated that compared with traditional examinations there was a 22% saving of time.

A variant of this approach within an examination in systems analysis included a question on a case study that was distributed before the examination. It contained the solution and the question was set to obtain criticisms of the solution and suggestions for improvement.

Another variation in the United States, where essay type questions were unusual, was their introduction into a junior/senior elective on Biomedical Electrical Systems (Blackwell, 1991). The four weeks of the course devoted to cardiac devices were run on a group discussion basis. Each group selected four topics from a possible list of eight. Each member of each group was given a packet of articles that included one paper that related to each topic the group had chosen. A list of questions relating to each topic was given to the groups. The questions were so arranged that each member must read the article that he/she chose to read. The groups were told that 70% of the questions covering this part of the course in the test would come from this list. The group activity was to provide answers to these questions, and this required questions that would force them to *"combine information out of several articles to answer each question, and were commonly required to make one or more assumptions on the way to their answer."* Such questions had to be open ended and he gave the following example:

"Present a design for a Lown-waveform defibrillator which meets the following criteria: - maximum of 8 second charge time under allowable conditions of the power line and discharge energy up to 400 joules, includes all safety factors present in articles you have seen."

Blackwell noted that the demands of this part of the course were considerable but the results were good. Average grades increased by 13% when compared with those on the standard course. Improvement in grades does not, of course, imply an improvement in learning (understanding).

Several papers testify to the importance of question design. Traditional explicit problem solving questions test limited skill and do not necessarily test engineering ability, the art, suggested Howard (1999), is to get the students to 'explore' more, and this can be achieved by implicit problem statements that force them to work out what the problem is. To put it in another way, discovery learning in the classroom as opposed to the laboratory.[31]

16.5. Oral Examinations and Presentations.

Although oral examinations are commonplace in medicine, they are not often used in engineering.[32] However, it has become the practice to get students either individually or in teams to present orally the results or project work that they have done. This has been extended to take into account knowledge and skill. At Purdue University three teachers listened to each student's report and rated it on five dimensions. These were Understanding, Presentation, Operation, Testing, and Construction. Each of these was written on a five point scale, (out of 20), for which descriptors were written. Schultz (1999), who reported this approach, found that for 124 projects or 372 individual evaluations, the mean deviation was about 6% of the possible score. He felt that there, were large disagreements between the assessors, this could be accounted for by an unconventional project. Otherwise he thought the agreement was reasonable enough at this level of subjectivity. It is certainly in line with the experience of those who moderated the engineering science projects (see Section 9.12). He suggested that profiles of those who marked easily and those who marked hard should be obtained and that the teams should contain one easy marker and one hard marker.

In Sweden, Lundgren (1998) described how an oral examination had been introduced midway through a compulsory course in semi-conductor devices. Its purpose had been to provide a challenge to the students because less than half of the students had an interest in semi-conductor devices. The traditional written examination that took place at the end of the course was of four hours duration, during which the students were expected to answer 10 short questions on facts, 3 numerical problems, and 3 problems to determine that there was a coherent understanding of concepts and their relationships.

The oral examination was introduced midway into this course on a voluntary basis. Those who took it could gain a bonus of up to 10% of the total score of the final written examination. About 60 students of the 100 students in each year who took the course also took this oral examination. The exam *"tests the student's abilities in a significantly different way than a written exam. The focus will not be on formal details but on the meaning of concepts and their interrelations, and the inherent interactivity of the dialogue will enable a rather thorough examination of student conceptions. In our meaning go the word understanding is more explicitly tested in the oral examination than is feasible in a written exam."*[33]

Lundgren and his colleagues fully understood the assumptions they made when they initiated this development. First among them was the fact that the procedure was more likely to attract the motivated students. This meant that it would not catch students who were at risk. The problem was not to make the oral examination compulsory, but to find means for making it attractive to all students. They found that students who took the oral did significantly better in their final examination than those who did not. Fifty nine percent said they studied more than they would otherwise have done, and thirty six percent said that they had approached their study with a view to understanding. Forty four percent said that during the oral they realized that they had not fully understood and needed to do more study.

Eleven of the orals were video taped, and it was reported that *"The Oral Examination thus makes it possible not only to judge whether the student knows his subject or not, but also enables a description of how the student understands the subject."*

At the University of Bradford, first-year students in electrical engineering had to take a course in communications including oral communication. They were required to make an oral presentation in front of an audience. After a detailed briefing the students were asked to give a talk of 9 minutes duration later in the term (semester). They could choose their own topic. This did not have to be of a technical nature because they were first-year students. They had the opportunity to participate in a video-taped rehearsal. The presentation was chaired by the student's personal tutor. There was a specialist assessor, and after each talk the student's strengths and weaknesses were in confidence (Bowron, 1990). No formal evaluation was reported except that 75% of the students thought the course was worthwhile and that it had it had not increased their workload unreasonably.

Polack-Wahl (2000) reported that at Mary Washington University each student supplied the teacher with a VHS tape at the beginning of the semester. The students presentations are all put on this tape. *"When the students are presenting, it is best to do a 'quick evaluation.' The quick evaluation allows the instructor to make notes on style, content and dynamics. A quick evaluation may be different for each instructor. If the instructor prefers to listen intently to the speaker the quick evaluation can be list of positive and negative points that the instructor circles on a schedule that*

---

[31] It is important to note the development of intelligent questioning systems that is taking place e.g., Zaharian (2001).

[32] Reference has already been made above to their use in peer assessment by Magin and Helmore.

[33] Cowan has pointed out that this is a good example of Vygotsky's zone of proximal development. In that Vygotsky's theory, the child's (student's) actual developmental level observed. When a child (student) is working with an adult the potential of the child under optimum circumstances can be observed. The difference between these two levels of functioning in the zone of proximal development. The purpose of instruction is to develop those functions in the zone of proximal development that allow the child (student) to grow.

distinguishes between dynamics and format". "Other types of *"quick evaluation"* included written evaluations, Likert scale evaluations, or any combination of the previously described. If no evaluation is done, the instructor will have to watch the tape twice later on, once to evaluate the presentation and once to grade the presentation. Whatever evaluation technique is used, the evaluation assists in the video grading.

Afterwards, the presentation video was dubbed by the instructor with audio comments. A grade sheet was given to the student at the end of the exercise.[34]

16.6.   Grading

Apart from research, grading is probably the most important task that the teacher undertakes. No wonder there is a vast literature on the topic. Grades influence admissions and progress during college. In some institutions, in spite of the fact that often there is only a moderate correlation between final engineering grades and early performance, some students may be screened out at an early stage (Willingham, 1964). LeBold, while demonstrating that retention is a function of achievement, has nevertheless shown that when students are given an appropriate treatment (course), they can make gains and retention can be reduced (see above).

Because grades are important, The ERM division of ASEE took part in a national study of the variability of test scoring by different instructors (Work, 1976) The participants were given a sample test to mark. The study found that there was wide variation in grades assigned for a given student performance. This diversity was attributed to different objectives and philosophies of teaching and testing.[35] In the United Kingdom other studies produced similar results. McVey (1975, 1976a, b) of the Department of Electrical and Electronic Engineering at the University of Surrey in a series of studies came to largely similar but less pessimistic conclusions. He involved his colleagues in the determination of the standard error of his papers. He asked his colleagues to design two papers instead of the usual one that the students would sit. Each of the papers was to be of the same standard and to cover the same area of the syllabus. They were vetted by a committee that also looked at all the papers set in the examination. The two papers were set to the same group of candidates in place of those that they usually sat, at intervals of between one and four days. The scripts of each pair were marked by the examiners. Eleven pairs and 578 scripts were marked over a period of three years. Of the differences in marks obtained between the examiners, 52% were 10 marks or less, 18% exceeded 20 marks, and 5% exceeded 30. He found the standard error to be 7.64 marks, which, he thought, given the limitations of the experiment, was too optimistic!

In a subsequent experiment McVey tried to distinguish between marker error and paper error. The two are interrelated because the paper error must contribute to the marker error, especially in the circumstances where ambiguous questions are set. In essay or in question problem solving papers where the number of questions to be answered is small, the content of the syllabus that is likely to be covered may be small compared with what had to be studied by the student. Therefore a student who has "spotted" (predicted) the questions on a paper may be at an advantage compared with one who has not.

McVey concluded that paper error is greater than marker error. He relied on paid student volunteers to take the two examinations that were necessary because of the need to remove paper error. James (1977), in a later replication of this experiment, was able to administrate the examinations as a normal part of course. His findings were similar to those of McVey.

McVey also established that when the papers were marked by an independent person, if the marks of the first rater remained on the paper, the correlation between them was high. However, if the first raters marks were removed before the second rater marked the script, then the correlation between them became much weaker. Like so many studies of this kind they suffered from small samples. There were similar findings in the United States, and these influenced Creighton et al., (2001) in their preparation for ABET EC2000.

There were in America in the 1970s and 1980s a number of papers on grading practices. One approach to the problem of variability is to compile standard scores. T Scores or Z scores can be used for this purpose, although T scores are preferred. Cheshier (1975), who gave full details of his approach, found that his students approved of this method and had asked other tutors to do likewise.[36] Cheshier's paper caused a debate, and Danner (1978) opposed standardization. Danner considered that the statistical assumptions underlying Cheshier's approach were weak. These related to the assumption that the method depended on the test scores being normally distributed, that the standardization procedure was a sampling procedure, and that tests that were being averaged were equally reliable. These points were refuted by Thomas (1983), who for support used work by Ebel (1974) one of the doyen of educational testing. Ellerton (1980) also supported the use of T scores in grading and an algorithm for test grading was proposed by Lando (1986). Karunamoorthy and Andres (1991) described an adaptation of Cheshier's method of transformation. Thomas (1986) also provided a substantial introduction to the problems of reliability. Another problem related to the transformation of letter grades (Boyd, 1978; Ellerton, 1980).

---

[34] There is a detailed description of how this should and should not be done in the paper.

[35] The test the participants were asked to mark is given in full in the paper.

[36] This might be because they were engineering students. In my department where all the examinations were standardised some students did not understand the procedure. This was probably due to the fact that a number of the graduate teacher trainees had an inadequate statistical background.

Perhaps the most interesting and most controversial of the papers published during this period was by Kuhlmann-Wilsdorf (1975). She argued that the "standard" that a teacher chose to meet was expressed by the amount of subject matter presented to the students in a fixed period of time, i.e., the number of lectures. For example, *"if in an introductory course, a professor aims for a very high standard, he selects a textbook containing a goodly amount of mathematical formulation and many pages of detailed derivations, descriptions and examples. He then proceeds in his lectures to cover as much of the material presented in the book as physically as possible. Conversely, a professor aiming at a low standard selects a slim textbook with a minimum of mathematical formulation, giving little more than highlights and the most basic consequences."* It follows from these examples that the standard is a simple function of the rate of teaching. Kuhlmann-Wisdorf went on to argue that the standard achieved would be different in the two approaches. If the standard aimed for is low, the student stands the chance of understanding and retaining everything whereas if it is high, then at some stage beyond an optimum the student will not be able to understand and gets "left behind." This is a common experience even among groups of students that could be labeled bright. For some the rate is to high, for others too low. It is possible to plot the learning curves for all the students in the class and from them to determine the optimum rate of teaching.

The major point of her paper was to argue that grades were related to the rate of teaching. Curves were presented to demonstrate this point. In fast teaching, the students are taught beyond their optimum assimilation rate; consequently, few A's are awarded. In contrast, a slow rate will yield a lot of A's. The optimum rate in her example of 13 students yielded one fail, one D, one C, two B's, and 9 A's using the convention of 4,3,2,1,0 for each of the letter grades. The hypothesis did not depend on the marking scheme used. She argued that the failing student could have been helped by extra instruction and that the typical student of grade A or B standing gained nearly the maximum knowledge that could have been transferred at any rate of teaching. One suspects that this argument still applies in some cases.

Kuhlmann-Wisdorf found that her colleagues differed as to their views of the amount of knowledge actually transferred in their lectures. She found that the averages were in fair agreement with grading system used in England and the Commonwealth countries. That is, they believed that a student retained 70% of the material taught. In those courses the course material was covered as uniformly as possible; they were conducted to enable a candidate to obtain 100% only by consistent and fluent work, free of errors during the whole examination period. This view was somewhat idealized and it is only mentioned here because the paper is in sufficient detail to give some insight into the two approaches to grading. She found support for her use of the English scale in arriving at A's, etc.

One of the problems that worried institutions in that period and continues to worry them is that of grade inflation. It could, for example, influence academic award selection (Cook, 1985). It could misrepresent the quality of graduates; and even Harvard was recently criticized for inflating grades.[37]

Grade inflation is important because it can cause engineering to be perceived to be a tough subject if engineering students obtain lower grades. At the University of Utah, de Nevers (1984) reported that the average GPA of engineering students was 2.8, compared with 3.5 for other students. This had brought complaints from business recruiters. The students also complained because they believed they had to do much more work than the students in other colleges with whom they had been at high school. When the engineering department examined the problem, they found that there was evidence of grade inflation in other subjects, in particular with respect to the number of *summa cum laude* awards offered. The study enabled them to persuade the university to change the awarding system.

There was also a considerable debate about mastery learning and grading (see Chapter 14).

16.6.1. Holistic Grading

At a more specific level there has been a debate about holistic versus traditional marking in the grading of reports This debate has not been confined to engineering. They provide tutors with a problem in grading. Dyrud (1994) distinguished between traditional and holistic approaches to grading. In the former the assessor awarded up to 100 points for a technical report. These points are arrived at in response to a domain based system of scoring that awarded so many marks for organization, so many for grammar, etc. Much effort and time is expended on marking a technical report in this way.

Dyrud argued that a holistic scheme greatly reduced the time for the essay. In such a scheme, criteria for excellent, acceptable, and unacceptable papers are decided by the tutor. The tutor reads the paper and, if necessary, writes comments in the margins. Where there is an emphasis on revision, those students who do not get an excellent have the opportunity to revise their papers for a better mark.

It is argued that holistic marking is realistic because that is how judgments are made at work. From the tutors' perspective, holistic marking is quick. From the students' perspective, they are able to learn about the process and take responsibility for the detail (spelling/grammar).

Sharp (1994) defined holistic marking as *"grading the paper as a whole without marking each error."* Grammatical and stylistic errors are only evaluated in general. She described a student conference that seemed to be the equivalent of an "Oxbridge tutorial." The *"purpose of grading conference is to teach*

---

[37] Article by Patrick Healy in the *Boston Globe* 7:10: 2001; 31:1:2002 and others. Boston Globe/on line/Harvard looks to raise bar for graduating with honors.

students to notice and correct their own errors. After noting and explaining one type of error, the instructor can ask the student to identify the same error in another passage and to correct it. The instructor does not need to mark all the errors of the same kind". Sharp suggested that grading sheets could be helpful as, for example, organization and development (30%); coherence and sentence structure (30%); usage and vocabulary (20%); punctuation, capitalization, and spelling (10%); and neatness, readability, and visual impact (10%). This in contrast to Dyrud's scheme that was based on descriptions of expected performance at three levels.[38]

16.7.   Profiles

In the United Kingdom and the countries of the old British Empire, degree results are reported in a single phrase or number i.e. one, two one or first, second class, first division, etc. This represents the averaged aggregation of the marks for all the examinations that the graduate took. It is assumed that every one knows what these terms mean. But it has been shown repeatedly in the literature, and it is evident from the discussions in this review that many factors contribute to both achievement and potential. Success is obtained in many ways. For this reason, a single grade as a measure of a person's overall performance is regarded as unsatisfactory or, to use Jackson's (1985), term 'hazardous' or, as lawyers would say, 'unsafe.' Profiles may therefore provide a means for overcoming this difficulty, and may also be used to give information about personal qualities and interests. This is something more than the profile that is the transcript of courses attended by the American student and the grade point average.

Assiter and Fenwick (1992) distinguished between three types of profile that might overlap, and they were interlinked. The first is the prescribed *learning outcome profile*, that, is a summative assessment of what a student has achieved in terms of learning outcomes. It may be graded, but the assessment criteria would have to describe what constitutes achievement at each grade. These are similar to, if not the same as, the criterion profiles that have long been used in technical and professional education.

The second is the negotiated outcomes profile. This is similar to the first with the exception that the student would play a role in determining what educational objectives they wished to achieve. Assiter and Fenwick consider that such profiles would be appropriate for the work-based components of a program. They would also be appropriate for a course of independent study negotiated by student. In engineering design, this could be a project. The third is the personal development profile. It is used for the formative development of students. Such profiles are often similar to diaries, journals, and logbooks.

A criterion or prescribed learning outcome profile may be used as an indicator of 'graduateness,' provided that the parameters are well defined. In the United States, McGuire (1967) developed a profile for assessing performance in orthopaedic surgery. These were used by Freeman and Byrne (1976) to derive a profile for the assessment of performance in general practice. In their profile there were 9 criteria. Each of them described the behavioral objectives for an acceptable trainee and an unacceptable trainee. They found that when the profile ratings of the same trainees were compared for different tutors, there was a high degree of correlation among the tutors about the performance of the best trainees. However, discrepancies occurred in the middle range of performance, as well as in the rating given to the poorest students. Freeman et al., (1982) found that the best trainees were found to be those who were less rigid and authoritarian. This suggests that as with holistic scoring, students should be assessed by two examiners. They would have to agree the final award. In that study, criterion profiles were not used by themselves but with other forms of assessment.

In the United Kingdom, the engineering professors' standards and benchmarks are profiles. There is, already, much experience of the assessment of practical work, in particular, projects. Unfortunately, there are few evaluations. Evaluation of the multiple strategy examination in engineering science examination showed that good students did equally well in all components of the examination, so for this group the profile had little meaning. Some teachers think that there is a case for providing students with a profile irrespective of the grade awarded (Carter et al., 1980).

Experience suggests that it will difficult to decide what the profiles should be and what they should be called. Anyone who has had experience of the design of performance based profiles will testify to that fact. Early research showed simple mastery approaches did not work. Teachers wish to be able to differentiate because they perceive their students to differ in their responses to what it is they are asked to do. It was also found that loosely structured schemes did not work in public examinations and that schemes like those used in engineering science were to be preferred (Heywood, 1977). Miller and Olds (2001) met the same kind of difficulties when they designed their rubric for the assessment of a unit laboratory in chemical engineering. They followed the same procedures that had been used in the earlier work and found that using scales like "exceeds standards", "meets standards", "does not meet standards" did not enable them to differentiate between acceptable and unacceptable performance. Moreover, they found that assessors had difficulties with the term 'standard'. It *"seemed to denote for some faculty the notion of 'minimum standard' which then erroneously implied some sort of 'lowest common denominator graduation requirement' that absolutely every student would have to achieve."*

Miller and Olds changed their rubric to include four levels of performance that they called 'exemplary',

---

[38]Success in writing may relate to attitudes toward writing thus in evaluations of this kind instruments such that developed by Rhoads et al., (1998) might provide rewarding information.

'proficient,' 'apprentice.' and 'novice.' Ideally, it might be said for formative evaluation, but since the possibility of movement from novice to expert is implied, the titles are hardly those should preside over a summative profile!

16.8.   The Formative Evaluation of Assessment

George and Cowan (1999) argued that improvement in formal assessment procedures (.i.e., assessment for grading) and in course provision was more likely if assessment was the subject of analysis and formative evaluation. They listed and discussed 11 factors that ought to be evaluated. In question form these were:

1. *Is the assessed syllabus the same as the declared one?*
2. *Does the assessment covered the listed learning outcomes?*
3. *In what parts of the syllabus are the candidates obtaining their marks?*
4. *Do the students know what is required of them?*
5. *Do the students understand the questions?*
6. *Can and do the students think in examinations?*
7. *Are there real differences in quality across the range of performance?*
8. *What does the assessed work suggest about the presence of common weaknesses?*
9. *Do examiners know how candidates react to their questions and tasks?*
10. *How reliable is the marking process?*
11. *Does the assessment confirm that enduring learning has taken place?*

16.9.   Examination Anxiety

A recent study of examination anxiety among a small group of sophomore students at McMaster University in Canada came to conclusions that were very similar to those found by Ryle (1969) in the 1960s for the general student population in Great Britain (see also Malleson, 1965). Using the *Alpert-Haber Anxiety Achievement Inventory* Roney and Woods (2003) found that while the debilitation score was related to short and long term memory (as measured by the *Kellner-Sheffield Inventory*) and self-image it was not related to study skills, or avoidance to engage with difficult problems. Workshops designed to help students address self-image and the problems of anxiety had some short term success. Because other measures of assessment such as term work, projects, and self assessment were associated with significant improvements in performance, they advocated the use of measures that gave students more control over their performance including the possibility of contracting the weight of the final examination. Like the studies of the 1960s, this study leads to a multiple strategy approach to assessment. This is supported by what should be self evident, that is that is, that term and final tests cannot test all the objectives engineering educators would wish to test.

The idea of self assessment was not around in the 1960s, but in this study it was found that it was successful for all students irrespective of level of anxiety.

Roney and Woods pointed out that each individual student was unique, and that profiles could be produced for individual students that would be helpful guides to instructors.

Given the small sample and the implications for testing, it is important that this study should be replicated, and the effect of relating different kinds of assessment to objectives be evaluated.

16.10.   Concluding Remarks

The American National Research Council's report on assessment pointed out that:

"Every assessment, regardless of its purpose, rests on three pillars: a model of how students represent knowledge and develop competence in the subject domain, tasks or situations that allow one to observe students' performance, and an interpretation method for drawing inferences from the performance evidence thus obtained" (p. 53. Pellegrino, Chudowsky, and Glaser, 2001).

It is now understood, better than it ever has been, that assessment is not an isolated activity. It exerts a powerful influence on learning, and it must be aligned with the curriculum, teaching and learning. When assessment is seen by the student, to be a matter of valuable research, then that students learning will be enhanced at a deep level. Because the curriculum has many objectives assessment like teaching will be multiple-strategy, each method being chosen for the objective that it is most likely to achieve. For this reason, non-traditional (authentic) as well as traditional measures will be required if a person's performance is to be satisfactorily judged. There is growing experience of this pedagogy of assessment among engineering educators. Some have been prepared to take risks in the quest for greater validity with the type of tests they use. There is plenty of room for experimentation and innovation in the methodologies of assessment.

References.

Allen, M (1991) *Issues in Assessment*. Report of the Personal Skills Unit, University of Sheffield, Sheffield.

Anderson, E (1993) (ed). *Campus use of the Teaching Portfolio* with an introduction by Pat Hutchings. American Association for Higher Education, Washington, DC.

Ashworth, P et al (1996). Unpublished conference report.

Ashworth, P and U. Lucas (2000) Achieving empathy and engagement: a practical approach to the design, conduct and reporting of phenomenographic research. *Studies in Higher Education*, 25, (3), 29 – 308.

Assiter, A., and A. Fenwick (1992) *Profiling in Higher Education: an interim report*. CNAA Project Report 35. Council for National Academic Awards, London.

Baillie, C., and S. Toohey (1997). The 'power test': its impact on student learning in a materials science course for engineering students. *Assessment and Evaluation in Higher Education*. 22, (1), 33–47.

Baume, D., and M. Yorke (2002). The reliability of assessment by portfolio on a course to develop and accredit teachers in higher education. *Studies in Higher Education*, 27, (1), 7–25.

Bedard, R (1974). Partly tailored examinations. *Alberta Journal of Educational Research*, 20, (1), 15–23.

Besterfield Sacre, N., Amaya, N. Y., Shuman, L. J., Atman, C. J., and R. L. Porter (1998). Understanding student confidence as it relates to first year achievement. *Proceedings Frontiers in Education Conference*, 1, 258–263.

Biggs, J. B., and K. F. Collis (1982). *Evaluating the Quality of Learning. The SOLO Taxonomy*. Academic Press, New York.

Blackwell, G. R (1991). Group discussion techniques in a technical course. *Proceedings Frontiers in Education Conference*, 430–431.

Bloom, B et al (1956). *The Taxonomy of Educational Objectives: Cognitive Domain*. Longmans Green, New York

Boud, D (1986). *Implementing Student-Staff Assessment*. University of New South Wales. Higher Education Society of Australasia.

Boud, D (1989) The role of self-assessment in student grading. *Assessment and Evaluation in Higher Education*, 14, 20–30.

Boud, D (1995). *Enhancing Learning through Self-Assessment*. Kogan Page, London.

Boud, D., Churches, A. E., and E. M. Smith (1986). Student self-assessment in an engineering design course: an evaluation. *International Journal of Applied Engineering Education* 2, (2), 83–90.

Boud, D., and W. H. Holmes (1981) Self and Peer marking in undergraduate engineering course. *IEEE Transactions on Education* E. 24 (4), 267–274.

Bowron, P (1990). Teaching communication skills in electrical engineering degree courses. *International Journal of Electrical Engineering Education*. 27, 3 – 12.

Boyd, H., and J. Cowan (1986) A case for self-assessment based on recent studies of student learning. *Assessment and Evaluation in Higher Education*, 10, (3), 225–235.

Boyd, D. W (1978). A formal method for assigning letter grades. *Engineering Education*, 69, (2), 207–210.

Bramhall, M. D., Eaton, D. E., Lawson, J. S. and I. M. Robinson (1991). An integrated engineering degree program: student centered learning. In R. A. Smith (ed). *Innovative Teaching in Engineering*. Ellis Horwood.

Brown, R. (2001). Multi-choice versus descriptive examinations. *Proceedings Frontiers in Education Conference*, 1, T3A-13 to 18.

BTEC (1992). *Common Skills and Core Themes. General Guidelines*. Business and Technician Council, London.

Burgoyne, J. G (1975). The judgment process in management students' evaluation of their learning experiences. *Human Relations*, 28, (6), 543–569.

Burkhardt, J., and P. R. Turner (2001). Student teams and jigsaw techniques in an undergraduate CSE project course. *Proceedings Frontiers in Education Conference*. 2, F3D-12 to 17.

Butcher, A. C., Stefani, L. A. J., and V. N. Tariq (1995) Analysis of peer, self and staff assessment in group project work. *Assessment in Education; Principles , Policies and Practice*. 2, (2), 165-186.

Canelos, J., and G. Catchen (1989). Testing intellectual skills in engineering; test design methods for learning. *International Journal of Applied Engineering Education*, 5, (1), 3–12.

Carroll, S., Beyerlein, S., Ford, M and D. Apple (1996). A learning assessment journal as a tool for structured reflection in process education. *Proceedings Frontiers in Education Conference*, 310–313.

Carter, G., Armour, D. G., Lee, L. S., and R. Sharples (1980) Assessment of undergraduate electrical engineering laboratory studies. *Institution of Electrical Proceedings*, 127, A7, 460–474.

Carter, G., Heywood, J., and D. T. Kelly (1986). *A Case Study in Curriculum Development. Engineering Science at 'A' Level*. Roundthorn, Manchester.

Che, X (1999) Development of an on-line teaching portfolio for freshman design. *Proceedings Frontiers in Education Conference*, 13b1-26 to 30.

Cheshier, S. R (1975), Assigning grades more fairly. *Engineering Education*. 65, (4), 343–348.

Claxton, G (1995). What kind of learning does self-assesssment drive? Developing a 'nose' for quality: comments on Klenowski. *Assessment in Education; Principles, Policy and Practice.*, 2, (3), 339–344.

Colton, D. A. et al (1997). *Reliability Issues with Performance Assessments: A Collection of Papers*. ACT Research report 97-3. American College Testing Program. Iowa City.

Cook, K. M (1985) Grade inflation and grading standards: their effect on student academic award selection. *Engineering Education*, 74, (4), 235–237.

Cowan, J (1998). *On Becoming an Innovative University Teacher. Reflection in Action*. Open University Press, Society for Research into Higher Education, Buckingham.

Creighton, S. D., Johnson, R. L., Penny, J., and E. Ernst (2001).A comprehensive system for student program assessment: lessons learned. *International Journal of Engineering Education*, 17 (1), 81–87.

Cress, D and B. J. McCullogh-Cress (1995). Reflective assessment :portfolios in engineering courses. *Proceedings Frontiers in Education Conference*, 4C1- 7 to 9.

Danner, C. H (1978). Some limitations on using standardized grades to assign grades. *Engineering Education*, 68, (8), 836–837.

Dempsey, G. L., Anakwa, W. K. N., Higgins, B. D., and J. H. Irwin "(2003) Electrical and computer engineering assessment via senior mini-project. *IEEE Transactions on Education*, 46, (3), 350v–358.

De Nevers N. (1984). An engineering solution to grade inflation. *Engineering Education*, 74, (7), 661–683.

Dobson, P. (1989) Self and Peer assessment. In P. Herriott (ed) *Assessment and Selection in Organizations: Methods and Practice for Recruitment and Appraisal*. Wiley, Chichester.

Duerden, S et al (1997). Trendy technology or a learning tool? Using electronic journal on Webnotes TM for curriculum integration in the freshman program in engineering at ASU. *Proceedings Frontiers in Education Conference*, 3, 1549–1556.

Dyrud, M. A (1994). Holistic grading: an alternative approach. *Proceedings Frontiers in Education Conference*, 721–723.

Earl, S. E (1986) staff and peer assessment: measuring an individual's contribution to group performance. *Assessment and Evaluation in Higher Education*, 11, (1), 60–69.

Ebel, R. L (1965) *Measuring Educational Achievement*. Prentice Hall, Englewood Cliffs, NJ.

Ellerton, R. W (1980). Another look at assigning grades. *Engineering Education*, 70, (8), 837–839.

Eschenbach, E. A (2001). Improving technical writing via web-based peer review of final reports. *Proceedings Frontiers in Education Conference*, 2, F3A-1 to 5

Excell, P. S (2000). Experiments in the use of multiple choice examinations for electromagnetics related topics. *IEEE Transactions on Education*, 43, (3), 250–256.

Fabb, W. E. and J. E. Marshall (1983). *The Assessment of Clinical Competence in General Family Practice*. MTP Press, Lancaster.

Falchikov, N (1986). Product comparisons and process benefits of peer group and self-assessments. *Assessment and Evaluation in Higher Education*, 11, (2), 146–186

Fan, J. P., Tina, K. M., and L. Y Shue (1996). Development of a knowledge based computer system. International Conference on Software Engineering: Education and Practice. Dunedin, New Zealand.

Feldman, J. M. and J. Jones.(1997) Semi automatic testing of student software under UNIX(R). *IEEE Transactions on Education*, 40, 158–161.

Frair, L (1995). Student peer evaluations using the analytic hierarchy process method. *Proceedings Frontiers in Education Conference*, 4c3–1 to 5.

Freeman, J., Carter, G and T. A. Jordan (1978). Cognitive styles, personality factors, problem solving skills and teaching approach in electrical engineering. *Assessment in Higher Education*, 3, 86.

Freeman, J., Roberts, J., Metcalfe, D., and V. Hillier (1982*) The Influence of Trainers on Trainees in General Practice*. Occasional Paper No 21. Royal College of General Practitioners, London.

Freeman, J., and P. Byrne (1976) *The Assessment of General Practice*, 2nd Edition. Society for Research into Higher Education, London.

Gentili, K. L et al (1999). Assessing student's design capabilities in an introductory design class. *Proceedings Frontiers in Education Conference*, 3, 13b-1-8 to 10.

George, J., and J. Cowan (1999). *A Handbook of Techniques for Formative Evaluation*. Kogan Page, London.

Gibbs, G., Habeshaw, T., and S. Habeshaw (1986), 1993).*53 Interesting Ways to Assess Your Students*. Technical and Educational Services, Bristol.

Gibbs, G., and L. Lucas (1995). Research to Improve Student Learning in large Classes. International Improving Student learning Symposium. Mimeo.

Goldfinch, J., and R. Raeside (1990) Development of peer assessment technique for obtaining individual marks on a group project. *Assessment and Evaluation in Higher Education*, 15, (3), 210–231.

Hamilton-Jones , J., and T. Svane (2003). Developing research using reflective diaries. *Proceedings Frontiers in Education Conference* 1, T3A-14 to 19.

Hanrahan, H. E (1992). Effective examining using short questions. *International Journal of Electrical Engineering Education,*29, 205–211.

Helfers, C., Duerden, S., Garland, J., and D. Evans (1999). An effective peer revision method for engineering students in first-year English courses. *Proceedings Frontiers in Education Conference,* 3, 13a6- 7 to 12

Heywood, J (1977). *Examining in Second Level Education.* Association of Secondary Teachers of Ireland, Dublin.

Heywood, J (2000). *Assessment in Higher Education. Student learning, Teaching, Programs and Institutions.* Jessica Kingsley, London.

Hestenes, D., Wells, M., and G. Swackhamer (1992). Force Concept Inventory. *The Physics Teacher,* 30, 141.

Hodges, B et al (1996). Evaluating communication skills in the objective structures clinical examination format: reliability and generalizability. *Medical Education,* 30, 281–286.

Houston, W., Raymond, M., and J. Svec (1991) Adjustment for rater effects in performance assessment. *Applied Psychological Measurement,* 15, 409–421.

Howard, B (1999). Enough of science and mathematics: lets do some engineering. *Proceedings Frontiers in Education Conference,* 3, 13d2-8–10.

Hwang, G. J (1998). A tutoring strategy support system for distance learning networks. *IEEE Transactions on Education,* 41.

Hwang, G. J (2003). A test-sheet-generating algorithm for multiple assessment requirements. *IEEE Transactions on Education,* 46, (1), 3, 329–337.

John, O. P. and R. W. Robins (1994). Accuracy and bias in self-perception: individual differences in self-enhancement and the role of narcissism. *Journal of Personality and Social Psychology,* 66, 206–219.

Karunamoorthy, S and R. M. Andres (1991). A new perception to the transformed score. *Proceedings Frontiers in Education Conference,* 41–44.

Kashy, D. A., et al. (2001). Individualized interaction exercises. A promising role for network technology. *Proceedings Frontiers in Education Conference,*F1E-8 to 13.

Klenowski, V (1995). Student self evaluation processes in student-centered teaching and learning contexts in Australia and England. *Assessment in Education. Principles, Policy and Practice,* 2, (2), 145–154.

Kuhlmann-Wilsdorf, D (1975). Academic standards and grades. *Engineering Education,* 66, (2), 160–164.

Lando, C. A (1986) A computer algorithm for scaling. *Engineering Education,* 76, (4), 225-226.

LeBold, W. K., Budny, D. D., and S. K. Ward (1998). Understanding of mathematics and science: efficient models for student assessment. *IEEE Transactions on Education,* 41, (1), 8–16.

Lejk, M., Wyvill, M., and S. Farrow (1996). A survey of methods of deriving individual grades from group assessment. *Assessment and Evaluation in Higher Education,* 21, (3), 267–280.

LeMahieu, P. G., Gitomer, D. H., and J. T. Eresh (1995) *Portfolio's Beyond the Classroom. Date, Quality and Qualities.* Educational Testing Service, Princeton, NJ.

Lennartsson, B., and E, Sundin (2001). Fronesis- The third dimension of knowledge, learning, and evaluation. *Proceedings Frontiers in Education Conference,* 1, T2B-14 to 19.

Leuba, R. J (1986a). Machine scored testing I. Purposes, Principles, and Practices. *Engineering Education,* 77, (2), 89-95

Leuba, R. J (1986b). Machine scored testing II. Creativity and item analysis. *Engineering Education,* (2), 181–186.

Lira, P., Bronfman, M., and J. Eyzaguirre (1990). MULTITEST II. A program for the generation, correction, and analysis of multiple choice tests. *IEEE Transactions on Education.* 33, 320–325.

Lubkin, J. L (1975). Improving innovative teaching with computer generated exams. *Engineering Education,* 65, (5), 408 – 414.

Lundgren, P (1998) Effects of elective oral examinations in a semiconductor devices course for computer engineering students. *International Journal of Engineering Education,* 14, (4), 294–299.

Lundström, T. S., and S. A. Booth (2002). Journals based applications: an attempt to improve students' learning about composite materials. *European Journal of Engineering Education,* 27, (2), 195–208.

Magin, D., and P. Helmore (2001). Peer and teacher assessments of oral presentation skills: how reliable are they? *Studies in Higher Education,* 26, (3), 287–298.

Marshall, P (1994). Open-exams: an experiment in student assessment. *Engineering Science and Education Journal, February,* 15–20.

McGuire, C (1967). *An Evaluation Model for Professional Education: Medical Education.* College of Medicine, Chicago.

McKenna, A., MacMartin, F., Terada, Y., Sirivedhin, V and A. Agogino (2001). Paper 1330. Annual Conference Proceedings of the American Society for Engineering Education.

McVey, P. J (1975). The errors in marking examination scripts. *International Journal of Electrical Engineering Education,* 12, (3), 203.

McVey, P. J (1976a). Standard error of the mark of an examination paper in electronic engineering. *Proceedings Institution of Electrical Engineers,* 123, (8), 843–844.

McVey, P. J (1976b) The paper error of two examinations in electronic engineering. *Physics Education,* 11, 58–60.

Mafi, M (1989) Involving students in a time-saving solution to the homework problem. *Engineering Education,* 79, (3), 444–446.

Malleson, N (1965) *A Handbook of British Student Health Services.* Pitman, London.

Miller, R. L and B. M. Olds (1994). Encouraging critical thinking in an interactive chemical engineering laboratory environment. *Proceedings Frontiers in Education Conference,* 506–510.

Miller, R. L., and B. M. Olds (2001) Performance assessment of EC 2000 student outcomes in the Unit Operations Laboratory. *Proceedings Annual Education Conference,* ASEEE Session 3513.

Moon, J. (1999). *Learning Journals.* Kogan Page, London,

Mourtos, N. J (1997). Portfolio assessment in aerodynamics. *Proceedings Frontiers in Education Conference* 91–94.

Mutharasan, R., Magee, W., Wheatley, M., and Y. Lee (1997). Multimedia assisted instruction in upper level engineering courses. *Proceedings Frontiers in Education Conference,* 2, 1175–1178.

Nelson, C. C., Hughes, B. J., and R. E. Virgo (1986). CAI Applications in Statics. *Engineering Education,* 77, (2), 96–100.

Nelson, S. (2000) Teaching collaborative writing and peer review techniques to engineering and technology undergraduates. *Proceedings Frontiers in Education Conference,* 3, S2B-1-S2B-5.

Nystrand, M., Cohen, A. S., and N. M. Dowling (1993). Addressing reliability problems in the portfolio assessment of college writing. *Educational Assessment,* 1, 515-520.

Olds, B (1997). The use of portfolios in outcomes assessment. *Proceedings Frontiers in Education Conference,* 262–265.

Orsmond, P., Merry, S., and K. Reiling (1996). The importance of marking criteria in the use of peer assessment. *Assessment and Evaluation in Higher Education* 21, (3), 239–250.

Payne, R. N., Bramhall, M. D., Lawson, J. S., Robinson, I and C. Short (1993). Portfolio assessment in practice in engineering. *International Journal of Technology and Design Education,* 3, (3), 37–42.

Pellegrino, J. W., Chudowsky, N., and R. Glaser (2001) (eds.). *Knowing What Students Know. The Science and Design of Educational Assessment.* National Academy Press. Washington, DC.

Penny, A. J and C. Grover (1996) An analysis of student grade expectations and marker consistency. *Assessment and Evaluation in Higher Education,* 21, (2), 173–184.

Petro D. W (2001). Cross-checking and good scores go together: students shrug. *Proceedings Frontiers in Education Conference,* 1, T3A- 7 to 12.

Polack-Wahl, J. A (2000). It is time to stand up and communicate. *Proceedings Frontiers in Education Conference,* 2, F1G –16

Polizzotto, L and W. R. Michalson (2001) The technical, process and business considerations for engineering design. *Proceedings Frontiers in Education Conference* 2, FIG- 19t o 24.

Posey, C. J (1965). Partial credit for wrong answers. *Engineering Education,* 56, (2), 39.

Puk, T (1995) Creating a quatum design scheme integrating extra rational and rational learning processes. *International Journal of Technology and Design Education,* 5, 255-266.

Rada, R., and K. Hu (2002). Patterns in student-student commenting. *IEEE Transactions on Education.* 45, (3), 262–267.

Rafiq, Y., and H. Fullerton (1996). Peer assessment of group projects in civil engineering. *Assessment and Evaluation in Higher Education*, 23, (3), 313–324.

Rhoads, T. R., Duerden, S. J., and J. Garland (1998). Views about writing survey- a new writing attitudinal survey applied to engineering students. *Proceedings Frontiers in Education Conference,* 973–979.

Rhoads, T. R., and R. J. Roedel (1999). The Wave Concept Inventory-A cognitive instrument based on Bloom's Taxonomy. *Proceedings Frontiers in Education Conference,* 3, 13c1-14 to 18.

Riley, K (1999). Seven habits of highly effective writers. *IEEE Transactions on Professional Communication*, 42, (1), 47-51.

Roedel, R. J., El Ghazaly, S., Rhoads, T. E. and E. El-Sharawy (1998). Wave Concepts Inventory- An assessment tool for courses in electromagnetic engineering. *Proceedings Frontiers in Education Conference*, 647–656.

Rogers, G. M., and J. K. Sando (1996). *Stepping Ahead: An Assessment Plan Development Guide.* Rose-Hulman Institute, Terre Haute, Indiana.

Rokeach, M. (1960). *The Open and Closed Mind.* Basic Books, New York

Roney, S. D., and D. R. Woods (2003). Ideas to minimize examination anxiety. *Journal of Engineering Education*, 92, (3), 249–256.

Rover, D. T., and P. D. Fisher (1998). Student self-assessment in upper level engineering courses. *Proceedings Frontiers in Education Conference*, 2, 980–986.

Rumpf, D. L. and S. Mehra (1988). Student journals in engineering education: Do they work? *Engineering Education*, 78, (5), 313–316.

Ryle, A (1969). *Student Casualties.* Allen Lane/, London.

Sander, M. E (2000). Web-based portfolios for technology education. *The Journal of Technology Studies*, 26, (1). 1–17.

Schultz, T. W. (1999). Synchronizing project assessments. *Proceedings Frontiers in Education Conference*, 12a1-1 to 4.

Schweiker, M., Moore, D. J., and D. R. Voltmer (2002). The design of an enhanced curricular evaluation+ portfolio (ECE + P) software system. *Proceedings Frontiers in Education Conference*, 1, T1BB-3 to 16.

Segers, M., and P. Dochy (2001). New assessment forms in problem-based learning: the value added of the students' perspective. *Studies in Higher Education*, 26 (3), 327–343.

Senge, P. M (1990). *The Fifth Discipline: The Art and Practice of the Learning Organization.* Doubleday, New York.

Senge, P. M, Roberts, C., Ross, R. B., Smith, B. J and A. Kleiner (1994). *The Fifth Discipline Fieldbook.* Doubleday, New York.

Sharp, J. E (1994). Grading technical papers during student conferences. *Proceedings Frontiers in Education Conference*, 724–728.

Sharp, J. E (1997). Using portfolios in the classroom. *Proceedings Frontiers in Education Conference*, 272 – 279.

Slater, T. F (1996). Portfolio assessment strategies in grading first-year university physics students in the USA. *Physics Education*, 31, (5), 329–333.

Slater, T. F., and P. M. Astwood (1995). Strategies for grading and using student assessment portfolios. *Journal of Geology Education*, 45, 216–220.

Sobek II, D. K (2002). Representation in design: data from engineering journals. *Proceedings Frontiers in Education Conference*, 2, Fd-11 to 16.

Storms, B. A., Sheingold, K., Nuzez, A. M. and J. I. Heller (1998). *The Feasibility, Comparability and Value of Local Scorings of Performance Assessments.* Educational Testing Service, Princeton, NJ.

Streveler, R. A., and R. L. Miller (2001). Investigating student misconceptions in the design process using multidimensional scaling. Session 2630. *Proceedings Annual Conference of the American Society for Engineering Education.*

Terwilliger, J (1997). Semantics, Psychometrics, and assessment reform. A close look at authentic assessment. *Educational Researcher*, 26, (98) 24–27.

Thomas, C. R (1983). A re-examination of standard scores used in grade assignment. *Engineering Education.* November, 114–116.

Thomas, C. R (1986) Examination reliability and reliability-weighted composite score. *Engineering Education*, 76, (4), 227–231.

Thompson, G (1992). On the assessment of student design ability. *International Journal Mechanical Engineering Education*, 21, 1, 72- 80.

Thompson, R. S (2001). Relative validity of peer and self-evaluation in self-directed interdependent work teams. *Proceedings Frontiers in Education Conference* 1, T4A-9 to 14.

Topping, K (1998) Peer assessment between students in colleges and universities. *Review of Educational Research.* 68, 249–276.

Upchurch, R. C and J. E. Sims-Knight (2002) Portfolio use in software engineering education an experience report. *Proceedings Frontiers in Education Conference*, 3, S26–1 to 5.

Vygotsky, L. S (1978). *Mind in Society. The Development of Higher Psychological Processes.* Translation. Harvard University Press, Cambridge, MA.

Wankat, P. C., and F. S. Oreovicz (1993). *Teaching Engineering.* McGraw Hill, New York.

Wellington, S. J., and R. E. Collier (2002). Experiences using student workbooks for formative and summative assessment. *International Journal of Electrical Engineering Education*, 39, (3), 263–268.

Wergin, J. F., Boland, D., and T. W. Haas (1986). Televising graduate engineering courses: results of an instructional experiment. *Engineering Education*, 77, (2), 109–112.

Wheeler, P. A (1996). Using the WWW in advanced digital design courses. *Proceedings Frontiers in Education Conference*, 3, 1039–1041.

Wiggins, G (1993). *Assessing Student Performance.* Jossey-Bass, San Francisco.

Wiliam, D (1995), Combination, aggregation and reconciliation: evidential and consequential bases. *Assessment in Education. Principles Policy and Practice*, 2, 1, 53–73.

Williams, J. M (2002). The engineering portfolio; Communication, reflection, and student learning outcomes assessment. *International Journal of Engineering Education.* 18, (2), 199.

Willingham, W. W (1964). Freshman grades and educational decisions. *Engineering Education.* 54, (10), 329–332.

Wolf, A (1998). Portfolio assessment in national policy. The National Council for Vocational Qualifications and its quest for pedagogical revolution. *Assessment in Education. Principles, Policy and Practice.* 5, (3), 413–446.

Woods, D. R., Haymark, A. N., and R. R. Marshall (1988). Self-assessment in the context of the McMaster problem-solving skills. *Assessment and Evaluation in Higher Education*, 13, (2), 107–127.

Work, C. E (1976). A national study of the variability of test scoring by different instructors. *Engineering Education*, 67, (3), 24 –248.

Wright, J. C (1993). Measuring CPD. *Engineering Science and Education Journal*, 23–30, February.

Yaeger, P. M., Marra, R. M., Costanzo, F., Gray, G. L and D. Sathianathan (1999). Interactive dynamics: effects of student centered activities on learning. *Proceedings Frontiers in Education Conference,* 1, 11a2-13 to 18.

Yokomoto, C. F (1993a) Using Journals in the engineering classroom. *Proceedings Frontiers in Education Conference*, p 120.

Yokomoto, C. F (1993b).What pre-exam and post-exam quizzes can tell us about test construction. *Proceedings Frontiers in Education Conference*, 2c1.6 to 8.

Yokomoto, C. F (2000). Promoting depth of knowledge through a new quiz format to improve problem solving abilities. *Proceedings Frontiers in Education Conference*, 2, F2B-8 to11.

Yokomoto, C. F and R. Ware (1995). What pre-exam and post-exam quizzesz can tell us about test construction. *Proceedings Frontiers in Education Conference*, 2c1- 6 to 8.

Zaharian, S. A. et al (2001). Question model for intelligent questioning systems in engineering education. *Proceedings Frontiers in Education Conference*, 1, T2B- 7 to 12.

Zaina, L. A. M., Bressan, G and W. V. Ruggierio (2002). Tool to develop and apply objective tests. *Proceedings Frontiers in Education Conference*, 1, T1B-1 to 6.

CHAPTER 17: ATTRITION AND RETENTION

Summary and Introduction

When this report was planned, the intention was to conclude it with a Chapter on admissions and retention. In retrospect, it seems that the conclusions that would have emerged have been implicitly, if not explicitly, expressed in the previous chapters. Nevertheless, discussion of admission and retention can bring focus even though there may be some overlap with previous chapters, to what is, in essence, part of an epilogue since it concludes with a summary of things that have been found to enhance learning and teaching.

The first part of the chapter draws attention to the problem of the supply of students to engineering departments from high school. This has been a continuing issue during the last forty-five years; and school teachers have been continually exhorted to persuade their pupils to become engineers-without very much success it would seem.

Schools have been encouraged to engage in design and make projects in the hope that this would interest their pupils in engineering. In Great Britain, Engineering Science was introduced into the school's examination curriculum and had little success. The engineering professors' gave little support to this curriculum, preferring to emphasize the merits of physics. During the period, with little or no assistance from the engineering profession, a world movement emerged from the industrial arts in design and technology, the emphasis of which tended to be on design. Like engineering, it suffered from a problem of identity. The implications of these developments for engineering departments are discussed in the light of opposing views to the effect that engineering educators on the one hand should, and on the other hand should not, intervene in the school curriculum. Some interventions in the United States have been shown to be successful, especially those directed at women and minorities.

It is argued that in any case there is a general obligation to help schools with technological literacy, but this should be undertaken for its educational merits and not for the social engineering purpose of increasing the supply of students. Attention is drawn to the fact that research on children learning to design has implications for engineering education.

A worldwide problem is the large number of students whose mathematical proficiency is relatively poor. In some countries this is a result of misalignments between the secondary school and engineering curricula. There is no easy fix, and engineering schools may have to change the organization of their curriculum where this is a problem, or introduce types of supplementary instruction.

The phenomenon of large rates of attrition during the first year is also a worldwide problem. There is a need to ease the problems associated with the transition from school to university, and some innovations to that end are described. These evidently have as their goal the creation of learning communities.

On the basis of face validity, it is argued that, overall this review supports the findings made by Astin from his extensive studies of liberal arts students. Engineering is not a special case. The more teachers know about their students and how they learn, the more effective their curriculum planning and teaching will be. For many it will involve a substantial change in role.

17. The Supply of Engineers and Technology Interventions in the School Curriculum

Throughout the nearly fifty years of engineering education that is encompassed by this review, the engineering profession has been bothered by what it has perceived to be a shortage of able[1] students wanting to study engineering.[2] In Great Britain, in 1963, among several reports on the attitudes of post primary (elementary) children to engineering, one of them which suggested that the entrants to engineering were less able than those who entered the 'pure sciences' shook the engineering establishment (Hutchings, 1963). It was particularly traumatic because it came it came at a time when a government committee was about to report on the future of higher education.[3]

Solutions to this problem were sought during the next twenty years and several government committees were convened to consider the more general issue of the supply of qualified manpower.[4] The engineering educators felt that school teachers should do more to persuade their students that engineering was an attractive career but provided them with precious little evidence to justify that claim. Among the suggestions was, that since adolescents might favor careers in 'pure science' because they had to study science subjects for their entrance to university, they should also be exposed to engineering in the school curriculum in the hope of achieving a similar outcome. But, what is engineering?

Attempts to answer this question produced not only a committee of enquiry[5] but also alternative views. The first of these argued that participation in engineering project activities in schools would change student attitudes. The second argued that if engineering were to acquire status, it would have to be an examined subject of the General Certificate of Education. Within both schools of thought there were those who thought that their proposals had educational merit irrespective of the supply problem. it is interesting to note that at the time there were reports of high schools in the United States teaching engineering concepts (EJCA, 1965).

---

[1] As measured by the grade obtained in advanced level examinations of the General Certificate of Education.

[2] I put it this way because a substantial paper by a British economist has argued that market forces dictate whether or not there is a shortage, and that in Great Britain the market has been satisfied (Marris, 1986).

[3] The Robbins Committee (1963).

[4] e.g., The Dainton report (1968) viewed the swing to the arts and social studies with alarm.

[5] Established by the Institution of Mechanical Engineers. Report by Page (1965).

In the event the majority of the engineering professors supported the project approach, and it became the first curriculum development supported by the Schools Council (Project Technology). The professors who supported an examination found a home for their work in the Joint Matriculation Board, and development of this subject received support from Project Technology! This project also published a set of books on engineering science topics. (See Chapter 2 for some details of this examination)

Although, in the long run, this examination failed because of the small numbers of candidates, it was a major and pioneering development in English education (Carter, Heywood, and Kelly, 1986). While it did not succeed in providing a flow of able students into engineering, it did demonstrate the need for multiple strategy approaches to the assessment of student learning as well as for evaluation.

The development of this examination met resistance from two sources. The first was the Engineering Professors' Conference.[6] Although engineering science had been set up as equivalent to physics, the conference did not wish to recommend it to engineering departments because it believed that physics was preferable. It wanted highly qualified candidates in mathematics and physics, but this was to support a cultural climate in which physics was perceived to be superior to engineering. Edels (1968), who led the development, found few takers for the philosophical rationale of the differences between engineering science and physics that he presented in support of this new examination.

The other objectors were the teachers of woodwork and metalwork (the industrial arts in the United States) in the geographical area served by the Joint Matriculation Board's examinations.[7] These subjects were threatened with extinction because of falling numbers. Their teachers hoped that engineering science would give them the status they sought. Unfortunately, they found the subject was too mathematical and too scientific. No one considered offering them retraining, but from the experience of training and retraining teachers for 'Technologie" in France and the difficulties encountered in Ireland there is reason to believe that it would not have been successful. The upshot was that this group of teachers found a new home in design, which was a curriculum area that was growing rapidly while engineering science floundered. Engineering Science also had the difficulty of recruiting teachers and had to rely mainly on those who had physics qualifications. This compounded the conflict inherent in the selection system because engineering science was designed to be equivalent to, and therefore an alternative to physics.

During the next ten years the idea that technology should accompany design was promoted independently of the engineering profession. Technology was interpreted as a systems approach to the teaching of electronics, mechanisms, and hydraulics. The arithmetical component was limited. The traditional approach to teaching the skills of metalwork and woodwork were dropped in favor of design and make projects. It is evident that those who developed the subject did not see it as a route to the study of engineering; after all, engineering departments had not accepted woodwork and metal work for their entry requirements.[8] In any case the emphasis in the subject was on design. These teachers came primarily from teacher education colleges, and their goals would not have been the enhancement of the supply of students to engineering since they themselves were not trained to be engineers. (Gradwell, 1996).[9] This view is reinforced by the fact that neither Gradwell nor Lewis in their comparative studies of developments in design and technology curricula in the United Kingdom and United States make a reference to the Page report or to the development of engineering science or the support it received from Project Technology.

By the middle of the 1980s, there was a world-wide movement in design and technology education in which those who had supported this approach in the United Kingdom were much sought after as consultants. By the end of the 1980s, design and technology, in one guise or another, was a compulsory subject in many countries. A world organization for technology organizations was launched at a conference in Weimar supported by the Technical Foundation of America (Blandow and Dyrenfurth, 1992).

In the United States these developments were accompanied by radical changes in the university departments of the industrial arts, including changes of name. The American based International Technology Education Association took a lead in establishing the Technology for All Americans project with the aid of funding from NASA and NSH (Dugger, 1995). Prior to that, National Science Education Standards had been developed and Fadali and Robinson (2000) examined them to see if they (a) generated enough interest in engineering and technology and (b) provided adequate preparation for engineering and technology. They

---

[6]Professors in the British context are the senior members of an engineering department. They would have a considerable say in admissions policy, and their advice would be sought by the professional institutions.

[7]The Midlands and North of England.

[8]With the exception of the Department of Engineering at the University of Leicester.

[9]Teacher training in woodwork and metalwork and other crafts was mostly undertaken in colleges specifically designated for this purpose. At the time there was a shake up of teacher training colleges per se and most of the free-standing colleges were merged with university departments of education or polytechnics. These specialist colleges were forced to evaluate their role and that of the subjects they taught. Technology was already impacting on the use of these materials, and separate high skill training was no longer perceived, to meet the needs of work. There was a need for a multi media approach through design that met the needs of teachers not primarily skilled in mathematics and physics (Gradwell, 1996).

concluded that while the standards would lead to an improvement in the science and math backgrounds of the students, which would be advantageous for engineering, they did not provide for sufficient exposure to engineering and technology. Moreover, the aspects of engineering covered would not be familiar to K-12 teachers. Surely one might ask; Isn't this the role of the technology standards?

Quite clearly, as indicated above, these developments were not made with a view to increasing the supply of students to engineering. It is doubtful if many of the teachers involved thought of themselves as teaching for engineering. Where these subjects were made a compulsory part of the curriculum, governments were responding to an economic view that the population ought to be technologically literate (Lewis, 1996). Insofar as engineering is concerned, this creates a muddle, because how does a technologist differ from an engineer. It is particularly difficult in the United States because a Bachelor of Technology degree is a lower level qualification than that of the Bachelor of Engineering degree. It corresponds to what is an upper level technician qualification in the United Kingdom.[10]

Unfortunately for this development, and in spite of its success, very many teachers confuse it with information technology. The subject also suffered from a lack of clear definition.[11] This issue, like the analogous issue in engineering has produced a profusion of papers about the nature of technology, technological capability, and technological literacy. One model, developed in Ireland, was clearly influenced by engineering, but in spite of substantial laboratory research on its teaching, the authors were unable to persuade the Minister to accept their work (Heywood, 1986). In Ireland, as in England, the Minister had to have an avenue for the existing woodwork and metalwork teachers. However, in the context of engineering, in Slovenia, a project-based course in mechatronics was introduced into the school technology program to integrate electronics, mechanical control and computer engineering (Kocijancic, 2001). Some Swedish social scientists used the undirected play of 6-7-year-old children to study the learning that happened with robotics and led them to suggest integrated play systems. They gave an example of moveable computers with separate open-ended gadgets (Aderklou et al., 2002).

A view of school technology suggested by a Canadian research worker could almost apply to engineering. Hill (1998) defined it as a study in elementary and secondary schools: *"where students are provided the opportunity to use a variety of materials and processes to solve real-life technological problems; to develop technological skills and concepts and the ability to use tools (including computers) to acquire an understanding of various technological systems and processes: to evaluate the impact of technology on people and the environment; and to develop the confidence to be risk takers in technological problem-solving."*

The trouble with that definition is there is no mention of science, and for some teachers these activities could be interpreted as an art. To accommodate engineering, it would have to clearly state that it was about the art and science of making things.

In the United Kingdom there was, within this debate about technology in schools, an important argument as to whether there should be a national test in technology.

In the late nineteen 1970s the government decided to check school standards in English, Math and Science at several different age levels. For this purpose it created an Assessment in Performance Unit (APU). Some technology educators thought there should be a test in technology, and the APU called together a group of technology and science educators to consider this proposition. At the meeting it was argued that technology was a problem solving activity. Some scientists took exception to this view and argued that in science problems were solved in the same way (i.e., generating hypotheses; gathering data; choosing from alternatives; implementing; and evaluating). The implication was that it was unnecessary to have a technology test since these skills were measured in science. Technology could not, therefore, be defined by problem solving alone.

In the event the development of a test in technology was approved, and its report should be a landmark in the evaluation of the assessment of student learning (Kimbell et al., 1991; Kimbell, 1994). It investigated how students progress toward achieving technological capability.

At the same time, the subject made new ground in that it became process- and not product-oriented. Later the subject became incorporated in the new national curriculum. It was based on the problem solving model and emphasized design and make projects. It gave pre-eminence to design at the expense of other technological processes such as modeling and systems (Medway cited by Lewis, 1996). Nevertheless, since it was characterized by problem solving it was relatively easy to embrace home economics within the new curriculum (e.g., food technology, textile technology, design), business, art, and design. In Britain this resolved the dilemma of home economics and business teachers who had found themselves without a home in the new compulsory curriculum; but it would seem to have broadened the definition of technology beyond what would have been perceived to be engineering or, for that matter, technology. Unlike the French curriculum, it lacked an epistemological foundation. It had grown from a number of social determinants that had brought together craft, design, and technology at a time when Great Britain was seeking economic regeneration. The Engineering Council criticized the 1990 Statutory Order on Design and Technology because the subject lacked a clear route into higher education, but what did they want? They had, or at least the Engineering Professors had, already missed the opportunity to back engineering science, and since they

---

[10] In the UK persons with appropriate qualifications may register with the Institution of Incorporated Engineers.

[11] See Lewis, (1996).

continued to demand physics and mathematics, it is difficult to see how it could have been modified to meet their needs without a massive retraining of teachers. It is also difficult to see how teachers would be persuaded away from a subject in whose development they had participated.

17.1.   Other Interventions, Women and Minorities

Yet, in Great Britain the engineering profession continues to debate the role of schools in the supply of engineering students, and it has made some interventions. For example at Kings College (of the University of London) the Department of Electrical Engineering held five day workshops in July of each year, the purpose of which was to introduce high school students to the work that engineers do. Three days of the workshop were held in college and two days in industry (Jolly and Turner, 1979). Surveys of four of these courses suggested that about a third of participants *"acknowledged a positive change in what had previously been a slight or even negligible interest in engineering."* The Department had been stimulated to provide this workshop because it had found that students with little aptitude for mathematics and the physical sciences were being encouraged to look at engineering as a possible career.

Another venture was the provision by a few universities of one year conversion courses for able high school students who had decided that they would like to try a career in engineering but did not have the qualifications in mathematics and physics to enable them to pursue such a career. The courses were not designed to replicate A level but to give them a flavor of engineering while at the same time enabling them to establish an adequate foundation in maths and physics. About a hundred and sixty students entered the first courses (Bronwitt, 1990). There were also courses designed for adults who did not hold formal entry qualifications, to help them enter science and technology programs. These ACCESS courses were available across the curriculum of higher education. Parry (1990) reported that they had not been particularly successful in science and technology, where there was a high rate of attrition. He thought that this was in part due to the curriculum strategies used.

There were many other interventions, some of them sponsored by government and the engineering institution. In this respect Australia, which inherited British attitudes to engineering, was no different and numerous attempts have been made to make children aware of science and technology. McDermott, Göl, and Nafalski (2003) in Australia described some of these developments. Interestingly, they made no reference to the work that is being done in technology education in schools. They argued that if there is to be a change in quality of entrants to engineering the status of the engineer will have to be raised: a familiar story in the United Kingdom. Moreover, they argued that at all levels of government there would have to be changes in priorities in resource allocation and attitudes. Engineering

educators will have to learn that traditional ways of learning will no longer suffice.

Other interventions were specifically aimed at women, as, for example, the Engineering Council's Women into Science and Engineering (WISE) project. In the United States there are many recorded interventions by engineers and engineering departments in schools'[12]. Some of these have been also specifically concerned to attract more women and minorities into engineering. It has been seen as a worldwide problem, as many documents show.

One idea taken up by the New Jersey Institute of Technology was to add to an existing program for grade 4–9 students a unit in biomedical engineering. The reasoning behind this approach was that since females gravitate toward the professions that help humanity, they would be able to see engineering as a problem-solving activity that helped solve medical problems (Koppel, Cano and Heyman, 2002). It was reported that as a result of the unit, many of the students expressed an interest in pursuing careers in the biomedical field; but this is hardly an effective evaluation. As Wigal et al., (2002) found, pre-and post-questionnaires are unlikely to provide the data that are necessary. They hoped to obtain a sufficiently large sample for this to be achieved. Their program at the University of Tennessee-Chattanooga comprised a one week summer camp, a one-day camp, sessions in school throughout the year, and fairs conducted at schools.

Arizona State University has also run summer programs for girls and recruitment and retention data for three programs was disclosed in 2002 (Newell, Fletcher, and Anderson-Rowland, 2002). The program is of three days duration, including evening activities, and designed to introduce girls to the twelve engineering programs available at the university. Pre and post test surveys were used to determine initial and post interest in engineering. The participants evaluated the laboratories and activities attended during the program. Staff counselors also evaluated the effectiveness of these laboratories and activities. Since the inception of this program the percentage of women in the College of Engineering and Applied Science has risen from 17.8% to 20.2%, which is above the national average. Of 201 female students known to be eligible for college, 32% enrolled at the university; of these, 64% enrolled in a math, science, or engineering major. In 1999, scholarships were introduced and eleven of the twelve recipients joined engineering and applied science programs. Eight were from underrepresented minority groups. Unfortunately, although the authors reported that prior intervention interest data were available, it was not presented in the paper.

In another investigation with the Arizona WISE program, it was found that females needed to have quality experiences in math and science together with exposure

---

[12] Each year there are one or two sessions devoted to K–12 education at the Frontiers in Education Conference, and a division is being established by ASEE.

to engineering role models to whom they could relate and from whom they could find out about what engineers do (Blaisdell, 1998). This supports the view of those who believe that engineers should visit schools and involve themselves in the career decision process.[13]

More generally it has been found that minority students in the United States who are not encouraged and have lowered expectations are often placed in less rigorous environments in high school, with the result that they are not adequately prepared for higher education (Johnson and Sheppard, 2002).

There is clearly a need for teachers to understand the personality characteristics that distinguish Afro-American students from white students in engineering. Brown, Cross, and Selby (1990) found that Afro-American students tended to be less competitive than their white counterparts. They pointed out that while the engineering curriculum is arranged to support achievement, it does not necessarily prepare students for the world. Many other commentators have taken this view. They pointed out that one of the personality traits of Afro-American students is their ability to work effectively within groups. They have patience and are willing to listen to all points of view. Group work may help the Afro-American student to align his/her expectations with those of the class, but not all competition should be discarded. This links with their other finding that Afro-American persisters tended to be less assertive and assumed the initiative less often. If they are not called on in class, they might believe that their contribution is not valued. This will cause them to feel left out, and if they feel alienated, they may well opt to leave the course. This is similar to what many women experience when teachers tend to question and respond to questions from males rather than from females. Much has been accomplished since 1990, and it would be interesting if a similar study were to be carried out now.

17.2.   Contrasting Positions in the United Kingdom

In Great Britain two views have surfaced about the value of these interventions. First, it is held that if students are to be successfully recruited from schools, it is important for schools to foster positive attitudes to science and technology from a very young age. This view was expressed by Tomkinson, Warner, and Renfrew (2002) who argued for certain kinds of intervention. They believed that WISE had failed but they made no reference to the role that design and technology might play in the scheme of things. They did mention a lack of teachers who were accomplished in mathematics, science, and technology. Perhaps this is why they do not mention the role of design and technology in schools. They suggested, among other things, that universities should form links with feeder schools and prepare students for the kind of learning that is undertaken in universities. They were particularly concerned with mismatches between the particular mathematics curriculum pursued in schools and university teacher expectations.

Edward (2002) expressed a somewhat contrary view. His paper is of interest, not least because he works in the Scottish Education System that differs from the English curriculum in that it is much less specialized in years 10 through 12. He surveyed engineering students' perceptions and reflections on their courses at The Robert Gordon University, and he came to conclusions that were similar to those of Seymour and Hewitt (1997).

The perceptions that both undergraduates and graduates had of their courses were found to be similar. They believed that they had had too little engineering practice and that the engineering applications were inadequate. The graduates were somewhat more generous than the undergraduates. On coming up to university *"the students did expect to have to learn theory and showed anxiety about the maths this would involve. But they were expecting a practical approach with background theory. Instead they reported finding what they viewed as a highly abstract theory with occasionally largely disconnected labs."*

Edward argued that if this was a common view among school students, then to try and attract them to engineering would only lead to greater disenchantment and attrition. This was exactly what Seymour and Hewitt had found. Edward went on to argue that *"courses should be changed to conform to the expectations of the majority of our entrants."* We should recognize *"that our courses do not greatly resemble the functions performed by a professional engineer and that the majority of our graduates find their role exciting and challenging. By reflecting these functions in our courses we might both better prepare our graduates and by exciting our students go some way towards resolving our retention problems."*

Edward was, therefore, arguing that engineering should put its own house in order, but as Seymour and Hewitt pointed out, this would require a substantial change in attitude because it is so easy to place the blame for attrition and poor performance on the students and not on their teachers. A considerable investment by the National Science Foundation in the United States in the engineering coalitions was required to begin to change to a more consumer friendly curriculum in the first year.

17.3.   Prospects

Taking these two commentaries together, what then should be the attitude to school interventions and the school curriculum?

First, it is unlikely that interventions will stop. Some, particularly those with women and minorities in the United States, appear to have been successful. In any event we live in a technological society, and engineering departments possess a vast knowledge that is not readily available to school teachers. Interventions in schools can help teachers acquire this knowledge as can summer

---

[13]The term WISE is used in both the United Kingdom and the United States for programs that have roughly similar objectives.

schools and the provision of other forms of in-service training. Engineering educators should undertake interventions for their educational merits, and not because they are seeking to increase the supply of students. Second, there is a newly developing subject of design and technology that would benefit from a rapprochement with engineering educators. This should be a two way process because some of the research that is being done on children's learning in technology has significance for the teaching of engineering and the arrangement of the curriculum. Examples include the research by Welch (1998), Welch et al., (2000) on three-dimensional modeling and sketching, the meaning of technology (De Vries and Tamir, 1997), problem solving in technology (McCormick, Murphy, and Hennessy, 1994), children's approaches to design (Davies, 1996), and children's play (Aderklou et al., 2002). Engineering educators have as much to learn from schools, as they have to give.

The involvement of university teachers in primary (elementary) and secondary education is an acknowledgment of the fact that education is a continuum, and that what happens in one sector has a direct effect on other sectors. There is as yet no comprehensive theory of development. It is as if secondary education begins and ends with Piaget, and higher education begins and ends with Perry. But the findings of Davies and Roth suggest that young children have 'technological skills' and knowledge that they use in everyday life. The question is, What happens to these skills and knowledge in secondary education? Why is it that these 'skills' have according to industrialists to be re-learnt in industry? Some theory of the kind suggested by Whitehead (1932) might help us better understand how the curriculum-as a continuum should be organized.

Third, we should encourage the development of new types of degree in which students undertaking an engineering program can also obtain teacher certification. At Michigan Technological University, this is possible within the Bachelor of Science in Engineering program. This program is fully accredited by ABET and by the Michigan State Education Department (Sorby and Oberto, 2002). There is a similar degree at the University of Glasgow, but while this program is recognized for teaching design and technology in schools the department has not sought more general recognition from the profession.

It needs to be remembered that in countries like England, traditionally the last two years of secondary school have been a stepping block to university study. Failure to offer a curriculum that enables university teaching to carry on in a continuum has promoted complaints about school education, especially mathematics, rather than caused adaptation within engineering departments. This is a complex problem since, in the United Kingdom outside of Scotland the government has wished to retain a three-year degree program and at the same time broaden the education students receive in these last two years.

In the United Kingdom traditional students coming from school expect and are expected to complete their degree programs on a full time basis and to complete them in three years. Thus, to maintain 'standards,' engineers would argue that they must have received a specialist education in maths, and physics in high school that is equivalent to first year in universities elsewhere. If standards are changed, by which is meant lowered, then the universities would expect to have students for four years instead of three, as is the case in Ireland and Scotland. In the case of the four year M.Eng, this would have to become a five-year program. In this case they would be emulating a new program at MIT (Williams, 2002). The problem is that the government has tried to broaden the high school program and current views are that this has failed and that a broad-based baccalaureate examination should be introduced. This would have profound implications for the subsequent teaching of engineering.

17.4.   Mathematics. Whose Responsibility?

As was shown in Chapter 3, there have been continuing complaints about the mathematics capabilities which students bring with them to university. The UK's Engineering Council reported that only 30% of entrants had the background in mathematics thought necessary 10 to 20 years ago (EC, 1995). Yet as long ago as 1963, Heywood (1969) found that a very large number of technology students in the Colleges of Advanced Technology had required help with mathematics. It is evidently a perennial problem. The situation found by the Engineering Council was largely confirmed by Armstrong and Croft (1999), who undertook a study at Loughborough University to identify the learning needs in mathematics of new entrants. Following a confidence test, that is, a test that asked the students how confident they were in certain aspects of mathematics, a multiple-choice diagnostic test was developed. It was set to the students before they had had any mathematics teaching in their program. The result of these investigations was the finding that significant numbers of entrants to degree programs in engineering required considerable help. There was a group of students who did not believe they needed help who nevertheless lacked basic ability and knowledge across the range of topics. More than 10% of the students required help with "graph of the logarithmic function; cartesian coordinates; and polar coordinates."

Armstrong and Croft argued that urgent attention needed to be paid to *"the nature, purpose and standards of post-16 qualifications in mathematics (primarily A level)."* At present *"many entrants to mathematics dependent programs were disadvantaged because they lacked fluency and skill in basic mathematical techniques."*

They argued that until such problems were resolved, universities would have to make special provision for these entrants. Since they published that paper the debate about A level has led to the proposition that a baccalaureate exam replace A level. This would change standards and affect university programs. They also suggested that as the variations in the intake increased, it might be necessary to provide individually tailored courses through open learning. Mustoe (2002), of a different department in the same university,[14] suggested that the engineers and mathematicians should design mathematics modules that that could establish a headstart before the engineers require the mathematics. In the light of the proposals for a baccalaureate examination, an in depth comparative study of the systems of education in Ireland, Scotland, the United States, and the International Baccalaureate should indicate a way forward. Overall it would seem that the biggest change that will be required is that of teacher expectations in the universities.

17.5.   The Significance of the First Semester/Year

During the forty five-year period covered by this review, it has been shown that the reaction of the student in the first semester or year is crucial to subsequent performance (Budny, LeBold, and Bjedov, 1998; Malleson, 1965). Various techniques were developed for the prediction of students at risk in United States programs (e.g., Shuman, Gottfried, and Atman, 1996; Sullivan, Daghestani. and Parsaei, 1996; Thomas et al., 1996). In Great Britain there was much concern with wastage, (as the dropout phenomenon was then known) in the early 1970s (UQ, 1971)[15] and a paper on students leaving mechanical engineering was published as early as 1967 (Malleson, 1967). Malleson suggested from this study and other work that much more attention needed to be paid to study habits. At that time the overall dropout rate was between 11% and 14%, with at least half of that occurring during the first year. It also seemed that wastage increased as a function of the length of a program. Greater rates were recorded in engineering and technology programs. In the 1990s, as a result of government policy, there was a massive increase in the proportion of school leavers going on to tertiary study. This brought with it a renewed interest in retention and attention. It resurfaced in 1998 at a conference organized by the Higher Education Funding Council. This time it was under the heading of noncompletion, and two major studies were presented (Ozga and Sukhnandan, 1998; Yorke et al., 1998). Both of these reports suggested that better career advice and advice about higher education institutions needed to be made available in schools. In spite of the rigidity of the system, Yorke found that over half of those who had withdrawn had found their way back into higher education. Nearly forty years earlier, Dickenson (1963) had found this to be true of technology students; although many of them went back, lower level courses often helped by their employer.[16] Apart from the reports mentioned above and one or two others, the investigations were not subject specific[17] and the general findings relied on statistics collected by the University Grants Committee and subsequently the funding councils.

In 2001 an extensive survey of attrition in electrical and electronic engineering departments in the United Kingdom was reported by Cutler and Pulko (2002).[18] They found that the mean first-year attrition rate for pre-1992 universities was 15.5% in the range 3–30%, and in the post 1992 universities 21.8% in the range 10–35%.[19] The qualitative data they reported suggested that there was a mismatch between staff and student expectations. This seems to have been the case in both engineering and engineering technology courses in the United Kingdom. For example, Tizard (1995), who obtained the views of engineering technology teachers and their students, found that teachers believed that students lacked prior knowledge and basic skills, particularly numerical skills.[20] They were unable to manage their time, did not know how to set about solving problems or write reports, and were unable to transfer learning from one context to another, and were unable to identify their own strengths and weaknesses. There was agreement with the students on managing time, solving problems and writing reports. But the students said that tutors made unrealistic assumptions about what students knew, particularly at the beginning of the course; they said *"there needed to be more time to review and apply their learning because 'engineering doesn't just sink in."*

Cutler and Pulko obtained information about the strategies that might alleviate the situation and enhance retention. These were in the areas of:

- Pre-course admissions policies.
- Skills development for study habits, personal skills and, computer awareness.
- Pastoral care including personal development tutors, counselling after a few weeks, and diagnostic interviews at commencement.
- Program modifications, including *'attuning program content to labour market, harmonisation of module contents, and stratification of learning outcomes.'*
- Attendance monitoring.
- Tuition to include compulsory tutorials.
- Teaching innovations including a move away from examinations to project based learning, and peer assisted learning and collaboration.
- Assessment strategies to include supplementary vacation work to boost marks, mini-examinations during the year, and up to 30% for coursework Weekly progress tests and mid session diagnostic tests.

There were others including strategies for dealing with math (see above). The worldwide nature of the problem is illustrated by research done at the

---

[14] He makes no reference to the Armstrong and Croft study!

[15] This issue of *Universities Quarterly* provides a comprehensive review.

[16] i.e. industry based students on sandwich (cooperative) courses.

[17] In the sense of detailed studies within subjects.

[18] There was another conference on Student Progression and Retention in Engineering. University of Hull. October 2001, Cutler and Pulko cite Forsey, L and K. Marshall. Student perspectives on first year engineering education. Pp 223 – 227.

[19] Post-1992 universities refer to Polytechnic Institutions that were given university status in that year.

[20] The students were at the end of the first year of a two year full-time Ordinary National Diploma in Engineering. This would correspond to the first two years of an engineering technology degree.

University of Aveiro in Portugal, where it was found that the main variables that led to the large attrition due to failure in a programming course in the first year were the curriculum and teaching methods. Silva, Pacheco, and Tavares (2003) reported that changes had to be made in the approach to the curriculum to better motivate the students and obtain greater achievement. The pass rate improved considerably and the students achieved higher grades than previously. More generally, in a survey of 12 countries and 20 institutions, Baillie (1998) found that many of these strategies had been implemented successfully in one institution or another.

With respect to pre-admission policies, universities need to re-think what it is they want to know about students when they begin their studies. Throughout this review the value of learning styles and other psychometric tests has been examined. There is much to support their use, and also that of study habit and disposition inventories. There are other more mundane pieces of information that might be valuable, as, for example, the level of computer literacy (LeBold et al., 1998).

Data from Virginia Tech showed a clear relationship between performance and GPA, which led to the suggestion that students with a low GPA should be mandated to attend class and required to do extra credit homework (Sullivan, Daghestani, and Parsaei, 1996; see also Giesey and Manhire, 2003).

In the United States, supplemental instruction (SI) is a program designed to help students achieve mastery of course materials through the use of effective learning and study strategies [Arendale, (1994), cited by Marra and Litzinger, 1996)]. It is directed at specific courses. There are some reports of its use in engineering in the United States (Marra and Litzinger, 1997, see also Martin and Arendale, (1996). One of the points that came from the analysis of a program at Rensselaer was that such programs might usefully apply to all students however able. They found that some high school students who had coasted through their courses did not possess the study skills appropriate for the rigors of the college environment. Also, engineering problem solving is often a totally new exercise for new students from high school (Webster and Dee, 1996, see also Marra and Litzinger, 1996). Related to this is the point that when provision is made for remedial training for students at risk, they often do not avail of the offer; Henderson, Fadali, and Johnston (2002) found that with respect to weakness in mathematics the students, while having positive attitudes to engineering, *"did not voluntarily avail of the service."*

Their recommendations on teaching and examining suggested a move to toward best practice in Canada and the United States. Baillie commented that as yet institutions do not understand the role of assessment in driving learning and tuition. It is not just a matter of changing techniques but of choosing the techniques most appropriate for the objective to be attained (see Chapter 2). There is no mention of pre-college orientation courses or of induction courses, nor is there any discussion of the use of psychometric tests, and attention to learning styles

(see Chapter 5). For example, it has been demonstrated that spatial ability is essential not only for engineering but for mathematics as well. In the United States engineering students, male and female, have demonstrated a wide range of ability in spatial reasoning, and have shown that spatial reasoning interventions can reduce these differences and enhance retention (Agogino and Hsi, 1995 also see Chapter 5).

Over the same period in the United States there was much more attention to retention and attrition, both in the general system of higher education and engineering education in particular. To be fair to the system, the much quoted report by Seymour and Hewitt (1997) came at a time when the problem of the first year had been understood and the National Science Coalitions were underway. There remains the problem of overload. According to Adelman, (1998) the credit load required by engineering colleges does not differ greatly from the credit requirements in other fields.[21] Therefore, it is the perceptions that students have that are important, and they are a major factor in decisions to leave engineering. He also found that women who left engineering had higher grades than men who left and that the major cause of departure was academic dissatisfaction (see Chapter 4).

In common with the United Kingdom, as LeBold has often reported, the single most important predictor of success is level of prior achievement. Thus in Cutler and Pulko's study, those institutions that set high admissions criteria had lower attrition rates than those that did not, but this infers that university course requirements are constant for a given time in a program. This is not to say that students in difficulty may not be helped. It is also to say that universities might need to review their criteria as Cutler and Pulko suggest, and they may need to review the induction they give students. As Giesey and Manhire (2003) stated, increasing the admissions requirements has the possibility of decreasing enrollments in a profession where there is thought to be a scarcity of student in relation to socioeconomic demand. This raises questions about the purpose of the basic engineering degree (see Section 17.6 below).

17.6.   The transition from School to University

Much has been written about the problems which students' face when they transfer from elementary to secondary school. New students find masses of people everywhere and don't know anyone, they don't know the services that are available, and they find lecturers, lectures, and examinations scary. But there are also things that annoy students; these include expensive texts, variations in the quality of teaching, and excessive demands of lecturers (Hargreaves, 1998). At Queensland University of Technolgy the view was taken that *"a positive and motivated attitude toward university life is… very important from the first week or so."* This position is not dissimilar to that taken by Morgan (1974). Twenty

---

[21] This was the first major study that tracked students in a particular field.

years later Baillie (1998), as a result of her international survey was repeating the same axiom. Evidently it cannot be stressed too much.

Both Hargreaves and Morgan described orientation courses. The orientation program described by Hargreaves was for two days, and also its continuation with staff mentors and a two-part unit on technology and society was linked to the orientation. The purpose of the first day of the orientation was to introduce the student to the faculty and the school. Morgan's first day was to get the freshmen *"to feel an important part of the school of engineering and to feel accepted by faculty and fellow students."*

The second day of the program at Queensland was to achieve goals similar to those described by Morgan through interactive exercises. "In order to 'break the ice,' students are asked to participate in a design exercise. Groups of about 10 students are given a box of Lego, and various other implements and asked to design and build a small device, for example to measure the girth of someone's chest." When the exercise was completed, the students returned to the lecture theater, where each design was explained and discussed. The winning group received a prize.

This activity was followed by a mock lecture on a topic related to mechanical engineering. Notes had to be taken by the students. Notes were also taken by the group leaders' (teachers) for discussion and comparison afterwards Tutorial questions were given by the lecturer; they were also discussed in the groups.

Hargreaves reported that this helped break down the student-perceived barriers between them and the university staff. A new course unit on Technology and Society was introduced that had as its objectives:

- *"To promote and develop learning and teamwork skills;*
- *To raise awareness of issues related to the environment and society as well as technical aspects of engineering;*
- *To develop an appreciation of how other professions, such as architecture, construction management, industrial design, property economics, surveying and town planning integrate into the conventional mechanical, civil and electrical disciplines".*

This course comprised two units. The first was on Learning at University, and the second was on an Introduction to the University and to Engineering.

Teacher mentors who had received an information/training session from counseling personnel were introduced into this course.[22] They were shown how to look for students at risk so that they could refer them for professional advice if necessary. They were each responsible for a group of about 10 students. Each student had to provide them with a résumé about themselves, *"to meet their mentor, [and] to write a short résumé about*

the mentor." The groups were expected to work together to complete the first assignment which was on the topic "get to know your university." The second assignment was to write a report on 'the need for appropriate technology in engineering solutions.' In the exercise the students were expected to take into account the needs of the stakeholders as well as the cultural, environmental and social needs of the community.

At Prairie A & M University the induction day was part of a Concepts Institute designed for entrants from high school. It carried with it nine hours of college credit. The institute comprised courses in engineering problems (computer programming), engineering graphics (basic concepts of communications through drawings), composition, and the concept of health. It was expected that work in the institute would uncover weaknesses in mathematics and language skills and provide for remediation. At the time the most frequent critical weakness was found to be in trigonometry. An increase in the rate of retention was associated with these institutes (Morgan, 1974).

In the United States, Budny (2001) cited nine major studies that highlighted the importance of interaction with freshman students during their first semester and reported that most colleges had pre-college orientation programs for their freshman students. His report is unusual in that, in this and another paper (Budny and Delaney, 2001),[23] he and his colleague discussed how the University of Pittsburgh involved parents in the transition process through student/parent workshops in a pre-orientation program. In these workshops, the academic, family and personal transitions are discussed. Among the tips for parents are that they should establish communication about basic academic goals, provide news from home, learn the names of friends and teachers, and become interested in campus life while respecting the student's independence. Budny and Delaney argued that these workshops were among the reasons for the steady decline in attrition rates at the University of Pittsburgh.

Not every university makes room in the timetable for adequate induction. It will be recalled that Tizard (1995) and others have reported that students have difficulty with problem solving when they arrive at university. At Pittsburgh, following the orientation of students and parents, a transition is made in the students' family structure by the introduction of counselors and advisors into a seminar course that had as its objectives the provision of parent figures and an explanation of university policies and procedures. Peer mentors were also introduced. The seminars, which the student had to attend, related more to culture and sports than to engineering, although there were three engineering oriented seminars among the 19 offered. The mentors, who were paid, facilitated the seminars and were involved in the planning of the course. It was found that the mentors took on the role coaching the students through the transition. They had to go through quite a

---

[22]An initial attempt to provide the students with mentors had partially failed because academic staff were not convinced of the need to act as mentors. *"The facilities are there, it is the students' responsibility to use them."*

[23]The latter paper is recommended reading. It is also supported by an extensive review of research.

sophisticated selection procedure. The students also had to take a problem solving course in engineering; and Budny reported on how these two courses had been integrated. *"Thus, in addition to enjoying activities related to their seminar theme, mentors also work with the Engineering Student Services Center advisors, to integrate topics on how to be successful in the engineering program. Lessons like how to have a life and be a great student, how to put together a decent schedule, how to get involved in a student or community organization, or simply how to have a great time balancing the rigor of engineering coursework with some of the activities the students enjoy doing."* The mentors also help with the collection of assignments and the grading of projects and presentations. These assignments are related to both courses. For example, a presentation on their project had to be made in the seminar course. The grade is incorporated in the engineering course.

Budny found that the new course was highly rated, and he believed that the mentors had provided a non-threatening counselor role during this critical period in the students' educational careers.

In Great Britain there has been a decline in the number of engineering enrolments. At the same time government policies have focused on widening participation in higher education. The problem faced by the new Department of Communication Systems at the University of Lancaster was how to provide a popular degree in what to undergraduates would appear to be a narrow specialisation. The Department believed that on the contrary the subject touched every area of society and addressed a wide range of skills required by industry.[24] In order to attract students the members of the department believed that they had to provide a first year undergraduate program that was *"accessible, fun, interesting and challenging"* (Edwards and Coulton, 2003). The course that was developed was conceptual rather than mathematical but covered every aspect of communications from Fourier transforms to video production.

The Lancaster curriculum requires all students in their first year, even though they are admitted to study a particular discipline, to study two other subjects (disciplines). It is a *"try-out-before-you buy"* system. The problem for departments is to make their first year courses attractive to a wide audience from technical and nontechnical backgrounds.

To this end, a combination of teaching methods were used. lectures, computer-based practicals, and seminars (50 hours, 50 hours, and 25 hours, respectively) The purpose of the seminars was to foster interest in the subject through small group work. Throughout the course, which is of 25 weeks duration, the students have to undertake a research on the internet that will lead to the formation of an opinion *"rather than a theory or concept to be learned by rote. [The] seminar topics were chosen to generate discussion and interest, for example 'are mobile phones bad for your health?' The intention of* these activities is to develop research skills and to increase awareness of an interest in technology and underlying issues, as well as the development of an understanding of how people from different backgrounds look at the same subject."*

The computer laboratory had to be designed so that every student could benefit. *"For example, the video project provides engineering students with practical experience of project management, and the use for technology they may later be called on to design or implement, for computing students the chance to learn and use new software packages, and for arts students the opportunity to apply their creative skills whilst gaining an appreciation of the technical skills required."* The software used (Hyper signal) enables students from all backgrounds *"to see the tasks as using another piece of software within a familiar environment."*

The first ten weeks of the course cover the fundamental concepts of communication systems; the second ten weeks cover computing, multimedia, and networking concepts; the final five weeks includes channel types and characteristics, optical communications, television broadcast systems, satellite systems, and point-to-point communications.

Statistical evidence suggests that standards comparable with other subjects have been attained and that the average point score for the class increases as students transfer. Moreover, the students came from a wide variety of backgrounds, among whom were a good proportion of nontraditional students. Transfer into the subject came from management science, electronic engineering, computer science, culture media and communication, and theater studies. In the first three years the number of undergraduate participants increased from 18 to 200.

17.7.   Toward Learning Communities

Although the importance of organizational structure was considered in Chapter 3 that chapter did not highlight the importance of learning communities, or discuss their creation. Those involved in the activities described in the last section were evidently trying to create learning communities, and those communities depended on positive student faculty interaction. As Astin (1997) has shown, such interactions promote educational attainment. But some authorities such as Newman (1851) hold that interactions between students outside of the classroom are as important for learning as the classroom. It is in the discussions they have that learning is accomplished, but he was not referring to engineering students but to mixed groups of students and he was concerned with education for life.

The simplest form of community among engineering students is when they are asked to meet regularly in small groups with a student monitor to discuss each week's homework problems. The monitor had to guide explanation towards accuracy. They met with the instructors once a week to consider the solutions and common errors that might arise in the explanations they might have to give. Hurley (1993) reported that

---

[24]The authors cited Hissey (2000) in support of this view.

when this was done the students found that it helped them to organize their study time. When each member of the group was asked to master one or two problems with a view to explaining them to the group, the students felt that the achievement of mastery in one two problems was *"more feasible than having to master all the problems on their own."* These groups also benefited from teamwork in a quiz section when under examination conditions they had to collaborate in groups of 3 or 4 to solve the problems presented. In the control group homework was discussed in the quiz section. Both the control group and the experimental group were taught by the same instructor but at different times.[25]

Hurley found that the grades of those participating in the groups were a grade higher than those obtained by a control group. Women and minorities also did better. Group work of this kind has the possibility of creating a community in the sense that meeting together is voluntary and self-sustaining.

At Texas A & M University a deliberate attempt was made to foster learning communities (Morgan and Kenimer, 2002; Morgan et al., 2002).[26] One of the intentions, as in the case of activities reported above, was to overcome the isolation students experienced in their first year. These learning communities were of groups of approximately 100 students taking the same engineering, math and science course in the room at the same time. It involved peer teaching.[27]

"The peer teachers were part of a teaching team consisting of one problem solving faculty; one graphics faculty; one graduate teaching assistant; and one undergraduate peer teacher. The peer teachers attended the engineering class; offered academic support two evenings a week on calculus, physics, chemistry and engineering and served as mentors and guides to first year students in their particular community/course cluster" (Morgan et al., 2002).

The sponsors reported that the peer teachers *"were instrumental in creating a sense of belonging."*

The pilot study involved some 900 students who completed the engineering course in sections with and without peer teaching. It was found that those students who completed the course with peer teachers obtained a GPA of 2.85 whereas those who did not obtained an average GPA of 2.61. Although the data for the second semester were not significant, it was reported that the *"impact of peer teachers appeared to provide a residual effect as students continued into the second semester."*

An organizational structure such as this leaves itself open to role conflict between teachers and peer teachers. Teachers have to be able to adapt, and the peer tutors have to be clear about their role. Morgan and his colleagues suggested that instructors should make time

available in class for peer teachers to make announcements about planned activities. At the same time, peer teachers have to commit themselves to engagement in the total classroom experience. When they had the trust of the students, they obtained feedback on course-related issues that would not have been given to the instructors.

Clearly, peer teachers are likely to benefit from training, and not every able student will make an adequate mentor. Thus, some form of selection might be necessary. There is, argued Morgan and his colleagues, a need to investigate the profile of the effective tutor. They did not comment on gender, although twelve of the peer teachers were female and only three were male. It was found that retention rates were greater for clustered students in both first and second years and that the non clustered students demonstrated less positive attitudes toward their education than the clustered. Overall there was a very positive response from faculty to clustering.

The impact of faculty involvement in engineering has not been investigated very often. One study at *Penn State University used the Classroom Activities and Outcomes Questionnaire* (Terenzini et al., 2001) to obtain data from students in an engineering design course. Factorial analysis generated four constructs. These were instructor interaction and feedback, collaborative learning activities, instructor climate, and peer climate. The learning outcomes rated were communication skills, problem solving skills, occupational awareness, and engineering competence.

It was found that the peer and instructional climates were not significantly related to perceptions of learning gains; but expected grade, participation in collaborative learning, and instructor interaction and feedback were significantly related to the reported gains in problem-solving skill. Collaborative learning, instructor interaction, and feedback were also significantly related to communication skills and occupational awareness. Instructor interaction and feedback was the only variable that was significantly related each of the learning outcomes.[28] *"Students reported the greatest gains in all four learning outcomes when they interacted with and received feedback from the instructor 'almost always."*

Similar results were obtained by Olds and Miller (2004) from their longitudinal study of an integrated course in engineering. As indicated in Chapter 8, they found that students who felt they belonged were more likely to persist than those who did not.

The learning environment has to be structured to obtain results such as these, and design projects integrated with collaborative learning are likely to produce much more faculty involvement than is obtained from traditional lecture structures.

In Chapter 3, mention was made of a proposal by Marbury and colleagues in 1991 for an engineering

[25]The first attempt did not produce significant differences. The results mentioned are those of a second attempt after the procedures had been modified.
[26]See also Everitt, Imbrie, and Morgan, (2000)
[27]The peer teachers worked 10 hours per week: 6 in the classroom and 4 in help sessions. They were paid at the rate $10 per hour.

[28]They discuss the characteristics of feedback and refer to a paper by Vines and Rowland (1995) on an instructional feedback model presented at the Frontiers in Education Conference in 1995.

class based on the single room school of the nineteenth century. The idea was that the lead professor would work with a small group of students in their major courses during their junior, senior, and graduate years. The program would lean on regular courses and faculty to supply the technical content of some major courses and all minor courses. They wanted to create a dedicated interactive group that would get over the problems of the information and technology explosions. It was a context that would encourage the interaction that research finds enhances learning. They found an actual arrangement of this kind at the University of Missouri-Kansas City in the school of medicine. They argued that their model incorporated *"more or less some aspects of conventional and unconventional educational approaches. We have extracted and extrapolated from the Chicago Plan (Hutchins) the conventional course examination/grade programs, the unique Parson philosophy, the Oxford school tutor method, the Goddard system (laissez-faire), the 'docent' (medical) system, and the 'magnet' school systems."*

Beyond the classroom is the college and university environment. It is not, Astin (1997) found, *"the institutional structure, as such, that is the key ingredient; rather, it is the kinds of peer groups and faculty environments that tend to emerge under these different structures."* But communities need to be defined. The 1998 MIT task force report defined a community as *"students, faculty members, staff and alumni who have come together on campus for the common purpose of developing the qualities that define an educated individual"* (Williams, 2002, p. 162). In 1851 Newman saw them as contributing to *"the enlargement of the mind."* Astin saw the need for large institutions to develop communities within them and cited some examples.

In engineering, one such community is to be found at Arizona State University, where a Hall of Residence has come to play a major role in the Inclusive Learning Communities Program of the College of Engineering and Applied Sciences. The arrangements were initiated in part as a means of enhancing retention. It was thought that a support system was required for the 1000 or so freshmen, most of whom did not live on campus. Part of this support was provided through clustered housing in which all the residential students from the college were located in one Hall of Residence. This made possible the development of study groups in which students were grouped together by interest, which, in its turn, made possible the development of a learning community. It also made possible the extension of the orientation program into the academic year with socials and events with the professors. A questionnaire was developed over several years that enabled roommates to be selected (Roommate Preference Questionnaire). It was found that the two most important items in the questionnaire were (a) the preference for a roommate who was outgoing, flexible or reserved, and (b) the type of music they liked and how loud they liked it played (Anderson-Rowland et al., 2002).

This organizational arrangement came to be considered part of the Inclusive Learning Communities Program which was in two parts. The first part was an integration of English, Calculus I, Introduction to Engineering, and Physics. The second part was for students in cohorts of 20 to participate in three classes in common; Academic Mentoring; Career Mentoring; Web based support for student dialogue and faculty involvement. Over 60% of the freshmen participated in this program in the fall of 2001.

It was hoped that the study groups would ensure that recommended study times were kept i.e., 2–4 hours per day spent in class. The students were strongly recommended to study within groups. However, a survey of patterns of behavior revealed that only 53% of the students studied with other students in the residence hall. Of these about 55% met every other day. In a survey of the previous year the figure was 60%, and 70% reported that they spent less than 5 hours per week in study groups compared with 64% in the previous year. Overall the total number of hours studied was lower than the previous year.

Academic mentoring and free tutoring was available in the hall, but only 16% availed of this tutoring. Seventeen percent did not seek any tutoring at all. Anderson-Rowland and her colleagues found it strange that 62% of the students were satisfied or somewhat satisfied with their academic performance compared with half of the previous year's students, given that the number hours of private studied had been reported to be lower. However, 94% compared with 83% said that the Hall of Residence experience was positive. It was found that there was a greater awareness of events in the college than in previous years.

These results may tend to give a negative picture of the activity, but Anderson-Rowland and her colleagues were pleased with the development including the socials and the pizzas with the professors. Of course there is more to be done and many more comparisons to be made over the period that students remain in the program if a detailed comparison is to be made with Astin's longitudinal studies.

In some engineering environments the creation of a community of males and females may be a problem. In Chapter 3 it was reported that at Heriot-Watt University that male teachers did not take women engineers seriously, although the fact that sexism existed did not deter women from persisting in a predominantly male culture. And this culture was reinforced by traditional approaches to teaching and assessment (Cronin, Foster, and Lister, 1999). To try and overcome these problems an attempt was made to build a community by changing approaches to teaching and assessment, and it was found that the changes in curriculum content, assessment techniques, and group work appealed to both male and female students. Thus, changes in the curriculum that were attractive to females were likely to be attractive to males. Nevertheless, there remained concerns that had to be addressed, especially when women form a very small minority in a department.

Teachers will not change by edict, they have to be helped to make change. This particular enquiry confirmed the view that the curriculum suggested by Belenky et al., (1986) for females would prove equally attractive to males.

There is a possibly a bigger problem, and that is the creation of communities in web-based learning. The question is, does computer-supported collaborative learning environments provide genuine opportunities for learning processes that rely on social interaction? Kreijns and Kirschner (2001) of the Open University in the Netherlands, who asked this question, considered that one of the factors why the expectations of learners and educators had not been fulfilled was because it was assumed that social interaction can be taken for granted. But, if it does not happen in face-to-face settings, then there is no reason why it should happen in asynchronous settings.[29] Social interaction has to be supported and structured as Anderson-Rowland and her colleagues demonstrated.

Texas Tech University took the view that it was *"imperative that students should have access to reliable people for on-line mentoring."* To achieve this goal they trained peer mentors, and in the belief that *"learning occurs on line because of the learning community"* (citing Pallof and Pratt), they tried to establish a sense of community not only among the students but among the peer mentors as well (Fontenot, Hagler, and Chandler, 2001). *"It is very important that the mentors feel that they belong to a community and that their community is separate from their students' communities. They are just as much in a learning process and need the learning community just as much as the students; they are learning to manage, to be responsible for others, and to be accountable in a manner that might be quite different from early forms of accountability."* Therefore, the training given to the mentors had to include team building.

To return to the Anderson Rowland study, it is not an academic myth to suggest that the variations between the years are what are commonly experienced in other institutions. The graduate assistant who lived in Hall and provided tutoring considered that the biggest challenge was student apathy. Again that is a common experience of those, certainly in England, who have tried to follow in Newman's footsteps. It is also the problem of individualism in our society, as well as society's failure to value interdependence and support community. As Williams (2002) made clear as a result of her study of MIT, the change from individualism to community required a deep cultural transformation. Often it requires, as Hesseling (1966) pointed out, a *Chocs des opinions*. In the case of MIT, this was the well-publicized suicide of a freshman student.

"The dilemma is that "building community", to use that favorite phrase of the task force, makes demands

---

[29]Kreijns and Kirschner review research in this area and using the concept of social affordances suggest a theoretical framework for achieving social interaction.

on the life-world. Each human link one tries to make, each connection, each message, each effort to reach out and touch someone happens both in space and in time. The framework of the life-world will continue to degrade until it is recognized that the provision of common time and space is part of politics" (Williams, 2002, p. 194).

The same has to be said about the demand that students develop skill in reflective practice. Without time there is no possibility for reflection.

17.8.   Beyond First Year

Mention has already been made elsewhere in this review of longitudinal studies by Felder and his colleagues (e.g., in Chapter 15). These are important because there is a tendency to forget that at all stages in a student's career a variety of factors may intervene and affect performance (Malleson, 1965). In the United States, there is also some attrition in these subsequent years, and students get delayed in completion. It has been found that these factors are particularly important in their effects on women and minorities. As part of the Carnegie Foundations enquiry into the state of engineering education, Johnson and Sheppard (2002) tracked the high school class of 1990 through the engineering pipeline, and they paid special attention to women and minorities. They found there were three critical decision points that affected the participation rates of these students. They begin with the decision to enrol in a full-time undergraduate institution; this is followed by a decision to enrol full-time in an engineering program, and then finally to graduate with a bachelor's degree.

Apart from inadequate funding, a major reason not to enrol was insufficient high school math and science. Insofar as engineering was concerned, *"disillusionment with engineering and lack of interest in the associated lifestyle were common reasons that deterred females from enrolling in engineering programs.... In addition, the perceived lack of faculty contact, role models, and peer support were described as key factors that caused both female and minority students not to persist."* (For other enquiries see Section 3.10).

A study in the electrical engineering department at Ohio State University highlights a problem that has been discussed worldwide. That is, how long should an engineering course be? (Giesey and Manhire, 2003). In the particular circumstances of the United States these investigations found that the average student took 5.15 years and 15.6 quarters to graduate. Their findings supported those of other studies relating to higher education more generally. These were to the effect that withdrawing from and repeating courses, enrolling in insufficient number of hours per quarter, and taking free electives were major causes of the problem. Transferring from institutions and changing majors also caused problems. Those with high GPA's finished more quickly than others (see Section 17.3 above). These results led them to suggest that *"one final approach might be to change the perceived purpose of the engineering bachelors degree from its current status as the all encompassing entry-level degree to the engineering profession and render it a truly four-year degree that was considered the first step towards the profession. The bachelor's degree would focus on providing students with the knowledge and skills necessary to continue their education through a master's degree and other formal and informal means lasting their entire career."* This is directly analogous with what happened in the United Kingdom when the master's degree was introduced as a fourth year addition to the traditional three-year degree.

At Temple University they have taken some steps toward the development of a normal engineering program that is spread over five years and accompanied by online learning communities. The purpose is to increase the number of working students obtaining science, math, engineering, and technology degrees from an urban commuter college. The results from small pilot studies were encouraging. This approach retains the same content but spread over a longer period, and as such is in contrast to those who argue that content should be reduced. It is unlikely that the issue of what constitutes an engineering degree will go away (see below and epilogue).

17.9.   Concluding Remarks

Astin's study involved data from 500,000 liberal arts students at 1300 institutions. Two-thirds of those with high school grade averages of A minus could expect to complete college in 4 years. Those with C minus had only a one in five chance of finishing in 4 years. The study showed that *"time devoted to studying and homework, tutoring, cooperative learning, independent research projects, giving class presentations, taking essay exams, and having class papers critiqued by professors"* was associated with favorable student outcomes. On the negative side, taking multiple-choice exams, watching television, working full-time, and commuting were among the factors that led to an increase in attrition.

No attempt has been made in this review to undertake a meta-study of the papers studied in terms of attrition, but a face-validity inspection of the Chapters would seem to confirm Astin's findings. It is difficult to contend that engineering is a special case. If there is one thing to add, it is that the more teachers know about their students and the way they learn, the more effective will be their teaching. For some this will involve a considerable change of role.

References

Adelman, C (1998) *Women and men of the Engineering Path. A Model for the Analyses of Undergraduate Careers.* Department of Education and National Institute of Science Education, Washington, DC

Aderklou, C et al (2002). Pedatronics, :robotic toys as a source to evoke young girls' technological interest. *Proceedings Frontiers in Education Conference,* 2, F1C-19 to 24.

Agogino, A. M., and S. Hsi (1995). Learning style based innovations to improve retention of female engineering students in the synthesis coalition. *Proceedings Frontiers in Education Conference,* 4a2.1 to 4.

Anderson-Rowland, M. R., Urban, J. E., Ighodaro, O., and A. Muchinsky (2002). Refining a living and learning community for first year enginineering students. The ASU perspective. *Proceedings Frontiers in Education Conference,* 3, S2C-5 to 10.

Arendale, D. R (1994) Understanding the supplemental instruction model. *New Directions for Teaching and Learning,* 60, (4), 11–22.

Armstrong, P. K. and A. C. Croft (1999). Identifying the learning needs in mathematics of entrants to undergraduate engineering in an English university. *European Journal of Engineering Education,* 24, (1), 59–72.

Astin, A. W (1997). *What Matters in College? Four Critical years Revisited.* Jossey Bass, San Francisco.

Baillie, C. (1998). First year issues in engineering education. *European Journal of Engineering Education,* 23, (4), 453–465.

Belenky, M. F., Clinchy, B. M., Goldberger, N. R., and J. M. Carule (1986) *Women's ways of Knowing.* Basic Books, New York.

Bjorklund, S. A., Parente, J. M., and D. Sathianathan (2002). Effects of faculty interaction and feedback on gains in student skills. *Proceedings Frontiers in Education Conference,* 3, S1B-9 to 15.

Blaisdell, S (1998). Predictors of women's entry into engineering: why academic preparation is not sufficient. *Proceedings Frontiers in Education Conference,* 1, 221–225.

Blandow, D., and M. Dyrenfurth (1992) (eds) *Technological Literacy, Competence and Innovation in Human Resource Development.* Proceedings of a Conference. Technical Foundation of America, San Marcos, TX

Bronwitt, B (1990). Steps courses in the universities. In G. Parry (ed). *Engineering Futures. New Audiences and Arrangements for Engineering Higher Education.* Engineering Council, London.

Brown, N. W., Cross, E. J., and G. V. Selby (1990). *Proceedings Frontiers in Education Conference,* 165–167.

Budny, D (2001) Integrating the freshman seminar and freshman problem solving courses. *Proceedings Frontiers in Education Conference,* 2, F4B- 21 to 26.

Budny, D., and C. A. Delaney (2001). Working with students and parents to improve the freshman retention. *Proceedings Frontiers in Education Conference,* 1, T3E- 5 to 10.

Budny, D., LeBold, W and G. Bjedov (1998). Asssesment of the impact of engineering courses. *Journal of Engineering Education.* 87, (4), 405-411.

Carter, G., Heywood, J., and D. T. Kelly (1986). *A Case Study in Curriculum Assessment. GCE Engineering Science (Advanced).* Roundthorn, Manchester.

Cronin, C., Foster, M., and E. Lister (1999). SET for the future: working towards inclusive science, engineering and technology curricula in higher education. *Studies in Higher Education,* 24, (2), 165–181.

Cutler, G. L., and S. H. Pulko (2002). Investigating UK undergraduate electrical and electronic engineering attrition. *International Journal of Electrical Engineering Education,* 39, (3), 181-191.

Dainton, Lord. Chairman of Committee. *Enquiry into the Flow of Candidates in Science and Technology into Higher Education.* Cmnd 3541. HMSO, London.

Davies, D (1996) Professional design and primary children. *International Journal of Technology and Design Education,* 6, 45–59.

De Vries, M. J., and A. Tamir (eds.) Shaping Concepts of technology. From Philosophical Perspective to Mental Images. Vol 7. Issues 1 and 2. *The International Journal of Technology and Design Education.*

Dickenson, H (1963). Students in a CAT: Qualifications and success. *Universities Quarterly,* 18, 407.

Dugger, W. E. Jr. (1995). Technology for all Americans. *The Technology Teacher,* 54, (5), 3–7.

EC. (1995) *The Changing Mathematics of Undergraduate Engineers.* Engineering Council, London.

Edels, H (1968). Technology in the sixth form. *Trends in Education.* No. 10. April. Department of Education, London.

Edward, N (2002). Preaching to the converted. *International Journal of Electrical Engineering Education,* 39, (3), 230 – 237.

Edwards, R., and P. Coulton (2003) Conceptualising engineering subjects for wider participation. *Proceedings Frontiers in Education Conference,* 2, F2D-14 to 18.

EJCA. (Engineers Joint Council of America) (1965). High Schools teach engineering concepts. *Engineer,* 6, 2 Summer – Fall.

Everitt, L., Imbrie, P. K., and J. R. Morgan (2000) Development of an integrated first year curriculum for engineers. *Journal of Engineering Education.* 89, (2),

Fadali, M. S., and M. Robinson (2000). How do the national science education standards support the teaching of engineering principles and design? *Proceedings Frontiers in Education Conference.* 1, 12E-6 to 10.
Fontento, A. D., Hagler, M. O., and J. R. Chandler (2001). Training peer-mentors to manage on-line class participation. *Proceedings Frontiers in Education Conference,* F2F-1 to 6.

Gradwell, J. B (1996). Philosophical and practical differences in the approaches taken to technology education in England, France and the United States. *International Journal of Technology and Design Education,* 6, (3), 239–262.
Giesey, J. J., and B. Manhire (2003). An analysis of BSEE degree completion time at Ohio University. *Journal of Engineering Education,* 92, (3), 275–280.

Hargreaves, D. J (1998). Addressing the transition to tertiary engineering. *European Journal of Engineering Education,* 23, (1), 79–88.
Henderson, N., Fadali, M. S., and J. Johnston (2002). An investigation of first-year engineering students' attitude toward peer-tutoring. *Proceedings Frontiers in Education Conference,* 2, F3B- 1 to 5.
Hesseling, P (1966). *A Strategy of Evaluation Research.* Van Gorcum, Aassen.
Heywood, J. (1969) An Evaluation of Certain Post-war Developments in Higher Technological Education. Thesis. University of Lancaster Library, Lancaster.
Heywood, J (1986) Toward technological literacy in Ireland: an opportunity for an inclusive approach in J. Heywood and P. Matthews (eds). *Technology, Society and the School Curriculum. Practice and Theory in Europe.* Roundthorn, Manchester.
Hill, A. M (1998). Problem solving in real-life contexts: an alternative for design in technology education, *International Journal of Technology and Design Education,* 8, (3), 203–220.
Hissey, T. W (2000). Education and careers 2000: Enhanced skills for engineers. *IEE Proceedings* 88 (No 8).
Hurley, C. N (1993). Cooperative learning in the quiz section in general chemistry. *Proceedings Frontiers in Education Conference,* 162–166.
Hutchings, D. G. (1963). *Technology and the Sixth Form Boy.* Oxford University, Department of Education, Oxford.

Johnson, M. J., and S. D. Sheppard (2002). Students entering and exiting the engineering-pipeline: identifying key decision points and trend. *Proceedings Frontiers in Education Conference,* 3, S3C-13 to 19.
Jolly, W. P., and C. W. Turner (1979). The transition from school to university: some experimental induction programs for engineering students. *Studies in Higher Education,* 4, (1), 39–46.

Kimbell, R (1994). Progression in learning and the assessment of children's attainments in technology. *International Journal of Technology and Design Education,* 4, (1), 65–74.
Kimbell, R., Stables, K., Wheeler, T., Wosniak, A., and V. Kelly (1991). *The Assessment of Performance in Design and Technology.* School Examinations and Assessment Council, London.
Kreijns, K., and P. A. Kirschner (2001). The social affordances of computer supported collaborative learning environments. *Proceedings Frontiers in Education Conference,* 1, T1F-12 to 17.
Kocijancic, S (2001). Mechatronics as a challenge for teaching technology in secondary education. *Proceedings Frontiers in Education Conference,* 1, T2E-1 to 4.
Koppel, N. B., Cano, R. M., and S. B. Heyman (2002). An attractive engineering option for girls. *Proceedings Frontiers in Education Conference,* F1C-2 to 7.

LeBold, W. K. et al (1998) Assessing computer literacy and achievement using self-concepts. *Proceedings Frontiers in Education Conference,* 1, 1 – 7.
Lewis, T (1996). Comparing technology education in the US and UK. *International Journal of Technology and Design Education,* 6, (3), 221–238.

McCormick, R., Murphy, P., and S. Hennessy (1994) Problem solving processes in technology education: a pilot study. *International Journal of Technology and Design Education,* 4, (1), 5–34.
McDermott, K. J. Göl, O and A. Nafalski (2003). Initiatives to increase number of entrants into engineering programs- an Australian perspective. *Proceedings Frontiers in Education Conference,* 2, F3D-24 to 28.
Marris, R (1986). Higher education and the mixed economy: the concept of competition. *Studies in Higher Education,* 11, (2), 131–154.
Malleson, N (1965) *A Handbook of British Student Health Services.* Pitman, London.
Malleson, N (1967). Students leaving mechanical engineering courses. *Universities Quarterly,* 22, 74
Marbury, C. H., Barnes, F. S., Lawsine, L., and N. C. Nicholson (1991) A one room schoolhouse plan for engineering education. *IEEE Transactions on Education,* 34, (4), 303–308.
Marra, R. M. and T. A. Litzinger (1997). A model for implementing "supplemental instruction" in engineering. *Proceedings Frontiers in Education Conference,* 1, 109–115.
Martin, D. C., and D. Arendale (1996) (eds) *Supplemental Instruction. Increasing Achievement and Retention.* Jossey Bass, San Francisco.
Medway, P (1992). Constructions of technology: reflections on a new subject. J. Beynon and H. McKay (eds). *Technology Literacy and the Curriculum.* Falmer Press, Basingstoke.
Morgan, J., and A. L. Kenimer (2002). Clustering courses to build student community. *Proceedings Frontiers in Education Conference,* 3, S1A-13 to 16.
Morgan, J., Kenimer, A., Kohutek, T., Riehart, J., and M. Lee (2002). Peer teachers from an instructors perspective. *Proceedings Frontiers in Education Conference,* 3, S2C-11 to 15.
Morgan, L. B (1974). Improving the retention of engineering students. *Engineering Education,* 65, (2), 166–169.
Mustoe, L (2002). The mathematics background of undergraduate engineers. *International Journal of Electrical Engineering Education,* 39, (3), 192–200.

Newell, D. C., Fletcher, S. L. and M. R. Anderson-Rowland (2002). The women in applied science and engineering (WISE) recruitment programs: investing in the future. *Proceedings Frontiers in Education Conference,* 2, F1C- 15 to 18.
Newman, J. H (1851-1947 edition) *The Idea of a University,* Longmans Green, London.

Olds, B. M., and R. L. Miller (2004). The effect of a first-year integrated engineering curriculum on graduation rates and student satisfaction: a longitudinal study. *Journal of Engineering Education,* 93, (1), 23–37.
Ozga, J., and L. Sukhnandan (1998). *Undergraduate Non-completion.* In Undergraduate Non-Completion in Higher Education. Higher Education Funding Council, Bristol.

Page, G. T (1965). *Engineering Among the Schools.* Institution of Mechanical Engineers, London.
Palloff, R. M and K. Pratt (1999) *Building Learning Communities in Cyberspace. Effective Strategies for the Online Classroom.* Jossey Bass, San Francisco.
Parry, G (1990) Access courses in post-school education. In G. Parry (ed). *Engineering Futures. New Audiences and Arrangements for Engineering Higher Education.* Engineering Council, London.

Robbins, Lord (1963) Chairman of a Committee. *Higher Education.* Cmnd 2165. HMSO, London.

Sendaula, M. H., and S. J. Biswas (2004). Curriculum deceleration and on-line communities for working students. *Proceedings Frontiers in Education Conference,* 1 T1E-8 to 12.
Seymour, E., and N. M. Hewitt (1997) *Talking about Learning. Why Undergraduates Leave the Sciences.* Westview Press, Boulder, CO
Shuman, L. J., Gottfried, B. S., and C. J. Atman (1996).The freshman engineering experience: two courses and assessment methodology. 1996 *ABET National Meeting Proceedings,* San Diego pp 118–125.

Silva, I. H., Pacheco, S., and J. Tavares (2003). Effects of curriculum adjustemtns on first-year programming courses: students performance and achievement. *Proceedings Frontiers in Education Conference,* T4c-10 to 14.

Sorby, S. A. and L. J. Oberto (2002). A Program combining engineering and teacher certification. *Proceedings Frontiers in Education Conference*, 2, F2C-11 to 15.

Sullivan, W. G., Daghestani, S. F., and H. R. Parsaei (1996). Multivariate analysis of student performance in large engineering Taconomy classes. *Proceedings Frontiers in Education Conference*, 1, 180–184.

Terenzini, P. T., Cabrera, A. F., Colbeck, C. L., Bjorklund, S. A. and J. M. Parente (2001). Racial and ethnic diversity: does it promote student learning? *Journal of Higher Education*, 72, (5), 509–531.

Thomas, E. W et al., (1996). Using discriminant analysis to identify students at risk. *Proceedings Frontiers in Education Conference*, 185–188.

Tizard, J. (1995) Will core skills improve engineering programs. *International Journal of Electrical Engineering Education,* 32, 99–107.

Tomkinson, B., Warner, R., and A. Renfrew (2002). Developing a strategy for student retention. *International Journal of Electrical Engineering Education*, 39, (3), 210–218.

UQ (1971). *Universities Quarterly*, Spring issue is devoted to the topic of wastage.

Vines, D. L., and J. R. Rowland (1995). An instructional feedback model for improved learning and mentoring. *Proceedings Frontiers in Education Conference*, 3C3–14 to 17

Webster, T., and K. C. Dee (1996). Supplemental instruction benefits students in an introductory engineering course. *Proceedings Frontiers in Education Conference*, 101–108.

Welch, M (1998). Students' use of three-dimensional modelling while designing and making a solution to a technological problem. *International Journal of Technology and Design Education*, 8, (3), 141–260.

Welch, M., Barlex, D., and H. S. Lim (2000). Sketching; friend or foe to the novice designer. *International Journal of Technology and Design Education*. 10, 125 –148.

Whitehead, A. N (1932). *The Aims of Education*. Benn, London.

Wigal, C. M. et al (2002). ACES: introducing girls and building interest in engineering and computer science. *Proceedings Frontiers in Education Conference* 2, F1C-8 to 13.

Williams, R (2002). *Retooling. A Historian confronts Technological Change*. MIT Press, Cambridge, MA.

Yorke, M et al (1998). Undergraduate non-completion in England in Undergraduate Non-Completion in Higher Education. Higher Education Funding Council, Bristol

EPILOGUE

In the mid 1990s the British Government responded to the reports of two official committees on higher education in the context of its quality assurance approach to higher education, and it proposed that University teachers should be trained in pedagogy. At the time I took the view that such training should be similar to that given in a good one-year post-graduate course for training secondary teachers that integrated theory with practice. A pedagogy of higher education had emerged in the United Kingdom and the United States and there was a substantial literature on which such training could be based. Research on in-career training in industry, in which personnel from different companies or parts of an organization came together for short periods of training, showed that there was no guarantee that when that person returned to the organization, he/she would have any influence on developments. Moreover, much valuable time had to be spent in ensuring that the course would meet the needs of a mixed bag of individuals. The same problem existed in teacher education and in traditional courses. It was solved, so it was thought, by making a distinction between the foundations of education in history, philosophy, psychology and sociology, and the methodology of teaching specific subjects. Depending on the program there might also be a course in curriculum theory, assessment and statistics. There was no guarantee that attending these courses would guarantee a transfer of practice to the classroom, because the culture of schools has a powerful influence on the socialization of teachers into the classroom in schools or universities. This has been convincingly demonstrated in the United States by Cohn and Kottkamp.[1] In Ireland, where the public examinations cause 'teaching to the test,' there was pressure on young teachers to use traditional methods because it was believed that these ensured that students could remember the facts required by the examination.

Taking these factors together, I was of the opinion that each profession should take responsibility for its own training, and in that way the possibility of climate change might be ensured. Teachers who were willing to experiment with new pedagogical methods would be encouraged, and note would be taken of the effectiveness of their efforts. If this were to be the case then there had to be a pedagogical literature within the subject. To examine if this were the case in engineering, I searched the literature back to 1960. By 1971 an annotated bibliography of British Technological Education and Training that included some American articles ran to 150 pages.[2] While there were very few research papers reported, it showed the extent of public interest in the area. By 1992, I had come to the conclusion that there were about 169 articles, mainly American and British, that a tutor would be able to use in a course on teaching and learning in engineering.[3] They covered all of the areas of teacher training listed above, and an article was found on a summer school on effective teaching in engineering in 1964, although not included in this analysis.[4] These figures suggested a growth in the literature since LeBold had published an overview of research in engineering education in 1980.[5] Grayson and LeBold had suggested, earlier, that although there was little research, there was plenty of innovation,[6] as they announced the founding of *Annals of Engineering Education* to publish *"first rate research"*. That review had made no reference to research in the United Kingdom which, as Carter and Jordan were to show, was not inconsiderable during that period.[7] Subsequently the publication in 1993 of *Teaching Engineering* by Wankat and Oreovicz confirmed this finding.[8] At the same time, it seemed that some help from teacher educators would be required.

Since then there has been a massive explosion in the amount of eligible material. *Engineering Education* was revamped and became the *Journal of Engineering Education,* and the annual *Proceedings of the Frontiers in Education Conference* has grown from one volume to three.[9] The *IEEE Transactions on Education* is also a major source. The British originated journals in Electrical and Mechanical Engineering Education continued to be published. *A European Journal for Engineering Education* was established, and an *International Journal of Applied Engineering Education* was also created. It has since lost the 'applied' from the title. Several new journals in the area of technology and design education have been created, and academic journals like *Assessment and Evaluation in Higher Education* and *Studies in Higher Education* have accepted research papers on topics in engineering education. With each succeeding Frontiers in Education Conference, there is an increase in the amount of material that can be used. Many other articles are to be found in the other publications in engineering, manufacturing, management, and the human sciences; but those named give the essence of what has

[1] Cohn, M. M., and R. B. Kottkamp (1993). *Teachers. The Missing Voice in Education.* State University Press of New York, Albany.

[2] *British Technological Education and Training* (1971). Hutchinson, London.

[3] Details were given in *Proceedings Frontiers in Education Conference*, 2, 2a3. 8 to 13. Toward the improvement of quality in engineering education

[4] Northrop, D. C (1965). Summer school on effective teaching for university teachers of engineering, Manchester 1964. *International Journal of Electrical Engineering Education*, 2, 683–684.

[5] LeBold, W.K (1980). Research in Engineering Education: an overview. *Engineering Education*, 70, (5), 406 to 409 & 422.

[6] Grayson, L. P. and W. K. LeBold (1976). Research in engineering education. *Engineering Education*. 67, (3), 217.

[7] Carter, G., and T. Jordan (1986). Student Centered Learning in Engineering. *Engineering Enhancement in Higher Education Prospects and Problems*. Monograph. Mimeo. University of Salford, Salford.

[8] Wankat, P., and F. S. Oreovicz (1993). *Teaching Engineering*. McGraw Hill, New York.

[9] For a review of the first 30 years of FIE see Jones, E. C. (2000) A journey through the FIE bookshelf −1971 to 2000. *Proceedings Frontiers in Education Conference*, 1, T4G- 1 to 7.

been happening in engineering education, and this review has been based primarily on them

The majority of these publications emanated in the United States, but there were significant contributions that were Australian and British based. In Great Britain the authorities toyed with higher education when three research units were set up at the Universities of Essex, Lancaster and Manchester. These had remits in teaching and learning as well as the social aspects of university life. Lancaster, and Manchester undertook research in engineering education and contributed to the first ever teacher training week for engineers. When these units died, other ventures followed in other places. Like the original ones, they were intended to serve the university. It is of some interest to note that some of the individuals involved in these activities moved to Australia to establish similar units, and Boud in particular made significant contributions to engineering education, among other things. Some Australians working in the field have now found their way to the British Isles.

A Staff Educational Development Association (SEDA) was founded to provide the professional status required, and it examined university teachers by means of a portfolio. As indicated in Chapter 1 in the late 1990s an Institute of Learning and Teaching (ILT) was founded with a government remit to provide a professional qualification for university teachers through membership. It achieves this by validating qualifications offered by Universities at certificate, diploma, and masters levels. The portfolio is an important vehicle in the assessment, and members of SEDA have contributed to its work.

Although there was one professor of engineering education at Heriot-Watt University, that appointment was a personal chair and lapsed when the incumbent moved to another post. Until recently, there was no focus center for engineering education that could offer a specific qualification in engineering education or provide the academic critique of curriculum and pedagogy that is the function of university discussion in research. To be fair, the Department of Chemical Engineering at Imperial College offered a post-graduate programme in teaching and learning.[10]

Recently (2000), in all subjects of the university curriculum, there have been established Learning and Teaching Support Networks (LTSN). The engineering network is based at Loughborough and comprises 24 subject centers. The general program director is based at the Institute for Learning and Teaching. The engineering network has conducted focus groups of students, and the findings are in keeping with many of those of this report.[11] As indicated in Chapter 1, the ILT and the LTSNs are being incorporated in a Higher Education Academy which has replaced the Institute for Learning and Teaching (ILT).

Likewise in the United States, there has been a growth in the number of centers dedicated to research and teaching and learning in engineering education. Some of these are long standing, as, for example, the Center at Arizona State University. One or two institutions also have a long standing record of supporting research in their Institutions, as, for example, the Colorado School of Mines, the Engineering School at North Carolina State University-Raleigh, the Department of Mechanical Engineering (design division) at Stanford, and the Engineering School at the University of Texas-Austin. Substantial research over the last decade was completed at the University of Pittsburgh, and one of its members has developed a major research unit at the University of Washington Seattle. Throughout much of the period, there was a continuous flow of papers from Purdue University. Several of those working in engineering education have come from the education and social sciences, and their contributions have been welcomed. In drawing attention to the big names, I am conscious that I do an injustice to the many individuals working in other universities to improve the pedagogy of engineering education, and that after all is what this review is about. Substantial experience of helping graduate teaching assistants to teach has been obtained at the University of Virginia,[12] and credits are being given for courses at the University of Wisconsin Madison[13] and the Colorado School of Mines.[14]

Training by itself does not ensure change. That is the experience of teacher training. It is further the experience of teacher and management training that the culture of the organization can inhibit a teacher from experimentation. If the organization's primary judgment of a person for promotion is the number of papers published and research grants obtained, then teaching can become a very poor second. No truer words were written than those by Patricia Cross when she said that teaching would not acquire status until teachers treated their classrooms as laboratories for research.[15] Subsequently, she, together with Angelo and Steadman,[16] made a distinction between classroom assessment and classroom

---

[10]Alpay, E and M. A. Mendes-Tatsis (2000). Postgraduate training in student learning and teaching. *European Journal of Engineering Education*, 25, (1), 83–97.

[11] The results of the first survey are in Davis, L (2002) Students focus on what they want. *International Journal of Electrical Engineering Education*, 39, (3), 238 - 244

[12]Richards, L. G (2000). Teaching GTAs how to teach. *Proceedings Frontiers in Education Conference*, 2, .F34F-14 to17 Richards, L. G (2001) A graduate seminar on learning to teach. *Proceedings Frontiers in Education Conference*, 3, S3D- 8 to 12.

[13] A summary of courses in the US was made by Smith, K. A and O. V. Kritskaya (1999). Design of a pedagogy course for graduate students and beginning faculty. *Proceedings Frontiers in Education Conference*. 12a5-7.

[14]Streveler, R. A., Moskal, B. M., and R. L. Miller (2001). The Center for engineering education at the Colorado School of Mines: using Boyer's four types of scholarship. *Proceedings Frontiers in Education Conference*, 2, F4b- 11 to 14.

[15] Cross, K. P (1986) A proposal to improve teaching. *AAHE Bulletin* September. 9 – 15.

[16]Angelo, T and K. P. Cross (1993). *Classroom Assessment Techniques*. Jossey Bass, San Francisco. Cross, K. P. and M. P. Steadman (1996). *Classroom Research. Implementing the Scholarship of Teaching*. Jossey Bass, San Francisco.

research. Fifty quite simple assessment exercises that would help the instructor to evaluate his teaching were suggested and illustrated. There are some reports in the literature of teachers using some of these techniques

Undoubtedly, others do these kinds of thing but do not think they are worth reporting. Engineering does not have its equivalent of *College Education* where the reporting such activities is valued. A person who does this in spite of opposition is leading himself/herself and acquiring the pedagogy of experience that can be explained to beginning teachers. It is a first level of curriculum leadership.

A second level of personal curriculum leadership is when that person undertakes more rigorous classroom research. The literature shows that activities of this kind are on the increase. The majority of studies follow the so-called scientific approach in one way or another, but there are a small but increasing number of case studies based on ethnography. In many cases they are more revealing than studies based on the scientific model. A few studies have been reported in which the methods are mixed. Such studies require a much greater understanding of the literature than the classroom assessment techniques, and they may require help from educators and social scientists. There are quite a number of studies that have resulted from collaboration with others outside of engineering. Moreover, a number of quite well known names working within engineering schools on matters of educational concern come from the humanities and psychology. The advantage of having such colleagues is that they can help us stand outside our frame of reference and reflect on what we are doing. An interesting trend is in the large number of women that are involved in the field.

The knowledge gained from such studies can put the investigator in the position where the department wants to be advised or led in taking a departmental initiative. The person involved is then operating at a third level of curriculum leadership. There are examples in the literature that show how a number of engineers went through all these stages and have become curriculum leaders.

There is a fourth level of curriculum leadership and that is to lead in policy forming. Because engineering education is in a state of flux, it is likely to continue to change. Such leaders will have to be versed in the theories of change and understand that not only are some faculty likely to be resistant to change, but so are students. Among the papers reviewed, there are models of the change process,[17] studies of the process of change in one of NSF coalitions,[18] the role of TQM in overcoming resistance to change,[19] and student resistance to change at MIT.[20]

Leadership depends in no small way on the perceptions that those seeking help have of the experience of the person sought. In the academic community, that is often judged by the research record of that person and the knowledge that he/she is perceived to have. After all, knowledge is controlled. The person who has knowledge has power. The literature shows that there is an increasing number of engineers with that knowledge. One of the purposes of this review has been to provide a compendium of the knowledge now available in engineering education. Without claiming that it is complete, the major areas of controversy, discussion, and development were considered.

It is evident that when there is a change from traditional to non-traditional methods of teaching, the instructor often has to make considerable changes in her/his perceptions of role. In most cases it means a shift from the control of learning to the management or facilitation of learning. Often this is not accomplished without difficulty. Equally often the reports either infer or state directly that training was needed. Often, neither teachers nor administrators appreciate the time required to implement a new method of instruction. Time is not on the side of the engineering educator,[21] inevitably this shortage inhibits the reflection necessary for educational connoisseurship.

Interviews with deans, chairs, faculty, industry leaders, and association leaders in the United States identified changes in educational practice in five areas. These were; the incorporation of design throughout the curricula; an emphasis on effective teaching; the influx of computer technology in the classroom and beyond; the need for broad-based curricula, and a new interest in assessment.[22] These changes can only be implemented through faculty, and any change requires commitment on the part of both the administration and the teachers; as was found in the survey, these senior administrators thought that faculty reward structures, and workshops on educational practice might encourage faculty to adapt. But workshops by themselves would not ensure the deep cultural change that may be needed. It is for this reason that this writer has promoted the idea of curriculum leaders within departments and schools of engineering. The successful promotion of change requires curriculum leadership at the fourth level.

[17]Walkington, J (2002). Curriculum change in engineering education. *European Journal of Engineering Education*, 27, (2), 133-148

[18]Froyd, J., Penberthy, D., and K. Watson (2000) good educational experiments are not necessarily good change processes. *Proceedings Frontiers in Education Conference*, 2, F1G- 1 to 6. Merton, P., Clark, C., Richardson, J., and J. Froyd (2001). Engineering curricular change across the Foundation Coalition: Lessons from qualitative research. *Proceedings Frontiers in Education Conference*, 2, F4B.

[19]Tomovic, C. L (1996) Managing resistance to classroom and student-learning assessment: Lessons learned from the past. *Proceedings Frontiers in Education Conference*, 802–805.

[20]Williams, R (2002). *Retooling. A Historian Confronts Technological Change*. MIT Press, Cambridge, MA.

[21] ibid.

[22]Bjorklund, S. A., and C. L. Colbeck (1999). The view from the top; leaders' perspectives on how to involve faculty in improving engineering education. *Proceedings Frontiers in Education Conference*, 2, 12a5-12 to 17.

Most of the literature assumes that it knows what constitutes effective teaching, yet the concept is problematic. It depends in no small measure on the role that the teacher assumes. There is at least one paper that investigated the characteristics of an effective teacher in engineering.[23] There is room for much more research on this dimension of teaching, and especially on the teacher's view of students and learning. There was one study in the Philippines that compared teacher's self-assessments with student perceptions of efficiency and effectiveness.[24] It identified areas where some training might help.

At the more general level of the overall curriculum, the period has been characterized by much change. In general, this is in response to changes in technology, the response to which, is more often than not, either a new degree program or a new course or courses within an existing program. To some extent the choice is dependent on economics in that for a new program to function, it has to have a steady supply of students and jobs for them to have. Manpower forecasting is notoriously difficulty and this is the reason that the core disciplines of civil, mechanical, and electrical/electronic remain the large disciplines. Different cultures (nations) have responded to the demands of technological change in different ways, but departments may be influenced by international competition between universities in the development of technologies.

It is unlikely that engineering education will have a long period of stability without demands for more change, and the debates about the nature and role of engineering will continue.

For example, in 2002 the European Society for Engineering Education held a conference on the *"renaissance engineer"* or, more correctly, *"reshaping the engineer for the third millenium"* Some of the papers given were recorded in the *European Journal of Engineering Education* (Vol. 28, Issue 2, 2003). Like many of those emanating from the United States, there is a concern that engineers in the future will have to be more flexible and trained for interdisciplinarity.[25] It was also argued that in order to prevent future catastrophes engineers would have to go beyond technology to consider the causes of vulnerabilities and examine if and how engineering can address matter that are often embedded in the fabric of society.[26] Jones (2003)[27]

pointed out that in the Renaissance those who practised engineering in Italy (Brunelleschi, di Giorgio, and da Vinci) had a breadth of vision that encompassed many fields that have now become specialized. It is he argued, difficult to maintain current knowledge in these fields, and because of the demand for increasing specialization there are inherent conflicts that run through the profession that are shaped by expecation and reality. Project management has to resolve such conflicts and coordinate the work of independent specialists. He did not envisage specific degree programs in project management but considered more generally the aims of engineering education in relation to lifelong and continuing professional development. But the value of courses in project management with engineering programs has surely been well demonstrated by Smith and his colleagues at the University of Minnesota.[28]

It is significant that the Institution of Engineers of Australia should have asked the question "does engineering still reflect community values and goals, or have these changed while engineering stood still?" Its answer to this question was that the horizons of engineering education would have to be broadened. It would have to develop a more holistic approach (McDermott, Göl, and Nafalski, 2003).[29]

In the United Kingdom the President of the Institution of Electrical Engineers in relation to the field of electronic engineering wrote *"the proliferation of detail and subject area within our field and the disappearance of boundaries between it and most sectors of endeavour reflect the critical importance it enjoys in a modern economy but will continue to provide difficult choices as to what to study and what not to at every stage of a career. Against this background simple notions of 'qualification' lose their meaning and become increasingly ephemeral and this in turn challenges our traditional approach to registration."[30]

To a large extent, this position underlines the view of those writing on their vision for ECE education in 2013 in a special section in the *IEEE Transactions on Education* (Vol. 46, issue 4, 2003). In that issue, Moore and Voltmeter[31] reminded their readers that engineering is a *"service profession"* but that in the last century it had concentrated on technology to the detriment of the *"soft skills"* that professionals need to be able to serve.

Elsewhere in his Presidential address, he argued that it was essential to deliver degree programs at affordable prices and this would require a restructuring of degree programs. One of the problems that departments

[23]Martinazzi, R., and J. Samples (2002). Characteristics and traits of an effective professor. *Proceedings Frontiers in Education Conference,* 2, F3F-7 to 12.

[24]Reyes, R. S. J (1999). The efficiency and effectiveness of engineers as full-time and part-time teachers in selected colleges of engingineering of higher learning. An assessment. *Proceedings Frontiers in Education Conference,* 2, 12a5–18 to 23.

[25]Melville, P (2003). The Renaissance engineer: Ideas from physics. *European Journal of Engineering Education,* 28, (2), 139–144.

[26]Akay, A (2003). The Renaissance engineer: Educating engineers in the post 9/11 world. *European Journal of Engineering Education,* 28, (2), 145–150.

[27]Jones, M. E. (2003). The renaissance engineer: a reality for the 21st Century. *European Journal of Engineering Education* 28, (2), 169–178.

[28]Smith, K. A. (2004). *Teamwork and Project Management.* 2nd Edition. McGraw-Hill, New York.

[29]McDermott, K. J., Göl, O., and A. Nafalski (2003). Initiatives to increase number of entrants into engineering programs- an Australian perspective. *Proceedings Frontiers in Education Conference,* 2, F3D-24 to 28.

[30]Midwinter, J. E (2000). Something old, something new and something just in time: Dilemmas for EE education and training. *Engineering Science and Education Journal,* October, 9, (95), 219–230.

[31]Moore, D. J. and D. R. Voltmer (2003). Curriculum for engineering renaissance. *IEEE Transactions on Education,* 46, (4), 452–445.

faced in the United Kingdom was that they were required to offer a wide range of specialist courses. This was costly because often the number of students in each of these courses was small compared with many overseas competitors. This led him to the view that universities should provide a two-year core program and that specialist options in the last two years would be *"closely tailored to specific company interests."* The students would participate in projects in companies for some of that time. He suggested that these two years might be structured on a sandwich (cooperative) basis (i.e., six months in industry followed by six months in college). He argued that students might be of value to industry. This was found to be the case in the Diploma in technology courses of the 1960s. If the students worked in industry on project work, there would be no need for it to be done in college time and this would reduce costs. A similar view has been put forward by Vaz and Orr (2003), who argued that the American four-year degree should be regarded as pre-professional.[32]

Earlier in his address, Midwinter argued that in electronic engineering the innovative, society-changing breakthroughs are multidisciplinary, and his approach to curriculum was based on generalized systems. *"It suggests common ground between engineering and most other disciplines. That engineering, science, business and law share common ground comes as no surprise but what about engineering and the liberal arts, or the social sciences? Yet many of engineering's greatest failures have come from the failure to take into account the human dimension."* But he does not follow this up whereas Rosalind Williams of MIT does.

In Chapter 3, I stressed the role of philosophy, psychology and sociology in determining the aims of a curriculum; little mention was made of history. Yet, as Rosalind Williams in her recent history of the last decade at MIT shows, history provides a powerful *chocs des opinions* to engineering educators. The short article *The Chronicle of Higher Education,* from which engineering educators learned about her thesis, does not do justice to her book because the article focuses on only one dimension of several that are discussed in the book.[33] However, the essence of the article is that the very technologies that engineering has created have caused engineering to lose its identity. It is no longer involved in *"the conquest of nature but the creation and management of self-made habitat."*

*"What engineers are being asked to learn keeps expanding along with the scope and complexity of the hybrid world. Engineering has evolved into an open-*ended profession of everything in a world where technology shades into science, art, and management, with no strong institutions to define an overarching mission. All the forces that pull engineering in different directions-toward science, toward the market, toward design, toward systems, toward socialization- add logs to the curricula jam."*

"Inevitably the profession formerly known as engineering will multiply into a much wider variety of grades, types, and levels because engagement with technology has far outgrown any one occupation. The future of engineering lies in accepting rather than this multiplicity."

"In terms of education that means that the trend toward cramming more and more into the engineering curriculum runs in exactly the wrong direction. Few students will want to commit themselves to an educational track that is nearly all-consuming. What we now call engineering education should be lowering the threshold of entry, mixing itself with the larger world rather than trying to keep expanding its own world. Students are trying to do this mixing on their own, but in too many cases they are trying to pour new educational wine into old institutional containers."

This view derives from what Midwinter called the multidisciplinary nature of projects that have technological, economic, managerial, social and human dimensions; this differs little from the view expressed by Jones above. But what do these views mean for the undergraduate curriculum? Does it mean a transdisciplinary approach of the kind suggested by Ertas and his colleagues (2003)[34] or is it to be acquired through a process of continuing professional development, or, in the case of Renaissance engineer, does it mean a broader curriculum that embraces the circle of knowledge? For Williams, the answer is the latter. For her it means that there will be a convergence between technological and liberal arts education which she believes will be *"deep, long term, and irreversible."* Students have to be prepared for a life in which all these different dimensions of knowledge and ways of knowing within them *"are all mixed together. Only a hybrid educational environment will prepare engineering students for handling technoscientific life in a hybrid world."*

It is a view that is little different from that held by Newman when he wrote the regulations for the Catholic University in Dublin in 1854; but as McGrath noted, he did not succeed in reconciling the liberal with the professional in a way that was successful.[35] Nor has anyone since. There are in America requirements that engineering students undertake some liberal education but there is little evidence to show that the majority recognize the importance of, or like, such studies. To achieve that goal, there will have to be a paradigm shift in what is meant by engineering that is easily understood by

[32] Their proposed structure is 1.5 years of maths science and engineering fundamentals; 1 year of humanities and social sciences; and computer, and information science and electrical and computer engineering. Vaz, R. F and J. A. Orr (2003). ECE as a pre-professional undergraduate program. *IEEE Transactions on Education,* 46, (4), 429 – 433.

[33] Williams, R (2003) Education for the profession formerly known as engineering. *The Chronicle of Higher Education.* Issue January 24th. Williams, R (2002). *Retooling: A Historian Confronts Technological Change.* MIT Press. Cambridge, MA.

[34] Ertas, A., Maxwell, T., Rainey, V. P. and M. M. Tanik (2003). The transdisciplinary approach in engineering. *IEEE Transactions on Engineering,* 46, (2), 289–295.

[35] McGrath. F (1951). *The Consecration of Learning.* Gill, Dublin.

applicants and that might mean the exchange of the term engineer to that of, say- Technologist! That is the challenge that Williams presents; but there remains in the system the same hostility that Hankins (1977) found in his attempt to introduce a technology and society course.[36] Newberry and Farison (2003)[37] reported that in the United States only 10 to 15 accredited programs provided a serious alternative to the traditional format. Thus, the question "Will the changes that have been be enough?"[38]-assumes some importance. The debate will surely come, and change there will surely be. The President of the National Academy of Engineering has called for a major overhaul of engineering education[39] but Feisel, a vice-president of IEEE, did not think that meaningful change could be brought about unless the whole of the profession was involved. This brought him full circle to Williams' position because[40] he found a fragmentation that when all the engineers in the components were added up did not make a whole profession, rather it was a *"profession in repose... it just lies there."* Among his recommendations were that *"faculty should learn something about the theory of education and practice it."* Evidently there are some, but it is a relatively small number who have, and the results have been profound. The need for curriculum leadership at this time is deep.

---

[36]Hankins, G (1977). Evaluating student and faculty attitudes toward a course in technology and society. *Engineering Education*. February. 400–402.

[37]Newberry, B and J.Farison (2003). A look at the past and present of general engineering and engineering science programs. *Journal of Engineering Education,* 92, (3), 217–226.

[38] Splitt, F. G (2003). The challenge of change: on realizing the new paradigm for engineering education. *Journal of Engineering Education,* 92, (2), 181 – 188.

[39] Wulf, W. A (2002) The Urgency of Engineering Education Reform. Excerpts from the Laboratory for Innovative Technology and Engineering Education 2002 Distinguished Lecture. 3/3&4 July-December 2002.

[40] Feisel, L (2002). A profession in repose. *The Interface. IEEE.* November, 1 & 2.

AUTHOR INDEX

SUBJECT INDEX